$$r^2 = \frac{b^2[\Sigma x_i^2 - (\Sigma x_i)^2/n]}{\Sigma y_i^2 - (\Sigma y_i)^2/n}$$

Sample coefficient of determination, simple linear regression

$$r = \frac{n\Sigma x_i y_i - (\Sigma x_i)(\Sigma y_i)}{\sqrt{n\Sigma x_i^2 - (\Sigma x_i)^2}\ \sqrt{n\Sigma y_i^2 - (\Sigma y_i)^2}}$$

Sample correlation coefficient

$$X^2 = \sum_{i=1}^{k}\left[\frac{(O_i - E_i)^2}{E_i}\right]$$

Statistic approximately distributed as χ^2, used as a test statistic in tests of goodness of fit, independence, and homogeneity

$$(r - 1)(c - 1)$$

Degrees of freedom for χ^2 in tests of independence and homogeneity (r = number of rows, c = number of columns)

Key to Exercise Symbols

 Accounting

 Health/Safety

 Production/Operations

 Agribusiness

 Management

 Real Estate

 Economics

 Marketing

 Research and Development

 Education/Training

 Personnel/Human Resources

 Transportation/Distribution

 Government

c Suitable for Computer Solution

BUSINESS STATISTICS

FOR MANAGEMENT AND ECONOMICS

BUSINESS STATISTICS

FOR MANAGEMENT AND ECONOMICS

SEVENTH EDITION

WAYNE W. DANIEL

Georgia State University

JAMES C. TERRELL

Georgia State University

HOUGHTON MIFFLIN COMPANY
BOSTON   TORONTO
Geneva, Illinois   Palo Alto   Princeton, New Jersey

Sponsoring Editor: Denise Clinton
Associate Project Editor: Magdalena Hernandez
Production/Design Coordinator: Jill Haber
Senior Manufacturing Coordinator: Marie Barnes
Marketing Manager: Charles Baker

Cover design and illustration: Judy Arisman, Arisman Design

Printed in the U.S.A.

Library of Congress Card Catalog Number: 94-76499

Exam copy ISBN: 0-395-71671-3

Student text ISBN: 0-395-71231-9

23456789-RM-97 96 95

CONTENTS

PREFACE

The seventh edition of *Business Statistics for Management and Economics* retains the best features of the first six editions. It also incorporates new material that our own experience and that of users of the previous editions and reviewers indicate will make for an improved text. With this edition, we continue our expanded computer coverage, integrating MINITAB commands and solutions, and adding to the exercises and Statistics at Work cases. Our objectives have remained the same as before: (1) to make the subject matter clear and understandable to the student and (2) to provide the instructor with the most teachable text possible.

RECENTLY ADDED TOPICS RETAINED

The following topics, introduced in the sixth edition, have been retained for the present edition.

- **Model Building.** The chapter "Regression Analysis—Model Building" follows the chapter on multiple regression. The topics covered include an overview of model building, curvilinear regression models, nonlinear regression models, and variable selection procedures. In the section on variable selection procedures we cover all possible regressions, stepwise regression, forward selection, and backward elimination. Solving problems using the computer is emphasized throughout the chapter, specifically through use of the STAT+/ DATA+ and MINITAB software packages. Five interesting real data sets are provided in the Statistics at Work section for student practice.

- **Harmonic mean and geometric mean.** In response to many requests we added a discussion of the harmonic mean and the geometric mean. These topics should be of benefit to students who take courses in finance and economics later on in their college careers.

- **Nonparametric regression.** In our efforts to provide as many nonparametric techniques as is practical, we included a discussion of Theil's method of regression analysis.

- **Coefficient of variation.** In the section on measures of dispersion, we introduce the concept of the coefficient of variation and show how it is computed.

- **Outliers in regression analysis.** We define *outliers* and discuss methods for their detection and treatment. We state some of their possible causes. We show how MINITAB can be used to detect and deal with outliers.

- **Influential points in regression analysis.** We define *influential points* and discuss methods for their detection and treatment. We discuss the calculation of leverages. We show how to use MINITAB to identify and deal with influential points.

- **Box-Jenkins forecasting procedure.** We greatly expanded our discussion of the Box-Jenkins forecasting procedure without going into the technical details of its use.

NEW MATERIAL

- **New Chapter.** Chapter 1 of previous editions has been deleted. It is replaced with a new Chapter 1 that combines some new material with material that previously appeared in other chapters. This new chapter includes an introduction to business statistics, definitions of important statistical terminology, a discussion of measurement and measurement scales, comments on the role of computers in statistics, and an overview of simple random sampling. In Chapter 1 we emphasize the dependence of statistical activities on the nature and availability of data. Some important sources of data are listed.

- **Expanded Coverage of Quality Control.** Our discussion of quality control in Chapter 17 has been expanded for this seventh edition of the text to include the following topics: total quality, total quality management, and process capability. In addition, the introduction to the topic has been expanded to provide a better balance between the mechanical aspects and the philosophical issues of quality control.

REAL DATA AND CASE APPLICATIONS

To show the relevance and application of statistics, we have devoted much effort to expanding our use of real data and the emphasis on applications.

- **Statistics at Work.** We now have 76 Statistics at Work case studies at the ends of the chapters. Most of these have real data sets that students may use in the application of the various statistical skills they have learned. Data come from a variety of publications and organizations, such as the *Journal of Marketing Research*, the U.S. Environmental Protection Agency, and active researchers in the fields of business. We believe that students and instructors will find these cases both interesting and challenging. Sources for additional real data sets may be found in the article "Improving the Teaching of Applied Statistics: Putting the Data Back Into Data Analysis," by Judith D. Singer and

John B. Willett, that appears in the August 1990 issue of *The American Statistician*, pages 223–330.

- **Real data.** The approximately 100 exercises that make use of real data appearing in earlier editions are retained in the present edition. The *Forbes* data on six variables for 785 of the country's largest firms have been updated with the latest available figures.

- **Large data sets.** Nine large data sets containing from 600 to 2,100 observations, including the *Forbes* data, are available on a diskette for use with microcomputers in conjunction with STAT+, the statistical software package that is also available free to adopters of the text. The larger data sets also appear in print in Appendix IV. Many student exercises in the book are designed to make use of these large data sets.

PEDAGOGICAL AIDS

Most students find the study of statistics to be a difficult undertaking. In an attempt to make the subject as easy to grasp as possible, we provide many features written and designed to aid and support their learning efforts.

- **Chapter objectives.** Each chapter begins by identifying the key concepts and points that will be covered. The purpose of this overview is to give students a glimpse of the forest before they begin looking at individual trees.

- **Margin annotations.** Sprinkled throughout the chapters, margin annotations add helpful hints, insights, and highlights to the text discussion.

- **Worked-out examples.** Key statistical techniques are clearly described and then followed by examples with worked-out solutions.

- **Example solutions highlighted.** For the convenience of the student and the instructor, the solution to each of the worked-out examples is prominently displayed in color.

- **Challenge Exercises.** The Review Exercises at the ends of the chapters contain one or more "Challenge Exercises" that may be assigned by the instructor to further enrich students' knowledge of statistics. These challenge exercises, highlighted with an asterisk, discuss a topic not covered in the text, present a worked-out example, and then provide an exercise for the student to work. These challenge exercises are ideal as bonus exercises, exercises for more highly motivated students, extra-credit exercises, and exercises for use with an honors course. In-text and end-of-chapter exercises now total over 1,350.

- **Summary.** Each chapter ends with a summary of important points and concepts, corresponding directly to the chapter objectives.

- **Suggestions for Further Reading.** For students and instructors who want to explore particular topics more thoroughly, a list of additional readings is provided at the end of each chapter.

INCREASED COMPUTER COVERAGE

- **MINITAB integration.**   We have included printouts of MINITAB commands and solutions for many of the worked-out examples in the computer analysis sections. An expanded MINITAB appendix highlights the major MINITAB commands as well. (MINITAB is a registered trademark. Further information on this software package may be obtained from MINITAB Data Analysis Software, 3081 Enterprise Drive, State College, PA 16801; telephone: 814-238-3280; telex: 881612.)

- **STAT+ integration.**   As with the last edition, for many of the worked-out examples we also display printouts from STAT+, a software program designed specifically for this book.

- **DATA+.**   To assist users of our STAT+ package, we provide many of the large data sets on our DATA+ disk.

- **Computer analysis.**   More emphasis is placed on the usefulness of the computer in performing analytic tasks. Strategically located computer analysis sections illustrate computer solutions for previously worked-out examples. These sections reinforce the idea that the computer is a convenient and efficient computational tool.

- **Computer coded exercises.**   Many of the end-of-section and end-of-chapter exercises (identified by Ⓒ) are especially suitable for solving with a computer. These exercises provide students numerous opportunities to practice their computer skills.

SUPPLEMENTARY MATERIALS

- **Solutions manual.**   The solutions manual, available free to adopters of the text, contains step-by-step solutions to all the student exercises. This is also available, for sale, to students upon professor's request.

- **Study Guide.**   The study guide has a programmed-instruction format that enables students to check their ability to use computational techniques by comparing their step-by-step solutions on the right side of a given page with step-by-step answers that appear on the left side. To check their mastery of statistical concepts, students complete fill-in-the-blank questions. Again the answers are conveniently provided in the left column of the page.

- **Instructor's Resource Manual and Test Bank.**   The instructor's resource manual and test bank, provided free to adopters of the text, contains more than 2,300 test items categorized by type as follows: fill-in-the-blank, computational, multiple choice, and true/false. This volume also contains over 135 transparency masters for classroom use.

- **Computerized Test Generator.**   For use with IBM-PCs and compatibles, the computerized test generator is easy to use, menu-driven, and allows instructors to edit existing questions, create and add their own questions, and provide multiple versions of the same test. Tests can be saved and stored, and multiple print options are available.

- **Computer Software.** The following statistical software packages are now available free to adopters of the text.

  STAT+. Designed specifically for use with this textbook, STAT+ will run on IBM and IBM-compatible microcomputers. It contains programs that perform the calculations necessary to obtain solutions to exercises presented in the chapters on descriptive statistics and inferential statistics. The package will also construct many of the graphs that are discussed in the book. This package is free to adopters of the text.

  DATA+. DATA+ is a system of programs developed to support the use of sampling in concert with STAT+. It contains all the large data sets presented in the book, including the *Forbes* data. Users may use the random number generating capability of DATA+ to automatically select simple random samples from these data sets. The samples can, in turn, be transported to the STAT+ system for the desired analysis. In addition, DATA+ allows the user to store additional data bases, demonstrate the function of the central limit theorem, and generate custom-made binomial tables to supplement published tables. It is capable of tabulating binomial probabilities for sample sizes from 1 to 500 and values of p from 0.001 to 0.999. This package is free to adopters of the text.

- **Generic Data Sets.** Available in IBM and Macintosh versions and free to adopters, these disks contain all the data sets contained on the DATA+ software. These generic data sets are configured for use with virtually all commercial statistical software programs.

Business Statistics for Management and Economics, seventh edition, may be used in either a one- or two-term course in business statistics. When used as the text for a two-term course, instructors will probably want to cover the material in the first seven chapters during the first term. For the second term instructors may select topics from among the remaining chapters to provide a course to meet the particular needs of their students.

When the text is used for a one-term course instructors again have considerable flexibility in designing a course especially for their students. Some instructors may wish to cover the first seven chapters in detail. Others may wish to omit some of the topics in the first seven chapters in order to provide enough time to include selected topics from Chapters 8 through 17.

The text is equally appropriate for instructors who wish to use computers extensively and for those who do not. The text contains generous amounts of raw data that are especially appropriate for computer analysis. On the other hand, instructors who do not wish to make use of a computer also will find the text suitable for their needs.

We retain in this edition the chapter and section numbering system that we employed in all previous editions. Sections are numbered consecutively with the section numbers separated from the chapter numbers by a period. Within sections, examples, exercises, figures, and tables are each numbered consecutively and their numbers are separated from the section number with a period. Thus, for example, Exercise 9.4.5 identifies the fifth exercise in Section 4 of Chapter 9.

We are deeply indebted to many people who have contributed to the production of this seventh edition of *Business Statistics for Management and Economics*.

We are especially grateful to members of the faculty of the Department of Decision Sciences at Georgia State University, who used previous editions in their classes and made invaluable suggestions for improvement. We particularly appreciate the efforts of Professors Brian Schott and Geoffrey Churchill, who wrote the computer programs to produce the binomial, Poisson, and normal distribution tables found in Appendix I.

We would like to thank Professor Carl Quitmeyer of Virginia Polytech and State University, who contributed some of the student exercises. Dr. Laszlo Pallos, Senior Statistician, Agency for Toxic Substances and Disease Registry, U.S. Public Health Service, Atlanta, made valuable suggestions for the improvement of the chapter on model building. We appreciate his help. Finally, we wish to acknowledge the cooperation of Minitab, Inc., for making available to us the latest version of the MINITAB software package for illustrating the use of the microcomputer in statistical analysis.

We would like to acknowledge the individuals who aided in developing and reviewing this and earlier editions of *Business Statistics for Management and Economics*. For their help and assistance, we extend our sincere thanks to

Mary Alquire
University of Arkansas
at Fayetteville

Steven Bajgier
Drexel University

Richard E. Bennett
Kent State University

Elizabeth Charron
Springfield College

Dalen Chiang
Cleveland State University

Allin Cottrell
Elon College

John Dunkelberger
Shippensburg University

Jerry Ehman
Franklin University

Patsy Eiland
Auburn University

Jamie Eng
San Francisco State University

Margaret Gavin
Seton Hall University

Jeffrey Green
Ball State University

Paul Guy
California State University at Chico

David Warren Haley
Miami University at Oxford

Mary Hirsch
University of Arkansas

Hui-Kuang Hseih
University of Massachusetts

Norman Kaye
Marquette University

Martin Kotler
Pace University

Lee Larsen
St. Norbert College

Avinash Mainkar
Tulane University

Jerrold May
University of Pittsburgh

Donald Miller
St. Mary's College

Jeffery Mock
Diablo Valley College

Eugene Murkison
Georgia Southern College

Kevin Murphy
Oakland University

Buddy Myers
Kent State University

Dennis Oberhelman
University of South Carolina

Thomas Obremski
University of Denver

E. A. Parent
George Mason University

Hong Park
Saginaw Valley State University

Derek Penney
South Bank Polytechnic

Joseph Pentecoste
Indiana University,
Northwest Campus

Len Presby
William Patterson College

Peter Royce
University of New Hampshire

Yitzchak Sabban
Baruch College

Daniel Sands
Pennsylvania State University

John Schank
George Mason University

Joseph Sessum
Kennesaw State College

Carl Silver
Drexel University

John Sims
Auburn University

Raphael Solis
California State University at Fresno

Patricia Smith
University of Michigan, Dearborn

Toni Somers
Wayne State University

William Soule
University of Maine

Pandu Tadikamalla
University of Pittsburgh

Vern Vincent
Pan American University

George Vlahos
University of Dayton

Jenny Wagner
University of Massachusetts
at Boston

Joseph R. Williams
Irawamba Community College

Rick Wing
San Francisco State University

Joseph Williams
Itawamba Community College

Peggy Young
George Mason University

Chris Zappe
Bucknell University

Finally, we express sincere gratitude to the people at Houghton Mifflin for their ideas, support, and expertise. We especially thank Denise Clinton, Sponsoring Editor; Magdalena Hernandez, Associate Project Editor; Joan Horan, Editorial Assistant; and Charles Baker, Marketing Manager.

W.W.D
J.C.T.

BUSINESS STATISTICS

FOR MANAGEMENT
AND ECONOMICS

1

Introduction to Business Statistics

Chapter Objectives: This chapter serves to introduce you to the field of statistics. It is here that you obtain an idea of what statistics is about and how a knowledge of statistics can be useful to you in the business field. From reading this chapter you learn the basic vocabulary of statistics and gain insight into the source and nature of the raw materials of statistical analysis. After studying this chapter, you should be able to

1. Define statistics.
2. Understand and be able to use vocabulary necessary for successful communication with others about statistics.
3. Discuss and give examples of the different kinds of variables.
4. Discuss and give examples of the different measurement scales.
5. Distinguish between descriptive and inferential statistics.
6. Explain the difference between a population and a sample.
7. Use MINITAB, STAT+, and/or some other statistical software package to select a simple random sample.

1.1 INTRODUCTION

Most students of business are required to take at least one course in statistics. There is a good reason for this requirement. Statistics is a widely used tool in the world of business. The techniques and concepts of statistics are used both in business research and in day-to-day business transactions. The proper use of statistics yields information that helps the businessperson make wise decisions.

The purpose of this book is twofold: (1) to provide students of business with the basic concepts and techniques that will enable them to use statistics as a tool in whatever career they choose after graduation and (2) to give these students a background in statistics that will help them understand the results of the statistical techniques employed by others. Such applications of statistics may be found in annual reports and in the literature of business research.

The concepts and techniques of applied statistics can be conveniently grouped under two broad headings: *descriptive statistics* and *inferential statistics*. Under the heading of descriptive statistics, we examine ways of organizing, summarizing, and presenting statistical data. Under the heading of inferential statistics, we deal with the concepts and techniques involved in reaching conclusions (making inferences) about a body of data when we examine only part of the data. Chapter 2 introduces the more important methods and concepts of descriptive statistics. Chapters 3 and 4 present basic concepts necessary for understanding statistical infernce, the subject of most of the remainder of the book.

In this chapter we define some of the basic words and terms that will help businesspeople better understand the statistical information they encounter in their work. A knowledge of statistical terminology enables those who are employed in the business field to use statistical information more effectively in making day-to-day business decisions. This chapter also covers the concept of data, which are the raw material from which statistical information is derived. Finally, this chapter introduces you to the basic concepts of sampling, a frequently used method by which the data are obtained.

1.2 SOME BASIC CONCEPTS

Like all fields of learning, statistics has its own vocabulary. In this section we present some of the basic terms that you will need to be familiar with before you study the sections and chapters that follow. Some terms will be unfamiliar to those who have never before been exposed to statistics. Other terms that are familiar will have different meanings when they are used in the context of statistics. We will use the following terms extensively in the remainder of this book.

Data The raw material of statistics are numbers which we call *data*. There are two kinds of numbers that we are concerned with in statistics: (1) numbers that result when we take a measurement and (2) numbers that result from the process of counting. When we measure something and record the observation, we have taken a *measurement*. When we count the number of something and record the result, we have a *count*. Each measurement and each count is a *datum*. A collection of measurements and/or counts is called *data*.

Statistics Statistics is the field of study that is concerned with the following activities: (1) collecting, organizing, summarizing, and analyzing data, (2) making inferences about a body of data when only a part of the data is observed, and (3) interpreting and communicating the results of the first two activities. In summary we may say that data are numbers, numbers contain information, and the purpose of statistics is to determine the nature of this information.

Sources of Data Those who engage in statistical activities are motivated to do so by the need to answer a question. Examples of such questions include the following: What is the best way to increase productivity? How can consumers be persuaded to purchase our product? How can we improve the quality of our product? How can we improve employee morale? How can we cut costs without compromising other facets of our organization?

When we determine that statistics provides suitable tools for answering some question, the search begins for suitable data to serve as the raw material for the required application of statistics. The necessary data are usually available from one or more of the following sources:

1. *Routinely Kept Records* Business firms and other organizations are noted for the volume of paperwork that accompanies their everyday activities. The information that this paperwork generates winds up in file cabinets and computer storage devices. In these repositories one may be able to find data that will help answer questions about such topics as employee characteristics, customer demographics, the competition, customer satisfaction, vendor reliability, and so on.

2. *Surveys* When the data needed to answer a question are not available from an organization's routinely kept records, the investigator must turn to other sources. A survey may provide the data needed to answer the question. The manager of a shopping mall, for example, may wish to know the age breakdown of the mall's shoppers. A survey of shoppers would be a logical way to obtain such data.

3. *Experiments* Frequently the data needed to answer a question are available only as the result of an experiment. A manager might conduct an experiment to determine the best strategy for improving employee morale. The experiment might involve trying different strategies with different groups of employees. Subsequent evaluation of the responses to the different strategies might enable the manager to decide which one is most effective.

4. *External Sources* In many instances the data needed to answer a question are already available in the form of published reports, commercially available data banks, or the research literature.

Additional terms that you will encounter in your study of statistics include the following:

Entity When we make observations about persons, places, and things, we call that which is being observed an *entity*, regardless of the type of unit involved.

Variable A characteristic that assumes different values for different entities is called a *variable*. By contrast, a characteristic that retains the same value from entity to entity is called a *constant*. Examples of variables are heights of adult army volunteers, number of customers entering a store each day, and the color of people's eyes. The different values of a variable that one observes (or measures) are called *observations*.

Random Variable If one can specify, for a given variable, a mathematical expression, called a *function*, which gives the relative frequency of occurrence of the values that the variable can assume, the function is called a *probability function* and the variable is called a *random variable*. The values that a random variable assumes in a given situation are thought of as arising from chance factors. Consequently the values vary in an uncertain and unpredictable manner. Consider, for example, your monthly electric bill. In general, the amount is not the same each month. The amount you pay for electricity each month is the result of such chance factors as temperature, how much time you spend at home, the number of appliances you own, how much you use these appliances, and so on. Your monthly electric bill, then, is a random variable. The term *variate* is frequently used as a synonym for random variable. Although this definition of random variable is not a rigorous one, it suffices for our purposes here.

Quantitative Variable A quantitative variable is one whose values are expressible as numerical quantities, such as measurements or counts. Height, which is a measurement, and number of customers, which is a count, are examples of quantitative variables. A measurement taken on a quantitative variable conveys information regarding amount.

Qualitative Variable A qualitative variable is one that is not measurable, in the sense that height is measured, or countable, as are people entering a store. Many characteristics can be *classified* only. Examples are designating items of a firm's output as defective or not defective and saying that the color of a person's eyes is blue, green, or brown. Such a variable is a qualitative variable. A measurement taken on a qualitative variable conveys information regarding attribute.

Discrete Variable A discrete variable is one that can assume only certain values within an interval. The number of customers that enter a store on a given day is an example of a discrete variable, since we cannot speak meaningfully of 1.5 customers or 2.78 customers. A discrete variable is characterized by "interruptions" between the values that the variable can assume.

Continuous Variable The interruptions, or gaps, that are characteristic of a discrete variable do not occur with a continuous variable. There is a continuum of values that a continuous variable can assume—all the whole numbers and all values in between. Height, for example, is a continuous variable, since people do not come in heights expressed by only certain values. One person may be 72.12341 inches tall (assuming that there is a measuring device that will give such a precise reading). Another person may be slightly taller, and the measuring device may show this person to be 72.12345 inches tall. No matter how close together two people's heights may be, it is always possible, theoretically, to find another person whose height is somewhere in between.

Population The largest collection of values of some variable in which there is interest constitutes the population of these values. If the heights of all college students in the United States are of interest, the population consists of all these heights. If interest does not extend beyond, say, a particular classroom of college students, the number of people involved has decreased considerably, but we are still talking about a population because we are interested in the heights of the students in only this classroom. Thus, a population is created merely by defining the collection of values of interest.

The word *population* can also refer to a collection of entities. It is often better to refer to entities (such as persons) rather than to the measurements (values) taken on these entities. In any case, the ultimate interest is always in the measurements taken on the entities, not in the entities themselves. It is always clear from the context whether the reference is to a collection of entities or to a collection of numerical values.

Sample A sample is a part of a population. If the population is defined as the heights of all college students in the United States, the heights of students in a college classroom in Michigan would constitute a sample from that population.

When we make statistical inferences, for example, the population is the body of data about which we make inferences, and the sample is the part of the data that is examined.

Random Sample A random sample is a sample drawn in such a way that the results of an analysis of it may be used to make inferences about the population from which it was drawn. There are many methods of selecting a sample from a population, but not all of them yield samples that provide a good basis for making inferences about the population from which the sample was drawn. Consider, for example, the population of all students enrolled at a college during a given term. A particular class—say, a class in statistics—would be a sample from this population. Do the students in the class provide a sample that is suitable for making an inference about all students enrolled at the college? The answer, of course, is no. The students are in the class for predetermined reasons—some students must take the class at that particular time of day, whereas others are in the class because they are, say, upperclassmen, because they are majoring in business, because they need it as an elective, and so on. Their presence in the class is not a chance, or random, event. The collection of students, then, is not a random sample.

1.3 MEASUREMENT AND MEASUREMENT SCALES

When most people hear or read the word *measurement* they think of such activities as using a tape measure to determine the length, width, or circumference of some object; weighing an object or person; and determining the volume of some substance as when a cook mixes the amounts of ingredients specified in a recipe. The word *measurement*, however, may be given a more scientific definition than is customary. A whole body of scientific literature is devoted to the subject of measurement. Part of this literature is concerned with the nature of the numbers that result from measurements. In this section we define measurement and the four measurement scales that are widely accepted as appropriate ways of classifying numbers resulting from measurement processes.

We may define *measurement* as "the assignment of numerals to objects or events according to rules." Here *numeral* is used to mean any symbol, not necessarily a number, that we may assign to an object or event. The use of different rules for the assignment of numerals leads to different types of measurement, which, in turn, lead to different *measurement scales*. There are four measurement scales: *nominal, ordinal, interval,* and *ratio.* We discuss each one briefly here.

The Nominal Scale The weakest of the four measurement scales is the *nominal* scale. We use this when we distinguish one object or event from another by names. For example, the names *desk, chair,* and *file cabinet* are assigned to objects in an office to distinguish one from another. Assigning numerals to football players for identification purposes also exemplifies nominal measurement. When objects or events are measured on a nominal scale, we can say that one is *different* from the other.

The Ordinal Scale When one object not only differs from another with respect to some characteristic, but also has more or less of the characteristic than another, we have at least an *ordinal* scale. There are many instances in business in which we use an ordinal measurement scale. We may categorize accounts receivable as large, medium, and small. We may label typists as fast, average, and slow. We may rate different sources of raw material for the manufacture of some product as good, better, and best. We may rank salespersons according to the strength of their personalities. When we rank items, it is possible to tell which ones have more or less of the characteristic on which the ranking is based (except in the case of ties). But it is not possible to tell how much more or less of the characteristic one object has than another.

The Interval Scale When we can say not only that one object is greater or less than another, but also that one is greater or less by a specified amount, we have achieved measurement on at least an *interval scale*. A characteristic of the interval scale is the presence of a *unit of measurement*. Temperature as measured on a Fahrenheit thermometer is an example of measurement on an interval scale. We can say that it is warmer today than yesterday. We can also say that it is five degrees warmer.

Another characteristic of the interval scale is the fact that the location of zero is an arbitrarily chosen point. For example, a reading of zero on a Fahrenheit or centigrade thermometer is not an indication of the total absence of heat. The arbitrary zero and unit of measurement characteristics of the interval scale allow us to compare two interval-scale measurements in terms of "more than" or "less than," but not in terms of "times as much" or "times as many." Suppose, for example, that on a given day the temperature in Montreal is 40°F and in Miami it is 80°F. We can say that it is 40 degrees warmer in Miami than in Montreal, but we cannot say that it is twice as warm in Miami as in Montreal.

The Ratio Scale The *ratio scale* is characterized by the use of both a unit of measurement and a true zero point. For example, we measure weight on a ratio scale. When a weighing device shows 0, this indicates an absence of weight. Measurement on a ratio scale allows us to say that one object is so many times as great as another, and that it is so many units more than another. For example, suppose that a man weighs 180 pounds and his child weighs 60 pounds. We can say (1) that the father weighs *three times as much* as the child and (2) that the father weighs 120 pounds *more than* the child. The ratio scale is the "strongest" of the four measurement scales.

1.4 COMPUTERS AND BUSINESS STATISTICS

The relatively recent widespread use of computers has had a tremendous impact on business research in general and statistical analysis in particular. The computer has greatly reduced the need for laborious hand calculations. Computers can perform more calculations faster—and far more accurately—than humans. Through the efficient use of computers, business managers can now devote more time to improving the quality of raw data and interpreting the results.

Many computer software packages are available to the decision-maker.

There are computer programs available that perform most of the descriptive and inferential statistical procedures that the business decision-maker is likely to need. Some widely used "packages" of statistical procedures are *BMDP: Biomedical Computer Programs, SPSS Statistical Package for the Social Sciences, The ISML Library, MINITAB,* and *SAS.*

The American Statistician regularly features a special section on statistical computing. This section gives (1) summaries of selected committee reports dealing with statistical computing, (2) announcements of new and/or newly updated program packages, (3) sources of further information, and (4) announcements and reviews of new computing products of interest to statisticians.

PERSONAL COMPUTERS

Along with the current widespread use of personal computers has come the development of a large number of statistical software packages for use with these machines. Potential customers looking for a statistical software package for a personal computer are likely to be overwhelmed by the wide variety of packages from which to choose. Computer-oriented magazines frequently publish articles that aid in making a selection.

Directory of Statistical Microcomputer Software by Woodward et al[1] is a helpful book for those shopping for statistical software. This book lists approximately 140 statistical software packages alphabetically by name. Each entry contains detailed facts, such as hardware and software requirements, ordering and price information, available documentation and phone support, statistical functions, graphic capabilities, and listings of published reviews.

USING COMPUTERS WITH THIS TEXT

Statistical programs differ with respect to their input requirements, their output formats, and the specific calculations they perform. If you wish to use a computer to obtain solutions to the exercises in this book, you should become familiar with the programs available at your computer installation. If you own a computer, you may wish to consider purchasing a statistical software package. You must determine, first of all, whether there is an existing program that will do the required calculations. Once you locate an appropriate program, study its input requirements so that you can enter the data of the exercises into the computer correctly. Finally, study the program's output format to ensure that you will interpret the results properly. If you have studied a computer language, you may, in some instances, wish to write your own computer programs for use with the exercises.

The programs in statistical program packages can perform the calculations for many of the exercises in this book. In particular, the computer is a useful tool for calculating descriptive measures and constructing various distributions from large sets of data.

STAT+

STAT+ is a statistical software package designed specifically for use with this textbook. The programs in STAT+ run on IBM and IBM-compatible microcomputers. STAT+ will perform the calculations necessary to obtain the descriptive measures detailed in Chapter 2 and those required for most of the techniques

---

[1]Wayne A. Woodward, Alan C. Elliott, Henry L. Gray, and Douglas C. Matlock, *Directory of Statistical Microcomputer Software*, 1988 ed., Marcel Dekker, New York, 1987.

discussed in the chapters that follow. The package will also construct many of the graphs that are discussed in this book.

DATA+

DATA+ is a system of programs developed principally to support the use of sampling in conjunction with the STAT+ statistical analysis system. Consisting of either two 5.25-inch diskettes or one 3.5-inch diskette, DATA+ contains the large data sets that are found in this book. Other DATA+ features include

1. instructions for creating data sets other than the ones in the book.
2. the Saint Petersburg Paradox game.
3. a demonstration of the central limit theorem.
4. bionomial tables.

MINITAB

Solutions to many of the examples in this book are illustrated by means of MINITAB computer printouts. In addition, specific commands are given for the execution of the statistical program used in the solution of the problem. Appendix VI contains a glossary of MINITAB data-handling commands. (MINITAB is a registered trademark of Minitab, Inc., 3081 Enterprise Drive, State College, PA 16801. Telephone: 814/238–3280. Telex: 881612.)

LARGE DATA SETS

This edition of our text emphasizes computer applications. Appendix II presents a "population" of 1,000 fictitious heads of households. For each one, we give recorded values of ten variables: sex, marital status, age, occupation, education, commuting distance to work, number of years with current employer, annual income, size of family, and size of residence. This data base offers you many chances to simulate actual research projects. Appendix III contains data on the "Forbes 500s." It presents data on six variables for 785 of the country's largest business firms. There are also several large data sets (each containing measurements on 500 or more subjects) in Appendix IV. These large data sets are for use in solving some of the Review Exercises, and provide numerous opportunities to use a computer in performing the various statistical analyses described in the text.

1.5 SIMPLE RANDOM SAMPLING

One of the purposes of this book is to teach the concepts of statistical inference, which may be defined as follows:

> *Statistical inference* is the procedure whereby we reach a conclusion about a population on the basis of the information contained in a sample drawn from that population.

It seems logical that useful inferences can be made only if, in some sense, the sample is representative of the population. Proper sampling techniques ensure that in the long run the sample we select for inference purposes will be appropriately representative of the population about which we wish to make an inference. We cannot rely for valid inferences on just any kind of sample that may happen to be conveniently available. For our inferences to be valid, they must be based on the information contained in a scientifically selected sample. One of the purposes of this chapter is to acquaint you with a sampling procedure on which valid inferences may be based.

It is important first to distinguish between two types of sample, the *probability sample* and the *nonprobability sample*.

> A *probability sample* is a sample of elements drawn from a population of elements in such a way that every element in the population has a known and nonzero chance of being selected.

All other methods of selecting a sample are known as *nonprobability* methods. The only type of sample we consider in this text is the probability sample. This is because only for probability samples are there statistically sound procedures that allow us both to infer from a sample to the population from which it is drawn and to obtain estimates of the sampling error involved.

We usually sample large populations. We usually do not sample small populations. Instead, when we need to know their characteristics, we examine them in their entirety. As a rule, we use sampling only when the population of interest is so large that examining it completely is impractical.

There are several types of probability samples. The simplest of these is the *simple random sample*. For the time being, this is the only type of sample with which we will be concerned. If we use the letter N to designate the size of a finite population and the letter n to designate the size of a sample, we may define a simple random sample as follows.

> If a sample of size n is drawn from a population of size N in such a way that every possible sample of size n has the same chance of being selected, the sample is called a *simple random sample*.

The mechanics of drawing a sample that satisfies the definition of a simple random sample is called *simple random sampling*. When drawing a simple ran-

We usually sample without replacement.

dom sample, we can sample *with replacement* or *without replacement*. In practice, sampling is almost always done without replacement.

In selecting a simple random sample from a population, we must use some objective method in order to ensure true randomness. One such procedure involves the use of a *table of random numbers,* such as Table D of Appendix I. Using such a table ensures that every observation in the sampled population has an equal and independent chance of being selected. This is because each digit in the random-number table was generated in such a way that the values 0 through 9 had an equal and independent probability of occurring.

EXAMPLE 1.5.1   The population of interest consists of 200 workers at Brannan Transportation, Inc. We want to draw a simple random sample from this population in order to find out how many units these employees produced during the past week.

SOLUTION   For each employee, there is a card on which the production record is recorded. These cards, which are filed alphabetically in a card file, are also numbered in sequence from 001 to 200. Table 1.5.1 represents this population of interest.

We can use Table D to draw a sample of size 10 without replacement from this population. Some samplers like to select a random starting point in the table of random numbers. However, since all the digits in the table are random, there is nothing wrong with starting with the very first number in the table. If we draw another sample from the same population later and use the same table of random numbers, we begin drawing random numbers where we left off. This prevents us from drawing the same sample twice. Since we have 200 cards from which to choose, we can use only those three-digit numbers between 001 and 200, inclusive.

The first three-digit number in Table D is 859, a number we cannot use. As we proceed downward, we find that we can use the second number, 074. Therefore, employee number 074 is the first employee we select for inclusion in the sample. This employee produced 49 units, as shown in Table 1.5.1. We record both the random number used and the number of units produced. (We record the random number so that we can keep track of the numbers used. Since we are sampling without replacement, we do not want to use the same random number twice.) Moving downward in this manner, we obtain the random numbers and corresponding numbers of units produced that are shown in Table 1.5.2. Note that when we get to the bottom, we merely shift five digits to the right and move upward. This is one of many alternatives. For example, we could start at the top of the next group of five digits.

This completes the drawing of our simple random sample. From now on, when we use the term *simple random sample,* we mean a sample that was drawn in this or an equivalent manner. Chapter 15 discusses other types of sampling.

Many computer programs have the capability of generating random numbers. Rather than using printed tables of random numbers, you may use a computer to generate random numbers. Actually, the "random" numbers generated by computers are *pseudorandom* numbers. They are the result of a deterministic formula. However, the numbers appear to serve satisfactorily for many practical purposes.

TABLE 1.5.1   Number of units produced by 200 employees

001. 30	041. 59	081. 65	121. 47	161. 62
002. 38	042. 56	082. 42	122. 64	162. 29
003. 33	043. 65	083. 73	123. 55	163. 37
004. 49	044. 50	084. 44	124. 50	164. 27
005. 33	045. 54	085. 54	125. 65	165. 36
006. 43	046. 61	086. 67	126. 53	166. 43
007. 60	047. 57	087. 49	127. 32	167. 30
008. 31	048. 55	088. 38	128. 44	168. 41
009. 34	049. 26	089. 59	129. 38	169. 59
010. 61	050. 41	090. 42	130. 37	170. 63
011. 49	051. 64	091. 46	131. 53	171. 55
012. 64	052. 25	092. 30	132. 44	172. 32
013. 62	053. 28	093. 64	133. 27	173. 32
014. 37	054. 49	094. 28	134. 40	174. 31
015. 25	055. 53	095. 64	135. 43	175. 35
016. 38	056. 25	096. 46	136. 45	176. 33
017. 65	057. 33	097. 59	137. 33	177. 58
018. 56	058. 28	098. 60	138. 60	178. 31
019. 55	059. 25	099. 46	139. 62	179. 38
020. 43	060. 60	100. 27	140. 30	180. 29
021. 58	061. 34	101. 59	141. 51	181. 43
022. 38	062. 25	102. 43	142. 49	182. 56
023. 71	063. 61	103. 50	143. 31	183. 53
024. 47	064. 42	104. 51	144. 29	184. 64
025. 65	065. 48	105. 39	145. 36	185. 38
026. 54	066. 57	106. 59	146. 50	186. 36
027. 74	067. 26	107. 33	147. 54	187. 59
028. 36	068. 55	108. 60	148. 38	188. 68
029. 62	069. 36	109. 26	149. 60	189. 26
030. 31	070. 33	110. 72	150. 65	190. 72
031. 48	071. 63	111. 25	151. 36	191. 29
032. 35	072. 48	112. 44	152. 25	192. 32
033. 26	073. 37	113. 58	153. 28	193. 73
034. 62	074. 49	114. 49	154. 56	194. 63
035. 51	075. 46	115. 31	155. 51	195. 69
036. 67	076. 31	116. 56	156. 53	196. 57
037. 30	077. 26	117. 37	157. 40	197. 38
038. 57	078. 28	118. 66	158. 33	198. 50
039. 50	079. 63	119. 55	159. 26	199. 60
040. 62	080. 37	120. 66	160. 42	200. 28

TABLE 1.5.2 Sample of ten employees, showing number of units produced (from population of Table 1.5.1)

Random number	074	037	091	018	189	119	145	025	167	176
Sequence in sample	1	2	3	4	5	6	7	8	9	10
Uni ts	49	30	46	56	26	55	36	65	30	33

COMPUTER **ANALYSIS**

As an alternative to using the table of random numbers in Appendix I, we may use either STAT+ or MINITAB in selecting a simple random sample. STAT+ will automatically select a simple random sample from any of the large data sets found in this book and on the DATA+ disk. With STAT+, we do not see the actual random numbers used in the process. When we use MINITAB, we first obtain the desired number of random numbers containing the desired number of digits. This set of random numbers tells us which members of the population are to be in the sample. The numbers are selected without replacement.

Suppose, for example, that we wish to select a simple random sample of size $n = 25$ from a population of size $N = 1,000$. Figure 1.5.1 shows the commands used and the random numbers that were selected and stored in column 1. The first line of the printout tells MINITAB the size of the sample and in which column to store the random numbers. The second line provides information regarding the size of the population, and the third line requests a printout of the selected random numbers. The random numbers that were generated tell us which members of the population are to be in the sample.

FIGURE 1.5.1 MINITAB commands for generating a set of random numbers and a resulting set of 25 random numbers

```
MTB > RANDOM 25 C1;
SUBC> INTEGER 1 1000.
MTB > PRINT C1
C1
    729    79   859   291   312   963   260   445   528   936   981
    536   960   939   301   563   257    77   567   841    50   172
    471   785    62
```

When we actually go to the population to select the sample, it usually will be more convenient if the random numbers are in order from smallest to largest. Figure 1.5.2 shows how an ordered array of the random numbers is obtained and stored in column 2.

FIGURE 1.5.2   Illustration of the use of MINITAB to sort, store, and print the random numbers shown in Figure 1.5.1

MINITAB	MTB > SORT C1 C2

```
MTB > SORT C1 C2
MTB > PRINT C2
C2
    50    62    77    79   172   257   260   291   301   312   445
   471   528   536   563   567   729   785   841   859   936   939
   960   963   981
```

EXERCISE

1.5.1   Use the table of random numbers or MINITAB to select another sample of size 10 from the population in Table 1.5.1. If you use the table of random numbers in Appendix I, select a new random starting point.

SUMMARY

This chapter deals with the basic concepts and vocabulary of statistics. You learned that the main sources of data are (1) routinely kept records, (2) surveys, (3) experiments, and (4) external sources such as published reports. The concept of measurement was introduced and the following four measurement scales were described: (1) nominal, (2) ordinal, (3) interval, and (4) ratio. You learned that the basic type of sample for making inferences about a population is the simple random sample. You also learned how to select a simple random sample using either a table of random numbers or an appropriate computer software package.

REVIEW EXERCISES

1. Explain the difference between descriptive statistics and inferential statistics.

2. Define the following terms:

   (a) variable
   (b) random variable
   (c) quantitative variable
   (d) qualitative variable
   (e) discrete variable
   (f) continuous variable
   (g) population
   (h) sample
   (i) random sample
   (j) measurement
   (k) count
   (l) entity

3. Define statistics in terms of the activities in which a statistician engages.

4. Name, describe, and give an example of two kinds of numbers.

5. What are data?

6. List and describe four sources of data.

7. List, describe, and give an example of the four measurement scales.

8. What is a probability sample?

9. What is a simple random sample?

10. Selecting a simple random sample can be a tedious and time-consuming task. Under certain circumstances it is possible to use a simpler procedure that results in a sample that is equivalent to a simple random sample. The technique, called *systematic sampling*, is discussed in Chapter 15. Read the section on systematic sampling in that chapter and do the following: locate a population that you think satisfies the conditions that make a systematic sample selected from the population equivalent to a simple random sample. Identify a variable for which measurements on the selected population are available. Select a systematic sample and estimate the mean. Consult Section 15.9 to help you decide how large your sample should be.

SUGGESTIONS FOR FURTHER READING

The following are a few of the several sources of business data that are available.

Dun's Business Rankings, Dun's Marketing Services, Parsippany, New Jersey.

Industry Norms and Key Business Ratios, Dun & Bradstreet Credit Services, New York.

Troy, Leo (1971). *Almanac of Business and Industrial Financial Ratios*. Prentice-Hall, Englewood Cliffs, New Jersey.

The Value Line Investment Survey, Value Line, Inc., New York.

The following two publications contain lists of other sources of business data.

James Woy, ed. 1991–1992. *Encyclopedia of Business Information Sources*, 8th ed. Gale Research Company, Detroit, Michigan.

Frank, Nathalie D., and John V. Ganly (1983). *Data Sources for Business and Market Analysis*. Scarecrow Press, Metuchen, New Jersey.

CD-ROM data bases, such as the following, provide information from additional sources of business data.

Disclosure—Contains information extracted from SEC filings, such as the 10-Ks and annual reports for more than 12,000 publicly traded U.S. companies.

Investext—Contains the full text of selected reports produced by 180 investment companies.

For further discussion of measurement scales, see the following book.

Williams, Frederick (1979). *Reasoning with Statistics*, 2nd ed. Holt, Rinehart and Winston, New York.

Additional sampling concepts and techniques are covered in the following publication.

Scheaffer, Richard L., William Mendenhall, and Lyman Ott (1986). *Elementary Survey Sampling*, 3rd ed. Duxbury Press, Boston.

The following is a nontechnical discussion of the use of statistics by managers and decision-makers.

Williams, Ken, ed. (1973). *The Statistician and the Manager*. Charles Knight & Co., Ltd., London.

2

Organizing and Summarizing Data

Chapter Objectives: This chapter teaches you some of the basic techniques used in describing and summarizing important characteristics of a set of data. It will help you to understand and be able to use these techniques. These skills are essential for handling much of the material in the remainder of the text. After studying the chapter and working the exercises, you should be able to

1. Organize and summarize data so that they can be better understood.
2. Communicate, by means of graphs, the important information contained in a set of data.
3. Compute numerical quantities that measure the central tendency and dispersion of a set of data.
4. Use exploratory data analysis techniques, such as stem-and-leaf displays and box-and-whisker plots, to communicate the information contained in a data set.
5. Understand and construct index numbers.
6. Use the MINITAB and STAT+ statistical software packages to compute descriptive measures.

2.1 INTRODUCTION

The concepts and techniques of applied statistics can be conveniently grouped under two broad headings: *descriptive statistics* and *inferential statistics*. Under the heading of descriptive statistics, we examine ways of organizing, summarizing, and presenting statistical data. Under the heading of inferential statistics, we deal with the concepts and techniques involved in reaching conclusions (making inferences) about a body of data when we examine only part of the data. This chapter introduces the more important methods and concepts of descriptive statistics. Chapters 3 and 4 present basic concepts necessary for understanding statistical inference, the subject of most of the remainder of the book.

In this chapter you learn that data must be organized and summarized before the information they contain can be easily determined and understood. You then learn how to organize and summarize data through the construction of graphs and tables.

In this chapter you will become acquainted with the ultimate summarization device—a single number that conveys information about some important characteristic of a set of data. Numbers that are computed for this purpose are called *descriptive measures*, and each one has a different name, depending on the characteristic about which it provides information. You will learn how to compute these measures and how to interpret them.

2.2 COMMUNICATION AND STATISTICS

The ability to communicate effectively is an important attribute to be cultivated by both those who use and those who supply statistical information. Before a person produces statistical information for someone else's use, this person must understand the nature of the information desired by the consumer. Thus managers and decision-makers who delegate the production of statistical information must articulate clearly and meaningfully the questions to which they want answers. Once the producers of statistical information understand the question, they must be able to communicate their findings effectively and meaningfully to the manager and the decision-maker. It is therefore important that both the consumer and the producer of statistical information be effective communicators.

In addition to narration, there are three basic tools for the communication of statistical information: (1) graphs, (2) tables, and (3) descriptive measures. In the sections that follow we discuss each of these in considerable detail. The objective of these sections is to provide you with concepts and techniques that you can use to communicate the output you generate as you apply the techniques learned in the succeeding chapters.

2.3 SUMMARIZING DATA: THE ORDERED ARRAY

Data from a special study or from routine business records are usually available to a decision-maker or manager as an unorganized mass of observations.

If the number of observations is not too great, a frequent first step in organizing the data is the preparation of an *ordered array*. An ordered array is a list of the

TABLE 2.3.1   Ages of 100 employees

60	39	23	30	29	26	29	41	40	32
63	22	32	52	46	35	25	28	33	33
20	25	42	34	29	43	41	31	30	36
58	21	24	55	51	28	18	40	44	38
32	21	30	31	25	49	31	26	33	36
43	34	35	22	33	38	34	34	33	34
23	26	57	23	26	36	39	31	35	34
34	51	40	50	35	45	28	36	32	39
26	48	17	45	45	25	25	30	36	30
43	25	27	21	53	25	38	33	37	33

observations in order of magnitude. The order may be from the smallest value to the largest value or from the largest to the smallest. By looking at an ordered array, the decision-maker can get a feel for the magnitude of the observations. If more calculations and further organization of the data have to be done with a pencil, paper, and a calculator, these operations will be much easier if an ordered array is first prepared. On the other hand, if all calculations are done by a computer, preparation of an ordered array may not be desirable.

EXAMPLE 2.3.1   The Albion Manufacturing Company wants to analyze the characteristics of its employees (entities). A sample of 100 employees is selected, and the age of each at nearest birthday is determined. The ages are obtained from individual employee records filed alphabetically in the personnel department. Table 2.3.1 shows the ages as recorded. Table 2.3.2 shows the ordered array prepared from the original list. According to this ordered array, the youngest employee in the sample is 17 and the oldest is 63. This information is hidden in Table 2.3.1. The ordered array also facilitates the tabular presentation of data, as we shall see in the next section.

TABLE 2.3.2   Ordered array prepared from 100 ages in Table 2.3.1

17	23	26	29	32	33	35	38	43	50
18	24	26	30	32	34	35	39	43	51
20	25	26	30	32	34	36	39	43	51
21	25	26	30	32	34	36	39	44	52
21	25	27	30	33	34	36	40	45	53
21	25	28	30	33	34	36	40	45	55
22	25	28	31	33	34	36	40	45	57
22	25	28	31	33	34	37	41	46	58
23	25	29	31	33	35	38	41	48	60
23	26	29	31	33	35	38	42	49	63

2.4   SUMMARIZING DATA: THE FREQUENCY DISTRIBUTION

Although the ordered array helps to convey the information contained in a set of data, it is hard to grasp a large number of observations, even when they are ordered according to magnitude. We can summarize further by grouping the data into *class intervals*.

> *Class intervals* are contiguous, nonoverlapping intervals selected in such a way that they are mutually exclusive and exhaustive. That is, each and every value in the set of data can be placed in one, and only one, of the intervals.

For example, we can summarize the individual incomes of a group of employees by showing the number falling into each of several class intervals, such as

$$< \$ \ 5,000$$
$$\$ \ 5,000–\$ \ 9,999$$
$$\$10,000–\$14,999$$
$$\$15,000–\$19,999$$
$$\$20,000–\$24,999$$
$$\$25,000–\$29,999$$
$$\$30,000 \text{ and over}$$

After we have determined the class intervals, we examine the data and count the number of values falling into each interval. The result is a *frequency distribution*. It can be displayed as either a table or a graph. We can define it as follows:

Usually, between 6 and 15 class intervals are required.

> A *frequency distribution* is any device, such as a graph or table, that displays the values that a variable can assume along with the frequency of occurrence of these values, either individually or as they are grouped into a set of mutually exclusive and exhaustive intervals.

One of the first things to consider when data are to be grouped is the *number of intervals* to include. We designate the number of class intervals by the letter k. Using too few intervals results in an excessive loss of information. Using too many defeats the purpose of summarization. You usually should not use fewer than 6 intervals or more than 15. When deciding how many class intervals to have, you need to be familiar with the data and to understand the purposes of grouping.

Those who wish more specific guidelines for determining the number of class intervals may use a formula given by Sturges. If we let k equal the number of class intervals and n equal the number of observations, *Sturges' rule* tells us that the number of class intervals should be

(2.4.1)
$$k = 1 + 3.322(\log_{10} n)$$

We *should not* regard the number of class intervals indicated by Sturges' rule as final. The actual number of class intervals we use may be more or less than the number k obtained using the formula if this will make for greater convenience and clarity. Suppose, for example, that we wish to construct a frequency distribution from 150 observations. Application of Sturges' rule yields

$$k = 1 + 3.322(\log_{10} 150) = 1 + 3.322(2.1761) \approx 8$$

$W \approx R/k$

Another decision to be made when grouping data concerns the *width of the intervals, W.* As a general rule, all the intervals should be the same width. We should also select a width that is convenient to work with.

We may approximate the width of the class intervals by dividing the *range* by k. The range is the difference between the largest and the smallest values in a set of data. Let R be the range. The approximate width of the class interval is given by R/k. The class-interval width determined in this manner is often not an integer and must be rounded up or down. Also R/k frequently yields a class-interval width that is undesirable because it is inconvenient to work with or because it is one that is not customarily used with the data under consideration. Class-interval widths of 5 units, 10 units, or some multiple of 5 units or 10 units are desirable, since people can grasp them more readily.

EXAMPLE 2.4.1 To understand how to group data, consider the employee ages in Table 2.3.2. An examination of these data indicates that 5-year intervals, beginning with the interval 15 through 19, would adequately summarize the data.

Now let us see how closely the results obtained by applying Sturges' rule agree with our subjective judgment.

SOLUTION By Sturges' rule, we have

$$k = 1 + 3.322(\log_{10} 100) = 1 + 3.322(2) \approx 8$$

From Table 2.3.2, we see that $R = 63 - 17 = 46$, so that

$$\frac{R}{k} = \frac{46}{8} = 5.75 \approx 6$$

Since we prefer intervals whose widths are 5 units or some multiple of 10 units, we have a choice here between using 5-year intervals and using 10-year intervals. If we were to use interval widths of 10 years, we would have only 5 class intervals, one fewer than the recommended minimum of 6. Hence 5-year intervals seem best here.

Specifying the intervals as suggested and counting the number of observations that fall into each gives the frequency distribution shown in Table 2.4.1. This table enables us to ascertain, at a glance, various features of the data. For example, there are more employees in the age group 30–34 than in any other group. The number in each group decreases in both directions from this interval. In Table 2.4.1, the numbers 15, 20, 25, 30, and so on, are the *lower class limits.* The numbers 19, 24, 29, 34, and so on, are the *upper class limits.* These numbers determine the magnitude of the observations that go into a given interval.

The choice of class limits reflects the extent to which the values being grouped are rounded off. The employee ages in the present example are rounded to the nearest year, since it was the age at the nearest birthday that was recorded. An employee between 24 and 24.5 would be counted in the second class interval,

TABLE 2.4.1 Frequency distribution of the ages of 100 employees

Age (in years)	Frequency
15–19	2
20–24	10
25–29	19
30–34	27
35–39	16
40–44	10
45–49	6
50–54	5
55–59	3
60–64	2
Total	100

whereas one who is between 24.5 and 25 would be counted in the third. Thus, 24.5 is really the boundary between the second and third class intervals. Similar boundaries between the other class intervals may be determined. These are sometimes referred to as the *class boundaries* or *true class limits*. For the employee ages, they are

14.5–19.5	19.5–24.5	24.5–29.5	29.5–34.5	34.5–39.5
39.5–44.5	44.5–49.5	49.5–54.5	54.5–59.5	59.5–64.5

Sometimes one wants a *cumulative frequency distribution*. Table 2.4.2 shows this for the 100 employee ages. We obtain the entries in the cumulative frequency column by adding the number of observations in a given interval to the cumulated number of observations from the first interval through the preceding interval, inclusive. The cumulative frequency distribution tells us quickly how many observations are below a certain value. For example, Table 2.4.2 shows that 74 employees are under 39.5 years old.

TABLE 2.4.2 Cumulative frequency distribution of the ages of 100 employees

Age (in years)	Frequency	Cumulative Frequency
15–19	2	2
20–24	10	12
25–29	19	31
30–34	27	58
35–39	16	74
40–44	10	84
45–49	6	90
50–54	5	95
55–59	3	98
60–64	2	100
Total	100	

TABLE 2.4.3 Relative frequency and cumulative relative frequency distributions of the ages of 100 employees

Age (in years)	Relative Frequency	Cumulative Relative Frequency
15–19	0.02	0.02
20–24	0.10	0.12
25–29	0.19	0.31
30–34	0.27	0.58
35–39	0.16	0.74
40–44	0.10	0.84
45–49	0.06	0.90
50–54	0.05	0.95
55–59	0.03	0.98
60–64	0.02	1.00
Total	1.00	

RELATIVE FREQUENCIES

We may at times wish to know what proportion of the observations under study fall within a certain class interval. We find this by dividing the number of values in that class interval by the total number of values. In Example 2.4.1, we find the proportion of observations in the class interval 15–19 by dividing 2 by 100. That is, $2 \div 100 = 0.02$. We refer to this as the *relative frequency* of occurrence of observations in that interval.

Just as we can construct cumulative frequency distributions, we can also construct *cumulative relative frequency* distributions. We can obtain cumulative relative frequencies in one of two ways: we can cumulate individual relative frequencies, or we can divide cumulative frequencies by the total number of observations. Table 2.4.3 shows the relative frequency and cumulative relative frequency distributions for Example 2.4.1.

EFFECTS OF TOO FEW OR TOO MANY CLASS INTERVALS

Let us now illustrate the effects of having too few or too many class intervals. Suppose that, in Example 2.4.1, we had used class-interval widths of 20. Table 2.4.4 shows the resulting frequency distribution. We can see that using only three class intervals results in too much loss of detail.

Now consider the same example, this time using 3-year class intervals. Table 2.4.5 shows the results of using too many class intervals. The frequency distribution in Table 2.4.5 does not condense the original data enough to make clear the information they contain.

TABLE 2.4.4   Frequency distribution of ages of 100 employees using 20-year class intervals

Age (years)	15–34	35–54	55–74	
Frequency	58	37	5	Total: 100

UNEQUAL CLASS INTERVALS

As noted earlier, all class intervals for a frequency distribution should usually be of the same width. Sometimes, however, it may be impossible or undesirable to have class intervals of equal width. Unequal class intervals are preferred, for example, when there are one or two extremely small or extremely large values in the set of data. In such cases, we may use an initial class interval labeled "less than ..." or a terminal class interval labeled "greater than. ..." This avoids having one or more equal class intervals that contain zero frequencies. The disadvantage of such *open-end class intervals* is that there is no way of knowing their true widths unless we use some special notation to convey this information. In some instances, we may need to use unequal class intervals at places other than at the ends of a distribution to better communicate the true nature of the data.

TABLE 2.4.5   Frequency distribution of the ages of 100 employees using 3-year class intervals

Age (years)	Frequency	Age (years)	Frequency
15–17	1	42–44	5
18–20	2	45–47	4
21–23	8	48–50	3
24–26	13	51–53	4
27–29	7	54–56	1
30–32	13	57–59	2
33–35	18	60–62	1
36–38	9	63–65	1
39–41	8		
		Total:	100

2.5   SUMMARIZING DATA: THE HISTOGRAM AND FREQUENCY POLYGON

A frequency distribution may be portrayed graphically. This method of representing data has the usual advantages of graphical presentations. We can see the salient features of the data without having to interpret a column of numbers.

FIGURE 2.5.1   Histogram of the ages of 100 employees

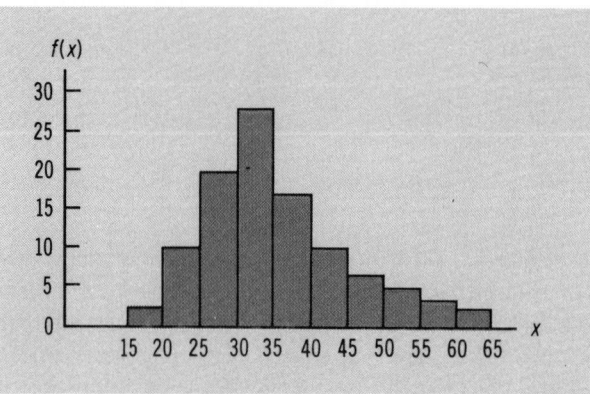

HISTOGRAM

One way of graphically representing a frequency distribution or a relative frequency distribution is by means of a special kind of bar graph called a *histogram*.
In a histogram, we plot the variable under consideration on the horizontal axis
and the frequency (or relative frequency) on the vertical axis. We locate the class
intervals on the horizontal axis, and above each we erect a vertical bar, or cell.
The height of a bar corresponds to the frequency (or relative frequency) of observations in the class interval above which it is erected. We also make the
adjacent cells of a histogram contiguous.

Figure 2.5.1 shows the histogram for the data in Table 2.4.1. Since there are
2 ages in the 15–19 interval, the height of the cell for that interval is 2 units.
The next cell is 10 units high, since there are 10 ages in the interval 20–24. The
lower limits of the intervals show, on the horizontal axis, the points of separation
between adjacent cells.

We may also use the true class limits to label the horizontal axis of a histogram.
However, we may find it more meaningful to use the lower class limits (as in
Figure 2.5.1), the upper class limits, or both.

FREQUENCY POLYGON

An alternative kind of graph for a frequency distribution is a special kind of line
graph called a *frequency polygon*. To construct this graph, we place a dot above
the center of each class interval at a height corresponding to the frequency for
that interval. We then connect the dots with straight lines.

FIGURE 2.5.2   Frequency polygon and histogram of the ages of 100 employees

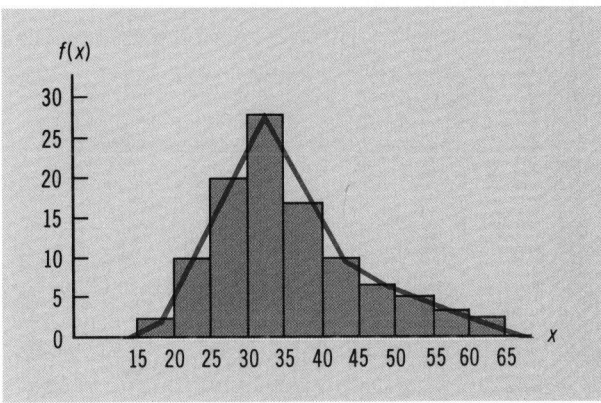

We can make a frequency polygon touch the horizontal axis at both ends by extending it to the center of an imaginary class interval at each end. Figure 2.5.2 shows a frequency polygon for the data in Table 2.4.1 superimposed over the corresponding histogram. This figure illustrates the relationship between these two graphic devices. Generally, the two graphs are not shown together in this manner. They are shown separately when both are desired, or alone when only one is wanted. Figure 2.5.3 shows, by itself, the frequency polygon for the frequency distribution of Table 2.4.1.

Note: We did not use true class limits to label the horizontal axis in Figures 2.5.1 and 2.5.2. Therefore, these graphs are shifted one-half unit to the right.

FIGURE 2.5.3   Frequency polygon of the ages of 100 employees

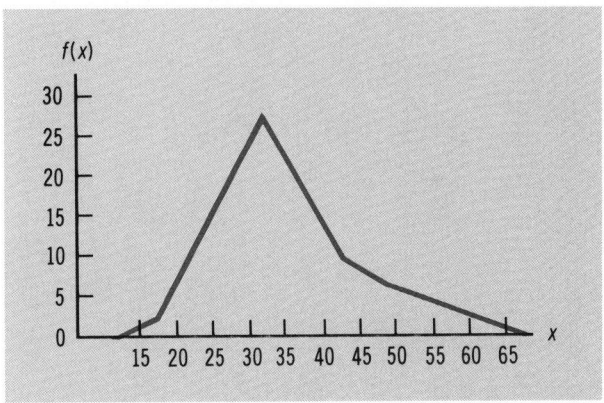

For example, the true limits for the first interval are 14.5–19.5, whereas the figures use the limits 15–20.

We may also use a frequency polygon to represent a relative frequency distribution. In this case we use the vertical axis to represent relative frequencies rather than frequency counts.

OGIVE

Graphs of cumulative frequency distributions often help to describe the nature of the data under analysis. This type of graph, which resembles a frequency polygon, is called an *ogive*. To construct an ogive, we place a dot above each lower class limit on the horizontal axis at a height corresponding to the cumulative frequency through the previous interval. We then connect these dots by straight lines. Any point on the ogive represents the number of observations that are less than the value directly below that point on the horizontal axis. Figure 2.5.4 shows the ogive for the cumulative frequency distribution of Table 2.4.2.

The histogram is an example of a bar graph or bar chart. Histograms differ from bar graphs in general in that the bars of a histogram are contiguous. For

FIGURE 2.5.4   Ogive for cumulative frequency distribution of Table 2.4.2

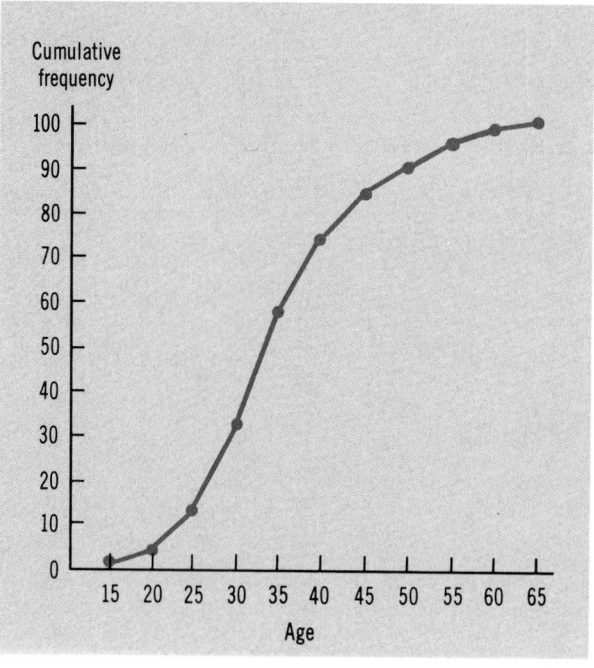

other kinds of bar graphs, this is not necessary. Frequency polygons and ogives are examples of line graphs. Other kinds of graphs can also be used to advantage in presenting quantitative data.

COMPUTER **ANALYSIS**

Many computer software packages that perform statistical analyses also contain routines for the construction of histograms. Figure 2.5.5 shows a computer-constructed histogram for the data in Table 2.3.2. The STAT+ package was used to construct this histogram.

MINITAB also constructs histograms, but their appearance is quite different from those constructed by STAT+. When we use MINITAB to construct histograms we may specify the width of the intervals by means of the INCREMENT subcommand. The subcommand START specifies the midpoint for the first class interval. After the data in Table 2.3.2 have been entered into column 1 of MINITAB, the following commands will produce the histogram of Figure 2.5.6:

MINITAB

```
MTB > HISTOGRAM C1;
SUBC> INCREMENT = 5;
SUBC> START = 17.
```

FIGURE 2.5.5   Computer-constructed histogram for the data in Table 2.3.2 (software package STAT +)

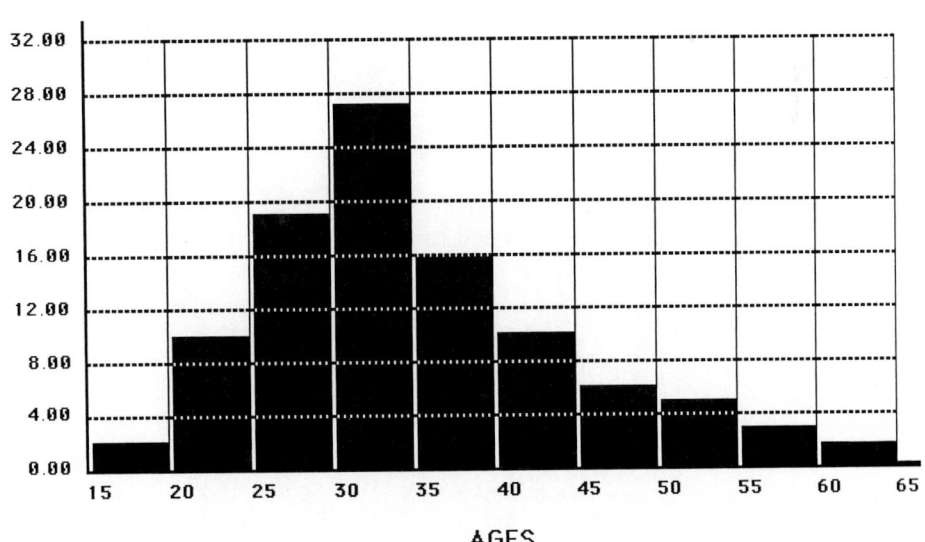

FIGURE 2.5.6   Computer-constructed histogram of the data in Table 2.3.2 (MINITAB printout)

```
   Histogram of C1              N = 100
      Midpoint     Count
       17.00         2      * *
       22.00        10      * * * * * * * * * *
       27.00        19      * * * * * * * * * * * * * * * * * * *
       32.00        27      * * * * * * * * * * * * * * * * * * * * * * * * * * *
       37.00        16      * * * * * * * * * * * * * * * *
       42.00        10      * * * * * * * * * *
       47.00         6      * * * * * *
       52.00         5      * * * * *
       57.00         3      * * *
       62.00         2      * *
```

EXERCISES

2.5.1   Ⓒ The following figures are the number of miles (rounded to the nearest 1,000) driven during a certain year by 110 salespeople with Baldwin Industries. Prepare an ordered array, a frequency distribution, a cumulative frequency distribution, a histogram, and a frequency polygon for these data.

40	26	41	40	39	34	61	42	47	23	18
43	29	93	46	32	44	71	45	62	36	22
49	31	35	36	84	81	51	51	52	66	34
55	44	18	33	38	28	42	11	48	55	42
65	54	97	67	88	44	39	42	35	50	90
73	60	41	40	29	24	58	47	53	45	84
30	31	32	34	48	76	38	52	63	41	73
36	50	31	56	35	15	26	28	41	45	61
32	27	75	30	68	24	37	30	20	50	52
10	65	52	20	36	38	38	43	21	55	48

2.5.2   Ⓒ The following is an ordered array of the amounts of money (in millions of dollars) on deposit in each of 100 banks on a certain date. Prepare a frequency distribution, a cumulative frequency distribution, a histogram, and a frequency polygon for these data.

0.9	2.3	5.0	6.0	8.6	10.3	13.7	16.1	21.2	27.5
1.1	2.4	5.1	6.1	8.7	10.5	13.9	16.3	21.3	28.3
1.5	2.5	5.2	6.1	8.8	11.1	14.0	16.4	22.4	28.3
1.7	2.7	5.2	6.5	9.3	11.2	14.2	17.1	23.6	29.0
1.8	3.0	5.4	6.8	9.4	11.8	14.4	17.2	23.8	29.4
1.9	3.2	5.5	6.9	9.5	12.1	14.5	18.8	24.0	30.0
1.9	3.7	5.6	7.1	9.6	12.2	14.6	19.0	24.2	30.1
2.0	4.2	5.7	7.3	9.8	13.5	15.1	19.5	25.2	30.5
2.0	4.6	5.8	7.4	9.8	13.6	15.3	20.4	25.4	33.2
2.1	4.9	5.8	8.2	10.1	13.6	15.6	20.5	26.2	34.4

2.5.3   [C] As part of its screening process in hiring new assembly-line employees, Cameron Clothing Company gives each applicant an aptitude test. The following are the scores made by the last 100 applicants. Prepare a frequency distribution, a cumulative frequency distribution, a histogram, and a frequency polygon for these data.

49	86	40	45	48	93	97	58	58	98
58	82	52	56	50	85	80	60	62	80
62	72	65	60	64	70	78	67	69	88
60	72	66	66	65	75	78	62	64	74
68	72	67	61	62	72	79	71	74	73
76	69	73	78	73	78	78	74	73	69
76	65	74	75	78	60	62	72	74	72
70	66	77	78	77	64	65	77	82	61
88	51	87	84	84	54	50	82	88	65
81	46	87	83	94	41	49	90	98	52

2.5.4   [C] In a study of the history of small business firms in a certain area, researchers collected data on the length of time (in years) that 120 such firms existed before going out of business. The results are shown in the following table.   (a) Construct a frequency distribution, a relative frequency distribution, a cumulative relative frequency distribution, and a histogram from these data.   (b) Construct an ogive from the data.

3	4	4	3	8	15	5	10	15	25	4	6
3	5	1	4	7	15	1	10	14	23	8	2
5	4	4	1	6	11	1	10	14	23	11	25
1	5	4	5	8	11	1	10	15	21	16	24
3	5	2	4	6	14	3	6	15	18	22	17
1	5	5	2	6	14	4	7	17	24	27	12
2	1	3	3	6	12	1	6	16	18	28	7
1	3	4	5	7	14	2	7	16	20	22	2
4	3	4	4	9	14	4	7	20	19	17	4
4	4	5	2	10	15	5	8	20	19	13	9

2.5.5   [C] The following are the lengths of service, in years, of 137 employees of The Danbury Chemical Company. Only employees with 10 or more years of service are included. From these data, construct the following: (a) a frequency distribution,   (b) a cumulative frequency distribution,   (c) a relative frequency distribution,   (d) a cumulative relative frequency distribution,   (e) a histogram, and   (f) an ogive.

10	10	19	17	21	22	20	24	25	33
12	13	19	15	24	21	22	26	29	32
11	12	17	16	23	21	24	26	27	31
12	12	17	17	20	24	24	29	25	33
12	10	17	15	22	22	20	25	27	31
10	14	19	19	22	22	22	25	27	34
11	13	17	15	20	20	24	29	28	37
11	13	17	18	20	20	23	29	26	35
14	11	16	18	20	20	22	26	28	35
14	19	19	17	24	24	20	26	27	44
13	15	15	23	21	21	20	26	29	42
14	19	15	23	20	20	21	27	31	
14	17	18	20	20	23	24	28	32	
11	15	18	22	24	24	20	27	33	

2.6 SUMMARIZING DATA: STEM-AND-LEAF DISPLAYS

Another graphical technique that is useful for representing quantitative data is the *stem-and-leaf* display. A stem-and-leaf display looks a lot like a histogram and serves the same purpose. That is, the display reveals the range of the data set, shows where the highest concentration of values occurs, provides information about the presence or absence of symmetry, and can indicate the degree to which the data are homogeneous.

In a stem-and-leaf display, each numerical value in a data set is partitioned into two parts. The first part is called the *stem*, and the second part is called the *leaf*. All the partitioned numbers are then shown together in a single display. The stem consists of one or more of the initial digits of the number, and the leaf is composed of one or more of the remaining digits.

Consider the number 12,375. In one situation, we might make 12 the stem and 375 the leaf. The number, along with the other numbers in the data set, would be displayed as follows:

Stem	Leaf
12	375

In a different situation, we might want to ignore the last two digits and form the following display:

Stem	Leaf
12	3

Numbers with the same stem are recorded in the same row of the completed display.

Suppose that the data set containing the number 12,375 also contains the number 12,376. Its stem is also 12, but its leaf is 376. In the first situation, the two numbers would appear as

Stem	Leaf	
12	375	376

and in the second situation, they would appear as

Stem	Leaf	
12	3	3

In the completed display, the stems are arranged in order, from smallest to largest. If a data set contains the numbers 12,375, 12,376, and 13,250, these numbers might appear in a stem-and-leaf display as

Stem	Leaf
12	375 376
13	250

or as

Stem	Leaf
12	3 3
13	2

Although a stem-and-leaf display and a histogram communicate essentially the same information, there are some advantages to using a stem-and-leaf display. In the first place, when we use all the digits of a number in the display, the identities of the individual values can be readily determined by inspection. In a histogram, the individual identities of the numbers are obscured. A second advantage of using a stem-and-leaf display is the fact that its preparation automatically yields an ordered data set with respect to the digits used as stems. The choice of digits to serve as the stem is a matter of judgment; it depends, in part, on the sizes of the individual measurements and on the number of measurements in the data set. Stem-and-leaf displays are most effective with relatively small data sets.

As a rule, stem-and-leaf displays are not suitable for use in annual reports or other communications aimed at the general public. They are primarily of value for in-house use, as tools for helping managers and other decision-makers to understand the nature of their data. Histograms are more appropriate for externally circulated publications.

EXAMPLE 2.6.1   Table 2.6.1 shows the number of employees under the supervision of 30 government department heads who responded to a survey. We wish to prepare a stem-and-leaf display from these data.

SOLUTION   The stem-and-leaf display is shown in Figure 2.6.1.

TABLE 2.6.1   Number of employees under direct supervision of 30 government department heads

53	39	37	55	44	35
45	43	45	45	55	56
23	21	54	36	46	45
64	32	12	22	22	57
10	35	60	34	38	36

FIGURE 2.6.1   Stem-and-leaf display for the data in Table 2.6.1

Stem	Leaf
1	0 2
2	3 1 2 2
3	9 2 5 7 6 4 8 5 6
4	5 3 5 5 4 6 5
5	3 4 5 5 6 7
6	4 0

STEM-AND-LEAF DISPLAYS WITH MINITAB

We may use MINITAB to construct stem-and-leaf displays. We stored the data of Table 2.6.1 in column 1 of the MINITAB workspace. We then issued the following command and subcommand:

MINITAB

```
MTB > STEM-AND-LEAF C1;
SUBC> INCREMENT = 10.
```

The subcommand INCREMENT specifies the distance from one stem to the next. Figure 2.6.2 shows the stem-and-leaf display produced by MINITAB from the data in Table 2.6.1. The leftmost column in Figure 2.6.2 is called the *depth* of the line. A number in this column indicates how many leaves lie on the line in which it appears and the lines above or below that line. In other words, each number in the depth column is either cumulative or decumulative. For example, in Figure 2.6.2, the first 15 tells us that there are a total of 15 leaves in the first three lines of the display. The second 15 tells us that there are 15 leaves in the last three lines of the display.

FIGURE 2.6.2   Computer-generated stem-and-leaf display (MINITAB printout)

```
Stem-and-leaf of C1      N = 30
Leaf Unit = 1.0

      2      1 02
      6      2 1223
     15      3 245566789
     15      4 3455556
      8      5 345567
      2      6 04
```

EXERCISES

2.6.1 The following are the number of microcomputers in use in a sample of 25 business firms in a large metropolitan area. Firms located in suburban office parks are marked with asterisks.

7	21*	36*	26	35*
30	42*	40*	30	21
12	34	20*	46*	30
18*	35*	30	51*	30
25	27	17	27	16

Construct a stem-and-leaf display from these data and discuss the results. What does the display suggest regarding the firms located in suburban office parks as compared with the other firms?

2.6.2 The following are the paid circulations of a sample of 35 weekly newspapers. Those marked with an asterisk have been in existence 30 years or less.

5545*	5678	6414*	7549*	5908
1168	8165*	3949	6806*	4349
4268	4298	4004	7772*	7566
6001*	4853*	3112	2607	4780
3339	2892	3440	4145	9989*
8494*	3808	7701*	1998	3023
2891	5699*	4191	2485	6015

Construct a stem-and-leaf display from these data. What does the display suggest with respect to the "younger" newspapers as compared with the others?

2.6.3 The following are the annual dollar sales per square foot of floor space as reported by a sample from each of two types of apparel store.

Adult Male				
171.10	191.40	214.40	201.20	217.90
222.00	225.50	202.50	239.80	229.80
212.50	213.30	249.10	245.70	233.90
201.70	195.10	222.20	213.00	209.70
184.90	214.30	205.90	238.80	248.30

Adult Female				
125.50	135.40	166.70	167.70	186.00
190.40	190.30	150.20	203.40	184.00
165.70	154.60	212.40	186.70	199.50
152.00	145.30	178.60	155.30	173.20
143.50	154.70	168.90	195.90	214.10

Construct a stem-and-leaf display for each set of data. What does a comparison of the two displays suggest regarding the two types of store?

2.7 GRAPHICAL REPRESENTATION OF QUALITATIVE DATA

When the variable in which we are interested is qualitative, the measurement procedure consists of determining the category of the variable to which a subject (or object) belongs. Suppose, for example, that the qualitative variable of interest is marital status. For each subject in the sample or population under study, we might determine whether he or she should be counted in the married, the never married, the widowed, or the divorced category. The numbers available for analysis, then, are the frequencies for the various categories. The resulting information can be presented either in the form of a frequency (or relative frequency) table or as a graph.

A *frequency table* for qualitative data consists of a list of the categories of the variable of interest, along with the number (frequency) of subjects (or objects) that belong in each category.

EXAMPLE 2.7.1   In a survey of 40 business executives, respondents were asked to specify the primary business activity of their firm. The categories were manufacturing (M), transportation (T), communications (C), utilities (U), and other (O). The results are shown in Table 2.7.1. We wish to construct a frequency table from these data.

TABLE 2.7.1   Primary business activity of 40 firms

Respondent	Activity	Respondent	Activity
1	C	21	T
2	T	22	M
3	M	23	C
4	C	24	M
5	T	25	M
6	M	26	O
7	C	27	C
8	M	28	T
9	U	29	O
10	T	30	M
11	T	31	C
12	M	32	O
13	M	33	T
14	C	34	M
15	M	35	M
16	O	36	C
17	M	37	T
18	C	38	U
19	M	39	M
20	U	40	C

TABLE 2.7.2 Frequency table for the data of Table 2.7.1

Primary Business Activity	Frequency
Manufacturing	15
Communications	10
Transportation	8
Utilities	3
Other	4
Total	40

SOLUTION   The frequency table for the data is shown as Table 2.7.2.

A *relative frequency table* for qualitative data contains a list of the categories of the qualitative variable of interest, along with the proportion of subjects (or objects) that belong in each category.

The relative frequency table for the data of Example 2.7.1 is shown as Table 2.7.3.

BAR CHARTS

The information contained in Tables 2.7.2 and 2.7.3 can be presented effectively in graphic form as a *bar chart*. When we prepare a bar chart for qualitative data, we may represent the variable involved on either the horizontal or the vertical axis. The frequencies (or relative frequencies) are represented on the other axis. We list the various categories of the variable along the appropriate axis. When the horizontal axis is used to represent the variable, we place bars of equal width above the category labels; the bars are placed to the side of the category labels when the vertical axis is used to represent the variable. The height (or length) of a given bar is proportional to the frequency (or relative frequency) of the corresponding category. With qualitative data, the order in which the bars are placed is usually of no concern. Unlike in a histogram, the bars of a graph representing qualitative data should not touch each other.

TABLE 2.7.3 Relative frequency table for the data of Table 2.7.1

Primary Business Activity	Relative Frequency
Manufacturing	0.3750
Communications	0.2500
Transportation	0.2000
Utilities	0.0750
Other	0.1000
Total	1.0000

FIGURE 2.7.1 Bar charts for the data of Table 2.7.1

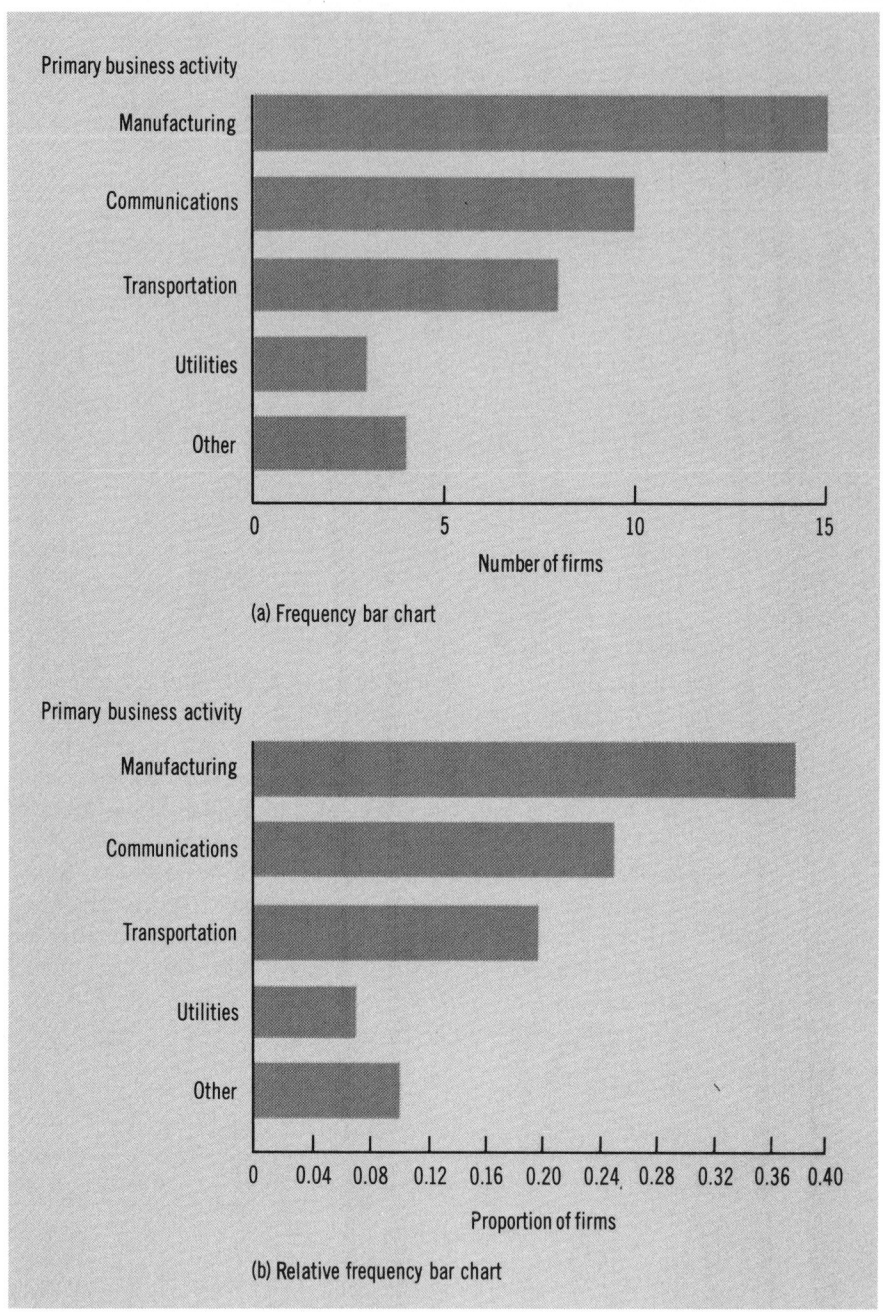

EXAMPLE 2.7.2 Figure 2.7.1 shows a frequency bar chart and a relative frequency bar chart for the data of Table 2.7.1.

There are many effective ways of using bar charts to highlight important features of a set of data.

Grouped Bar Charts Appropriate grouping of bars makes it possible to compare more than one characteristic for a given category at the same time. Figure 2.7.2 is an example of a grouped bar chart.

100% Bar Charts Sometimes it is useful to portray in a single bar the percentages that various components are of a whole. This may be done in a single graph for the several levels of a qualitative variable. The result, called a *100% bar chart*, is illustrated in Figure 2.7.3.

Paired Bar Charts Two different types of data may be represented effectively by a *paired bar chart*. Such a chart is shown in Figure 2.7.4.

Deviation Bar Charts When we wish to portray both positive and negative values in the same graph, we can use a *deviation bar chart*. Such a chart is suitable for showing the percentage change in some quantity from one year to the next. When possible, the bars in a deviation bar chart should be arranged in descending order of magnitude, as illustrated in Figure 2.7.5.

FIGURE 2.7.2 Ethnic groups of assembly-line employees at the five plants of a certain manufacturing firm

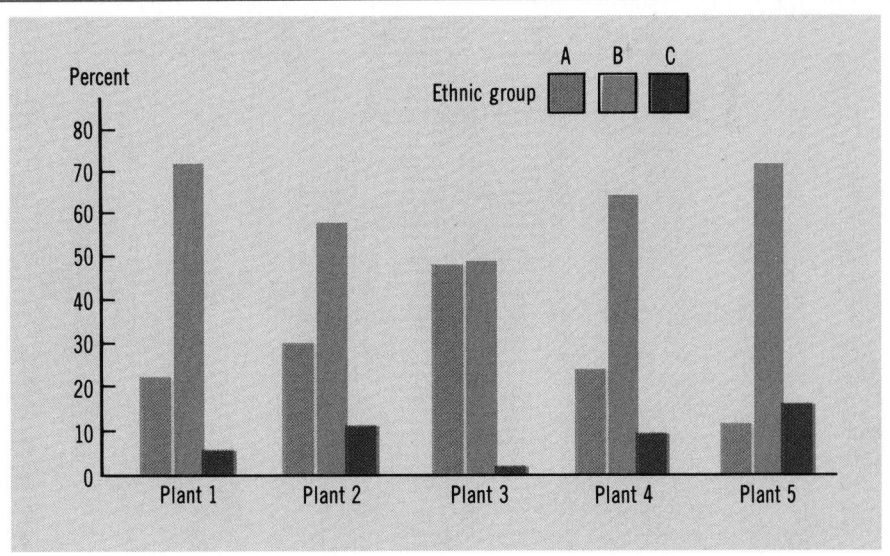

FIGURE 2.7.3   Educational background of a sample of business executives by type of firm

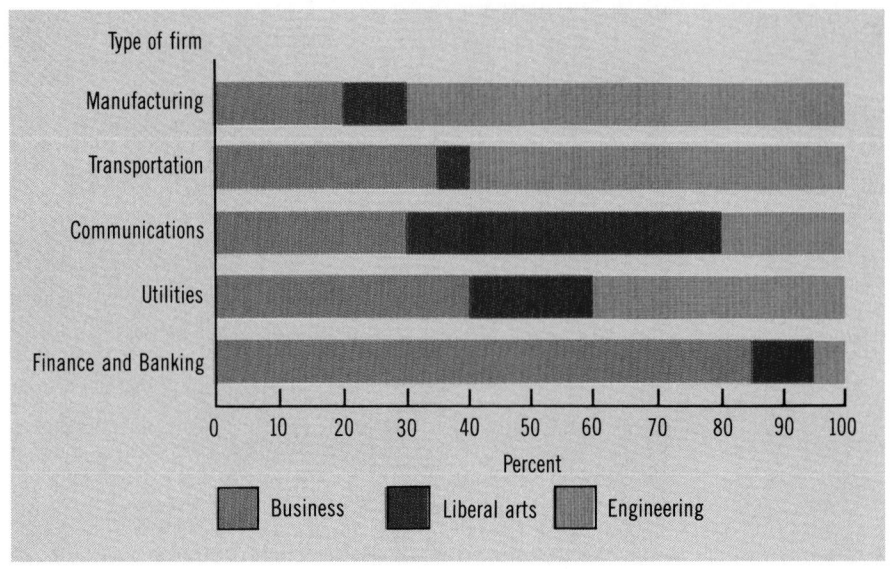

FIGURE 2.7.4   Number of items produced and number of items replaced under warranty for the five plants of a manufacturing company

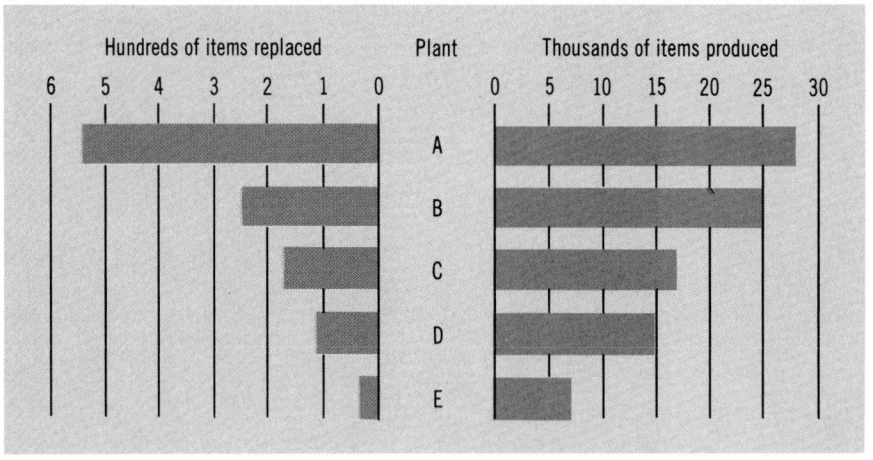

FIGURE 2.7.5   Percent change in number of sickness and accident insurance claims filed by employees of ten large business firms, 1987–1988

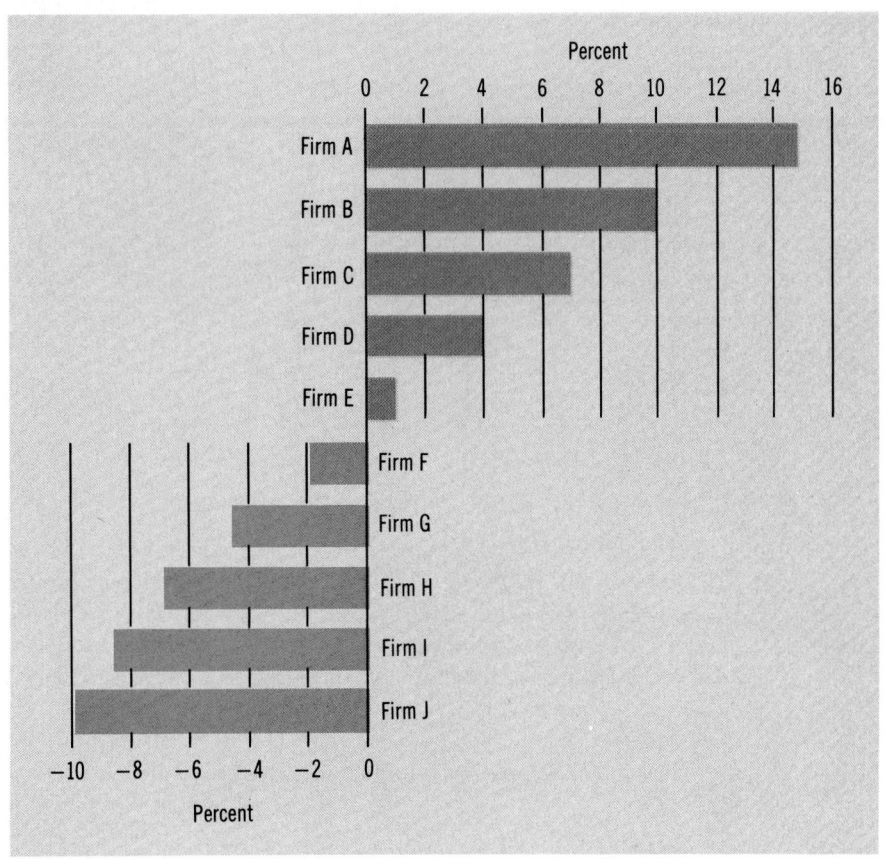

PIE CHARTS

An alternative to the 100% bar chart is the *pie chart*, which conveys the same information, but in a different form. In a pie chart, the whole is represented by a circle, or "pie," and the component parts are represented by "slices" of the pie. The size of a slice is proportional to the relative frequency of the component it represents. Since a complete circle contains 360 degrees, a component representing 25% of the total number of measurements, for example, will contain $(0.25)(360) = 90$ degrees. When possible, the largest slice of the pie should begin at the 12 o'clock position, and the other slices should follow in a clockwise direction according to size, with the smallest slice last. This rule may have to be violated when two or more pies are used, for comparison purposes, in the same

FIGURE 2.7.6 Estimated market penetration (percent of sales) of five brands of bath soap in two geographic regions

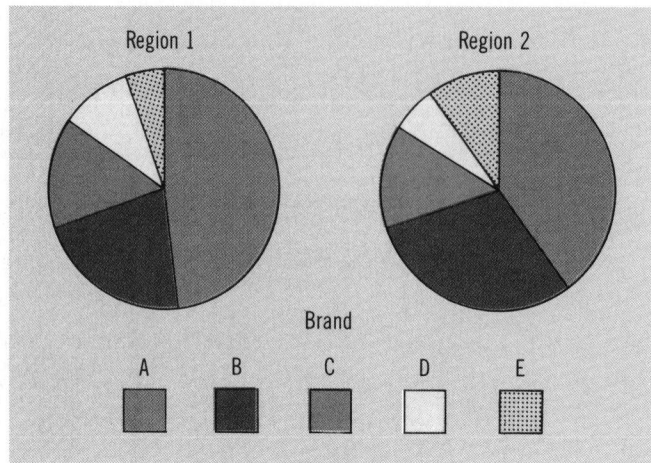

graph. Normally, the number of slices should not exceed five, and no slice should contain less than 5% (18 degrees) of the total pie. Figure 2.7.6 provides an example of the use of pie charts.

There are many other kinds of graphs that can be used to portray qualitative and quantitative data. When used properly, they are effective tools for bringing out the important characteristics of data sets. If they are not constructed and presented properly, however, they can create, in the minds of those who view them, false impressions about the data they represent.

EXERCISES

 2.7.1 The following are Eldorado Limited's quarterly sales in thousands of dollars in each of three major markets.

	Market		
Quarter	A	B	C
1	225	110	350
2	175	180	290
3	120	100	425
4	210	220	510

Using these data, construct the kind of bar chart that you think best communicates the information.

 2.7.2 In a survey, the employees of Forsyth Trucking Company were asked to state their opinion of the firm's health insurance plan. Of the 2,500 female employees, 650 said that they were satisfied, 975 said that they were dissatisfied, and the remainder had no opinion. Of the 4,300 male employees, 2,279 said that they were satisfied, 1,720 said that they were dissatisfied, and the remainder had no opinion. (a) Use what you consider to be the best type of bar chart to represent these data. (b) Use a pie chart to portray the data. (c) Which type of graph do you think is better for representing the data? Why?

2.7.3 The following housing data were reported by officials of 15 rural counties. Construct a single graph that you think best portrays this information.

Number of Housing Units

County	Owner-occupied	Renter-occupied	Vacant
A	3828	1304	360
B	3838	1847	42
C	3708	2249	195
D	1358	800	413
E	5003	2471	100
F	3195	818	159
G	2896	1422	369
H	4127	1251	340
I	3054	898	191
J	4875	1760	404
K	4147	1104	254
L	4992	1307	125
M	2794	792	393
N	2688	974	488
O	2876	1412	318

2.7.4 The following are the number of employees of ten business firms on July 1, 1987 and 1988. Construct a single graph that you think best portrays this information.

	Number of Employees on July 1	
Firm	1987	1988
A	859	1031
B	962	977
C	491	481
D	973	924
E	904	904
F	285	295
G	252	265
H	287	270
I	847	847
J	410	381

2.7.5 The following table shows the number of housing units located in each of 12 geographic regions and the size of each region. Construct a single graph that you think best portrays these data.

Region	Area (sq. mi.)	Number of Housing Units	Region	Area (sq. mi.)	Number of Housing Units
A	520	5,813	G	372	3,346
B	268	12,240	H	414	4,682
C	260	3,206	I	355	6,947
D	566	12,958	J	259	3,409
E	285	7,388	K	441	3,566
F	400	4,152	L	252	4,096

2.8   SUMMARIZING DATA: DESCRIPTIVE MEASURES

In addition to tabular and graphical methods of summarizing data, it is also useful to summarize data by methods that lead to numerical results, called *descriptive measures*. We discuss two types of descriptive measures: *measures of central tendency* and *measures of dispersion*. They may be computed from the data contained in a sample or from the data of a finite population. In order to distinguish between the two types on the basis of whether they refer to a sample or a population, we use the following definitions:

> A descriptive measure computed from or used to describe a sample of data is called a *statistic*.

> A descriptive measure computed from or used to describe a population of data is called a *parameter*.

Always be aware of the difference between a population and a sample. As stated earlier, a population is the largest collection of observations in which we have an interest in a given situation. Frequently, it is impractical to analyze an entire population, because of its size or for some other reason. Instead, we examine a part of the population. This part of the population is called a *sample*. Throughout this text, we use different symbols to distinguish between descriptive measures that relate to a population and those that relate to a sample. Later you will learn how to reach decisions about population characteristics on the basis of an analysis of a sample drawn from that population.

As you will learn when we study statistical inference, we frequently use statistics as estimators of parameters. For example, suppose we wish to know the numerical value of a population mean, which is a parameter. We may draw a sample from the population, compute the sample mean, which is a statistic, and use this statistic to estimate the unknown population parameter.

A Limitation of Descriptive Measures   As we have seen, when we group measurements into class intervals to construct frequency distributions, there is a considerable loss of detail because measurements lose their identity. Even more detail is lost when we compute a descriptive measure to represent the central tendency or the dispersion of a data set. You should keep this limitation in mind when you use a descriptive measure—a single numerical value—to convey information about a data set that contains many individual measurements.

MEASURES OF CENTRAL TENDENCY

Even when you draw a collection of data from a common source, individual observations are not likely to have the same value. It is impractical to keep in mind all the values that may be present in a set of data. What we need is some single value that we may consider typical of the set of data as a whole. The need for such a single value is usually met by one of the three measures of central tendency: the *arithmetic mean,* the *median,* and the *mode.*

The Arithmetic Mean The most familiar measure of central tendency is the arithmetic mean. Popularly known as the average, it is sometimes called the *arithmetic average,* or simply the *mean.* We find it by adding all the values in a set of data and dividing the total by the number of values that were summed.

EXAMPLE 2.8.1 The Goddard Bus Company uses extra drivers to handle demands for service beyond its routine schedule. A sample of five extra drivers drove the following number of hours during a certain week:

Driver	A	B	C	D	E
Hours driven	17	28	35	42	45

Find the mean number of hours driven by this sample of drivers.

SOLUTION We add the five numbers showing the hours driven and divide by 5. Thus, we have

(2.8.1)
$$\text{Sample mean} = \frac{\text{sum of all values in the sample}}{\text{number of values in the sample}}$$

For the present example, we have

$$\text{Mean hours driven} = \frac{17 + 28 + 35 + 42 + 45}{5} = \frac{167}{5} = 33.4$$

X designates the variable of interest.

We can represent the calculation of the sample mean in a more concise way by using the capital letter X to designate the variable of interest, which here is the hours driven by extra drivers during a week. Particular values of this variable may be represented by lower-case letters as follows: $x_1, x_2, \ldots, x_n$, where the subscripts refer to the location of the value in the sequence of data. For example, x_1 refers to the first value, x_2 to the second value, and so on, to x_n, which represents the last value in a set of sample data. For the present example, $x_1 =$

17, $x_2 = 28$, $x_3 = 35$, $x_4 = 42$, and $x_5 = 45$. Note that the subscript n also indicates the size of the sample. If $\bar{x}$ denotes the mean of the sample, we can write Equation 2.8.1 as

$$(2.8.2) \qquad \bar{x} = \frac{\sum_{i=1}^{n} x_i}{n}$$

where the symbol

$$\sum_{i=1}^{n} \qquad \text{("summation from } i = 1 \text{ to } i = n\text{")}$$

x_i designates a particular value of X

tells us to add the values of X from the first to the last. The subscript i on the x following Σ indicates a typical value from the series of values under study. From now on, we will omit the $i = 1$ and the n when it is clear from the context what they should be. We can write the formula for the sample mean, then, as

$$(2.8.3) \qquad \bar{x} = \frac{\Sigma x_i}{n}$$

$\bar{x}$ = sample mean

A more complete discussion of summation notation appears in Appendix V.

Other capital letters, such as Y and Z, may also be used to designate variables of interest.

On occasion, we may have some finite population of values for which we want to compute the mean. The procedure for calculating the population mean is exactly the same as that for calculating the sample mean.

μ = population mean

To distinguish a sample mean from a population mean, we designate the population mean by the Greek letter μ (pronounced "mu"), and use the letter N to indicate the size of a finite population. Thus, the formula for calculating the mean of a finite population is given by

$$(2.8.4) \qquad \mu = \frac{\sum_{i=1}^{N} x_i}{N}$$

or simply

$$(2.8.5) \qquad \mu = \frac{\Sigma x_i}{N}$$

$\bar{x}$ is the balance point of a data set

You can think of the mean as the *balance point* of a set of data. Think of the number line as a balance bar and the different values in the data set as cubes of equal weight. If you place each of the "cubes" on the "balance bar" at a position corresponding to its numerical value, and if you place a fulcrum at a point on the balance bar corresponding to the numerical value of the mean, the bar will be in perfect balance.

EXAMPLE 2.8.2   Suppose that we want to find the mean of the following sample of values: 1, 1, 2, 5, 2, 2, 8.

SOLUTION   By Equation 2.8.3, we find that

$$\bar{x} = \frac{1 + 1 + 2 + 5 + 2 + 2 + 8}{7} = \frac{21}{7} = 3$$

Figure 2.8.1 illustrates the concept that the mean is the balance point for the data. We can see here that the sum of the distances of the observations to the left of the mean plus the sum of the distances of the observations to the right of the mean equals zero. That is,

$$[3(-1) + 2(-2)] + [1(+2) + 1(+5)] = -7 + (+7) = 0$$

This demonstrates another property of the arithmetic mean: *the sum of the deviations $(x_i - \bar{x})$ of a set of observations about their mean is equal to zero.* We may express this property symbolically as follows:

$$\Sigma(x_i - \bar{x}) = 0$$

For our present example, we have

$$\begin{aligned}\Sigma(x_i - \bar{x}) &= (1 - 3) + (1 - 3) + (2 - 3) + (5 - 3) + (2 - 3) \\ &\quad + (2 - 3) + (8 - 3) \\ &= (-2) + (-2) + (-1) + (+2) + (-1) + (-1) + (+5) \\ &= 0\end{aligned}$$

Since $\bar{x}$ is computed from a sample, it is called a *statistic*, whereas μ, computed from a population of data, is called a *parameter*.

FIGURE 2.8.1   The mean is the balance point of a data set

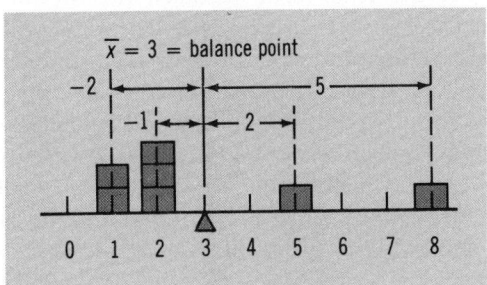

The properties of the arithmetic mean include the following:

1. For a given set of data, there is one, and only one, arithmetic mean.
2. Its meaning is easily understood.
3. Since every value goes into its computation, it is affected by the magnitude of each value. Because of this property, the arithmetic mean may not be the best measure of central tendency when one or two extreme values are present in a set of data.
4. The mean, unlike some descriptive measures whose values may be determined by inspection, is a computed measure, and therefore it can be manipulated algebraically. This property makes it an especially useful measure for statistical inference purposes.

The Weighted Mean When the frequency of occurrence of the individual measurements to be averaged varies, we may compute the mean quickly by multiplying each measurement by its frequency of occurrence, adding these products, and dividing by the sum of the frequencies. Suppose, for example, that we wish to find the mean age $\bar{x}$ of a sample of ten students whose ages x_i, in years, are as follows: 19, 19, 20, 20, 20, 21, 21, 21, 21, 22. We see that there are two 19s, three 20s, four 21s, and one 22. Multiplying each different age by its frequency and adding the products yields

$$2(19) + 3(20) + 4(21) + 1(22) = 204$$

The sum of the frequencies is $2 + 3 + 4 + 1 = 10$, and $\bar{x} = 204/10 = 20.4$. Thus, we see that in the computation of the mean each different measurement is *weighted* by its frequency of occurrence. Consequently, we may refer to the frequencies as weights and to the resulting mean as a *weighted mean.*

In general, if we designate the weights by w_i, a formula for computing a weighted sample mean $\bar{x}_w$ may be expressed as follows:

$$\bar{x}_w = \frac{\Sigma w_i x_i}{\Sigma w_i}$$

A weighted population mean is computed in the same manner.

Sometimes the measurements to be averaged vary in importance rather than frequency of occurrence. In such cases, a weighted mean will provide an average that reflects the relative importance of the individual measurements.

A familiar example of measurements that frequently vary in importance is the grades assigned to the various components of a student's final course grade. Suppose that the final grade in a course is to be based on three tests, which count 25% each, a final exam, which counts 20%, and a term project, which counts 5%. The weights, then, are 25, 25, 25, 20, and 5, and the sum of the weights is 100. If a student makes scores of 80, 85, and 90 on the three tests, 75 on the final exam, and 90 on the term project, the student's final grade will be

$$\mu_w = \frac{\Sigma w_i x_i}{\Sigma w_i} = \frac{25(80) + 25(85) + 25(90) + 20(75) + 5(90)}{100}$$

$$= \frac{8325}{100} = 83.25$$

The Median   The *median* is that value above which half the values lie and below which the other half lie. If the number of items is odd, the median is the value of the middle item of an ordered array, when the items are arranged in ascending (or descending) order of magnitude. If the number of items is even, none of the items has an equal number of values above and below it. In this event, the median is equal to the mean, or average, of the two middle values.

EXAMPLE 2.8.3   Five households have total annual incomes of $10,000, $24,500, $15,000, $21,500, and $13,000. We wish to find the median total income for these five households.

SOLUTION   We first arrange the values in order of magnitude:

$10,000   13,000   15,000   21,500   24,500

The median is the middle value, $15,000. Suppose that there had been a sixth value of $9,000. The ordered array would have been

$9,000   10,000   13,000   15,000   21,500   24,500

and the median would have been ($13,000 + $15,000)/2 = $14,000.
    Properties of the median include the following:

1. The median always exists in a set of numerical data. For a given set of data, there is only one median.
2. The median is not often affected by extreme values, whereas the mean is. Because of this property, the median is frequently the central tendency measure of choice for a data set that is skewed.
3. The median can be used to characterize qualitative data. For example, a product might be marketed in three quality categories—good, better, and best— where the quality of the product falling in the "better" category is considered "average."
4. The median is easy to calculate unless a large number of values are involved.
5. The median for a data set can be located even when the data are incomplete, provided that the number and general location of all the measurements are known and that exact information regarding the magnitude of measurements near the center of the data set is available.

The Mode   The mode for ungrouped discrete data is the value that occurs most frequently. If all the values in a set of data are different, there is no mode. In the preceding family income example, there is no mode because all the values are different.

EXAMPLE 2.8.4   Here is a set of data that does have a mode. A clerical pool consists of 10 employees whose ages are 18, 19, 21, 22, 22, 22, 26, 32, 35, and 36. The most frequently occurring, or *modal*, age is 22. Some sets of data may have two modes, in which case the data are said to be *bimodal*. If the ages of the employees had been 18, 19, 21, 22, 22, 22, 26, 32, 32, and 32, the two modes would be 22 and 32. A set of data can have more than two modes, but the usefulness of indicating a large number of modes is questionable.

In a symmetrical distribution the mean median, and mode are equal.

In symmetrical distributions, the mean and median are identical in value. In asymmetrical distributions, these values are not equal. If the mean is larger than the median, the distribution is skewed to the right. If the mean is smaller than the median, the distribution is skewed to the left. Figure 2.8.2 shows the relative positions of the mean, median, and mode for a symmetrical and for some asymmetrical distributions. When a distribution has a graph that looks like Figure 2.8.2*b*, we say that the distribution is *skewed to the left*. A distribution whose graph looks like Figure 2.8.2*c* is said to be *skewed to the right*. A symmetrical distribution, such as the one shown in Figure 2.8.2*a*, is not skewed.

Population measures of central tendency are often called *location parameters*, since they "locate" the position of a population's frequency distribution on the horizontal axis. Consider two population distributions with means μ_A and μ_B such that μ_A is smaller than μ_B. If you graph the two populations on the same horizontal axis, the population with mean μ_A will be located to the left of the population with mean μ_B. Although the mode is a location parameter, it does not always indicate the center of a population.

Of the three measures of central tendency we have discussed, the mean plays the most important role in the type of statistics presented in this text.

THE GEOMETRIC MEAN

There are some problems requiring the calculation of an average for which none of the averages discussed so far is appropriate. For example, when we wish to obtain the average value of a series of ratios, percentages, or rates of change, the arithmetic mean proves to be an inadequate choice for the job. The measure needed in these situations is the *geometric mean*.

The *geometric mean* of a series of *n* measurements is the *n*th root of the product of the *n* measurements.

To find the geometric mean of three measurements, for example, we multiply the three measurements together and take the cube root of the resulting product. Suppose that we wish to find the geometric mean of the measurements 4, 8, and

FIGURE 2.8.2   Locations of mean, median, and mode for different distributions

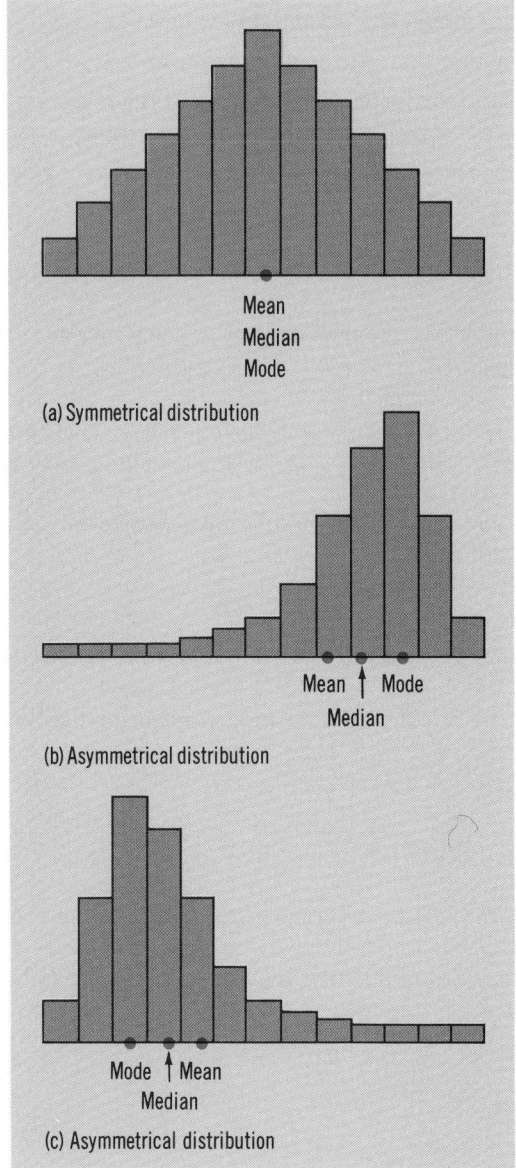

(a) Symmetrical distribution

(b) Asymmetrical distribution

(c) Asymmetrical distribution

16. The product of these three numbers is $4 \times 8 \times 16 = 512$. The geometric mean, then, is the cube root of 512, which is 8.

Calculating the geometric mean according to its basic definition can be a laborious task. By the use of logarithms, however, the measure may be computed with relative ease.

The following are some characteristics of the geometric mean:

1. It is not unduly influenced by extreme values.
2. It is always smaller than the arithmetic mean.
3. It is a meaningful measure only when all of the measurements are positive.
4. The product of a series of measurements remains unchanged if the geometric mean of the measurements is substituted for each measurement in the series.

THE HARMONIC MEAN

Another average that is preferred over other such measures in certain situations is the *harmonic mean*.

The *harmonic mean* of a series of measurements is the reciprocal of the arithmetic mean of the reciprocals of the individual measurements.

Consider, for example, the n sample measurements $x_1, x_2, \ldots, x_n$. The harmonic mean (H) of these measurements is

$$H = \frac{1}{[(1/x_1) + (1/x_2) + \cdots + (1/x_n)]/n} = \frac{1}{\Sigma(1/x_i)/n} = \frac{n}{\Sigma(1/x_i)}$$

To illustrate, let us calculate the harmonic mean for the three measurements 4, 8, and 16. We have

$$H = \frac{1}{[(1/4) + (1/8) + (1/16)]/3} = \frac{1}{(7/16)/3} = \frac{3}{7/16} = 6.86$$

The harmonic mean is the average of choice when the average of time rates is required. It has decided advantages when the data to be averaged are certain types of price data. Consequently, the harmonic mean finds frequent use in the field of economics.

MEASURES OF DISPERSION

Once we have computed the mean of a set of data, we want to know the extent to which the values differ from this mean. We use the term *dispersion* to describe the degree to which a set of values vary about their mean. Other terms that convey this same concept are *variation, scatter,* and *spread*. When the values in a sample or population are all close to the mean, they exhibit less dispersion than when some of the values are much larger and/or much smaller than the mean. Figure 2.8.3 shows frequency polygons for two frequency distributions. They

FIGURE 2.8.3 Two frequency distributions with equal means but different amounts of dispersion

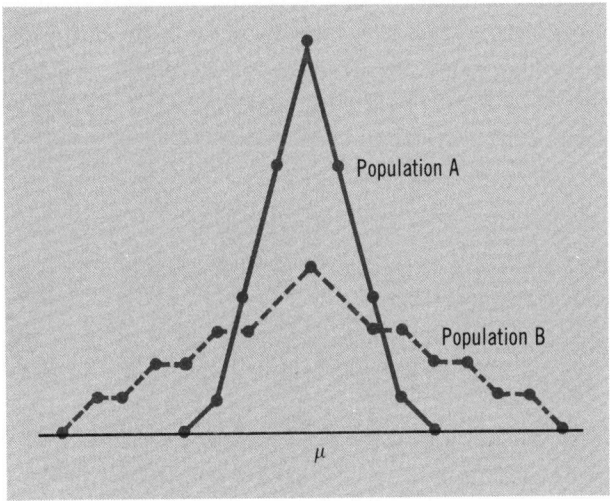

both have the same mean, but they differ with respect to variability. Four descriptive measures used to express the amount of dispersion present in a set of data are the *range*, the *average deviation*, the *variance*, and the *standard deviation*.

The Range The *range* is the difference between the largest and the smallest values in a set of data.

EXAMPLE 2.8.5 Ten typists applying for a job with The Harris Bank and Trust Company made the following scores on a typing speed test.

Applicant	1	2	3	4	5	6	7	8	9	10
Speed (words/min)	54	55	79	70	86	81	75	89	72	68

SOLUTION We wish to get an idea of the variation in typing speeds. We compute the range by subtracting the smallest score from the largest score. That is, for these data, Range = 89 − 54 = 35.

The range is easy to compute. However, it is usually an unsatisfactory measure of dispersion, since only two values in a set of data are used in computing it. In other words, the range does not use all the information available in the data it is supposed to describe.

The Average Deviation The *average deviation* expresses the average amount by which the values in a sample or population differ from their mean. When computed from a sample, the average deviation takes into account the deviation of each value from the mean, $x_i - \bar{x}$. However, the sum of these deviations, and hence their mean, is always equal to 0, as shown in Example 2.8.2. Therefore, to get a valuable measure of dispersion, we must modify the procedure. An appropriate modification is to take the mean of the deviations while ignoring the signs. That is, we add the absolute values of the deviations and divide by n to obtain the average deviation. The procedure is expressed in the following formula:

(2.8.6)
$$\text{Average deviation} = \frac{\Sigma \, |x_i - \bar{x}|}{n}$$

EXAMPLE 2.8.6   Let us use the data of Example 2.8.5 to show how to compute the average deviation.

SOLUTION   Since the mean of these data is 72.9, we have

$$\text{Average deviation} = \frac{|54 - 72.9| + |55 - 72.9| + \cdots + |68 - 72.9|}{10}$$

$$= \frac{18.9 + 17.9 + \cdots + 4.9}{10} = 9.1$$

Thus, we can say that, on the average, the values differ from their mean by 9.1 words per minute.

The average deviation is an intuitively satisfying measure of dispersion. But its usefulness is limited because it does not lend itself to further mathematical manipulation. Consequently, it is seldom used as a measure of dispersion.

The Variance   The *variance*, like the average deviation, uses all the deviations of values from their mean, that is, $x_i - \bar{x}$. In computing the variance, however, we avoid negative differences by squaring, rather than by taking absolute values. We may compute the variance of a sample of data, then, from the formula

(2.8.7)
$$\text{Sample variance} = \frac{\Sigma(x_i - \bar{x})^2}{n}$$

(As we explain in more detail later, we use the sample variance computed by this formula for descriptive purposes only.) Thus, the variance is also a kind of average. It is the average of the squares of the deviations of the individual values from their mean. The numerator of Equation 2.8.7 is called the *sum of squares about the mean. Note:* For any set of values, the sum of squared deviations from the mean is smaller than the sum of squared deviations from any other point.

The sample variance has two functions in statistical analysis. First, it is used as a measure of the dispersion present in the sample. Second, it is used to *estimate* the variance of the population from which the sample was drawn. You will use the sample variance for this purpose when you study statistical inference. When we use it as a measure of the dispersion present in a sample, the sample variance should be computed by Equation 2.8.7. However, when we use the sample variance as an estimate of the population variance, it is better to divide the sum of squares about the mean by $n - 1$ rather than n. (Chapter 6 discusses this subject more fully.) Since the main object of computing a sample variance is usually to estimate the population variance, the following formula is almost always used in defining the sample variance:

Sample variance =
$$s^2 = \frac{\sum (x_i - \bar{x})^2}{n - 1}$$

(2.8.8)
$$s^2 = \frac{\Sigma(x_i - \bar{x})^2}{n - 1}$$

Unless otherwise specified, we will use Formula 2.8.8 to calculate the sample variance.

The Standard Deviation   The variance is expressed in square units. If the data are measured in feet, the variance is expressed in feet *squared*. In statistical analysis, you often want to have a measure of dispersion that is expressed in the same units as the original observations. We obtain such a measure, called the *standard deviation*, by taking the positive square root of the variance. That is, the sample standard deviation is equal to

(2.8.9)
$$s = \sqrt{\frac{\Sigma(x_i - \bar{x})^2}{n - 1}}$$

EXAMPLE 2.8.7   Let us compute the variance and standard deviation for the typing speed scores given in Example 2.8.5.

SOLUTION

$$s^2 = \frac{(54 - 72.9)^2 + (55 - 72.9)^2 + \cdots + (68 - 72.9)^2}{10 - 1}$$

$$= \frac{1248.9}{9} = 138.77$$

$$s = \sqrt{138.77} = 11.8$$

These formulas for the standard deviation and variance are known as *definitional* or *conceptual* formulas because they are literal representations of the definitions and concepts involved. Learning these formulas helps convey the concepts.

The computational formula may save time.

When the computations involve a large number of values, using the definitional formulas without a computer may be tedious. There are alternative, less cumbersome formulas, called *computational formulas*, that yield exactly the same results as the definitional formulas. These are not approximations, but shortcut formulas algebraically derived from the definitional formulas. Their purpose is to lighten your computational burden, especially when you are making computations on a desk calculator or by hand.

There are three shortcut formulas for the sample variance. They are

(2.8.10)
$$s^2 = \frac{\Sigma x_i^2 - \dfrac{(\Sigma x_i)^2}{n}}{n - 1}$$

(2.8.11)
$$s^2 = \frac{n\Sigma x_i^2 - (\Sigma x_i)^2}{n(n - 1)}$$

(2.8.12)
$$s^2 = \frac{\Sigma x_i^2 - n\bar{x}^2}{n - 1}$$

EXAMPLE 2.8.8 Let us compute the variance for the data of Example 2.8.5 by each of the three equations.

SOLUTION

By Equation 2.8.10,

$$s^2 = \frac{(54^2 + 55^2 + \cdots + 68^2) - (54 + 55 + \cdots + 68)^2/10}{9}$$

$$= \frac{(54{,}393) - (729)^2/10}{9} = 138.77$$

By Equation 2.8.11,

$$s^2 = \frac{10(54^2 + 55^2 + \cdots + 68^2) - (54 + 55 + \cdots + 68)^2}{(10)(9)} = 138.77$$

By Equation 2.8.12,

$$s^2 = \frac{(54{,}393) - 10(72.9)^2}{9} = 138.77$$

The standard deviation, as before, is

$$s = \sqrt{138.77} = 11.8$$

In Equation 2.8.8, the numerator, as we see, is a sum of squared quantities. The quantities squared are the differences between the sample mean $\bar{x}$ and the individual observations x_i. For short, we call the numerator of Equation 2.8.8 the *sum of squares*. The denominator, $n - 1$, is called the *degrees of freedom*. The concept of degrees of freedom is rooted in mathematical theory that is beyond the scope of this text.

σ^2 = population variance

Population Variance and Standard Deviation The variance and standard deviation of a *population* are designated, respectively, by the symbols σ^2 and σ. We may compute the variance σ^2 of a finite population by any one of the following formulas:

$$(2.8.13) \qquad \sigma^2 = \frac{\Sigma(x_i - \mu)^2}{N}$$

$$(2.8.14) \qquad \sigma^2 = \frac{\Sigma x_i^2 - \frac{(\Sigma x_i)^2}{N}}{N}$$

$$(2.8.15) \qquad \sigma^2 = \frac{N\Sigma x_i^2 - (\Sigma x_i)^2}{N \cdot N}$$

or

$$(2.8.16) \qquad \sigma^2 = \frac{\Sigma x_i^2}{N} - \mu^2$$

We find the standard deviation of the population by taking the positive square root of σ^2. Suppose, for example, that we have a population of size $N = 4$ consisting of the values 10, 4, 3, and 7. By Equation 2.8.15, we find that

$$\sigma^2 = \frac{4(10^2 + 4^2 + 3^2 + 7^2) - (10 + 4 + 3 + 7)^2}{4(4)} = 7.5$$

The standard deviation, then, is $\sigma = \sqrt{7.5} = 2.74$.

COEFFICIENT OF VARIATION

Sometimes the need arises to compare the variability present in two sets of data. This usually can be done satisfactorily by comparing the two variances or standard deviations if the data satisfy two conditions: (1) the same unit of measurement is employed in both data sets and (2) the means of the two data sets are approximately equal. If either of these conditions is not met, we need a relative measure of dispersion for use in comparing the variability of the two data sets. Such a relative measure of dispersion is the *coefficient of variation*.

The sample *coefficient of variation* (CV) is equal to the ratio of the standard deviation to the mean. That is,

$$CV = s/\bar{x}$$

Suppose, for example, that we wish to compare the variability in dwelling size of dwelling units in Area A with the variability of those in Area B. We have the following information:

Area A: $\bar{x} = 1,000$ square feet, $s = 50$ square feet
Area B: $\bar{x} = 3,000$ square feet, $s = 300$ square feet

If we use the standard deviations to compare the variability, we find that the standard deviation for Area B is six times as large as the standard deviation for Area A. Now let us compute the coefficient of variation for the two areas:

$$CV(A) = 50/1,000 = 0.05, \quad CV(B) = 300/3,000 = 0.10$$

We see that when we use the coefficients of variation as measures of variability the dwelling unit sizes in Area B are only twice as variable as those in Area A.

The coefficient of variation is frequently multiplied by 100 and expressed as a percent. Note that the coefficient of variation is independent of the unit of measurement. Since both the mean and standard deviation are expressed in the same measurement units, these units cancel out in the calculation of the ratio.

COMPUTER **ANALYSIS**

Descriptive measures such as means, medians, variances, and standard deviations can be computed much more rapidly and with greater accuracy on a computer than by hand or on a calculator. This is particularly true when large data sets are involved. You are encouraged to use a computer, whenever possible, to work the exercises in this chapter that require the calculation of descriptive measures. The STAT+ microcomputer software package, for example, computes the mean, median, range, variance, and standard deviation for both grouped and ungrouped data.

To use STAT+ for computing descriptive measures, we make appropriate choices from a series of menus, enter the data, and request the calculations. Figure 2.8.4 shows the STAT+ printout for the typing speed data of Example 2.8.5. As you see, there are two sets of descriptive measures in the printout. In the first set, labeled "To Describe This Data Set," the variance and standard deviation are computed with the formula that has n as the denominator. In the set labeled "To Estimate the Parent Population," the variance and standard deviation are computed with the formula that has $n - 1$ as the denominator.

When the data to be described are in column 1, we use the command DESCRIBE C1 to obtain the descriptive measures from the MINITAB software package. The resulting printout for the data of Example 2.8.5 is shown in Figure 2.8.5.

On the MINITAB printout, TRMEAN stands for *trimmed mean*. The trimmed mean, instead of the arithmetic mean, is sometimes used as a measure of central

FIGURE 2.8.4   Computer-generated descriptive measures for the typing speed data of Example 2.8.5 (STAT+ printout)

```
        FOR DATA SET SPEED WITH 10 OBSERVATIONS
        (ALL ESTIMATES BASED ON UNGROUPED DATA)
            To Describe this Data Set...
    RANGE                       35.0000    MEDIAN    73.5000
    VARIANCE                   124.8900    MEAN      72.9000
    STANDARD DEVIATION          11.1754
            To Estimate the Parent Population...
    VARIANCE                   138.7667    MEAN      72.9000
    STANDARD DEVIATION          11.7799
```

FIGURE 2.8.5   Computer-generated descriptive measures for the typing speed data of Example 2.8.5 (MINITAB printout)

```
          N      MEAN     MEDIAN    TRMEAN    STDEV    SEMEAN
C1       10     72.90      73.50     73.25    11.78      3.73

         MIN      MAX         Q1        Q3
C1     54.00    89.00      64.75     82.25
```

tendency. It is computed after some of the extreme values have been discarded. The trimmed mean, therefore, does not have the disadvantage of being influenced unduly by extreme values, as is the case with the arithmetic mean. The term SEMEAN stands for *standard error of the mean*. This measure, as well as Q1 (the first quartile) and Q3 (the third quartile), is discussed later in the text.

CHEBYSHEV'S THEOREM

We noted earlier that when all the values in a set of data are located near their mean they exhibit a small amount of variation or dispersion. And those sets of data in which some values are located far from their mean have a large amount of dispersion. Expressing these relationships in terms of the standard deviation, which measures dispersion, we can say that when the values of a set of data are concentrated near their mean, the standard deviation is small. When the values of a set of data are scattered widely about the mean, the standard deviation is large. If the standard deviation computed from a set of data is small, the values are concentrated near the mean. If the standard deviation is large, the values from which it is computed are dispersed widely about their mean.

A useful rule illustrating the relationship between dispersion and standard deviation is given by *Chebyshev's theorem*, named after the Russian mathematician P. L. Chebyshev (1821–1894). This theorem enables us to calculate for any set of data (either sample or population) the minimum proportion of values that can be expected to lie within a specified number of standard deviations of the mean. The theorem tells us that at least 75% of the values in a set of data can be expected to fall within *two* standard deviations of the mean, at least 88.9% within *three* standard deviations of the mean, and at least 96% within *five* standard deviations of the mean. Chebyshev's theorem may be stated in general terms as follows:

> Given a set of n observations $x_1, x_2, x_3, \ldots, x_n$ on the variable X, the probability is at least $(1 - 1/k^2)$ that X will take on a value within k (where $k > 1$) standard deviations of the mean of the set of observations.

Chebyshev's theorem is applicable to any set of observations, so we can use it for either samples or populations. Let us now see how we can apply it in practice.

Suppose that a set of data has a mean of 150 and a standard deviation of 25. By Chebyshev's theorem, the probability is at least $1 - 1/(2)^2 = 0.75$ that X will take on a value within two standard deviations of the mean. Since $2(25) = 50$, the probability is at least 0.75 that X will take on a value between $150 - 50 = 100$ and $150 + 50 = 200$. Consequently, we can say that we can expect at least 75% of the values to be between 100 and 200. By similar calculations, we find that we can expect at least 88.9% to be between 75 and 225, and at least 96% to be between 25 and 275. Suppose that another set of data has the same mean, 150, but a standard deviation of 10. Applying Chebyshev's theorem, for this set of data we can expect at least 75% of the values to be between 130 and 170, at least 88.9% to be between 120 and 180, and at least 96% to be between 100 and 200. Thus, the intervals computed for the latter set of data are all narrower than those for the former. Therefore, we see that for a set of data with a small standard deviation a larger proportion of the values will be concentrated near the mean than for a set of data with a large standard deviation. We discuss Chebyshev's theorem again later in the text.

EXERCISES

2.8.1 [C] The Iola Office Supply Company has a fleet of 100 trucks, which it uses for making local deliveries. The following are the number of miles that each truck in a sample of 10 was driven during a recent month. Compute the following descriptive measures: (a) the mean, (b) the median, (c) the mode, (d) the range, (e) the variance, and (f) the standard deviation.

Truck number	1	2	3	4	5	6	7	8	9	10
Miles driven ($\times 100$)	23	34	20	18	30	30	30	38	25	27

2.8.2 [C] The following are the amounts for food and lodging claimed on the expense accounts of a sample of 12 salespersons for the same day. For these data, compute: (a) the mean, (b) the median, (c) the mode, (d) the range, (e) the variance, (f) the standard deviation, and (g) the average deviation.

Salesperson	1	2	3	4	5	6	7	8	9	10	11	12
Amount, $	55	84	63	57	52	70	56	68	74	66	68	64

2.8.3 Ⓒ The following are the prices (in thousands of dollars) of 15 condominiums in a sample selected from those in a new complex: 59, 52, 54, 56, 62, 62, 56, 56, 58, 55, 60, 54, 59, 55, 59. For these data, find: (a) the mean, (b) the median, (c) the mode, (d) the range, (e) the variance, and (f) the standard deviation.

2.8.4 Ⓒ The following are the number of miles between home and office of a sample of 10 people who work for Jarvis Properties: 3, 16, 12, 11, 14, 5, 7, 14, 9, 8. For these data, find: (a) the mean, (b) the median, (c) the mode, (d) the range, (e) the variance, and (f) the standard deviation.

2.8.5 A grocer has determined that the mean daily sales of eggs is 100 dozen, with a standard deviation of 10. (a) What minimum percentage of the time can the grocer expect to sell between 80 and 120 dozen per day? (b) Between what two bounds can the grocer expect daily sales to lie at least 96% of the time?

2.9 DESCRIPTIVE MEASURES COMPUTED FROM GROUPED DATA

It is sometimes necessary or convenient to compute descriptive measures from grouped data.

One sometimes needs to compute the various descriptive measures from data that have been grouped into class intervals and presented as a frequency distribution, such as the one shown in Table 2.4.1. If the data consist of a large number of values, and if the computations have to be made by hand or on a calculator, you can save yourself a great deal of labor by grouping the data before you compute the descriptive measures. If you have access to a computer, however, having a large number of values to analyze poses no particular problem. You can usually enter the raw data into the computer with little inconvenience.

Sometimes original data are inaccessible, but a frequency distribution based on the data is available in some published source, such as an annual report. In this case, if you need descriptive measures, use the techniques given in this section.

When data are grouped into class intervals, each observation loses its identity. We can determine the number of observations falling in each of the various class intervals from a frequency distribution, but we cannot determine the actual values associated with the observations. For this reason, when we compute descriptive measures from grouped data, we must make certain assumptions regarding the data. As a consequence of making these assumptions, we must regard the values of the descriptive measures computed in this manner as approximations to the true values. We will indicate the assumptions that have to be made as we consider each measure.

THE MEAN

When we compute the mean from grouped data, we make the assumption that each observation falling within a given class interval is equal to the value of the midpoint of that interval. The midpoint of a class interval is called the *class*

To compute the mean, assume that all values in an interval are equal to the class mark.

mark. We obtain the class mark by adding the respective class limits and dividing by 2. Consider the data on employee ages in Table 2.4.1. To calculate the mean for this frequency distribution, we assume that the 2 observations in the first class interval are both equal to 17, the 10 observations in the second class interval are equal to 22, and so on. Of course, for a given frequency distribution, it is unlikely that all the observations in the class intervals have values that are actually equal to the class marks. We make this assumption with the hope that the errors that it introduces will average out. Experience has shown that the assumption is generally satisfactory, as are the assumptions made about the other descriptive measures computed from grouped data.

Since each observation takes on the value of the class mark of the interval in which it falls, we compute the mean by multiplying each class mark by its corresponding frequency. Then we add the resulting products and divide the total by the number of observations. We may express the procedure for sample data by

$$\bar{x} = \frac{\sum_{i=1}^{k} x_i f_i}{n}$$

(2.9.1)

where k = the number of class intervals, x_i = the class mark of the ith class interval, and f_i = the frequency of the ith class interval.

Note that Equation 2.9.1 resembles Equation 2.8.2, the formula for computing the mean from ungrouped data. The numerator of Equation 2.9.1 illustrates an alternative way of finding the sum of a set of numbers when some of them are duplicated. For example, suppose we have the numbers 2, 2, 2, 3, 3, 6, 6, 6, 6. We can find the sum of these numbers by simple addition:

$$2 + 2 + 2 + 3 + 3 + 6 + 6 + 6 + 6 = 36$$

This is the procedure followed in obtaining the numerator of Equation 2.8.2. Alternatively, we can find the sum as follows:

$$3(2) + 2(3) + 4(6) = 6 + 6 + 24 = 36$$

This is the procedure followed in computing the numerator of Equation 2.9.1.

The mean computed by Equation 2.9.1 is an example of a weighted mean. It is a mean of the class marks in which each is weighted by the frequency with which it is represented in the frequency distribution.

To compute the variance and standard deviation, assume that all values in a class interval are equal to the class mark.

THE VARIANCE AND STANDARD DEVIATION

We make the same assumption regarding the values assumed by the observations when we compute the variance and standard deviation from grouped data. Consequently, the definitional or conceptual formula for the sample variance is

TABLE 2.9.1 Intermediate calculations for computing descriptive measures for the frequency distribution of Table 2.4.1

Class Interval	Class Mark (x_i)	Frequency (f_i)	$x_i f_i$	$x_i^2 f_i$
15–19	17	2	34	578
20–24	22	10	220	4,840
25–29	27	19	513	13,851
30–34	32	27	864	27,648
35–39	37	16	592	21,904
40–44	42	10	420	17,640
45–49	47	6	282	13,254
50–54	52	5	260	13,520
55–59	57	3	171	9,747
60–64	62	2	124	7,688
Total		100	3,480	130,670

(2.9.2)
$$s^2 = \frac{\sum_{i=1}^{k} (x_i - \bar{x})^2 f_i}{n - 1}$$

and the computational formula is

(2.9.3)
$$s^2 = \frac{n\sum_{i=1}^{k} x_i^2 f_i - (\sum_{i=1}^{k} x_i f_i)^2}{n(n - 1)}$$

We find the standard deviation by taking the square root of s^2.

We may use the data of Table 2.4.1 to show how to compute the mean, variance, and standard deviation. Table 2.9.1 gives the necessary intermediate calculations. For the mean, we have

$$\bar{x} = \frac{3480}{100} = 34.8$$

For the variance, we have

$$s^2 = \frac{100(130,670) - (3480)^2}{(100)(99)} = 96.63$$

and for the standard deviation,

$$s = \sqrt{96.63} = 9.8$$

The formulas in this section have implied that the values used in the calculations are those of a sample. To convert these formulas to formulas for computing the corresponding descriptive measures from a finite population, substitute μ for

$\bar{x}$, σ^2 for s^2, and N for n and $n - 1$ wherever they appear in Equations 2.9.1 through 2.9.3. That is,

$$\mu = \frac{\sum_{i=1}^{k} x_i f_i}{N}$$

$$\sigma^2 = \frac{\sum_{i=1}^{k} (x_i - \mu)^2 f_i}{N}$$

$$= \frac{N\sum_{i=1}^{k} x_i^2 f_i - (\sum_{i=1}^{k} x_i f_i)^2}{N \cdot N}$$

THE MEDIAN

We may also compute the median from grouped data. We defined this measure of central tendency earlier as the value in a set of data above and below which half the values lie. This definition holds when the data are in the form of a frequency distribution. But since the individual values in a frequency distribution are not identifiable, we cannot find the exact value of the median.

> The *median* for a frequency distribution is that value, or point, on the horizontal axis of the histogram of the distribution at which a perpendicular line divides the area of the histogram into two equal parts.

To compute the median, assume that the values in a class interval are evenly distributed over the interval.

For this definition to be valid, we must assume that the values in each class interval are evenly distributed over the entire interval. Figure 2.9.1 shows the location of the median of a set of data represented by a histogram.

The first step in computing the median for a frequency distribution is to determine the class interval in which it is located. We do this by finding which interval contains the $n/2$ value. For the employee-ages example, $n/2 = 50$. Table

FIGURE 2.9.1 Histogram showing median

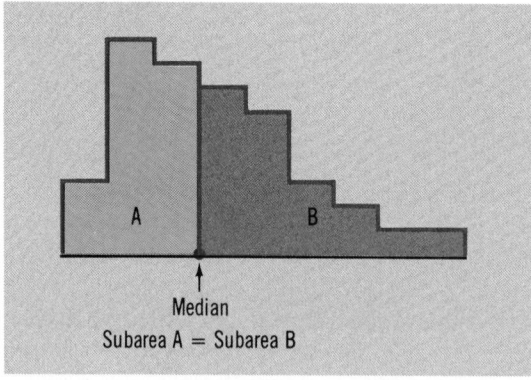

Median
Subarea A = Subarea B

2.4.2, the cumulative frequency distribution, shows that the 50th value is located in the fourth class interval. In Table 2.4.2, 31 values are less than 29.5, the *true* upper limit of the third interval. Thus, that point is only $50 - 31 = 19$ values away from the median. Assume that the values in the fourth class interval are evenly distributed throughout the interval. Then, since there are 27 values in the fourth interval, we can reason that the median is that value which is 19/27 of the way into the fourth interval. To obtain the value of the median, we multiply 19/27 by 5, the width of the class interval, and add the product to 29.5, the true lower limit of the fourth class interval. We have, then, for the employee-ages data,

$$\text{Median} = 29.5 + \frac{19}{27}(5) = 33.0$$

In general, we find the median of a set of data, either a sample or a population, from

(2.9.4)
$$\text{Median} = L + \frac{j}{f}W$$

where L = the true lower limit of the class interval in which the median is located

j = the number of values still needed to reach the median after the lower limit of the interval containing the median has been reached

f = the frequency in the class interval containing the median

W = the width of the class interval

To summarize the calculation of the median from grouped data, we present the following example.

EXAMPLE 2.9.1   Table 2.9.2 shows the frequency distribution of the number of years with their last employer of 70 persons who recently retired from their jobs. We wish to compute the median.

TABLE 2.9.2   Number of years with last employer of 70 recently retired persons and information for calculation of the median number of years

Number of Years	f	Cumulative f
0– 9	8	8
10–19	13	21
20–29	15	36
30–39	21	57
40–49	10	67
50–59	3	70
Total	70	

FIGURE 2.9.2   Assumed location of the 27 observations in the fourth class interval of Table 2.4.2

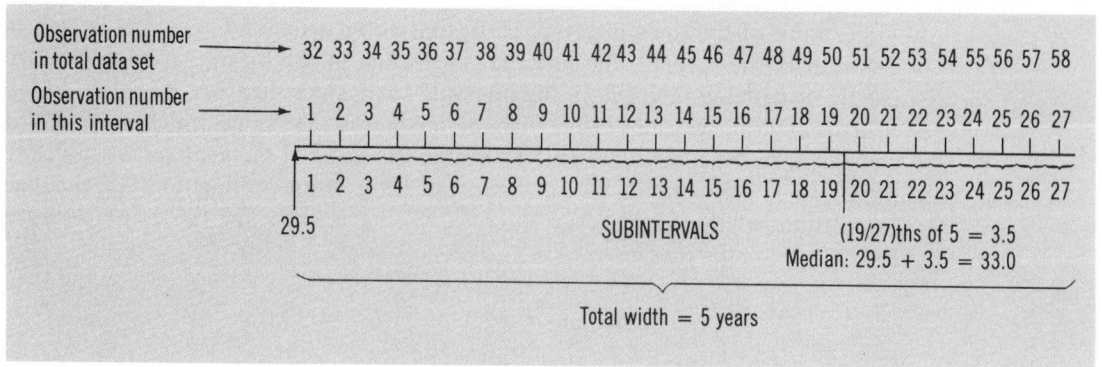

SOLUTION   Table 2.9.2 gives the information necessary for the calculation of the median number of years with last employer for the group.

$$\frac{70}{2} = 35 \qquad M = 19.5 + \frac{14}{15}(10) = 28.83$$

It may seem to you that we should use $(n + 1)/2$, rather than $n/2$, to locate the median. In the employee-ages example, it may appear that $100/2 = 50$ locates the fiftieth observation, rather than an observation that is halfway between the fiftieth and the fifty-first. To show that $100/2 = 50$ locates an observation halfway between the fiftieth and the fifty-first, we must recall that when we calculate the median from grouped data, we assume that the observations in any interval are evenly distributed over the interval. In Example 2.4.1, the 27 observations in the fourth class interval (see Table 2.4.2) are assumed to be evenly distributed over that interval. That is, we think of the interval as being divided into 27 subintervals, each with a width of $5/27$ of a year. One observation is thought of as being located at the midpoint of each of these subintervals. This concept is illustrated in Figure 2.9.2.

When we locate the fiftieth observation in the total data set, we find that it is the nineteenth observation in the fourth class interval. We also see that this fiftieth observation is located at the midpoint of the nineteenth subinterval of the fourth class interval. Moving $19/27$ of the total distance into the class interval, as shown in Figure 2.9.2, brings us to the end of the nineteenth subinterval. This, we see, is a point that is halfway between the fiftieth and fifty-first observations.

THE MODE

When we want to find the mode of a frequency distribution, we usually just specify the *modal class*, which is defined as the *class interval containing the largest number of values*. The modal class for the employee-ages example is the fourth

FIGURE 2.9.3   Histograms that differ with respect to number of modes

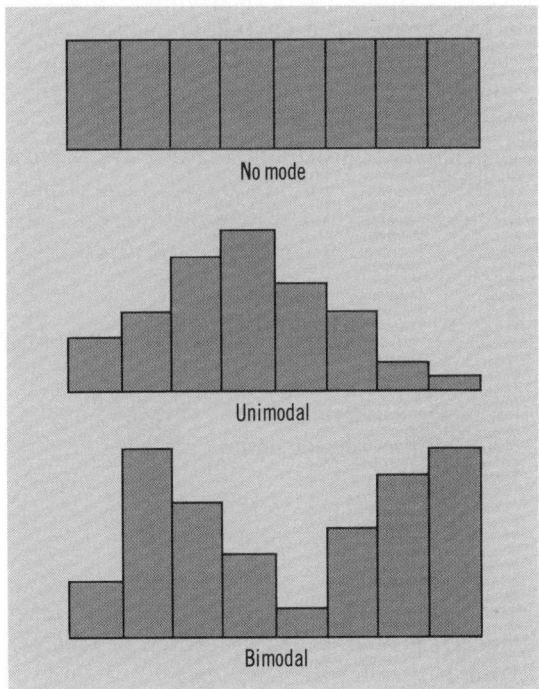

interval, whose limits are 30 and 34. Figure 2.9.3 shows histograms for three sets of data: one that has no mode, one that has one mode, and one that has two modes.

PERCENTILES AND QUARTILES

The mean and median are special cases of a family of parameters called *location parameters*. These parameters "locate" a distribution on the horizontal axis by designating certain positions in terms of the variable assigned to that axis when the distribution is graphed. For example, a distribution with a median of 50 is located to the right of a distribution with a median of 25 when the two distributions are graphed. Other location parameters include *percentiles* and *quartiles*. We define a percentile as follows:

> Given a set of observations $x_1, x_2, \ldots, x_n$, the pth *percentile P* is the value of X such that p percent of the observations are less than P and $(100 - p)$ percent are greater than P.

To distinguish one of the 99 possible percentiles from another, we use appropriate subscripts on P. For example, the tenth percentile is P_{10}, the sixty-fifth percentile is P_{65}, and so on. The median is the fiftieth percentile: P_{50}.

Sometimes, rather than speaking of a percentile, we prefer to speak of a *quantile*. The pth percentile is the $(0.01p)$th quantile. For example, the ninety-fifth percentile is also sometimes called the 0.95th quantile.

Suppose that we wish to find the sixtieth percentile of the distribution given in Table 2.4.1. Since 60% of 100 (the sample size) is 60, the sixtieth observation, when the observations are ordered, is P_{60}, the sixtieth percentile. When we consult the cumulative frequency distribution (Table 2.4.2), we note that the sixtieth observation is in the class interval 35–39. We assume that the values falling in an interval are uniformly distributed over the interval. To find the sixtieth percentile, we use the procedure for computing the median:

$$P_{60} = 34.5 + \frac{60 - 58}{16}(5) = 35.125$$

We say that 60% of the observations are below and 40% are above 35.125. In general, the location of the kth percentile P_k is given by

(2.9.5)
$$P_k = \frac{k}{100}(n + 1)$$

The twenty-fifth percentile is often called the *first quartile* Q_1. The fiftieth percentile (the median) is often called the second or *middle quartile* Q_2, and the seventy-fifth percentile is called the *third quartile* Q_3.

For ungrouped data, the quartiles may be conveniently found as follows:

$$Q_1 = \frac{n + 1}{4}\text{th} \qquad \text{ordered observation}$$

$$Q_2 \text{ (the median)} = \frac{2(n + 1)}{4} = \frac{n + 1}{2}\text{th} \qquad \text{ordered observation}$$

$$Q_3 = \frac{3(n + 1)}{4}\text{th} \qquad \text{ordered observation}$$

BOX-AND-WHISKER PLOTS

The information about a data set that the quartiles provide can be portrayed graphically by what is known as a *box-and-whisker plot*. To construct a box-and-whisker plot, we proceed as follows:

1. The variable of interest is represented on the horizontal axis.

2. A box is drawn in the space above the horizontal axis in such a way that the left end of the box aligns with the first quartile Q_1 and the right end of the box is aligned with the third quartile Q_3.

TABLE 2.9.3   Downtime in hours of 30 machines

4	4	1	4	1	4
6	10	5	5	8	2
1	6	10	3	13	5
8	4	3	9	4	9
1	4	4	11	8	9

3. The box is divided into two parts by a vertical line that aligns with the median.

4. A line, called a *whisker*, is extended from the left end of the box to a point that aligns with the smallest measurement in the data set.

5. Another line, or whisker, is extended from the right end of the box to a point that aligns with the largest measurement in the data set.

The following example illustrates the construction of a box-and-whisker plot.

EXAMPLE 2.9.2   Table 2.9.3 shows the downtime, in hours, recorded for 30 machines owned by a large manufacturing company. The period of time covered was the same for all machines. We wish to construct a box-and-whisker plot for these data.

SOLUTION   The smallest and largest measurements are 1 and 13, respectively. The first quartile is the $(30 + 1)/4 = 7.75$th ordered measurement and is equal to 3.75. The median is the $(30 + 1)/2 = 15.5$th measurement, or 4.5, and the third quartile is the $3(30 + 1)/4 = 23.25$th ordered measurement, which is 8.25. The resulting box-and-whisker plot is shown in Figure 2.9.4.

By looking at a box-and-whisker plot, we can quickly form impressions regarding the amount of spread, location of concentration, and symmetry of the represented data set. A glance at Figure 2.9.4, for example, reveals that 50% of the measurements are between 4 and about 8. The median is 5, and the range is 12. Since the median line is closer to the left end of the box, we conclude that the data are skewed to the right. (In a perfectly symmetrical data set, the median

FIGURE 2.9.4   Box-and-whisker plot of machine downtime

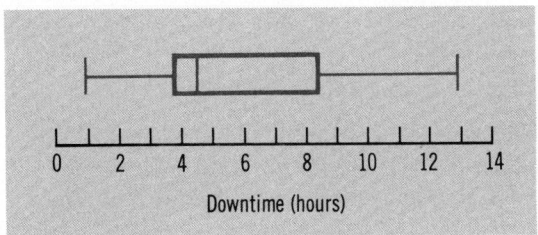

line will be exactly halfway between the two ends of the box, and in a data set that is skewed to the left, the median line will be closer to the right end of the box.)

COMPUTER **ANALYSIS**

MINITAB can construct box-and-whisker plots. To illustrate, let us use the data of Example 2.9.2. We first enter the data into column 1 of the MINITAB workspace. We then issue the following command and subcommands.

MINITAB

```
MTB > BOXPLOT C1;
SUBC > INCREMENT = 3;
SUBC > START = 0 [14].
```

The resulting box-and-whisker plot is shown in Figure 2.9.5. The subcommand INCREMENT is the distance between tick marks (the plus signs) on the horizontal axis. That is, the INCREMENT subcommand specifies the scale on the horizontal axis. The subcommand START specifies the first tick mark on the horizontal axis. The number in brackets indicates the last tick mark to be shown on the horizontal axis.

FIGURE 2.9.5 Computer-generated box-and-whisker plot (MINITAB printout)

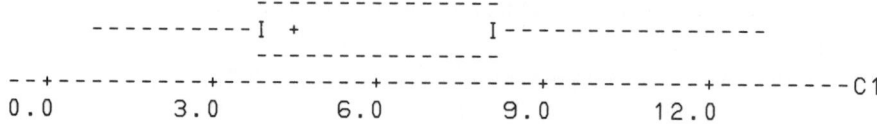

EXERCISES

2.9.1 ⓒ Refer to Exercise 2.5.1. Treat the data as a sample and compute the mean, median, variance, and standard deviation by the methods of this section.

2.9.2 ⓒ Repeat Exercise 2.9.1 using the data of Exercise 2.5.2.

2.9.3 ⓒ Repeat Exercise 2.9.1 using the data of Exercise 2.5.3.

2.9.4 ⓒ The following are the monthly salaries ($\times 10$) quoted on the last 100 listings for junior executive positions filed with the Keystone Employment Agency. Treat these data as a sample and compute the mean, median, variance, and standard deviation. Use the formulas for ungrouped data.

119	183	147	148	143	153	163	169	149	153
126	191	143	156	145	151	163	166	135	152
139	200	133	151	143	161	157	169	137	143
130	202	136	161	143	173	152	162	142	143
142	190	123	191	124	176	142	155	140	137
140	180	117	184	134	184	143	143	150	144
158	171	122	175	130	187	137	146	156	139
159	164	139	160	140	172	132	143	154	145
162	157	139	151	148	164	145	144	154	148
170	152	149	150	155	151	147	148	154	153

2.9.5 Ⓒ Refer to Exercise 2.9.4. Prepare an ordered array, a frequency distribution, a histogram, and a frequency polygon.

2.9.6 Ⓒ Refer to Exercise 2.9.4. Using grouped data formulas, compute the mean, median, variance, and standard deviation. Use intervals of size 10, beginning with 110.

2.9.7 Ⓒ Refer to Exercise 2.9.4. Construct from the data a frequency distribution using class-interval widths of 20. Begin with 100 as the lower limit of the first class interval. Using the formulas for grouped data, compute the mean, median, variance, and standard deviation.

2.9.8 Ⓒ The following is the distribution of commissions earned during a week by 160 salespersons. (a) Compute the mean, median, variance, and standard deviation for these data. (b) Determine the first and third quartiles and the ninety-fifth percentile.

Class interval, $	100–149	150–199	200–249	250–299	300–349	350–399	400–449	450–499
Frequency	19	25	30	25	20	17	14	10

2.9.9 The following are the odometer readings (in thousands of miles) for the last 40 cars that Longwood Motors accepted as trade-ins. Construct a box-and-whisker plot from these data. Describe the data set in the light of your graph.

36	64	76	68	64
76	34	31	53	67
93	40	46	69	32
19	25	67	65	54
81	39	41	54	37
41	79	69	55	55
36	48	46	54	36
57	70	35	51	31

2.10 INDEX NUMBERS

This section introduces another summary statistic, the *index number*, which is useful in describing changes in economic variables over time. Index numbers, essentially, are relative numbers that express the relationship between two figures, one of which is called the *base*. They are used to describe changes in business and economic activity—for example, changes over time in production, wages, prices, and employment.

THE CONSUMER PRICE INDEX

The best known example of an index number is the Consumer Price Index (CPI) for Urban Wage Earners and Clerical Workers. This is the most generally accepted measure of changes in purchasing power. Although there were earlier studies of the cost of living for wage earners, the CPI, formerly called the Cost-of-Living Index, was started by the U. S. government at the time of World War I. From the beginning, the CPI has been used in the evaluation and adjustment of wages by union and management negotiators. It has also been used in other types of contract-escalation provisions: leases, service contracts, annuities and pensions, welfare allowances, and alimony payments. The CPI is also widely used as a guide to decisions about economic policy.

The *CPI Detailed Report* describes the CPI as follows: The Consumer Price Index is a measure of the average change in prices over time in a fixed market basket of goods and services. The Bureau of Labor Statistics (BLS) publishes CPIs for two population groups: (1) a CPI for All Urban Consumers (CPI-U), which covers approximately 80% of the total population, and (2) a CPI for Urban Wage Earners and Clerical Workers (CPI-W), which covers 32% of the total population. The CPI-U includes, in addition to wage earners and clerical workers, groups such as professional, managerial, and technical workers, the self-employed, short-term workers, the unemployed, and retirees and others not in the labor force.

The CPI is based on prices of food, clothing, shelter, and fuels, transportation fares, charges for doctors' and dentists' services, medicines, and the other goods and services that people buy for day-to-day living. Prices are collected in 91 urban areas across the country from about 60,000 housing units and approximately 21,000 retail establishments—department stores, supermarkets, hospitals, filling stations, and other types of stores and service establishments. All taxes directly associated with the purchase and use of the items are included in the index. Prices of food, fuels, and a few other items are obtained every month in all 91 locations. Prices of most other commodities and services are collected every month in the 5 largest geographic areas and every other month in other areas. Prices of most goods and services are obtained by personal visits of the bureau's trained representatives. Mail questionnaires are used to obtain public utility rates, some fuel prices, and prices of certain other items.

In calculating the index, price changes for the various items in each location are averaged together with weights that represent their importance in the spending of the appropriate population group. Local data are then combined to obtain a U.S. city average. Separate indexes are also published by size of city, by region of the country, for crosscalculations of regions and population-size classes, and for 27 local areas. Area indexes do not measure differences in the level of prices among cities; they only measure the average change in prices for each area since the base period.

The indexes measure price change from a designated reference date whose prices equal 100.0. An increase of 203%, for example, is shown as 303.0. This change can also be expressed in dollars as follows: the price of a base period "market basket" of goods and services in the CPI has risen from $10 in 1967 to $30.30.[1]

For further details, see BLS Handbook of Methods, Vol. II, "The Consumer Price Index," Bulletin 2134-2, April 1984, and "The Consumer Price Index: 1987 Revision," BLS Report 736, January 1987.

In addition to the *Consumer Price Index*, there are other indexes that are useful to businesspeople and economists. They include the Federal Reserve's *Industrial Production* index and *Producer Price Indexes* published by the U.S. Department of Labor's Bureau of Labor Statistics.

THE INDUSTRIAL PRODUCTION INDEX

This index is a measure of industrial production expressed as a percentage of output in a reference period. The changes in the physical output of the nation's factories, mines, and electric and gas utilities are represented by 252 individual series in the index. For each individual series, index series relatives are calculated first and are then aggregated in two ways: first, by market groupings, such as consumer goods, equipment, intermediate products, and materials, from which the seasonally adjusted total index is derived; and second, by industry groupings and major aggregates of these groupings, such as durable and nondurable manufacturing, mining, and utilities.

THE PRODUCER PRICE INDEXES

The producer price indexes (PPI) measure average changes in prices received by domestic producers of commodities in all stages of processing. Most of the information used in calculating the indexes is obtained by systematically sampling nearly every industry in the manufacturing and mining sectors of the economy. The PPI program also includes some information from other sectors, such as agriculture, fishing, forestry, services, and gas and electricity. Because producer price indexes are designed to measure only the change in prices received for the output of domestic industries, imports are not included. The sample currently contains about 3,100 commodities and 75,000 quotations per month.

There are three primary systems of indexes within the PPI program. They are (1) stage-of-processing indexes, (2) commodity indexes, and (3) indexes for the net output of industries and their products. The stage-of-processing structure organizes products by class of buyer and degree of fabrication. The entire output of various industries is sampled to derive price indexes for the net output of industries and their products. The commodity structure organizes products by similarity of end use or of material composition.

---

[1]*CPI Detailed Report* (U.S. Department of Labor, Bureau of Labor Statistics), November 1987.

EXERCISES

2.10.1 Consult the "Explanatory Note" section of a recent *Federal Reserve Statistical Release*. Write a brief review of the section covering the following points: market groupings, timing, source data, seasonal adjustment, weights, the formula used, and reliability.

2.10.2 Consult the most recent copy of *Producer Price Indexes*. Select one item from each of the tables and report on the index for each.

2.10.3 Consult the "Technical Notes" section of a recent issue of *Producer Price Indexes*. Write a brief review of the section covering the following points: calculating index changes and seasonally adjusted and unadjusted data.

2.10.4 Read and write a review of the following article: "Revision of the Consumer Price Index Now Under Way," *Monthly Labor Review*, April 1985, pages 27–38. Be sure to answer the following questions:

(a) Why are periodic revisions of the index needed?
(b) What is the geographic coverage?
(c) What is meant by the term "rolling-in" samples?
(d) What are the advantages of these samples?
(e) What improvements in the index did the author anticipate for the revision?

2.10.5 Read and write a review of the following article: "New Basket of Goods and Services Being Priced in Revised CPI," *Monthly Labor Review*, January 1987, pages 3–22. Be sure to answer the following questions:

(a) What are the changes in the expenditure weight definitions?
(b) What were some of the factors that contributed to changes in expenditures for the items in the CPI market basket between the 1972–1973 period and the 1982–1984 period?
(c) What were some of the causes of changes in the market basket?

2.10.6 Read and write a review of the following article: "Indexing—It Grows on You," *Business Horizons*, May/June 1982, pages 3–8. Be sure to answer the following questions:

(a) What does the author mean when he writes that "Indexing, of course, provides no cure"?
(b) What does the author mean by the term "politics of indexing"?
(c) What does the author consider to be the social ramifications of indexing?

2.10.7 Read and write a review of the following article: "Comparison of the Revised and the Old CPI," *Monthly Labor Review*, November 1987, pages 3–6.

2.10.8 Read and write a review of the following publication: *The Consumer Price Index: Concepts and Content over the Years,* U.S. Department of Labor, Bureau of Labor Statistics, May 1978 (Revised), Report 517. Be sure to cover the following points: (a) uses of the CPI, (b) CPI concepts, (c) early history of the CPI, and (d) the various revisions.

TYPES OF ECONOMIC INDEX NUMBERS

There are three important types of economic index numbers: (1) *price indexes* measure the changes in prices paid and prices received by producers and consumers; (2) *quantity indexes* measure changes in production and shipment; and

(3) *value indexes* measure changes in the value of various commodities and activities.

We can construct index numbers from a single series, such as the price of a single commodity. An index number of this type is called a *simple index* or *price relative*. We are often more interested in index numbers that combine figures relating to several variables, such as the prices of several commodities. Index numbers constructed in this manner are called *composite indexes*. We limit our discussion to this type of index.

We may further categorize index numbers on the basis of the mathematical method used in their construction. We construct the *aggregative* type of index by summing (aggregating) figures for one time period, called the *nonbase period*. We compare them with a similar aggregate of figures for another period, called the *base period*. We obtain an *average-of-relatives index* by first calculating a relative for each item and then taking the average of the relatives. We can further classify both aggregative and average-of-relatives indexes as either *weighted* or *unweighted*, depending on whether or not we assign specific weights to the items in the computational process. Actually, the term *unweighted index* may be a misnomer, since all items are weighted equally in the absence of formal weighting factors. The weighting scheme is inherent in the method of calculation. For this reason, some writers refer to the index for which the analyst does not assign weights as a *simple index*.

2.11 AGGREGATIVE PRICE INDEXES

This section discusses the methods of constructing aggregative price indexes. We consider first the unweighted and then the weighted index.

UNWEIGHTED AGGREGATIVE PRICE INDEX

The unweighted aggregative price index is given by

(2.11.1)
$$\left(\frac{\Sigma P_n}{\Sigma P_0}\right) 100$$

where P_0 is the price in the base period and P_n is the price in the nonbase period.

EXAMPLE 2.11.1 To illustrate the construction of an unweighted aggregative price index, consider a collection of five foods consumed by a typical family in a certain city. The base year is 1976 and the nonbase year is 1986. Table 2.11.1 shows the data, which are fictitious.

SOLUTION From the data, we can use Equation 2.11.1 to calculate the following unweighted aggregative index for 1986 on 1976 as a base:

$$\left(\frac{\Sigma P_{86}}{\Sigma P_{76}}\right) 100 = \left(\frac{\$8.83}{\$6.84}\right) 100 = 129.1$$

TABLE 2.11.1 Unit prices for selected food commodities, 1976 and 1986

Food Commodity	Unit Price	
	1976 P_{76}	1986 P_{86}
Meat	$2.12	$2.59
Milk	1.65	2.00
Eggs	0.69	1.00
Bread	0.63	0.90
Coffee	1.75	2.34
Total	$6.84	$8.83

Since

$$\left(\frac{\Sigma P_{76}}{\Sigma P_{76}}\right) 100 = \left(\frac{\$6.84}{\$6.84}\right) 100 = 100$$

the base year index equals 100.

We can interpret the index figure of 129.1 as follows: it would have cost 29.1% more in 1986 than in 1976 to buy the goods in Table 2.11.1. Stated another way, the cost of the items in 1986 is 129.1% of the cost of the same items in 1976.

Generally, the unweighted aggregative index is an unsatisfactory measure because of two limitations. First, the index is unduly influenced by high-priced items. Suppose, for example, that Table 2.11.1 had contained a sixth item that cost $6.50 in 1976 and $4.00 in 1986. The totals for 1976 and 1986 would have been $13.34 and $12.83, respectively. The index, therefore, would have been 100($12.83/$13.34) = 96.2, indicating a decline in price of 3.8%. Thus, one high-priced item would have enough influence to cause the overall index to show a decline, even though five out of six items actually increased in price.

The unweighted aggregative index has some limitations.

The second limitation of the unweighted aggregative index is the effect of the arbitrary nature of the units of measurement for the items. When, for example, the unit for milk is a gallon, the price index is different from the index that results when the unit is a quart.

These limitations indicate a need for a more satisfactory measure. Such a measure is provided by the *weighted aggregative index*.

WEIGHTED AGGREGATIVE INDEX, BASE-YEAR WEIGHTS (LASPEYRES INDEX)

We can overcome the limitations of the aggregative price index just described by the proper use of weights. We can get a better index for the data of Table 2.11.1 by assigning to each item a weight that reflects the amount of each item that the typical family actually buys. These weights, which reflect the amounts or quantities of the items under consideration, are called *quantity weights*.

TABLE 2.11.2   Unit prices, 1976 and 1986, and average weekly quantities bought in 1976, selected food commodities

Food Commodity	Unit Price		Quantity		
	1976 P_{76}	1986 P_{86}	1976 Q_{76}	$P_{76}Q_{76}$	$P_{86}Q_{76}$
Meat	$2.12	$2.59	2	$4.24	$5.18
Milk	1.65	2.00	3	4.95	6.00
Eggs	0.69	1.00	1	0.69	1.00
Bread	0.63	0.90	3	1.89	2.70
Coffee	1.75	2.34	1	1.75	2.34
Total	$6.84	$8.83		$13.52	$17.22

Weights may represent quantities of items bought during either the base period or the nonbase period. Appropriate base-period weights for the data of Table 2.11.1 would be average amounts of each item consumed per week during 1976. If the base-period weights are denoted by Q_0 (for quantity), the weighted aggregative index with base-period weights is given by

(2.11.2)
$$\left(\frac{\Sigma P_n Q_0}{\Sigma P_0 Q_0}\right) 100$$

This index, which measures the change in the total cost of a fixed bill of goods, is also known as the *Laspeyres index*, after the German statesman and economist Etienne Laspeyres (1834–1913), who first proposed the use of the formula.

EXAMPLE 2.11.2   To illustrate the calculation of a weighted aggregative index using base-period weights, assume that in 1976 the average weekly purchased quantities of the items in Table 2.11.1 were as shown in Table 2.11.2.

SOLUTION   The last two columns of Table 2.11.2 show that in 1986 it would cost $17.22 to buy the same goods that cost $13.52 in 1976. The weighted aggregative index for the example, then, is

$$\left(\frac{\$17.22}{\$13.52}\right) 100 = 127.4$$

Thus, it costs 27.4% more in 1986 to purchase the same goods.

One deficiency of the weighted aggregative index is that it assumes a fixed consumption pattern. That is, it assumes that the quantities of items bought in the nonbase period are the same as those in the base period. If the base period and the nonbase period are close together, this may not pose a very serious problem. If, however, the time interval between the base period and the nonbase period is great, the assumption may be unrealistic, and the index may lose much of its usefulness.

WEIGHTED AGGREGATIVE INDEX, NONBASE-PERIOD WEIGHTS (PAASCHE INDEX)

Suppose that instead of using base-period weights, we use weights that reflect the quantities of the index items bought during the nonbase period. If these weights are denoted by Q_n, the weighted aggregative index is given by

(2.11.3)
$$\left(\frac{\Sigma P_n Q_n}{\Sigma P_0 Q_n}\right) 100$$

The use of current- (nonbase-) period weights in calculating the aggregative index was first proposed by Herman Paasche (1851–1925), another German economist. Therefore, the index given by Formula 2.11.3 is known as the *Paasche index*.

One disadvantage of the Paasche index is that we cannot make year-to-year comparisons of price changes when we use current-period weights. Another limitation is the need to obtain new weights for each current period of interest. The practical difficulties involved in gathering data on current purchasing habits for each new time period are overwhelming. As a consequence, the Paasche index is not widely used.

WEIGHTED ARITHMETIC MEAN OF RELATIVES INDEX

Just as we can compute aggregative indexes, we can compute indexes based on averages. As with aggregative indexes, indexes computed by an averaging process may be weighted or unweighted. The most useful and widely used index based on averages is a weighted index. Thus, we limit our discussion to that index.

Although we can use any method of averaging in computing an index, we ordinarily use the arithmetic mean. The index we are considering, then, is called the *weighted arithmetic mean of relatives index*. The weights used in this index are called *values*, since they reflect the values of the items consumed, produced, shipped, purchased, and so on. Table 2.11.2, for example, shows that the quantity of meat consumed is two units. The value for meat is obtained by multiplying the quantity by the unit price in 1976, $2.12, to obtain the 1976 value of $4.24. In general, then, value = price × quantity.

Note also that the weights used need not be for the base period to which the prices pertain. It is desirable, however, that the weights be fixed—that is, not based on the current period—in order to allow for period-to-period comparisons.

If the weights are denoted by W, the weighted arithmetic mean of relatives index is given by

(2.11.4)
$$\frac{\Sigma \left(\frac{P_n}{P_0} \cdot 100\right) W}{\Sigma W}$$

TABLE 2.11.3   Data needed to calculate the weighted arithmetic mean of relatives index, Example 2.11.3

Food Commodity	Price 1976 P_{76}	Price 1986 P_{86}	Price Relatives $\left(\dfrac{P_{86}}{P_{76}}\right)100$	Quantity 1976 Q_{76}	Weight $W = P_{76}Q_{76}$	Weighted Price Relatives $\left(\dfrac{P_{86}}{P_{76}} \cdot 100\right)W$
Meat	$2.12	$2.59	122.2	2	$ 4.24	$ 518.13
Milk	1.65	2.00	121.2	3	4.95	599.94
Eggs	0.69	1.00	144.9	1	0.69	99.98
Bread	0.63	0.90	142.9	3	1.89	270.08
Coffee	1.75	2.34	133.7	1	1.75	233.98
Total					$13.52	$1,722.11

EXAMPLE 2.11.3   We can illustrate the construction of a weighted arithmetic mean of relatives index using the data from Example 2.11.1.

SOLUTION   Table 2.11.3 reproduces the data, along with some additional necessary calculations. Using Formula 2.11.4, we find the weighted arithmetic mean of relatives index for the present example to be

$$\frac{\$1722.11}{\$13.52} = 127.4$$

Note that this result is the same as the Laspeyres index obtained by Formula 2.11.2. A little manipulation of Formula 2.11.4 shows that when the fixed weights of Formula 2.11.4 are base-period values this formula reduces to Formula 2.11.2. Thus, we interpret the results of the two methods in the same way.

There is a reason for having two methods of arriving at the same result. In certain situations, value weights may be more readily available than quantity weights. Or price data may be available in the form of relative rather than absolute values. In such cases, Formula 2.11.4 is better than Formula 2.11.2.

THE FISHER IDEAL PRICE INDEX

Irving Fisher, in his book *The Making of Index Numbers* (Houghton Mifflin, 1922), proposed an index that has come to be known as the *Fisher ideal price index*. As part of his treatise on the construction of index numbers, Fisher proposed a list of tests against which index numbers should be judged. The ideal price index passes more of the tests than do the Laspeyres and the Paasche indexes.

The Fisher ideal price index is the geometric mean of the Laspeyres and the Paasche indexes. We recall from an earlier discussion some properties of the geometric mean. The geometric mean of a set of k positive numbers is the kth root of their product. If the numbers are all identical, the geometric mean and the arithmetic mean are equal. For other cases, the geometric mean is less than the arithmetic mean. The geometric mean is used mostly for finding the averages of ratios, rates of change, and index numbers. We may, then, write the formula for the Fisher ideal price index as follows:

(2.11.5)

$$\sqrt{\left(\frac{\Sigma P_n Q_0}{\Sigma P_0 Q_0}\right) 100 \left(\frac{\Sigma P_n Q_n}{\Sigma P_0 Q_n}\right) 100}$$

We see that the first term under the radical is the Laspeyres index expressed as a ratio (Formula 2.11.2) and the second term is the Paasche index, also expressed as a ratio (Formula 2.11.3).

The Fisher ideal price index passes four of the five tests that good index numbers are expected to pass. Many economists consider the fifth test optional. The Fisher index passes the following tests:

1. *Identity Test.* When one year is compared with itself, the index shows no change.
2. *Proportionality Test.* When all prices move in proportion, so does the index.
3. *Change-of-units Test.* The index is unchanged by any change in the money or physical units in which individual prices are measured.
4. *Time-reversal Test.* The index gives the same ratio between one point (in time) of comparison and the other point, no matter which of the two is taken as the base. That is, reversing the bases makes one index the reciprocal of the other.

The unweighted price index, as well as the Laspeyres and Paasche indexes, fails test 4. The general consensus is that the Fisher ideal index makes economic sense since it is a cross between the basic aggregative index numbers and meets a maximum number of the test criteria.

EXAMPLE 2.11.4 Use the data in Table 2.11.2 and Table 2.11.3 to construct the Fisher ideal price index.

SOLUTION Since the Laspeyres and Paasche indexes have already been computed, we may use them and Formula 2.11.5 to obtain the following results

$$\sqrt{(127.4)(127.4)} = 127.4$$

Since the Laspeyres and Paasche indexes were the same, we find, as expected, that the Fisher ideal index is also the same.

The following example illustrates the calculations when the Laspeyres and Paasche indexes are not the same.

EXAMPLE 2.11.5 A market basket of commodities yielded a Laspeyres index of 145.87 and a Paasche index of 140.05. Construct the Fisher ideal price index.

SOLUTION By Formula 2.11.5, we have

$$\sqrt{(145.87)(140.05)} = 142.94$$

USE OF PRICE INDEXES TO DEFLATE DOLLAR FIGURES

Price indexes are frequently used to adjust a series of dollar figures for changes in levels of prices. The procedure is referred to as *deflation*. The resulting figures are said to be measured in "constant dollars." A useful application of the technique is in the calculation of "real wages" as opposed to "money wages" for wage earners. Presumably, wage earners should be more interested in what their wages will buy than in the actual dollar amounts of these wages. The joy of a 20% raise over last year's salary can be severely dampened by the realization by wage earners that during the same period of time the prices of the things they have to buy have increased by 40%. A convenient and meaningful way to calculate real wages—wages that reflect actual buying power given the price of goods to be bought—is to divide actual money wages by an appropriate price index. The following example illustrates the procedure.

EXAMPLE 2.11.6 In 1980, in a large city, the average weekly wage for a certain group of wage earners was $302.25. In 1988, the average weekly paycheck for the same group of wage earners showed an earning of $483.60. In 1988, the consumer price index using 1980 as a base was 165. We wish to calculate the real average weekly wage for this group of wage earners in 1988.

SOLUTION To obtain the answer, we divide $483.60 by 165 and multiply the result by 100. That is, ($483.60/165)(100) = $293.09. Thus, we see that these wage earners, in terms of what their money would buy, were worse off in 1988 than in 1980, despite a 60% increase in weekly wages.

PROBLEMS IN THE CONSTRUCTION AND USE OF INDEX NUMBERS

C. Frederick Eisele, in a booklet entitled *The Consumer Price Index: Description and Discussion* (The University of Iowa, 1975), discusses in some detail a number of problems and limitations of the CPI. They include the following:

1. *Upward Bias.* When the index increases, not all prices of items in the market basket increase by the same percentage. The author explains how consumers, through manipulation of their individual market baskets, may experience a cost of living increase that is less than the official one.
2. *Changes in Quality.* Over a period of time, the quality of many consumer goods

increases faster than their price. The author believes that attempts to solve this problem have not been totally successful.

3. *Consumer Tastes.* Over time, the market basket on which the index is based may become less representative of consumer preferences as a result of trends and fads.

4. *Seasonal Adjustments.* The fact that certain consumer goods vary in price according to the season of the year is a problem that has been addressed. The author reports, however, that the results have not been widely published.

5. *Sampling Error.* The fact that the CPI is based on a sample introduces technical problems that the author feels are dealt with in a way that may lead to misleading interpretations of the index.

6. *List Prices Versus Actual Prices.* When the index is based on list prices that are different from actual prices the potential for error is present, but the author concludes that for the CPI errors of this type are probably not large.

7. *Representativeness of Sample Locations.* Indexes for the nation as a whole are based on a sample of cities. One should be concerned with the question of how representative the sample is of the whole. The author states that the error likely introduced by the sampling procedure employed is virtually impossible to estimate.

8. *Adequacy of the Market Basket.* The items in the market basket are also a sample of all possible items. The possibility of error in this regard should be kept in mind.

Eisele states that a consideration of these problems "suggests that one should be cautious in interpreting and using the CPI."

EXERCISES

2.11.1 The following prices and quantities reflect the average weekly buying habits of a typical family in 1978 and 1983. Construct the following: (a) price relatives for each item; (b) an unweighted aggregative index for 1983 on 1978 as a base; (c) a weighted aggregative index with base-period weights (Laspeyres index); (d) a weighted aggregative index with nonbase-period weights (Paasche index); and (e) a weighted arithmetic mean of relatives index. Explain the meaning of each of the computed indexes.

	1978		1983	
Item	Unit Price	Quantity	Unit Price	Quantity
Apples	$0.15	2	$0.25	1
Milk	0.30	2	0.35	2
Bread	0.30	3	0.40	3
Eggs	0.50	1	0.65	1

2.11.2 A manufacturer uses four raw materials in the production of a product. The following table shows the average prices and quantities of the four raw materials used in 1978 and 1983. Construct the following: (a) price relatives for each raw material; (b) an unweighted aggregative index for 1983 on 1978 as a base; (c) a weighted aggregative index with base-period weights; (d) a weighted aggregative index with nonbase-period weights; and (e) a weighted arithmetic mean of relatives index. Explain the meaning of each of the computed indexes.

	1978		1983	
Raw Material	Price	Quantity	Price	Quantity
A	$10	10	$12	15
B	3	20	5	25
C	5	50	10	60
D	2	30	5	40

2.11.3 Read pages 7–11 of *The Consumer Price Index* by C. Frederick Eisele and write a detailed report on the problems and limitations of the CPI that he mentions.

SUMMARY

This chapter deals with techniques for organizing and summarizing data. People who wish to understand the true nature of their data and to communicate to others the information that the data contain must be able to use these techniques.

You learned in this chapter that making an ordered array may be a good first step toward summarizing data. Frequency distributions, relative frequency distributions, and cumulative distributions make possible further organization and summarization of data. We can effectively communicate the information contained in large sets of data by using graphic procedures such as histograms, frequency polygons, ogives, and stem-and-leaf displays. You learned that graphs are also an effective way to represent qualitative data, and you learned how to construct several kinds of graphs for this purpose.

You learned how to compute several descriptive measures that provide useful summary information about sets of data. The two broad categories of descriptive measures covered here are *measures of central tendency* (or measures of location) and *measures of dispersion*. You learned to compute and understand the meaning of the *mean*, the *median*, and the *mode* as measures of central tendency. The most important measures of dispersion you learned about in this chapter are the *variance* and the *standard deviation*. You learned to compute these descriptive measures using both grouped and ungrouped data. You learned how to construct box-and-whisker plots to communicate information contained in a data set.

This chapter also covers the concepts and methods involved in the construction and interpretation of index numbers. It presents methods for calculating weighted and unweighted aggregative indexes and the weighted arithmetic mean of relatives index.

REVIEW EXERCISES

1. Explain why users and producers of statistical information should be good communicators.

2. Define the following terms:

(a) ordered array
(b) frequency distribution
(c) histogram
(d) frequency polygon
(e) statistic
(f) parameter
(g) ogive
(h) relative frequency distribution

(i) percentile
(j) quartile
(k) Sturges' rule
(l) Chebyshev's theorem
(m) class-interval width
(n) class mark
(o) class limits
(p) stem-and-leaf display

(q) bar chart
(r) grouped bar chart
(s) 100% bar chart
(t) paired bar chart
(u) deviation bar chart
(v) pie chart
(w) box-and-whisker plot

3. Compare and contrast the mean, median, and mode as measures of central tendency.

4. What is meant by the term *dispersion*?

5. Discuss the range, the average deviation, and the variance as measures of dispersion.

6. Explain how Chebyshev's theorem can be used to answer questions about a set of data.

7. Give two reasons why it is useful to be able to compute descriptive measures from grouped data.

8. State the assumptions made in computing each of the following descriptive measures from grouped data: (a) the mean,   (b) the mode,   (c) the variance, and   (d) the median.

9. What is an index number?

10. Define   (a) price index,   (b) quantity index,   (c) value index,   (d) price relative, (e) simple index, and   (f) composite index.

11. Explain in words the method of constructing the Laspeyres index.

12. What are the disadvantages of the Laspeyres index?

13. Explain in words the method of constructing the Paasche index.

14. What are the disadvantages of the Paasche index?

 15. Two regionally distributed general-interest magazines solicit advertising from the same clientele. The advertising rates and the total number of subscribers are the same for both magazines. The following table shows the age distributions of subscribers to the two magazines, in thousands of subscribers.   (a) Construct a histogram for each set of data. (b) Prepare the relative frequency distribution for each set of data.   (c) Prepare the cumulative relative frequency distribution for each set of data.   (d) Suppose that you are a manufacturer of baby food. In which magazine would you advertise? Why?   (e) Suppose that you are a real estate agent for a retirement community. In which magazine would you advertise? Why?

Age (years)	10–19	20–29	30–39	40–49	50–59	60–69	70–79
Magazine A	10	48	58	38	28	10	8
Magazine B	8	18	18	28	54	46	28

16. A contest sponsored by radio station WSAD draws 10,000 responses. The following table shows the age distribution of the contestants.   (**a**) Construct a histogram from these data.   (**b**) What is the approximate mean age of the contestants?   (**c**) What proportion of the contestants are between 20 and 39 years of age, inclusive?   (**d**) What proportion of the contestants are under 30 years of age?   (**e**) What proportion are 40 or over?

Age (years)	10–14	15–19	20–24	25–29	30–34	35–39	40–44	45–49	50–54	55–59
Contestants (×100)	4	8	15	19	21	12	8	6	4	3

17. Ⓒ Malone Market-Research Analysts conducts a household survey in a certain community. One question asked is "Number of rooms per dwelling unit." The following table shows the results. Compute the mean, median, variance, and standard deviation.

3	2	4	4	1	6	3	6	6	6	7	6
5	7	5	2	7	5	4	6	8	4	5	7
4	3	6	6	4	3	6	5	5	6	7	6
5	5	2	5	8	6	6	3	7	7	7	5
6	1	5	6	5	4	3	4	3	6	5	4

18. Ⓒ The weights, in micrograms, of 20 one-inch specimens of a certain synthetic fiber randomly selected from a day's production of the Nimrod Company are as follows: 3.7, 3.1, 2.0, 2.8, 2.3, 4.5, 3.6, 3.0, 3.0, 2.3, 3.1, 2.6, 3.4, 4.8, 3.8, 4.2, 4.5, 3.5, 3.1, 4.6. Compute the measures that would be appropriate for describing these data.

19. Ⓒ In a survey of small bakeries in the Southeast, 10 bakeries report the following numbers of employees: 15, 14, 12, 19, 13, 14, 15, 18, 13, 19. Find the mean, median, variance, and standard deviation.

20. Ⓒ A sample of the records of Optimum Appliances reveals the following ages (in years) for 15 refrigerators at the time of their first service call: 9.1, 2.5, 9.5, 1.1, 7.8, 7.0, 2.2, 4.4, 8.0, 6.4, 2.9, 7.4, 7.2, 4.3, 5.9. Compute the mean, median, variance, and standard deviation.

21. Ⓒ A random sample of 10 college students reveals the following current balances in their bank accounts (in hundreds of dollars): 3.4, 1.8, 1.4, 3.6, 1.8, 3.7, 3.4, 2.9, 4.2, 2.8. Compute the mean, median, variance, and standard deviation.

22. Ⓒ The following are the current prices per share (in dollars) of 20 stocks: 59, 97, 53, 83, 45, 47, 88, 51, 76, 64, 66, 92, 97, 55, 85, 108, 62, 55, 136, 51. Find the mean, median, variance, and standard deviation.

23. Ⓒ For its quality-control program, the makers of Pineywoods spark plugs periodically draw samples of size 100 from the assembly line and inspect them. The numbers of defective spark plugs found in 25 such samples are as follows: 0, 1, 0, 0, 1, 5, 3, 0, 5, 5, 0, 0, 4, 4, 0, 3, 5, 0, 2, 3, 4, 2, 1, 5, 4. Find the mean, median, variance, and standard deviation.

24. C In a survey of urban employees designed to learn more about their eating and drinking habits, 15 secretaries reported the number of cups of coffee they drank each day to be as follows: 4, 2, 1, 3, 5, 6, 6, 3, 3, 2, 4, 3, 2, 0, 1. Compute the measures that would be appropriate for describing these data.

25. C The quality-control division of the Quigley Company, a light-bulb manufacturer, conducted forced-life tests on a sample of 25 bulbs. The bulbs' lifetimes, in thousands of hours, were as follows: 1.1, 1.1, 1.2, 1.1, 1.4, 0.9, 1.2, 1.2, 1.3, 0.8, 1.2, 1.2, 1.2, 1.7, 1.5, 1.2, 0.8, 1.3, 0.9, 1.7, 1.3, 1.2, 1.2, 1.4, 1.0. Compute the mean, median, variance, and standard deviation.

26. C A sample of 20 car registrations selected by the Regis County Tax Office reveals the following ages of cars (to the nearest year): 1, 3, 3, 3, 8, 7, 4, 6, 8, 5, 5, 5, 9, 9, 10, 10, 4, 2, 4, 2. Compute the mean, median, variance, and standard deviation.

27. C The following are the tensile strengths of 15 specimens of plastic: 37, 46, 45, 31, 32, 48, 44, 45, 35, 42, 42, 33, 35, 26, 47. The data have been coded for ease of calculation. Compute the mean, median, variance, and standard deviation.

28. C A sample of 20 cartons of household fuses reveals the following numbers of defectives per carton: 7, 6, 3, 4, 3, 9, 4, 4, 5, 5, 9, 4, 6, 9, 7, 0, 6, 1, 3, 0. Compute the mean, median, variance, and standard deviation.

29. An estimator of timber yield selects a sample of 20 trees from a tract of land and estimates the following yields in board feet per tree: 385, 317, 326, 309, 595, 228, 241, 582, 411, 418, 305, 463, 482, 208, 503, 386, 329, 251, 193, 368. Compute the mean, median, variance, and standard deviation.

30. C A survey of 20 households reveals the following ages of refrigerators: 1, 1, 2, 2, 2, 2, 3, 3, 3, 3, 3, 3, 4, 4, 4, 5, 5, 6, 7, 8, 10.   (a) What is the mean age of the 20 refrigerators? (b) What is the median age?   (c) Compute the variance and standard deviation of the ages.

31. C The following are the times in seconds that a sample of 16 assembly-line employees at the Sequoia Company took to perform a certain operation: 5.9, 7.2, 8.8, 7.0, 8.7, 6.3, 7.1, 5.1, 10.0, 8.5, 8.9, 9.3, 6.3, 6.9, 9.8, 6.7. Compute the mean, median, variance, and standard deviation.

32. C The following are the number of days elapsing between date of purchase and date of return of the first 110 items returned to Trenton Department Store during the current fiscal year.

10	10	2	11	6	20	7	14	24	24	12
2	11	4	10	8	21	5	14	23	22	14
11	11	2	5	6	24	6	10	24	21	13
6	4	2	8	5	8	8	13	11	22	6
20	2	11	9	10	5	14	8	14	11	8
7	2	12	19	11	9	14	5	14	10	5
14	12	11	16	11	19	14	5	19	11	17
24	14	10	26	11	18	18	17	14	29	16
24	11	18	28	21	17	19	18	30	26	19
12	13	18	29	22	34	18	28	34	29	25

Summarize these data in the ways that you think would be appropriate for presentation to management.

33. Ⓒ The following are the annual salaries (in thousands of dollars) of the heads of households in two communities.

Community A

10	28	29	36	53	11	33	10	13	11	41	19	19	15	11
22	24	15	69	58	56	22	33	17	15	17	22	30	46	41
37	10	46	40	32	63	28	14	10	17	42	15	14	11	13
42	52	48	61	27	53	61	24	10	22	18	31	25	55	51
63	48	39	12	33	48	16	18	12	14	61	15	17	17	19
51	54	72	21	25	33	42	10	19	34	14	32	62	23	60
77	32	14	54	22	46	69	18	11	18	51	16	19	18	14

Community B

75	69	94	47	60	56	28	69	51	34	46	18	27	57	60
14	62	61	25	59	32	41	71	15	38	55	53	72	62	52
58	57	36	31	39	56	18	24	44	49	30	35	60	72	72
60	18	76	53	29	71	49	46	48	20	43	18	36	76	70
98	49	71	50	31	73	76	71	67	45	18	26	44	23	36
20	54	67	73	68	45	69	75	64	67	31	68	19	78	76
74	73	76	42	31	70	16	75	51	49	52	78	54	40	56
29	26	50	14											

(a) Organize and summarize these data as you would for presentation to the client of a market research firm.

(b) The client, which specializes in expensive home furnishings, wants to open a new retail outlet in one of these communities. Which community would you recommend for the new store? Why?

(c) Is the mean or the median a more appropriate measure of central tendency for the data of Community A? Community B?

(d) Which set of data is more variable?

34. Ⓒ Refer to the population of employed heads of households given in Appendix II. Use descriptive measures to compare the widowed or divorced males and females with respect to annual income.

35. Ⓒ Refer to Data Set 1 in Appendix IV, which shows the number of hours that 600 new Ultra Light photocopy machines operated before having to undergo unscheduled servicing. Construct a frequency distribution from these data.

36. Ⓒ Compute the mean for the grouped data in Exercise 35.

37. Ⓒ Compute the variance and standard deviation for the grouped data in Exercise 35. Treat the data both as a sample and as a population and compare the two results.

38. Ⓒ Construct a histogram and frequency polygon from the results of Exercise 35.

39. Ⓒ Use the results of Exercise 35 to construct a relative frequency distribution.

40. Ⓒ Compute the median for the grouped data in Exercise 35.

41. The following table gives the details of an investment portfolio consisting of five stocks. From these data, construct appropriate indexes to aid in evaluating the performance of the portfolio to date.

Stock	Purchase Price per Share ($)	Current Price per Share ($)	Number of Shares
A	18.80	20.75	450
B	21.25	24.65	375
C	32.50	31.00	250
D	44.70	54.40	320
E	23.50	20.00	200

42. From the list of companies in Appendix III, select every tenth company, beginning with the company determined by the following procedure. If the day of the month on which you were born ends with a 1, begin with the first company; if it ends with a 2, begin with the second company; if 3, begin with the third company; and so on through the ninth company. If the day of the month ends with zero, begin with the tenth company. For each company in your sample, record the information on assets, sales, market value, net profits, cash flow, and number employed. Using the data on assets, do the following and compare your results with those of other students in your class: **(a)** construct a frequency distribution;   **(b)** construct a relative frequency distribution;   **(c)** construct a cumulative frequency distribution;   **(d)** construct a cumulative relative frequency distribution;   **(e)** draw a histogram;   **(f)** draw a frequency polygon; and   **(g)** use grouped data methods to compute the mean, median, variance, and standard deviation.

43. Repeat Exercise 42 using the data on sales.

44. Repeat Exercise 42 using the data on market value.

45. Repeat Exercise 42 using the data on net profit.

46. Repeat Exercise 42 using the data on cash flow.

47. Repeat Exercise 42 using the data on the number employed.

48. The following are the lengths of life, in thousands of miles of driving, for a sample of 15 automobile water hoses of a certain brand: 38.5, 52.5, 62.1, 45.3, 45.9, 40.7, 40.3, 40.3, 61.7, 64.7, 45.9, 56.9, 50.1, 59.9, 56.3. Compute the mean, median, variance, and standard deviation from the data of this sample.

49. Refer to Exercise 48. Subtract 10 from each of the 15 values and use the new numbers to compute the mean, median, variance, and standard deviation. Compare the results with those obtained in Exercise 48. How do you account for the differences?

50. Refer to Exercise 48. Divide each value by 2 and use the new numbers to compute the mean, median, variance, and standard deviation. Compare the results with those obtained in Exercise 48. How do you account for the differences?

51. The following is a frequency distribution of the semiannual bonuses received by a sample of 78 salespersons. Compute the mean, median, and standard deviation for these data. (For the sake of calculating convenience, round the midpoint of each class interval to the nearest dollar.)

Class Interval ($)	Frequency
0– 999.99	3
1000–1999.99	15
2000–2999.99	32
3000–3999.99	12
4000–4999.99	9
5000–5999.99	7

52. A random sample of business executives reported the following data on airline miles flown during the previous year.

Class Interval (mi.)	Frequency
0– 4,999.99	24
5,000– 9,999.99	37
10,000–14,999.99	41
15,000–19,999.99	29
20,000–24,999.99	17
25,000–29,999.99	12
30,000–34,999.99	3

(a) What is your best estimate of the mean airline miles flown each year by the sampled population of business executives?
(b) What is your best estimate of the population standard deviation?
(c) Calculate the seventieth percentile.
(d) At least how far do 90% of the executives in the sample fly every year? For calculating convenience, round the midpoint of each class interval to the nearest mile.

53. A sample of 137 families reported the total dollar amount that they had available as a liquid cash reserve. The survey data are as follows:

Class Interval ($)	Number of Families
0– 1,999	29
2,000– 3,999	42
4,000– 5,999	35
6,000– 7,999	18
8,000– 9,999	7
10,000–11,999	4
12,000–13,999	2

(a) Estimate the mean and standard deviation of the sampled population.
(b) A family selected at random from the population ranks in the ninetieth percentile. You know that this family's cash reserve is at least how large?

54. The following frequency distribution was constructed from data provided by a sample of homeowners who recently borrowed money from a bank using their home as collateral. The tabulated variable is the amount of the loan's unpaid balance.

Class Interval ($)	Frequency	Class Interval ($)	Frequency
0– 999	7	7,000– 7,999	51
1,000–1,999	21	8,000– 8,999	36
2,000–2,999	26	9,000– 9,999	28
3,000–3,999	32	10,000–10,999	17
4,000–4,999	41	11,000–11,999	9
5,000–5,999	38	12,000–12,999	5
6,000–6,999	46	13,000–13,999	3

(a) Calculate estimates of the population mean, standard deviation, median, and ninetieth percentile.

(b) Recalculate the estimates of the population mean, standard deviation, median, and ninetieth percentile using $2,000 intervals. For calculating convenience, round the midpoint of each class interval to the nearest dollar.

55. The following is a frequency distribution of the ages of 130 salespersons with the Voorhees Company. Compute the mean, median, variance, and standard deviation.

Age:	25	28	30	33	38	40	45	48	50	57
Frequency:	26	7	12	11	16	20	24	5	6	3

56. There are a total of 115 houses in the Wistful Woods subdivision. Of these, 33 have 6 rooms, 28 have 7 rooms, 25 have 8 rooms, 15 have 9 rooms, and 14 have 10 rooms. What is the mean number of rooms per house in this subdivision? The median number? Compute the variance and standard deviation.

57. Ⓒ The following are the measurements taken on the thrust of 25 rockets:

1,074.8	962.8	973.6	904.7	920.7
1,037.8	1,091.6	1,018.5	955.8	981.5
1,018.9	1,027.6	1,024.0	1,073.8	971.9
989.8	940.8	969.8	966.4	1,076.8
1,025.6	985.5	1,094.9	1,060.9	936.2

Compute the mean, median, variance, and standard deviation for these data.

58. Ⓒ The following are the times in seconds between the arrivals of 160 automobiles at a certain checkpoint during a midmorning time period.

0.6	4.8	0.8	3.9	2.1	1.4	0.9	1.1	0.5	0.8	0.9
2.8	0.9	9.9	4.7	1.8	1.5	2.5	1.8	12.4	1.8	0.9
0.8	1.7	3.8	0.9	2.3	12.5	1.2	2.8	1.7	1.2	2.3
1.3	3.9	3.3	4.0	2.0	1.6	2.3	1.3	0.4	2.5	8.6
1.7	3.5	7.9	3.0	5.4	1.0	0.9	0.8	1.8	3.3	0.9
1.2	4.9	0.8	1.5	1.2	1.2	1.8	6.6	2.8	0.6	0.9
0.6	3.0	6.6	2.8	1.0	5.1	13.2	1.7	2.8	4.4	8.7
0.8	2.7	6.1	4.3	10.2	2.9	1.9	1.4	11.4	3.8	9.2
0.9	12.3	2.3	1.0	1.3	1.0	3.7	1.0	1.1	0.9	2.4
2.9	0.7	0.4	1.7	2.8	1.8	2.1	3.8	0.7	0.7	1.5
0.7	1.4	2.7	0.8	10.7	1.4	1.6	1.0	3.5	0.6	2.3
3.1	0.7	1.0	0.8	1.0	4.2	1.0	1.5	1.3	0.8	3.0
0.8	3.9	1.0	4.9	0.8	4.4	3.3	9.0	4.0	5.5	1.6
0.7	0.7	1.2	1.5	9.6	0.7	0.6	1.7	2.4	3.5	4.6
5.0	7.0	7.7	10.1	11.2	0.8					

Construct a frequency distribution and histogram for these data. Use class interval widths of two seconds. How would you describe this distribution?

59. Ⓒ Refer to Exercise 58. Compute the mean, median, variance, and standard deviation.

60. A recent newspaper story stated that Americans are buying more electronic devices for use in the home. A telephone survey of 500 homes asked which of 5 electronic devices were owned by a member of the household. The results were as follows:

Device	Number of households owning the device
Home computer	115
Cordless telephone	125
Answering machine	155
Compact disc player	95
Videocassette recorder	340

Construct a graph that effectively conveys the information obtained in the survey.

61. You select a sample from a population for the purpose of estimating the population's parameters. You compute $s^2 = 100$. The sum of squares about the mean is 2,500. What is the size of the sample?

62. Ten servers at the Wildflower Restaurant reported the following numbers of patrons who tipped more than 15% on a recent Saturday evening: 4, 5, 4, 2, 8, 8, 1, 4, 2, 6. (a) Compute the variance for these observations. (b) The following Saturday evening, each server found that the number of patrons tipping more than 15% was exactly two more than the previous Saturday evening. Compute the variance for the observations for the following Saturday evening. Compare this result with that obtained in (a). (c) Last Saturday evening a large convention was in progress in a hotel near the Wildflower Restaurant. Each server at the restaurant reported that during the convention evening twice as many patrons as those on the initial Saturday evening reported tipped more than 15%. Calculate the variance for the observations for the convention Saturday night. Compare the result with that obtained in (a). (d) The results of the calculations in (a), (b), and (c) illustrate two important properties of the variance. Can you state these two properties in general terms?

63. C The following are the assets (in millions of dollars) of a sample of 60 money market funds. Construct a stem-and-leaf display from these data.

233	379	120	333	275	452	485	151	749	914	243	401
102	754	800	523	112	923	133	128	299	173	687	601
421	342	120	105	529	178	622	586	129	157	371	485
279	518	376	461	248	112	155	828	337	246	254	107
388	424	340	878	164	345	187	487	493	707	264	376

64. C A sample of 117 quality control technicians who participated in a survey were asked to report the number of years they had been with their present employer. The results follow. From these data construct a frequency distribution, a relative frequency distribution, cumulative frequency and cumulative relative frequency distributions, a histogram, and a frequency polygon.

23	29	26	27	26	29	4	2	2	2	4	2	2
4	3	3	1	1	1	5	6	8	6	5	8	5
9	5	8	12	11	10	11	12	9	7	5	6	8
7	9	9	5	14	3	4	2	3	4	3	1	3
4	1	4	4	4	11	14	11	11	12	14	14	7
6	8	5	8	5	11	2	3	2	3	4	3	2
1	4	3	1	2	4	10	12	19	17	15	17	17
19	18	18	17	15	16	4	3	2	2	3	8	9
8	6	7	9	7	7	23	21	24	22	20	23	24

65. Wabash Industries has 35 salespersons who work in Territory A, 20 who work in Territory B, and 28 who work in Territory C. Last month the mean numbers of units sold per salesperson per territory were (A), 897; (B), 1244; and (C), 989. What was the mean number of units sold per salesperson in the three territories combined?

*66. A sometimes useful descriptive measure that may be computed for a set of data is the interquartile range (IQR), which is the difference between the first and the third quartiles. That is, $IQR = Q_3 - Q_1$. The quality-control manager for Gomez Manufacturing Company recorded in minutes the times required for 30 employees to perform the same assembly-line task. The results were as follows:

38	37	49	45	51	38	55	44	36	50	54	38	52	43	31
41	51	51	36	37	52	50	34	51	43	36	48	34	48	58

(a) Compute the IQR for these data. **(b)** What percent of the measurements are included in the IQR? **(c)** Six months after the initiation of an incentive program, the same 30 employees were timed again on the same task. The interquartile range for the new measurements was 6. What can you conclude about the incentive program?

1. WOMEN IN SCIENCE AND ENGINEERING

According to a National Science Foundation publication, employment of women and minorities in science and engineering increased much more rapidly than that of men and the majority during the 1976–1988 period. The following table is one of many summary tables contained in the publication.

Proportion of men and women in management who are primarily engaged in R&D management by field: 1986

Field	Men	Women
	Percent	
TOTAL	32.0	23.5
Scientists, total	31.9	22.4
Physical	60.0	40.4
Mathematical	43.0	34.7
Computer specialists	38.5	34.6
Environmental	35.2	26.3
Life	28.0	23.7
Psychologists	13.7	15.0
Social	15.9	18.2
Engineers, total	32.0	32.6
Aeronautical/astronautical	67.5	25.0
Chemical	36.6	30.0
Civil	8.6	4.8
Electrical/electronics	47.2	48.0
Mechanical	34.5	37.5
Other	26.0	35.7

Prepare a graph of these data that effectively communicates the information contained in the table.

Source: *Women and Minorities in Science and Engineering*, Washington, D.C.: National Science Foundation, January 1988, p. 9.

2. DEATH ROW INMATES

The following are the ages at first arrest of 146 California death row inmates.

17	13	14	13	15	16	11	15	18	17	14	14	26
17	30	15	15	18	18	16	16	20	25	14	18	17
21	18	23	18	13	25	21	21	18	39	22	42	17
16	25	18	24	18	21	19	18	17	15	20	39	14
25	18	37	20	15	15	15	14	19	18	16	17	15
13	20	14	19	18	15	17	18	26	18	19	20	27

14	24	15	19	11	23	27	14	14	17	18	34	17
15	30	23	19	25	17	15	18	16	16	19	16	19
18	29	31	20	18	32	15	19	19	18	15	17	15
14	14	15	19	17	24	19	30	17	30	19	20	17
19	12	16	18	18	18	19	17	18	19	21	21	20
16	20	18										

Use these data to construct a frequency distribution. Compute the mean, median, variance, and standard deviation.

Source: California Department of Justice, Bureau of Criminal Statistics. Used by permission.

3. FOREST RESEARCH IN THE SOUTHEAST

The following table shows the amount of federal funds allocated in 1986 to the Southeastern Forest Experiment Station at Asheville, North Carolina, for research by functional activity.

Functional activity	Allocated funds (thousands of dollars)
Fire	$1,111
Insect and disease research	2,363
Renewable resources evaluation	4,003
Renewable resources economics	315
Timber management	3,241
Forest products utilization	642
Other	1,427

Construct a graph to show the allocation of funds to the various functional activities.

Source: *The South's Fourth Forest: Alternatives for the Future* (1988). Forest Resource Report No. 24, U.S. Department of Agriculture, Forest Service, Washington, D.C.

4. TRANSPORTATION

Data Set 2 in Appendix IV gives the number of vehicles owned by bus companies and transit agencies in the continental United States that own fewer than 1,000 vehicles. Construct a frequency distribution, relative frequency distribution, and histogram from these data. Compute the mean, median, variance, and standard deviation.

5.   EMPLOYMENT OF SCIENTISTS AND ENGINEERS

The data on the employment of scientists and engineers shown in the following table were published by the National Science Foundation.

Use these data to do the following:

(a). Construct a pie chart to show the percentage of scientists employed in the seven subcategories (physical scientists, mathematical scientists, and so on) in 1986.

(b). Construct a single bar graph to show the trend in employment of all scientists and the seven subcategories during the period from 1976 through 1986.

(c). Construct a pie chart to show the percentage of all engineers employed in each of the engineer subcategories in 1986.

(d). Construct a single bar graph to show the trend in employment of all engineers and the subcategories during the period from 1976 through 1986. Use only those subcategories for which data are available for all six reported years.

(e). Construct a bar graph that shows the average annual employment growth rates for all scientists and each of the subcategories.

(f). Construct a bar graph that shows the average annual growth rate for all engineers and each of the subcategories. Use only those subcategories for which data are available for all six reported years.

Source: National Science Foundation (1988). *Profiles—Computer Science: Human Resources and Funding* (NSF 88–324), Washington, D.C., p. 57.

Employment of scientists and engineers by field: 1976, 1978, 1980, 1982, 1984, and 1986

Field	1976	1978	1980	1982	1984	1986
Total, all fields	2,331,200	2,609,800	2,860,400	3,253,100	3,995,500	4,626,500
Total scientists	959,500	1,071,000	1,184,500	1,405,700	1,781,400	2,186,300
Physical scientists	188,900	208,300	215,200	227,400	254,100	288,400
Chemists	132,800	143,000	148,800	154,100	168,600	184,700
Physicists/astronomers	44,300	46,400	47,200	47,600	61,200	72,600
Other physical scientists	11,800	18,800	19,300	25,600	24,300	31,100
Mathematical scientists	48,600	53,700	64,300	79,400	100,400	131,000
Mathematicians	43,400	46,300	53,400	62,500	83,900	110,700
Statisticians	5,200	7,300	11,000	16,900	16,500	20,300
Computer specialists	119,000	177,000	207,800	299,000	436,800	562,600
Environmental scientists	54,800	68,900	77,600	87,200	98,100	111,300
Earth scientists	46,500	54,000	64,000	73,600	82,300	93,700
Oceanographers	4,400	7,300	5,100	3,400	3,200	4,200
Atmospheric scientists	3,800	7,600	8,500	10,300	12,600	13,500
Life scientists	213,500	244,100	287,500	337,100	353,300	411,800
Biological scientists	139,400	164,000	198,300	233,800	236,600	273,300
Agricultural scientists	40,700	49,600	59,300	73,800	88,700	103,300
Medical scientists	33,300	30,500	29,900	29,500	27,900	35,200
Psychologists	112,500	121,700	128,100	138,400	209,500	253,500
Social scientists	222,300	197,400	204,000	237,200	329,200	427,800
Economists	62,500	62,100	75,000	103,100	125,600	163,600
Sociologists/anthropologists	33,900	40,900	48,300	57,000	77,700	93,400
Other social scientists	125,900	94,400	80,700	77,200	125,900	170,800
Total engineers	1,371,700	1,538,800	1,675,900	1,847,300	2,214,100	2,440,100
Aeronautical/astronautical	56,800	62,000	69,500	80,800	97,200	110,500
Chemical	77,500	84,200	94,500	107,700	140,100	149,000
Civil	188,200	211,700	232,100	258,200	312,700	346,300
Electrical/electronics	283,000	341,500	383,100	437,700	500,700	574,500
Industrial	NA	NA	NA	113,100	131,700	137,700
Materials	NA	NA	NA	39,200	51,300	53,100
Mechanical	276,200	299,300	322,600	357,900	445,600	492,600
Mining	NA	NA	NA	14,200	16,500	17,300
Nuclear	NA	NA	NA	18,200	22,100	22,700
Petroleum	NA	NA	NA	27,700	33,300	30,800
Other engineers	490,000	540,100	574,100	392,500	463,000	505,600

NA = Not available
NOTE: Detail may not add to total because of rounding

6.   FATALITIES AMONG CONSTRUCTION WORKERS

The following table, published by the Occupational Safety and Health Administration, shows the fatality rates among construction workers in ten regions of the United States for the years 1985 through 1989. For each region compute the mean rate and standard deviation across the five years. For each year compute the mean and standard deviation across the ten regions. Which appears to be more variable, rates across years or rates across regions?

Fatality Rate*

	1985	**1986**	**1987**	**1988**	**1989**
Region I	16.3	9.3	16.9	10.0	11.4
Region II	10.8	11.8	11.9	16.3	7.6
Region III	18.6	12.9	16.5	15.6	13.5
Region IV	16.3	19.6	17.7	17.1	16.8
Region V	21.6	19.8	18.3	16.7	18.6
Region VI	23.8	18.1	18.4	18.1	17.2
Region VII	20.7	17.8	19.1	19.9	16.3
Region VIII	15.1	19.2	19.0	16.1	20.1
Region IX	14.8	11.6	28.5**	7.8	26.8**
Region X	24.4	18.4	18.9	18.2	15.2

* $\dfrac{\text{Number of fatalities}}{\text{Number of construction workers in region}} \times 100{,}000$

**Excluding California

Source: U.S. Department of Labor, Occupational Safety and Health Administration, Office of Construction and Engineering, *Analysis of Construction Fatalities—The OSHA Data Base 1985–1989*, Washington, D.C., November 1990.

7.   INDUSTRY AND THE ENVIRONMENT

Hertzman et al. conducted a study to identify determinants of elevated lead levels in the blood of preschool children; to compare the current situation with past information; to determine historical trends in environmental lead contamination in a Canadian community; and to find a basis for identifying appropriate precautions and protection against future lead exposure. Subjects were children between the ages of two and five years, inclusive, who resided in a Canadian community that is the site of one of North America's largest lead-zinc smelters. Subjects were divided into two catagories: (1) cases, consisting of children who had blood lead levels of 18µg/ml or greater, and (2) controls, consisting of children whose blood lead levels were 10 µg/dl or less. Lead levels were ascertained for samples of drinking water, paint, household dust, home-grown vegetables, and soil at the subjects' residences. The following table shows the soil lead levels for the cases (coded 1) and the controls (coded 0). For each group, cases and controls, construct frequency, relative frequency, cumulative frequency, and cumulative relative frequency distributions. Construct a histogram and a frequency polygon. Compare the distributions and graphs of the two groups and comment on the comparisons.

Subject Category	Soil Lead Level (ppm)	Subject Category	Soil Lead Level (ppm)	Subject Category	Soil Lead Level (ppm)
1 = case	1290	1	61	1	1455
0 = control	90	1	1290	0	977
1	894	1	1409	1	624
0	193	1	880	1	392
1	1410	1	40	1	427
1	410	1	40	1	1000
1	1594	0	68	1	1009
0	321	0	777	0	1010
0	40	1	1975	1	3053
0	96	1	1237	0	1220
0	260	0	133	0	46
0	433	0	269	0	181
0	260	0	357	0	87
0	227	0	315	0	131
0	337	0	315	0	131
1	867	0	255	1	1890
1	1694	0	422	1	221
0	302	0	400	1	221
1	2860	0	400	0	79
1	2860	0	229	1	1570
1	4320	1	229	1	909
1	859	0	768	1	1720
0	119	0	886	1	308
1	115	1	58	1	97
0	192	0	508	0	200
1	1345	1	811	0	1135
0	55	1	527	0	320
0	55	1	1753	1	5255
1	606	0	57	0	176
1	1660	0	769	0	176
0	82	0	677	0	100
0	1470	1	677	0	328

1	600	1	424
1	2120	1	2230
1	569	0	421
0	105	1	628
1	503	1	1406
0	161	1	378
0	161	1	812
1	1670	1	812
0	132	1	852
1	974	0	137
1	3795	0	137
0	548	0	125
1	622	1	562
0	788	0	325
1	2130	1	1317
0	197	1	2125
1	916	1	2635
1	755	1	2635
1	59	0	544
1	1720	1	731
1	574	1	815
1	403		

Source: Dr. Clyde Hertzman. These data were a part of the study described in Clyde Hertzman, Helen Ward, Nelson Ames, Shona Kelly, and Cheryl Yates, "Childhood Lead Exposure in Trail Revisited," *Canadian Journal of Public Health*, 82 (November/December 1991): 385–391.

SUGGESTIONS FOR FURTHER READING

Berk, Kenneth N., "Effective Microcomputer Statistical Software," *The American Statistician, 41,* 1987, pp. 222–228.

Butler, Darrell L. and William Neudecker, "A Comparison of Inexpensive Statistical Packages for Microcomputers Running MS-DOS," *Behavior Research Methods, Instruments, & Computers, 21,* 1989, pp. 113–120.

Carpenter, James, Dennis Deloria, and David Morganstein, "Statistical Software for Microcomputers," *Byte,* April 1984, pp. 234–264.

Eisele, C. Frederick (1975). *The Consumer Price Index: Description and Discussion.* Center Report Series No. 3, Center for Labor and Management, College of Business Administration, University of Iowa, Iowa City.

Hoagland, David C., Frederick Mosteller, and John W. Tukey (1983). *Understanding Robust and Exploratory Data Analysis.* Wiley, New York.

Meyers, Cecil H. (1970). *Handbook of Basic Graphs: A Modern Approach.* Dickenson Publishing Company, Belmont, Calif.

Muller, Mervin E. (1980). "Aspects of Statistical Computing: What Packages for the 1980s Ought to Do," *The American Statistician,* 34:159–168.

Schmid, Calvin F., and Stanton E. Schmid (1979). *Handbook of Graphic Presentation*, 2nd ed. Wiley, New York.

Selby, Peter H. (1979). *Using Graphs and Tables*. Wiley, New York.

Spear, Mary Eleanor (1969). *Practical Charting Techniques*. McGraw-Hill, New York.

Tufte, Edward R. (1983). *The Visual Display of Quantitative Information*. Graphic Press, Cheshire, Conn.

Tukey, John W. (1977). *Exploratory Data Analysis*. Addison-Wesley, Reading, Mass.

3

Some Elementary Probability Concepts

Chapter Objectives: This chapter introduces you to the basic concepts and techniques of probability. These skills provide a mechanism that can help you to understand much of the variability and complexity in the business world. This is the first of three chapters that tie together descriptive and inferential statistics. After studying this chapter and working the exercises, you should be able to

1. Understand the basic concepts of set theory.
2. Determine the number of permutations that can be made from n objects taken r at a time.
3. Determine the number of combinations that can be made from n objects taken r at a time.
4. Construct a tree diagram to represent the possible choices available to a decision-maker, along with the associated possible outcomes.
5. Understand the three recognized views of probability.
6. Understand the elementary properties of probability.
7. Compute the probability of an event.
8. Use Bayes' theorem, an important formula that is useful for computing certain probabilities.

3.1 INTRODUCTION

The next three chapters introduce the basic concepts of statistical inference. We can think of these chapters as bridging the gap between descriptive statistics (the topic of Chapter 2) and statistical inference.

The *theory of probability* is a branch of mathematics concerned with the concept and measurement of uncertainty. We cannot cover such a large subject in depth in a single chapter. However, since statistical inference is based on probability theory, we need a rudimentary understanding of probability in order to understand it. The objective of this chapter, then, is to present the basic concepts of probability needed for an understanding of statistical inference. We shall introduce the subject by discussing probabilities that are based on observed data.

We obtain the observations that we use in calculating probabilities in a variety of ways.

The process whereby we obtain these observations is called an *experiment*.

For many people the word *experiment* evokes visions of a scientific laboratory populated with technicians dressed in white coats scrutinizing test tubes and recording the behavior of white mice. We use the word here, however, in a much broader sense. For example, an experiment may consist of determining which brand of detergent a shopper in a certain area prefers. Recording the gasoline consumed by a car during a given week is another example.

The result of an experiment is called an *outcome*.

If an experiment consists of determining which brand of detergent a shopper prefers, the outcome might be "Brand A" or "Brand B" or any one of the brands that are available. If an experiment involves the assessment of an automobile's performance in terms of miles driven per gallon of gasoline, the outcome might be 20 or perhaps 25 or, in the case of superior performance, 40.

An *event* is a collection of one or more outcomes considered as a group.

An event is said to occur if an experiment yields at least one of its outcomes. Suppose, for example, that an experiment consists of determining the ages (at the nearest birthday) of shoppers at a grocery store on a given day. Possible outcomes would include 16, 20, 30, 35, 50, 60, and so on. The event of interest to the experimenter might consist of the outcomes "30 and under." If, during the day, only one person 30 years of age or under shopped at the store, the event would consist of one outcome. If 20 people in the designated age group shopped at the store while the experiment was in progress, the event would be composed of 20 outcomes.

The collection of all possible outcomes that may result when an experiment is conducted is called the *sample space* for that experiment.

In our example about grocery-store shoppers, the sample space consists of all possible ages, but in reality it might include only the ages 12 through 85 or 15 through 75 or some similar range.

We may now define probability as follows:

Probability is a number between 0 and 1 inclusive that measures the likelihood of the occurrence of some event.

The more likely the event, the closer the number is to 1. The more unlikely the event, the closer the number is to 0. An event that cannot occur has a probability of 0. An event that is certain to occur has a probability of 1.

Here are some examples of events for which we may be interested in computing probabilities: a defective item coming off an assembly line; the purchase of Product A; the arrival of a shipment of goods on time; or Salesperson A selling more than 500 items during a given week.

3.2   SET CONCEPTS AND NOTATION (BASIC NOTIONS)

In this section, we present some ideas and notation from set theory that will help you to understand probability and to calculate probabilities.

Set theory was introduced in the latter part of the nineteenth century by Georg Cantor (1845–1918). It is an important tool that is useful in many branches of mathematics, including probability theory. For this reason, we include set concepts in this chapter. We will cover only a minimum of the basic concepts.

A *set* is a collection of definite, distinct objects called elements or members of the set.

We shall follow the convention of designating a set by a capital letter, usually chosen arbitrarily. We may describe a set either by listing all the elements in the set or by describing the type of element of which the set is composed.

The following are examples of sets for which all members of the set are specified:

A = {Salespersons Jones, Smith, Williams, and Adams}
B = {Products A, B, C, D, and E}
C = {Johnson, King, Phillips, Brown}
K = {Atlanta, Chicago, Denver, Seattle, San Diego}

For each of these sets, we could describe the elements of which it is composed:

A = {The four top salespersons in a certain company}
B = {The five products manufactured by a certain company}
C = {All the secretaries in the shipping department of a certain company}
K = {The cities in which a certain firm has branch offices}

Some additional concepts relating to sets are as follows:

1. A *unit set* is a set composed of only one element.
2. A set that contains *no* elements is called the *empty set*, or *null set*. It is designated by the symbol ∅.
3. The set of all elements in which there is interest in a given discussion is called the *universal set*. It is designated by the capital letter *U*.
4. If every element of *A* is an element of *B*, then *A* is said to be a *subset* of *B*. Every set is a subset of itself.
5. The null set is a subset of every other set, by definition.
6. Two sets are equal if, and only if, they contain the same elements.

The *union* of two sets *A* and *B* is another set, consisting of elements belonging to *either A* or *B* or *both A* and *B*. The symbol ∪ designates the union of two sets.

Examples 3.2.1 through 3.2.5 illustrate some useful set operations. Where appropriate, we use a device called a *Venn diagram* to portray the relationships among sets.

EXAMPLE 3.2.1   In one city, the radio stations that play country music compose set A, where A = {radio stations 1,2,3,4,5}. In the same city, the radio stations that play rock music make up set B, where B = {radio stations 2,4,6,7}. We may write the union of these two sets A ∪ B = {radio stations 1,2,3,4,5,6,7} = {all radio stations in the city that play country music or rock music or both}. Sets A and B are *conjoint* because they have at least one element in common. In this case, the common elements are radio stations 2 and 4. Figure 3.2.1 uses Venn diagrams to show the three sets. (Note that A ∪ B is the total shaded area in the rectangle on the right.) If two sets have no elements in common, they are said to be *disjoint*.

EXAMPLE 3.2.2   In a certain city, there are 12 AM radio stations. Of these stations, 4 have a daytime broadcasting power of 1,000 watts or less. The remaining 8 have a daytime broadcasting power greater than 1,000 watts. From this information, we may define the following two sets:

A = {All radio stations in the city with a daytime broadcasting power of 1,000 watts or less}

FIGURE 3.2.1   Venn diagram showing the union of two conjoint sets

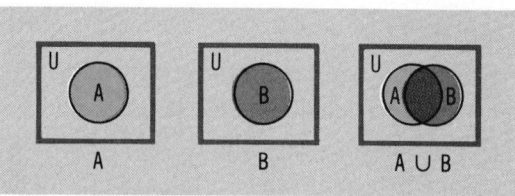

A   B   A ∪ B

FIGURE 3.2.2   Venn diagram showing the union of two disjoint sets

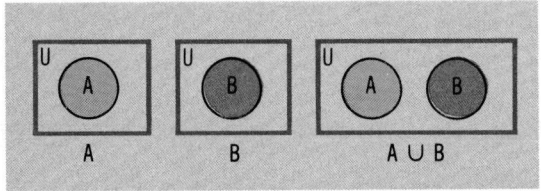

B = {All radio stations in the city with a daytime broadcasting power greater than 1,000 watts}

A ∪ B = {All radio stations in the city}

Here the sets A and B are disjoint since a radio station cannot belong to both set A and set B. Figure 3.2.2 shows the union of two disjoint sets.

The *intersection* of two sets *A* and *B* is another set, consisting of all elements in both *A* and *B*. The symbol ∩ designates the intersection of two sets.

EXAMPLE 3.2.3   In Example 3.2.1, the intersection of sets A and B would be written A ∩ B = {radio stations 2 and 4} = {radio stations that play both country and rock music}. In Figure 3.2.1, A ∩ B is the doubly shaded area that represents the overlapping of sets A and B. The intersection of two disjoint sets is the null set, as illustrated by Figure 3.2.2.

If set *A* is a subset of the universal set *U*, the *complement* of *A* is another subset of *U* consisting of the elements in *U* that are not in *A*. The complement of *A* is designated $\overline{A}$ (called "A bar"). Note that *A* and $\overline{A}$ are disjoint sets and that $A \cup \overline{A} = U$.

EXAMPLE 3.2.4   Of the 250 workers employed by Acadia Construction Company, 150 have been with the firm 10 years or longer. Let us designate the 250 employees as the universal set *U*, and the subset of 150 who have been with the firm 10 years or longer as set A. Then the complement of set A is set $\overline{A}$, consisting of the 100 employees who have been with the firm less than 10 years. Figure 3.2.3 illustrates the complement of a set.

FIGURE 3.2.3   Venn diagram showing the complement of a set

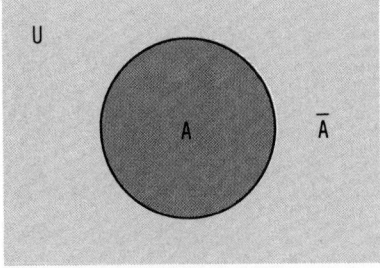

TABLE 3.2.1 300 trucking firms classified by location of home office and type of cargo hauled

| | Home Office Location | | | | | |
Type of Cargo	A_1 New England	A_2 Middle Atlantic	A_3 South	A_4 Midwest	A_5 West	Total
B_1 Household goods	20	40	25	35	30	150
B_2 Agricultural products	8	8	20	30	12	78
B_3 Building materials	7	4	4	5	10	30
B_4 General freight	10	6	10	10	6	42
Total	45	58	59	80	58	300

We often want to identify sets and subsets that are represented by cross-tabulated data, as shown in Table 3.2.1. When we indicate the number of elements in a set, we enclose the set symbol in parentheses and prefix it by the letter n. For example, $n(A) = 30$ indicates that there are 30 elements in set A.

EXAMPLE 3.2.5 Table 3.2.1 classifies 300 trucking firms by location of home office and type of cargo hauled. Sets A_1 through A_5 consist of trucking firms in each of the geographic regions. Sets B_1 through B_4 consist of firms that haul various types of cargo. We may specify other sets by using the concepts of intersection, union, and complement. For example, the set $B_1 \cap A_4$ consists of trucking firms that haul household goods and whose home office is in the Midwest. The number of trucking firms in this set, $n(B_1 \cap A_4)$, is 35.

The set $B_2 \cup A_2$ consists of firms that haul agricultural products or are located in the Middle Atlantic states or both. And $n(B_2 \cup A_2) = 78 + 58 - 8 = 128$. In calculating $n(B_2 \cup A_2)$, we subtract the 8 firms that both haul agricultural products *and* have home offices in the Middle Atlantic states because this subset has been counted twice. That is, these 8 are included in both subtotals 78 and 58.

The complement of A_5, $\overline{A_5}$, consists of all trucking firms not located in the West, and $n(\overline{A_5}) = 300 - 58 = 242$.

EXERCISES

3.2.1 The Banft Distributing Company has 231 employees classified by age and job category as follows:

| | Age Category | | | | | |
Job Category	A_1 ≤20	A_2 21–25	A_3 26–30	A_4 31–35	A_5 >35	Total
B_1 Clerical	20	20	15	10	5	70
B_2 Custodial	3	6	3	2	1	15
B_3 Craft workers	15	30	35	20	10	110
B_4 Salespeople	1	5	10	5	2	23

Job Category	A₁ ≤20	A₂ 21–25	A₃ 26–30	A₄ 31–35	A₅ >35	Total
	Age Category					
B₅ Junior executives	0	1	5	2	0	8
B₆ Executives	0	0	2	2	1	5
Total	39	62	70	41	19	231

Based on this table, explain in words the following sets and give the number of employees in each: **(a)** $B_1 \cap A_5$, **(b)** $A_2 \cap B_6$, **(c)** $B_4 \cap A_5$, **(d)** $A_1 \cup B_6$, **(e)** $A_3 \cup A_5$, **(f)** $B_2 \cup B_3$, **(g)** $\overline{A}_4$, **(h)** $(A_1 \cup A_2) \cap B_3$, **(i)** $(B_3 \cup B_4) \cap A_5$.

How many employees satisfy each of the following conditions?

(j) The person is neither an executive nor a junior executive.
(k) The person is both an executive and a junior executive.
(l) The person is more than 30 years old and is clerical or custodial.
(m) The person is a salesperson and/or between 21 and 25 years old, inclusive.
(n) The person is a craft worker 35 years old or younger.
(o) The person is a craft worker or a salesperson and is between 21 and 30 years old, inclusive.
(p) The person is clerical or custodial and is more than 30 years old.

 3.2.2 A salesperson with a three-product line calls on 200 customers over a period of time. These 200 customers place orders as follows:

100 ordered Product A	55 ordered Products A and C
95 ordered Product B	30 ordered Products B and C
85 ordered Product C	20 ordered Products A and B and C
50 ordered Products A and B	

Determine the number of customers who order **(a)** at least one product, **(b)** no products, **(c)** exactly one product, **(d)** exactly two products, **(e)** exactly three products. Use a Venn diagram to illustrate.

3.2.3 Given two sets: A = {0, 1, 2, 3}, B = {3, 4, 5}. Find $A \cup B$ and $A \cap B$.

3.2.4 Given the following sets:

$$A = \{5,6,7,8,9,10\} \quad B = \{7,8,9,10,11,12\} \quad C = \{11,12,13,14,15\}$$

Find: **(a)** $A \cup B$ **(b)** $A \cap B$ **(c)** $A \cup C$ **(d)** $A \cap C$ **(e)** $(A \cup B) \cap C$

3.3 COUNTING TECHNIQUES – PERMUTATIONS AND COMBINATIONS

Suppose that we are computing the probability of some event, or the probability of a combination of events, when the total number of possible events is large. We find it convenient to have some method of counting the number of such events. Let us now look at some techniques to facilitate the counting of events. These techniques are useful for counting the number of events composing the numerator and/or the denominator of a probability.

THE mn COUNTING RULE

The most basic counting rule is the *mn rule*. Suppose that a general merchandise discount store chain has $m = 5$ stores in a metropolitan area. Each store has $n = 8$ departments supervised by department heads. To determine the total number of department heads that the chain employs in the area, we use the *mn* rule. That is, there are $mn = 5 \times 8 = 40$ department heads.

We can think of the chain store example as a two-stage situation. The *mn* rule may be expanded to include any number of stages. If we designate the number of elements at each stage by n_1, n_2, n_3, and so on, we can find the total number of elements of interest by computing the product of n_1, n_2, n_3, and so on. For example, suppose that a national firm has offices in each of $n_1 = 4$ regions. Within each region, branch offices are located in each of $n_2 = 5$ cities. Each branch office has $n_3 = 3$ major divisions. A person hired by the firm may be assigned to any one of the four regional offices. The regional manager, in turn, assigns the employee to one of the five branch offices. Finally, the branch manager assigns the employee to one of the three major divisions. To find the total number of possible assignments, we use an extension of the *mn* rule. That is, the total number of possible assignments is $n_1 \times n_2 \times n_3 = 4 \times 5 \times 3 = 60$.

FACTORIALS

Given the positive integer n, the product of all the whole numbers from n down through 1 is called n *factorial* and is written n!.

The following are examples of factorials:

$$10! = 10 \cdot 9 \cdot 8 \cdot 7 \cdot 6 \cdot 5 \cdot 4 \cdot 3 \cdot 2 \cdot 1$$
$$5! = 5 \cdot 4 \cdot 3 \cdot 2 \cdot 1$$
$$2! = 2 \cdot 1$$

In general, $n! = n(n - 1)(n - 2)(n - 3) \cdots 1$. By definition, $0! = 1$. Note that $10! = 10 \cdot 9!$, $5! = 5 \cdot 4!$, $n! = n(n - 1)!$.

By means of factorials, we can find the number of ways in which objects or persons can be arranged in a line.

EXAMPLE 3.3.1 At the Carleton Company, four secretaries' desks are arranged in a line against a wall. Each secretary can sit at any desk. How many seating arrangements are possible?

FIGURE 3.3.1   Tree diagram showing the possible arrangements of 4 objects taken 4 at a time

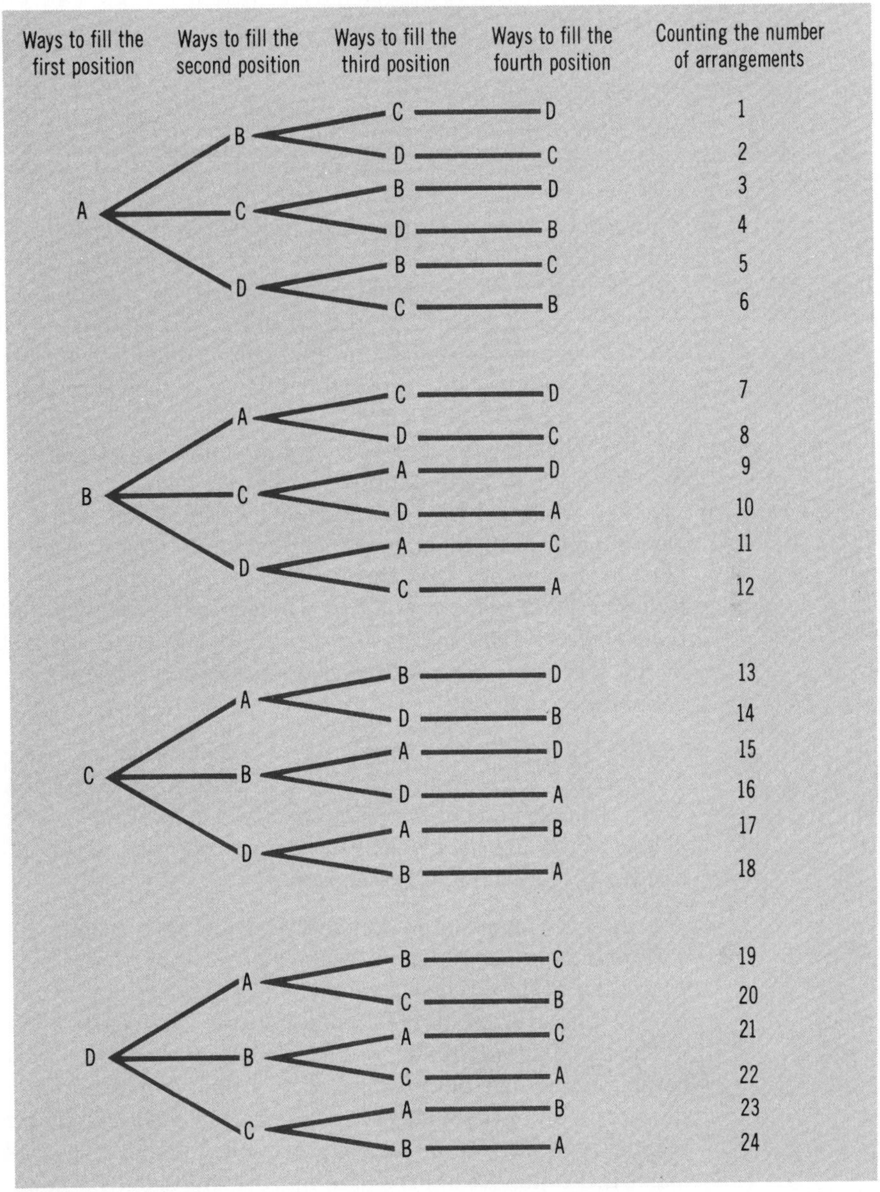

Ways to fill the first position	Ways to fill the second position	Ways to fill the third position	Ways to fill the fourth position	Counting the number of arrangements

SOLUTION   The answer is 4! = 4 · 3 · 2 · 1 = 24 seating arrangements.

Using a graphic aid called a *tree diagram*, we can show the possibilities. Let us designate the positions as the first, second, third, and fourth positions, and the four secretaries as A, B, C, and D. Figure 3.3.1 is a tree diagram representing the possible arrangements.

PERMUTATIONS

A *permutation* is an ordered arrangement of objects.

The 24 arrangements of secretaries shown in Figure 3.3.1 are the possible permutations of 4 objects taken 4 at a time. In certain situations, there may be more objects available than positions to be filled. For example, we may wish to know how many permutations are possible if we have 5 objects and wish to take only 2 at a time. We may think of this problem as one in which we have 2 positions to fill and 5 objects from which to make selections to fill them. We can get the answer using the following line of reasoning: We can fill the first position in one of 5 ways, since initially there are 5 objects from which to select. Once we have selected an object to fill the first position, there are 4 remaining objects from which we can make a selection to fill the second position. Hence, by the *mn* rule, there is a total of 20 ways (5 × 4) of filling the two positions. Each of these ways of filling the two positions is a permutation, and consequently we may say that there are 20 permutations of 5 objects taken 2 at a time.

In permutations, order counts.

A key word in the definition of a permutation is the word "ordered." In determining the number of possible permutations in a given situation, we say that "order counts." By this we mean, for example, that a pair of adjacent positions filled with the objects *a* and *b* and the same pair of adjacent positions filled with the objects in the order *b* then *a* are two different permutations of the same two objects. Rearranging the order of two objects creates a new permutation.

| **EXAMPLE 3.3.2** | The telephone switchboard in the company referred to in Example 3.3.1 requires two operators whose chairs (positions) are side by side. When the telephone operators go to lunch, two of the four secretaries take their places. If we make a distinction between the two operators' positions, in how many ways can the four secretaries fill them?

| SOLUTION | We can answer this question by determining the number of possible permutations of 4 things taken 2 at a time. There are 4 secretaries, A, B, C, and D, to fill the first position. Once that position has been filled, there are only 3 secretaries to fill the second position. See Figure 3.3.2.

The tree diagram in Figure 3.3.2 illustrates that there are 4 · 3 = 12 possible permutations of 4 things taken 2 at a time. Suppose that *n* is the number of distinct objects from which an ordered arrangement is to be derived, and *r* is the number of objects in the arrangement. The number of possible ordered arrangements is the number of permutations of *n* things taken *r* at a time. This is written symbolically as $_nP_r$. In general,

(3.3.1)
$$_nP_r = n(n - 1)(n - 2) \cdots (n - r + 1)$$

We multiply the right-hand side of Equation 3.3.1 by $(n - r)!/(n - r)!$. This is equivalent to multiplying by 1. We obtain

FIGURE 3.3.2   Tree diagram showing the number of permutations of 4 objects taken 2 at a time

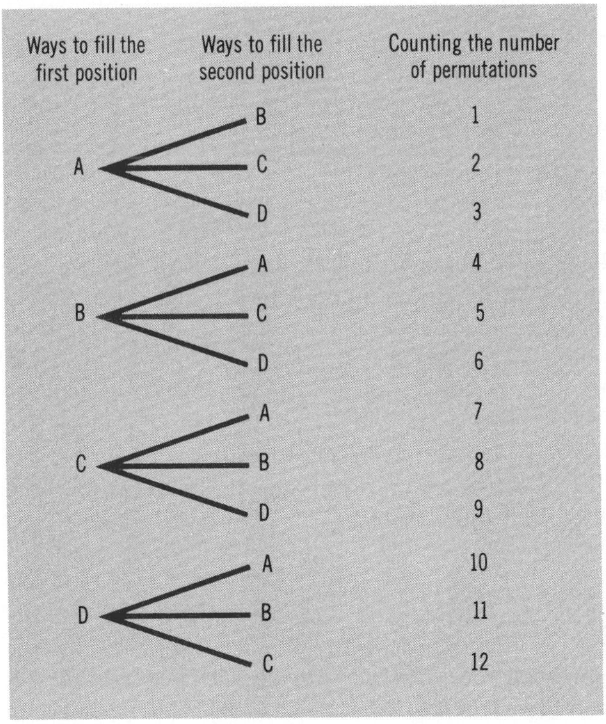

$$
\begin{aligned}
{}_nP_r &= n(n - 1)(n - 2) \cdots (n - r + 1) \, \frac{(n - r)!}{(n - r)!} \\
&= \frac{n(n - 1)(n - 2) \cdots (n - r + 1)(n - r)!}{(n - r)!} \\
&= \frac{n!}{(n - r)!}
\end{aligned}
$$

(3.3.2)

EXAMPLE 3.3.3   In a stock room, five adjacent bins are available for storing five different items. The stock of each item can be stored satisfactorily in any bin. In how many ways can we assign the five items to the five bins?

SOLUTION   We get the answer by evaluating ${}_5P_5$, which is

$$
{}_5P_5 = \frac{5!}{(5 - 5)!} = 5 \cdot 4 \cdot 3 \cdot 2 \cdot 1 = 120
$$

Suppose that there are 6 different parts to be stocked, but only 4 bins are available. To find the number of possible arrangements, we need to determine the number of permutations of 6 things taken 4 at a time, which is

$$_6P_4 = \frac{6!}{(6-4)!} = \frac{6 \cdot 5 \cdot 4 \cdot 3 \cdot 2!}{2!} = 360$$

COMBINATIONS

A *combination* is an arrangement of objects without regard to order.

The number of combinations of n things taken r at a time may be written as $_nC_r$.
  In Figure 3.3.2, the permutations of 4 things taken 2 at a time consist of the following 12 arrangements:

$$\begin{array}{cccccc}
AB & AC & AD & BA & BC & BD \\
CA & CB & CD & DA & DB & DC
\end{array}$$

In this list, 6 of the arrangements are the same as the other 6, except for the order in which the letters occur. They are

$$\begin{array}{cccccc}
AB & AC & AD & BC & BD & CD \\
BA & CA & DA & CB & DB & DC
\end{array}$$

In combinations, order does not count.

Sometimes we may not need to distinguish between, for example, arrangement AB and arrangement BA. We may consider them to be the same subset. That is, their order does not count. In that case, we refer to the arrangements as *combinations*. In the case of the 4 secretaries occupying 2 switchboard positions, there are 12 permutations but only 6 combinations. That is, there are 2 permutations for each combination. In general, there are $r!$ permutations for each combination of n things taken r at a time. In other words, there are always $r!$ times as many permutations as combinations. We express this symbolically as

(3.3.3)
$$_nP_r = r! \, _nC_r$$

When we solve Equation 3.3.3 for $_nC_r$, the result is

$$_nC_r = \frac{_nP_r}{r!}$$

We rewrite the numerator of this last expression as the right-hand side of Equation 3.3.2 to get the formula for the number of combinations of n things taken r at a time:

(3.3.4)
$$_nC_r = \frac{n!}{r!(n-r)!}$$

Now let us use Equation 3.3.4 to obtain the number of combinations of 4 things taken 2 at a time. As expected, we get 6:

$$_4C_2 = \frac{4!}{2!2!} = \frac{4 \cdot 3 \cdot 2!}{2 \cdot 1 \cdot 2!} = 6$$

EXAMPLE 3.3.4   The Powerful Perfume Manufacturing Company makes 10 fragrances. The company wants to prepare a gift package containing 6 fragrances. How many combinations of fragrances are available?

SOLUTION   The answer is

$$_{10}C_6 = \frac{10!}{6!4!} = \frac{10 \cdot 9 \cdot 8 \cdot 7 \cdot 6!}{6! \cdot 4 \cdot 3 \cdot 2 \cdot 1} = 210$$

PERMUTATIONS OF OBJECTS THAT ARE NOT ALL DIFFERENT

In our discussion of permutations, we considered the case in which all the objects being permuted were different. Sometimes, in the set of objects to be permuted, one or more subsets of items are indistinguishable. The problem then is to determine how many permutations, or distinguishable arrangements, are possible under these circumstances. Logic tells us that the number should be smaller than when all the objects are different.

EXAMPLE 3.3.5   On a certain day, the Cheerful Cafeteria wants to serve two white, one green, and two yellow vegetables. How many distinguishable arrangements of these vegetables can be made on the serving line if we distinguish between vegetables only on the basis of color?

SOLUTION   The possible color sequences for the 5 vegetables are as follows:

WWYYG	WYWYG	YYWWG	YWYWG	YWWYG	WYYWG
WWYGY	WYWGY	YYWGW	YWYGW	YWWGY	WYYGW
WWGYY	WYGWY	YYGWW	YWGYW	YWGWY	WYGYW
WGWYY	WGYWY	YGYWW	YGWYW	YGWWY	WGYYW
GWWYY	GWYWY	GYYWW	GYYWW	GYWWY	GWYYW

Thus, there are 30 possible sequences. If the vegetables had all been different colors, there would have been $_5P_5 = 5! = 120$ possible color sequences.

Let us say that the two white vegetables are cauliflower and potatoes, and the two yellow ones are squash and corn. We can distinguish between them on this basis by the following method: We indicate the differences by using subscripts, W_1, W_2, Y_1, and Y_2. We can then take any one of the sequences previously listed and obtain three additional sequences by permuting the subscripts. We permute two subscripts for white, leaving the yellows unchanged. There are 2! such permutations. We obtain 2! additional sequences by permuting the subscripts of the yellows and leaving the whites unchanged. Since there is only one green, we are not concerned with its effect on the number of permutations. We simply note that there is 1! permutation of the single green. (If, however, there were two distinguishable greens, we would have to take the resulting 2! possible permutations into account.) Let us use the first sequence, WWYYG, to illustrate. The four possible sequences, when we distinguish between the whites and the yellows, are

$$W_1W_2Y_1Y_2G \quad\quad W_2W_1Y_1Y_2G \quad\quad W_1W_2Y_2Y_1G \quad\quad W_2W_1Y_2Y_1G$$

Since we can obtain 3 additional sequences for each of the 30 original sequences, there are $30 \cdot 2! \cdot 2! \cdot 1! = 120$ sequences when all objects are different. This equals $_5P_5 = 120$, the result previously obtained.

Suppose that $_nP_{n_1,n_2,...,n_k}$ equals the number of distinguishable sequences that can be formed from n objects taken n at a time. Say that n_1 are of one type, n_2 are of a second type, . . . , n_k are of a kth type, and $n = n_1 + n_2 + \cdots + n_k$. We can generalize the previous result as follows:

$$n! = (_nP_{n_1,n_2,...,n_k})n_1!n_2! \ldots n_k!$$

When we solve for $_nP_{n_1,n_2,...,n_k}$, we obtain

(3.3.5)

$$_nP_{n_1,n_2,...,n_k} = \frac{n!}{n_1!n_2! \ldots n_k!}$$

Now, using our example, we have

$$_5P_{2,2,1} = \frac{5!}{2!2!1!} = \frac{120}{4} = 30$$

This is the number of sequences previously listed.

EXAMPLE 3.3.6 A developer of a residential subdivision has five house styles and wants to build on ten adjacent lots. How many distinguishable arrangements are possible if the developer decides to build two houses of each style?

SOLUTION We get the answer by evaluating Equation 3.3.5. That is,

$$_{10}P_{2,2,2,2,2} = \frac{10!}{2!2!2!2!2!} = 113,400$$

An important special case of Equation 3.3.5 occurs when there are only two types of objects, that is, when r objects are of one type and $n - r$ objects are of another type:

(3.3.6)
$$_nP_{r,n-r} = \frac{n!}{r!(n - r)!} = {}_nC_r$$

Thus, the number of distinct permutations of n things of which r are of one type and $n - r$ are of another type is equal to the number of combinations of n different things taken r at a time.

EXERCISES

3.3.1 Evaluate the following: **(a)** $_8P_2$, **(b)** $_5P_3$, **(c)** $_9P_9$, **(d)** $_{10}P_4$, **(e)** $_6P_2$, **(f)** $_{10}C_3$, **(g)** $_{10}C_7$, **(h)** $_7C_3$, **(i)** $_5C_1$, **(j)** $_8C_4$

3.3.2 An office suite consists of four offices located side by side. These are to be occupied by four junior executives, A, B, C, and D. In how many ways can these executives be assigned to the four offices?

3.3.3 A supervisor has seven workers available from which to form a four-member production team. How many different teams are possible?

3.3.4 An advertising artist has eight photographs from which to choose in designing a full-page magazine ad containing three photographs. The position on the page is immaterial. How many designs using different combinations of photographs are possible?

3.3.5 The president of a firm that produces five different kinds of soap has a sample of each displayed in a row on a credenza in her office. **(a)** In how many different ways can she display the five products? **(b)** Suppose that she wants to display only three of the products at a time (in a row). How many distinguishable arrangements are possible?

3.3.6 A salesperson has seven products that he wishes to display at a national convention. He can display only four. The order in which he displays the products is immaterial. How many displays does he have to choose from?

3.3.7 An airline has six flights that it wishes to advertise in one-page ads in a Sunday newspaper. It wants to feature a different flight each Sunday for six Sundays. **(a)** How many different sequences of ads can the airline run? **(b)** Suppose that the airline decides at the last minute to run only four ads. How many sequences of ads can it run?

3.3.8 A firm has 5 different positions to fill and 15 applicants from which to choose. All applicants are equally qualified for all 5 positions. In how many ways can the firm fill the positions?

3.4 DIFFERENT VIEWS OF PROBABILITY

There are two types of objective probability: classical and relative frequency.

We can discuss probability from two points of view: the *objective* and the *subjective*. Until recently, most statisticians have held the objective point of view. We can also classify objective probability into two categories: (1) *a priori* or *classical* probability, and (2) *a posteriori* or the *relative frequency* concept. Classical probability has its origins in the seventeenth century and in the games of chance that were popular at that time. Examples from those games illustrate the principles. When a fair coin is tossed, the probability of observing a head is equal to one-half. This is also equal to the probability of observing a tail. When a perfectly balanced die is rolled, the probability of observing a one equals one-sixth. The probability is the same for the other five faces. One can compute the probabilities of such events through abstract reasoning. One does not have to rely on the results of any experiment. A coin need never be tossed, nor a die rolled, in order to be able to calculate these probabilities. We can define probability from the classical point of view as follows:

If some event can occur in N mutually exclusive and equally likely ways, and if m of these ways have characteristic E, the *probability* of the occurrence of E is equal to m/N.

We can write this definition as a formula:

(3.4.1)
$$P(E) = \frac{m}{N}$$

Here $P(E)$ is read as "the probability of E."

MUTUALLY EXCLUSIVE AND EQUALLY LIKELY EVENTS

Key phrases in the classical definition of probability are *mutually exclusive* and *equally likely*.

Two events are *mutually exclusive* if they cannot occur simultaneously. Two events are *equally likely* when there is no reason to expect one event rather than the other to occur.

The following examples illustrate the classical concept of probability.

EXAMPLE 3.4.1 A magazine advertised that it would give a prize to 50 persons selected at random from those returning a completed entry form enclosed as part of an advertising brochure. As of the closing date for receipt of entries, the magazine had received 10,000 completed entry forms. What is the probability that a given individual who entered the contest will win a prize?

SOLUTION Using the classical concept of probability expressed by Equation 3.4.1,

$$P(\text{Winner}) = \frac{\text{number of prizes to be awarded}}{\text{total number of entries}} = \frac{50}{10,000}$$

EXAMPLE 3.4.2   A business executive is attending a convention in an unfamiliar city. A Chamber of Commerce brochure lists six restaurants, A, B, C, D, E, and F, within walking distance of his hotel. From the brochure descriptions, the restaurants all appear to be equally attractive. In the absence of further information, the executive decides to roll a die to determine which restaurant he will visit for his first evening meal. What is the probability that the executive will dine at Restaurant C?

SOLUTION   Suppose that we represent each restaurant by one of the six faces of the die as follows:

Restaurant	Die Face Shows
A	1
B	2
C	3
D	4
E	5
F	6

We assume that the die is fair. That is, we assume that each die face is equally likely to occur on a given roll. In that case, $P(C) = P(3) = 1/6$.

THE CONCEPT OF RELATIVE FREQUENCY

There is another definition of probability, the *relative frequency* definition. It is similar to the classical definition. The relative frequency approach to probability depends on the repeatability of some process and the ability to count the number of such repetitions along with the number of times that some event of interest occurs. From the relative frequency point of view, we can define probability as follows:

Suppose that some process is repeated a large number of times n, and some resulting event with characteristic E occurs m times. The *relative frequency* of occurrence of E, m/n, will be approximately equal to the probability of E.

We can express this definition as a formula:

(3.4.2)
$$P(E) = \frac{m}{n}$$

EXAMPLE 3.4.3   A researcher with the Gaspé soft drink company wants to estimate the probability that a customer of a certain grocery store will buy one of its products. A total of 1,500 customers are observed over a period of time. Of these, 600 bought one or more of the firm's products. On the basis of this information, what is the best estimate of the desired probability?

SOLUTION By Equation 3.4.2,

$$P(E) = \frac{600}{1,500} = 0.4$$

Bear in mind that m/n in Equation 3.4.2 is only an estimate of $P(E)$, the true probability of occurrence of event E.

SUBJECTIVE PROBABILITY

The subjective approach to probability, which first received extensive attention in the early 1950s, holds that probability measures the confidence that a certain individual has in the truth of a certain proposition.

This view of probability does not depend on the repeatability of any process. In fact, we can apply this approach to events that can happen only once. An example would be the probability that the Los Angeles Rams will win the Super Bowl game this year. As another example, consider Salesperson A, who assesses the probability of winning the company sales contest this year to be 0.9. The sales manager assesses this salesperson's probability of winning to be only 0.5. The true probability is unknown. We say only that the salesperson is more optimistic than the sales manager. This view of probability is enjoying increased attention, especially in an area known as *Bayesian decision theory* (see Chapter 16). However, it has not been fully embraced by traditionally oriented statisticians.

3.5 ELEMENTARY PROPERTIES OF PROBABILITY

The following elementary properties of probability form the basis of all probability calculations.

1. *Given some process (or experiment) with n possible outcomes O_1, O_2, . . . , O_n, each event O_i is assigned a nonnegative number such that*

(3.5.1)
$$0 \le P(O_i) \le 1$$

Equation 3.5.1 is called the probability of outcome O_i. Simply stated, this property says that all outcomes must have a probability that is between 0 and 1, inclusive. This is a reasonable requirement, inasmuch as the concept of a negative probability has little intuitive appeal.

The *probability of an event* is equal to the sum of the probabilities of the outcomes of which the event is composed. Given any event E_i, it is also true that $0 \le P(E_i) \le 1$.

2. *If all possible events E_1, E_2, . . . , E_n are mutually exclusive, the sum of their probabilities is equal to 1.*

(3.5.2) $$P(E_1) + P(E_2) + \cdots + P(E_n) = 1$$

This is the property of *exhaustiveness*. It refers to the fact that the observer of a probabilistic experiment must allow for all possible events. When all these events are taken together, their total probability is 1. The requirement that the events be mutually exclusive specifies that the events $E_1, E_2, \ldots, E_n$ be *disjoint*, that is, that they do not overlap.

3. *Given any two mutually exclusive events E_i and E_j, the probability of the occurrence of either E_i or E_j is equal to the sum of their probabilities.*

(3.5.3) $$P(E_i \text{ or } E_j) = P(E_i) + P(E_j)$$

To see the implications of this property more easily, think about what would be true if the two events were not mutually exclusive. What if E_i and E_j could happen at the same time? If we tried to find the probability of the occurrence of either E_i or E_j, we would find the problem of an overlap. Then it would not be so easy to calculate the probability. Given that E_i and E_j *cannot* occur at the same time—that they are mutually exclusive—we simply add the individual probabilities to find $P(E_i \text{ or } E_j)$. In Section 3.6, we learn how to calculate $P(E_i \text{ or } E_j)$ when E_i and E_j are not mutually exclusive.

EXAMPLE 3.5.1   A group of employees consists of Employees A, B, and C. Each has the same chance (probability) of being selected for promotion. One of them is definitely going to be promoted. What is the probability that Employee A will be promoted? Employee B? Employee C?

SOLUTION   Each employee has one chance out of three of being promoted. Thus, the probabilities are 1/3 for Employee A, 1/3 for Employee B, and 1/3 for Employee C. We can see that each of these probabilities is a number between 0 and 1.

Since only one person is to be promoted, the three possible events are mutually exclusive. Therefore, their sum is equal to 1. That is, $1/3 + 1/3 + 1/3 = 1$.

The probability that either Employee A or Employee B will be promoted is equal to the sum of their individual probabilities since the events are mutually exclusive. Thus, the probability that either Employee A or Employee B will be promoted is equal to $1/3 + 1/3 = 2/3$.

3.6   CALCULATING THE PROBABILITY OF AN EVENT

Let us now use the concepts and techniques introduced in the previous sections to solve practical problems involving the calculation of specific probabilities.

We must first distinguish between two types of probability, *conditional probability* and *unconditional probability*. Suppose that all the possible outcomes of some experiment constitute the universal set. We compute the probability of the occurrence of an event by forming the ratio of the number of favorable outcomes to the number of all possible outcomes. This probability is called an *uncondi-

TABLE 3.6.1   Household appliances classified by color and style

Style	C_1 (White)	C_2 (Copper)	C_3 (Green)	Total
		Color		
S_1	1,400	450	900	2,750
S_2	1,300	350	800	2,450
S_3	900	700	750	2,350
S_4	1,000	250	1,200	2,450
Total	4,600	1,750	3,650	10,000

tional probability. The discussion in this section assumes that each outcome is equally likely.

At times the set of all possible outcomes may constitute a subset of the universal set. The population of interest may be reduced by some set of conditions not applicable to the total population.

When we calculate probabilities using a subset of the universal set as the denominator, the result is a *conditional probability*.

EXAMPLE 3.6.1   Table 3.6.1 shows 10,000 household appliances cross-classified by color and style. Suppose that we want to calculate the probability that an appliance picked at random will be white.

SOLUTION   The desired probability is an unconditional probability, since we have placed no restrictions on the set of all possible outcomes. We compute the probability as follows:

$$P(C_1) = \frac{n(C_1)}{n(U)} = \frac{4,600}{10,000} = 0.46$$

Note that we calculate the probability by forming the ratio of two numbers. The denominator consists of the total number of applicances that could be selected $n(U)$. The numerator is the number of appliances with the characteristic of interest $n(C_1)$. This example illustrates the use of Equation 3.4.1.

CONDITIONAL PROBABILITY

Now suppose that we reduce the set of all possible outcomes to S_1 appliances. What is the probability that an appliance picked at random will be white, given that it is type S_1? This is a conditional probability. In Table 3.6.1, there are 2,750 members of set S_1. Of these, 1,400 are white. These 1,400 belong to the set $C_1 \cap S_1$. The probability sought is given by $P(C_1|S_1)$, where the vertical line between C_1 and S_1 is read "given." The entire expression is read "the probability of C_1 given S_1." Thus, we have

$$P(C_1|S_1) = \frac{n(C_1 \cap S_1)}{n(S_1)} = \frac{1,400}{2,750} = 0.51$$

We may compute the conditional probability $P(C_1|S_1)$ another way. Divide both the numerator and the denominator in the preceding equation by $n(U)$, the number in the universal set, or the total number of appliances. The result is

$$P(C_1|S_1) = \frac{\dfrac{n(C_1 \cap S_1)}{n(U)}}{\dfrac{n(S_1)}{n(U)}}$$

Here the numerator is the probability that an appliance picked at random from all appliances will be both white and style S_1. We can write it $P(C_1 \cap S_1)$. The denominator is the probability that an appliance picked at random will be style S_1. We can write it $P(S_1)$. We can rewrite the entire expression as

$$P(C_1|S_1) = \frac{P(C_1 \cap S_1)}{P(S_1)} = \frac{\dfrac{1,400}{10,000}}{\dfrac{2,750}{10,000}} = \frac{0.14}{0.275} = 0.51$$

The following example further illustrates conditional probability.

EXAMPLE 3.6.2   A class consists of 30 students, of whom 10 are men and 20 are women. Five of the women and none of the men are out-of-state students. Thus, the events "male" and "out-of-state" are mutually exclusive.

(a) A student is selected at random from the class. What is the probability that the one selected will be an out-of-state student? The answer is $5/30 = 0.17$.
(b) Now suppose that the student selected is a woman. What is the probability that she will be an out-of-state student? Men are now no longer of interest, since one of the 20 women has been drawn. Since 5 of the women are out-of-state students, the probability that the one selected is from out of state is $5/20 = 0.25$. The occurrence of one event (a woman) increased the probability of the occurrence of the second event (an out-of-state student).
(c) Suppose that the student selected is a man. What is the probability that he is an out-of-state student? Now women are eliminated from consideration in the calculation of the probability. Since no men are from out of state, the probability we seek is $0/10 = 0$. This time the occurrence of the first event decreases the probability of the occurrence of the second event.

Now think about the three probabilities that we have just computed. Why are they different? The probability computed in (a) is an *unconditional probability*.

FIGURE 3.6.1   Situation for calculation of conditional probabilities described in Example 3.6.2

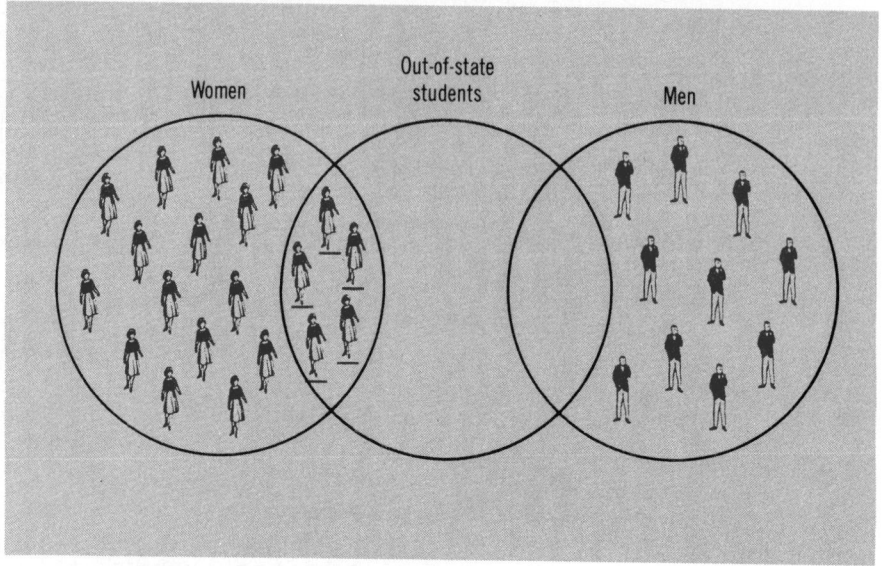

No "conditions" were stipulated. The denominator of the probability consisted of all 30 students in the class.

The probabilities computed in (b) and (c) are *conditional probabilities*. We computed them under the stipulated "condition" that some preceding event had occurred. The denominators for these probabilities are subsets of the original 30 students. Figure 3.6.1 shows the situation described in this example.

The following is a general definition of conditional probability:

> The *conditional probability* of A given B is equal to the probability $A \cap B$ divided by the probability of B, provided that the probability of B is not 0.

That is,

$$(3.6.1) \qquad P(A|B) = \frac{P(A \cap B)}{P(B)}, \qquad P(B) \neq 0$$

JOINT PROBABILITY

A probability such as $P(A \cap B)$ is called a *joint probability* since it gives the probability of the *joint*, or simultaneous, occurrence of two events or characteristics. Referring to Table 3.6.1, we see that $P(C_1 \cap S_1) = 1,400/10,000$ is a joint probability since it shows the probability of the joint occurrence of color C_1 and style S_1.

MARGINAL PROBABILITY

To illustrate the concept of marginal probability, let us again refer to Example 3.6.1. When we ask for the probability that an appliance in Table 3.6.1 is style S_1, we are asking for a *marginal probability*. Interest centers on a probability associated with a marginal total. We disregard any other criterion of classification. When we compute

$$P(S_1) = \frac{2,750}{10,000} = 0.275$$

this implies that we are not interested in the color. Similarly, if we are interested in the probability that an appliance picked at random is white, we use the marginal total, 4,600, and ignore the style classification. This suggests the following definition:

When we ignore one or more criteria of classification in computing a probability, the resulting probability is a *marginal probability*.

To gain further insight into the nature of marginal probabilities, let us refer again to Table 3.6.1. From the first row of the table, we may compute the following joint probabilities:

$$P(C_1 \cap S_1) = \frac{1,400}{10,000} = 0.14$$

$$P(C_2 \cap S_1) = \frac{450}{10,000} = 0.045$$

$$P(C_3 \cap S_1) = \frac{900}{10,000} = 0.09$$

If we add these probabilities, we get $0.14 + 0.045 + 0.09 = 0.275$, which is the marginal probability we computed earlier. This result is not a coincidence, since, alternatively, we may define a marginal probability as follows:

A *marginal probability* is the sum of two or more joint probabilities taken over all values of one or more variables.

THE ADDITION RULE

The probability of the occurrence of either one or the other of two mutually exclusive events is equal to the sum of their individual probabilities. When two events are *not* mutually exclusive, we use the *addition rule*, which may be stated as follows:

> Given two events A and B, the probability that event A or event B or both occur is equal to the probability that event A occurs, plus the probability that event B occurs, minus the probability that both events occur.

We can write this as

(3.6.2)
$$P(A \cup B) = P(A) + P(B) - P(A \cap B)$$

Refer to Table 3.6.1 again. We compute the probability that an appliance picked at random will be either style S_1 or white or both. Using Equation 3.6.2, we obtain

$$P(C_1 \cup S_1) = P(C_1) + P(S_1) - P(C_1 \cap S_1)$$
$$= \frac{4,600}{10,000} + \frac{2,750}{10,000} - \frac{1,400}{10,000} = \frac{4,600 + 2,750 - 1,400}{10,000}$$
$$= \frac{5,950}{10,000} = 0.595$$

The 1,400 appliances that are *both* white *and* style S_1 are included in the 2,750 that are style S_1 and also in the 4,600 that are white. Since in computing this probability we have added these 1,400 into the numerator twice, we must subtract them once to overcome the effect of duplication, or overlapping.

THE MULTIPLICATION RULE

Another useful rule for computing the probability of an event is the *multiplication rule*. This rule is suggested by the definition of conditional probability. Recall that we compute the conditional probability of A given B from

$$P(A|B) = \frac{P(A \cap B)}{P(B)}, \qquad P(B) \neq 0$$

We may rewrite this equation to obtain

(3.6.3)
$$P(A \cap B) = P(B)P(A|B)$$

This is the symbolic statement of the multiplication rule. In words, it is

> The probability of the joint occurrence of event A and event B is equal to the conditional probability of A given B times the marginal probability of B.

As noted previously, this type of probability, which is the probability of the simultaneous occurrence of two events, is called a joint probability.

To illustrate the use of the multiplication rule, let us use Equation 3.6.3 to find the probability that an appliance picked at random from all appliances is both white and style S_1. The desired probability is

$$P(C_1 \cap S_1) = P(S_1)P(C_1|S_1) = \frac{2{,}750}{10{,}000} \cdot \frac{1{,}400}{2{,}750} = \frac{1{,}400}{10{,}000} = 0.14$$

We can also calculate this joint probability directly from the data of Table 3.6.1, as follows:

$$P(C_1 \cap S_1) = \frac{n(C_1 \cap S_1)}{n(U)} = \frac{1{,}400}{10{,}000} = 0.14$$

INDEPENDENT EVENTS

Suppose that, in Equation 3.6.3, we are told that event B has occurred, but that this fact has no effect on the probability of A. That is, suppose that the probability of event A is the same regardless of whether or not B occurs. In this situation, $P(A|B) = P(A)$. We say that A and B are *independent events*. The multiplication rule for two independent events, then, may be written as

(3.6.4)
$$P(A \cap B) = P(B)P(A)$$

Thus, we see that if two events are independent, the probability of their joint occurrence is equal to the product of the probabilities of their individual occurrences.

Note that when two events are independent, each of the following statements is true:

$$P(A|B) = P(A), \qquad P(B|A) = P(B), \qquad P(A \cap B) = P(A)P(B)$$

In fact, two events are not independent unless all these statements are true.

As an illustration of independence, consider the following example.

EXAMPLE 3.6.3 A government agency employs 100 clerk-typists, classified by sex and marital status as shown in Table 3.6.2. If an employee is picked at random from the 100 employees, the probability that he or she is single is $P(S) = (24 + 16)/100 = 40/100 = 0.4$. What is the probability that an employee picked at random is single, given that the employee is male?

SOLUTION Using the formula for computing a conditional probability (Equation 3.6.1),

TABLE 3.6.2   Data for Example 3.6.3

	Marital Status		
Sex	Single	Married	Total
Male	16	24	40
Female	24	36	60
Total	40	60	100

$$P(S|M) = \frac{P(S \cap M)}{P(M)} = \frac{16/100}{40/100} = 0.4$$

Thus, the additional information that a randomly selected employee is male does not alter the probability that the employee is single, and $P(S) = P(S|M)$. Consequently, we can say that the two events—being single and being male—are, for this group, independent.

JOINT PROBABILITY OF TWO INDEPENDENT EVENTS

We can show the calculation of the joint probability of two independent events by means of a tree diagram.

EXAMPLE 3.6.4   At the Acton Fabricating Company, an average of 1 out of every 20 items coming off an assembly line is defective. The quality-control supervisor wants to know the probabilities of the following joint events for two items randomly selected from the assembly line:

1. Both items are defective.
2. The first item is defective and the second is not.
3. The first item is not defective and the second is.
4. Neither item is defective.

The quality-control supervisor believes that whether or not a given item is defective is independent of whether or not any other item is defective.

SOLUTION   We designate the probability of a defective item by $P(D)$ and the probability of a nondefective item by $P(\overline{D})$. We have $P(D) = 1/20$ and $P(\overline{D}) = 19/20$. If the assumption of independence is correct, these probabilities hold for every item drawn from the assembly line. The four desired probabilities, then, are

1. $P(D \cap D) = P(D)P(D) = (1/20)(1/20) = 1/400$
2. $P(D \cap \overline{D}) = P(D)P(\overline{D}) = (1/20)(19/20) = 19/400$
3. $P(\overline{D} \cap D) = P(\overline{D})P(D) = (19/20)(1/20) = 19/400$
4. $P(\overline{D} \cap \overline{D}) = P(\overline{D})P(\overline{D}) = (19/20)(19/20) = 361/400$

FIGURE 3.6.2   Tree diagram for Example 3.6.4

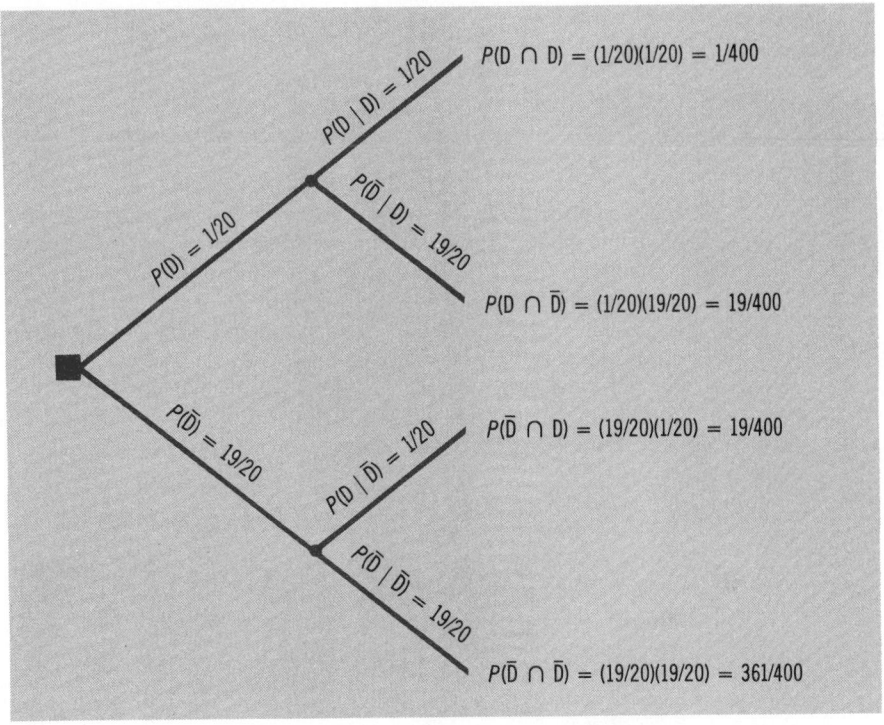

The total of the probabilities for these four mutually exclusive events is

$$\frac{1}{400} + \frac{19}{400} + \frac{19}{400} + \frac{361}{400} = \frac{400}{400} = 1$$

Figure 3.6.2 is a tree diagram representing these probabilities.

COMPLEMENTARY EVENTS

We must consider one more concept here. The probability of an event A is equal to 1 minus the probability of its complement $\overline{A}$, and therefore

$$P(\overline{A}) = 1 - P(A)$$

(3.6.5)

This result follows from the third property of probability, since the event A and its complement $\overline{A}$ are mutually exclusive.

Suppose, for example, that for some population the probability $P(A)$ that a person is a college graduate is 0.25. Then, for this population, the probability that a person is not a college graduate is

$$P(\overline{A}) = 1 - P(A) = 1 - 0.25 = 0.75$$

EXERCISES

3.6.1   The following table classifies 1,000 college graduates by area of concentration in college and type of employer for whom they went to work after graduation.   (a) A graduate is picked at random from this group. Calculate the probability that he or she was (1) an accounting major, (2) employed by a banking and finance firm, (3) an accounting major employed by a banking and finance firm, (4) an accounting major, given that he or she was employed by a banking and finance firm, (5) an accounting major or an engineering major, (6) an accounting major or employed by a banking and finance firm.   (b) Evaluate the following probabilities: (1) $P(B_3)$, (2) $P(A_4)$, (3) $P(B_3 \cap A_4)$, (4) $P(A_4)P(B_3|A_4)$, (5) $P(A_4 \cup B_3)$, (6) $P(A_4 \cup A_3)$, (7) $P(A_1|B_1)$.   (c) Is type of employer independent of area of concentration? How do you support your answer mathematically?

	Type of Employer					
	Public Accounting A_1	Banking & Finance A_2	Electronics A_3	Merchandising A_4	All Others A_5	Total
Major						
Accounting B_1	60	15	10	5	10	100
General business B_2	20	50	10	65	5	150
Humanities B_3	1	2	2	10	60	75
Social science B_4	2	20	8	20	70	120
Engineering B_5	2	5	188	5	50	250
All Others	30	50	55	60	110	305
Total	115	142	273	165	305	1,000

3.6.2   The Bailey and Benbow Company has two vacancies at the junior executive level. Ten people, seven men and three women, are eligible and equally qualified. The company has decided to draw two names at random from the list of eligibles. What is the probability that   (a) both positions will be filled by women,   (b) at least one of the positions will be filled by a woman,   (c) neither of the positions will be filled by a woman?

3.6.3   There are 300 homes in a neighborhood. At 100 of these, on a certain evening, no one is at home. Of the remaining homes, the occupants of 50 will not participate in telephone surveys. On a particular evening, a person conducting a telephone survey calls one of these homes at random. What is the probability that   (a) the surveyor will call a home in which no one is present,   (b) the surveyor will call a home in which someone is present, but the person will not participate in the survey,   (c) the call will result in participation in the survey?

3.6.4   At the Cabot Candy Company, the probability that an employee picked at random will be over 30 years of age is 0.58. What is the probability that an employee picked at random will be 30 years old or younger?

3.6.5   Refer to Exercise 3.2.1. Compute the probability than an employee picked at random will belong to each of the sets specified in (a) through (i).

3.7   BAYES' THEOREM

Thomas Bayes (1702–1761) was an English clergyman interested in mathematics. His name is associated with an area of probability that concerns a method of estimating the probabilities of the causes that may have produced an observed event. The method is summarized in a theorem that bears Bayes' name. It may be stated as follows:

Given $B_1, B_2, \ldots, B_n$ mutually exclusive events whose union is the universe, and let A by an arbitrary event in the universe, such that $P(A) \neq 0$; then

(3.7.1)
$$P(B_j|A) = \frac{P(A|B_j)P(B_j)}{\Sigma_{i=1}^{n} P(A|B_i)P(B_i)}$$

where $i = 1, 2, \ldots, n, j = 1, 2, \ldots,$ or n

Equation 3.7.1 is called the formula for the probability of *causes*. It enables us to find the probability of a particular B_j, or "cause," that may have brought about event A. It is sometimes written in another form:

(3.7.2)
$$P(B_j|A) = \frac{P(A \cap B_j)}{\Sigma_{i=1}^{n} P(A \cap B_i)}$$
$$= \frac{P(A \cap B_j)}{P(A \cap B_1) + P(A \cap B_2) + \cdots + P(A \cap B_n)}$$

Note that the probabilities computed by Equations 3.7.1 and 3.7.2 are conditional probabilities.

EXAMPLE 3.7.1   In an office, three clerks process incoming copies of a certain form. The first clerk, B_1, processes 40% of the forms. The second clerk, B_2, processes 35%. The third clerk, B_3, processes 25%. The first clerk has an error rate of 0.04, the second has an error rate of 0.06, and the third has an error rate of 0.03. A form selected at random from a day's output is found to have an error. The supervisor wishes to know the probability that it was processed by the first, second, or third clerk, respectively.

SOLUTION   Let A designate the event that a form containing an error is selected at random. Let B_1, B_2, and B_3 be the event that the form was processed by the first, second, and third clerk, respectively. Using our usual notation, we want to compute the following conditional probabilities: $P(B_1|A)$, $P(B_2|A)$, and $P(B_3|A)$. From the information given, we have the following unconditional probabilities: $P(B_1) = 0.40$, $P(B_2) = 0.35$, and $P(B_3) = 0.25$. These probabilities, which we can obtain without additional information, are called *prior probabilities*.

We are also told that the conditional probabilities of finding a record with an error, given that it was processed by one of the three clerks, are $P(A|B_1) = 0.04$, $P(A|B_2) = 0.06$, and $P(A|B_3) = 0.03$. These probabilities are called the *likelihood*. From them, we can calculate the three joint probabilities:

$$P(A \cap B_1) = P(A|B_1)P(B_1) = (0.04)(0.40) = 0.016$$
$$P(A \cap B_2) = P(A|B_2)P(B_2) = (0.06)(0.35) = 0.021$$
$$P(A \cap B_3) = P(A|B_3)P(B_3) = (0.03)(0.25) = 0.0075$$

We can now use Equation 3.7.2 to obtain the desired probabilities.

$$P(B_1|A) = \frac{P(A \cap B_1)}{P(A \cap B_1) + P(A \cap B_2) + P(A \cap B_3)}$$

$$= \frac{0.016}{0.016 + 0.021 + 0.0075} = \frac{0.016}{0.0445} = 0.36$$

$$P(B_2|A) = \frac{P(A \cap B_2)}{0.0445} = \frac{0.021}{0.0445} = 0.47$$

$$P(B_3|A) = \frac{P(A \cap B_3)}{0.0445} = \frac{0.0075}{0.0445} = 0.17$$

We call these *posterior probabilities* because they were calculable after it was known that the form was one that had an error. Table 3.7.1 summarizes these calculations. Figure 3.7.1 is a graphic representation (not drawn to scale) of the calculations in Table 3.7.1.

Today Bayes' theorem is considered the cornerstone of modern decision theory, sometimes called Bayesian decision theory (see Chapter 16). Its use in this regard, however, has some critics. The criticism focuses not on its mathematical integrity, but on the way in which the prior probabilities are sometimes determined. These prior probabilities frequently are arrived at subjectively or intuitively, rather than being based on objective data.

TABLE 3.7.1   Summary of calculations illustrating the use of Bayes' theorem, Example 3.7.1

Event	Prior Probability $P(B_i)$	Likelihood $P(A|B_i)$	Joint Probability $P(A \cap B_i)$	Posterior Probability $P(B_i|A)$
B_1	0.40	0.04	0.0160	0.36
B_2	0.35	0.06	0.0210	0.47
B_3	0.25	0.03	0.0075	0.17
Total	1.00	—	0.0445	1.00

FIGURE 3.7.1   Graphic representation of Bayes' theorem in Example 3.7.1

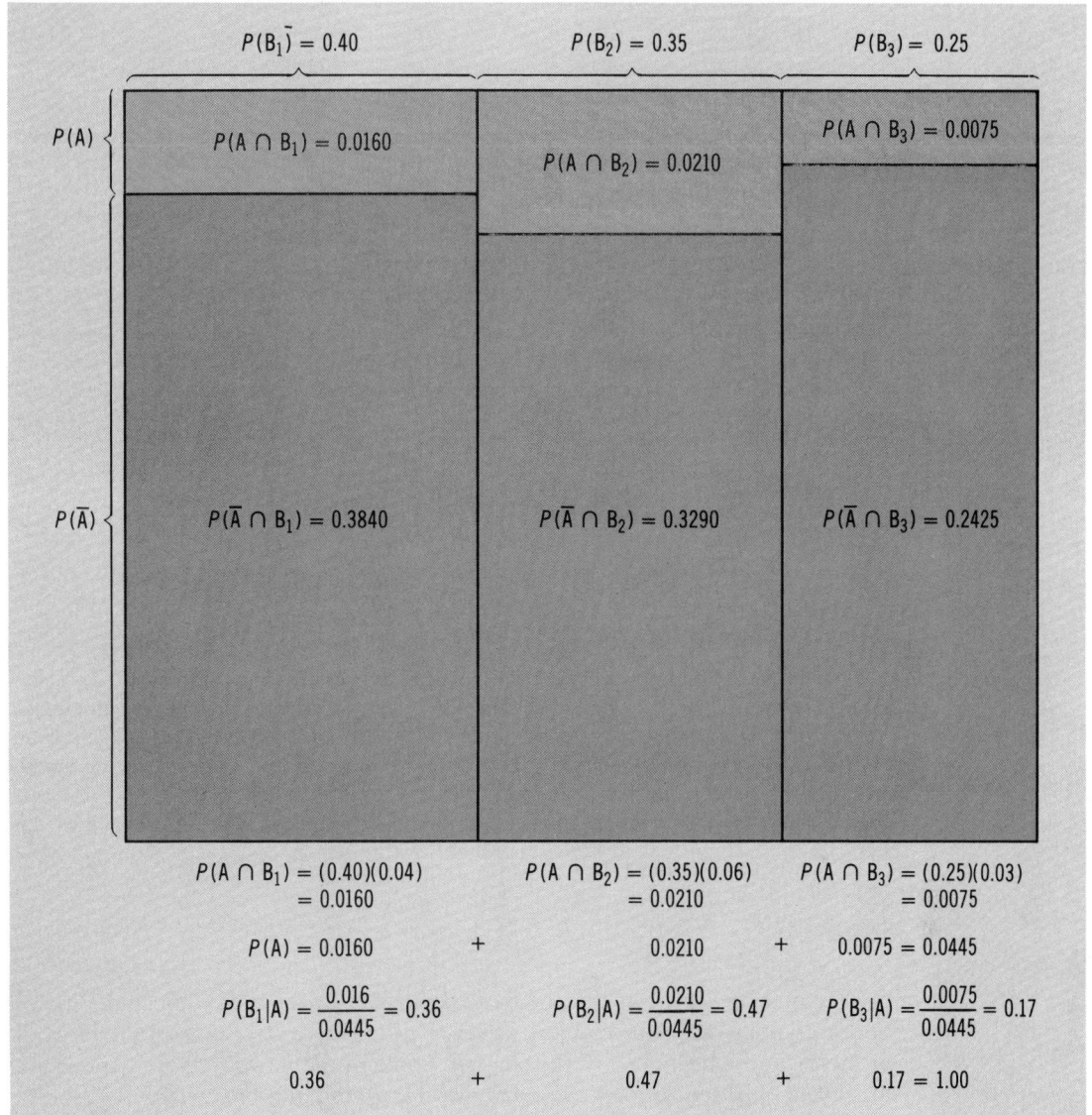

EXERCISES

3.7.1   In a survey conducted by Candid Canvassers, 1,000 adult males are cross-classified by father's occupational status and by whether or not they have surpassed their fathers in occupational status. The following table shows the results. A man is selected at random from this group for further interviews. It is found that he has surpassed his father's occupational status. What is the probability that his father   (a) was an unskilled laborer,   (b) was a semiskilled or skilled laborer,   (c) held a clerical or sales job,   (d) held a semi-professional or low-level-management job?

		Son	
Father's Occupational Status	Surpassed	Not Surpassed
Unskilled labor	250	100
Semiskilled and skilled labor	150	100
Clerical and sales	115	110
Semiprofessional and low-level management	70	105

3.7.2 Gourmet Goodies, a mail-order business, receives orders from four areas of the country, as shown in the following table. Ten percent of the orders from the East, 25% of those from the South, 5% from the Midwest, and 15% from the West are for more than $10. An order picked at random from the files is found to be for more than $10. What is the probability that it came from   (a) the East,   (b) the South,   (c) the Midwest,   (d) the West?

Area	**Percent of Orders**
East	30
South	40
Midwest	20
West	10

3.7.3 In a suburban community, 30% of the households use Brand A toothpaste, 27% use Brand B, 25% use Brand C, and 18% use Brand D. In the four groups of households, the proportions of residents who learned about the brand they use through television advertising are as follows: Brand A, 0.10; Brand B, 0.05; Brand C, 0.20; and Brand D, 0.15. In a household selected at random from the community, it is found that residents learned about the toothpaste through television advertising. What is the probability that the brand of toothpaste used in the household is   (a) A,   (b) B,   (c) C,   (d) D?

SUMMARY

This chapter presents some of the basic concepts of probability. Since the use of set terminology makes probability easier to discuss, we give some of the ideas of set theory at the beginning of the chapter. Some of the terms that are defined are *set, subset, null set, disjoint set, universal set, union,* and *intersection.*

You learned that various sets and subsets can be portrayed visually by a graphic device known as a *Venn diagram.*

To ease the task of counting certain events in order to compute their associated probabilities, the chapter introduces some counting rules. You learned how to determine the number of permutations that can be made from *n* objects taken *r* at a time. You also learned about another type of arrangement, called a *combination.* We show how to find the number of combinations that can be made from *n* things taken *r* at a time.

You learned that we can discuss probability from three different points of view: the *a priori* or classical, the *a posteriori* or relative frequency, and the subjective.

You learned three elementary properties of probability for a given set of mutually exclusive events $E_1, E_2, \ldots, E_n$:

1. $0 \leq P(E_i) \leq 1$
2. $P(E_1) + P(E_2) + \cdots + P(E_n) = 1$
3. $P(E_i \text{ or } E_j) = P(E_i) + P(E_j)$

In calculating probabilities, you need to understand the concepts of mutually exclusive events, independent events, unconditional probability, conditional probability, marginal probability, and joint probability.

You learned the addition rule and the multiplication rule, two rules that are helpful in calculating certain probabilities.

Finally, this chapter discusses Bayes' theorem, which provides a formula for computing a conditional probability. This theorem is called the formula for the probability of "causes," since it enables us to find the probability of a particular B_i, or "cause," that may have brought about event A.

REVIEW EXERCISES

1. Define the following:

(a) probability
(b) objective probability
(c) subjective probability
(d) classical probability
(e) relative frequency
(f) mutually exclusive events
(g) independence

(h) marginal probability
(i) joint probability
(j) conditional probability
(k) experiment
(l) outcome
(m) event
(n) sample space

2. Name and explain the three properties of probability.

3. What is a set? Give three examples of sets.

4. Define the following: (a) unit set, (b) subset, (c) empty set, (d) disjoint set, (e) universal set, (f) complement.

5. Under what condition are two sets considered equal?

6. Define and give an example of the union of two sets.

7. Define and give an example of the intersection of two sets.

8. What is a Venn diagram?

9. Describe and illustrate the following: (a) multiplication rule, (b) addition rule, (c) combination, (d) permutation, (e) factorial.

10. Make up a realistic problem from your area of interest to illustrate the use of Bayes' theorem.

11. A firm interviews 15 applicants for a position on its sales force. One question on the application form concerns leisure-time activities. Six applicants say that they spend a major portion of their leisure time playing golf. Ten mention bowling. Three do not mention sports at all. How many applicants spend their leisure time both golfing and bowling? Illustrate with a Venn diagram. [*Hint*: $n(A \cup B) = n(A) + n(B) - n(A \cap B)$.]

12. At a convention, four men and two women are to be seated at the head table. How many different arrangements are possible if the six persons are distinguished only with respect to sex?

13. A final examination consists of 20 questions. A student who takes the exam is told to select and answer 15. How many possible tests does a student have from which to choose?

14. Of 1,000 items produced in a day at Dakin Manufacturers, 400 are produced on the first shift, 350 on the second, and 250 on the third. An item is picked at random. What is the probability that it was produced on (a) the first shift, (b) the second shift, (c) the third shift, (d) either the first or the second shift?

15. In Exercise 14, suppose that the proportions of defective items produced on the first, second, and third shifts are 0.01, 0.02, and 0.04, respectively. An item is picked at random. (a) What is the probability that it is defective? (b) What is the probability that it is defective, given that it was produced on the third shift? (c) What is the probability that it is defective and also was produced on the first shift?

16. A race driver uses Make A cars 50% of the time, Make B cars 30% of the time, and Make C cars 20% of the time. Of the 25 races that he has entered with Make A cars, he has won 5. Of the 15 races with Make B cars, he has won 4. Of the 10 races with Make C cars, he has won 4. He has just won a race. What is the probability that the car he was driving was (a) Make A, (b) Make B, (c) Make C?

17. Set C consists of the employees of a certain firm who voted in favor of a new insurance plan. Set D consists of the employees of the same firm who have children in school. Define (a) $C \cup D$, (b) $C \cap D$, (c) $\bar{C}$, (d) $\bar{D}$.

18. Express each of the following sets by a single symbol: (a) $A \cap \varnothing$, (b) $A \cap \bar{A}$, (c) $A \cup \varnothing$, (d) $A \cup \bar{A}$.

19. Express each of the following sets by a different symbol: (a) $\bar{U}$, (b) $(\bar{A})$, (c) $\bar{\varnothing}$, (d) $(\overline{A \cup \varnothing})$.

20. One hundred business people are asked to specify the type of magazine they prefer. The following table shows the 100 responses, cross-classified by educational level and type of magazine preferred. Specify the number of members of each of the following sets: (a) S, (b) $V \cup C$, (c) A, (d) $\bar{W}$, (e) U, (f) $\bar{B}$, (g) $T \cap B$, (h) $(\overline{T \cap C})$.

		Educational Level		
Type of Magazine	High School (A)	College (B)	Graduate School (C)	Total
Sports (S)	15	8	7	30
General news (T)	3	7	20	30
Travel (V)	5	5	15	25
Business news (W)	10	3	2	15
Total	33	23	44	100

21. An athletic team has 12 members. It plans to elect 4 officers—a captain, a co-captain, a manager, and a treasurer—by secret write-in ballot. All 12 members are eligible and willing to serve. How many possible sets of 4 members can serve? (Ignore the office held.)

22. In the Eames Company's computer center there are seven microcomputer operators who must sit at machines that are placed one behind the other. In how many ways can the seven operators be assigned to the machines?

23. A salesperson has ten clients to visit in a week. The clients are three manufacturers, four retail stores, two office-supply firms, and one government agency. How many distinguishable visiting arrangements can the salesperson prepare if he or she wishes to distinguish among the clients only on the basis of type of business?

24. The probability that a salesperson will make a sale is 0.8. What is the probability (assuming independence) that on two calls made in a day the salesperson will make two sales?

25. The following table shows the outcome of 500 interviews attempted during a survey of opinions about big business held by residents of a certain city. The data are also classified by the area of the city in which the interview was attempted. A questionnaire is selected at random from the 500.   (a) What is the probability that (1) the questionnaire was completed? (2) the potential respondent was not at home? refused to answer? (3) the potential respondent lived in area A? B? D? E? (4) the questionnaire was completed, given that the potential respondent lived in area B? (5) the potential respondent refused to answer the questionnaire or lived in area D or both?   (b) Calculate the following probabilities: (1) $P(A \cap R)$, (2) $P(B \cup C)$, (3) $P(\overline{D})$, (4) $P(N|D)$, (5) $P(B|R)$, (6) $P(C)$.

Outcome of Interview

Area of City	Completed (C)	Not at Home (N)	Refused (R)	Total
A	100	20	5	125
B	115	5	5	125
D	50	60	15	125
E	35	50	40	125
Total	300	135	65	500

26. In a large city, 70% of the households receive a daily newspaper, and 90% have a television set. Suppose that these two events are independent. What is the probability that a randomly selected household will be one that receives a daily newspaper and has a televison set?

27. At the Faraday Electric Company, 10% of the assembly-line employees have only a fourth-grade education or less. The educational status of the remainder is as follows: completed Grade 5, 6, or 7, 50%; completed Grade 8 or higher, 40%. Of the first group, 20% are under 25 years old. Of the second group, 50% are under 25. Of the third group, 70% are under 25. An employee picked at random from this population is found to be under 25. What is the probability that the employee has a fourth-grade education or less? Find the probabilities for the other two groups.

28. Of the persons employed by Gaillard Industries, 45% come from one area of the city, Area A; 30% from a second area, B; and 25% from a third area, C. Within one year, 30% of the employees from Area A, 20% from Area B, and 10% from Area C leave the firm. A record is picked at random from the firm's files. It is found that the person under consideration left the firm within one year. What is the probability that the person was from Area A? Area B? Area C?

29. At the Hammond Company, the probability that an employee picked at random is a college graduate is 0.55. What is the probability that an employee picked at random is not a college graduate?

 30. In a government agency, 30% of the employees take public transportation to work. Also, 60% of the employees are female. It is assumed that these two characteristics are independent. Draw a tree diagram to illustrate and find the probability than an employee picked at random from this population will be   (a) female and take public transportation to work;   (b) female and not take public transportation to work;   (c) male and take public transportation to work;   (d) male and not take public transportation to work.

 31. At the Ibsen Construction Company, six persons (four females and two males) are eligible for promotion to two higher-paying positions.   (a) How many different combinations of these employees are eligible for promotion? List them.

Assume that the persons who will be promoted are to be selected at random. Find the probability that   (b) at least one of the persons promoted will be a female,   (c) exactly one female will be promoted,   (d) no more than one female will be promoted,   (e) no female will be promoted.

 32. There are 50 applicants for a job. Ten are members of Ethnic Group A, 15 of Ethnic Group B, and 25 of Ethnic Group C. The numbers of females (F) in the three groups are 2, 9, and 15, respectively. A person is selected at random to fill the job. Find the probability that this person will be   (a) A and F,   (b) A or F or both,   (c) F given B,   (d) A and B, (e) F and C.

33. Suppose that there are two events E_1 and E_2 such that $P(E_1) = 0.20$ and $P(E_2) = 0.30$.   (a) Given that E_1 and E_2 are independent, what is $P(E_1 \cap E_2)$?   (b) Given that E_1 and E_2 are mutually exclusive, what is $P(E_1 \cup E_2)$?

34. At the Jacobs Ladder Company, 60% of the employees are males. Furthermore, 80% of the females and 60% of the males are high school graduates. Find the probability that an employee picked at random will be   (a) a male high school graduate,   (b) a female high school graduate.

 35. An office supervisor claims to be a good judge of human intelligence. To test this claim, a psychologist asks the supervisor to pick the three most intelligent workers from a group of nine and rank them in order of intelligence. Suppose that the supervisor actually has no special ability to evaluate intelligence.   (a) What is the probability that the supervisor makes a correct selection and ranking?   (b) What is the probability that the supervisor will select at least one of the three most intelligent workers?

 36. A personnel director has found that she can fill a certain type of position within one week 70% of the time. But she finds that 60% of the time all applicants for the position are high school dropouts. The other 40% of the time none of them are dropouts. When all applicants *are* high school dropouts, the position is filled within one week only 56% of the time.   (a) What is the probability that the position is filled within one week, given that the applicants are not high school dropouts?   (b) Is filling the position within a week independent of whether the applicants are high school dropouts?

 37. The human resources director at the Kane Insurance Company has determined the following probabilities for the length of time a certain type of employee remains with the firm after being hired. Find the probability that a newly hired employee of this type will be with the firm   (a) less than five years,   (b) three years or more,   (c) at least two but less than four years,   (d) at least four years.

Length of Stay	Probability
Less than 1 year	0.05
1 year but less than 2	0.10
2 years but less than 3	0.10
3 years but less than 4	0.15
4 years but less than 5	0.20
5 years or longer	0.40
	1.00

38. In a survey of business managers, 90% said that they were covered by whole life insurance and 70% said that they were covered by term insurance. In addition, 65% said that they were covered by both types of insurance. Assume that these percentages apply to the sampled population.   (a) What is the probability that a person selected at random from the sampled population will be covered by one or the other of the two types of insurance?   (b) A person selected at random from the sampled population is covered by whole life insurance. What is the probability that he or she is also covered by term insurance?   (c) What is the probability that a person randomly selected from the population will be covered by whole life insurance if he or she is covered by term insurance?

39. An instructor has a test bank consisting of 300 easy true-false questions, 200 difficult true-false questions, 500 easy multiple-choice questions, and 400 difficult multiple-choice questions. If a question is selected at random from the test bank, what is the probability that it will be   (a) an easy question,   (b) an easy multiple-choice question,   (c) an easy question, given that it is a multiple-choice question?

40. A market analyst claims to have an uncommon ability to predict the success of new products. He is asked to rank six new products in order of future success. If, in fact, he has no special ability to predict a product's success, what is the probability that he will correctly rank the products?

41. A personnel director must select from among ten persons to fill four job openings. Four of the candidates belong to a minority group. If the four positions are filled at random from among the candidates, what is the probability that no minority group member will be selected?

42. Refer to Exercise 41. What is the probability that at least one minority group member will be selected?

43. The manager of the Gulp fast-food restaurant chain found that 75% of the customers order a dessert with their meal, 60% order a certain brand of cola, and 40% order both. (a) What is the probability that a customer will order either a dessert or the particular brand of cola or both?   (b) What is the probability that a customer who orders a dessert will also order the particular brand of cola?   (c) What is the probability that a customer who orders the particular brand of cola will also order a dessert?

44. At Lamont Consultants, Inc., 80% of the technical employees have met the training requirements for promotion, 70% have met the experience requirements, and 60% have met both requirements. If an employee is selected at random from the population, find the probability that the employee will   (a) meet at least one of the requirements;   (b) not meet either of the requirements;   (c) meet the training requirement, given that he or she meets the experience requirement.

45. In a survey of senior executives, it was found that 30% were recruited from outside their current firm; 20% of all the executives surveyed said that they would like to change firms, and 60% of those who said that they would like to change firms were recruited from outside their current firm. If we select an executive at random from this group, find the probability that he or she   (a) would like to change firms and was recruited from outside his or her current firm;   (b) would like to change firms or was recruited from out .de his or her current firm or both;   (c) would like to change firms, given that he or she was recruited from outside his or her current firm.

46. $P(A) = 0.7$ and $P(B) = 0.4$. Calculate $P(A \cap B)$, $P(A|B)$, and $P(B|A)$ and determine whether A and B are either independent or mutually exclusive when   (a) $P(A \cup B) = 0.96$,   (b) $P(A \cup B) = 0.82$.

47. In how many ways can 5 people be selected from among 15 people   (a) if order counts,   (b) if order does not count?

48. In how many ways can 12 people be selected from among 18 people   (a) if order counts,   (b) if order does not count?

49. There are three urns of Type A and nine urns of Type B. The three urns of Type A each contain two red (R) and eight white (W) balls. The nine urns of Type B each contain seven red and three white balls. Find the probabilities of the following events: (a) $P(A)$,   (b) $P(B)$,   (c) $P(A|W)$,   (d) $P(B|W)$, and the prior probabilities   (e) $P(W)$ and   (f) $P(R)$.

50. If we use the digits 0 through 9, how many distinct 3-digit numbers can we write if (a) each number can be used more than once,   (b) each number can be used only once?

51. $P(A) = 0.25$, $P(A \cap B) = 0.15$, and $P(A \cup B) = 0.7$. Find the following: (a) $P(A \cap \overline{B})$,   (b) $P(A \cup \overline{B})$,   (c) $P(A|\overline{B})$.   (d) Are A and B independent?   (e) Are A and B mutually exclusive?

52. $P(A) = 0.4$, $P(B) = 0.3$, and $P(B|\overline{A}) = 0.5$. Find the following: (a) $P(A|B)$,   (b) $P(A \cap \overline{B})$,   (c) $P(\overline{A} \cup \overline{B})$.   (d) Are A and B independent?   (e) Are A and B mutually exclusive?

53. The following table shows 1,000 unemployed adult males classified according to three levels of education (E, F, G) and three levels of job skills (R, S, T). Calculate the following probabilities: (a) $P(E)$,   (b) $P(F \cap T)$,   (c) $P(T|E)$,   (d) $P(R \cup G)$,   (e) $P(E \cup \overline{F})$.

	R	S	T	
E	160	40	50	250
F	75	90	225	390
G	210	100	50	360
	445	230	325	1,000

54. A firm has three salespersons, A, B, and C. The average number of customers that each salesperson visits per day is 7 for A, 9 for B, and 4 for C. The probabilities of completing a sale on any given visit are 0.4 for A, 0.3 for B, and 0.5 for C. The manager of the firm has just received a letter indicating that a sale has been completed. Based on this information, determine the probability that this sale was completed by each of the three salespersons, A, B, and C.

55. An urn contains one red, two white, and three blue balls. Balls are drawn without replacement. Given that the second ball drawn was red (R_2), calculate the probability that the first ball drawn was (a) red (R_1), (b) white (W_1), (c) blue (B_1). (d) Calculate the prior probability of drawing a red on the second draw.

56. With a single roll of a pair of dice, determine the probability of getting the following: (a) the sum of 7, (b) the sum of 7, given that at least one of the dice is a 5, (c) a 4, 5, or 6 on at least one of the dice, (d) a 4, 5, or 6 on both dice, (e) a sum that is odd or more than 5, (f) a sum that is odd and more than 5.

57. It is required that five men and four women be seated in a row in such a way that the women occupy the even places. (a) How many seating arrangements are possible? (b) Given that all possibilities are equally likely, what is the probability that Frank and Jane will sit next to each other?

58. Bill, Mary, and Joe belong to a club of 19 people. A committee of 12 is to be selected at random. What is the probability that these 3 will all be on the committee? (*Hint*: Think of the total set of 19 people as consisting of two subsets, one subset composed of Bill, Mary, and Joe, and the other composed of the remaining 16 people. Then determine the number of ways in which the 3 people can be selected, without replacement, from the set of 3, and the number of ways the other 9 members of the committee can be selected from the set of 16 that does not include Bill, Mary, and Joe.)

59. Consider a family with two children and assume that each child is as likely to be a boy as a girl. What is the conditional probability that both children are boys, given that (a) the older child is a boy, (b) at least one of the children is a boy?

60. One out of eight people employed by Company A is a college graduate. The ratio of college graduates at Company B is twice as large. If one person from each company is selected at random, calculate the probability that (a) both are graduates, (b) Company A's employee is a graduate but Company B's employee is not, (c) at least one of them is a graduate, (d) at most one of them is a graduate. [*Hint*: You may wish to construct a tree diagram and use the fact that $P(A) = P(B)P(A|B) + P(\bar{B})P(A|\bar{B})$.]

61. $P(A \cup B) = 0.9$, $P(A|B) = 0.625$, and $P(A|\bar{B}) = 0.5$. Calculate: (a) $P(A)$, (b) $P(B)$, (c) $P(A \cap B)$, (d) $P(B|A)$, (e) $P(B|\bar{A})$, (f) $P(\bar{A} \cup \bar{B})$.

62. Two committees, one with 6 and one with 7 people, are to be selected from a group of 18 people, with no one person serving on both committees at the same time. (a) In how many different ways can this be done? (b) If you are a member of the group, what is the probability that you will be selected to serve on one of the two committees?

63. When one forms all possible arrangements of r items from a total of n available items, are there more or fewer combinations than permutations?

64. Given: $P(A \cap B) = 0.3$, $P(A|B) = 0.5$. What is $P(B)$?

65. Given: $P(A \cap D) = 0.10$, $P(B \cap D) = 0.12$, $P(C \cap D) = 0.08$, $P(A) + P(B) + P(C) = 1$. Find $P(D)$.

66. Given: $P(A) = 0.25$, $P(B) = 0.50$, $P(A \cap B) = 0.15$. Find $P(A \cup B)$.

67. Given: $P(B) = 0.20$, $P(A|B) = 0.1515$. Find $P(A \cap B)$.

68. Given: $P(A) = 0.55$. Find $P(\bar{A})$.

69. A class of 30 students meets in a classroom that has 6 front-row seats. Each time the class meets, the instructor assigns seats in such a way that a different arrangement of 6 students occupies the front-row seats. For how many periods would the class have to meet in order for the instructor to lecture to every different possible arrangement of 6 front-row students?

70. The following table shows a sample of voters cross-classified according to place of residence and their preference for four candidates for governor of their state. The data were obtained from a pre-election survey.

Place of Residence

Preferred Candidate	Urban	Suburban	Rural	Total
A	100	30	30	160
B	60	40	70	170
C	50	90	10	150
D	30	40	50	120
Total	240	200	160	600

Suppose that we use the results of this survey to estimate preference and residence probabilities in the sampled population. What is the estimated probability that a voter picked at random will be a suburban dweller and will prefer Candidate C?

71. Refer to Exercise 70. A voter picked at random prefers Candidate A. What is the estimated probability that he or she is an urban dweller?

72. Refer to Exercise 70. What is the estimated probability that a voter picked at random will be either a rural dweller or will prefer Candidate D?

73. Refer to Exercise 70. What is the estimated probability that a randomly selected voter will not be an urban resident?

74. Refer to Exercise 70. How many marginal probabilities can we compute from the data?

75. Refer to Exercise 70. How many joint probabilities can we compute from the data?

76. Refer to Exercise 70. How many conditional probabilities can we compute from the data?

*77. A frequently used probability concept is the notion of odds. Simply stated, the odds of a success are equal to the ratio of the number of successes to the number of failures when the total number of relevant events can be classified as either a success or a failure. If the total number of events is n and the number of these that are successes is s, then the odds of a success are $s/(n - s)$. Suppose there are 50 students of whom 30 are female and 20 are male. Suppose we select a student at random from the 50. The odds in favor of a female's being selected are 30 to 20, or 30/20, or 3 to 2. While this is a statement of the odds in favor of a female, the probability that a female will be selected is 30/50 or 0.6. But the odds in favor of a female are equal to the ratio of the probability that a female will be selected to the probability that a male will be selected. That is, the odds in favor of a female are equal to $(30/50)/(20/50) = 30/20 =$ odds of 3 to 2.

A total of 100 people have applied for a single job opening with the Thebes Advertising Agency. Of these, 70 have an MBA degree. (a) If the position is to be filled by selecting a person at random from among the applicants, what are the odds in favor of a person with an MBA degree being selected? (b) What is the probability that a person with an MBA will be selected? (c) What is the probability that a person who does not have an MBA will be selected? (d) Use probabilities to find the odds in favor of a person with an MBA. (e) Based on your knowledge of odds, what appears to be true about the numerator and denominator of an odds as compared to the numerator and denominator of a probability when the same numbers are relevant to the calculations?

STATISTICS AT WORK

STATISTICS AT WORK

STATISTICS AT WORK

STATISTICS AT WORK

1. WOMEN EXECUTIVES AND PERFUME

According to the book *100% American*, 36% of American women executives say that wearing perfume helps a woman's career. Suppose that we ask a randomly selected American woman executive if she thinks that wearing perfume helps a woman's career. What is the probability that she will answer no?

Source: Daniel Evan Weiss, *100% American*, New York, Poseidon Press, 1988.

2. MINORITY ENTERPRISE LOANS

The following table shows, by type of loan and region, the number of minority enterprise loans approved by the Small Business Administration in 1971.

Number of minority enterprise loans approved—FY 1971

	All ME Loans	7(a) Loans
Total SBA	7,776	2,123
Region I—Boston	342	148
II—New York	1,809	484
III—Philadelphia	588	177
IV—Atlanta	873	171
V—Chicago	938	372
VI—Dallas	945	241
VII—Kansas City	467	92
VIII—Denver	253	54
IX—San Francisco	1,181	333
X—Seattle	380	51

	EOL Loans	DBL and LDC Loans
Total SBA	5,451	202
Region I—Boston	191	3
II—New York	1,289	36
III—Philadelphia	398	13
IV—Atlanta	641	61
V—Chicago	538	28
VI—Dallas	691	13
VII—Kansas City	368	7
VIII—Denver	184	15
IX—San Francisco	833	15
X—Seattle	318	11

7(a) loan = loan to an operating small business
EOL = economic opportunity loan
DBL = displaced business loan
LDC = local development company

Suppose that a loan is picked at random for review from those approved in 1971. Find the probability that the loan will be

(a) a 7(a) loan approved for Region V.

(b) an EOL loan, given that it was approved for Region X.

(c) an EOL or a 7(a) loan.

(d) one approved for Region IV or Region V.

(e) one approved for Region VII or will be an EOL loan.

Source: *SBA Economic Review*, Annual Issue 1972, Small Business Administration, Office of Planning, Research and Analysis.

3. CONSTRUCTION FATALITIES

Construction is considered one of the most hazardous industries. Each year thousands of construction workers are killed and injured during the course of their day's work. The following table shows the causes of 3,496 construction fatalities investigated by the Occupational Safety and Health Administration for the period 1985 to 1989.

Cause	Number of Fatalities
Struck by	781
Caught in/between	639
Fall (from elevation)	1148
Inhalation	62
Cardiovascular/Respiratory	109
Electrical shock	580
Other	177
Total	3496

Suppose that from these we select a fatality report at random.

(a) What is the probability that the report will be for a fall-from-elevation fatality?

(b) What is the probability that the report will be for a fall-from-elevation or an electrical-shock fatality?

Source: U.S. Department of Labor, Occupational Safety and Health Administration, *Analysis of Construction Fatalities—The OSHA Data Base 1985–1989*, Washington, D.C., November 1990.

4. WORKING MEN AND WOMEN: THEIR OCCUPATIONS

The following table shows the percent distribution of the employed by occupation and sex in 1990.

(a) Suppose we select a female at random from the work force. What are the odds against her being employed in an administrative support position? (See Review Exercise 77.)

(b) Suppose we select a male at random from the work force. What are the odds against his being employed in an administrative support position? (See Review Exercise 77.)

Percent Distribution of the Employed by Occupation and Sex, 1990 Average

Occupation	Women	Men
Total, 16 years and over (thousands).........	53,479	64,435
Percent	100.0	100.0
Executive, administrative, and managerial	11.1	13.8
Professional specialty.........................	15.1	12.0
Technicians and related support	3.5	3.0
Sales occupations	13.1	11.2
Administrative support, including clerical	27.8	5.9
Service occupations..........................	17.7	9.8
Precision production, craft, and repair	2.2	19.4
Operators, fabricators, and laborers..........	8.5	20.6
Farming, forestry, and fishing.................	1.0	4.4

Source: U.S. Department of Labor, Bureau of Labor Statistics, *Working Women: A Chartbook*, Bulletin 2385, August 1991.

SUGGESTIONS FOR FURTHER READING

Blake, Ian F. (1979). *An Introduction to Applied Probability*. Wiley, New York.

Dauben, Joseph W. (1979). *Georg Cantor*. Harvard University Press, Cambridge, Mass.

Enderton, Herbert (1977). *Elements of Set Theory*. Academic Press, New York.

Hrbacek, Karel, and Thomas Jech (1978). *Introduction to Set Theory*. Marcel Dekker, New York.

Khazanie, Ramakant (1976). *Basic Probability Theory and Applications*. Goodyear, Pacific Palisades, Calif.

Moschovakis, Yiannis (1980). *Descriptive Set Theory*. North-Holland, Amsterdam.

Pfeiffer, Paul E., and David A. Schum (1973). *Introduction to Applied Probability*. Academic Press, New York.

Pinter, Charles C. (1971). *Set Theory*. Addison-Wesley, Reading, Mass.

Ross, Sheldon M. (1985). *Introduction to Probability Models*, 3rd ed. Academic Press, New York.

4

Some Important Probability Distributions

Chapter Objectives: This chapter deals with the basic concepts you need to understand random variables and probability distributions. These concepts and techniques provide the foundation for the statistical inference procedures that we discuss later. You will learn to use theoretical distributions that help you to get approximations of many probability distributions found in business situations. Distributions such as these are a necessary background for understanding a special type of probability distribution that we encounter in Chapter 5. After studying this chapter and working the exercises, you should be able to

1. Distinguish between discrete and continuous random variables.
2. Construct a probability distribution from raw data.
3. Compute the mean and variance of a probability distribution.
4. Use the binomial, Poisson, hypergeometric, normal, and uniform distribution models to calculate probabilities for appropriate random variables.
5. Determine which model—the binomial, Poisson, hypergeometric, normal, or uniform—is appropriate for describing a given situation.
6. Use appropriate computer software packages (either DATA+ or MINITAB) to generate probability distributions and to calculate probabilities when the distribution of the variable of interest can be represented by a probability distribution with known properties.

4.1 INTRODUCTION

In Chapter 3, you studied the basic concepts of probability theory, as well as methods for computing the probability of an event. This chapter builds on those methods and concepts. It introduces techniques for calculating the probability of an event under more complicated circumstances.

We discuss the topic of this chapter, probability distributions, under two headings: probability distributions of *discrete random variables* and probability distributions of *continuous random variables*. You learned in Chapter 1 that a random variable is a variable for which we can specify a function that gives the relative frequency of occurrence of the values that the variable can assume.

Many of the problems confronting the business decision-maker can be expressed through the use of mathematical concepts. By employing appropriate mathematical symbols and operations, decision-makers can obtain solutions to their problems that are expressible in quantitative terms. *Modeling* is the term we use to refer to the procedures by which a decision-maker selects a mathematical concept and its accompanying symbols and operations to represent a problem or process. We call the mathematical concept selected to represent a problem or process the *model* for that problem or process. The purpose of studying probability distributions is to learn how they provide adequate models for many of the problems encountered by business decision-makers. The examples and exercises that follow illustrate many typical business decision-making problems and the models that can be employed to solve them.

4.2 PROBABILITY DISTRIBUTIONS OF DISCRETE RANDOM VARIABLES

Let us begin with the following definition:

> The *probability distribution of a discrete random variable* is a table, graph, formula, or other device used to specify all possible values of the discrete random variable, along with their respective probabilities.

As you learned in Chapter 1, a discrete variable is one that can assume only certain values within a specified interval. The number of daily admissions to a hospital is an example of a discrete variable.

EXAMPLE 4.2.1 Macadoo Electronics employs 50 salespersons. We wish to construct the probability distribution of the random variable X, the number of new customers each salesperson obtained during the past year.

SOLUTION We construct a table in which one column lists the possible values x_i that X can assume. Another column lists $P(X = x_i)$, the probability of X assuming each value. Table 4.2.1 shows the probability distribution of X for our

TABLE 4.2.1   Probability distribution of the number of new customers obtained by 50 salespersons

x_i	Frequency of occurrence of x_i	$P(X = x_i)$
0	1	1/50
1	2	2/50
2	4	4/50
3	3	3/50
4	6	6/50
5	8	8/50
6	10	10/50
7	7	7/50
8	5	5/50
9	3	3/50
10	1	1/50
Total	50	50/50

firm. The entries in the last column are the relative frequencies of occurrence of values of X.

Alternatively, we may represent the probability distribution by a graph. In Figure 4.2.1, the length of each vertical line indicates the probability for the corresponding value of x in this example. The values of $P(X = x_i)$ are all positive, they are all less than 1, and their sum is equal to 1. These characteristics are not peculiar to this particular example. They are the essential properties of the prob-

FIGURE 4.2.1   Probability distribution of the number of new customers obtained by 50 salespersons

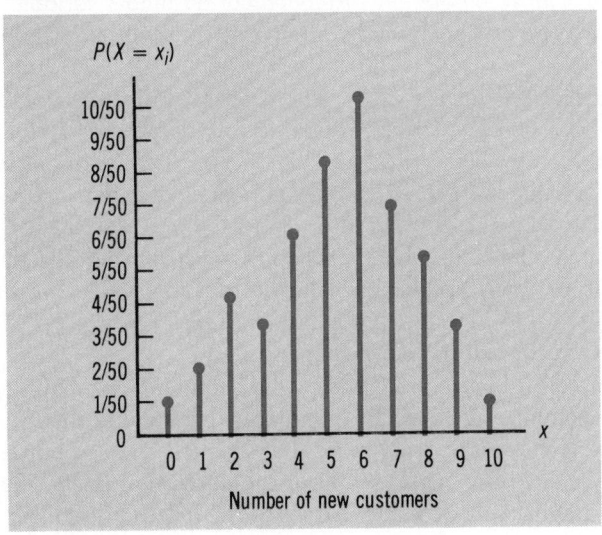

ability distribution of a discrete random variable. This may be expressed more formally as follows:

> Given a discrete random variable X that can assume only the k different values $x_1, x_2, \ldots, x_k$, the probability distribution of X must satisfy the following two conditions:

(4.2.1)
$$0 \leq P(X = x_i) \leq 1, \quad i = 1, 2, \ldots, k$$

(4.2.2)
$$\sum_{i=1}^{k} P(X = x_i) = 1$$

A probability distribution gives us $P(X = x)$.

We can make probability statements about the random variable X once we know its probability distribution. Suppose, for example, that a salesperson is picked at random from the 50. What is the probability of selecting a salesperson who got 4 new customers? The last column of Table 4.2.1 shows that the answer is $6/50 = 0.12$, that is, $P(X = 4) = 6/50 = 0.12$.

What is the probability that a salesperson selected at random is one who got either 5 or 6 new customers? To answer this question, we use the addition rule. The probability of selecting a salesperson who got 5 new customers is 8/50. The probability of selecting a salesperson who got 6 new customers is 10/50. Thus, the probability of selecting a salesperson who got either 5 or 6 new customers is $8/50 + 10/50 = 0.16 + 0.20 = 0.36$. We express this more compactly as $P(X = 5 \text{ or } 6) = P(X = 5) + P(X = 6) = 0.36$.

Cumulative Distributions At times it will be more convenient to compute probabilities using the *cumulative probability distribution* of a random variable.

> The *cumulative probability distribution* of a random variable X gives the probability that X is less than or equal to x_0, some specified value of X.

Suppose that we have $P(X = x)$, the probability distribution of the random variable X. The cumulative probability distribution of X for x_0, some specified value of X, may be written as $P(X \leq x_0)$, and we obtain it by summing the individual values of $P(X = x)$ over all values of x that are less than or equal to x_0. That is, $P(X \leq x_0) = \Sigma P(X = x)$ for all $x \leq x_0$.

To obtain the cumulative probability distribution for the discrete variable whose probability distribution is given in Table 4.2.1, we successively add the probabilities $P(X = x_i)$ in the last column. Table 4.2.2 shows the resulting cumulative probability distribution.

A cumulative probability distribution gives us $P(X \leq x)$.

The graph in Figure 4.2.2 shows the cumulative probability distribution of X for this example. We call the cumulative probability distribution $F(x)$. That is, $F(x) = P(X \leq x)$, the probability that X is less than or equal to any value of x. The graph of $F(x)$ consists solely of the horizontal lines. The vertical lines only give the graph a connected appearance. The length of each vertical line represents the same probability as that of the corresponding line in Figure 4.2.1. For ex-

TABLE 4.2.2   Cumulative probability distribution of number of new customers obtained by 50 salespersons

x	Frequency of occurrence of x	P(X = x)	P(X ≤ x)
0	1	1/50	1/50
1	2	2/50	3/50
2	4	4/50	7/50
3	3	3/50	10/50
4	6	6/50	16/50
5	8	8/50	24/50
6	10	10/50	34/50
7	7	7/50	41/50
8	5	5/50	46/50
9	3	3/50	49/50
10	1	1/50	50/50
Total	50	50/50	

ample, the length of the vertical line at $X = 6$ in Figure 4.2.2 represents the same probability as the length of the line erected at $X = 6$ in Figure 4.2.1, or 10/50 units on the vertical scale.

The cumulative probability distribution lets us answer such questions as the following:

1. What is the probability that a salesperson picked at random got fewer than 4 new customers during the past year? To answer this question, we need to find $P(X < 4)$, or $P(X \leq 3)$. We can find this in Table 4.2.2 by noting the value of $P(X \leq x)$ for $x = 3$. We find this to be $10/50 = 0.20$.

FIGURE 4.2.2   Cumulative probability distribution of the number of new customers obtained by 50 salespersons

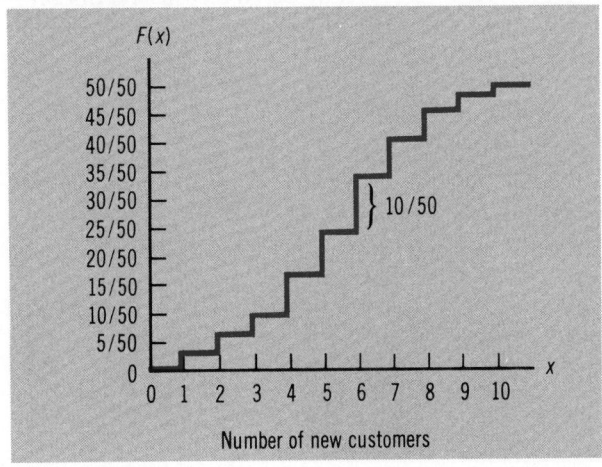

Number of new customers

2. What is the probability that a randomly selected salesperson got four or more new customers during the past year? The answer is the complement of the answer to the previous question. Since we have already found $P(X < 4) = 0.20$, we have $P(X \geq 4) = 1 - P(X < 4) = 1 - 0.20 = 0.80$.

3. What is the probability that a salesperson selected at random got between five and eight new customers, inclusive? To answer this, we need $P(5 \leq X \leq 8)$, which is equal to $P(X \leq 8) - P(X < 5)$. From Table 4.2.2, we find that $P(X \leq 8) = 46/50$ and $P(X < 5) = 16/50$, so that $P(5 \leq X \leq 8) = 46/50 - 16/50 = 30/50 = 0.60$.

The probability distribution in Table 4.2.1 was developed from actual experience. To find another variable that followed this distribution would be a coincidence. However, the probability distribution of a discrete random variable of interest often follows, or approximates, some probability distribution that has been named and extensively studied. The next three sections introduce three well-known distributions—the binomial distribution, the Poisson distribution, and the hypergeometric distribution.

THE MEAN AND VARIANCE OF DISCRETE PROBABILITY DISTRIBUTIONS

We introduce the concepts of mean and variance in Chapter 2 and discuss there the calculation of these measures for samples and finite populations. This section treats these concepts in terms of discrete probability distributions.

> The mean of a probability distribution is the *expected value* of the random variable that has the specified distribution.

For example, the expected value of a discrete random variable X is merely the arithmetic mean. Therefore, it may be labeled μ. To obtain it, we multiply each value of the random variable by its probability of occurrence and sum the products. We express this procedure symbolically as follows:

(4.2.3)
$$E(X) = \Sigma x P(X = x) = \mu$$

Similarly, we define the variance of the probability distribution of the random variable X as the expected value of the squared deviations of the values of X from their mean. In symbols, we write this as

(4.2.4)
$$E(x - \mu)^2 = \Sigma(x - \mu)^2 P(X = x) = \sigma^2$$

Alternatively, we may write the variance of X as

(4.2.5)
$$\sigma^2 = E(X^2) - [E(X)]^2$$

where $E(X^2) = \Sigma x^2 P(X = x)$.

TABLE 4.2.3 Calculations for obtaining the mean and variance of the random variable X by Equations 4.2.3 and 4.2.4

x	$P(X = x)$	$x - \mu$	$(x - \mu)^2$	$xP(X = x)$	$(x - \mu)^2 P(X = x)$
1	1/6	-2	4	1/6	4/6
2	1/6	-1	1	2/6	1/6
3	2/6	0	0	6/6	0
4	1/6	1	1	4/6	1/6
5	1/6	2	4	5/6	4/6
Total	1			$\Sigma xP(X = x) = 3$	$\Sigma(x - \mu)^2 P(X = x)$ = 10/6 = 1.67

EXAMPLE 4.2.2 We wish to find the mean and variance of the random variable X that has the probability distribution shown in the first two columns of Table 4.2.3.

SOLUTION We compute the mean and variance of X as follows:

By Equation 4.2.3, we have

$$\mu = E(X) = \Sigma xP(X = x)$$
$$= 1(1/6) + 2(1/6) + 3(2/6) + 4(1/6) + 5(1/6) = 3$$

By Equation 4.2.4, we compute

$$\sigma^2 = E(x - \mu)^2 = \Sigma(x - \mu)^2 P(X = x)$$
$$= (1 - 3)^2(1/6) + (2 - 3)^2(1/6) + (3 - 3)^2(2/6)$$
$$+ (4 - 3)^2(1/6) + (5 - 3)^2(1/6)$$
$$= 10/6 = 1.67$$

A summary of the calculations appears in Table 4.2.3.

If we wish to use Equation 4.2.5 to compute σ^2, we first compute

$$E(X^2) = 1^2 \left(\frac{1}{6}\right) + 2^2 \left(\frac{1}{6}\right) + 3^2 \left(\frac{2}{6}\right) + 4^2 \left(\frac{1}{6}\right) + 5^2 \left(\frac{1}{6}\right)$$
$$= \frac{64}{6} = 10.67$$

By Equation 4.2.5, then, we may compute

$$\sigma^2 = 10.67 - (3)^2 = 1.67$$

This result agrees with that obtained using Equation 4.2.4.

The calculation of $E(X^2)$ appears in Table 4.2.4.

EXAMPLE 4.2.3 Table 4.2.5 shows the results of a survey in which respondents were asked the number of times that they had changed jobs during the past five years. We wish to find the mean and variance.

TABLE 4.2.4 Calculations for obtaining the variance of the random variable X of Example 4.2.2 using Equation 4.2.5

x	P(X = x)	x²	x²P(X = x)
1	1/6	1	1/6
2	1/6	4	4/6
3	2/6	9	18/6
4	1/6	16	16/6
5	1/6	25	25/6
Total	1		64/6

SOLUTION   Using the information in Table 4.2.5, we compute the mean and variance as follows:

$$\mu = E(X) = \Sigma xP(X = x) = 0(0.30) + 1(0.40)$$
$$+ 2(0.20) + 3(0.05) + 4(0.03) + 5(0.02) = 1.17$$
$$\sigma^2 = E(X - \mu)^2 = \Sigma(x - \mu)^2 P(X = x)$$
$$= (0 - 1.17)^2(0.3) + (1 - 1.17)^2(0.4)$$
$$+ (2 - 1.17)^2(0.2) + (3 - 1.17)^2(0.05) + (4 - 1.17)^2(0.03)$$
$$+ (5 - 1.17)^2(0.02)$$
$$= 1.2611$$

Equations 4.2.3 and 4.2.4 are examples of weighted arithmetic descriptive measures in which the weights are probabilities. The calculations are similar to those for computing the mean and variance of grouped data, discussed in Chapter 2.

For the probability distribution of a continuous random variable, we find the mean and variance by integrating $xf(x)$ and $(x - \mu)^2 f(x)$ over the possible values of x. The computations are analogous to Equations 4.2.3 and 4.2.4.

TABLE 4.2.5 Probability distribution for Example 4.2.3

Number of job changes	0	1	2	3	4	5
Proportion of respondents	0.30	0.40	0.20	0.05	0.03	0.02

EXERCISES

4.2.1   The following table shows the distribution of the number of days of sick leave taken by 100 employees during a year.   (a) Construct and graph the probability distribution of X = days of sick leave taken.   (b) Construct and graph the cumulative probability distribution.   (c) Find the mean and variance.

x_i (Days of sick leave taken)	0	1	2	3	4	5	6	7	8	9	10
Number of employees	5	8	10	12	18	14	10	9	8	4	2

4.2.2   Find, for Exercise 4.2.1, the probability that a randomly selected employee will be one who took   (a) three days sick leave,   (b) more than five days sick leave,   (c) six to eight days (inclusive) sick leave,   (d) either nine or ten days sick leave.

4.2.3   For Exercise 4.2.1, find   (a) $P(X = 0)$,   (b) $P(X = 10)$,   (c) $P(X \geq 6)$,   (d) $P(X < 6)$,   (e) $P(3 \leq X \leq 7)$.

4.2.4   The following table shows the distribution of on-the-job accidents that befell 500 factory employees during a given year.   (a) Construct and graph the probability distribution of X = number of accidents.   (b) Construct and graph the cumulative probability distribution.   (c) Find the probability that a randomly selected employee will be one who had (1) no accident, (2) more than three accidents, (3) between two and four accidents, inclusive, (4) fewer than four accidents, and (5) four or more accidents.   (d) Find the mean and variance.

Number of accidents	0	1	2	3	4	5	6
Number of employees	300	100	60	20	10	5	5

4.2.5   A sample of 80 customers at Napiers Department Store were interviewed regarding their buying habits. One question asked was, "How many times did you shop at this store during the preceding month?" The responses are shown in the table that follows.   (a) Construct and graph the probability distribution of X = number of times shopped.   (b) Construct and graph the cumulative probability distribution.   (c) Find the probability that a randomly selected customer shopped (1) more than once, (2) zero times, (3) more than four times, (4) fewer than three times.   (d) Find the mean and variance.

X_i (Number of times shopped)	0	1	2	3	4	5	6	7
Number of customers	15	27	14	12	6	4	1	1

4.2.6   A credit union has 400 members. A review of the membership account records reveals the information regarding the number of transactions that occurred during the past quarter shown in the table below.   (a) Construct and graph the probability distribution of X = number of transactions.   (b) Construct and graph the cumulative probability distribution.   (c) Find the probability that a randomly selected account record will have had (1) no transactions, (2) at least one transaction, (3) more than five transactions, (4) fewer than six transactions.   (d) Find the mean and variance.

X_i (Transactions)	0	1	2	3	4	5	6	7	8	9	10
Number of members	146	97	73	34	23	10	6	3	4	2	2

4.3   THE BINOMIAL DISTRIBUTION

The *binomial distribution* is one of the most widely encountered probability distributions in applied statistics. It is derived from a process known as a *Bernoulli trial*, named for the Swiss mathematician James Bernoulli (1654–1705), who made many contributions to probability theory.

A *Bernoulli trial* is a trial of some process or experiment that can result only in one of two mutually exclusive outcomes, such as defective or not defective, correct or incorrect, present or absent, acceptable or not acceptable.

We may think of a Bernoulli trial as taking a measurement on some variable that can assume only one of two possible values.

A population of such measurements—of which some are of one kind and the remainder are of another kind—is called a *dichotomous population*.

BERNOULLI PROCESS

A sequence of Bernoulli trials forms a *Bernoulli process* when the following conditions are met:

1. Each trial results in one of two possible, mutually exclusive outcomes. One of the possible outcomes is denoted (arbitrarily) as a success and the other as a failure.
2. The probability of a success, p, remains constant from trial to trial. (The probability of a failure, $1 - p$, is denoted by q.)
3. The trials are independent, that is, the probabilities associated with any particular trial are not affected by the outcome of any other trial.

In n repetitions of a Bernoulli trial, the number of successes possible is 0, 1, 2, ..., n. We want to be able to determine the probability of each possible number of successes in n repetitions, or trials. The distribution from which we determine these probabilities is called the *binomial distribution*.

EXAMPLE 4.3.1   A horticulturist knows from experience that 90% of a certain kind of seedling will survive being transplanted. A random sample of five seedlings is selected from current stock. What is the probability that exactly three will survive?

SOLUTION   The probability of survival for each seedling is 0.90. Let us call survival a *success* and nonsurvival a *failure*. Also, let us assign a value of 1 to a success (survival) and a value of 0 to a failure (nonsurvival). The actual random selection of a seedling is a Bernoulli trial.

Suppose that the first seedling survives (S), the second seedling fails to survive (F), the third and fourth survive, and the fifth fails to survive. We record the following sequence of outcomes: SFSSF. Using zeros and ones, we may write the sequence of outcomes as 10110. We find the probability of this sequence of outcomes using the multiplication rule. It is given by

$$P(1, 0, 1, 1, 0) = pqppq = q^2p^3$$

We are looking for the probability of a success, a failure, a success, a success, and a failure, in that order. In other words, we want the joint probability of the

TABLE 4.3.1   Additional sequences for 3 successes and 2 failures

Sequence number	Sequence	Sequence number	Sequence
2	11100	6	10101
3	10011	7	01110
4	11010	8	00111
5	11001	9	01011
		10	01101

five outcomes. (For simplicity's sake, we have used commas, rather than intersection notation, to separate the outcomes of the events in the probability statement.)

The resulting probability is the probability of obtaining the specific sequence of outcomes in the order shown. But we are not interested in the order in which the successes and failures occur. Rather, we are interested in the probability of the occurrence of *exactly* three successes (survivals) out of five randomly selected seedlings. In addition to the given sequence (call it sequence 1), three successes and two failures could also occur in any one of the sequences in Table 4.3.1. Each of these sequences has the same probability of occurring, q^2p^3.

A single sample of size 5, drawn from the population specified, yields only one sequence of successes and failures. The question we must answer is: What is the probability of getting sequence 1, *or* sequence 2, . . . , *or* sequence 10? To find the answer, we use the addition rule to calculate the sum of the individual probabilities. In this example, we need to find the sum of the 10 q^2p^3's or, equivalently, multiply q^2p^3 by 10.

We can now answer the original question: What is the probability that in a random sample of size 5, drawn from the specified population, there are three successes (survivals) and two failures (nonsurvivals)? Since $p = 0.90$ and $q = (1 - p) = (1 - 0.90) = 0.10$, the answer is

$$10(0.10)^2(0.90)^3 = 10(0.01)(0.729) = 0.0729$$

Figure 4.3.1 illustrates the solution to this problem with a tree diagram. The probability of each individual event (S or F) is given in parentheses on the branch representing the event.

As the size of the sample increases, it becomes more and more difficult to construct a tree diagram or list the various sequences. We need an easy method of counting them. Since a sequence of outcomes consists of n things, some of which are of one type and the rest of another type, we can use Equation 3.3.6 to count the number of sequences. Using this equation, we find the number of sequences to be

$$_5C_3 = \frac{5!}{3!2!} = \frac{120}{12} = 10$$

FIGURE 4.3.1 Tree diagram for Example 4.3.1

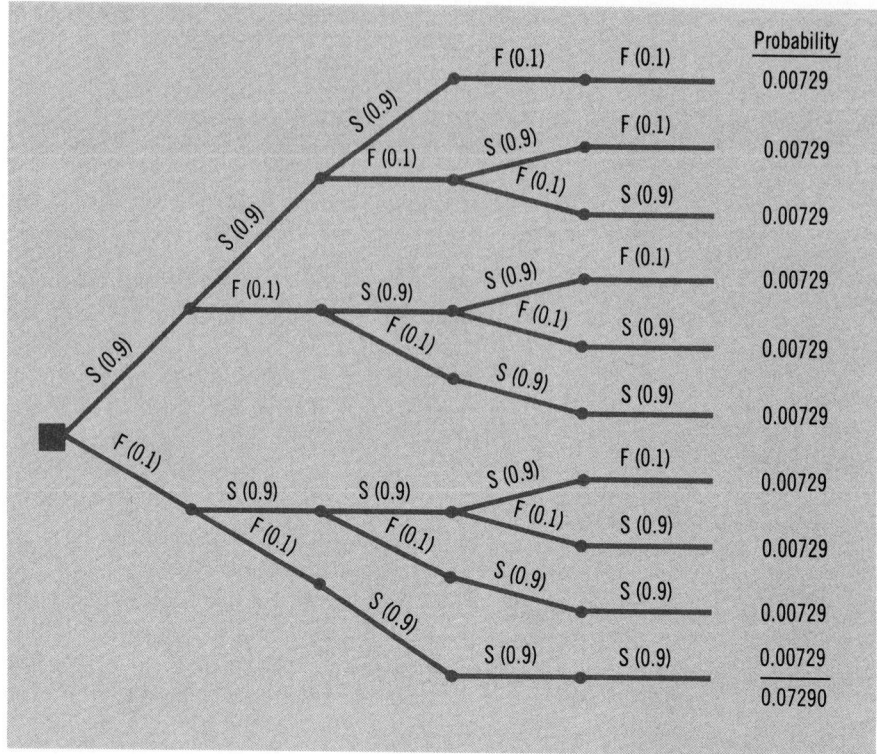

In general, if n equals the total number of objects, x the number of objects of one type, and $n - x$ the number of objects of the other type, the number of sequences is equal to

$$_nC_x = \frac{n!}{x!(n-x)!}$$

which is equal to the number of combinations of n things taken x at a time.

We thus can write the probability of obtaining exactly x successes in n trials as

(4.3.1)
$$f(x) = {}_nC_x q^{n-x}p^x = {}_nC_x p^x q^{n-x} \qquad \text{for } x = 0, 1, 2, \dots, n$$
$$= 0 \qquad \text{elsewhere}$$

This expression is the *binomial distribution*. In Equation 4.3.1, $f(x) = P(X = x)$, where X is the random variable, number of successes in n trials. We use $f(x)$ rather than $P(X = x)$ not only because it is shorter, but also because it is commonly used.

Table 4.3.2 shows the binomial distribution in tabular form.

To establish the fact that Equation 4.3.1 has the two essential properties of a

TABLE 4.3.2   The binomial distribution

Number of successes x	Probability $f(x)$
0	$_nC_0 q^{n-0} p^0$
1	$_nC_1 q^{n-1} p^1$
2	$_nC_2 q^{n-2} p^2$
$\vdots$	$\vdots$
x	$_nC_x q^{n-x} p^x$
$\vdots$	$\vdots$
n	$_nC_n q^{n-n} p^n$
Total	1

probability distribution, consider the following:

1. $f(x) \geq 0$ for all real values of x. This follows from the fact that n and p are both nonnegative, and hence

$$\binom{n}{x}, \; p^x, \text{ and } (1 - p)^{n-x}$$

are all nonnegative. Consequently their product is greater than or equal to 0.

2. $\Sigma f(x) = 1$. To see that this is true, we must recognize that

$$\sum_{x=0}^{n} {}_nC_x q^{n-x} p^x = [(1 - p) + p]^n = 1^n = 1$$

the familiar binomial expansion. Expansion of the binomial $(q + p)^n$ yields

$$(q + p)^n = q^n + nq^{n-1}p^1 + \frac{n(n - 1)}{2} q^{n-2}p^2 + \cdots + nq^1 p^{n-1} + p^n$$

Suppose that we compare the terms in this expansion term for term with the $f(x)$ in Table 4.3.2. We see that they are equivalent, since

$$f(0) = {}_nC_0 q^{n-0}p^0 = q^n$$
$$f(1) = {}_nC_1 q^{n-1}p^1 = nq^{n-1}p^1$$
$$f(2) = {}_nC_2 q^{n-2}p^2 = \frac{n(n - 1)}{2} q^{n-2}p^2$$
$$\vdots \qquad \vdots \qquad \vdots$$
$$f(n) = {}_nC_n q^{n-n}p^n = p^n$$

EXAMPLE 4.3.2 In a certain community, on a given evening, someone is at home in 85% of the households. Suppose that a researcher conducting a telephone survey randomly selects 12 households to call that evening. What is the probability that someone will be at home in exactly 7 households?

SOLUTION The answer, by Equation 4.3.1, is

$$f(7) = {}_{12}C_7(0.85)^7(0.15)^{12-7} = \frac{12!}{5!7!}(0.320577)(0.00007594) = 0.0193$$

THE BINOMIAL TABLE

When the sample size is large, using Equation 4.3.1 to calculate probabilities is tedious. Fortunately, probabilities for different values of n, p, and x have been tabulated. Thus, instead of calculating the probabilities, we may consult a table to find the desired result. Table A of Appendix I is one such table. This table gives the probability that X is *less than or equal to* some specified value. To use Table A, we first locate the page containing the size of the sample under consideration. We next locate the relevant value of p, found in the column headings of the table. Finally, the desired value of x is located in the leftmost column of the table. For a given value of n, the number at the intersection of the row labeled with the desired value of x and the column labeled with the desired value of p is the probability we seek. Suppose, for example, that we have a sample of size $n = 12$ drawn from a population in which the probability of a success is $p = 0.25$. Suppose that we want to know the probability of observing three or fewer successes in our sample. We may state the desired probability in compact notation as follows:

$$P(X \le 3 | n = 12, p = 0.25)$$

We first locate the page containing $n = 12$. Then we find the column labeled 0.25 and the row labeled 3. We find that the number at the intersection of this row and column is 0.6488. Thus,

$$P(X \le 3 | n = 12, p = 0.25) = 0.6488$$

Some additional examples illustrate the use of Table A.

EXAMPLE 4.3.3 The Ochs Insurance Company has found that 8% of its claims are for damages resulting from burglaries. What is the probability that a random sample of 20 claims will contain 5 or fewer that are for burglary damages?

SOLUTION We seek the probability that $X \le 5$ when $n = 20$, $p = 0.08$, and $q = 0.92$. The table gives the probability that $X \le x$, so we only need to locate the entry corresponding to $n = 20$, $p = 0.08$, and $X = 5$. We find this to be

0.9962. We can write the problem and its solution in a more compact notation as

$$P(X \leq 5|n = 20, p = 0.08) = 0.9962$$

EXAMPLE 4.3.4   In the previous example, what is the probability that a sample of 20 claims will contain more than 5 claims for damages resulting from burglaries?

SOLUTION   The answer to this question is the complement of the probability found in Example 4.3.3. Thus,

$$P(X > 5|n = 20, p = 0.08) = 1 - P(X \leq 5|n = 20, p = 0.08)$$
$$= 1 - 0.9962 = 0.0038$$

EXAMPLE 4.3.5   In Example 4.3.3, let us determine

$$P(2 \leq X \leq 5|n = 20, p = 0.08)$$

SOLUTION   In this example, we want the probability associated with an interval. To obtain the answer, we must find the probability that $X \leq 5$ and subtract from it the probability that $X < 2$ (or $X \leq 1$). Therefore, when $n = 20$ and $p = 0.08$,

$$P(2 \leq X \leq 5) = P(X \leq 5) - P(X \leq 1) = 0.9962 - 0.5169 = 0.4793$$

EXAMPLE 4.3.6   In Example 4.3.2, suppose that the researcher calls a random sample of 12 households in a community on the night that 85% of the households have someone at home. Use Table A to find the probability that the person conducting the telephone survey finds someone at home in exactly 7 households.

SOLUTION   Table A does not give probabilities for values of p greater than 0.5. We may obtain such probabilities from Table A, however, by restating the problem in terms of the probability of a failure, $1 - p$, rather than in terms of the probability of a success, p. For such a restatement, we must also think in terms of the number of failures, $n - x$, rather than the number of successes, x. We may summarize this idea as follows:

$$P(X = x|n, p > 0.50) = P(X = n - x|n, 1 - p)$$

In this example, we restate the problem as follows: What is the probability that the person conducting the telephone survey gets no answer from exactly 5 calls out of 12, if no one is at home in 15% of the households? We find the answer as follows:

$$P(X = 5|n = 12, p = 0.15) = P(X \leq 5) - P(X \leq 4)$$
$$= 0.9954 - 0.9761 = 0.0193$$

This is the same answer we obtained previously. Thus, the probability of finding someone at home in exactly 7 households is equal to the probability of finding no one at home in exactly 5 households, given the conditions in the example.

When p is greater than 0.5, we may obtain cumulative probabilities from Table A by using the following relationship:

$$P(X \leq x|n, p > 0.5) = P(X \geq n - x|n, 1 - p)$$

To illustrate, let us refer to Example 4.3.6 and find the probability that the telephone surveyor will find someone at home in 5 or fewer households. The probability we want is

$$
\begin{aligned}
P(X \leq 5|n = 12, p = 0.85) &= P(X \geq 12 - 5|n = 12, p = 0.15) \\
&= P(X \geq 7|n = 12, p = 0.15) \\
&= 1 - P(X \leq 6|n = 12, p = 0.15) \\
&= 1 - 0.9993 = 0.0007
\end{aligned}
$$

Finally, to use Table A to find the probability that X is greater than or equal to some x when $p > 0.5$, we use the following relationship:

$$P(X \geq x|n, p > 0.5) = P(X \leq n - x|n, 1 - p)$$

Suppose that we want to find the probability that the telephone surveyor in Example 4.3.6 will find someone at home in eight or more households. The probability we seek is

$$P(X \geq 8|n = 12, p = 0.85) = P(X \leq 4|n = 12, p = 0.15) = 0.9761$$

There is a different binomial distribution for each different value of n or p.

The binomial distribution is really a family of distributions. Each different value of either n or p specifies a different distribution. In this distribution, n and p are called parameters. Figure 4.3.2 shows how the binomial distribution varies for different values of p and n. Regardless of the value of n, the distribution is symmetrical when $p = 0.5$. When p is greater than 0.5, the distribution is asymmetrical and the peak occurs to the right of center. When p is less than 0.5, the distribution is asymmetrical and the peak occurs to the left of center.

In theory, the binomial distribution can be applied only when the sample is drawn from an infinite population, or from a finite population when sampling is with replacement. (When sampling is with replacement, a selected unit is returned to the population before the next unit is selected.)

In practice, samples are usually drawn from finite populations. Given this circumstance, the question naturally arises as to whether the binomial distribution is appropriate. The answer depends on how constant p remains as succeeding observations are drawn. It is generally agreed that when n is small relative to the

FIGURE 4.3.2   Binomial distribution for selected values of p and n

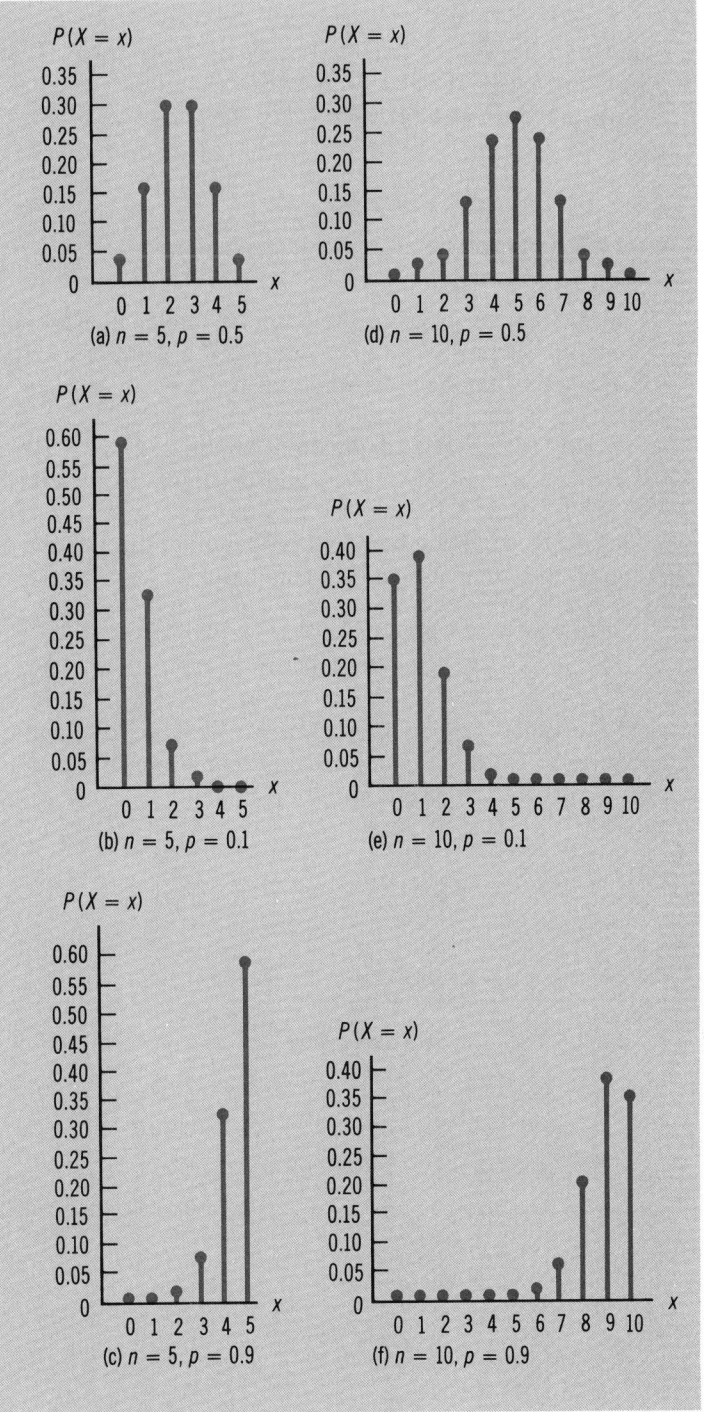

population size N, the binomial model is appropriate. That is, the constancy of p is not seriously affected. Some writers say that n is small relative to N if N is at least ten times as large as n.

COMPUTER **ANALYSIS**

As an alternative to using the binomial tables in Appendix I, we may obtain binomial probabilities through the use of a computer software package. Figure 4.3.3 contains binomial distributions for $n = 12$ and $0 = 0.85$, the parameters designated in Example 4.3.6, obtained by using DATA+. As we see in Figure 4.3.3, DATA+ gives individual probabilities, $P(X = x)$; cumulative probabilities, $P(X \leq x)$ and $P(X < x)$; and decumulative probabilities, $P(X > x)$ and $P(X \geq x)$. Figure 4.3.4 shows a graph of $P(X = x)$ constructed by DATA+.

One may also obtain binomial probabilities through the use of MINITAB. For example, the command and subcommand

MINITAB

```
PDF;
BINOMIAL N = 12, P = .85.
```

yield individual probabilities $P(X = x)$ for the distribution with the specified parameters. To obtain cumulative probabilities $P(X \leq x)$ for the same parameters, we use the command and subcommand

MINITAB

```
CDF;
BINOMIAL N = 12, P = .85.
```

FIGURE 4.3.3   Computer-generated probabilities (DATA+ printout)

```
    Binomial Probabilities for n = 12 and p = 0.85000
 x    P( = x)   P(X <= x)   P(X < x)   P(X > x)   P(X >= x)
 0   0.000000   0.000000   0.000000   1.000000   1.000000
 1   0.000000   0.000000   0.000000   1.000000   1.000000
 2   0.000000   0.000000   0.000000   1.000000   1.000000
 3   0.000005   0.000005   0.000000   0.999995   1.000000
 4   0.000066   0.000072   0.000005   0.999928   0.999995
 5   0.000600   0.000672   0.000072   0.999328   0.999928
 6   0.003969   0.004642   0.000672   0.995358   0.999328
 7   0.019280   0.023922   0.004642   0.976078   0.995358
 8   0.068284   0.092206   0.023922   0.907794   0.976078
 9   0.171976   0.264182   0.092206   0.735818   0.907794
10   0.292358   0.556540   0.264182   0.443460   0.735818
11   0.301218   0.857758   0.556540   0.142242   0.443460
12   0.142242   1.000000   0.857758   0.000000   0.142242
```

FIGURE 4.3.4   Computer-generated graph of individual binomial probabilities (STAT+ printout)

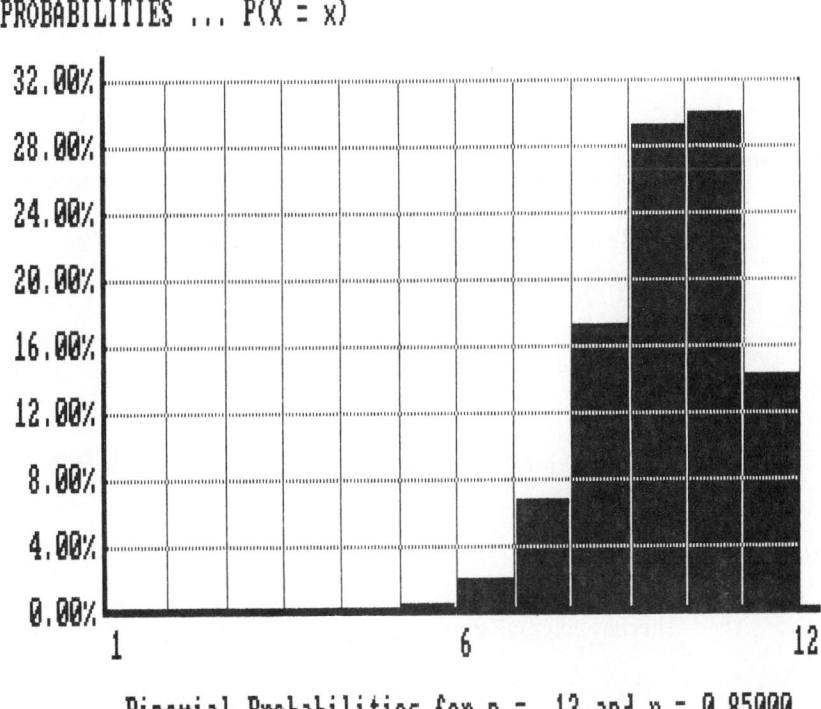

PROBABILITIES ... P(X = x)

Binomial Probabilities for n = 12 and p = 0.85000

THE MEAN AND VARIANCE OF THE BINOMIAL DISTRIBUTION

The mean and variance of the binomial distribution are

(4.3.2)
$$\mu = np$$

and

(4.3.3)
$$\sigma^2 = np(1 - p)$$

respectively, where n is the number of trials, p is the probability of a success for each trial, and the trials are independent. Thus, we find the mean of the binomial distribution by multiplying the number of trials by the probability of a success on an individual trial. In other words, we *expect*, in the long run, to observe np successes out of n Bernoulli trials.

To find the variance of the binomial distribution, as indicated by Equation 4.3.3, we multiply the number of trials n by the probability of a success. We then multiply this product by the probability of a failure.

USE OF CHEBYSHEV'S THEOREM

Chapter 2 shows how to use Chebyshev's theorem to calculate the proportion of values in a set of data that we can expect to fall within a specified distance (as measured in standard deviations) of the mean. The following is a statement of this theorem in probabilistic terms:

Given the probability distribution of the random variable X with mean μ and standard deviation σ, the probability of observing a value of X within k standard deviations of μ is at least $1 - 1/k^2$.

We may express Chebyshev's theorem in symbols as follows:

$$P\left(|x - \mu| \leq k\sigma\right) \geq 1 - \frac{1}{k^2}$$

Alternatively, we may state Chebyshev's theorem as follows:

Given the probability distribution of the random variable X with mean μ and standard deviation σ, the probability of observing a value of X that differs from μ by k or more standard deviations cannot exceed $1/k^2$.

We may use Chebyshev's theorem to answer questions about a binomial distribution.

EXAMPLE 4.3.7   In a certain population, 60% are said to prefer a particular brand of toothpaste. We interview a random sample of 500 persons from this population. Within what interval would we expect the number of successes (persons who prefer the particular brand of toothpaste) out of these 500 trials to lie with a probability of 0.96?

SOLUTION   Since $1 - 1/k^2 = 0.96$ when $k = 5$, the probability is at least 0.96 that the number of successes we would observe is within 5 standard deviations of the mean. The probability that a given person prefers the brand of toothpaste is 0.6. And the number of successes out of 500 trials (interviews) is a random variable having a binomial distribution with $n = 500$ and $p = 0.6$. From Equations 4.3.2 and 4.3.3, we find the mean and standard deviation to be

$$\mu = np = (500)(0.6) = 300$$

and

$$\sigma = \sqrt{np(1 - p)} = \sqrt{(500)(0.6)(0.4)} = 10.95$$

Since $5(10.95) = 54.75$, the interval we want is 300 ± 54.75, or about 245 to 355.

Suppose that we find that only 240 of the 500 persons prefer the brand of toothpaste. What conclusion might we draw from this? We might question the truth of the statement that 60% of the population prefers the brand, since 240 is more than 5 standard deviations from the mean. Chebyshev's theorem tells us that the probability of this occurring is equal to $1/k^2 = 1/5^2 = 0.04$ or less.

Chebyshev's theorem applies to all random variables. However, it may provide weak information for the specific variable of interest. For many random variables, the probability of observing a value within 2 standard deviations of the mean is far greater than $1 - 1/2^2 = 0.75$. We have devoted so much time to the theorem in order to shed some light on the nature and importance of the standard deviation as a measure of dispersion.

EXERCISES

(In each of the following exercises, assume that N is sufficiently large relative to n, and use the binomial distribution to find the desired probabilities.)

4.3.1 Over a long period of time, a salesperson has found that the probability of making a sale when calling on a customer is 0.5. If this salesperson calls on five customers on a given day, find the probability of making (a) exactly three sales, (b) three or more sales, (c) fewer than three sales, (d) no sales, (e) five sales.

4.3.2 For a certain group of people, it is estimated that 40% use a particular type of credit card primarily for installment buying. Suppose that this estimate is correct, and 25 persons picked at random from this group are questioned on the matter. What is the probability that the number using the credit card in this manner is (a) 5 or fewer, (b) between 10 and 15, inclusive, (c) 15 or more?

4.3.3 Given $n = 6$, $p = 0.2$, find (a) $P(X > 3)$, (b) $P(X \leq 4)$, (c) $P(2 \leq X \leq 4)$.

4.3.4 Given $n = 15$, $p = 0.3$, determine (a) $P(X \geq 10)$, (b) $P(X < 5)$, (c) $P(X > 12)$, (d) $P(7 \leq x \leq 10)$.

4.3.5 Refer to Exercise 4.3.2. Suppose that we review the records of 1,000 holders of the credit card and find that 500 of them use the card primarily for installment buying. Is this sufficient evidence to indicate that the estimate of the true number using this credit card primarily for installment buying should be revised? (*Hint*: Use Chebyshev's theorem.)

4.3.6 In a certain town, 35% of the residents are opposed to the widening of Main Street. In a simple random sample of 20 residents, what is the probability that the number opposed to the widening is (a) more than 10, (b) between 15 and 18, inclusive, (c) fewer than 8, (d) at least 12, (e) no more than 13?

4.3.7. Suppose that 72% of a certain population of drivers regularly use seat belts. You take a simple random sample of 15 of these drivers. What is the probability that the number regularly using seat belts is (a) more than 10, (b) fewer than 8, (c) at least 11, (d) 7 or more?

4.3.8 Suppose that 60% of the members of a credit union have loans with the credit union. If you select a random sample of ten members, what is the probability that **(a)** all have loans, **(b)** more than five have loans, **(c)** none has a loan, **(d)** fewer than six have loans, **(e)** at least one has a loan?

4.3.9 The manager of Palmer's restaurant claims that only 3% of the customers are dissatisfied with the service. If this claim is true, what is the probability that the number of dissatisfied customers in a random sample of 25 customers will be **(a)** 0, **(b)** at least 1, **(c)** between 1 and 5, inclusive, **(d)** greater than 5, **(e)** 25?

4.3.10 A manufacturer claims that 6% of her product is defective. If the claim is true, what is the probability that the number of defective products in a random sample of 20 will be **(a)** exactly 2, **(b)** 2 or more, **(c)** 0, **(d)** fewer than 5, **(e)** between 2 and 5, inclusive?

4.3.11 In a survey of M.B.A. students, 75% said that they expect to be promoted within a month after receiving their degree. If this proportion holds for the population, find, for a sample of size 15, the probability that the number expecting a promotion within a month after graduation is **(a)** 6, **(b)** at least 7, **(c)** no more than 5, **(d)** between 6 and 9, inclusive.

4.4 THE POISSON DISTRIBUTION

A second important discrete distribution is the *Poisson distribution*. It is named for the French mathematician Simeon Denis Poisson (1781–1840), who published its derivation in 1837.

The Poisson distribution is given by

$$(4.4.1) \qquad f(x) = \frac{e^{-\lambda}\lambda^x}{x!} \qquad x = 0, 1, 2, \ldots$$

This formula represents the probability that a discrete variable X assumes the value x. That is, $f(x) = P(X = x)$. The Greek letter λ (lambda) is called the parameter of the distribution. It is the average number of occurrences of a random event in an interval of time or space. The number of occurrences of the random event in the interval is indicated by x. The symbol e is the constant (to four decimals) 2.7183.

> The *Poisson distribution* provides a suitable model for a situation where we can observe the number of times an event occurs but where it is not meaningful to speak of the number of times the event did not occur.

For example, people who travel a lot by automobile may tell us how many flat tires they have had over the past several years. They would not be able to tell us how many flat tires they have not had during the same period of time. The phenomenon we are describing is an example of the occurrence of isolated events in a continuum over a specified interval of time or space. The Poisson distribution provides a suitable model for such a phenomenon. Other examples of situations for which the Poisson distribution might provide a suitable model include the

FIGURE 4.4.1   Poisson distribution for selected values of λ

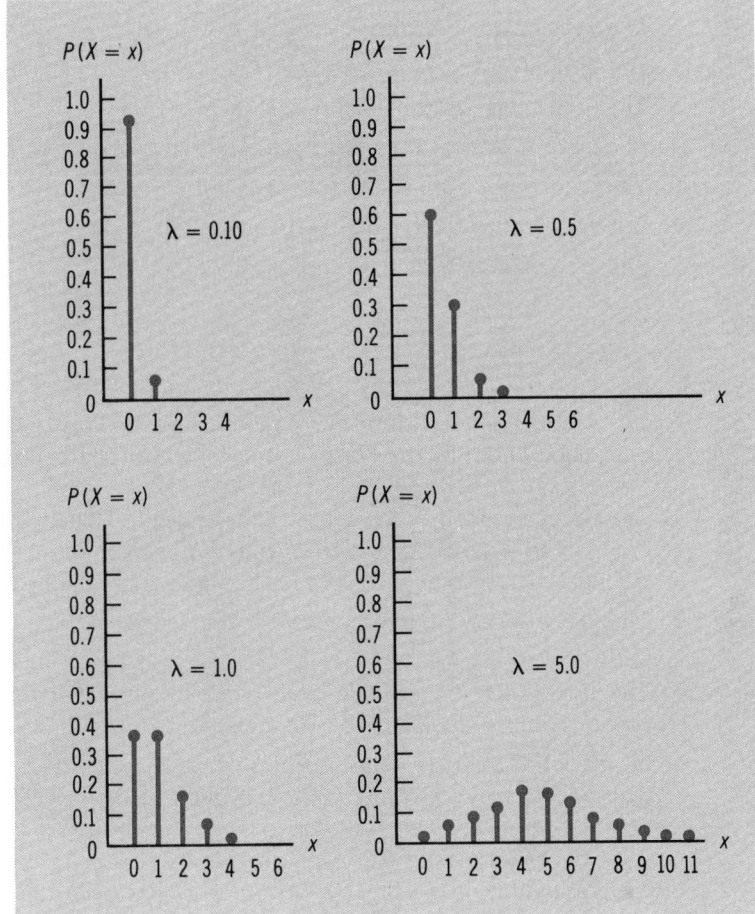

number of accidents in a factory over a period of time, the number of tornadoes occurring in a certain geographic area over a period of time, the number of observed mutations per acre of some crop, and the number of particles of some pollutant per volume of air collected in a city as part of an environmental monitoring program.

The Poisson distribution has been extensively tabulated. Table B in Appendix I gives the cumulative Poisson distribution for various values of λ. This table gives the probability that X is less than or equal to some specified value x_0 for a distribution with a given λ. It can be shown that $f(x) \geq 0$ for every x, and that $\Sigma f(x) = 1$. Thus, the distribution satisfies the requirements for a probability distribution.

Figure 4.4.1 shows the form of the Poisson distribution for selected values of λ.

The Poisson distribution applies in *many* areas. Here are some examples:

1. The demand for a product
2. Typographical errors in a book
3. The occurrence of accidents in a factory
4. The pattern of arrival of store customers at a check-out counter
5. The occurrence of flaws in a bolt of fabric
6. The emission of radioactive particles
7. The arrival of calls at a switchboard

THE POISSON PROCESS

Random occurrences of some event that follow the Poisson distribution are said to be brought about by the *Poisson process*, whose characteristics are as follows:

1. The occurrences of the event are independent. That is, the occurrence of an event in an interval of space or time has no effect on the probability of a second occurrence of the event in the same, or any other, interval.
2. Theoretically, an infinite number of occurrences of the event must be possible in the interval.
3. The probability of a single occurrence of the event in a given interval is proportional to the length of the interval.
4. In any infinitesimally small portion of the interval, the probability of more than one occurrence of the event is negligible.

When the conditions of a Poisson process are reasonably satisfied, we can view the determination of whether or not an event has occurred as a Bernoulli trial. For example, suppose that we want to use the Poisson model to study the demand for a certain item sold in a retail store. We observe the store's sales for a short period of time, and we assume that there can be no more than one call for the item during this time period. In each observed time period, there will be either a demand (success) or no demand (failure) for the item.

An interesting characteristic of the Poisson distribution is the fact that the mean and variance are both equal to λ.

EXAMPLE 4.4.1 A long-term study of accidents at a Quincy shoe factory led management to conclude that the number of accidents per person during a year (X) is distributed according to the Poisson law. The average number of accidents per person per year was 0.3. What is the probability that a randomly selected employee will not have an accident during the coming year?

SOLUTION We need to evaluate Equation 4.4.1 for $X = 0$. That is, we need to evaluate

$$P(X = 0) = f(0) = \frac{e^{-0.3}0.3^0}{0!}$$

If we enter Table B with $X = 0$ and $\lambda = 0.3$, we find the desired probability to be 0.741.

EXAMPLE 4.4.1   *continued*   What is the probability that a randomly selected employee will have at least one accident during the coming year?

SOLUTION   What we need here is the complement of the probability just obtained. That is,

$$P(X \geq 1) = 1 - P(X = 0) = 0.259$$

EXAMPLE 4.4.1   *continued*   What is the probability that an employee will have exactly one accident?

SOLUTION   To answer this question, we find

$$P(X = 1) = P(X \leq 1) - P(X = 0) = 0.963 - 0.741 = 0.222$$

EXAMPLE 4.4.2   Assume that the number of cars arriving at a certain freeway entrance ramp is Poisson distributed. If the assumption is correct, and if the average number of cars arriving during an hour is five, what is the probability that in a given hour no cars will arrive at the ramp?

SOLUTION   To answer this question, we need to evaluate

$$f(0) = \frac{e^{-5}5^0}{0!}$$

We enter Table B with $X = 0$ and $\lambda = 5$ and find the probability to be 0.007.

EXAMPLE 4.4.2   *continued*   What is the probability that exactly five cars will arrive in an hour?

SOLUTION   We use Table B and proceed as follows:

$$P(X = 5) = P(X \leq 5) - P(X \leq 4) = 0.616 - 0.440 = 0.176$$

EXAMPLE 4.4.2   *continued*   What is the probability that more than five cars will arrive in an hour?

SOLUTION   Again, we use Table B to find

$$P(X > 5) = 1 - P(X \leq 5) = 1 - 0.616 = 0.384$$

THE POISSON DISTRIBUTION AS AN APPROXIMATION TO THE BINOMIAL DISTRIBUTION

The binomial distribution is cumbersome to work with for certain combinations of n and p. We can use the Poisson distribution to approximate the binomial distribution when n is large and p is small. When these conditions are met, we can express the relationship as follows:

$$(4.4.2) \qquad {}_nC_x q^{n-x} p^x \approx \frac{e^{-np}(np)^x}{x!}$$

This expression shows that when the Poisson distribution is used to approximate the binomial distribution, the value of λ is taken to be np. What is meant by large n and small p is not precise. A generally accepted rule of thumb is that the approximation may be used if $n \geq 20$ and $p \leq 0.05$. Usually, the approximation is very good when $n \geq 100$ and $np \leq 10$.

EXAMPLE 4.4.3 Suppose that the probability that a certain type of seed does not germinate is 0.04. If 25 of these seeds are planted, what is the probability that 5 or fewer do not germinate?

SOLUTION If we use the binomial distribution, we find that when $n = 25$ and $p = 0.04$

$$P(X \leq 5) = 0.9996$$

Now let us use the Poisson distribution. We let $\lambda = np = (25)(0.04) = 1$. We then find from Table B that

$$P(X \leq 5) = 0.999$$

EXAMPLE 4.4.4 Consider Example 4.3.3, in which $p = 0.08 =$ the proportion of insurance claims that are for burglary damages. The insurance company wants to determine the probability that in a random sample of 20 claims 5 or more are for burglary damages.

SOLUTION Using the binomial distribution, we found an answer of 0.0183. Now we let $\lambda = np = (0.08)(20) = 1.6$ and use the Poisson distribution. We find from Table B that

$$P(X \geq 5) = 0.024$$

Thus, we see that even with $p > 0.05$, the results of the two methods are close. They are the same when the answers are rounded to two decimal places.

COMPUTER **ANALYSIS**

We may use MINITAB to generate Poisson probabilities. To illustrate, let us refer to Example 4.4.1, where the number of accidents in a factory are believed to be distributed according to the Poisson law, with the mean number of accidents per person per year being 0.3. Suppose that we want to find the probability that a randomly selected worker will have 0 accidents per year. The following MINITAB commands and subcommand will yield the desired probability.

MINITAB

```
MTB > SET C1
DATA> 0
DATA> END
MTB > PDF C1;
SUBC> POISSON .3.
```

The resulting printout is as follows:

MINITAB

```
     K          P( X = K )
   0.00           0.7408
```

If we do not specify the value of X for which we wish to have a probability computed, MINITAB will calculate all individual probabilities that are greater than 0.0005. The following command and resulting printout illustrates this feature.

MINITAB

```
MTB > PDF;
SUBC> POISSON .3.
POISSON WITH MEAN = 0.300
     K          P( X = K )
     0            0.7408
     1            0.2222
     2            0.0333
     3            0.0033
     4            0.0003
     5            0.0000
```

If we want to obtain cumulative Poisson probabilities with MINITAB, we substitute the term CDF for PDF in the commands.

EXERCISES

4.4.1 The number of defects per square foot of a certain manufactured fabric is Poisson distributed, with $\lambda = 0.08$. If a square foot of fabric is inspected, what is the probability that the number of defects observed is (a) 0, (b) at least 1, (c) exactly 2?

4.4.2 Suppose that the number of persons per car arriving at the entrance to an amusement park is Poisson distributed, with $\lambda = 2.4$. What is the probability that a car arriving at the entrance contains (a) no persons, (b) only one person, (c) more than one person, (d) eight persons, (e) more than eight persons?

4.4.3 Of the items produced by Pickens Products Company, 3% are defective. A sample of 25 items is selected for inspection. Use both the binomial and the Poisson distributions to answer the following questions, and compare the results. (a) What is the probability that exactly four defectives are found? (b) What is the probability that three or more defectives are found?

4.4.4 In the Royal Ridge resort area, the number of vacant motel rooms follows a Poisson distribution. The expected vacancy rate is 10 rooms per night. Find the probability that on a given night the number of vacant rooms will be (a) none, (b) 1, (c) 7, (d) 6 or more, (e) 5 or fewer, (f) between 5 and 12, inclusive, (g) more than 12.

4.4.5 In a certain large population, 5% suffer from emotional disorders. In a simple random sample of 60, what is the probability that the number suffering from emotional disorders will be (a) more than 6, (b) at least 10, (c) between 5 and 15, inclusive?

4.4.6 In a certain population of executives, 3% belong to a particular ethnic group. In a simple random sample of 40 of these executives, what is the probability that the number who belong to the ethnic group will be (a) more than 2, (b) at least 4, (c) 5 or more?

4.5 THE HYPERGEOMETRIC DISTRIBUTION

In Section 4.3, you learned that if analysis based on the binomial model is to be valid the probability of a success p must remain constant throughout the sampling operation. That is, p must be the same each time we select an element from the population. As we noted, this condition is met when sampling is from an infinite population. If the sampled population is finite, p will not be the same on successive drawings of elements if sampling is *without replacement*. When sampling is without replacement, the population is decreased by one each time we select an element.

For example, suppose that we have a population of 27 people, of whom 15 are males and 12 are females. Suppose further that we wish to draw a random sample of size 5 from this population. Before we select the first person, the probability that this person will be a female (a success) is $p = 12/27$. After we select the first person but before we select the second person, the probability that the person we select will be a female is either $12/26$ or $11/26$, neither of which is equal to $12/27$. The probability that the second person we select will be female is $p = 12/26$ if the first person we select is male and $11/26$ if the first person we select is female. Figure 4.5.1 shows sampling without replacement from a population of 15 males and 12 females.

FIGURE 4.5.1 Pictorial representation of sampling without replacement from a small population

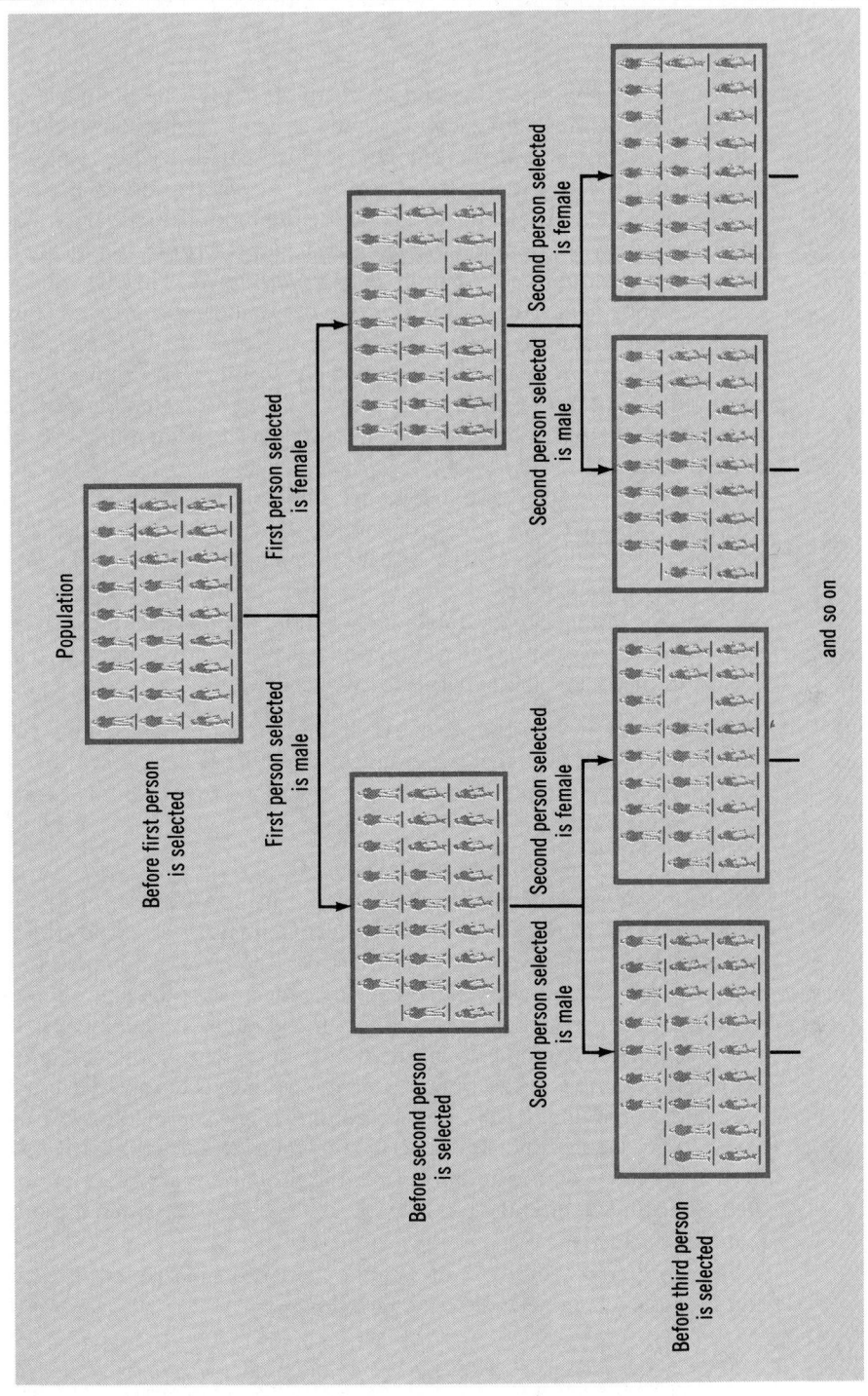

As noted in Section 4.3, when we sample from very large finite populations, we usually need not be concerned with the fact that the binomial model is not strictly valid. If the sample contains only a small proportion of the finite population, say 10% or less, the binomial model usually yields results that closely approximate those that we would realize if the population were infinite.

We may have a problem if we try to use the binomial model with a very small population or with a sample that contains a large proportion of the population. One solution would be to sample *with replacement*. That is, we would return each element to the population after we drew and examined it. This procedure would ensure a constant value of p, the proportion of successes, throughout the sampling operation. It would be equivalent to sampling from an infinite population. In situations of practical importance, however, sampling with replacement is difficult to justify. Consequently, we conduct most sampling operations without replacement.

When sampling is without replacement from a small dichotomous (0, 1) population, the hypergeometric distribution may provide a suitable model.

Fortunately we have another model available for many of the situations in which we cannot use the binomial model. We can use this model, known as the *hypergeometric* model, when we need to sample without replacement from a small population. In fact, the hypergeometric model is appropriate any time we are sampling without replacement from a finite population and wish to determine the probability of a specified number of successes and/or failures. This example illustrates the use of the hypergeometric model.

EXAMPLE 4.5.1   A carton of six flashlight batteries contains two that are defective (D) and four that are nondefective (N). If we select three batteries at random from the carton, what is the probability that the sample contains exactly one defective battery?

SOLUTION   The tree diagram in Figure 4.5.2 shows the ways in which we can obtain one defective item when we sample from a population of size six that contains two defective and four nondefective items. Not all possible samples of size three will contain exactly one defective. The heavy branches in Figure 4.5.2 represent the samples with exactly one defective. Also, the figure shows the composition of the carton before each draw. It shows the probability associated with each outcome in parentheses on the branch representing the outcome.

There are three ways to obtain a sample with exactly one defective. Each has the same probability, 0.200, of occurring. A single sample drawn from the population may be the one shown as DNN, the one shown as NDN, or the one shown as NND. By the addition rule, the probability of obtaining one of these three outcomes is $0.200 + 0.200 + 0.200 = 0.600$, since the outcomes are mutually exclusive.

We can describe the type of sampling situation illustrated in Example 4.5.1 and Figure 4.5.2 in general terms as follows:

From a population of size N consisting of N_1 elements of one type (successes) and N_2 elements of another type (failures), select at random and without

FIGURE 4.5.2   Tree diagram for Example 4.5.1

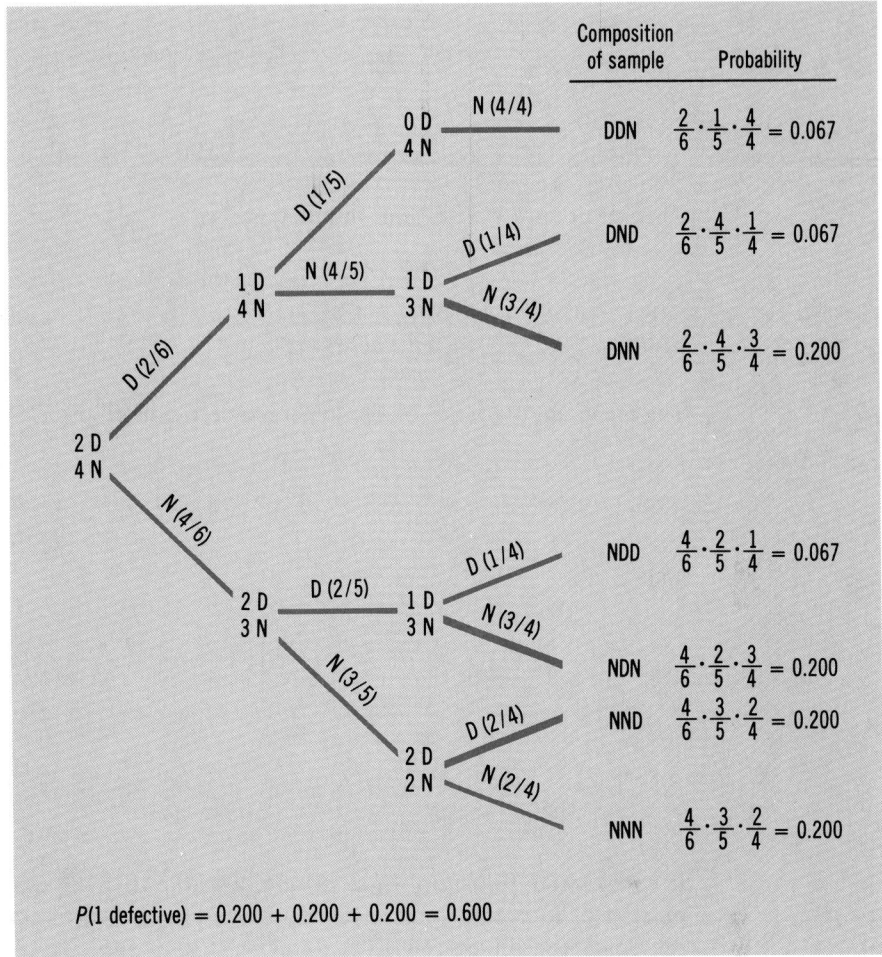

	Composition of sample	Probability
N (4/4)	DDN	$\frac{2}{6} \cdot \frac{1}{5} \cdot \frac{4}{4} = 0.067$
D (1/4)	DND	$\frac{2}{6} \cdot \frac{4}{5} \cdot \frac{1}{4} = 0.067$
N (3/4)	DNN	$\frac{2}{6} \cdot \frac{4}{5} \cdot \frac{3}{4} = 0.200$
D (1/4)	NDD	$\frac{4}{6} \cdot \frac{2}{5} \cdot \frac{1}{4} = 0.067$
N (3/4)	NDN	$\frac{4}{6} \cdot \frac{2}{5} \cdot \frac{3}{4} = 0.200$
D (2/4)	NND	$\frac{4}{6} \cdot \frac{3}{5} \cdot \frac{2}{4} = 0.200$
N (2/4)	NNN	$\frac{4}{6} \cdot \frac{3}{5} \cdot \frac{2}{4} = 0.200$

$P(1 \text{ defective}) = 0.200 + 0.200 + 0.200 = 0.600$

replacement a sample of size n. Determine the probability $P(X = x)$ that the sample will contain x successes.

The formula for $P(x)$ under these conditions is

(4.5.1)
$$P(X = x) = \frac{{}_{N_1}C_x \, {}_{N_2}C_{n-x}}{{}_{N}C_n}, \qquad x = 0, 1, 2, \ldots, n$$

To illustrate the use of Equation 4.5.1, let us refer again to Example 4.5.1, in which $N_1 = 2, N_2 = 4, N = 2 + 4 = 6, n = 3$, and $x = 1$. Proper substitution into the formula gives

$$P(X = 1) = \frac{{}_2C_1 \, {}_4C_2}{{}_6C_3} = \frac{\left(\dfrac{2!}{1!1!}\right)\left(\dfrac{4!}{2!2!}\right)}{\left(\dfrac{6!}{3!3!}\right)} = \frac{(2)(6)}{20} = 0.60$$

This result agrees with that obtained earlier.

MEAN AND VARIANCE OF THE HYPERGEOMETRIC DISTRIBUTION

The mean and variance of the hypergeometric distribution are, respectively,

(4.5.2)
$$\mu = E(X) = n \left(\frac{N_1}{N}\right)$$

and

(4.5.3)
$$\sigma^2 = n \left(\frac{N_1}{N}\right)\left(1 - \frac{N_1}{N}\right)\left(\frac{N - n}{N - 1}\right)$$

BINOMIAL PROBABILITIES AS APPROXIMATIONS TO HYPERGEOMETRIC PROBABILITIES

If we examine Equation 4.5.2 closely, we note that the term N_1/N is the proportion of successes, p, in a dichotomous population of size N. Consequently, the equation can be rewritten as $\mu = E(x) = np$, which is identical to the equation we use to calculate the mean of a binomial distribution. Similarly, examination of Equation 4.5.3 reveals that not only does the term $N_1/N = p$, the proportion of successes in a dichotomous population of size N, but the term $1 - N_1/N = 1 - p = q$, the proportion of nonsuccesses, or failures, in a dichotomous population of size N. Were it not, then, for the term $(N - n)/(N - 1)$ in Equation 4.5.3, the equation would be the same as the equation for computing the variance of the binomial distribution.

The fpc is $\dfrac{N - n}{N - 1}$

Taking a closer look at $(N - n)/(N - 1)$, we discover that if N is considerably larger than n, the term is numerically close to 1. For example, suppose that $N = 10,000$ and $n = 10$. In that case, $(N - n)/(N - 1) = (10,000 - 10)/(10,000 - 1) = 9,990/9,999 = 0.999$, which most people would agree is close to 1. Thus, we see that in that case multiplying $n(N_1/N)(1 - N_1/N)$ by $(N - n)/(N - 1) = 0.999$ would yield a result almost identical to that obtained by multiplying by 1. In other words, if in Equation 4.5.3 we ignore the factor $(N - n)/(N - 1)$ when it is equal to 0.999, the effect on the value of σ^2 is negligible. In general, then, when we compute the variance of a hypergeometric distribution for which N is large relative to n, we may ignore the term $(N - n)/(N - 1)$. This term is called the *finite population correction* (fpc), to call attention to the fact that sampling is from a finite population and without replacement. When $(N - n)/(N - 1)$ is ignored, Equation 4.5.3 becomes identical to the equation we use in calculating the variance of a binomial distribution. This relationship between hypergeometric distributions and binomial distributions allows us, when N is large relative to n, to use the binomial distribution formula and table to determine probabilities whose calculation would otherwise require the use of the hypergeometric formula and tables. Using the binomial distribution formulas and tables rather than those for the hypergeometric distribution is more convenient in many practical situations. A generally accepted rule of thumb is that N should be at least ten times as large as n—that is, $(N \geq 10n)$—for the approximation of hypergeometric probabilities by binomial probabilities to be acceptable. This is the same rule of thumb that we use to justify the appropriateness of the binomial model when sampling is from a finite population.

EXAMPLE 4.5.2 Suppose that $N = 25$, N_1 (the number of successes) $= 15$, $N_2 = 10$, $n = 2$, and sampling is without replacement. We wish to find the probability that $X = 0$, $X = 1$, and $X = 2$.

SOLUTION   If we use the hypergeometric formula of Equation 4.5.1, we compute

$$P(X = 0) = \frac{{}_{15}C_0 \, {}_{10}C_2}{{}_{25}C_2} = \frac{\left(\dfrac{15!}{0!15!}\right)\left(\dfrac{10!}{2!8!}\right)}{\left(\dfrac{25!}{2!23!}\right)} = 0.15$$

$$P(X = 1) = \frac{{}_{15}C_1 \, {}_{10}C_1}{{}_{25}C_2} = \frac{\left(\dfrac{15!}{1!14!}\right)\left(\dfrac{10!}{1!9!}\right)}{\left(\dfrac{25!}{2!23!}\right)} = 0.50$$

$$P(X = 2) = \frac{{}_{15}C_2 \, {}_{10}C_0}{{}_{25}C_2} = \frac{\left(\dfrac{15!}{2!13!}\right)\left(\dfrac{10!}{0!10!}\right)}{\left(\dfrac{25!}{2!23!}\right)} = 0.35$$

Since $N = 25$ is more than 10 times the size of $n = 2$, we can expect to get probabilities that are close to these if we use the binomial approximations. The binomial formula with $p = 15/25 = 0.6$ yields

$$P(X = 0|2,0.6) = {}_2C_0(0.6)^0(0.4)^2 = 0.16$$
$$P(X = 1|2,0.6) = {}_2C_1(0.6)^1(0.4)^1 = 0.48$$
$$P(X = 2|2,0.6) = {}_2C_2(0.6)^2(0.4)^0 = 0.36$$

We see that the probabilities obtained by using the binomial approximation are quite close to those obtained by using the hypergeometric formula.

EXERCISES

4.5.1   A population consists of eight persons, of whom three are married and five are single. Suppose that we draw a sample of size 4 without replacement from this population. What is the probability that exactly two members of the sample will be married?

 4.5.2   A population consists of seven people, of whom three drive foreign cars and four drive American-made cars. Suppose that we draw a sample of size three from the population. What is the probability that the sample will contain *exactly* one person who drives a foreign car? What is the probability that the sample will contain *at least* one person who drives a foreign car?

4.5.3   A box contains ten two-inch screws, of which four have a Phillips head and six have a regular head. Suppose that we select four screws randomly, without replacement, from the box. What is the probability that the number of Phillips-head screws in the sample will be   (a) exactly four,   (b) two or three,   (c) at least one?

 4.5.4   Sanger Services employs six microcomputer operators, of whom three are women. You choose four from the six, at random. What is the probability that of those chosen, the number of women will be   (a) exactly two,   (b) two or more,   (c) at least two?

4.5.5   A population consists of nine junior executives, of whom five have a master's degree. You select a random sample of six from this population. What is the probability that the number with a master's degree will be   (a) exactly three,   (b) between two and four, inclusive?   (c) no more than three?

4.6   PROBABILITY DISTRIBUTIONS OF CONTINUOUS RANDOM VARIABLES

The binomial, Poisson, and hypergeometric distributions are distributions of discrete random variables. In this section, we consider the general idea of the distribution of a continuous random variable. In the following section, we discuss in detail the most important special distribution of a continuous random variable—the *normal distribution*.

> The random variable X is *continuous* if it can assume all possible values between any two particular values x_a and x_b.

To understand the nature of the distribution of a continuous random variable, consider the following example.

TABLE 4.6.1   Distribution of lengths of 200 aluminum-coated steel sheets

Length (inches)	Frequency	Relative frequency
30.000–30.124	8	0.04
30.125–30.249	20	0.10
30.250–30.374	32	0.16
30.375–30.499	40	0.20
30.500–30.624	36	0.18
30.625–30.749	34	0.17
30.750–30.874	20	0.10
30.875–30.999	10	0.05
Total	200	1.00

EXAMPLE 4.6.1   Table 4.6.1 shows the frequency and relative frequency distributions of the lengths of a sample of 200 aluminum-coated steel sheets taken from a production lot at a factory operated by Freeman Industries. Since the probability associated with each interval of lengths shown in the first column is given by the relative frequency column, this column constitutes the probability distribution of the random variable, length of aluminum-coated steel sheet.

We can present the probability distribution as a histogram, as in Figure 4.6.1, or as a frequency polygon, as in Figure 4.6.2. The area within each cell of the histogram represents a certain proportion of the total area bounded by the histogram and the horizontal axis. The proportion of the total area contained within a particular cell is equal to the probability of observing a value between the boundaries of that cell. For example, Table 4.6.1 shows that the relative fre-

FIGURE 4.6.1   Histogram of lengths of 200 aluminum-coated steel sheets

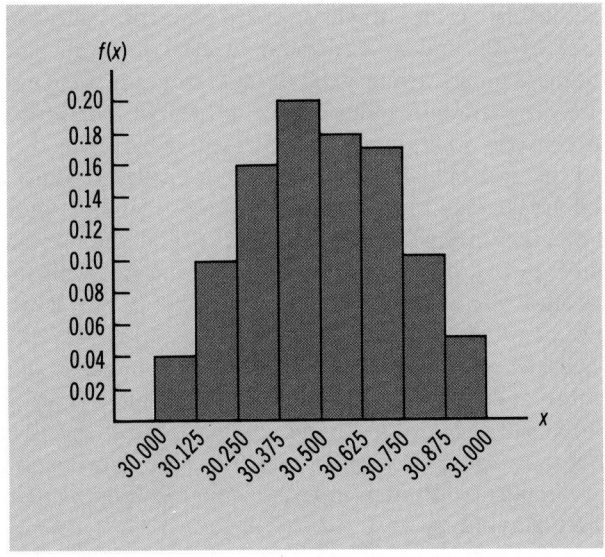

FIGURE 4.6.2   Relative frequency polygon of lengths of 200 aluminum-coated steel sheets

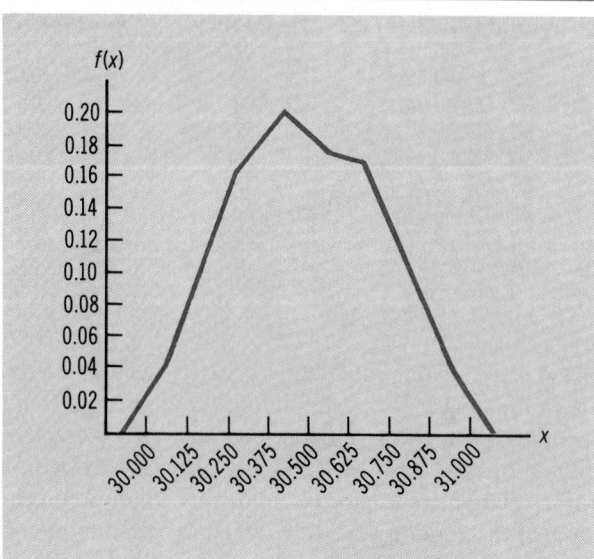

quency, or probability, of occurrence of values between 30.000 and 30.125 inches is 0.04. The corresponding cell in Figure 4.6.1 has 4% of the total area of the histogram.

Given any histogram of a probability distribution, we can find the probability of occurrence of values between any two points on the horizontal axis. We do this by determining what proportion of the total area we enclose when we erect vertical lines at these points. For example, to find the probability of occurrence of values between 30.500 and 30.625 in Figure 4.6.1, we determine what proportion of the histogram's area is enclosed by vertical lines erected at these points. The values 30.500 and 30.625 define a class interval. Since the vertical lines erected at these points define a cell of the histogram, we consult Table 4.6.1, and we find the proportion of area enclosed to be 0.18. The probability of occurrence of values between 30.500 and 30.625, then, is 0.18.

To find the area enclosed by two or more cells, we must find the sum of the individual areas. This total is equal to the probability associated with the corresponding class intervals. For example, to find the area between 30.500 and 30.750 in Figure 4.6.1, we add the areas of the two cells involved. From Table 4.6.1, we find this area to be $0.18 + 0.17 = 0.35$. Thus, the probability of occurrence of values between 30.500 and 30.750 is 0.35.

Now consider a situation in which the number of values of the random variable is very large and the width of the class intervals is very small. For example, suppose that we have 2,000 aluminum-coated steel sheets instead of 200. And suppose that we prepare a histogram for these data using much smaller class intervals, perhaps 0.010 inch in width. The resulting histogram might look like the one in Figure 4.6.3.

FIGURE 4.6.3   Histogram of lengths of 2000 aluminum-coated steel sheets (much smaller class intervals than in Figure 4.6.1)

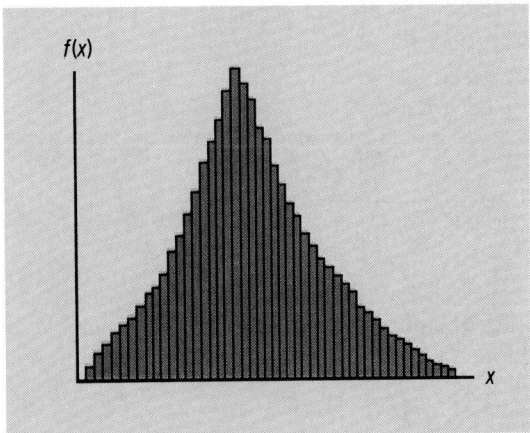

Suppose that we were to construct a frequency polygon from the histogram of Figure 4.6.3. The curve in this figure would be much smoother than the one in Figure 4.6.2. In fact, as the number of values n approaches infinity and the width of the class intervals approaches 0, the frequency polygon approaches a smooth curve, such as the one shown in Figure 4.6.4. We can use smooth curves as a graphical means of representing probability distributions of continuous random variables.

As with a histogram, the total area under a smooth curve used to represent a probability distribution is equal to 1. The probability of occurrence of values between any two points on the horizontal axis is equal to the area bounded by perpendicular lines erected at these points, the curve itself, and the horizontal axis. Figure 4.6.5 shows the graph of the probability distribution of a continuous random variable with the area between two points a and b shaded. This area is equal to the probability of occurrence of values between a and b.

FIGURE 4.6.4   Smooth curve approximating a histogram for data with large n and a large number of class intervals

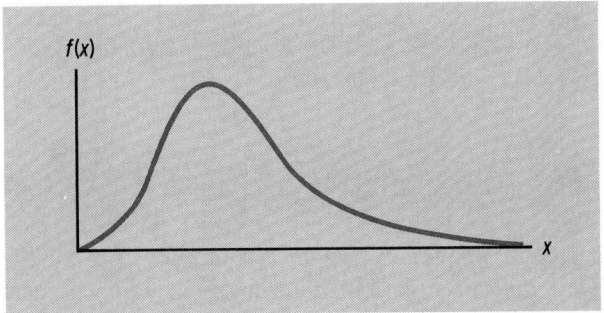

FIGURE 4.6.5   Probability distribution of the continuous random variable X showing $P(a \le x \le b)$

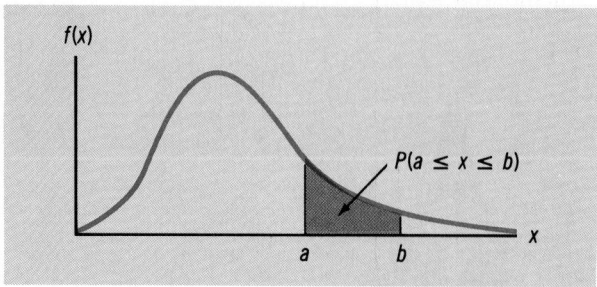

We can describe the curve used to represent the probability distribution of a continuous random variable, such as that shown in Figure 4.6.5, by a *probability density function*.

> A *probability density function* is a formula, or equation, used to represent the probability distribution of a continuous random variable.

We need to represent the distribution of a continuous random variable in this manner. Because of the variable's continuity, we cannot list its possible values along with the associated probabilities as we can for a discrete random variable.

We cannot find areas under a smooth curve the same way that we find areas under a histogram. A smooth curve does not have delineated subareas corresponding to the cells of a histogram. We use integral calculus to find subareas under smooth curves. That is, to find the area between points a and b in Figure 4.6.5, we integrate the probability density function, using a and b as the limits of integration. Methods of integral calculus are beyond the scope of this text. However, this is not a serious problem, since tables of values obtained by integration are available for those probability density functions of interest to us.

In the preceding discussion, we have implied the definition of a *probability distribution of a continuous random variable*. In a more compact form, it is as follows:

> A function $f(x)$, where $f(x) \ge 0$, is called a *probability distribution (or probability density function) of the continuous random variable X* if the total area bounded by its curve and the x axis is equal to 1, and if the subarea under the curve bounded by the curve, the x axis, and perpendiculars erected at any two points a and b gives the probability that X is between points a and b.

4.7   THE UNIFORM DISTRIBUTION

A useful though simple example of a continuous probability distribution is the *uniform distribution*. A variety of business-related phenomena may be quantified by means of a continuous random variable whose probability distribution conforms to the characteristics of a uniform distribution. Such a continuous random variable is one that is just as likely to assume a value within one interval as it is to assume a value in any other interval of equal width. Consider, for example, the arrival time of a plane that is just as likely to arrive at one time as another over a 30-minute period. The manufacturer of some product has determined that the ages of consumers of the product fall between 16 years and 30 years with equal frequency. The uniform distribution would be an appropriate model for this age variable, and given certain necessary information the manufacturer could use the model to answer probability questions about the ages of the product's consumers. Another example of a variable that follows a uniform distribution might be discovered in the examination of the annual incomes of a certain population of individuals. Such would be the case if one were to find that annual incomes occur with equal frequency between 25 and 50 thousand dollars. We call such a variable a *uniform random variable.*

> A *uniform random variable* is one whose measurements are not more highly concentrated around one value than they are around any of the other values. (In the case of a variable that has a mound-shaped distribution, for example, the values are more highly concentrated about some central value.) The measurements of a uniform random variable are evenly spread over the entire range of possible values.
>
> The probability distribution of a uniform random variable is called a *uniform distribution.*

The graph of the uniform distribution is a rectangle with width equal to the range R of the variable under consideration and height equal to $1/R$. For the uniform random variable X whose smallest value is a and whose largest value is b, the range is $R = b - a$ and

(4.7.1)
$$f(X) = \frac{1}{b - a} \quad \text{for } a \leq X \leq b; \text{ otherwise } f(X) = 0$$

The mean μ and standard deviation σ of the uniform distribution are

(4.7.2)
$$\mu = \frac{a + b}{2}$$

and

(4.7.3)
$$\sigma = \frac{b - a}{\sqrt{12}}$$

Figure 4.7.1 illustrates the characteristics of a uniform probability distribution. As Figure 4.7.1 suggests, the uniform distribution is symmetrical, it has no mode, and the mean and median are equal. The following example illustrates the use of the uniform distribution.

FIGURE 4.7.1   The uniform probability distribution

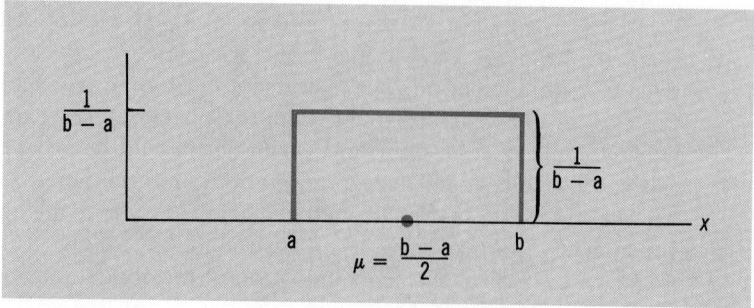

EXAMPLE 4.7.1   A fertilizer manufacturer buys a certain raw material by weight. Each batch of raw material purchased is weighed, and the weight is recorded to the nearest pound. It is assumed that the round-off error is uniformly distributed in the interval from -0.5 to $+0.5$. We wish to   (a) know the mean round-off error,   (b) know the standard deviation of the round-off error, (c) graph the distribution, and   (d) determine the proportion of batches of raw material in which the true weight exceeds the recorded weight by 0.3 pound or more.

SOLUTION

$$(a) \quad \mu = \frac{-0.5 + 0.5}{2} = \frac{0}{2} = 0$$

$$(b) \quad \sigma = \frac{0.5 - (-0.5)}{\sqrt{12}} = \frac{1}{\sqrt{12}} = 0.2887$$

(c) The uniform probability distribution is

$$f(X) = \frac{1}{b - a} = \frac{1}{0.5 - (-0.5)} = \frac{1}{1} = 1$$

The graph of the distribution is shown in Figure 4.7.2.   (d) The proportion of batches for which the true weight exceeds the recorded weight by more than 0.3 pound is equal to the probability that $0.3 \leq X \leq 0.5$. That is, we must find the area under the curve of the distribution between $x = 0.3$ and $x = 0.5$. The desired area is the area of a rectangle with a width of $0.5 - 0.3 = 0.2$ and a height of 1. The answer is $P(x \geq 0.3) = $ (width)(height) $= (0.2)(1) = 0.2$. The probability is shown in Figure 4.7.3.

The cumulative probability distribution of a continuous uniform random variable is given by

(4.7.4) $$P(X \leq x) = (x - a)/(b - a)$$

where $a \leq x \leq b$.

FIGURE 4.7.2   Graph of the uniform distribution described in Example 4.7.1

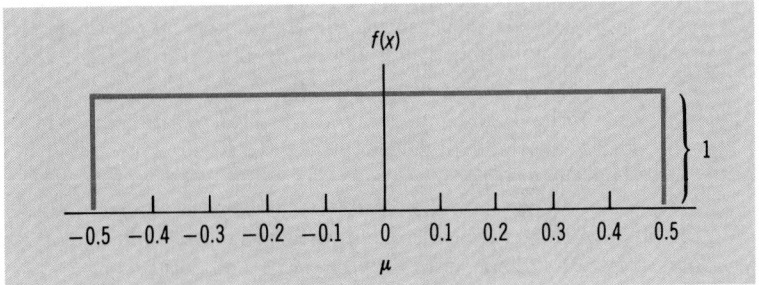

EXAMPLE 4.7.2   A city bank has just announced that customers using its teller windows will be served in 5 minutes or less after entering the service line. What bank officials didn't say in their announcement was the fact that they had determined that waiting times were uniformly distributed over the interval 0 to 5 minutes. What is the probability that a customer entering the service line will have to wait 3 minutes or less?

SOLUTION   We may answer the question by using Equation 4.7.4.

$$P(X \le 3) = (3 - 0)/(5 - 0) = 3/5 = 0.60.$$

THE DISCRETE UNIFORM DISTRIBUTION

Discrete random variables may also follow a uniform distribution called a *discrete uniform distribution*. A familiar example is the random numbers for use in selecting simple random samples as discussed in Chapter 1. Since theoretically each digit from 0 through 9 is equally represented, the distribution of a large number of random digits could be well approximated by a discrete uniform distribution. The distribution could be represented by a graph consisting of 10 vertical bars of equal height.

FIGURE 4.7.3   The uniform distribution described in Example 4.7.1 showing $P(x \ge 0.3)$

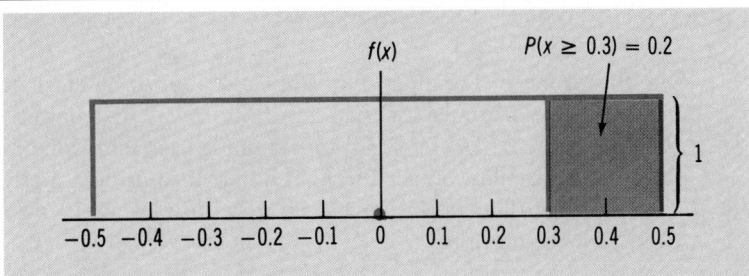

EXERCISES

4.7.1 During a particular experiment, the temperature at which a certain chemical reaction takes place is uniformly distributed in the interval from 250°F to 300°F.

(a) What is the mean temperature at which the reaction takes place?
(b) What is the standard deviation?
(c) Graph the distribution.
(d) What proportion of the reactions take place at temperatures below 260°F?
(e) If you conduct the experiment, what is the probability that the chemical reaction will take place at a temperature between 265°F and 280°F?

4.7.2 The manager of the home delivery department of the Speedy Eater fast-food chain believes that the time that elapses between the placement of an order and delivery of the order is uniformly distributed over the interval from 20 minutes to 60 minutes. Suppose that he is correct.

(a) If you place an order, how long can you expect to wait for delivery?
(b) What is the variance of the time that elapses between ordering time and delivery time?
(c) Draw a graph of the distribution.
(d) What proportion of the orders are delivered within 35 minutes?
(e) If you place an order, what is the probability that you will have to wait more than 30 minutes for delivery?

4.7.3 A rancher has a fence that extends in a straight line for five miles from his maintenance shed. Breaks in the fence are just as likely to occur at one place as another.

(a) Draw a graph of the probability distribution of X = distance from maintenance shed at which a break occurs.
(b) Compute the mean and variance of X.
(c) What proportion of breaks can be expected to occur between three and four miles from the maintenance shed?

4.8 THE NORMAL DISTRIBUTION

We now come to the most important distribution in statistics—the *normal distribution*. The formula for this distribution was first published by Abraham de Moivre (1667–1754) in 1733. Other mathematicians linked with the history of the normal distribution are Pierre Simon, Marquis de Laplace (1667–1754) and Carl Friedrich Gauss (1777–1855), in whose honor it is sometimes called the *Gaussian distribution*.

FIGURE 4.8.1   A normal distribution

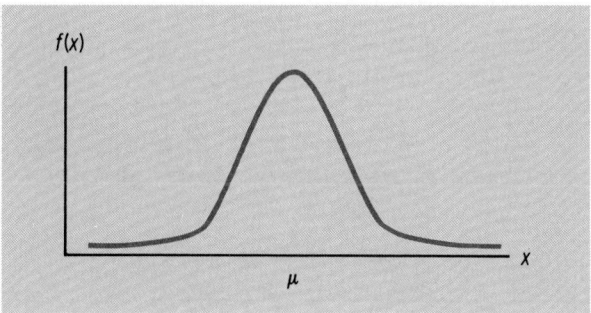

The normal density function is given by

$$(4.8.1) \qquad f(x) = \frac{1}{\sqrt{2\pi}\sigma} e^{-(x-\mu)^2/2\sigma^2}, \qquad -\infty < x < \infty$$

The parameters of the normal distribution are μ and σ.

where π and e are the familiar constants 3.14159 and 2.71828, respectively. The distribution has two parameters: μ, the mean, and σ, the standard deviation. The graph of the normal distribution is the familiar bell-shaped curve shown in Figure 4.8.1.

CHARACTERISTICS OF THE NORMAL DISTRIBUTION

The following are some important characteristics of the normal distribution:

1. It is symmetrical about its mean, μ. As seen in Figure 4.8.1, the curve on either side of μ is a mirror image of the other side.

2. The mean, the median, and the mode are all equal.

3. The total area under the curve above the x axis is equal to 1. Because of the symmetry of the normal curve, 50% of the area is to the right of a perpendicular line erected at the mean, and 50% is to the left.

4. Suppose that we erect vertical lines one standard deviation from the mean in each direction. The area enclosed by these lines, the x axis, and the curve will be equal to approximately 68% of the total area. If we erect these lateral boundaries two standard deviations from the mean in each direction, they will enclose approximately 95% of the area. Perpendiculars erected three standard deviations on either side of the mean will enclose approximately 99.7% of the total area. Figure 4.8.2 illustrates these approximate areas.

Interval	Approx-imate area
$\mu \pm \sigma$	0.68
$\mu \pm 2\sigma$	0.95
$\mu \pm 3\sigma$	0.997

FIGURE 4.8.2 Normal distributions, showing areas bounded by perpendiculars erected a distance of one, two, and three standard deviations on either side of the mean (areas are approximate)

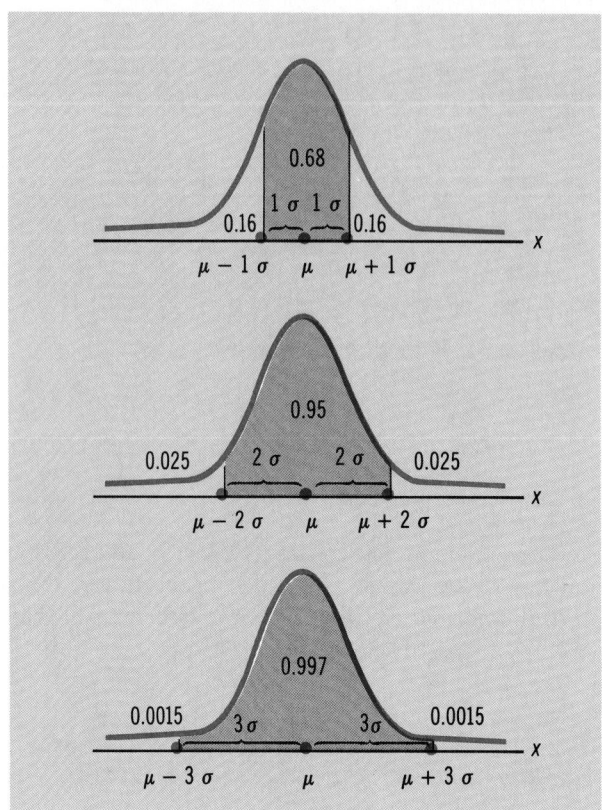

A *normally distributed* random variable is an example of a case in which Chebyshev's theorem provides weak information regarding the probability of observing a value within specified distances of the mean. Instead of the probabilities of 0.95 and 0.997, Chebyshev's theorem leads to probabilities of at least $1 - 1/2^2 = 0.75$ and at least $1 - 1/3^2 = 0.89$, respectively, of observing a value within two and three standard deviations from the mean. Chebyshev's theorem gives no information at all about the probability of observing a value within one standard deviation from the mean, since $1 - 1/k^2 = 0$ when $k = 1$. Thus, if we know that a random variable is normally distributed, we can make more powerful probability statements than we could using Chebyshev's theorem.

5. The normal distribution is completely determined by its parameters μ and σ. That is, each different value of μ or σ specifies a different normal distribution. Figure 4.8.3 shows how different values of μ cause the graph of the distri-

FIGURE 4.8.3   Three normal distributions with different means

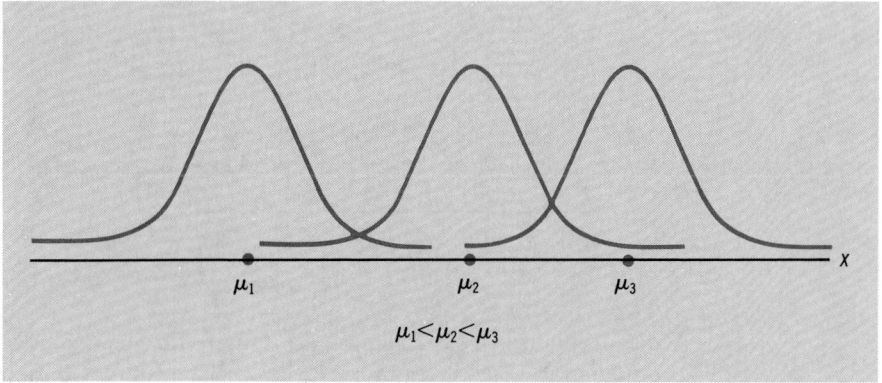

bution to be shifted along the x axis. Figure 4.8.4 shows how different values of the standard deviation σ, which is a measure of dispersion, determine the flatness or peakedness of the graph of the distribution.

THE STANDARD NORMAL DISTRIBUTION

The normal distribution is really a family of distributions in which one member is distinguished from another on the basis of the values of μ and σ. In other words, as already indicated, there is a different normal distribution for each different value of either μ or σ.

The most important member of this family of distributions is the *standard normal distribution*.

> The *standard normal distribution* has a mean of 0 and a standard deviation of 1.

FIGURE 4.8.4   Three normal distributions with different standard deviations

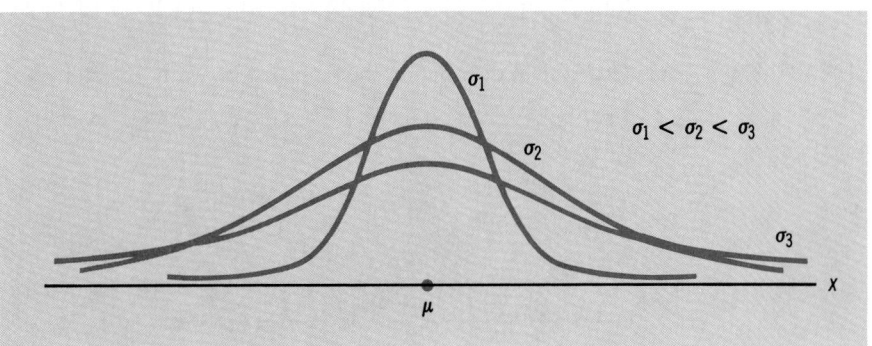

FIGURE 4.8.5   The standard normal distribution

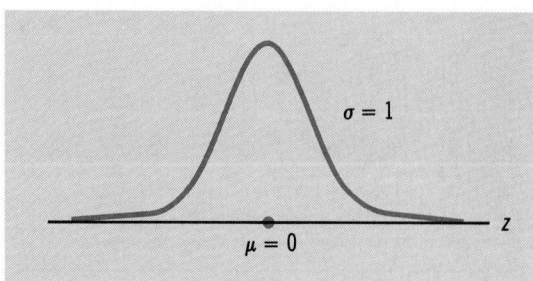

We can obtain it from Equation 4.8.1 by letting $\mu = 0$ and $\sigma = 1$. We usually use the letter z for the random variable that results. Consequently the equation for the standard normal distribution is written

(4.8.2)
$$f(z) = \frac{1}{\sqrt{2\pi}} e^{-z^2/2}, \qquad -\infty < z < \infty$$

Figure 4.8.5 shows the graph of the standard normal distribution.

The probability that z lies between any two points on the z axis, say z_0 and z_1, is determined by the area bounded by perpendiculars erected at each of these points, the curve, and the horizontal axis. We find areas under the curve of a continuous distribution by integrating the function between two values of the variable. Thus, to find the area between z_0 and z_1 of the standard normal distribution, we must evaluate the following integral:

$$\int_{z_0}^{z_1} \frac{1}{\sqrt{2\pi}} e^{-z^2/2} \, dz$$

There are tables that give the results of integrations in which we might be interested. Therefore, we do not need to perform the integration. Table C of Appendix I, for example, gives the areas under the standard normal curve between $-\infty$ and the values of z shown in the marginal column of the table. The shaded area in Figure 4.8.6 represents the area listed in the body of Table C as being between

FIGURE 4.8.6   Standard normal distribution showing area between $-\infty$ and z_0

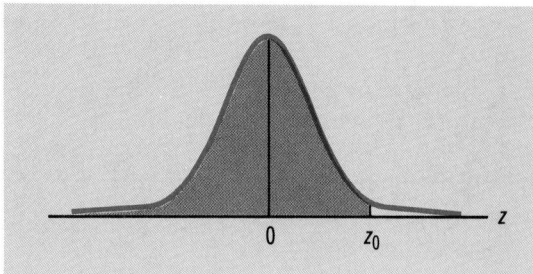

FIGURE 4.8.7   Standard normal distribution showing area between $-\infty$ and $z = 2.5$

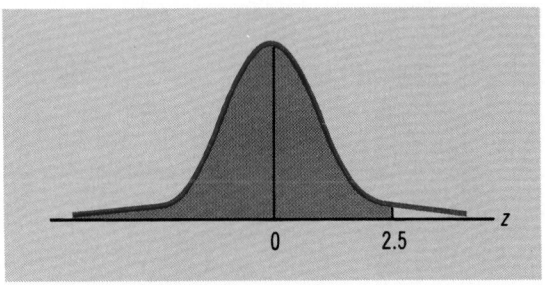

$-\infty$ and $z = z_0$. Thus, we see that Table C represents a cumulative probability distribution—more specifically, the cumulative normal distribution. The following examples illustrate the use of Table C.

EXAMPLE 4.8.1   Given the standard normal distribution, find the area under the curve above the z axis between $z = -\infty$ and $z = 2.5$.

SOLUTION   The area is shaded in Figure 4.8.7. Locating $z = 2.5$ in Table C and reading the corresponding entry in the body of the table, we find the desired area to be 0.9938. We can interpret this in several ways. It is the probability that a z picked at random from the population of z's will have a value between $-\infty$ and 2.5. It is also the relative frequency of occurrence (or proportion) of values of z between $-\infty$ and 2.5. Or we can say that 99.38% of the z's have a value between $-\infty$ and 2.5.

EXAMPLE 4.8.2   What is the probability that a z picked at random from the population of z's will have a value between -2.65 and $+2.65$?

SOLUTION   Figure 4.8.8 shows the desired area. We find the area between $-\infty$ and 2.65 by locating 2.65 in Table C. The table shows us that the area to the left of 2.65 is 0.9960. Similarly, we find the area from $-\infty$ to -2.65 to be 0.0040. We find the area we want by subtracting 0.0040 from 0.9960. That is,

$$P(-2.65 \leq z \leq 2.65) = 0.9960 - 0.0040 = 0.9920$$

FIGURE 4.8.8   Standard normal distribution showing area between $z = -2.65$ and $z = +2.65$

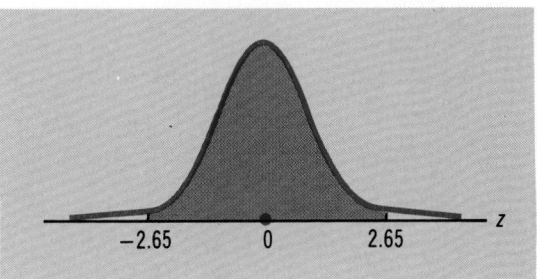

FIGURE 4.8.9 Standard normal distribution showing area between $z = -2.78$ and $z = +1.47$

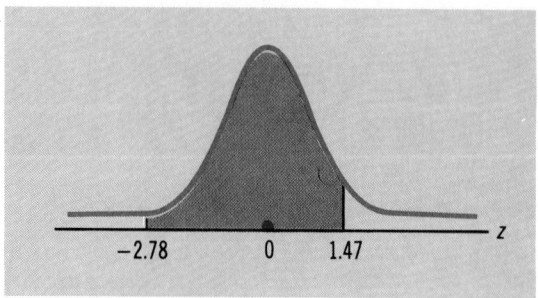

EXAMPLE 4.8.3 What proportion of z values are between -2.78 and 1.47?

SOLUTION Figure 4.8.9 shows the area desired. The area between $-\infty$ and 1.47 is 0.9292. The area between $-\infty$ and -2.78 is 0.0027. To find the desired area, we subtract 0.0027 from 0.9292 to obtain 0.9265. That is,

$$P(-2.78 \leq z \leq 1.47) = 0.9292 - 0.0027 = 0.9265$$

EXAMPLE 4.8.4 Given the standard normal distribution, find $P(z \geq 1.73)$.

SOLUTION Figure 4.8.10 shows the area desired. We can obtain the area to the right of $z = 1.73$ by subtracting the area between $-\infty$ and 1.73 from 1. Thus,

$$P(z \geq 1.73) = 1 - P(-\infty < z < 1.73) = 1 - 0.9582 = 0.0418$$

Note that $P(z < 1.73) + P(z \geq 1.73) = 1$ because the events $z < 1.73$ and $z \geq 1.73$ are complementary events.

Again, the probability that z is between two values z_a and z_b is equal to the area under the curve between perpendicular lines erected at z_a and z_b. The area above a point, say z_a, is equal to 0. Thus, the probability that $z = z_a = 0$. That is, $P(z = z_a) = 0$. Therefore, the probability that z is greater than or equal to

FIGURE 4.8.10 Standard normal distribution showing area to right of $z = 1.73$

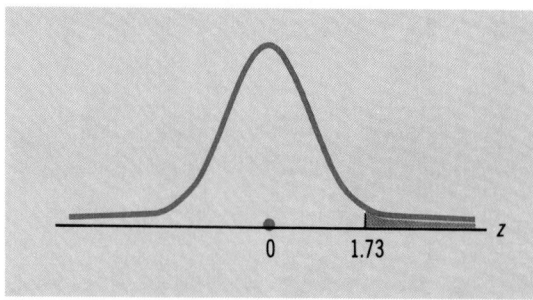

z_a is the same as the probability that z is greater than z_a. Using symbols, we can write $P(z \geq z_a) = P(z > z_a)$. For example, Table C tells us that $P(z \geq 1.5) = 0.0668$. Since $P(z = 1.5) = 0$, $P(z > 1.5) = 0.0668$ also. Similarly, $P(z_a \leq z \leq z_b) = P(z_a < z < z_b)$ and $P(z_a \leq z) = P(z_a < z)$.

The table of the standard normal distribution may be presented in many different forms. For example, the entire distribution as presented in Table Ca of Appendix I may be condensed into a single page, as shown in Table Cb, which follows Table Ca. In the condensed table, the leftmost column contains positive values of z in increments of 0.1. To obtain a z expressed in hundredths, we add an appropriate column heading. The numbers in the body of the table give the amount of area under the curve to the left of a specified z. For example, suppose we want to know how much area is to the left of $z = 1.55$. We locate $z = 1.50$ in the leftmost column of the condensed table and 0.05 as a column heading. The number at the intersection of the row labeled 1.50 and the column labeled 0.05 is 0.9394. Thus, we have found that the area to the left of $z = 1.55$ is 0.9394. That is, $P(z \leq 1.55) = 0.9394$. When finding probabilities (areas) associated with negative values of z, recall that the standard normal curve is symmetrical about zero. Therefore, the amount of area to the left of any positive value of z is equal to the amount of area to the right of the negative of that value of z. For example, $P(z \leq 1.55) = P(z \geq -1.55) = 0.9394$. Let us illustrate the application of Table Cb by using it to obtain the solutions to Examples 4.8.1 through 4.8.4.

EXAMPLE 4.8.1   *continued*   Find $P(z \leq 2.50)$.

SOLUTION   The number in the table at the intersection of the row labeled 2.50 and 0.00 is 0.9938. Therefore, as we found before, $P(z \leq 2.50) = 0.9938$.

EXAMPLE 4.8.2   *continued*   Find $P(-2.65 \leq z \leq 2.65)$.

SOLUTION $P(-2.65 \leq z \leq 2.65) = P(z \leq 2.65) - P(z \leq -2.65)$. Recall that $P(z \leq -2.65) = P(z \geq 2.65) = 1 - P(z \leq 2.65) = 1 - 0.9960 = 0.0040$. Therefore, $P(-2.65 \leq z \leq 2.65) = 0.9960 - 0.0040 = 0.9920$.

EXAMPLE 4.8.3   *continued*   Find $P(-2.78 \leq z \leq 1.47)$.

SOLUTION $P(-2.78 \leq z \leq 1.47) = P(z \leq 1.47) - P(z \leq -2.78) = 0.9292 - (1 - 0.9973) = 0.9265$.

EXAMPLE 4.8.4   *continued*   Find $P(z \geq 1.73)$.

SOLUTION $P(z \geq 1.73) = 1 - P(z \leq 1.73) = 1 - 0.9582 = 0.0418$.

COMPUTER **ANALYSIS**

We may use MINITAB to obtain $P(z \leq z_0)$ where z_0 is a specified value of the variable that is distributed as the standard normal. Suppose, for example, that we use MINITAB to find the solution to Example 4.8.4, in which we wish to find $P(z \geq 1.73)$. We first obtain $P(z \leq 1.73)$, as shown in the following printout:

MINITAB
```
MTB > SET C1
DATA> 1.73
DATA> END
MTB > CDF C1
        1.7300    0.9582
```

Finally, we subtract 0.9582 from 1 to obtain $P(z \geq 1.73) = 1 - 0.9582) = 0.0418$.

EXERCISES

Given the standard normal distribution, find

4.8.1   the area under the curve between $z = 0$ and $z = 1.54$.

4.8.2   the probability that a z picked at random has a value between $z = -2.07$ and $z = 2.33$.

4.8.3 $P(z \geq 0.65)$

4.8.4 $P(z \geq -0.65)$

4.8.5 $P(z < -2.33)$

4.8.6 $P(z < 2.33)$

4.8.7 $P(-1.96 \leq z \leq 1.96)$

4.8.8 $P(-2.58 \leq z \leq 2.58)$

4.8.9 $P(-3.10 \leq z \leq 1.25)$

4.8.10 $P(1.47 \leq z \leq 3.44)$

Given the following probabilities, find z_1:

4.8.11 $P(z \leq z_1) = 0.0055$

4.8.12 $P(-2.67 \leq z \leq z_1) = 0.9718$

4.8.13 $P(z > z_1) = 0.0384$

4.8.14 $P(z_1 \leq z \leq 2.98) = 0.1117$

4.8.15 $P(-z_1 \leq z \leq z_1) = 0.8132$

APPLICATIONS OF THE NORMAL DISTRIBUTION

The normal distribution is very important in statistical inference. We should realize, however, that it is not a natural law that we encounter each time we analyze a continuous random variable. The normal distribution is a theoretical, or ideal, distribution. No set of measurements conforms exactly to its specifications. Many sets of measurements, however, are *approximately* normally distributed. In such cases, the normal distribution is quite useful when we try to answer practical questions regarding these data.

In particular, whenever a set of measurements is approximately normally distributed, we can find the probability of occurrence of values within any specific interval, just as we can with the standard normal distribution. We can do this because we can easily transform any normal distribution with a known mean μ and standard deviation σ to the standard normal distribution. Once we have made this transformation, we can use a table of standard normal areas, such as Table C, to find relevant probabilities.

Any value of any normal distribution can be transformed to a value of the standard normal distribution.

We can transform a normal distribution to the standard normal distribution using the formula

(4.8.3)
$$z = \frac{x - \mu}{\sigma}$$

This transforms any value of x in an original distribution with mean μ and standard deviation σ to the corresponding value of z in the standard normal distribution.

The transformation of a normally distributed variable X to the standard normal variable z may be thought of as a two-step procedure. In the first step, we in effect subtract the mean of X from each value of X, which changes the location of the original distribution. Initially centered at μ, the distribution is now centered at 0. In the second step, we divide $X - \mu$ by σ, which changes the dispersion parameter. Whereas the original variable X had a variance of σ^2, the transformed variable z has a variance of 1. We may use such a transformation to find probabilities associated with values of X. For example, suppose that we have a normally distributed variable X with mean μ and standard deviation σ. If a and b are two values of X such that $a < b$, then

$$P(a < X < b) = P\left(\frac{a - \mu}{\sigma} < z < \frac{b - \mu}{\sigma}\right)$$

$$= P\left(z < \frac{b - \mu}{\sigma}\right) - P\left(z < \frac{a - \mu}{\sigma}\right)$$

Also,

$$P(X < a) = P\left(z < \frac{a - \mu}{\sigma}\right)$$

and

$$P(X > a) = P\left(z > \frac{a - \mu}{\sigma}\right) = 1 - P\left(z < \frac{a - \mu}{\sigma}\right)$$

FIGURE 4.8.11   Original distribution of X (approximately normal) and corresponding standard normal distribution

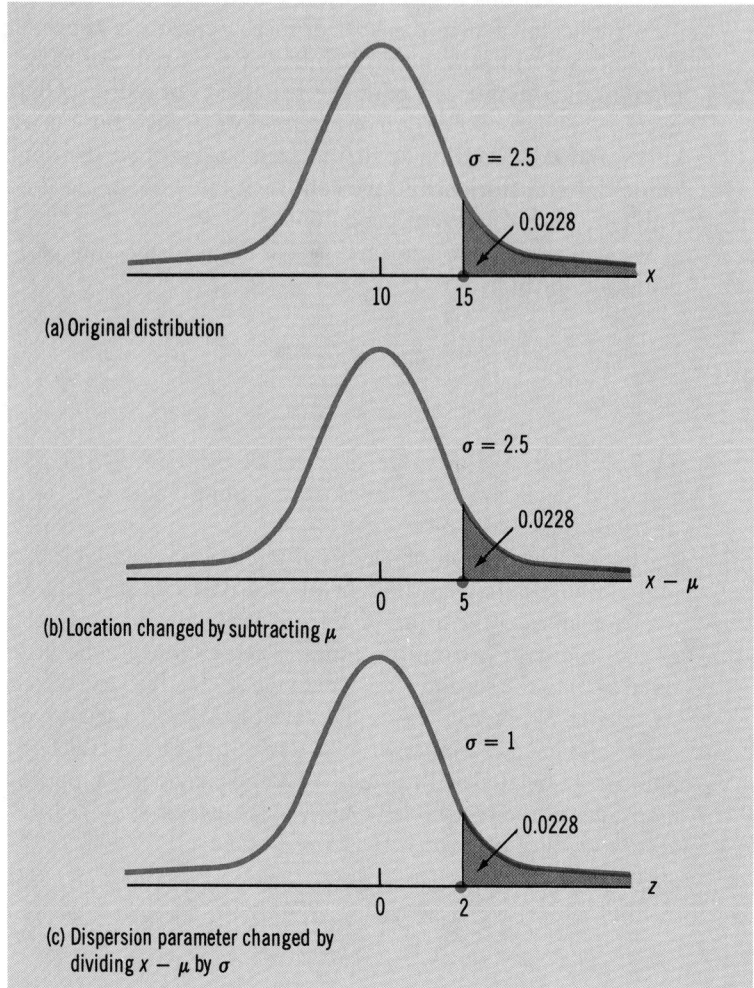

(a) Original distribution

(b) Location changed by subtracting μ

(c) Dispersion parameter changed by dividing $x - \mu$ by σ

Suppose, for example, that we have a population of measurements that are approximately normally distributed with a mean of 10 and a standard deviation of 2.5. Suppose, also, that we want to find the probability that a measurement selected at random from this population will have a value equal to or greater than 15. We first transform $x = 15$ to its corresponding z value. That is,

$$z = \frac{x - \mu}{\sigma} = \frac{15 - 10}{2.5} = \frac{5}{2.5} = 2$$

Figure 4.8.11 shows the relationship between the original distribution and the standard normal distribution, with the areas of interest shaded. The figure shows that the distance from the mean, 10, to the value of interest, 15, is $15 - 10 = 5$. This is a distance of 2 standard deviations. When x values are transformed to z values, the distance of a z value from its mean, 0, is equal to the distance of the corresponding x value from its mean in standard deviation units. In the present example, x is 2 standard deviations from its mean. In the z distribution, a standard deviation is equal to 1. Therefore the point on the z scale located 2 standard deviations from 0 is $z = 2$. This is the same result that we obtained using the formula. From Table C, the area to the right of $z = 2$ is 0.0228. We can summarize this discussion as follows:

$$P(X \geq 15) = P\left(z \geq \frac{15 - 10}{2.5}\right) = P(z \geq 2) = 0.0228$$

EXAMPLE 4.8.5   Refer to Example 4.6.1. Suppose that the population of lengths of aluminum-coated steel sheets is approximately normally distributed with a mean of $\mu = 30.5$ inches and a standard deviation of $\sigma = 0.2$ inch. What is the probability that a sheet selected at random from the population is between 30.250 and 30.750 inches long?

SOLUTION   First we transform each value of x to the corresponding value of z. Thus,

$$z_1 = \frac{30.250 - 30.500}{0.2} = \frac{-0.250}{0.2} = -1.25$$

and

$$z_2 = \frac{30.750 - 30.500}{0.2} = \frac{0.250}{0.2} = 1.25$$

Figure 4.8.12 shows the relationship between the original distribution and the standard normal distribution. The areas of interest are shaded. The probability

FIGURE 4.8.12   Normal distribution and corresponding standard normal distribution, Example 4.8.5

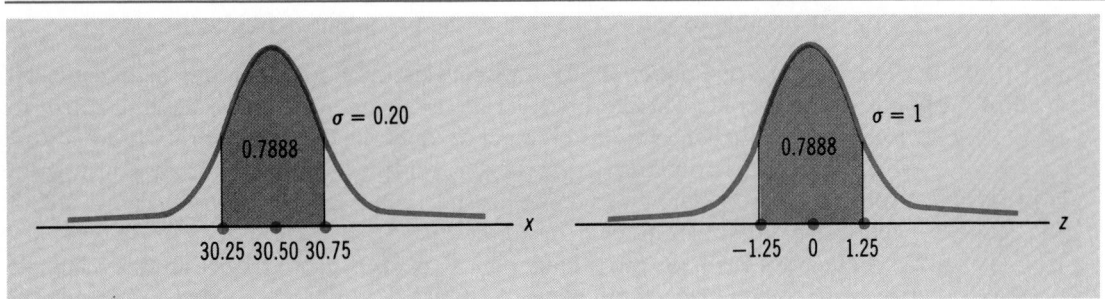

we seek is

$$P(30.250 \leq X \leq 30.750) = P(-1.25 \leq z \leq 1.25)$$
$$= P(z \leq 1.25) - P(z \leq -1.25)$$

Table C shows this to be $0.8944 - 0.1056 = 0.7888$.

COMPUTER **ANALYSIS**

Normal distribution probabilities needed to solve problems like the one posed in Example 4.8.5 may be obtained through the use of MINITAB. The following printout, for instance, illustrates the steps we go through to obtain these probabilities for Example 4.8.5.

MINITAB

```
MTB > SET C1
DATA> 30.250   30.750
DATA> END
MTB > CDF C1;
SUBC> NORMAL 30.5 [0.2].
     30.2500        0.1056
     30.7500        0.8944
```

Using these probabilities, we find that $P(30.250 \leq x \leq 30.750) = 0.8944 - 0.1056 = 0.7888$.

THE NORMAL APPROXIMATION TO THE BINOMIAL

The normal distribution gives a good approximation to the binomial distribution when n is large and p is not too close to 0 or 1. This enables us to calculate probabilities for large binomial samples for which binomial tables are not available. A good rule of thumb is that the normal approximation to the binomial is appropriate when np and $n(1 - p)$ are both greater than 5. To use the normal approximation, we use $\mu = np$ and $\sigma = \sqrt{np(1 - p)}$. We convert values of the original variable to values of z to find the probabilities of interest.

The Continuity Correction The normal distribution is continuous and the binomial is discrete. Therefore we get better results if we make an adjustment to account for this when we use the approximation. The need for such an adjustment, called the *continuity correction*, is evident when we compare a histogram constructed from binomial data with a superimposed smooth curve. Figure 4.8.13 illustrates this situation for $n = 20$ and $p = 0.3$.

In Figure 4.8.13, the probability that $X = x$ is equal to the area of the rectangle centered at x. For example, the probability that $X = 8$ is equal to the area of

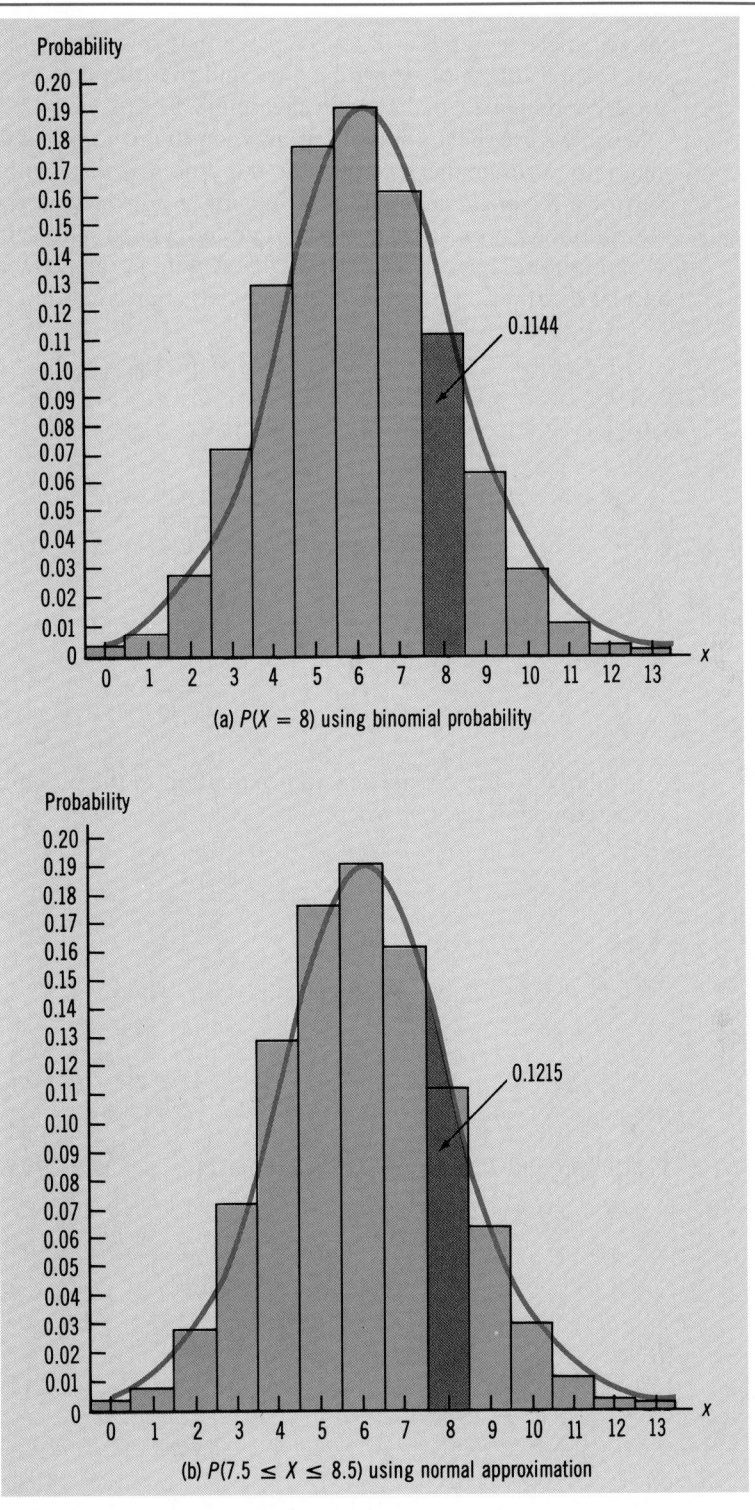

(a) $P(X = 8)$ using binomial probability

(b) $P(7.5 \leq X \leq 8.5)$ using normal approximation

the rectangle centered at 8. We can see that this rectangle extends from 7.5 to 8.5. From Table A of Appendix I we find that this area is equal to 0.1144. The corresponding area is shaded in Figure 4.8.13(a).

When we use the normal approximation to the binomial distribution, we must take into account the fact that for the binomial distribution, $P(X = x)$ is the area of a rectangle centered at x. When we convert values of x to values of z, the continuity correction consists of adding 0.5 to, and subtracting 0.5 from, x as appropriate. For a binomial variable X with parameters n and p, the standard normal distribution provides the following approximation to $P(x_a \leq X \leq x_b)$:

$$P(x_a \leq X \leq x_b) \simeq P(z_a \leq z \leq z_b)$$

where

$$z_a = \frac{(x_a - 0.5) - np}{\sqrt{npq}}$$

and

$$z_b = \frac{(x_b + 0.5) - np}{\sqrt{npq}}$$

Similarly, to use the normal approximation to the binomial to find $P(X \leq x_a)$, we determine $P(z \leq z_a)$, where

$$z_a = \frac{(x_a + 0.5) - np}{\sqrt{npq}}$$

To find $P(X \geq x_a)$, we determine $P(z \geq z_a)$, where

$$z = \frac{(x_a - 0.5) - np}{\sqrt{npq}}$$

Finally, to find $P(X = x_a)$, we compute $P(z_{a_1} \leq z \leq z_{a_2})$, where

$$z_{a_1} = \frac{(x_a - 0.5) - np}{\sqrt{npq}}$$

and

$$z_{a_2} = \frac{(x_a + 0.5) - np}{\sqrt{npq}}$$

To illustrate, let us use the continuity correction and normal approximation to find $P(X = 8 | n = 20, p = 0.3)$. Converting to z values, we have

$$z_a = \frac{(8 - 0.5) - 6}{\sqrt{(20)(0.3)(0.7)}} = \frac{1.5}{2.05} = 0.73$$

$$z_b = \frac{(8 + 0.5) - 6}{\sqrt{(20)(0.3)(0.7)}} = \frac{2.5}{2.05} = 1.22$$

From Table C, the probability we seek is 0.1215, which is reasonably close to the exact probability of 0.1144. The area under the normal curve corresponding to $P(7.5 \leq X \leq 8.5)$ is shaded in Figure 4.8.13(b).

Let us use this same example to find $P(5 \leq X \leq 10)$. Using binomial probabilities from Table A, we find the answer to be 0.7454. The corresponding area is shaded in Figure 4.8.14(a).

To use the normal approximation, we find

$$P(5 \leq X \leq 10 | n = 20, p = 0.3) = P\left[\frac{5 - 0.5 - 6}{2.05} \leq z \leq \frac{(10 + 0.5) - 6}{2.05}\right]$$
$$= P(-0.73 \leq z \leq 2.20)$$
$$= 0.9861 - 0.2327 = 0.7534$$

The corresponding area is shaded in Figure 4.8.14(b).

Again, we see that the normal approximation gives a result that is quite close to the exact probability. If we had not used the continuity correction, the normal approximation would have given

$$P(5 \leq X \leq 10) = P\left(\frac{5 - 6}{2.05} \leq z \leq \frac{10 - 6}{2.05}\right)$$
$$= P(-0.49 \leq z \leq 1.95)$$
$$= 0.9744 - 0.3121 = 0.6623$$

This approximation is not nearly as close to the true probability of 0.7454 as is the approximation obtained with the continuity correction. When n is large and p is not too close to 0 or 1, we usually omit the continuity correction when finding probabilities associated with such intervals as $P(x_a \leq X \leq x_b)$, $P(X \leq x)$, or $P(X \geq x)$.

EXERCISES

(In the following exercises, draw pictures to show areas and points of interest.)

4.8.16   Given a normally distributed population of values with a mean of 76 and a standard deviation of 10,   (a) what proportion of values are between 71 and 82;   (b) what pro-

FIGURE 4.8.14 Normal approximation to the binomial with $n = 20$, $p = 0.3$, and $\mu = np = 6$, showing $P(5 \leq X \leq 10)$

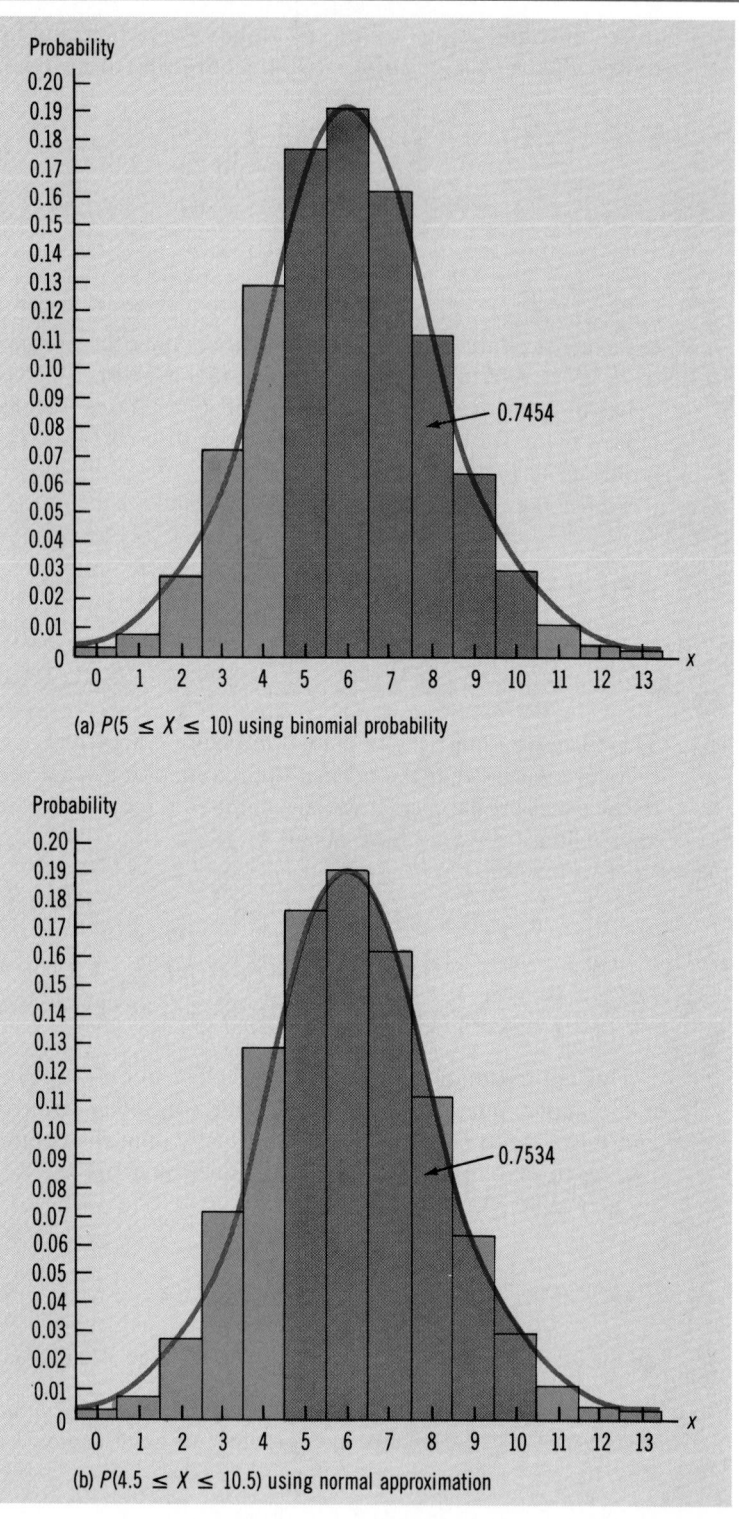

(a) $P(5 \leq X \leq 10)$ using binomial probability

(b) $P(4.5 \leq X \leq 10.5)$ using normal approximation

portion are greater than 75; (c) what is the probability that a value picked at random from this population is less than 78?

 4.8.17 The diameters of lids for tin cans produced by the Tinker Can Company are normally distributed with a mean of 4 inches and a standard deviation of 0.012 inch. What proportion of the lids produced are between 3.97 inches and 4.03 inches?

4.8.18 Given a normal distribution of values with a mean of 120 and a variance of 16, what proportion of the values are greater than 121?

 4.8.19 The weights of a certain melon are normally distributed with a mean of 14 ounces and a standard deviation of 1.22 ounces. What is the probability that a melon drawn at random from this population will weigh less than 12 ounces?

 4.8.20 A bank official finds that the lengths of time customers have to wait to be served by a teller are approximately normally distributed with a mean of 3 minutes and a standard deviation of 1 minute. (a) What proportion of customers have to wait longer than 2 minutes but less than $3\frac{1}{2}$ minutes? (b) What proportion of customers have to wait 1 minute or less? (c) You are about to enter the bank. What is the probability that you will have to wait longer than 5 minutes?

 4.8.21 A production supervisor finds that employees, on the average, complete a certain task in ten minutes. The times required to complete the task are approximately normally distributed with a standard deviation of three minutes. Find the following: (a) the proportion of employees completing the task in less than four minutes, (b) the proportion of employees requiring more than five minutes to complete the task, (c) the probability that an employee who has just been assigned the task will complete it within three minutes.

4.8.22 At Urban Developers, 30% of the employees are females. A random sample of 50 is selected from this population. What is the probability that the number of females is between 20 and 24, inclusive?

 4.8.23 Suppose that only 40% of the residents of a city favor a certain zoning petition. What is the probability that a random sample of 100 citizens will contain between 30 and 50, inclusive, who favor the petition?

4.8.24 Refer to Exercise 4.3.5. Use the normal approximation to the binomial to determine whether 500 out of 1,000 provides sufficient evidence to indicate that the estimate should be revised.

SUMMARY

This chapter introduced you to some important probability distributions. If you understand the basic concepts presented here, you will understand the ideas presented in the later chapters more easily. Chapter 3, this chapter, and the next chapter serve as a bridge connecting the methods and concepts of descriptive statistics with those of inferential statistics.

In this chapter, you learned about discrete probability distributions and continuous probability distributions. You learned that *the probability distribution of a discrete random variable is a table, graph, formula, or other device used to specify all possible values of a discrete random variable along with their respective probabilities.*

You learned that if a random variable X is continuous we cannot speak meaningfully of the probability that $X = x$. Thus, the probability distribution of a continuous random variable must be defined differently.

> A nonnegative function $f(x)$ is called a *probability distribution of the continuous random variable X* if the total area bounded by its curve and the x axis is equal to 1, and if the subarea under the curve bounded by the curve, the x axis, and perpendiculars erected at any two points a and b gives the probability that X is between the points a and b.

The discrete probability distributions covered in this chapter are the binomial, the Poisson, and the hypergeometric distributions. The binomial distribution provides an appropriate model for analysis when the available data consist of n repetitions of a Bernoulli trial. A Bernoulli trial is one of a sequence of trials, each of which can result only in one of two mutually exclusive outcomes.

The Poisson distribution is a good model for analyzing a variety of business problems, such as those concerned with product demand, the occurrence of accidents in a factory, and arrival patterns of customers at various types of service counters.

When we sample without replacement from a small population, the hypergeometric distribution often serves as the model for determining the probability of some predetermined number of successes. Using the hypergeometric formula to calculate probabilities is very tedious if the population is large. Fortunately, in most situations in which the population is large, the hypergeometric model is satisfactorily approximated by the binomial distribution. In turn, we frequently find it convenient to use either the Poisson distribution or the normal distribution to approximate the binomial distribution when we wish to answer probability questions about a process for which the binomial distribution provides an appropriate model. The following table summarizes the conditions under which the various approximations are usually used.

When the distribution used as the underlying model is the	And when	The distribution that provides an appropriate approximation is the
hypergeometric	$n \leq N/10$	binomial
binomial	$n \geq 20$, $p \leq 0.05$	Poisson (approximation better when $n \geq 100$ and $np \leq 10$)
binomial	$np \geq 5$, $n(1 - p) \geq 5$	normal (use of the continuity correction improves approximation)

The two continuous probability distributions covered in this chapter are the normal distribution and the uniform distribution. The normal distribution is the most important distribution we encounter in the study and practice of statistics. We use it often in later chapters.

REVIEW EXERCISES

1. What is a discrete random variable? Give three examples from the field of business.

2. What is a continuous random variable? Give three examples from the field of business.

3. Define the probability distribution of a discrete random variable.

4. Define the probability distribution of a continuous random variable.

5. What is a cumulative probability distribution?

6. What is a Bernoulli trial?

7. Describe the binomial distribution.

8. Give an example of a random variable that you think follows a binomial distribution.

9. Describe the Poisson distribution.

10. Give an example of a random variable that you think is distributed according to the Poisson law.

11. Describe the normal distribution.

12. Describe the standard normal distribution and tell how it is used in statistics.

13. Give an example of a random variable that you think is at least approximately normally distributed.

14. Using the example you gave in Exercise 13, demonstrate the use of the standard normal distribution in answering probability questions relating to this variable.

15. State Chebyshev's theorem and explain how it may be used.

16. Discuss the concept of expected value.

17. The following is the frequency distribution of the number of times each of 100 machines at Wallace Productions broke down during the past year. (a) Construct the probability distribution of the random variable X = number of machine breakdowns. (b) Draw a graph of the distribution. (c) Construct and graph the cumulative probability distribution of X.

x_i (Number of breakdowns)	0	1	2	3	4	5	6	7	8	9	10
Frequency of occurrence of x_i	10	15	20	25	15	5	3	2	2	2	1

18. In Exercise 17, find (a) the probability that a machine picked at random is one that broke down three times; (b) the probability that a randomly selected machine is one that broke down four or fewer times; (c) the probability that a machine picked at random is one that broke down between four and seven times, inclusive; (d) the probability that a randomly selected machine is one that broke down either one or two times; (e) $P(X > 5)$; (f) $P(X < 1)$; (g) $P(X \geq 5)$; (h) $P(0 < X \leq 3)$.

19. Customers entering a store have five brands (equal in price and weight) of a certain product from which to choose. Say that 30% of the customers prefer Brand A. What is the probability that, of 20 customers making a selection from the available brands, Brand A is selected by (a) at least half, (b) more than half, (c) between 5 and 10, inclusive, (d) 14 or more?

20. You know that 5% of all items produced at a certain factory are defective. You select 25 items at random from a day's production. What is the probability that the number of defectives in the sample is   **(a)** at least 1,   **(b)** no more than 5,   **(c)** between 3 and 7, inclusive,   **(d)** 10 or more,   **(e)** 0? Repeat (a) through (e) using an appropriate approximation.

21. The average number of calls made from a pay telephone during a given time interval is 3.2. What is the probability that during such a time interval the number of calls made from this telephone is   **(a)** no more than 2,   **(b)** more than 2,   **(c)** 5 or fewer,   **(d)** more than 5,   **(e)** 0,   **(f)** at least 1? What is necessary to make your results valid?

22. The mean number of calls for key rings at a variety store during a day is 2.4. What is the probability that on a given day the number of calls for key rings is   **(a)** 0,   **(b)** at least 1,   **(c)** more than 1,   **(d)** between 3 and 5, inclusive?

23. Given the standard normal distribution, find $P(-1.65 \leq z \leq 1.65)$.

24. Given the standard normal distribution, find $P(z = 0.75)$.

25. A population of values is normally distributed with a mean of 25.5. It is known that 75.49% of the values are less than 27.8. What is the standard deviation of the population?

26. The inside diameters of metal washers produced by the Young Manufacturing Company are normally distributed with a mean of 0.5 inch and a standard deviation of 0.01 inch. Of all washers produced, 0.8% are rejected because they are too small for a bolt used to test them. What is the diameter of the bolt used for the test?

27. The breaking strengths of plastic bottles are normally distributed with a variance of 25. Approximately 0.0197 of specimens produced are rejected because they fail a quality-control test that subjects them to 255 psi of pressure. What is the mean breaking strength of the bottles?

28. Agricultural experts have found that when a certain type of fertilizer is used, yields per acre of a certain grain are approximately normally distributed with a mean and standard deviation of 40 and 10 bushels per acre, respectively.   **(a)** When this fertilizer is used, what proportion of the acreage planted in this grain yields more than 50 bushels per acre?   **(b)** What is the probability that a randomly selected acre will yield less than 15 bushels?

29. Scores made by employees on a manual dexterity test are normally distributed with a mean of 600 and a variance of 10,000.   **(a)** What proportion of employees taking the test score below 300?   **(b)** An employee is about to take the test. What is the probability that the employee's score will be 850 or more?   **(c)** What proportion of employees score between 450 and 700?   **(d)** Management has decided that those employees whose scores are among the top 10% will be considered for promotion to a better job. What score must an employee make in order to be eligible for promotion?   **(e)** Suppose that management decides to consider for promotion only those employees who make a score of 800 or more. What percentage of the employees will be eligible to be considered for promotion?

30. In a household survey, the Zola market research firm found that family gasoline consumption per month was approximately normally distributed with a mean and standard deviation of 70 and 9 gallons, respectively.   **(a)** What proportion of families use between 55 and 79 gallons per month, inclusive?   **(b)** A family is picked at random from this population. What is the probability that it uses more than 76 gallons per month?   **(c)** What proportion of families in this population use less than 64 gallons per month?

31. In a suburban community, on a given weekday evening, the head of the household is at home in 65% of the households. A researcher conducting a telephone survey randomly selects 15 households to call in an evening. What is the probability that the researcher will find the head of the household at home in exactly 8 households?

32. You know that 80% of the people applying for a certain job have had no previous experience in this job. You select a random sample of five current applicants. What is the probability that exactly three have had no previous experience in the job?

33. It is estimated that 30% of a certain group of truck drivers eat at a certain truck stop. Suppose that this estimate is correct. You question 25 drivers picked at random from this group. What is the probability that the number eating at the truck stop will be (a) 5 or fewer, (b) between 15 and 19, inclusive, (c) 15 or more? Repeat (a) through (c) using a suitable approximation.

34. In a certain population of adolescents, the proportion of those who have their own cars is 0.40. A random sample of 20 is selected from the population. What is the probability that the number of those who have their own cars is (a) greater than 10, (b) fewer than 5, (c) between 5 and 15, inclusive?

35. In a population of executives, 40% are under 45. What is the probability that in a random sample of 15 of these executives, 8 or more are under 45?

36. You know that 20% of the salaried employees in a certain city have less than a high school education. You take a random sample of 20 of these employees. What is the probability that between 10 and 15, inclusive, have less than a high school education?

37. The standard deviation of employees' scores on an aptitude test is ten. What is the probability that the score of a randomly selected employee differs by more than two points from the mean score of all employees? Assume that scores are approximately normally distributed.

38. The mean breaking strength of Rough and Ready plastic trash bag is 10 pounds per square inch. Breaking strengths are approximately normally distributed with a standard deviation of 0.1. In a shipment of 10,000 bags, how many would we expect to find with breaking strengths below 9.8 pounds per square inch? The manufacturer says that if 1% or more of the bags have breaking strengths below 9.75 pounds per square inch, the firm will look for a stronger raw material. Should the firm do so at this time?

39. On the average, the Asbury Supermarket sells 250 quarts of milk per day. The standard deviation is 25. (a) On a given day, the supermarket stocks 300 quarts. What is the probability that all will be sold? Assume that the number of quarts sold per day is approximately normally distributed. (b) How many quarts should the supermarket stock if the proprietor wants the probability of not being able to meet the demand for quarts of milk to be 0.01?

40. Given the normally distributed random variable X, find the numerical value of k such that $P(\mu - k\sigma \leq X \leq \mu + k\sigma) = 0.754$.

41. Given the normally distributed random variable X with mean 100 and standard deviation of 15, find the numerical value of k such that (a) $P(X \leq k) = 0.0094$, (b) $P(X \geq k) = 0.1093$, (c) $P(100 \leq X \leq k) = 0.4778$, (d) $P(k' \leq X \leq k) = 0.9660$, where k' and k are equidistant from μ.

42. Given the normally distributed random variable X with $\sigma = 10$ and $P(X \leq 40) = 0.0080$, find μ.

43. Given the normally distributed random variable X with $\sigma = 15$ and $P(X \le 50) = 0.9904$, find μ.

44. Given the normally distributed random variable X with $\sigma = 5$ and $P(X \ge 25) = 0.0526$, find μ.

45. Given the normally distributed random variable X with $\mu = 25$ and $P(X \le 10) = 0.0778$, find σ.

46. Given the normally distributed random variable X with $\mu = 30$ and $P(X \le 50) = 0.9772$, find σ.

47. Let $n = 20$. Find μ and σ^2 of the binomial distribution when **(a)** $p = 0.1$, **(b)** $p = 0.2$, **(c)** $p = 0.3$, **(d)** $p = 0.4$, **(e)** $p = 0.5$, **(f)** $p = 0.6$, **(g)** $p = 0.7$, **(h)** $p = 0.8$, **(i)** $p = 0.9$. For which value of p is σ^2 smallest? Largest?

48. In a clothing factory, the average number of machines that are inoperable on a given day is three. What is the probability that on a given day **(a)** there are more than three inoperable machines, **(b)** there are fewer than three inoperable machines, **(c)** all machines are operable?

49. In a large office, the average number of employees smoking in any 15-minute time period is 5. What is the probability that during a randomly selected 15-minute period the number of employees smoking is **(a)** 3 or more, **(b)** between 5 and 8, inclusive, **(c)** fewer than 4?

50. In a large pine forest, the mean number of trees per acre infested with southern pine beetles is thought to be 0.2. If this is true, find the probability that on a randomly selected acre the number of infested trees is **(a)** 0, **(b)** more than 3, **(c)** either 1 or 2, **(d)** exactly 1.

51. An automobile salesperson sells on the average three cars per week. Find the probability that during a given week the salesperson sells **(a)** one car, **(b)** no cars, **(c)** two or more cars, **(d)** five or more cars. What assumptions must be made about sales?

52. At a certain intersection, there is an average of three accidents per week. What is the probability that in a given week there are **(a)** six or more accidents, **(b)** no accidents, **(c)** between three and seven accidents, inclusive, **(d)** three or fewer accidents?

53. At Balfour Brands Company, the number of employee absences averages 10 per day. On a randomly selected day, what is the probability that the number of employees absent is **(a)** more than 5, **(b)** more than 15, **(c)** between 5 and 15, inclusive, **(d)** fewer than 8, **(e)** fewer than 12?

54. The manufacturer of a certain prestige item has found that the expected demand for this product is five per month. Find the probability that in a given month the demand is **(a)** no items, **(b)** six or more items, **(c)** four or fewer items.

55. In a population of employees, 2% have completed college. Suppose that a random sample of 50 persons is selected from the population. What is the probability that 3 or more will be college graduates?

56. A population consists of 20 clerical workers. Of these workers, 12 have been with their present employer for more than 5 years. You select, without replacement, a random sample of 5 workers from this population. What is the probability that exactly 3 will have been with their present employer for more than 5 years?

57. In a population of heads of household, 38% own their homes. You select a simple random sample of size 15 from this population. What is the probability that the number of those in the sample who own their homes will be   (a) exactly 8,   (b) between 5 and 7, inclusive,   (c) at least 12,   (d) 9 or more?

58. In a population of executives, 10% have changed employers within the past two years. You select a simple random sample of 70 from this population. What is the probability that 12 or more in the sample will have changed employers within the past two years?

59. In a certain county, in 70% of the households there is at least one person who is over 40. You draw a random sample of 200 from this population. What is the probability that the number of households with a person over 40 is between 150 and 155, inclusive?

60. The probability of a success for a random variable is a constant 0.53. If 15 values of this variable are observed, calculate the probability that the number of successes will be greater than 6 and less than 12   (a) using the binomial probability distribution,   (b) using an appropriate approximation to the binomial.

61. For a certain random variable, the probability of a success is a constant 0.93. Find the probability of obtaining between 12 and 16 successes, inclusive, in 17 trials.

62. Bank customers arrive at a drive-through window independently at an average rate of 32.8 per hour. Find the probability that more than 10 will arrive during the next 15 minutes.

63. A fair coin is flipped 100 times. Find the probability of obtaining   (a) 55 or more heads,   (b) fewer than 60 heads,   (c) exactly 50 heads.

64. In a large city, 53% of the voters are registered as Democrats and 47% are registered as Republicans. A sample of 300 voters within the city is to be selected at random. Each person will be questioned concerning a controversial issue. Find the probability that, among the 300 voters polled, a majority will be persons who are registered as Republicans.

65. The probability of an adverse reaction to a drug is 0.0021. A team of doctors at a hospital plans to administer the drug to 800 persons. What is the probability that 3 or more of the 800 persons will develop an adverse reaction?

66. A box contains 18 clocks, of which all but 4 have no defects. You choose 10 of these clocks at random. Find the probability that at most 1 of the 10 clocks is defective.

67. Variable X is normally distributed with a mean of 56.5 and a standard deviation of 8.94. Find the probability that an individual value of X will be within the interval 50 to 60.

68. Nu-Vu television sets have an 88% chance of operating without need of repair during the one-year warranty period. Your store sold 22 of these sets last year. What is the probability that fewer than 4 of these 22 sets will require repair during the warranty period?

69. A fire station receives alarms at an average rate of 10.5 per 24-hour day. With the assumption that these alarms occur independently and at a constant rate throughout the day, find the probability that more than 4 calls will be received during any one 8-hour shift.

70. For a certain disease, an experimental drug has an 82% cure rate that is considered to be constant. Find the probability that fewer than 15 patients out of 18 who are given the drug will be cured.

71. Out of 4,000 items, it is known that exactly 3,840 are in good condition. If 200 are selected, the expected number of good items among these 200 is 192. **(a)** Identify the probability distribution that provides an appropriate model for this situation. **(b)** List the parameters and give the values for each. **(c)** What is the probability that a sample of 200 items will contain 192 that are in good condition? Set up the basic formula for solution, but do not solve. **(d)** Identify each additional probability distribution that may be used as a close approximation to solve the problem. For each, justify why it may be used and list the parameters required and their values. **(e)** Use each approximation to answer the probability question asked in (c).

72. The telephone directory of a small town lists 646 residential telephone numbers. Of these, 230 are listed under the name of a female. If, in a survey, 40 telephone numbers are selected at random, find the probability that 15 or fewer will be listed under a female's name.

73. In a city, an average of 34 serious crimes occur each evening between the hours of 6 p.m. and 6 a.m. Assuming that occurrences are independent and equally likely throughout the period, find the probability that more than 2 serious crimes will occur during the next 20 minutes.

74. Customers arrive independently at Berkeley's Variety Store at the rate of 25.75 per hour. What is the probability that 8 or more will arrive during the next 15 minutes?

75. In a certain population, 73% of the people fall into Category A, and 27% fall into Category B. If 283 people are sampled, find the probability that **(a)** more than 80 fall into Category B, **(b)** less than 70% fall into Category A.

76. There are 19 items in a box, of which 4 are defective. If you take out 15 of these items, what is the probability that no more than 1 of the 15 is defective?

77. Suppose that 76% of the people in a certain area rode a subway last year. What is the probability that, out of 20 people sampled, more than 75% will have ridden on a subway last year?

78. The probability that a tornado will occur in a particular area of the country is considered to be a constant 0.000222 per square mile per year. City A has an area of 76 square miles. What is the probability that City A will experience a tornado during the next 5 years?

79. The probability of any one person having a certain disease is 0.00193. Independence is assumed. Suppose that a cruise ship carries 475 passengers. Find the probability that 1 or more of its passengers, on any one cruise, will have the disease.

80. Suppose that X is a normally distributed variable with $\mu = -32.6$ and $\sigma = 8.29$. Find $P(-40 \leq X \leq -20)$.

81. A box contains 1,000 items, of which 327 are defective. Suppose that 300 of the items are selected at random. What is the probability that fewer than 100 of the items selected will be defective?

82. A box contains 1,000 items, of which 27 are defective. Suppose that 30 of the items are selected at random. What is the probability that at most 1 will be defective?

83. It has been found that 35% of the persons hired to do a certain job quit within a year of being hired. In a sample of 50 persons hired to do the job, what is the probability that between 25 and 30, inclusive, will quit within the first year?

84. One-fourth of the people hired to do a certain job have no prior experience in that job. In a sample of 150 people hired to do this job, what is the probability that 50 or more have had no prior experience?

85. It is estimated that in a certain population of smokers, 30% are trying to quit. If the estimate is true, what is the probability that, in a sample of 200, the number trying to quit will be 75 or fewer?

86. Suppose that 6% of the customers of Jiffy Joe's fast-food establishment order a dessert with their meal. In a sample of 70 customers, what is the probability that more than 5 will order a dessert?

87. The probability of death during a given year for a certain population of people is 0.002. If a life insurance company insures 3,000 of these people, what is the probability that during a given year the company will have to pay exactly 5 claims?

88. A mail-order book dealer is unable to completely fill 1% of its customers' orders. In a sample of 500 orders, find the probability that the number that cannot be filled completely is (a) 10, (b) more than 5, (c) 7 or more, (d) fewer than 10, (e) between 5 and 10, inclusive.

89. Given, $E(X) = 25$, $E(X^2) = 800$, find the variance of X.

90. Given, a binomial distribution with a mean of 180 and a probability of success equal to 0.60, find the sample size.

91. Given, a binomial distribution with a mean of 40 and a probability of success equal to 0.20, find the standard deviation.

92. Given, a normally distributed random variable X for which $P(70 \leq X \leq 130) = 0.8882$ and $P(X \leq 70) = 0.0559$, find the standard deviation.

93. Given, a normally distributed random variable X for which $P(X \leq 160) = 0.0548$ and the variance is 625, find the mean.

94. Given the following probability distribution, find the mean:

x:	20	25	30	35	40
P(X = x):	0.3	0.2	0.2	0.2	0.1

95. Given the following probability distribution, find the standard deviation:

x:	20	25	30	35	40
P(X = x):	0.5	0.3	0.1	0.05	0.05

*96. Besides those discussed in this chapter, there are many other probability distributions that provide useful models for a variety of business phenomena. One is the exponential distribution, which is closely related to the Poisson. Specifically, if the occurrences of some event can be modeled by the Poisson distribution, then the lengths of time between successive occurrences follow an exponential distribution. The mean length of time between successive occurrences is $1/\lambda$, where λ, the Poisson parameter described in Section 4.4, is the mean number of occurrences within a specified interval. The exponential probability model is used to describe those situations that involve demand for service over some period of time. It can be used to determine the probability that a customer will have to wait in line more than X minutes before being served, that the victim of an automobile accident will have to wait between X_1 and X_2 minutes before the arrival of police, or that you will be able to talk to a human being within X minutes of calling an 800 number to make a motel reservation. Such probabilities are calculated by means of the exponential cumulative probability function, which is $F(x) = P(X \leq x) = 1 - e^{-\lambda x}$. For example, suppose the mean waiting time, in minutes, at a grocery store checkout counter is an exponential variable with a mean waiting time of 2.5 minutes ($\lambda = 1/2.5 = 0.4$). We wish to know the probability that a customer will have to wait no more than five minutes before being served. We calculate this probability as $P(X \leq 5) = 1 - e^{-(0.4)(5)} = 1 - e^{-2} = 1 - .1353 = .8647$.

Suppose the length of satisfactory operation (in hours) between breakdowns of a photo-copy machine is exponentially distributed with a mean of 400 hours. Find the probability that the copier will operate satisfactorily for   (a) 200 hours or less,   (b) more than 650 hours, and   (c) between 350 and 700 hours.

STATISTICS AT WORK

STATISTICS AT WORK STATISTICS AT

1. THE POISSON DISTRIBUTION ON CAMPUS

In an innovative physics course, Lafleur and colleagues challenged their students to investigate any phenomenon that the students thought might follow a Poisson distribution. In one such investigation, a student counted the number of people in the entrance of a dormitory during the time it took the student to walk through it (30 seconds). The reported data conform well to the requirements for a Poisson distribution. From the student's data, we are able to compute a Poisson parameter of 2.67. Use this information to find the probability that one would observe

(a) no people in the dormitory entrance.

(b) between two and five people, inclusive, in the entrance.

(c) more than three people in the entrance.

Source: M. S. Lafleur, P. F. Hinrichsen, P. C Landry, and R. B. Moore, "The Poisson Distribution: An Experimental Approach to Teaching Statistics," *Physics Teacher*, 10 (1972), 314–321.

2. ALZHEIMER'S DISEASE AND THE NORMAL DISTRIBUTION

As part of a study of Alzheimer's disease, Dusheiko reported data that are compatible with the hypothesis that brain weights of victims of the disease are normally distributed. From the reported data, we may compute a mean of 1,076.80 grams and a standard deviation of 105.76 grams. If we assume that these results are applicable to all victims of Alzheimer's disease, find the probability that a randomly selected victim of the disease will have a brain that weighs

(a) less than 800 grams.

(b) more than 1,200 grams.

(c) between 800 and 1,200 grams.

In what area of business would this type of information be useful?

Source: S. D. Dusheiko, "Some Questions Concerning the Pathological Anatomy of Alzheimer's Disease," *Soviet Neurological Psychiatry*, 7 (Summer 1974), 56–64. Published by International Arts and Sciences Press, White Plains, N.Y.

3. MALE BIRTHS AND THE BINOMIAL DISTRIBUTION

Edwards and Fraccaro reported data on the number of males among the first 7 children born to 1,334 fathers. The data support the hypothesis that the number of male births is distributed as a binomial variable with $p = 0.51$. If we assume that these results apply to all male births, find the probability that in a sample of 20 births the number of males will be

(a)   0.

(b)   5 or fewer.

(c)   more than 10.

(d)   between 8 and 13, inclusive.

In what area of business would this information be of use?

Source: A. W. Edwards and M. Fraccaro, "Distribution and Sequences of Sexes in a Selected Sample of Swedish Families," *Annals of Human Genetics*, 24 (1960), 245–252.

4.   AGRIBUSINESS—A PROBABILITY DISTRIBUTION APPLICATION

The primary cause of a certain condition in alfalfa is Fraction 1 Protein (FR1P) which occurs when FR1P is above 1.8%. The following table shows the distribution of FR1P levels in 1,372 alfalfa seedlings. The mean and standard deviation are 4.3% and 0.81%, respectively. Make use of your knowledge of the normal distribution to see if you think, on the basis of these data, that FR1P levels in alfalfa might be normally distributed. In Chapter 12 you can learn about a technique that will allow you to reach a more informed conclusion.

FR1P class interval, % oven-dry weight	Number in class
0.61–1.20	1
1.21–1.80	3
1.81–2.40	4
2.41–3.00	65
3.01–3.60	180
3.61–4.20	328
4.21–4.80	408
4.81–5.40	284
5.41–6.00	83
6.01–6.60	13
6.61–7.20	1
7.21–7.80	1
7.81–8.40	0
8.41–9.00	1

Source: J. E. Miltimore, J. M. McArthur, B. P. Goplen, W. Majak, and R. E. Howarth, "Variability of Fraction 1 Protein and Heritability Estimates for Fraction 1 Protein and Total Phenolic Constituents in Alfalfa," *Agronomy Journal*, 66 (May–June 1974), 384–386.

SUGGESTIONS FOR FURTHER READING

Freund, John E., and Ronald E. Walpole (1987). *Mathematical Statistics*, 4th ed. Prentice-Hall, Englewood Cliffs, N.J.

Haight, Frank A. (1967). *Handbook of the Poisson Distribution*. Wiley, New York.

Hogg, Robert V., and Allen T. Craig (1978). *Introduction to Mathematical Statistics*, 4th ed. Macmillan, New York.

Larsen, Richard J., and Morris L. Marx (1981). *An Introduction to Mathematical Statistics and Its Application*. Prentice-Hall, Englewood Cliffs, N.J.

Mendenhall, William, and Richard L. Scheaffer (1973). *Mathematical Statistics with Applications*. Duxbury, North Scituate, Mass.

Mood, Alexander M., Franklin A. Graybill, and Duane C. Boes (1974). *Introduction to the Theory of Statistics*, 3rd ed. McGraw-Hill, New York.

Pearson, Karl (1924). "Historical Note on the Origin of the Normal Curve of Errors," *Biometrika* 16:402–404.

5

Some Important Sampling Distributions

Chapter Objectives: This chapter is the most important one in the book. It holds the key to statistical inference. Study this chapter very carefully. Pay special attention to the general discussion of sampling distributions. Before you can understand statistical inference, you must understand sampling distributions. After studying this chapter and working the exercises, you should be able to

1. Construct the sampling distribution of sample means computed from samples drawn from a small population.
2. Determine the mean, standard error, and functional form of the sampling distribution of the mean, the difference between two means, a proportion, and the difference between two proportions.
3. Explain the central limit theorem and discuss its importance in statistical inference.
4. Use your knowledge of sampling distributions to compute the probability associated with specified sample results when the statistic of interest is the mean, the difference between two means, a proportion, or the difference between two proportions.

5.1   INTRODUCTION

Let us pause here and review briefly the material that we have covered so far. Chapter 1 introduces you to the basic concepts and vocabulary of statistics. It is also concerned with the organization and summarization of data generated by the routine operation of a business firm or by special studies. Chapter 2 presents computations of the basic measures, such as the mean and standard deviation, used for describing a set of data. Chapter 3, the first of three chapters designed to lay the foundation for statistical inference, is devoted to the basic concepts of probability. Chapter 4 expands on these concepts and introduces the idea of a probability distribution. It discusses in detail three distributions of discrete variables—the binomial, the hypergeometric, and the Poisson—as well as the normal distribution and the uniform distribution. We refer to the normal distribution frequently in later chapters.

The present chapter is the last of the three chapters that link the descriptive material of Chapter 2 and the concepts of inference that we begin to explore in Chapter 6. You must understand the principles introduced here if you are to understand the inferential procedures that make up the major portion of this book.

USES OF SAMPLING DISTRIBUTIONS

As you will learn in this chapter, sampling distributions are merely probability distributions of some sample statistic such as the sample mean or the sample proportion. Sampling distributions are used for two purposes: to answer probability questions about a sample statistic and to provide the theoretical basis for statistical inference.

As we shall see in this chapter, for example, a knowledge of the sampling distribution of the sample mean allows us to answer questions such as this: If I select a sample of people from a population of people, and compute the mean age of the people in the sample, what is the probability that the sample mean will be less than 40 years?

In the next two chapters, we introduce the two types of statistical inference: interval estimation (Chapter 6) and hypothesis testing (Chapter 7). The validity of these two statistical procedures depends on the laws and concepts of sampling distributions, which in turn are based on probability laws and concepts. The uses of sampling distributions justify the amount of time you spent learning the basic concepts of probability presented in Chapter 3.

5.2   SIMPLE RANDOM SAMPLING

You learned in Chapter 1 that a population of values of a variable consists of the largest collection of such values in which we have an interest in a given situation. You learned also that a sample, simply defined, is a part of a population. Finally, you learned that a parameter is a descriptive measure computed from or used to describe a population, and that a statistic is a descriptive measure computed from or used to describe a sample.

The ideas presented in this chapter are based on the concept of *sampling*. The type of sampling assumed is simple random sampling as discussed in Chapter 1. It may be wise at this time for you to turn back to that chapter and review the section on simple random sampling.

5.3   SAMPLING DISTRIBUTIONS

We can define a *sampling distribution* as follows:

> The distribution of all possible values that can be assumed by some statistic, computed from samples of the same size randomly drawn from the same population, is called the *sampling distribution* of that statistic.

A knowledge of the characteristics of sampling distributions and how they are constructed serves two purposes. Such knowledge allows us to answer probability questions about a statistic, such as the sample mean, and helps us understand statistical inference.

STEPS IN CONSTRUCTING A SAMPLING DISTRIBUTION

We can construct sampling distributions empirically from discrete, finite populations. The construction of a sampling distribution consists of the following steps:

1. From a discrete, finite population of size N, randomly draw all possible samples of size n.
2. Compute the value of the statistic of interest for each sample.
3. List in one column the different observed values of the statistic. In another column, list the corresponding frequency of occurrence of each observed value of the statistic.

IMPORTANT CHARACTERISTICS OF A SAMPLING DISTRIBUTION

Given a sampling distribution, we want to know its mean, variance, and functional form.

Three characteristics of a given sampling distribution are of interest to us: its mean, its variance, and its functional form (how it looks when graphed).

We cannot construct exact sampling distributions empirically when the population we are sampling is infinite. In such a situation, we can only approximate the sampling distribution of the statistic of interest by taking a large number of samples. This is not a problem of any practical importance, since sampling distributions *per se* are of only theoretical interest.

Since we can derive sampling distributions mathematically, the empirical construction of a sampling distribution is of academic interest only. The procedures involved are not compatible with the mathematical level of this text. We treat the subject in some detail in this chapter simply to help you understand the nature of sampling distribution. For the more mathematical and theoretical aspects of sampling distributions, see the textbooks on mathematical statistics listed at the end of this chapter.

We emphasize that in practical situations we do not construct sampling distributions. As a rule, we select only one sample from a population about which we wish to make an inference and base our inference on the information provided by that one sample. We study sampling distributions because in order to understand statistical inference you must first understand sampling distributions.

5.4 DISTRIBUTION OF THE SAMPLE MEAN

As we have seen, the arithmetic mean is an important descriptive measure for characterizing the central tendency of a set of data. In many situations, we want to know the mean of a population. This information may not be available unless we draw a sample from the population and make an inference regarding the parameter μ based on analysis of the sample data. We consider this procedure in detail in Chapter 6. However, since the validity of this inferential procedure depends on knowing the sampling distribution of the statistic involved, that is, the sample mean, let us give some thought to this matter before we proceed.

The text that follows illustrates the construction of a sampling distribution of the sample mean, computed from samples drawn from a very small population. It is important that you realize that this is for instructional purposes only. In practice, we do not actually construct a sampling distribution as a preliminary to statistical inference.

EXAMPLE 5.4.1   A population consists of the ten salespersons employed by Waldo Properties. The random variable of interest, X, is the number of years a salesperson has been with the firm. The values of the variable are as follows: $X_1 = 3$, $X_2 = 6$, $X_3 = 2$, $X_4 = 4$, $X_5 = 8$, $X_6 = 7$, $X_7 = 9$, $X_8 = 5$, $X_9 = 1$, $X_{10} = 10$. For this population, we may compute the following parameters:

$$\mu = \frac{\Sigma x_i}{N} = \frac{55}{10} = 5.5 \qquad \sigma^2 = \frac{\Sigma(x_i - \mu)^2}{N} = 8.25$$

CONSTRUCTING THE SAMPLING DISTRIBUTION

To construct the sampling distribution of $\bar{x}$, computed from samples drawn from this population, we follow the steps outlined in Section 5.3.

TABLE 5.4.1   All possible samples of size $n = 2$ from a population of size $N = 10$

First draw	Second draw									
	1	**2**	**3**	**4**	**5**	**6**	**7**	**8**	**9**	**10**
1	1,1 (1)	1,2 (1.5)	1,3 (2)	1,4 (2.5)	1,5 (3)	1,6 (3.5)	1,7 (4)	1,8 (4.5)	1,9 (5)	1,10 (5.5)
2	2,1 (1.5)	2,2 (2)	2,3 (2.5)	2,4 (3)	2,5 (3.5)	2,6 (4)	2,7 (4.5)	2,8 (5)	2,9 (5.5)	2,10 (6)
3	3,1 (2)	3,2 (2.5)	3,3 (3)	3,4 (3.5)	3,5 (4)	3,6 (4.5)	3,7 (5)	3,8 (5.5)	3,9 (6)	3,10 (6.5)
4	4,1 (2.5)	4,2 (3)	4,3 (3.5)	4,4 (4)	4,5 (4.5)	4,6 (5)	4,7 (5.5)	4,8 (6)	4,9 (6.5)	4,10 (7)
5	5,1 (3)	5,2 (3.5)	5,3 (4)	5,4 (4.5)	5,5 (5)	5,6 (5.5)	5,7 (6)	5,8 (6.5)	5,9 (7)	5,10 (7.5)
6	6,1 (3.5)	6,2 (4)	6,3 (4.5)	6,4 (5)	6,5 (5.5)	6,6 (6)	6,7 (6.5)	6,8 (7)	6,9 (7.5)	6,10 (8)
7	7,1 (4)	7,2 (4.5)	7,3 (5)	7,4 (5.5)	7,5 (6)	7,6 (6.5)	7,7 (7)	7,8 (7.5)	7,9 (8)	7,10 (8.5)
8	8,1 (4.5)	8,2 (5)	8,3 (5.5)	8,4 (6)	8,5 (6.5)	8,6 (7)	8,7 (7.5)	8,8 (8)	8,9 (8.5)	8,10 (9)
9	9,1 (5)	9,2 (5.5)	9,3 (6)	9,4 (6.5)	9,5 (7)	9,6 (7.5)	9,7 (8)	9,8 (8.5)	9,9 (9)	9,10 (9.5)
10	10,1 (5.5)	10,2 (6)	10,3 (6.5)	10,4 (7)	10,5 (7.5)	10,6 (8)	10,7 (8.5)	10,8 (9)	10,9 (9.5)	10,10 (10)

Samples above or below the principal diagonal result when sampling is without replacement. Sample means are in parentheses.

1. We draw all possible samples of some size n. Suppose that we let $n = 2$. Table 5.4.1 shows the possible samples. Note that there are 100 samples. In general, when we sample with replacement, as we have done here, there will be N^n possible samples of size n.

2. We compute the mean $\bar{x}$ for each of these samples. The sample means are shown in parentheses in Table 5.4.1.

3. We list the different values of $\bar{x}$ that we observed, along with their frequencies of occurrence. The resulting table, Table 5.4.2, constitutes the sampling distribution of $\bar{x}$ for samples of size 2 from the specified population.

TABLE 5.4.2 Sampling distribution of $\bar{x}$ computed from samples in Table 5.4.1

$\bar{x}$	Frequency	Relative frequency	$\bar{x}$	Frequency	Relative frequency
1	1	1/100	6	9	9/100
1.5	2	2/100	6.5	8	8/100
2	3	3/100	7	7	7/100
2.5	4	4/100	7.5	6	6/100
3	5	5/100	8	5	5/100
3.5	6	6/100	8.5	4	4/100
4	7	7/100	9	3	3/100
4.5	8	8/100	9.5	2	2/100
5	9	9/100	10	1	1/100
5.5	10	10/100			
			Total	100	100/100

The individual probabilities (relative frequencies) shown in Table 5.4.2 are all greater than 0, and their sum is equal to 1. Thus, the requirements for a probability distribution are met.

Look at Figure 5.4.1 and compare the two distributions.

As stated earlier, we usually are interested in the *mean,* the *variance,* and the *functional form* of a sampling distribution.

We can compare the functional form of the distribution of $\bar{x}$ that we just constructed with the distribution of the original population. Figure 5.4.1 shows both distributions. Observe that the two figures are very different. The population distribution is a uniform distribution (that is, each value occurs with the same frequency). The distribution of $\bar{x}$ is a symmetrical distribution that is by no means uniform.

An impressive feature of the sampling distribution of $\bar{x}$, as Figure 5.4.1 shows, is the fact that the most frequently occurring value of $\bar{x}$ is 5.5. We also note the symmetrical shape of the sampling distribution. We shall see shortly that these characteristics are not unique to these particular data. This is a general pattern of behavior that is inherent in sampling distributions of sample means.

Now we compute the mean $\mu_{\bar{x}}$ of the sampling distribution by adding the 100 sample means given in Table 5.4.1 and dividing by 100. That is,

$$\mu_{\bar{x}} = \frac{\Sigma \bar{x}_i}{N^n} = \frac{550}{100} = 5.5$$

This formula is a special case of Formula 2.8.4, which shows how to compute μ, the mean of a population of original observations. In the present case we are computing $\mu_{\bar{x}}$, the mean of a population of sample means. Therefore, $\bar{x}_i$ in this formula has the same role as x_i in Formula 2.8.4, and N^n here has the same role as N in Formula 2.8.4.

Note that the mean of the sampling distribution of $\bar{x}$ is equal to the mean of the original population. That is, $E(\bar{x}) = \mu$.

FIGURE 5.4.1   Distribution of population and sampling distribution of $\bar{x}$ for $n = 2$

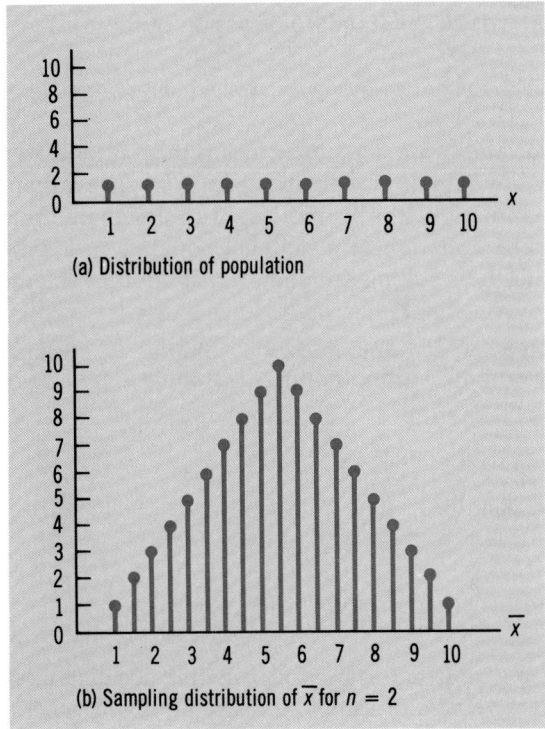

(a) Distribution of population

(b) Sampling distribution of $\bar{x}$ for $n = 2$

Finally, we compute the variance of $\bar{x}$, $\sigma_{\bar{x}}^2$, as follows:

$$\sigma_{\bar{x}}^2 = \frac{\Sigma(\bar{x}_i - \mu_{\bar{x}})^2}{N^n}$$

$$= \frac{(1 - 5.5)^2 + (1.5 - 5.5)^2 + \cdots + (10 - 5.5)^2}{100}$$

$$= \frac{412.5}{100} = 4.125$$

The variance of the sample mean is not equal to the variance of the population. However, the variance of the sample mean is equal to the *variance of the population divided by the size of the sample* used to obtain the sampling distribution. That is,

$$\sigma_{\bar{x}}^2 = \frac{\sigma^2}{n} = \frac{8.25}{2} = 4.125$$

The standard deviation of a sampling distribution is called the standard error.

The square root of the variance of the sampling distribution (that is, the standard deviation of the sampling distribution, $\sqrt{\sigma_{\bar{x}}^2} = \sigma/\sqrt{n}$) is called the *standard error of the sample mean* or, simply, the *standard error*. It is written $\sigma_{\bar{x}}$. Variation in a sampling distribution represents estimation errors for the various possible samples. Thus, we call the standard deviation of these errors the *standard error*.

The *standard error* measures the variability among sample means.

There is less variability among sample means than among original measurements. Therefore, for any sample size greater than 1, $\sigma_{\bar{x}}$ is less than σ.

Here is a summary of the symbols used to designate the mean, the variance, and the standard deviation of a sampled population, a single sample from the population, and the resulting sampling distribution of the sample mean.

Descriptive measure	Sampled population	Single sample	Sampling distribution of $\bar{x}$
Mean	μ	$\bar{x}$	$\mu_{\bar{x}}$
Variance	σ^2	s^2	$\sigma_{\bar{x}}^2$
Standard deviation	σ	s	$\sigma_{\bar{x}}$

NORMALLY DISTRIBUTED POPULATIONS

The fact that $\mu_{\bar{x}} = \mu$ and $\sigma_{\bar{x}}^2 = \sigma^2/n$ is not peculiar to this example. These results are characteristic of sampling distributions in general when sampling is with replacement from a finite population or when the sampled population is infinite. We can also describe a sampled population according to whether it is normally or nonnormally distributed. The sampling distribution of $\bar{x}$ is different in the two cases. Actually, as noted in Chapter 4, no variables are exactly normally distributed, since the normal distribution is a mathematical ideal that is not realized in practice. In this text, when we speak of a normally distributed population, we mean one that approximates a normal distribution well enough for us to use the properties of a normal distribution in describing it.

The following descriptions of the sampling distribution of $\bar{x}$ under the two conditions have been proved mathematically. For the proofs, see the mathematical statistics texts listed at the end of this chapter.

The sampling distribution of $\bar{x}$ when the population is normal

When sampling is from a normally distributed population, the sampling distribution of the sample mean will have the following properties:

1. The distribution of $\bar{x}$ will be normal, regardless of the size of the sample.

2. The mean $\mu_{\bar{x}}$ of the distribution of $\bar{x}$ will be equal to the mean of the population from which the samples were drawn.

3. The variance $\sigma_{\bar{x}}^2$ of the distribution of $\bar{x}$ will be equal to the variance of the population divided by the sample size.

In later chapters, when we make inferences about normally distributed populations, we use these properties of the sampling distribution of $\bar{x}$. Sometimes we may have some doubt as to whether the population of interest is normally distributed. Chapter 12 discusses a procedure that you can use to help you determine whether a population of unknown form is likely to be normally distributed.

THE CENTRAL LIMIT THEOREM

In many situations, the normal distribution so poorly approximates the population of interest that, if we based our analyses on this distribution, we would get misleading results. Consequently, when the sampled population is not normally distributed, we must know the nature of the sampling distribution of the sample mean.

Knowledge of the sampling distribution of $\bar{x}$ when sampling is from a nonnormally distributed population comes from the proof of an important mathematical theorem, the *central limit theorem*. We can summarize this theorem as follows:

The sampling distribution of $\bar{x}$ when the population is not normal and n is large

> Given an infinite population with a distribution of any nonnormal functional form with a mean μ and finite variance σ^2, the sampling distribution of $\bar{x}$, computed from simple random samples of size n from this population, will be approximately normally distributed with mean μ and variance σ^2/n when the sample size is large.

The central limit theorem guarantees that if we sample from a nonnormally distributed population we will get approximately the same results as we would if the population were normally distributed, provided that we take a large sample. This is an important result. It is useful in applying the techniques of statistical inference.

To study the effect of the central limit theorem, we could draw k large sets of samples of varying sizes, $n_1 < n_2 < \cdots < n_k$, from a nonnormally distributed population and compare the resulting sampling distributions. We would find that the larger the value of n, the more closely the sampling distribution resembles a normal distribution. Figure 5.4.2 illustrates the general results of such a procedure.

THE MEANING OF "A LARGE SAMPLE"

The phrase "when the sample size is large" that appears in our statement about the central limit theorem requires explanation. The size of the sample needed to achieve an approximately normal sampling distribution of $\bar{x}$ depends on how nonnormal the original population is. The greater the departure of the population

FIGURE 5.4.2 Illustration of the effect of the central limit theorem on the sampling distribution of $\bar{x}$

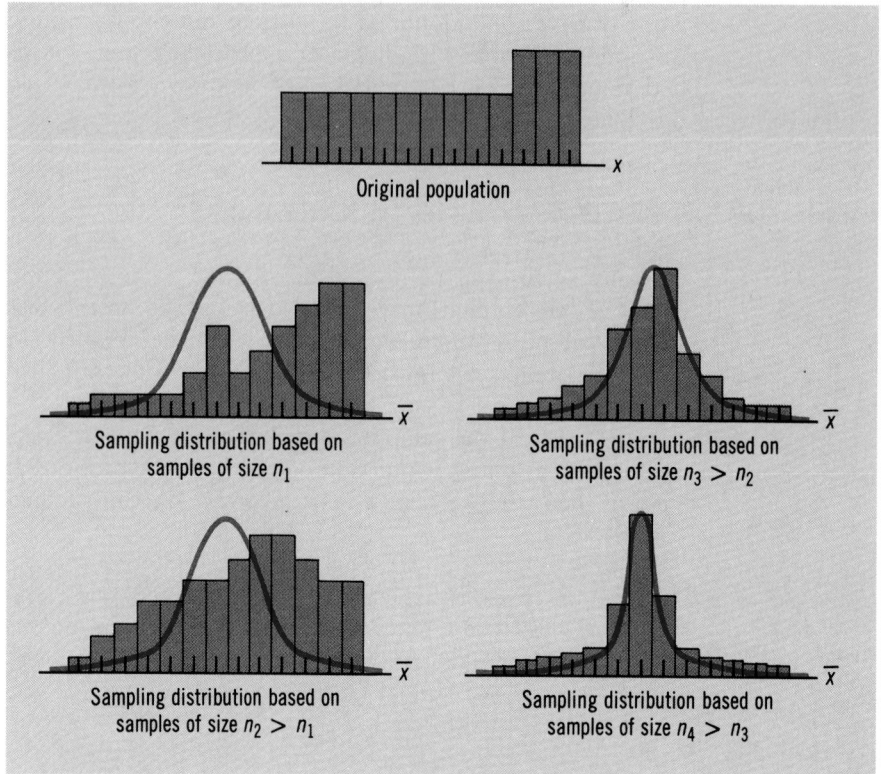

distribution from normal, the larger the sample must be. One rule of thumb states that the sample size should be 30 or more. We adopt this rule for the sake of convenience in later chapters when we apply inferential procedures.

SAMPLING WITHOUT REPLACEMENT

The previous results assume that the sample is drawn either from an infinite population or from a finite population with replacement. As we have pointed out, we do not sample with replacement in most practical situations. Because of this, we need to know how the sampling distribution of $\bar{x}$ behaves when we sample without replacement from a finite population. When we do so, we can describe the distribution of the sample means as follows:

When sampling is without replacement from a finite population, the sampling distribution of the sample mean will have a mean $\mu_{\bar{x}}$ equal to the population mean μ and a variance $\sigma_{\bar{x}}^2$ equal to $[\sigma^2/n][(N-n)/(N-1)]$. When the sample size is large enough, the central limit theorem applies, and the sampling distribution will be approximately normally distributed.

It should be noted that on very rare occasions the central limit theorem may not apply. Researchers have shown that when sampling is from a finite population, both n and $N - n$ must be large for the central limit theorem to apply. Both quantities, n and $N - n$, should be greater than or equal to 30. In most practical situations, if $n \geq 30$, $N - n$ will also be greater than or equal to 30.

Let us now try to verify the results relating to the mean and variance with a sampling experiment using the data of Example 5.4.1. We cannot verify that $\bar{x}$ is approximately normally distributed, since from a population of size 10 it is impossible to draw samples large enough to apply the central limit theorem. We should, however, be able to verify the statements about $\mu_{\bar{x}}$ and $\sigma_{\bar{x}}^2$.

If we take samples of size 2 without replacement, the resulting sample means are those shown above the principal diagonal in Table 5.4.1. The possible sample means are also shown below the diagonal, but with the order of drawing values reversed. We see that there are 45 of these. We can compute the means below the diagonal from the samples that result when the order of selection is the reverse of that which yields the sample means above the diagonal. You may verify that you can also obtain the following means and variances if you use all 90 of the off-diagonal means in Table 5.4.1. In performing these calculations, we have ignored, for simplicity's sake, the order in which the elements of the samples were drawn.

When sampling is without replacement, $_NC_n$ different simple random samples of size n can be drawn from a population of size N.

In general, when we draw samples of size n from a finite population of size N without replacement, if we ignore the order in which the elements are selected, the number of possible samples is given by the combination of N things taken n at a time. In our present example,

$$_NC_n = \frac{N!}{n!(N - n)!} = \frac{10!}{2!8!} = \frac{10 \cdot 9 \cdot 8!}{2 \cdot 1 \cdot 8!} = 45$$

The mean of these 45 sample means is

$$\mu_{\bar{x}} = \frac{\Sigma \bar{x}_i}{_NC_n} = \frac{1.5 + 2 + \cdots + 9.5}{45} = \frac{247.5}{45} = 5.5$$

Thus, we again see that $\mu_{\bar{x}} = \mu = 5.5$. The variance of this sampling distribution is found to be

$$\sigma_{\bar{x}}^2 = \frac{\Sigma(\bar{x}_i - \mu_{\bar{x}})^2}{_NC_n}$$

$$= \frac{(1.5 - 5.5)^2 + (2 - 5.5)^2 + \cdots + (9.5 - 5.5)^2}{45} = \frac{165}{45} = 3.67$$

This time the variance of the sampling distribution is not equal to the population variance divided by the sample size, since $\sigma_{\bar{x}}^2 = 3.67 \neq 8.25/2 = 4.125$.

But

$$\frac{\sigma^2}{n} \cdot \frac{N-n}{N-1} = \frac{8.25}{2} \cdot \frac{8}{9} = \frac{66}{18} = 3.67$$

and we have verified the fact that in this example

$$\sigma_{\bar{x}}^2 = \frac{\sigma^2}{n} \cdot \frac{N-n}{N-1}$$

Ignore the fpc when $n/N < 0.05$.   We may ignore the *finite population correction* (fpc), $(N-n)/(N-1)$, when the sample size is small compared with the population size. When the population is much larger than the sample, the difference between σ^2/n and $[\sigma^2/n][(N-n)/(N-1)]$ is negligible. Suppose that a sample of size 25 is drawn from a population containing 10,000 observations. The finite population correction would be equal to $(10,000 - 25)/(9,999) = 0.9976$. The product of 0.9976 and σ^2/n is almost equal to the product of σ^2/n and 1. Most statisticians do not use the finite population correction when the sample contains less than 5% of the observations in the population. Note that $\sigma_{\bar{x}}^2$ is always smaller when sampling is without replacement than when sampling is with replacement.

We may briefly summarize the key concepts of this section as follows. Given a population with mean μ and standard deviation σ, the sampling distribution of $\bar{x}$, computed for samples of size n, has the following characteristics:

1. The mean of the sampling distribution has a mean equal to the population mean. That is,

$$\mu_{\bar{x}} = E(\bar{x}) = \mu$$

2. The standard error of the sampling distribution is

$$\sigma_{\bar{x}} = \frac{\sigma}{\sqrt{n}}$$

when the population is infinite or when sampling is with replacement, and

$$\sigma_{\bar{x}} = \frac{\sigma}{\sqrt{n}} \sqrt{\frac{N-n}{N-1}}$$

when the population is finite and of size N and sampling is without replacement.

3. If the population is normally distributed, the sampling distribution of $\bar{x}$ will be normally distributed.

4. If the population is not normally distributed and infinite or if sampling is with replacement, the sampling distribution of $\bar{x}$ will be approximately normally distributed if n is sufficiently large for the central limit theorem to apply.

5. If the sample is small relative to the population,

$$\frac{\sigma}{\sqrt{n}} \sqrt{\frac{N-n}{N-1}} \approx \frac{\sigma}{\sqrt{n}}$$

That is, the finite population correction $\sqrt{(N-n)/(N-1)}$ can be ignored.

APPLICATIONS

We have discussed the sampling distribution of $\bar{x}$ in detail here so that you will be able to apply the concept confidently later, in making inferences. We need not wait for Chapter 6, however, to apply this material. We can now answer questions such as this: "Given a population with mean μ and variance σ^2, what is the probability that a simple random sample of size n will yield a sample mean $\bar{x}$ as large as or larger than some specified value $\bar{x}_0$?"

EXAMPLE 5.4.2   The pressure, in pounds per square inch, required to rupture a certain type of fuel tank is an approximately normally distributed random variable with a mean of 2,800 psi and a variance of 9,216 psi^2. Suppose that we select a simple random sample of size 10 from this population and test each tank until it ruptures. What is the probability that the mean pressure required to rupture the tanks in the sample will be 2,750 psi or less?

SOLUTION   The single sample under consideration is one of the possible samples of size 10 that we can draw from the population. The mean of this sample is one of the $\bar{x}$'s from the sampling distribution of $\bar{x}$ that, theoretically, we could derive from this population.

If the population is approximately normally distributed, this assures us that the sampling distribution of $\bar{x}$ is, for all practical purposes, normally distributed. The mean and standard deviation of the sampling distribution are equal to 2,800 and $\sqrt{9216/10} = 30.36$, respectively. We assume that the population is large relative to the sample, and so we can ignore the finite population correction.

From Chapter 4, we know that we can transform any normally distributed random variable to the standard normal distribution by using a simple formula. In the present example, the random variable is $\bar{x}$, and the mean and standard deviation of its distribution are $\mu_{\bar{x}} = \mu$ and $\sigma_{\bar{x}} = \sigma/\sqrt{n}$, respectively.

Appropriate modification of the formula for z gives us the following formula for transforming the normal distribution of $\bar{x}$ to the standard normal distribution:

(5.4.1)
$$z = \frac{\bar{x}_0 - \mu_{\bar{x}}}{\sigma_{\bar{x}}} = \frac{\bar{x}_0 - \mu}{\sigma/\sqrt{n}}$$

FIGURE 5.4.3   Distribution of a population, the sampling distribution of $\bar{x}$, and the standard normal distribution (Example 5.4.2)

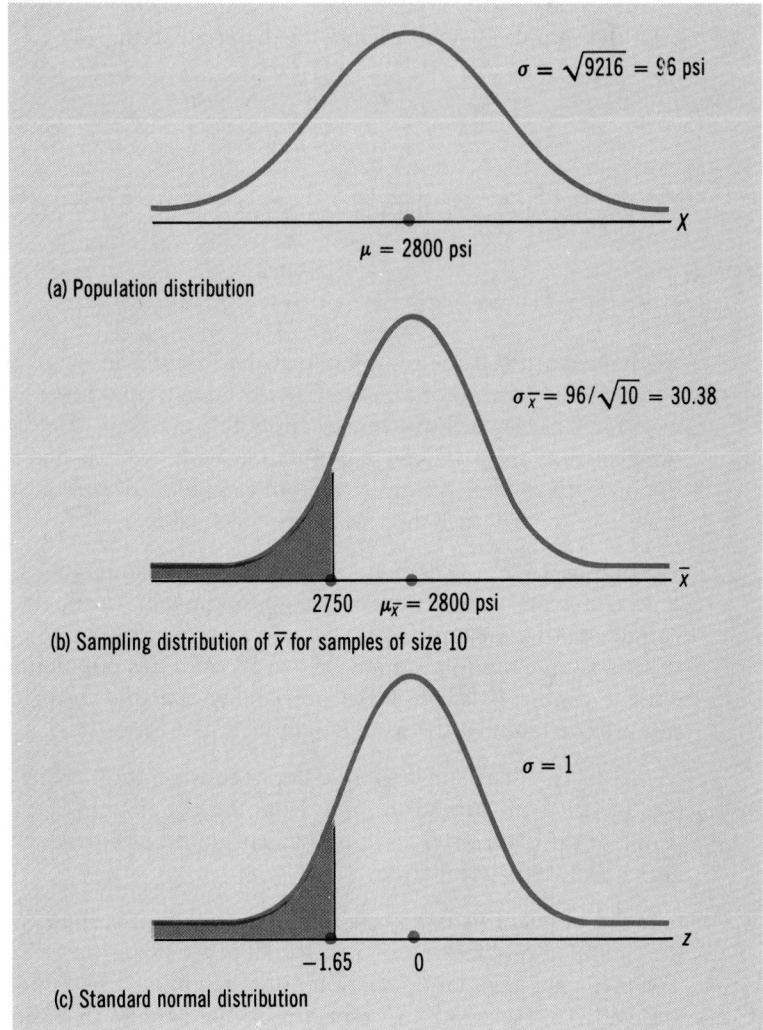

(a) Population distribution

(b) Sampling distribution of $\bar{x}$ for samples of size 10

(c) Standard normal distribution

In this example, the probability is represented by the area to the left of $\bar{x} = 2,750$ under the curve of the sampling distribution. This area is equal to the area to the left of

$$z = \frac{2750 - 2800}{\sqrt{9216}/\sqrt{10}} = \frac{-50}{96/3.16} = -1.65$$

Table C of Appendix I indicates that the area to the left of -1.65 is 0.0495. Thus, we can say that the probability of drawing, from the specified population, a sample with a mean of 2,750 or less is 0.0495. Figure 5.4.3 shows the relationship between the original population, the sampling distribution of $\bar{x}$, and the standard normal distribution.

EXAMPLE 5.4.3   The mean life of a certain saw blade is 41.5 hours, with a standard deviation of 2.5 hours. What is the probability that a simple random sample of 50 saw blades has a mean of between 40.5 and 42 hours?

SOLUTION   We are not told that the population of lives is normally distributed. However, this does not prevent us from using the standard normal distribution, as in Example 5.4.2. Because the sample size is large, the central limit theorem tells us that the sampling distribution of $\bar{x}$ is at least approximately normally distributed, regardless of how the population is distributed. The mean and standard deviation of the sampling distribution of $\bar{x}$ are $\mu_{\bar{x}} = 41.5$ and $\sigma_{\bar{x}} = 2.5/\sqrt{50} = 0.35$, respectively. The probability we seek is

$$P(40.5 \leq \bar{x} \leq 42) = P\left(\frac{40.5 - 41.5}{0.35} \leq z \leq \frac{42 - 41.5}{0.35}\right)$$
$$= P(z \leq 1.43) - P(z \leq -2.86)$$
$$= 0.9236 - 0.0021 = 0.9215$$

The desired probability is shown in Figure 5.4.4.

FIGURE 5.4.4   Probability calculation for Example 5.4.3

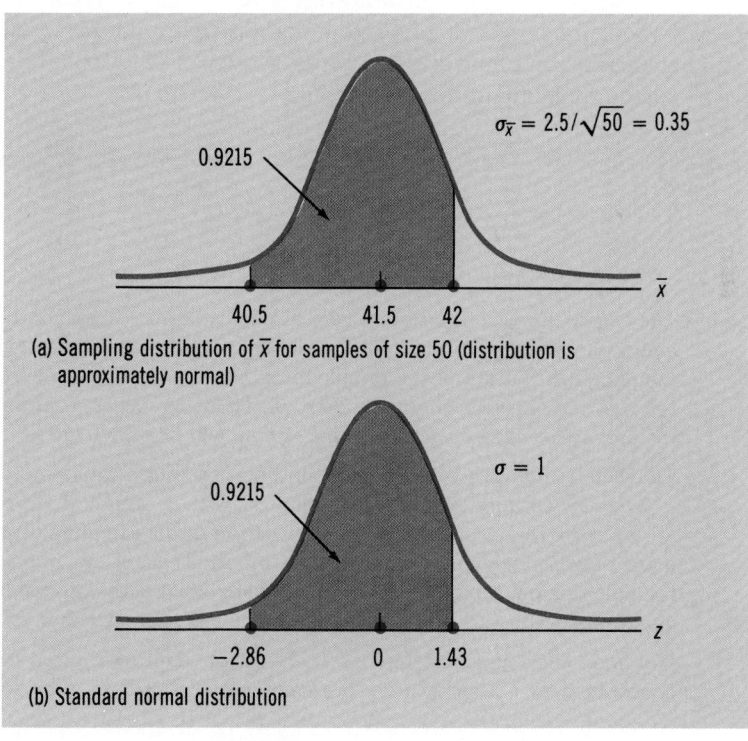

(a) Sampling distribution of $\bar{x}$ for samples of size 50 (distribution is approximately normal)

(b) Standard normal distribution

To illustrate the use of the fpc, let us suppose that the population referred to in Example 5.4.3 consists of 800 saw blades. The standard error in that case would be

$$\sigma_{\bar{x}} = \sqrt{\frac{(2.5)^2(800 - 50)}{50(800 - 1)}} = \sqrt{(0.125)(0.938673)} = 0.34$$

The desired probability, then, would be

$$P(40.5 \leq \bar{x} \leq 42) = P\left(\frac{40.5 - 41.5}{0.34} \leq z \leq \frac{42 - 41.5}{0.34}\right)$$
$$= 0.9292 - 0.0016 = 0.9276$$

The result that we obtain by using the fpc is not very different from the result that we obtain without it, even though the sample contains 6.25% of the population.

COMPUTER **ANALYSIS**

STAT+ contains a program that allows the user to demonstrate performance of the central limit theorem. The user describes a simple frequency distribution of virtually any shape, which is converted by the program to a probability distribution. Simulated sampling from that distribution is performed, and the resulting empirical sampling distribution is shown. The distributions may be graphed, computer configuration permitting.

EXERCISES

5.4.1   The tensile strength of a certain type of wire is normally distributed with a mean of 99.8 and a standard deviation of 5.48.   (a) What are the mean and standard deviation of the sampling distribution of the sample mean based on simple random samples of size 100? (b) You draw a single simple random sample of 16 values from this population. What is the probability that the mean of this sample will be between 98.8 and 100.9?

5.4.2   Caldwell Temporary Services has found that the mean time required for a job applicant to take an aptitude test is 24.5 minutes, with a standard deviation of 4.5 minutes. (a) What are the mean and standard deviation of the sampling distribution of the sample mean based on simple random samples of size 81 from this population?   (b) You draw a simple random sample of 81 applicant files. What is the probability that the mean time applicants in this sample need for taking the test is greater than 25 minutes?

5.4.3   Hill and Dale Nurseries employs 1,500 people. During a given year, the mean amount contributed to a charity drive per employee was $25.75. The standard deviation was

$5.25. What is the probability that a simple random sample of 100 employees yields a mean between $25.00 and $27.00?

5.4.4   In a population of 1,200 executives, the mean amount spent on lunch per day is $6.50. The standard deviation is $6.00. What is the probability that a simple random sample of 36 executives from this population yields a mean between $5.00 and $10.00?

5.4.5   Select a simple random sample of 125 subjects from the population of employed heads of households given in Appendix II. Use commuting distance to work as the variable of interest. Construct a frequency distribution, a histogram, and a frequency polygon. Compute the mean commuting distance and the variance. Compare your results with those of your classmates.

5.4.6   A population consists of the values 2, 4, 6, 8, and 10. Construct the sampling distribution of $\bar{x}$ based on samples of size 2 selected without replacement. Find the mean and variance of the original population and of the sampling distribution.

5.4.7   In a population of assembly-line workers, the mean length of employment with their present firm is 2.5 years. The standard deviation is 3 years. A simple random sample of 40 is drawn from this population. What is the probability that the mean will be more than 3.5 years?

5.4.8   © Use the central limit theorem simulation program in STAT+ to demonstrate the performance of the central limit theorem with the following population frequency distribution.

x	0	1	2	3	4	5	6	7	8	9
Frequency	60	40	25	20	12	8	5	4	3	2

Perform the simulation with samples of size 5, 10, 15, and 30. For each different sample size, perform the simulation with 200, 300, and 500 samples. Graph your results. Do your results support the central limit theorem?

5.5   DISTRIBUTION OF THE DIFFERENCE BETWEEN TWO SAMPLE MEANS

In practical situations, we are often interested in the difference between two population means. To make inferences about this difference from sample data, we need to know the properties of the sampling distribution of the difference between two sample means, $\bar{x}_1 - \bar{x}_2$.

The samples must be independent.   In practice, we would not try to actually construct the sampling distribution of the difference between two means. We can, however, easily conceptualize its construction when the two populations of interest are finite. First we select, without replacement, from population 1 all possible simple random samples of size n_1 and compute the mean for each sample. There are $_{N_1}C_{n_1}$ such samples, where N_1 is the population size and n_1 is the size of the sample drawn from population 1. Next we select, without replacement, all possible simple random samples of size n_2 from population 2 and compute the mean for each of these. Then we form all possible pairs of sample means, taking one mean from popu-

TABLE 5.5.1 Working table for constructing the distribution of the difference between the two sample means

Samples from population 1	Samples from population 2	Sample means, population 1	Sample means, population 2	All possible differences between means
n_{11}	n_{12}	$\bar{x}_{11}$	$\bar{x}_{12}$	$\bar{x}_{11} - \bar{x}_{12}$
n_{21}	n_{22}	$\bar{x}_{21}$	$\bar{x}_{22}$	$\bar{x}_{11} - \bar{x}_{22}$
				$\vdots$
n_{31}	n_{32}	$\bar{x}_{31}$	$\bar{x}_{32}$	$\bar{x}_{21} - \bar{x}_{12}$
$\vdots$	$\vdots$	$\vdots$	$\vdots$	$\vdots$
$n_{N_1'1}$	$n_{N_2'2}$	$\bar{x}_{N_1'1}$	$\bar{x}_{N_2'2}$	$\bar{x}_{N_1'1} - \bar{x}_{N_2'2}$

$N_1' = {}_{N_1}C_{n_1}$ = the number of samples drawn from population 1, $N_2' = {}_{N_2}C_{n_2}$ = the number of samples drawn from population 2

lation 1 and one mean from population 2. The samples composing each pair are independent. We then compute the difference between each of these possible pairs of means. Table 5.5.1 shows the results.

The distribution we seek is the distribution of the differences between these pairs of sample means. Assume that the two populations are approximately normally distributed. If we plotted the sample differences against their frequency of occurrence, the result, for all practical purposes, would be a normal distribution with a mean equal to $\mu_1 - \mu_2$, the difference between the true population means, and a variance equal to $(\sigma_1^2/n_1) + (\sigma_2^2/n_2)$.

This procedure is valid when the sample sizes n_1 and n_2 are either equal or different, and when the population variances σ_1^2 and σ_2^2 are either equal or different. Although we can construct the exact sampling distribution only with finite populations, the results of the outlined procedure also apply to infinite populations. We may summarize:

> Given two normally distributed populations with means μ_1 and μ_2 and variances σ_1^2 and σ_2^2, respectively, the sampling distribution of the difference $\bar{x}_1 - \bar{x}_2$ between the means of independent samples of size n_1 and n_2 drawn from these populations is normally distributed with mean $\mu_{\bar{x}_1 - \bar{x}_2} = \mu_1 - \mu_2$ and variance $\sigma_{\bar{x}_1 - \bar{x}_2}^2 = (\sigma_1^2/n_1) + (\sigma_2^2/n_2)$.

Figure 5.5.1 illustrates the sampling distribution of the difference between two sample means. This description specifies that the samples be *independent*. Two samples are independent if the selection of elements to be included in one sample is in no way influenced by the selection of elements to be included in the other

FIGURE 5.5.1 Two normal distributions and the sampling distribution of the difference between sample means

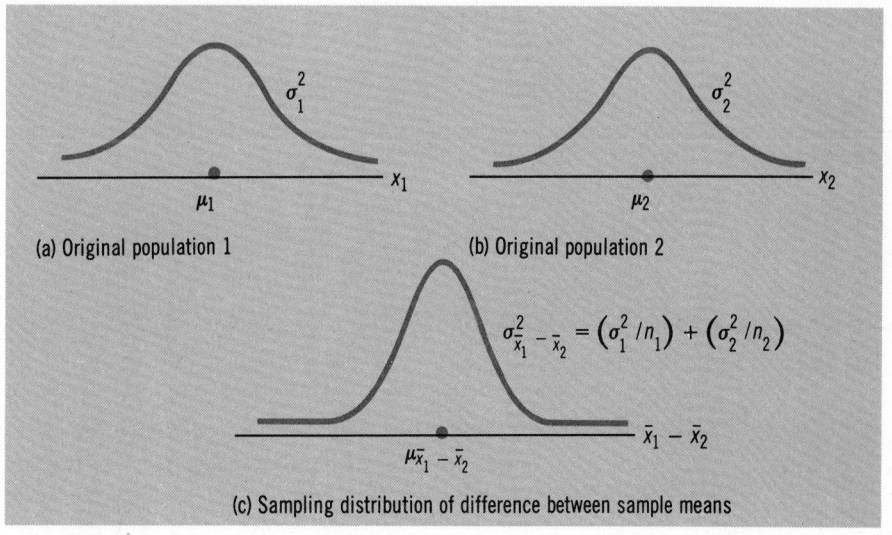

(a) Original population 1

(b) Original population 2

$$\sigma^2_{\bar{x}_1 - \bar{x}_2} = \left(\sigma^2_1/n_1\right) + \left(\sigma^2_2/n_2\right)$$

(c) Sampling distribution of difference between sample means

sample. Note that in Table 5.5.1, $_{N_1}C_{n_1}$ = the number of samples drawn from population 1, and $_{N_2}C_{n_2}$ = the number of samples drawn from population 2.

EXAMPLE 5.5.1 Two companies manufacture high-temperature lubricants aimed at the same market. Company A claims that the mean temperature at which its product ceases to be effective is 505°F. It quotes a standard deviation of 10°. Company B states that corresponding data for its product are a mean of 475°F and a standard deviation of 7°. Experience has shown that temperatures at failure for both products are approximately normally distributed. Suppose that a simple random sample of 20 specimens of Company A's product and an independent simple random sample of 25 specimens of Company B's product are tested. What is the probability that the difference between the mean temperature at failure for the two samples will be between 25 and 35 degrees?

SOLUTION From the data given here, we know that the sampling distribution of $\bar{x}_A - \bar{x}_B$ is normally distributed with mean $\mu_A - \mu_B$ and variance (σ_A^2/n_A) $+ (\sigma_B^2/n_B)$. To find the desired probability, we transform this normal distribution to the standard normal distribution using an adaptation of an earlier formula. The new formula is

(5.5.1)
$$z = \frac{(\bar{x}_1 - \bar{x}_2) - (\mu_1 - \mu_2)}{\sqrt{\dfrac{\sigma_1^2}{n_1} + \dfrac{\sigma_2^2}{n_2}}}$$

For the present example, we compute two values of z as follows:

$$z_1 = \frac{25 - (505 - 475)}{\sqrt{\dfrac{(10)^2}{20} + \dfrac{(7)^2}{25}}} = -1.89 \qquad z_2 = \frac{35 - (505 - 475)}{\sqrt{\dfrac{(10)^2}{20} + \dfrac{(7)^2}{25}}} = 1.89$$

The probability we seek, then, is

$$P(-1.89 \leq z \leq 1.89) = P(z \leq 1.89) - P(z \leq -1.89)$$
$$= 0.9706 - 0.0294 = 0.9412$$

The probability for this example is shown in Figure 5.5.2.

SAMPLING FROM TWO NONNORMAL POPULATIONS

In practice, the following problems often arise: (1) the need to sample from a nonnormally distributed population and (2) the need to sample from a population of unknown functional form. We solve these problems by taking large samples. When the sample sizes are large, the central limit theorem applies. The distribution of the difference between two sample means is then approximately normally distributed with a mean equal to $\mu_1 - \mu_2$ and a variance of $(\sigma_1^2/n_1) + (\sigma_2^2/n_2)$. To find the probabilities associated with specific values of the statistic, then, we proceed just as we do when sampling from populations that are normally distributed.

EXAMPLE 5.5.2 Two methods of performing a certain task in a manufacturing plant, Method A and Method B, are under study. The variable of interest is length of time needed to perform the task. It is known that σ_A^2 is 9 min^2 and σ_B^2 is 12 min^2. A simple random sample of 35 employees performed the task by Method A. An independent simple random sample of 35 employees, similar in all important aspects to the first group, performed the task by Method B. The average time the first group needed to complete the task was 25 minutes. The average time for the second group was 23 minutes. What is the probability of a difference $\bar{x}_A - \bar{x}_B$ this large or larger if there is no difference in the true average lengths of time needed for the task?

SOLUTION Since the functional form of the population is not specified, and since the sample sizes are large (greater than 30), we can use the central limit theorem. We compute

$$z = \frac{(25 - 23) - 0}{\sqrt{\dfrac{9}{35} + \dfrac{12}{35}}} = 2.58$$

FIGURE 5.5.2   Probability calculation for Example 5.5.1

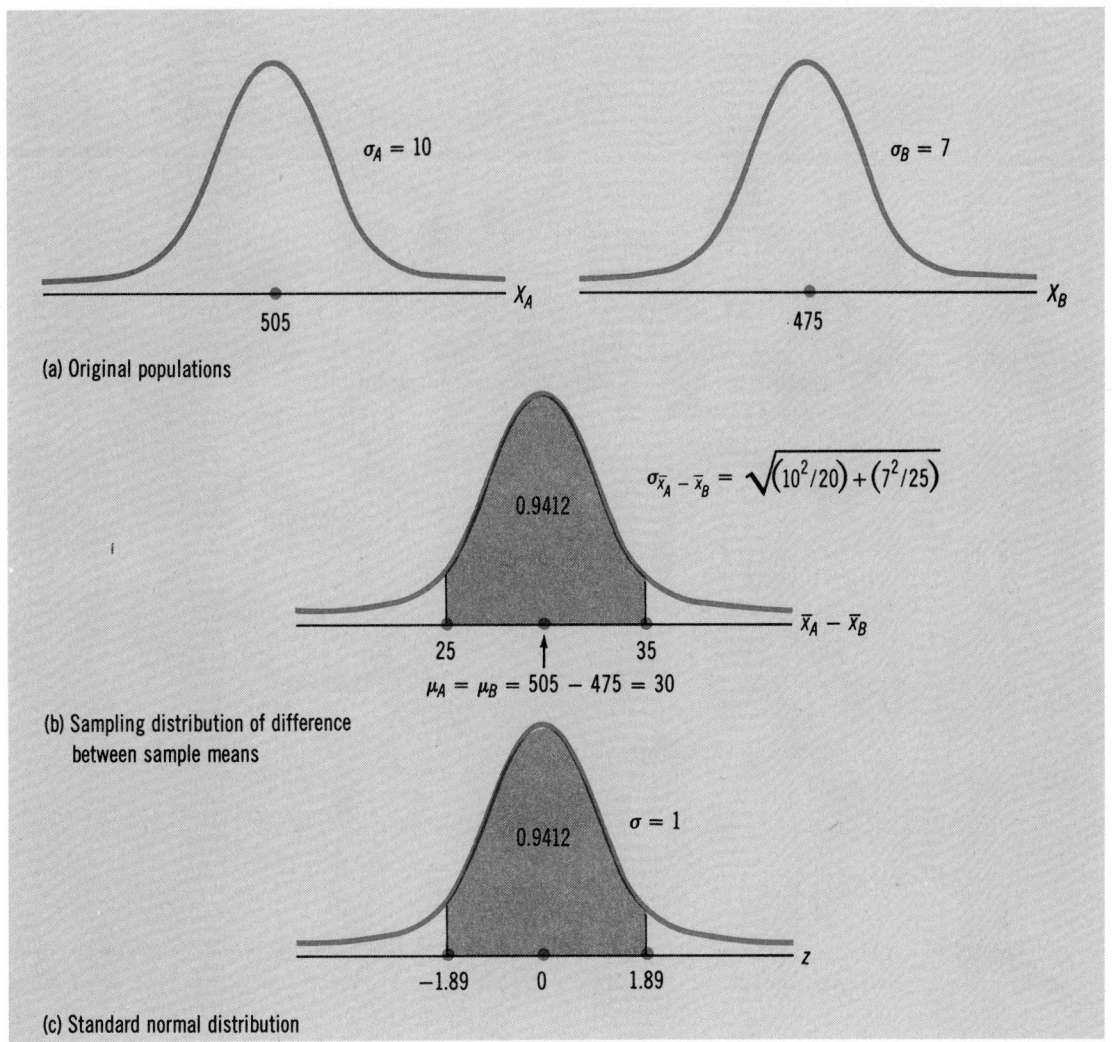

(a) Original populations

(b) Sampling distribution of difference between sample means

(c) Standard normal distribution

Table C in Appendix I shows that the area to the right of $z = 2.58$ is 0.0049. Thus, a difference between sample means as large as and in the same direction as the one observed in this case is rather rare when the population means are equal.

This probability is shown in Figure 5.5.3.

FIGURE 5.5.3   Probability calculation for Example 5.5.2

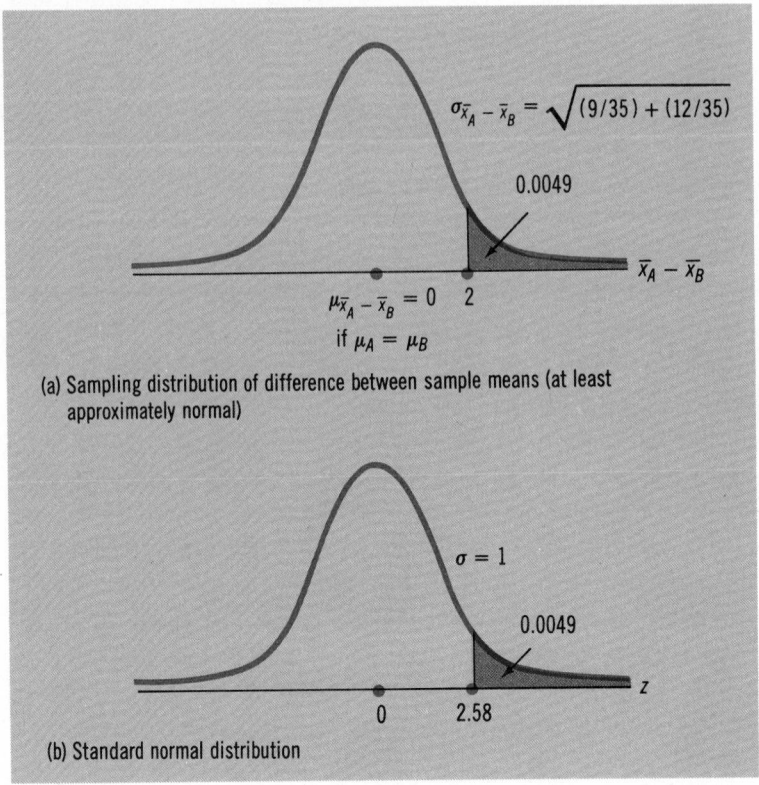

$\sigma_{\bar{x}_A - \bar{x}_B} = \sqrt{(9/35) + (12/35)}$

0.0049

$\bar{x}_A - \bar{x}_B$

$\mu_{\bar{x}_A - \bar{x}_B} = 0$ 2
if $\mu_A = \mu_B$

(a) Sampling distribution of difference between sample means (at least approximately normal)

$\sigma = 1$

0.0049

0   2.58

z

(b) Standard normal distribution

EXERCISES

5.5.1   A market analyst studying the length of time shoppers spend in two types of grocery store observes a sample of 75 shoppers in each store. The mean time the sample of shoppers spend in Store A is 55 minutes. The mean time the sample of shoppers spend in Store B is 49 minutes. What is the probability of observing a sample difference $\bar{x}_A - \bar{x}_B$ at least as large as and in the same direction as this if there is no difference in the true mean time that shoppers spend in the two stores and if the standard deviation is 15 minutes for both populations? What assumptions are made regarding the samples?

5.5.2   An accountant for Eaton's Department Store is studying the characteristics of customers who have charge accounts. A customer may choose between two types of account, A or B. A simple random sample of 50 customers with Type A charge accounts has a mean age of 38 years. The mean age of an independent simple random sample of 50 customers with Type B accounts is 33 years. If both populations have the same mean age and a standard deviation of 10 years, what is the probability of drawing two samples with a difference $\bar{x}_A - \bar{x}_B$ in means at least as large as and in the same direction as the one this accountant observed?

5.5.3 Scores on a motor-performance test for employees who hold nonsedentary jobs (Group 1) are normally distributed with a mean and variance of 60 and 100, respectively. Scores for employees who hold sedentary jobs (Group 2) are normally distributed with a mean of 50 and a variance of 121. A random sample of 10 employees is selected from Group 1. An independent random sample size of 11 is selected from Group 2. What is the probability that the difference between sample means $\bar{x}_1 - \bar{x}_2$ is between 8 and 14?

 5.5.4 Researchers have determined that hostility scores among blue-collar workers are approximately normally distributed, with a variance of 400 for both high school dropouts and those who have finished high school. Random samples of 15 dropouts and 20 high school graduates yielded sample means of $\bar{x}_d = 77.50$ and $\bar{x}_g = 62.75$, respectively. Assume that there is no difference between the population means. What is the probability of obtaining sample results as large as, or larger than (in either direction), what was observed in these samples?

5.6 DISTRIBUTION OF THE SAMPLE PROPORTION

Sections 5.4 and 5.5 discuss the sampling distributions of measured variables. However, we often want to know the sampling distribution of statistics that arise from data that consist of counts. An example of such a statistic is the *sample proportion,* which is a special case of the sample mean. Suppose that we know that in some population the proportion of elements with a particular characteristic is p. We refer to such a population as a dichotomous population because each subject or object in the population either has $(X = 1)$ or does not have $(X = 0)$, the characteristic of interest. We may use graphs to represent dichotomous populations, as shown in Figure 5.6.1. We are often interested in finding the probability of observing in a sample of size n from this population a proportion of elements with the characteristic of interest as extreme as or more extreme than some specified value p_0. To do this, we need to know the properties of the sampling distribution of the sample proportion $\hat{p}$.

This problem is related to the problems in Chapter 4 that we solved by means of the binomial distribution. Those problems involved determining the probability of observing a certain number of elements with some characteristic in a sample of size n from a population in which a proportion p of the elements had that characteristic. Here we are interested in the proportion, rather than the number, that have the characteristic of interest. The two problems are related, since the sample proportion is equal to the number in the sample that have the characteristic divided by the sample size.

When the entities in a population can assume only one of two values, we usually call these values success and failure. Suppose that we give the value 1 to an element in the sample that has the characteristic of interest (success), and the value 0 to an element in the sample that does not have the characteristic (failure). We compute the sample proportion $\hat{p}$ by

The sample proportion is equal to the number of sample elements with the characteristic of interest divided by the total number of elements in the sample.

(5.6.1)

$$\hat{p} = \frac{\Sigma x_i}{n}$$

FIGURE 5.6.1   Graphical representation of three dichotomous populations

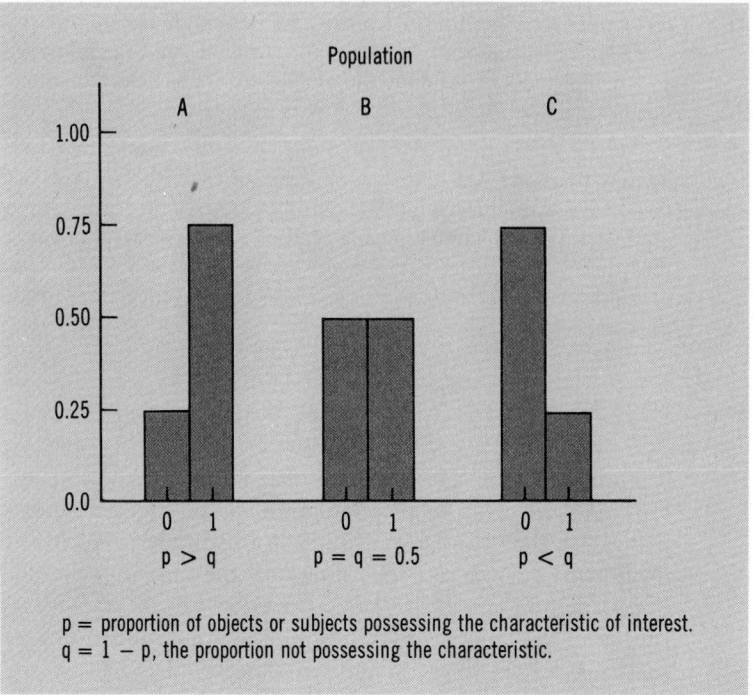

p = proportion of objects or subjects possessing the characteristic of interest.
q = 1 − p, the proportion not possessing the characteristic.

The numerator of Equation 5.6.1 is merely a count of the elements with the characteristic of interest (successes, or 1s). For example, suppose that in a simple random sample of 10 secretaries, 4 are married. The proportion married is given by

$$\hat{p} = \frac{\Sigma x_i}{n} = \frac{4}{10}$$

Observe the similarity between Equations 5.6.1 and the formula for the sample mean. In fact, since the sample proportion is a special case of the sample mean, it is not surprising that there are similarities between the sampling distributions of $\hat{p}$ and $\bar{x}$.

We can construct the sampling distribution of a sample proportion experimentally. We use the same method that we used to construct the sampling distributions of the arithmetic mean and the difference between two means. From the population, assumed to be finite, we take all possible random samples of a given size. For each sample, we compute the sample proportion $\hat{p}$. We then prepare a frequency distribution of $\hat{p}$. Table 5.6.1 shows the results if the samples are drawn without replacement. We can summarize the characteristics of the sampling distribution presented in Table 5.6.1 as follows:

TABLE 5.6.1   Sampling distribution of a sample proportion

Sample	Sample size $n_1 = n_2 = \cdots = n_{{}_NC_n}$	Sample proportion	$f(\hat{p}_i)$
1	n_1	$\hat{p}_1$	$f(\hat{p}_1)$
2	n_2	$\hat{p}_2$	$f(\hat{p}_2)$
3	n_3	$\hat{p}_3$	$f(\hat{p}_3)$
$\vdots$	$\vdots$	$\vdots$	$\vdots$
$_NC_n$	$n_{{}_NC_n}$	$\hat{p}_{{}_NC_n}$	$f(\hat{p}_{{}_NC_n})$

When the sample size is large, the distribution of sample proportions is approximately normally distributed by virtue of the central limit theorem. The mean of the distribution $\mu_{\hat{p}}$—that is, the average of all the possible sample proportions—is equal to the true population proportion p. The variance of the distribution $\sigma_{\hat{p}}^2$ is equal to $[p(1 - p)]/n$.

Figure 5.6.2 shows the relationship between a dichotomous population with parameter p and the sampling distribution of $\hat{p}$ computed from samples of size n drawn from the population.

The sampling distribution of $\hat{p}$ is only *approximated* by a normal distribution. For this approximation to be achieved, n must be large. A common rule of thumb states that we should use the approximation only when both np and $n(1 - p)$ are greater than 5.

FIGURE 5.6.2   A dichotomous population with parameter p and the sampling distribution of $\hat{p}$ computed from samples of size n drawn from the population

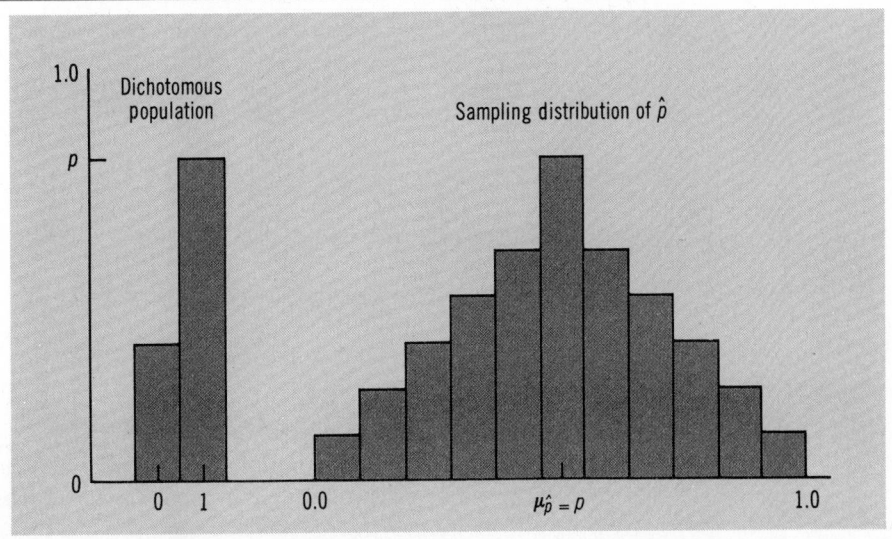

These results are known as the *normal approximation to the binomial,* which is discussed in Chapter 4.

There we note that when sampling is without replacement from a finite population in which the variable can assume only one of two values the actual sampling distribution is the *hypergeometric distribution,* not the binomial distribution. The binomial distribution results only when sampling is from an infinite population or from a finite population with replacement. The reason is that it is only under these circumstances that p remains constant from draw to draw. When the population is very large, we can use the binomial distribution to approximate the hypergeometric distribution when sampling is without replacement under the conditions specified in Section 4.3. In turn, we can use the normal distribution to approximate the binomial distribution. In dealing with proportions, we assume in this book that the binomial distribution is an appropriate approximation.

EXAMPLE 5.6.1 The Finlay Iron Works, manufacturer of nails, has found that 3% of the nails produced are defective. Suppose that a random sample of 300 nails is examined. What is the probability that the proportion defective is between 0.02 and 0.035?

SOLUTION Since $(0.03)(300) = 9$ is greater than 5, we may use the normal approximation. We conclude that $\hat{p}$ is approximately normally distributed with a mean of $\mu_{\hat{p}} = 0.03$ and a variance of $\sigma_{\hat{p}}^2 = p(1 - p)/n$. We can transform any value of $\hat{p}$ to a value of the standard normal distribution using the following modification of a now-familiar formula:

(5.6.2)
$$z = \frac{\hat{p} - p}{\sqrt{\dfrac{p(1 - p)}{n}}}$$

Applying this formula, we obtain the following two values of z:

$$z_1 = \frac{0.02 - 0.03}{\sqrt{\dfrac{(0.03)(0.97)}{300}}} = -1.02 \qquad z_2 = \frac{0.035 - 0.03}{\sqrt{\dfrac{(0.03)(0.97)}{300}}} = 0.51$$

The probability we seek, then, is

$$P(-1.02 \leq z \leq 0.51) = P(z \leq 0.51) - P(z \leq -1.02)$$
$$= 0.6950 - 0.1539 = 0.5411$$

which is found by referring to Table C.

This probability is shown in Figure 5.6.3.

Just as with the sampling distributions of $\bar{x}$, you should use the finite population correction factor in computing $\sigma_{\hat{p}}^2$ when n is more than 5% of N. When

FIGURE 5.6.3   Probability calculation for Example 5.6.1

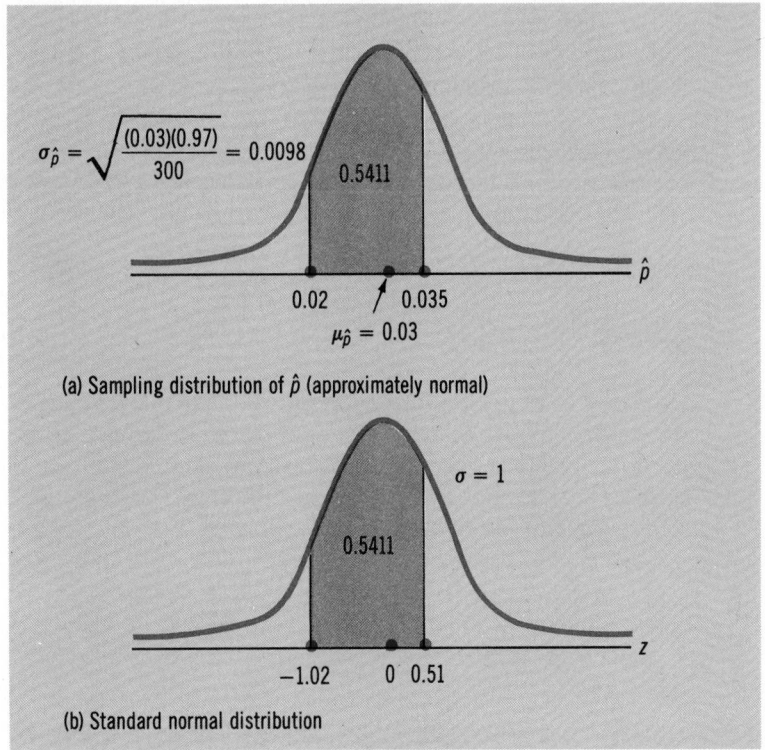

(a) Sampling distribution of $\hat{p}$ (approximately normal)

(b) Standard normal distribution

the finite population correction factor has to be used,

$$\sigma_{\hat{p}}^2 = \frac{p(1 - p)}{n} \cdot \frac{N - n}{N - 1}$$

EXERCISES

5.6.1   The Garrick, Hadley, and Irwin accounting firm has found that 60% of its clients' customers respond to initial requests for confirmation of their account balances. A simple random sample of 24 customers is sent requests for confirmation. What is the probability that 50% or more respond?

5.6.2   We know that 5% of the forms processed by a clerical pool contain at least one error. If we examine a simple random sample of 475 forms, what is the probability that the proportion containing at least one error is between 0.03 and 0.075?

5.6.3   It is known that 25% of the people who saw a certain television program thought it contained too much violence. A random sample of 200 is selected from this population. What is the probability that the proportion in the sample with this opinion is between 0.24 and 0.28?

5.6.4　The Joffre-Kyne Advertising Agency claims that 20% of the members of a certain adult population have never heard a certain slogan created by the agency. In a random sample of 100 adults drawn from this population, 24 say that they have never heard the slogan. If the agency's claim is true, what is the probability of obtaining results as large as or larger than those found in this sample?

5.6.5　Malory Opinion Polls selects a simple random sample of size 250 from a population of 4000 households. Of the households in the sample, 143 report the presence of more than one television set. If the true population proportion is 0.55, what is the probability of obtaining a proportion as large as or larger than that obtained in this survey?

5.7　DISTRIBUTION OF THE DIFFERENCE BETWEEN TWO SAMPLE PROPORTIONS

Often there are two population proportions of interest, and we wish to determine the probability associated with an observed difference between two sample proportions, where we draw an independent sample from each of the two populations. The relevant sampling distribution is the *sampling distribution of the difference between two sample proportions*. We can describe it as follows.

Suppose that independent random samples of size n_1 and n_2 are drawn from two populations, where the proportions of observations with the characteristic of interest in the two populations are p_1 and p_2, respectively. When n_1 and n_2 are large, the *distribution of the difference between sample proportions* $\hat{p}_1 - \hat{p}_2$ is approximately normal, with mean

$$\mu_{\hat{p}_1 - \hat{p}_2} = p_1 - p_2 \quad \text{and variance} \quad \sigma^2_{\hat{p}_1 - \hat{p}_2} = \frac{p_1(1 - p_1)}{n_1} + \frac{p_2(1 - p_2)}{n_2}$$

We consider n_1 and n_2 sufficiently large when $n_1 p_1$, $n_2 p_2$, $n_1(1 - p_1)$, and $n_2(1 - p_2)$ are all greater than 5.

To answer probability questions about the difference between two sample proportions, we transform values of $\hat{p}_1 - \hat{p}_2$ to values of the standard normal distribution using the following formula:

(5.7.1)
$$z = \frac{(\hat{p}_1 - \hat{p}_2) - (p_1 - p_2)}{\sqrt{\dfrac{p_1(1 - p_1)}{n_1} + \dfrac{p_2(1 - p_2)}{n_2}}}$$

To construct the sampling distribution of the difference between two proportions for finite populations, we follow the same procedure used for the construction of the sampling distribution of the difference between two sample means.

EXAMPLE 5.7.1　It is claimed that 30% of the households in Community A and 20% of the households in Community B have at least one teen-ager. A simple random sample of 100 households from each community yields the following results: $\hat{p}_A = 0.34$, $\hat{p}_B = 0.13$. What is the probability of observing a difference this large or larger if the claims are true?

SOLUTION   We assume that if the claims are true the sampling distribution of $\hat{p}_A - \hat{p}_B$ is approximately normally distributed, with a mean of

$$\mu_{\hat{p}_A - \hat{p}_B} = 0.3 - 0.2 = 0.1$$

and a variance of

$$\sigma^2_{\hat{p}_A - \hat{p}_B} = \frac{(0.3)(0.7)}{100} + \frac{(0.2)(0.8)}{100} = 0.0037$$

The observed difference in sample proportions is

$$\hat{p}_A - \hat{p}_B = 0.34 - 0.13 = 0.21$$

The probability we want is represented by the area to the right of 0.21 in the sampling distribution of $\hat{p}_A - \hat{p}_B$. To find this area, we compute

$$z = \frac{0.21 - 0.10}{\sqrt{0.0037}} = \frac{0.11}{0.06} = 1.83$$

and consult Table C. We find that the area to the right of $z = 1.83$ is 0.0336. Thus, if the claim is true, the probability of observing a difference as large as or larger than that actually observed is 0.0336. This probability is shown in Figure 5.7.1.

EXERCISES

5.7.1   A research group states that 16% of the firms of Type A increased their market research budgets in the past five years. For Type B firms, the figure was 9%.   (a) What are the mean and standard deviation of the sampling distribution of the difference between sample proportions, based on independent simple random samples of 100 firms of each type? (b) What proportion of the sample differences $\hat{p}_A - \hat{p}_B$ would be between 0.05 and 0.10? (c) Suppose that you took a simple random sample of size 100 from each industry. What is the probability that the difference you would observe would be equal to or less than 0.02?

5.7.2   In a certain community, it is felt that 40% of the householders prefer a grocery store of a particular chain. In another community, it is felt that only 14% of the householders prefer a store of this chain. If these figures are correct, what is the probability that simple random samples of 100 from each community would yield a difference $\hat{p}_1 - \hat{p}_2$ of 0.42 or more in the proportion of householders preferring this type of store?

FIGURE 5.7.1 Probability calculation for Example 5.7.1

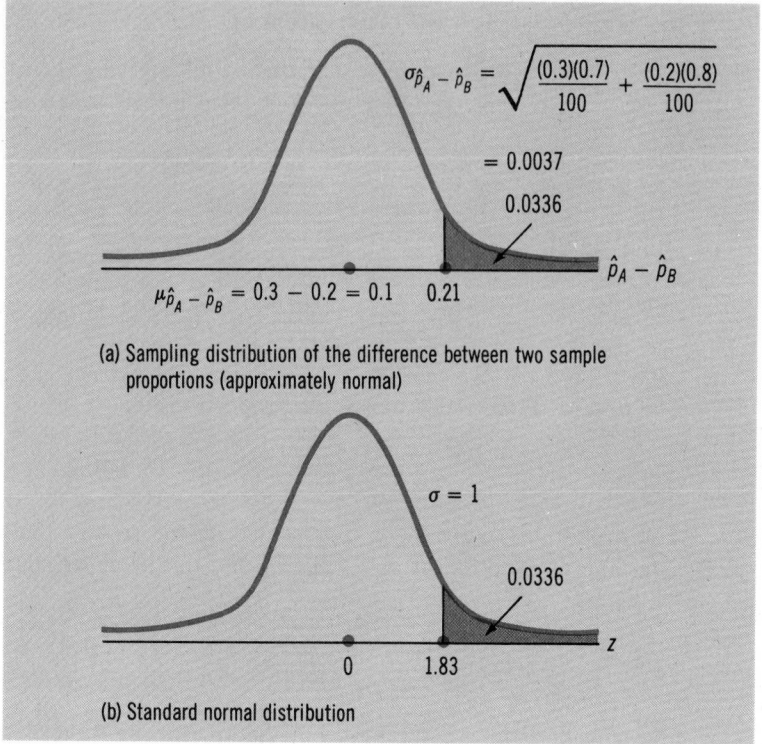

(a) Sampling distribution of the difference between two sample proportions (approximately normal)

(b) Standard normal distribution

5.7.3 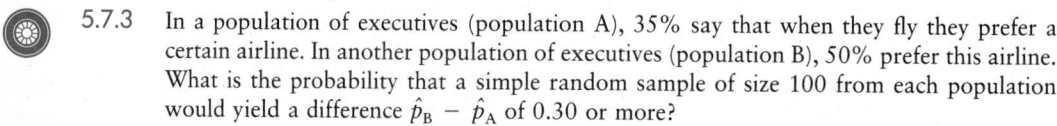 In a population of executives (population A), 35% say that when they fly they prefer a certain airline. In another population of executives (population B), 50% prefer this airline. What is the probability that a simple random sample of size 100 from each population would yield a difference $\hat{p}_B - \hat{p}_A$ of 0.30 or more?

5.7.4 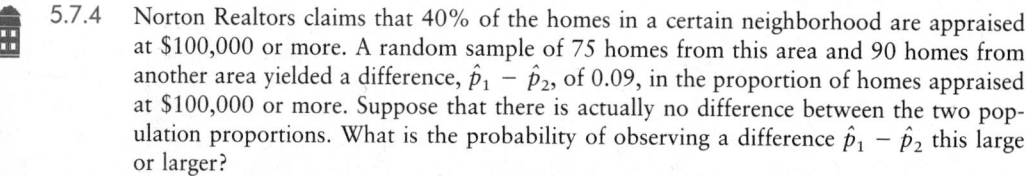 Norton Realtors claims that 40% of the homes in a certain neighborhood are appraised at $100,000 or more. A random sample of 75 homes from this area and 90 homes from another area yielded a difference, $\hat{p}_1 - \hat{p}_2$, of 0.09, in the proportion of homes appraised at $100,000 or more. Suppose that there is actually no difference between the two population proportions. What is the probability of observing a difference $\hat{p}_1 - \hat{p}_2$ this large or larger?

5.7.5 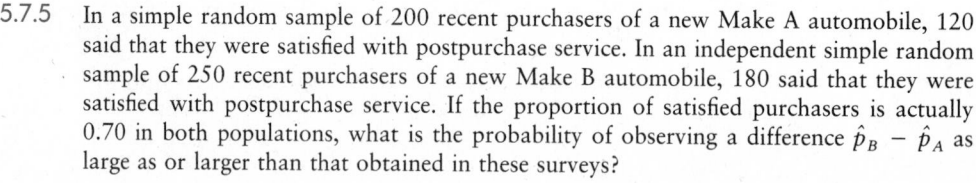 In a simple random sample of 200 recent purchasers of a new Make A automobile, 120 said that they were satisfied with postpurchase service. In an independent simple random sample of 250 recent purchasers of a new Make B automobile, 180 said that they were satisfied with postpurchase service. If the proportion of satisfied purchasers is actually 0.70 in both populations, what is the probability of observing a difference $\hat{p}_B - \hat{p}_A$ as large as or larger than that obtained in these surveys?

SUMMARY

This chapter is the most important one in the book. Unless you understand the concepts presented here, you can never truly understand statistical inference. For this reason, you should review this chapter carefully before you proceed further. Clear up *now* any points that you do not understand. Remember that knowing how to get correct answers to exercises does not mean that you understand the concepts they illustrate. The *why* of the exercise is just as important as the *how*.

This chapter introduced you to the concept of a probability sample. The statistical inference procedures discussed in the rest of this book depend for their validity on the assumption that the samples being analyzed are probability samples. You should now be familiar with the simple random sample, one of several kinds of probability samples. In Chapters 6 and 7, we assume that the samples on which our inferences are based are simple random samples.

The main concern of this chapter is sampling distributions. You should know what a sampling distribution is, and how to construct one from a small finite population. You should also know the mean, the standard error, and the functional form for the sampling distributions discussed. If you have not yet grasped these concepts, study this chapter some more before you begin Chapter 6.

Another important concept that you should now understand is the central limit theorem.

Finally, in this chapter you learned the characteristics of the sampling distributions of four statistics: the mean, the difference between two means, a proportion, and the difference between two proportions. You will encounter these sampling distributions again in Chapters 6 and 7.

REVIEW EXERCISES

1. What are the two types of sampling?

2. Why is nonprobability sampling not covered in this text?

3. Define or explain   (a) probability sample,   (b) simple random sample,   (c) sampling with replacement,   (d) sampling without replacement,   (e) sampling distribution.

4. Explain how to construct a sampling distribution from a finite population.

5. Describe the sampling distribution of the sample mean when sampling is with replacement from a normally distributed population.

6. Explain the central limit theorem.

7. How does the sampling distribution of the sample mean when sampling is *without* replacement differ from the sampling distribution obtained when sampling is *with* replacement?

8. Describe the sampling distribution of the difference between two sample means.

9. Describe the sampling distribution of the sample proportion when large samples are drawn.

10. Describe the sampling distribution of the difference between two sample means when large samples are drawn.

11. Explain the procedure you would follow in constructing the sampling distribution of the difference between sample proportions based on large samples from finite populations.

12. Using a table of random numbers, from some real population of at least 100 observations, draw a simple random sample of size 10.

13. A population has a mean and standard deviation of 32 and 12, respectively. Consider the sampling distribution of the sample mean based on simple random samples of size 64. **(a)** What are the mean and standard deviation of the sampling distribution? **(b)** What proportion of sample means is between 30 and 35? **(c)** What is the probability that the mean of a single sample is greater than 35? **(d)** Less than 30? **(e)** Draw a picture of the sampling distribution and label the areas and points of interest as specified in (a) through (d). **(f)** What assumption is made about the sample specified in (c)?

14. Two normally distributed populations have the following parameters: population I, $\mu = 60$, $\sigma = 8$; population II, $\mu = 50$, $\sigma = 10$. A simple random sample of size 16 from population I and an independent simple random sample of size 20 from population II yield means of 61 and 45, respectively. What is the probability of observing a difference $\bar{x}_I - \bar{x}_{II}$ this large or larger between the sample means?

15. A recent report states that 10% of all employees of a certain type who are fired during a certain period are fired because they violated company policy. In a simple random sample of 100 of these discharged employees, what is the probability that the proportion fired for violation of company policy is 0.15 or more?

16. Given the following population proportions: $p_1 = 0.6$, $p_2 = 0.5$. **(a)** Describe the sampling distribution of the difference $\hat{p}_1 - \hat{p}_2$ between sample proportions when $n_1 = 100$ and $n_2 = 50$. (Assume that the sample sizes are small relative to the population sizes.) **(b)** What proportion of sample differences would be between 0.03 and 0.24? **(c)** What is the probability that samples of these sizes would yield a difference in sample proportions greater than 0.31?

17. The mean time that city bus drivers require to complete a round trip via Route 1 is 80 minutes, with a standard deviation of 3 minutes. For Route 2, the mean and standard deviation are 75 and 2, respectively. What is the probability that a random sample of 40 trips from Route 1 and an independent sample of 50 trips from Route 2 yield a difference $\bar{x}_1 - \bar{x}_2$ between sample means of 6 or more?

18. A random sample of 50 reports by householders in City 1 yields a mean monthly utilities payment of $180. An independent random sample of 45 reports by householders in City 2 yields a mean monthly payment of $175. Suppose that there is no difference in the true mean monthly utilities payments for the two cities. What is the probability of observing a difference between sample means $\bar{x}_1 - \bar{x}_2$ as large as or larger than $5? Assume that $\sigma^2 = 225$ for both cities.

19. The mean yield per acre of a certain grain in one locality is 100 pounds. The yield in another locality is 75 pounds. Suppose that yields per acre in the two localities are normally distributed with a standard deviation of 20 pounds. What is the probability that independent random samples of 20 acres from each locality will yield a difference $\bar{x}_1 - \bar{x}_2$ between sample means of 10 or less?

20. Physical fitness scores of a certain population of executives are normally distributed with a mean and standard deviation of 75 and 10, respectively. What is the probability that a random sample of 25 such executives has a mean score between 70 and 78?

21. The mean number of years of experience of a certain population of salespersons is 10 years. The standard deviation is 3 years. What is the probability that a random sample of 81 of these salespersons yields a mean greater than 10 years and 8 months?

22. In a certain town, 18% of the teen-age boys regularly ride a motorcycle. A random sample of 100 teen-age boys is selected from this town. What is the probability that between 15% and 25% are regular motorcycle riders?

23. A study of a certain suburb reveals that 70% of the families moved into the town during the past 5 years. A random sample of 200 families is drawn from this town. What is the probability that the proportion who have moved into the town within the past 5 years is between 0.65 and 0.75? What is the probability that the proportion is greater than 0.75?

24. Of the 1,150 middle managers in a certain area, 60% hold M.B.A. degrees. You select a random sample of 150 of them. What is the probability that the proportion in the sample with M.B.A. degrees is between 0.50 and 0.65?

25. It is believed that 0.16 of the households in Metropolitan Area I have at least one preschool child. The proportion in Metropolitan Area II is believed to be 0.11. If these figures are accurate, what is the probability that a random sample of 200 households from Area I and an independent simple random sample of 225 households from Area II will yield a difference in sample proportions $\hat{p}_I - \hat{p}_{II}$ as large as or larger than 0.10?

26. In a random sample of 150 children from Area A, 45 report that they regularly eat a certain breakfast cereal. In an independent random sample of 200 children from Area B, 20 say that they regularly eat the cereal. Suppose that the proportion who regularly eat the cereal is actually 0.15 in each population. What is the probability of observing sample results $\hat{p}_A - \hat{p}_B$ this large or larger?

27. Two drugs, A and B, are believed to be equally effective in preventing insomnia. The proportion of persons for whom the drugs are effective is believed to be 0.70. In a random sample of 100 persons who are given Drug A, 75 experience relief. Drug B is effective with 105 of an independent random sample of 150 subjects. Suppose that the two drugs are, in fact, equally effective, as believed. What is the probability of observing a value of $\hat{p}_A - \hat{p}_B$ as large as or larger than that reported here?

28. It is believed that 15% of the members of population A have tried a certain brand of shampoo, but only 8% of the people in population B have tried it. Suppose that these figures are accurate. What is the probability that a random sample of 120 people from population A and an independent random sample of 130 people from population B will yield a value of $\hat{p}_A - \hat{p}_B$ equal to or greater than 0.16?

29. The weights of a certain kind of steel product are approximately normally distributed, with a mean of 2,800 pounds and a variance of 9,000 pounds.[2] Suppose that a random sample of size 10 is to be selected from this population. What is the probability that the mean weight of the sample is 2,750 pounds or less?

30. The mean weight gain of a certain breed of dog fed a given puppy chow for a year is 24.5 pounds with a standard deviation of 4.5 pounds. (a) What are the mean and standard deviation of the sampling distribution of the sample mean, based on random samples of size 81 from this population? (b) A random sample of 81 puppies is fed the chow for a year. What is the probability that the mean weight gain in this sample is greater than 25 pounds?

31. From Table D, select a simple random sample of 30 one-digit numbers. Compute the mean and variance for your sample. Using your results and those of the other students in your class, construct a frequency distribution of the sample means. Plot the distribution as a histogram. Compute the mean and variance of the sample means obtained by the class. Compare your results with the mean and variance of the true sampling distribution based on samples of size 30. They are $\mu_{\bar{x}} = 4.5$ and $\sigma_{\bar{x}}^2 = 8.25/30 = 0.275$.

32. For a population consisting of 1,000 employees, the variable of interest is number of days of accrued annual leave. Suppose that the mean and variance are 12 and 144, respectively. What is the probability that a sample of size 100 will yield a mean greater than 9?

33. What is the probability that a sample of size 225 will yield a mean of 30 or less, given that the sampled population has a mean of 35 and a standard deviation of 30? The population size is 1,500.

34. ☐ Data Set 3 in Appendix IV shows the sizes, in square feet of living space rounded to the nearest hundred square feet, of the 724 dwelling units that compose a city housing development. Select a simple random sample of size 35 from this population.

35. ☐ Compute the mean and standard deviation for the sample you drew in Exercise 34. Compare your results with those of your classmates.

36. ☐ Select a simple random sample of size 10 from the population in Exercise 34. Compute the mean and variance for this sample and compare the results with those of Exercise 35.

37. A poll of shoppers in City A reveals that 112 of a sample of 330 purchasers of toothpaste selected the push-button dispenser rather than the conventional tube. In City B, 35 of a sample of 150 shoppers made a similar selection. Suppose that the proportion of those who select the push-button dispenser is 0.30 in both populations. What is the probability of obtaining results as extreme as or more extreme than those obtained in the two samples?

38. Osborne Tire Manufacturing Company makes two types of automobile tires, A and B. We wish to know whether the two types differ with respect to mean life in miles of wear. The variances of the lifetime are known to be $\sigma_A^2 = 2,600,000$ and $\sigma_B^2 = 2,100,000$. Simple random samples yielded the following information. Suppose that the population mean lifetimes for the two types of tires are the same. What is the probability of getting results as extreme as or more extreme than those found?

Type	$\bar{x}$	n
A	31,500	35
B	30,300	40

39. The variable X is normally distributed, with a mean of 94.8 and a standard deviation

of 18.7. Calculate (a) $P(X > 100)$, (b) $P(\bar{x} > 100)$, if $\bar{x}$ is obtained from a sample size of 100, (c) n such that $P(\bar{x} > 100) = 0.10$.

40. In a simple random sample of 230 heads of household, the average age was 42.6 years with a standard deviation of 14.9 years. Find the probability that this sample mean is within 1 year of the true population mean for all heads of household in the population.

 41. The average weight of all passengers traveling by air on the Peacock Airline is 177.3 pounds with a standard deviation of 19.6 pounds. What is the probability that a random sample of 100 passengers on such a flight will weigh more than 18,000 pounds?

42. The random variable X is normally distributed with a mean of 30 and a standard deviation of 5. Find the following: (a) $P(28 \le X \le 32)$, (b) $P(28 \le \bar{x} \le 32)$, $n = 100$ (c) A such that $P(X < A) = 0.67$, (d) B such that $P(\bar{x} < B) = 0.67$, $n = 100$, (e) the Σx that will be exceeded 5% of the time $(n = 100)$.

43. The random variable X is normally distributed with a mean of 294.6 and a standard deviation of 31.8. Find the following: (a) $P(X > 300)$, (b) $P(\bar{x} > 300)$ if $n = 40$, (c) $P(\bar{x} > 300)$ if $n = 90$, (d) $P(\bar{x} > 300)$ if $n = 200$, (e) $P(\bar{x} > 300)$ if $n = 800$, (f) the sample size n such that $P(\bar{x} > 300) = 0.05$.

 44. A passenger ferry boat is rated safe for carrying 130 people. Suppose that a load of more than 19,500 pounds is unsafe. If the average weight of people is 143.9 pounds with a standard deviation of 23.7, what is the probability that the boat will have an unsafe load when 130 people are aboard?

 45. The wage earners in cities A and B are assumed to have identical incomes, with an average annual income of \$18,322 and a standard deviation of \$5,428. If this is so, find the probability that a sample of 80 wage earners from City A and an independent sample of 100 wage earners from City B will have average wages that differ by more than \$2,000.

46. The random variable X is normally distributed with a standard deviation of 6.73. The population mean, which is unknown, will be estimated by the sample mean. Find the sample size such that the probability is 0.95 that the sample mean will differ from the population mean by no more than (a) 10, (b) 5, (c) 1, (d) 0.5.

 47. A new transoceanic commercial aircraft is being developed by the Ramsay Aircraft Corporation. Excluding a significant safety margin, the weight allocated to passengers and their luggage is 70,000 pounds. If transoceanic passengers, plus their luggage, weigh an average of 226.7 pounds with a standard deviation of 28.3 pounds, how many passengers should the aircraft be designed to hold if the probability of exceeding 70,000 pounds is to be limited to 0.0001? (*Note:* The answer requires obtaining the solution to a quadratic equation.)

48. From a large finite population, we select a simple random sample of size 20. From the sample, we compute a mean of 150 and a standard deviation of 30. From previous experience, we know that the mean and standard error of the relevant sampling distribution are 160 and 15, respectively. We may ignore the finite population correction. What is the mean of the population from which the sample was drawn?

49. From a large finite population, we select a simple random sample of size 30. From the sample, we compute a mean of 200 and a standard deviation of 30. We also know that the mean and standard error of the relevant sampling distribution are 225 and 5, respectively. We may ignore the finite population correction. What is the standard deviation of the population from which the sample was drawn?

50. From a large finite population, we select a simple random sample. From this sample, we compute a mean of 250 and a standard deviation of 70. We know that the mean and standard error of the relevant sampling distribution are 230 and 20, respectively, and that the population standard deviation is 80. We may ignore the finite population correction. What is the size of the sample?

51. There are 30 students in a statistics class. The instructor randomly selects 5 students from the class to work together on a special class project. What is the probability that the 5 students selected will be Arnold, Betty, Carolyn, Donald, and Eleanor?

52. In a certain community, 55% of the homes have a telephone answering machine. The sampling distribution of the sample proportion has a standard error of 0.02872. What is the sample size on which the sampling distribution is based?

53. In a certain population of urban residents, 40% have a telephone in their car. What is the mean of the sampling distribution of the sample proportion based on samples of size 500?

54. In a certain population of executives, 60% report that they are involved in a physical fitness program. Consider the sampling distribution of the sample proportion based on samples of size 175 drawn from this population. What is the standard error of the sampling distribution?

*55. Generally, the concept of the sampling distribution is applicable to any statistic. Theoretically, we may also construct the sampling distribution of any statistic by following the three-step procedure discussed in this chapter. Consider, for example, the sampling distribution of the sample median. When sampling is from a normally distributed population with median M and the sample size is large (say $n \geq 30$), the distribution of the sample median is approximately normal with expected value equal to the population median and with variance approximately equal to $\pi\sigma^2/2n$. With these results, we may answer probability questions about a sample median, m, by computing $z = (m - M)/\sqrt{\pi\sigma^2/2n}$ and finding relevant probabilities in the table of the standard normal distribution. Suppose, for example, that a normally distributed variable has a mean of 300 and a standard deviation of 30. What is the approximate probability that a sample of size 150 will have a median ≥ 308? We compute $z = (308 - 300)/\sqrt{3.14159265(30^2)/2(150)} = 2.61$. Reference to Table C of Appendix I reveals that the probability of z being greater than or equal to 2.61 is 0.0045, and that is the answer to our question. A population is normally distributed with a mean of 125 and a standard deviation of 15. What is the approximate probability that a sample of size 90 drawn from the population will have a median somewhere between 122 and 126?

SUGGESTIONS FOR FURTHER READING

Cochran, William G. (1977). *Sampling Techniques,* 3rd ed. Wiley, New York. Cochran points out that the use of the central limit theorem may not be valid for certain populations when sampling is without replacement.

Freund, John E., and Ronald E. Walpole (1980). *Mathematical Statistics,* 3rd ed. Prentice-Hall, Englewood Cliffs, N.J.

Hogg, Robert V., and Allen T. Craig (1978). *Introduction to Mathematical Statistics,* 4th ed. Macmillan, New York.

Mood, Alexander M., Franklin A. Graybill, and Duane C. Boes (1974). *Introduction to the Theory of Statistics,* 3rd ed. McGraw-Hill, New York.

Plane, Donald R., and Kenneth R. Gordon (1982). "A Simple Proof of the Non-applicability of the Central Limit Theorem to Finite Populations," *The American Statistician* 36:175–176.

Plane, Donald R., and Edward B. Oppermann (1986). *Business and Economic Statistics,* 3rd ed. Business Publications, Inc., Plano, Tex. See page 189 for a discussion of the sample size requirements for applicability of the central limit theorem when sampling is from a finite population.

6

Statistical Inference I: Estimation

Chapter Objectives: This chapter discusses estimation, one of the two kinds of statistical inference procedures. (We discuss the other type — hypothesis testing — in Chapter 7.) There are two kinds of estimation: point estimation and interval estimation. Interval estimation is the more useful of the two. This chapter also gives you a chance to apply what you learned earlier about probability, probability distributions, and sampling distributions. After studying this chapter and working the exercises, you should be able to

1. Define statistical inference.
2. Discuss the properties of a good estimator.
3. Construct confidence intervals for the following parameters: (a) a population mean, (b) a population proportion, (c) a population variance, (d) the difference between two population means, (e) the difference between two population proportions, (f) the ratio of two population variances, and (g) a mean of a population of paired differences.
4. Determine how large a sample to draw from a population when the objective is to estimate either a population mean or a population proportion.
5. Describe the *t* distribution and discuss when its use is appropriate.
6. Choose the correct reliability factor (z or t) for constructing a confidence interval.
7. Explain the difference between probabilistic and practical interpretations of a confidence interval.
8. Use a computer software package to construct confidence intervals.

6.1 INTRODUCTION

We discuss the foundations of statistical inference in Chapters 3, 4, and 5, which focus on the concepts of probability, probability distributions, and sampling distributions.

In Chapter 2, we say that the motivation for analyzing data is the desire for insight into the nature of the data at hand. We compute a mean and a variance in order to describe a given set of data. Any conclusions we reach relate only to those data. The calculation of a mean and a variance (and a standard deviation) takes on a new dimension in the area of *statistical inference*. Our interest now centers on what these measures can tell us about some larger body of data. Statistical inference, then, is defined as follows:

> *Statistical inference* is the procedure whereby we reach a conclusion about a population on the basis of the information contained in a sample drawn from that population.

WHY SAMPLE?

There are several reasons why you may want to draw and analyze a sample in order to reach a conclusion about a population. A population may be so large that examining it in its entirety would demand prohibitive amounts of money, time, or resources. Or the process of taking a measurement may be destructive. Consider, for example, a manufacturer of light bulbs who wants information on the average lifetime of the product. The impracticality of testing every element (light bulb) of the population is obvious. The manufacturer can get the desired information only by means of sampling and inference.

There are two types of statistical inference: (1) *estimation* and (2) *hypothesis testing*. We discuss estimation in this chapter and hypothesis testing in Chapter 7.

Before we begin our discussion of estimation, consider the following examples of situations in which we might use sampling for the purpose of making inferences.

1. A firm is considering the establishment of a mobile home park in a certain area. The firm needs to know the average monthly rental fees for mobile homes in order to reach a decision on whether to develop the park.

2. The manager of a retail grocery chain is interested in knowing what proportion of the customers in a given week are regular shoppers at the chain's stores.

3. The human resources manager of a large organization wishes to know the average amount of time per week that its employees spend watching television.

4. An advertising executive wants to know what proportion of subscribers to a certain magazine remember a particular ad.

5. An employment agency wishes to know the average salary being paid to people employed in a certain job classification.

SAMPLED POPULATIONS AND TARGET POPULATIONS

In applying statistical inference, you must know the difference between the *sampled population* and the *target population*.

> The *sampled population* is the population from which we actually draw the sample.

> The *target population* is the population about which we want information.

The two may or may not be the same. Statistical inference, properly used, lets us make inferences about a (properly) sampled population. Statistical procedures do not help us to reach decisions about a target population if that target population is different from the sampled one.

Suppose that you wish to know what percentage of the households in a certain city have central air conditioning. Someone might propose that you select a simple random sample of households from the telephone book and base an inference about the population of households in the city on the information provided by this sample. You should ask yourself whether, in this case, the target population (households in the city) and the proposed sampled population (households listed in the phone book) are the same. A little reflection will probably convince you that they are not. What about households without phones? What about households with unlisted phone numbers? Is the telephone book up-to-date?

The sampled population and the target population are not necessarily the same.

In many situations, the target population and the sampled population are the same. Then inferences about the target population are straightforward. You should, however, be aware that the two populations may be different so that you do not fall into the trap of making unwarranted inferences about a population that is different from the one that you sampled.

6.2 PROPERTIES OF GOOD ESTIMATORS

We can distinguish two types of estimates: *point estimates* and *interval estimates*.

Estimate = numerical value

> A *point estimate* is computed from the data of a sample. It consists of a single value (of a statistic) used as the best conjecture as to what the corresponding population value (parameter) may be.

We define an interval estimate in Section 6.3.

Note that an estimate is a specific numerical value. We make a distinction between an estimate and an *estimator*. An *estimator* is the procedure or rule, usually expressed as a mathematical formula, that tells how an estimate is com-

Estimator = procedure used to obtain estimate

puted. An example of an estimator is

$$\overline{x} = \frac{\Sigma x_i}{n}$$

which is the estimator used to obtain an estimate of a population mean.

One aspect of point estimators has to do with whether a particular estimator is good or poor. Estimators are usually judged on the basis of the following criteria: (1) *unbiasedness*, (2) *consistency*, (3) *efficiency*, and (4) *sufficiency*. A rigorous treatment of these criteria is beyond the mathematical level of this text. However, a brief discussion will be of value. (If you want to explore the topic more fully, see the mathematical statistics texts cited in Chapter 5.)

UNBIASEDNESS

An estimator is said to be an *unbiased* estimator of a population parameter if the mean value of the statistic computed from all possible simple random samples of a given size drawn from that population is equal to the corresponding parameter. That is, the estimator is unbiased if the *expected value* of the statistic is equal to the parameter. If θ is the parameter being estimated and $\hat{\theta}$ (read "theta hat") is an unbiased estimator of θ, we express this fact symbolically as

$$E(\hat{\theta}) = \theta$$

The left-hand term reads, "the expected value of $\hat{\theta}$." The sample arithmetic mean $\overline{x}$ is an unbiased estimator of the population mean μ, since $E(\overline{x}) = \mu$. In Chapter 5, the example showing the construction of the sampling distribution of the sample mean illustrates this fact.

The sample variance computed by

$$\frac{\Sigma_{i=1}^{n} (x_i - \overline{x})^2}{n}$$

is not an unbiased estimator of σ^2. The sample variance calculated by this formula serves only as a measure of dispersion for the sample data. When we want to use sample data to compute an unbiased estimate of the population variance, we alter the estimator slightly. We divide the sum of the squared deviations of the values from their mean by $n - 1$ rather than n. To illustrate the fact that

$$s^2 = \frac{\Sigma(x_i - \overline{x})^2}{n - 1}$$

provides an unbiased estimate of the population variance, refer to the sampling distribution of $\overline{x}$ that we have constructed in Section 5.4. The population there

TABLE 6.2.1   Sample variances computed from the samples shown in Table 5.4.1

First Draw	Second Draw									
	1	2	3	4	5	6	7	8	9	10
1	0	0.5	2	4.5	8	12.5	18	24.5	32	40.5
2	0.5	0	0.5	2	4.5	8	12.5	18	24.5	32
3	2	0.5	0	0.5	2	4.5	8	12.5	18	24.5
4	4.5	2	0.5	0	0.5	2	4.5	8	12.5	18
5	8	4.5	2	0.5	0	0.5	2	4.5	8	12.5
6	12.5	8	4.5	2	0.5	0	0.5	2	4.5	8
7	18	12.5	8	4.5	2	0.5	0	0.5	2	4.5
8	24.5	18	12.5	8	4.5	2	0.5	0	0.5	2
9	32	24.5	18	12.5	8	4.5	2	0.5	0	0.5
10	40.5	32	24.5	18	12.5	8	4.5	2	0.5	0

consists of the values 1, 2, 3, 4, 5, 6, 7, 8, 9, and 10, and the following measure of dispersion is computed from these data:

$$\sigma^2 = \frac{\Sigma(x_i - \mu)^2}{N} = 8.25$$

If we compute, for each of the samples shown in Table 5.4.1, the sample variance

$$s^2 = \frac{\Sigma(x_i - \bar{x})^2}{n - 1}$$

we obtain the sample variances shown in Table 6.2.1.

Consider first the case in which sampling is with replacement. To obtain the expected value of s^2, we find the mean of all the sample variances in Table 6.2.1. That is,

$$E(s^2) = \frac{\Sigma s_i^2}{N^n} = \frac{0 + 0.5 + \cdots + 0}{100} = \frac{825}{100} = 8.25$$

For this example, when sampling is with replacement, $E(s^2) = \sigma^2$ and s^2 is an unbiased estimator of σ^2.

Now consider the case in which sampling is without replacement. If we ignore the order in which the elements were selected in obtaining the samples, we get the expected value of s^2 by computing the mean of the 45 variances above (or below) the principal diagonal. Thus,

$$E(s^2) = \frac{\Sigma s_i^2}{{}_N C_n} = \frac{0.5 + 2 + \cdots + 0.5}{45} = \frac{412.5}{45} = 9.17$$

which is not equal to σ^2.

We may ask whether there is some parameter to which $E(s^2)$ is equal. The answer is yes. If we define the population variance slightly differently, we find a parameter to which $E(s^2)$ is equal. Let us define the population variance as

(6.2.1)
$$S^2 = \frac{\Sigma(x_i - \mu)^2}{N - 1}$$

In other words, we find the measure of dispersion defined by S^2 by dividing the sum of squared deviations (of observations from their mean) by $N - 1$ rather than by N.

When we compute S^2 for the population described in Example 5.4.1, we have

$$S^2 = \frac{(3 - 5.5)^2 + (6 - 5.5)^2 + \cdots + (10 - 5.5)^2}{10 - 1} = 9.17$$

Thus, we see that, for this example, when sampling is without replacement, $E(s^2) = S^2$.

Again, s^2 is an unbiased estimator of the population variance if the latter is defined as S^2. We obtain the same results when we consider all 90 of the off-diagonal sample variances in Table 6.2.1.

These results are examples of general principles that can be proved mathematically. They can be summarized as follows:

$E(s^2) = \sigma^2 \qquad$ when sampling is with replacement
$E(s^2) = S^2 \qquad$ when sampling is without replacement from a finite population

where

$$s^2 = \frac{\sum_{i=1}^{n}(x_i - \bar{x})^2}{n - 1} \qquad \sigma^2 = \frac{\sum_{i=1}^{N}(x_i - \mu)^2}{N} \qquad \text{and} \qquad S^2 = \frac{\sum_{i=1}^{N}(x_i - \mu)^2}{N - 1}$$

These results justify using $s^2 = \Sigma(x_i - \bar{x})^2/(n - 1)$ to compute the sample variance.

As noted previously, the denominator $(n - 1)$ is called the *degrees of freedom*. We can explain the concept of degrees of freedom as it applies to the calculation of the sample variance on an intuitive basis as follows: since the sum of the deviations $(x_i - \bar{x})$ must add to 0, only $n - 1$ of these deviations are independent. The last deviation is automatically specified when $n - 1$ of them are known.

Thus, we say that only $n - 1$ degrees of freedom are available for estimating the population variance. You will encounter the concept of degrees of freedom *many* times in this text.

When N is large, $N - 1$ and N will be approximately equal. Consequently, σ^2 and S^2 will also be approximately equal. However, although s^2 is an unbiased estimator of σ^2, s is not an unbiased estimator of σ. The bias diminishes rapidly as n increases.

CONSISTENCY

A statistic is said to be a *consistent* estimator if, as the sample size increases, the estimator more closely approaches the population parameter being estimated.

We have seen that the variance of $\bar{x}$, $\sigma_{\bar{x}}^2$, is equal to σ^2/n. This indicates that as n increases we can expect the sample means to be closer to μ. Consequently, $\bar{x}$ is a consistent estimator of μ.

An estimator is consistent if it is unbiased and if its variance approaches 0 as the sample size approaches infinity. The estimator $\bar{x}$ fulfills these conditions. As already pointed out, it is unbiased, and certainly σ^2/n approaches 0 as n approaches infinity. It can also be shown that s^2 is a consistent estimator of σ^2.

EFFICIENCY

The *efficiency* of an estimator depends on its variance: One estimator is more efficient than another if the variance of the former is less than the variance of the latter in repeated sampling. We can compute a measure of relative efficiency by forming the ratio of the variances of two estimators. In general, the relative efficiency of an unbiased estimator $\hat{\theta}_1$ with respect to another unbiased estimator $\hat{\theta}_2$ is given by

$$\frac{\text{Variance } (\hat{\theta}_2)}{\text{Variance } (\hat{\theta}_1)}$$

As an example, compare the sample mean with the sample median for efficiency in the estimation of the mean of a normal population. We know that the variance of $\bar{x}$ is σ^2/n. The variance of the median (which, like the mean, is unbiased) is approximately equal to $\pi\sigma^2/2n$.

The efficiency of the median relative to the mean, then, is

$$\frac{\text{Variance } (\bar{x})}{\text{Variance (median)}} = \frac{\sigma^2/n}{\pi\sigma^2/2n} = \frac{2}{\pi} = 0.64$$

This shows that, for the same sample size n, the variance of $\bar{x}$ is less than the variance of the median. Hence, $\bar{x}$ is a more efficient estimator than the median. (This discussion of efficiency assumes that the estimators are unbiased.)

SUFFICIENCY

An estimator is said to be *sufficient* if it utilizes all the information about the parameter being estimated that is contained in the sample. Admittedly, this is a rather vague statement. To be more specific, however, would require a more complex mathematical explanation than is desirable in this text. It is important to remember that if a sufficient estimator exists it is useless to consider any other nonsufficient estimator. The sufficient estimator has exhausted all the information in the sample that is relevant to the estimation of the parameter of interest. The sample mean $\bar{x}$ and sample proportion $\hat{p}$ are sufficient estimators, respectively, of μ and p.

6.3   ESTIMATING THE POPULATION MEAN — KNOWN POPULATION VARIANCE

In contrast to a point estimate, an *interval estimate* consists of an interval that we are willing to say, with varying degrees of conviction, contains the parameter being estimated. We may obtain both "one-sided" and "two-sided" interval estimates. However, since two-sided intervals are more often used, we consider only these. The bounds of a two-sided interval consist of two possible values of the parameter being estimated. It is a characteristic of point estimates that no statement of confidence can be attached to them. As we show later, this is not true of interval estimates. We can obtain an interval to satisfy any degree of confidence that the interval does contain the parameter of interest.

To consider the most extreme case, we may say with 100% confidence that the unknown mean of some population is contained in the interval $-\infty$ to $+\infty$. The uselessness of such an interval is obvious. Fortunately, we can obtain much narrower and, therefore, more useful intervals. The price we pay for a more useful interval is a reduction in confidence that it contains the parameter being estimated.

Since we can attach a statement of confidence to each interval estimate that we obtain, we can refer to interval estimates as *confidence intervals* and to the bounds of the interval as *confidence limits*.

OBTAINING USEFUL CONFIDENCE INTERVALS — NORMALLY DISTRIBUTED POPULATIONS

To obtain a useful interval estimate, we draw on our knowledge of sampling distributions. For example, if we want to obtain an interval estimate of a population mean, we recall what we know about the sampling distribution of $\bar{x}$, the estimator of the population mean. Chapter 5 shows that when sampling is from

FIGURE 6.3.1   Sampling distribution of $\bar{x}$, showing $\mu_{\bar{x}} - 2\sigma_{\bar{x}}$ and $\mu_{\bar{x}} + 2\sigma_{\bar{x}}$

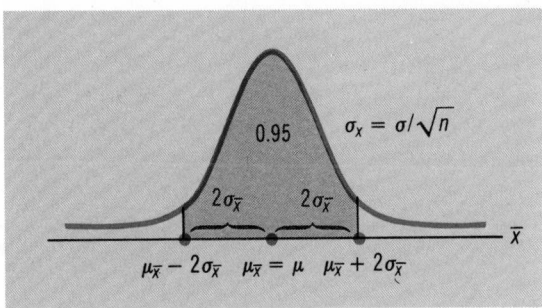

a normally distributed population the sampling distribution of $\bar{x}$ is normally distributed with mean $\mu_{\bar{x}} = \mu$ and standard deviation $\sigma_{\bar{x}} = \sigma/\sqrt{n}$. Knowing that $\bar{x}$ is normally distributed lets us make further statements about the distribution of $\bar{x}$. For example, approximately 95% of all the values of $\bar{x}$ are within 2 standard errors of the mean μ, regardless of its numerical value. In other words, the interval bounded by $\mu - 2\sigma_{\bar{x}}$ and $\mu + 2\sigma_{\bar{x}}$ has μ as its center and contains approximately 95% of all values of $\bar{x}$.

Suppose that we were to draw a sketch of the sampling distribution of $\bar{x}$, showing the points that are 2 standard deviations from the mean. In any practical situation, this would not be feasible, since μ, and hence $\mu_{\bar{x}}$, would be unknown. With $\mu_{\bar{x}}$ unknown, we would not know where on the $\bar{x}$ axis to center the distribution. In the general case, however, we can sketch the distribution as in Figure 6.3.1.

In a practical situation, the expression $\mu \pm 2\sigma_{\bar{x}}$ is not by itself informative, since μ is unknown. But if μ is replaced by its estimator $\bar{x}$, the picture changes completely. In $\bar{x} \pm 2\sigma_{\bar{x}}$, we have an interval estimate of μ. Furthermore, the nature of this interval is such that we can attach to it a statement of our degree of confidence that it actually contains the unknown parameter μ. We can change our degree of confidence simply by changing the value of the numerical coefficient accompanying $\sigma_{\bar{x}}$.

As you try to understand this confidence interval, consider the situation in which a confidence interval of the form $\bar{x} \pm 2\sigma_{\bar{x}}$ is computed for every possible value of $\bar{x}$. (If the population is infinite, imagine computing a large number of these confidence intervals.) The result would be a large number of intervals, all with widths equal to the width of the interval about the unknown μ. The centers of 95% of these intervals would fall within the interval about μ. Each of these intervals, therefore, would contain μ. Figure 6.3.2 shows the concept. It shows that $\bar{x}_1$, $\bar{x}_3$, and $\bar{x}_4$ all fall within the $2\sigma_{\bar{x}}$ interval about μ. Thus, the $2\sigma_{\bar{x}}$ intervals about these sample means "cover," or include, μ. The sample means $\bar{x}_2$ and $\bar{x}_5$ do not fall within the $2\sigma_{\bar{x}}$ interval about μ. Therefore, the $2\sigma_{\bar{x}}$ intervals about these sample means do not include μ.

FIGURE 6.3.2 Sampling distribution of $\bar{x}$, showing several confidence intervals for μ

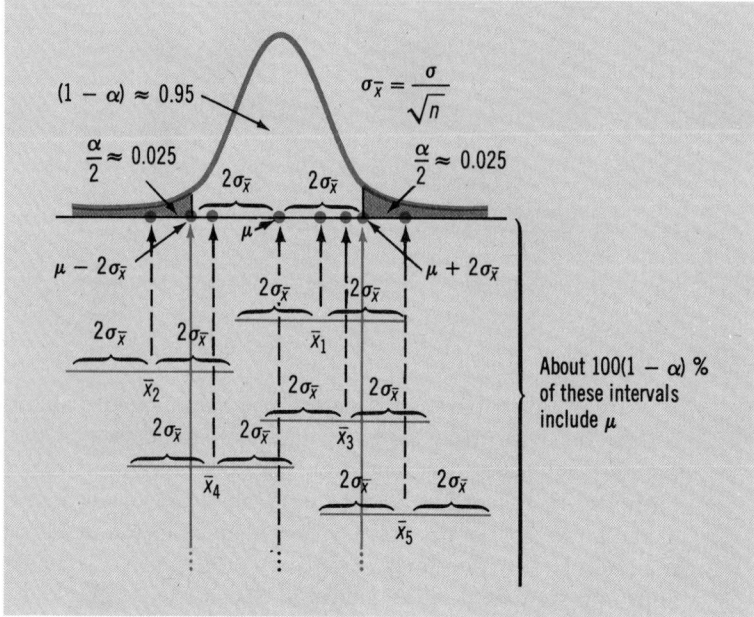

COMPONENTS OF A CONFIDENCE INTERVAL

Let us examine the composition of the interval estimate $\bar{x} \pm 2\sigma_{\bar{x}}$. The center of this interval is $\bar{x}$, the point estimator of μ. The 2 is a value from the standard normal distribution that indicates within how many standard errors of the mean lie approximately 95% of the possible values of $\bar{x}$. This value of z is referred to as the *reliability factor*. The value of the reliability factor depends on the value of the *confidence coefficient,* which specifies the degree of confidence that we can attach to the interval estimate. If the reliability factor is 2, the level of confidence is approximately 95%, and the confidence coefficient is approximately 0.95. In general, the confidence coefficient is equal to $1 - \alpha$, where α is the area under the curve of the sampling distribution of $\bar{x}$ that lies outside the interval about the unknown μ. This means that $1 - \alpha$ is equal to the area under the curve that is included in the interval about μ. See Figure 6.3.2.

The last component of the interval estimate, $\sigma_{\bar{x}}$, is the standard error, or standard deviation of the estimator $\bar{x}$. In general, we may express a two-sided interval estimate as follows:

(6.3.1)   Estimate $\pm$ (reliability factor) $\times$ (standard error)

In particular, when sampling is from a normal distribution with a known variance, an interval estimate for μ is given by

FIGURE 6.3.3   Standard normal distribution, showing $z_{1-\alpha/2}$ and $z_{\alpha/2}$ for $\alpha = 0.05$

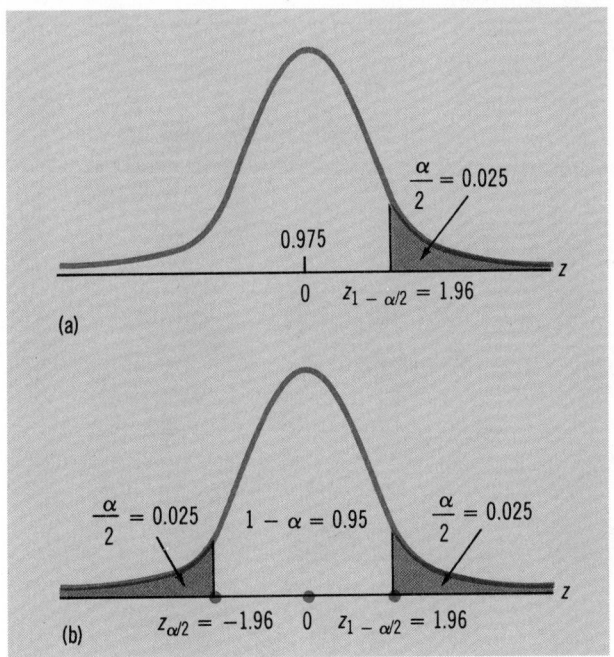

$$(6.3.2) \qquad \bar{x} \pm z_{1-\alpha/2}\sigma_{\bar{x}}$$

where $z_{1-\alpha/2}$ is the value of z to the right of which lies $\alpha/2$ of the area under the standard normal curve. Figure 6.3.3a shows $z_{1-\alpha/2}$ for the situation in which $\alpha = 0.05$. Table C of Appendix I shows that when $\alpha = 0.05$, $z_{1-\alpha/2} = z_{0.975} = 1.96$. That is, 0.975 of the area under the curve is to the left of 1.96. We see in Figure 6.3.3b that, when $\alpha = 0.05$, an area equal to $1 - \alpha = 0.95$ is centered over 0, leaving $\alpha/2$ of the area in the left tail of the distribution. The value of z that has $\alpha/2$ of the area to its left is called $z_{\alpha/2}$ and is equal to -1.96 when $1 - \alpha = 0.95$.

SELECTING THE CONFIDENCE COEFFICIENT

Thus, for an exact 95% confidence interval, we would use a reliability factor of 1.96 rather than 2, which gives only an approximate 95% confidence interval. When constructing a confidence interval, we may select any level of confidence we wish. The most commonly used confidence coefficients, however, are 90%, 95%, and 99%. When we construct a two-sided confidence interval for the mean of a normally distributed population, these confidence coefficients yield z values

Confidence coefficient	z
0.90	±1.645
0.95	±1.96
0.99	±2.58

FIGURE 6.3.4 Selection of z for 90%, 95%, and 99% confidence intervals for the mean of a normally distributed population

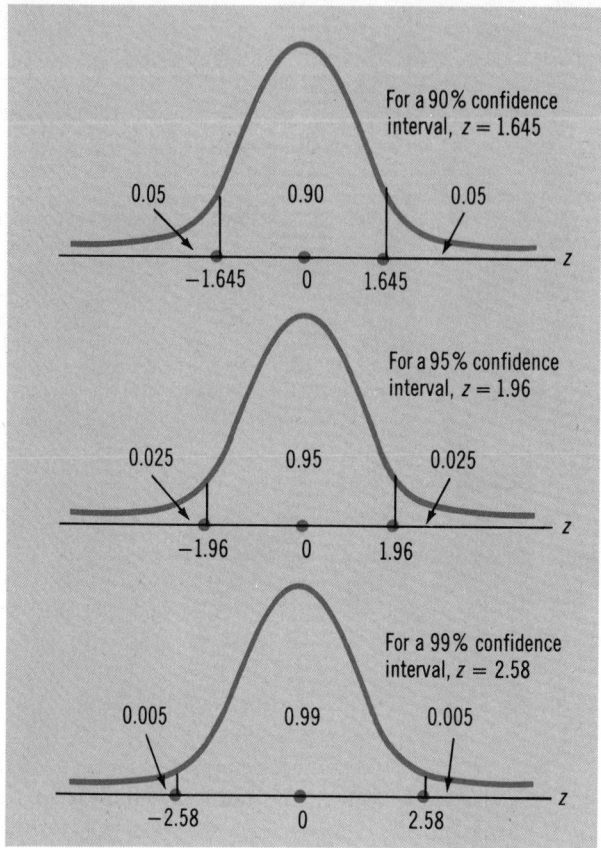

of ± 1.645, ± 1.96, and ± 2.58, respectively, as shown in Figure 6.3.4. We also see in Figure 6.3.4 that, when all other things are equal, the more confidence we desire, the wider our confidence interval.

INTERPRETING THE CONFIDENCE INTERVAL

We can interpret the confidence interval in one of two ways. The first, called the *probabilistic interpretation*, is based on the probability of occurrence of intervals about $\bar{x}$ that include μ. This interpretation may be stated as follows:

In repeated sampling from a normally distributed population, $100(1 - \alpha)\%$ of all intervals of the form $\bar{x} \pm z_{1-\alpha/2}\sigma_{\bar{x}}$ that may be constructed from simple random samples of size n will, in the long run, include the population mean μ.

The other interpretation, called the *practical interpretation*, may be stated as follows:

> We are $100(1 - \alpha)\%$ confident that the single interval $\bar{x} \pm z_{1-\alpha/2}\sigma_{\bar{x}}$, computed from a simple random sample of size n from a normally distributed population, contains the population mean μ.

If we have constructed a 95% confidence interval, for example, that means that we are 95% confident that this single interval contains the population mean. We can make this statement because we know that 95% of all possible intervals constructed in this manner will contain μ.

The following example illustrates the construction of a confidence interval. (In this chapter we assume, unless otherwise indicated, that the population is large enough relative to the sample that the finite population correction can be ignored.)

EXAMPLE 6.3.1   The quality-control supervisor for Rolfe Wire Manufacturing Company periodically selects a sample of wire specimens to test for breaking strength. Experience has shown that the breaking strengths of a certain type of wire are normally distributed with a standard deviation of 200 pounds. A random sample of 16 specimens yields a mean of 6,200 pounds. The supervisor wants a 95% confidence interval for the mean breaking strength of the population.

SOLUTION   The point estimate of μ is $\bar{x} = 6200$ pounds, the z value corresponding to a confidence coefficient of 0.95 is 1.96, and the standard error of the estimate is $\sigma/\sqrt{n} = 200/\sqrt{16} = 50$. The population from which the sample was drawn is normally distributed. Thus, Equation 6.3.2 can be used to obtain

$$6200 \pm 1.96(50), \quad 6102, 6298$$

We are 95% confident that the population mean is contained in the interval 6102 to 6298. We can make this statement because we know that, in repeated sampling, 95% of the intervals that we can construct in this manner using data from a sample of size 16 will, in the long run, contain the population mean. We emphasize that it is incorrect to say that the probability is 0.95 that the population mean will lie between 6102 and 6298.

This procedure for constructing the confidence interval for a population mean applies as long as the departure from normality is not too severe. If the sampled population deviates substantially from a normal distribution, we must take a further precaution, which we discuss later.

PRECISION

In Equations 6.3.1 and 6.3.2, we refer to the product we obtain by multiplying the reliability factor by the standard error as the *precision* of the estimator.

That is,

(6.3.3)   Precision = (reliability factor)(standard error)

Different situations require different levels of precision. In one case, in which the mean, expressed in dollars, is the parameter we wish to estimate, we might want the precision to be within $1. In another case, a precision of $5 might suffice.

A high level of confidence leads to a large reliability factor. A large reliability factor, when multiplied by a given standard error, yields a large product, which indicates low precision. High precision is indicated by a small numerical value of the product (reliability factor)(standard error). Remember that the standard error is equal to the population standard deviation divided by the square root of the sample size. For fixed values of both the reliability factor and the population standard deviation, the precision can be high or low, depending on the sample size. Larger samples result in higher (more) precision. Smaller samples result in lower (less) precision. For example, let the confidence coefficient be 0.95 (the reliability factor is 1.96), let $\sigma = 30$, and let $n = 25$. The precision is

$$\text{Precision} = 1.96 \left(\frac{30}{\sqrt{25}} \right) = 1.96(6) = 11.76$$

Now suppose that we keep the same confidence coefficient and population σ, but increase the sample size to $n = 100$. We then have

$$\text{Precision} = 1.96 \left(\frac{30}{\sqrt{100}} \right) = 1.96(3) = 5.88$$

CONFIDENCE INTERVALS FOR MEANS OF NONNORMALLY DISTRIBUTED POPULATIONS

In many, perhaps most, practical cases, it is neither possible nor wise to assume that the population of interest is normally distributed, or even approximately normally distributed. This is not a problem as far as the use of Formula 6.3.2 is concerned, as long as it is possible to take a large sample. We are interested in the sampling distribution. We know that the sampling distribution of $\bar{x}$ is approximately normally distributed regardless of the functional form of the sampled population, provided that the sample size is large. This result is based on the use of the central limit theorem (recall Chapter 5).

When we rely on the central limit theorem to provide us with an approximately normally distributed sampling distribution of sample means, our interpretations of the confidence intervals we construct must be modified. From the probabilistic point of view, only *approximately* $100(1 - \alpha)\%$ of all possible intervals that could be constructed would include the population mean. Consequently, we must be aware that for a given confidence interval that we have constructed we are only *approximately* $100(1 - \alpha)\%$ confident that it contains the population mean we are estimating.

EXAMPLE 6.3.2   A counselor for Saroyan Personnel Services draws a simple random sample of previous applicants in order to estimate the mean score that all previous applicants made on an aptitude test. The sample, which consists of 150 applicants, yields a mean score of $\bar{x} = 68$. The counselor knows from experience that the population variance is 100. The counselor also has evidence from experience that the population is not normally distributed. A 99% confidence interval for μ is desired.

SOLUTION   Here we need to ask about the size of the population, to see whether we should use the finite population correction factor, discussed in Section 5.4. Suppose that the population consists of 1,000 previous applicants. The sample then contains more than 5% of the population, and we should use the finite population correction factor. The sample size is large, the central limit theorem applies, and we may use Formula 6.3.2, with $\sigma_{\bar{x}}$ adjusted by the finite population correction factor, to obtain the following interval:

$$\bar{x} \pm z_{1-\alpha/2} \sqrt{\frac{\sigma^2}{n}} \sqrt{\frac{N - n}{N - 1}}$$

$$68 \pm 2.58 \sqrt{\frac{100}{150}} \sqrt{\frac{1000 - 150}{1000 - 1}}, \quad 68 \pm 2.58(0.82)(0.92), \quad 66.05, 69.95$$

We say that we are approximately 99% confident that the population mean is contained in the interval 66.05 to 69.95. But now suppose that the population had been much larger, say $N = 10,000$. We would not have needed the finite population correction factor, and the interval would have been

$$68 \pm 2.58(0.82), \quad 65.88, 70.12$$

COMPUTER **ANALYSIS**

When confidence intervals are desired, we can save a lot of time by using a computer. The following example illustrates the use of a computer and the STAT+ software package to construct a confidence interval.

EXAMPLE 6.3.3   The number of units of a certain impurity found in 35 specimens of an experimental drug are as follows: 0.360, 1.189, 0.614, 0.788, 0.273, 2.464, 0.517, 1.827, 0.537, 0.374, 0.449, 0.262, 0.448, 0.971, 0.372, 0.898, 0.411, 0.348, 1.925, 0.550, 0.622, 0.610, 0.319, 0.406, 0.413, 0.767, 0.385, 0.674, 0.521, 0.603, 0.533, 0.662, 1.177, 0.307, 1.499. Suppose that we know the population variance to be 0.36.

FIGURE 6.3.5   Sample descriptive measures computed by STAT+

```
                    TO DESCRIBE THIS DATA SET . . .

Range                    2.202         Median      .537
Variance                 .253821*      Mean        .7164286
Standard Deviation       .5038065*


                TO ESTIMATE THE PARENT POPULATION. . .

Variance                 .2612863**    Mean        .7164286
Standard Deviation       .5111617**
```

 *Obtained by dividing by *n*.
**Obtained by dividing by *n* − 1.

| SOLUTION | It is not necessary to assume that the sampled population of values is normally distributed, since the sample size is sufficiently large for the central limit theorem to apply. When we enter the data into the computer and select an appropriate STAT+ menu, we obtain the printout shown in Figure 6.3.5.

We note that in Figure 6.3.5 the variance and standard deviation "to describe this data set . . ." are computed by dividing the sum of squares by n. The sample variance and standard deviation "to estimate the parent population . . ." are obtained by dividing the sum of squares by $n - 1$.

To obtain the 95% confidence interval for the population mean, we use the appropriate STAT+ program. Figure 6.3.6 shows the information requested by

---

FIGURE 6.3.6   Computer printout showing input requirements and computed 95% confidence interval for a population mean using STAT+ (user responses underlined)

```
              CONFIDENCE INTERVAL CONCERNING ONE MEAN

Is your dispersion measure a S)tandard deviation or a V)ariance? V
Is Sigma^2 known (Y/N) ? Y
Sample size n for mean = 35
Sample mean Xbar = .7164286
The population Sigma^2 = .36
We will draw inferences using the z distribution.
1-Alpha is the level of confidence. What 1-Alpha do you want ? .95

           95% CONFIDENCE INTERVAL CONCERNING ONE MEAN
Sample:

Xbar = .7164286     Sigma = .6      n = 35
Std error of the estimator = 0.1014

Inference:

You are 95% confident that the interval
    0.5176, 0.9152
encloses the true population mean, using
z(1-.0500/2) = 1.960
```

the program, the appropriate user responses (underlined), and the final confidence interval computed by STAT+.

We may also use MINITAB to construct confidence intervals with any desired confidence coefficient for population means when the population variance is known. Suppose we wish to construct a 99% confidence interval for a population mean when our sample data are in column 1 and the population standard deviation is 10. The appropriate command is

MINITAB   MTB > ZINTERVAL 99 10 C1

The printout includes the sample size, the sample mean, the sample standard deviation, the standard error of the mean, and the lower and upper limits of the confidence interval. If a confidence coefficient is not specified, MINITAB automatically chooses 0.95.

EXERCISES

6.3.1   Low-Temp Frozen Food Company wishes to know the mean length of ears of corn received in a large shipment. A random sample of 200 is collected and the ears measured. The arithmetic mean of the lengths is found to be 8.8 inches. The population has a standard deviation of 1.5 inches. What are the 95% confidence limits for μ?

6.3.2   The Stanley Telephone Answering service, at the end of each call, completes a report in which the length of the call is recorded. A simple random sample of 9 reports yields a mean length of call of 1.2 minutes. Construct the 99% confidence interval for the population mean. It is known that the population is normally distributed with a standard deviation of 0.6 minute.

6.3.3   The quality-control supervisor with Tedder and Associates, a large manufacturing firm, wishes to estimate the mean weight of 5,500 packages of raw material. A simple random sample of 250 packages yields a mean of 65 pounds. The population standard deviation is 15 pounds. Construct a confidence interval for the unknown population mean μ. Assume that a 95% confidence interval is satisfactory.

6.3.4   Ⓒ A physical fitness research team wishes to estimate, for males between the ages of 17 and 21, the mean consumption of oxygen after a standard set of exercises. Previous research has indicated that the population variance is 0.0512. A random sample of 25 subjects yields the following results, in liters per minute: 2.87, 2.05, 2.90, 2.41, 2.93, 2.94, 2.26, 2.21, 2.20, 2.88, 2.51, 2.51, 2.56, 2.59, 2.52, 2.51, 2.50, 2.58, 2.52, 2.58, 2.44, 2.48, 2.43, 2.46, 2.46. Assume that the variable of interest is normally distributed. Obtain a 95% confidence interval for the population mean.

6.3.5   A psychologist with Viviani Industries wants to estimate the mean age of a certain population of female employees. She draws a random sample of 60 females from the population. The sample yields a mean age of 23.67 years. She knows that the population of ages is not normally distributed and that the population standard deviation is 15 years. Construct a 99% confidence interval.

6.4 ESTIMATING THE POPULATION MEAN – UNKNOWN POPULATION VARIANCE

The procedures in Section 6.3 for constructing a confidence interval for a population mean depend on knowing the numerical value of the population variance. But often we know neither the value of a population variance nor the value of the mean. In the typical situation, both will be unknown.

When we do not know the population variance, we cannot use Formula 6.3.2 to construct a confidence interval for μ because we need σ to compute $\sigma_{\bar{x}} = \sigma/\sqrt{n}$. In that case, we compute the sample standard deviation s and use it to estimate σ, a procedure that leads to the following estimate of $\sigma_{\bar{x}}$:

(6.4.1)
$$s_{\bar{x}} = s/\sqrt{n}$$

We may now substitute $s_{\bar{x}}$ for $\sigma_{\bar{x}}$ in the formula for the confidence interval for μ.

This procedure, however, does not completely solve the problem. The reliability factor z in the formula is no longer available, since it is obtained from the relation

(6.4.2)
$$z = \frac{\bar{x} - \mu_{\bar{x}}}{\sigma_{\bar{x}}} = \frac{\bar{x} - \mu_{\bar{x}}}{\sigma/\sqrt{n}}$$

and z is normally distributed. In other words, we can no longer determine the appropriate z value accurately, since σ is unknown.

STUDENT'S t DISTRIBUTION

When we use $s_{\bar{x}}$ to estimate $\sigma_{\bar{x}}$ in Equation 6.4.2, the resulting variable is

(6.4.3)
$$t = \frac{\bar{x} - \mu_{\bar{x}}}{s_{\bar{x}}} = \frac{\bar{x} - \mu_{\bar{x}}}{s/\sqrt{n}}$$

which we use in place of z in the confidence interval for μ.

The next problem is to obtain a numerical value for t in a specific situation. We must consider the nature of the distribution of t. In other words, suppose that we take a very large number of samples of size n from a normally distributed population and use the mean and standard deviation of each to compute a value of t. The problem relates to the manner in which these values of t would be distributed.

The nature of the distribution of

$$t = \frac{\bar{x} - \mu_{\bar{x}}}{s/\sqrt{n}}$$

was first investigated and reported by William Sealy Gossett (1876–1937). Gossett published under the pseudonym "Student." Consequently, the distribution of t is frequently referred to as *Student's distribution.*

Properties of the* t *Distribution The properties of this distribution are as follows:

1. It has a mean of 0.

2. It is symmetrical about its mean.

3. In general, it has a variance greater than 1, but the variance approaches 1 as the sample size increases. For df > 2, the variance of the t distribution is df/(df $-$ 2), where df is the degrees of freedom. Alternatively, for $n > 3$ we may write the variance of the t distribution as $(n - 1)/(n - 3)$.

4. The variable t takes on values between $-\infty$ and ∞.

5. The t distribution is really a family of distributions, since there is a different distribution for each degrees-of-freedom value. In the one-sample case, this is $n - 1$, the divisor used in computing s^2.

6. In general, the t distribution is less peaked at the center and higher in the tails than the standard normal distribution.

7. The t distribution approaches the standard normal distribution as n increases.

Figure 6.4.1 compares the t distribution and the normal distribution.

The t distribution, like the standard normal distribution, has been extensively tabulated. Table E in Appendix I is an example of one such table. To use it, we need to know the value of the confidence coefficient and the degrees of freedom.

The general procedure for constructing confidence intervals for μ is not affected by the fact that we must obtain the reliability coefficient from the t table rather than from the z table. We still use the fact that we can express a confidence interval by the general relationship

$$\text{Estimate} \pm (\text{reliability factor}) \times (\text{standard error})$$

To be more specific, when we are sampling from a normally distributed population with unknown σ, the $100(1 - \alpha)\%$ confidence interval for the population

FIGURE 6.4.1   The standard normal distribution and the t distribution

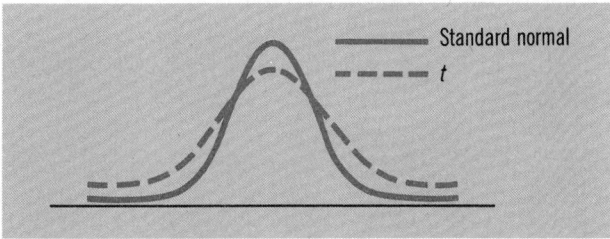

mean is given by the following expression (in which $t_{1-\alpha/2}$ is the reliability factor):

$$\bar{x} \pm t_{1-\alpha/2}\, s/\sqrt{n} \tag{6.4.4}$$

In theory, we should use this formula only when sampling is from a normally distributed population. Experience has shown, however, that moderate departures from this assumption do not appreciably affect the results. Therefore, the t distribution is widely used even when it is known that the sampled population is not normally distributed. Most researchers require that the distribution of the population be at least mound-shaped. In Chapter 12, we discuss a procedure for determining whether or not it is likely that a population is normally distributed. The following example shows the use of the t distribution.

EXAMPLE 6.4.1 In an effort to establish a standard time needed to perform a certain task, a production engineer at Waugh Enterprises randomly selects 16 experienced employees to perform the task. The mean time required by the 16 employees is 13 minutes. The standard deviation is 3 minutes. The production engineer wishes to construct a 95% confidence interval for the true mean length of time required by the population of employees to perform the task.

SOLUTION Let us assume that these 16 measurements constitute a simple random sample from a normally distributed population of times required to perform the task. These assumptions allow us to use Formula 6.4.4. The point estimate is 13 minutes. The standard error of the estimate is $s/\sqrt{n} = 3/\sqrt{16} = 0.75$. To find the reliability factor, we enter Table E with $n - 1 = 15$ degrees of freedom. The column containing the appropriate value of t is the one labeled $t_{0.975}$, since this is the one that contains t values with 0.025 of the area under the curve to their right. (The negatives of these values have 0.025 of the area under the curve to their left.) The appropriate t value is 2.1315. The desired interval is

$$13 \pm 2.1315(0.75), \qquad 11.4,\ 14.6$$

Based on the evidence from this sample, we can be 95% confident that the true mean time required to perform the task is between 11.4 and 14.6 minutes. We can say this because of probabilistic interpretation. According to this interpretation in repeated sampling, 95% of the intervals that can be constructed in the same manner include the true population mean.

COMPUTER **ANALYSIS**

If we wish to use STAT+ to construct a confidence interval for a population mean when the population variance is unknown, we use the same menus that we use to construct a confidence interval when the population variance is known.

The program determines what procedure to follow based on the responses to its questions.

To use MINITAB, the command is TINTERVAL. A value for the population standard deviation is, of course, omitted from the command.

CONFIDENCE INTERVALS FOR MEANS OF NONNORMALLY DISTRIBUTED POPULATIONS— UNKNOWN POPULATION VARIANCE

We have said that if we are to use Formula 6.4.4 the distribution of the sampled population must not deviate too much from a normal distribution. When sampling is from a nonnormally distributed population, the central limit theorem guarantees at least an approximately normally distributed sampling distribution of $\bar{x}$ when the sample size is large ($n \geq 30$). We have said earlier that when you are sampling from a nonnormally distributed population you should draw a large sample and use Formula 6.3.2. But Formula 6.3.2 requires knowledge of σ, which is unknown under conditions of the type we are now discussing. Again, we may use the sample standard deviation to estimate σ and use the resulting modification of Formula 6.3.2, which is as follows:

(6.4.5)
$$\bar{x} \pm z_{1-\alpha/2}\, s/\sqrt{n}$$

We can do this because we assume that, since the sample size is large, it provides an adequate estimate of σ. In fact, many people use Formula 6.4.5 when σ is unknown and n is large, whether or not they assume the population to be normally distributed. In other words, the size of the sample, rather than whether σ is known or unknown, is often used as the criterion for determining whether to use z or t as the reliability factor when constructing confidence intervals. This is reasonable because the t distribution approaches the standard normal distribution as the size of the sample increases.

EXAMPLE 6.4.2 Wingate and Associates, a real estate firm, wants to develop a new shopping center. It wishes to know the average size of grocery stores in existing shopping centers. The firm's researchers are unwilling to assume that the population of store sizes is normally distributed. To obtain an interval estimate of μ, therefore, they decide to take a large sample. Then the central limit theorem will apply, and they can use the standard normal distribution to obtain their reliability factor. The population standard deviation is unknown, but they feel that a large sample will yield a satisfactory estimate of σ. The researchers draw a random sample of 50 grocery stores. They find the sample mean and standard deviation to be 10,000 and 4,800 square feet, respectively. They choose a confidence coefficient of 0.95.

SOLUTION   Under the circumstances, the appropriate formula for constructing a confidence interval for μ is Formula 6.4.5. Using this formula gives the following 95% confidence interval:

$$10,000 \pm 1.96 \left(\frac{4800}{\sqrt{50}} \right), \qquad 8669; \; 11,331$$

PAIRED OBSERVATIONS

There are many ways to obtain paired observations.

A special case of statistical inference about a single population mean occurs when the data for analysis consist of *paired observations*. We can generate paired observations in a variety of ways. We can take measurements on subjects before and after some intervening treatment, environmental alteration, and so forth. For example, we might gather individual production data on assembly-line employees before and after the initiation of measures designed to improve their working conditions. In the laboratory, we may divide individual specimens of material into two parts and subject each half to a different experimental procedure. For example, we can record tensile strengths for batches of plastic prepared according to the same formula, except that the two halves of each batch receive different amounts of a key ingredient. Another way to obtain paired observations is to match pairs of subjects according to as many relevant characteristics as possible. Then we apply one treatment to one member of each pair and a different treatment to the other member. For example, we pair salespersons by matching them according to age, years of experience, education, level of initiative, and so forth. Then we assign one member of each pair to a training course taught by one method and the other member to a training course taught by another method.

In such situations, we are interested in the difference between the results produced under each of the two different conditions. We may, for example, want to determine the extent to which a change in working conditions causes a change in production volume. For individual employees, we can compare the number of units produced in a week before the change with the number produced during a week after the change. From the difference between these two observations, we can tell whether an individual employee's weekly production has increased, decreased, or remained the same. To assess the overall effect of the change, we examine the difference in production for the group as a whole. A measure that seems particularly relevant is the mean of the individual differences between before- and after-production figures. Indeed, this is a measure of considerable interest in analyzing paired observations.

A CONFIDENCE INTERVAL FOR A MEAN DIFFERENCE

Let d_i denote the difference between two paired observations x_{1i} and x_{2i}. We may define the sample mean of the differences (*mean difference*) as

(6.4.6)
$$\bar{d} = \frac{\Sigma d_i}{n}$$

where n is the number of pairs of observations. The sample variance, denoted by s_d^2, may be computed as follows:

(6.4.7)
$$s_d^2 = \frac{\Sigma(d_i - \bar{d})^2}{n-1} = \frac{n\Sigma d_i^2 - (\Sigma d_i)^2}{n(n-1)}$$

We can use the sample mean difference $\bar{d}$ as a point estimator of the population mean difference μ_d. Note that $\mu_d = \mu_1 - \mu_2$, the difference between the population mean of X_1 and the population mean of X_2. When the population of differences is normally distributed with unknown variance, a $100(1 - \alpha)\%$ confidence interval for μ_d is given by

(6.4.8)
$$\bar{d} \pm t_{1-\alpha/2}\frac{s_d}{\sqrt{n}}$$

where $s_d/\sqrt{n}$ is the estimated standard error of the mean difference. The degrees of freedom for t are $n - 1$. If the central limit theorem is applicable, we can use z in place of t in Equation 6.4.8.

EXAMPLE 6.4.3   A simple random sample of ten electronics firms is asked in a questionnaire to state the amount of money spent on employee training programs during the year just ended and during a year a decade ago. Table 6.4.1 gives the results (adjusted for inflation).

We wish to construct a 95% confidence interval for the mean difference in expenditures for employee training programs by the ten firms.

SOLUTION   From the last column of Table 6.4.1, we compute

$$\bar{d} = \frac{2 + 3 + \cdots + 1}{10} = \frac{15}{10} = 1.5$$

$$s_d = \sqrt{\frac{10(2^2 + 3^2 + \cdots + 1^2) - (15)^2}{(10)(9)}} = \sqrt{5.17} = 2.3$$

$$s_{\bar{d}} = \frac{2.3}{\sqrt{10}} = 0.73$$

TABLE 6.4.1   Amount of money spent on employee training by ten firms ($\times \$1,000$)

Firm	A	B	C	D	E	F	G	H	I	J
Past year (X_1)	12	14	8	12	8	10	8	9	10	10
Decade ago (X_2)	10	11	8	7	9	6	10	9	7	9
d_i	2	3	0	5	-1	4	-2	0	3	1

The 95% confidence interval for μ_d is

$$1.5 \pm 2.2622(0.73), \qquad -0.2, 3.2$$

When constructing confidence intervals for population means, we must decide whether to use z or t as the reliability factor. We can use Figure 6.4.2 as a guide in making the correct choice.

Example 6.4.3 demonstrates an important characteristic of the data that are appropriate for analysis by the technique described. The data in their original form consist of paired observations, with one member of the pair coming from one sample and the other member of the pair coming from the other sample. The two samples are called *related samples,* or *paired samples.* When we take the difference between the members of each pair of observations, we reduce the data to a single sample of differences. The statistical analysis, as we have seen, is performed on the differences between the pairs of observations that constitute a single sample. The analytical technique, then, is a special case of the one-sample procedure. In the sections that follow, we show you how to construct confidence intervals for an appropriate population parameter when there are two independent, or unrelated, samples available for analysis.

FIGURE 6.4.2 Flow chart for deciding between z and t when making inferences about population means

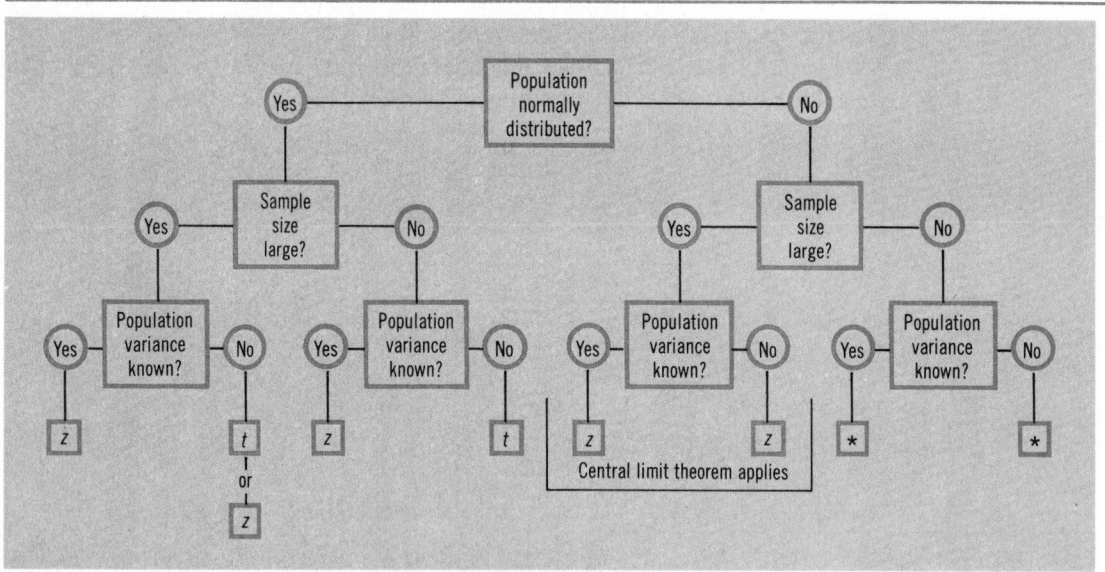

* = use a nonparametric procedure (Chapter 13)

EXERCISES

6.4.1 In a study to determine the feasibility of using a flexible plastic hose on a certain piece of machinery, engineers want to estimate the mean pressure to which the hose will be subjected. They take 9 pressure readings at random intervals throughout a 24-hour period of operation. The sample mean and standard deviation are 362 and 45, respectively. Assume that pressure readings are approximately normally distributed. Construct the 99% confidence interval for the true mean pressure.

6.4.2 A simple random sample of 16 radio stations is selected in order to estimate the average charge for the same fixed-length spot announcement. The sample mean and standard deviation are $15.50 and $8, respectively. Assume that the charges made by all radio stations of the type sampled are approximately normally distributed. Construct the 95% confidence interval for the population mean.

6.4.3 A record club wishes to know the average age of its members. A random sample of 100 members yields a mean age of 26 years with a standard deviation of 5 years. Assume that the population of ages is not normally distributed. Find the 95% confidence interval for μ.

6.4.4 © A soft-drink manufacturer wants to know the extent of customer preference for twist-off resealable tops for 32-ounce bottles. To investigate this, the manufacturer sets up a study in which the regular 32-ounce bottles are replaced with bottles with twist-off resealable tops in 16 randomly selected supermarkets in a certain area for a period of 1 month. The sales volume for each store for that month is compared with the same store's sales volume for the preceding month. The results (in hundreds of bottles) are as shown in the table. Construct a 95% confidence interval for μ_d based on $d_i = x_{1i} - x_{2i}$.

Store #	1	2	3	4	5	6	7	8	9	10	11	12	13	14	15	16
Test month (X_1)	44	61	46	55	49	50	45	64	40	62	53	54	57	55	61	52
Preceding month (X_2)	47	62	56	39	45	51	56	47	48	40	44	52	51	60	61	57

6.5 ESTIMATING THE DIFFERENCE BETWEEN TWO POPULATION MEANS—KNOWN POPULATION VARIANCES

We often want to know the difference between two population means $\mu_1 - \mu_2$. In the absence of direct knowledge of this difference, we estimate it from sample data. Chapter 5 shows that $\bar{x}_1 - \bar{x}_2$ is an unbiased estimator of $\mu_1 - \mu_2$. It also shows that, when two populations are normally distributed, the sampling distribution of $\bar{x}_1 - \bar{x}_2$, computed from *independent random samples*, is normally distributed, with a standard error given by

$$\sigma_{\bar{x}_1 - \bar{x}_2} = \sqrt{\frac{\sigma_1^2}{n_1} + \frac{\sigma_2^2}{n_2}}$$

We can construct a $100(1 - \alpha)\%$ confidence interval for $\mu_1 - \mu_2$, then, by

(6.5.1)

$$(\bar{x}_1 - \bar{x}_2) \pm z_{1-\alpha/2} \sqrt{\frac{\sigma_1^2}{n_1} + \frac{\sigma_2^2}{n_2}}$$

This applies when the sampled populations are normally distributed, the population variances are known, and the samples are randomly and independently drawn from the two populations. Here is an example of the construction of such an interval.

EXAMPLE 6.5.1   Xavier Manufacturing Company produces a synthetic fiber at two factories located in different parts of the country. Every effort is made to maintain uniformity of production between the two factories with respect to the mean breaking strength of the fiber. To determine whether the two factories are maintaining uniformity of production, the manufacturer selects a sample of 25 specimens from Factory 1 and a sample of 16 specimens from Factory 2. The objective is to construct a confidence interval for the difference between the two population means. The mean breaking strength of the sample from Factory 1 is 22 pounds. The mean of the sample from Factory 2 is 20 pounds. The variance in both factories is known to be 10 lb^2. The populations are normally distributed. The desired confidence coefficient is 0.95.

SOLUTION   The following 95% confidence interval is constructed using Formula 6.5.1:

$$(22 - 20) \pm 1.96 \sqrt{\frac{10}{25} + \frac{10}{16}}, \qquad 0.0, 4.0$$

The usual probabilistic and practical interpretations may be given to this interval.

EXERCISES

6.5.1   The York Petroleum Company wishes to compare credit-card holders in one area with those in another area. One question is how long the customers have held credit cards. A random sample of 100 card holders is selected from each area. The sample means are 156 months (Area 1) and 96 months (Area 2). The population variances for the two areas are 900 and 700, respectively. Construct a 95% confidence interval for the difference between population means.

6.5.2   A bank official who wants to know the difference between the average amount of money that customers have on deposit in two branch banks selects a random sample of 25 customers from each branch. The sample means are Branch A, \$450; Branch B, \$325. The two populations are normally distributed with variances $\sigma_A^2 = 750$ and $\sigma_B^2 = 850$. **(a)** Construct a 95% confidence interval for $\mu_A - \mu_B$.   **(b)** Construct a 99% confidence interval.

6.5.3   A firm hires a team of psychologists to study the difference between the characteristics of employees who attended a special training course and those who did not. The researchers examine a simple random sample of 50 employees who attended the course and an independent simple random sample of 60 who did not. At the end of 6 months, they give the employees a job-satisfaction test. Those who attended the course have a mean score of 4.50. Those who did not attend have a mean score of 3.75. Construct a 95% confidence interval for the difference between population means. On the basis of experience, the researchers assume that the two populations are approximately normally distributed. The variances are 1.8 for the population that attended the course and 2.1 for the population that did not.

6.5.4   [C] A researcher wants to construct a 95% confidence interval for the difference between the mean IQs of two groups of employees. The two populations of IQ scores are approximately normally distributed with variances of $\sigma_1^2 = 100$ and $\sigma_2^2 = 144$. Independent simple random samples of sizes $n_1 = 25$ and $n_2 = 16$ yield the following results.

Sample 1	108	107	101	108	103	109	103	116	116	115	111	116	109
	111	120	102	119	124	101	114	128	111	115	129	126	
Sample 2	116	98	94	89	124	99	114	114	99	89	110	117	99	94	92
	117												

What are the upper and lower limits of the desired confidence interval?

6.5.5   A counselor with Auden Fitness Centers wishes to compare the muscular power of young executives who exercise regularly with that of executives of the same age and sex who do not exercise regularly. The subjects consist of 40 randomly selected exercisers and 50 randomly selected nonexercisers. The means of the muscular endurance scores are 17.35 for exercisers and 15.19 for nonexercisers. The counselor feels that these scores are normally distributed. Experience shows that the variance for each group is about 2.25. The counselor would like to construct a 95% confidence interval for the difference between population means.

6.6   ESTIMATING THE DIFFERENCE BETWEEN TWO POPULATION MEANS — UNKNOWN POPULATION VARIANCES

Section 6.5 explains how to construct a confidence interval for the difference between two population means when the sampled populations are both normally distributed and the two population variances are known. But in real life, conditions are usually quite different. Sampled populations may be nonnormally distributed and/or population variances may be unknown. Here we consider three possible situations.

1. The populations are normally distributed, and the population variances are unknown but equal.

2. The populations are normally distributed, and the population variances are unknown and *un*equal.

3. The populations are not normally distributed, and the population variances are unknown.

NORMALLY DISTRIBUTED POPULATIONS, UNKNOWN BUT EQUAL VARIANCES

When we want to estimate the difference between two population means, we cannot use Formula 6.5.1 if the population variances are unknown. Suppose that the populations are normally distributed, the *population variances are unknown, but known to be equal,* and we draw independent random samples from each of the two populations of interest. We may then construct a confidence interval for $\mu_1 - \mu_2$ by using the t distribution to obtain a reliability factor and by estimating the population variances from sample data. Chapter 7 gives a procedure for determining whether or not two population variances are likely to be equal.

Pooling Sample Variances Say that the assumption of equal population variances is justified. Each of the sample variances computed from the two samples will be an estimate of the common variance σ^2. We capitalize on this fact by pooling the two sample estimates to obtain a single estimate of σ^2. To do this, we compute the weighted average of the two sample variances, where the weights are the degrees of freedom. If the sample sizes are equal, the weighted average is merely the arithmetic mean of the two sample variances. If, however, the two sample sizes are unequal, the weighted average takes advantage of the additional information provided by the larger sample. The pooled estimate of the common σ^2 is given by

(6.6.1)
$$s_p^2 = \frac{(n_1 - 1)s_1^2 + (n_2 - 1)s_2^2}{n_1 + n_2 - 2}$$

The estimated standard error of the estimator, $\overline{x}_1 - \overline{x}_2$, then, is

$$\sqrt{\frac{s_p^2}{n_1} + \frac{s_p^2}{n_2}}$$

s_p^2 is a weighted average of sample variances in which the weights are degrees of freedom

It can be shown that

$$t = \frac{(\overline{x}_1 - \overline{x}_2) - (\mu_1 - \mu_2)}{\sqrt{\frac{s_p^2}{n_1} + \frac{s_p^2}{n_2}}}$$

follows the t distribution with $n_1 + n_2 - 2$ degrees of freedom. This justifies the use of t as a reliability factor in the confidence interval for $\mu_1 - \mu_2$ under the conditions mentioned.

In summary, we may state the following:

When random and independent samples of size n_1 and n_2, respectively, are drawn from two normally distributed populations with unknown but equal variances, the $100(1 - \alpha)\%$ confidence interval for $\mu_1 - \mu_2$ is given by

(6.6.2)
$$(\bar{x}_1 - \bar{x}_2) \pm t_{1-\alpha/2}\sqrt{\frac{s_p^2}{n_1} + \frac{s_p^2}{n_2}}$$

EXAMPLE 6.6.1 Experimenters with Bancroft Chemicals test two types of fertilizer for possible use in the cultivation of cabbages. They grow the cabbages in two different fields. One of the two fertilizers is applied in each field. At harvest time they select a random sample of 25 cabbages from the crop grown with Fertilizer I. They randomly select 12 cabbages from the crop grown with Fertilizer II. The sample mean and variance of the weights of cabbages grown with Fertilizer I are 44.1 oz and 36 oz^2. The mean weight computed from the second sample is 31.7 oz, and the variance is 44 oz^2. The experimenters assume that the two populations of weights are normally distributed. They also assume that the two population variances are equal.

SOLUTION   We first compute the following pooled estimate of σ^2:

$$s_p^2 = \frac{24(36) + 11(44)}{25 + 12 - 2} = \frac{864 + 484}{35} = \frac{1348}{35} = 38.51$$

Formula 6.6.2 is used to compute the 95% confidence interval for $\mu_I - \mu_{II}$.

$$(44.1 - 31.7) \pm 2.0301\sqrt{\frac{38.51}{25} + \frac{38.51}{12}}, \qquad 8.0, 16.8$$

UNEQUAL POPULATION VARIANCES

When the population variances are unequal, we may not use the t distribution as previously outlined to construct confidence intervals for the difference between two means, even if the populations are normally distributed. This is a problem of no small consequence, since it seems reasonable that in many practical cases we cannot expect two population variances to be equal.

The problem results from the fact that the quantity

$$\frac{(\bar{x}_1 - \bar{x}_2) - (\mu_1 - \mu_2)}{\sqrt{\frac{s_1^2}{n_1} + \frac{s_2^2}{n_2}}}$$

does not follow a t distribution with $n_1 + n_2 - 2$ degrees of freedom when the population variances are not equal. Consequently, we cannot use the table of the t distribution in the usual way to obtain the reliability factor for the confidence interval for the difference between the means of two populations that have unequal variances. A solution to this problem, proposed by W. G. Cochran, consists of computing the reliability factor $t'_{1-\alpha/2}$ by the following formula:

When population variances are not equal, we use a special formula to obtain the reliability factor.

(6.6.3)
$$t'_{1-\alpha/2} = \frac{w_1 t_1 + w_2 t_2}{w_1 + w_2}$$

where $w_1 = s_1^2/n_1$, $w_2 = s_2^2/n_2$, $t_1 = t_{1-\alpha/2}$ for $n_1 - 1$ degrees of freedom, and $t_2 = t_{1-\alpha/2}$ for $n_2 - 1$ degrees of freedom.

An approximate $100(1 - \alpha)\%$ confidence interval for $\mu_1 - \mu_2$ is given by

(6.6.4)
$$(\bar{x}_1 - \bar{x}_2) \pm t'_{1-\alpha/2} \sqrt{\frac{s_1^2}{n_1} + \frac{s_2^2}{n_2}}$$

We interpret a confidence interval obtained using Equation 6.6.4 in the usual manner, but we should remember that the limits are only approximate.

EXAMPLE 6.6.2   Refer to Example 6.6.1. Assume, for illustrative purposes, that the two population variances are not equal.

SOLUTION   In preparing to use Equation 6.6.4 to construct a confidence interval for $\mu_1 - \mu_2$, we proceed as follows.

In Table E of Appendix I, we find that for 95% confidence, $t_1 = 2.0639$ and $t_2 = 2.2010$. We compute $w_1 = 36/25 = 1.44$ and $w_2 = 44/12 = 3.6667$. By Equation 6.6.3, we compute

$$t' = \frac{(1.44)(2.0639) + (3.6667)()2.2010)}{1.44 + 3.6667}$$

$$= 2.1623$$

The approximate 95% confidence interval for $\mu_1 - \mu_2$ is

$$(44.1 - 31.7) \pm 2.1623 \sqrt{\frac{36}{25} + \frac{44}{12}}, \quad 7.5, 17.3$$

NONNORMALLY DISTRIBUTED POPULATIONS AND UNKNOWN VARIANCES

When we seek a confidence interval for the difference between two means, we may find that not only are the two population variances unknown, but the populations are not normally distributed. However, if n_1 and n_2 are both large, the central limit theorem applies, and we may use s_1^2 and s_2^2 to estimate σ_1^2 and σ_2^2. Under these circumstances, an approximate $100(1 - \alpha)\%$ confidence interval for $\mu_1 - \mu_2$ is given by

(6.6.5)
$$(\bar{x}_1 - \bar{x}_2) \pm z_{1-\alpha/2} \sqrt{\frac{s_1^2}{n_1} + \frac{s_2^2}{n_2}}$$

FIGURE 6.6.1 Flow chart for deciding between *z* and *t* when making inferences about the difference between two population means

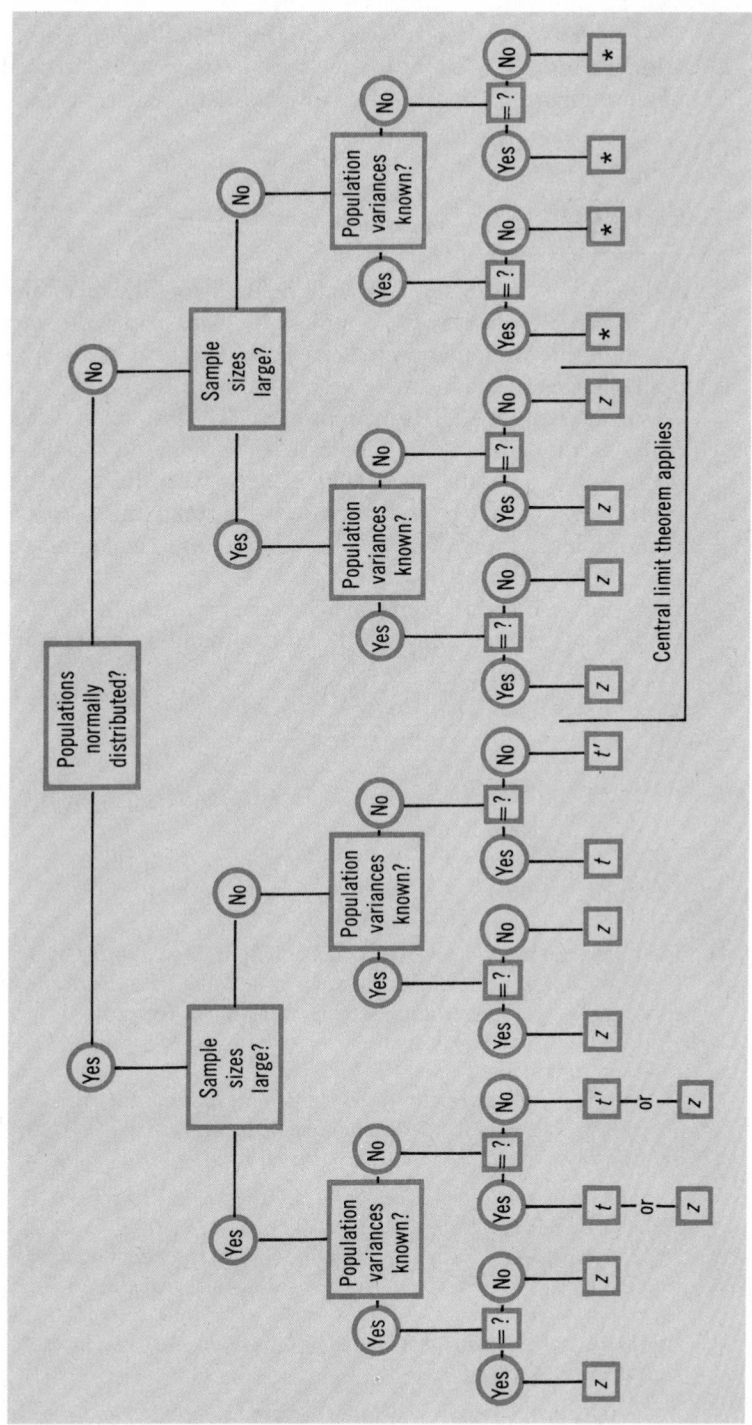

* = use a nonparametric procedure (Chapter 13)

When constructing confidence intervals for the difference between two population means, we must decide whether to use z or t as the reliability factor. We may use Figure 6.6.1 as a guide in making the correct choice.

COMPUTER **ANALYSIS**

Both STAT+ and MINITAB may be used to construct confidence intervals for the difference between two population means under the various conditions discussed in this section and the preceding section. Where necessary, as determined from the user's responses to the questions it asks, STAT+ automatically pools the sample variances. When you use MINITAB to construct a confidence interval in the two-independent-sample case, the command should include a confidence coefficient if one other than 0.95 is desired. If the sample variances should be pooled, this should be indicated in a subcommand. Suppose that we have the data of sample 1 and the data of sample 2 stored in columns 1 and 2, respectively of a MINITAB worksheet. For a 99% confidence interval for the difference between two population means when the two unknown population variances are assumed to be equal, the MINITAB command and subcommand are

MINITAB

```
MTB > TWOSAMPLE 0.99 C1 C2;
SUBC > POOLED.
```

EXERCISES

6.6.1 The difference in the ages of patients admitted to two different hospitals is of interest to The Booth Insurance Company, which is studying patterns of use of health facilities in a certain area. A simple random sample of discharge records is drawn from the files of each of the two hospitals, with the following results: for Hospital A, $n = 22$, $\bar{x} = 54.5$, $s^2 = 256$; and for Hospital B, $n = 20$, $\bar{x} = 39.4$, $s^2 = 200$. It is felt that the two populations are approximately normally distributed. (a) Assume that the two population variances are equal. Construct the 95% confidence interval for $\mu_A - \mu_B$. (b) Assume that $\sigma_A^2 \neq \sigma_B^2$. Construct the 95% confidence interval for $\mu_A - \mu_B$.

6.6.2 A telephone answering service completes a report on each call received, noting the length of the call. The answering service serves only two types of clients. A simple random sample of 225 records for the Type A client and an independent, simple random sample of 100 records for the Type B client give the following means and variances for length of call: $\bar{x}_A = 121.4$ seconds, $\bar{x}_B = 93.5$ seconds, $s_A^2 = 900$, $s_B^2 = 1200$. Assume that the populations are not normally distributed and have unequal variances. Compute the 90% confidence interval for $\mu_A - \mu_B$.

6.6.3 At Carter Ironworks, two machines are used to produce metal rods. A random sample of 11 rods from Machine A and a random sample of 21 rods from Machine B give these results with respect to the lengths of metal rods produced: $\bar{x}_A = 5.95$ in., $\bar{x}_B = 6.01$ in.,

$s_A^2 = 0.018$, $s_B^2 = 0.020$. Assume that the populations are approximately normally distributed. (a) Assume that the population variances are equal. Construct the 95% confidence interval for $\mu_A - \mu_B$. (b) Do part (a) on the assumption that the two population variances are not equal.

6.6.4 A research team wishes to know by how much, on the average, employees who have problems with alcohol and those who do not differ with respect to self-control. The researchers give a test designed to measure self-control to $n_1 = 21$ employees who do not have problems with alcohol and $n_2 = 16$ problem drinkers. The results are as follows: $\bar{x}_1 = 29.75$, $s_1^2 = 68.06$, $\bar{x}_2 = 24.50$, $s_2^2 = 47.61$. The researchers believe that the test yields scores that are approximately normally distributed. The sample variances are not equal, but the researchers believe that the population variances are equal. Construct a 95% confidence interval for the difference between population means.

6.7 ESTIMATING A POPULATION PROPORTION

In many business situations, we want to know what proportion of items in a population have a certain characteristic. A firm may want to find out what proportion of its customers would respond favorably to a change in the way service is provided. A company may want to know what proportion of its employees have not completed high school. A manufacturer may want to know what proportion of rejected items are rejected because of defective material.

To estimate a population proportion, we do the same things we did when we estimated a population mean. We randomly draw a sample of size n from the population of interest and compute the sample proportion $\hat{p}$. We use this sample proportion as a point estimate of the population proportion. We obtain a confidence interval for the population proportion by the general formula

Estimate ± (reliability factor) × (standard error)

For estimating p, the reliability factor is z.

Chapter 5 shows that when both np and $n(1-p)$ are greater than 5, the sampling distribution of $\hat{p}$ is approximately normal, with mean p and standard error $\sigma_{\hat{p}} = \sqrt{p(1-p)/n}$. Since we are looking for an estimate of p, it must be unknown. Therefore, in practical situations, we use $\hat{p}$ rather than p in the formula for the standard error. We obtain the estimate $s_{\hat{p}} = \sqrt{\hat{p}(1-\hat{p})/n}$. When we can consider the sampling distribution of $\hat{p}$ as approximately normal, we can obtain the reliability factor in the formula for the confidence interval from the table of the standard normal distribution. As indicated in Chapter 5, if the sample constitutes more than 5% of the population, we should use the finite population correction factor. The examples and exercises that follow assume that n is sufficiently small relative to N that the correction factor is not needed.

In summary, then, we may state the following:

When np and $n(1 - p)$ are both greater than 5 and when n is small relative to the size of the population, the approximate $100(1 - \alpha)\%$ confidence interval for p is given by

(6.7.1)

$$\hat{p} \pm z_{1-\alpha/2} \sqrt{\frac{\hat{p}(1-\hat{p})}{n}}$$

This interval is given the usual probabilistic and practical interpretations.

EXAMPLE 6.7.1   The personnel director at Desmond Dairy Products is trying to find out what proportion of all persons who have ever been interviewed for any position have been hired. A 95% confidence interval is desired. A random sample of 500 interview records reveals that 76 (or 0.152) of the persons in the sample have been hired.

SOLUTION   The 95% confidence interval for the population proportion, by Equation 6.7.1, is

$$0.152 \pm 1.96 \sqrt{\frac{(0.152)(0.848)}{500}}, \quad 0.152 \pm 0.031, \quad 0.121, 0.183$$

The interpretation of this interval is the same as the interpretation of the confidence interval for the arithmetic mean. In the long run, 95% of the intervals constructed in this manner will include the population proportion. We are therefore 95% confident that the interval actually constructed contains the population proportion.

COMPUTER **ANALYSIS**

STAT+ constructs confidence intervals for population proportions. The required input is n, $\hat{p}$, and the confidence coefficient.

EXERCISES

6.7.1   A consultant for an association of personnel directors wants to find out what proportion of clerical personnel who change jobs do so because they are bored with their work. The consultant queries a random sample of 400 clerical workers who recently changed jobs. Two hundred state that they changed jobs because they were bored. The consultant prepares a 95% confidence interval for the proportion in the population changing jobs because of boredom. What are the lower and upper limits of this interval?

6.7.2   The Ellis Manufacturing Company wishes to estimate the proportion of its employees who have read with retention a safety leaflet that was distributed the previous week to all employees. A random sample of 300 employees is given a test to measure retention of the contents of the leaflet. Of those tested, 75 make a passing score. Construct a 95% confidence interval for the proportion in the population retaining sufficient knowledge of the contents of the leaflet to make a passing score.

6.7.3 In a study of the reasons for employee turnover, an investigator draws a sample of 200 from a population of former employees of a firm. Of the 200, 140 say that they left because they could not get along with their supervisors. Construct a 95% confidence interval for the proportion in the population who left the firm for this reason.

6.7.4 When you interview a random sample of 175 adults, 79 tell you that they feel that their community's most pressing social problem is drug and alcohol abuse. Construct a 95% confidence interval for the proportion in the population who hold that opinion.

6.8 ESTIMATING THE DIFFERENCE BETWEEN TWO POPULATION PROPORTIONS

It is often worthwhile to have some idea of the magnitude of the difference between two population proportions. For example, we may wish to compare—with respect to some characteristic of interest—men and women, two age groups, two types of firms, two socioeconomic groups, or two factories.

To estimate $p_1 - p_2$, the difference between the population proportions, we draw a simple random sample from each of the populations and use $\hat{p}_1 - \hat{p}_2$, the difference between the sample proportions. We may construct an interval estimate in the usual manner.

Chapter 5 shows that when n_1 and n_2 are both large, and the population proportions are not too close to 0 or 1, the sampling distribution of $\hat{p}_1 - \hat{p}_2$ for independent samples is approximately normally distributed with mean $p_1 - p_2$ and standard error

$$\sigma_{\hat{p}_1 - \hat{p}_2} = \sqrt{\frac{p_1(1 - p_1)}{n_1} + \frac{p_2(1 - p_2)}{n_2}}$$

Since p_1 and p_2 are unknown, the standard error has to be estimated by

$$s_{\hat{p}_1 - \hat{p}_2} = \sqrt{\frac{\hat{p}_1(1 - \hat{p}_1)}{n_1} + \frac{\hat{p}_2(1 - \hat{p}_2)}{n_2}}$$

For estimating $p_1 - p_2$, the reliability factor is z.

Under the given conditions, then, an approximate $100(1 - \alpha)\%$ confidence interval for $p_1 - p_2$ is given by

(6.8.1)
$$(\hat{p}_1 - \hat{p}_2) \pm z_{1-\alpha/2} \sqrt{\frac{\hat{p}_1(1 - \hat{p}_1)}{n_1} + \frac{\hat{p}_2(1 - \hat{p}_2)}{n_2}}$$

EXAMPLE 6.8.1 The Foxe-Slye ad agency conducts a survey to study the characteristics of subscribers to two newspapers. A random sample of 500 subscribers to Newspaper A reveals that 300 have annual incomes in excess of $50,000. In the case of Newspaper B, 200 out of a random sample of 500 subscribers have annual incomes in excess of $50,000. Construct a 95% confidence interval for the difference between the two proportions of subscribers with annual incomes in excess of $50,000.

SOLUTION   From the information given, we compute $\hat{p}_A = 300/500 = 0.6$ and $\hat{p}_B = 200/500 = 0.4$. Substituting in Equation 6.8.1 gives the desired interval:

$$(0.6 - 0.4) \pm 1.96 \sqrt{\frac{(0.6)(1 - 0.6)}{500} + \frac{(0.4)(1 - 0.4)}{500}}$$

$$0.2 \pm 1.96(0.03), \quad 0.14, 0.26$$

We are 95% confident that the true difference is between 0.14 and 0.26 because in the long run approximately 95% of the intervals constructed in this manner would include the true difference.

COMPUTER **ANALYSIS**

STAT+ constructs confidence intervals for the difference between two proportions. The required input is n_1, n_2, $\hat{p}_1$, $\hat{p}_2$, and the confidence coefficient.

EXERCISES

6.8.1   Doctors who have developed a new drug for the treatment of a certain disease treat a sample of 400 patients suffering from the disease with the new drug. They treat another sample of 400 patients with an alternative drug. At the end of two weeks, 320 of the patients receiving the new drug recover, whereas 240 of those taking the alternative drug recover. Construct a 95% confidence interval for the difference between the two population proportions of patients who might be expected to respond to the two drugs.

6.8.2   A random sample of 350 salespersons and an independent random sample of 325 executives are questioned about their reading habits. Of the 350 salespersons, 105 say that they subscribe to car magazines. Of the executives, 130 say that they subscribe to car magazines. Construct a 90% confidence interval for the difference between the two population proportions subscribing to car magazines.

6.8.3   In a study of the types of errors made by employees in two factories owned by the same firm, researchers note the following facts. Construct a 95% confidence interval for $p_A - p_B$.

Factory	A	C
n	200	225
Proportion of errors due to employee carelessness	0.32	0.25

6.8.4   A random sample of 200 female clerical workers and an independent random sample of 200 male clerical workers participate in a study conducted by a psychologist. In this study, 32 of the men and 11 of the women exhibit an intense dislike for their jobs. Construct a 99% confidence interval for the difference between the two population proportions.

6.9 DETERMINING SAMPLE SIZE FOR ESTIMATING MEANS

Up to this point, the problems and exercises have specified the sample size being used. But they have not mentioned how a particular sample size was decided on. We need a method for determining how large a sample to take. Suppose that we want to estimate, with a confidence interval, the mean of a population. One of the first questions to arise is, How large should the sample be? We must consider this question seriously. It is a waste of resources to take a larger sample than we need to achieve the desired results. Similarly, if the sample is too small, the results may be of no practical value. The key questions that bear on this problem are these:

To determine *n* for estimating μ, we need to know
1. desired precision.
2. desired confidence.
3. σ^2.

1. What precision is desired? That is, how close do we want our estimate to be to the true value? In other words, how wide would we like to make the confidence interval that we want to construct?

2. How much confidence do we want to place in our interval? That is, what confidence coefficient do we wish to employ?

3. How much variability is present in the population to be sampled?

These questions bring to mind the nature of the confidence interval that we will eventually construct. This interval will be of the form

$$\bar{x} \pm z \frac{\sigma}{\sqrt{n}}$$

if we can ignore the finite population correction factor. The quantity

$$z \frac{\sigma}{\sqrt{n}}$$

is equal to one-half the confidence interval. If we can answer the first question, we can set up the following equation:

(6.9.1)
$$d = z \frac{\sigma}{\sqrt{n}}$$

where *d* indicates how close to the true mean we want our estimate to be. Stated another way, we may think of *d* as the amount of discrepancy that we are willing to tolerate between the true value of the parameter we are estimating and our estimate. That is, *d* is equal to one-half the desired interval width. If we solve Equation 6.9.1 for *n*,

(6.9.2)
$$n = \frac{z^2 \sigma^2}{d^2}$$

Thus, if we can specify d, z, and σ^2 in advance, it is a simple matter to find n. We merely substitute the specified values into Equation 6.9.2.

The value we specify for d varies from case to case. If we want a narrow interval, d will be small. The value of z depends on the level of confidence we want. For example, if the level of confidence is $1 - \alpha$, the z value is $z_{1-\alpha}$. And σ^2 depends on the variability present in the population of interest. As a general rule, σ^2 is unknown and has to be estimated.

ESTIMATING σ^2

The most frequently used methods of estimating σ^2 are the following:

Possible sources of estimates of σ:
1. Pilot sample
2. Similar studies
3. R/6

1. We may use the variance computed from a *pilot* or preliminary sample, drawn from the population of interest, as an estimate of σ^2. We may count observations used in the pilot sample as part of the final sample. Therefore, the number of observations we need after drawing the pilot sample is equal to $n - n_1$, where n is equal to the computed sample size and n_1 is the number of observations in the pilot sample.

2. We may have estimates of σ^2 from previous or similar studies.

3. If we feel that the population from which the sample is to be drawn is approximately normally distributed, we may use the fact that the range is approximately equal to 6 standard deviations to compute $\sigma \approx R/6$. This method requires some knowledge of the smallest and largest values of the variable in the population.

When sampling is without replacement from a finite population, the finite population correction is appropriate. Equation 6.9.1 becomes

(6.9.3)
$$d = z \frac{\sigma}{\sqrt{n}} \sqrt{\frac{N - n}{N - 1}}$$

which, when solved for n, gives

(6.9.4)
$$n = \frac{Nz^2\sigma^2}{d^2(N - 1) + z^2\sigma^2}$$

If we ignore the finite population correction, Equation 6.9.4 reduces to Equation 6.9.2.

EXAMPLE 6.9.1 The Grant-Harding advertising firm wants to estimate the average amount of money that a certain type of store spent on advertising during the past year. Experience has shown the population variance to be about 1,800,000. How large a sample should the advertising firm take in order for the estimate to be within $500 of the true mean with 95% confidence?

SOLUTION   Substituting the given data into Equation 6.9.2, we have

$$n = \frac{(1.96)^2(1,800,000)}{(500)^2} = 27.65 \approx 28$$

The advertising firm should take a sample of 28 establishments. (Note that n is always rounded up. For example, if the formula yields 27.1, we round up to 28.)

The Two-Sample Case By a straightforward extension of the method used to develop a formula for determining the sample size needed to estimate a single population mean, we also may derive a sample-size formula for the two-independent-sample case. We assume either that the two populations to be sampled are normally distributed or that the sample sizes will be large enough so that we can apply the central limit theorem. We also assume that the finite population correction factor is not needed.

We again designate one-half of the desired interval width by d. We write

(6.9.5)

$$d = z \sqrt{\frac{\sigma_1^2}{n_1} + \frac{\sigma_2^2}{n_2}}$$

Squaring both sides of this equation yields

$$d^2 = z^2 \left(\frac{\sigma_1^2}{n_1} + \frac{\sigma_2^2}{n_2} \right)$$

Let us assume that n_1 and n_2 are equal, that is, $n_1 = n_2 = n$. We have

$$d^2 = z^2 \left(\frac{\sigma_1^2 + \sigma_2^2}{n} \right) \qquad \text{or} \qquad nd^2 = z^2(\sigma_1^2 + \sigma_2^2)$$

When we solve for n, we have

(6.9.6)

$$n = \frac{z^2(\sigma_1^2 + \sigma_2^2)}{d^2}$$

To find n for a given application, we need only specify d, the level of confidence desired (in order to determine z), and the values of σ_1^2 and σ_2^2. The population variances, usually unknown, may be estimated by the usual methods.

The following example illustrates the use of Formula 6.9.6.

EXAMPLE 6.9.2   A researcher wishes to know whether the mean length of employment with the current firm at time of retirement is different for men and women. The researcher would like to have a confidence-interval estimate of the difference between the two population means. The specifications are a confidence-interval width of 1 year ($d = 0.5$) and 95% confidence. Pilot samples yielded variances of 5 and 7. The researcher wants samples of equal size. What size sample should be drawn from each population?

SOLUTION   By Equation 6.9.6, we have

$$n = \frac{(1.96)^2(5 + 7)}{(0.5)^2} = 184.4 \approx 185$$

We need a sample of 185 men and an independent sample of 185 women. Again, note that d is equal to one-half the width of the desired confidence interval. Thus, since the desired interval width is 1 year, d is equal to 0.5 year.

EXERCISES

6.9.1   A plastics firm wishes to estimate the mean impact strength of a spool. How many spools should the company test if it wishes to be within 20 psi of the true value with 99% confidence? Previous experience indicates that an acceptable estimate of σ^2 is 4,900.

6.9.2   A consultant for the Kemble motel chain wants to estimate the average number of miles driven per day by families on vacation. The consultant obtains the names and addresses of vacationing families who stayed at motels in the chain during the past year. How large a sample should the consultant select in order to estimate the average daily mileage to within 25 miles with 95% confidence? It is felt that a reasonable estimate of σ^2 is 18,000.

6.9.3   A researcher with a company that employs 2,500 workers wishes to estimate the mean travel time between the company and the employees' homes. The investigator wants a 99% confidence interval and an estimate that will be within 1 minute of the true mean. A small pilot sample yields a variance of 25 minutes squared. What size sample should the researcher draw?

6.9.4   A psychologist wants to construct an interval estimate of the mean IQ of a certain population of employees. The estimate is to be within 5 points of the true mean with 95% confidence. Previous experience indicates that the IQs for the population of interest are approximately normally distributed with a variance of 100. The psychologist wants to know how large a sample to draw from the population.

6.9.5   A realtor wishes to estimate, for Areas A and B, the difference in the mean number of days elapsing between the time houses are placed on the market and the time they are sold. A confidence coefficient of 0.95 and an interval width of 10 days are desired. Pilot samples from the two areas yielded $s_A = 21$ and $s_B = 24$. What size sample should be selected from each area ($n_1 = n_2$)?

6.9.6   A market research firm wishes to estimate the difference in the mean number of cigarettes smoked per week by two populations of cigarette smokers. A confidence coefficient of 0.99 and an interval width of 20 are desired. Estimates of the population variances are 225 and 250. What size sample should be drawn from each population ($n_1 = n_2$)?

6.10   DETERMINING SAMPLE SIZE FOR ESTIMATING PROPORTIONS

When we estimate a population proportion, we determine the sample size in about the same way as that described for estimating a population mean. We set half the desired interval d equal to the product of the reliability factor and the standard error. The assumption of random sampling and conditions warranting approximate normality of the distribution of $\hat{p}$ lead to the following formula for n, when sampling is with replacement or is from an infinite population:

(6.10.1)

$$n = \frac{z^2 pq}{d^2}$$

where $q = 1 - p$. If sampling is *without* replacement, the proper formula for n is

(6.10.2)

$$n = \frac{Nz^2 pq}{d^2(N - 1) + z^2 pq}$$

When N is large in comparison to n (that is, $n/N \leq 0.05$), we may ignore the finite population correction, and Equation 6.10.2 reduces to Equation 6.10.1.

To determine n for estimating p, we need to know
1. desired precision.
2. desired confidence.
3. an estimate of p.

Both formulas require a knowledge of p, the proportion of elements in the population with the characteristic of interest. This is the parameter to be estimated. Obviously, it is unknown. Again, we may take a pilot sample and compute an estimate to use in place of p in the formula for n. Alternatively, we may have a good notion of the likely value of p that we can use in the formula. For example, a personnel director who wants to estimate the proportion of employees who have not completed high school may feel that p is about 0.10. In the formula for n, 0.10 would be used for p.

If we cannot obtain a better estimate, we may set p equal to 0.5 in the formula for n. This gives a sample of sufficient size for the desired reliability and interval width since it yields the maximum sample size. It may be larger than we need, however, in which case the sample will be more expensive than it would have been had we had a better estimate of p available. Use this procedure only if you cannot obtain a better estimate of p.

EXAMPLE 6.10.1   The Lincoln and Lind market research firm wants to estimate the proportion of households in a certain area that have color television sets. The firm would like to estimate p to within 0.05 with 95% confidence. No estimate of p is available.

SOLUTION   Since no better estimate of p is available, we must use 0.5. When appropriate substitutions are made in Equation 6.10.1, we have

$$n = \frac{(1.96)^2 (0.5)(0.5)}{(0.05)^2} = 385$$

The Two-Sample Case In a manner similar to that used to derive a sample-size formula for estimating the difference between two population means, we may derive a sample-size formula for estimating the difference between two population proportions. We assume that the populations to be sampled are large enough for us to apply the normal approximation to the binomial distribution. We also assume that the samples are of equal size. From the relationship

(6.10.3)

$$d = z \sqrt{\frac{p_1(1 - p_1)}{n_1} + \frac{p_2(1 - p_2)}{n_2}}$$

we derive, when $n_1 = n_2 = n$,

(6.10.4)

$$n = \frac{z^2[p_1(1 - p_1) + p_2(1 - p_2)]}{d^2}$$

where d is, as usual, one-half the desired interval width. The parameters p_1 and p_2 are estimated in the usual ways.

EXAMPLE 6.10.2   For two populations of consumers, a researcher wants to estimate the difference between the proportions of those who have used a particular brand of coffee. A confidence coefficient of 0.95 and an interval width of 0.10 are desired. Estimates of p_1 and p_2 are 0.20 and 0.25, respectively. How large should the sample sizes be ($n_1 = n_2$)?

SOLUTION   By Equation 6.10.4, we have

$$n = \frac{1.96^2[(0.20)(0.80) + (0.25)(0.75)]}{(0.05)^2} = 533.9824 \approx 534$$

The researcher should draw a sample of size 534 from each population.

EXERCISES

6.10.1   An urban university will offer Saturday classes if student demand is sufficiently high. What size sample of students should you poll in order to estimate with 95% confidence, and to within 0.05, the proportion of students who would register for Saturday classes if they were offered? Assume that no estimate of p is available.

6.10.2   A specialist in industrial medicine wants to determine what proportion of all shoe factories require an employee to provide a doctor's certificate for three or more days' absence for illness. What size sample should the researcher take in order to be within 0.05 of the true value with 95% confidence? The researcher feels that the true proportion cannot be more than 0.30.

6.10.3   A market research analyst wishes to know how large a sample of the homes in a certain community to draw in order to find out in what proportion of the homes at least one member has seen a certain newspaper ad. There are 500 homes in the community. The analyst wants to be within 0.04 of the true proportion with 90% confidence. In a pilot sample of 20 homes, 35% of the respondents indicate that someone in the home has seen the ad. How large a sample should be drawn?

6.10.4   For two populations of drivers, an insurance executive wants to estimate the difference in the proportions of those who regularly wear seat belts. A confidence coefficient of 0.95 and an interval width of 0.12 are desired. Estimates of p_1 and p_2 are 0.25 and 0.18, respectively. How large should the samples be ($n_1 = n_2$)?

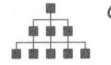

6.10.5   For two populations of employees, an industrial psychologist wishes to estimate the difference in the population proportions of those who have been sexually harassed at their place of employment. A confidence coefficient of 0.90 and an interval width of 0.14 are desired. How many employees should be selected from each population ($n_1 = n_2$)? Estimates of p_1 and p_2 are 0.10 and 0.28, respectively.

6.11 ESTIMATING THE VARIANCE OF A NORMALLY DISTRIBUTED POPULATION

We often want to know the magnitude of a population variance. Manufacturers of household appliances, for example, want to know the variability in the quality of their product in order to establish warranty periods. A drug manufacturer, in order to prepare truthful advertising copy, needs to know the variability of patient response to a given drug.

We usually do not know population variances. Consequently we must estimate them from sample data. In the typical case, interval estimates are more useful than point estimates. We usually base confidence intervals for σ^2 on the sampling distribution of $(n - 1)s^2/\sigma^2$.

THE SAMPLING DISTRIBUTION OF $(n - 1)s^2/\sigma^2$

We can approximate the sampling distribution of $(n - 1)s^2/\sigma^2$ empirically, using the following steps.

1. Draw a large number of simple random samples of size n from a normally distributed population with a known variance σ^2.
2. Compute s^2 from the data of each sample.
3. Use each value of s^2 to compute $(n - 1)s^2/\sigma^2$.
4. Construct the frequency distribution of $(n - 1)s^2/\sigma^2$.

The resulting sampling distribution is an approximation of the sampling distribution of $(n - 1)s^2/\sigma^2$. This is distributed as a well-known distribution called the *chi-square distribution*. If we were to graph this sampling distribution, it would resemble a chi-square distribution with $n - 1$ degrees of freedom. The larger the number of samples drawn, the closer the graph of the empirical sampling distribution is to the corresponding chi-square distribution. Computer simulation is a very effective method of constructing empirical sampling distributions of this type. We discuss the chi-square distribution, designated by the Greek letter χ^2, in greater detail in Chapter 12.

Note that the chi-square distribution, unlike the normal and t distributions, is asymmetrical. Like the t distribution, the chi-square distribution is a family of distributions. There is a different distribution for each possible value of degrees of freedom, $n - 1$.

Chi-square distributions are asymmetrical.

Figures 6.11.1 and 6.11.2 show some chi-square distributions for several values of degrees of freedom. Table F gives percentiles of the chi-square distribution.

To construct a $100(1 - \alpha)\%$ confidence interval for σ^2, we first obtain an interval about $(n - 1)s^2/\sigma^2$. We select two values of χ^2 from Table F in Appendix I in such a way that $\alpha/2$ is to the left of the smaller value and $\alpha/2$ is to the right of the larger value. If we call these two values $\chi^2_{\alpha/2}$ and $\chi^2_{1-\alpha/2}$, respectively, the following probability statement is true:

(6.11.1)
$$P\left[\chi^2_{\alpha/2} < \frac{(n - 1)s^2}{\sigma^2} < \chi^2_{1-\alpha/2}\right] = 1 - \alpha$$

We can rewrite Equation 6.11.1 in such a way that we get an expression with σ^2 alone as the middle term. First we divide each term by $(n - 1)s^2$ to get

(6.11.2)
$$P\left[\frac{\chi^2_{\alpha/2}}{(n - 1)s^2} < \frac{1}{\sigma^2} < \frac{\chi^2_{1-\alpha/2}}{(n - 1)s^2}\right] = 1 - \alpha$$

Taking the reciprocal of Equation 6.11.2 yields

(6.11.3)
$$P\left[\frac{(n - 1)s^2}{\chi^2_{\alpha/2}} > \sigma^2 > \frac{(n - 1)s^2}{\chi^2_{1-\alpha/2}}\right] = 1 - \alpha$$

Taking reciprocals changes the direction of the inequalities. If we reverse the order of the terms, the result is

(6.11.4)
$$P\left[\frac{(n - 1)s^2}{\chi^2_{1-\alpha/2}} < \sigma^2 < \frac{(n - 1)s^2}{\chi^2_{\alpha/2}}\right] = 1 - \alpha$$

The lower limit of the confidence interval for σ^2 is

$$\frac{(n - 1)s^2}{\chi^2_{1-\alpha/2}}$$

The upper limit is

$$\frac{(n - 1)s^2}{\chi^2_{\alpha/2}}$$

We say, then, that we are $100(1 - \alpha)\%$ confident that the population variance, σ^2, is somewhere between

$$\frac{(n - 1)s^2}{\chi^2_{1-\alpha/2}} \quad \text{and} \quad \frac{(n - 1)s^2}{\chi^2_{\alpha/2}}$$

FIGURE 6.11.1   Chi-square distributions for selected degrees of freedom

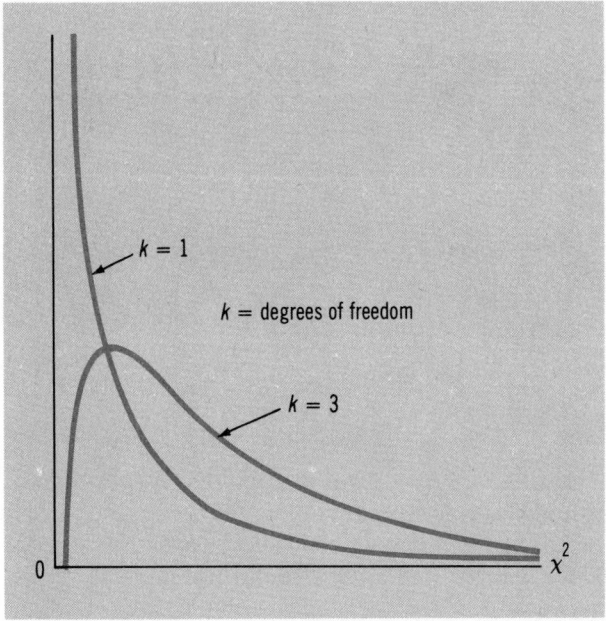

FIGURE 6.11.2   Chi-square distributions for selected degrees of freedom

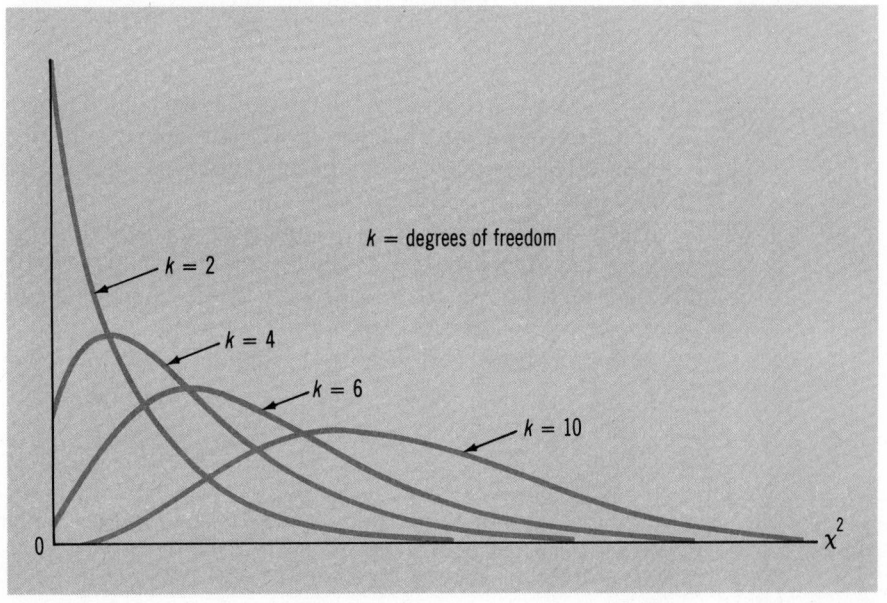

Taking the square root of each term in Equation 6.11.4 yields the following probability statement about σ, the population standard deviation:

(6.11.5)
$$P\left[\sqrt{\frac{(n-1)s^2}{\chi^2_{1-\alpha/2}}} < \sigma < \sqrt{\frac{(n-1)s^2}{\chi^2_{\alpha/2}}}\right] = 1 - \alpha$$

The lower limit of the confidence interval is

$$\sqrt{\frac{(n-1)s^2}{\chi^2_{1-\alpha/2}}}$$

and the upper limit is

$$\sqrt{\frac{(n-1)s^2}{\chi^2_{\alpha/2}}}$$

EXAMPLE 6.11.1 As part of its quality-control program, a firm that makes wrought-iron sheets wants to estimate the variance of weight per square foot of its product. A random sample of 51 specimens yields a variance of 0.021 pounds squared. We want to find a 95% confidence interval for σ^2.

SOLUTION The χ^2 values for 50 degrees of freedom are $\chi^2_{1-\alpha/2} = 71.420$ and $\chi^2_{\alpha/2} = 32.357$. When we substitute these values and the information from the example into the formulas for the lower and upper limits, we obtain the following interval:

$$\frac{(50)(0.021)}{71.420}, \frac{(50)(0.021)}{32.357}; \qquad 0.0147, 0.0325$$

To obtain a 95% confidence interval for σ, we take the square root of each limit of the interval for σ^2. This gives lower and upper limits of 0.1212 and 0.1803, respectively. We are 95% confident that the population standard deviation is somewhere between 0.1212 and 0.1803.

This method of constructing confidence intervals for σ^2 is widely used, but it is not without its drawbacks. The assumption of the normality of the population being sampled is crucial. Results are likely to be misleading if the assumption of normality is not met. Another difficulty stems from the fact that this method does not yield the shortest possible confidence intervals.

EXERCISES

6.11.1 A random sample of 10 specimens of a certain material is tested for tensile strength. The variance computed from these data is 4. Construct the 95% confidence interval for σ^2. What assumption underlies the construction of this interval?

6.11.2   A production manager needs to know the time required to complete a certain task in a manufacturing plant. A study is designed in such a way that a random sample of 25 observations is made available for analysis. The variance computed from the sample data is 0.3 hr^2.   (a) Construct the 95% confidence interval for σ^2.   (b) Construct the 99% confidence interval.   (c) Construct the 90% confidence interval.   (d) What assumption must we make in order to construct a valid confidence interval?

6.11.3   An ecologist measures the amount of pollutants in 15 samples of water from a stream located in an industrial area. She obtains $\Sigma(x_i - \bar{x})^2 = 508.06$. Construct a 95% confidence interval for the population variance.

6.12 ESTIMATING THE RATIO OF THE VARIANCES OF TWO NORMALLY DISTRIBUTED POPULATIONS

We often need to compare two population variances. For example, we may wish to compare the variances of the tensile strengths of steel wires manufactured by two different suppliers. Generally, we prefer the product with the smaller variance. Suppose that each of the two suppliers of wire provides a product whose tensile strength is normally distributed with equal means. Suppose that we cannot use a segment of wire with a tensile strength less than k pounds per square inch. If the tensile strengths of Supplier A's wire vary more than those of Supplier B's wire, a larger proportion of Supplier A's wire will be unusable. Figure 6.12.1 illustrates the truth of this statement. We see that the area to the left of k is greater for Supplier A's product (the more variable product) than for Supplier B's. Since area represents proportion of items, we see that the proportion of items less than k is greater for A's product than for B's.

One way of comparing two population variances is to form the ratio σ_1^2/σ_2^2, which, if the two variances are equal, is equal to 1. As a general rule, we do not

FIGURE 6.12.1   Two normal distributions, showing that the area to the left of k is greater for the more variable distribution

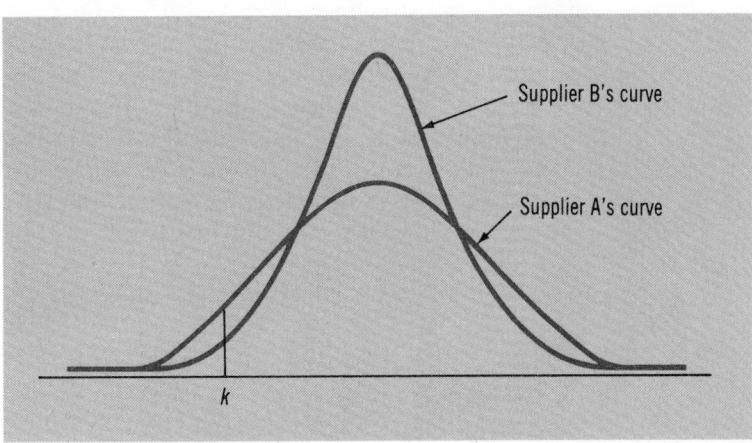

know the population variances. We have to base our comparisons on sample variances. Since we can infer the magnitude of the ratio σ_1^2/σ_2^2 from the sample results, the procedure depends on an appropriate sampling distribution.

We can use the distribution of $(s_1^2/\sigma_1^2)/(s_2^2/\sigma_2^2)$ provided that certain assumptions are met. The assumptions are that s_1^2 and s_2^2 are computed from independent samples of size n_1 and n_2, respectively, and that the samples are each drawn from a normally distributed population. If these assumptions are met, $(s_1^2/\sigma_1^2)/(s_2^2/\sigma_2^2)$ follows a distribution known as the F distribution. See Table G of Appendix I.

THE SAMPLING DISTRIBUTION OF $(s_1^2/\sigma_1^2)/(s_2^2/\sigma_2^2)$

We can approximate the sampling distribution of $(s_1^2/\sigma_1^2)/(s_2^2/\sigma_2^2)$ empirically by using the following steps:

1. Draw a large number of simple random samples of size n_1 from a normally distributed population with known variance σ_1^2.
2. Draw the same number of simple random samples of size n_2 (n_2 may or may not be equal to n_1) from a second normally distributed population with known variance σ_2^2.
3. Compute s_1^2 from the data of each sample of step 1.
4. Compute s_2^2 from the data of each sample of step 2.
5. For every possible pair of sample variances s_1^2 and s_2^2, form the ratio $(s_1^2/\sigma_1^2)/(s_2^2/\sigma_2^2)$.
6. Construct the frequency distribution of the values computed in step 5.

The resulting frequency distribution is an approximation of the sampling distribution of $(s_1^2/\sigma_1^2)/(s_2^2/\sigma_2^2)$, which is distributed as the F distribution. As noted in the discussion of the sampling distribution of $(n - 1)s^2/\sigma^2$, we can use computer simulation in constructing this empirical sampling distribution.

Chapter 8 discusses the F distribution more completely. To obtain a value of F from the table, we specify two degrees-of-freedom values, one corresponding to the value of $n_1 - 1$ used in computing s_1^2, the other corresponding to the value of $n_2 - 1$ used in computing s_2^2. These quantities are referred to as the *numerator degrees of freedom* and the *denominator degrees of freedom*, respectively.

Figure 6.12.2 shows F distributions for various sets of values of degrees of freedom. Note that, like chi-square distributions, F distributions are asymmetrical.

To find the $100(1 - \alpha)\%$ confidence interval for σ_1^2/σ_2^2, we begin with the following probability statement

F distributions are asymmetrical.

(6.12.1)
$$P\left(F_{\alpha/2} < \frac{s_1^2/\sigma_1^2}{s_2^2/\sigma_2^2} < F_{1-\alpha/2}\right) = 1 - \alpha$$

FIGURE 6.12.2   The F distribution for various degrees of freedom

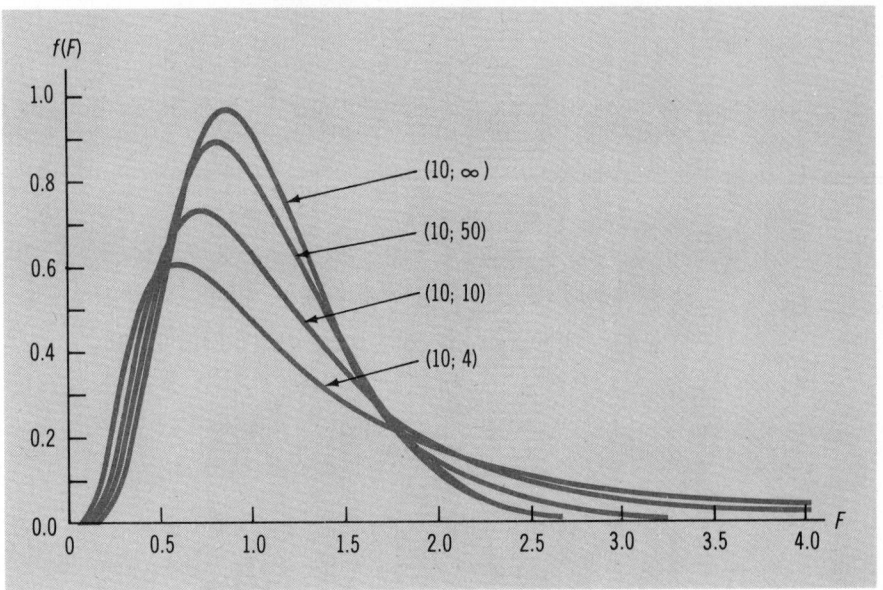

(From *Documenta Geigy, Scientific Tables*, 7th ed., 1970. Courtesy of Ciba-Geigy Limited, Basel, Switzerland)

where $F_{\alpha/2}$ and $F_{1-\alpha/2}$ are the values from the F table (Table G of Appendix I) to the left and right of which, respectively, lies $\alpha/2$ of the area under the curve.

In Equation 6.12.1, we let s_1^2 be the larger of the two sample variances. Since

$$\frac{(s_1^2/\sigma_1^2)}{(s_2^2/\sigma_2^2)} = \left(\frac{s_1^2}{s_2^2}\right) \div \left(\frac{\sigma_1^2}{\sigma_2^2}\right)$$

we may rewrite the middle term of Equation 6.12.1 so that the entire expression is

(6.12.2)
$$P\left(F_{\alpha/2} < \frac{s_1^2}{s_2^2} \cdot \frac{\sigma_2^2}{\sigma_1^2} < F_{1-\alpha/2}\right) = 1 - \alpha$$

Dividing through by s_1^2/s_2^2 gives

(6.12.3)
$$P\left(\frac{F_{\alpha/2}}{s_1^2/s_2^2} < \frac{\sigma_2^2}{\sigma_1^2} < \frac{F_{1-\alpha/2}}{s_1^2/s_2^2}\right) = 1 - \alpha$$

If we take the reciprocals of the three terms, we obtain

(6.12.4)
$$P\left(\frac{s_1^2/s_2^2}{F_{\alpha/2}} > \frac{\sigma_1^2}{\sigma_2^2} > \frac{s_1^2/s_2^2}{F_{1-\alpha/2}}\right) = 1 - \alpha$$

Reversing the order of the terms gives

(6.12.5)
$$P\left(\frac{s_1^2/s_2^2}{F_{1-\alpha/2}} < \frac{\sigma_1^2}{\sigma_2^2} < \frac{s_1^2/s_2^2}{F_{\alpha/2}}\right) = 1 - \alpha$$

Recall that s_1^2 is the larger of the two sample variances.
The lower limit of the confidence interval for $\dfrac{\sigma_1^2}{\sigma_2^2}$ is

$$\frac{s_1^2/s_2^2}{F_{1-\alpha/2}},$$

and the upper limit is

$$\frac{s_1^2/s_2^2}{F_{\alpha/2}}.$$

Table G does not contain entries for $\alpha/2$. We can get the value of F corresponding to $\alpha/2$ by taking the reciprocal of the F value corresponding to $1 - \alpha/2$ when the numerator and denominator degrees of freedom have been interchanged. Suppose, for example, that $\alpha = 0.05$, and the numerator and the denominator degrees of freedom are 5 and 10, respectively. From Table G we find $F_{1-\alpha/2,5,10} = F_{0.9075,5,10} = 4.24$. When we reverse the numerator and denominator degrees of freedom, the tabulated value of F is $F_{1-\alpha/2,10,5} = 6.62$. We now compute $F_{\alpha/2,5,10} = 1/6.62 = 0.15$.

EXAMPLE 6.12.1 The Manning Manufacturing Company conducts an experiment to compare the life of a certain product produced by two different methods. The variance of the lives of a random sample of 16 items produced by Method 1 is 1,200 hours squared. A random sample of 21 items produced by Method 2 gives a variance of 800 hours squared. A 95% confidence interval for σ_1^2/σ_2^2 is desired.

SOLUTION We use the formulas for the upper and lower limit to obtain the following interval:

$$\frac{1200/800}{2.57}, \frac{1200/800}{1/2.76}; \qquad 0.58, 4.14$$

We give this interval the usual probabilistic and practical interpretations.

EXERCISES

6.12.1 We are comparing two brands of transistors with respect to output. The variance of Brand A, based on a random sample of size 21, is 110. For Brand B, $n_B = 25$ and $s_B^2 = 185$. Construct the 99% confidence interval for the ratio of the two population variances. What assumptions must we make?

6.12.2 A random sample of 31 apples is stored under standard conditions. A random sample of 25 apples is stored under what purport to be improved conditions. The variable of interest is the number of months elapsing before the onset of deterioration. The sample variance under standard conditions is 4 months squared. Under the new conditions, the variance is 1.5 months squared. Construct the 95% confidence interval for the ratio of the two population variances. What assumptions must we make?

6.12.3 Following an exercise program, a physician gives two groups of executives tests of their muscular endurance. The scores of Group 1, consisting of 16 subjects, yield a sample variance of 4685.40. For Group 2, consisting of 25 subjects, the sample variance is 1193.70. The physician is willing to assume that the two groups of scores constitute independent simple random samples from normally distributed populations. Construct a 95% confidence interval for σ_1^2/σ_2^2.

SUMMARY

This chapter introduces statistical inference procedures. The previous chapters provide the basic foundation for this and for the material in later chapters. In this chapter, the inference procedure discussed is estimation.

We first consider point estimation and the properties of good estimators. You learned that a *point estimate* consists of a single numerical value computed from a sample. Since you cannot attach a statement of confidence to a point estimate alone, it is of limited value. *Interval estimates* or confidence intervals are of much greater use, since you can explicitly state the confidence you have that the interval contains the parameter you are estimating. The degree of confidence is equal to the percentage (or proportion) of all similarly constructed intervals that contain the parameter.

You learned that in many instances the general formula for a two-sided confidence interval is

$$\text{Estimate} \pm (\text{reliability factor}) \times (\text{standard error})$$

In this formula, the degree of confidence we need determines the reliability factor. We compute the estimate and usually the standard error from sample data.

This chapter also introduces two possible *reliability factors*, z and t. Which reliability factor you should use depends on the specific situation. You learned the criteria for choosing between the two. You may consult Figures 6.4.2 and 6.6.1 when choosing between z and t.

We can interpret a confidence interval in two ways. The *probabilistic interpretation* is stated in terms of the proportion of all similarly constructed intervals that contain the estimated parameter. The *practical interpretation* is stated in terms of the degree of confidence that we attach to the single interval that is computed.

In this chapter, you learned to construct confidence intervals for population means, population proportions, population variances, the difference between two population means, the difference between two population proportions, the ratio of two population variances, and a mean of a population of paired differences.

You also learned how to compute the sample size you need to obtain a confidence interval for a population mean, a population proportion, the difference between two means, and the difference between two proportions.

REVIEW EXERCISES

1. What is statistical inference?

2. Why is estimation an important type of inference?

3. What is a point estimate?

4. Explain the meaning, as applied to estimators, of   (a) unbiasedness,   (b) efficiency, (c) sufficiency,   (d) consistency.

5. Define the following: (a) reliability factor,   (b) confidence coefficient,   (c) standard error,   (d) estimator,   (e) precision.

6. Give the general formula for a confidence interval.

7. State the probabilistic and practical interpretations of a confidence interval.

8. Of what use is the central limit theorem in estimation?

9. Describe the *t* distribution.

10. What are the assumptions underlying the use of the *t* distribution in estimating a single population mean?

11. What is the finite population correction? When can it be ignored?

12. What assumptions underlie the use of the *t* distribution to estimate the difference between two population means?

13. What assumption underlies the construction of   (a) a confidence interval for a population variance,   (b) a confidence interval for the ratio of two population variances?

14. What is the rationale underlying the pooling of sample variances when one is testing the difference between means?

15. The widths of metal bars produced by Nomura Industries are normally distributed with a standard deviation of 0.02 inches. A random sample of 25 bars is measured, and a mean of 2.49 inches is computed. Construct the 95% confidence interval for μ.

16. A quality-control engineer with the Ofway Paper Company wishes to estimate the mean diameter of a large shipment of logs. From a random sample of 49 logs, the engineer computes a mean of 32 inches and a standard deviation of 3.5 inches.   (a) Construct the 95% confidence interval for μ.   (b) Construct the 99% confidence interval. (c) Construct the 90% confidence interval.

17. Describe a situation from your particular area of interest in which a confidence

interval for a mean difference would be meaningful. Use real or realistic data to obtain a sample of paired observations. Construct a 95% confidence interval for the mean difference.

18. A manufacturer designs a study to assess the effectiveness of an additive in prolonging the shelf life of bath salts. Two independent simple random samples consisting of 100 specimens with and 100 specimens without the additive are stored under identical conditions. The average life of the specimens with the additive is 32 months ($s^2 = 90$). For the specimens without the additive, the mean and variance are 24 and 160, respectively. The researcher is unwilling to assume that the populations are normally distributed. (a) Construct the 95% confidence interval for the difference between the population means. (b) Construct the 90% confidence interval. (c) Construct the 99% confidence interval.

19. A random sample of 200 items produced by the Peale Company is inspected for defectives. Ten defective items are discovered. Construct the 95% confidence interval for the true proportion defective.

20. A random sample of 100 people in a small town is asked to evaluate two brands of coffee. Of the sample, 70 say they prefer Brand A. (a) Construct the 95% confidence interval for the true proportion preferring Brand A. (b) Construct the 90% confidence interval. (c) Construct the 99% confidence interval.

21. Two apple orchards are sprayed with two different insecticides to prevent infestation of the mature fruit by fruit flies. At harvest time, a random sample of 500 apples from each orchard is examined, with the following results: of the 500 apples from trees sprayed with Insecticide A, 50 are infested; of those from trees sprayed with Insecticide B, 25 are infested. Construct the 95% confidence interval for the difference in the true proportions infested.

22. A firm specializing in direct-mail questionnaires has developed a new format and technique that it believes will get a higher response rate than the standard procedure. How large a sample of a particular type of respondent should the firm use in order to estimate within 0.03 the true proportion of those who would respond to the new procedure? The desired confidence level is 95%. Of those included in a pilot sample, 80% responded.

23. Each member of a random sample of 36 sixth-grade children keeps a record for one week of the amount of time spent watching television. The mean and standard deviation computed from the results are 15 hours and 6 hours, respectively. Construct a 99% confidence interval for the population mean.

24. A random sample of 100 records kept by Redmond Utilities on wooden utility poles placed in service since 1900 reveals a sample mean life and standard deviation of 10.5 years and 5 years, respectively. Construct a 95% confidence interval for the population mean.

25. A researcher selects a random sample of 150 wooden utility poles currently in service. The survey reveals that 15% of the poles need to be replaced. Construct a 99% confidence interval for the population proportion in need of replacement.

26. A random sample of 169 households in a certain area is selected as part of a study of the recreation habits of community residents. The respondents indicate a mean amount spent annually for recreation of $350 per family. The sample standard deviation is $65. Construct a 95% confidence interval for the population mean.

27. Of the households referred to in Exercise 26, 60% had two or more children. Construct the 95% confidence interval for the proportion of households in the area with two or more children.

28. In a survey of adult residents of a rural area, 80 out of 150 respondents say they prefer a certain type of music. Construct a 99% confidence interval for the population proportion.

29. © A manufacturer of fire alarm systems makes an alarm that is sensitive to smoke. The quality-control department tests a random sample of 15 alarms to determine the level of smoke concentration required for activation. The results, coded for ease of calculation, are as follows: 3, 8, 8, 9, 9, 6, 9, 6, 2, 5, 6, 4, 8, 7, 5. Construct a 95% confidence interval for the population mean.

30. A radio station conducts a survey to determine what local citizens perceive to be the most pressing national problems. Of 350 adults contacted, 80 say that they consider declining moral standards to be the most serious problem. Construct the 90% confidence interval for the population proportion that holds this opinion.

31. The editor of the *Selkirk Scribe* wishes to know what proportion of the subscribers regularly read the business news section. In a random sample of 500 subscribers, 200 state that they are regular readers of the business news. Construct a 90% confidence interval for the proportion of all subscribers in the population who regularly read the business news.

32. The mean weight of a sample of 100 trucks weighed at a highway weigh station is found to be 50,000 pounds with a standard deviation of 3,600 pounds. Construct a 95% confidence interval for the population mean.

33. During a winter shortage of natural gas, citizens are asked to lower the thermostats in their homes to 65° or less. A random sample of 150 households in a midwestern town reveals that 130 have thermostats set at 65° or lower. Construct the 95% confidence interval for the proportion of all households in the community that have lowered thermostats.

34. A survey of 800 regular listeners to a popular radio station reveals that 600 are teenagers. Construct the 90% confidence interval for the population proportion of teen-agers in the audience.

35. In a random sample of 100 households in a suburb, selected as part of a study of energy consumption, the mean amount spent for electricity during December is $42, with a standard deviation of $50. Construct a 90% confidence interval for the population mean.

36. Of 29 applicants for a position as mechanic with Tilden Motors, 13 have just completed a six-month training course at a county vocational school, whereas 16 have learned their trade through on-the-job experience. Each applicant is given the same mechanical proficiency test. The variance of the scores for the first group is 525. For the second group, the variance is 350. Construct a 90% confidence interval for the ratio of the two population variances. What assumptions are necessary?

37. A researcher with Udall Textiles randomly divides 21 specimens of fabric into two groups. Each group is treated by a different method to make the fabric water repellent. The specimens are tested for ability to repel water, with the following results: $n_1 = 11$, $s_1^2 = 280$, $n_2 = 10$, $s_2^2 = 200$. Assume that the data constitute independent simple random samples from normally distributed populations, and construct a 90% confidence interval for the ratio of the two population variances.

38. A research chemist wishes to estimate the mean amount of oxygen (in liters) required to bring about a particular chemical reaction when the oxygen is mixed with a fixed amount of sulfur. The researcher wants to be within 0.10 liter of the true mean with 95% confidence. Previous studies indicate that the variance of the oxygen requirements for this type of chemical reaction is about 0.09. What size sample does this investigator need?

39. A student working for a doctorate in education wishes to draw a sample of high school freshmen in order to estimate the average amount of time per day they spend studying. A standard deviation of 20 minutes is reported by a researcher who conducted a similar study. The student wants a 95% confidence interval for the population mean. How large should the sample be if the estimate is to be within 3 minutes of the true value?

40. The following data give the means and standard deviations of nonverbal IQ scores obtained from independent simple random samples drawn from two populations of factory employees: for sample I, $n = 19$, $\bar{x} = 110$, and $s = 10$; for sample II, $n = 23$, $\bar{x} = 95$, and $s = 15$. Assume that each of the two populations of nonverbal IQ scores is approximately normally distributed with equal variances. Construct the 95% confidence interval for the difference between the two population means.

41. New employees hired to perform highly technical tasks are randomly assigned to one of two classes for training. Class A uses a computer-assisted instruction technique to teach employees the fundamentals of the job. Instruction in Class B follows traditional patterns. Performance tests are administered to each employee in the study after six months on the job. The results are as follows: for Class A, $n = 35$, $\bar{x} = 85$, and $s = 10$; for Class B, $n = 32$, $\bar{x} = 71$, and $s = 15$. Construct a 95% confidence interval for $\mu_A - \mu_B$.

42. Ⓒ A manufacturer who wishes to increase employee production selects a department with 12 employees for an experiment. The manufacturer tries to improve working conditions in this department through renovation and employee incentives. The following table shows the mean number of items produced per day by the employees one month before and one month after the changes are made. Construct the 95% confidence interval for the population mean difference.

Mean number of items produced per day

Employee	1	2	3	4	5	6	7	8	9	10	11	12
Before	75	61	62	68	58	70	59	79	68	80	64	75
After	82	70	74	80	65	80	70	88	77	90	75	87

43. An economist is studying the attitudes of local citizens toward the national energy program. As part of the proposed interview, respondents will be asked to indicate whether they agree or disagree with the statement, "The federal government should establish a strong energy department." She wants to know how large a sample to take in order to estimate the true proportion of citizens who agree with the statement. She wishes to be within 0.025 of the true value with 95% confidence. Researchers who conducted a similar study in another locality found that 60% of the people interviewed agreed with the statement. How large should the sample be?

44. The personnel director of Winthrop Environmental Services wants to estimate the proportion of the 2,000 employees of the firm who plan to go out of state during vacation.

How large a sample should the personnel director take if the estimate is to be within 0.05 of the true value with 99% confidence? The previous year 70% of the employees polled went out of state during their vacations.

45. Researchers at Yamada Agricultural Products deliberately infect 200 plants with a certain disease. Then they treat half the plants with Chemical A and half with Chemical B. Of the plants treated with Chemical A, 75 survive. Of those treated with Chemical B, 64 survive. Construct a 90% confidence interval for $p_A - p_B$.

46. A random sample of 300 blue-collar workers in a certain city reveals that 75% are planning to vote for a particular candidate for mayor. Of a random sample of 200 white-collar workers, 66% state that they are planning to vote for the candidate. Construct a 95% confidence interval for the difference between the two population proportions.

47. As part of an experiment, scientists weigh a random sample of 20 mice. The sample yields $\Sigma(x_i - \bar{x})^2 = 72.25$. Construct a 95% confidence interval for σ^2. What assumptions must you make?

48. The following are the tensile strengths of 10 specimens of yarn selected at random from a day's production at a textile plant, coded for ease of computation: 66, 37, 18, 31, 85, 63, 73, 83, 65, 80. Assume that tensile strengths are normally distributed. Construct a 99% confidence interval for σ^2.

49. Ⓒ A simple random sample of 15 employees who work downtown reports the following distances (in miles) traveled to work each day: 13, 21, 35, 10, 24, 35, 19, 11, 25, 17, 25, 11, 11, 6, 6. Construct a 95% confidence interval for the mean distance traveled by the population of employees from which the sample was drawn.

50. Ⓒ Each of a random sample of nine automobiles of a certain make is test-driven. The number of miles obtained per gallon of gasoline is recorded for each. The results are as follows: 23, 25, 21, 22, 23, 22, 21, 24, 22. Construct a 99% confidence interval for the population mean.

51. Ⓒ During a local health fair, a simple random sample of ten business executives suffering from hypertension yields the following systolic blood pressure readings: 171, 190, 157, 181, 178, 176, 167, 165, 198, 165. Construct a 90% confidence interval for the population mean.

52. For two populations of employees, a researcher wishes to estimate the difference between the proportions of those who have ever been fired from a job. A confidence coefficient of 0.99 and an interval width of 0.10 are desired. Estimates of p_1 and p_2 are 0.12 and 0.28, respectively. What equal-sized samples should be drawn?

53. Ⓒ Researchers have found that it is not profitable for your firm to try to sell a new product to persons who live in houses that have fewer than 7 rooms. In fact, the researchers have recommended that at least 30% of houses in prospective market areas should have 7 rooms or more. You want to know whether you should enter a new market area. You ask a market research firm to conduct a survey of households in the area to find out the number of rooms per dwelling unit. The results, for a random sample of 60 dwelling units, are as follows:

3	2	4	4	5	7	5	2	4	3	6	6	5	5	2	5	6	1	5	6
1	6	3	6	7	5	4	6	4	3	6	5	8	6	6	3	5	4	3	4
6	6	7	6	8	4	5	7	5	6	7	6	7	7	7	5	3	6	5	4

Construct a 95% confidence interval for the proportion of dwelling units in the population with 7 or more rooms. Should you market your product in the area?

54. Ⓒ A sample of 25 apples from a truckload shipment yields the following weights in ounces: 16, 11, 14, 20, 16, 13, 14, 17, 10, 18, 11, 20, 14, 15, 19, 16, 10, 15, 16, 14, 15, 20, 18, 18, 20.   (a) Compute the mean weight of the apples in the sample.   (b) Compute the median weight.   (c) Compute the sample variance and standard deviation.   (d) Use these data to construct a 95% confidence interval for the population mean.   (e) Before you vouch for the legitimacy of the inference procedure in part (d), is there any further information you would like to have?   (f) The owner of the orchard in which the apples were grown claims that the mean weight of the apples in the truck is 16 ounces. Do you think that these data support the owner's claim? Explain.

55. Ⓒ Quality-control experts with the Yarrow Shirt Company have found that, on the average, an employee performs 30 defective operations in a week when morale is high. When morale is low, the number of defective operations is higher. During a recent week a random sample of 12 employees performed the following number of defective operations: 40, 37, 32, 34, 31, 36, 34, 32, 33, 31, 35, 33. Construct a 99% confidence interval for the mean number of defective operations performed by the employees in the sampled population. On the basis of these data, does it appear that morale may be low?

56. Ⓒ A sales manager has found that salespeople who spend more time per customer call are more successful. The most successful salespeople spend, on the average, 50 minutes per customer call. A random sample of 20 sales calls from the records of a new salesperson reveals the following amounts of time in minutes spent per sales call: 35, 41, 24, 26, 25, 53, 41, 40, 34, 39, 57, 23, 28, 53, 30, 79, 81, 90, 79, 88. Construct a 95% confidence interval for the population mean. Does it appear from these data that the new salesperson may become one of the firm's more successful salespeople?

57. A researcher wants to estimate, for a large population of employees, the proportion of those who have ever sought professional help for an emotional or mental problem. Another researcher found the proportion in a similar population to be 0.15. The present researcher, who wants to be within 0.03 of the true proportion with 99% confidence, wants to know how large a sample to draw.

58. For two populations of employees, an insurance investigator wants to estimate the difference in the mean number of accidents in which the employees have been involved during the past ten years. A confidence coefficient of 0.90 and an interval width of 4 are desired. Estimates of the population variances are 28 and 20. How large should the sample sizes be ($n_1 = n_2$)?

59. Ⓒ Select a simple random sample of size 50 from the population of employed heads of household given in Appendix II. Construct a 95% confidence interval for the proportion of women in the population. Compare your results with those of your classmates and determine how many of the intervals constructed by the class include the population proportion, which is 0.20.

60. Ⓒ Select a simple random sample of size 50 from the population of employed heads of households given in Appendix II. Then do the following.   (a) Construct a 95% confidence interval for the population mean commuting distance from work, using the finite population correction factor.   (b) From the same data, construct a 95% confidence interval for the same population mean, but ignore the finite population correction factor. Compare this interval with the one you found in part (a).   (c) Construct a 95% confidence interval for the mean annual salary of the persons in the population.

61. C In a survey of office workers in a large city, each subject in a random sample of 35 is asked to report the number of times during the previous month that he or she has eaten an evening meal at a restaurant other than a fast-food establishment. The results were as follows:

5	0	9	1	9	8	5	5	2	6	4	9	0	3
7	1	9	7	2	3	5	2	8	5	9	4	7	3
1	3	4	3	8	1	7							

Construct a 95% confidence interval for the mean of the sampled population. Who do you think might be interested in the results of this survey? Define the sampled population.

62. In a survey of college students who own automobiles, a random sample of 100 students is asked to report information on the following variables:

1. Gender—male, female

2. Residence—on campus, off campus

3. Type of car owned—foreign (F), American-made (A)

4. Number of miles driven during previous week

	1	**2**	**3**	**4**
Subject	Gender	Live on campus?	Type of car	Number of miles driven
1	F	Yes	A	43
2	M	Yes	A	77
3	M	No	F	91
4	F	No	A	48
5	F	Yes	F	39
6	M	No	A	72
7	M	No	A	99
8	F	Yes	A	56
9	M	No	A	100
10	M	Yes	A	86
11	M	No	A	99
12	M	No	F	78
13	F	Yes	A	45
14	F	No	F	64
15	F	Yes	F	67
16	M	No	F	99
17	M	Yes	A	88
18	M	No	F	81
19	M	No	A	98
20	F	Yes	F	67
21	M	No	A	88
22	M	Yes	A	98
23	M	No	A	85
24	F	Yes	F	58
25	M	No	A	99
26	F	No	A	58
27	M	Yes	F	84

Subject	**1** Gender	**2** Live on campus?	**3** Type of car	**4** Number of miles driven
28	M	Yes	A	73
29	M	No	A	76
30	M	No	F	87
31	F	Yes	F	55
32	M	Yes	F	72
33	M	No	F	81
34	F	Yes	A	68
35	M	Yes	A	61
36	F	Yes	A	67
37	M	No	F	85
38	M	Yes	A	68
39	M	No	F	99
40	F	Yes	A	40
41	M	Yes	A	70
42	M	No	F	90
43	F	Yes	A	44
44	F	No	F	51
45	F	No	A	64
46	F	Yes	A	47
47	M	Yes	A	75
48	M	No	A	91
49	F	Yes	A	39
50	M	No	A	102
51	M	Yes	F	87
52	M	No	A	97
53	F	Yes	A	54
54	M	No	F	89
55	M	No	A	87
56	F	No	F	82
57	M	Yes	A	64
58	M	No	A	40
59	F	Yes	A	62
60	M	No	F	78
61	M	No	A	82
62	M	No	A	78
63	F	Yes	F	52
64	M	Yes	A	56
65	M	Yes	F	57
66	M	Yes	A	56
67	M	No	A	75
68	F	Yes	F	47
69	F	Yes	A	45
70	M	Yes	A	59
71	F	No	F	60
72	M	Yes	A	47
73	M	No	A	75
74	F	Yes	A	42
75	F	Yes	A	38

Subject	1 Gender	2 Live on campus?	3 Type of car	4 Number of miles driven
76	F	No	A	90
77	F	Yes	A	54
78	M	Yes	F	50
79	M	No	A	68
80	F	No	F	75
81	F	Yes	A	66
82	M	Yes	A	30
83	F	No	A	58
84	M	No	A	54
85	M	No	A	64
86	F	Yes	F	56
87	F	Yes	A	60
88	M	Yes	F	26
89	M	No	A	73
90	M	Yes	A	27
91	M	No	A	80
92	F	Yes	F	51
93	M	No	A	62
94	M	Yes	F	20
95	F	Yes	F	60
96	M	Yes	A	28
97	M	No	A	59
98	F	Yes	A	38
99	F	No	F	38
100	F	No	A	62

Define the sampled population. Who do you think would be interested in the information collected in this survey? Explain how you think a survey of this type could best be conducted.

63. Ⓒ Refer to the data in Exercise 62. Construct a 95% confidence interval for the proportion of females in the sampled population.

64. Ⓒ Refer to the data in Exercise 62. Construct a 95% confidence interval for the proportion of males in the sampled population.

65. Ⓒ Refer to the data in Exercise 62. Construct a 90% confidence interval for the proportion of students in the population who drive foreign cars.

66. Ⓒ Refer to the data in Exercise 62. Construct a 90% confidence interval for the proportion of students in the population who drive American-made cars.

67. Ⓒ Refer to the data in Exercise 62. Assume that the males constitute a simple random sample from one population and the females an independent simple random sample from another population. Define these two populations. From the information given, what is the best point estimate of the population proportion of males who drive foreign cars? What is the best point estimate of the population proportion of females who drive foreign cars?

68. Ⓒ Construct a 90% confidence interval for the difference between the two population proportions for which point estimates were computed in Exercise 67.

69. [C] Refer to Exercise 62. Construct a 95% confidence interval for the mean number of miles driven during the previous week by the sampled population.

70. [C] Refer to Exercise 62. Assume that the females are a simple random sample from one population and the males are an independent simple random sample from another population. Define these two populations. What is the best point estimate of the mean number of miles driven by the population of females? What is the best point estimate of the mean number of miles driven by the population of males?

71. [C] Construct a 99% confidence interval for the mean number of miles driven by the population of females defined in Exercise 70.

72. [C] Construct a 99% confidence interval for the mean number of miles driven by the population of males defined in Exercise 70.

73. [C] Construct a 99% confidence interval for the difference between the mean number of miles driven by the two populations defined in Exercise 70.

74. [C] Refer to Exercise 70. For the population of females, construct a 95% confidence interval for the proportion who live on campus.

75. [C] Refer to Exercise 70. For the population of males, construct a 95% confidence interval for the proportion who live on campus.

76. [C] Construct a 95% confidence interval for the difference between the proportions who live on campus for the two populations defined in Exercise 70.

77. [C] The director of a city tourist bureau conducts a survey of a random sample of out-of-state tourists who visited the city during the previous year. The sampled population consists of individuals and families who traveled by automobile and stayed in motels or hotels. Among the questions asked on the survey were the following:

1. How many miles did you travel while on vacation last year?

2. What type of accommodations did you patronize?
    1 Economy-priced motel or hotel
    0 Regular-priced or luxury motel or hotel

The results are shown in Data Set 4 in Appendix IV. Construct a 95% confidence interval for the mean number of miles driven by the respondents in the sampled population.

78. [C] Construct a 95% confidence interval for the population proportion who stayed at economy-priced hotels and motels.

79. [C] Pretend that the data in Exercise 77 are for a population rather than a sample. Select a simple random sample of 15 respondents from this population. Construct a 95% confidence interval for the mean number of miles driven by the population. Does your confidence interval contain the true population mean? Compare your results with those of your classmates. What proportion of the intervals constructed by class members contain the true population mean?

80. [C] Pretend that the data in Exercise 77 are for a population. Select a simple random sample of 35 respondents from this population. Construct a 95% confidence interval for the proportion of the population that stayed at economy-priced motels and hotels.

81. Pretend that the data in Exercise 77 are for two populations: (1) vacationers who stayed at economy-priced motels and hotels, and (2) vacationers who stayed at regular-priced or luxury motels and hotels. Select a simple random sample of size 15 from the respondents who stayed at economy-priced motels and hotels. Select an independent simple random sample of size 10 from the respondents who stayed at regular-priced or luxury motels and hotels. Construct a 95% confidence interval for the difference between the two population means. On the basis of your confidence interval, do you believe that the population means are different? Compare your results with those of your classmates.

82. Ⓒ Select a simple random sample from the list of companies in Appendix III. (Ask your instructor how large your sample should be.) For each company in your sample, record the data on each of the six variables. Construct a 95% confidence interval for the population mean assets. *Reminder*: You may need to use the finite population correction factor.

83. Ⓒ Refer to Exercise 82. Construct a 95% confidence interval for the population mean sales.

84. Refer to Exercise 82. Construct a 95% confidence interval for the population mean market value.

85. Ⓒ Refer to Exercise 82. Construct a 95% confidence interval for the population mean net profits.

86. Ⓒ Refer to Exercise 82. Construct a 95% confidence interval for the population mean cash flow.

87. Ⓒ Refer to Exercise 82. Construct a 95% confidence interval for the population mean number employed.

88. Ⓒ Refer to Exercise 82. Construct a 95% confidence interval for the proportion of companies in the population with assets of $1 billion or more.

89. Ⓒ Refer to Exercise 82. Construct a 95% confidence interval for the proportion of companies in the population with sales of $1 billion or more.

90. Ⓒ Refer to Exercise 82. Construct a 95% confidence interval for the proportion of companies in the population with a market value of $1 billion or more.

91. Ⓒ Refer to Exercise 82. Construct a 95% confidence interval for the proportion of companies in the population with net profits of $100 million or more.

92. Ⓒ Refer to Exercise 82. Construct a 95% confidence interval for the proportion of companies in the population with a cash flow of $1 billion or more.

93. Ⓒ Refer to Exercise 82. Construct a 95% confidence interval for the proportion of companies in the population with 50,000 or more employees.

94. A research firm wishes to estimate the mean travel time of persons who live in a suburban location and work at a large industrial complex. (a) If a rough estimate of the standard deviation of the travel time is 9 minutes, what sample size should the firm use to obtain a 99% confidence interval with a maximum estimate error of 2 minutes? (b) A sample of 150 workers yields a mean of 22.8 minutes and a standard deviation of 8.36 minutes. Construct a 99% confidence interval for the population mean.

95. A pre-election poll is to be taken in a city to determine voter preference on an issue. How many voters should be sampled if the desired maximum error between the sample proportion and the population proportion is 2% with a confidence of 98%?

96. In a simple random sample of 2,000 voters, 1,120 are in favor of a particular candidate for office. Construct a 95% confidence interval for the proportion of voters in the population in favor of this candidate.

97. A simple random sample of 43 bus drivers yields a mean driving time between two cities of 5.37 hours and a standard deviation of 0.69 hours. Construct a 95% confidence interval for the population mean driving time between the two cities.

98. Ⓒ Two methods are available for estimating the percentage of impurities present in a certain compound. One method (the standard method) is expensive and time consuming. A newer method is less expensive but may not be as accurate. To determine whether the two methods give comparable results, both were employed on 20 specimens of the compound, with the following results:

Specimen	Standard Method	New Method
1	13.8	11.5
2	16.6	16.94
3	13.7	10.57
4	13.8	12.2
5	18.71	14.6
6	10.84	13.16
7	11.1	9.33
8	13.64	15.86
9	11.57	12.7
10	14.5	13.82
11	8.9	10.09
12	13.8	9.53
13	17.96	11.57
14	11.7	15.14
15	12.37	15.66
16	7.4	7.74
17	14.94	18.49
18	10.84	13.16
19	14.5	13.82
20	16.6	16.94

Construct a 95% confidence interval for the mean difference between the two methods.

99. From a normally distributed population with unknown variance, you select a simple random sample of size 25. From the sample data, you compute a mean of 175 and a standard deviation of 15. You construct a 95% confidence interval for the population mean. What is the precision of the estimate?

100. You select a simple random sample of size 300 from a dichotomous population. You observe 120 successes. You construct a 90% confidence interval for the proportion of successes in the population. What is the precision of the estimate?

*101. In this chapter, our discussion of confidence intervals is limited to two-sided intervals. When we have a two-sided interval we are able to state how much confidence we have that a population parameter is between the interval's lower limit and its upper limit. In certain situations, one-sided confidence intervals are desired. We might want to say, for example, that we are 95% confident that a population mean is greater than or equal to some value (or, equivalently, that the population mean is between a specified value and $+\infty$). This type of interval is called a lower-limit confidence interval. In another situation we might want to say that we are 99% confident that a population mean is less than or equal to some value (or, equivalently, that the population mean is between a specified value and $-\infty$). Such an interval is referred to as an upper-limit confidence interval. When sampling is from a normally distributed population with unknown variance, the upper-limit confidence interval for the population mean is obtained by computing $\bar{x} + t(s/\sqrt{n})$, and the lower-limit interval is obtained by computing $\bar{x} - t(s/\sqrt{n})$, where the value of t is found in Appendix I Table E at the intersection of the row labeled df $= n - 1$ and the column labeled t_α (rather than $t_{\alpha/2}$). A manufacturing firm wishes to establish a 99% lower confidence interval on the breaking strength of its product. A sample of 26 specimens yields a mean breaking strength of 180 psi with a standard deviation of 11 psi. (a) Construct the desired interval. (b) State the practical interpretation of the interval. (c) Rewrite the formulas for the upper and lower confidence limits for the following situations: (1) The sampled population is normally distributed with a known variance. (2) The sampled population is not normally distributed, but the sample size is greater than 30. (3) The parameter to be estimated is the population proportion.

STATISTICS AT WORK

STATISTICS AT WORK S

1. EFFECT OF MARATHON GROUP THERAPY ON DRUG ABUSE PATIENTS

The responsible manager is concerned with both the physical and the mental well-being of employees. Employees with personal problems—either physical or mental—constitute a drain on productivity because of absenteeism and because of their inefficiency while on the job. An ability to recognize the symptoms of personal problems among employees, plus a knowledge of available therapeutic resources, enhances the effectiveness of the manager.

One personal problem with which the modern manager often has to cope is drug abuse among subordinates. Therapists have advanced the idea that drug-rehabilitation programs need to focus on changing the behavior and attitudes of persons with drug problems. Page and Mannion conducted a study to assess the effects of a 16-hour marathon therapy group, conducted with patients in a residential drug-treatment center. Twenty-eight subjects were randomly assigned to either a marathon therapy group ($n = 12$) or a control group ($n = 16$). The control group received no therapy. After the marathon therapy, an evaluative test was given to all 28 subjects at the same time. The investigators assessed the effects of the marathon group therapy on the attitudes of the participants through the use of the semantic differential technique (C. E. Osgood, G. T. Suci, and P. H. Tannenbaum, *The Measurement of Meaning*, Urbana, Ill., University of Illinois Press, 1957). The mean scores and standard deviations on the group-counseling (E) subscale of the semantic differential were as follows.

	$\bar{x}$	s
Marathon group	5.85	0.75
Control group	5.25	0.76

Construct a 95% confidence interval for the difference between population means. What assumptions are necessary for this inferential procedure to be valid?

Source: Richard C. Page and John Mannion, "Marathon Group Therapy with Former Drug Users," *Journal of Employment Counseling*, 17 (1980): 307–313.

2. TEEN-AGERS AND COMPACT CARS

In a survey of teen-agers, Allan F. Williams and his coresearchers found that 30% of 2,626 who have their own cars drive compact cars. Of 2,023 teen-agers who do not have their own cars, 36% drive compact cars. Consider these data as samples from two populations of teen-agers—those who have their own cars and those who do not. Construct a 95% confidence interval for the difference between the proportions of those who drive compact cars in the two populations.

Source: Allan F. Williams, et al, "Cars Owned and Driven by Teenagers," *Transportation Quarterly*, 41 (April 1987), 177–188.

3. COLLEGE STUDENTS AND GETTING BY

According to a newspaper article, 53% of college teachers responding to a survey agreed that most undergraduates at their schools "only do enough to get by." Suppose that you conducted your own survey of 500 college teachers and obtained the same results. Construct the 95% confidence interval for the population proportion of those who hold this opinion.

Source: *The Atlanta Journal and Constitution*, November 6, 1989, p. C–5.

4. GETTING TO WORK

A newspaper article states that, according to a national sample survey, the average American worker travels 21 minutes to work each day. Suppose that you conducted your own survey of 60 workers and obtained the same results, plus a sample standard deviation of 10. Construct the 95% confidence interval for the population mean.

Source: *The Atlanta Journal and Constitution*, November 6, 1989, p. C–5.

5. BUSINESS ETHICS

Miesing and Preble conducted a study of 487 adult, MBA, and undergraduate business students on business philosophies of Machiavellianism, Objectivism, Social Darwinism, Ethical Relativism, and Universalism. The authors describe the philosophies in considerable detail. The following are some components of the philosophies. *Machiavellianism:* Success results when expediency takes precedence over virtue. *Objectivism:* The moral guide for objectivism is rational self-interest. *Social Darwinism:* Biological laws, such as survival of the fittest, can be applied to the world of business. *Ethical Relativism:* Behavior sanctioned by group norms is acceptable and leads to the business concept of commonly accepted practice. *Universalism:* There are certain absolute codes of behavior that are applicable in all situations. The research of Miesing and Preble revealed that prospective managers were less ethical than practicing managers, women were more ethical than men, and those who reported having a strong religious conviction tended to be more ethical than those without such a conviction. The means and standard deviations of the scores made by the subjects on the scales designed to measure their standing with respect to the five philosophies were as follows:

Philosophy	$\bar{x}$	s
Machiavellianism	2.28	0.56
Objectivism	2.60	0.52
Social Darwinism	2.37	0.54
Ethical Relativism	2.32	0.71
Universalism	3.61	0.65

Construct a 95% confidence interval for each population mean.

Source: Paul Miesing and John F. Preble, "A Comparison of Five Business Philosophies," *Journal of Business Ethics,* 4 (1985), 465–476.

SUGGESTIONS FOR FURTHER READING

Good, I. J. (1973). "What Are the Degrees of Freedom?" *American Statistician* 27:227–228.

Gossett, W. S. [Student](1908). "The Probable Error of a Mean," *Biometrika* 6:1–25.

Walker, Helen M. (1940). "Degrees of Freedom," *The Journal of Educational Psychology* 31:253–269.

7

Statistical Inference II: Hypothesis Testing

Chapter Objectives: In this chapter, we discuss the second type of statistical inference, hypothesis testing. You will note some similarities as well as some differences between hypothesis testing and interval estimation, about which you learned in Chapter 6. The same parameters are of interest. However, in this chapter, you will analyze sample data to see whether they support or fail to support a speculation (hypothesis) about the magnitudes of the parameters. In Chapter 6, you were not concerned with preanalysis conjectures about parameters. Instead, you used sample data to help you form an opinion about the magnitudes of parameters.

After studying this chapter and working the exercises, you should be able to

1. List seven steps that you can follow in testing a hypothesis.
2. Conduct tests of hypotheses about values of the following parameters: (a) a population mean, (b) a population proportion, (c) a population variance, (d) the difference between two population means, (e) the difference between two population proportions, (f) the ratio of two population variances, and (g) a mean of a population of paired differences.
3. Compute a p value for each test.
4. Calculate the power of a test for a specific alternative hypothesis about the population mean.
5. Determine the sample size required if a test is to meet certain specified conditions.
6. Use a computer software package to perform calculations in a hypothesis test.

7.1 INTRODUCTION

There are two types of statistical inference—estimation, which is covered in Chapter 6, and hypothesis testing, which is the subject of this chapter.

> The purpose of *hypothesis testing*, like that of estimation, is to help one reach a decision about a population by examining the data contained in a sample from that population.

In the examples and exercises of this chapter, the samples we refer to are simple random samples. In Section 7.2, we cover some general concepts of hypothesis testing. In succeeding sections, we shall cover specific tests of hypotheses in detail.

Again, remember that *the sampled population may not always be the same as the target population.* When testing hypotheses, you should exercise the same caution in distinguishing between these two kinds of population that we suggested in connection with estimation.

7.2 HYPOTHESIS TESTING—SOME GENERAL CONSIDERATIONS

A hypothesis is a statement about one or more populations.

We may define a *hypothesis* as simply *a statement about one or more populations.* The hypotheses of interest here are those concerned with one or more parameters of the population or populations about which we are making the statement. An advertising executive may hypothesize that a certain type of newspaper ad attracts a larger proportion of readers than some other type of ad. A production supervisor may hypothesize that employees trained in a certain way need less time to do a task than employees trained in some other way. A quality-control engineer may hypothesize that the variance of the measurements generated by some process is equal to some specific value σ_0^2. A marketing analyst may hypothesize that the mean family income in a certain area is some specific value μ_0. Or a company president may hypothesize that 60% of the company's employees have completed at least one year of college.

Given enough time, money, and other resources, each of these investigators could determine the truth of the hypothesis beyond doubt by examining the entire population to which the statement refers. But such an undertaking would cost a great deal. So investigators welcome a more economical means of testing the reasonableness of their hypotheses. They are also willing to settle for some degree of uncertainty in their conclusions.

The cases just described are typical of situations in which the concepts and techniques of sampling work well. The motivation for sampling may be a need to obtain estimates of population parameters, as discussed in Chapter 6, or to test hypotheses, as we see in this chapter. The advantages of sampling mentioned in Chapter 6 also apply in hypothesis testing. Therefore, we do not repeat them. Here is a seven-step procedure for hypothesis testing.

STEPS IN HYPOTHESIS TESTING

1. Statement of the hypotheses
2. Identification of the test statistic and its distribution
3. Specification of the significance level
4. Statement of the decision rule
5. Collection of the data and performance of the calculations
6. Making the statistical decision
7. Drawing a conclusion

There is nothing sacred about this format. It just breaks the hypothesis-testing process into its basic components of acts and decisions. We can then analyze and understand each separately.

1. *Statement of the hypotheses.* You will ordinarily be concerned with two statistical hypotheses, the *null* hypothesis (designated H_0) and the *alternative hypothesis* (designated H_1).

> The *null hypothesis* is the hypothesis that is tested.

The null hypothesis usually specifies one of the parameters of the population of interest. For example, the statement, or hypothesis, that 60% of the employees in a firm have had at least one year of college specifies that the parameter, the proportion of employees with at least one year of college, is 0.60. The null hypothesis is the hypothesis that is assumed to be true throughout the statistical analysis. The analysis is based on this assumption. Only after the analysis is complete, and there is evidence to warrant our doing so, do we entertain the idea that the null hypothesis is not true.

The null hypothesis includes a statement of equality.

The term *null hypothesis* reflects the concept that this is a *hypothesis of no difference*. For this reason, the null hypothesis always includes a statement of equality. When it is presented symbolically, it contains an equals sign.

> The *alternative hypothesis* is the alternative available when the null hypothesis is rejected.

In the case of the company president's hypothesis about the education of the employees, we may state the alternative hypothesis in one of three ways: (1) the true proportion is not 0.60; (2) the true proportion is greater than 0.60; or (3) the true proportion is less than 0.60. The statement of the alternative hypothesis implies either a condition of not equal or an inequality. In the first case, if we reject the null hypothesis, we conclude that the true condition of the population with regard to the parameter is something other than that specified in the null hypothesis. However, this alternative does not indicate whether the true proportion is greater or less than that specified in the null hypothesis. In the second and third cases, when we reject the null hypothesis, we conclude either that the true proportion is greater than 0.60 or that it is less than 0.60, depending on the alternative hypothesis. Which of the three alternative hypotheses we use is dictated by the nature of the problem.

FORMULATING THE HYPOTHESES

An investigator may originally formulate a hypothesis in the null form or as the alternative. Thus, the proportion of employees who have completed at least one year of college can be stated as 0.6 (null form) or not 0.6 (alternative form). Regardless of how we state the original hypothesis, we must specify both appropriate null and alternative hypotheses before we collect any data. In general, if we hypothesize that a population parameter θ is equal to some value θ_0, we may display the null and alternative hypotheses formally as follows:

$$H_0: \theta = \theta_0, \qquad H_1: \theta \neq \theta_0$$

What you expect to conclude goes in the alternative hypothesis.

When setting up the null and alternative hypotheses, you must determine what you are trying to conclude. You should state this in the alternative hypothesis, unless this would violate the rule that the null hypothesis includes a statement of equality. You should state what you are trying to conclude in the alternative hypothesis because we want to reject the null hypothesis if at all possible.

Consider a situation in which you need to test a hypothesis about a population. If you want to know whether your sample data provide sufficient evidence to indicate that the population mean is not equal to some value μ_0, your alternative hypothesis is

$$H_1: \mu \neq \mu_0$$

and the null hypothesis, being the complement of the alternative, is

$$H_0: \mu = \mu_0$$

The alternative hypothesis $H_1: \mu \neq \mu_0$ is an example of what is known as a two-sided alternative. You form a one-sided alternative if the question you want answered is one of the following: (1) Do the sample data provide sufficient evidence to indicate that the population mean is greater than μ_0? In this case the alternative hypothesis is $H_1: \mu > \mu_0$ and the null hypothesis is $H_0: \mu \leq \mu_0$. (2) Do the sample data provide sufficient evidence to indicate that the population mean is less than μ_0? In this case the alternative hypothesis is $H_1: \mu < \mu_0$ and the null hypothesis is $H_0: \mu \geq \mu_0$. We say more about two-sided and one-sided alternative hypotheses later in this chapter.

The null hypothesis and the alternative hypothesis are complements of each other.

When deciding which statement to put in the null hypothesis and which to put in the alternative hypothesis, you will usually find it more convenient to state the alternative hypothesis first, and then make the statement in the null hypothesis the complement of the statement in the alternative hypothesis.

If we reject the null hypothesis, we can conclude with a high degree of conviction that the alternative hypothesis is true. If we cannot reject the null hypothesis, however, we do not conclude that the null hypothesis is true. We merely conclude that it *may be true*. This is because, in general, evidence compatible with a hypothesis is never conclusive, whereas contradictory evidence is sufficient to cast doubt on a hypothesis.

Consider an example. A firm that makes a headache remedy claims that the product always cures headaches within 15 minutes. This is the firm's hypothesis. You develop a headache and take the remedy. Your headache is gone within 15 minutes. You would not conclude that the firm's hypothesis is true. If you had similar results with your next 25 headaches, would you conclude that the hypothesis is true? Although the evidence in favor of the hypothesis is now substantial, it is not sufficient for concluding that the manufacturer's hypothesis is true. On your twenty-seventh headache, relief does not come for 30 minutes. You can then conclude that the hypothesis is not true. This conclusion is based on a rejected hypothesis. You needed only one piece of contradictory evidence to reach this decision, whereas 26 pieces of evidence in favor of the hypothesis failed to establish its truth.

Decisions about statistical hypotheses of the type we consider here are never as clear-cut as in the headache example. The concept, however, is the same. To summarize, a decision based on a rejected null hypothesis is more conclusive than a decision based on evidence that is compatible with a null hypothesis. You will come to understand the meaning of this statement as you gain additional insight into the general nature of hypothesis testing.

The following rules of thumb may be useful in helping you decide how to state null and alternative hypotheses:

(a) What you hope or expect to be able to conclude as a result of the test usually should be placed in the alternative hypothesis.
(b) The null hypothesis should contain a statement of equality, either $=$, $\leq$, or $\geq$.
(c) The null hypothesis is the hypothesis that is tested.
(d) The null and alternative hypotheses are complementary. That is, the two together exhaust all possibilities regarding the value that the hypothesized parameter can assume.

The test statistic serves as a decision-maker.

2. *Identification of the test statistic and its distribution.* A *test statistic* is a statistic that is used in statistical hypothesis testing. From sample data we compute a numerical value of the test statistic. Generally, the test statistic may assume many possible values. The particular value observed depends on the particular sample drawn. The test statistic serves as a decision-maker, since the decision to reject or not reject the null hypothesis depends on its magnitude.

When one is testing a hypothesis about a population mean, a possible test statistic is

$$z = \frac{\bar{x} - \mu_0}{\sigma/\sqrt{n}}$$

where μ_0 is the hypothesized value of the population mean. The subscript zero is used to indicate a hypothesized value of a parameter. This quantity follows the standard normal distribution when certain assumptions are met and the population mean is μ_0 as hypothesized. Some other test statistics that will concern us are

$$t = \frac{\bar{x} - \mu_0}{s/\sqrt{n}}$$

a possible test statistic when we are testing a hypothesis about a population mean, and

$$t = \frac{(\bar{x}_1 - \bar{x}_2) - (\mu_1 - \mu_2)_0}{\sqrt{\dfrac{s_p^2}{n_1} + \dfrac{s_p^2}{n_2}}}$$

when the parameter of interest is the difference between population means. Under certain conditions, both of these statistics follow a t distribution.

When we test a hypothesis about a population proportion, the test statistic is

$$z = \frac{\hat{p} - p_0}{\sqrt{\dfrac{p_0(1 - p_0)}{n}}}$$

which is approximately normally distributed when certain conditions are met. Many of the test statistics that we encounter will be of this form:

$$\text{Test statistic} = \frac{\text{sample statistic} - \text{hypothesized parameter value}}{\text{standard error of the statistic}}$$

3. *Specification of the significance level.* When the results are in, there are two possible actions: (1) *reject* H_0 or (2) *fail to reject* H_0. A hypothesis that is not rejected may be true or false. Likewise, a rejected hypothesis may be either true or false. Thus, there are *four* possible outcomes when we test a hypothesis: (1) rejecting a false null hypothesis, (2) rejecting a true null hypothesis, (3) failing to reject a false null hypothesis, and (4) failing to reject a true null hypothesis. Outcomes (2) and (3) are undesirable. Outcomes (1) and (4) are

desirable. We may classify the possible outcomes by the action taken and by the condition of the population relative to the null hypothesis. We may think of the two undesirable outcomes as incorrect actions, or errors, and distinguish them by referring to them by type. That is, we may call the act of rejecting H_0 when it is true a Type I error, and the act of failing to reject H_0 when it is false a Type II error. In tabular form, this two-way classification and the resulting errors are as follows:

		Possible Condition of Null Hypothesis	
		True	False
Possible action	Fail to reject H_0	Correct	Incorrect (Type II error)
	Reject H_0	Incorrect (Type I error)	Correct

Bear in mind that in a hypothesis-testing situation there is always the probability that you will commit one or the other of these errors. We call the probability of committing a Type I error α, and the probability of committing a Type II error β. The larger α is, the more likely it is that we will commit a Type I error. That is, the more likely it is that we will reject a true null hypothesis. The larger β is, the more likely it is that we will commit a Type II error and fail to reject a false null hypothesis. We would like the probability of committing both errors to be as small as possible. As the examples will show, for a given sample size, decreasing α causes an increase in β. Conversely, decreasing β causes an increase in α. The only way to reduce the likelihood of both types of error is to increase the sample size.

CHOOSING α

As we have noted, α is the probability of committing a Type I error. The quantity α is also called the *level of significance*. Before we collect the data, we specify that the level of significance, or probability of committing a Type I error, be some small probability. The value of α chosen by the decision-maker indicates the amount of risk of committing a Type I error that he or she is willing to tolerate. The greater the decision-maker's desire to avoid rejecting a true null hypothesis (committing a Type I error), the smaller will be the value of α that he or she selects.

When we have computed the test statistic, we determine the probability of obtaining a value as extreme as or more extreme than ours when the null hypothesis is true. If this probability is less than or equal to α, we reject H_0 in favor of H_1. We then say that the computed test statistic is *significant*. If the probability associated with the computed test statistic is greater than α, we cannot reject the null hypothesis. The value of the test statistic is then *not significant*.

Although we could use any value of α between 0 and 1, the most common values are 0.05 and 0.01. These choices of α, though somewhat arbitrary, are based on tradition.

CONSEQUENCES OF A TYPE I ERROR

We choose the value of α in reference to the consequences of a Type I error. Consider the possible consequences of committing the two errors in an actual situation. Suppose that a firm that makes calculators has a policy of refusing to accept any shipment of microchips if there is reason to believe that more than 7% of them are of inferior quality. The manager selects a sample of microchips from each shipment and uses an appropriate hypothesis-testing procedure. Sometimes the hypothesis test indicates that a shipment should be rejected. By rejecting a shipment, the manager may commit a Type I error. Assume that when a shipment is rejected, the only alternative is to buy microchips from another supplier at a higher price. If the manager rejects a shipment of cheaper microchips that in fact do meet the specifications, and buys more expensive ones, this increases the cost of the calculators. A cost increase, then, is the consequence of rejecting a true null hypothesis in this case. If, on the other hand, the firm accepts a shipment as satisfactory, it may be committing a Type II error. That is, it may be accepting a shipment of inferior microchips, thus increasing the chance of producing inferior calculators. This may result in an added cost later if the firm has to make good its warranties. If it places too many inferior calculators on the market, the company may also face consumer ill will.

The manager must decide which of the two errors is more costly and then try either to minimize the probability of the more expensive error or to strike a balance between the two errors on the basis of the costs involved.

Select α early.

Note that we select α early in the investigation. If we select α after we have completed the test, the results may influence our choice, and this would detract from the objectivity of the investigation.

REJECTION AND NONREJECTION REGIONS

The distribution of a test statistic includes all values that the statistic can assume when H_0 is true. In other words, we can imagine the set of all values of the test statistic that are possible when the null hypothesis is true. We call the subset of values of the statistic that are unlikely if the null hypothesis is true the *rejection region*. We call the remaining values the *nonrejection region*. (However, avoid such phrases as "accept the null hypothesis." The word "accept" implies a greater degree of conviction than we should accord decisions based on hypotheses that we cannot reject. When we cannot reject the null hypothesis, we should characterize our action by saying that we "fail to reject the null hypothesis.") We call the values of the test statistic that separate the nonrejection region from the rejection region *critical values*. The value of α determines the location of rejection and nonrejection regions, in conjunction with the value of the hypothesized pa-

Critical values separate rejection regions from nonrejection regions.

rameter and the relevant sampling distribution. This will become clearer when we consider a specific example.

4. *Statement of the decision rule.* The decision rule is a guide that we follow when deciding whether to reject or not to reject the null hypothesis. We may state the decision rule, which is made before the data are gathered, in probabilistic terms, as follows:

If, when the null hypothesis is true, the probability of obtaining a value of the test statistic as extreme as or more extreme than the one actually obtained is less than or equal to α, we reject the null hypothesis. Otherwise, we do not reject the null hypothesis.

We may express this rule in terms of the computed test statistic, as follows:

If the computed value of the test statistic falls in the rejection region, we reject the null hypothesis. If the computed value of the test statistic falls in the nonrejection region, we do not reject the null hypothesis. If the computed value of the test statistic is equal to the critical value, we reject the null hypothesis.

Regardless of how we state the decision rule, it will, if followed, lead to the same decision.

5. *Collection of the data and performance of the calculations.* For our conclusions about a population to be valid, we must obtain the data to be analyzed according to sound scientific principles. We cannot stress this point too much. The quality of a final decision depends on the quality of the raw data on which it is based. We discuss ways to improve the quality of basic data by using proper planning techniques in more detail in Chapter 8, the chapter on analysis of variance, and in Chapter 15, where we discuss the design of sample surveys. If the inferential procedures discussed here and in previous chapters are to be valid, *the sample must be random.*

Collect the data with the analysis in mind. Plan the analysis in detail before collecting the data in accordance with the steps outlined in Chapter 1. The nature of the calculations depends on the question being answered or the problem being solved. The method of analysis depends on the complexity of the calculations and the amount of data to be processed. For simpler problems, a calculator may suffice. But more complicated surveys, involving a large amount of data, will probably require a computer.

6. *Making the statistical decision.* We evaluate the computed test statistic in the light of the decision rule. The statistical decision consists of rejecting or not rejecting the null hypothesis based on this evaluation.

7. *Drawing a conclusion.* If we reject the null hypothesis, we conclude that *the*

alternative hypothesis is true. If we fail to reject the null hypothesis, we conclude that the *null hypothesis may be true.*

To summarize the steps of a hypothesis test, let us consider a situation in which we wish to test a hypothesis about a population mean μ.

1. *Hypotheses.*

$$\left.\begin{array}{l} H_0: \mu = \mu_0 \\ H_1: \mu \neq \mu_0 \end{array}\right\} \quad \text{or} \quad \left.\begin{array}{l} H_0: \mu \leq \mu_0 \\ H_1: \mu > \mu_0 \end{array}\right\} \quad \text{or} \quad \left.\begin{array}{l} H_0: \mu \geq \mu_0 \\ H_1: \mu < \mu_0 \end{array}\right\}$$

(Two-sided alternative)   (One-sided alternatives)

μ_0 is the hypothesized value of μ.

FIGURE 7.2.1   Flow chart for hypothesis-testing procedure

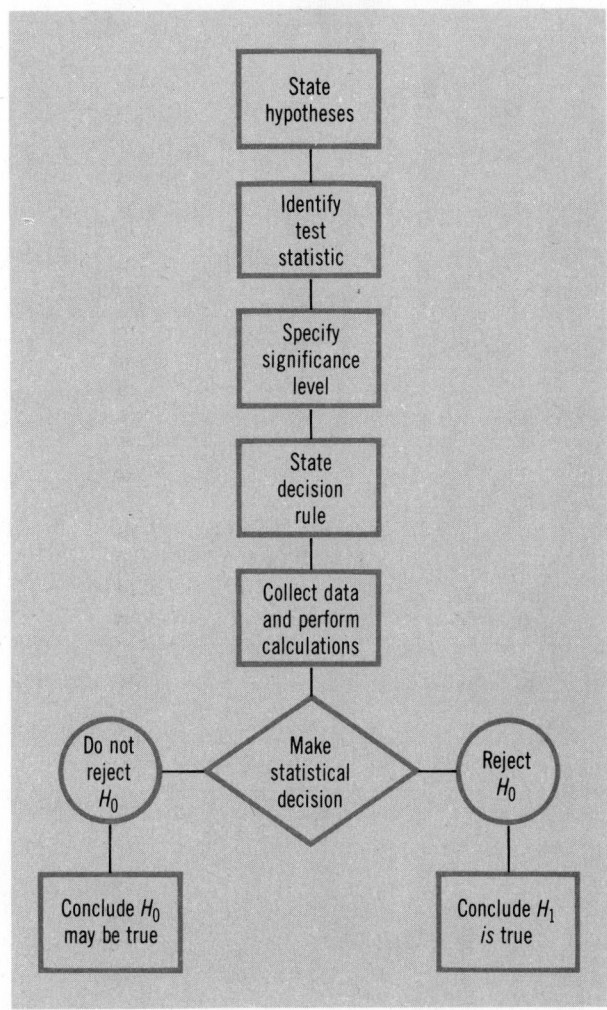

TABLE 7.2.1 Guide to construction of confidence intervals and testing of hypotheses

Case	Sample Statistic	Parameter	Normal Population(s)?	Large Sample Size(s)?	Variance(s) Known?	Standard Error		Test Statistic
1	$\bar{x}$ or $\bar{d}$	μ or μ_d	Yes	Yes	Yes	$\sigma_{\bar{x}} = \sigma/\sqrt{n}$	$\sigma_{\bar{d}} = \sigma_d/\sqrt{n}$	z
2	$\bar{x}$ or $\bar{d}$	μ or μ_d	Yes	Yes	No	$s_{\bar{x}} = s/\sqrt{n}$	$s_{\bar{d}} = s_d/\sqrt{n}$	z or t
3	$\bar{x}$ or $\bar{d}$	μ or μ_d	Yes	No	Yes	$\sigma_{\bar{x}} = \sigma/\sqrt{n}$	$\sigma_{\bar{d}} = \sigma_d/\sqrt{n}$	z
4	$\bar{x}$ or $\bar{d}$	μ or μ_d	Yes	No	No	$s_{\bar{x}} = s/\sqrt{n}$	$s_{\bar{d}} = s_d/\sqrt{n}$	t
5	$\bar{x}$ or $\bar{d}$	μ or μ_d	No	Yes	Yes	$\sigma_{\bar{x}} = \sigma/\sqrt{n}$	$\sigma_{\bar{d}} = \sigma_d/\sqrt{n}$	z
6	$\bar{x}$ or $\bar{d}$	μ or μ_d	No	Yes	No	$s_{\bar{x}} = s/\sqrt{n}$	$s_{\bar{d}} = s_d/\sqrt{n}$	z
7	$\bar{x}$ or $\bar{d}$	μ or μ_d	No	No	Yes	Use nonparametric test (Chapter 13)		
8	$\bar{x}$ or $\bar{d}$	μ or μ_d	No	No	No	Use nonparametric test (Chapter 13)		
9	$\bar{x}_1 - \bar{x}_2$	$\mu_1 - \mu_2$	Yes	Yes	Yes ($=$ or $\neq$)	$\sigma_{\bar{x}_1 - \bar{x}_2} = \sqrt{(\sigma_1^2/n_1) + (\sigma_2^2/n_2)}$		z
10	$\bar{x}_1 - \bar{x}_2$	$\mu_1 - \mu_2$	Yes	Yes	No ($=$)	$s_{\bar{x}_1 - \bar{x}_2} = \sqrt{(s_1^2/n_1) + (s_2^2/n_2)}$ or $sx_2 = \sqrt{(s_p^2/n_1) + (s_p^2/n_2)}$		z or t^*
11	$\bar{x}_1 - \bar{x}_2$	$\mu_1 - \mu_2$	Yes	Yes	No ($\neq$)	$s_{\bar{x}_1 - \bar{x}_2} = \sqrt{(s_1^2/n_1) + (s_2^2/n_2)}$		z or t'
12	$\bar{x}_1 - \bar{x}_2$	$\mu_1 - \mu_2$	Yes	No	Yes ($=$ or $\neq$)	$\sigma_{\bar{x}_1 - \bar{x}_2} = \sqrt{(\sigma_1^2/n_1) + (\sigma_2^2/n_2)}$		z
13	$\bar{x}_1 - \bar{x}_2$	$\mu_1 - \mu_2$	Yes	No	No ($=$)	$s_{\bar{x}_1 - \bar{x}_2} = \sqrt{(s_p^2/n_1) + (s_p^2/n_2)}$		t^*
14	$\bar{x}_1 - \bar{x}_2$	$\mu_1 - \mu_2$	Yes	No	No ($\neq$)	$s_{\bar{x}_1 - \bar{x}_2} = \sqrt{(s_1^2/n_1) + (s_2^2/n_2)}$		t'
15	$\bar{x}_1 - \bar{x}_2$	$\mu_1 - \mu_2$	No	Yes	Yes ($=$ or $\neq$)	$\sigma_{\bar{x}_1 - \bar{x}_2} = \sqrt{(\sigma_1^2/n_1) + (\sigma_2^2/n_2)}$		z
16	$\bar{x}_1 - \bar{x}_2$	$\mu_1 - \mu_2$	No	Yes	No ($=$ or $\neq$)	$s_{\bar{x}_1 - \bar{x}_2} = \sqrt{(s_1^2/n_1) + (s_2^2/n_2)}$		z
17	$\bar{x}_1 - \bar{x}_2$	$\mu_1 - \mu_2$	No	No	Yes ($=$ or $\neq$)	Use nonparametric test (Chapter 13)		
18	$\bar{x}_1 - \bar{x}_2$	$\mu_1 - \mu_2$	No	No	No ($=$ or $\neq$)	Use nonparametric test (Chapter 13)		
19	$\hat{p}$	p	No, dichotomous data	Yes	No	$s_{\hat{p}} = \sqrt{\hat{p}(1 - \hat{p})/n}$		z^{**}
20	$\hat{p}_1 - \hat{p}_2$	$p_1 - p_2$	No, dichotomous data	Yes	No	$s_{\hat{p}_1 - \hat{p}_2} = \sqrt{[\hat{p}_1(1 - \hat{p}_1)/n_1] + [\hat{p}_2(1 - \hat{p}_2)/n_2]}$		z^{***}

Size for large samples
$\bar{x}$: $n \geq 30$
$\bar{x}_1 - \bar{x}_2$: $n_1, n_2 \geq 30$
$\hat{p}$: $n\hat{p}, n(1 - \hat{p}) \geq 5$
$\hat{p}_1 - \hat{p}_2$: $n_1\hat{p}_1, n_1(1 - \hat{p}_1), n_2\hat{p}_2, n_2(1 - \hat{p}_2) \geq 5$

$^*s_p^2 = \dfrac{(n_1 - 1)s_1^2 + (n_2 - 1)s_2^2}{n_1 + n_2 - 2}$

**For hypothesis test
$s_{\hat{p}} = \sqrt{p_0(1 - p_0)/n}$
***When testing H_0: $p_1 = p_2$

$s_{\hat{p}_1 - \hat{p}_2} = \sqrt{\dfrac{\bar{p}(1 - \bar{p})}{n_1} + \dfrac{\bar{p}(1 - \bar{p})}{n_2}}$ where $\bar{p} = \dfrac{n_1' + n_2'}{n_1 + n_2}$

This table is based on a table designed by Professor Glenn Milligan, Ohio State University.

2. *Test statistic.* We decide between z and t.
3. *Significance level.* We select a value of α.
4. *Decision rule.*
5. *Calculations.* We compute a z or t value.
6. *Statistical decision.* We decide whether or not to reject H_0.
7. *Conclusion*

Figure 7.2.1 is a flow chart of the steps in testing a hypothesis. When testing hypotheses about population means and proportions, you must choose either z or t as the appropriate test statistic. The criteria for choosing between the two (as reliability factors) when constructing confidence intervals also apply in hypothesis-testing situations. Table 7.2.1 and Figures 6.4.2 and 6.6.1 summarize these criteria for cases in which the mean and the difference between two means are the parameters of interest.

The following sections are devoted to some specific hypothesis tests. The examples and exercises of this chapter assume that the population is large enough relative to the sample so that the finite population correction can be ignored.

7.3 A TEST FOR THE MEAN OF A NORMALLY DISTRIBUTED POPULATION — KNOWN POPULATION VARIANCE

This section considers examples of hypothesis testing that require the drawing of only one sample. We are interested in knowing whether or not the sample drawn is likely to have come from a population that has a specified mean.

EXAMPLE 7.3.1   Ypsilanti Gifts, a mail-order company that deals in small gifts, charges a flat rate for postage, regardless of the weight of the package. This policy is based on the results of a study conducted several years ago. The study revealed that the mean weight of mailed packages was 17.5 ounces with a standard deviation of 3.6 ounces. The total flat postage rate is the current postage rate per ounce times 17.5. The company management assumed that in the long run the firm would break even on postage costs. The accounting department feels that the mean weight of packages being mailed today may not be 17.5 ounces and that the flat rate charged perhaps should be changed. It suggests that this hypothesis be tested. The volume of business has grown so large that undertaking a complete study, as was done previously, would be impractical. Therefore, management decides to take a random sample of the weights of 100 packages mailed and base the decision on the results from the sample. It is assumed that the weights of packages are approximately normally distributed.

SOLUTION   We can reach a decision by following the seven steps of hypothesis testing discussed in Section 7.2.

1. *Hypotheses.* We wish to reject or not reject the hypothesis that the mean weight of packages being mailed today is the same as it was previously. The implied

alternative hypothesis makes no suggestion as to the direction of any change. It merely suggests that the mean is now different from 17.5. We may state the null and alternative hypotheses symbolically as follows:

$$H_0: \mu = 17.5, \qquad H_1: \mu \neq 17.5$$

We state the two hypotheses in this manner because the firm presumably wants to reject the null hypothesis if the mean has either increased or decreased. That is, the firm wants to adjust its postage charges up or down, depending on the true state of affairs.

2. *Test statistic.* Since the parameter of interest is the population mean μ, the relevant statistic to be computed from the sample is $\bar{x}$. We know from Chapter 5 that when the sampled population is normally distributed the sampling distribution of $\bar{x}$ is normal, with mean μ and variance σ^2/n. Therefore, the test statistic that we can compute from the sample data is

(7.3.1)

$$z = \frac{\bar{x} - \mu_0}{\sigma/\sqrt{n}}$$

which has the standard normal distribution if H_0 is true and the assumptions are met.

3. *Significance level.* Assume that the consequences of committing a Type I error, rejecting H_0 when it is true, are such that we are willing to take a 1 in 20, or 5 in 100, chance of committing this type of error. If the mean weight is 17.5, as stated in the null hypothesis, the investigator does not want the null hypothesis to be rejected, and so he or she makes the probability of rejecting the null hypothesis if it happens to be true fairly small (0.05). If the null hypothesis is rejected because the sample mean is sufficiently larger than 17.5, the firm will be justified in raising the postage rate. Such an act will be unattractive to customers and could possibly drive some of them away. On the other hand, if the null hypothesis is rejected because the sample mean is sufficiently smaller than 17.5, the firm would be justified in lowering the postage rate, an act that would reduce profits. The decision-maker, therefore, selects the level of significance with care. These considerations set the level of significance at $\alpha = 0.05$. Reference to the null and alternative hypotheses reveals that both sufficiently large and sufficiently small values of the test statistic will cause rejection of the null hypothesis. This is because the hypothesized sampling distribution of $\bar{x}$ is centered on 17.5, the hypothesized value of μ. Values of $\bar{x}$ sufficiently far from 17.5 in either direction, above or below, cause z to fall in the rejection region. In other words, if the sample yields a sufficiently large value of $\bar{x}$, we shall compute a sufficiently large value of z. And if we obtain a sufficiently small value of $\bar{x}$ from the sample data, we shall compute a sufficiently small value of z. We know that in the standard normal distribution, "large" values of z are located in the right tail and "small" ones in the left tail. Half of α, therefore, is assigned to each tail of the distribution. A hypothesis test of this type is called a *two-sided test.*

FIGURE 7.3.1   Standard normal distribution, showing nonrejection and rejection regions for $\alpha = 0.05$ for a two-sided test

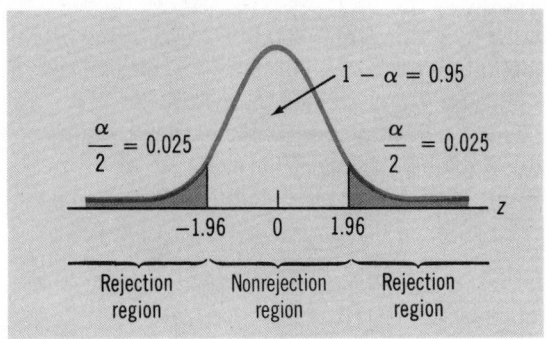

In a two-sided test about μ, $\alpha/2$ is assigned to each tail of the distribution of the test statistic.

    The specification of α fixes the line of demarcation between the nonrejection region and the rejection region. In other words, the values of z that have $\alpha/2 = 0.05/2 = 0.025$ of the area under the standard normal curve to their left and right, respectively, are -1.96 and $+1.96$. These are called the *critical values* of z. The rejection region consists of z values greater than or equal to $+1.96$ and smaller than or equal to -1.96. The nonrejection region consists of the remaining values of z. Figure 7.3.1 shows the nonrejection and rejection regions for $\alpha = 0.05$.

4. *Decision rule.* In the present example, we have a two-sided test. Thus, $\alpha = 0.05$ is divided equally between the two tails of the distribution of the test statistic. We must reflect this in the statement of the decision rule. In probabilistic terms, we may state the decision rule in two parts.

(a) If the data yield a value of the test statistic so *large* that the probability of the occurrence of a value this large or larger when H_0 is true is less than or equal to $\alpha/2 = 0.025$, we reject the null hypothesis.

The decision rule may be stated in terms of probability or in terms of values of the test statistic.

(b) If the data yield a value of the test statistic so *small* that the probability of the occurrence of a value this small or smaller when H_0 is true is less than or equal to $\alpha/2 = 0.025$, we reject the null hypothesis.

    As we have already noted, the critical values of the test statistic are ± 1.96. We may state the decision rule in terms of these values as follows: *If the computed value of the test statistic is either greater than or equal to $+1.96$ or less than or equal to -1.96, we reject the null hypothesis.*

5. *Calculations.* The next step is to collect the data and perform the calculations. We have already decided to draw a sample of 100 packages to be weighed. The statistic of interest is the arithmetic mean $\bar{x}$. Suppose that the value of $\bar{x}$ computed from the sample is 18.4 ounces. From the sample, we may compute the following value of the test statistic:

$$z = \frac{18.4 - 17.5}{3.6/\sqrt{100}} = 2.5$$

6. *Statistical decision.* From the table of the standard normal distribution, the probability of obtaining a value of the test statistic this large or larger when the null hypothesis is true is less than 0.025. In fact, the probability of obtaining a value of 2.5 or larger is 0.0062. According to the decision rule, then, we reject the null hypothesis. Alternatively, we can say that we reject the null hypothesis because 2.5 is greater than 1.96.

7. *Conclusion.* The conclusion compatible with the results of the study is that the mean weight of mailed packages has changed. The firm should consider changing the amount charged for postage.

RELATIONSHIP BETWEEN HYPOTHESIS TESTING AND INTERVAL ESTIMATION

At this point, let us consider the relationship between hypothesis testing and interval estimation. Specifically, we can use the interval-estimation procedures discussed in Chapter 6 to test hypotheses. For example, suppose that we wish to test

$$H_0: \mu = \mu_0 \quad \text{against the alternative} \quad H_1: \mu \neq \mu_0$$

for some level of significance α. Instead of following the procedure just discussed, we can test this hypothesis by constructing the $100(1 - \alpha)\%$ confidence interval for μ. If μ_0 is contained in this interval, we fail to reject H_0. If, on the other hand, μ_0 is not contained in the interval, we reject H_0.

We can illustrate this by using the data of Example 7.3.1. The 95% confidence interval for μ in this example is

$$\bar{x} \pm 1.96 \frac{\sigma}{\sqrt{n}}, \quad 18.4 \pm 1.96 \left(\frac{3.6}{\sqrt{100}} \right), \quad 18.4 \pm 0.7, \quad 17.7, 19.1$$

Since the interval does not contain $\mu_0 = 17.5$, we reject H_0. This is the same result we obtained by following the seven-step hypothesis-testing procedure.

A ONE-SIDED TEST

The test illustrated by Example 7.3.1 is a two-sided test. Now here is an example of a hypothesis test when a *one-sided* test is appropriate.

EXAMPLE 7.3.2 The quality-control department of Atherton Mills specifies that the mean net weight per package of cereal should not be less than 20 ounces. Experience has shown that the weights are approximately normally distributed with a standard deviation of 1.5 ounces. A random sample of 15 packages yields a mean weight of 19.5 ounces. Is this sufficient evidence to indicate that the true mean weight of the packages has decreased?

SOLUTION   We shall use a hypothesis test to help us answer this question.

1. *Hypotheses.* We can say that the sample data provide sufficient evidence that the mean has decreased if we can reject the null hypothesis that the mean has either remained the same or increased. This reasoning suggests the following hypotheses:

$$H_0: \mu \geq 20, \qquad H_1: \mu < 20$$

Note one way in which these hypotheses differ from the hypotheses for the two-sided test: in the two-sided test, the null hypothesis specifies only *one* value of the parameter, whereas the null hypothesis of the one-sided test specifies a large number of values. Theoretically, then, in the case of a one-sided test, a large number of tests would be needed. Generally, we perform only one test—a test at the point of equality. It can be shown, however, that if we reject H_0 at the point of equality, we will also reject H_0 for any other value implied by the null hypothesis.

2. *Test statistic.* Since the population is approximately normally distributed and we know the population standard deviation, we can compute the following test statistic:

$$z = \frac{\bar{x} - \mu_0}{\sigma/\sqrt{n}}$$

3. *Significance level.* Assume that a 0.05 level of significance is satisfactory.

4. *Decision rule.* The fact that there is an inequality in the alternative hypothesis indicates that this is a one-sided test. All of $\alpha = 0.05$, therefore, will be in one tail of the distribution of the test statistic. Since computed values of the test statistic that are sufficiently small will cause rejection of the null hypothesis, the region of rejection will be in the left tail. The critical value of z, then, is that value of z to the left of which lies 0.05 of the area under the standard normal curve. Table C in Appendix I shows the critical value of the test statistic to be -1.645 when we interpolate. We may state the decision rule as follows: if the value of z computed from the sample data is less than or equal to -1.645, we reject H_0; otherwise we do not reject H_0. Figure 7.3.2 shows the rejection and nonrejection regions for this example.

In a one-sided test about μ, all of α is assigned to one tail of the distribution of the test statistic.

5. *Calculations.* A random sample of size 15 yielded a mean of 19.5. From these data, we compute the following value of the test statistic:

$$z = \frac{19.5 - 20}{1.5/\sqrt{15}} = -1.29$$

6. *Statistical decision.* Since -1.29 is greater than -1.645, we cannot reject the null hypothesis.

FIGURE 7.3.2 Standard normal distribution, showing nonrejection and rejection regions for $\alpha = 0.05$ for a one-sided test

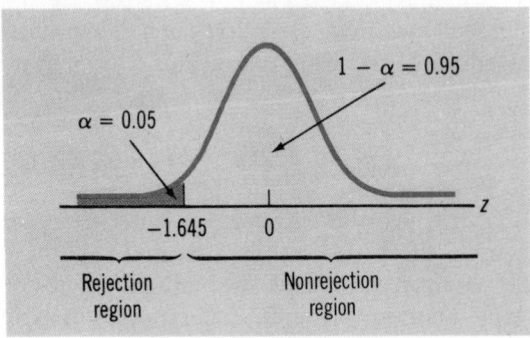

7. _Conclusion._ Even though the sample mean is less than 20, the test result does not provide sufficient evidence to indicate that the true mean has decreased.

SELECTED CRITICAL VALUES OF z

From Examples 7.3.1 and 7.3.2, we learn that when a test is one-sided we need only one critical value of the test statistic and when a test is two-sided we need two critical values of the test statistic. Table 7.3.1 shows the critical values of z for both one-sided and two-sided tests for selected values of α.

p VALUES

In scientific journals, researchers usually report, as part of their research findings, a quantity known as the p value. A p value is a probability associated with a statistical hypothesis test.

> A p value is the probability of obtaining a value of the test statistic as extreme as or more extreme (in the appropriate direction) than that actually obtained given that the tested null hypothesis is true. It is also the smallest level of significance at which H_0 can be rejected.

When you read an article in _The Journal of Marketing Research_, for example, you are likely to see such compact statements as $p < 0.01$, $0.025 < p < 0.05$, and so on. The statement $p < 0.01$, for example, tells you that if the null hypothesis is true the probability of obtaining a value of the test statistic (such as z) as extreme as or more extreme than that actually observed is less than 0.01. We interpret such a finding as evidence supporting the rejection of the null hypothesis and the acceptance of the alternative hypothesis.

TABLE 7.3.1 Critical values of z for selected values of α

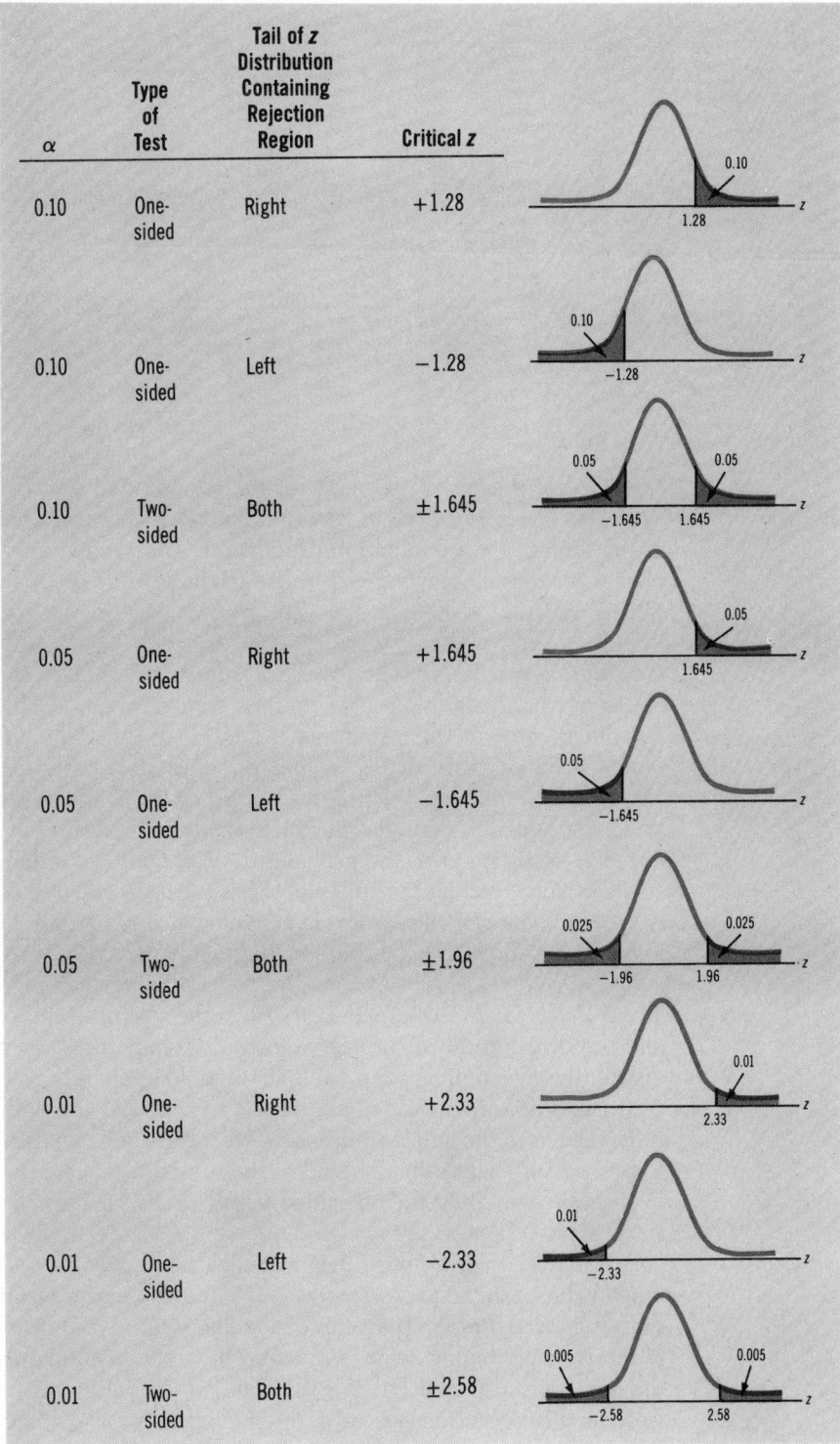

α	Type of Test	Tail of z Distribution Containing Rejection Region	Critical z	
0.10	One-sided	Right	+1.28	
0.10	One-sided	Left	−1.28	
0.10	Two-sided	Both	±1.645	
0.05	One-sided	Right	+1.645	
0.05	One-sided	Left	−1.645	
0.05	Two-sided	Both	±1.96	
0.01	One-sided	Right	+2.33	
0.01	One-sided	Left	−2.33	
0.01	Two-sided	Both	±2.58	

FIGURE 7.3.3 p value for Example 7.3.2

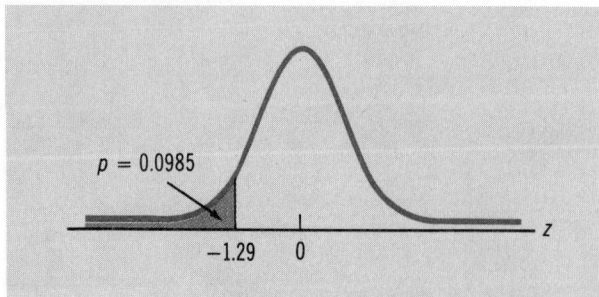

A variety of symbols are used for the p value. We use the lower-case letter p, since this seems to be the most common. Do not confuse this p with the p used as the symbol for a population proportion. The context in which it appears will always make it clear whether p refers to the p value or to a population proportion.

Calculating a p Value   The p value associated with a given hypothesis test depends on three conditions: (1) the test statistic used, (2) the magnitude of the computed value of the test statistic, and (3) whether the alternative hypothesis is one-sided or two-sided. We find p values in a table of the applicable test statistic. As an example, let us refer to Example 7.3.2, in which we had a one-sided test and we computed the value of the test statistic as $z = -1.29$. From Table C in Appendix I, the probability of obtaining a value of z as small as or smaller than -1.29, if the null hypothesis is true, is equal to 0.0985. Since 0.0985 is greater than our chosen level of significance, 0.05, we would not reject H_0. Figure 7.3.3 shows the p value for Example 7.3.2.

The p Value for a Two-sided Test   When the alternative hypothesis is two-sided and the distribution of the test statistic is symmetrical, as in the case of the z distribution, we double the p value that would apply if the alternative hypothesis were one-sided. A two-sided alternative hypothesis, you will recall, allows for a difference from the null hypothesis in either direction. That is, either a sufficiently large or a sufficiently small value of the test statistic causes rejection of the null hypothesis. Doubling the one-sided p value reflects this characteristic of a two-sided hypothesis test.

> For a two-sided test, double the probability found in one tail of the z distribution.

Let us refer to Example 7.3.1, in which the test was two-sided and the computed value of the test statistic was 2.5. The sample data resulted in a test statistic that was located in the right tail of the distribution. However, we did not know that this would happen when we set up the test. To allow for the possibility that the test statistic would fall in either tail, we made the test two-sided. Just as α is divided between the two tails, the p value must also come from both tails. In

FIGURE 7.3.4   *p* value for Example 7.3.1

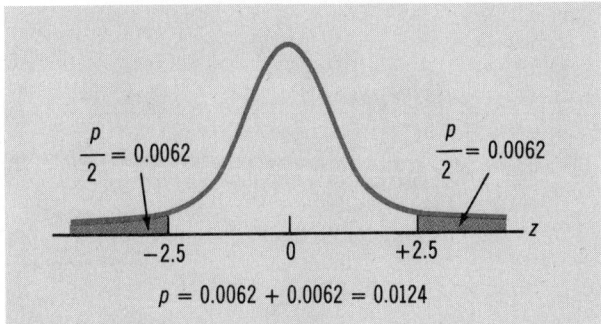

$$\frac{p}{2} = 0.0062 \qquad \frac{p}{2} = 0.0062$$

$$-2.5 \qquad 0 \qquad +2.5$$

$$p = 0.0062 + 0.0062 = 0.0124$$

this case, the p value is equal to the area under the z curve to the right of $+2.5$ plus the area to the left of -2.5. When we consult Table C, we find that $p = 0.0062 + 0.0062 = 0.0124$. Since 0.0124 is less than 0.05, we reject H_0. Figure 7.3.4 shows the p value for Example 7.3.1.

Advantage of Reporting **p** *Values*   When researchers report a p value as part of their research findings, we can set our own level of significance. We can then use our own criterion, rather than that of the researcher, to reject or not reject the null hypothesis. The researcher who reports merely that the null hypothesis was rejected at, say, the 0.05 level is withholding information. This deprives the reader of the ability to make an independent decision on whether or not to reject the null hypothesis. One should, however, avoid the temptation to adjust his or her level of significance after seeing the p value.

Table 7.3.2 provides a concise summary of the steps involved in finding a p value.

EXERCISES

Carry out the seven-step hypothesis-testing procedure at the indicated level of significance and compute the p value for each test.

7.3.1   A population is normally distributed with a standard deviation of 50. A random sample of size 25 is drawn from the population, and a sample mean of 70 is computed. Test at the 0.01 level of significance the null hypothesis that $\mu = 100$.

7.3.2   Bartlett Bolts claims that the mean length of its product is 4.500 inches with a standard deviation of 0.020 inches. A random sample of 16 bolts yields a mean of 4.512 inches. Do these data provide sufficient evidence to indicate that the population mean length is greater than the manufacturer claims? Assume that the dimensions are normally distributed. Let $\alpha = 0.01$.

7.3.3   Dubois Chemicals produces a certain compound by adding distilled water to fixed amounts of other ingredients. The amount of water needed depends on the purity of the

TABLE 7.3.2 Steps for finding the p value for a hypothesis test when the test statistic is z or t

When the alternative hypothesis is a statement of	The p value is	Example
>	located to the right of the computed value of the test statistic.	
<	located to the left of the computed value of the test statistic.	
≠	divided into two parts. Half ($p/2$) is to the right of the computed value of the test statistic if it is positive. Double this $p/2$ value to obtain p.	
	If the computed value of the test statistic is negative, half of the p value ($p/2$) is to its left. Double this $p/2$ value to obtain p.	

other ingredients. As a result of using quality-control techniques, the manufacturer has determined that the mean amount of water needed to meet product standards is 6 liters with a standard deviation of 1 liter. A random sample of 9 batches required, on the average, 7 liters of water. Do these data provide sufficient evidence to indicate that quality-control standards are not being met? Let $\alpha = 0.05$.

 7.3.4 Ⓒ A psychologist is conducting a project in which the subjects are employees with a certain type of physical handicap. On the basis of past experience, the psychologist believes that the mean sociability score of the population of employees with this handicap is greater than 80. The population of scores is known to be approximately normally distributed, with a standard deviation of 10. A random sample of 20 employees selected from the population yields the following results: 99, 69, 91, 97, 70, 99, 72, 74, 74, 76, 96, 97, 68, 71, 99, 78, 76, 78, 83, 66. The psychologist wants to know whether this sample result provides sufficient evidence to indicate that this belief about the population mean sociability score is correct. Let $\alpha = 0.05$.

7.4 A TEST FOR THE MEAN OF A NORMALLY DISTRIBUTED POPULATION—UNKNOWN POPULATION VARIANCE

We often need to test hypotheses about population means when we do not know the population variance. In such cases, even though the population may be approximately normally distributed, we cannot compute the test statistic

$$z = \frac{\overline{x} - \mu_0}{\sigma/\sqrt{n}}$$

because we do not know σ. When this is the case, we use the test statistic

(7.4.1)
$$t = \frac{\overline{x} - \mu_0}{s/\sqrt{n}}$$

As we have seen, this is distributed as Student's t with $n - 1$ degrees of freedom.

In all respects other than choice of test statistic, the hypothesis-testing procedure appropriate under these conditions is the same as that outlined in Section 7.3.

EXAMPLE 7.4.1 Chatham Tire and Rubber Company claims that the average life of a certain grade of tire is greater than 25,000 miles under normal driving conditions on a car of a certain weight. A random sample of 15 tires is tested. A mean and standard deviation of 27,000 and 5,000 miles, respectively, are computed. Assume that the lives of the tires in miles are approximately normally distributed. Can we conclude from these data that the manufacturer's product is as good as claimed?

SOLUTION

1. *Hypotheses.* We are asking whether we can conclude that μ, the population mean, is greater than 25,000. Thus, a statement to this effect should go in the alternative hypothesis. The appropriate hypotheses, then, are

$$H_0: \mu \leq 25{,}000, \qquad H_1: \mu > 25{,}000$$

2. *Test statistic.* The population is approximately normally distributed, and the population standard deviation is unknown. Therefore, the appropriate test statistic is

$$t = \frac{\bar{x} - \mu_0}{s/\sqrt{n}}$$

This is distributed as Student's t with $n - 1$ degrees of freedom if H_0 is true.

3. *Significance level.* Assume that a significance level of 0.05 is satisfactory.

4. *Decision rule.* The test is a one-sided test. Since only sufficiently large values of t will cause us to reject H_0, the region of rejection is in the upper, or right, tail of the distribution. The critical value of the test statistic, then, is the value of t with $n - 1 = 14$ degrees of freedom that has to its right 0.05 of the area under the curve of t. From Table E of Appendix I, we find this value to be 1.7613. The decision rule, then, may be stated as follows: if the computed value of t is greater than or equal to 1.7613, we reject H_0.

5. *Calculations.* From the information given in the statement of the problem, we compute the following value of the test statistic:

$$t = \frac{27{,}000 - 25{,}000}{5000/\sqrt{15}} = 1.55$$

6. *Statistical decision.* Since $1.55 < 1.7613$, we cannot reject H_0.

7. *Conclusion.* Since we do not reject the null hypothesis, the data do not support the conclusion that the true mean life of the tires is as great as the manufacturer claims. Any action the tire firm takes that is incompatible with the hypothesis that $\mu \leq 25{,}000$ would not be warranted on the basis of these data, even though the sample mean is greater than 25,000.

DETERMINING THE CRITICAL VALUES OF t

The appropriate critical values of t depend on the number of degrees of freedom, the value of α, and whether the test is one-sided or two-sided. If the test is one-sided, all of α will be in the right tail of the t distribution when H_1 contains the symbol $>$, and all of α will be in the left tail when H_1 contains the symbol $<$.

TABLE 7.4.1 Location of critical t for one-sided and two-sided tests

| Type of Test | α is | Column in Table E Containing Critical t | | | | |
| | | α | | | | |
		$t_{0.90}$	$t_{0.95}$	$t_{0.975}$	$t_{0.99}$	$t_{0.995}$
One-sided	In one tail	0.10	0.05	0.025	0.01	0.005
Two-sided	Divided between the two tails	0.20	0.10	0.05	0.02	0.01

If the test is two-sided, $\alpha/2$ will be in the right tail and $\alpha/2$ will be in the left tail. For example, if df $= 10$, $\alpha = 0.05$, H_1 contains the symbol $>$, and the test is one-sided, we obtain the critical value of t from Table E by looking in the column headed by $t_{0.95}$. The critical value is 1.8125. If H_1 contains the symbol $<$, the critical value of t is -1.8125.

For a two-sided test with df $= 10$ and $\alpha = 0.05$, the area in each tail of the t distribution is $0.05/2 = 0.025$. There are two critical values of t, and we obtain them from Table E by looking in the column labeled $t_{0.975}$. The critical values are $+2.2281$ and -2.2281.

Table 7.4.1 shows which columns of Table E contain the critical values of t for one-sided and two-sided tests.

CALCULATING THE p VALUE

When we use the t distribution, p is usually an interval.

Readily available tables of the t distribution do not provide us with enough detail to determine the exact p value associated with the computed value of the test statistic. Student's t distribution in Table E, for example, gives values of t only for selected percentiles: 0.90, 0.95, 0.975, 0.99, and 0.995. Unless the computed value of t happens to be exactly equal to a tabulated value, we cannot determine an exact p value from these tables. Thus, when the test statistic is a Student's t, the p value is usually reported as an interval, for example, $p < 0.05$ or $0.025 < p < 0.05$.

Let us consider the value $t = 1.55$ that we computed in Example 7.4.1. When we enter Table E with 14 degrees of freedom, we find that 1.55 falls between 1.345 and 1.7613. If H_0 is true, the probability of obtaining a value of t as large as or larger than 1.345 is 0.10. The probability of obtaining a value as large as or larger than 1.7613 is 0.05. Then the probability, if H_0 is true, of obtaining a value of t as large as or larger than 1.55 is somewhere between 0.10 and 0.05. That is, for this test, $0.10 > p > 0.05$. Figure 7.4.1 shows the calculation of the p value for Example 7.4.1. See Table 7.3.2 for the steps to follow in finding the p value for a test.

FIGURE 7.4.1 p value for Example 7.4.1

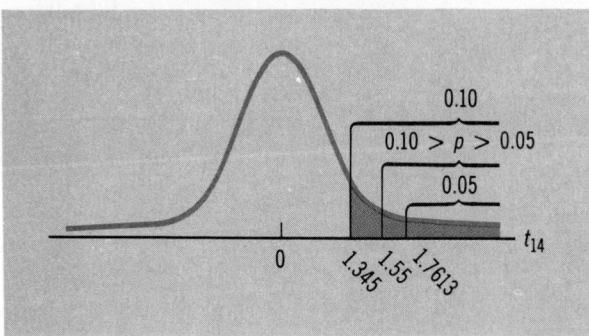

PAIRED OBSERVATIONS

Chapter 6 shows that in statistical inference interest may focus on a population mean difference and explains the construction of a confidence interval for the mean difference using paired sample observations. We may also test hypotheses about the mean difference μ_d in a manner like that described in this section. We sometimes call such a test a *paired-comparisons test* or a *paired-difference test*. Recall that the data for analysis consist of sample differences $d_i = x_{1i} - x_{2i}$, where x_{1i} and x_{2i} are observations taken on the ith pair of subjects under condition 1 and condition 2, respectively. As we saw in Chapter 6, when the data for analysis consist of differences, we have a single sample of measurements. The procedures we follow in testing hypotheses, then, are the ones we use for testing hypotheses in the single sample case.

We may formulate any one of the following pairs of hypotheses:

1. $H_0: \mu_d = \mu_{d_0}$, $H_1: \mu_d \neq \mu_{d_0}$
2. $H_0: \mu_d \leq \mu_{d_0}$, $H_1: \mu_d > \mu_{d_0}$
3. $H_0: \mu_d \geq \mu_{d_0}$, $H_1: \mu_d < \mu_{d_0}$

When the population is normally distributed and the true variance of the difference is known, the test statistic is

(7.4.2)
$$z = \frac{\overline{d} - \mu_{d_0}}{\sigma_{\overline{d}}}$$

When the variance is unknown, the test statistic is

(7.4.3)
$$t = \frac{\overline{d} - \mu_{d_0}}{s_{\overline{d}}}$$

In practice, the most frequently used value of μ_{d_0} is 0.

TABLE 7.4.2 Scores made by nine pairs of salespersons, each member of which was trained by a different method

Pair	Method A	Method B	$d_i = (x_{Ai} - x_{Bi})$
1	90	85	5
2	95	88	7
3	87	87	0
4	85	86	−1
5	90	82	8
6	94	82	12
7	85	70	15
8	88	72	16
9	92	80	12

EXAMPLE 7.4.2 Nine pairs of salespeople are matched as to age, years of experience, level of initiative, and other variables. One member of each pair is randomly assigned to a training course taught by Method A. The other is assigned to the same type of training course taught by Method B. At the end of the course, each salesperson is given an examination to test retention of the material presented. Table 7.4.2 shows the results. The investigator wishes to know whether Method A is better than Method B.

SOLUTION If the methods are equally effective, we would expect, in the long run, to observe an equal number of differences above and below 0. That is, we would expect the true mean difference μ_d to be 0. If, however, Method A is better than Method B, we would expect, in the long run, to find that Method A scores are higher than Method B scores. In this case μ_d, the mean of all $d_i = x_{Ai} - x_{Bi}$, will be greater than 0. The investigator in this example is asking whether this is so.

We carry out the hypothesis test by means of the following familiar steps.

1. *Hypotheses.* Since, in Table 7.4.2, $d_i = x_{Ai} - x_{Bi}$, we have the following hypotheses:

$$H_0: \mu_d \leq 0, \qquad H_1: \mu_d > 0$$

2. *Test statistic.* Assume that the population of differences is approximately normally distributed. Then the test statistic is given by Equation 7.4.3.
3. *Significance level.* Let $\alpha = 0.05$.
4. *Decision rule.* H_1 indicates a one-sided test, with the rejection region in the upper tail of the distribution of t. Since there are 9 paired observations, we have $9 - 1 = 8$ degrees of freedom, and the critical value of t is 1.8595. If the computed t is greater than or equal to 1.8595, we reject H_0. Otherwise we do not reject H_0.

5. _Calculations._ From the data of Table 7.4.2, we compute

$$\bar{d} = \frac{\Sigma d_i}{n} = \frac{5 + 7 + \cdots + 12}{9} = \frac{74}{9} = 8.2$$

$$s_d = \sqrt{\frac{n\Sigma d_i^2 - (\Sigma d_i)^2}{n(n-1)}} = \sqrt{\frac{9(5^2 + 7^2 + \cdots 12^2) - (74)^2}{(9)(8)}} = 6.12$$

$$s_{\bar{d}} = \frac{s_d}{\sqrt{n}} = \frac{6.12}{\sqrt{9}} = 2.04$$

By Equation 7.4.3, we compute the following value of the test statistic:

$$t = \frac{8.2 - 0}{2.04} = 4.02$$

6. _Statistical decision._ Since the computed value of t exceeds the critical value of t, we reject H_0.
7. _Conclusion._ Since we reject H_0, we conclude that on the basis of these data Method A instruction is superior to Method B. Since $4.02 > 3.3554$, $p < 0.005$.

A Reminder Remember that this hypothesis-testing procedure rests on the assumption that the distribution of differences is at least approximately normal. All is not lost, however, if this assumption is not tenable. We may resort to one of two other options. If the sample size is equal to or greater than 30, we can use the procedures of Section 7.5 regardless of the form of the population of differences. If the population of differences is not at least approximately normally distributed and it is not possible to draw a large sample, we may use a test known as the _sign test._ This test, which does not depend on the functional form of the parent population, is discussed in Chapter 13.

COMPUTER **ANALYSIS**

Computers may be used effectively to test hypotheses. Once we have written an appropriate program or located an existing one in a software package, we enter the raw data, give the computer the required commands, and obtain the resulting output. To illustrate the use of computers in testing hypotheses, consider the following example.

EXAMPLE 7.4.3   The following are the weights, in ounces, of 15 bags of raw nuts: 33.38, 32.15, 33.99, 34.10, 33.97, 34.34, 33.95, 33.85, 34.23, 32.73, 33.46, 34.13, 34.45, 34.19, 34.05. We wish to test H_0: $\mu = 34.5$ against H_1: $\mu \neq 34.5$.

SOLUTION   We presume that the assumptions for use of the *t* statistic are met. To perform the hypothesis test, we use the appropriate STAT+ program. Figure 7.4.2 is the computer printout showing the information requested by the program, the appropriate user responses (underlined), and the results of the hypothesis test.

We also may use MINITAB to test hypotheses about a population mean for the single sample case and the paired-comparisons case. For Example 7.4.3, in which the test is two-sided and the sample data are in column 1, the MINITAB command is

MINITAB

MTB > TTEST 34.5, C1

The resulting printout is as follows:

MINITAB

```
TEST OF MU = 34.500 VS MU N.E. 34.500
        N      MEAN    STDEV    SE MEAN          T    P VALUE
C1     15    33.798    0.630      0.163      -4.31     0.0007
```

FIGURE 7.4.2   Computer printout showing STAT+ hypothesis-testing procedure (user responses are underlined)

```
              HYPOTHESIS TESTING CONCERNING ONE MEAN
                        The Hypothesis

Hypothetical Mean : Mu = 34.5
Possible Alternative Hypotheses:
  L) H1: Mu < 34.5
  N) H1: Mu # 34.5
  G) H1: Mu > 34.5
Please select L)ess than, N)ot equal, or G)reater than : N
Alpha (significance level) = .05
                          The Sample

Is your dispersion measure a S)tandard deviation or a V)ariance ? V
Is Sigma^2 known (Y/N) ? N
Sample size n for mean = 15
Sample mean Xbar = 33.798
The sample s^2 = .397274
We will draw inferences using the t distribution with 14 degrees of
freedom.
Press enter key and wait for computation of t values
                          The Test

Ho : Mu = 34.5    H1 : Mu # 34.5
Alpha = .05
Decision rule :
If the observed t <= - 2.1448 or >= 2.1448 then reject Ho
                        The Decision

Observed t = -4.313
Critical t = +/- 2.1448
Based on a random sample of 15 observations with sample s = 0.630297
and Xbar = 33.798, we reject the null hypothesis.
The P value (smallest Alpha to reject Ho) = .001
```

For a one-sided t test, we indicate the type of alternative hypothesis by means of a subcommand. When the alternative hypothesis contains the symbol $>$, the subcommand is $+1$. When the alternative hypothesis contains the symbol $<$, the subcommand is -1. If the conditions call for a z test statistic, the command for a two-sided test is

MINITAB

MTB > ZTEST MU K, C1

where MU is the hypothesized value of the population mean, K is the known or estimated population standard deviation, and C1 specifies that the column containing the sample data is column 1. For one-sided tests, subcommands $+1$ and -1 are used as appropriate.

EXERCISES

Carry out the seven-step hypothesis-testing procedure at the indicated level of significance and compute the p value for each test.

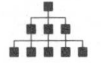

7.4.1 The mean operating temperature of a heat-sensing device, according to the manufacturer, is 190°F. A mean and standard deviation of 195° and 8°, respectively, are computed from the operating temperatures of a random sample of 16 devices. Do these data provide sufficient evidence to indicate that the mean operating temperature is higher than claimed? Let $\alpha = 0.05$, and assume that operating temperatures are approximately normally distributed.

7.4.2 ⓒ Evans Petroleum Company has developed a gasoline additive, which, it expects, will improve gasoline mileage. To obtain information to support the planned marketing program, the firm hires a testing organization to conduct a paired-comparisons test involving 16 pairs of cars. Each pair is identical with respect to make, model, engine size, and other relevant characteristics. One car of each pair is randomly selected and driven over a test course using gasoline with the additive. The other car of the pair is driven over the same course using a comparable gasoline without the additive. The mileage per gallon on the test course is shown here for all cars tested. Use the difference in gasoline mileage for a pair of cars as the variable of interest. Do the data provide sufficient evidence to indicate that the additive does increase gas mileage? Let $\alpha = 0.05$.

Pair #	With additive (X_1)	Without additive (X_2)	Pair #	With additive (X_1)	Without additive (X_2)
1	17.1	16.3	9	10.8	10.1
2	12.7	11.6	10	14.9	13.7
3	11.6	11.2	11	19.7	18.3
4	15.8	14.9	12	11.4	11.0
5	14.0	12.8	13	11.4	10.5
6	17.8	17.1	14	9.3	8.7
7	14.7	13.4	15	19.0	17.9
8	16.3	15.4	16	10.1	9.4

7.4.3 C A study is conducted to investigate how effective street lighting placed at various locations is in reducing automobile accidents in a certain town. The following table shows the median number of nighttime accidents per week at 12 locations one year before and one year after the installation of lighting. Do these data provide sufficient evidence to indicate that lighting does reduce nighttime automobile accidents? Let $\alpha = 0.05$.

Location	A	B	C	D	E	F	G	H	I	J	K	L
# before	8	12	5	4	6	3	4	3	2	6	6	9
# after	5	3	2	1	4	2	2	4	3	5	4	3

7.4.4 A random sample of 25 hamburger patties sold by Hamburger Heaven yields a mean weight of 3.8 ounces with a standard deviation of 0.5 ounce. Can we conclude from these data that the population mean is less than 4 ounces? Let $\alpha = 0.05$. Weights of hamburger patties are approximately normally distributed.

7.4.5 C The following are the weights of a random sample of 10 employees working in the shipping department of Flanagan Grocery Company: 154, 154, 186, 243, 159, 174, 183, 163, 192, 181. On the basis of these data, can we conclude that the firm's shipping department employees have a mean weight greater than 160 pounds? Let $\alpha = 0.05$.

7.4.6 C A hospital administrator states that emergency-room charges for a certain procedure must average at least $25 if the hospital is not to lose money on its emergency service. The hospital charged the following amounts (rounded to the nearest dollar) for treating a sample of patients with the procedure in the emergency room during a one-year period: 26, 20, 33, 25, 27, 30, 23, 27, 22, 38, 51, 60, 38, 56, 31. On the basis of these data, can we conclude at the 0.01 significance level that the mean charge for the sampled population of patients is greater than $25?

7.5 A TEST FOR THE MEAN OF A POPULATION THAT IS NOT NORMALLY DISTRIBUTED

Needless to say, not all populations are normally—or even approximately normally—distributed. Suppose that the sample on which a hypothesis test is based has been drawn from a population that is not normally distributed. If the sample is large (say, $n \geq 30$), we take advantage of the central limit theorem and use

$$z = \frac{\bar{x} - \mu_0}{\sigma/\sqrt{n}}$$

as the test statistic. If we do not know the standard deviation of the population, we use the sample standard deviation as an estimate. We reason that the large sample, which is necessary if the central limit theorem is to apply, will yield a satisfactory estimate of σ.

EXAMPLE 7.5.1 Gilman Marketing Services is interested in the amount that households in a certain town spend on groceries each week. The firm believes that the average amount spent per household each week is less than $90. A random sample of 100 households yields a mean of $88 and a standard deviation of $10. Do these data support the firm's belief?

SOLUTION — We can use the results of a hypothesis test to answer the question.

1. *Hypotheses.*

$$H_0: \mu \geq \$90, \qquad H_1: \mu < \$90$$

2. *Test statistic.* The functional form of the population is not specified. However, since the sample size is large, we know that the sampling distribution of $\bar{x}$ is at least approximately normally distributed because of the central limit theorem. If σ were known, the test statistic would be

$$z = \frac{\bar{x} - \mu_0}{\sigma/\sqrt{n}}$$

However, since the sample size is large, it ought to yield a satisfactory estimate of σ. The test statistic we compute, then, is

$$z = \frac{\bar{x} - \mu_0}{s/\sqrt{n}}$$

We assume that this statistic will follow a normal distribution well enough for us to use a value from the standard normal distribution as the critical value of the test statistic.

3. *Significance level.* Let $\alpha = 0.05$.
4. *Decision rule.* If the computed value of z is less than or equal to -1.645, we reject H_0.
5. *Calculations.* From the information given, the computed value of the test statistic is

$$z = \frac{\$88 - \$90}{10/\sqrt{100}} = -2.0$$

6. *Statistical decision.* Since $-2.0 < -1.645$, we reject H_0.
7. *Conclusion.* Since we reject H_0, we conclude that the data support the firm's belief. For this test, $p = 0.0228$.

EXERCISES

Carry out the seven-step hypothesis-testing procedure at the indicated level of significance and compute the p value for each test.

7.5.1 An accountant with the Hudson Group has been told that in her section of the country the average weekly salary of typists is $175. She wants to know whether she should doubt this information. She calls on you for help. You decide to use the procedures of hypothesis testing. Use the seven steps of hypothesis testing to arrive at a decision. Let $\alpha = 0.05$, use a sample of size 100, and use the sample standard deviation, $s = \$25$, to estimate the population standard deviation.

If your sample yielded an $\bar{x}$ of \$170, what advice would you give the accountant?

 7.5.2 A real estate agent claims that the average value of homes in a certain neighborhood is greater than \$45,000. A random sample of 36 homes has a mean value of \$48,000 and a standard deviation of \$12,000. Do these data support the agent's claim at the 0.05 level of significance?

 7.5.3 The manager of Ingersoll Shopping Malls hypothesizes that cars in mall parking lots remain there, on the average, more than 90 minutes on weekends. A random sample of 100 cars arriving on weekends yields a mean parking time of 96 minutes with a standard deviation of 30 minutes. Do these data provide sufficient evidence to support the manager's contention? Let $\alpha = 0.05$.

 7.5.4 An industrial psychologist who serves as consultant to many electronics firms has accused production supervisors of promoting unskilled assembly-line employees to a certain job for which they have no aptitude. A random sample of 40 of these employees yields the following aptitude scores. The population variance is known to be 280, and the population of scores is not normally distributed. The production supervisors contend that the mean aptitude score of all the employees they promoted is greater than 60. Do these data provide sufficient evidence to support their claim? Let $\alpha = 0.05$. Find the p value.

73	57	96	78	74	42	55	44	91	91
50	65	46	63	82	60	97	79	85	79
92	50	42	46	86	81	81	83	64	76
40	57	78	66	84	96	94	70	70	81

 7.5.5 Ⓒ Jowett Roofing Company wants the percentage of impurities in its roofing tar not to exceed an average of 3%. A random sample of 30 one-gallon cans yields the following percentages of impurities. On the basis of these data, can one conclude that the population mean is less than 3%? Let $\alpha = 0.01$.

3	3	1	1	0.5	2	2	4	5	4	5	3	1	3	1
4	1	1	4	2	5	3	1	1	1	0.75	1.5	3	3	2

7.6 A TEST FOR THE DIFFERENCE BETWEEN THE MEANS OF TWO NORMALLY DISTRIBUTED POPULATIONS

The difference between two population means often interests researchers and managers. If we do not have direct knowledge of the true parameters, we make an inference on the basis of sample data. Two independent random samples, one from each of two populations, provide data on which we base the inference. In the most common situation involving the difference between two population means, we want to find whether it is reasonable to conclude that the two are not equal. In this situation the test may be either one-sided or two-sided. For the two-sided case, the hypotheses are of the form

$$H_0: \mu_1 - \mu_2 = 0, \qquad H_1: \mu_1 - \mu_2 \neq 0$$

and in the one-sided case, the hypotheses are formulated as

$$H_0: \mu_1 - \mu_2 \leq 0, \qquad H_1: \mu_1 - \mu_2 > 0$$

or

$$H_0: \mu_1 - \mu_2 \geq 0, \qquad H_1: \mu_1 - \mu_2 < 0$$

However, in these hypotheses we can replace 0 with any value of interest. For example, we might want to test the null hypothesis that $\mu_1 - \mu_2 = 10$.

We discuss hypothesis tests involving the difference between two population means under three different circumstances: (1) when sampling is from normally distributed populations with known population variances; (2) when sampling is from normally distributed populations with unknown population variances; and (3) when sampling is from populations that are not normally distributed. This section covers the first two situations, and Section 7.7 the third situation.

KNOWN POPULATION VARIANCES

For testing the difference between two population means when the populations are normally distributed and the population variances are known, the appropriate test statistic is

(7.6.1)
$$z = \frac{(\bar{x}_1 - \bar{x}_2) - (\mu_1 - \mu_2)_0}{\sqrt{\dfrac{\sigma_1^2}{n_1} + \dfrac{\sigma_2^2}{n_2}}}$$

This follows from our knowledge of the sampling distribution of $\bar{x}_1 - \bar{x}_2$, the difference between two sample means. Neither the sample sizes nor the variances need be equal.

EXAMPLE 7.6.1   Two procedures can be used to manufacture wire. Experience has shown that the tensile strengths that result from both procedures are approximately normally distributed. The standard deviation for Procedure 1 is 6 psi. For Procedure 2 the standard deviation is 8 psi. Management wishes to know whether the mean tensile strengths of wire produced by the two methods are different.

SOLUTION   We can decide by means of the following hypothesis test.

1. *Hypotheses.*

$$H_0: \mu_1 - \mu_2 = 0, \qquad H_1: \mu_1 - \mu_2 \neq 0$$

2. *Test statistic.* The test statistic is

$$z = \frac{(\bar{x}_1 - \bar{x}_2) - 0}{\sqrt{\dfrac{\sigma_1^2}{n_1} + \dfrac{\sigma_2^2}{n_2}}}$$

which is distributed as the standard normal if H_0 is true and the assumptions are met.

3. *Significance level.* Let $\alpha = 0.05$.
4. *Decision rule.* Reject H_0 if the computed value of the test statistic is either greater than or equal to $+1.96$ or less than or equal to -1.96.
5. *Calculations.* A random sample of 12 pieces of wire made by Procedure 1 gives a mean of 40 psi. A random sample of 16 pieces made by Procedure 2 yields a mean of 34 psi. From these data, we can compute the following value of the test statistic:

$$z = \frac{(40 - 34) - 0}{\sqrt{\dfrac{36}{12} + \dfrac{64}{16}}} = 2.27$$

6. *Statistical decision.* Since $2.27 > 1.96$, we reject H_0.
7. *Conclusion.* On the basis of the sample data, we conclude that the two population means are different. That is, we conclude that the two procedures, on the average, do not yield wire with the same tensile strength. For this test, $p = 2(1 - 0.9884) = 2(0.0116) = 0.0232$.

UNKNOWN POPULATION VARIANCES

In testing a hypothesis about the difference between the means of two normally distributed populations when the population variances are unknown, we distinguish between two cases: (1) the case in which the population variances are equal, and (2) the case in which they are not equal. We make the same distinction in Chapter 6 when we discuss interval estimation of the difference between two population means. Let us consider each case separately.

Equal Population Variances Suppose that the population variances, though unknown, are equal. Then the correct test statistic for testing hypotheses about the difference between the means of two normally distributed populations is

$$t = \frac{(\bar{x}_1 - \bar{x}_2) - (\mu_1 - \mu_2)_0}{\sqrt{\dfrac{s_p^2}{n_1} + \dfrac{s_p^2}{n_2}}}$$

(7.6.2)

where

$$s_p^2 = \frac{(n_1 - 1)s_1^2 + (n_2 - 1)s_2^2}{n_1 + n_2 - 2}$$

is the pooled estimate of the common population variance. We discuss the rationale for pooling sample variances in Section 6.6.

EXAMPLE 7.6.2 Two machines are used in the making of steel rings. The quality-control department asks whether it should conclude that Machine 1 is producing rings with a larger inside diameter than Machine 2. Assume that the diameters are approximately normally distributed and $\sigma_1^2 = \sigma_2^2$.

SOLUTION

1. *Hypotheses.*

$$H_0: \mu_1 - \mu_2 \le 0, \qquad H_1: \mu_1 - \mu_2 > 0$$

2. *Test statistic.* Under the assumption that the two populations are normally distributed with equal variances, the appropriate test statistic is

$$t = \frac{(\bar{x}_1 - \bar{x}_2) - 0}{\sqrt{\dfrac{s_p^2}{n_1} + \dfrac{s_p^2}{n_2}}}$$

which, if H_0 is true, is distributed as Student's t with $n_1 + n_2 - 2$ degrees of freedom.

3. *Significance level.* Let $\alpha = 0.01$.

4. *Decision rule.* If the computed value of t is greater than or equal to the critical t for $n_1 + n_2 - 2$ degrees of freedom and $\alpha = 0.01$, reject H_0.

5. *Calculations.* A random sample of 10 rings from Machine 1 and 15 rings from Machine 2 gives the following results: $\bar{x}_1 = 1.051$, $\bar{x}_2 = 1.036$, $s_1^2 = 0.000441$, and $s_2^2 = 0.000225$. The pooled estimate of the common population variance is

$$s_p^2 = \frac{9(0.000441) + 14(0.000225)}{23} = 0.000310$$

The value of the test statistic that we may compute from the sample data is

$$t = \frac{(1.051 - 1.036) - 0}{\sqrt{\dfrac{0.000310}{10} + \dfrac{0.000310}{15}}} = 2.09$$

6. *Statistical decision.* Since the computed t of 2.09 is less than the critical t of 2.5, we cannot reject the null hypothesis.
7. *Conclusion.* Since we did not reject H_0, the quality-control department cannot conclude from the test results that Machine 1 is producing steel rings with a larger inside diameter than Machine 2. Since $2.0687 < t < 2.500$, then $0.025 > p > 0.01$.

Unequal Population Variances When the population variances are not equal, there is, of course, no basis for pooling s_1^2 and s_2^2. The test statistic, then, is

(7.6.3)
$$t' = \frac{(\bar{x}_1 - \bar{x}_2) - (\mu_1 - \mu_2)_0}{\sqrt{\dfrac{s_1^2}{n_1} + \dfrac{s_2^2}{n_2}}}$$

The critical value of t' for an α level of significance and a two-sided test is approximately

(7.6.4)
$$t'_{1-\alpha/2} = \frac{w_1 t_1 + w_2 t_2}{w_1 + w_2}$$

where $w_1 = s_1^2/n_1$, $w_2 = s_2^2/n_2$, $t_1 = t_{1-\alpha/2}$ for $n_1 - 1$ degrees of freedom, and $t_2 = t_{1-\alpha/2}$ for $n_2 - 1$ degrees of freedom. The critical value of t' for a one-sided test is found by computing $t'_{1-\alpha}$ by Equation 7.6.4 using $t_1 = t_{1-\alpha}$ for $n_1 - 1$ degrees of freedom and $t_2 = t_{1-\alpha}$ for $n_2 - 1$ degrees of freedom.

For a one-sided test with the rejection region in the right tail of the sampling distribution, reject H_0 if the computed t' is equal to or greater than the critical t'. For a one-sided test with a left-tail rejection region, reject H_0 if the computed value of t' is equal to or smaller than the negative of the critical t' computed by the indicated adaptation of Equation 7.6.4.

When we wish to test a hypothesis about the difference between the means of two populations that have unequal variances, the Mann-Whitney two-sample test described in Chapter 13 provides a possible alternative technique.

EXAMPLE 7.6.3 In Example 7.6.2, suppose that we do not know whether the population variances are equal and that we are unwilling to assume that they are equal.

SOLUTION The critical value of the test statistic for $\alpha = 0.01$ (one-sided test) is found as follows:

$$t_1 = t_{1-0.01,\, 9} = 2.821$$
$$t_2 = t_{1-0.01,\, 14} = 2.624$$
$$w_1 = 0.000441/10 = 0.0000441$$
$$w_2 = 0.000225/15 = 0.000015$$
$$t' = \frac{0.0000441(2.821) + 0.000015(2.624)}{0.0000441 + 0.000015} = 2.771$$

The value of the test statistic that we can compute from the sample data is

$$t' = \frac{(1.051 - 1.036) - 0}{\sqrt{\dfrac{0.000441}{10} + \dfrac{0.000225}{15}}} = 1.95$$

Since $1.95 < 2.771$, we cannot reject H_0 on the basis of this test.

COMPUTER **ANALYSIS**

Both STAT+ and MINITAB, as well as other statistical software packages, contain routines for performing the calculations necessary for testing hypotheses about the difference between two population means. The following example illustrates the use of MINITAB for this purpose.

EXAMPLE 7.6.4   We wish to know if female retail sales personnel have better communications skills than their male counterparts. Scores made on a communications skills test by a sample of female and male retail salespersons are stored in column 1 and column 2, respectively, of a MINITAB worksheet.

SOLUTION   Figure 7.6.1 shows the stored data, the necessary commands, and the output from the MINITAB program for testing the null hypothesis that, on the average, the female population has the same or poorer communications skills than the male population.

FIGURE 7.6.1   Computer printout for Example 7.6.4 (MINITAB printout)

MINITAB
```
MTB > SET C1
DATA> 53 32 58 43 47 41 39 46 51 56 46 35
DATA> END
MTB > SET C2
DATA> 52 61 46 23 35 42 38 39 36 37 51 49 37 34 17
DATA> TWOSAMPLET C1 C2;
SUBC> POOLED;
SUBC> ALTERNATIVE = +1.

TWOSAMPLE T FOR C1 VS C2
          N         MEAN        STDEV      SE MEAN
C1       12        45.58        8.07         2.3
C2       15        39.8         11.2         2.9

95 PCT CI FOR MU C1 - MU C2: (-2.1, 13.7)

TTEST MU C1 = MU C2 (VS GT): T= 1.50 P=0.072 DF= 25

POOLED STDEV =          9.92
```

EXERCISES

Carry out the seven-step hypothesis-testing procedure at the indicated level of significance and compute the p value for each test.

7.6.1 Knox Textiles can buy a certain type of yarn from one of two vendors. The vendors' products appear to be compatible in all respects except price and, possibly, breaking strength. The manufacturer will buy from Vendor 1 (whose price is lower) unless there is reason to believe that Vendor 1's product has a lower mean breaking strength than Vendor 2's. Random samples are drawn from the two vendors' stocks, with the following results. Assume that breaking strengths are approximately normally distributed. (a) Based on an appropriate hypothesis test with $\alpha = 0.05$, would you advise the manufacturer to buy the cheaper yarn? Assume that the population variances are equal. (b) Repeat part (a) under the assumption that the population variances are not equal.

Vendor 1	$n = 10$	$\bar{x} = 94$	$s^2 = 14$
Vendor 2	$n = 12$	$\bar{x} = 98$	$s^2 = 9$

7.6.2 The following data are based on random samples taken from two shifts at La Follette Technologies. The variable of interest is the length of time needed to do a certain task. Do these data provide sufficient evidence to indicate that the average time needed on Shift 2 is less than that on Shift 1? Let $\alpha = 0.05$. Specify all assumptions that you have to make in order to validate your procedure.

Shift 1	$n = 10$	$\bar{x} = 26.1$	$s^2 = 144$
Shift 2	$n = 8$	$\bar{x} = 17.6$	$s^2 = 110$

7.6.3 McKinley Drugs is comparing the effectiveness of a new sleeping pill formula, B, with formula A, which is now on the market. For three nights, 25 subjects try Formula B, and 25 subjects in an independent sample try Formula A. The variable of interest is the average number of additional hours of sleep (compared with the nights when no drug is taken) the subjects get for the three nights. The results are as follows. Do these data provide sufficient evidence to indicate that Formula B is better than Formula A? Let $\alpha = 0.01$.

Medicine	A	B
$\bar{x}$	1.4	1.9
s^2	0.09	0.16

7.6.4 [C] An industrial psychologist feels that a big factor in job turnover among assembly-line workers is the individual employee's self-esteem. He thinks that workers who change jobs often (population A) have, on the average, lower self-esteem, as measured by a standardized test, than workers who do not (population B). To determine whether he can support his belief with statistical analysis, he draws a simple random sample of employees from each population and gives each a test measuring self-esteem. The results are as follows. The psychologist believes that the relevant populations of scores are normally distributed, with equal, although unknown, variances. At the 0.01 level of significance, what should he conclude? What use can he make of his findings?

Group A	60	45	42	62	68	54	52	55	44	41								
Group B	70	72	74	74	76	91	71	78	76	78	83	50	52	66	65	53	52	

7.6.5   [C] In a university economics class, an argument arises over the contention of some members of the class that men have a better knowledge of the stock market than women. To settle the argument, the instructor gives a test to measure knowledge of the stock market to a random sample of 15 male students and an independent random sample of 15 female students. The results are as follows. Can one conclude on the basis of these data that male students, on the average, have a better knowledge of the stock market than female students? Let $\alpha = 0.05$. What assumptions are necessary?

Women	73	96	74	55	91	50	46	82	43	79	79	50	46	81	83
Men	57	78	42	44	91	65	63	60	97	85	92	42	86	81	64

7.7 A TEST FOR THE DIFFERENCE BETWEEN MEANS OF TWO POPULATIONS NOT NORMALLY DISTRIBUTED

When samples are drawn from nonnormally distributed populations, we can use the results of the central limit theorem if the sample sizes are large. This lets us use normal theory, since the sampling distribution will be approximately normally distributed.

The appropriate test statistic for hypothesis-testing purposes is

(7.7.1)
$$z = \frac{(\bar{x}_1 - \bar{x}_2) - (\mu_1 - \mu_2)_0}{\sqrt{\dfrac{\sigma_1^2}{n_1} + \dfrac{\sigma_2^2}{n_2}}}$$

If the population variances are unknown, we use the sample variances as estimates. We do not pool the sample variances, however, since we do not need to assume equality of population variances when we use the z statistic.

EXAMPLE 7.7.1   Moody Marketing Systems wishes to know whether it can conclude that the mean number of hours of television viewing per week by families in a certain type of community (Type A) is less than that in another type of community (Type B). Independent random samples give the following information:

	Type A	Type B
Number of families interviewed	100	75
Average number of hours of television viewing per week	18.50	27.25
Standard deviation	10	14

SOLUTION   The results of the following hypothesis test will help answer the question.

1. *Hypotheses.*

$$H_0: \mu_A \geq \mu_B, \qquad H_1: \mu_A < \mu_B$$

2. *Test statistic.* The functional forms of the populations are not given. However, since the sample sizes are large, we rely on the central limit theorem and assume that the statistic $\bar{x}_A - \bar{x}_B$ is approximately normally distributed. If σ_A^2 and σ_B^2 were known, the appropriate test statistic would be given by Equation 7.7.1. Since these parameters are unknown, we compute

$$z = \frac{(\bar{x}_A - \bar{x}_B) - 0}{\sqrt{\dfrac{s_A^2}{n_A} + \dfrac{s_B^2}{n_B}}}$$

which is approximately normally distributed if H_0 is true.
3. *Significance level.* Let $\alpha = 0.05$.
4. *Decision rule.* If the computed value of the test statistic is less than or equal to -1.645, reject H_0.
5. *Calculations.* From the data given in the problem statement, we may compute the following value of the test statistic:

$$z = \frac{(18.50 - 27.25) - 0}{\sqrt{\dfrac{100}{100} + \dfrac{196}{75}}} = -4.60$$

6. *Statistical decision.* Since $-4.60 < -1.645$, we reject H_0.
7. *Conclusion.* Since we reject H_0, we can conclude that μ_A is less than μ_B. For this test, $p < 0.001$.

Here we have seen that, when two populations are not normally distributed, we can test the hypothesis that the two population means are equal if the samples are large enough to apply the central limit theorem. When the data consist of small samples drawn from populations that are not normally distributed, we need a hypothesis test appropriate for such a situation. Chapter 13 presents such a test, the *Mann-Whitney test.*

EXERCISES

Carry out the seven-step hypothesis-testing procedure at the indicated level of significance and compute the p value for each test.

7.7.1   Neurath Paper Company is thinking of buying one of two tracts of timberland. The size of the trees on each tract is important. Measurements of trunk diameter for a random sample of 50 trees from each tract give the following results. Do these data provide sufficient evidence at the 0.05 level of significance to indicate that trees on Tract B are, on the average, smaller than trees on Tract A?

Tract A	$\bar{x} = 28.25''$	$s^2 = 25$
Tract B	$\bar{x} = 22.50''$	$s^2 = 16$

7.7.2 An analyst is studying the advertising practices of two types of retail firms. One variable is the amount spent on advertising during the preceding year. An independent random sample is drawn from each type of firm, with the following results. Can we conclude from these data that Type A firms spent more for advertising, on the average, than Type B firms? Let $\alpha = 0.05$.

Type A	$n = 60$	$\bar{x} = \$14,800$	$s^2 = 180,000$
Type B	$n = 70$	$\bar{x} = \$14,500$	$s^2 = 133,000$

7.7.3 A random sample of 100 families from Community A and a random sample of 150 families from Community B yield the following data on length of residence in current homes. Do these data provide sufficient evidence to indicate that, on the average, families in Community A have been living in their current homes for less time than families in Community B have? Let $\alpha = 0.05$.

Community A	$\bar{x} = 33$ months	$s^2 = 900$
Community B	$\bar{x} = 49$ months	$s^2 = 1,050$

7.7.4 An advertising analyst interviews a random sample of male executives and a random sample of married, unemployed, middle-class adult females regarding their exposure to advertising through radio, television, newspapers, and magazines. One variable is the number of ads to which each subject is exposed on a typical weekday. The results are shown in the following table. Do these data provide sufficient evidence to indicate that, on the average, the sampled female population is exposed to more ads than the sampled population of male executives? Let $\alpha = 0.01$.

Group	n	Mean number of ads to which exposed	Standard deviation
Male executives	100	200	50
Unemployed females	144	225	60

7.7.5 [C] Oxford Electrical Products wants to compare two types of electrical wire with respect to resistance per unit length. Thirty specimens of Wire 1 and 35 specimens of Wire 2 yield the following measurements in ohms $\times 10^2$. Can we conclude on the basis of these data that the populations differ with respect to mean resistance? Let $\alpha = 0.05$.

Wire 1	55.2	53.5	52.3	54.1	52.4	50.5	53.5	46.9	52.9	57.1	55.7	51.2	55.2
	57.4	53.9	58.1	50.6	59.4	51.8	50.8	56.9	56.3	59.1	52.7	56.1	58.2
	53.1	50.6	53.1	59.7									
Wire 2	46.9	50.6	47.3	48.0	49.2	48.4	48.5	48.6	48.2	50.2	47.2	50.3	49.1
	48.2	47.4	48.1	49.4	47.4	49.7	49.1	49.3	50.3	50.8	48.3	47.7	48.5
	51.1	50.9	49.5	49.7	51.4	48.1	49.7	50.9	48.6				

7.7.6 [C] A manufacturer wants to compare the viscosity of two brands of motor oil. Thirty-two randomly selected specimens of each brand are analyzed, with the following results. (The data are coded for ease of computation.) Can we conclude on the basis of these data that the mean viscosity of the two brands differs? Let $\alpha = 0.05$.

Brand A	13	21	60	35	38	10	36	24	35	35	45	19	42	11	35	39	25
	17	51	25	52	25	11	11	55	44	25	41	16	47	50	18		
Brand B	46	52	66	65	71	67	47	48	58	42	66	69	60	80	45	47	69
	75	43	46	74	73	43	70	51	72	65	45	76	48	56	64		

7.8 A TEST FOR A POPULATION PROPORTION

We come now to hypothesis testing when the parameter of interest is the proportion of elements that have a given characteristic. We call the elements with the characteristic "successes" and designate the proportion of successes by p.

Chapter 4 shows that the binomial probability distribution is the correct model when we are considering the number of elements out of a total of n elements that have a certain characteristic.

When we test hypotheses about p, and n is large, the test statistic is z.

When n is large, the work it takes to find the probability of some specified number of successes using the binomial formula is less than appealing. However, as we point out in Chapter 5, when np and $n(1 - p)$ are both greater than 5, the binomial distribution may be approximated by the normal distribution. When n/N is also ≤ 0.05, the appropriate test statistic for testing hypotheses about population proportions is

(7.8.1)
$$z = \frac{\hat{p} - p_0}{\sqrt{\dfrac{p_0 q_0}{n}}}$$

where p_0 is the hypothesized proportion, $q_0 = 1 - p_0$, and $\hat{p}$ is the sample proportion. This statistic is distributed approximately as the standard normal if H_0 is true. When n is large relative to N, we use a finite population correction in Equation 7.8.1. As we have noted, in the examples and exercises of this chapter, we assume that n is small relative to N, so that we can ignore the correction factor. We use p_0 rather than $\hat{p}$ in the denominator of Equation 7.8.1 because we assume H_0 to be true while we are conducting the test.

EXAMPLE 7.8.1   The president of Peabody Power and Light Company, concerned about the safety record of the firm's employees, sets aside \$15,000 a year for safety education. The firm's accountant believes that more than 75% of similar firms spend more than \$15,000 a year on safety education. The president asks the accountant for evidence to support this belief.

SOLUTION   The accountant bases his response on the following hypothesis test.

1. *Hypotheses.*

$$H_0: p \leq 0.75, \qquad H_1: p > 0.75$$

2. *Test statistic.* The accountant decides to obtain information from a simple random sample of 60 firms. This sample is large enough to enable the accountant to use Equation 7.8.1.
3. *Significance level.* Let $\alpha = 0.05$.
4. *Decision rule.* If the computed value of the test statistic is greater than or equal to 1.645, reject H_0.
5. *Calculations.* Of the 60 firms, 50 state that they spend more than $15,000 per year on safety education. Therefore $\hat{p} = 50/60 = 0.83$, and the computed value of the test statistic is

$$z = \frac{0.83 - 0.75}{\sqrt{\dfrac{(0.75)(0.25)}{60}}} = 1.43$$

6. *Statistical decision.* Since $1.43 < 1.645$, we cannot reject the null hypothesis.
7. *Conclusion.* Even though the sample proportion is greater than 0.75, the test results do not support the accountant's hypothesis. We should conclude that the true proportion with the characteristic of interest may be less than or equal to 0.75. For this test, $p = 1 - 0.9236 = 0.0764$.

EXERCISES

Carry out the seven-step hypothesis-testing procedure at the desired level of significance and compute the p value for each test.

 7.8.1 A self-help club is considering the promotion of a home study course leading to a high school diploma for members who have not finished high school. The president of the club thinks that fewer than 25% of the members have not completed high school, and would like to support this belief with an appropriate hypothesis test. Of a random sample of 200 members, 42 indicate that they have not completed high school. Do these data support the president's belief at the 0.05 significance level?

 7.8.2 A college with an enrollment of approximately 10,000 students wants to build a new student parking garage. The administration believes that more than 60% of the students drive cars to school. If, in a random sample of 250 students, 165 indicate that they drive a car to school, is the administration's position supported? Let $\alpha = 0.05$.

 7.8.3 The head accountant at Raglan Resources is concerned over the clerical errors on outgoing invoices and suspects that more than 20% of these invoices contain at least one error. In a random sample of 400 invoices, 100 are found to contain at least one error. Do these data support the accountant's view? Let $\alpha = 0.05$.

 7.8.4 In a study of job turnover, a researcher interviews a random sample of 200 top-level employees who have changed jobs during the past year. Thirty state that they changed jobs because they did not see much prospect for advancement at their old jobs. Do these data provide sufficient evidence at the 0.05 level of significance to indicate that less than 20% of such employees change jobs for this reason?

7.9 A TEST FOR THE DIFFERENCE BETWEEN TWO POPULATION PROPORTIONS

When n_1 and n_2
are large and we
test hypotheses
about $p_1 - p_2$, the
test statistic is z.

The manager or the researcher is often interested in the difference between two population proportions. We can test the null hypothesis that the difference between two population proportions is equal to any given value. However, the hypothesis we find most often in practice is that the difference is 0. The correct test statistic for testing hypotheses about the difference between two population proportions is

(7.9.1)
$$z = \frac{(\hat{p}_1 - \hat{p}_2) - (p_1 - p_2)_0}{\sqrt{\dfrac{p_1(1 - p_1)}{n_1} + \dfrac{p_2(1 - p_2)}{n_2}}}$$

where the samples are independent simple random samples. Since p_1 and p_2, the true population proportions, are unknown, we must estimate them. The best available estimates usually are the sample proportions.

Pooling Sample Results The null hypothesis that $p_1 - p_2 = 0$ is equivalent to the hypothesis that the two population proportions are equal. We may use this as justification for combining the results of the two samples. We thus obtain a pooled estimate of the hypothesized common proportion, which is given by

(7.9.2)
$$\bar{p} = \frac{n_1' + n_2'}{n_1 + n_2}$$

where n_1' and n_2' are the number in the first and second sample, respectively, with the characteristic of interest. We use this pooled estimate of $p = p_1 = p_2$ to compute the following standard error:

(7.9.3)
$$s_{\hat{p}_1 - \hat{p}_2} = \sqrt{\frac{\bar{p}(1 - \bar{p})}{n_1} + \frac{\bar{p}(1 - \bar{p})}{n_2}}$$

The test statistic, then, is

(7.9.4)
$$z = \frac{(\hat{p}_1 - \hat{p}_2) - 0}{s_{\hat{p}_1 - \hat{p}_2}}$$

which is distributed approximately as the standard normal if the null hypothesis is true.

Always pool the
samples when n_1
and n_2 are
unequal.

Suppose that n_1 and n_2 are fairly close in size and neither p_1 nor p_2 is too close to 0 or 1. Then the results we obtain by pooling will, as a rule, not differ very much from the results we obtain when the data are not pooled. It is never wrong to pool the data under $H_0: p_1 = p_2$. Since in some cases it may make a difference, it is advisable always to pool the data when n_1 and n_2 are unequal.

EXAMPLE 7.9.1 A researcher studies the grocery-shopping habits of city residents. Interviews with the principal shopper in each of 400 households reveal the following: of 225 shoppers with rural backgrounds and 175 shoppers with urban backgrounds, 54 and 52, respectively, state that they do most of their grocery shopping at chain stores. We want to decide, on the basis of this sample, whether the two groups differ with respect to where they do most of their grocery shopping.

SOLUTION

1. *Hypotheses.*

$$H_0: p_1 = p_2, \qquad H_1: p_1 \neq p_2$$

2. *Test statistic.* The test statistic is given by Equation 7.9.4.
3. *Significance level.* Let $\alpha = 0.05$.
4. *Decision rule.* If the computed value of the test statistic is greater than or equal to $+1.96$ or less than or equal to -1.96, we reject H_0.
5. *Calculations.* From the information given in the problem statement, we compute the value of the test statistic as follows. By Equation 7.9.2, we have

$$\bar{p} = \frac{54 + 52}{225 + 175} = \frac{106}{400} = 0.265$$

The test statistic, by Equation 7.9.4, is

$$z = \frac{(0.240 - 0.297) - 0}{\sqrt{\dfrac{(0.265)(0.735)}{225} + \dfrac{(0.265)(0.735)}{175}}} = -1.28$$

6. *Statistical decision.* Since $-1.28 > -1.96$, we do not reject the null hypothesis.
7. *Conclusion.* On the basis of the data given, we conclude that the two proportions may be equal. These data do not allow us to accept the alternative hypothesis. For this test, $p = 2(0.1003) = 0.2006$.

Let us now test the hypothesis using the unpooled estimate of the standard error. That is, let us base the test statistic on Equation 7.9.1.

$$z = \frac{(0.240 - 0.297) - 0}{\sqrt{\dfrac{(0.240)(0.760)}{225} + \dfrac{(0.297)(0.703)}{175}}} = -1.27$$

We see that, in the present example, pooling has had a negligible effect.

Sometimes the hypothesized difference between population proportions is other than 0. In these cases, it is not correct to pool the sample data. The following example shows this.

EXAMPLE 7.9.2   A market researcher believes that Area A's proportion of households with two or more cars exceeds by more than 0.05 the proportion of Area B's households with two or more cars.

To see whether the facts support this hypothesis, the researcher conducts a survey among Area A and Area B households, with the following results.

Area	Sample Size	Number of Households with Two or More Cars
A	$n_A = 150$	113
B	$n_B = 160$	104

SOLUTION

1. *Hypotheses.*

$$H_0: p_A - p_B \leq 0.05, \qquad H_1: p_A - p_B > 0.05$$

2. *Test statistic.* The relevant statistic is $\hat{p}_A - \hat{p}_B$. If H_0 is true, the mean of the distribution is 0.05 or less (we test at 0.05). The test statistic is as follows:

$$z = \frac{(\hat{p}_A - \hat{p}_B) - 0.05}{\sqrt{\dfrac{\hat{p}_A(1 - \hat{p}_A)}{n_A} + \dfrac{\hat{p}_B(1 - \hat{p}_B)}{n_B}}}$$

When H_0 is true, the test statistic is distributed approximately as the standard normal.

3. *Significance level.* Let $\alpha = 0.05$.

4. *Decision rule.* If the computed value of the test statistic is greater than or equal to 1.645, reject H_0.

5. *Calculations.* From the sample data, we compute $\hat{p}_A = 113/150 = 0.75$ and $\hat{p}_B = 104/160 = 0.65$.

The standard error is

$$s_{\hat{p}_A - \hat{p}_B} = \sqrt{\frac{(0.75)(0.25)}{150} + \frac{(0.65)(0.35)}{160}} = 0.05$$

which allows us to compute

$$z = \frac{(0.75 - 0.65) - 0.05}{0.05} = 1.00$$

6. *Statistical decision.* Since the computed z of 1.00 is less than 1.645, we do not reject H_0.

7. *Conclusion.* We may not conclude, on the basis of these data, that the market researcher's hypothesis is true. For this test, we have $p = 1 - 0.8413 = 0.1587$.

EXERCISES

Carry out the seven-step hypothesis-testing procedure at the desired level of significance and compute the p value for each test.

7.9.1 Rockingham Floor Coverings is seeking a carpeting material that can withstand temperatures of up to 250°F. Two materials, one a natural material and the other a synthetic (and cheaper) material, are equally satisfactory in all respects except, possibly, heat tolerance. Simple random samples of 225 specimens of each of the two materials are tested for this characteristic. The samples are independently drawn. Thirty-six specimens of the natural material and 45 specimens of the synthetic material fail at temperatures below 250°F. Can we conclude from these data that the two materials differ with respect to heat tolerance? Let $\alpha = 0.05$.

7.9.2 The Sankey Corporation finds that 63% of the 150 salespeople who have never had a self-improvement course would like such a course. The firm had done a similar study ten years before. Then only 58% of 160 salespeople wanted a self-improvement course. At the 0.05 level of significance, test the null hypothesis that salespeople are no more eager for self-improvement courses this year than they were ten years ago. The groups are assumed to constitute two independent simple random samples.

7.9.3 A simple random sample of 200 Type A industrial firms shows that 12% of them spend more than 1% of their total sales for advertising. An independent simple random sample of the same size from Type B firms shows that 15% spend more than 1% of their sales for advertising. Let $\alpha = 0.05$, and test

$$H_0: p_B \leq p_A \quad \text{against the alternative} \quad H_1: p_B > p_A$$

7.9.4 You conduct a study of the leisure-time activities of businesspeople in a certain city. A simple random sample of 400 salespersons and an independent simple random sample of 400 businesspeople *not* engaged in selling yield the following results: 288 salespersons and 260 nonsales businesspeople say that their leisure-time activities are mainly sports-oriented. Would you conclude on the basis of these data that a smaller proportion of nonsales businesspeople than of salespersons spend their leisure time in sports-oriented activities? Let $\alpha = 0.05$.

7.10 A TEST FOR THE VARIANCE OF A NORMALLY DISTRIBUTED POPULATION

Chapter 6 shows how to construct a confidence interval for the variance of a normally distributed population. We may use the same general principles to test a hypothesis about a population variance. The appropriate test statistic for testing $H_0: \sigma^2 = \sigma_0^2$ is

(7.10.1)

$$\chi^2 = \frac{(n-1)s^2}{\sigma_0^2}$$

To test a hypothesis about σ^2, we use the χ^2 distribution.

where s^2 is computed from a random sample of size n from a normally distributed population. When the null hypothesis is true, the test statistic is distributed as χ^2 with $n - 1$ degrees of freedom. We may make both one-sided and two-sided tests.

To repeat, *this procedure requires that the sampled population be normally distributed.* Violation of this assumption can yield misleading results.

EXAMPLE 7.10.1 Specifications for a certain type of steel plate state that the variance in weight shall not exceed 0.016 pounds squared. A random sample of 25 plates yields a variance of 0.025 pounds squared. Can we conclude from these data that specifications are not being met?

SOLUTION We can conclude that specifications are not being met if we can reject the null hypothesis that the population variance is less than or equal to 0.016.

To reach a conclusion, we use the seven-step hypothesis-testing procedure.

1. *Hypotheses.*

$$H_0: \sigma^2 \le 0.016, \qquad H_1: \sigma^2 > 0.016$$

2. *Test statistic.* Equation 7.10.1 gives the test statistic. We assume that the population of weights is approximately normally distributed.
3. *Significance level.* Let $\alpha = 0.05$.
4. *Decision rule.* For $\alpha = 0.05$ and 24 degrees of freedom, the critical value of χ^2 is 36.415. If the computed value of χ^2 is greater than or equal to 36.415, reject H_0.
5. *Calculations.* From the information given in the problem, we can compute the following value of the test statistic:

$$\chi^2 = \frac{24(0.025)}{0.016} = 37.5$$

6. *Statistical decision.* Since $37.5 > 36.415$, we reject H_0.
7. *Conclusion.* The data indicate that the variance specifications are not being met.

For this test, $0.05 > p > 0.025$, since $36.415 < 37.5 < 39.364$. When the alternative hypothesis is two-sided, a complication arises in the calculation of the p value associated with a chi-square statistic. Since the chi-square distribution is not symmetrical, it is not correct to double the one-sided p value, as we have done for two-sided tests based on symmetrical distributions. For two-sided tests based on asymmetrical distributions, we may report the one-sided p value accompanied by a statement indicating the direction of the observed departure from the null hypothesis.

EXERCISES

Carry out the seven-step hypothesis-testing procedure at the desired level of significance and compute the p value for each test.

7.10.1 A simple random sample of size 21 from a normally distributed population gives a variance of 10. Test the null hypothesis that $\sigma^2 = 15$ against the alternative that $\sigma^2 \neq 15$. Let $\alpha = 0.05$.

7.10.2 The inside diameters of metal washers have a variance of 0.00005 in² or less when the process by which they are made is under control. A random sample of 31 washers taken from the assembly line yields a variance of 0.000061 in². Do these data provide sufficient information to indicate that the process is out of control? Let $\alpha = 0.05$. What assumption must we make in order to answer the question?

7.10.3 The tensile strength of a synthetic fiber must have a variance of 5 or less before it is acceptable to a certain manufacturer. A random sample of 25 specimens taken from a new shipment gives a variance of 7. Does this provide sufficient grounds for the manufacturer to refuse the shipment? Let $\alpha = 0.05$ and assume that tensile strength of the fiber is approximately normally distributed.

7.11 A TEST FOR THE RATIO OF THE VARIANCES OF TWO NORMALLY DISTRIBUTED POPULATIONS

The use of the t distribution in constructing confidence intervals and testing hypotheses for the difference between two population means assumes that the population variances are equal. We compute estimates of the population variances from samples taken from the two populations. We want to know whether the observed difference between the sample variances indicates a difference in the population variances. Or could the difference have come about because of chance alone when the population variances are, in fact, equal? Suppose that we examine the sample variances and conclude that the two population variances are not equal. We either discard the t test or use the modification for unequal variances.

Two machines may produce items that are equal with respect to the mean value of some critical measurement. However, the variability among items produced by one of the machines may be greater. We would like some method on which to base a decision as to whether this is likely to be so. This example shows a case in which we want to know whether or not two population variances are equal.

To test for equality of population variances, we use the F distribution.

Decisions about the equality of two population variances are based on the *variance ratio* or *F test*. Recall from Chapter 6 that when certain assumptions are met, the quantity $(s_1^2/\sigma_1^2)/(s_2^2/\sigma_2^2)$ is distributed as F with $n_1 - 1$ numerator degrees of freedom and $n_2 - 1$ denominator degrees of freedom. We assume that $H_0: \sigma_1^2 = \sigma_2^2$ is true, in which case the two population variances cancel out. This leaves s_1^2/s_2^2, which follows the same F distribution. The test statistic, then, for testing $H_0: \sigma_1^2 = \sigma_2^2$ is

(7.11.1)
$$F = \frac{s_1^2}{s_2^2}$$

For a two-sided test, we place the larger sample variance in the numerator. We then find the critical value of F for $\alpha/2$ and the appropriate degrees of freedom. However, for a one-sided test, which of the two sample variances to put in the numerator is predetermined by the statement of the null hypothesis. For example, for the null hypothesis that $\sigma_1^2 \le \sigma_2^2$, with $H_1: \sigma_1^2 > \sigma_2^2$ the appropriate test statistic is $F = s_1^2/s_2^2$. The critical value of F is obtained for α (not $\alpha/2$) and the appropriate degrees of freedom. Similarly, if the null hypothesis is that $\sigma_1^2 \ge \sigma_2^2$, with $H_1: \sigma_1^2 < \sigma_2^2$, the appropriate test statistic is $F = s_2^2/s_1^2$.

Thus, we see that in both cases the larger of the two sample variances will usually be in the numerator of the test statistic. If the sample variance in the numerator happens to be smaller than the one in the denominator, there is no need to proceed with the hypothesis test because the computed value of the test statistic would be less than 1 and the hypothesis could not be rejected. When the sample variance in the numerator is larger than the one in the denominator, the computed value of the test statistic will be greater than 1. The burden of the hypothesis test, then, is to determine if the computed value of the test statistic is sufficiently large (that is, greater than or equal to the critical value of F) to cause rejection of the null hypothesis.

In all cases, the decision rule is to reject the null hypothesis if the computed F is equal to or greater than the critical value of F.

EXAMPLE 7.11.1 Tamerlane Brands, Inc., has two types of training programs for new employees. New employees are assigned alternately to one program or the other. At the end of the training period, each is given the same examination. There are 22 in the first group and 25 in the second group. Assume that the populations are approximately normally distributed. A t test is used to test whether the mean scores of the two groups are significantly different. The variance for the first group is $s_1^2 = 70.3$. The variance for the second group is $s_2^2 = 225.5$. Do these data cast doubt on the assumption of equal variances necessary for the valid use of the t test?

SOLUTION We may use the results of a hypothesis test to help answer the question.

1. *Hypotheses.*

$$H_0: \sigma_1^2 = \sigma_2^2, \qquad H_1: \sigma_1^2 \neq \sigma_2^2$$

2. *Test statistic.* The equation $F = s_2^2/s_1^2$ gives the appropriate test statistic, under the assumption that the samples came from normally distributed populations.
3. *Significance level.* Let $\alpha = 0.05$.
4. *Decision rule.* If the computed value of F is greater than or equal to the critical F for $\alpha = 0.05$ and 24 and 21 degrees of freedom, we reject H_0. Since we have a two-sided alternative, we select from the table the value of F that has $\alpha/2 = 0.025$ of the area under the curve to its right. From Table G of Appendix I, we find the critical value of F to be 2.37.
5. *Calculations.* From the information given in the problem statement, we compute the following value of the test statistic:

$$F = \frac{225.5}{70.3} = 3.21$$

6. *Statistical decision.* Since $3.21 > 2.37$, we reject H_0 and conclude that the assumption of equal population variances is not met. In other words, we feel that a variance ratio as large as that observed did not come about as a result of chance alone, but is the result of a false null hypothesis.
7. *Conclusion.* We should use the test statistic t'.

Since we have a two-sided alternative hypothesis and since the F distribution is asymmetrical, we report the one-sided p value, along with a statement of the direction of the departure from H_0. Since 3.21 is greater than 3.15, the value of $F_{0.995}$ for 24 and 21 degrees of freedom, the one-sided p value is less than 0.005. Thus, we can say that $p < 0.005$. Since we placed the larger sample variance in the numerator of the ratio, we know that the p value is a right-tail probability.

EXERCISES

Carry out the seven-step hypothesis-testing procedure at the desired level of significance and compute the p value for each test.

7.11.1   A person is considering the use of the t test to test the difference between two means. Two samples of size 16 yield variances of 28.5 and 9.5, respectively. Do the data indicate that the t test is inappropriate on the basis of the assumption of equality of population variances? Let $\alpha = 0.05$.

7.11.2   A pilot sample ($n = 25$) yields a variance of 96.0, which is used in determining the sample size needed for a survey. The variance computed from the sample survey data ($n = 121$) is 144. Do these results indicate that the estimate of the pilot-sample variance may have been too low? Let $\alpha = 0.05$.

7.11.3 A study is designed to compare two drugs for relieving tension among employees in stressful jobs. A medical team collects data on levels of tension of the subjects in two treatment groups at the end of the first two months of treatment. The variances computed from the sample data are $s_I^2 = 2916$ and $s_{II}^2 = 4624$. There are 8 subjects in each group. At the 0.05 level of significance, do these data provide sufficient evidence to suggest that the variability in tension levels is different in the two populations represented by the samples? State all necessary assumptions.

7.12 THE TYPE II ERROR AND THE POWER OF A TEST

In our discussion of hypothesis testing so far, we have said a lot about α, the probability of committing a Type I error (rejecting a true null hypothesis). We have said little about β, the probability of committing a Type II error (failing to reject a false null hypothesis). This is because, for a given test, α is a single number that the investigator assigns. β, on the other hand, may assume one of many values. Consider the null hypothesis that some population parameter is equal to some specified value. If H_0 is false and we fail to reject it, we commit a Type II error. The value of β, the probability that we will commit a Type II error, depends on the true value of the parameter of interest, the hypothesized value of the parameter, α, and n, given that the hypothesized value is not the true value. Thus, before we perform a hypothesis test, we may compute many β's by postulating many values for the parameter of interest, for fixed α and n, given that the hypothesized value is false.

An important fact about a particular hypothesis test has to do with how well the test controls Type II errors. For a given test in which H_0 is false, we would like to know the probability that we will reject it. The *power* of a test, $1 - \beta$, gives information relevant to this point. It gives the probability that we will reject a false null hypothesis. We see that $1 - \beta$, which can be computed for any alternative value of a parameter, represents the probability that we will take the correct action when H_0 is false because the true parameter is equal to the one for which we computed $1 - \beta$. We may, for a given test, construct a *power function* that gives possible values of the parameter of interest along with the corresponding values of $1 - \beta$. The graph of a power function, called a *power curve*, is a useful device for quickly assessing the nature of the power of a given test.

Power = $1 - \beta$ = the probability of rejecting a false null hypothesis.

EXAMPLE 7.12.1 To show the procedures we use to analyze the power of a test, let us refer again to Example 7.3.1. In this example, $n = 100$, $\sigma = 3.6$, and $\alpha = 0.05$. The hypotheses were

$$H_0: \mu = 17.5, \qquad H_1: \mu \neq 17.5$$

SOLUTION When we investigate the power of a test, it is convenient to locate the acceptance and rejection regions on the $\bar{x}$ scale rather than the z scale. We find the critical values of $\bar{x}$ for a two-sided test using the following formulas:

$$\bar{x}_U = \mu_0 + z \frac{\sigma}{\sqrt{n}} \qquad \text{and} \qquad \bar{x}_L = \mu_0 - z \frac{\sigma}{\sqrt{n}}$$

where $\bar{x}_U$ and $\bar{x}_L$ are the upper and lower critical values, respectively, of $\bar{x}$; $+z$ and $-z$ are the critical values of z; and μ_0 is the hypothesized value of μ. For the present example, we have

$$\bar{x}_U = 17.50 + 1.96 \frac{(3.6)}{(10)} = 17.50 + 1.96(0.36)$$

$$= 17.50 + 0.7056 = 18.21$$

and

$$\bar{x}_L = 17.50 - 1.96(0.36) = 17.50 - 0.7056 = 16.79$$

Suppose that H_0 is false, that is, that μ is not equal to 17.5. In that case, μ is equal to some value other than 17.5. We do not know the actual value of μ. However, if H_0 is false, μ is one of the many values that are greater than or smaller than 17.5. Suppose that the true population mean is $\mu_1 = 16.5$. Then the sampling distribution of $\bar{x}_1$ is also approximately normal, with $\mu_{\bar{x}} = \mu = 16.5$. We may call this sampling distribution $f(\bar{x}_1)$, and the sampling distribution under the null hypothesis $f(\bar{x}_0)$.

Now β, the probability of the Type II error of failing to reject a false null hypothesis, is the area under the curve of $f(\bar{x}_1)$ that overlaps the acceptance region specified under H_0. To determine the value of β, we need to find the area under $f(\bar{x}_1)$, above the $\bar{x}$ axis, and between $\bar{x} = 16.79$ and $\bar{x} = 18.21$. The value of β is equal to $P(16.79 \leq \bar{x} \leq 18.21)$ when $\mu = 16.5$. This is the same as

$$P\left(\frac{16.79 - 16.5}{0.36} \leq z \leq \frac{18.21 - 16.5}{0.36}\right) = P\left(\frac{0.29}{0.36} \leq z \leq \frac{1.71}{0.36}\right)$$

$$= P(0.81 \leq z \leq 4.75)$$

$$\approx 1 - 0.7910 = 0.2090$$

This means that the probability of taking an appropriate action (that is, rejecting H_0) when the null hypothesis states that $\mu = 17.5$, but in fact $\mu = 16.5$, is $1 - 0.2090 = 0.7910$. As we noted, μ may be one of a large number of possible values when H_0 is false. Figure 7.12.1 shows several such possibilities graphically. Table 7.12.1 shows the corresponding values of β and $1 - \beta$ (which are approximate), along with the values of β for some additional alternatives.

Note that in Figure 7.12.1 and Table 7.12.1 those values of μ under the alternative hypothesis that are closer to the value of μ specified by H_0 have larger associated β values. For example, when $\mu = 18$ under the alternative hypothesis, $\beta = 0.7190$; and when $\mu = 19.0$ under H_1, $\beta = 0.0143$. The power of the test for these two alternatives, then, is $1 - 0.7190 = 0.2810$ and

FIGURE 7.12.1   Size of β for selected values for H_1 for Example 7.12.1

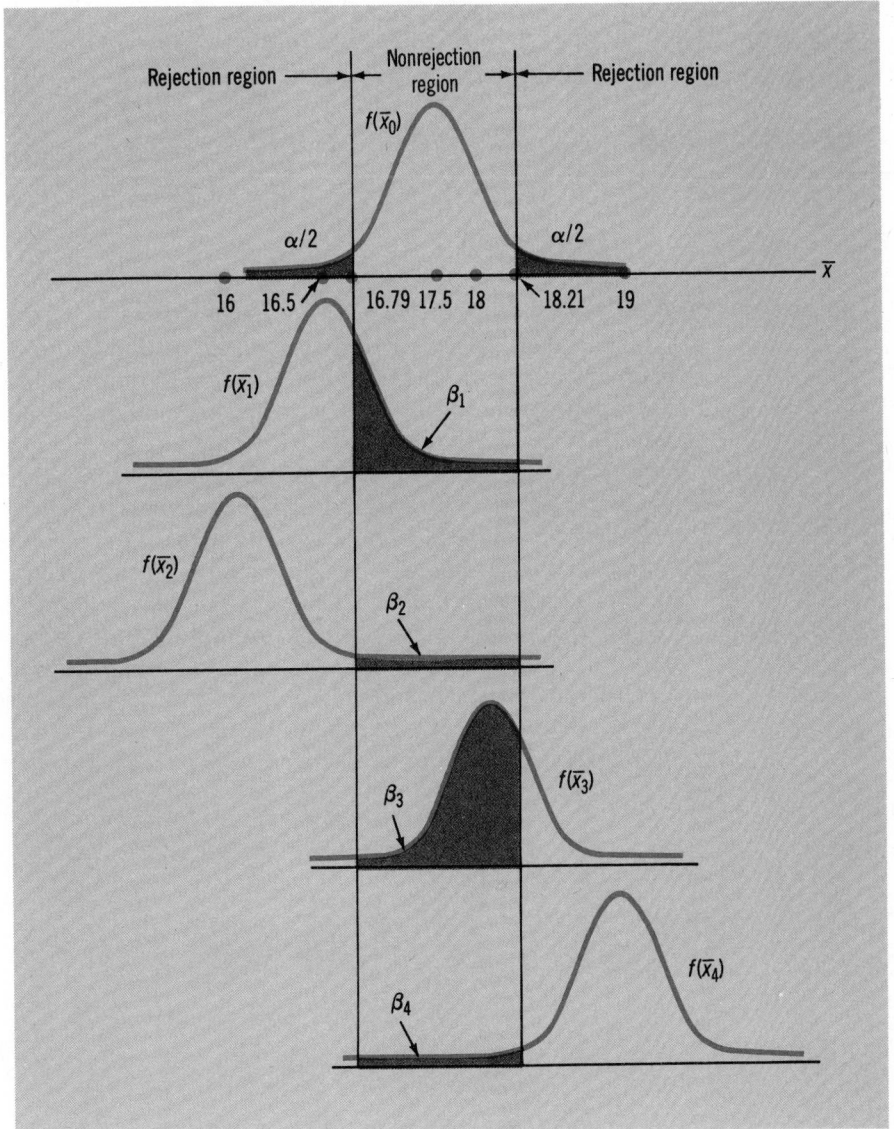

$1 - 0.0143 = 0.9857$, respectively. We may show the power of the test graphically in a power curve, as in Figure 7.12.2. Note that the higher the curve, the greater the power.

Thus, although only one value of α is associated with a given hypothesis test, there are many values of β, one for each possible value of μ if $μ_0$ is not the true value of μ as hypothesized. Also, unless alternative values of μ are much larger

TABLE 7.12.1   Values of β and $1 - \beta$ for selected alternative values of μ_1, Example 7.12.1

Possible values of μ under H_1 when H_0 is false	β	$1 - \beta$
16.5	0.2090	0.7910
16.0	0.0143	0.9857
18.0	0.7190	0.2810
18.5	0.2090	0.7910
19.0	0.0143	0.9857
17.0	0.7190	0.2810

or smaller than μ_0, β is relatively large compared with α. In general, we use hypothesis-testing procedures more often in those cases in which, when H_0 is false, the true value of the parameter is fairly close to the hypothesized value. In most cases, β, the computed probability of failing to reject a false null hypothesis, is larger than α, the probability of rejecting a true null hypothesis. These conditions are compatible with our earlier statement that a decision based on a rejected null hypothesis is more conclusive than a decision based on a null hypothesis that is not rejected. The probability of being wrong in the latter case is generally larger than the probability of being wrong in the former case.

Figure 7.12.2 shows the V-shaped appearance of a power curve for a two-sided test. In general, a two-sided test that discriminates well between the value of the parameter in H_0 and values in H_1 results in a narrow V-shaped power curve. A wide V-shaped curve indicates that the test discriminates poorly over a relatively wide interval of alternative values of the parameter.

FIGURE 7.12.2   Power curve for Example 7.12.1

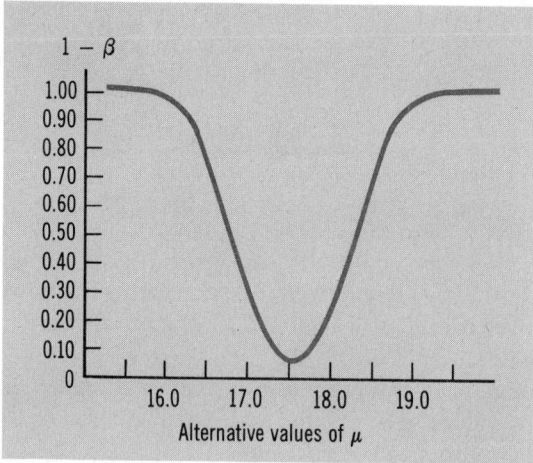

POWER CURVES FOR ONE-SIDED TESTS

The power curve for a one-sided test with the rejection region in the upper tail appears as an elongated S. When the rejection region of a one-sided test is located in the lower tail of the distribution, the power curve takes the form of a reverse elongated S. The following example shows the nature of the power curve for a one-sided test.

EXAMPLE 7.12.2   The mean time assembly-line employees at Van Loon Industries now take to do a certain task on a machine is 65 seconds, with a standard deviation of 15 seconds. The times are approximately normally distributed. The manufacturers of a new machine claim that their product will reduce the mean time taken to perform the task. The quality-control engineers design a test to determine whether or not they should believe the claim of the makers of the new machine. They choose a significance level of $\alpha = 0.01$ and randomly select 20 employees to perform the task on the new machine. The hypotheses are

$$H_0: \mu \geq 65, \qquad H_1: \mu < 65$$

The quality-control engineers also wish to construct a power curve for the test.

SOLUTION   The engineers compute, for example, the following value of $1 - \beta$ for the alternative $\mu = 55$. The critical value of $\bar{x}$ for the test is

$$65 - 2.33 \left(\frac{15}{\sqrt{20}} \right) = 57$$

We find β as follows:

$$\beta = P(\bar{x} > 57 | \mu = 55) = P \left(z > \frac{57 - 55}{15/\sqrt{20}} \right) = P(z > 0.60)$$

$$= 1 - 0.7257 = 0.2743$$

FIGURE 7.12.3 β calculated for $\mu = 55$

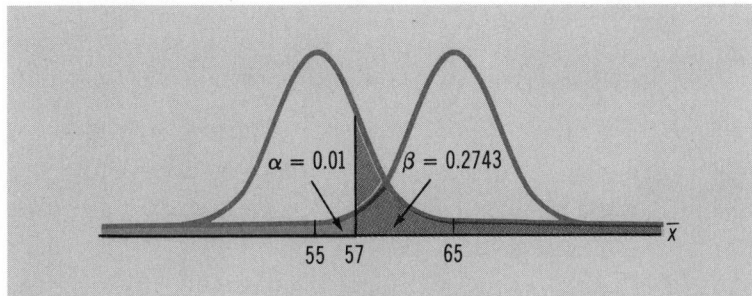

FIGURE 7.12.4   Power curve for Example 7.12.2

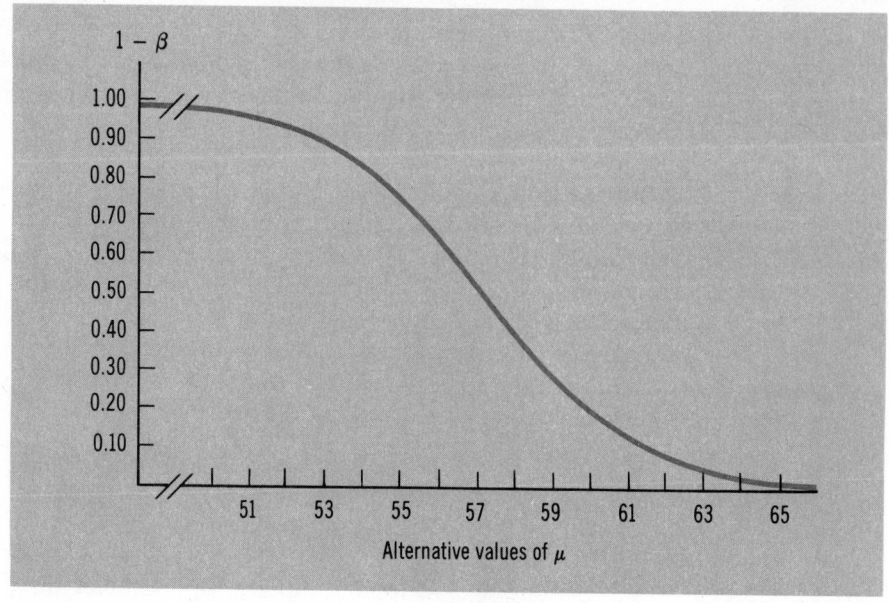

Consequently, $1 - \beta = 1 - 0.2743 = 0.7257$. Figure 7.12.3 shows the calculation of β. Similar calculations for other alternative values of μ also yield values of $1 - \beta$. When plotted against the values of μ, these give the power curve shown in Figure 7.12.4.

OPERATING CHARACTERISTIC CURVES

An alternative way of evaluating a test is to look at its *operating characteristic curve,* or OC curve. When we construct an OC curve, we plot values of β, rather than $1 - \beta$, along the vertical axis. In other words, an OC curve is the complement of the corresponding power curve.

EXERCISES

Construct and graph the power function for each of the following situations.

7.12.1 $H_0: \mu \le 516$, $H_1: \mu > 516$, $n = 16, \sigma = 32, \alpha = 0.05$.

7.12.2 $H_0: \mu = 3$, $H_1: \mu \ne 3$, $n = 100, \sigma = 1, \alpha = 0.05$.

7.12.3 $H_0: \mu \le 4.25$, $H_1: \mu > 4.25$, $n = 81, \sigma = 1.8, \alpha = 0.01$.

7.12.4   Refer to Exercise 7.12.1. Calculate β if $\mu = 535$.

7.12.5   Refer to Exercise 7.12.3. Calculate β if $\mu = 5.0$.

7.13   DETERMINING SAMPLE SIZE TO CONTROL BOTH TYPE I AND TYPE II ERRORS

In Chapter 6, you learned how to find the sample size needed to construct an interval estimate for either a population mean or a population proportion with a specified confidence coefficient. In Section 7.3, you also learned that confidence intervals can be used to test hypotheses. Since a confidence coefficient is equal to $1 - \alpha$, the method of determining sample size presented in Chapter 6 takes into account the probability of a Type I error, but not a Type II error.

In many applications of statistical inference, we want to consider Type II errors as well as Type I errors in determining sample sizes. To illustrate the procedure, let us refer again to Example 7.12.2.

EXAMPLE 7.13.1   In Example 7.12.2, the hypotheses are

$$H_0: \mu \geq 65, \qquad H_1: \mu < 65$$

The population standard deviation is 15, and the probability of a Type I error is set at 0.01. Now suppose that we want the probability of failing to reject H_0 (β) to be 0.05 if H_0 is false because the true mean is 55 rather than the hypothesized 65. We wish to know how large a sample we need in order to realize, simultaneously, the desired levels of α and β.

SOLUTION   For $\alpha = 0.01$ and $n = 20$, β is equal to 0.2743. The critical value is 57. Under the new conditions, the critical value is unknown. Let us call this new critical value C. We also let μ_0 be the hypothesized mean and μ_1 the mean under the alternative hypothesis. We can transform each of the relevant sampling distributions of $\bar{x}$, the one with a mean of μ_0 and the one with a mean of μ_1, to a z distribution. Consequently we can convert C to a z value on the horizontal scale of each of the two standard normal distributions. When we transform the sampling distribution of $\bar{x}$ that has a mean of μ_0 to the standard normal distribution, we call the z that results z_0. When we transform the sampling distribution of $\bar{x}$ that has a mean of μ_1 to the standard normal distribution, we call the z that results z_1. Figure 7.13.1 represents the situation described so far.

We can express the critical value C as a function of z_0 and μ_0 and also as a function of z_1 and μ_1. This gives the following equations:

(7.13.1)
$$C = \mu_0 - z_0 \frac{\sigma}{\sqrt{n}}$$

(7.13.2)
$$C = \mu_1 + z_1 \frac{\sigma}{\sqrt{n}}$$

We can set the right-hand sides of these equations equal to each other and solve for n, to obtain

FIGURE 7.13.1   Graphic representation of relationships in determination of sample size to control both Type I and Type II errors

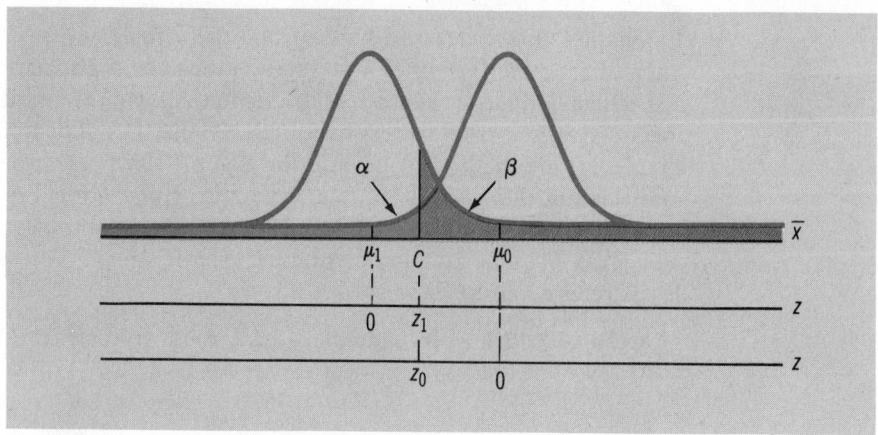

$$(7.13.3) \qquad n = \left[\frac{(z_0 + z_1)\sigma}{(\mu_0 - \mu_1)} \right]^2$$

To find n for our illustrative example, we substitute into Equation 7.13.3. We have $\mu_0 = 65$, $\mu_1 = 55$, and $\sigma = 15$. From Table C of Appendix I, the value of z that has 0.01 of the area to its left is -2.33. The value of z that has 0.05 of the area to its right is 1.645. Both z_0 and z_1 are taken as positive. We determine whether C lies above or below either μ_0 or μ_1 when we substitute into Equations 7.13.1 and 7.13.2. Thus, we compute

$$n = \left[\frac{(2.33 + 1.645)(15)}{(65 - 55)} \right]^2 = 35.55$$

We need a sample of size 36 to achieve the desired levels of α and β when we choose $\mu_1 = 55$ as the alternative value of μ.

We now compute C, the critical value for the test, and state an appropriate decision rule. To find C, we may substitute known numerical values into either Equation 7.13.1 or Equation 7.13.2. For illustrative purposes, we solve both equations for C. First we have

$$C = 65 - 2.33 \left(\frac{15}{\sqrt{36}} \right) = 59.175$$

From Equation 7.13.2, we have

$$C = 55 + 1.645 \left(\frac{15}{\sqrt{36}} \right) = 59.1125$$

The discrepancy between the two results is due to rounding error.

The decision rule, when we use the first value of C, is as follows.

Select a sample of size 36 and compute $\bar{x}$. If $\bar{x} \leq 59.175$, reject H_0. If $\bar{x} > 59.175$, do not reject H_0.

For the sake of brevity, we have limited our discussion of the Type II error and the power of a test to the case involving a population mean. These concepts may be extended to cases involving other parameters.

EXERCISES

7.13.1 Refer to Exercise 7.12.1. Let $\beta = 0.10$ and $\mu_1 = 520$, and find n and C. State the appropriate decision rule.

7.13.2 Refer to Exercise 7.3.2. Let $\beta = 0.05$ and $\mu_1 = 4.52$, and find n and C. State the appropriate decision rule.

7.13.3 Refer to Exercise 7.12.3. Let $\beta = 0.03$ and $\mu_1 = 5.00$, and find n and C. State the appropriate decision rule.

SUMMARY

This chapter covers the basic concepts of hypothesis testing, the second type of statistical inference procedure. You learned that the hypothesis-testing procedure may be broken down into seven sequential steps.

1. Statement of the hypotheses
2. Identification of the test statistic and its distribution
3. Specification of the significance level
4. Statement of the decision rule
5. Collection of the data and performance of the calculations.
6. Making the statistical decision
7. Drawing a conclusion

You learned how to carry out the seven-step hypothesis-testing procedure when the parameter of interest is one of the following:

1. The mean of a normally distributed population for which the population variance is known
2. The mean of a normally distributed population for which the population variance is unknown
3. The mean of a population that is not normally distributed (large-sample case)
4. The difference between the means of two normally distributed populations

5. The difference between the means of two populations that are not normally distributed (large-sample case)

6. A population proportion (large-sample case)

7. The difference between two population proportions (large-sample case)

8. The variance of a normally distributed population

9. The ratio of the variances of two normally distributed populations

You learned that in many hypothesis-testing procedures, we may compute the test statistic using the general formula

$$\text{Test statistic} = \frac{\text{sample statistic} - \text{hypothesized parameter value}}{\text{standard error of the statistic}}$$

You also learned how to determine a p value for each test conducted.

Finally, for the case in which the normal distribution is the appropriate sampling distribution, you learned how to compute the power of a statistical test for specified alternative values of the population mean and how to determine the sample size needed to control both Type I and Type II errors.

REVIEW EXERCISES

Where appropriate, carry out the seven-step hypothesis-testing procedure at the indicated level of significance and compute the p value for the test.

1. What is the purpose of hypothesis testing?

2. What is a hypothesis?

3. List and explain each step in the seven-step hypothesis-testing procedure.

4. What is a Type I error?

5. What is a Type II error?

6. Explain how to decide what statement goes into the null hypothesis and what statement goes into the alternative hypothesis.

7. What are the assumptions underlying the use of the t statistic in testing hypotheses about (a) a single mean, (b) the difference between two means?

8. When may the z statistic be used in testing hypotheses about (a) a single population mean, (b) the difference between two population means, (c) a single population proportion, (d) the difference between two population proportions?

9. In testing a hypothesis about the difference between two population means, what is the rationale behind pooling the sample variances?

10. What is meant by the power of a test?

11. Give an example from your field of interest in which it would be appropriate to test a hypothesis about the difference between two population means. Use real or realistic data and carry out the seven-step hypothesis-testing procedure.

12. Do Exercise 11 for a single population mean.

13. Do Exercise 11 for a single population proportion.

14. Do Exercise 11 for the difference between two population proportions.

15. Do Exercise 11 for a population variance.

16. Do Exercise 11 for the ratio of two population variances.

17. A manufacturer of strapping tape claims that the tape has a mean breaking strength of 500 psi. Experience has shown that breaking strengths are approximately normally distributed, with a standard deviation of 48 psi. A random sample of 16 specimens is drawn from a large shipment of tape, and a mean of 480 psi is computed. Can we conclude from these data that the mean breaking strength for this shipment is less than that claimed by the manufacturer? Let $\alpha = 0.05$.

18. The mean length of time required to perform a certain assembly-line task at Warren Electronics has been established at 15.5 minutes, with a standard deviation of 3 minutes. A random sample of 9 employees is taught a new method. After the training period, the average time these 9 employees take to perform the task is 13.5 minutes. Do these results provide sufficient evidence to indicate that the new method is faster than the old? Let $\alpha = 0.05$. Assume that the times required to perform the task are normally distributed.

19. A certain type of yarn is manufactured under specifications that the mean tensile strength must be 20 pounds. A random sample of 16 specimens yields a mean tensile strength of 18 pounds and a standard deviation of 3.2 pounds. Can we conclude from these data that the mean tensile strength for the population is less than 20 pounds? Assume that the tensile strengths are approximately normally distributed. Let $\alpha = 0.05$.

20. A manufacturer of electrical products will not accept a shipment of a certain part from a vendor if there is reason to believe that the mean resistance is not 70 ohms. A random sample of 25 selected from a large shipment yields a mean and standard deviation, respectively, of 66 and 10 ohms. Should the shipment be accepted? Let $\alpha = 0.05$. Assume that the resistances are approximately normally distributed.

21. The credit manager of the Adler department store chain believes that the average age of charge-account customers is less than 30 years. A random sample of 100 charge-account customers reveals a mean age of 27 years and a standard deviation of 10 years. Do these data provide sufficient evidence to support the credit manager's belief? Let $\alpha = 0.05$.

22. A random sample of size 81 gives a mean and standard deviation, respectively, of 485 and 45. (a) Test the null hypothesis that $\mu = 500$. Let $\alpha = 0.01$. (b) Test the null hypothesis that $\mu \leq 500$ ($\alpha = 0.01$).

23. We test two brands of electrical fuse by subjecting each to a fixed load and measuring the subsequent life of the fuse in seconds. We find the following test results. Can we conclude from these data that Brand B fuses have longer life, on the average, than Brand A fuses? Let $\alpha = 0.05$. What assumptions are necessary in order to carry out a valid hypothesis test?

Brand A	$n = 7$	$\bar{x} = 75$	$s^2 = 20$
Brand B	$n = 10$	$\bar{x} = 85$	$s^2 = 16$

24. The following results are based on independent simple random samples drawn from two normally distributed populations with variances $\sigma_1^2 = 135$ and $\sigma_2^2 = 91$. Can we conclude from these data that $\mu_2 < \mu_1$? Let $\alpha = 0.05$.

| Sample 1 | $n = 15$ | $\bar{x} = 62$ |
| Sample 2 | $n = 13$ | $\bar{x} = 50$ |

25. Explain the conditions under which a paired-comparisons test is appropriate.

26. The following data are obtained from independent simple random samples from two populations. Can we conclude from these data that the population means are different? Let $\alpha = 0.01$.

| Population A | $n = 50$ | $\bar{x} = 100$ | $s^2 = 650$ |
| Population B | $n = 50$ | $\bar{x} = 107$ | $s^2 = 600$ |

27. An official with Bartram Paint and Varnish, Inc., believes that more than one-third of ordered raw materials are not delivered on time. She compares the actual delivery date with the promised delivery date on a random sample of 100 orders, and finds that 38 orders were not delivered on time. Do these data support her belief? Let $\alpha = 0.01$.

28. A simple random sample of size 210 yields a $\hat{p}$ of 0.7. Test the null hypothesis that $p = 0.75$. Let $\alpha = 0.01$.

29. It is hypothesized that the proportion of executives reared in cities of 100,000 or less population is greater for Industry A than for Industry B. Do the following sample results support this hypothesis at the 0.01 level?

	Industry A	**Industry B**
Sample size	150	100
Number of executives reared in cities of 100,000 or less population	78	48

30. An account executive with Caxton Opinion Polls has two mailing lists available for the distribution of a questionnaire. A simple random sample of 200 names and addresses is selected from each list, and a questionnaire covering general-interest topics is mailed to each person. Of the questionnaires sent to the sample from Mailing List A, 52% are returned, whereas only 40% of those sent to the B sample are returned. Do these data provide sufficient evidence to indicate that people on Mailing List A are more apt to respond to this type of questionnaire? Let $\alpha = 0.05$.

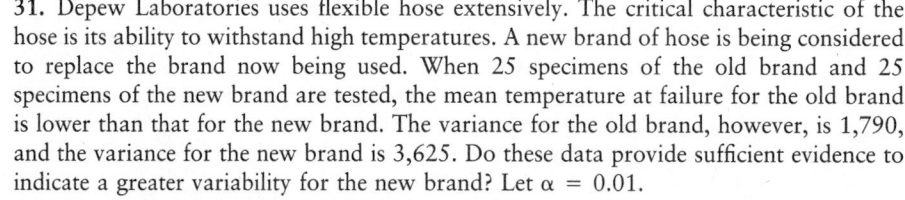

31. Depew Laboratories uses flexible hose extensively. The critical characteristic of the hose is its ability to withstand high temperatures. A new brand of hose is being considered to replace the brand now being used. When 25 specimens of the old brand and 25 specimens of the new brand are tested, the mean temperature at failure for the old brand is lower than that for the new brand. The variance for the old brand, however, is 1,790, and the variance for the new brand is 3,625. Do these data provide sufficient evidence to indicate a greater variability for the new brand? Let $\alpha = 0.01$.

32. According to specifications, the variance of the shear strength of a particular spot weld must be 324 pounds squared or less. A random sample of 11 welds tested for shear strength gives a variance of 400 pounds squared. On the basis of these data, should we conclude that the specifications are not being met? Let $\alpha = 0.05$. What assumption must you make to validate your method?

33. A random sample of 64 bank depositors reveals a mean checking account balance of $375, with a standard deviation of $80. Can we conclude from these data that the population mean is less than $400? Let $\alpha = 0.01$.

34. A sample of 9 high school seniors in a school system reports a mean of 5 hours worked at part-time jobs during a recent week. The sample standard deviation was 3 hours. Do these data provide sufficient evidence to indicate that the mean for the population is less than 8 hours? Assume a normally distributed population.

35. Draw a simple random sample of 30 one-digit numbers from Table D of Appendix I. Test the null hypothesis that $\mu = 4.5$ at the 0.05 level. Let $\sigma^2 = 8.25$. Compare your results with those of the other members of your class. Repeat the exercise, but this time use the sample variance in computing the standard error. Compare the results from the two procedures.

 36. The owner of the Ellenborough Shopping Center claims that more than 50% of the households within a three-mile radius of the shopping center have at least one member who shops at the center at least once a week. In a sample of 300 households in the area, an investigator found that members of 171 households did so. Do these data provide sufficient evidence to support the shopping center owner's claim? Let $\alpha = 0.01$.

 37. Noting the declining popularity of public billiard parlors, a recreation specialist hypothesizes that more than 10% of the homes in a certain area have pool tables. In a random sample of 100 homes in the area, 18 are found to have pool tables. Do these data support the recreation specialist's contention? Let $\alpha = 0.05$.

38. Draw a simple random sample of 20 one-digit numbers from Table D of Appendix I. Compute $\hat{p}$ = number of odd digits/20. Test the null hypothesis that $p = 0.5$. Let $\alpha = 0.05$. Compare your results with those of the other members of your class.

 39. A researcher with Fuller's Nursery conducts an experiment to compare the characteristics of two kinds of tomato plants. The heights at a certain age are determined for a sample of each of the two kinds grown under conditions that are as nearly identical as possible. The results are as follows: For Type A, $n = 15$, $\bar{x} = 11.5$, and $s = 3.2$. For Type B, $n = 22$, $\bar{x} = 13.2$, and $s = 3.8$. Do these data provide sufficient evidence to indicate that Type B plants are, on the average, taller than Type A plants at this age? Let $\alpha = 0.05$.

 40. A psychologist investigates the differences between high-performing and low-performing salespersons with respect to certain psychological factors. A random sample is selected from each of the two groups, and sampled subjects are given a battery of tests. The results of one such test, designed to measure subjects' need for security, are as follows: For the 16 high performers, $\bar{x} = 4.75$ and $s^2 = 2.25$. For the 21 low performers, $\bar{x} = 3.25$ and $s^2 = 2.00$. Can we conclude from these data that the two populations differ with respect to mean level of need for security? Let $\alpha = 0.05$.

41. Draw two simple random samples of one-digit numbers from Table D of Appendix I, letting $n_1 = n_2 = 30$ and $\sigma_1^2 = \sigma_2^2 = 8.25$. Test the null hypothesis that $\mu_1 - \mu_2 = 0$ at the 0.05 level of significance. Compare your results with those of other members of your class. Repeat the exercise, but this time use sample variances in computing the standard error. Compare the results from the two procedures.

 42. C A factory manager with Garfield Products wishes to know whether the efficiency of employees working in a high-noise area could be improved by reducing the noise level. The following table gives efficiency ratings taken before and after noise-reduction measures were introduced for 15 affected employees. Can we conclude from these data that reducing the noise level raises the efficiency level of employees? A higher number indicates a higher efficiency. Let $\alpha = 0.01$.

Employee	Efficiency Rating Before	Efficiency Rating After	Employee	Efficiency Rating Before	Efficiency Rating After
1	21	32	9	22	40
2	35	35	10	35	48
3	40	58	11	28	38
4	38	57	12	20	33
5	23	37	13	39	39
6	27	40	14	28	41
7	28	39	15	34	44
8	39	58			

43. C A sample of 12 pairs of brothers, no more than two years apart in age, take part in a study conducted by a high school guidance counselor. During his senior year in high school, each boy is given a business-knowledge test. The younger brothers, when they are seniors, all take a course in business practices that the older brothers did not take when they were seniors. The following table shows the scores. Should we conclude from these data that the course in business practices raises the level of a student's knowledge of business? Let $\alpha = 0.01$.

Pair	Older Brother	Younger Brother	Pair	Older Brother	Younger Brother
1	104	113	7	150	151
2	223	214	8	143	146
3	241	246	9	205	210
4	103	104	10	185	191
5	145	150	11	104	111
6	156	160	12	225	234

44. A random sample of 500 is selected from among the subscribers of *Spectator Sports* magazine. The sample is then divided at random into two subsamples, A and B, of 250 each. Each subject is mailed a questionnaire seeking his or her opinions of certain sports teams. Each subject in subsample A is sent a dollar bill with the questionnaire. Subjects in subsample B are sent only the questionnaire. Then 212 persons in subsample A and 150 in subsample B return a completed questionnaire. Do these data provide sufficient evidence to indicate that paying people causes an increase in the rate of response to mailed questionnaires? Let $\alpha = 0.05$.

45. Harmsworth Advertising, while testing its commercials, inserts a Format A test commercial for a detergent into the normal Monday morning programming of a local radio station. The next day the agency telephones 100 listeners. Asked whether they recall the commercial, 25 out of the 100 say they do recall it. The following Monday morning the ad agency inserts a Format B commercial for the same detergent into the radio station's normal programming. The next day the agency follows it up with telephone calls to 110 listeners. Of these, 40 were able to recall the Format B commercial. Do these data provide sufficient evidence to indicate that Format B is more easily recalled than Format A?

46. A random sample of households is selected from each of two communities, A and B. Each head of household is asked the question, "Is anyone in this household bothered by air pollution?" In Community A, 80 out of 240 answer yes. In Community B, 90 out of 250 answer yes. Do these data provide sufficient evidence to indicate a difference in population proportions between the two communities?

47. An executive with the Judd Ad Agency believes that the proportion of adult females in Area A who regularly watch a certain soap opera on television exceeds by more than 0.10 the proportion of those in Area B who regularly watch it. Independent random samples of adult females from the two areas give the following information. In Area A, the sample size $n_A = 150$, and the number of respondents who regularly watch the program is 98. In Area B, the sample size $n_B = 200$, and the number who watch regularly is 80. Do these data provide sufficient evidence to support the advertising executive's belief? Let $\alpha = 0.05$.

48. An industrial psychologist with Kondo Industries believes that a certain employee orientation program will reduce the turnover rate among new employees by more than 15%. During a certain year, by random assignment, 100 new employees are chosen to participate in the orientation program. Another 100 new employees, by random assignment, are chosen as a control group. Both groups are followed for a period of five years. At the end of this time, 22 persons in the experimental group and 45 in the control group have left the firm. Is the psychologist's belief about the orientation program justified? Let $\alpha = 0.05$.

49. A chemist with the Sprayless Pest Control Company believes that the variance of the life of a termite exposed to a poison is 625 minutes squared. A random sample of 11 exposed termites yields a variance of 1,225 minutes squared. Do these data provide sufficient evidence to indicate that the chemist's assessment of the variability is wrong? Let $\alpha = 0.05$.

50. A time-and-motion expert believes that the variance of the time that clerical employees need for a certain task is 9 minutes squared. A random sample of 6 employees who perform the task yields a sample variance of 25 minutes squared. Do these data provide sufficient evidence to indicate that the variance is greater than the time-and-motion expert believes? Let $\alpha = 0.05$.

51. Two groups of executives are given a test to measure their levels of extroversion. Group I consists of 25 executives who started their careers as salespersons. Group II consists of 31 executives who started their careers as accountants. The variances computed from the sample data are $s_I^2 = 81$ and $s_{II}^2 = 36$. Do these data suggest, at the 0.05 level of significance, that the population of scores represented by Group I is more variable than that represented by Group II? Let $\alpha = 0.05$. State all necessary assumptions.

52. A random sample of 16 college freshmen who plan to major in marketing and a random sample of 13 who plan to major in accounting are given a sales aptitude test. The variance of the scores of the marketing majors is 7.29. The variance of the scores of the accounting majors is 39.69. Do these data provide sufficient evidence to indicate, at the 0.01 level of significance, that the two population variances are different? State all necessary assumptions.

53. [C] Langmuir Pharmaceuticals wants to know whether two methods of producing headache tablets result in a difference in mean thickness. A researcher draws a random sample from the items produced by the two methods and records the following results (coded for computational convenience). Do these data provide sufficient evidence to indicate that the two population means are different? Let $\alpha = 0.05$.

Method A	39	46	35	38	36	45	42	54	52	55					
Method B	50	41	44	47	51	43	57	40	51	43	44	51	60	59	40

54. [C] Simple random samples are selected from among male factory workers in two industries. The variable of interest is a measure of lung health. The results are as follows. Can we conclude from these data that the two population means differ? Let $\alpha = 0.10$.

Industry A	3.44	3.81	2.05	3.01	2.42	2.12	2.83	3.26	3.69	2.46	2.72	3.39
	2.64	3.65	3.64	3.65								
Industry B	3.94	2.96	4.14	2.55	3.52	2.92	2.92	3.33	2.62	3.76	3.94	4.19
	2.62	4.31	2.55	3.51	4.31	4.15	3.51	3.14	3.89			

55. [C] The Mansfield-Pompey Company makes soap using two different formulas. The firm wants to know the specific gravity of the soap produced by the two formulas. To compare the two formulas with respect to the specific gravity of the product, a chemist draws simple random samples from production lots representing the two formulas. The results (coded for computational convenience) are as follows. Can we conclude from these data that the two population means are different? Let $\alpha = 0.05$.

Formula A	4	6	4	8	5	3	2	7	6	4				
Formula B	7	5	8	6	6	10	10	9	10	6	9	9	8	8	4

56. [C] Select a simple random sample of size 50 from the population of employed heads of households in Appendix II. Perform a hypothesis test to see whether you can conclude that the proportion of single persons in the population is greater than 0.20. Let $\alpha = 0.05$.

57. [C] In a study comparing the attitudes of white-collar and blue-collar workers toward paid religious holidays, researchers with a large firm selected a random sample of 150 white-collar workers and an independent random sample of 120 blue-collar workers. Of these, 29 of the white-collar and 34 of the blue-collar workers said that they thought paid religious holidays were very important. Do these data provide sufficient evidence to indicate, at the 0.05 level, that the proportions of workers who think paid religious holidays are important are different in the two sampled populations?

58. [C] Consider the population of employed heads of households in Appendix II. Select a simple random sample of size 30 from this population. Perform an appropriate hypothesis test to see whether you can conclude that the mean age of the subjects in the population is greater than 30. Let $\alpha = 0.05$. Compare your results with those of your classmates.

59. [C] An industrial psychologist believes that the mean test score for manual dexterity of a population of employees with a certain handicap is greater than 75. The population of scores, which has a standard deviation of 9, is assumed to be normally distributed. A random sample of 20 of these employees yields the following data: 77, 99, 96, 89, 85, 63, 51, 52, 54, 81, 91, 69, 91, 92, 98, 70, 53, 76, 90, 64. Do these data provide sufficient evidence to support the psychologist's belief? Let $\alpha = 0.01$.

60. Ⓒ O'Connor Drugs, a pharmaceuticals manufacturer, is concerned with the side effects of a depressant drug when used by normal adults. A researcher would like to find a dosage that would produce sedation but not be strong enough to cause serious side effects. A random sample of 16 subjects taking part in an experiment with the drug achieved sedation with the following dosages, in milligrams per kilogram of body weight: 1.6, 1.8, 7.3, 5.7, 3.0, 1.6, 3.8, 3.1, 7.8, 7.4, 4.2, 1.6, 2.1, 2.1, 5.5, 4.4. Do these data provide sufficient evidence to indicate that the mean dosage required to produce sedation is greater than 2.5 milligrams per kilogram of body weight? Let $\alpha = 0.05$.

61. Ⓒ Two researchers wish to know whether they can conclude that high school seniors with a high aptitude for a career in law have higher IQs than seniors with a low aptitude for a law career. The subjects of their study consist of 12 pairs of seniors. Each pair was matched on as many relevant variables as possible. The subjects within each pair differed with respect to their aptitude for a law career. The following table shows the IQs of the sample subjects. Do these data provide sufficient evidence to indicate that seniors with a high aptitude for law have, on the average, higher IQs than those who have a low aptitude for it? Let $\alpha = 0.05$.

Pair	1	2	3	4	5	6	7	8	9	10	11	12
High aptitude	129	103	123	118	99	95	126	115	110	122	127	135
Low aptitude	127	94	115	114	90	92	129	105	101	110	125	134

62. Ⓒ The amount of a certain chemical in the raw material used to produce linoleum is a critical factor in the linoleum's durability. A researcher for a linoleum manufacturer believes that the mean concentration of the chemical is different in the raw material obtained from two suppliers. To find out whether or not this belief can be supported by objective data, the researcher takes random samples from the raw material provided by the two suppliers, and determines the concentration of the chemical in each specimen. The results are as follows. Do the data support the researcher's belief? Let $\alpha = 0.05$. State any assumptions that are necessary.

Supplier A	60.9	49.8	65.3	40.6	51.6	69.7	58.0	59.6	47.8	46.9	47.6	67.3
Supplier B	72.9	67.3	81.4	89.4	86.5	51.1	72.9	74.0	77.8	86.4	82.0	77.6
	74.8	50.7	61.0	57.4	61.0	57.8	74.7	89.4				

63. Ⓒ Researchers give each of a random sample of 15 employees with high absenteeism records (Group A) a test to measure level of hostility. They give the same test to an independent random sample of 22 employees with low absenteeism records (Group B). The results are as follows. Do these data provide sufficient evidence to indicate that, on the average, employees who are often absent are more hostile than employees who are not? A high score indicates a high level of hostility. Let $\alpha = 0.01$. What use can the researchers make of their findings? What assumptions are necessary?

Group A	62	93	71	90	69	90	71	76	86	71	81	84	65	61	69
Group B	55	56	57	60	48	60	53	65	64	46	41	67	66	64	42	59	70
	75	69	72	74	55										

64. A Phillips Marketing International wants to find out whether the annual average household consumption of diet mayonnaise differs in two large market areas. The firm selects random samples of 100 households in each area, with the following results. What

should the firm conclude from these results? Let $\alpha = 0.01$. What use can the researchers make of these results?

Area 1	$\bar{x}_1 = 10$ units	$s_1 = 6$
Area 2	$\bar{x}_2 = 14$ units	$s_2 = 8$

65. Ⓒ A sample of 100 orders received during a year by Happy Hobbies, specializing in hobby and craft supplies, showed the following receipts, rounded to the nearest dollar. Can we conclude on the basis of these data that the mean value of the company's receipts is greater than $20? Let $\alpha = 0.05$.

8	12	9	14	8	10	7	17	18	18	20	10	23	12	27	11	27	15	15	16
21	14	22	14	29	28	26	16	19	24	21	14	23	21	28	27	29	18	19	32
23	13	24	22	28	27	32	16	19	36	24	10	21	21	27	29	31	16	19	36
22	13	22	22	25	26	32	15	15	37	23	14	21	24	26	34	34	15	16	34
23	14	20	24	27	37	33	19	19	33	9	11	9	21	6	38	9	18	18	32

66. Ⓒ A random sample of persons who regularly shop at Riverside Mall (A) and an independent random sample of persons who regularly shop at Lakeview Mall (B) participated in a survey. Each person in the two samples answered the following questions:

1. About how many hours per day do you spend watching television?
2. How long have you lived at your present address?
3. How many cars are owned by members of your household?

The results are as follows:

Subject	Shopping Mall	Hours of TV per Day	Length of Residence	No. of Cars
1	A	2	1	1
2	A	3	6	2
3	A	2	16	3
4	A	2	0.5	3
5	A	6	9	4
6	A	5	7	2
7	A	4	7	3
8	A	4	2	3
9	A	2	7	4
10	A	1	9	2
11	A	4	2	5
12	A	1	0.5	4
13	A	0	9	5
14	A	2	2	2
15	A	5	8	2
16	A	5	19	3
17	A	5	8	4
18	A	6	5	4
19	A	1	7	2
20	A	4	7	2
21	A	4	5	2

Subject	Shopping Mall	Hours of TV per Day	Length of Residence	No. of Cars
22	A	2	8	3
23	A	5	8	3
24	A	4	3	4
25	A	0	9	4
26	A	5	8	3
27	A	6	18	1
28	A	0.5	1	2
29	A	0	7	2
30	A	3	3	3
31	A	0.5	14	2
32	A	5	2	3
33	A	1	13	2
34	A	9	12	3
35	A	2	3	3
36	A	6	7	2
37	A	0	16	2
38	A	0	5	3
39	A	0.5	12	3
40	A	1	2	2
41	A	6	11	2
42	A	7	16	3
43	A	0	5	3
44	A	2	2	3
45	A	4	7	3
46	A	0	3	3
47	A	2	5	3
48	A	4	15	3
49	A	7	15	2
50	A	1	10	2
1	B	6	0.5	1
2	B	5	15	2
3	B	7	7	2
4	B	7	1	3
5	B	7	16	2
6	B	3	13	2
7	B	7	4	3
8	B	6	3	1
9	B	4	15	2
10	B	7	3	2
11	B	7	16	3
12	B	2	11	4
13	B	3	11	2
14	B	5	12	3
15	B	4	15	1
16	B	4	10	3
17	B	6	2	2
18	B	11	7	2
19	B	7	10	2
20	B	2	17	4
21	B	8	13	1
22	B	5	10	1

Subject	Shopping Mall	Hours of TV per Day	Length of Residence	No. of Cars
23	B	2	16	2
24	B	7	2	3
25	B	2.5	8	2
26	B	2.5	15	2
27	B	3	11	3
28	B	8	6	2
29	B	6	10	3
30	B	6	8	2
31	B	2	15	2
32	B	5	2	3
33	B	5	9	3
34	B	2	14	4
35	B	6	14	2
36	B	6	10	3
37	B	4	5	1
38	B	9	13	2
39	B	2	7	2
40	B	4	13	4
41	B	8	7	2
42	B	2	15	4
43	B	6	10	3
44	B	4	12	2
45	B	8	15	2
46	B	3	15	2
47	B	3	10	4
48	B	9	13	3
49	B	8	7	3
50	B	9	8	2

Calculate the variance and the mean for the number of hours per day spent watching television by the respondents in sample A. Do the same for sample B.

67. C Refer to Exercise 66. For the respondents in sample A, compute the variance and the mean for length of residence at present address. Do the same for sample B.

68. C Refer to Exercise 66. For the respondents in sample A, calculate the proportion of those who have more than two cars. Do the same for sample B.

69. Refer to Exercise 66. Can we conclude from these data that the population of shoppers at Mall A, on the average, spend less time per day watching television? Let $\alpha = 0.05$, and find the p value.

70. Refer to Exercise 66. On the basis of these sample data, can we conclude that the population of shoppers at Mall B, on the average, have lived at their present residences for a greater number of years than have shoppers at Mall A? Let $\alpha = 0.05$, and find the p value.

71. Refer to Exercise 66. Can we conclude on the basis of these sample data that, for the population of shoppers at Mall B, the proportion of those who own more than two cars is less than that for the population of Mall A shoppers? Let $\alpha = 0.05$, and find the p value.

 72. C An executive with Richter Insurance Company wishes to study the characteristics of hospitalization policyholders aged 65 or over who filed claims during the previous year.

A simple random sample of size 700 was selected from the relevant population. Two items of information collected from claims records were the number of days of hospitalization and whether or not the patient had surgery. The results appear in Data Set 5 of Appendix IV. (1 = yes, surgery was performed; 0 = no, surgery was not performed) Calculate the mean number of days spent in the hospital by the patients in the sample. Calculate the sample standard deviation.

73. Ⓒ Refer to Exercise 72. What proportion of the patients in the sample had surgery?

74. Ⓒ Refer to Exercise 72. Can we conclude from these data that the mean number of days of hospitalization for the sampled population is greater than 7? Let $\alpha = 0.05$, and determine the p value.

75. Ⓒ Refer to Exercise 72. Can we conclude on the basis of these data that for the sampled population of patients, the proportion who had surgery is less than 0.75? Let $\alpha = 0.05$, and determine the p value.

76. Ⓒ Refer to Exercise 72. Pretend that the data represent two populations: a population of patients who had surgery, and a population of patients who did not have surgery. Select a simple random sample of 10 patients from those who did not have surgery, and select an independent simple random sample of 15 patients from those who had surgery. On the basis of these data, can we conclude that the mean length of hospitalization for the two populations is different? Let $\alpha = 0.05$, and find the p value. Compare your results with those of your classmates.

For Exercises 77 through 88, do the following: Select a simple random sample from the population of companies listed in Appendix III. (Ask your instructor what size sample you should select.) For each company in your sample, record the data on each of the six variables.

77. Ⓒ Formulate and test an appropriate null hypothesis about the population mean assets. Select your own significance level, and follow the seven-step hypothesis-testing procedure. Find the p value for your test.

78. Ⓒ Repeat Exercise 77 using the sales variable.

79. Ⓒ Repeat Exercise 77 using the market value variable.

80. Ⓒ Repeat Exercise 77 using the net profits variable.

81. Ⓒ Repeat Exercise 77 using the cash flow variable.

82. Ⓒ Repeat Exercise 77 using the number employed variable.

83. Ⓒ Formulate and test an appropriate null hypothesis about the proportion of companies in the population with assets of $1 billion or more. Select your own significance level, and follow the seven-step hypothesis-testing procedure. Find the p value for your test.

84. Ⓒ Repeat Exercise 83 with a hypothesis about the proportion of companies in the population with sales of $1 billion or more.

85. Ⓒ Repeat Exercise 83 with a hypothesis about the proportion of companies in the population with a market value of $1 billion or more.

86. Ⓒ Repeat Exercise 83 with a hypothesis about the proportion of companies in the population with net profits of $100 million or more.

87. Ⓒ Repeat Exercise 83 with a hypothesis about the proportion of companies in the population with a cash flow of $1 billion or more.

88. ⟨C⟩ Repeat Exercise 83 with a hypothesis about the proportion of companies in the population with 50,000 or more employees.

89. Researchers conduct a test to determine the braking distance required for an automobile using a particular brand of tire and traveling at 55 miles per hour. The seven recorded distances, in feet, are 114, 122, 117, 109, 121, 115, and 112. At a 0.05 level of significance, do these data support a claim that, on the average, the tire provides braking capability of less than 120 feet for similar cars traveling at 55 miles per hour?

90. The average GMAT test score of a sample of 125 students at University A is 6.2 points higher than the average GMAT test score of a sample of 142 students at University B. Use a two-sided test and a level of significance of 0.05 to determine whether this difference is significant. The standard deviation of test scores at University A is 26.3. The standard deviation of scores at University B is 29.8.

91. When a simple random sample of 16 relays from Manufacturer A is tested, the mean time to failure is 2,781.3 hours, with a standard deviation of 238.9 hours. A sample of 11 relays from Manufacturer B yields a mean time to failure of 2,939.8 hours, with a standard deviation of 254.1 hours. **(a)** At the 1% level of significance, can we conclude that the two population variances are not equal? **(b)** Consider the results of your test concerning the population variances, and conduct a test to see whether you can conclude that the two population means are not equal. Let $\alpha = 0.05$.

92. Scheer Plastics plans to switch to a new material in the manufacture of plastic containers if a hypothesis test indicates that the new material is stronger. The material currently in use has a breaking strength of 150 psi. You are asked to conduct the test at the 0.05 level of significance. You select a sample of 10 containers manufactured from the new material and observe the pressures at failure to be 149, 157, 160, 147, 156, 148, 153, 152, 150, and 154 psi. What is your conclusion?

93. United Consumers wishes to test a manufacturer's claim that at least 80% of all dentists recommend the use of one or more of the manufacturer's products. The agency wishes to protect itself by limiting to 1% the probability of filing a false claim against the manufacturer. The agency selected a simple random sample of 200 dentists. Of these, 148 indicated that they recommended the use of one or more of the manufacturer's products. What should be the conclusion of the consumer protection agency?

94. Using $\alpha = 0.05$, we wish to test the null hypothesis that the mean time to assemble a product is 1 hour or more against the alternative that it takes less than 1 hour. **(a)** Calculations based on a sample of 46 yield a mean assembly time of 57.61 minutes, with a standard deviation of 9.52 minutes. Use these results to perform the test. **(b)** Use the hypothesis test as designed and the sample standard deviation as your best estimate of the population standard deviation, and determine the probability of failing to reject the null hypothesis if the population mean assembly time is actually 3 minutes under an hour.

95. You are asked to test at the 0.10 level of significance the null hypothesis that the mean weekly wage of a population of employees is $200. The population standard deviation is assumed to be $18, and a sample of size 36 is selected. Find the probability of failing to reject $200 as the correct value of the population mean when the true value of the population mean deviates from $200 by $10.

96. Refer to Exercise 7.3.2, in which we have H_1: $\mu > 4.5$, $\sigma = 0.02$, $n = 16$, and $\alpha = 0.01$. Find the probability of committing a Type II error if $\mu = 4.52$.

97. Refer to Exercise 7.8.3, in which we have H_1: $p > 0.20$, $n = 400$, and $\alpha = 0.05$. Find the probability of committing a Type II error if the true population proportion is 0.25.

98. Refer to Exercise 7.8.4, in which we have H_1: $p < 0.20$, $n = 200$, and $\alpha = 0.05$. Find the probability of failing to reject a false null hypothesis if $p = 0.15$.

99. Refer to Review Exercise 28, in which we have H_1: $p \neq 0.75$, $n = 210$, and $\alpha = 0.01$. Find the probability of failing to reject a false null hypothesis if the true population proportion is 0.85.

100. Given a normally distributed population with unknown variance, you wish to test the null hypothesis that the population mean is equal to 200. From the sample, you compute a mean of 195. The probability of committing a Type I error is 0.05 and the p value for the test is greater than 0.10. Should the null hypothesis be rejected? Why?

101. From a normally distributed population with unknown variance, you select a sample of size 20. From the sample data, you compute a mean of 215 and a variance of 625. You wish to test the null hypothesis that the population mean is equal to 200. What is the computed value of the test statistic?

102. You wish to test the null hypothesis that a population mean is equal to 100. From the data of a sample of size 21 drawn from the population, you compute a value of the test statistic of $t = -2.416$. What is the p value for the test?

103. From a normally distributed population with unknown variance, you select a sample of size 24. You wish to test the null hypothesis that the population mean is greater than 150, with a level of significance of 0.01. From the sample, you compute a mean of 125 and a standard deviation of 50. What is (are) the critical value(s) for the test?

104. You wish to test the null hypothesis that $p = 0.35$ at the 0.01 level of significance. From the population, you select a simple random sample of size 200. You observe 60 successes. What is the computed value of the test statistic?

***105.** Situations are sometimes encountered in which the binomial distribution is not adequately approximated by the normal distribution. These situations may occur when p, the probability of a success, is not close to 0.5 and the sample size is small. If, under these circumstances, we wish to test a hypothesis about the binomial parameter p (the number of successes in n trials), an alternative test to the one based on large samples discussed in Section 7.8 is needed. Such an alternative is provided by the binomial test. If the conditions of the binomial distribution discussed in Chapter 4 are met, we may use the binomial test to test the following null hypotheses against their respective alternatives (p_0 is some hypothesized value of p): (a) (Two-sided test) H_0: $p = p_0$, H_1: $p \neq p_0$, (b) (One-sided test) H_0: $p \leq p_0$, H_1: $p > p_0$, (c) (One-sided test) H_0: $p \geq p_0$, H_1: $p < p_0$.

The test statistic is x, the number of observed successes in n trials. The decision rule in each case is "Reject H_0 if the p value for the test is equal to or less than α." Bear in mind that in the two-sided test, either sufficiently large or sufficiently small values of x will cause rejection of H_0 and the p value and α will be split (as nearly equally as possible) between the two extremes. For test b, only sufficiently large values of x will cause rejection of H_0; and for test c, only sufficiently small values of x will allow us to reject H_0. Consider the following example. Some health professionals (Andrew L. Dannenberg and Jon S. Vernick, "A Proposal for the Mandatory Inclusion of Helmets with New Children's Bicycles," *American Journal of Public Health,* 83 [1993], 644–646) have made a proposal, to be enforced by regulation or legislation, requiring that a helmet be included in the retail price of each new child's bicycle sold. Suppose we conduct a survey of a random sample of 10 consumers and find that 8 are in favor of such a requirement. May we conclude, on the basis of these data and at the 0.05 significance level, that in the sampled population the proportion of consumers in favor of the requirement is not 0.5? Reference to Table A in Appendix I reveals that for $n = 10$ and $p = 0.5$, a value of $x \geq 8$ has an associated probability of 0.0107, which we interpret as half the p value. The p value for the test, then, is $2(0.0107) = 0.0214$. Since 0.0214 is less than 0.05, we reject H_0 and conclude that the population proportion in favor of the requirement is not 0.5. The sample data are compatible with the notion that more than 50% of the population are in favor of the requirement. In a survey of employers, a professor of nursing (Patty J. Hale, "Employer Response to AIDS in a Low-Prevalence Area," *Family & Community Health,* 13, No. 2 [1990], 38–45) found that 20% had a documented policy on AIDS. Suppose you conduct a similar survey among employers in another part of the country and find that 6 out of 15 have a documented policy on AIDS. On the basis of these data could we conclude at the 0.05 level of significance that more than 20% of the surveyed employers have a documented policy on AIDS?

1. POPULAR RECORD MARKETING

Two researchers in marketing, Meenaghan and Turnbull, reviewed the theory of product life cycle with respect to a specific product. They conducted a research project to determine the applicability of the theory to popular records.

As part of the study, they collected extensive information on a sample of 12 records judged (on the basis of certain well-defined criteria) to be successes and a sample of 10 judged to be failures. They collected data on each record for a period of 16 weeks from its date of release. One item of information that they collected on each was a measure of radio airplay. Measurement of this variable yielded the following means and standard deviations for the two samples of records.

Successes	$\bar{x} = 179{,}595$	$s = 54{,}231$
Failures	$\bar{x} = 15{,}268$	$s = 21{,}722$

Can one conclude, on the basis of these data, that successful and unsuccessful records differ with respect to mean amount of airplay? Let $\alpha = 0.01$. Find the p value for the test. What assumptions are required?

Source: A. Meenaghan and Peter W. Turnbull, "The Application of Product Life Cycle Theory to Popular Record Marketing," *European Journal of Marketing*, 15, 5 (1981):1–50.

2. RAISING CAPITAL and CORPORATE REPORTING POLICIES

The main purpose of a corporate annual report is to give information about the company's affairs to outside persons. Michael Firth conducted a study that examined the changes a company makes in the quality and extent of voluntary financial disclosure in its annual report when it is trying to find additional capital in the stock market.

Firth paired each money-raising company with a control (non-money-raising) firm of the same size in the same industry. He hypothesized that the change in the extent of financial disclosure in corporate reports of companies raising money in the stock market is greater than that of control companies *not* concerned with doing so. He calculated a disclosure-index score for each firm in the matched samples by assigning points for each of 48 items disclosed in the firm's annual report.

He examined three paired samples of British firms: (1) firms that made new issues (those that raised equity capital on the stock market for the first time); (2) small firms that made rights issues (that is, that sought additional capital on the stock market); and (3) large firms that made rights issues. Firth compared the annual reports of these firms at three different times: (a) three years prior to issuing stock ($t - 3$); (b) one year prior to issuing stock ($t - 1$); and (c) immediately after issuing stock (t).

Suppose that you wish to repeat the study with a sample of 12 firms making new stock issues (and their matched control firms). Let us say that you use Firth's index, with the following results. (A higher score indicates greater disclosure.) For each of the time periods, state appropriate hypotheses, analyze the data, and state your conclusions. Let $\alpha = 0.05$ for all tests. What assumptions do you need to make?

Disclosure Index Score at Time					
$t - 3$		$t - 1$			
Equity-raising Firm	Control Firm	Equity-raising Firm	Control Firm	Equity-raising Firm	Control Firm
15.38	15.00	20.35	15.10	21.22	15.12
5.21	5.50	10.00	5.55	11.54	5.70
17.78	17.95	21.98	18.00	23.90	18.10
6.31	6.30	11.30	6.30	12.41	7.35
6.21	6.22	11.32	6.22	12.11	7.10
16.77	17.00	21.78	17.20	23.02	18.25
16.05	16.00	21.15	16.00	23.10	17.00
8.24	8.35	13.27	8.42	14.24	8.45
7.52	7.00	12.00	7.10	13.10	8.60
17.67	18.00	23.67	18.10	24.21	19.20
9.24	10.00	14.50	10.25	16.00	10.50
12.47	12.45	17.30	12.00	18.30	12.10

Source: Michael Firth, "Raising Finance and Firms' Corporate Reporting Policies," Abacus, 16 (December 1980):100–115.

3. ADVERTISING WITH AND WITHOUT SAMPLING

Marks and Kamins conducted research to see if they could conclude that belief confidence will be higher for subjects exposed to product sampling (that is, being given a free sample of the product or allowed to use the product) in the absence of advertising than for subjects exposed to advertising in the absence of sampling. The variable of interest was scores made on a test to measure belief confidence. Subjects for the experiment were graduate and undergraduate university students. As part of the investigators' research, the following information was reported.

Advertising in the absence of sampling: $\bar{x} = 5.20$, $s = 0.98$, $n = 45$.
Sampling in the absence of advertising: $\bar{x} = 5.58$, $s = 1.29$, $n = 45$.

Use these data to perform an appropriate hypothesis test. Find the p value for the test. What do you conclude on the basis of your test?

Source: Lawrence J. Marks and Michael A. Kamins, "The Use of Product Sampling and Advertising: Effects of Sequence of Exposure and Degree of Advertising Claim Exaggeration on Consumers' Belief Strength, Belief Confidence, and Attitudes," Journal of Marketing Research, 25 (August 1988), 266–281.

WORK

STATISTICS AT WORK

STATISTICS AT WORK

STATISTIC

4. EMPLOYEE HEALTH RISK APPRAISAL

In a study designed to identify the current health habits and risk factors of employees of a large hospital and to motivate the employees to make changes in their health habits, investigators Pilon and Renfroe report their results with respect to a sample of 387 employees. Among their findings were a mean serum cholesterol level of 220.9 at the beginning of the study and a mean of 216.2 after a year of intervention that included feedback on risk factors, private counseling, and risk reduction education. The investigators, who used a paired *t* test to analyze their data, reported a standard deviation of the differences of 32.4. For a test of the null hypothesis that the mean difference is equal to zero, compute *t* and find the *p* value.

Source: Bonita Ann Pilon and Darlene Renfroe, "Evaluation of an Employee Health Risk Appraisal Program," *American Association of Occupational Health Nurses*, 38 (May 1990), 230–235.

5. EFFECTS OF OFFICE INFORMATION SYSTEMS

Rice and Contractor (Ronald E. Rice and Noshir S. Contractor, "Conceptualizing Effects of Office Information Systems: A Methodology and Application for the Study of Alpha, Beta, and Gamma Changes," *Decision Sciences*, 21 [1990], 301–317) conducted a study to determine whether the implementation of a new office information system with networking capabilities changes the way organizational members conceptualize office work. Subjects were office staff in an organization that implemented a system of desktop personal computers linked to an electronic mail package by a local area network. Three sets of measurements of subjects' perceptions of their performance effectiveness with respect to eight office activities were obtained: before implementation (T1), after implementation (T2), and after implementation, but reflecting the subjects' retrospective perceptions of their effectiveness before implementation (T3). The following are the T2 and T3 scores of 23 subjects responding to questions about record-keeping activity. Use a paired-comparisons procedure to test for significance. Let $\alpha = 0.01$. Can you conclude on the basis of these data that implementation of the new office information system changes the way organizational members conceptualize record-keeping activity?

Subject	T2	T3
1	2	2
2	5	3
3	4	3
4	3	3
5	3	4
6	4	4
7	3	3
8	4	3

Subject	T2	T3
9	3	3
10	4	2
11	5	3
12	5	4
13	5	4
14	2	4
15	4	3
16	5	4
17	4	3
18	4	3
19	4	1
20	4	3
21	5	4
22	5	3
23	4	4

Source: Professor Ronald E. Rice. Used with permission.

6. DYSFUNCTIONAL ORGANIZATIONAL TURNOVER AMONG RETAIL STORE BUYERS

Susan M. Keaveney reported the results of an empirical study of dysfunctional organizational turnover conducted among a nationwide probability sample of retail buyers. Subjects were classified as stayers or leavers according to whether they were still employed with their organization nine months after the survey. Among the variables on which measurements were obtained was job satisfaction. The mean job satisfaction score for 177 stayers was 17.59 with a standard deviation of 3.45. The 36 leavers yielded a mean job satisfaction score of 16.31 with a standard deviation of 3.64. On the basis of these data may we conclude that leavers tend to have a lower level of job satisfaction than stayers? Let $\alpha = 0.05$.

Source: Susan M. Keaveney, "An Empirical Investigation of Dysfunctional Organizational Turnover Among Chain and Non-Chain Retail Store Buyers," *Journal of Retailing*, 68 (Summer 1992), 145–173.

SUGGESTIONS FOR FURTHER READING

The following four articles will help you to understand better the concepts involved in formulating hypotheses.

Daniel, Wayne W. (1977). "Statistical Significance Versus Practical Significance," *Science Education* 61:423–427.

Lurie, William (1958). "The Impertinent Questioner: The Scientist's Guide to the Statistician's Mind," *American Scientist* 46:57–61.

Wilson, Warren, H. Miller, and J. S. Lower (1967). "Much Ado About the Null Hypothesis," *Psychological Bulletin* 67:188–196.

Wilson, Warren R., and H. Miller (1964). "A Note on the Inconclusiveness of Accepting the Null Hypothesis," *Psychological Review* 71:238–242.

The following book discusses hypothesis testing at a more rigorous level.

Lehmann, E. L. (1959). *Testing Statistical Hypotheses*. Wiley, New York.

For a better understanding of Type I and Type II errors, see the following article.

Feinberg, William E. (1971). "Teaching the Type I and Type II Errors: The Judicial Process," *American Statistician* 25 (June):30–32.

For a more detailed discussion of p values, see the following three articles.

Bahn, Anita K. (1972). "P and the Null Hypothesis," *Annals of Internal Medicine* 76:674.

Daniel, Wayne W. (1977). "What Are p Values? How Are They Calculated? How Are They Related to Levels of Significance?" *Nursing Research* 26:304–306.

Gibbons, Jean D., and John W. Pratt (1975). "P Values: Interpretation and Methodology," *The American Statistician* 29:20–25.

8

Analysis of Variance

Chapter Objectives: Now that you have learned the basic concepts and techniques of statistical inference, you can use these ideas and skills in more complex situations. In this chapter, you learn to test the null hypothesis that several population means are equal. To do so, you will use a technique known as *analysis of variance.*

After studying this chapter and working the exercises, you should be able to

1. Describe the following experimental designs and use the appropriate analysis-of-variance technique to analyze the data generated by these designs: (a) the completely randomized design, (b) the randomized complete block design, (c) the Latin square design, and (d) the factorial experiment.
2. Test for a significant difference between individual pairs of sample means.
3. Use a computer software package to perform the calculations for analysis of variance.

8.1   INTRODUCTION

We may view the preceding chapters, which cover the basic concepts and techniques of descriptive and inferential statistics, as providing the foundation for this and later chapters. The objective of this portion of the book is to help you understand some of the more widely used tools of statistical analysis.

This chapter is concerned with *analysis of variance* (ANOVA). The techniques and concepts of analysis of variance are used most frequently to test hypotheses about the equality of three or more population means. In this chapter, you will learn that analysis of variance provides a useful extension of the techniques for testing hypotheses about the equality of two population means and hypotheses about a population mean difference, which you studied in Chapter 7.

Analysis of variance may be defined as follows:

> *Analysis of variance* is a technique whereby the total variation present in a set of data is partitioned into several components. Associated with each of these components is a specific source of variation, so that, in the analysis, it is possible to ascertain the magnitude of the contribution of each of these sources to the total variation.

The introduction and development of the techniques of analysis of variance are due to R. A. Fisher, whose contributions over the years 1912 to 1962 had a tremendous influence on modern statistical thought.

Analysis of variance is most often used to analyze data derived from designed experiments. Its use, however, is not restricted to this type of data. As some of the examples and exercises of this chapter show, we can also use analysis-of-variance techniques to analyze data from surveys.

When we design experiments with an analysis in mind—before we conduct the experiment—we identify those sources of variation that we consider important. We then choose a design that will let us measure the extent to which these sources contribute to the total variation.

The assumptions underlying ANOVA techniques are important.

We use analysis of variance to estimate and test hypotheses about both population variances and population means. Although this text deals only with testing hypotheses about population means, the conclusions depend on the magnitudes of the observed variances.

The valid use of analysis of variance depends on a set of fundamental assumptions. We state these briefly in the sections that follow. Not all the assumptions will be met perfectly in a given situation. Thus, it is important to be aware of the underlying assumptions and to be able to recognize serious departures from them. Analysis-of-variance results must be considered approximate, rather than exact, because experiments in which all the assumptions are perfectly met are rare.

We discuss analysis of variance in the context of three different experimental designs: the completely randomized, the randomized complete block, and the

Latin square. We present the concept of a factorial experiment through its use in a completely randomized design.

To illustrate analysis-of-variance techniques, we use the seven-step hypothesis-testing procedure introduced in Chapter 7.

At the start, let us define two terms: we define other terms as we introduce them. The term *treatment* is broadly used in the design of experiments.

A *treatment* is any factor that the experimenter controls. It may refer, for example, to a type of drug, one of several concentrations of a single drug, a new type of house paint, an advertising technique, or a particular training program.

The term *treatment* originated in the early days of analysis of variance, when different groups had different treatments (in the usual sense of the word) applied to their respective experimental units.

The entity that receives a treatment is called an *experimental unit*.

An experimental unit may be, for example, an individual, a single white mouse, a group of white mice, a plot of ground, a segment of the consuming public, a group of trainees, or an item of production. We may also think of it as that entity on which we take a measurement in order to obtain a value for the variable of interest.

In this chapter, we frequently use the expression "mean square" synonymously with the word "variance." Thus, when we are speaking of a measure of variability for a data set, we may speak of the mean square of the set of data rather than the variance of the set of data.

8.2   THE COMPLETELY RANDOMIZED DESIGN

When we use the *completely randomized design*, we assign the treatments at random to the experimental units. Suppose, for example, that we want to road-test four brands of tires, A, B, C, and D, to determine whether there are any differences among the brands with respect to expected tire mileage. We can assign 10 tires of each brand at random to the 40 rear wheels of 20 cars. We can then drive the cars until a predetermined amount of tread wear occurs. At that time we record the number of miles driven. We then use an analysis of variance to decide whether the brands differ with respect to expected tire mileage. The two sources of variation that we isolate are (1) *variation due to treatment* (brand) *differences* and (2) *residual variation*. Residual variation measures the variation resulting from all sources other than the tire brands.

We analyze data from an experiment using the completely randomized design by what is known as *one-way analysis of variance*. The term *one-way* refers to the fact that we classify the experimental units (and consequently the measure-

---

Marginal notes:

A treatment is any factor that the experimenter controls.

Treatments are applied to experimental units.

Mean square = variance.

We use one-way ANOVA to analyze data from a completely randomized design.

ments obtained) according to only one criterion—the treatment group to which they belong.

We may also use one-way analysis of variance to analyze data from a sample survey in which we draw a random sample from each of several populations. In fact, one-way analysis of variance, which enables one to test for a significant difference among several means, is an extension of the t test for the difference between two means (discussed in Chapter 7).

ONE-WAY ANOVA MODEL

In trying to understand analysis of variance, it is helpful to consider the concept of the *analysis-of-variance model*. A model is a symbolic representation of a typical value from a set of data. We may identify such a value by the symbol x_{ij}, where the subscript ij indicates the ith value from the jth population. Within a given population, a specific value is equal to the mean μ_j of the population, plus some amount that prevents the individual value from being equal to the mean (unless the amount is 0, in which case the individual value is equal to the mean).

In other words, if we add some amount (which may be negative, positive, or 0) to the mean, we get the particular value x_{ij}. We may call this amount the error and designate it by e_{ij}. We can write this relationship as

(8.2.1)
$$x_{ij} = \mu_j + e_{ij}$$

Solving for e_{ij}, we have

(8.2.2)
$$e_{ij} = x_{ij} - \mu_j$$

Suppose that there are k finite populations of equal size. We can obtain the grand mean μ of all the observations in the k populations together by calculating the mean of the k population means:

(8.2.3)
$$\mu = \sum_{j=1}^{k} \mu_j / k$$

We may designate the difference between any μ_j and μ as

(8.2.4)
$$\tau_j = \mu_j - \mu$$

We usually refer to this term as the jth population effect, or jth *treatment effect*. It is a measure of the average effect that the jth treatment has on an individual observation.

We may solve Equation 8.2.4 for μ_j to obtain

(8.2.5)
$$\mu_j = \mu + \tau_j$$

Substituting the right-hand portion of Equation 8.2.5 into Equation 8.2.1, we have

(8.2.6)
$$x_{ij} = \mu + \tau_j + e_{ij}$$

and the model is specified.

Thus, a typical observation from the set of data under study is composed of the grand mean μ, a treatment effect τ_j, and an error term that represents the deviation of the observation from its population mean.

ONE-WAY ANOVA ASSUMPTIONS

The assumptions underlying analysis of variance depend on the manner in which we select the treatments. We may identify two cases. We usually refer to them as the *fixed-effects model*, or *model I*, and the *random-effects model*, or *model II*. We use the fixed-effects model when we are interested in the k populations represented by the sample data. And we use the random-effects model when we consider these k populations to be a sample of size k from a population of treatments.

In the fixed-effects model, our inferences are limited to the specific treatments that appear in the experiment. The following are some examples of situations in which the fixed-effects model applies.

Examples in which the fixed-effects model applies

(a) We have three methods of teaching management skills to department supervisors. Trainees are randomly assigned to one of the methods. At the end of the training period, we compare the mean scores of the three groups and make inferences about the three methods' relative effectiveness.
(b) We have five kinds of fertilizer. Each is used to fertilize ten randomly selected tomato plants. We measure the mean yield of each group of ten plants and make inferences about the relative quality of the five fertilizers.
(c) We have four factories. We select a random sample of employees from each. Then we determine the mean amount of time that these employees spend per day watching television. We wish to make inferences about the equality of the four population means.

When we randomly assign treatments to experimental units, we may use the sample results to make inferences about causation. For example, in situation (b), the five fertilizers are randomly assigned to the tomato plants. Thus, we may, as we said earlier, make inferences about their relative quality. Situation (c), however, is different. In that case, factories are not randomly assigned to employees. Therefore, our inference is limited to a statement about the differences among the population means. We cannot infer that the factories are the cause of any observed differences among means.

In the random-effects model, the populations represented in the experiment are a sample of populations from a larger set of populations. The following are examples of situations in which the random-effects model is applicable.

Examples in which
the random-effects
model applies

(a) We have 50 kinds of fertilizer. We select a random sample of 5 for an experiment. We wish to make an inference about the entire set of 50 fertilizers based on the performance of the 5 in our experiment.

(b) We have 200 factories. We select a random sample of 10 factories. We wish to use the results of a survey in these 10 factories to make inferences about the set of 200 factories.

(c) We have 50 drugs that are potential competitors for the treatment of a certain disease. We randomly select 6 for use in an experiment. Our objective is to draw conclusions about the set of 50 drugs.

The calculations are identical, regardless of the model. However, we make a distinction in the interpretation of the results when the parameters of interest are means. We assume the fixed-effects model in the examples and exercises of this chapter.

Fixed-Effects Model Assumptions The assumptions for the fixed-effects model are as follows:

(a) The k sets of observed data constitute k independent random samples from the specified populations.

(b) Each of the populations represented by a sample is normally distributed, with mean μ_j and variance σ_j^2.

(c) Each of the populations has the same variance. That is, $\sigma_1^2 = \sigma_2^2 = \cdots = \sigma_k^2 = \sigma^2$, the common variance.

(d) The τ_j's are unknown constants. Since (by Equation 8.2.4) $\tau_j = \mu_j - \mu$ and since the sum of all deviations of values of a variable from their mean is equal to 0, we may write $\Sigma\tau_j = 0$.

Three consequences of the relationship

$$e_{ij} = x_{ij} - \mu_j$$

specified in Equation 8.2.2 are as follows:

(a) The e_{ij} have a mean of 0. This follows from the fact that the mean of the x_{ij} is μ_j.

(b) The e_{ij} have a variance equal to the variance of the x_{ij}, since the e_{ij} and x_{ij} differ only by a constant. In other words, the variance of the e_{ij} is equal to σ^2, the common variance specified in assumption (c).

(c) The e_{ij} are normally (and independently) distributed.

As already noted, the fixed-effects model implies that our interest is limited to the k populations represented by the sample data. Any inferences that we make apply only to these populations. For example, suppose that the treatments represented by the sample data are three methods of packaging a product. Any inferences we make under model I are limited to these three methods. They are not extended to any larger set of methods.

Violations of the assumptions of equal population variances and normally distributed populations tend to increase the probability of rejecting a true null hypothesis. Violating the assumption of equal population variances usually causes a worse problem than violating the assumption that the populations are all normally distributed. The consequences of unequal variances are less severe when the sample sizes are equal.

ONE-WAY ANOVA HYPOTHESES

Under the present model, we may test the null hypothesis that all treatment, or population, means are equal against the alternative that there is at least one inequality among them. In general, we may state the hypotheses symbolically as follows:

$$H_0: \mu_1 = \mu_2 = \cdots = \mu_k, \qquad H_1: \text{not all } \mu_j \text{ are equal}$$

If the population means are equal, each treatment effect is equal to 0. Alternatively, we may state the hypotheses as

$$H_0: \tau_j = 0, \qquad j = 1, 2, \ldots, k, \qquad H_1: \text{not all } \tau_j = 0$$

ONE-WAY ANOVA CALCULATIONS

As noted earlier, when we perform an analysis of variance, we partition the total variability in a set of sample data into two or more components, each of which is associated with a specified source of variability. Furthermore, as also previously noted, when we use one-way ANOVA, we partition the total variability into two components: (1) variability due to the treatment and (2) variability due to all other sources, called the residual, or error, variability.

For each of these sources, as well as for the total variability, we compute a sample variance, or mean square, as the quantity is called in the ANOVA context. As you learned in Chapter 2, a sample variance (or mean square) is equal to a sum of squares divided by the appropriate degrees of freedom. The treatment mean square MSTr in one-way ANOVA involving k treatments is equal to the treatment sum of squares SSTr divided by $k - 1$ degrees of freedom. That is,

$$\text{MSTr} = \frac{\text{SSTr}}{k - 1}$$

In one-way ANOVA, the residual, or error, mean square (MSE) computed from a total of n observations resulting from the application of k treatments is equal to the error sum of squares SSE divided by $n - k$ degrees of freedom.

That is,

$$MSE = \frac{SSE}{n - k}$$

The total sum of squares computed from a total of n observations is designated SST and has associated with it $n - 1$ degrees of freedom.

Calculating these mean squares manually or on a calculator using the definitional formulas is a tedious and lengthy procedure. Short-cut formulas that are especially efficient with calculators save time. However, most ANOVA calculations are now performed by some type of computer, so that those employing the techniques need not concern themselves with the formulas. We assume that most users of this text have access to a computer. For those who, by either choice or necessity, perform the calculations on a calculator, the necessary formulas are given in Section 8.7. The use of STAT+ and MINITAB to perform the calculations for one-way analysis of variance is illustrated at the end of Section 8.3.

ONE-WAY ANOVA TABLE

When the population means are all equal, we can show that the sample SSTr and SSE, when divided by their respective degrees of freedom, yield independent and unbiased estimates of σ^2, the variance that is assumed to be common to all populations.

Let us suppose that the null hypothesis is true, that is, that there are no treatment effects. All population means are equal. Then the two estimates of σ^2 ought to be fairly close in size, since they are independent estimates of the same parameter. Suppose, however, that the null hypothesis is false. Then the treatment mean square, which reflects variability among treatment or sample means, ought to be larger than the error mean square, which is an unbiased estimate of the common population variance even when H_0 is not true.

There is a reason for expecting the estimate of the treatment mean square to be larger than the estimate of the error mean square. The estimate of the treatment mean square includes an estimate of the common variance, along with an estimate of any variation that exists among the population (treatment) means. That is,

$$MSTr = \text{estimate of } \sigma^2 + \begin{array}{l} \text{estimate of the variability} \\ \text{among population means} \end{array}$$

On the other hand,

$$MSE = \text{estimate of } \sigma^2 \text{ only}$$

When H_0 is true (that is, when the population means are all equal),

$$\text{MSTr} = \text{estimate of } \sigma^2 \text{ only}$$

and tends to be approximately equal to MSE. But when H_0 is not true (when the population means are not all equal), the MSTr estimate also contains an estimate of the additional variation among population (treatment) means and tends to be larger than MSE. These facts make it possible for us to reach a conclusion about the equality of population means by using a statistic that compares the magnitudes of two sample variances.

THE F STATISTIC

Chapter 7 shows that we can compare two variances by forming their ratio. At present we are interested in the following variance ratio:

$$(8.2.7) \qquad F = \frac{\text{treatment mean square}}{\text{error mean square}} = \frac{\text{MSTr}}{\text{MSE}}$$

If the numerator and denominator of Equation 8.2.7 are about equal, the variance ratio is close to 1. Then the hypothesis of equal population means is supported. If, however, the treatment mean square is much larger than the error mean square, the variance ratio is much greater than 1. In this case, the hypothesis of equal population means becomes suspect.

Even when the null hypothesis is true (all population means are equal), it is unlikely that the two estimates of σ^2 will be equal, because of the uncertainty (variation) of sampling. We must decide, then, how much greater than 1 the computed variance ratio has to be before we can conclude that something other than sampling fluctuation is operating. In other words, we wish to know how large F must be before we are willing to conclude that the observed difference between the two estimates of σ^2 is not due to chance alone, but is due instead to a lack of equality among population means.

Critical values in ANOVA come from the table of the F distribution.

Chapter 7 shows that the ratio of two sample variances, such as the quantity defined by Equation 8.2.7, follows a distribution known as the F distribution when the sample variances are computed from samples that have been randomly and independently drawn from normally distributed populations with equal variances. We need, then, to determine the appropriate F distribution by observing the degrees of freedom associated with the numerator and denominator of F. Once we have done so, the size of the observed F that will cause rejection of the hypothesis of equal population means will depend on the critical value selected. This, in turn, will depend on the significance level. In other words, if the computed value of F is equal to or exceeds the critical value of F, we reject the null hypothesis of equal population means and conclude that at least one population mean is different from at least one of the others.

Table 8.2.1, which is an analysis-of-variance (ANOVA) table, summarizes the calculations involved in one-way analysis of variance.

TABLE 8.2.1 ANOVA table for one-way analysis of variance

Source of variation	Sum of squares (SS)	Degrees of freedom (df)	Mean square (MS)	F
Treatments	SSTr	$k - 1$	$MSTr = SSTr/(k - 1)$	$F = MSTr/MSE$
Error	SSE	$n - k$	$MSE = SSE/(n - k)$	
Total	SST	$n - 1$		

ONE-WAY ANOVA DECISION

Suppose that the computed value of F in the last column of Table 8.2.1 is equal to or greater than the critical value of F. Then we reject the null hypothesis of equal population means. As with all hypothesis tests, this critical value depends on the significance level chosen. We treat the hypothesis test in analysis of variance as a one-sided test, even though the hypotheses as stated are like those for a two-sided test. As we have noted, if H_0 is false, we expect the numerator of F to be larger than the denominator. Thus, it seems logical that the rejection region should be in the right tail of the F distribution. This line of reasoning indicates that the p value should be one-sided.

Here is an example of the type of business problem for which one-way analysis of variance would be appropriate.

EXAMPLE 8.2.1 Tibbett Plastics, Ltd., wants to know what effect three formula ingredients have on the elasticity of its plastic products. Each of the ingredients is randomly assigned to batches of experimental material. Table 8.2.2 shows the results (in coded form) of elasticity tests made on each specimen of the product. The manufacturer wishes to know whether the ingredients have a differential effect on the elasticity of the plastic.

SOLUTION Figure 8.2.1 shows the sample observations, represented by dots; the sample means, represented by squares; and the grand mean $\bar{x}_{..}$, represented by the heavy horizontal line. This figure visually represents the variability of the three sample observations about their respective means and the variability of the sample means about the grand mean. In Figure 8.2.1, for example, $\hat{e}_{4,B}$ shows the amount by which the fourth observation in sample B, $x_{4,B}$, deviates from the mean of sample B.

TABLE 8.2.2 Elasticity of plastic produced with three different formula ingredients (coded data)

													Total		Mean	
A	5	6	5	8	6	7	6	5	6	7			61		6.1	
B	8	9	8	7	9	9	10	8					68		8.5	
C	10	10	9	8	8	9	10	9	8	9	10	8	108		9.0	
													237	= Grand total	7.9	= Grand mean

FIGURE 8.2.1 The data of Example 8.2.1, showing the variability within samples and the variability among sample means

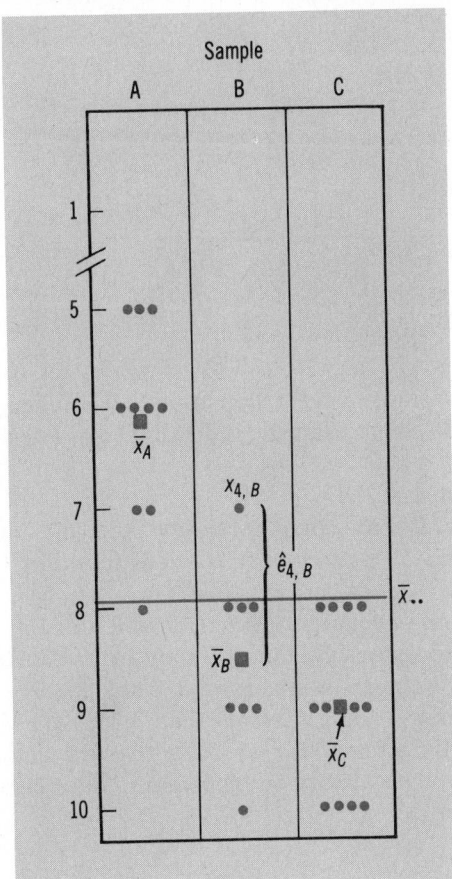

We assume that the one-way analysis-of-variance model is appropriate and that its underlying assumptions are met. We then apply the seven-step hypothesis-testing procedure learned in Chapter 7.

1. Hypotheses.

$$H_0: \mu_A = \mu_B = \mu_C, \qquad H_1: \text{at least one equality does not hold}$$

Figure 8.2.2 shows the case in which the assumptions are met and H_0 is true. Figure 8.2.3 shows the case in which the assumptions are met, but H_0 is false because none of the population means are equal. If any one of the three population means is not equal to the other two, the null hypothesis is also false.

FIGURE 8.2.2   Picture of each of the populations represented by Example 8.2.1 when H_0 is true and the assumptions are met

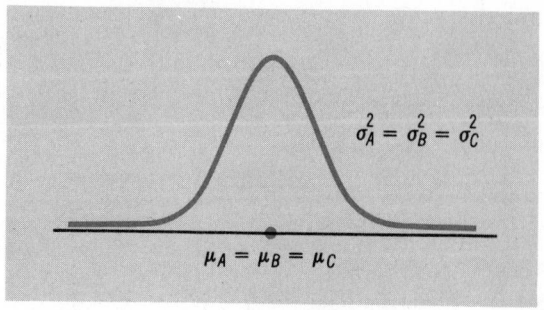

2. *Test statistic.* The test statistic is F of Equation 8.2.7. When H_0 is true and the assumptions are met, the test statistic is distributed as F with 2 and 27 degrees of freedom.

3. *Significance level.* Let $\alpha = 0.05$.

4. *Decision rule.* Reject H_0 if the computed F is ≥ 3.35, the critical value of F for $\alpha = 0.05$ and 2 and 27 degrees of freedom as found in Table G of Appendix I.

5. *Calculations.* The sums of squares calculations will probably be done either on a calculator or by computer. Section 8.7 shows the calculations using short-cut formulas. The results are summarized in Table 8.2.3.

6. *Statistical decision.* Since 29.358 is greater than 3.35, we reject H_0.

7. *Conclusion.* The manufacturer may conclude that the ingredients do have a differential effect on the elasticity of the product. Since 29.358 is greater than 6.49, $p < 0.005$.

FIGURE 8.2.3   Picture of the populations represented in Example 8.2.1 when the assumptions of equal variances and normally distributed populations are met, but H_0 is false because no two of the population means are equal

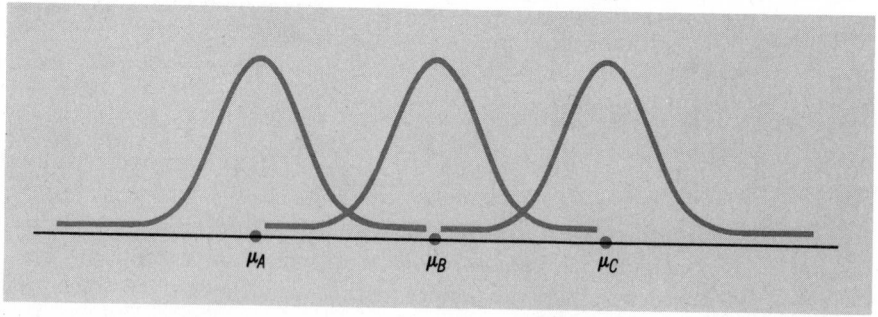

TABLE 8.2.3   ANOVA table for Example 8.2.1

Source	SS	df	MS	F
Treatments	49.8	2	24.9	29.358
Error	22.9	27	0.84815	
Total	72.7	29		

ONE-WAY ANOVA AND THE t DISTRIBUTION

The completely randomized experimental design extends to three or more treatments the two-independent-samples design for detecting a difference between two population means (discussed in Chapter 7). The one-way analysis of variance for three or more samples replaces the t test used to detect a significant difference between two sample means. Here is an example that shows the relationship between analysis of variance and the t test.

EXAMPLE 8.2.2   Untermeyer Chemicals wishes to compare the effectiveness of two formulas for rat poison. Wild rats are randomly assigned to receive one of the two formulas. The variable of interest is the rats' survival time, in minutes, after eating a fixed amount of the poison. Table 8.2.4 shows the results. We want to test the null hypothesis that the mean survival time is the same for both poisons.

TABLE 8.2.4   Survival time in minutes of 22 wild rats fed a fixed amount of one of two poisons

Poison A	38.7	42.4	34.8	46.6	48.0	36.4	51.1	42.1	43.3	43.9	43.3	46.6
Poison B	35.1	36.0	38.7	34.4	40.8	35.4	41.5	37.4	43.5	39.6		

SOLUTION   To reach a conclusion, we test

$$H_0: \mu_A = \mu_B \quad \text{against the alternative} \quad H_1: \mu_A \neq \mu_B$$

Let $\alpha = 0.05$. To test the null hypothesis by means of the t test, we first compute

$$\bar{x}_A = 43.10 \qquad s_A^2 = 22.53273$$
$$\bar{x}_B = 38.24 \qquad s_B^2 = 9.47822$$

We pool the sample variances, by Equation 6.6.1, to obtain

$$s_p^2 = \frac{11(22.53273) + 9(9.47822)}{20} = 16.658201$$

We now compute

$$t = \frac{43.10 - 38.24}{\sqrt{\dfrac{16.658201}{12} + \dfrac{16.658201}{10}}} = 2.78$$

Since 2.78 is greater than 2.0860, the critical value of t for $\alpha = 0.05$ and 20 degrees of freedom, we reject H_0. We conclude that the two poisons do result in different mean survival times.

Now let us use one-way analysis of variance to test the null hypothesis of equal population means. The sums of squares calculations are given in Section 8.7. From these results, we compute

$$\text{MSTr} = \frac{128.834}{1} = 128.834$$

$$\text{MSE} = \frac{333.164}{20} = 16.6582$$

$$F = \frac{128.834}{16.6582} = 7.73$$

Since 7.73 is greater than 4.35, the critical value of F for $\alpha = 0.05$ and 1 and 20 degrees of freedom, we reject H_0. We conclude that the two population means are not equal.

As tests for the equality of two population means, the t test and one-way ANOVA are equivalent.

We see that the statistical decision we reach using analysis of variance is the same as the statistical decision we reach when we use the t test. This is not a coincidence. For the two-sample case, the two tests are equivalent. Note that the critical F value, 4.35, is equal to the critical t value squared. That is, $4.35 = (2.0860)^2$. Also, the computed F, 7.73, is equal to the computed t squared. That is, $7.73 = (2.78)^2$. In general, for the same α, F with 1 and $n - k$ degrees of freedom is equal to the square of t (two-sided test) with $n - k$ degrees of freedom. It is this relationship between the t and the F distributions that makes the two tests equivalent.

Often you may feel that one or more of the assumptions underlying one-way analysis of variance are not met. In this case, a procedure known as the *Kruskal-Wallis one-way analysis of variance* may provide a suitable alternative test. Chapter 13 discusses this procedure in detail.

EXERCISES

Carry out the seven-step hypothesis-testing procedure at the indicated level of significance and compute the p value for the test.

8.2.1 ⓒ Vancouver Products is testing customer acceptance of a new product using four different counter displays, A, B, C, and D. It selects 36 stores, matched on all relevant criteria. Each display is used in 9 of the stores. Total sales (coded) at the end of a week are as follows. At the 0.05 level of significance, test the null hypothesis of no difference among the four means.

A	5	6	7	7	8	6	7	7	6
B	2	2	2	3	3	2	3	3	2
C	2	2	3	3	2	2	2	3	3
D	6	6	7	8	8	8	6	6	6

8.2.2 ⓒ The following data give the production costs, in cents per pound, of broilers produced in three production areas, A, B, and C, as reported by ten producers randomly selected from each area. Do these data provide sufficient evidence to indicate a difference in mean cost among the three regions? Let $\alpha = 0.05$.

A	11	10	12	10	11	9	8	13	12	12
B	12	10	9	11	10	12	12	14	8	9
C	12	13	15	14	14	11	15	14	14	15

8.2.3 ⓒ The following table gives the production cost per dollar of net sales for 24 firms with different asset sizes. Do these data provide sufficient evidence to indicate that firms of different sizes have different mean costs? Let $\alpha = 0.05$. (Assets given in millions of dollars.)

$10–$19.9	69	72	72	66	76	72	70	72
$20–$49.9	75	70	80	74	68	80	72	76
$50 and over	83	77	80	74	86	75	85	80

8.2.4 ⓒ The following table shows the results, in miles per gallon, of an experiment conducted to compare three brands of gasoline. Each brand was used with seven different cars of the same weight and engine size, driven under similar conditions. Do these data provide sufficient evidence at the 0.01 level of significance to indicate a difference between brands of gasoline?

Brand A	14	19	19	16	15	17	20
Brand B	20	21	18	20	19	19	18
Brand C	20	26	23	24	23	25	23

8.3 TESTING FOR SIGNIFICANT DIFFERENCES BETWEEN INDIVIDUAL PAIRS OF MEANS

In those cases in which we obtain a significant F and conclude that "not all population (treatment) means are equal," we may want to perform a test of significance on each pair of treatment means. There is a problem inherent in this procedure, however, because of the probabilities involved.

Consider, for example, an experiment with five treatments. To find which of all the possible pairs of means are significantly different would require

$$_5C_2 = 10$$

tests. Suppose that there is no difference among the treatments. That is, suppose that the population means are all equal. If we conduct the tests at the 5% level of significance, the probability of rejecting a true null hypothesis is 0.05 for each test individually. As long as we conduct a single test, no problem arises. If we carry out all ten tests, however, the probability of rejecting at least one true hypothesis is greater than 0.05. If the tests are independent, the probability of rejecting at least one true null hypothesis in ten tests is $1 - (0.95)^{10} = 0.4013$, which is considerably larger than 0.05. Tests involving all possible pairs of means in an analysis-of-variance context are not independent. The probability of rejecting at least one true null hypothesis in this case is hard to obtain. However, it seems reasonable to expect that, as the number of dependent tests increases, the probability of rejecting at least one true hypothesis also increases.

PAIRWISE COMPARISONS

Interest is usually focused on *pairwise comparisons*.

A *pairwise comparison* is the difference between two means without regard to the algebraic sign.

Investigation of comparisons between pairs of means may take the form of a hypothesis test of the difference between two means. Or we may want to construct a confidence interval for the difference. We may encounter either of two situations involving comparisons.

(a) Before we conduct a study, we may decide that it is worthwhile to compare only certain pairs of sample treatment means to see whether they are significantly different. We call such comparisons *planned*, or *a priori*, comparisons. We may make *a priori* comparisons whether or not the computed F in the analysis of variance is significant. We plan *a priori* comparisons *before*, or *prior to*, analyzing the sample data, as the term implies.

(b) At other times we may have no basis for planning comparisons among means before we conduct the study. If the F value computed in the analysis of variance is not significant, this indicates that there is no evidence of a treatment effect. Thus, we probably will not be interested in comparing individual pairs of means. However, if the computed F *is* significant, we are likely to want to find which pairs of sample treatment means are significantly different.

Comparisons made after the initial analysis of variance are called *a posteriori*, or *post hoc*, comparisons.

When the fixed-effects model applies, there are several procedures that we can use to make all possible pairwise comparisons among means, whether or not these comparisons were planned in advance. Using these procedures, we can make a large number of comparisons routinely. Or, after the experiment, we can select the comparisons that appear most interesting.

TUKEY'S HSD TEST

In 1953, J. W. Tukey proposed a procedure for making all *pairwise* comparisons among means. This method, which is now widely used, is called the *HSD* (honestly significant difference) *test* or the *w procedure*. When Tukey's test is used with equal sample sizes, we compute a single value with which we compare all differences. This value, called the HSD, is given by the following formula:

$$(8.3.1) \qquad \mathrm{HSD} = q_{\alpha, k, n-k} \sqrt{\frac{\mathrm{MSE}}{n_j}}$$

where q is obtained from Table H (in Appendix I) for significance level α, k means in the experiment, and $n - k$ error degrees of freedom. Any difference between pairs of means that exceeds HSD is declared significant. Note that the HSD statistic requires that all sample sizes be equal; that is, $n_1 = n_2 = \cdots = n_j$. Let us use an example to illustrate the way this procedure works.

EXAMPLE 8.3.1   Table 8.3.1 presents data from an experiment designed to compare four methods (A, B, C, and D) used in the production of a cleaning compound. The variable of interest is the percentage of solid content of the compound. There are six observations for each method. The computed F is significant at $\alpha = 0.01$, the significance level selected before the analysis. The logical question now is, where do the significant differences occur?

SOLUTION   Tukey's HSD test provides the answer we seek. When we apply this method to the data of Table 8.3.1, we first display the absolute values of the differences between means, as in Table 8.3.2. The sample treatment means arranged in ascending order of magnitude provide the row and column labels.

TABLE 8.3.1   Analysis-of-variance table, Example 8.3.1

Source	SS	df	MS	F
Treatments	1,045.44	3	348.49	6.026
Error	1,156.56	20	57.8281	
	2,202.00	23		
Method	A	B	C	D
Mean	75.67	78.83	69.17	87.50

TABLE 8.3.2 Differences between all pairs of means, Example 8.3.1

	$\overline{x}_C$	$\overline{x}_A$	$\overline{x}_B$	$\overline{x}_D$
$\overline{x}_C = 69.17$	—	6.50	9.66	18.33*
$\overline{x}_A = 75.67$		—	3.16	11.83
$\overline{x}_B = 78.83$			—	8.67
$\overline{x}_D = 87.50$				—

*Significant at the 0.01 level

The body of the table gives the corresponding differences. If we choose a significance level of $\alpha = 0.01$, we find $q_{0.01,4,20}$ in Table H to be 5.02. From Table 8.3.1, MSE = 57.8281, and we compute

$$\text{HSD} = 5.02 \sqrt{\frac{57.8281}{6}} = 15.58$$

When we compare the differences between means shown in Table 8.3.2 with 15.58, we realize that only one pair of means is significantly different, $|\overline{x}_C - \overline{x}_D| = 18.33$.

When the samples are not all of the same size, we cannot apply the Tukey HSD test given by Equation 8.3.1. We may, however, extend Tukey's method to the case in which the sizes of samples are different. It can be applied in experiments that involve three or more treatments and significance levels of 0.05 or less. The method consists of replacing n_j in Equation 8.3.1 with n_j^*, the smallest of the samples whose means we are comparing. We call the new quantity HSD*. We then have as the new test criterion

$$\text{HSD}^* = q_{\alpha,k,n-k} \sqrt{\frac{\text{MSE}}{n_j^*}}$$

We call "significant" any absolute value of the difference between two sample means that exceeds the proper HSD*.

To see the use of the HSD* statistic at the $\alpha = 0.05$ level, refer to Example 8.2.1. The sample means, as shown in Table 8.2.2, are 6.1, 8.5, and 9.0. These means are computed from samples of size 10, 8, and 12, respectively. The absolute values of the differences between all possible pairs of means are

$$|6.1 - 8.5| = 2.4$$
$$|6.1 - 9.0| = 2.9$$
$$|8.5 - 9.0| = 0.5$$

The value of $q_{0.05,3,27}$, obtained by interpolation from Table H, is 3.51. To test H_0: $\mu_A = \mu_B$, we have

$$HSD^* = 3.51 \sqrt{\frac{0.84815}{8}} = 1.14$$

Since 2.4 is greater than 1.14, we reject H_0. To test H_0: $\mu_A = \mu_C$, we compute

$$HSD^* = 3.51 \sqrt{\frac{0.84815}{10}} = 1.02$$

Since 2.9 is greater than 1.02, we reject H_0. Finally, to test H_0: $\mu_B = \mu_C$, we compute

$$HSD^* = 3.51 \sqrt{\frac{0.84815}{8}} = 1.14$$

Since 0.5 is not greater than 1.14, we cannot reject H_0 this time. We conclude, then, that μ_A is different from μ_B and μ_C, but that μ_B and μ_C may be equal.

Multiple-comparison procedures are usually not appropriate when the treatments are quantitative rather than qualitative. In some instances "treatments" that appear to be qualitative are in fact quantitative. Consider a study of characteristics of department stores. If the "treatments" are formed by grouping stores on the basis of size, measured by floor space or sales volume, they are quantitative.

COMPUTER **ANALYSIS**

Computers make the calculations you need for analysis of variance much easier to do. You can work the exercises in this chapter by using one of the computer statistical packages that are available. The input requirements and output formats for the various statistical packages vary somewhat, but anyone familiar with the general concepts of analysis of variance can easily understand them.

Figure 8.3.1 shows the output for Example 8.2.1 provided by a one-way analysis-of-variance program found in the STAT+ package. Compare the ANOVA table on the printout with the one given in Table 8.2.3. You can see that the printout uses the label "Among groups" instead of "Treatments." The printout also gives the three sample means and standard deviations.

You may use STAT+ to perform Tukey's HSD test. The output, as shown in Figure 8.3.2, includes a table of differences between all possible pairs of sample means, as well as a table that shows which differences are significantly different. Differences given in the first table that are not significantly different are replaced by zeros in the second table.

Finally, STAT+ will give you a plot of the individual sample values, along with the sample means. Figure 8.3.3 shows this graph for our present example.

FIGURE 8.3.1 Computer output for analysis of variance of data of Example 8.2.1 using STAT+ statistical package

```
ONE  WAY  ANALYSIS  OF  VARIANCE
                 Sum of      Degrees of      Mean       Fisher's
     Source      Squares      Freedom       Square         F
Among Groups      49.80          2           24.90        29.36
Error             22.90         27            0.85
Total             72.70         29

                                         Standard
              Group      Mean           Deviation
                A        6.1000          0.9944
                B        8.5000          0.9258
                C        9.0000          0.8528
```

FIGURE 8.3.2 Tukey's HSD Test performed by STAT+ for Example 8.2.1

```
    DIFFERENCES  BETWEEN  GROUP  MEANS
           FOR  THE  HSD*  TEST
       Group        B          C
         A        2.4000     2.9000
         B                   0.5000


    SIGNIFICANT  DIFFERENCES
      BETWEEN  GROUP  MEANS
        FOR  THE  HSD*  TEST
       Group        B          C
         A        2.4000     2.9000
         B                   0.0000
```

The nonzero values above, if any, are the paired
group mean differences for the groups found to
be honestly significantly different for
alpha = .05 using the HSD* Test

FIGURE 8.3.3 STAT+ graph of individual sample values and sample means for Example 8.2.1

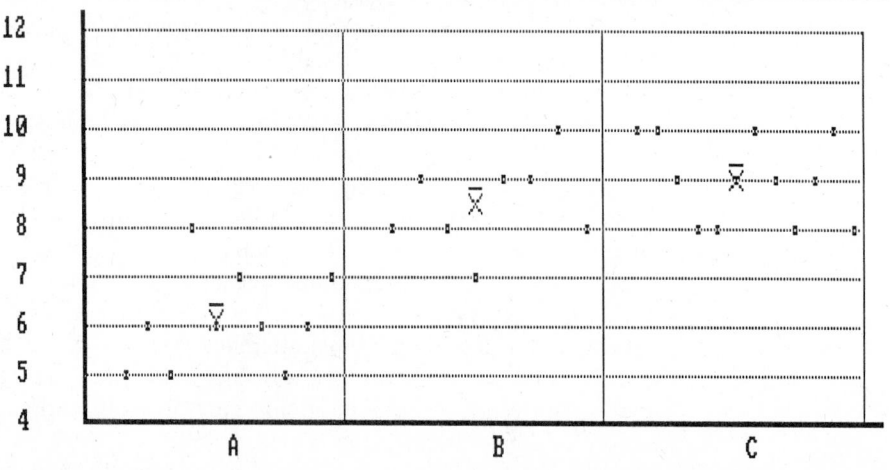

Points and means from one-way ANOVA data

FIGURE 8.3.4 Computer printout of one-way analysis of variance for Example 8.2.1 (MINITAB Printout)

```
MTB > AOVONEWAY C1-C3
ANALYSIS OF VARIANCE
SOURCE    DF      SS       MS        F       P
FACTOR     2   49.800   24.900   29.36   0.000
ERROR     27   22.900    0.848
TOTAL     29   72.700
                                INDIVIDUAL 95 PCT CI'S FOR MEAN
                                BASED ON POOLED STDEV
LEVEL     N     MEAN    STDEV   -----+---------+---------+---------+-
C1       10   6.1000   0.9944   (----*----)
C2        8   8.5000   0.9258                      (----*----)
C3       12   9.0000   0.8528                           (----*----)
                                -----+---------+---------+---------+-
POOLED STDEV = 0.9209            6.0      7.2      8.4      9.6
```

To illustrate the use of MINITAB in performing the calculations for one-way analysis of variance, we first enter the data of Example 8.2.1 into columns 1, 2, and 3. Figure 8.3.4 shows the necessary command and the resulting printout.

EXERCISES

8.3.1 Apply Tukey's test to the data of Exercise 8.2.1. Which counter display should be chosen?

8.3.2 Apply Tukey's test to the data of Exercise 8.2.2.

8.3.3 Apply Tukey's test to the data of Exercise 8.2.4. State the statistical hypotheses to be tested.

8.4 THE RANDOMIZED COMPLETE BLOCK DESIGN

A paint manufacturer wants to compare the hiding quality of paint produced by six different formulas but wants to eliminate from the experimental error the variability that would result if the paint were applied to different surfaces. What experimental design is appropriate? The objectives suggest that we use the *randomized complete block design*. This design is both easily understood and computationally simple. It is appropriate (a) when we can meaningfully cross-classify the experimental units according to two criteria, or (b) when we can apply treatments to different kinds of experimental material. One of the criteria of classification is called *treatments*; the other, *blocks*.

The objective is to remove from the error term the variability due to blocks.

In the randomized complete block design, each treatment must be applied to each different kind of experimental material, called a block. We achieve randomization by randomly assigning the treatments within the blocks according to a table of random numbers or any other randomization procedure. The primary objective of the randomized complete block design is to isolate and remove from the error variation the variation attributable to the blocks, while at the same time ensuring that treatment means are free of block effects. The effectiveness of the design depends on how well we achieve homogeneous blocks of experimental units. This, in turn, depends on knowing the experimental material well.

In industrial applications, we may use different kinds of raw material as a blocking factor. In comparing different metal-processing machines, for example, we can use each machine on several types of metal. As another example, suppose that our objective is to compare the performances of different operators. We may want to eliminate differences caused by such possible blocking factors as experience or training. We may also use the randomized complete block design when we must carry out an experiment in more than one factory (block), or when we need several days (blocks) to complete it. In the problem at the beginning of this section, the "treatments" are the six paint formulas, and the "blocks" are the different types of surfaces to which the paint is applied.

Two-way analysis of variance

The analysis-of-variance technique used in the analysis is called *two-way analysis of variance*, since we classify each observation according to two criteria: the treatment and the block. We use the letter k to designate the number of treatments and the letter n to designate the number of blocks in a given experiment.

THE RANDOMIZED COMPLETE BLOCK MODEL

By an argument similar to that used in Section 8.2, we can establish the following model for the randomized complete block design:

(8.4.1)
$$x_{ij} = \mu + \beta_i + \tau_j + e_{ij}, \qquad 1 \le i \le n; \, 1 \le j \le k$$

where x_{ij} is a typical value from the overall population

μ is an unknown constant

β_i represents a block effect, reflecting the fact that the experimental unit fell in the ith block

τ_j represents a treatment effect, reflecting the fact that the experimental unit received the jth treatment

e_{ij} is a residual component representing all sources of variation other than treatments and blocks

RANDOMIZED COMPLETE BLOCK ASSUMPTIONS

We make three assumptions when we use the randomized complete block design. (a) Each observed x_{ij} constitutes an independent random sample of size 1 from one of the kn populations represented. (b) Each of these kn populations is normally distributed with mean μ_{ij} and the same variance σ^2. This assumption, along with (a), implies that the e_{ij} are independently and normally distributed with mean 0 and variance σ^2. (c) The block and treatment effects are *additive*. To state this assumption another way, we say that there is no *interaction* between treatments and blocks. When there is no interaction, the effect of a particular block-treatment combination is neither greater nor less than the sum of their individual effects. (We discuss interaction in more detail in Section 8.6.) We can show that when this assumption is met,

$$\sum_{j=1}^{k} \tau_j = \sum_{i=1}^{n} \beta_i = 0$$

If the assumption of additivity is not met, the analysis of variance may produce misleading results. We need not be concerned, however, unless the largest mean is more than 50% greater than the smallest. If we feel that the additivity assumption is not met, we use appropriate procedures for handling the situation. (See the Suggestions for Further Reading at the end of this chapter.)

When the given assumptions hold, the τ_j and β_i are a set of fixed constants, and the data fit the fixed-effects model. We often consider the blocks to be a random sample from some population of blocks. When this is true, and when the treatments are fixed, the model is known as the *mixed model*. When both blocks and treatments are random samples from populations of blocks and treatments, respectively, we have the random-effects model.

RANDOMIZED COMPLETE BLOCK HYPOTHESES

In general, we test

$$H_0: \mu_1 = \mu_2 = \mu_3 = \cdots = \mu_k \text{ versus}$$
$$H_1: \text{at least one equality does not hold}$$

In other words, we test the null hypothesis that the treatment means are all equal or, equivalently, that there are no differences in treatment effects.

Although we can test hypotheses about block means, we are seldom interested in such tests when the fixed-effects model applies, since our primary interest is in treatment effects. We introduce the blocks merely to eliminate a source of extraneous variation. Furthermore, although we randomly assign experimental units to treatments, we usually obtain blocks in a nonrandom manner.

RANDOMIZED COMPLETE BLOCK CALCULATIONS

The calculations necessary to analyze the data from an experiment using the randomized complete block design can be done best on a computer. The needed quantities are the total sum of squares SST, the sum of squares for blocks SSB, the sum of squares for treatments SSTr, and the error sum of squares SSE. When these sums of squares are divided by the appropriate degrees of freedom, we have the mean squares necessary for computing the F statistic. For an experiment involving k treatments and n blocks, the degrees of freedom are computed as follows:

$$
\begin{array}{ccccc}
\text{Total} & \text{Treatments} & \text{Blocks} & & \text{Error} \\
kn - 1 = & (k - 1) & + (n - 1) & + & (n - 1)(k - 1)
\end{array}
$$

We find the error degrees of freedom, like the error sum of squares, by subtraction:

$$
\begin{aligned}
(kn - 1) - (k - 1) - (n - 1) &= kn - 1 - k + 1 - n + 1 \\
&= n(k - 1) - 1(k - 1) = (n - 1)(k - 1)
\end{aligned}
$$

Short-cut formulas for computing the required sums of squares are given in Section 8.7.

RANDOMIZED COMPLETE BLOCK ANOVA TABLE

We can display the results of the calculations for the randomized complete block design in an analysis-of-variance table such as Table 8.4.1.

RANDOMIZED COMPLETE BLOCK DECISION

When the fixed-effects model applies and the null hypothesis of equal treatment effects (all $\tau_j = 0$) is true, both the error mean square and the treatments mean square are estimates of the common variance σ^2. Consequently, when the null hypothesis is true, the ratio

$$
F = \frac{\text{MSTr}}{\text{MSE}}
$$

follows the F distribution with $k - 1$ numerator degrees of freedom and with $(n - 1) \times (k - 1)$ denominator degrees of freedom. We compare the computed ratio with the critical value of F. If this ratio is equal to or exceeds the critical value of F, we reject the null hypothesis.

TABLE 8.4.1 ANOVA table for a two-way analysis of variance

Source	SS	df	MS	F
Treatments	SSTr	$k - 1$	MSTr = SSTr/$(k - 1)$	MSTr/MSE
Blocks	SSB	$n - 1$	MSB = SSB/$(n - 1)$	
Error	SSE	$(n - 1)(k - 1)$	MSE = SSE/$(n - 1)(k - 1)$	
Total	SST	$kn - 1$		

Here is an example that shows the analysis of variance for a randomized complete block design.

EXAMPLE 8.4.1   Refer to the case at the beginning of this section. Suppose that the paint manufacturer conducts the experiment to see whether the six paint formulas differ with respect to hiding quality. In this experiment, the types of paint (paint formulas) are considered treatments. The blocking factor is the type of surface to which the paint is applied. Figure 8.4.1 shows how the experiment might be conducted in a laboratory. Each rectangular bar represents one of the five surfaces, or blocks. Each surface is divided into six equal parts, and one of the types of paint is applied to each of these parts. We use a randomization procedure to determine which type of paint to apply to each part of each surface. Table 8.4.2 shows the results of the experiment. We assume that the randomized complete block model and assumptions apply.

SOLUTION   To determine whether we can conclude that the six paints differ with respect to hiding quality, we proceed as follows.

1. *Hypotheses.* Since we are not interested in comparing surface effects, our hypotheses relate to the formulas, or treatments. Thus, we have

FIGURE 8.4.1   Diagram of experiment described in Example 8.4.1

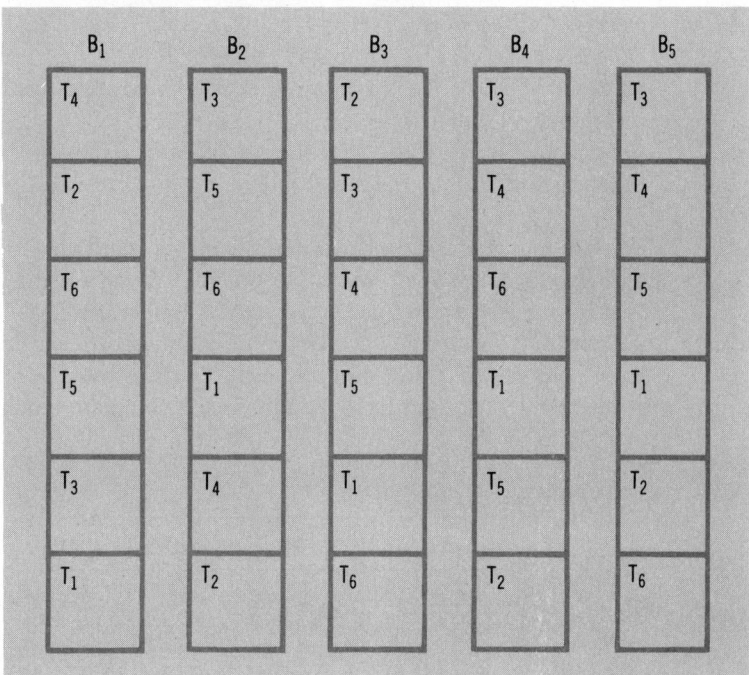

TABLE 8.4.2 Measurements of hiding quality taken on six types of paint, each applied to five different surfaces

| | **Type of paint** | | | | | | |
Surface	T_1	T_2	T_3	T_4	T_5	T_6	**Total**
B_1	20	12	20	10	14	8	84
B_2	22	10	20	12	6	7	77
B_3	24	14	18	18	10	10	94
B_4	16	4	8	6	18	9	61
B_5	26	22	16	20	10	8	102
Total	108	62	82	66	58	42	418
Means	21.6	12.4	16.4	13.2	11.6	8.4	13.93

$$H_0: \mu_1 = \mu_2 = \mu_3 = \mu_4 = \mu_5 = \mu_6$$
$$H_1: \text{at least one equality does not hold}$$

2. *Test statistic.* The test statistic is $F = \text{MSTr/MSE}$. If H_0 is true and the assumptions for the randomized complete block design are met, the test statistic is distributed as F with 5 and 20 degrees of freedom.
3. *Significance level.* Let $\alpha = 0.05$.
4. *Decision rule.* Reject H_0 if the computed F is ≥ 2.71.
5. *Calculations.* The calculations may be done on a computer or on a calculator, as shown in Section 8.7. The results are summarized in Table 8.4.3.
6. *Statistical decision.* The computed value of F, 5.41, is greater than the critical value of F, 2.71. We therefore reject the null hypothesis that the treatment means are all equal.
7. *Conclusion.* We conclude that the six types of paint do differ with respect to hiding quality. Since $5.41 > 4.76$, we have for this test $p < 0.005$.

Suppose that the assumptions underlying the randomized complete block design as presented in this section are not met. Then we may use an alternative, known as the *Friedman two-way analysis of variance*, as a hypothesis-testing procedure. We discuss this procedure in detail in Chapter 13.

An adaptation of Tukey's multiple-comparison procedure is available for use with the analysis of data from a randomized complete block design.

TABLE 8.4.3 ANOVA table, paint experiment

Source	SS	df	MS	F
Treatments	519.07	5	103.81	5.41
Blocks	166.87	4	41.72	
Error	383.93	20	19.20	
Total	1069.87	29		

COMPUTER **ANALYSIS**

Both STAT+ and MINITAB may be used to perform the calculations for two-way analysis of variance with data generated by a randomized complete block experimental design. When we use MINITAB, we set up a worksheet consisting of three columns. Column 1 contains the observations, column 2 contains a number that identifies the block to which the observation belongs, and column 3 contains a number that identifies the treatment to which the observation belongs. Table 8.4.4 shows how the MINITAB worksheet for Example 8.4.1 looks. Figure 8.4.2 shows the MINITAB command and the resulting printout.

When we use STAT+ to do the calculations for two-way analysis of variance, we select 2) INTERMEDIATE STATISTICS from the System Menu. From subsequent menus, we select 2) ANALYSIS OF VARIANCE and 2) TWO-WAY ANOVA and respond to the STAT+ prompts.

TABLE 8.4.4   MINITAB worksheet for the data in Table 8.4.2

ROW	C1	C2	C3
1	20	1	1
2	12	1	2
3	20	1	3
.	.	.	.
.	.	.	.
.	.	.	.
7	22	2	1
8	10	2	2
9	20	2	3
.	.	.	.
.	.	.	.
.	.	.	.
28	20	5	4
29	10	5	5
30	8	5	6

FIGURE 8.4.2   MINITAB command and printout for two-way analysis of variance, Example 8.4.1

MINITAB

```
MTB > TWOWAY C1, C2, C3
ANALYSIS OF VARIANCE C1
SOURCE      DF        SS         MS
C2           4      166.9       41.7
C3           5      519.1      103.8
ERROR       20      383.9       19.2
TOTAL       29     1069.9
```

EXERCISES

Carry out the seven-step hypothesis-testing procedure at the indicated level of significance and compute the p value for the test.

8.4.1   C The data below show the charges made by radio stations for a fixed-length spot announcement by size of radio station and trade area in which the station is located. After eliminating the effect of size, do these data suggest a difference in charges among the five trade areas? Let $\alpha = 0.05$.

			Trade area		
Size (watts)	I	II	III	IV	V
500	7	5	2	5	2
1,000	16	11	8	6	5
5,000	18	17	10	12	8
10,000	60	24	16	15	12

What action(s) would you suggest to advertisers as a result of your statistical analysis? Would you consider redoing this analysis after dividing each cost figure by the given radio station's wattage? How would your ANOVA table differ?

8.4.2   C Batches of homogenous raw material are analyzed in four laboratories for the presence of lead. Three methods are used. The following table shows the reported amounts of lead per unit volume of raw material. After eliminating laboratory effects, do these data suggest a difference in detection ability among the three methods? Let $\alpha = 0.05$.

		Method	
Laboratory	A	B	C
I	4	5	8
II	5	5	7
III	3	6	9
IV	4	4	9

What method of detection would you suggest? Does the cost of the method make a difference?

8.4.3   C The following table shows the density (coded) of a certain solution by temperature and by the technician who prepared the solution. After eliminating the effects of different technicians, do these data suggest a difference in mean density at different temperatures? Let $\alpha = 0.05$.

	Temperature (in degrees Celsius)			
Technician	10	20	30	40
A	7	7	8	10
B	8	8	7	10
C	8	8	7	9
D	9	8	8	9
E	8	7	8	9

8.4.4   C An engineer with Westcott Industries compares the tensile strength of a certain material produced by four machines at four different temperatures. The effects of the machines are eliminated by blocking. The results (coded) are as follows. Do these data provide sufficient evidence at the 0.01 level of significance to indicate that temperature has an effect on tensile strength?

		Temperature		
Machine	A	B	C	D
I	12	26	24	23
II	15	29	23	25
III	15	27	25	24
IV	18	38	33	31

8.5 THE LATIN SQUARE DESIGN

A researcher with a plastics firm wants to compare the tensile strength of plastic sheets made by four different processing methods. The researcher thinks that there are two main sources of extraneous variation: the technician who mixes the formula and the equipment used in the manufacturing process. What experimental design should be used? Since there are two identifiable sources of extraneous variation, the researcher needs a design that will isolate and remove both sources from the residual. The *Latin square design* is such a design.

Each treatment occurs once, and only once, in each row and each column.

In the Latin square design, we assign one source of extraneous variation to the columns of the square and the second source of extraneous variation to the rows of the square. We then assign the treatments, designated by capital letters, in such a way that each treatment occurs once and only once in each row and each column. The number of rows, the number of columns, and the number of treatments, therefore, are all equal. Table 8.5.1 shows a typical Latin square. We use the letter r to designate the number of rows, as well as the number of columns and the number of treatments, since all three occur an equal number of times. The Latin square design is so named because (1) the number of rows must equal the number of columns, thereby forming a square, and (2) Latin letters, A, B, C, and so on, are used to identify the treatments assigned to the cells of the square.

TABLE 8.5.1   A typical Latin square

			Columns		
Rows	1	2	3	4	5
1	B	A	E	C	D
2	D	C	A	B	E
3	C	B	D	E	A
4	A	E	C	D	B
5	E	D	B	A	C

ADVANTAGES OF THE LATIN SQUARE DESIGN

The Latin square design has the following advantages:

1. Eliminating two sources of extraneous variation often leads to a smaller error mean square than we would obtain using the randomized complete block design.
2. The analysis of variance is simple.
3. There are simple procedures for handling certain complications that may arise in the course of the experiment.

A minimum-size square of 5 × 5 is recommended.

Small Latin squares provide only a small number of degrees of freedom for the error mean square. So a minimum size of 5 × 5 is usually recommended. For a 4 × 4 square, for example, there are only 6 degrees of freedom associated with the error mean square. For a 5 × 5 square, there are 12 error degrees of freedom. Since there must be as many rows and columns as treatments, a Latin square larger than 12 × 12 is seldom practical.

We get randomization in the Latin square by randomly selecting a square of the desired dimension from all possible squares of that dimension. One method of doing this is to randomly assign a different treatment to each cell in each column, with the restriction that each treatment must appear once, and only once, in each row.

THE LATIN SQUARE MODEL

We write the model for the Latin square design as

$$(8.5.1) \qquad x_{ijk} = \mu + \alpha_i + \beta_j + \tau_k + e_{ijk}, \qquad 1 \leq i, j, k \leq r$$

where x_{ijk} = a typical value generated by the experiment

μ = an unknown constant

α_i = a row effect, reflecting the fact that the experimental unit appeared in the ith row

β_j = a column effect, reflecting the fact that the experimental unit appeared in the jth column

τ_k = a treatment effect, reflecting the fact that the experimental unit received the kth treatment

e_{ijk} = a residual component representing all sources of variation other than rows, columns, and treatments.

LATIN SQUARE ASSUMPTIONS

We make the following assumptions when we use the Latin square design. (a) Each observation constitutes an independent random sample of size 1 from the population defined by the cell in which the observation occurs. In general, there are r^2 such populations. (**b**) Each of the r^2 populations is normally distributed. (**c**) The variances of the r^2 populations are all equal. (**d**) The row, column, and treatment effects are additive. That is, there is no interaction among rows and columns; rows and treatments; columns and treatments; or rows, columns, and treatments.

LATIN SQUARE HYPOTHESES

We want to know whether the results of the experiment provide evidence of a true difference in treatment effects. At some significance level α, therefore, we test the null hypothesis that all treatment means are equal against the alternative that there is a difference between at least one pair of means. We state the hypotheses formally as follows.

$$H_0: \mu_1 = \mu_2 = \mu_3 = \cdots = \mu_r,$$
$$H_1: \text{not all treatment means are equal}$$

LATIN SQUARE CALCULATIONS

The calculations for the Latin square design can be done best with the aid of a computer. If the calculations are not done on a computer, we may use the short-cut formulas given in Section 8.7.

LATIN SQUARE ANOVA TABLE

Table 8.5.2 is the ANOVA table for the Latin square design.

LATIN SQUARE DECISION

When the given assumptions hold, we can test the hypothesis of equal treatment means by comparing the computed $F = \text{MSTr/MSE}$ with the critical value of F for α with $r - 1$ numerator degrees of freedom and $r^2 - 3r + 2$ denominator

TABLE 8.5.2 Analysis-of-variance table for the Latin square design

Source	SS	df	MS	F
Rows	SSR	$(r - 1)$	$\text{MSR} = \text{SSR}/(r - 1)$	
Columns	SSC	$(r - 1)$	$\text{MSC} = \text{SSC}/(r - 1)$	
Treatments	SSTr	$(r - 1)$	$\text{MSTr} = \text{SSTr}/(r - 1)$	MSTr/MSE
Error	SSE	$r^2 - 3r + 2$	$\text{MSE} = \text{SSE}/(r^2 - 3r + 2)$	
Total	SST	$r^2 - 1$		

TABLE 8.5.3 Tensile strength (coded) of 16 plastic specimens, by technician and equipment

Rows (technician)	Columns (equipment) 1	2	3	4	Row totals	Row means
1	A = 13	C = 13	D = 7	B = 15	48	12.00
2	B = 12	A = 13	C = 11	D = 9	45	11.25
3	C = 11	D = 9	B = 13	A = 14	47	11.75
4	D = 7	B = 13	A = 12	C = 11	43	10.75
Column totals	43	48	43	49	183	
Column means	10.75	12.00	10.75	12.25		11.44

Treatment totals: A = 52, B = 53, C = 46, D = 32.
Treatment means: A = 13.00, B = 13.25, C = 11.50, D = 8.00.

degrees of freedom. If the computed F equals or exceeds the critical value of F, we reject the null hypothesis.

The following example illustrates the analysis of variance for the Latin square design.

EXAMPLE 8.5.1   Recall the case at the beginning of this section, in which a researcher wishes to compare the tensile strength of plastic after eliminating the effects of technician and equipment. Table 8.5.3 shows the results of the experiment. We presume that the Latin square model applies and that the assumptions of this model are met.

SOLUTION   To determine whether we should conclude that the population mean tensile strength is the same for all methods, we proceed as follows.

1. *Hypotheses.* We state the following hypotheses regarding treatments:

$$H_0: \mu_A = \mu_B = \mu_C = \mu_D, \qquad H_1: \text{at least one equality does not hold}$$

2. *Test statistic.* The test statistic is $F = \text{MSTr/MSE}$. If H_0 is true and the assumptions are met, this statistic follows the F distribution with 3 and 6 degrees of freedom.
3. *Significance level.* Let $\alpha = 0.05$.
4. *Decision rule.* Reject H_0 if the computed F is ≥ 4.76.
5. *Calculations.* We may use a computer to perform the necessary calculations, or we may use the short-cut formulas given in Section 8.7. The results are given in Table 8.5.4.
6. *Statistical decision.* Since the computed F of 58.5 is larger than the critical value of 4.76, we reject the null hypothesis.
7. *Conclusion.* The evidence from this sample indicates that there is a difference in the treatment means. That is, we conclude that the processing methods do have a differential effect. For this test, $p < 0.005$, since $58.5 > 12.92$.

TABLE 8.5.4 Analysis-of-variance table for Example 8.5.1

Source	SS	df	MS	F
Rows (technicians)	3.69	3	1.23	
Columns (equipment)	7.69	3	2.56	
Treatments	70.19	3	23.40	58.5
Error	2.37	6	0.40	
Total	83.94	15		

EXERCISES

Carry out the seven-step hypothesis-testing procedure at the indicated level of significance and compute the p value for the test.

8.5.1 C The quality of a certain plastic product depends to some extent on the number of breaks per 100 pounds of material that occur during one of the phases of production. The manufacturer tests four methods of treatment designed to reduce breakage: A, B, C, and D. The treatments are applied to the raw material before the critical phase of production. To eliminate environmental effects, such as temperature and humidity, the 24-hour work-day is divided into four 6-hour periods. Each treatment is used once in each period. Four makes of machine are normally used in the process. Thus, each treatment is used once on each machine. The following table shows the number of breaks per 100 pounds of material for each treatment, by time period and machine. Do these data suggest a differential treatment effect at the 0.05 level of significance? At the 0.01 level?

		Time period		
Machine	I	II	III	IV
1	A(2)	B(6)	C(16)	D(9)
2	B(8)	D(9)	A(3)	C(16)
3	C(16)	A(3)	D(10)	B(7)
4	D(6)	C(12)	B(7)	A(4)

8.5.2 C An engineer who wants to evaluate four brands of lubricating oil uses a Latin square design, as shown in the following table. The columns represent the four seasons of the year, and the rows represent four makes of car. The variable of interest is the consumption of fuel, in gallons per 100 miles traveled. Test at the 0.05 level of significance the null hypothesis of no difference between treatment means.

		Seasons		
Vehicle Make	F	W	Sp	Su
1	A(12)	B(10)	C(10)	D(12)
2	B(10)	A(12)	D(12)	C(10)
3	C(10)	D(11)	B(10)	A(12)
4	D(11)	C(10)	A(13)	B(10)

8.5.3   C To study the effect of packaging on the sales of Asoka Cereals, a researcher tries three different packaging methods (treatments) at three different times of the week (columns) in three different supermarket chains (rows). The variable of interest is daily sales. The following table shows the results of the study. Do these data show a significant difference in shoppers' response to the different packaging methods? Let $\alpha = 0.05$.

	Time of week		
Store	First	Middle	End
I	C(30)	A(45)	B(75)
II	B(50)	C(40)	A(50)
III	A(35)	B(65)	C(50)

8.6 THE FACTORIAL EXPERIMENT

The manufacturer of a new product wishes to study the effect on sales of the product of different packaging and the effect of availability in different types of stores. Five different kinds of packages are to be tested. The four types of stores are grocery stores, drugstores, convenience stores, and variety stores. The price and quantity per package are the same, and other variables are felt to be satisfactorily controlled. The experimental format used is that known as the *factorial experiment*. This type of experiment allows two or more *factors* to be studied simultaneously.

> A *factor* is a kind of treatment.

Stores and packages are the two factors of interest in the present example. A factor is represented by two or more *levels* of the factor.

> A *level* is a treatment category within a factor.

In the present example, there are four levels of the store factor and five levels of the package factor. Each type of store is a level of the store factor, and each package type is a level of the package factor. Let us call the two factors Factor A and Factor B, respectively. Then Factor A occurs at four levels, a_1, a_2, a_3, and a_4. Factor B occurs at five levels, b_1, b_2, b_3, b_4, and b_5. In a factorial experiment, not only can we investigate the effects of the individual factors, but when we conduct the experiment properly, we can also study the *interaction* between the two factors.

INTERACTION

We say that

There is *interaction* between two factors (say A and B) if a change in one of the factors (say B) produces a change in response at one level (say level 1) of the other factor (say A) different from that produced at other levels (say level 2) of this second factor (A), where a level is one of the treatments within a factor.

The following example illustrates the concept of interaction.

EXAMPLE 8.6.1   Suppose that we are studying how well factory employees learn safety rules. Let us say that we know the true relationship between three methods of instruction and the educational level of the employees. Suppose further that workers' education can be classed at two levels—"less than high school" and "high school or higher." If we know the true relationship between the two factors, we also know, for the three methods of instruction, the mean effect on learning of subjects in the two education groups. We measure that effect in terms of scores made on a test taken immediately after instruction. Suppose that these means are as shown in Table 8.6.1. The following features of the data in Table 8.6.1 are important in understanding interaction.

1. For both levels of Factor A, the difference between the means for any two levels of Factor B is the same. That is, for both levels of Factor A, the difference between means for levels 1 and 2 of Factor B is 15, the difference for levels 2 and 3 is 30, and the difference for levels 1 and 3 is 45.

2. For all levels of Factor B, the difference between means for the two levels of Factor A is the same. In the present case, the difference is 15 at all three levels of Factor B.

3. We see a third characteristic when we plot the data, as in Figure 8.6.1. The curves corresponding to the different levels of a factor are all parallel.

When population data have these three characteristics, we say that there is no interaction present.

Interaction between two factors affects the characteristics of data in a variety of ways, depending on the nature of the interaction. Table 8.6.2 shows the data of Table 8.6.1 altered to show the effect of one type of interaction.

The following characteristics of the data in Table 8.6.2 are important in understanding interaction:

TABLE 8.6.1   Scores of subjects in two education groups at three methods of instruction levels

Factor A: Education	Factor B: Method of instruction		
	$j = 1$	$j = 2$	$j = 3$
Less than high school ($i = 1$)	$\mu_{11} = 15$	$\mu_{12} = 30$	$\mu_{13} = 60$
High school or higher ($i = 2$)	$\mu_{21} = 30$	$\mu_{22} = 45$	$\mu_{23} = 75$

FIGURE 8.6.1   Effects of method of instruction and education, no interaction present

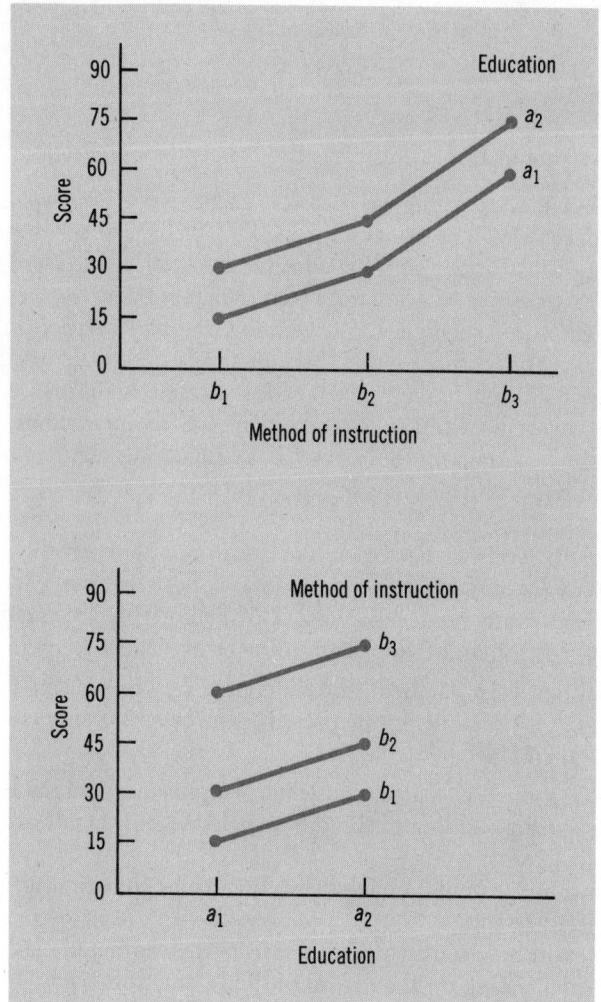

TABLE 8.6.2   The data of Table 8.6.1 altered to show the effect of one type of interaction

	Factor B: Method of instruction		
Factor A: Education	$j = 1$	$j = 2$	$j = 3$
Less than high school ($i = 1$)	$\mu_{11} = 15$	$\mu_{12} = 30$	$\mu_{13} = 60$
High school or higher ($i = 2$)	$\mu_{21} = 45$	$\mu_{22} = 30$	$\mu_{23} = 15$

FIGURE 8.6.2   Effects of education and method of instruction, interaction present

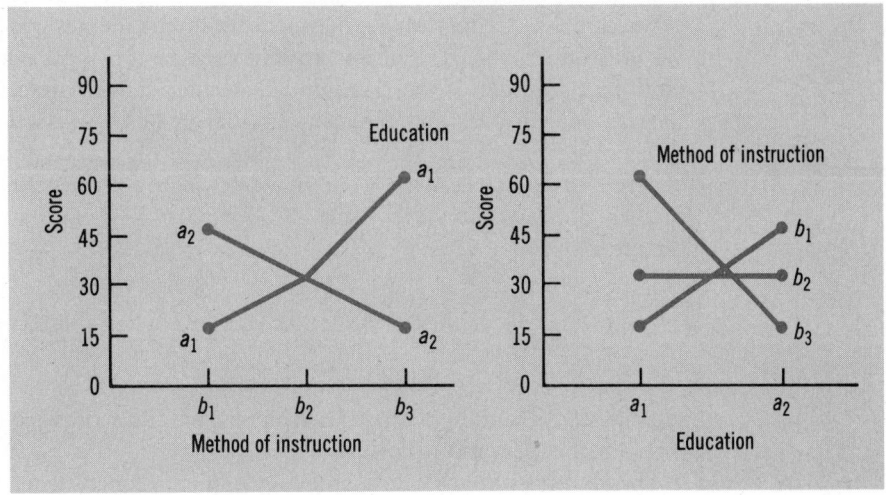

1. The difference between means for any two levels of Factor B is not the same for both levels of Factor A. In Table 8.6.2, for example, the difference between levels 1 and 2 of Factor B is -15 for the less-than-high-school group and $+15$ for the high-school-or-higher group.

2. The difference between means for both levels of Factor A is not the same at all levels of Factor B. The differences between Factor A means are -30, 0, and $+45$ for levels 1, 2, and 3, respectively, of factor B.

3. Figure 8.6.2 shows that the factor-level curves are not parallel.

When population data have these characteristics, we say that there is inter-action between the two factors. We emphasize that the kind of interaction illus-trated by this example is only one of many types of interaction that may occur between two factors.

ADVANTAGES OF THE FACTORIAL EXPERIMENT

One advantage of the factorial experiment is that using all the observations to study the effects of each of the factors under investigation saves time and effort. When we are investigating two factors, we can use a single factorial experiment rather than the two different experiments that we would otherwise need—one to study each of the two factors. If we conduct two separate experiments, we need more experimental units to achieve the level of accuracy of a factorial experiment. Thus, one two-factor experiment is more efficient than two one-factor experiments. Another advantage of the factorial experiment is that, since the various factors are combined in one experiment, the results have a wider range of application.

We can adapt a factorial experiment to any of the designs we have described. We illustrate the analysis of a factorial experiment using a two-factor completely randomized design. We can present the results of such an experiment in a table, such as Table 8.6.3. This table shows a levels of Factor A, b levels of Factor B, and n observations for each combination of levels. Each of the ab combinations of levels of Factor A with levels of Factor B is a treatment. In addition to the totals and means shown in Table 8.6.3, we may designate the total and mean of the ijth cell by

$$T_{ij.} = \sum_{k=1}^{n} x_{ijk} \qquad \text{and} \qquad \bar{x}_{ij} = T_{ij.}/n$$

respectively. The subscript i runs from 1 to a and j runs from 1 to b. The total number of observations is nab.

The analysis of variance for the factorial experiment is as follows.

TABLE 8.6.3 Sample data from a two-factor completely randomized experiment

Factor A	Factor B 1	2	$\cdots$	b	Total	Means
1	x_{111} $\vdots$ x_{11n}	x_{121} $\vdots$ x_{12n}	$\cdots$ $\vdots$ $\cdots$	x_{1b1} $\vdots$ x_{1bn}	$T_{1..}$	$\bar{x}_{1..}$
2	x_{211} $\vdots$ x_{21n}	x_{221} $\vdots$ x_{22n}	$\cdots$ $\vdots$ $\cdots$	x_{2b1} $\vdots$ x_{2bn}	$T_{2..}$	$\bar{x}_{2..}$
$\vdots$	$\vdots$	$\vdots$	$\vdots$	$\vdots$	$\vdots$	$\vdots$
a	x_{a11} $\vdots$ x_{a1n}	x_{a21} $\vdots$ x_{a2n}	$\cdots$ $\vdots$ $\cdots$	x_{ab1} $\vdots$ x_{abn}	$T_{a..}$	$\bar{x}_{a..}$
Total	$T_{.1.}$	$T_{.2.}$	$\cdots$	$T_{.b.}$	$T_{...}$	
Means	$\bar{x}_{.1.}$	$\bar{x}_{.2.}$	$\cdots$	$\bar{x}_{.b.}$		$\bar{x}_{...}$

THE FACTORIAL EXPERIMENT MODEL

For the sake of brevity, we consider only one type of factorial experiment—the fixed-effects, two-factor, completely randomized design. Under the general heading of factorial experiment, we could also consider the random model, the mixed model, and the experiment in which more than two factors are involved. For discussion of these topics, see the textbooks on experimental design listed at the end of this chapter.

We may write the model for the present case as

(8.6.1)
$$x_{ijk} = \mu + \alpha_i + \beta_j + (\alpha\beta)_{ij} + e_{ijk}$$

where x_{ijk} is a typical observation, μ is a constant, α represents an effect due to Factor A, β represents an effect due to Factor B, $(\alpha\beta)$ represents an effect due to the interaction of factors A and B, and e_{ijk} represents the experimental error.

FACTORIAL EXPERIMENT ASSUMPTIONS

The assumptions for the factorial experiment are threefold. (**a**) The observations in each of the *ab* cells constitute an independent random sample of size *n* drawn from the population defined by the particular combination of the levels of the two factors. (**b**) Each of the *ab* populations is normally distributed. (**c**) The populations all have the same variance.

FACTORIAL EXPERIMENT HYPOTHESES

We can compute three mean squares, other than the residual mean square, from data generated by a factorial experiment of the type under discussion. These are the mean squares associated with Factor A, Factor B, and the interaction AB. Consequently, we can compute three variance ratios, using each mean square in turn in the numerator and the residual mean square in each denominator. There are, then, three separate hypotheses that we may test. They are

Three hypotheses may be tested.

(a) H_0: $\alpha_i = 0$, H_1: not all $\alpha_i = 0$, $i = 1, 2, \ldots, a$

The null hypothesis in this case states that the various levels of Factor A all have the same effect.

(b) H_0: $\beta_j = 0$, H_1: not all $\beta_j = 0$, $j = 1, 2, \ldots, b$

This null hypothesis states that the various levels of Factor B all have the same effect.

(c) H_0: $(\alpha\beta)_{ij} = 0,$ H_1: not all $(\alpha\beta)_{ij} = 0,$
$i = 1, 2, \ldots, a;$ $j = 1, 2, \ldots, b$

This null hypothesis states that there is no interaction between Factor A and Factor B.

Before collecting the data, we may decide to test only one of the three hypotheses. In this case, we select the one to be tested, along with the desired significance level α. Usually, the hypothesis of no interaction is the one that is tested.

If, on the other hand, we wish to test all three hypotheses, a problem arises because the three tests are not independent in the probability sense. Suppose that α is the significance level associated with the test as a whole, and α', α'', and α''' are the significance levels associated with hypotheses a, b, and c, respectively. Then

$$\alpha < 1 - (1 - \alpha')(1 - \alpha'')(1 - \alpha''')$$

If $\alpha' = \alpha'' = \alpha''' = 0.05$, then $\alpha < 1 - (0.95)^3$, or $\alpha < 0.143$. This result indicates that the probability of rejecting one or more of the three hypotheses is something less than 0.143 when a significance level of 0.05 has been chosen for each hypothesis and all are true. To demonstrate the hypothesis-testing procedure for each case, we perform all three tests. However, you should keep in mind the problem involved in interpreting the results.

FACTORIAL EXPERIMENT CALCULATIONS

If the calculations for the factorial experiment are not done on a computer, we may use the short-cut formulas given in Section 8.7. The initial quantities needed are the total sum of squares SST, the treatment sum of squares SSTr, the Factor A sum of squares SSA, the Factor B sum of squares SSB, the interaction sum of squares SSAB, and the error sum of squares SSE. When we divide SSA, SSB, SSAB, and SSE each by the appropriate degrees of freedom, we obtain the mean squares necessary for computing the F test statistic.

FACTORIAL EXPERIMENT ANOVA TABLE

In general, we can display the results of the calculations for a two-factor completely randomized fixed-effects model experiment as shown in Table 8.6.4. The degrees-of-freedom column in Table 8.6.4 shows that, to carry out the analysis of variance for this type of factorial experiment, there must be more than one observation per cell. If there is only one, the degrees of freedom are all expended on the two factors and interaction. As a result, there are no degrees of freedom with which to compute the error mean square, a necessary factor in the computation of the variance ratio.

TABLE 8.6.4   Analysis-of-variance table for a two-factor completely randomized experiment (fixed-effects model)

Source	SS	df	MS	F
A	SSA	$a - 1$	$MSA = SSA/(a - 1)$	MSA/MSE
B	SSB	$b - 1$	$MSB = SSB/(b - 1)$	MSB/MSE
AB	SSAB	$(a - 1)(b - 1)$	$MSAB = SSAB/(a - 1)(b - 1)$	MSAB/MSE
Treatments	SSTr	$ab - 1$		
Error	SSE	$ab(n - 1)$	$MSE = SSE/(ab)(n - 1)$	
Total	SST	$abn - 1$		

FACTORIAL EXPERIMENT DECISION

If the assumptions stated earlier hold and if each null hypothesis is true, each of the variance ratios in table 8.6.4 is distributed as F with the indicated degrees of freedom. Any variance ratio equal to or greater than the critical value of F causes rejection of the associated null hypothesis. When we reject H_0: $\alpha_1 = \alpha_2 = \cdots = \alpha_a$, we conclude that there are differences in effects among the levels of A. If we reject H_0: $\beta_1 = \beta_2 = \cdots = \beta_b$, we conclude that there are differences in effects among the levels of B. When we reject H_0: $(\alpha\beta)_{ij} = 0$, we conclude that Factors A and B interact.

When we reject the hypothesis of no interaction, we are usually interested in the effects of interaction rather than the levels of Factors A and B. In other words, we are interested in learning what combinations of levels are significantly different. We do not deal with this problem in this text.

Remember that if we make all three tests simultaneously the probability of rejecting at least one null hypothesis when all are true is greater than the probability associated with each individual test.

The following example illustrates the analysis of variance for the factorial experiment.

EXAMPLE 8.6.2   Table 8.6.5 shows the results of the experiment described at the beginning of this section. In this experiment, we wish to study the effects on sales of type of store and type of package.

SOLUTION   If we can assume that the model for the factorial experiment applies and that the assumptions underlying the model are met, we can carry out the analysis of variance of the data shown in the table as follows.

1. *Hypotheses.* To demonstrate the hypothesis-testing procedure for each of the possible hypotheses, we perform all three tests. Recall, however, the problem involved in interpreting the results. For this example, we can test the following hypotheses.

   (a) H_0: $\alpha_I = \alpha_{II} = \alpha_{III} = \alpha_{IV} = 0$ (the row [store] effects are all 0)
   H_1: not all $\alpha_i = 0$ (they are not all 0)

TABLE 8.6.5 Sample data, Example 8.6.2

Factor A (store type) levels	Factor B (package type)					Total	Mean
	Levels						
	1	2	3	4	5		
I	5	6	4	9	3	93	6.20
	6	8	3	10	7		
	4	7	5	12	4		
II	7	5	3	4	12	103	6.87
	8	5	6	4	14		
	8	6	4	6	11		
III	3	6	8	9	10	97	6.47
	2	6	9	8	7		
	4	5	6	7	7		
IV	8	12	4	10	7	128	8.53
	9	11	7	12	8		
	9	10	3	12	6		
Total	73	87	62	103	96	421	
Mean	6.08	7.25	5.17	8.58	8.00		7.02

Cell	a_1b_1	a_1b_2	a_1b_3	a_1b_4	a_1b_5
Total	15	21	12	31	14
Mean	5.00	7.00	4.00	10.33	4.67

Cell	a_2b_1	a_2b_2	a_2b_3	a_2b_4	a_2b_5
Total	23	16	13	14	37
Mean	7.67	5.33	4.33	4.67	12.33

Cell	a_3b_1	a_3b_2	a_3b_3	a_3b_4	a_3b_5
Total	9	17	23	24	24
Mean	3.00	5.67	7.67	8.00	8.00

Cell	a_4b_1	a_4b_2	a_4b_3	a_4b_4	a_4b_5
Total	26	33	14	34	21
Mean	8.67	11.00	4.67	11.33	7.00

(b) H_0: $\beta_1 = \beta_2 = \beta_3 = \beta_4 = \beta_5 = 0$ (the column [package] effects are all 0)

H_1: not all $\beta_j = 0$ (they are not all 0)

(c) H_0: $(\alpha\beta)_{ij} = 0$ (the interaction effects are all 0)

H_1: not all $(\alpha\beta)_{ij} = 0$ (they are not all 0)

2. *Test statistic.* The test statistic for each hypothesis test is F.
3. *Significance level.* Let $\alpha = 0.05$ for each test.
4. *Decision rule.* The decision rules for hypothesis tests *a*, *b*, and *c* are as follows:

TABLE 8.6.6   ANOVA table, Example 8.6.2

Source	SS	df	MS	F
A	49.38	3	16.46	10.29
B	93.23	4	23.31	14.57
AB	268.37	12	22.36	13.98
Treatments	410.98	19		
Error	64.00	40	1.60	
Total	474.98	59		

(a) Reject H_0 if the computed F is ≥ 2.84, the critical value of F for $\alpha = 0.05$ and 3 and 40 degrees of freedom.

(b) Reject H_0 if the computed F is ≥ 2.61, the critical value of F for $\alpha = 0.05$ and 4 and 40 degrees of freedom.

(c) Reject H_0 if the computed F is ≥ 2.00, the critical value of F for $\alpha = 0.05$ and 12 and 40 degrees of freedom.

5. *Calculations.* The calculations are shown in Section 8.7. Table 8.6.6 shows the analysis-of-variance table for this example.

6. *Statistical decision.* The statistical decisions for the three sets of hypotheses are as follows:

(a) Reject H_0, since $10.29 > 2.84$.

(b) Reject H_0, since $14.57 > 2.61$.

(c) Reject H_0, since $13.98 > 2.00$.

7. *Conclusion.* The conclusions for the three tests are as follows:

(a) Different types of stores have different mean sales values.

(b) The different types of packages result in different mean sales values.

(c) There is interaction between the type of package used and the type of store in which the product is sold. For each test we have $p < 0.005$.

We have discussed only the case in which the number of observations in each cell is the same. When the number of observations in each cell is *not* the same, the analysis is more complicated.

COMPUTER **ANALYSIS**

We may use MINITAB to perform the calculations for a factorial experiment. We first prepare a worksheet by storing information in columns 1, 2, and 3. Column 1 contains the observations, column 2 contains a number that identifies the level of factor A to which the measurement belongs, and column 3 contains a number that identifies the level of factor B to which the observation belongs. Table 8.6.7 shows how the worksheet for Example 8.6.2 would look.

TABLE 8.6.7 MINITAB worksheet for the data in Table 8.6.5

ROW	C1	C2	C3
1	5	1	1
2	6	1	2
3	4	1	3
4	9	1	4
5	3	1	5
.	.	.	.
.	.	.	.
.	.	.	.
16	7	2	1
17	5	2	2
18	3	2	3
19	4	2	4
20	12	2	5
.	.	.	.
.	.	.	.
.	.	.	.
56	9	4	1
57	10	4	2
58	3	4	3
59	12	4	4
60	6	4	5

Figure 8.6.3 shows the necessary command for performing the calculations and the resulting printout.

FIGURE 8.6.3 MINITAB command for performing calculations for a factorial experiment and the resulting printout for Example 8.6.2

MINITAB
```
MTB > TWOWAY C1, C2, C3
ANALYSIS OF VARIANCE C1
SOURCE        DF      SS       MS
C2             3     49.38    16.46
C3             4     93.23    23.31
INTERACTION   12    268.37    22.36
ERROR         40     64.00     1.60
TOTAL         59    474.98
```

EXERCISES

Carry out the seven-step hypothesis-testing procedure at the indicated level of significance and compute the p value for the test.

8.6.1   C The temperature and pressure used in molding a certain plastic affect its tensile strength. The following table shows the tensile strength (coded) in pounds per square inch of specimens of plastic molded at three different temperatures and under three different pressures. Complete the analysis of variance for these data, using a 0.05 significance level.

		Temperature	
Pressure	I	II	III
	8	9	10
	9	9	10
A	9	10	11
	9	9	11
	9	10	11
	10	10	8
	11	10	8
B	12	9	8
	12	8	9
	12	9	9
	8	12	9
	9	12	8
C	9	11	9
	8	11	9
	8	11	8

8.6.2   C The following table shows the weights of salmon caught by species and area. Complete the analysis of variance of these data, using a 0.05 significance level.

			Species		
Area	King	Red	Coho	Pink	Chum
	12	5	7	3	8
	13	5	8	4	10
1	13	6	6	4	9
	12	5	7	5	9
	13	6	7	4	9
	20	5	6	3	8
	24	6	7	4	9
2	22	6	7	4	8
	23	6	7	4	8
	22	6	7	3	8
	12	5	7	3	7
	11	5	7	4	8
3	12	5	8	4	7
	12	6	7	4	7
	12	5	7	4	8

How might you carry out random sampling in this experimental design? Are you surprised that there is an interaction between the two factors, area and species? What is your interpretation of this phenomenon? What fact(s) could make fishing for king salmon in Area 2 undesirable? What approximate overall level of significance does your statistical test have when you test both main effects and the effect of interaction between species and area? How many treatments would be required if this experiment were performed as a one-way ANOVA? Could a one-way ANOVA detect the effects of interaction?

8.6.3   Ⓒ Yasuda Camera Company introduces a new kind of camera into four geographic regions. Within each region, three subareas with different levels of competitive activity are identified. The following table shows the weekly sales (coded) of the product in each subarea for a period of four weeks. Complete the analysis of variance of these data, using a 0.05 level of significance.

Level of competitive activity	Geographic region			
	1	2	3	4
I	4	8	10	3
	3	7	14	2
	2	6	13	1
	3	6	15	2
II	8	3	3	15
	8	2	3	16
	6	1	2	12
	7	4	4	14
III	12	6	3	8
	10	7	2	7
	9	8	3	7
	11	7	4	6

8.7 ANOVA CALCULATIONS

In this section, we present the computational formulas for calculating the various sums of squares needed for the experimental designs discussed in this chapter.

THE COMPLETELY RANDOMIZED DESIGN (ONE-WAY ANOVA)

To facilitate the calculations, we may display experimental or survey data that are to be analyzed by one-way analysis of variance, as in Table 8.7.1. We define the symbols used in Table 8.7.1 as follows:

$$x_{ij} = \text{The } i\text{th observation that receives the } j\text{th treatment,}$$
$$i = 1, 2, \ldots, n_j, j = 1, 2, \ldots, k$$

n_j = the number of observations in the jth sample

TABLE 8.7.1   Sample data for analysis by one-way analysis of variance

	Population sampled				
	1	2	3	$\cdots$	k
	x_{11}	x_{12}	x_{13}	$\cdots$	x_{1k}
	x_{21}	x_{22}	x_{23}	$\cdots$	x_{2k}
	x_{31}	x_{32}	x_{33}	$\cdots$	x_{3k}
	.	.	.	.	.
	.	.	.	.	.
	.	.	.	.	.
	$x_{n_1 1}$	$x_{n_2 2}$	$x_{n_3 3}$		$x_{n_k k}$
Total	$T_{.1}$	$T_{.2}$	$T_{.3}$	$\cdots$	$T_{.k}$ $T_{..}$
Mean	$\bar{x}_{.1}$	$\bar{x}_{.2}$	$\bar{x}_{.3}$	$\cdots$	$\bar{x}_{.k}$ $\bar{x}_{..}$

$$T_{.j} = \sum_{i=1}^{n_j} x_{ij} = \text{total of the } j\text{th column}$$

$$\bar{x}_{.j} = \frac{T_{.j}}{n_j} = \text{mean of the } j\text{th column}$$

$$T_{..} = \sum_{j=1}^{k} T_{.j} = \sum_{j=1}^{k} \sum_{i=1}^{n_j} x_{ij} = \text{total of all observations}$$

$$\bar{x}_{..} = \frac{T_{..}}{n}$$

We also let $\quad n = \sum_{j=1}^{k} n_j$

The Total Sum of Squares We define analysis of variance as an arithmetic process by which we partition the *total variation* in a set of data into components attributable to different sources. Variation used in this context refers to a *sum of squared deviations of values from their mean*, or *sum of squares*. The *total sum of squares* that we may compute from a set of data is the sum of the squares of the deviations of each observation from the mean of all the observations taken together. We define this total sum of squares as

(8.7.1)
$$\text{SST} = \sum_{j=1}^{k} \sum_{i=1}^{n_j} (x_{ij} - \bar{x}_{..})^2$$

where $\Sigma_{i=1}^{n_j}$ tells us to add the squared deviations for each group and $\Sigma_{j=1}^{k}$ instructs us to sum the k group totals obtained by applying $\Sigma_{i=1}^{n_j}$.

We may rewrite Equation 8.7.1 in a form that is more convenient for computing purposes:

(8.7.2)
$$\text{SST} = \sum_{j=1}^{k} \sum_{i=1}^{n_j} x_{ij}^2 - \frac{\left(\Sigma_{j=1}^{k} \Sigma_{i=1}^{n_j} x_{ij}\right)^2}{n}$$

We can show by appropriate algebraic manipulation that

(8.7.3)
$$\text{SST} = \sum_{j=1}^{k} n_j(\bar{x}_{.j} - \bar{x}_{..})^2 + \sum_{j=1}^{k} \sum_{i=1}^{n_j} (x_{ij} - \bar{x}_{.j})^2$$

The Treatment Sum of Squares The first term on the right of Equation 8.7.3 tells us to find the difference between each treatment mean and the grand mean, square each of these differences, multiply by the sample size, and find the sum of these products. This quantity reflects the amount of variation among the sample means. It is referred to as the *treatment sum of squares*, or SSTr. The computing formula for this quantity is

(8.7.4)
$$\text{SSTr} = \sum_{j=1}^{k} n_j(\bar{x}_{.j} - \bar{x}_{..})^2$$

$$= \left(\frac{T_{.1}^2}{n_1} + \frac{T_{.2}^2}{n_2} + \cdots + \frac{T_{.k}^2}{n_k} \right) - \frac{\left(\sum_{j=1}^{k} \sum_{i=1}^{n_j} x_{ij} \right)^2}{n}$$

which, when all samples are equal in size, reduces to

(8.7.5)
$$\text{SSTr} = \frac{\sum_{j=1}^{k} T_{.j}^2}{n_j} - \frac{\left(\sum_{j=1}^{k} \sum_{i=1}^{n_j} x_{ij} \right)^2}{n}$$

The Error Sum of Squares The second term on the right of Equation 8.7.3 is the pooled sum of squares computed from the values in each sample. This procedure extends to several samples the pooling procedure for two samples that we described in Chapter 6. This component of variation is called the *error sum of squares*, or SSE. It is sometimes called the *within-treatments sum of squares* or the *residual sum of squares*. Although we can compute the error sum of squares directly, it is more convenient to subtract the treatment sum of squares from the total sum of squares. That is,

(8.7.6)
$$\text{SSE} = \text{SST} - \text{SSTr}$$

Note that Equation 8.7.2 and Equation 8.7.4 both contain the factor

$$C = \frac{\left(\sum_{j=1}^{k} \sum_{i=1}^{n_j} x_{ij} \right)^2}{n} = \frac{T_{..}^2}{n}$$

This term, called the *correction term* C, may be computed only once and used as needed.

SUMS OF SQUARES CALCULATIONS FOR EXAMPLE 8.2.1

$$C = \frac{(237)^2}{30} = 1872.3$$

By Equation 8.7.2,

$$SST = 5^2 + 6^2 + \cdots + 8^2 - 1872.3 = 72.7$$

and by Equation 8.7.4,

$$SSTr = \frac{61^2}{10} + \frac{68^2}{8} + \frac{108^2}{12} - 1872.3 = 49.8$$

By subtraction, we find that

$$SSE = 72.7 - 49.8 = 22.9$$

SUMS OF SQUARES CALCULATIONS FOR EXAMPLE 8.2.2

$$C = \frac{(899.6)^2}{22} = 36{,}785.462$$

$$SST = (38.7)^2 + (42.4)^2 + \cdots + (39.6)^2 - 36{,}785.462$$
$$= 37{,}247.46 - 36{,}785.462 = 461.998$$

$$SSTr = \frac{(517.2)^2}{12} + \frac{(382.4)^2}{10} - 36{,}785.462 = 128.834$$

$$SSE = 461.998 - 128.834 = 333.164$$

THE RANDOMIZED COMPLETE BLOCK DESIGN (TWO-WAY ANOVA)

We can display the data generated by a randomized complete block design as shown in Table 8.7.2.

TABLE 8.7.2   Sample data for analysis by two-way analysis of variance

Blocks	Treatments					Total	Mean
	1	2	3	$\cdots$	k		
1	x_{11}	x_{12}	x_{13}	$\cdots$	x_{1k}	$T_{1.}$	$\bar{x}_{1.}$
2	x_{21}	x_{22}	x_{23}	$\cdots$	x_{2k}	$T_{2.}$	$\bar{x}_{2.}$
3	x_{31}	x_{32}	x_{33}	$\cdots$	x_{3k}	$T_{3.}$	$\bar{x}_{3.}$
$\vdots$	$\vdots$	$\vdots$	$\vdots$	$\vdots$	$\vdots$	$\vdots$	$\vdots$
n	x_{n1}	x_{n2}	x_{n3}	$\cdots$	x_{nk}	$T_{n.}$	$\bar{x}_{n.}$
Total	$T_{.1}$	$T_{.2}$	$T_{.3}$	$\cdots$	$T_{.k}$	$T_{..}$	
Mean	$\bar{x}_{.1}$	$\bar{x}_{.2}$	$\bar{x}_{.3}$	$\cdots$	$\bar{x}_{.k}$		$\bar{x}_{..}$

Table 8.7.2 introduces the following new notation:

$$k = \text{the number of treatments,} \qquad n = \text{the number of blocks}$$

$$\text{Total of the } i\text{th block} = T_{i.} = \sum_{j=1}^{k} x_{ij}$$

$$\text{Mean of the } i\text{th block} = \bar{x}_{i.} = \frac{\sum_{j=1}^{k} x_{ij}}{k}$$

$$\text{Grand total} = T_{..} = \sum_{j=1}^{k} T_{.j} = \sum_{i=1}^{n} T_{i.}$$

Note: We can find the grand total by adding either row totals or column totals.

We partition the total sum of squares (SST) for the randomized complete block design into three components, one each attributable to treatments (SSTr), blocks (SSB), and error (SSE). We may express the partitioned sum of squares by the following equation:

(8.7.7)
$$\sum_{j=1}^{k} \sum_{i=1}^{n} (x_{ij} - \bar{x}_{..})^2 = \sum_{j=1}^{k} \sum_{i=1}^{n} (\bar{x}_{.j} - \bar{x}_{..})^2 + \sum_{j=1}^{k} \sum_{i=1}^{n} (\bar{x}_{i.} - \bar{x}_{..})^2$$
$$+ \sum_{j=1}^{k} \sum_{i=1}^{n} (x_{ij} - \bar{x}_{i.} - \bar{x}_{.j} + \bar{x}_{..})^2$$

That is,

(8.7.8)
$$\text{SST} = \text{SSTr} + \text{SSB} + \text{SSE}$$

The computing formulas for the quantities in Equations 8.7.7 and 8.7.8 are

(8.7.9)
$$SST = \sum_{j=1}^{k} \sum_{i=1}^{n} x_{ij}^2 - C$$

(8.7.10)
$$SSB = \frac{\sum_{i=1}^{n} T_{i.}^2}{k} - C$$

(8.7.11)
$$SSTr = \frac{\sum_{j=1}^{k} T_{.j}^2}{n} - C$$

(8.7.12)
$$SSE = SST - SSB - SSTr$$

We compute the correction term as follows:

(8.7.13)
$$C = \frac{\left(\sum_{j=1}^{k} \sum_{i=1}^{n} x_{ij}\right)^2}{kn} = \frac{T_{..}^2}{kn}$$

CALCULATIONS FOR EXAMPLE 8.4.1

$$C = \frac{418^2}{(6)(5)} = 5824.13$$

$$SST = 20^2 + 12^2 + \cdots + 8^2 - 5824.13$$
$$= 6894 - 5824.13 = 1069.87$$

$$SSTr = \frac{108^2 + 62^2 + \cdots + 42^2}{5} - 5824.13 = 519.07$$

$$SSB = \frac{84^2 + 77^2 + \cdots + 102^2}{6} - 5824.13 = 166.87$$

$$SSE = 1069.87 - 519.07 - 166.87 = 383.93$$

THE LATIN SQUARE DESIGN

We display sample data resulting from a Latin square design in a table such as Table 8.7.3.

In this table, the first subscript refers to the row, the second to the column, and the third to the treatment. We assign treatments randomly to the cells defined by the intersections of particular rows and columns. The treatment appearing in a given cell depends on the particular randomization scheme. We use the letter k to refer to a particular treatment. A value from the ith row and the jth column receiving treatment k is designated as x_{ijk}. The subscripts all run from 1 to r.

TABLE 8.7.3 Sample data from the Latin square design

		Columns				Row totals	Row means
Rows	1	2	3	$\cdots$	r		
1	x_{11t}	x_{12t}	x_{13t}	$\cdots$	x_{1rt}	$T_{1..}$	$\bar{x}_{1..}$
2	x_{21t}	x_{22t}	x_{23t}	$\cdots$	x_{2rt}	$T_{2..}$	$\bar{x}_{2..}$
3	x_{31t}	x_{32t}	x_{33t}	$\cdots$	x_{3rt}	$T_{3..}$	$\bar{x}_{3..}$
$\vdots$	$\vdots$	$\vdots$	$\vdots$	$\vdots$	$\vdots$	$\vdots$	$\vdots$
r	x_{r1t}	x_{r2t}	x_{r3t}	$\cdots$	x_{rrt}	$T_{r..}$	$\bar{x}_{r..}$
Column totals	$T_{.1.}$	$T_{.2.}$	$T_{.3.}$	$\cdots$	$T_{.r.}$	$T_{...}$	
Column means	$\bar{x}_{.1.}$	$\bar{x}_{.2.}$	$\bar{x}_{.3.}$	$\cdots$	$\bar{x}_{.r.}$		$\bar{x}_{...}$

Since the number of rows, columns, and treatments are equal, we write the kth treatment total and kth treatment mean, respectively, as

$$T_{..k} \quad \text{and} \quad \bar{x}_{..k}$$

It can be shown that we can partition the total sum of squares for the Latin square design into the following components:

(8.7.14)
$$\sum_{i,j,k=1}^{r} (x_{ijk} - \bar{x}_{...})^2 = \sum_{i,j,k=1}^{r} (\bar{x}_{i..} - \bar{x}_{...})^2 + \sum_{i,j,k=1}^{r} (\bar{x}_{.j.} - \bar{x}_{...})^2$$

$$+ \sum_{i,j,k=1}^{r} (\bar{x}_{..k} - \bar{x}_{...})^2$$

$$+ \sum_{i,j,k=1}^{r} (x_{ijk} - \bar{x}_{i..} - \bar{x}_{.j.} - \bar{x}_{..k} + 2\bar{x}_{...})^2$$

We may also write Equation 8.7.14 as

(8.7.15)
$$\text{SST} = \text{SSR} + \text{SSC} + \text{SSTr} + \text{SSE}$$

where SSR and SSC are the sums of squares computed from the values in the rows and columns, respectively. The computational formulas are as follows:

(8.7.16)
$$\text{SST} = \sum_{i,j,k=1}^{r} x_{ijk}^2 - C$$

(8.7.17)
$$\text{SSR} = \frac{\sum_{i=1}^{r} T_{i..}^2}{r} - C$$

$$(8.7.18) \qquad SSC = \frac{\Sigma_{j=1}^{r} T_{.j.}^2}{r} - C$$

$$(8.7.19) \qquad SSTr = \frac{\Sigma_{k=1}^{r} T_{..k}^2}{r} - C$$

$$(8.7.20) \qquad SSE = SST - SSR - SSC - SSTr$$

The correction factor C is given by

$$(8.7.21) \qquad C = \frac{(\Sigma_{i,jk=1}^{r} x_{ijk})^2}{r^2} = \frac{T_{...}^2}{r^2}$$

CALCULATIONS FOR EXAMPLE 8.5.1

$$C = 2093.06$$

From the data of Table 8.5.3, we may compute the following sums of squares:

$$SST = 13^2 + 12^2 + \cdots + 11^2 - \frac{183^2}{16} = 2177 - 2093.06 = 83.94$$

$$SSR = \frac{48^2 + 45^2 + 47^2 + 43^2}{4} - 2093.06 = 3.69$$

$$SSC = \frac{43^2 + 48^2 + 43^2 + 49^2}{4} - 2093.06 = 7.69$$

$$SSTr = \frac{52^2 + 53^2 + 46^2 + 32^2}{4} - 2093.06 = 70.19$$

$$SSE = 83.94 - 3.69 - 7.69 - 70.19 = 2.37$$

THE FACTORIAL EXPERIMENT

The equations and formulas that follow use the notation presented in Table 8.6.3. By an adaptation of the procedure used in the completely randomized design, we can partition the total sum of squares under the present model into two parts, as follows:

$$(8.7.22) \qquad \sum_{i=1}^{a} \sum_{j=1}^{b} \sum_{k=1}^{n} (x_{ijk} - \bar{x}_{...})^2 = \sum_{i=1}^{a} \sum_{j=1}^{b} \sum_{k=1}^{n} (\bar{x}_{ij.} - \bar{x}_{...})^2$$
$$+ \sum_{i=1}^{a} \sum_{j=1}^{b} \sum_{k=1}^{n} (\bar{x}_{ijk} - \bar{x}_{ij.})^2$$

or

(8.7.23)
$$SST = SSTr + SSE$$

We can partition the sum of squares for treatments into three parts, as follows:

(8.7.24)
$$\sum_{i=1}^{a} \sum_{j=1}^{b} \sum_{k=1}^{n} (\bar{x}_{ij.} - \bar{x}_{...})^2 = \sum_{i=1}^{a} \sum_{j=1}^{b} \sum_{k=1}^{n} (\bar{x}_{i..} - \bar{x}_{...})^2$$
$$+ \sum_{i=1}^{a} \sum_{j=1}^{b} \sum_{k=1}^{n} (\bar{x}_{.j.} - \bar{x}_{...})^2$$
$$+ \sum_{i=1}^{a} \sum_{j=1}^{b} \sum_{k=1}^{n} (\bar{x}_{ij.} - \bar{x}_{i..} - \bar{x}_{.j.} + \bar{x}_{...})^2$$

or

(8.7.25)
$$SSTr = SSA + SSB + SSAB$$

The computing formulas for the various components are as follows:

(8.7.26)
$$SST = \sum_{i=1}^{a} \sum_{j=1}^{b} \sum_{k=1}^{n} x_{ijk}^2 - C$$

(8.7.27)
$$SSTr = \frac{\sum_{i=1}^{a} \sum_{j=1}^{b} T_{ij.}^2}{n} - C$$

(8.7.28)
$$SSE = SST - SSTr$$

(8.7.29)
$$SSA = \frac{\sum_{i=1}^{a} T_{i..}^2}{bn} - C$$

(8.7.30)
$$SSB = \frac{\sum_{j=1}^{b} T_{.j.}^2}{an} - C$$

and

(8.7.31)
$$SSAB = SSTr - SSA - SSB$$

In these equations,

(8.7.32)
$$C = \frac{\left(\sum_{i=1}^{a} \sum_{j=1}^{b} \sum_{k=1}^{n} x_{ijk} \right)^2}{abn} = \frac{T_{...}^2}{abn}$$

CALCULATIONS FOR EXAMPLE 8.6.2

$$C = 2954.02$$

$$SST = 5^2 + 6^2 + \cdots + 6^2 - \frac{421^2}{60} = 3429 - 2954.02 = 474.98$$

$$SSTr = \frac{15^2 + 21^2 + \cdots + 21^2}{3} - 2954.02 = 410.98$$

$$SSE = 474.98 - 410.98 = 64.00$$

$$SSA = \frac{93^2 + 103^2 + 97^2 + 128^2}{15} - 2954.02 = 49.38$$

$$SSB = \frac{73^2 + 87^2 + 62^2 + 103^2 + 96^2}{12} - 2954.02 = 93.23$$

$$SSAB = 410.98 - 49.38 - 93.23 = 268.37$$

SUMMARY

This chapter covers the basic concepts and techniques of analysis of variance that we use to test for significant differences among several means. We discuss the completely randomized, the randomized block, and the Latin square designs, and the factorial experiment. In addition, the chapter discusses the problem of multiple tests of significance between pairs of means. Tukey's test is demonstrated by an example.

You learned that you can use a technique known as blocking to eliminate extraneous sources of variability in an experiment. The objective in blocking is to reduce the size of the error term in order to improve the chance of detecting any differences between population means that may exist. We use the randomized block design to eliminate *one* source of extraneous variation. We use the Latin square design when we wish to eliminate *two* sources of extraneous variation.

You also learned that we sometimes want to design an experiment in such a way that we can measure the effects of interaction. An experiment of this type is called a factorial experiment.

In the interest of brevity, this chapter omits many related topics. The following brief comments introduce you to some additional important topics in the analysis of variance. Further information is available in the texts on experimental design and analysis of variance listed in the Suggestions for Further Reading at the end of this chapter.

Missing Data In the course of an experiment, accidents that result in the loss of some of the observations are not uncommon. When this happens, we need some method of dealing with the problem.

Efficiency We often want to know how much improvement we may expect in an experiment as a whole if we use one type of design instead of some other type. To answer this question, we must determine the relative efficiency of the two designs.

Transformations If the data do not meet the assumptions underlying the analysis of variance, an alternative procedure is to perform a *transformation* on the data, so that the assumptions are more nearly met. Most texts on general statistics and experimental design discuss transformations to some extent.

Nonparametric Alternatives Alternatively, when the assumptions underlying analysis of variance are not met, we may use *nonparametric* methods of analysis. We discuss these methods more fully in Chapter 13 and present appropriate nonparametric alternatives to some of the procedures discussed in this chapter.

REVIEW EXERCISES

Where appropriate, do an analysis of variance at the indicated level of significance and compute a p value for the test. If no level of significance is indicated, compute the p value and state whether or not you think the null hypothesis should be rejected.

1. Define analysis of variance.

2. For each of the following experimental designs, describe a situation in your particular field of interest in which that design would be appropriate. Use real or realistic data and do the appropriate analysis of variance for each. (a) Completely randomized design, (b) randomized complete block design, (c) Latin square design (d) completely randomized design with a factorial experiment.

3. What are the fundamental assumptions underlying the analysis of variance?

4. Explain the difference between the fixed-effects model and the random-effects model.

5. What is the correction factor? How is it computed? How is it used?

6. What are two other names for the error sum of squares?

7. When is the randomized complete block design appropriate?

8. How is randomization achieved in the randomized complete block design?

9. What is the primary objective in using the randomized complete block design?

10. Explain the various components of the randomized complete block model.

11. What is *interaction*?

12. What is meant by *level*?

13. Explain the components of the factorial model.

14. In the factorial experiment, why is there always more than one observation on the variable of interest for each experimental condition?

15. Explain the essential features of the Latin square design.

16. What are the assumptions underlying the Latin square design?

17. How is randomization achieved when the Latin square design is used?

18. Ⓒ The following table shows the unit cost of producing a certain product by size of firm. Can we conclude at the 0.05 level of significance that there are differences among the three sizes of firm with respect to mean unit production cost?

Small	8	7	7	6	6	6	6	8	8	8
Medium	3	4	4	4	2	4	5	3	4	3
Large	4	5	5	5	3	4	5	4	5	6

19. Ⓒ A psychologist is hired to compare the levels of job satisfaction of salespersons at three large companies. Ten salespersons are selected at random from each firm and given in-depth tests to ascertain their level of job satisfaction. The results appear in the following table. Do these data provide sufficient evidence to indicate a difference in mean job satisfaction among the three firms? Let $\alpha = 0.01$.

Firm A	67	65	59	59	58	61	66	53	51	64
Firm B	66	68	55	59	61	66	62	65	64	74
Firm C	87	80	67	89	80	84	78	65	72	85

20. Ⓒ The following table shows the results of an experiment designed to compare the tensile strength of a certain product produced from raw material from five different vendors. The investigator wishes to eliminate the effects of (a) the size stock from which the product is manufactured and (b) the assembly line on which the processing took place. The data in the table have been coded for easy computation. Test at the 0.05 level of significance the null hypothesis of no difference in tensile strength among the different vendors.

| Assembly line | Stock size | | | | |
	1	2	3	4	5
I	A(23)	E(21)	C(29)	B(25)	D(20)
II	D(22)	C(30)	E(22)	A(24)	B(23)
III	E(19)	A(22)	B(24)	D(22)	C(27)
IV	C(25)	B(20)	D(21)	E(20)	A(23)
V	B(21)	D(23)	A(23)	C(31)	E(27)

21. Ⓒ The following table shows the results, in miles per gallon, of an experiment designed to compare four brands of gasoline. The experiment uses four makes of cars. Cars serve as a blocking factor. After eliminating car effects, do these data provide sufficient evidence to indicate that there are differences among the brands of gasoline? Let $\alpha = 0.05$.

| Make of automobile | Gasoline | | | |
	A	B	C	D
I	17	18	15	20
II	21	20	16	21
III	25	24	20	19
IV	15	22	15	18

22. Ⓒ Wyatt/Stokes Advertising conducts an experiment to try to assess the effectiveness of various formats of television commercials. Fifty regular television viewers are randomly assigned to view one of five formats of a TV commercial for a cold remedy. On the basis of an interview after the viewing, a score measuring the impact of the commercial on the participant is recorded. The results are as follows. Can we conclude on the basis of these data that the formats differ in their effectiveness? Let $\alpha = 0.05$.

TV commercial format

A			B			C			D			E		
20	23	21	28	27	22	33	34	25	33	29	31	49	41	41
23	26	24	28	23	29	26	27	33	29	27	25	39	41	48
26	23	20	27	25	28	25	32	25	26	26	33	43	43	46
24			21			34			32			35		

23. Use Tukey's multiple-comparison test in order to determine which pairs of means in Exercise 22 differ significantly. Let $\alpha = 0.05$.

24. Ⓒ A study is conducted to compare the job-satisfaction levels of assembly-line employees whose working environments are structured to different degrees. Also of interest is the relationship of length of employment to job satisfaction. The researchers wish to study the interaction between length of employment and the extent to which the working environment is structured and the effect of this interaction on job satisfaction.

The following table shows job-satisfaction scores from the study. The data are coded for ease of calculation. Do an appropriate analysis of variance of these data.

	Nature of working environment		
Length of employment (years)	Highly structured	Moderately structured	Unstructured
<5	12	10	8
	15	10	7
	15	9	7
	14	10	8
	12	9	6
5–10	12	10	10
	14	10	11
	12	14	12
	10	14	10
	11	10	14
11 or more	9	10	12
	10	11	14
	9	10	15
	9	10	15
	10	12	18

25. Refer to Exercise 19 and use Tukey's test to make all pairwise comparisons. Let $\alpha = 0.01$.

26. C In a random sample of 30 junior executives, each is classified by potential for promotion as good, poor, or uncertain. Each is then given a test to measure his or her level of anxiety. The results (coded for ease of computation) are as follows. What are your conclusions about this study? Let $\alpha = 0.05$.

Potential	Level of anxiety											
Good	3	4	3	2	2	5	3	2	5	4	4	4
Poor	4	8	7	10	10	4	8	8				
Uncertain	4	5	3	4	3	3	4	4	6	5		

27. C Industrial psychologists conduct an experiment to evaluate three methods of motivating employees in a factory. The researchers want to use a design that allows blocking by education. Scores (coded) on a test designed to measure effectiveness of the methods are as follows. Do these data indicate that there is a difference in treatment effects? Let $\alpha = 0.05$.

Education group	Treatment group		
	A	B	C
1	8	9	7
2	5	8	7
3	3	9	5
4	4	8	5

28. C Austin Fabrics & Fibers experiments to compare the effects of 4 different processing methods on the strength of a synthetic fiber. The investigator uses the randomized complete block design, with the 4 sources of raw material serving as blocks. The following table gives the strengths (coded) of 16 specimens prepared during the experiment. After eliminating block effects, can the manufacturer conclude that the different processing methods do have different effects on fiber strength? Let $\alpha = 0.01$.

Block	Processing method			
	A	B	C	D
1	11	10	13	14
2	12	10	16	14
3	16	17	18	18
4	17	15	18	18

29. C A different brand of floor tile is installed in each of five areas of a public building. Five different cleaning agents are used in such a way that a Latin square design results. The following table shows measures of deterioration and wear for each brand of tile at the end of one year. Do these data provide sufficient evidence to indicate a difference in durability among the brands? Let $\alpha = 0.05$.

Area	Cleaning agents				
	1	2	3	4	5
I	A(58)	B(62)	C(77)	D(94)	E(66)
II	B(48)	A(76)	D(103)	E(58)	C(99)
III	C(74)	D(113)	E(70)	A(105)	B(93)
IV	E(66)	C(95)	A(111)	B(108)	D(150)
V	D(110)	E(63)	B(113)	C(126)	A(160)

30. $\boxed{C}$ A study is designed to evaluate four advertising strategies, A, B, C, and D. Investigators use a Latin square design in which the columns represent the four seasons of the year and the rows represent four areas of the country. The variable of interest is consumer knowledge of the product advertised. The results (coded) are as follows. Test, at the 0.05 level of significance, the null hypothesis of no difference among treatment means.

Area	Season			
	Fall	Winter	Spring	Summer
1	A(12)	B(10)	C(10)	D(12)
2	B(10)	A(12)	D(12)	C(10)
3	C(10)	D(11)	B(10)	A(12)
4	D(11)	C(10)	A(13)	B(10)

31. $\boxed{C}$ The following table shows the neuroticism scores of 27 employees classified on the basis of the stressfulness of their jobs and length of employment. Perform an appropriate analysis of variance of these data.

Length of employment (in years) (Factor A)	Stressfulness of job (Factor B)		
	Very stressful	Moderately stressful	Not stressful
<5	25	18	17
	28	23	24
	22	19	19
5–10	28	16	18
	32	24	22
	30	20	20
>10	25	14	10
	35	16	8
	30	15	12

32. $\boxed{C}$ A research team hired by Consolidated Fertilizer Company conducts an experiment to study the yield of a certain grain using 3 different levels of fertilizer—low, medium, and high. Three varieties of seed are used in the experiment, making a total of 9 treatment combinations. Each treatment combination is assigned at random to one of 27 plots of ground, so that 3 plots receive each treatment. The yields (coded) are as follows. Perform an appropriate analysis of variance of these data.

		Fertilizer level	
Variety	Low	Medium	High
A	5	8	10
	8	8	12
	7	10	10
B	6	10	15
	8	12	14
	6	11	14
C	7	12	16
	8	12	16
	10	14	18

33. Ⓒ Conrad Astor Marketing Services designs a study to compare the characteristics of people with high exposure to various media. Through intensive interviewing, they classify 40 randomly selected adults on the basis of the extent of their exposure to radio, TV, newspapers, and magazines. They include only subjects with "high" exposures to each medium. For each subject, they obtain scores on a wide range of demographic and psychographic variables. The following table shows the subjects' scores on a test designed to measure knowledge of current events. Test for a difference among population means at the 0.05 level. Prepare a report on the results of this study for the president of the market research firm.

	High exposure to										
Radio			TV			Newspapers			Magazines		
11	13	16	18	21	22	11	14	20	15	15	18
14	13	17	16	15	21	16	19	13	10	14	14
17	11	15	22	25	19	15	16	15	15	18	18
11			16			14			13		

34. Ⓒ Researchers wish to study the effect of crowding on the productivity of office workers. Office workers of the same age, sex, and level of training and experience are randomly assigned to one of three groups representing three levels of crowding: severe, moderate, or none. The following table shows the results. Can we conclude from these data that crowding affects productivity? Let $\alpha = 0.05$. What use can we make of the results of this experiment?

Severe	22	49	32	37	32	22
Moderate	31	30	43	30	46	
None	68	73	78	47	56	59

35. Ⓒ Beardsley Publications hires a reading specialist to assess the effects of different typefaces—A, B, and C—on reading comprehension scores of schoolchildren. The following table shows, for 20 subjects randomly assigned to a treatment, the difference in the reading scores of children given material set in a standard typeface and those given material set in experimental typefaces. The material was of equal difficulty. Can we conclude from these data that typeface has an effect on reading comprehension? Let $\alpha = 0.05$. What use can we make of the results of this experiment?

A	12	13	7	15	7			
B	15	11	15	15	14	17	18	
C	16	18	24	18	24	23	24	22

36. [C] Researchers conducted an experiment designed to evaluate the effectiveness of four different methods—A, B, C, and D—of teaching problem solving. The following table shows, by teaching method, the scores made by the participating subjects (who were randomly assigned to one of the treatments) when they were forced to solve problems following this training. Do these data provide sufficient evidence to indicate that the four teaching methods differ in effectiveness? Let $\alpha = 0.05$. Do the results of this experiment have any relevance to the world of business? Explain.

A	48	38	20	16	95		
B	91	37	53	91	80	38	
C	67	61	33	85	99	95	81
D	57	62	50	43	59	60	70

37. [C] Four different groups of kittens were given food with four different flavors—A, B, C, and D. Kittens of the same age, sex, and species were randomly assigned to one of the four flavors. The following table shows the amount (coded) of food consumed by each kitten in each group during a 24-hour period. Test to determine whether the kittens' acceptance of the four flavors differs. Let $\alpha = 0.05$. How might management use the results of this experiment in deciding which flavor or flavors to market? Could the results of this experiment be used in advertising? Explain.

A	12	14	18	11	19	10
B	23	20	17	23	20	
C	29	27	30	35	33	
D	38	33	40	34	34	37

38. [C] Researchers compare three brands of automobile tires of the same size. The criterion is length of life in thousands of miles. Six tires of each brand are tested. The following table shows the results. Can we conclude from these data that the three brands are not equal in quality? Let $\alpha = 0.05$. Prepare a report on the results of this experiment for the management of the firm that manufactures Brand B tires. Prepare advertising copy for Brand B tires using the results of this experiment.

Brand A	43	44	42	50	46	48
Brand B	51	49	52	45	48	50
Brand C	47	41	42	45	43	42

39. [C] Researchers conduct a study to compare the characteristics of assembly-line employees at the Brieux watch factory. Employees are categorized into five achievement groups: very high, moderately high, average, low, and very low. The researchers select a random sample from each group and interview and test them in depth. The following table shows the self-concept scores of subjects in the five groups. Do these data provide sufficient evidence to indicate that the populations differ with respect to the mean level of self-concept? Let $\alpha = 0.05$. What use can management make of the results of this experiment?

Very high	90	90	90	95	90	88		
Mod. high	79	83	85	75	93			
Average	77	66	85	87	67	73	75	82
Low	97	81	92	85				
Very low	66	63	83	65	74	64		

40. Complete the following ANOVA table and state which design was used.

Source	SS	df	MS	F	p
Treatments	154.9199	4			
Error					
Total	200.4773	39			

41. Complete the following ANOVA table and state which design was used.

Source	SS	df	MS	F	p
Treatments		3			
Blocks	183.5	3			
Error	26.0				
Total	709.0	15			

42. Complete the following ANOVA table and state which design was used.

Source	SS	df	MS	F	p
Rows	7420				
Columns	1295				
Treatments	2050				
Error		20			
Total	12,250	35			

43. Consider the following ANOVA table.

Source	SS	df	MS	F	p
A	12.3152	2	6.15756	29.4021	<0.005
B	19.7844	3	6.59481	31.4898	<0.005
AB	8.9417	6	1.49027	7.11596	<0.005
Treatments	41.0413	11			
Error	10.0525	48	0.209427		
Total	51.0938	59			

(a) What sort of analysis was employed?   (b) What can we conclude from the analysis? Let $\alpha = 0.05$.

44. Consider the following ANOVA table.

Source	SS	df	MS	F
Treatments	5.05835	2	2.52917	1.0438
Error	65.42090	27	2.4230	

(a) What design was employed? (b) How many treatments were compared? (c) How many observations were analyzed? (d) At the 0.05 level of significance, can we conclude that there is a difference among treatments? Why?

45. Consider the following ANOVA table.

Source	SS	df	MS	F
Treatments	231.5054	2	115.7527	2.824
Blocks	98.5000	7	14.0714	
Error	573.7500	14	40.9821	

(a) What design was employed? (b) How many treatments were compared? (c) How many observations were analyzed? (d) At the 0.05 level of significance, can we conclude that the treatments have different effects? Why?

46. © The manager of the Catullus Health Clubs wishes to compare four physical fitness programs designed for young adult females. Thirty new members are given physical fitness tests at the time they join. Each is then randomly assigned to one of the four programs. At the end of six months, each subject is again given the physical fitness test. The following table shows the gains in scores made by the 30 subjects. Construct an analysis-of-variance table from these data and compute the four sample means.

	Program		
A	B	C	D
13	11	12	22
24	13	19	26
19	20	9	22
18	14	14	22
9	11	21	26
21	21	7	19
17	14	6	
22	8		
24			

47. © Refer to Exercise 46. Can the manager conclude from the sample results that the four programs differ in effectiveness? Let $\alpha = 0.05$, and find the p value.

48. Refer to Exercise 46. Use Tukey's test to determine which pairs of the sample means are significantly different. Let $\alpha = 0.05$.

49. © A manufacturer of hearing aids wishes to compare three proposed designs prepared by the company's research and development department. Four hearing-impaired subjects had their hearing tested first without a hearing aid and then while wearing a prototype of each of the three hearing aids. The following table shows the amount of hearing improvement each subject experienced with each hearing aid. Construct an analysis-of-variance table from these data.

Subject	Hearing aid type		
	A	B	C
1	16	26	22
2	16	20	23
3	17	21	22
4	28	29	36

50. Ⓒ Refer to Exercise 49. Can we conclude, on the basis of the analysis, that the four types of hearing aid are not equally effective? Let $\alpha = 0.05$, and find the p value.

51. Ⓒ The manager of Dawson Dairies wishes to compare the bacterial counts in raw milk supplied by five different dairy farms—A, B, C, D, and E. A Latin square design is employed in which the two blocking factors are day of week and time of day when the counts are taken. The results are shown in the following table, in which the measurements are the logarithms of the bacterial counts per cubic millimeter. Construct an ANOVA table from these data.

Time of day	Day				
	1	2	3	4	5
8 A.M.	A = 2.0	B = 1.1	C = 0.6	D = 2.1	E = 2.2
10 A.M.	D = 2.2	C = 1.9	E = 0.5	B = 2.5	A = 2.4
Noon	C = 2.0	A = 1.6	D = 1.6	E = 1.0	B = 2.9
2 P.M.	B = 2.8	E = 1.0	A = 1.3	C = 1.7	D = 2.5
4 P.M.	E = 1.7	D = 2.0	B = 1.9	A = 2.5	C = 2.4

52. Ⓒ Refer to Exercise 51. Can we conclude on the basis of the analysis that the farms differ with respect to mean bacterial count? Why? Let $\alpha = 0.05$.

53. Ⓒ The director of the Central City University physical fitness center wishes to develop an effective total program to help obese students lose weight. To compare different combinations of diets and exercise routines, the director conducts the following experiment. Seventy-two students, overweight to approximately the same extent, are randomly assigned to one of 24 different programs consisting of different combinations of 4 diets and 6 exercise routines. There are 3 students in each combination. The number of pounds lost by each student at the end of the experimental period is shown in the following table. Construct an ANOVA table from these data.

Exercise routine	Diet			
	A	B	C	D
	11.0	9.4	12.5	13.2
I	9.6	9.6	11.5	13.2
	10.8	9.6	10.5	13.5

(continues on next page)

Exercise routine	Diet			
	A	B	C	D
II	10.5	10.8	10.5	15.0
	11.5	10.5	11.8	14.6
	12.0	10.5	11.5	14.0
III	12.0	11.5	11.8	12.8
	11.5	11.5	11.8	13.7
	11.8	12.3	12.3	13.1
IV	11.5	9.4	13.7	14.0
	11.8	9.1	13.5	15.0
	10.5	10.8	12.5	14.0
V	11.0	11.2	14.4	13.0
	11.2	11.8	14.2	14.2
	10.0	10.2	13.5	13.7
VI	11.2	10.8	11.5	11.8
	10.8	11.5	10.2	12.8
	11.8	10.2	11.5	12.0

54. Refer to Exercise 53. Can we conclude on the basis of the analysis that the diets have different effects? Can we conclude that the exercise routines differ with respect to their effect on weight loss? Can we conclude that diets and exercise routines interact? Let $\alpha = 0.05$, and find the p value for each test.

55. Ⓒ Data Set 6 in Appendix IV contains data on the following four populations of subjects. The measurements given in this table are scores made on a test designed to measure the level of stress experienced by the subjects. Select four independent simple random samples, one sample from each of the four populations, and perform an analysis to determine whether we may conclude that the four population means are not equal. Let $\alpha = 0.05$, and find the p value. Compare your results with those of your classmates.

56. Ⓒ Refer to Exercise 55. Use Tukey's test to compare, at the 0.05 level, all possible pairs of sample means. Compare your results with those of your classmates.

57. Ⓒ The following sample data are the responses of 17 subjects to one of three treatments—A, B, or C. At the 0.05 level of significance, can we conclude that there is a difference between population means? **(a)** Construct the ANOVA table. **(b)** State the null and alternative hypotheses. **(c)** State the decision rule. **(d)** What is the statistical decision? **(e)** What is the standard deviation of these 17 values?

A	B	C
53	44	Not observed
48	50	51
51	45	55
50	52	54
46	57	56
49	47	53

58. Ⓒ You have measured the driving time from home to the office using four alternative routes. The results in minutes are as follows. Consider each of these sets of measurements as a simple random sample of measurements from a population of measurements that would result if each of the routes were driven many, many times. At the 0.05 level of significance, can we conclude that there is a difference in the population mean driving times among these four routes? (a) Construct the ANOVA table. (b) State the null and alternative hypotheses. (c) State the decision rule and the statistical decision. (d) What is your conclusion? (e) What is the standard deviation of the 20 values?

A	B	C	D
23	35	28	34
28	42	38	29
31	38	33	31
18	37	36	38
26	29	32	
	36		

 59. Ⓒ We wish to know the effect, if any, that the temperature at which an alloy is produced has on the strength of the alloy. The following table shows the strengths of alloy specimens produced at three different temperatures.

Temperature

A	B	C
40.2	41.3	40.0
40.4	41.3	39.0
40.0	42.1	39.5
40.7	41.5	39.1
40.7	41.8	39.4

What should we conclude from these data? Let the probability of committing a Type I error be 0.01.

 60. Ⓒ In the manufacture of a laminated fabric, machines are used to apply resin to the surface of the materials being laminated. We wish to know if four machines differ with respect to the mean amount of resin that they apply per square unit of surface. The following table shows the amount of resin applied to the same square unit of surface by each of the machines in ten replications each of the lamination process. What should we conclude from these data? Let $\alpha = 0.05$.

Machine

A	B	C	D
2.9	6.5	4.6	4.4
1.4	5.1	3.3	5.1
3.6	6.6	3.6	5.2
4.8	6.7	5.6	5.1
2.2	4.7	4.1	4.2
3.5	3.6	5.6	3.7
1.4	6.7	6.0	3.5
3.3	2.6	6.3	5.7

*61. An experiment designed in such a way that the same subjects or objects are exposed to all the treatments under study is often called a *repeated measures design*. This design is frequently employed in business research. The technique was used by Bretz and Thomas (Robert D. Bretz, Jr., and Steven L. Thomas, "Perceived Equity, Motivation, and Final-Offer Arbitration in Major League Baseball," *Journal of Applied Psychology*, 77 [June 1992], 280–287) in a study of major league baseball arbitration, by Andrews and Franke (Rick L. Andrews and George R. Franke, "The Determinants of Cigarette Consumption: A Meta-Analysis," *Journal of Public Policy & Marketing*, 10 [Spring 1991], 81–100) in a study of the determinants of cigarette consumption, and by Pulakos et al. (Elaine D. Pulakos, Leonard A. White, Scott H. Oppler, and Walter C. Borman, "Examination of Race and Sex Effects on Performance Ratings," *Journal of Applied Psychology*, 74 [October 1989], 770–780) in a study of the effects of race and sex on performance ratings. Repeated measures designs are particularly appropriate when the behavior of subjects over time is of interest. Keppel (Geoffrey Keppel, *Design and Analysis: A Researcher's Handbook* [Englewood Cliffs, N.J.: Prentice Hall, 1973], 404–406) describes an experiment of this type. Researchers who use a repeated measures design usually consider the subjects or objects receiving the treatments to be a random sample from a population. When this is the case and the treatments are fixed, the design is analogous to the randomized complete block design discussed in this chapter, and the analysis of the data is carried out in the manner described for this design. Describe a research situation in your field of interest in which a repeated measures design would be appropriate. Collect real data or make up realistic data and analyze them to reach a conclusion about the equality of the treatment effects.

*62. As noted earlier, an adaptation of Tukey's procedure may be employed to test for significant differences among sample means resulting from the ANOVA of a randomized complete block experimental design. The criterion statistic is $T = (1/\sqrt{n})q_{\alpha,k,(n-1)(k-1)}$ where k and n are as defined in Section 8.4 and q is obtained from Table H of Appendix I as described in Section 8.3. Any difference between pairs of sample means whose absolute value exceeds the computed value of T is significant. Refer to Example 8.4.1 and determine which pairs of treatment means are significantly different. Let $\alpha = 0.05$.

1. EFFECT OF PROGRAM CONTENT ON VIEWERS' RESPONSES TO TV COMMERCIALS

Advertising agencies are concerned with the extent of viewers' involvement in the content of various programs and how much this involvement has to do with the effectiveness of television commercials. Two investigators, Soldow and Principe, proposed four hypotheses about viewers' responses to commercials. One hypothesis was that viewers will recall more brand names when they see commercials embedded in "less involving" programs than in "more involving" ones.

The following 3 groups, composed of 29 subjects each, participated in the experiment:

1. Those exposed to commercials in more involving programs

2. Those exposed to commercials in less involving programs

3. Those who watched commercials only (the control group)

The mean brand-recall scores for the 3 groups were as follows.

Group	1	2	3
Mean	1.21	2.24	2.28

An analysis of variance of the data yielded the following sums of squares: among-groups, 21.40; within-groups, 85.86.

What can one conclude from these results? Let $\alpha = 0.05$. What is the p value for the test? Compare all possible pairs of means. What assumptions are required?

Source: Gary F. Soldow and Victor Principe, "Response to Commercials as a Function of Program Content," *Journal of Advertising Research*, 21 (April 1981), 59–65.

2. JOB TRAINING AND WORKER SATISFACTION

The satisfaction of workers is a subject of perennial concern to managers. Most managers assume that if they provide workers with more training and education the workers will be more satisfied with their jobs. Drexler and Lindell conducted a study on (1) whether an objective, specific measure of training/job fit (the worker does the job for which he or she is trained) is directly related to the worker's satisfaction with that job and (2) whether the social aspects of work environments are more strongly related to satisfaction when people work in jobs for which they are not trained.

Subjects of the study were 2,286 army personnel. Drexler and Lindell divided subjects into two treatment groups: (a) those who were now working in their primary military occupational specialty (MOS) and (b) those who were not. Drexler and Lindell considered membership in group (a) as an indication of training/job fit. They obtained a happiness score by using a seven-item measure that touched on the subjects' satisfaction with their pay, their supervisor, their coworkers, the organization, their opportunities for advancement, and the job itself.

One of the analyses Drexler and Lindell performed was one-way analysis of variance, using 2,232 subjects. They tested the null hypothesis of no difference between subjects in group (a) and group (b) with respect to mean level of job satisfaction. They obtained a between-groups mean square of 13.29 and a within-groups mean square of 0.88.

What are the between-groups and within-groups degrees of freedom for this test? What is the computed value of F? Should the null hypothesis be rejected at the 0.05 level? Why? What is the p value for the test? What conclusions can one draw from these results? Construct an ANOVA table for these results. What assumptions are necessary?

Source: John A. Drexler, Jr., and Michael K. Lindell, "Training/Job Fit and Worker Satisfaction," *Human Relations*, 34(1981), 907–915.

3. WAITING FOR A PHONE

Ruback, Pape, and Doriot, in a series of studies, found that users of public telephones tended to spend more time on the phone when someone was waiting for them to finish than when they were alone. In an experiment, the investigators measured the length of time (in seconds) that subjects spent on the telephone under one of three conditions: when alone (A), when one person was using an adjacent telephone (B), or when one person was using an adjacent telephone and another person was waiting to use one of the two telephones (C). The study was conducted in an alcove of a shopping mall, an area that contained only the two adjacent telephones. The following table shows, by experimental condition, how long the 56 subjects (35 females and 21 males) spent on the telephone.

Experimental Condition			Experimental Condition		
A	B	C	A	B	C
52	55	794	135	312	236
33	73	54	38	83	72
55	56	138	54	99	79
149	49	67	79	43	308
145	323	71	142	111	1,319
34	97	259	36	60	180
47	149	124	70	114	
59	131	51	224	52	
86	94	43		53	
43	128	104			
68	57	137			

Can we conclude, on the basis of these data, that the mean time people spend on a telephone differs under the three conditions? Let the probability of committing a Type I error be 0.05.

Source: R. Barry Ruback, Karen D. Pape, and Philip Doriot (1989). "Waiting for a Phone: Intrusion on Callers Leads to Territorial Defense," *Social Psychology Quarterly* 52:232–241. Data provided by senior author and used by permission.

4.   CONSUMER INVOLVEMENT AND COGNITIVE RESPONSE TO BROADCAST ADVERTISING

Buchholz and Smith (Laura M. Buchholz and Robert E. Smith, "The Role of Consumer Involvement in Determining Cognitive Response to Broadcast Advertising," *Journal of Advertising*, 20 [1991], 4–17) investigated the role of involvement in determining consumer response to radio and TV commercials. Subjects, who were undergraduate seniors at a large midwestern university, were randomly assigned to one of the four treatment conditions. The treatment variables were type of commercial (Media: 1 = TV, 2 = radio) and level of involvement (Involvmt: 1 = low, 2 = high). The dependent variables were: (1) number of elaborations produced (Elabtot), (2) brand recognition score (Brandcog), and (3) ad recognition score (Adcog). *Elaboration* refers to the condition in which a subject connects an ad's content to his or her own life in some meaningful way. The following are the data collected by the investigators.

Media	Involvmt	Elabtot	Brandcog	Adcog
1	2	0	1	4
1	2	0	0	3
1	2	0	1	3
1	2	0	1	4
1	2	0	1	3
1	2	0	1	5
1	2	0	1	4
1	2	1	1	4
1	2	0	1	4
1	2	1	1	4
1	2	0	1	4
1	2	0	1	3
1	2	0	1	4
1	2	1	1	4
1	2	0	1	5
1	2	1	1	4
1	2	1	1	4
1	2	0	1	5
1	2	0	1	4

(continues on next page)

Media	Involvmt	Elabtot	Brandcog	Adcog
1	2	0	1	4
1	1	0	1	2
1	1	0	1	2
1	1	0	0	2
1	1	0	1	3
1	1	1	1	3
1	1	0	1	3
1	1	0	1	4
1	1	2	1	3
1	1	0	0	2
1	1	0	1	3
1	1	0	1	3
1	1	1	1	5
1	1	2	1	3
1	1	0	1	3
1	1	1	1	3
1	1	1	1	4
1	1	0	1	3
1	1	1	1	4
1	1	0	1	3
1	1	0	1	2
2	2	2	1	4
2	2	2	1	4
2	2	0	1	4
2	2	2	1	3
2	2	0	1	3
2	2	0	1	4
2	2	5	1	4
2	2	0	1	3
2	2	3	1	4
2	2	0	1	5
2	2	1	1	4
2	2	0	1	3
2	2	4	1	4
2	2	0	1	2
2	2	2	1	3
2	2	0	0	4
2	2	0	1	5
2	2	0	1	2
2	2	1	1	5
2	2	0	1	4
2	1	0	1	2
2	1	0	0	0
2	1	3	1	2
2	1	0	0	0
2	1	0	0	1
2	1	0	0	1
2	1	0	0	1
2	1	0	0	2

Media	Involvmt	Elabtot	Brandcog	Adcog
2	1	3	1	2
2	1	0	0	0
2	1	0	1	2
2	1	1	1	3
2	1	0	1	2
2	1	0	1	3
2	1	0	1	4
2	1	2	0	3
2	1	1	1	1
2	1	0	1	3
2	1	1	1	2
2	1	0	1	4

Set up appropriate hypotheses regarding each of the dependent variables. Analyze the data as a factorial experiment, compute p values, and state your conclusions.

Source: Professor Robert E. Smith. Used with permission.

5. ELECTRONIC BRAINSTORMING

Gallupe and his colleagues have written that brainstorming groups have consistently produced fewer ideas than have the equivalent number of individuals working by themselves (R. Brent Gallupe, Lana M. Bastianutti, and William H. Cooper, "Unblocking Brainstorms," *Journal of Applied Psychology*, 76 [1991], 137–142). The authors conducted a study to determine the effect of a software tool called *Electronic Brainstorming* on the generation of ideas. Subjects were bachelor of commerce and master of business administration students at a Canadian university. The independent variables were group type (Grp: interacting — subjects recorded their ideas while interacting with others; nominal — subjects recorded their ideas without interacting with others) and technology (Tech: subjects entered their ideas into computers). The four resulting treatment groups were electronic nominal, electronic interacting, nonelectronic nominal, and nonelectronic interacting. Among the dependent variables on which data were collected was the subjects' response to the statement "I had more ideas than I actually expressed." Scores ranged from 1 (strongly disagree) to 7 (strongly agree). The following data were collected on this variable.

Subject #	Grp 1 = Interacting 2 = Nominal	Tech 1 = Interacting 2 = Nominal	More Ideas? 1 = strg disagree 7 = strg agree
1	1	1	4
2	1	1	6
3	1	1	2
4	1	1	3
5	1	1	4
6	1	1	2
7	1	1	5
8	1	1	5
9	2	2	3
10	2	2	6
11	2	2	3
12	2	2	1
13	2	1	1
14	2	1	2
15	2	1	4
16	2	1	1
17	2	2	1
18	2	2	1
19	2	2	1
20	2	2	6
21	1	2	4
22	1	2	3
23	1	2	7
24	1	2	3
29	1	2	3
30	1	2	4
31	1	2	5
32	1	2	5
37	2	2	1
38	2	2	3
39	2	2	2
40	2	2	3
41	1	1	2
42	1	1	7
43	1	1	5
44	1	1	3
45	1	1	1
46	1	1	1
47	1	1	6
48	1	1	2
49	2	1	6
50	2	1	3
51	2	1	3
52	2	1	2
53	2	1	3
54	2	1	1
55	2	1	2

Subject #	Grp 1 = Interacting 2 = Nominal	Tech 1 = Interacting 2 = Nominal	More Ideas? 1 = strg disagree 7 = strg agree
56	2	1	4
57	2	2	2
58	2	2	3
59	2	2	3
60	2	2	1
73	1	2	2
74	1	2	2
75	1	2	3
76	1	2	3
77	2	1	5
78	2	1	5
79	2	1	3
80	2	1	3
81	2	2	2
82	2	2	3
83	2	2	3
84	2	2	2
85	1	2	5
86	1	2	7
87	1	2	3
88	1	2	3
89	1	2	6
90	1	2	6
91	1	2	2
92	1	2	2
93	2	1	2
94	2	1	3
95	2	1	2
96	2	1	2
101	1	1	3
102	1	1	5
103	1	1	3
104	1	1	5

State appropriate hypotheses, analyze the data as a factorial experiment, compute p values, and state your conclusions.

Source: Professor Brent Gallupe. Used with permission.

6. QUESTION SEQUENCE AND EXAM PERFORMANCE

The objective of a study by Canlar and Jackson was to investigate the effects of three different versions of the same exam (regular order, reverse order, and random order) on student performance. Subjects were 193 students enrolled in introductory financial accounting at a northeastern college. Final examination scores of the students were analyzed using one-way analysis of variance. The sum of squares for total and treatment were 81,806 and 3,255, respectively. Can one conclude, on the basis of these results, that question sequencing has an effect on final exam scores in introductory financial accounting? State appropriate hypotheses, construct an ANOVA table, and find the p value. Let $\alpha = 0.05$. What do you think are the implications of these results for accounting educators?

Source: Mehmet Canlar and William K. Jackson, "Alternative Test Question Sequencing in Introductory Financial Accounting," *Journal of Education for Business*, 67 (November/December 1991), 116–119.

SUGGESTIONS FOR FURTHER READING

The following books provide a general introduction to analysis of variance and experimental design and cover in more detail the topics discussed in this chapter, as well as additional topics.

Cochran, William G., and G. M. Cox (1968). *Experimental Designs*, 2nd ed. Wiley, New York.

Davies, Owen L., ed. (1978). *The Design and Analysis of Industrial Experiments*, 2nd ed. Longman Group, New York.

Finney, D. J. (1955). *Experimental Design and Its Statistical Basis*. University of Chicago Press, Chicago.

——— (1976). *An Introduction to the Theory of Experimental Design*. University of Chicago Press, Chicago.

Hicks, Charles R. (1982). *Fundamental Concepts in the Design of Experiments*, 3rd ed. Holt, Rinehart and Winston, New York.

Kirk, Roger E. (1968). *Experimental Design: Procedures for the Behavioral Sciences*. Brooks/Cole, Belmont, Calif.

Lee, Wayne (1975). *Experimental Design and Analysis*. Freeman, San Francisco.

Lindman, Harold R. (1974). *Analysis of Variance in Complex Experimental Designs*. Freeman, San Francisco.

Mendenhall, William (1968). *Introduction to Linear Models and the Design and Analysis of Experiments*. Wadsworth, Belmont, Calif.

Montgomery, Douglas C. (1976). *Design and Analysis of Experiments*. Wiley, New York.

Neter, John, and William Wasserman (1985). *Applied Linear Statistical Models*, 2nd ed. Richard D. Irwin, Inc., Homewood, Ill.

Winer, B. J. (1971). *Statistical Principles in Experimental Design*, 2nd ed. McGraw-Hill, New York.

A thorough discussion of the assumptions underlying analysis of variance and the consequences of their violation can be found in the following two papers.

Cochran, William G. (1947). "Some Consequences When the Assumptions for the Analysis of Variance Are Not Satisfied." *Biometrics* 3:22–38.

Eisenhart, Churchill (1947). "The Assumptions Underlying the Analysis of Variance," *Biometrics* 3:1–21.

An interesting and helpful graphical respresentation of the various sums of squares computed in analysis of variance is given in the following book.

Li, C. C. (1964). *Introduction to Experimental Statistics*. McGraw-Hill, New York.

The following references contain discussions of various multiple-comparisons procedures, including comparative studies and a bibliography.

Bancroft, T. A. (1968). *Topics in Intermediate Statistical Methods*, vol. I. Iowa State University Press, Ames.

Chen, Ta-chuan (1960). "Multiple Comparisons of Population Means." Unpublished master's thesis. Iowa State University, Ames.

Daniel, Wayne W. (1980). *Multiple Comparison Procedures: A Selected Bibliography*. Vance Bibliographies, Monticello, Ill.

Daniel, Wayne W., and Carol E. Coogler (1975). "Beyond Analysis of Variance, A Comparison of Some Multiple Comparison Procedures," *Physical Therapy* 55:144–150.

Gill, J. L. (1973). "Current Status of Multiple Comparisons of Means in Designed Experiments," *Journal of Dairy Science* 56:973–977.

McCall, Chester H., Jr. (1960). "Linear Contrasts, Part I," *Industrial Quality Control* 17 (July):19–21.

———— (1960). "Linear Contrasts, Part II," *Industrial Quality Control* 17 (August):12–16.

———— (1960). "Linear Contrasts, Part III," *Industrial Quality Control* 17 (Sept.):5–8.

Mead, R., and D. J. Pike (1975). "A Review of Response Surface Methodology from a Biometric Viewpoint," *Biometrics* 31:803–851.

Peterson, R. G. (1977). "The Use and Misuse of Multiple Comparison Procedures," *Agronomy Journal* 69:205–208.

Spjøtvoll, Emil, and Michael R. Stoline (1973). "An Extension of the *T* Method of Multiple Comparison to Include the Cases with Unequal Sample Sizes," *Journal of the American Statistical Association* 68:975–978.

The following two papers discuss the nonadditivity problem in analysis of variance. The one by Tukey gives a test that is widely used to detect a violation of the nonadditivity assumption.

Mandel, John (1971). "A New Analysis of Variance Model for Non-Additive Data," *Technometrics* 13:1–18.

Tukey, J. W. (1949). "One Degree of Freedom for Non-Additivity," *Biometrics* 5:232–242.

9

Simple Linear Regression and Correlation

Chapter Objectives: This chapter introduces you to two of the most widely used of all statistical techniques—regression analysis and correlation analysis. After studying this chapter and working the exercises, you should be able to

1. State and discuss applications of the simple linear regression and correlation models.
2. State the assumptions underlying the two methods of analysis.
3. Obtain an equation that you can use for prediction and estimation.
4. Perform hypothesis tests to determine whether you should conclude that two variables are linearly related.
5. Compute a measure of the strength of the correlation between two variables.
6. Perform a hypothesis test to determine whether you should conclude that two variables are correlated.
7. Construct a confidence interval for a population measure of correlation.
8. Use a computer software package to perform the calculations for regression analysis.

9.1 INTRODUCTION

In analyzing data generated by a business or industrial operation, we often want to know something about the relationship between two variables, X and Y. Is there a relationship between the sales of a certain product and the age of persons in the various market areas? Do employees who score high on a certain aptitude test perform well on the job? What is the nature of the relationship between the amount of a certain chemical in some material and its optical density? Between the price of a product and demand for that product? Between the hardness and the tensile strength of a certain metal? The list of pairs of variables with a relationship of potential interest is almost limitless.

One approach to studying such relationships is to use analysis of variance, discussed in Chapter 8. Now we show that we can also examine the nature of the relationships between variables such as those listed using *regression analysis* and *correlation analysis*. Although regression and correlation are related, they serve different purposes.

We use regression to predict and to estimate.

Regression analysis helps one determine the probable *form* of the relationship between variables. The objective of this method of analysis is usually to *predict* or *estimate* the value of one variable corresponding to a given value of another variable. The English scientist Sir Francis Galton (1822–1911) first proposed the ideas of regression in reports of his research in the area of heredity—first in sweet peas and later in human stature. Galton used first the word *reversion* and later the word *regression* to describe a tendency of adult offspring, even those with short or tall parents, to revert toward the average height of the general population.

Correlation measures the strength of a relationship.

Correlation analysis is concerned with measuring the *strength* of the relationship between variables. When we compute measures of correlation from a set of bivariate data, our interest focuses on the degree of *correlation* between the variables. The concepts and terminology of correlation analysis also originated with Galton, who first used the word *correlation* in 1888.

In this chapter, we limit our discussion of regression and correlation to studying the form and strength of the relationship between two variables. The order of presentation is as follows:

1. The regression model
2. The assumptions underlying simple linear regression
3. Obtaining the regression equation
4. Evaluating the regression equation
5. Using the regression equation
6. The correlation model
7. A measure of the strength of a relationship
8. Considerations in deciding between regression and correlation
9. Some precautions

In Chapter 10, we consider relationships among three or more variables.

9.2   THE SIMPLE LINEAR REGRESSION MODEL

The typical regression problem is like most problems in applied statistical inference. We have available for analysis a sample of observations from some real or hypothetical population. On the basis of our analysis of these data, we want to reach decisions about the population from which we presume the sample was drawn. In order to handle the analysis intelligently and interpret the results properly, we must understand the nature of the population from which the sample was drawn. We should know enough about the population to be able either to construct a mathematical model to represent it or determine whether it fits some established model reasonably well.

Suppose, for example, that we want to study the relationship between workers' aptitude for a certain job and their satisfaction in that job. After we observe that employees who have a greater aptitude for the job also seem to be better satisfied with the job, we might suspect that the relationship between the two variables is linear. If we can learn enough about this suspected relationship, we may be able to predict a prospective employee's level of job satisfaction on the basis of a knowledge of his or her level of aptitude for the job. The variable *aptitude* may be designated by X and the variable *job satisfaction* by Y. To obtain data on which to base our study of the relationship between the two variables, we would select a random sample of employees. We would give each of them two tests—one to measure aptitude for the job and one to measure level of job satisfaction.

Most statistical models that are of practical value do not conform perfectly to the real world. A model that fits the situation at hand perfectly is usually too complicated for practical use. On the other hand, an analysis that has forced the sample data into a model that is not applicable is worthless. Fortunately, we can get useful results from a model that falls somewhere between these two extremes.

Measurements are made on the unit *of association.*

The type of relationship between the two variables X and Y that is of concern here is a *linear* relationship. This implies that the relationship of interest has something to do with a straight line. The measurements that are available for analysis come in pairs, (x_1, y_1), (x_2, y_2), . . . , (x_n, y_n), where the measurements (x_i, y_i) are taken on the same entity, called the *unit of association*.

Two variables X and Y are linearly related if their relationship can be expressed by the following *simple linear model:*

(9.2.1)
$$y_i = \alpha + \beta x_i + e_i$$

where y_i is the value of the Y variable for a typical unit of association from the population, x_i is the value of the X variable for that same unit of association, α and β are parameters called the *regression constant* and the *regression coefficient*, respectively, and e_i is a random variable with a mean of 0 and a variance of σ^2. The error term is present for two reasons. (1) There are often other variables besides the one in the model that also affect Y. Since they are not individually specified in the model, their effect is contained in the error term. (2) In most instances, even though the relationship between X and Y is strong, the relationship is not exactly linear. This lack of precision in the relationship is reflected in the error term. If the relationship between X and Y were exactly linear and no other variables affected Y, the error term would be 0.

Note the similarity between the model of Equation 9.2.1 and the one-way analysis-of-variance model of Equation 8.2.6. The reason for this similarity is that regression analysis and analysis of variance are essentially the same. In fact, we can get the same results obtained in Chapter 8 through analysis of variance by using appropriate regression models, in which treatments, blocks, factors, and so on are identified as variables, either qualitative or quantitative. A further discussion of this point would be too complex for this text.

To understand the model of Equation 9.2.1, we must consider the assumptions underlying simple linear regression.

9.3 THE ASSUMPTIONS UNDERLYING SIMPLE LINEAR REGRESSION

As we have said, simple linear regression analysis is concerned with the relationship between two variables, X and Y. For reasons that will become apparent, the variable X is called the *independent variable*, and Y is called the *dependent variable*. In discussing the linear relationship between X and Y, given in Equation 9.2.1, we speak of the *regression of Y on X*.

REGRESSION ASSUMPTIONS

The following assumptions underlie the simple linear regression model of Equation 9.2.1:

1. Values of the independent variable X may be either "fixed" or random. That is, we may select the values of X in advance ("fixed"), so that as we collect the data we control the values of X. Or we may obtain the values of X without imposing any restrictions, in which case X is a random variable. When the X's are nonrandom, we refer to the regression model as the *classic regression model,* which is model I of Chapter 8. When X is a random variable, we have model II of Chapter 8. As Section 9.7 will show, this is the model required for correlation analysis.

2. The variable X is measured without error. From a practical point of view, this means that the magnitude of the measurement error in X is negligible.

3. For each value of X, there is a subpopulation of Y values. For the inferential procedures of interval estimation and hypothesis testing to be valid, these subpopulations must be normally distributed. To demonstrate inferential procedures, we assume in the example and exercises that follow that the Y values are normally distributed.

4. The variances of the subpopulations of Y are all equal.

5. The means of the subpopulations of Y all lie on the same straight line. This assumption is known as the *assumption of linearity*. It may be expressed symbolically as

(9.3.1)
$$\mu_{y|x} = \alpha + \beta x_i$$

where $\mu_{y|x}$ is the mean of the subpopulation of Y values assumed to exist for x_i, a particular value of X. When viewed geometrically, as in Figure 9.3.1, α and β represent the Y intercept and slope, respectively, of the line on which all the subpopulation means are assumed to lie.

When $\beta = 0$, the line is horizontal, and we say that there is no linear relationship between X and Y. Note that if $\beta = 0$, X vanishes from Equation 9.3.1, and X is of no value in making predictions and estimates about Y.

FIGURE 9.3.1   Representation of the simple linear regression model

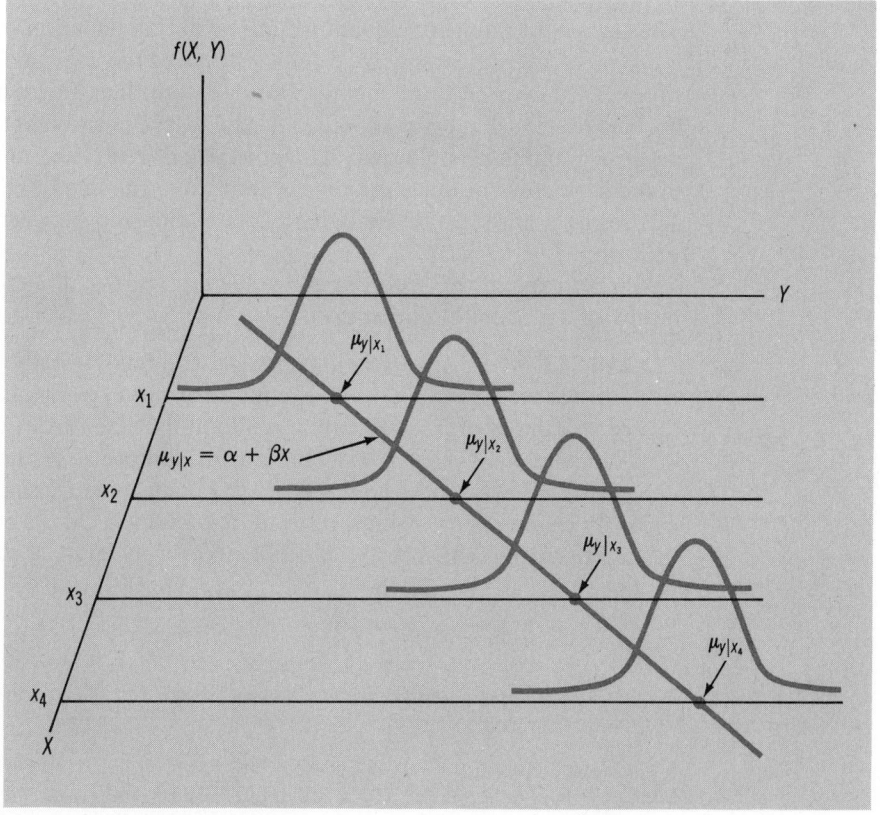

6. The Y values are statistically independent. This means that in drawing the sample, the values of Y observed at one value of X in no way depend on the values of Y observed at another value of X.

We are now in a position to shed some more light on the term e_i in the simple linear model. Solving Equation 9.2.1 for e_i, we have

(9.3.2)
$$e_i = y_i - (\alpha + \beta x_i)$$

Thus, e_i shows the amount by which y_i deviates from the mean of the subpopulation of Y values from which it is drawn, since, by Equation 9.3.1, $\mu_{y|x} = \alpha + \beta x_i$. The subpopulations of Y values are assumed to be normally distributed with equal variances. When this is the case, the e_i's for each subpopulation are also normally distributed, with a variance equal to σ^2, the common variance of the subpopulations of Y values. The e_i's are assumed to be independent, and their distribution has a mean of 0.

9.4 OBTAINING THE SAMPLE REGRESSION EQUATION

The regression model of Equation 9.2.1 is not an equation for a straight line. It is a symbolic representation of a typical value of the dependent variable Y. Equation 9.3.1, however, *is* an equation for a straight line. It is the line that describes the true relationship between X and $\mu_{y|x}$. The true position of this line is unknown because α and β are unknown. The objective of regression analysis is to estimate α and β in order to make inferences about the true line of regression of Y on X. The result is an equation describing the relationship between the sample values of X and Y.

We can explain the procedures involved in regression analysis more easily by means of a numerical illustration.

EXAMPLE 9.4.1   An operations analyst conducts a study to analyze the relationship between production and manufacturing expenses in the electronics industry. A sample of $n = 10$ firms, randomly selected from within the industry, yields the data in Table 9.4.1. "Manufacturing expenses" is considered to be the dependent variable and "production" the independent variable. Manufacturing expenses change as the volume of production varies. On the other hand, a change in manufacturing expenses would not necessarily cause a change in volume of production.

TABLE 9.4.1   Production (X) and manufacturing expenses (Y) for ten selected firms

X (thousands of units)	40	42	48	55	65	79	88	100	120	140
Y (thousands of dollars)	150	140	160	170	150	162	185	165	190	185

Note that X, as well as Y, is a random variable here, since we made no effort to collect sales figures only for firms with preselected values of the independent variable, production. In this example, we call the firm the *unit of association*.

> The *unit of association* is the entity on which we take measurements of the variables of interest. It is important that we preserve the pairwise identity of the measurements throughout the analysis.

A scatter diagram is helpful.

A good first step in a study of the relationship between two variables is to make a *scatter diagram,* a graph of the observed pairs of observations. We assign values of the independent variable X to the horizontal axis. We use the vertical axis to represent the dependent variable Y. We place a dot on the graph at the intersection of each pair of values of X and Y. Figure 9.4.1 shows the scatter diagram for these data. The pattern made by the points on the scatter diagram usually suggests the basic nature of the relationship between two variables. The points in Figure 9.4.1, for example, appear to be scattered around an invisible straight line. The scatter diagram also shows that, in general, firms with high production tend to have high manufacturing costs. These impressions suggest that the relationship between production and manufacturing expenses may be described by a straight line crossing the Y axis above the origin and making less than a 45-degree angle with the X axis.

FIGURE 9.4.1   Scatter diagram for Example 9.4.1

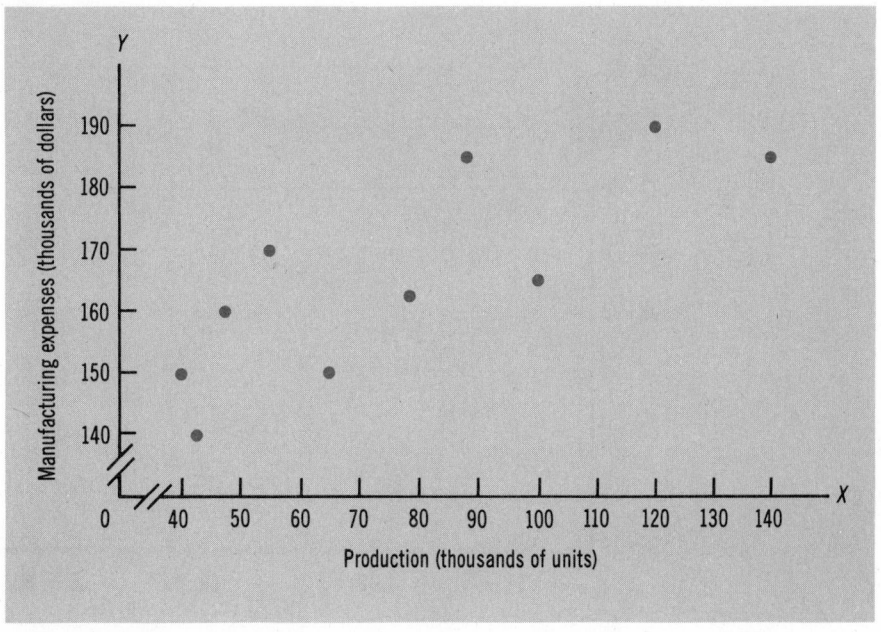

COMPUTER **ANALYSIS**

We may use either STAT+ or MINITAB to construct a scatter diagram. When we use STAT+ for this purpose, we merely make appropriate selections from the menus and respond to the prompts. Figure 9.4.2 shows the scatter diagram for Example 9.4.1 as constructed by STAT+. We note that the sample regression line is also plotted on the graph.

When we use MINITAB to construct a scatter diagram, we use the plot command. For Example 9.4.1, the procedure is as follows:

1. Store the observations on the dependent variable Y = manufacturing expenses in column 1. Store the observations on the independent variable X = production in column 2.
2. To obtain labels for the vertical and horizontal axes, we assign the name EXP to column 1 and the name PROD to column 2.
3. Finally, we use the appropriate plot command to instruct MINITAB to construct the scatter diagram.

Figure 9.4.3 illustrates the procedure, along with the resulting scatter diagram.

FIGURE 9.4.2   Computer-constructed scatter diagram for Example 9.4.1 (STAT+ printout)

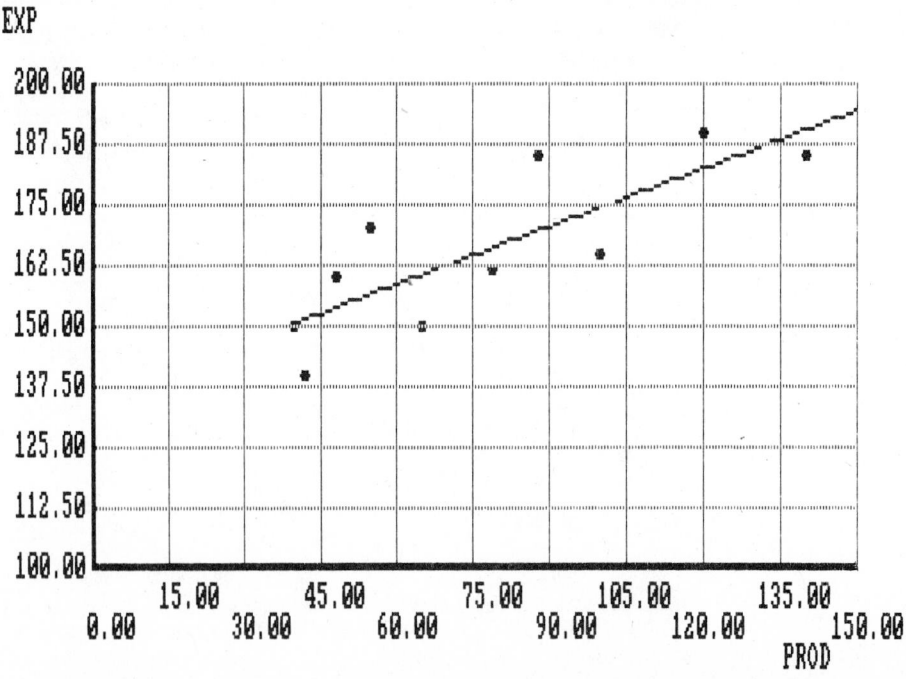

FIGURE 9.4.3   Computer constructed scatter diagram for Example 9.4.1 (MINITAB printout)

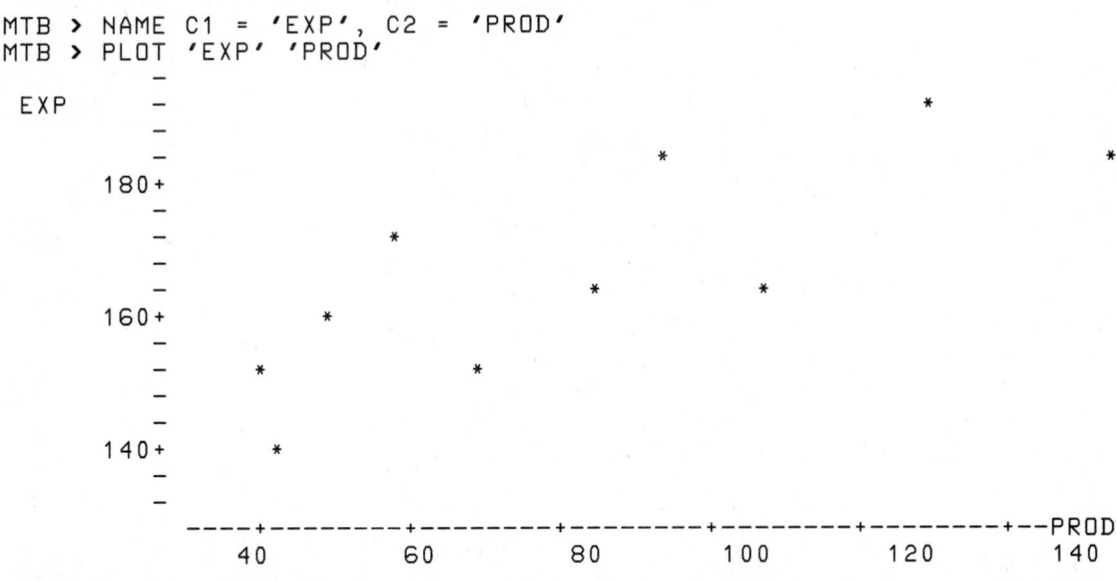

```
MTB > NAME C1 = 'EXP', C2 = 'PROD'
MTB > PLOT 'EXP' 'PROD'
           -
EXP        -                                                    *
           -
           -                                        *                        *
    180+
           -
           -                      *
           -
           -                                 *              *
    160+
           -              *
           -        *                  *
           -
           -
    140+        *
           -
           -
        ----+---------+---------+---------+---------+---------+--PROD
           40        60        80       100       120       140
```

We could draw a freehand line through the data. The question is, Would this be the best possible line for describing the relationship that exists? It probably would not be. Any such freehand line would be subjective and would reflect any defects in the vision or judgment of the person drawing it. We need some objective method of drawing a line that, by some criterion, we could call the *best line* to describe the relationship between the variables.

THE LEAST-SQUARES LINE

The objective method that we use here to find a line to describe the relationship between the variables is called the *method of least squares*.

The line obtained by the method of least squares is called the *least-squares line*.

We may write the equation for a straight line as

(9.4.1)
$$y = a + bx$$

Here a is the point at which the line crosses the Y axis and b is the amount by which Y changes for each unit change in X. We refer to a as the Y *intercept* and to b as the *slope* of the line. To draw a straight line for the sample data, then, we need only numerical values for a and b. Once we have these values, we can

FIGURE 9.4.4   A linear regression equation illustrating the geometrical interpretations of *a* and *b*

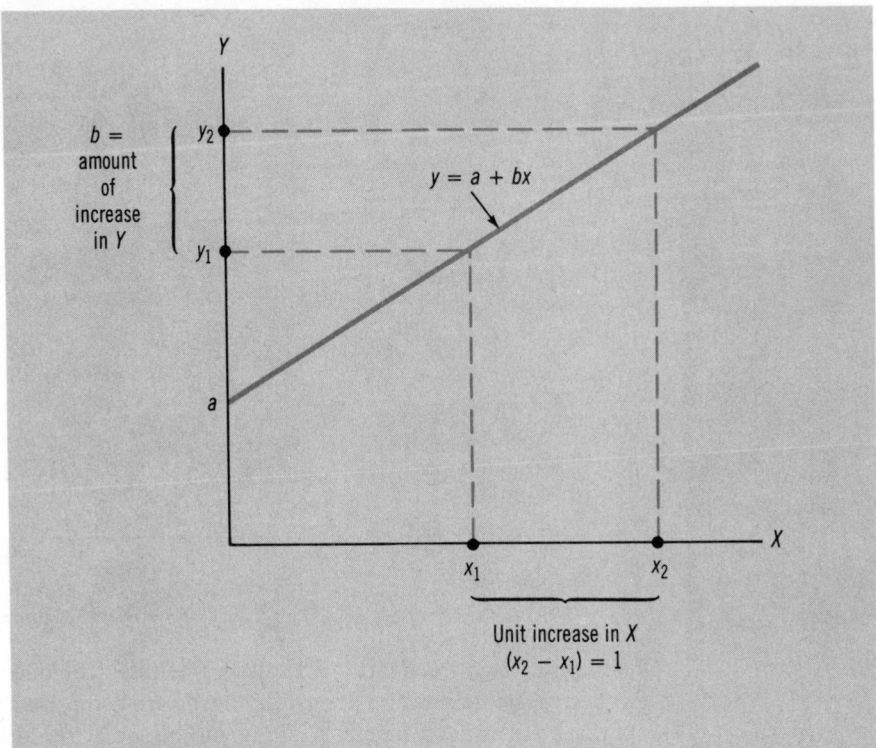

substitute two different values of X into the equation and get corresponding values of Y. If we plot the resulting coordinates (x_1, y_1) and (x_2, y_2) on the graph and connect them, we have a straight line.

Figure 9.4.4 is a graph of a straight line. Here we see the geometric relationships between the slope, the Y intercept, and a unit change in *x*.

THE MEANING OF THE SLOPE AND Y INTERCEPT

Examination of Figure 9.4.4 reveals that if *y* does not change when *x* changes by one unit, $b = 0$. That is, there is no slope and the line is horizontal. When such is the case in regression analysis, we say that there is no linear relationship between X and Y. If, when X increases by one unit, Y also increases, *b* is positive. In that case, as we emphasize again, we say that there is a *direct* linear relationship between X and Y. If, when X increases by one unit, Y decreases, *b* is negative, and we say that the relationship between X and Y is *inverse*.

The Y intercept may also be positive, negative, or zero. When the Y intercept is positive, as is the case in Figure 9.4.4, the regression line crosses the Y axis above the origin. When the Y intercept is negative, the regression line crosses the Y axis below the origin. When the Y intercept is zero, the regression line crosses the Y axis at the origin. We may also think of the Y intercept as the value of Y when $x = 0$. We may verify this by substituting 0 for x in any equation of the form 9.4.2 below.

As noted previously, a computer is particularly convenient for obtaining the numerical values of a and b, the y intercept and slope of a sample regression line. If a computer is not available, you can perform the calculations described in Section 9.11 to obtain a and b. The resulting equation is of the form

(9.4.2)
$$\hat{y}_i = a + bx_i$$

where $\hat{y}_i$ denotes the calculated value of Y for a given X, and a and b are estimates of α and β, respectively. We emphasize: a and b are the coefficients of the fitted sample regression line and are estimates of the parameters α and β of the population regression line specified in Equation 9.3.1.

The equation for the least-squares line that describes the relationship between the sample values of production and manufacturing expenses in the present example is

$$\hat{y}_i = 134.79 + 0.3978x$$

If we let $x_i = 0$, $\hat{y}_i = 134.79$. And if $x_i = 100$, $\hat{y}_i = 174.57$. These two points are sufficient for plotting the line, as we have done in Figure 9.4.5. This line is the sought-after "best" line for describing the relationship between the sample values of X and Y. Before we say by what criterion we judge it to be best, let us look at Figure 9.4.5. None of the points actually fall on the line that was drawn. That is, the points *deviate* from the line. It is obvious that we cannot draw a straight line that will pass through all the points. Some deviation of points from any straight line is inevitable. The line drawn through the points, therefore, is best in this sense:

> The sum of the squared deviations of the observed data points y_i from the least-squares line is smaller than the sum of the squared deviations of the data points from any other straight line that can be drawn through the data points.

Suppose that we square the vertical distance from each observed point y_i to the least-squares line and add these squared distances over all points. The total we get will be smaller than the similarly computed total for any other straight line that we could draw through the original points. This is why we call the line the *least-squares line*.

If, in our sample regression equation, we set x_i equal to $\bar{x}$, the mean of X, we find that $\hat{y}_i$ is equal to $\bar{y}$, the mean of Y. Hence we see that the plotted line passes through the point $(\bar{x}, \bar{y})$.

FIGURE 9.4.5   Scatter diagram and least-squares line for Example 9.4.1

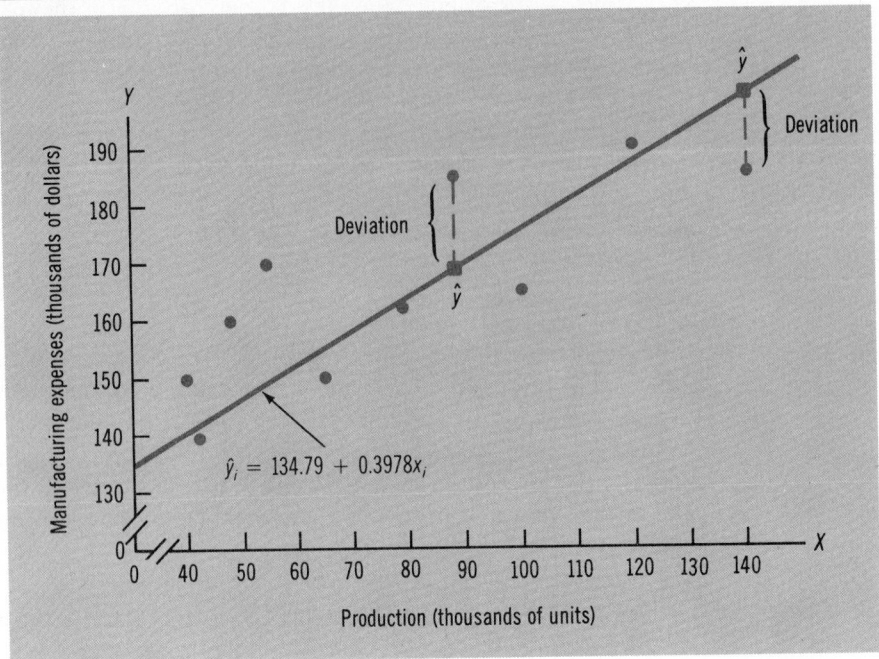

The least-squares formulas for computing the slope and Y intercept of the regression line can be derived by means of calculus. The resulting formulas, which can be evaluated by simple arithmetic, are given in Section 9.11. Those who use a computer to obtain numerical values of the slope and Y intercept, of course, enjoy the convenience of bypassing this exercise in arithmetic.

In summary, the method of least squares yields values of the slope and Y intercept of the line that best fits the data because the sum of the squared vertical distances of the observed values of Y from this line is smaller than any other similarly computed sum with respect to any other line.

The minimum sum of squares corresponding to the sample slope and Y intercept computed by the method of least squares is known by several names: *sum of squares about the regression line,* the *residual sum of squares,* and the *sum of squares due to error.*

EXERCISES

In these exercises,   (a) plot the data as a scatter diagram,   (b) obtain the least-squares regression equation, and   (c) draw the regression line on the scatter diagram.

9.4.1 ⓒ Emerson Office Supplies wants to expand. The head of the firm wants to know what sales volume can be expected in various market areas. Regression analysis, with sales as the dependent variable, is suggested. It is decided that effective buying income would be the best independent variable. A sample of 15 market areas in which the firm now does business gives the following results.

Amount of sales (Y) (× $100,000)	Effective buying income (X) (× $1,000,000)
0.5	11
2.3	69
9.4	168
1.1	22
2.9	38
2.5	30
3.0	51
3.4	61
5.8	83
6.1	91
6.8	101
6.9	124
7.2	159
11.4	176
14.3	201

$$\Sigma x_i = 1385 \qquad \Sigma y_i = 83.6 \qquad \Sigma x_i y_i = 10{,}917.6$$
$$\Sigma x_i^2 = 179{,}661 \qquad \Sigma y_i^2 = 681.32$$

In the regression equation $\hat{y}_i = a + bx_i$, what do the values of a and b mean to the executive in the context of this problem?

9.4.2 ⓒ An analyst is studying the relationship between shopping center traffic and a department store's daily sales. The analyst develops an index to measure the daily volume of traffic entering the shopping center, and an index of daily sales. The following table shows the index values for ten randomly selected days.

Traffic index (X):	71	82	111	85	89	110	111	121	129	132
Sales index (Y):	250	280	301	325	328	390	410	420	450	475

$$\Sigma x_i = 1041 \qquad \Sigma y_i = 3629 \qquad \Sigma x_i y_i = 390{,}918$$
$$\Sigma x_i^2 = 112{,}359 \qquad \Sigma y_i^2 = 1{,}369{,}435$$

In the regression equation $\hat{y}_i = a + bx_i$, what do the values of a and b mean to the shopping center manager in the context of this problem?

9.4.3 ⓒ The following data show the daily wages (X) and amount of monthly rent payments (Y) for a random sample of 15 unskilled workers who live alone.

(Y), $	120	130	135	138	142	149	155	158	160	169	170	175	182	190	195
(X), $	34	37	39	42	41	45	40	52	50	62	68	65	70	68	75

$$\Sigma x_i = 788 \quad \Sigma y_i = 2368 \quad \Sigma x_i y_i = 128{,}592 \quad \Sigma x_i^2 = 44{,}162 \quad \Sigma y_i^2 = 380{,}858$$

9.4.4   C The following table shows the hardness (in Brinell hardness numbers) and the tensile strength (in thousands of pounds per square inch) of ten specimens of a certain alloy.

Hardness (X)	20	30	40	50	60	70	80	90	100	25
Tensile strength (Y)	10	16	22	30	35	40	45	50	60	15

9.5 EVALUATING THE SAMPLE REGRESSION EQUATION

After we have determined the regression equation, we must evaluate it to find out whether it adequately describes the relationship between the two variables and to see whether we can use it effectively for prediction and estimation.

COMPUTER **ANALYSIS**

Both the STAT+ and MINITAB statistical software packages provide output containing the information necessary for evaluating a sample regression equation. With the observations on the dependent variable in column 1 and the observations on the independent variable in column 2, the MINITAB command for simple regression analysis is REGRESS C1 1 PREDICTOR C2. To obtain the maximum amount of output, type BRIEF 3 before entering the command.

The multiple regression program in STAT+ provides the maximum amount of regression-analysis output available from that package. Figure 9.5.1 shows the complete STAT+ multiple-regression output for Example 9.4.1. The various components of the output will be cited and explained in the discussion that follows.

Note in Figure 9.5.1 that the statistic beta appearing at the beginning of the printout is a standardized regression coefficient obtained by dividing the standard deviation of X by the standard deviation of Y and multiplying the result by the slope. For the present example, we have

$$\text{Beta} = \frac{32.45012}{15.98158}(0.397822) = 0.807766$$

Beta is not the same as the symbol β that is used to designate the slope coefficients in the population regression equation.

PARTITIONING THE TOTAL SUM OF SQUARES

One method of evaluating the regression equation is to compare the scatter of the points about the regression line with the scatter about $\bar{y}$, the mean of the

```
VariableI      B(I)       BETA(I)       XBAR(I)       S(I)
EXP      1    134.7892    N.D.          165.7000     15.98158
PROD     2    0.397822    0.807766      77.70000     32.45012

INDEX OF DETERMINATION (R-SQ) = 0.65249

CORRELATION COEFFICIENT (R) =    0.80777
           CORRELATION MATRIX
              EXP              PROD
EXP          1.0000           0.8078
PROD         0.8078           1.0000
                  ANALYSIS OF VARIANCE
   Source         SS        DF         MS          F
REGRESSION   1,666.524352    1    1,666.524352   15.021   **
ERROR          887.585754    8      110.948219
TOTAL        2,554.110107    9

STANDARD DEVIATION OF ERROR TERM   10.533196

**   SIGNIFICANT AT 1% LEVEL

                                                   95%
                                                Confidence
                                                  Limits
Variable  Coefficient STD Error  T Statistic    (+, -)
PROD     2   0.397822   0.10265    3.87565       0.23670

D.F.= 8

DURBIN-WATSON STATISTIC =     2.8666

ACTUAL VS CALCULATED
  Actual      Calculated      Residual       PCT Residual
 150.0000      150.7021       -0.7021      -0.4000
 140.0000      151.4978      -11.4978      -8.2000
 160.0000      153.8847        6.1153                     3.8000
 170.0000      156.6694       13.3306                     7.8000
 150.0000      160.6477      -10.6477      -7.0000
 162.0000      166.2172       -4.2172      -2.6000
 185.0000      169.7976       15.2024                     8.2000
 165.0000      174.5714       -9.5714      -5.8000
 190.0000      182.5279        7.4721                     3.9000
 185.0000      190.4843       -5.4843      -2.9000

CONFIDENCE INTERVALS ON EXP

 Enter observed value of X2, PROD         50

THE 95% CONFIDENCE LIMITS ON THE EXPECTED VALUE OF X1
(EXP) ARE:

X1= 154.6803 +/- 10.099        UPPER = 164.7792
LOWER = 144.5814

THE 95% PREDICTION LIMITS ON THE EXPECTED VALUE OF X1
(EXP) ARE:

X1= 154.6803 +/- 26.305        UPPER = 180.9857
LOWER = 128.3750
```

FIGURE 9.5.2 Scatter diagram for Example 9.4.1, showing deviations about $\bar{y}$ and the regression line

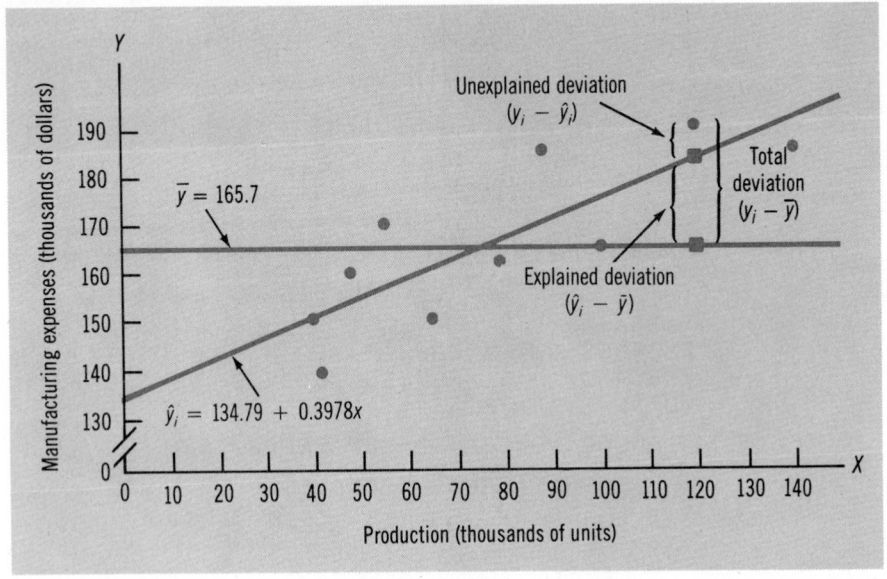

sample values of Y. Figure 9.5.2 shows the regression line and the relative magnitudes of the scatter of the points from $\bar{y}$ for Example 9.4.1. It shows the line representing $\bar{y}$ as a horizontal line. This is because, regardless of the value of X, $\bar{y}$ remains constant. For these data, the dispersion of the points about the regression line is much less than the dispersion about the $\bar{y}$ line. So it seems that the regression line provides a good fit for the data.

THE TOTAL DEVIATION

We get the amount by which any observed value of Y, y_i, deviates from $\bar{y}$ by measuring the vertical distance between y_i and $\bar{y}$, as shown in Figure 9.5.2.

The difference $y_i - \bar{y}$ is called the *total deviation*.

Consider, for example, the ninth value of Y. You will find it in Table 9.4.1 to be $y_9 = 190$. Since $\bar{y} = 165.7$, the total deviation of this Y value is $190 - 165.7 = 24.3$. Figure 9.5.3 shows the total deviation for each observation.

THE EXPLAINED DEVIATION

The vertical distance from the regression line to the $\bar{y}$ line, $\hat{y}_i - \bar{y}$, is called the *explained deviation*.

FIGURE 9.5.3   Total deviations $y_i - \bar{y}$ for Example 9.4.1

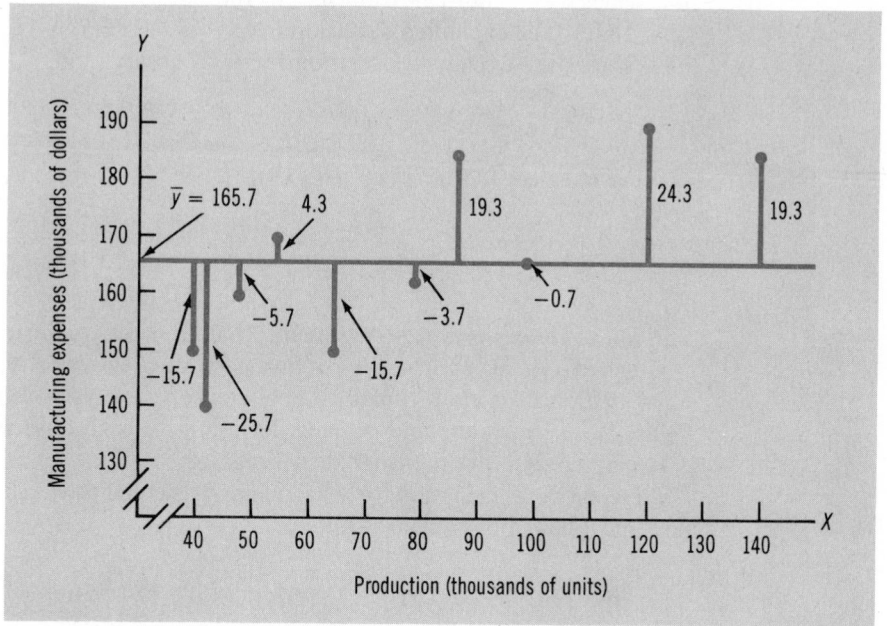

FIGURE 9.5.4   Explained deviations $\hat{y} - \bar{y}$ for Example 9.4.1

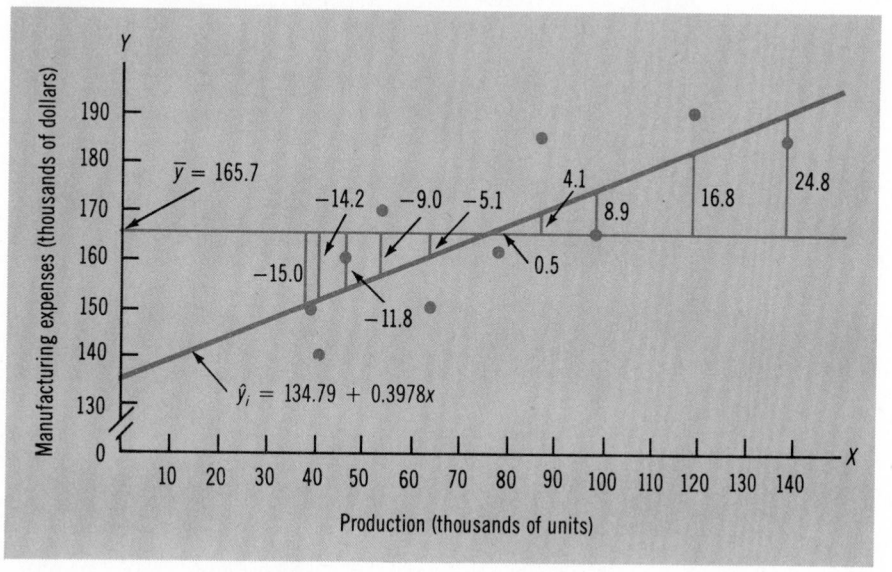

The *explained deviation* shows the amount by which we reduce the total deviation when we fit the regression line to the points. For example, for $y_9 = 190$, $\hat{y}_9 = 182.5$. The explained deviation is $\hat{y}_9 - \bar{y} = 182.5 - 165.7 = 16.8$. Figure 9.5.4 shows the explained deviation for each observation.

THE UNEXPLAINED DEVIATION

The vertical distance of the observed Y from the regression line, $y_i - \hat{y}_i$, is called the *unexplained deviation*.

The *unexplained deviation* represents that portion of the total deviation not "explained" or accounted for by fitting of the regression line. In the case of $y_9 = 190$, there is an unexplained deviation of $y_9 - \hat{y}_9 = 190 - 182.5 = 7.5$. Figure 9.5.5 shows the unexplained deviation for each observation.

Figure 9.5.2 shows the three deviations for y_9.

Thus, the total deviation for a particular y_i is equal to the sum of the explained and unexplained deviations. That is,

$$(9.5.1) \qquad (y_i - \bar{y}) = (\hat{y}_i - \bar{y}) + (y_i - \hat{y}_i)$$

$$\underset{\text{Total deviation}}{\phantom{(y_i - \bar{y})}} \qquad \underset{\text{Explained deviation}}{\phantom{(\hat{y}_i - \bar{y})}} \qquad \underset{\text{Unexplained deviation}}{\phantom{(y_i - \hat{y}_i)}}$$

FIGURE 9.5.5   Unexplained deviations $y_i - \hat{y}$ for Example 9.4.1

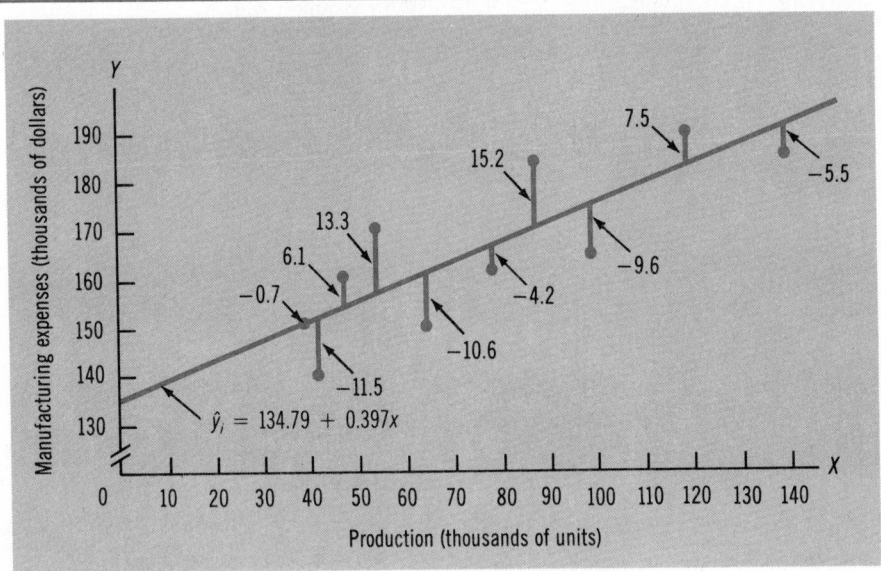

In the case of $y_9 = 190$, we have $24.3 = 16.8 + 7.5$. We can perform similar calculations for each y_i.

If we square each of the deviations in Equation 9.5.1 and sum for all observations, we get three sums of squared deviations. Their relationship may be expressed as follows:

(9.5.2)

$$\Sigma(y_i - \bar{y})^2 = \Sigma(\hat{y}_i - \bar{y})^2 + \Sigma(y_i - \hat{y}_i)^2$$

| Total sum | Explained sum | Unexplained sum |
| of squares | of squares | of squares |

THE TOTAL SUM OF SQUARES

Each of the terms in Equation 9.5.2 is a measure of dispersion.

> The *total sum of squares* measures the dispersion of the observed values of Y about their mean $\bar{y}$.

That is, the total sum of squares is a measure of the total variation in the observed value of Y. It is the numerator of the familiar formula for the sample variance.

THE EXPLAINED SUM OF SQUARES

> The *explained sum of squares* is a measure of the total variability in the observed values of Y that is accounted for by the linear relationship between the observed values of X and Y.

The explained sum of squares is sometimes referred to as the *sum of squares due to linear regression*.

THE UNEXPLAINED SUM OF SQUARES

> The *unexplained sum of squares* measures the dispersion of the observed Y values about the regression line.

The unexplained sum of squares is sometimes referred to as the *sum of squares of deviations from linearity*. The unexplained sum of squares is the quantity that we minimize when we find the least-squares line. It is usually called the *error sum of squares*. We may write Equation 9.5.2 in a more compact form as follows:

(9.5.3)

$$SST = SSR + SSE$$

where SST = total sum of squares

        SSR = sum of squares due to regression (explained sum of squares)

        SSE = error sum of squares (unexplained sum of squares)

CALCULATING THE SUMS OF SQUARES

If you need numerical values of the sums of squares, you can obtain them most conveniently with a computer. If you do not have access to a computer, you can use the formulas given in Section 9.11.

ANALYSIS OF VARIANCE

When the assumptions we gave in Section 9.3 hold, we may use analysis of variance to test for the presence of a linear relationship between X and Y. In this process, the total sum of squares $\Sigma(y_i - \bar{y})^2$ is a measure of the total *variability* present in the data. The explained sum of squares $\Sigma(\hat{y}_i - \bar{y})^2$ is a measure of the *variability due to linear regression*. And the unexplained sum of squares $\Sigma(y_i - \hat{y}_i)^2$ is a measure of *variability left unexplained* after regression has been considered. This last sum of squares is also called the *deviations from regression* or *error sum of squares*. We can also subdivide the total degrees of freedom $n - 1$ into two components, 1 for regression and $(n - 1) - 1 = n - 2$ associated with the error sum of squares.

We always have 1 degree of freedom for regression in simple linear regression analysis because we have only one independent variable. As we see in Chapter 10, when we are using multiple-regression analysis, we have more than 1 degree of freedom for regression because in multiple-regression analysis we have more than one independent variable. In fact, the number of degrees of freedom for regression is always equal to the number of independent variables in the regression equation.

Dividing the sums of squares by their associated degrees of freedom yields corresponding mean squares. If there is no linear regression (that is, if $\beta = 0$), and if the stated assumptions about the model apply, the ratio of the regression mean square to the error mean square is distributed as F with 1 and $n - 2$ degrees of freedom. Therefore, in the test of the hypothesis of no linear relationship between X and Y in the population, we obtain the critical value for the test from the table of the F distribution (Table G) in Appendix I. To obtain the critical value of F, we enter the table with our chosen level of significance and 1 and $n - 2$ degrees of freedom.

We can thus test the null hypothesis that $\beta = 0$ using analysis of variance. Table 9.5.1 shows the analysis-of-variance table that we can construct.

TABLE 9.5.1 ANOVA table for simple linear regression

Source of variation	SS	df	MS	F
Linear regression	SSR	1	MSR = SSR/1	MSR/MSE
Deviation from linearity (error)	SSE	$n - 2$	MSE = SSE/$(n - 2)$	
Total	SST	$n - 1$		

EXAMPLE 9.4.1 *continued* For the situation described in Example 9.4.1, we wish to test H_0: $\beta = 0$.

SOLUTION

1. *Hypotheses.*
   H_0: There is no linear regression between X and Y ($\beta = 0$).
   H_1: There is a linear regression of Y on X ($\beta \neq 0$).
2. *Test statistic.* The test statistic is $F = $ MSR/MSE, which, if H_0 is true and the assumptions are met, follows the F distribution with 1 and 8 degrees of freedom.
3. *Significance level.* Let $\alpha = 0.05$.
4. *Decision rule.* Reject H_0 if the computed value of F is ≥ 5.32.
5. *Calculations.* Table 9.5.2 shows the analysis-of-variance table that we can construct from the sample data. When we use a computer in regression analysis, the ANOVA table is usually part of the computer output. The ANOVA table produced by STAT+ is shown in Figure 9.5.1. When we use a calculator to perform regression analysis calculations, the formulas in Section 9.11 yield the sums of squares given in the table.
6. *Statistical decision.* Since $15.02 > 5.32$, we reject H_0.
7. *Conclusion.* We conclude that the data of this sample provide sufficient evidence of the presence of regression. Since $15.02 > 14.69$ (the value of $F_{0.995}$ for 1 and 8 degrees of freedom in Table G of Appendix I), we have, for this test, $p < 0.005$.

When we cannot reject H_0: $\beta = 0$, we cannot be certain that X and Y are unrelated. Aside from the fact that we may have committed a Type II error, we must be aware that, although they may not be linearly related, X and Y may

TABLE 9.5.2 Analysis of variance for Example 9.4.1

Source	SS	df	MS	F
Regression	1666.33	1	1666.33	15.02
Error	887.77	8	110.97	
Total	2554.10	9		

have a nonlinear relationship. Even when we can reject H_0: $\beta = 0$, we cannot be certain that the strongest form of relationship between X and Y is a linear one. The two variables may be more strongly related in a nonlinear way, although a linear model gives a satisfactory approximation to the true relationship. Of course, a rejected null hypothesis that $\beta = 0$ may very well indicate that there is a true linear relationship between X and Y. By using t as our test statistic, we may also test the null hypothesis that β is equal to any nonzero constant. A discussion of this procedure follows.

ANOTHER HYPOTHESIS TEST ABOUT β

An alternative way to evaluate the sample regression equation is to use b, the slope of the sample line, as a basis for testing the null hypothesis of no regression.

When the assumptions in Section 9.3 are met, a and b are unbiased point estimators, respectively, of α and β. When, under these assumptions, the subpopulations of Y values are normally distributed, the sampling distributions of a and b are each normal, with means and variances as follows:

(9.5.4)
$$\mu_a = \alpha$$

(9.5.5)
$$\sigma_a^2 = \frac{\sigma_{y|x}^2 \Sigma x_i^2}{n\Sigma(x_i - \bar{x})^2}$$

(9.5.6)
$$\mu_b = \beta$$

(9.5.7)
$$\sigma_b^2 = \frac{\sigma_{y|x}^2}{\Sigma(x_i - \bar{x})^2}$$

In Equations 9.5.5 and 9.5.7, $\sigma_{y|x}^2$ is the variance about the population regression line. We also call $\sigma_{y|x}^2$ the *unexplained variance of the population*. It is the common variance σ^2 of the subpopulations of Y as specified in the initial assumptions. The definitional equation for this quantity, for a finite population of size N, is

(9.5.8)
$$\sigma_{y|x}^2 = \frac{\Sigma_{i=1}^N(y_i - \mu_{y|x})^2}{N}$$

Variables may be related directly or inversely.

When the assumptions are met, then, we can construct confidence intervals for, and test hypotheses about, α and β in the usual way. In most cases, inferences about α are not of great interest. We have already discussed, in terms of sample results, the meaning of a positive slope, a negative slope, and a slope that is equal to 0. Here we wish to emphasize that these explanations of b may be extended to β, the slope of the population regression line, which is the parameter that the statistic b estimates.

The parameter β, however, *is* of great interest. If β = 0, the regression line is horizontal, and an increase or decrease in X is not associated with a predictable change in Y, since any change in X is just as likely to be accompanied by an increase in Y as by a decrease. In this situation, we conclude that X and Y are not linearly related.

A positive β indicates that, generally, Y tends to increase as X increases.

When β is positive in this situation, we say that there is a *direct linear relationship* between X and Y.

A negative β indicates that values of Y tend to decrease as values of X increase.

When β is negative, we say that there is an *inverse linear relationship* between X and Y.

Figure 9.5.6 illustrates these three situations.

We want to determine whether the sample data provide sufficient evidence to indicate that β is different from 0. Suppose that we can reject the null hypothesis that β = 0. Then we can conclude that β is not equal to 0 and therefore that there is a linear relationship between X and Y. Whether this suggested linear relationship is presumed to be direct or inverse depends on the sign of b, the estimate of β.

The test statistic, when $\sigma_{y|x}^2$ is known, is

(9.5.9)
$$z = \frac{b - \beta_0}{\sigma_b}$$

FIGURE 9.5.6   Scatter diagrams showing different types of linear relationships

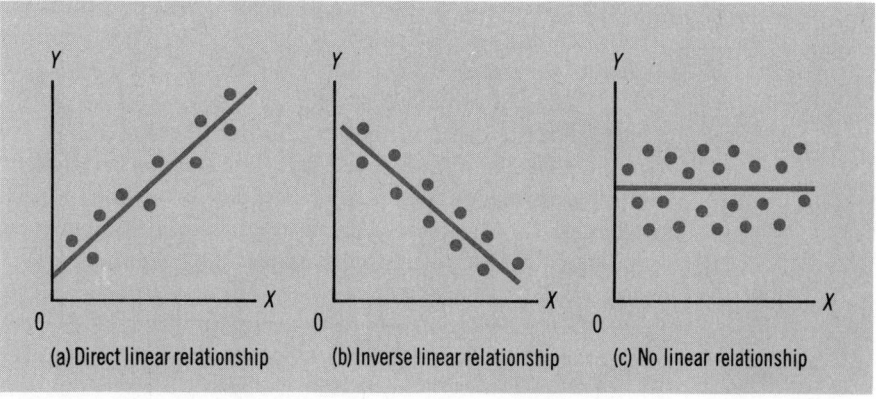

(a) Direct linear relationship   (b) Inverse linear relationship   (c) No linear relationship

In the usual case, $\sigma^2_{y|x}$ is unknown and the test statistic is

(9.5.10)
$$t = \frac{b - \beta_0}{s_b}$$

where s_b is the estimator of σ_b. The associated degrees of freedom are $n - 2$, the error degrees of freedom from the ANOVA table. Section 9.11 contains a formula for calculating s_b, the standard error of the sample slope coefficient.

EXAMPLE 9.4.1   *continued*   Let us now use the example of production and manufacturing expenses (Example 9.4.1) to show how to test the null hypothesis that $\beta = 0$ with the t statistic.

SOLUTION

1. *Hypotheses.*

$$H_0: \beta = 0, \qquad H_1: \beta \neq 0$$

2. *Test statistic.* The test statistic is t, as given by Equation 9.5.10. If H_0 is true and the assumptions are met, it follows the t distribution with 8 degrees of freedom.
3. *Significance level.* Let $\alpha = 0.05$ as before.
4. *Decision rule.* Reject H_0 if the computed t is ≤ -2.3060 or ≥ 2.3060.
5. *Calculations.* The sample slope b is 0.3978, and $s_b = 0.102$, as calculated in Section 9.11. The test statistic that we may compute, then, is

$$t = \frac{0.3978 - 0}{0.102} = 3.9$$

6. *Statistical decision.* We reject H_0, since $3.9 > 2.3060$.
7. *Conclusion.* We conclude that β is not 0 and that there is a linear relationship between X and Y. Since b is positive, we conclude that the relationship is direct, not inverse. Since $3.9 > 3.3554$, $p < 2(0.005) = 0.01$.

Note that the decision that results from testing $H_0: \beta = 0$ by means of the t test is the same as that reached using analysis of variance. In fact, the value of t computed from Equation 9.5.10 is equal to the square root of the F computed in the analysis of variance. (In practice, small differences may occur because of rounding.) The t statistic for Example 9.4.1 computed by STAT+ is shown in Figure 9.5.1.

We can use Equation 9.5.10 to test the null hypothesis that β is equal to some value other than 0. The hypothesized value for β, β_0, replaces 0 in the equation. All other quantities, computations, degrees of freedom, and methods of determining significance are the same as in the example.

A CONFIDENCE INTERVAL FOR β

Alternatively, we can test the null hypothesis that $\beta = 0$ by means of a confidence interval for β. We use the general formula for a confidence interval,

$$\text{Estimate} \pm (\text{reliability factor}) \times (\text{standard error})$$

When we construct a confidence interval for β, the estimator is b. The reliability factor is some value of z or t (depending on whether or not $\sigma^2_{y|x}$ is known). And the standard error of the estimator is

$$\sigma_b = \sqrt{\frac{\sigma^2_{y|x}}{\Sigma(x_i - \bar{x})^2}}$$

When $\sigma^2_{y|x}$ is unknown, we estimate σ_b by

$$s_b = \sqrt{\frac{s^2_{y|x}}{\Sigma(x_i - \bar{x})^2}}$$

Thus, in most practical cases, the $100(1 - \alpha)\%$ confidence interval for β is given by

(9.5.11)
$$b \pm t_{1-\alpha/2}s_b$$

If the confidence interval that we construct includes 0, we conclude that 0 is a candidate for β. Therefore, we cannot rule out the possibility that β is 0. This conclusion corresponds to the statistical decision of failing to reject H_0: $\beta = 0$. If, on the other hand, the interval does not contain 0, we reject the null hypothesis that $\beta = 0$. We conclude that X and Y are linearly related. The strength of this conclusion is related to the confidence coefficient selected in constructing the interval.

Let us construct a 95% confidence interval for β, using the data from Example 9.4.1. We can construct the following 95% confidence interval using Expression 9.5.11:

$$0.3978 \pm 2.306(0.102)$$
$$0.3978 \pm 0.2352, \quad 0.1626, 0.6330$$

We interpret this interval in the usual way. From the probabilistic point of view, we say that, if we were to draw samples of size 10 repeatedly from the population and compute a confidence interval for β, 95% of these intervals would, in the long run, include the parameter β. From a practical standpoint, we say that we are 95% confident that the single interval that we have constructed includes β.

The interval 0.1626 to 0.6330 does not include 0. We therefore conclude that

β is not 0 and that there is a linear relationship between X and Y. This is the same conclusion that we reached by means of the hypothesis tests described earlier. The three inferential procedures always lead to the same conclusion. The precision for our estimate of β for this example as calculated by STAT+ appears under the heading "95% CONFIDENCE LIMITS $(+, -)$" in Figure 9.5.1. The computed value of 0.23670 differs slightly from our value of 0.2352.

THE COEFFICIENT OF DETERMINATION

A frequently used measure of how well the least-squares line fits the observed data is the *coefficient of determination*. If you interpret this descriptive measure properly, it helps you decide whether the regression equation you have obtained is likely to be useful for prediction and estimation.

Let us define the sample coefficient of determination as

(9.5.12)
$$r^2 = \frac{\Sigma(\hat{y} - \bar{y})^2}{\Sigma(y_i - \bar{y})^2} = \frac{\text{SSR}}{\text{SST}}$$

A useful computing formula for r^2 is given by

(9.5.13)
$$r^2 = \frac{b^2\Sigma(x_i - \bar{x})^2}{\Sigma(y_i - \bar{y})^2} = \frac{b^2[\Sigma x_i^2 - (\Sigma x_i)^2/n]}{\Sigma y_i^2 - (\Sigma y_i)^2/n}$$

In words, we say that the coefficient of determination is equal to the ratio of the explained (or regression) sum of squares to the total sum of squares.

> The coefficient of determination shows what proportion of the total variation in Y is explained by the regression of Y on X.

Thus, since we compute r^2 from sample data, it measures a characteristic of these sample data, and it is not the measure of that characteristic for the total population of data. The population counterpart of r^2 is usually designated by ρ^2. Thus, we use r^2 to estimate ρ^2, the population coefficient of determination.

INTERPRETATIONS OF r^2

We can interpret the sample coefficient of determination in the following ways.

r^2 measures closeness of fit

1. We may interpret r^2 as a *measure of the closeness of fit of the regression equation to the sample data.* The better the fit of the *computed* regression line, the closer r^2 will be to 1. In other words, if the regression line provides a perfect fit, the total variation in Y is completely explained, and r^2 is exactly

equal to 1. If, in Equation 9.5.2, the unexplained sum of squares is 0, the total sum of squares and the explained sum of squares are equal. Figure 9.5.7a shows this situation. On the other hand, if the regression line is very close to the $\bar{y}$ line, it will explain a small proportion of the total variation in Y, and r^2 will approach 0. Figure 9.5.7b illustrates this concept.

r^2 measures relative reduction in SST

2. We may also think of r^2 as a *measure of the relative reduction in the total sum of squares achieved by fitting a regression line.* As we have implied, the relative reduction may be 0, 1, or any amount in between.

r^2 measures linearity

3. Finally, we may interpret r^2 as a *measure of the linearity of the data points.* When the regression line fits the data well, the data points are such that their scatter diagram gives the impression of a straight line. On the other hand, when the fit is not good, the points are so widely scattered that the diagram does not suggest a straight line. Figure 9.5.8a and b illustrates this. This interpretation requires that the points have a distribution and that $b \neq 0$. When all values of Y are the same, $b = 0$, y is a constant, the variables X and Y are unrelated, and $r^2 = 0$. In other words, if $y_i = \bar{y}$ for all y_i, then $\Sigma(y_i - \bar{y})^2$, the denominator of the formula for r^2, is equal to 0, and r^2 has no meaning. Figure 9.5.8c illustrates this.

> **EXAMPLE 9.4.1** *continued* Let us illustrate the calculation of r^2 using the data on production and manufacturing expenses in Example 9.4.1. *Table 9.11.1* gives the needed preliminary calculations.

> **SOLUTION** By Equation 9.5.13, we compute

$$r^2 = \frac{(0.3978)^2[70{,}903 - (777)^2/10]}{277{,}119 - (1657)^2/10} = 0.65$$

FIGURE 9.5.7 Scatter diagrams illustrating different values of r^2

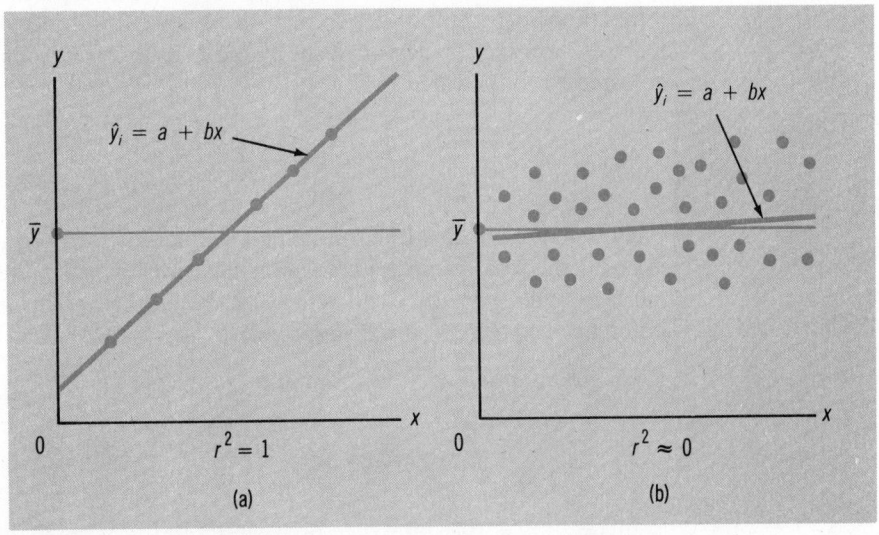

(a)   (b)

FIGURE 9.5.8   Scatter diagrams illustrating different degrees of closeness of fit of observed values of Y to a regression line

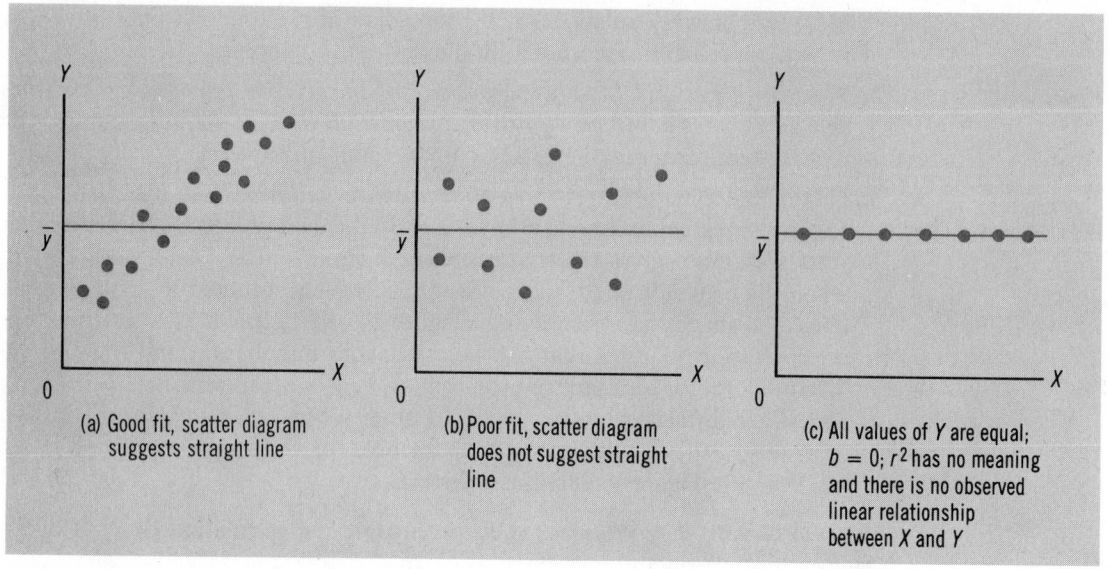

(a) Good fit, scatter diagram suggests straight line

(b) Poor fit, scatter diagram does not suggest straight line

(c) All values of Y are equal; $b = 0$; r^2 has no meaning and there is no observed linear relationship between X and Y

Thus, the regression of Y on X explains 65% of the total variability in Y. The coefficient of determination for this example computed by STAT+ appears in Figure 9.5.1 as "INDEX OF DETERMINATION (R-SQ) = 0.65249."

USING r^2 TO ESTIMATE ρ^2

The sample coefficient of determination provides a point estimator of ρ^2, the population coefficient of determination. When the number of degrees of freedom is small, however, r^2 is positively biased. An unbiased estimator, which we call adjusted r^2, is provided by

(9.5.14)
$$\tilde{r}^2 = 1 - \frac{\Sigma(y_i - \hat{y})^2/(n - 2)}{\Sigma(y_i - \bar{y})^2/(n - 1)}$$

The numerator of this fraction is the unexplained mean square, and the denominator is the total mean square. Thus, the difference between r^2 and $\tilde{r}^2$ is due to the factor $(n - 1)/(n - 2)$. When n is large, this factor approaches 1 and the difference between r^2 and $\tilde{r}^2$ approaches 0.

For the example, we may compute

$$\tilde{r}^2 = 1 - \frac{(887.77)/8}{(2554.10)/9} = 0.61$$

In this example, the difference between r^2 and $\tilde{r}^2$ is small.

RESIDUAL PLOTS

As noted in Section 9.3, for the valid use of inferential procedures in regression analysis, certain assumptions about the sampled population must be met. We may state these assumptions in terms of e_i of Equation 9.2.1. We refer to the e_i component of the model as the *error term*. The calculated residuals are estimates of the error term in the model. The residuals in a given application are the unexplained components of the individual total deviations. That is, $\hat{e}_i = y_i - \hat{y}$. Figure 9.5.5 graphs the residuals for Example 9.4.1.

If, then, we wish to determine whether or not the data satisfy the assumptions, we focus on the residuals. Succeeding chapters will present statistical tests that you can use to test the following assumptions:

1. The population e_i values are normally distributed with a mean of 0 (see Chapter 12)

2. The subpopulations of Y values for given X values all have the same variance, σ^2 (see Chapter 13)

3. The e_i are independent (see Chapter 13)

We may, however, use a simple technique to help us decide whether or not it appears likely that the assumptions are violated. The technique consists of plotting the residuals. We may plot the residuals in many ways. One way is to plot them against the independent variable X. That is, we plot values of X on the horizontal axis and the residuals on the vertical axis.

Residual plots provide clues about the nature and strength of the relationship between variables.

If a scatter diagram of sample residuals has a pattern that suggests a horizontal band centered on 0, this is taken as a lack of evidence that the assumptions are violated. Figure 9.5.9a shows a scatter diagram that is compatible with the assumptions. You must realize that we are not saying that such a scatter diagram indicates that the assumptions are met. Rather, we are saying that this particular plot does not indicate that they are violated.

As a first step in reaching a conclusion regarding the normality or lack of normality of the distribution of the dependent variable, we may plot the residuals as a histogram, as illustrated in Figure 9.5.10. An asymmetrical histogram suggests the possibility that the assumption of normality is violated. A symmetrical histogram suggests that the dependent variable may be normally distributed. You should not base a final conclusion on the histogram alone, however. An appropriate statistical test should also be employed. One such test is the chi-square goodness-of-fit test discussed in Chapter 12.

A scatter diagram that conforms to the pattern in Figure 9.5.9b suggests that the variances in the subpopulations are not all equal. This scatter diagram suggests that $\sigma^2_{y|x}$ increases as X increases. When the scatter diagram resembles Figure 9.5.9c, this indicates that the relationship between X and Y is curvilinear rather than linear. That is, Figure 9.5.10c suggests that the relationship between X and Y can be represented best by some kind of curved line rather than a straight line.

When error terms are correlated, the correlation is often due to a dependence between successive values. This type of correlation is called *autocorrelation* or *serial correlation*. If we suspect that the assumptions are violated because of

FIGURE 9.5.9 Some typical residual plots

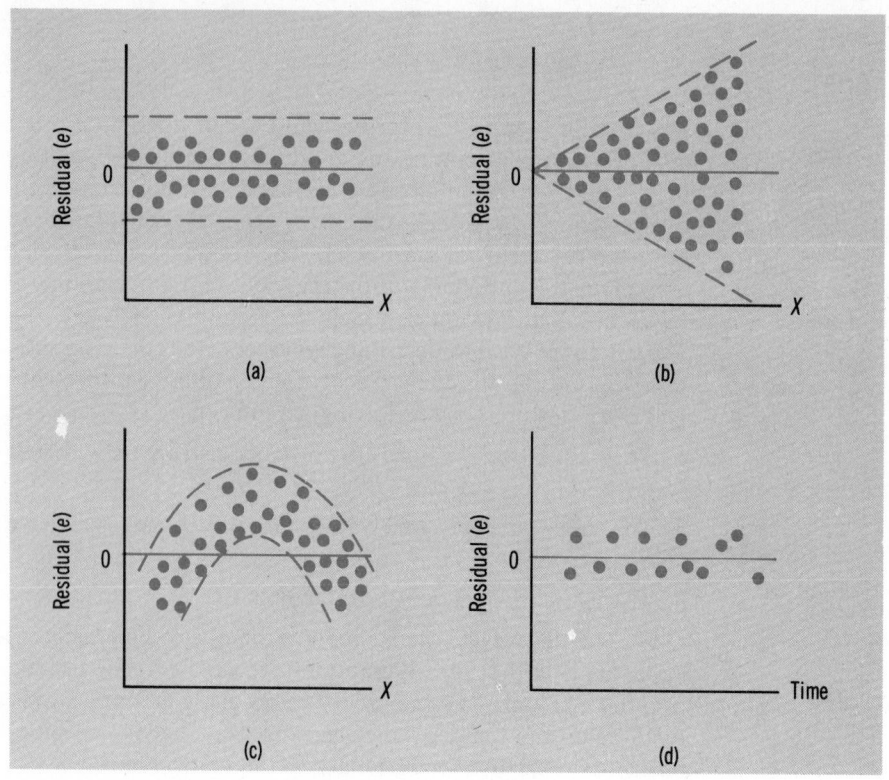

FIGURE 9.5.10 Histograms of residuals

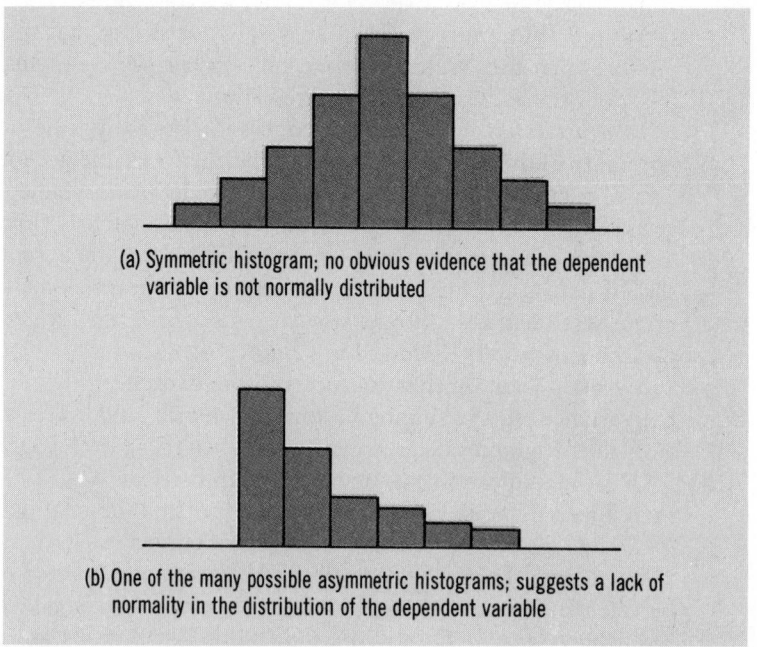

(a) Symmetric histogram; no obvious evidence that the dependent variable is not normally distributed

(b) One of the many possible asymmetric histograms; suggests a lack of normality in the distribution of the dependent variable

autocorrelation, a plot of the residuals against time may prove helpful. A scatter diagram resembling that of Figure 9.5.9d suggests the presence of autocorrelated error terms.

Suppose that when we examine the residuals, we doubt that our assumptions apply to the data at hand. Must we then discontinue the analysis? Not necessarily. Moderate departures from the assumption of normality do not invalidate the results, since the inferential procedures are not overly sensitive to violations of that assumption. When confronted by marked violations of the assumption of normality, as illustrated by Figure 9.5.10a, we should consider the use of an alternative method of analysis. Nonparametric regression analysis, described in Chapter 13, usually provides an appropriate alternative. Violations of the assumptions of equal variances and/or correlated error terms, however, usually call for some type of remedial action. Usually a proper transformation of the dependent variable Y solves the problems introduced by these violations. For a discussion of transformations, see Chapter 11.

To illustrate a plot of sample residuals, let us refer to the residuals of Example 9.4.1, which are shown in Figure 9.5.5. When we plot these residuals, we have the scatter diagram shown in Figure 9.5.11. This scatter diagram suggests that the subpopulation variances may not be equal, but tend to decrease as X increases.

FIGURE 9.5.11   Residual plot for Example 9.4.1

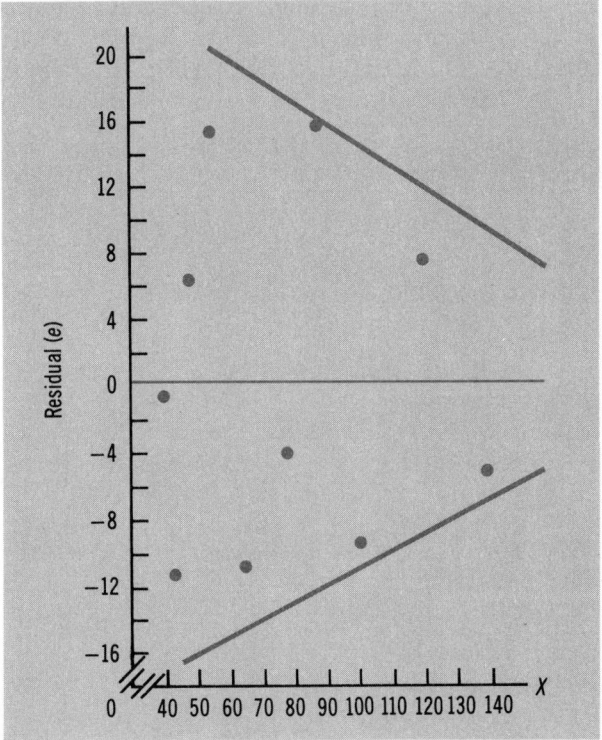

OUTLIERS

Residual plots provide a convenient means for detecting *outliers*.

> An *outlier* is a value of the dependent variable, which, in some way, is inconsistent with the other sample values of the dependent variable.

More specifically, we define an outlier as a dependent-variable observation whose actual value differs sufficiently from the predicted value to yield a residual that can be labeled as "unusually large" when compared with other such residuals. Points on a scatter diagram that appear to be a long distance from the bulk of the data points should be considered as potential outliers. The following example illustrates a situation in which a potential outlier is identified.

EXAMPLE 9.5.1   One of the data sets contained in the MINITAB software package is labeled TREES. It consists of the following three variables:

DIAMETER—diameter in inches at 4.5 feet above ground level
HEIGHT—height of tree in feet
VOLUME—volume of tree in cubic feet

The purpose of the data set is to provide data for developing a regression equation that can be used to predict the volume of a tree from a knowledge of its diameter and/or height. By means of the RETRIEVE command the data are retrieved and put in columns 1 (DIAMETER), 2 (HEIGHT), and 3 (VOLUME). The sample data for VOLUME and DIAMETER are shown in Table 9.5.3.

FIGURE 9.5.12   Computer generated scatter diagram for Example 9.5.1 (MINITAB printout)

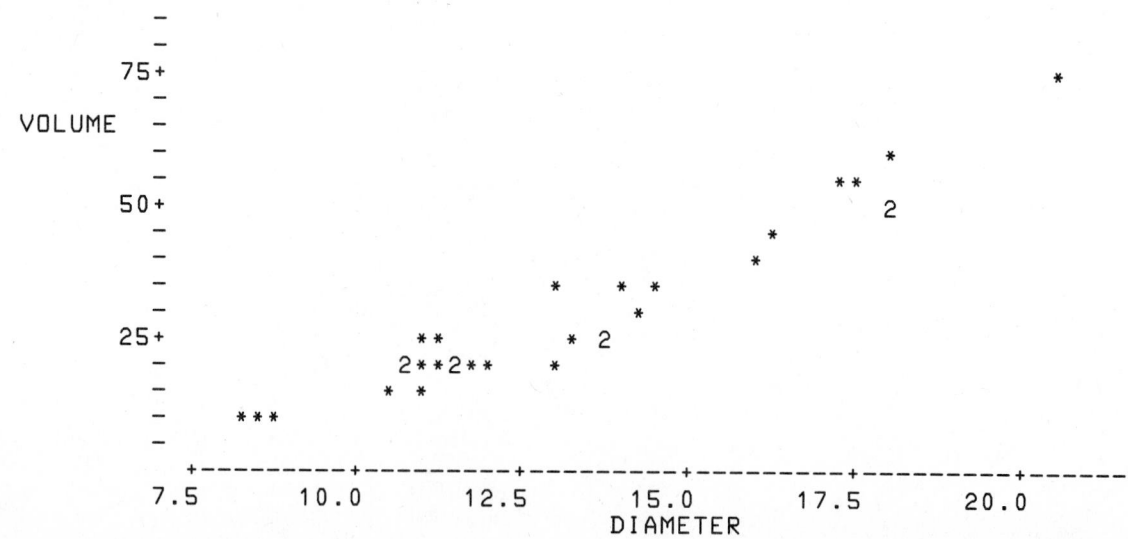

TABLE 9.5.3   Data for Example 9.5.1

Row	Volume	Diameter
1	10.3	8.3
2	10.3	8.6
3	10.2	8.8
4	16.4	10.5
5	18.8	10.7
6	19.7	10.8
7	15.6	11.0
8	18.2	11.0
9	22.6	11.1
10	19.9	11.2
11	24.2	11.3
12	21.0	11.4
13	21.4	11.4
14	21.3	11.7
15	19.1	12.0
16	22.2	12.9
17	33.8	12.9
18	27.4	13.3
19	25.7	13.7
20	24.9	13.8
21	34.5	14.0
22	31.7	14.2
23	36.3	14.5
24	38.3	16.0
25	42.6	16.3
26	55.4	17.3
27	55.7	17.5
28	58.3	17.9
29	51.5	18.0
30	51.0	18.0
31	77.0	20.6

Through the command PLOT C3 VS C1, we obtain the scatter diagram shown in Figure 9.5.12. We identify the point plotted in the upper right-hand corner of the scatter diagram as a possible outlier. The vertical distance between this point and its nearest neighbor is greater than the distance between any other two adjacent points. We note that this point is the one plotted for the last pair of data points and represents a tree with a volume of 77 and a diameter of 20.6.

INVESTIGATION OF OUTLIERS

Since outliers can affect the estimates and predictions for which we plan to use a regression equation, they should be thoroughly investigated. The following are the steps to be followed in the investigation of outliers:

1. Specify how large a residual has to be before it is to be labeled an outlier.

2. Identify any outliers that may be present in the data set being analyzed.

3. Determine, if possible, the cause of the outlier.

4. Decide whether an observation that has been labeled an outlier should be deleted from the data set prior to conducting any further analysis.

Different investigators use different criteria for labeling an observation an outlier. The MINITAB statistical package, for example, labels an observation an outlier if its standardized residual is either less than -2 or greater than $+2$.

We standardize a residual by dividing it by its estimated standard deviation. Suppose that we let $e_i = y_i - \hat{y}_i$, the residual associated with the ith observation on the dependent variable. The estimated standard deviation of e_i is

$$(9.5.15) \qquad s_{e_i} = s_{y|x} \sqrt{1 - \frac{1}{n} + \frac{(x_i - \bar{x})^2}{\sum_{i=1}^{n} (x_i - \bar{x})^2}}$$

where x_i is the ith value of x in the data set.

MINITAB routinely standardizes the residuals as part of the regression analysis. It automatically flags with the letter R those standardized residuals that are either less than -2 or greater than $+2$.

POSSIBLE CAUSES OF OUTLIERS

Once an observation has been identified as an outlier, we try to determine the reason for its being so labeled. The explanation may be as simple as an error made in recording a measurement. The person taking the observation may have made a measurement error. On the other hand, an outlier may indicate the presence of some previously unknown or unconsidered characteristic of the sampled population. It may be that for some reason the observation identified as an outlier really belongs to another population.

If an observation achieves outlier status as the result of a clerical error or measurement error, the error should be corrected if possible. If the error cannot be corrected, the offending observation should be deleted from the data set before further analyses are conducted. If an observation is identified as an outlier for some other reason, it should be given further consideration before a decision is made as to whether it should be kept or deleted. The investigator faced with this problem will find helpful the papers by Anscombe and by Anscombe and Tukey listed in the Suggestions for Further Reading at the end of this chapter.

| **EXAMPLE 9.5.1** | *continued* We continue our investigation of the observation in the TREES data that we identified as a potential outlier. By means of the following MINITAB commands, we obtain the regression analysis shown in Figure 9.5.13.

FIGURE 9.5.13   Computer-generated regression analysis for Example 9.5.1 (MINITAB printout)

```
The regression equation is
VOLUME = - 36.9 + 5.07 DIAMETER

Predictor      Coef       Stdev       t-ratio       p
Constant     -36.943      3.365       -10.98      0.000
DIAMETER      5.0659      0.2474       20.48      0.000

s = 4.252      R-sq = 93.5%      R-sq(adj) = 93.3%

Analysis of Variance

SOURCE        DF       SS       MS        F        p
Regression     1     7581.8   7581.8   419.36    0.000
Error         29      524.3    18.1
Total         30     8106.1

Unusual Observations
Obs. DIAMETER VOLUME  Fit    Stdev.Fit Residual St. Resid
  31    20.6   77.000 67.413   1.972     9.587    2.55RX

R denotes an obs. with a large st. resid.
X denotes an obs. whose X value gives it large
influence.
```

MINITAB

```
MTB > BRIEF 3
MTB > REGR C3 1 C1;
SUBC > HI C4;
SUBC > RESIDUALS C5.
```

The subcommand HI C4 will be explained later. The subcommand RESIDUALS C5 instructs MINITAB to store the residuals in column 5. We see in Figure 9.5.13 that the last observation is flagged with an R, indicating that it is indeed an outlier. We see that the standardized residual is 2.55.

By means of an appropriate plot command, we plot the residuals stored in column 5 against the DIAMETER observations stored in column 1. The graph is shown in Figure 9.5.14. We see in Figure 9.5.14 that the residual corresponding to an observed tree volume of 77 (the last observation in the data set) is conspicuous by its great distance from the rest of the residuals. This is compatible with our previous identification of the observation as an outlier.

INFLUENTIAL POINTS

You learned in Chapter 2 that the mean is influenced by extreme values, that is, values that are either much larger or much smaller than most of the other values in the data set. A similar situation exists in simple linear regression analysis. In simple linear regression analysis a value of the independent variable that is far removed from the other values of the independent variable has an undue influence on the slope of the line representing the relationship between the dependent

FIGURE 9.5.14 Computer-generated scatter diagram of residuals for Example 9.5.1 (MINITAB printout)

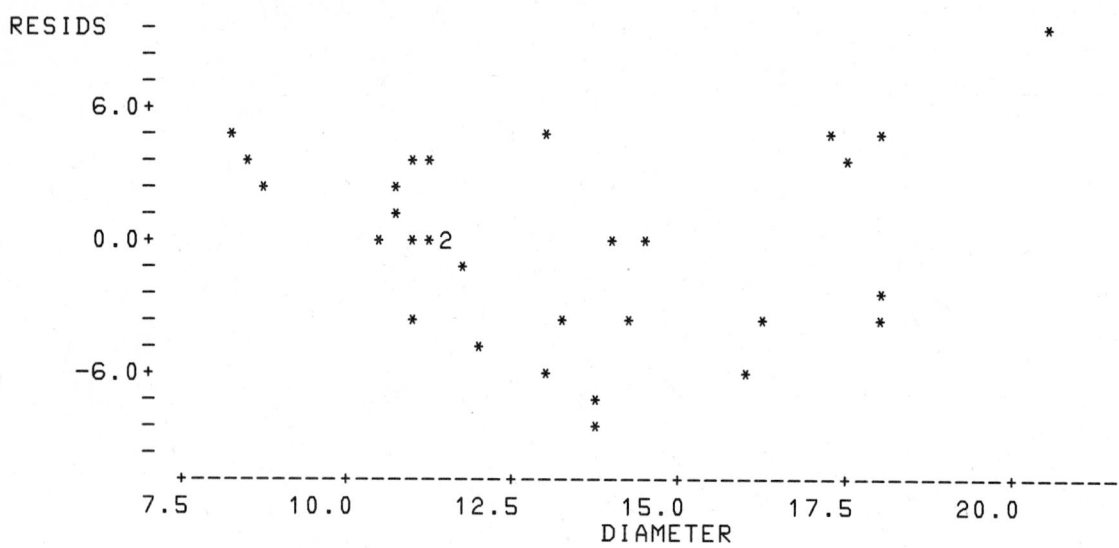

variable and the independent variable. In general, the greater the distance of a value of the independent variable from the mean of the independent-variable values, the greater is the influence of that value on the regression results.

> A value of the independent variable, X, that is located sufficiently far, according to some criterion, from the mean of the X values is called an *influential point* or a *high leverage point*.

Like outliers, potentially influential points need to be identified as part of the regression analysis. Usually, we can detect potentially influential points through inspection of the scatter diagram of our data. Points far removed horizontally from most of the data points are suspect. Some objective criterion should provide the basis for labeling an observation an influential point. The usual procedure consists of computing for each value of the independent variable a measure of the distance of the value from the mean of all the values of the independent variable. Any value of the independent variable whose computed distance measure is greater than some specified value is labeled an influential value. The MINITAB software package follows this procedure and flags influential points by printing an X beside the associated standardized residual value. In response to a subcommand under the REGRESS command, MINITAB stores the computed distances, called *leverages*, in a designated column. They can then be printed for closer scrutiny. MINITAB flags with an X any observation whose leverage value is greater than $3p/n$, where p is the number of variables under study and n is the sample size. The following example illustrates the identification and measurement of influential points.

EXAMPLE 9.5.2   Refer to Example 9.5.1, in which the objective is to develop a regression equation to predict the volume of a tree from a knowledge of its diameter. We wish to know if there are any influential points in the data of our independent variable.

SOLUTION   While we are inspecting the scatter diagram of Figure 9.5.12 for potential influential points, the point in the upper right-hand corner attracts our attention. Its horizontal distance from its closest neighbor is greater than the horizontal distance between any other two adjacent points. We consider this point a potentially influential point. We get the same impression when we inspect the residual plot of Figure 9.5.14.

Through the use of the subcommand HI C4, we instruct MINITAB to store the leverages in column 4. The printout of the regression analysis, shown in Figure 9.5.13, reveals that the last observation ($x = 20.6$) is flagged with an X, indicating that it is an influential point and confirming our prior suspicions. A printout of the leverages is shown in Table 9.5.3.

TABLE 9.5.3   Leverages for Example 9.5.2

0.115140	0.105395	0.099237	0.057826	0.054240	0.052549	0.049369
0.049369	0.047881	0.046460	0.045108	0.043822	0.043822	0.040373
0.037533	0.032669	0.032669	0.032267	0.032948	0.033288	0.034170
0.035323	0.037560	0.057886	0.063779	0.087822	0.093443	0.105497
0.108680	0.108680	0.215194				

EXERCISES

9.5.1   C Refer to Exercise 9.4.1.   (a) Compute the coefficient of determination.   (b) Prepare an ANOVA table and test the null hypothesis of no linear relationship between the two variables.   (c) Test the null hypothesis that $\beta = 0$ using a 0.05 level of significance.   (d) State your conclusions in terms of the problem.   (e) Construct the 95% confidence interval for β.   (f) Determine the p value for each test.   (g) Arrange the residuals in the order of their corresponding X values and sketch the relationship.

9.5.2   C Repeat steps (a) through (f) of Exercise 9.5.1 using the data of Exercise 9.4.2. Assume that the sample values were collected in the sequence 1, 2, 3, . . . , 10 (time = 1, 2, 3, . . . , 10) and sketch the residuals accordingly, with time as the independent variable.

9.5.3   C Repeat steps (a) through (f) of Exercise 9.5.1 using the data of Exercise 9.4.3.

9.5.4   C Repeat steps (a) through (f) of Exercise 9.5.1 using the data of Exercise 9.4.4.

9.5.5   Refer to Example 9.4.1. Calculate the explained, the unexplained, and the total deviations for $x = 88$. Locate and label these deviations on the scatter diagram in Figure 9.4.2.

9.5.6   C Refer to Exercise 9.4.1. Use the MINITAB software package to identify any outliers and influential points.

9.5.7   C Repeat Exercise 9.5.6 using the data of Exercise 9.4.2.

9.5.8   C Repeat Exercise 9.5.6 using the data of Exercise 9.4.3.

9.5.9   C Repeat Exercise 9.5.6 using the data of Exercise 9.4.4.

9.5.10   C The following are the measurements on the variables height and volume stored in the MINITAB worksheet TREES. Use the MINITAB software package to perform a regression analysis of these data to see how well you might be able to predict the volume of a tree from a knowledge of its height. Identify any outliers and influential points and compute the leverages.

Height	70	65	63	72	81	83	66	75	80	75	79	76	76	69	75	74
	85	86	71	64	78	80	74	72	77	81	82	80	80	80	87	
Volume	10.3	10.3	10.2	16.4	18.8	19.7	15.6	18.2	22.6	19.9	24.2	21.0	21.4	21.3	19.1	22.2
	33.8	27.4	25.7	24.9	34.5	31.7	36.3	38.3	42.6	55.4	55.7	58.3	51.5	51.0	77.0	

9.5.11   C The following are the midterm and final examination scores for 21 students enrolled in an elementary statistics course. Perform a regression analysis of these data to see how well you might be able to predict a student's final examination score from a knowledge of the student's midterm grade. Use the MINITAB software package to identify outliers and influential points. Compute the leverages.

Midterm	98	80	85	65	85	88	78	82	95	100	70	88	82	82	85	80	78	80	88	85	75
Final	91	91	91	58	73	97	85	85	88	100	79	73	81	67	88	76	55	79	91	79	79

9.6 USING THE SAMPLE REGRESSION EQUATION

Once we have decided that the data at hand provide sufficient evidence to indicate a linear relationship between X and Y, we can use the sample regression equation. We can use it in two ways. First, we can use it to *predict* what value Y is likely to assume for a given value of X. When the assumptions of Section 9.3 are met, we can construct a *prediction interval* for Y. Second, we can use it to *estimate* the mean of the subpopulation of Y values for a particular value of X. Again, if the assumptions of Section 9.3 are met, we can construct a confidence interval for the mean.

We make predictions about individual subjects.

When we use a regression equation to make an inference about the Y value of a single subject (or other entity), given the subject's X value, we call the procedure *predicting*.

For example, suppose that we have a regression equation that describes the relationship between the grade-point averages (Y) of college students and their scores on the Scholastic Aptitude Test (X). We may wish to use the equation and a student's SAT score to *predict* the student's grade-point average in college.

We make estimates about populations.

When we use a regression equation to make an inference about the mean Y score of a population of subjects, all of whom have the same X value, we call the procedure *estimating*.

We may, for example, want to use the regression equation describing the relationship between college students' grade-point averages and their SAT scores to estimate the mean grade-point average of a population of college-bound students, all of whom have the same SAT score.

For any given value of X, the predicted value of Y and the point estimate of the mean of the subpopulation of Y are numerically the same. However, the two intervals are not of the same width. This seems reasonable, since the estimate of the mean ought to be subject to less variation than the estimate of a single value. Most statistical software packages provide point estimates and point predictions, as well as prediction intervals and confidence intervals, for values of X supplied by the user.

PREDICTING Y FOR A GIVEN X

We get a point prediction of the value that Y is likely to assume when $X = x_p$ by substituting a particular value of X, x_p, into the sample regression equation and solving for $\hat{y}_i$. We may also construct a prediction interval. The interval is of the form

Predictor $\pm$ (reliability factor) $\times$ (standard error of the predictor)

in which the predictor is $\hat{y}$. Note the similarity of this interval to the general expression for a confidence interval.

If the assumptions of Section 9.3 are met and if $\sigma^2_{y|x}$ is unknown, the $100(1 - \alpha)\%$ prediction interval for Y is given by

(9.6.1)
$$\hat{y}_i \pm t_{1-\alpha/2} s_{\hat{y}}$$

where

$$s_{\hat{y}} = s_{y|x} \sqrt{1 + \frac{1}{n} + \frac{(x_p - \bar{x})^2}{\Sigma(x_i - \bar{x})^2}}$$

we can evaluate the denominator, $\Sigma(x_i - \bar{x})^2$, by means of the formula

$$\Sigma x_i^2 - \frac{(\Sigma x_i)^2}{n}$$

The degrees of freedom used in selecting t are $n - 2$.

EXAMPLE 9.4.1   *continued*   Suppose that, in Example 9.4.1, we wish to predict the manufacturing expenses for a firm that produces 50,000 units.

SOLUTION   Substituting $x_p = 50$ for x in the sample regression equation gives

$$\hat{y}_i = 134.79 + 0.3978(50) = 155$$

Where $\hat{y}_i$ is the point prediction of Y when $x_p = 50$.

Using Expression 9.6.1 and the data from Tables 9.11.1 and 9.5.2, we construct the following 95% prediction interval:

$$\$155 \pm 2.306(\sqrt{110.97})\sqrt{1 + \frac{1}{10} + \frac{(50 - 77.7)^2}{70{,}903 - (777)^2/10}}$$

$$\$155 \pm \$26, \quad \$129, \$181$$

Interpreting a prediction interval is like interpreting a confidence interval. If we repeatedly draw samples, do a regression analysis, and construct prediction intervals for manufacturing expenses for firms that produce 50,000 units, 95% of the intervals will include the manufacturing expenses. This is the probabilistic interpretation. The practical interpretation is that we are 95% confident that the single prediction interval constructed includes the true manufacturing expenses. Figure 9.5.1 shows the point prediction, the precision and the upper and lower prediction limits for this example as computed by STAT+.

ESTIMATING THE MEAN OF Y FOR A GIVEN X

To estimate the mean $\mu_{y|x}$ of a subpopulation of Y values when $X = x_p$, we substitute x_p into the sample regression equation and solve for $\hat{y}_i$.

To obtain a confidence interval for $\mu_{y|x}$, we use the general expression for a confidence interval,

$$\text{Estimate} \pm (\text{reliability factor}) \times (\text{standard error})$$

where the estimator is $\hat{\mu}_{y|x}$.

The $100(1 - \alpha)\%$ confidence interval for $\mu_{y|x}$, when $\sigma^2_{y|x}$ is unknown and the assumptions of Section 9.3 are met, is given by

(9.6.2)
$$\hat{\mu}_{y|x} \pm t_{1-\alpha/2} s_{\hat{\mu}_{y|x}}$$

where

$$s_{\hat{\mu}_{y|x}} = s_{y|x}\sqrt{\frac{1}{n} + \frac{(x_p - \bar{x})^2}{\Sigma(x_i - \bar{x})^2}}$$

EXAMPLE 9.4.1 *continued* Suppose that, for the example of the production and manufacturing expenses, we wish to estimate the mean of the subpopulation of Y values for firms that produce 50,000 units.

SOLUTION We obtain the point estimate as follows:

$$\hat{\mu}_{y|x} = 134.79 + 0.3978(50) = 155$$

$\hat{\mu}_{y|x}$ is the point estimate of the mean of the population of Y values when $x_p = 50$.

TABLE 9.6.1   95% confidence limits, selected values of X, Example 9.4.1

X	40.0	50.0	60.0	77.7	100.0	120.0	140.0
Lower limit	139	145	150	158	166	170	173
Upper limit	163	165	168	174	184	196	207

Using Expression 9.6.2, we obtain the 95% confidence interval for $\mu_{y|x}$:

$$\$155 \pm 2.306(\sqrt{110.97})\sqrt{\frac{1}{10} + \frac{(50 - 77.7)^2}{70,903 - (777)^2/10}}$$

$$\$155 \pm \$10, \qquad \$145, \$165$$

If we repeatedly drew samples of size 10 from the population, performed a regression analysis, and constructed confidence intervals for $\mu_{y|x}$ for $X = 50$, 95% of such intervals would include the true mean. Thus, we are 95% confident that the single interval constructed contains the true mean. Figure 9.5.1 shows the point estimate, the precision, and the upper and lower confidence limits for this example as computed by STAT+.

CONSTRUCTING A CONFIDENCE BAND FOR $\mu_{y|x}$

Suppose that we construct confidence intervals for several subpopulation means and plot the upper and lower limits on the same scatter diagram with the regression line. We may construct a *confidence band* by connecting all the upper limits with one curve and all the lower limits with another curve. Table 9.6.1 gives the upper and lower 95% confidence limits for $\mu_{y|x}$ for selected values of X in the example of production versus manufacturing expenses. Figure 9.6.1 shows the 95% confidence band that results when we plot these values.

Note that the confidence band of Figure 9.6.1 is wider at the ends than in the middle. In fact, the band is narrowest for $x_p = \bar{x}$, since the quantity under the radical of Expression 9.6.2 is smallest when we use the mean of the X values as the particular value of X. As x_p increases or decreases, the quantity under the radical becomes larger and the corresponding intervals become wider. We can construct *prediction bands,* using prediction intervals, in a similar manner.

COMPUTER **ANALYSIS**

The regression analysis printout available with STAT+ is illustrated in Figure 9.5.1, which shows the analysis for Example 9.4.1. By way of contrast, Figure 9.6.2 shows the MINITAB printout for the same example. The MINITAB instructions for producing the printout are as follows:

MINITAB

```
MTB > NAME C1 = 'EXP' C2 = 'PROD'
MTB > BRIEF 3
MTB > REGRESS 'EXP' ON 1 PREDICTOR 'PROD';
SUBC> PREDICT 50.
```

EXERCISES

In each of these exercises, construct (a) the 95% confidence interval and (b) the 95% prediction interval using the indicated value of X to obtain $\hat{y}$.

9.6.1 Refer to Exercise 9.4.1 and let $X = 50$.

9.6.2 Refer to Exercise 9.4.2 and let $X = 100$.

9.6.3 Refer to Exercise 9.4.3 and let $X = 60$.

9.6.4 Refer to Exercise 9.4.4 and let $X = 75$.

9.6.5 Construct the 95% confidence band for Exercise 9.4.4.

9.6.6 Refer to Figure 9.6.2, which contains the MINITAB regression analysis for Example 9.4.1. Identify the following entries and compare them with the corresponding entry on the STAT+ printout shown in Figure 9.5.1: (a) y-intercept, (b) slope, (c) predicted y for $x = 50$, (d) the 95% prediction limits on y for $x = 50$, (e) the 95% confidence limits for the mean y value when $x = 50$.

FIGURE 9.6.1 Regression line and 95% confidence band for Example 9.4.1

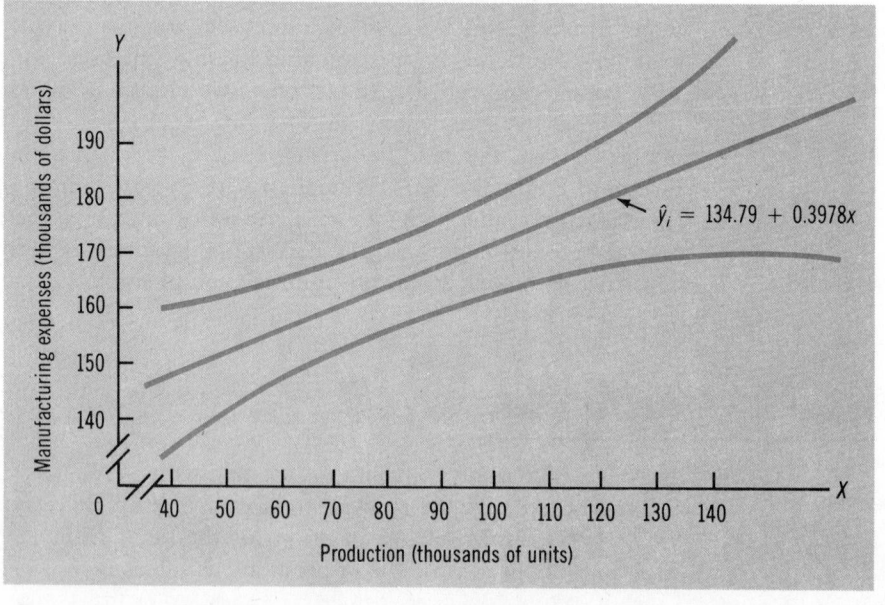

FIGURE 9.6.2   Computer generated regression analysis for Example 9.4.1 (MINITAB printout)

```
The regression equation is
EXP = 135 + 0.398 PROD
Predictor        Coef        Stdev        t-ratio         p
Constant      134.789        8.643         15.59       0.000
PROD           0.3978       0.1026          3.88       0.005
s = 10.53     R-sq = 65.2%      R-sq(adj) = 60.9%
                    ANALYSIS OF VARIANCE
   Source         DF          SS          MS          F           p
Regression        1        1666.5      1666.5      15.02       0.005
Error             8         887.6       110.9
Total             9        2554.1
Obs.     PROD       EXP         Fit      Stdev.Fit     Residual     St.Resid
  1       40      150.00      150.70       5.11         -0.70        -0.08
  2       42      140.00      151.50       4.95        -11.50        -1.24
  3       48      160.00      153.88       4.52          6.12         0.64
  4       55      170.00      156.67       4.06         13.33         1.37
  5       65      150.00      160.65       3.58        -10.65        -1.07
  6       79      162.00      166.22       3.33         -4.22        -0.42
  7       88      185.00      169.80       3.49         15.20         1.53
  8      100      165.00      174.57       4.04         -9.57        -0.98
  9      120      190.00      182.53       5.47          7.47         0.83
 10      140      185.00      190.48       7.21         -5.48        -0.71
  Fit          Stdev.Fit          95% C.I.                  95% P.I.
154.68           4.38        ( 144.58, 164.78)        ( 128.37, 180.99)
```

9.7 THE LINEAR CORRELATION MODEL

The classic regression model requires that only Y be a random variable. The variable X under this model is nonrandom. We have pointed out, however, that we can perform a regression analysis when X is random. For the *correlation model,* which is the model we assume when we want to obtain a measure of the strength of the correlation between two variables, both X and Y must be random variables.

For correlation analysis, both X and Y must be random variables.

When we choose correlation analysis, we obtain sample observations by selecting a random sample of units of association and taking a measurement of both X and Y on each. In this procedure, values of X are not selected in advance but occur at random, depending on the unit of association randomly selected in the sample.

In regression analysis, you will recall, one variable is referred to as the dependent variable and the other as the independent variable. Correlation analysis involving two variables implies that both variables have equal status. It does not distinguish between them on the basis of dependence and independence. In fact, we can fit a straight line to the data by minimizing either $\Sigma(y_i - \hat{y}_i)^2$ or $\Sigma(x_i - \hat{x}_i)^2$. In other words, we may do a regression of X on Y or Y on X. The fitted lines in the two cases, in general, will be different. Thus, a logical question arises as to which line to fit.

If our objective is only to measure the strength of the relationship between the two variables, it does not matter which line we fit, since the computed measure of correlation will be the same in either case. If, however, we wish to use the equation describing the relationship between the two variables for estimation and prediction, which line we fit does make a difference. We should treat the variable for which we wish to estimate means or make predictions as the dependent variable. That is, we should regress this variable on the other variable.

Figure 9.7.1 shows a scatter diagram of sample data from a bivariate population and the two regression lines that we can obtain from the data.

Sampling from a bivariate normal distribution is necessary for valid inferences about correlation.

Under the correlation model, X and Y vary together in a *joint distribution*. If the form of the joint distribution of X and Y is normal, the joint distribution is called a *bivariate normal distribution*. When we sample from a bivariate normal distribution, we can make inferences about the population on the basis of our analysis of the sample. If, on the other hand, the joint distribution of the population is not normal, we cannot make inferences about it. However, we can compute descriptive measures of correlation for the sample.

ASSUMPTIONS FOR INFERENCES ABOUT CORRELATION

When sampling is from a bivariate distribution, the following assumptions are necessary if inferences about the population are to be valid.

1. For each value of X, there is a normally distributed subpopulation of Y values.

2. For each value of Y, there is a normally distributed subpopulation of X values.

3. The joint distribution of X and Y is a normal distribution called the bivariate normal distribution.

FIGURE 9.7.1   Scatter diagram of sample data from a bivariate distribution, showing regression lines of Y on X and X on Y

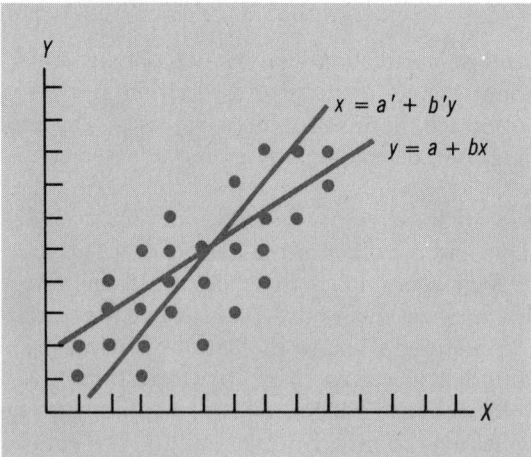

FIGURE 9.7.2   Three views of a bivariate normal distribution

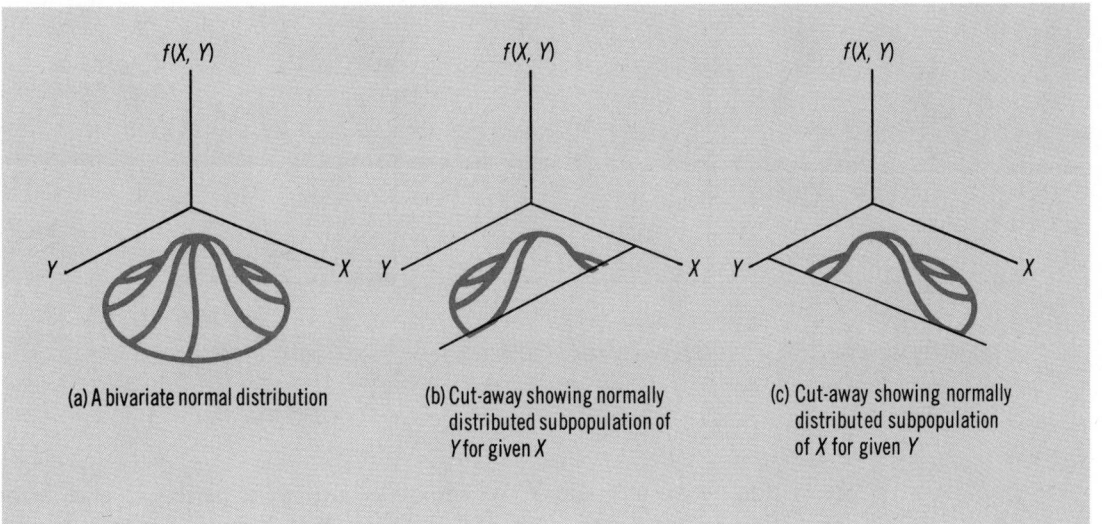

(a) A bivariate normal distribution

(b) Cut-away showing normally distributed subpopulation of Y for given X

(c) Cut-away showing normally distributed subpopulation of X for given Y

Figure 9.7.2 is a graph of the bivariate normal distribution. It shows that if we slice the mound parallel to Y at some value of X we will see the corresponding normal distribution of Y. Similarly, a slice through the mound parallel to X at some value of Y reveals the corresponding normally distributed subpopulation of X.

9.8   THE CORRELATION COEFFICIENT

The bivariate normal distribution discussed in Section 9.7 has five parameters: σ_x, σ_y, μ_x, μ_y, and ρ. The first four of these are, respectively, the standard deviations and means associated with the individual distributions. The other parameter, ρ, is called the population *correlation coefficient*.

The *correlation coefficient* measures the strength of the linear relationship between X and Y.

The population correlation coefficient is the square root of ρ^2, the population coefficient of determination, which we discussed in Section 9.5.

IMPORTANT PROPERTIES OF THE CORRELATION COEFFICIENT

1. Since ρ^2 can assume values between 0 and 1, inclusive, ρ can take on values between -1 and $+1$, inclusive. When $\rho = +1$, there is perfect direct linear

FIGURE 9.8.1   Scatter diagrams illustrating different values of the sample correlation coefficient

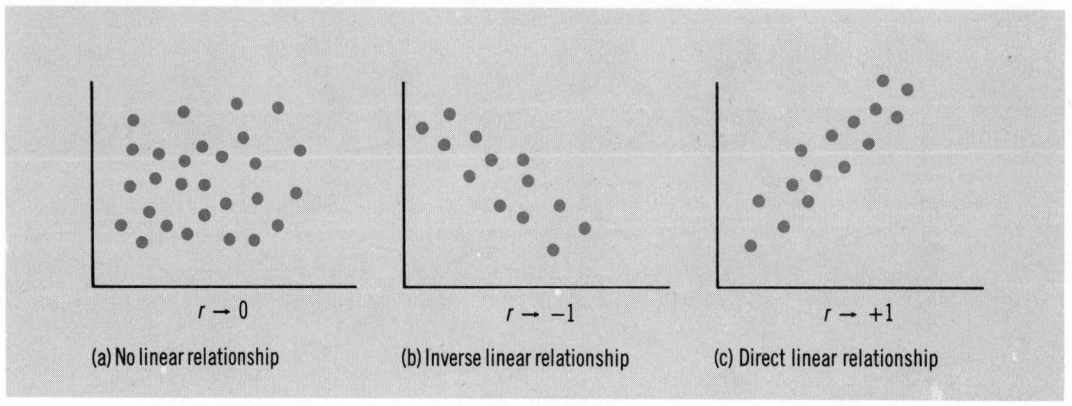

(a) No linear relationship   (b) Inverse linear relationship   (c) Direct linear relationship

correlation between X and Y. When $\rho = -1$, there is perfect inverse linear correlation between them. A ρ of 0 indicates that X and Y are not linearly correlated.

2. The sign of ρ is always the same as the sign of β, the slope of the regression line for X and Y. Similarly, for the sample, r and b always have the same sign. The sample correlation coefficient r, the square root of the sample coefficient of determination, measures the strength of the relationship between the sample observations on two variables in the same way that ρ describes the relationship in a population. The scatter diagrams in Figure 9.8.1 represent situations in which r is approaching 0, -1, and $+1$, respectively.

3. The correlation coefficient is a dimensionless measure. That is, the correlation coefficient is independent of the units of measurement of X and Y.

r and b always have the same sign

A HYPOTHESIS TEST FOR ρ

We usually want to know whether a set of sample data provides sufficient evidence to indicate that $\rho \neq 0$. If we can reject the null hypothesis that $\rho = 0$, we can conclude that there is a linear relationship between X and Y.

We illustrate the procedures with an example.

EXAMPLE 9.8.1   A study is made of the relationship between annual sales volume and size of shopping centers. Table 9.8.1 shows data on a sample of ten shopping centers. Here X denotes thousands of square feet of building space and Y denotes volume of sales in millions of dollars. Can we conclude on the basis of these data that X and Y are correlated?

SOLUTION   To find out whether we can conclude that shopping center size and sales volume are correlated, we conduct the following hypothesis test.

TABLE 9.8.1   Sales volume and size of shopping center, selected shopping centers for a given year

X	40	600	60	72	400	90	200	70	80	84	Total: 1,696
Y	3.5	25.0	4.8	3.5	30.0	5.0	12.0	4.5	5.0	6.0	Total: 99.3

$\Sigma x_i^2 = 596,840$ $\Sigma y_i^2 = 1,822.79$ $\Sigma x_i y_i = 31,749$

1. _Hypotheses._

$$H_0: \rho = 0, \qquad H_1: \rho \neq 0$$

2. _Test statistic._ We compute the test statistic by the following equation:

(9.8.1)
$$t = r \sqrt{\frac{n-2}{1-r^2}}$$

If H_0 is true and the assumptions are met, the test statistic is distributed as Student's t with $n - 2$ degrees of freedom. For this example, $n - 2 = 8$.

3. _Significance level._ Let $\alpha = 0.05$.
4. _Decision rule._ Reject H_0 if the computed t is either ≤ -2.306 or ≥ 2.306.
5. _Calculations._ When one uses a computer for correlation analysis, the computed values of r and t are usually part of the output. Formulas for r are given in Section 9.11. For this example, r is 0.9227. (This is computed in Section 9.11.)
   The computed value of the test statistic is

$$t = 0.9227 \sqrt{\frac{10-2}{1-0.8514}} = 6.7701$$

When $\beta_0 = 0$, the t value computed by Equation 9.8.1 is identical to the t computed by Equation 9.5.10. That is, in simple linear correlation and regression analysis, the t statistic for testing $H_0: \beta = 0$ is equivalent to the t statistic for testing $H_0: \rho = 0$.

6. _Statistical decision._ Since $6.7701 > 2.306$, we reject H_0.
7. _Conclusion._ We conclude that X and Y are correlated; $p < 0.010$.

Since F with 1 and $n - 2$ degrees of freedom is equal to t^2 with $n - 2$ degrees of freedom, we can carry out an alternative test of $H_0: \rho = 0$. We use as the test statistic

$$F = t^2 = \left(r \sqrt{\frac{n-2}{1-r^2}} \right)^2 = r^2 \left(\frac{n-2}{1-r^2} \right) = \frac{r^2(n-2)}{1-r^2}$$

This is the F we found in the analysis of variance in Table 9.5.1. For this example, we have

$$F = (6.7701)^2 = \frac{0.8514(8)}{1 - 0.8514} = 45.8358$$

FISHER'S Z

When ρ is not close to 0, it may not be appropriate to use the normal distribution to approximate the sampling distribution of r. Therefore, we shall use the t statistic of Equation 9.8.1 only for testing H_0: $\rho = 0$. If we want to test H_0: $\rho = \rho_0$, where ρ_0 is some value other than 0, we should use another approach. R. A. Fisher has suggested the following procedure. First we transform r to z_r as follows:

(9.8.2)
$$z_r = \frac{1}{2} \ln \frac{1 + r}{1 - r}$$

where ln is a natural logarithm. It can be shown that z_r is approximately normally distributed with a mean of

$$z_\rho = \frac{1}{2} \ln \frac{1 + \rho}{1 - \rho}$$

and estimated standard deviation of

(9.8.3)
$$\hat{\sigma}_{z_r} = \frac{1}{\sqrt{n - 3}}$$

To test the null hypothesis that ρ is equal to some value other than 0, the test statistic is as follows (where z_{ρ_0} is the value from Appendix Table I of Appendix I for the hypothesized value of ρ):

(9.8.4)
$$Z = \frac{z_r - z_{\rho_0}}{\hat{\sigma}_{z_r}}$$

The statistic Z follows approximately the standard normal distribution.

To determine z_r for an observed r and z_ρ for a hypothesized ρ, we can consult Table I to avoid the direct use of natural logarithms.

Suppose, for Example 9.8.1, that we wish to test

$$H_0: \rho = 0.95 \quad \text{against} \quad H_1: \rho \neq 0.95$$

at the 0.05 level of significance. Table I shows that for $r = 0.93$, $z_r = 1.65839$, and for $\rho = 0.95$, $z_\rho = 1.83178$. The test statistic, then, is

$$Z = \frac{1.65839 - 1.83178}{1/\sqrt{10 - 3}} = -0.46$$

Since $-1.96 < -0.46 < 1.96$, we cannot reject H_0. We must conclude that ρ may be 0.95.

For sample sizes of less than 25, Fisher's z transformation is usually not recommended. We may use an alternative method for sample sizes equal to or greater than 10. With this method, we use the following transformation of r (symbolized by z^*):

(9.8.5)
$$z^* = z_r - \frac{3z_r + r}{4n}$$

The standard deviation of z^* is

(9.8.6)
$$\sigma_{z^*} = \frac{1}{\sqrt{n - 1}}$$

The test statistic is

(9.8.7)
$$Z^* = \frac{z^* - \zeta^*}{1/\sqrt{n - 1}} = (z^* - \zeta^*)\sqrt{n - 1}$$

where ζ^* (pronounced *zeta star*) $= z_\rho (3z_\rho + \rho)/4n$. We obtain critical values from the standard normal distribution.

In the present example, if we test H_0: $\rho = 0.95$ against H_1: $\rho \neq 0.95$, with $\alpha = 0.05$, we have

$$z^* = 1.65839 - \frac{3(1.65839) + (0.93)}{4(10)} = 1.51076$$

and

$$\zeta^* = 1.83178 - \frac{3(1.83178) + 0.95}{4(10)} = 1.67065$$

We may use these results to compute

$$Z^* = (1.51076 - 1.67065)\sqrt{10 - 1} = -0.48$$

Since -0.48 is greater than -1.96, we cannot reject H_0. We reach the same conclusion we did with Fisher's transformation.

CONFIDENCE INTERVAL FOR ρ

We can use Fisher's transformation to construct $100(1 - \alpha)\%$ confidence intervals for ρ. We use the general formula for a confidence interval,

$$\text{Estimate} \pm (\text{reliability factor}) \times (\text{standard error})$$

We convert the estimator r to z_r, and construct a confidence interval about z_ρ. We reconvert the limits to obtain a $100(1 - \alpha)\%$ confidence interval about ρ. The general formula for a confidence interval for z_ρ is given by

(9.8.8)
$$z_r \pm z\hat{\sigma}_{z_r}$$

For this example, the 95% confidence interval for z_ρ is

$$1.65839 \pm 1.96(1/\sqrt{10 - 3})$$
$$1.65839 \pm 0.74080, \qquad 0.91759, \ 2.39919$$

Converting these limits, which are values of z_r, into values of r gives the following 95% confidence interval for ρ:

$$0.725, \ 0.983$$

Because of the limited number of entries in Table I, we must consider this interval, obtained by rough interpolation, as only approximate.

When the correlation assumptions of this chapter are not met, we can compute a measure of correlation known as the *Spearman rank correlation coefficient*. We discuss the procedure in Chapter 13.

EXERCISES

9.8.1   Ⓒ The following table shows the amount spent for insurance and safety during a year (Y) and volume of business in tons hauled (X) for a random sample of trucking firms of a certain type. All figures are in thousands.

Y, $	13	18	14	18	23	21	14	25	23	14
X, tons	10	16	12	18	17	17	9	19	17	11

$\Sigma x_i = 146 \qquad \Sigma y_i = 183 \qquad \Sigma x_i y_i = 2804 \qquad \Sigma x_i^2 = 2254 \qquad \Sigma y_i^2 = 3529$

(a) Plot the data as a scatter diagram. (b) Test H_0: $\rho = 0$ at the 0.05 significance level. (c) Test H_0: $\rho = 0.95$. (d) Determine the p value for each test. (e) Interpret r^2. (f) Discuss the way the sampling scheme in this case makes correlation analysis, as well as regression analysis, appropriate.

9.8.2 C The following table shows the scores on a clerical aptitude test (X) and grades in a clerical skills course (Y) for ten business students.

X	60	70	65	72	75	75	82	84	90	95
Y	68	72	76	78	80	86	82	90	96	93

$\Sigma x_i = 768$ $\Sigma x_i y_i = 63,885$ $\Sigma y_i^2 = 68,153$ $\Sigma x_i^2 = 60,064$ $\Sigma y_i = 821$

(a) Plot the data as a scatter diagram.   (b) Perform the correct hypothesis test to determine whether the data provide sufficient evidence to indicate that X and Y are linearly correlated. Let $\alpha = 0.05$.   (c) Test H_0: $\rho = 0.98$.   (d) Determine the p value for each test.

9.8.3 C The following table shows the expenditures for equipment maintenance (X) and net income before taxes (Y) for a random sample of ten firms of a certain type. All figures are coded for ease of calculation.

X, $	10	20	25	30	36	42	54	62	74	82
Y, $	12	24	14	18	18	28	26	40	38	54

$\Sigma x_i = 435$ $\Sigma y_i = 272$ $\Sigma x_i y_i = 14,438$ $\Sigma x_i^2 = 24,045$ $\Sigma y_i^2 = 8984$

(a) Plot the data as a scatter diagram.   (b) Determine whether we can conclude from these data that the two variables are linearly related. Let $\alpha = 0.05$.   (c) Test H_0: $\rho = 0.95$. (d) Determine the p value for each test.

9.9   CONSIDERATIONS IN DECIDING BETWEEN REGRESSION AND CORRELATION

The nature of our questions is the primary determining factor in choosing between regression analysis and correlation analysis. As previously noted, we use regression analysis when we want to determine the nature of the relationship between two variables (for example, to determine whether they are linearly related), to predict what value Y is likely to assume for a given value of X, and to estimate means of subpopulations of Y values.

Correlation analysis requires that both X and Y be random.

If we are interested only in assessing the strength of the relationship between two variables, then correlation analysis will suffice. We emphasize that the correlation model requires that both X and Y be random variables. In order for inferential procedures to be fully valid, the two variables must follow a bivariate normal distribution. Typically, we obtain the data for correlation analysis by randomly drawing a sample of subjects (units of association) from the population of interest and taking a measurement on each of the two variables, X and Y. We therefore conduct our analysis on all the observed values. That is, we place no restriction on what values of either variable may enter into the analysis.

For regression analysis, X does not have to be random.

Regression analysis has broader applications, since it does not require that both variables be random. For example, an investigator interested in studying the nature of the relationship between family income and propensity to save may feel that studying only families whose incomes are of certain specified magnitudes would be meaningful and practical. To obtain the data for such an analysis, the investigator would select for study only families with the specified incomes. When data are gathered in this manner, the investigator is considered to have "control" over one of the variables. In this example, the variable of family income is controlled. As we have seen, the variable that is controlled is called the independent variable.

In correlation analysis, where no control is exercised on any variable, we do not speak of "independent" and "dependent" variables. Thus, in regression analysis, the independent variable does not have to represent either the complete set of values that might occur or the proper relative frequencies with which the selected values occur. Correlation analysis, on the other hand, should be based on a sample selected from the entire set of values that occur in the given situation.

9.10 SOME PRECAUTIONS

When properly used, regression and correlation analysis are powerful statistical techniques. Their inappropriate use, however, can lead only to meaningless results. We offer the following suggestions:

1. Carefully review the assumptions underlying regression and correlation analysis before you collect the data. It is rare for assumptions to be met to perfection. However, you should have some idea of the magnitude of the gap between the data to be analyzed and the assumptions of the proposed model. That way, you can decide whether you should choose another model, proceed with the analysis but use caution in interpreting the results, or use the chosen model with confidence.

   One alternative, when the assumptions of this chapter are not met, is to use a nonparametric technique for analysis. We discuss this alternative in greater detail in Chapter 13, on nonparametric statistics.

2. No matter how strong the indication of a relationship between two variables, do not interpret it as one of cause and effect. For example, suppose that you observe a significant sample correlation coefficient between two variables X and Y. This can mean one of several things: (a) X causes Y; (b) Y causes X; (c) some third factor, either directly or indirectly, causes both X and Y; (d) an unlikely event has occurred, and a large sample correlation coefficient has been generated by chance from a population in which X and Y are in fact not correlated; or (e) the correlation is purely nonsensical, a situation that may arise when measurements of X and Y are not taken on a common unit of association.

3. Do not use the sample regression equation to predict or estimate outside the range of values of the independent variable represented in the sample. This practice, called *extrapolation,* can have dangerous consequences. The true relationship between two variables may be linear over an interval of the in-

FIGURE 9.10.1   Example of possible danger of using extrapolation in linear regression

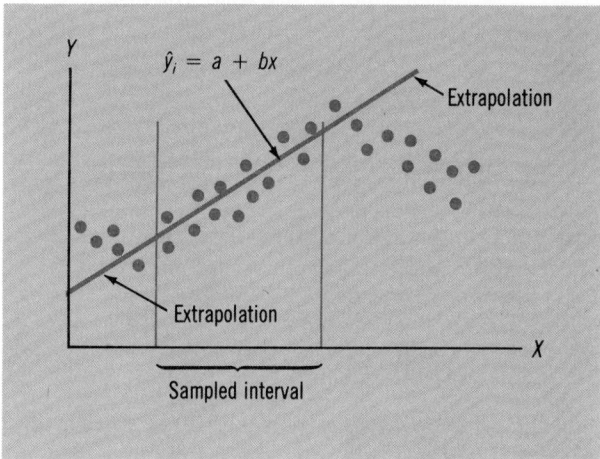

dependent variable, but may best be described as a curve outside this interval. If the sample happens to be drawn only from the interval in which the relationship is linear, it provides only a limited representation of the population. To project the sample results beyond the interval represented by the sample may lead to false conclusions. Figure 9.10.1 shows one of the possible pitfalls of extrapolation.

4. As we have seen, researchers often find that, among the data they have collected as part of an experiment or a sample survey, there are one or more observations that seem to be "unusual" relative to the majority of the observations. These unusual observations are variously called "spurious," "unrepresentative," "mavericks," and "outliers." They may be either much smaller or much larger than most of the observations collected. The presence of outliers may cause misleading results. Analyzing residuals makes the detection of outliers easier. What to *do* about outliers has bothered researchers for more than 100 years. Areas of concern are   (a) how can one be sure that a given observation is a true outlier, that is, that it does not "belong" to the set of data under consideration;   (b) what is the cause of a confirmed outlier; and   (c) what should one do with confirmed outliers? Attempts to answer the questions posed by outliers have generated a large body of literature, dating back to the mid-1800s.

5. When constructing a model in which X will be used to predict Y, the model builder should make sure that appropriate values of X for predicting Y will be knowable at the time the prediction is to be made. If the appropriate value of X for predicting Y is one that will not be known until the true Y value for which the prediction is desired is also known, the model will not serve its purpose.

6. When choosing an independent variable, do not choose one that is inherently a component of the dependent variable. For example, you should not try to predict revenue (Y) using either price or quantity as the independent variables, since each is a component factor of revenue.

9.11   SIMPLE LINEAR REGRESSION CALCULATIONS

In this section, we present the computational formulas for calculating the various quantities needed in simple linear regression analysis.

CALCULATING a AND b

We can find the numerical values of a and b for any set of data, such as that in Table 9.4.1, by simultaneously solving the following two equations:

(9.11.1)
$$\Sigma y_i = na + b\,\Sigma x_i$$

(9.11.2)
$$\Sigma x_i y_i = a\,\Sigma x_i + b\,\Sigma x_i^2$$

These equations, obtained by differential calculus, are called the *normal equations*. Their solution yields the equation for the least-squares line describing the relationship between X and Y.

When we solve Equations 9.11.1 and 9.11.2, we obtain the following formulas

(9.11.3)
$$b = \frac{\Sigma x_i y_i - \dfrac{\Sigma x_i \Sigma y_i}{n}}{\Sigma x_i^2 - \dfrac{(\Sigma x_i)^2}{n}} = \frac{n\Sigma x_i y_i - \Sigma x_i \Sigma y_i}{n\Sigma x_i^2 - (\Sigma x_i)^2}$$

(9.11.4)
$$a = \frac{\Sigma y_i}{n} - b\left(\frac{\Sigma x_i}{n}\right) = \bar{y} - b\bar{x}$$

Table 9.11.1 gives the values of Σy_i, Σx_i, $\Sigma x_i y_i$, Σx_i^2, and n, which are needed to solve the equations. Substituting values from Table 9.11.1 into Equations 9.11.3 and 9.11.4 gives

$$b = \frac{132{,}938 - \dfrac{(777)(1657)}{10}}{70{,}903 - \dfrac{(777)^2}{10}} = 0.3978$$

$$a = 165.7 - 0.3987(77.7) = 134.79$$

TABLE 9.11.1   Intermediate computations for normal equations, Example 9.4.1

	x_i	y_i	x_i^2	xy	y_i^2
	40	150	1,600	6,000	22,500
	42	140	1,764	5,880	19,600
	48	160	2,304	7,680	25,600
	55	170	3,025	9,350	28,900
	65	150	4,225	9,750	22,500
	79	162	6,241	12,798	26,244
	88	185	7,744	16,280	34,225
	100	165	10,000	16,500	27,225
	120	190	14,400	22,800	36,100
	140	185	19,600	25,900	34,225
Total	777	1,657	70,903	132,938	277,119

CALCULATING THE SUMS OF SQUARES

We can compute the total sum of squares by the following formula:

(9.11.5)
$$\text{SST} = \Sigma(y_i - \bar{y})^2 = \Sigma y_i^2 - \frac{(\Sigma y_i)^2}{n}$$

The formula for the explained sum of squares is

(9.11.6)
$$\text{SSR} = \Sigma(\hat{y}_i - \bar{y})^2 = b^2 \Sigma(x_i - \bar{x})^2 = b^2 \left[\Sigma x_i^2 - \frac{(\Sigma x_i)^2}{n} \right]$$

We can get the unexplained sum of squares by subtraction. That is,

$$\text{SSE} = \text{SST} - \text{SSR}$$

CALCULATING THE SUMS OF SQUARES FOR EXAMPLE 9.4.1

From the data on production and manufacturing expenses (Example 9.4.1), we may compute

$$\text{SST} = 277,119 - \frac{(1,657)^2}{10} = 2,554.10$$

Alternatively, we may compute SST by squaring and summing the individual total deviations $(y_i - \bar{y})$, as shown in Figure 9.5.2. When we do this, we have

$$(-15.7)^2 + (-25.7)^2 + \cdots + (19.3)^2 = 246.49 + 660.49 + \cdots$$
$$+ 372.49 = 2{,}554.10$$

By Equation 9.11.6, the explained sum of squares, or sum of squares due to regression, is

$$SSR = (0.3978)^2 \left[70{,}903 - \frac{(777)^2}{10} \right] = 1{,}666.33$$

Or we can get the explained sum of squares by squaring and summing the explained deviations $(\hat{y}_i - \bar{y})$, shown in Figure 9.5.3, to give

$$SSR = (-15)^2 + (-14.2)^2 + \cdots + (24.8)^2$$
$$= 225.0 + 201.64 + \cdots + 615.04 = 1{,}666.44$$

The unexplained, or error, sum of squares, obtained by subtraction, is

$$SSE = 2{,}554.10 - 1{,}666.33 = 887.77$$

As an alternative, we can compute SSE by squaring and summing the individual unexplained deviations $(y_i - \hat{y}_i)$, shown in Figure 9.5.4. Thus,

$$SSE = (-0.7)^2 + (-11.5)^2 + \cdots + (-5.5)^2$$
$$= 0.49 + 132.25 + \cdots + 30.25 = 886.54$$

Note a slight discrepancy due to rounding in the results for SSR and SSE computed by the two methods.

CALCULATING s_b^2

To find s_b^2, we must first estimate $\sigma_{y|x}^2$. An unbiased estimator of this is given by

(9.11.7)
$$s_{y|x}^2 = \frac{\Sigma(y_i - \hat{y}_i)^2}{n - 2}$$

An alternative formula for $s_{y|x}^2$ is

(9.11.8)
$$s_{y|x}^2 = \frac{\Sigma y_i^2 - a\,\Sigma y_i - b\,\Sigma x_i y_i}{n - 2}$$

The estimator, $s_{y|x}^2$, is the same as the error mean square appearing in the analysis-of-variance table. An unbiased estimator of σ_b^2, then, is

(9.11.9)
$$s_b^2 = \frac{s_{y|x}^2}{\Sigma(x_i - \bar{x})^2}$$

The following formula takes less work:

(9.11.10)
$$s_b^2 = \frac{s_{y|x}^2}{\Sigma x_i^2 - (\Sigma x_i)^2/n}$$

CALCULATING s_b^2 FOR EXAMPLE 9.4.1

By Equation 9.11.9, we have

$$s_b^2 = \frac{110.97}{70,903 - (777)^2/10} = 0.0105 \quad \text{and} \quad s_b = \sqrt{0.0105} = 0.102$$

The figures in the denominator of s_b^2 come from Table 9.11.1, and

$$s_{y|x}^2 = \text{MSE} = 110.97$$

is found in Table 9.5.2.

CALCULATING r, THE SAMPLE CORRELATION COEFFICIENT

To calculate r, proceed as follows:

1. Obtain b by solving Equation 9.11.3.
2. Compute r^2 by Equation 9.5.13 and take the square root. Be careful to give r the appropriate sign, which is the same as the sign of the sample slope b.

An alternative formula for r is

(9.11.11)
$$r = \frac{n\Sigma x_i y_i - (\Sigma x_i)(\Sigma y_i)}{\sqrt{n\Sigma x_i^2 - (\Sigma x_i)^2}\,\sqrt{n\Sigma y_i^2 - (\Sigma y_i)^2}}$$

When we use this formula, we do not need to compute b first. Equation 9.11.11 is usually better when we do not need the regression equation. When we use Equation 9.11.11, the value of r that results will have the correct sign.

CALCULATING r FOR EXAMPLE 9.8.1

1. Using Equation 9.11.3 and the data in Table 9.8.1 yields

$$b = \frac{10(31,749) - (1,696)(99.3)}{10(596,840) - (1,696)^2} = 0.048$$

2. Using Equation 9.5.13, we compute

$$r^2 = \frac{(0.048)^2[596,840 - (1,696)^2/10]}{1,822.79 - (99.3)^2/10} = 0.8514$$

and we wind up with

$$r = \sqrt{0.8514} = 0.9227$$

When we compute r by the alternative formula using the data of this example, we have

$$r = \frac{10(31,749) - (1,696)(99.3)}{\sqrt{10(596,840) - (1,696)^2}\ \sqrt{10(1,822.79) - (99.3)^2}} = 0.9268$$

Except for rounding error, this is the value we found using Equation 9.5.13.

SUMMARY

This chapter presents two important tools of statistical analysis, simple linear regression and correlation. It suggests the following outline for the application of these techniques:

1. Identify the model.
2. Review the assumptions.
3. Obtain the regression equation.
4. Evaluate the equation.
5. Use the equation.

You learned how you can use an analysis of residual plots to determine whether or not it is likely that the data violate the assumptions underlying regression analysis.

You saw that correlation analysis, though closely related to regression analysis, is used for a different purpose: to study the strength of the relationship between two variables. Correlation analysis is strictly valid only when both X and Y are continuous random variables. However, regression analysis is valid when X is either fixed or random. You learned that you can use regression analysis to predict the value that Y is likely to assume for a given X. You can also use it to estimate the mean of the subpopulation of Y values at a given value of X. The chapter discusses methods for testing hypotheses and constructing confidence intervals under both the regression and the correlation models.

This chapter deals with regression and correlation in which the model specifies a linear relationship between X and Y. However, sometimes we can best describe the relationship between two variables by a second-degree curve or by one that is even more complicated.

Sometimes we can predict a dependent variable more precisely by using two or more independent variables rather than one. There are also situations in which we are more interested in knowing the strength of the relationship among several variables than in knowing the relationship between only two variables. Chapter 10 explores these possibilities.

REVIEW EXERCISES

1. In the equation $\hat{y}_i = a + bx$, explain   (a) two ways we may interpret $\hat{y}_i$,   (b) the meaning of a, and   (c) the meaning of b.

2. What is a scatter diagram?

3. Why is the regression line called the least-squares line?

4. What are the basic assumptions underlying regression analysis?

5. Give three interpretations of the coefficient of determination.

6. For the following expression, explain each of the terms, express each term symbolically, and draw a picture to illustrate the relationship:

Total sum of squares = explained sum of squares + unexplained sum of squares

7. What is the function of the analysis of variance in regression analysis?

8. Describe three ways of testing the null hypothesis that $\beta = 0$.

9. What are the assumptions underlying simple correlation analysis when inference is an objective?

10. What is meant by the unit of association in regression and correlation analysis?

11. What are the possible explanations for a significant sample correlation coefficient?

12. Explain why it is risky to use a sample regression equation to predict or estimate outside the range of values of the independent variable represented in the sample.

13. Describe a situation in your area of interest in which simple regression analysis would be useful. Use real or realistic data and do a complete regression analysis.

14. Describe a situation in your area of interest in which simple correlation analysis would be useful. Use real or realistic data and do a complete correlation analysis.

 15. ⓒ The following table shows the age and efficiency rating of a random sample of 20 assembly-line employees.   (a) Obtain the equation describing the linear relationship between age and efficiency rating. (b) Compute r. (c) Do the data provide sufficient evidence to indicate that the two variables are correlated? (d) Determine the p value for the test.

Age	Efficiency rating	Age	Efficiency rating
44	61	51	60
44	41	50	78
45	89	61	78
43	76	47	74
40	79	62	82
52	67	34	70
43	73	51	60
47	94	48	67
54	96	51	72
43	77	57	80

 16. C A survey is conducted among customers holding charge cards from Engels Department Stores. Researchers ask each of a random sample of 16 customers to estimate the amount he or she charged at the store during the past month. The estimates and actual charges obtained from store records are as follows (amounts are rounded to the nearest dollar). (a) Compute r and test for significance at the 0.05 level. (b) Find the p value for the test.

Customer	Actual	Estimate	Customer	Actual	Estimate
1	85	85	9	84	75
2	96	100	10	41	50
3	49	50	11	67	75
4	97	100	12	72	75
5	90	75	13	92	100
6	28	50	14	29	30
7	25	30	15	74	60
8	28	35	16	75	90

 17. C Foley Suits wants to know the relationship between the age and annual maintenance costs of sewing machines. A sample of 16 machines reveals the following ages and maintenance costs during the past year. (a) Find the sample regression equation. (b) Do the data provide sufficient evidence at the 0.05 level to indicate that the two variables are related? Use ANOVA. (c) Determine the p value for the test. (d) What is the expected annual maintenance cost for a seven-year-old machine?

Age (years)	Maintenance costs (dollars)	Age (years)	Maintenance costs (dollars)
8	109	1	25
3	75	3	70
1	21	6	126
9	135	2	58
5	67	1	30
7	125	2	47
5	71	6	120
2	52	8	105

18. [C] The following are scores on a sales aptitude test made by 15 salespersons, and the salespersons' performance ratings as given by their supervisor. (a) Find the sample regression equation. (b) Use ANOVA to evaluate the equation. Let $\alpha = 0.05$. (c) Determine the p value for the test.

Aptitude test score (X)	Performance rating (Y)	Aptitude test score (X)	Performance rating (Y)
92	70	84	63
77	57	70	51
83	65	85	66
72	55	81	62
81	62	76	53
90	79	76	52
79	57	70	59
91	73		

19. [C] The following table shows the hardness, measured in units of Brinell hardness, and tensile strength, in thousands of pounds per square inch, of 15 specimens of a metal alloy. (a) Plot a scatter diagram of these data. (b) Find the sample regression equation. (c) Test the null hypothesis that $\beta = 0$. (d) Compute r^2. (e) Suppose that a new specimen has a hardness of 50. Estimate the tensile strength with a 95% confidence interval.

Hardness	Tensile strength	Hardness	Tensile strength
41	27	41	23
74	42	96	51
100	62	20	15
72	43	45	22
67	37	38	19
55	31	26	17
71	45	29	17
35	21		

20. [C] A professor is doing a study of the relationship between students' grades and their part-time work. She analyzes data from a random sample of 15 college students. The numbers of hours worked per week and the grade-point averages of these students are as follows. (a) Plot a scatter diagram of these data. (b) Find the least-squares regression equation. (c) Do these data provide sufficient evidence to indicate that there is a relationship between grade-point average and number of hours worked? (d) Determine the p value for the test.

Hours/week worked (X)	GPA (Y)	Hours/week worked (X)	GPA (Y)
10	2.5	32	3.9
22	3.0	29	2.7
24	2.3	29	1.4
28	3.5	5	2.4
9	4.0	25	1.8
10	1.8	9	1.7
7	2.8	17	2.9
7	3.2		

21. Ⓒ From Table D in Appendix I, select a random sample of 15 pairs of one-digit numbers. Compute the sample correlation coefficient. Test H_0: $\rho = 0$ against the alternative H_1: $\rho \neq 0$ at the 0.05 level of significance. Compare your results with those of other members of the class.

22. For each of the following situations, indicate whether one should use regression analysis or correlation analysis. **(a)** An industrial psychologist wants to know the relationship between intelligence and job satisfaction of assembly-line employees. **(b)** In a factory, there are two methods for measuring the durability of a certain product. One (the direct method) is expensive and hard to perform, but gives a true measure of durability. A second (the indirect method) provides an indirect measure of durability. Officials will switch to the less expensive indirect method if it can be shown that this method is a good predictor of the results that the direct method would give. **(c)** A drug company wants to know the average reduction in reaction time to a certain stimulus of people who take various strengths of their drug. The strengths are one-, two-, three-, and four-milligram doses. **(d)** Medical researchers wish to know whether high levels of exercise are associated with low levels of serum cholesterol in adults.

23. The president of Gardiner and Associates wants to find out the relationship between the effectiveness of salespersons, as measured in dollar volume of sales, and their aptitude for selling. Data are collected on a sample of 15 salespersons and analyzed by means of regression analysis. The independent variable is the salesperson's score on a sales aptitude test. The dependent variable is mean annual sales, in $10,000 units, over the past five years. The following computer printout shows the results of the analysis. **(a)** Write out the sample regression equation. **(b)** Should H_0: $\beta = 0$ be rejected at the 0.05 level of significance?

Variable I	B(I)	XBAR(I)	S(I)
1	4.78001	11.4667	2.47301
2	.897939E-01	74.4666	18.2939

Index of determination (R-SQ) = .441219
Correlation matrix

1	.664244
.664244	1

ACTUAL VS CALCULATED

Actual	Calculated	Residual	PCT Residual
11	12.2329	-1.23291	-10
13	13.3104	-.310435	-2.3
8	9.3595	-1.3595	-14.5
14	13.6696	.330389	2.4
14	11.1554	2.84462	25.4
15	12.1431	2.85689	23.5
10	10.0779	-.778542E-01	-.7
13	11.1554	1.84462	16.5
13	9.98806	3.01194	30.1
11	10.9758	.242071E-01	.2
6	9.4493	-3.4493	-36.5
8	8.64115	-.641151	-7.4
13	13.2206	-.220641	-1.6
11	12.9513	-1.95126	-15
12	13.6696	-1.66961	-12.2

```
A N A L Y S I S   O F   V A R I A N C E
Source        SS            DF            MS            F

Regression    40.476        1             40.476        10.2649**
Error         51.2608       13            3.94314
Total         91.7368       14

**Significant at 1% level

 Variable     Coefficient    STD Error      T Statistic

 2            .897939E-01    .280274E-01    3.20379
DF = 13
```

24. Ⓒ Select a simple random sample of size 40 from the population of employed heads of household in Appendix II. Do a complete regression analysis, using education as the independent variable and annual salary as the dependent variable.

 25. Ⓒ The measurements in the following table were made on 40 geographic regions. The variable X is a measure of the extent of industrialization (the higher the value of X, the greater the industrialization). The variable Y is an overall measure of the extent of air and water pollution (the higher the value of Y, the greater the pollution). Plot a scatter diagram of these data.

X	Y	X	Y	X	Y
85	118	82	101	48	50
73	90	80	89	86	82
88	123	76	85	68	89
52	74	86	82	76	88
85	98	55	52	77	96
68	91	91	105	91	97
109	113	81	92	89	102
47	62	67	76	69	80
79	76	63	73	74	84
60	63	73	82	87	87
54	67	69	81	81	84
71	78	71	93	77	95
62	74	61	75		
67	60	57	73		

26. Ⓒ Refer to Exercise 25. Obtain the least-squares regression equation for these data and plot the line on your scatter diagram.

27. Ⓒ Refer to Exercise 25. Compute the coefficient of determination for these data.

28. Ⓒ Refer to Exercise 25. Construct the ANOVA table. Can we conclude, at the 0.05 level of significance, that, in the population, X and Y are linearly related? What is the p value for the test?

29. Ⓒ Refer to Exercise 25. Use the t test to determine whether you may conclude that $\beta \neq 0$. Let $\alpha = 0.05$, and find the p value.

30. Ⓒ Refer to Exercise 25. Construct a 95% confidence interval for β.

31. Ⓒ Refer to Exercise 25. What is the correlation coefficient for these data? Do you think that the correlation coefficient is an appropriate measure in this case?

32. Ⓒ Refer to Exercise 25. Can we conclude that the correlation coefficient in the sampled population is not 0? Let $\alpha = 0.05$, and find the p value.

33. ©️ Refer to Exercise 25. Suppose that an area has an industrialization score of 80. What do you predict the pollution score to be?

34. ©️ Refer to Exercise 33. Construct the 95% prediction interval for the predicted Y.

35. ©️ Data Set 7 in Appendix IV contains a population of measurements on two variables. The data were collected as part of a study that Haber Technologies is conducting to analyze and subsequently estimate the costs associated with the repair of customer-returned products. The independent variable X is the amount of time involved in a major repair operation, in thousandths of an hour, and the dependent variable Y is the total cost of repair for each product. Select a simple random sample of size 25 from this population, and plot a scatter diagram of the resulting data points.

36. ©️ Refer to Exercise 35. Obtain the least-squares regression equation for your sample, and plot the line on your scatter diagram.

37. ©️ Refer to Exercise 35. Compute the coefficient of determination for your sample. Compare your results with those of your classmates.

38. ©️ Refer to Exercise 35. Construct the ANOVA table for your sample. Can we conclude, at the 0.05 level of significance, that, in the population, X and Y are linearly related? What is the p value for the test? Compare your results with those of your classmates.

39. ©️ Refer to Exercise 35. Use the t test to determine whether you can conclude that $\beta \neq 0$. Let $\alpha = 0.05$, and find the p value.

40. ©️ Refer to Exercise 35. Construct a 95% confidence interval for β.

41. ©️ Refer to Exercise 35. What is the correlation coefficient for your sample? Do you think that the correlation coefficient is an appropriate measure for these data?

42. Refer to Exercise 35. Can we conclude that the correlation coefficient in the sampled population is not 0? Let $\alpha = 0.05$, and find the p value.

43. ©️ Refer to Exercise 35. Predict Y for a selected value of X and construct the 95% prediction interval.

44. ©️ Refer to Exercise 35. Estimate the mean Y value for a subpopulation of time studies in which the value of X was the same. You choose the value of X. Construct the 95% confidence interval for the mean.

For Exercises 45 through 59, do the following. Select a simple random sample from the population of companies in Appendix III. (Ask your instructor how large your sample should be.) For each company in your sample, record the information on each of the six variables.

45. ©️ With sales as the dependent variable and assets as the independent variable, do a regression analysis that includes at least the following calculations and procedures. (a) Find the simple linear regression equation. (b) Compute r^2 and r. (c) Use ANOVA to determine whether you can conclude that, in the population, the two variables are linearly related. (d) Use the t test to test the null hypothesis that the population slope is equal to 0. (e) Construct a 95% confidence interval for the population slope. (f) Use the regression equation to predict Y for selected values of X. (g) Use the regression equation to estimate $\mu_{y|x}$ for selected values of X.

46. ©️ Repeat Exercise 45 with sales as the dependent variable and market value as the independent variable.

47. Ⓒ Repeat Exercise 45 with sales as the dependent variable and net profits as the independent variable.

48. Ⓒ Repeat Exercise 45 with sales as the dependent variable and cash flow as the independent variable.

49. Ⓒ Repeat Exercise 45 with sales as the dependent variable and number employed as the independent variable.

50. Ⓒ Repeat Exercise 45 with net profits as the dependent variable and assets as the independent variable.

51. Ⓒ Repeat Exercise 45 with net profits as the dependent variable and sales as the independent variable.

52. Ⓒ Repeat Exercise 45 with net profits as the dependent variable and market value as the independent variable.

53. Ⓒ Repeat Exercise 45 with net profits as the dependent variable and cash flow as the independent variable.

54. Ⓒ Repeat Exercise 45 with net profits as the dependent variable and number employed as the independent variable.

55. Ⓒ Repeat Exercise 45 with cash flow as the dependent variable and assets as the independent variable.

56. Ⓒ Repeat Exercise 45 with cash flow as the dependent variable and sales as the independent variable.

57. Ⓒ Repeat Exercise 45 with cash flow as the dependent variable and market value as the independent variable.

58. Ⓒ Repeat Exercise 45 with cash flow as the dependent variable and net profits as the independent variable.

59. Ⓒ Repeat Exercise 45 with cash flow as the dependent variable and number employed as the independent variable.

60. This ANOVA table was completed for a linear regression problem. Answer the following questions based on the information contained in the table. Let $\alpha = 0.05$.

ANOVA table

Source	df	SS	MS	F
Regression	1	2,547.3	2,547.3	17.89
Error	22	3,136.4	142.6	
Total	23	5,683.7	247.1	

(a) How many values of X were observed?   (b) How many values of Y were observed?   (c) How many coefficients are there?   (d) How many residuals?   (e) What is the value of the total sum of squares for Y?   (f) What is the standard deviation of all the values of Y?   (g) What is the standard deviation of all the residual values?   (h) What percentage of the variation in Y is explained by X?   (i) What is the value of t for testing H_0: $\beta = 0$?   (j) Can we conclude that X and Y are linearly related? Why?

61. We wish to perform a simple linear regression analysis. Use the following quantities to construct an ANOVA table and answer the questions. $\bar{x} = 10.08$, $\bar{y} = 13.36$,

$n = 50$. $\Sigma(x_i - \bar{x})^2 = 3{,}753.68$, $\hat{y} = 3.0 + 1.027x$, $s_{y|x} = 3.717$, $\Sigma(y_i - \bar{y})^2 = 4{,}625.25$.
(a) What is the standard deviation of Y?   (b) What is the standard deviation of the residuals?   (c) What is the standard deviation of b?   (d) What is the standard deviation of the predicted Y for $X = 20$?   (e) What is the value of r?   (f) What is the computed value of F?   (g) At the 0.05 level of significance, what is the statistical decision after testing H_0: $\beta = 0$ using the F statistic? Why?   (h) What is the computed value of t for testing H_0: $\beta = 0$?

62. Measurements on X and Y are obtained for 25 units of association. A linear regression model is assumed. The following quantities are calculated. Using these, perform the requested calculations and answer the questions that follow. $\Sigma y = 487$, $\Sigma y^2 = 9{,}849$, $n = 25$, $\Sigma x = 375$, $\Sigma x^2 = 6{,}925$, $\Sigma xy = 7{,}941$.   (a) $\Sigma(x - \bar{x})^2$,   (b) $\Sigma(y - \bar{y})^2$,   (c) $\Sigma(x - \bar{x})(y - \bar{y})$,   (d) slope,   (e) y intercept,   (f) SST,   (g) SSR,   (h) MSE,   (i) calculated F,   (j) critical F for $\alpha = 0.05$,   (k) $s_{y|x}$,   (l) s_b,   (m) computed t for testing H_0: $\beta = 0$.   (n) Is the computed t significant ($\alpha = 0.05$)?   (o) What is the value of $\hat{y}$ at $X = 20$?   (p) What is the standard deviation of the predicted Y for $X = 20$?   (q) What is the standard deviation of the expected value of Y for $X = 20$?   (r) At what value of X is the confidence interval for Y the narrowest?   (s) What is the expected value of Y at the point where the confidence interval for Y is narrowest?   (t) Find the 95% confidence interval for the mean of Y at $X = 20$.   (u) Find the 95% prediction interval for an individual observation of Y at $X = 20$.   (v) Which is wider, the confidence interval or the prediction interval? Why?

63. The following is a partial STAT+ regression analysis printout. Fill in the blanks.

```
Variable  I          (BI)      BETA(I)    XBAR(I)     S(I)
   Y       1       19.40822    N.D.       51.66667    9.540550
   X       2        0.989523   0.999715   32.60000    9.638816
```

INDEX OF DETERMINATION (R-SQ) = 0.99943

CORRELATION COEFFICIENT (R) = ____(a).

```
                ANALYSIS OF VARIANCE
  Source          SS           DF    MS            F
REGRESSION    1,364.551067      1    ____ (b.)    ____ (d.)**
ERROR             0.780354     13    ____ (c.)
TOTAL         1,365.331421     14
```

STANDARD DEVIATION OF ERROR TERM   0.2450045

** SIGNIFICANT AT 1% LEVEL

```
                                              95%
                                          Confidence
                        STD                 Limits
Variable   Coefficient  Error  T Statistic  (+, -)
   X     2  0.989523    0.00656  ____(e.)    0.01418
```

D.F. = 13

CONFIDENCE INTERVALS ON Y

Enter observed value of X2, X   40

THE 95% CONFIDENCE LIMITS ON THE EXPECTED VALUE OF X1 (Y) ARE:

X1= 58.98914 +/- 0.1723   UPPER = ____(f.)
LOWER = ____(g.)

```
THE 95% PREDICTION LIMITS ON THE EXPECTED VALUE OF X1
(Y) ARE:
X1= 58.98914 +/- 0.5566        UPPER = ____(h.)
LOWER = ____(i.)
```

64. The following is a MINITAB regression analysis printout. Fill in the blanks.

```
The regression equation is
Y = 225 + 15.7X

Predictor     Coef      Stdev      t-ratio              p
Constant      225.27    55.12      ____  (a.)      0.001
X             15.673    5.198      ____  (b.)      0.009

s = 106.5          R-sq = 39.4%      R-sq(adj) = 35.0%
               ANALYSIS OF VARIANCE

   Source     DF     SS        MS          F          p
Regression    1      103047    ____ (c.)   ____ (e.)  0.009
Error         14     158692    ____ (d.)
Total         15     261738

             UNUSUAL OBSERVATIONS

Obs.    X       Y      Fit     Stdev.Fit   Residual   St.Resid
 7     8.7    605.0   362.1     26.8        242.9       2.36R
R denotes an obs. with a large st. resid.
```

*65. Refer to the formula for the sample correlation coefficient given by Equation 9.11.11. The numerator of this equation, $n\Sigma x_i y_i - (\Sigma x_i)(\Sigma y_i)$, is the numerator of a measure called the *covariance* of x and y and written $\text{Cov}(x,y)$, which is a measure of the extent to which x and y vary together. The denominator of the sample $\text{Cov}(x,y)$ is $n - 1$. Rewrite Equation 9.11.11 to show explicitly that the correlation coefficient is the $\text{Cov}(x,y)$ divided by the geometric mean of the variances of x and y.

*66. In Section 9.7 we discussed the fact that given a bivariate sample, it is possible to regress Y on X or X on Y. In both cases the correlation coefficients are the same. The slopes of the regression lines, however, are generally different. Suppose, as usual, we use b to label the slope of the regression line obtained when we regress y on x. Let us use b' to designate the slope of the regression line obtained when we regress x on y. An interesting relationship between the two slopes is the fact that the correlation coefficient is the geometric mean of the two sample slopes. That is, $r = \sqrt{bb'}$. Refer to Review Exercise 17. Compute r, b, and b', and show that in this case $r = \sqrt{bb'}$.

STATISTICS AT WORK

STATISTICS AT WORK STATISTICS AT WORK

1. IS IGNORANCE BLISS?

Lee Sigelman subjected the old adage "Ignorance is bliss" to modern scientific scrutiny. He gave subjects in his study a shortened form of the Thorndike intelligence test, which measures happiness in terms of a three-point scale. Low scores indicate happiness; high scores unhappiness. Sigelman collected data on 2,650 subjects and reported a simple correlation coefficient between intelligence and happiness of -0.064. For testing $H_0: \rho = 0$ versus $H_1: \rho \neq 0$, what are the degrees of freedom? What value of the test statistic can one compute from the reported result? Can one reject H_0 at the 0.05 level? Why? What is the p value for this test? What can one conclude from the test of the hypothesis?

Source: Lee Sigelman, "Is Ignorance Bliss? A Reconsideration of the Folk Wisdom," *Human Relations* 34 (1981), 965–974.

2. THE POISONING OF LIVESTOCK BY INSECTICIDES

In recent years environmentalists and health professionals have been concerned about the ill effects on the environment of the widespread use of insecticides. Insecticides kill insects—and much else as well. They often find their way into the systems of animals, and even people. If human beings are to cope with the problem and make decisions about how to deal with it, they must understand the effect of insecticides on humans and other animals. In the kind of study often done to promote such understanding, Mount and Oehme investigated the effect of a commonly used insecticide on sheep. Among other statistical analyses, they derived the following linear regression equation ($n = 16$). This equation describes the relationship between the activity of a certain enzyme in the sheep's brain (Y) and the time (in hours) after the sheep has been exposed to the insecticide (X):

$$\hat{y}_i = 27.32 + 1.36x$$

Suppose that 30 hours have elapsed since a sheep has been exposed to the insecticide. What is the predicted value of Y? How would you describe the relationship between these two variables?

Mount and Oehme computed a coefficient of determination of 0.86 from their data. What conclusion can one draw about the true relationship between the two variables? Let $\alpha = 0.05$. Find the p value. What assumptions are necessary?

Source: Michael E. Mount and Frederick W. Oehme, "Diagnostic Criteria for Carbaryl Poisoning in Sheep," *Archives of Environmental Contamination and Toxicology* 10 (1981), 483–495.

3. CHARACTERISTICS OF ASPHALT

Brian H. Chollar et al. conducted a study in which they determined the characteristics of a group of asphalts used in highway pavements and related these characteristics to the physical properties of asphalts. Twenty-eight asphalt specimens were analyzed. Two of the characteristics on which the researchers collected data were large molecular size content measured as a percentage (LMS) and limiting stiffness temperature in degrees centigrade (LST). The data are shown in the following table. Do a regression analysis of these data with LMS as the dependent variable. Write a narrative description of the results. What conclusions can be drawn from the analysis?

Source: Brian H. Chollar, John G. Boone, Warren E. Cuff, and Ernest F. Bailey, "Chemical and Physical Characterization of Binder Materials," *Public Roads* 49(June 1985), 7–12.

LMS	LST	LMS	LST
32.23	−46	16.09	−53
32.15	−45	12.40	−41
27.01	−41	12.64	−56
12.70	−39	16.13	−46
9.43	−39	11.52	−34
23.96	−51	22.61	−46
17.75	−51	16.27	−40
17.24	−48	18.43	−33
15.98	−44	14.93	−36
8.79	−20	14.11	−35
15.57	−50	11.66	−35
23.07	−54	6.96	−30
26.88	−39	16.50	−23
14.58	−42	3.47	−22

4. BRIDGE SAFETY

Howard H. Bissell et al. state that safety on bridges has been shown to be related to the width of the bridge and the width of the roadway approach (travelway, plus the shoulder). The following table shows accident rates per 100 million vehicles (ACCIDENT) and the related bridge and roadway width differences in feet (WIDTH). Perform a regression analysis of these data with ACCIDENT as the dependent variable. Write a narrative summary of the results. What can one conclude from the analysis?

Source: Howard H. Bissell, George B. Pilkington II, John M. Mason, and Donald L. Woods, "Roadway Cross Section and Alinement," *Public Roads* 46(March 1983), 132–141.

WIDTH	−6	−4	−2	0	2	4	6	8	10	12
ACCIDENT	120	103	87	72	58	44	31	20	12	7

5. RETAIL ENVIRONMENTS

Ward et al. introduce a method to measure the prototypicality of retail environments and explore the relationship between environmental prototypicality, affect, and market share. Subjects were undergraduate students at a large campus in the Southwest. The study focused on fast-food restaurants. Among the variables on which data were collected were frequency of instantiation (FOI) and market share. To measure FOI, respondents were asked to rate how frequently they had encountered each of the restaurants in everyday life, in conversations, and in advertisements. The following table shows the measurements on FOI and market share for the 15 restaurants referred to in the study.

	FOI	Market Share
Wendy's	6.59	30
Long John Silver	2.18	6
Carl's Jr.	3.71	21
Whataburger	3.00	19
Dairy Queen	4.36	31
Church's	3.00	23
McDonald's	8.00	45
Kentucky Fried Chicken	5.16	38
Arby's	3.95	24
Jack in the Box	6.84	58
Ted's Hot Dogs	2.42	2
El Pollo Asado	4.53	24
Taco Bell	6.30	37
Burger King	7.53	51
Delectable Dog	1.12	3

We wish to know if we may conclude that there is a relationship between FOI and market share.

Source: James C. Ward, Mary Jo Bitner, and John Barnes, "Measuring the Prototypicality and Meaning of Retail Environments," *Journal of Retailing*, 68 (1992), 194–220.

SUGGESTIONS FOR FURTHER READING

Anscombe, F. J. (1960). "Rejection of Outliers," *Technometrics*, 2:123–147.

Anscombe, F. J., and John W. Tukey (1963). "The Examination and Analysis of Residuals," *Technometrics*, 5:141–160.

Draper, N. R., and H. Smith (1981). *Applied Regression Analysis*, 2nd ed. Wiley, New York.

Gunst, Richard F., and Robert L. Mason (1980). *Regression Analysis and Its Application*. Marcel Dekker, New York.

Kleinbaum, David G., and Lawrence L. Kupper (1988). *Applied Regression Analysis and Other Multivariable Methods,* 2nd ed. Duxbury, North Scituate, Mass.

Mendenhall, William, and James T. McClave (1981). *A Second Course in Business Statistics: Regression Analysis.* Dellen, San Francisco.

Montgomery, Douglas C., and Elizabeth A. Peck (1982). *Introduction to Linear Regression Analysis.* Wiley, New York.

Neter, John, and William Wasserman (1985). *Applied Linear Statistical Models,* 2nd ed. Irwin, Homewood, Ill.

————, and Michael H. Kutner (1988). *Applied Linear Regression Models,* 2nd ed. Irwin, Homewood, Ill.

Weisberg, Sanford (1985). *Applied Linear Regression,* 2nd ed. Wiley, New York.

Younger, Mary Sue (1979). *Handbook for Linear Regression.* Duxbury, North Scituate, Mass.

10

Multiple Regression and Correlation

Chapter Objectives: In Chapter 9, you studied techniques for investigating the relationships between two variables. In this chapter, we extend the discussion to include relationships among three or more variables. After studying this chapter and working the exercises, you should be able to

1. Write and explain the multiple regression model.
2. Obtain a multiple regression equation from sample data.
3. Evaluate a sample regression equation by means of analysis of variance.
4. Test null hypotheses about and construct confidence intervals for individual population regression coefficients.
5. Use a sample multiple regression equation for prediction and estimation.
6. Understand the concepts and techniques involved in the use of dummy variables.
7. Compute a coefficient of multiple correlation from sample data.
8. Test the sample multiple and partial correlation coefficients for significance.
9. Use a computer software package to perform multiple regression analysis calculations.

10.1 INTRODUCTION

Chapter 9 presents the concepts and techniques of regression and correlation as tools for analysis of the relationships between two variables. It shows that regression analysis, properly done, leads to an equation that we can use to predict the likely value of one variable, given the value of some other associated variable. Similarly, it shows that we can use correlation analysis to assess the strength of the relationship between two variables.

In multiple regression analysis, we study the relationships among three or more variables.

One would think that if we can predict the value of a variable on the basis of knowing *one* associated variable we might be able to make an even better prediction, given knowledge of *several* associated variables. We also often want to obtain some measure of the strength of the relationship among several variables rather than only two. A market analyst, for example, may correctly predict sales of a company's product in a given area from a knowledge of such things as the age composition of the population in the area, per capita income, population density, and the amount of money the firm spends on advertising. A personnel director may find that the productivity of employees is related to such factors as their experience, education, intelligence, emotional stability, and aptitude. A quality-control engineer may find that the quality of the product depends on such variables as the temperature, humidity, and pressure under which it is produced, as well as the quality of the raw material and the amount of some key ingredient.

We can study relationships such as these by means of *multiple regression* and *multiple-correlation* analysis. The techniques are logical extensions of those used in simple linear regression and correlation. Thus, the following discussion parallels that of Chapter 9. We first present the multiple regression model and its underlying assumptions. Then we look at ways to obtain and evaluate the multiple-regression equation. We also illustrate the use of the equation for predicting and estimating. Finally, we present the multiple-correlation model, its assumptions, and some of its uses.

10.2 THE MULTIPLE REGRESSION MODEL AND ITS UNDERLYING ASSUMPTIONS

You will recall that in Chapter 9 we wrote the simple linear regression model as

$$y_i = \alpha + \beta x_i + e_i$$

in which α and β are constants. In a discussion of multiple regression analysis, it is more convenient to use the Greek letter β to refer to all the constants in the model. The constants are distinguished from one another by subscripts. Consequently, we write the multiple regression model as follows:

(10.2.1)
$$y_j = \beta_0 + \beta_1 x_{1j} + \beta_2 x_{2j} + \cdots + \beta_k x_{kj} + e_j$$

where y_j is a typical value of Y, the dependent variable, from the population of interest; β_0, β_1, ..., β_k are the population *partial regression coefficients*; and x_{1j}, x_{2j}, ..., x_{kj} are observed values of the independent variables X_1, X_2, ..., X_k, respectively.

The model specified in Equation 10.2.1 is referred to as a *multiple linear regression model*. In the model, Y is a linear function of the k independent variables, $X_1, X_2, \ldots, X_k$.

A *linear model* is a model that is linear in the parameters.

The parameters of the model specified in Equation 10.2.1 are the partial regression coefficients, β_0, β_1, ..., β_k. We see that the model is linear because none of these regression coefficients is raised to a power greater than 1.

The reason for calling the parameters in Equation 10.2.1 partial regression coefficients is this: the parameter β_1, for example, is interpreted as the expected change in Y per unit change in X_1 while the other X's are held constant. The other β's may be interpreted in a similar manner.

ASSUMPTIONS

The following are the necessary assumptions underlying the multiple regression model when inference is an objective of the analysis:

1. The X_i may be either random or nonrandom (fixed) variables. Because of their role in explaining the variability in the dependent variable Y, they are sometimes referred to as *explanatory variables*. The X_i are also sometimes referred to as *predictor variables*, because of their role in predicting Y.
2. The independent variables, the X_i, are measured without error.
3. For each combination of X_i values, there is a normally distributed subpopulation of Y values.
4. The variances of the subpopulations of Y values are all equal.
5. The Y values are independent. This means that the value of Y observed for one value of X does not depend on the value observed for another value of X.
6. The e_j are normally and independently distributed, with mean 0 and variance σ^2.

THE REGRESSION SURFACE

You know that we can describe the linear relationship between two variables by a straight line. But how can we describe the linear relationship among *several* variables? We do so by means of a *regression surface*: a *plane* when three variables are involved or a *hyperplane* when there are more than three variables.

10.3 OBTAINING THE SAMPLE MULTIPLE REGRESSION EQUATION

We obtain the sample multiple regression equation by the method of least squares, in which the sum of the squared deviations of the observed data points about the regression surface is minimized. The calculations are best done on a computer. If a computer is not available, you may use the procedure described in Section 10.9. Regardless of the method used, the resulting sample regression equation is

(10.3.1)
$$\hat{y}_j = b_0 + b_1 x_{1j} + b_2 x_{2j} + \cdots + b_k x_{kj}$$

When the model contains only two independent variables, the sample regression equation is given by

(10.3.2)
$$\hat{y}_j = b_0 + b_1 x_{1j} + b_2 x_{2j}$$

The regression equation with two independent variables defines a plane.

where b_0 is the Y intercept of the plane, and b_1 and b_2 are the slopes of the plane associated with X_1 and X_2, respectively.

Figure 10.3.1 shows a typical scatter diagram of sample values and the corresponding regression plane for the case of two independent variables.

We illustrate the application of multiple regression analysis by means of the following example.

EXAMPLE 10.3.1   A market-research firm wants to predict weekend circulation of daily newspapers in various market areas. The firm selects two variables,

FIGURE 10.3.1   Scatter diagram and regression plane for multiple regression model

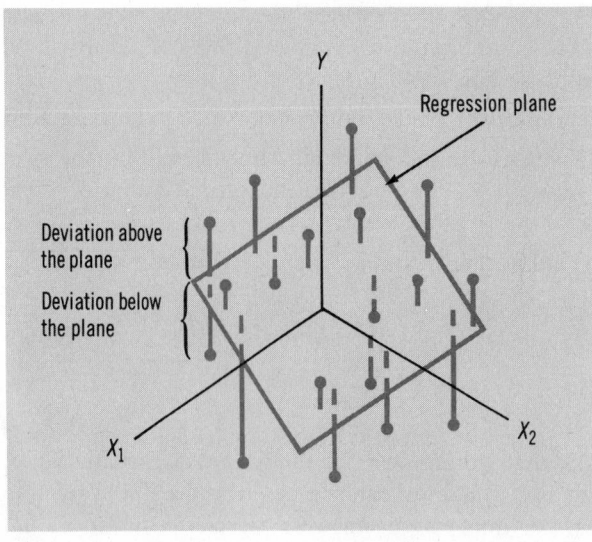

TABLE 10.3.1   Sample data, Example 10.3.1

Trade Area	Daily Newspapers, Weekend Circulation ($\times 1000$) y_j	Total Retail Sales ($1,000,000) x_{1j}	Population Per Sq. M x_{2j}
1	3.0	21.7	47.8
2	3.3	24.1	51.3
3	4.7	37.4	76.8
4	3.9	29.4	66.2
5	3.2	22.6	51.9
6	4.1	32.0	65.3
7	3.6	26.4	57.4
8	4.3	31.6	66.8
9	4.7	35.5	76.4
10	3.5	25.1	53.0
11	4.0	30.8	66.9
12	3.5	25.8	55.9
13	4.0	30.3	66.5
14	3.0	22.2	45.3
15	4.5	35.7	73.6
16	4.1	30.9	65.1
17	4.8	35.5	75.2
18	3.4	24.2	54.6
19	4.3	33.4	68.7
20	4.0	30.0	64.8
21	4.6	35.1	74.7
22	3.9	29.4	62.7
23	4.3	32.5	67.6
24	3.1	24.0	51.3
25	4.4	33.9	70.8
Total	98.2	739.5	1,576.6
Mean	3.928	29.580	63.064

total retail sales and population density, as the independent variables. A random sample of $n = 25$ trade areas gives the results shown in Table 10.3.1.

SOLUTION   After the sample data have been collected, the next step in multiple regresssion analysis is to obtain the sample regression equation. When the equation is obtained by computer, it appears as part of the output. When a computer is not available, we may use the formulas given in Section 10.9. By either method, the equation is

$$\hat{y}_j = 0.381 + 0.067x_{1j} + 0.025x_{2j}$$

We perform further analyses of the data in Table 10.3.1 in the sections that follow.

COMPUTER **ANALYSIS**

The use of a computer in multiple regression analysis is highly desirable. As the number of independent variables increases, the number and complexity of the calculations increase very rapidly. If the only computational aid you have is a calculator, you can easily become discouraged when you have to carry out a regression analysis involving several independent variables. The use of a computer also lets you include many independent variables in the analysis when other considerations suggest their inclusion. With a computer, you can escape the drudgery of monotonous calculations. You can redirect your energies to the more interesting and challenging jobs of improving the quality of the data and interpreting the analysis properly. Most of the many statistical software packages that are available for mainframe computers and microcomputers have programs that perform multiple regression analysis. Figure 10.3.2 shows the printout for a multiple regression analysis performed by STAT+. The input for the analysis was the data of Example 10.3.1, shown in Table 10.3.1.

FIGURE 10.3.2   STAT+ computer printout of analysis of data for Example 10.3.1

```
Variable  I      B(I)        BETA(I)      XBAR(I)       S(I)
CIRC      1    0.382148    N.D.         3.928000     0.548826
RETSAL    2    0.067754    0.581531     29.58000     4.710566
POP       3    0.024446    0.412238     63.06400     9.254804

INDEX OF DETERMINATION (R-SQ) = 0.98026

CORRELATION COEFFICIENT (R) = 0.99008
            CORRELATION MATRIX
            CIRC        RETSAL       POP
CIRC      1.0000      0.9875      0.9849
RETSAL    0.9875      1.0000      0.9848
POP       0.9849      0.9848      1.0000
            ANALYSIS OF VARIANCE
  Source        SS        DF       MS          F
REGRESSION    7.381612    2     3.690806    546.243      @
ERROR         0.148648   22     0.006757
TOTAL         7.530260   24

STANDARD DEVIATION OF ERROR TERM 0.0821992

@ BEYOND BOUNDS OF MY TABLE-CONSULT F TABLE TO
DETERMINE SIGNIFICANCE
                                              95%
                                          Confidence
                            STD    T        Limits
Variable   Coefficient    Error  Statistic  (+, -)
RETSAL    2  0.067754    0.02006  3.37751   0.04160
POP       3  0.024446    0.01021  2.39426   0.02118
```

FIGURE 10.3.2   (continued)

```
D.F. = 22
DURBIN-WATSON STATISTIC = 1.9624
                    ACTUAL VS CALCULATED
   Actual      Calculated    Residual      PCT Residual
 3.000000      3.020949    -0.020949    -0.600000
 3.300000      3.269121     0.030879                   0.0
 4.700000      4.793633    -0.093633    -1.900000   0.900000
 3.900000      3.992469    -0.092469    -2.300000
 3.200000      3.182158     0.017842
 4.100000      4.146627    -0.046628    -1.100000   0.500000
 3.600000      3.574078     0.025922
 4.300000      4.156196     0.143805                0.700000
 4.700000      4.655122     0.044878                3.300000
 3.500000      3.378434     0.121566                0.900000
 4.000000      4.104437    -0.104437    -2.600000   3.400000
 3.500000      3.496756     0.003244            0.0
 4.000000      4.060781    -0.060781    -1.500000
 3.000000      2.993710     0.006290                0.200000
 4.500000      4.600223    -0.100223    -2.200000
 4.100000      4.067208     0.032792                0.700000
 4.800000      4.625786     0.174214                3.600000
 3.400000      3.356570     0.043431                1.200000
 4.300000      4.324601    -0.024601    -0.500000
 4.000000      3.998896     0.001104            0.0
 4.600000      4.586461     0.013539                0.200000
 3.900000      3.906906    -0.006906    -0.100000
 4.300000      4.236731     0.063269                1.400000
 3.100000      3.262345    -0.162345    -5.200000
 4.400000      4.409815    -0.009815    -0.200000
CONFIDENCE INTERVALS ON CIRC
Enter observed value of X2, RETSAL      25
Enter observed value of X3, POP         52
THE 95% CONFIDENCE LIMITS ON THE EXPECTED VALUE OF X1
(CIRC) ARE:

X1 = 3.347212 +/- 0.0666    UPPER = 3.413826
LOWER = 3.280598

THE 95% PREDICTION LIMITS ON THE EXPECTED VALUE OF X1
(CIRC) ARE:

X1 = 3.347212 +/- 0.1830    UPPER = 3.530238
LOWER = 3.164186
```

On the computer printout, the dependent variable Y and the independent variables X_1 and X_2 are referred to as CIRC, RETSAL and POP, respectively. The correlation matrix on the printout shows the simple correlation coefficients for each pair of variables. The simple correlation between CIRC and RETSAL, for

FIGURE 10.3.3 MINITAB printout of multiple regression analysis of the data in Example 10.3.1

```
MINITAB    MTB > REGR 'CIRC' 2 'RETSAL' 'POP';
           SUBC> PREDICT 25 52.

           The regression equation is
           CIRC = 0.382 + 0.0678 RETSAL + 0.0244 POP

           Predictor     Coef        Stdev      t-ratio       p
           Constant      0.3822      0.1203      3.18        0.004
           RETSAL        0.06779     0.02006     3.38        0.003
           POP           0.02443     0.01021     2.39        0.026

           s = 0.08220       R-sq = 98.0%      R-sq(adj) = 97.8%
                          ANALYSIS OF VARIANCE
           Source        DF        SS          MS         F          p
           Regression     2      7.3818      3.6909     546.25     0.000
           Error         22      0.1486      0.0068
           Total         24      7.5304

           Source        DF      SEQ SS
           RETSAL         1      7.3431
           POP            1      0.0387

           Obs.  RETSAL  CIRC    Fit     Stdev.Fit  Residual  St.Resid
             1    21.7   3.0000  3.0209   0.0320    -0.0209    -0.28
             2    24.1   3.3000  3.2691   0.0279     0.0309     0.40
             3    37.4   4.7000  4.7937   0.0349    -0.0937    -1.26
             4    29.4   3.9000  3.9924   0.0392    -0.0924    -1.28
             5    22.6   3.2000  3.1821   0.0379     0.0179     0.25
             6    32.0   4.1000  4.1467   0.0311    -0.0467    -0.61
             7    26.4   3.6000  3.5741   0.0205     0.0259     0.33
             8    31.6   4.3000  4.1562   0.0180     0.1438     1.79
             9    35.5   4.7000  4.6551   0.0327     0.0449     0.60
            10    25.1   3.5000  3.3785   0.0268     0.1215     1.56
            11    30.8   4.0000  4.1044   0.0227    -0.1044    -1.32
            12    25.8   3.5000  3.4967   0.0211     0.0033     0.04
            13    30.3   4.0000  4.0607   0.0267    -0.0607    -0.78
            14    22.2   3.0000  2.9938   0.0469     0.0062     0.09
            15    35.7   4.5000  4.6003   0.0301    -0.1003    -1.31
            16    30.9   4.1000  4.0672   0.0179     0.0328     0.41
            17    35.5   4.8000  4.6258   0.0273     0.1742     2.25R
            18    24.2   3.4000  3.3565   0.0319     0.0435     0.57
            19    33.4   4.3000  4.3246   0.0277    -0.0246    -0.32
            20    30.0   4.0000  3.9989   0.0190     0.0011     0.01
            21    35.1   4.6000  4.5864   0.0271     0.0136     0.17
            22    29.4   3.9000  3.9069   0.0165    -0.0069    -0.09
            23    32.5   4.3000  4.2368   0.0224     0.0632     0.80
            24    24.0   3.1000  3.2624   0.0273    -0.1624    -2.09R
            25    33.9   4.4000  4.4098   0.0232    -0.0098    -0.12

           R denotes an obs. with a large st. resid.
            Fit    Stdev.Fit      95% C.I.            95% P.I.
           3.3473   0.0321    (3.2806, 3.4139)    (3.1642, 3.5303)
```

example, is 0.9875, and for CIRC and POP, $r = 0.9849$. The correlation coefficients are repeated below the diagonal of 1's.

The "actual" and "calculated" values are the observed and calculated values of Y. For each observed (actual) value of Y (y_j), the computer substitutes the accompanying observed values of X_1 and X_2 into the regression equation to obtain $\hat{y}$, the calculated value of Y. The "residuals" column contains the $y_j - \hat{y}_j$ values. The analysis-of-variance table allows the user to determine whether the overall regression is significant. The computer also does the calculations necessary to test the null hypothesis that each slope coefficient β_i is equal to 0. Finally, STAT+ provides point and interval estimates of the mean of Y and point and interval prediction limits for selected values of X_1 and X_2.

Figure 10.3.3 contains a printout of the multiple regression analysis of the data of Example 10.3.1 as produced by MINITAB. Preceding the printout of the analysis in Figure 10.3.3 are the MINITAB commands and subcommands necessary to obtain the analysis. Because of rounding errors, some of the results shown on the computer printouts differ from those given in the text, which were obtained by the use of a calculator.

EXERCISES

Find the multiple regression equation for the sample data in each of the following exercises.

10.3.1   Ⓒ In a study of the yield of a certain grain, in bushels per acre (Y), researchers obtain the following data from ten farms. Here X_1 is fertilizer applied, in pounds per acre, and X_2 is an index of soil quality.

Y	50	52	56	59	62	64	68	69	70	71	Total = 621
X_1	38	39	39	41	44	42	43	46	48	47	Total = 427
X_2	50	50	54	56	56	60	64	63	62	60	Total = 575

$$\Sigma y_j^2 = 39{,}087 \qquad \Sigma x_{2j}^2 = 33{,}297 \qquad \Sigma x_{2j} y_j = 36{,}039$$
$$\Sigma x_{1j}^2 = 18{,}345 \qquad \Sigma x_{1j} y_j = 26{,}742 \qquad \Sigma x_{1j} x_{2j} = 24{,}682$$

10.3.2   Ⓒ The following table shows the scores (Y) made by ten assembly-line employees on a test designed to measure job satisfaction. It also shows the scores made on an aptitude test (X_1) and the number of days absent (X_2) during the past year (excluding vacations). All employees were on the payroll during the entire year.

Y	70	60	80	50	55	85	75	70	72	64	Total = 681
X_1	6	6	8	5	6	9	8	6	7	6	Total = 67
X_2	1	2	1	8	9	0	1	1	1	2	Total = 26

$$\Sigma y_j^2 = 47{,}455 \qquad \Sigma x_{2j}^2 = 158 \qquad \Sigma x_{2j} y_j = 1{,}510$$
$$\Sigma x_{1j}^2 = 463 \qquad \Sigma x_{1j} y_j = 4{,}673 \qquad \Sigma x_{1j} x_{2j} = 153$$

$\$$ 10.3.3 $\boxed{C}$ The following table shows, for a particular week, the sales (Y) of a certain product, advertising expenditures (X_1), and population density (X_2) for ten market areas. Sales and advertising expenditures are in tens of thousands of dollars, and population density is in people per square mile.

Y	20	25	24	30	32	40	28	50	40	50	Total = 339
X_1	0.2	0.2	0.2	0.3	0.3	0.4	0.3	0.5	0.4	0.5	Total = 3.3
X_2	50	50	50	60	60	70	50	75	70	74	Total = 609

$$\Sigma y_j^2 = 12,509 \qquad \Sigma x_{2j}^2 = 38,101 \qquad \Sigma x_{2j} y_j = 21,620$$
$$\Sigma x_{1j}^2 = 1.21 \qquad \Sigma x_{1j} y_j = 122.8 \qquad \Sigma x_{1j} x_{2j} = 211.5$$

10.4 EVALUATING THE REGRESSION EQUATION

Before we can feel confident about using a sample multiple regression equation for prediction and estimation, we must be assured that it adequately represents the relationship among the variables. The *coefficient of multiple determination* provides an overall measure of the adequacy of the equation. We can also use analysis of variance and the F test as an overall significance test for regression. We can evaluate the importance of individual explanatory variables by examining the sample *partial regression coefficients* associated with each.

THE COEFFICIENT OF MULTIPLE DETERMINATION

The *coefficient of multiple determination* is defined as

(10.4.1)
$$R_{y.12...k}^2 = \frac{\Sigma(\hat{y}_j - \bar{y})^2}{\Sigma(y_j - \bar{y})^2} = 1 - \frac{\Sigma(y_j - \hat{y}_j)^2}{\Sigma(y_j - \bar{y})^2}$$

The numerator of the middle term is the explained sum of squares, or the *sum of squares due to regression*, SSR, as it is sometimes called. The denominator is the total sum of squares, SST. The subscript on R^2 indicates that Y is the dependent variable and $X_1, X_2, \ldots, X_k$ are independent variables.

Thus, we may write Equation 10.4.1 as

(10.4.2)
$$R_{y.12...k}^2 = \frac{\text{SSR}}{\text{SST}}$$

The *coefficient of multiple determination* tells us what proportion of the total variability in Y, the dependent variable, is explained by the independent variables.

Chapter 9 shows that r^2, the coefficient of determination for simple linear regression, is positively biased. Likewise, the coefficient of multiple determination is a positively biased estimator of the population coefficient of multiple determination. We can adjust for bias by computing, as follows, a measure, $\tilde{R}^2_{y.12...k}$, that we call adjusted R^2.

(10.4.3)

$$\tilde{R}^2_{y.12...k} = 1 - \frac{\dfrac{\Sigma(y_j - \hat{y}_j)^2}{(n - k - 1)}}{\dfrac{\Sigma(y_j - \bar{y})^2}{(n - 1)}}$$

Since the correction factor, $(n - 1)/(n - k - 1)$, approaches 1 as the size of the sample increases, the difference between $R^2_{y.12...k}$ and $\tilde{R}^2_{y.12...k}$ is negligible for large samples.

Computing formulas for SSR and SST are found in Section 10.9. When we perform the calculations on a computer, the coefficient of multiple determination usually appears as part of the computer output.

EXAMPLE 10.3.1 *continued* We wish to obtain the coefficient of multiple determination for the newspaper-circulation problem.

SOLUTION SST and SSR for Example 10.3.1 are computed in Section 10.9. When we substitute these numerical values into Equation 10.4.2, we have

$$R^2_{y.12} = \frac{SSR}{SST} = \frac{7.40}{7.53} = 0.9827 \approx 0.98$$

Thus, the regression of Y on X_1 and X_2 explains 98% of the total variation in Y. We also may interpret $R^2_{y.12}$ as a measure of the goodness of fit of the regression plane to the observed points.

We can display the results of these calculations in an analysis-of-variance table, such as Table 10.4.1. We then carry out an F test to determine whether the overall regression of Y on the independent variables is significant.

EXAMPLE 10.3.1 *continued* We illustrate the procedure for determining whether an overall regression is significant for the case of the newspaper-circulation data of Example 10.3.1.

TABLE 10.4.1 ANOVA table for multiple-regression analysis

Source of Variation	SS	df	MS	F
Regression	SSR	k	MSR = SSR/k	MSR/MSE
Error	SSE	$n - k - 1$	MSE = SSE/$(n - k - 1)$	
Total	SST	$n - 1$		

TABLE 10.4.2 ANOVA table, Example 10.3.1

Source of Variation	SS	df	MS	F
Regression	7.40	2	3.7000	627.12
Error	0.13	22	0.0059	
Total	7.53	24		

SOLUTION

1. *Hypotheses.*

> H_0: there is no linear relationship between Y and
> the set of independent variables
> H_1: there is a linear relationship between Y and
> the set of independent variables

2. *Test statistic.* The test statistic is $F = \text{MSR}/\text{MSE}$, which, if the assumptions are met and H_0 is true, is distributed as F with k and $n - k - 1$ degrees of freedom.
3. *Significance level.* Let $\alpha = 0.01$.
4. *Decision rule.* Reject H_0 if the computed F is ≥ 5.72, the critical value of F for $\alpha = 0.01$ and 2 and 22 degrees of freedom.
5. *Calculations.* The calculations are shown in Table 10.4.2.
6. *Statistical decision.* We see that the computed F is considerably larger than 5.72. Therefore, we reject the hypothesis of no regression.
7. *Conclusion.* We conclude that the data at hand provide evidence to support, at the 0.01 level of significance, the contention that there is a linear regression between Y and the two independent variables ($p < 0.005$).

When the analysis of variance leads to a significant computed F, we say that a significant proportion of the variation in Y is explained by the regression of Y on the independent variables. Or we simply say that $R^2_{y.12...k}$ is significant.

The analysis-of-variance tables for the data of Example 10.3.1 produced by STAT+ and MINITAB are shown in Figures 10.3.2 and 10.3.3.

INFERENCES ABOUT INDIVIDUAL PARTIAL REGRESSION COEFFICIENTS

We can make inferences about individual population partial regression coefficients when the assumptions in Section 10.2 apply. When these assumptions hold, the b_i are each normally distributed. To test the null hypothesis that β_i is equal to some particular value β_{i0}, we use the following test statistic:

(10.4.4)
$$t = \frac{b_i - \beta_{i0}}{s_{b_i}}$$

The test statistic is distributed as Student's t with $n - k - 1$ degrees of freedom when H_0 is true and the assumptions are met. When we use a computer for multiple regression analysis, we usually find that s_{b_i} is part of the computer printout. Some computer programs that are readily available will also compute the t statistic. A formula for s_{b_i} is given in Section 10.9 for those who do not have access to a computer. The calculations of the s_{b_i} for Example 10.3.1 are also given in Section 10.9.

| **EXAMPLE 10.3.1** | *continued*   To illustrate inferential procedures with respect to the β's, let us use the newspaper-circulation data of Example 10.3.1.

| SOLUTION |

1. *Hypotheses.*

$$H_0: \beta_1 = 0, \qquad H_1: \beta_1 \neq 0$$

2. *Test statistic.* The test statistic is given by Equation 10.4.4.
3. *Significance level.* Let $\alpha = 0.05$.
4. *Decision rule.* Reject H_0 if the computed t is either ≤ -2.0739 or ≥ 2.0739, the critical values for $\alpha = 0.05$ (two-sided test) and 22 degrees of freedom.
5. *Calculations.* Using Equation 10.4.4 and the value of s_{b_1} computed in Section 10.9, we can compute the following value of the test statistic:

$$t = \frac{b_1 - 0}{s_{b_1}} = \frac{0.067 - 0}{0.0187447} = 3.57$$

6. *Statistical decision.* Since 3.57 is greater than 2.0739, we reject H_0.
7. *Conclusion.* We conclude that X_1, total retail sales, is linearly related to newspaper circulation ($p < 0.01$). We conclude that this variable in the presence of X_2 is useful in predicting and estimating the dependent variable.

We can carry out a similar test for β_2. Suppose, for this example, that we test

$$H_0: \beta_2 = 0 \qquad \text{against} \qquad H_1: \beta_2 \neq 0$$

at the 0.05 level of significance. The computed value of the test statistic is

$$t = \frac{0.025}{0.0095408} = 2.62$$

Since the computed t of 2.62 is greater than 2.0739, we again reject the null hypothesis. We conclude that population density, when it is used as an explanatory variable in the presence of X_1, has a significant influence on weekend circulation of daily newspapers $(0.02 < p < 0.01)$.

We can construct confidence intervals for the β_i from the general formula

$$\text{Estimate} \pm (\text{reliability factor}) \times (\text{standard error})$$

That is,

$(10.4.5)$
$$b_i \pm t_{(1-\alpha/2, n-k-1)} s_{b_i}$$

For our newspaper-circulation example, the 95% confidence interval for β_1 is

$$0.067 \pm 2.0739(0.0187447)$$
$$0.067 \pm 0.039, \quad 0.028, 0.106$$

We interpret this interval in the usual ways.

In testing hypotheses about all the β_i, the same problem arises concerning multiple tests using the same data that arose in the discussion of analysis of variance. If multiple tests are performed, the actual level of significance is generally larger than that stated. We have the same problem when we construct confidence intervals. If we construct them for more than one β, they will not be independent. Thus, the tabulated reliability factor is not strictly appropriate.

Note that $R^2_{y.12}$ may be significant when only one or neither of the partial regression coefficients is significant. In fact, in multiple regression analysis, any one of the following situations may arise:

1. R^2 and all b_i significant
2. R^2 and some but not all b_i significant
3. R^2 but none of the b_i significant
4. All b_i significant but not R^2
5. Some but not all b_i significant and not R^2
6. Neither R^2 nor any b_i significant

EXERCISES

10.4.1 Ⓒ Refer to Exercise 10.3.1.   (a) Calculate the coefficient of multiple determination. (b) Perform an analysis of variance.   (c) Test the significance of each b_i.   (d) Construct a confidence interval for at least one β_i. Let $\alpha = 0.05$ for all tests of significance and confidence intervals. Determine the p value for each test.

10.4.2 Ⓒ Refer to Exercise 10.3.2. Do the analysis suggested in Exercise 10.4.1.

10.4.3 Ⓒ Refer to Exercise 10.3.3. Do the analysis suggested in Exercise 10.4.1.

10.5   USING THE SAMPLE MULTIPLE REGRESSION EQUATION

We use the sample multiple regression equation for the same purposes as the simple linear regression equation: (1) to *predict*, for a single unit of association, the value Y is likely to assume for given values of the independent variables, and (2) to *estimate* the mean of the subpopulation of Y values assumed to exist for a given combination of values of the independent variables.

When the assumptions of Section 10.2 are met, we may also construct *prediction intervals* and *confidence intervals* by methods that are straightforward extensions of those in Chapter 9.

PREDICTING Y FOR GIVEN VALUES OF THE INDEPENDENT VARIABLES

To predict, for a single unit of association, the value that Y is likely to assume for given values of the independent variables, we substitute the values of interest into the regression equation. We call the result the point prediction of Y. The $100(1 - \alpha)\%$ prediction interval for the three-variable case is given by

(10.5.1)
$$\hat{y}_j \pm t_{(1 - \alpha/2, n - k - 1)} s_{\hat{y}.12}$$

where $s_{\hat{y}.12}$ is the estimated standard error of the prediction. The formula for this quantity is rather long and is given in Section 10.9. Those who use a computer will get the quantity or the prediction interval, or both, as part of their output.

EXAMPLE 10.3.1   *continued*   To illustrate the use of the regression equation for prediction, let us go back to our newspaper-circulation example.

SOLUTION   The equation is

$$\hat{y}_j = 0.381 + 0.067x_{1j} + 0.025x_{2j}$$

Suppose that, from the population of trade areas from which the sample was drawn, we draw another trade area with total retail sales of \$25,000,000 and population density of 52 persons per square mile. We wish to predict the weekend circulation of daily newspapers for this trade area.

Substituting $X_1 = 25$ and $X_2 = 52$ into the regression equation gives

$$\hat{y} = 0.381 + (0.067)(25) + (0.025)(52) = 3.356$$

Our point prediction of the weekend circulation of daily newspapers for this trade area is 3356.

We may now use Expression 10.5.1 to construct a 95% prediction interval for Y. To the point prediction we add and subtract the product of the reliability factor and the estimated standard error of the prediction. When we enter Table E of Appendix I with 22 degrees of freedom, we find that the reliability factor is 2.0739. The estimated standard error of the prediction, which is calculated in Section 10.9, is 0.0824525. The 95% prediction interval, then, is

$$3.356 \pm 2.0739(0.0824525)$$
$$3.356 \pm 0.171, \qquad 3.185, 3.527$$

Our interpretation of this interval is as follows: given a single trade area with annual sales of $25,000,000 and a population density of 52 people per square mile, we are 95% confident that the weekend circulation of daily newspapers in the area is between 3,185 and 3,527. We say this because we know that if we fit a regression plane to sample data from this population repeatedly and predict circulation in a trade area in a similar manner, we expect 95% of such intervals to include the trade area's true circulation.

ESTIMATING THE MEAN OF A SUBPOPULATION OF Y VALUES

To get a point estimate $\hat{\mu}_{y.12}$ of the mean of a subpopulation of Y values, we substitute the X values into the sample regression equation. The numerical value of the estimate will be the same as that of the prediction for the same values of x_1 and x_2.

The $100(1 - \alpha)\%$ confidence interval for the mean of a subpopulation of Y values for the three-variable case is given by

$$(10.5.2) \qquad \hat{\mu}_{y.12} \pm t_{(1-\alpha/2,n-k-1)}s_{\hat{\mu}.12}$$

where $s_{\hat{\mu}_{y.12}}$ is the estimated standard error of the estimate.

EXAMPLE 10.3.1 *continued* Suppose that, for our newspaper-circulation example, we wish to estimate the mean circulation for all trade areas that have total retail sales of $25,000,000 and a population density of 52 persons per square mile.

SOLUTION   As we have seen, the point estimate is 3,356. To obtain the 95% confidence interval for the subpopulation mean, we add to and subtract from the point estimate the product of the reliability factor and the estimated standard error. As for the prediction interval, the reliability factor is 2.0739. The estimated standard error, calculated in Section 10.9, is 0.03001. The 95% confidence interval, then, is

$$3.356 \pm 2.0739(0.03001)$$
$$3.356 \pm 0.062, \qquad 3.294, 3.418$$

We interpret this interval as follows: we are 95% confident that the mean of the subpopulation of Y for the specified combination of X's is between 3,294 and 3,418. We can say this because, if we repeated the process of fitting a regression plane to sample data from this population many times and constructed confidence intervals in the way described, in the long run 95% of these intervals would include the true mean.

EXERCISES

Construct 95% confidence and prediction intervals for specified X_i.

10.5.1   C Refer to Exercise 10.3.1 and let $x_{1j} = 40$ and $x_{2j} = 50$.

10.5.2   C Refer to Exercise 10.3.2 and let $x_{1j} = 5$ and $x_{2j} = 1$.

10.5.3   C Refer to Exercise 10.3.3 and let $x_{1j} = 0.2$ and $x_{2j} = 60$.

10.6   QUALITATIVE INDEPENDENT VARIABLES

The independent variables considered in the preceding discussion are all quantitative; that is, they yield numerical values that are either counts or measurements in the usual sense of the word. For example, some of the independent variables used in our examples and exercises are advertising expenditures, aptitude test scores, and employee absences. Frequently, however, it is desirable to use one or more qualitative variables as independent variables in the regression model. Qualitative variables, as we have seen, are those variables whose "values" are categories that convey the concept of attribute rather than amount or quantity. The variable "marital status," for example, is a qualitative variable, whose categories are "single," "married," "widowed," and "divorced." Other examples of qualitative variables include sex (male or female), employment status, race, occupation, and place of residence (urban, suburban, or rural, for example). In certain situations, an investigator may suspect that including one or more variables of this type in the regression equation would contribute significantly to the reduction of the error sum of squares and thereby provide more precise estimates of the parameters of interest.

Qualitative variables convey the concept of attribute.

Suppose, for example, that we are studying the relationship between the dependent variable job satisfaction and the independent variables aptitude for the job and age. We might also want to include the qualitative variable sex as one of the independent variables. Or suppose that we wish to gain insight into the nature of the relationship between sales volume of some product and other relevant variables. Candidates for inclusion in the model might consist of such quantitative variables as advertising expenditures, number of competing brands, and the length of time the product has been on the market, along with qualitative variables like the type of store in which the product is sold and the geographic region in which it is sold.

In order to incorporate a qualitative independent variable in the multiple regression model, we must quantify it in some manner. We may accomplish this through the use of what are known as *dummy variables*.

A *dummy variable* is a variable that assumes only a finite number of values (such as 0 or 1) for the purpose of identifying the different categories of a qualitative variable.

The term "dummy" is used to indicate the fact that the numerical values (such as 0 and 1) assumed by the variable have no quantitative meaning but merely identify different categories of the qualitative variable under consideration. Dummy variables are also referred to as indicator variables.

The following are some examples of qualitative variables and the dummy variables used to quantify them.

Qualitative Variable	Number of Categories	Dummy Variable
Sex (male, female)	2	$X = \begin{cases} 1 \text{ for male} \\ 0 \text{ for female} \end{cases}$
Place of residence (urban, rural, suburban)	3	$X_1 = \begin{cases} 1 \text{ for urban} \\ 0 \text{ for rural or suburban} \end{cases}$ $X_2 = \begin{cases} 1 \text{ for rural} \\ 0 \text{ for urban or suburban} \end{cases}$
Employment status (employed, unemployed for six months or less, unemployed more than six months, never worked)	4	$X_1 = \begin{cases} 1 \text{ for employed} \\ 0 \text{ otherwise} \end{cases}$ $X_2 = \begin{cases} 1 \text{ for unemployed } (\leq 6 \text{ months}) \\ 0 \text{ otherwise} \end{cases}$ $X_3 = \begin{cases} 1 \text{ for unemployed } (>6 \text{ months}) \\ 0 \text{ otherwise} \end{cases}$

We can see that a qualitative variable with two categories requires one dummy variable. A qualitative variable with three categories requires two dummy variables, X_1 and X_2, used in combination as follows:

X_1	X_2	
1	0	Category 1 (urban in the example)
0	1	Category 2 (rural in the example)
0	0	Category 3 (suburban in the example)

A qualitative variable with four categories requires three dummy variables $(X_1, X_2, \text{ and } X_3)$, used in combination as follows:

X_1	X_2	X_3	
1	0	0	Category 1 (employed in the example)
0	1	0	Category 2 (unemployed ≤6 months in the example)
0	0	1	Category 3 (unemployed >6 months in the example)
0	0	0	Category 4 (never worked in the example)

Note that no more than one of the dummy variables receives a code of 1 to represent a given category.

A qualitative variable with k categories requires $k - 1$ dummy variables.

Note in these examples that when the qualitative variable has k categories we must define $k - 1$ dummy variables in order to code all the categories properly. This rule is applicable for any multiple regression equation that contains an intercept constant. We can quantify the variable "sex," with two categories, using only one dummy variable, whereas we need three dummy variables to quantify the variable "employment status," which has four categories.

The following examples illustrate some of the uses of qualitative variables in multiple regression. In the first example, we assume that there is no interaction between the independent variables. Since the assumption of no interaction is not realistic in many instances, we illustrate, in the second example, the analysis that is appropriate when interaction between variables needs to be accounted for.

EXAMPLE 10.6.1   The production manager for Hassam Manufacturing Company wishes to study the relationship between productivity and other characteristics of employees assigned to work in a newly opened branch plant located in the same city. One of the questions to which the production manager wants an answer is, Do employees who volunteer for a new work environment and those who are involuntarily assigned to the environment differ with respect to productivity? Employees who have been with the firm for at least a year are given an opportunity to volunteer to work in the new plant. From these, a random sample of 16 is selected for transfer. From among the employees who did not volunteer, an independent random sample of 16 is selected and assigned to work in the new plant. The data on these 32 employees, shown in Table 10.6.1, are collected during their second month in the new plant. The dependent variable is the average number of units produced per day during the second month that the new plant was open. One of the independent variables is job aptitude test score. The other independent variable, which is qualitative, indicates whether the employee volunteered to transfer to the new plant or whether he or she was involuntarily assigned by management to work there.

SOLUTION   For the analysis of the data, we will quantify assignment status by means of a variable that is coded 1 if the employee was involuntarily assigned (I) and 0 if the employee volunteered (V). The data in Table 10.6.1 are plotted as a scatter diagram in Figure 10.6.1. The scatter diagram suggests that in general, higher aptitude scores are associated with higher production levels.

TABLE 10.6.1   Data collected on a sample of 32 employees, Example 10.6.1

Employee	Number of Units Produced Y	Aptitude Test Score X_1	Assignment Status X_2
1	2940	38	I
2	3130	38	V
3	2420	36	I
4	2450	34	V
5	2760	39	I
6	2440	35	I
7	3226	40	V
8	3301	42	I
9	2729	37	V
10	3410	40	V
11	2715	36	I
12	3095	39	V
13	3130	39	I
14	3244	39	V
15	2520	35	V
16	2928	39	I
17	3523	41	V
18	3446	42	I
19	2920	38	V
20	2957	39	I
21	3530	42	V
22	2580	38	I
23	3040	37	V
24	3500	42	I
25	3200	41	I
26	3322	39	V
27	3459	40	V
28	3346	42	I
29	2619	35	V
30	3175	41	I
31	2740	38	I
32	2841	36	V

COMPUTER **ANALYSIS**

To obtain additional insight into the nature of these data, we may enter them into a computer and employ an appropriate program to perform further analyses. For example, we enter the observations $y_1 = 2940$, $x_{11} = 38$, $x_{21} = 1$ for the first employee; $y_2 = 3130$, $x_{12} = 38$, $x_{22} = 0$, for the second employee; and so on. Figure 10.6.2 shows the computer output obtained using the STAT+ multiple regression program.

We see in the printout that, after rounding, the multiple regression equation is

FIGURE 10.6.1   Productivity and job aptitude for 32 employees

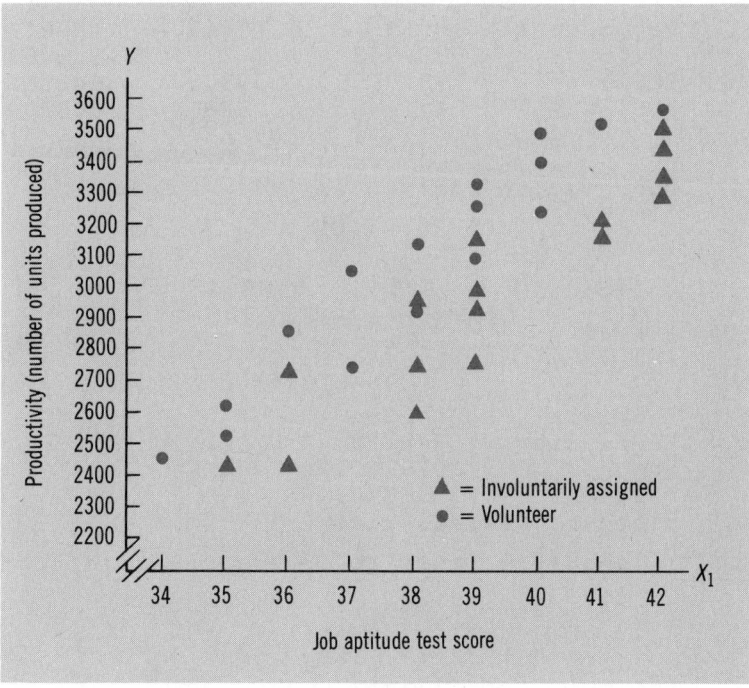

(10.6.1)
$$\hat{y} = b_0 + b_1 x_1 + b_2 x_2$$
$$\hat{y} = -2390 + 143x_1 - 245x_2$$

To observe the effect on this equation when we wish to consider only the productivity of involuntarily assigned employees, we let $x_2 = 1$. The equation then becomes

(10.6.2)
$$\hat{y} = -2390 + 143x_1 - 245(1)$$
$$= -2635 + 143x_1$$

which has a y intercept of $-2,635$ and a slope of 143. Note that the y intercept for the new equation is equal to $(b_0 + b_2) = [-2390 + (-245)] = -2,635$.

Now let us consider only the productivity of employees who volunteered. When we let $x_2 = 0$, our regression equation reduces to

(10.6.3)
$$\hat{y} = -2,390 + 143x_1 - 245(0)$$
$$= -2,390 + 143x_1$$

FIGURE 10.6.2 Computer printout for Example 10.6.1

```
Variable I     B(I)      BETA(I)      XBAR(I)      S(I)
UNITS       -2389.543    N.D.        3019.875    341.6797
TEST          143.0995   0.963093      38.65625    2.299584
ASSIGN       -244.5432  -0.357854       0.500000    0.500000
Index of Determination (R-SQ) = 0.89639
Correlation Coefficient (R) = 0.94678
              CORRELATION MATRIX
            Units      Test       Assign
UNITS       1.0000     0.8804     -0.1354
TEST        0.8804     1.0000      0.2310
ASSIGN     -0.1354     0.2310      1.0000
                ANALYSIS OF VARIANCE
    Source        SS         DF        MS           F
 Regression   3348770.000     2    1674385.000   125.448*
 Error         387070.000    29      13347.240
 Total        3735840.000    31
 Standard Deviation of Error Term    115.5303
 * Consult F Table to Determine Significance

                                              95%
                                          Confidence
                                            Limits
 Variable Coefficient Std Error  T Statistic  (+,-)
 TEST         143.0995    9.1281    15.677     18.667
 ASSIGN      -244.5432   41.9818    -5.825     85.853
 DF = 29
```

The slope of this equation is the same as the slope of the equation for involuntarily assigned employees, but the y intercepts are different. The y intercept for the equation associated with employees who volunteered is larger than the one for the involuntarily assigned employees. These results show that, for this sample, employees who volunteered were more productive, on the average, than those who were involuntarily assigned to the new plant when aptitude test scores are taken into account. The amount of the difference, on the average, is 245 units. Stated another way, we can say that, for this sample, employees who were involuntarily assigned produced, on the average, 245 fewer units than employees who volunteered, when job aptitude test scores are taken into account. Figure 10.6.3 shows the scatter diagram of the original data, along with a plot of the two regression lines (Equations 10.6.2 and 10.6.3).

FIGURE 10.6.3   Productivity and job aptitude test scores for 32 employees and the fitted regression lines

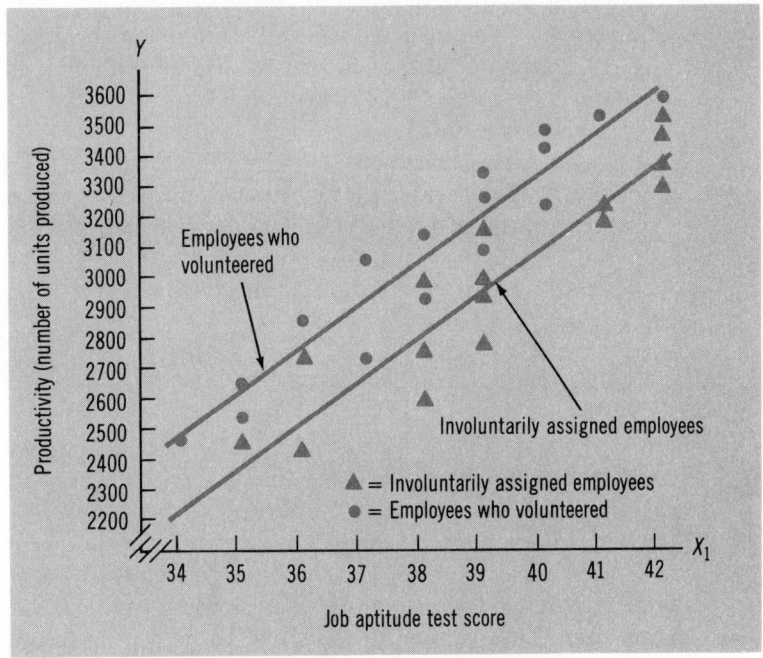

HYPOTHESIS TESTING

At this point, a question arises regarding what inferences we can make about the sampled population on the basis of these sample results. First of all, we may ask whether the sample difference of 245 is significant. In other words, does method of assignment have an effect on productivity? We may answer this question through the following hypothesis-testing procedure.

1. *Hypotheses.*

$$H_0: \beta_2 = 0, \qquad H_1: \beta_2 \neq 0$$

2. *Test statistic.* The test statistic is

$$t = \frac{b_2 - 0}{s_{b_2}}$$

3. *Significance level.* Let $\alpha = 0.05$.

4. *Decision rule.* We reject H_0 if the computed t is either greater than or equal to 2.0452 or less than or equal to -2.0452.

5. *Calculations.* The calculated value of the test statistic appears in Figure 10.6.2 as the t ratio for the coefficient associated with the variable appearing in column 3 of Table 10.6.1. This coefficient, of course, is b_2. We see that the computed t is -5.825.

6. *Statistical decision.* Since $-5.825 < -2.0452$, we reject H_0.

7. *Conclusion.* We conclude that whether employees volunteer to work at a new plant or are assigned to the new plant does have an effect on their productivity.

For this test, we have $p < 2(0.005)$, since -5.825 is less than -2.7564.

CONFIDENCE INTERVALS

Now that we are able to conclude that in the sampled population the assignment status of the employees does have an effect on their productivity, we may next inquire as to the magnitude of the effect. Our best point estimate of the average difference in productivity when aptitude test scores are taken into account is 245 units more for employees who volunteer to work in the new plant. We may obtain an interval estimate of the mean amount of the difference by using information from the computer printout and the following formula:

$$b_2 \pm ts_{b_2}$$

For a 95% confidence interval, we have

$$-244.5432 \pm 2.0452(41.9818)$$
$$-330.4044, \quad -158.6820$$

Thus, we are 95% confident that the difference is somewhere between about 159 units and 330 units.

ADVANTAGES OF USING DUMMY VARIABLES

You may have correctly surmised that an alternative analysis of the data of Example 10.6.1 would consist of fitting two separate regression equations: one to the subsample of employees who volunteered and another to the subsample of those who were involuntarily assigned. Such an approach, however, lacks some of the advantages of the dummy-variable technique and is a less desirable procedure when the dummy-variable technique is valid. If we can justify the assumption that the two separate regression lines have the same slope, we can get a better estimate of this common slope using dummy variables and pooling the data from the two subsamples. In Example 10.6.1, the estimate using a dummy variable is based on a total sample size of 32 observations, whereas separate estimates would each be based on a sample of only 16 observations. The dummy-variable approach also yields more precise inferences regarding other parameters, since more degrees of freedom are available for the calculation of the error mean square.

INTERACTION

Now let us consider the situation in which interaction between the variables is assumed to be present. Suppose, for example, that we have two independent variables: one quantitative variable X_1 and one qualitative variable with three response levels, yielding the two dummy variables X_2 and X_3. The model, then, would be

(10.6.4)
$$y_j = \beta_0 + \beta_1 X_{1j} + \beta_2 X_{2j} + \beta_3 X_{3j} + \beta_4 X_{1j} X_{2j} + \beta_5 X_{1j} X_{3j} + e_j$$

in which $\beta_4 X_{1j} X_{2j}$ and $\beta_5 X_{1j} X_{3j}$ are called *interaction terms* and represent the interaction between the quantitative and qualitative independent variables. Note that there is no need to include the term containing $X_{2j} X_{3j}$ in the model, since it will always be 0: when $X_2 = 1$, $X_3 = 0$, and when $X_3 = 1$, $X_2 = 0$. Only one level of the qualitative variable will exist for a given unit of association, and therefore no interaction between response levels is possible. This model allows for a different slope and Y intercept for each level of the qualitative variable. Suppose that we use the following dummy-variable coding to quantify the qualitative variable:

$$X_2 = \begin{cases} 1 \text{ for level 1} \\ 0 \text{ otherwise} \end{cases}$$

$$X_3 = \begin{cases} 1 \text{ for level 2} \\ 0 \text{ otherwise} \end{cases}$$

The three sample regression equations for the three levels of the qualitative variables, then, are as follows:

Level 1 ($X_2 = 1$, $X_3 = 0$):

(10.6.5)
$$\begin{aligned} \hat{y} &= b_0 + b_1 x_{1j} + b_2(1) + b_3(0) + b_4 x_{1j}(1) + b_5 x_{1j}(0) \\ &= b_0 + b_1 x_{1j} + b_2 + b_4 x_{1j} \\ &= (b_0 + b_2) + (b_1 + b_4) x_{1j} \end{aligned}$$

Level 2 ($X_2 = 0$, $X_3 = 1$):

(10.6.6)
$$\hat{y} = b_0 + b_1 x_{1j} + b_2(0) + b_3(1) + b_4 x_{1j}(0) + b_5 x_{1j}(1)$$
$$= b_0 + b_1 x_{1j} + b_3 + b_5 x_{1j}$$
$$= (b_0 + b_3) + (b_1 + b_5)x_{1j}$$

Level 3 ($X_2 = 0$, $X_3 = 0$):

(10.6.7)
$$\hat{y} = b_0 + b_1 x_{1j} + b_2(0) + b_3(0) + b_4 x_{1j}(0) + b_5 x_{1j}(0)$$
$$= b_0 + b_1 x_{1j}$$

The following example illustrates these results.

EXAMPLE 10.6.2   A drug manufacturer wishes to compare three drugs (A, B, and C), which it can produce for the treatment of severe depression. The investigator would also like to study the relationship between age and drug effectiveness and the interaction (if any) between age and drug. Each member of a simple random sample of 36 patients, comparable with respect to diagnosis and severity of depression, was randomly assigned to receive Drug A, B, or C. The results are shown in Table 10.6.2.

SOLUTION   The dependent variable Y is drug effectiveness, the quantitative independent variable X_1 is patient's age at nearest birthday, and the independent variable "drug" is a qualitative variable that occurs at three levels. The following dummy-variable coding is used to quantify the qualitative variable:

$$X_2 = \begin{cases} 1 \text{ if Drug A} \\ 0 \text{ if otherwise} \end{cases}$$

$$X_3 = \begin{cases} 1 \text{ if Drug B} \\ 0 \text{ if otherwise} \end{cases}$$

The scatter diagram for these data is shown in Figure 10.6.4. Table 10.6.3 shows the data as they were entered into a computer for analysis, and Figure 10.6.5 contains the printout of the analysis using the STAT+ multiple regression program.

INTERPRETING THE COMPUTER PRINTOUT

Now let us examine the printout to see what insight into the nature of the relationships among the variables it provides. The least-squares equation (with the constants rounded) is

$$\hat{y}_j = 6.21 + 1.03x_{1j} + 41.3x_{2j} + 22.7x_{3j} - 0.703x_{1j}x_{2j} - 0.510x_{1j}x_{3j}$$

TABLE 10.6.2   Data for Example 10.6.2

Measure of Effectiveness	Age	Drug
56	21	A
41	23	B
40	30	B
28	19	C
55	28	A
25	23	C
46	33	B
71	67	C
48	42	B
63	33	A
52	33	A
62	56	C
50	45	C
45	43	B
58	38	A
46	37	C
58	43	B
34	27	C
65	43	A
55	45	B
57	48	B
59	47	C
64	48	A
61	53	A
62	58	B
36	29	C
69	53	A
47	29	B
73	58	A
64	66	B
60	67	B
62	63	A
71	59	C
62	51	C
70	67	A
71	63	C

The three regression equations for the three drugs are as follows:

Drug A (Equation 10.6.5):

$$\hat{y}_j = (6.21 + 41.3) + (1.03 - 0.703)x_{1j}$$
$$= 47.51 + 0.327x_{1j}$$

FIGURE 10.6.4   Scatter diagram of data for Example 10.6.2

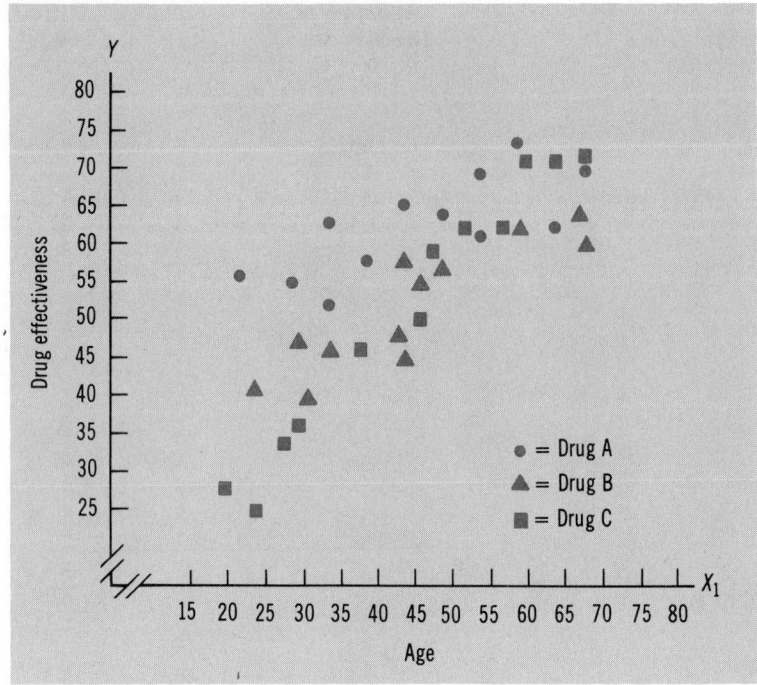

Drug B (Equation 10.6.6):

$$\hat{y}_j = (6.21 + 22.7) + (1.03 - 0.510)x_{1j}$$
$$= 28.91 + 0.520x_{1j}$$

Drug C (Equation 10.6.7):

$$\hat{y}_j = 6.21 + 1.03x_{1j}$$

Figure 10.6.6 shows the scatter diagram of the original data along with the regression equations for the three drugs. Visual inspection of Figure 10.6.6 suggests that Drugs A and B do not differ greatly with respect to their slopes, but their y intercepts are considerably different. The graph suggests that Drug A is better than Drug B for younger patients but that the difference is less dramatic with older patients. Drug C appears to be decidedly less desirable than either Drug A or Drug B for younger patients but is about as effective as Drug B for older patients. These subjective impressions are compatible with the contention that there is interaction between treatments and age.

What we see in Figure 10.6.6, however, are sample results. What can we conclude about the population from which the sample was drawn?

TABLE 10.6.3   Data of Example 10.6.2 coded for computer analysis

Y	X_1	X_2	X_3	X_1X_2	X_1X_3
56	21	1	0	21	0
55	28	1	0	28	0
63	33	1	0	33	0
52	33	1	0	33	0
58	38	1	0	38	0
65	43	1	0	43	0
64	48	1	0	48	0
61	53	1	0	53	0
69	53	1	0	53	0
73	58	1	0	58	0
62	63	1	0	63	0
70	67	1	0	67	0
41	23	0	1	0	23
40	30	0	1	0	30
46	33	0	1	0	33
48	42	0	1	0	42
45	43	0	1	0	43
58	43	0	1	0	43
55	45	0	1	0	45
57	48	0	1	0	48
62	58	0	1	0	58
47	29	0	1	0	29
64	66	0	1	0	66
60	67	0	1	0	67
28	19	0	0	0	0
25	23	0	0	0	0
71	67	0	0	0	0
62	56	0	0	0	0
50	45	0	0	0	0
46	37	0	0	0	0
34	27	0	0	0	0
59	47	0	0	0	0
36	29	0	0	0	0
71	59	0	0	0	0
62	51	0	0	0	0
71	63	0	0	0	0

MAKING INFERENCES ABOUT Y-INTERCEPT PARAMETERS

For an answer, let us look at the t ratios on the computer printout in Figure 10.6.5. Each of these is the test statistic

$$t = \frac{b_i - 0}{s_{b_i}}$$

FIGURE 10.6.5 Computer printout for Example 10.6.2

Variable I	B(I)	BETA(I)	XBAR(I)	S(I)
1	6.211048	N.D.	55.16667	12.24178
2	1.033398	1.217584	44.11112	14.42368
3	41.30451	1.590548	0.333333	0.471405
4	22.70717	0.874404	0.333333	0.471405
5	− 0.702890	−1.298073	14.94444	22.60770
6	− 0.509714	−0.921792	14.63889	22.13865

Index of Determination (R-SQ) = 0.91434

Correlation Coefficient (R) = 0.95621

CORRELATION MATRIX

1.0000	0.7967	0.4140	−0.1877	0.4639	−0.0567
0.7967	1.0000	0.0354	−0.0095	0.2307	0.1838
0.4140	0.0354	1.0000	−0.5000	0.9348	−0.4676
−0.1877	−0.0095	−0.5000	1.0000	−0.4674	0.9351
0.4639	0.2307	0.9348	−0.4674	1.0000	−0.4371
−0.0567	0.1838	−0.4676	0.9351	−0.4371	1.0000

ANALYSIS OF VARIANCE

Source	SS	DF	MS	F
Regression	4932.853	5	986.571	64.043 *
Error	462.147	30	15.405	
Total	5395.000	35		

Standard Deviation of Error Term   3.9249

* Consult F Table to Determine Significance

Variable	Coefficient	Std Error	T Statistic	95% Confidence Limits (+,−)
2	1.0334	0.0723	14.288	0.148
3	41.3045	5.0845	8.124	10.383
4	22.7072	5.0910	4.460	10.396
5	−0.7029	0.1090	−6.451	0.222
6	−0.5097	0.1104	−4.617	0.225

DF = 30

for testing H_0: $\beta_i = 0$. We can see by Equation 10.6.5 that the y intercept of the regression line for Drug A is equal to $b_0 + b_2$. Since the t ratio of 8.124 for testing H_0: $\beta_2 = 0$ is greater than the critical t of 2.0423 (for $\alpha = 0.05$), we can reject H_0: $\beta_2 = 0$ and conclude that the y intercept of the population regression line for Drug A is different from the y intercept of the population regression line for Drug C, which has a y intercept of β_0. Similarly, since the t ratio of 4.46 for testing H_0: $\beta_3 = 0$ is also greater than the critical t of 2.0423, we can conclude (at the 0.05 level of significance) that the y intercept of the population regression line for Drug B is also different from the y intercept of the population regression line for Drug C. (See the y intercept of Equation 10.6.6.)

MAKING INFERENCES ABOUT SLOPE PARAMETERS

Now let us consider the slopes. We see by Equation 10.6.5 that the slope for the regression line for Drug A is equal to b_1 (the slope of the line for treatment C) + b_4. Since the t ratio of -6.451 for testing $H_0: \beta_4 = 0$ is less than the critical t of -2.0423, we can conclude (for $\alpha = 0.05$) that the slopes of the population regression lines for Drugs A and C are different. Similarly, since the computed t ratio for testing $H_0: \beta_5 = 0$ is also less than -2.0423, we conclude (for $\alpha = 0.05$) that Drugs B and C have different slopes. (See the slope of Equation 10.6.6.) Thus, we conclude that there is interaction between age and drug. This is reflected by a lack of parallelism among the regression lines in Figure 10.6.6.

Another question of interest is this: is the slope of the population regression line for Drug A different from the slope of the population regression line for Drug B? Answering this question requires computational techniques beyond the scope of this text.

In Section 10.4, you were warned that there are problems involved in making multiple inferences from the same sample data. You can consult the Suggestions

FIGURE 10.6.6   Scatter diagram of data for Example 10.6.2 with the fitted regression lines

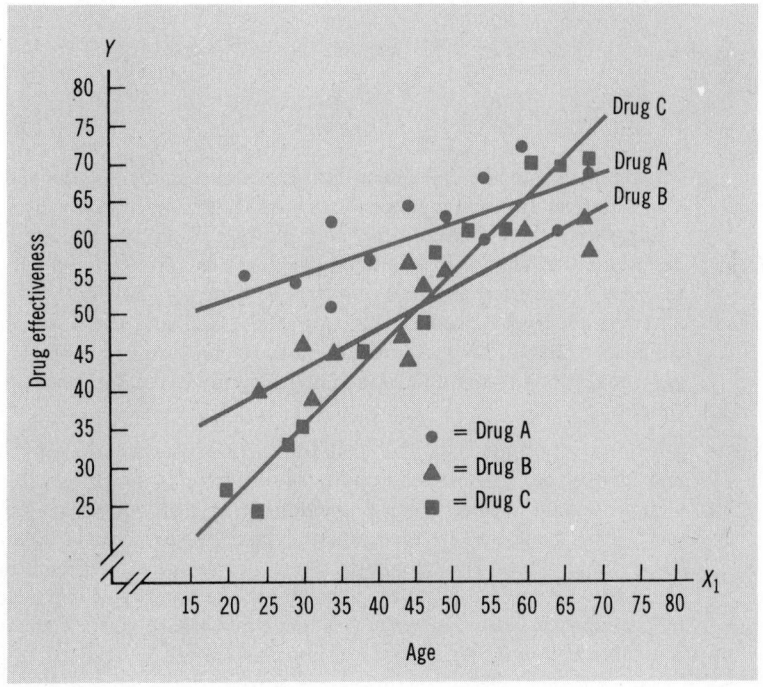

for Further Reading at the end of the chapter for procedures to follow when you want multiple inferences, such as those discussed in this section.

We have discussed only two situations in which the use of dummy variables is appropriate. More complex models involving the use of one or more qualitative independent variables in the presence of two or more quantitative variables may be appropriate in certain circumstances.

EXERCISES

10.6.1   Ⓒ Twenty-two business executives participated in a study designed to provide information about the relationship between overall health status and age. Ten of the subjects were hypertensive, and 12 had normal blood pressure levels. The following table shows the results.

Health Status (Y)	Age	Hypertensive?	Health Status (Y)	Age	Hypertensive?
30.1	32	yes	51.8	57	yes
27.0	36	no	22.1	35	no
46.1	57	no	30.3	46	no
45.3	45	yes	45.8	37	yes
59.9	73	no	51.8	67	no
38.2	32	yes	52.9	49	yes
29.1	42	no	16.0	41	no
60.0	62	yes	43.9	61	no
51.0	72	no	48.6	39	yes
32.5	38	yes	29.8	48	no
35.0	54	no	64.1	57	yes

Measurements on the dependent variable, health status, are derived in such a way that a larger number indicates a poorer quality of health. Use dummy-variable coding to quantify the qualitative variable and use multiple regression to obtain a least-squares equation describing the relationship between health status and age for the hypertensive group and the group with normal blood pressure. Can we conclude that blood pressure status has an effect on level of health? Let $\alpha = 0.05$, and find the p value. Construct the 95% confidence interval for the difference in the mean level of health for the two groups when age is taken into account. Draw a scatter diagram of the data, and plot the fitted regression equations.

10.6.2   Ⓒ A production manager at Iredell Tool Works studying the effect of background music and manual dexterity on the ability of assembly line workers to perform accurately a complicated task selects a simple random sample of workers to participate in an experiment. Fifteen subjects are then randomly assigned to perform the task in the presence of background music. The remaining subjects perform the task without background music. The following table shows, for each subject, the number of consecutive repetitions of the task completed before an error was made and the subject's manual dexterity test score. The table also indicates whether or not music was present.

Music/No Music	Manual Dexterity Score	Number of Repetitions (Y)	Music/No Music	Manual Dexterity Score	Number of Repetitions (Y)
M	87	106	N	162	73
M	212	76	M	211	75
M	112	100	M	136	70
N	199	49	N	100	100
M	137	75	M	100	100
N	149	50	N	88	87
N	180	55	N	87	106
M	25	115	N	101	91
N	142	50	M	90	105
M	77	112	N	245	51
N	137	89	M	150	52
N	171	52	M	251	75
M	225	88	N	102	75
M	88	102	M	90	112

Use dummy-variable coding and regression techniques to analyze these data. Draw a scatter diagram of the original data, and plot the fitted regression equations.

10.6.3 Ⓒ Juarez Clothing Company, which uses three makes of sewing machine, wishes to study the relationship between the ages of the machines and their reliability. Coordinators of the study select a simple random sample of 40 machines, service each one, and then record the number of continuous hours of operation before breakdown. The following table shows the results, along with the age (in months) and make of each machine.

Hours Before Breakdown	Age in Months	Make	Hours Before Breakdown	Age in Months	Make
205	59	A	220	22	B
236	48	A	260	30	A
260	25	B	45	69	B
176	39	C	210	30	C
245	20	A	225	40	A
123	66	A	126	45	B
176	40	B	200	26	C
150	62	C	115	71	A
148	70	C	65	69	B
265	20	B	240	25	A
200	52	A	194	33	B
45	75	B	156	48	C
110	75	C	100	75	A
216	25	B	240	21	B
176	63	A	170	56	A
90	75	C	116	58	C
176	69	A	120	50	B
112	65	C	240	37	A
230	30	B	88	56	B
280	23	A	120	67	A

Use dummy-variable coding to quantify the qualitative variable, and obtain the regression equation for each make of machine. What can we conclude from the results of the analysis? Is there interaction between age and make of machine? Plot the original data and the fitted regression equations. If there appears to be interaction between the two independent variables, how do you explain it?

10.7 THE MULTIPLE-CORRELATION MODEL

We have shown that the purpose of correlation analysis is to assess the strength of the relationship among several variables. The model that we assume in multiple-correlation analysis is the same as that given by the multiple regression model of Equation 10.2.1. There is an important difference, however, in the assumptions underlying the two models.

In the correlation model, we assume that *all* the variables, not just Y, are random. If inferential procedures are an objective of the analysis, we must assume that the joint distribution of the variables is a *multivariate normal distribution*.

> A *multivariate normal distribution* is composed of three or more normal distributions such that their joint distribution is also normal.

The concept of a multivariate normal distribution is an extension of the concept of a bivariate normal distribution. To show all the descriptive and inferential methods, we assume a multivariate normal distribution in the exercises and examples that follow.

All the other assumptions specified in Section 10.2 also apply to the correlation model. However, the concept of dependent and independent variables is not appropriate under the correlation model.

When the correlation model applies, we can carry out all the analyses we have discussed so far in this chapter. In addition, under this model, we can extend the analysis in two ways: (1) We can estimate the overall strength of the correlation between variables, and (2) we can assess the strength of the correlation between combinations of selected variables, when the effect of all other variables has been removed.

THE COEFFICIENT OF MULTIPLE CORRELATION

Under the correlation model, we can give the quantity $R^2_{y.12...k}$ an additional interpretation.

> We call the square root of $R^2_{y.12...k}$ the *sample coefficient of multiple correlation* and interpret it as a measure of the correlation between sample values of Y and all the X_i.

We may also think of $R_{y.12...k}$ as a measure of the correlation between observed values of Y and calculated values of Y. An estimate of the population coefficient of multiple correlation, $\rho_{y.12...k}$, is provided by $R_{y.12...k}$. Both $R_{y.12...k}$ and $\rho_{y.12...k}$ are always given a positive sign. If we wish to know whether sample data provide sufficient information to justify the conclusion that a set of variables is correlated, we test the null hypothesis that $\rho_{y.12...k} = 0$ against the alternative that $\rho_{y.12...k} \neq 0$. The test statistic is

10.7.1
$$F = \frac{R_{y.12...k}^2}{1 - R_{y.12...k}^2} \cdot \frac{n - k - 1}{k}$$

When the null hypothesis is true, this statistic is distributed as F with k and $n - k - 1$ degrees of freedom. This test is exactly equivalent to the F test for overall regression discussed in Section 10.4.

In our newspaper-circulation example, let us assume that the correlation model applies. This is not an unreasonable assumption, as the sample of trade areas was randomly selected (we did not single out specific values of the X's for study). There seems to be no reason to believe that there is anything inherent in any of the variables that would keep them from being random.

We may use the data from this example, then, to illustrate the calculation of the coefficient of multiple correlation and the test of the null hypothesis that $\rho_{y.12} = 0$. We have already found the coefficient of multiple determination for this example to be $0.9827 \approx 0.98$. The square root of this gives

$$R_{y.12} = \sqrt{0.98} = 0.99$$

The test statistic for the hypothesis test, from Equation 10.7.1, is

$$F = \frac{(0.9827)(22)}{(1 - 0.9827)(2)} = 624.84$$

We definitely reject the hypothesis, since the probability of obtaining a value of F as large as or larger than 624.84 when the null hypothesis is true is extremely small. Note that, because of rounding errors, the value of F differs from that obtained in the analysis-of-variance table.

PARTIAL CORRELATION

In multiple-correlation analysis, *partial correlation coefficients* are frequently of interest.

> A *partial correlation coefficient* is a measure of the contribution of an individual variable when the other variables are held constant.

In computing the partial correlation coefficient between two variables, we want to eliminate the influence of one or more other variables.

Suppose that we have three variables, Y, X_1, and X_2. The partial correlation coefficient measuring the correlation between Y and X_1 with X_2 held constant, for example, is written $r_{y1.2}$. In the subscript, the symbol to the right of the decimal indicates which variable is held constant, whereas the two symbols to the left of the decimal indicate which variables are being correlated. For the three-variable case, there are two other partial correlation coefficients that we may compute. They are $r_{y2.1}$ and $r_{12.y}$.

THE COEFFICIENT OF PARTIAL DETERMINATION

The *coefficient of partial determination* provides useful information about the interrelationships among variables.

> The *coefficient of partial determination* is the square of the partial correlation coefficient.

Consider $r_{y1.2}$, for example. Its square, $r_{y1.2}^2$, tells us what proportion of the remaining variability in Y is explained by X_1 after X_2 has explained as much of the total variability in Y as it can.

Partial correlation coefficients usually appear as part of the output when we use a computer for multiple regression and correlation analysis. Formulas for use when a computer is not available are given in Section 10.9.

EXAMPLE 10.3.1 *continued*

SOLUTION   Let us refer to the newspaper-circulation example to illustrate the concepts of partial correlation and determination. The partial correlation coefficients are

$$r_{y1.2} = 0.5810 \qquad r_{y2.1} = 0.4608 \qquad r_{12.y} = 0.4435$$

Since $r_{y1.2}^2 = (0.5810)^2 = 0.3376$, we learn that after X_2 (population density) has explained as much of the total variability in Y (weekend circulation) as it can, X_1 (total retail sales) explains 33.76% of the remaining variability in Y. STAT+ calculates partial correlation coefficients when requested to do so.

TESTING HYPOTHESES

For any one of these partial correlation coefficients, we may use the t test to test the null hypothesis that the corresponding population partial correlation coefficient is 0. For example, to test H_0: $\rho_{y1.2...k} = 0$, we compute

$$t = r_{y1.2...k} \sqrt{\frac{n - k - 1}{1 - r_{y1.2...k}^2}}$$

We compare the computed t with the critical value of t corresponding to the chosen level of significance and $n - k - 1$ degrees of freedom.

We can use the newspaper-circulation data to illustrate the procedure.

$$H_0: \rho_{y1.2} = 0, \qquad H_1: \rho_{y1.2} \neq 0$$

Let $\alpha = 0.05$.

$$t = 0.5810 \sqrt{\frac{25 - 2 - 1}{1 - (0.5810)^2}} = 3.348$$

Since $3.348 > 2.074$, the tabulated value of t for $\alpha = 0.05$ and 22 degrees of freedom, we reject the null hypothesis ($p < 0.01$).

We have limited this illustration to the three-variable case under the correlation model. But the concepts and techniques of analysis extend logically to four or more variables. Needless to say, the complexity of computation increases greatly as the number of variables increases.

EXERCISES

In each of the following exercises, (a) compute the multiple-correlation coefficient; (b) test H_0 that $\rho_{y.12} = 0$; (c) compute the partial correlation coefficients; (d) test H_0 that $\rho_{y1.2} = 0$. (Let $\alpha = 0.05$ for all tests, and determine the p value.)

10.7.1   C Lansbury Lumber Company hires forestry specialists to study timber yield on ten plots of ground of equal size. Three measurements are taken on each plot: age of trees in years (X_1), a measure of fertility (X_2), and yield per acre (Y). The following data are collected.

Plot	1	2	3	4	5	6	7	8	9	10	Totals
X_1	15	20	24	38	44	48	56	62	63	64	434
X_2	60	76	84	85	86	85	86	86	87	87	822
Y	0.8	1.2	2.3	3.2	4.3	4.8	5.0	5.5	6.3	7.2	40.6

$$\Sigma x_{1j}^2 = 21{,}930 \qquad \Sigma y_j^2 = 205.92 \qquad \Sigma x_{2j} y_j = 3459.7$$
$$\Sigma x_{2j}^2 = 68{,}208 \qquad \Sigma x_{1j} y_j = 2111.1 \qquad \Sigma x_{1j} x_{2j} = 36{,}727$$

10.7.2   C In a study of urban housing, the following measurements are made on 15 low-income residential areas. Here X_1 denotes average family income ($\times$ \$100), X_2 denotes number of miles from the central city, and Y denotes average monthly rental for a one-bedroom dwelling.

Area	1	2	3	4	5	6	7	8	9	10	11	12	13	14	15	Totals
X_1, \$	34	37	39	42	41	45	40	52	50	62	68	65	70	68	75	788
X_2	7.5	6.3	5.0	3.5	4.8	4.2	4.5	3.8	4.0	3.4	3.9	3.0	4.0	3.8	2.5	64.2
Y, \$	120	130	135	138	142	149	155	158	160	169	170	175	182	190	195	2368

$$\Sigma x_{1j}^2 = 44{,}162 \qquad \Sigma y_j^2 = 380{,}858 \qquad \Sigma x_{2j} y_j = 9822.4$$
$$\Sigma x_{2j}^2 = 297.02 \qquad \Sigma x_{1j} y_j = 128{,}592 \qquad \Sigma x_{1j} x_{2j} = 3190.4$$

10.7.3 $\boxed{C}$ A city treasurer is studying factors thought to be related to per capita public expenditures. The treasurer collects data for 11 wards in the city. In the following table, the wards are numbered 1 through 11. Y denotes annual per capita public expenditure ($\times$ \$1,000), X_1 denotes population density in persons per square mile, and X_2 denotes annual per capita income ($\times$ \$10,000).

	1	2	3	4	5	6	7	8	9	10	11	Totals
Y	0.02	0.06	0.04	0.05	0.03	0.05	0.04	0.05	0.03	0.04	0.03	0.44
X_1	133	7	61	15	32	32	19	12	64	29	99	503
X_2	1.6	1.9	1.8	2.0	1.5	2.0	1.7	1.5	2.1	1.4	2.2	19.7

$$\Sigma x_{1j}^2 = 38{,}975 \qquad \Sigma y_j^2 = 0.019 \qquad \Sigma x_{2j} y_j = 0.791$$
$$\Sigma x_{2j}^2 = 36.01 \qquad \Sigma x_{1j} y_j = 16.24 \qquad \Sigma x_{1j} x_{2j} = 921$$

10.8 CHOOSING INDEPENDENT VARIABLES FOR THE REGRESSION EQUATION

When we use regression analysis, we must decide *which* independent variables to include in the model. Usually, we base the decision on both statistical and nonstatistical considerations. We may have to omit some variables because of the difficulty or expense of obtaining measurements. We may also omit some variables because the results of statistical analyses cast doubt on their usefulness as predictor, or explanatory, variables. Some writers suggest that under some circumstances variables that fare poorly when subjected to statistical evaluation should remain in the model, either because measurements on them are easily obtained or because the logic of their presence is so strong.

VARIABLE SELECTION TECHNIQUES

Statistical criteria for excluding variables usually center on the magnitude and significance of R^2 and the b_i's. Ideally, we would regress Y on each subset of the independent variables and evaluate the results against the appropriate statistical criterion. This procedure would involve regressing Y on each independent variable alone, then on each possible pair, then on each possible triplet, and so on. If there are many independent variables, this can be time-consuming.

Two alternative approaches are the *step-up procedure* and the *step-down procedure*. In the step-up procedure, we regress Y on each independent variable separately. We retain the variable yielding the highest R^2. Next we regress Y on all possible pairs of variables that we can form from the variable retained in the first step and the $k - 1$ other variables. We retain the pair yielding the largest R^2 value. We continue this way until the R^2 we obtain is not significantly larger than the R^2 we obtained in the preceding step.

In the step-down procedure, we regress Y on all independent variables at once. We omit the least significant variable and regress Y on all the $k - 1$ remaining variables at once. We omit the least significant variable from these $k - 1$ variables. We continue this way until all retained variables are contributing significantly to the regression.

Each time an independent variable is added to the regression model, R^2 is increased to some extent. You should not, however, take this as a license to include every possible independent variable in the model. The magnitude of the increase in R^2 resulting from the addition of an independent variable may not justify the costs involved in collecting data on that variable.

Variable selection techniques are discussed in detail in Chapter 11.

Multicollinearity One of the problems that may arise in regression analysis is *multicollinearity*. We say that multicollinearity exists between two (or more) variables when the relationship between (among) them is perfectly (or almost perfectly) linear. When multicollinearity is present, estimates of parameters tend to have very large standard errors. They are also highly dependent on the particular data points observed in the sample. Methods for dealing with multicollinearity are discussed in the books and articles cited at the end of this chapter.

Residual Plots We discuss the importance of residual analysis in Chapter 9. You should not overlook the techniques of this valuable tool when you are performing multiple regression analysis. As we saw in Chapter 9, various graphs of the residuals can provide insight into the data under study and aid in the detection of problems that might result in poor predictions and estimates. The residual analysis procedures discussed in Chapter 9 are easily extended to the multiple-variable case.

10.9   MULTIPLE REGRESSION CALCULATIONS

This section contains the formulas needed for the calculations necessary for multiple regression analysis.

OBTAINING THE SAMPLE MULTIPLE REGRESSION EQUATION

To find the sample multiple regression equation, we must first get a set of normal equations. We get the normal equations by the method of differential calculus, in which the quantity

(10.9.1) $$\Sigma \hat{e}_j^2 = \Sigma (y_j - b_0 - b_1 x_{1j} - b_2 x_{2j} - \cdots - b_k x_{kj})^2$$

is minimized. Equation 10.9.1 represents the sum of the squared deviations of the observed values of Y from the regression surface. Thus, the *method of least squares* is used for multiple regression, just as it was for simple linear regression.

In the multiple regression case, the *sum of the squared deviations of the observed values from the regression surface is minimized.*

The normal equations for k variables are as follows:

(10.9.2)

$$nb_0 + b_1\Sigma x_{1j} + b_2\Sigma x_{2j} + \cdots + b_k\Sigma x_{kj} = \Sigma y_j$$
$$b_0\Sigma x_{1j} + b_1\Sigma x_{1j}^2 + b_2\Sigma x_{1j}x_{2j} + \cdots + b_k\Sigma x_{1j}x_{kj} = \Sigma x_{1j}y_j$$
$$b_0\Sigma x_{2j} + b_1\Sigma x_{2j}x_{1j} + b_2\Sigma x_{2j}^2 + \cdots + b_k\Sigma x_{2j}x_{kj} = \Sigma x_{2j}y_j$$
$$\cdots \quad \cdots \quad \cdots \quad \cdots \quad \cdots \quad \cdots \quad \cdots$$
$$b_0\Sigma x_{kj} + b_1\Sigma x_{1j}x_{kj} + b_2\Sigma x_{2j}x_{kj} + \cdots + b_j\Sigma x_{kj}^2 = \Sigma x_{kj}y_j$$

Note that the number of equations is the same as the number of parameters to be estimated. Solving these normal equations leads to the following sample regression equation:

(10.9.3)

$$\hat{y}_j = b_0 + b_1 x_{1j} + b_2 x_{2j} + \cdots + b_k x_{kj}$$

CALCULATIONS FOR EXAMPLE 10.3.1

We assume that the multiple regression model of Equation 10.2.1, for three variables, applies here. Since there are measurements on three variables, we need three normal equations. They are as follows:

(10.9.4)

$$nb_0 + b_1\Sigma x_{1j} + b_2\Sigma x_{2j} = \Sigma y_j$$
$$b_0\Sigma x_{1j} + b_1\Sigma x_{1j}^2 + b_2\Sigma x_{1j}x_{2j} = \Sigma x_{1j}y_j$$
$$b_0\Sigma x_{2j} + b_1\Sigma x_{1j}x_{2j} + b_2\Sigma x_{2j}^2 = \Sigma x_{2j}y_j$$

We divide the first normal equation by n and solve for b_0 to get

(10.9.5)

$$b_0 = \frac{\Sigma y_j}{n} - b_1 \frac{\Sigma x_{1j}}{n} - b_2 \frac{\Sigma x_{2j}}{n} = \bar{y} - b_1\bar{x}_1 - b_2\bar{x}_2$$

Substituting this result for b_0 in the second normal equation gives us

$$\left(\frac{\Sigma y_j}{n} - b_1 \frac{\Sigma x_{1j}}{n} - b_2 \frac{\Sigma x_{2j}}{n} \right) \Sigma x_{1j} + b_1\Sigma x_{1j}^2 + b_2\Sigma x_{1j}x_{2j} = \Sigma x_{1j}y_j$$

$$\frac{\Sigma x_{1j}\Sigma y_j}{n} - b_1 \frac{(\Sigma x_{1j})^2}{n} - b_2 \frac{\Sigma x_{1j}\Sigma x_{2j}}{n} + b_1\Sigma x_{1j}^2 + b_2\Sigma x_{1j}x_{2j} = \Sigma x_{1j}y_j$$

Rearranging terms, we get

(10.9.6)

$$b_1\left[\Sigma x_{1j}^2 - \frac{(\Sigma x_{1j})^2}{n} \right] + b_2\left[\Sigma x_{1j}x_{2j} - \frac{\Sigma x_{1j}\Sigma x_{2j}}{n} \right] = \Sigma x_{1j}y_j - \frac{\Sigma x_{1j}\Sigma y_j}{n}$$

Similarly, substituting for b_0 in the third normal equation and rearranging terms yields

$$(10.9.7) \qquad b_1 \left[\Sigma x_{1j} x_{2j} - \frac{\Sigma x_{1j} \Sigma x_{2j}}{n} \right] + b_2 \left[\Sigma x_{2j}^2 - \frac{(\Sigma x_{2j})^2}{n} \right] = \Sigma x_{2j} y_j - \frac{\Sigma x_{2j} \Sigma y_j}{n}$$

Table 10.9.1 gives the sums of squares and cross products needed to evaluate the normal equations for Example 10.3.1.

$$\Sigma x_{1j}^2 - \frac{(\Sigma x_{1j})^2}{n} = 22{,}429.15 - \frac{(739.5)^2}{26} = 554.74$$

$$\Sigma x_{2j}^2 - \frac{(\Sigma x_{2j})^2}{n} = 101{,}568.00 - \frac{(1576.6)^2}{25} = 2141.30$$

$$\Sigma x_{1j} x_{2j} - \frac{\Sigma x_{1j} \Sigma x_{2j}}{n} = 47{,}709.10 - \frac{(739.5)(1576.6)}{25} = 1073.27$$

$$\Sigma x_{1j} y_j - \frac{\Sigma x_{1j} \Sigma y_j}{n} = 2968.58 - \frac{(739.5)(98.2)}{25} = 63.82$$

$$\Sigma x_{2j} y_j - \frac{\Sigma x_{2j} \Sigma y_j}{n} = 6317.95 - \frac{(1576.6)(98.2)}{25} = 125.07$$

We substitute the results of these computations into Equations 10.9.6 and 10.9.7 to obtain

$$554.74 b_1 + 1073.27 b_2 = 63.82, \qquad 1073.27 b_1 + 2141.30 b_2 = 125.07$$

We solve these simultaneous equations for b_1 and b_2 and obtain $b_1 = 0.06741$ and $b_2 = 0.02462$. We find the constant b_0 from the following relationship, as shown in Equation 10.9.5:

$$b_0 = \bar{y} - b_1 \bar{x}_1 - b_2 \bar{x}_2$$

For our example, we have

$$b_0 = 3.928 - (0.06741)(29.58) - (0.02462)(63.064) = 0.381$$

Now, when we round to three places, we have our sample multiple regression equation:

$$\hat{y}_j = 0.381 + 0.067 x_{1j} + 0.025 x_{2j}$$

The notation for subsequent calculations will be greatly simplified if we transform each variable into a deviation from its mean. We call these deviations

TABLE 10.9.1 Sample data and additional calculations for Example 10.3.1

(1) Trade Area	(2) Daily Newspapers, Weekend Circulation (×1000) y_j	(3) Total Retail Sales ($1,000,000) x_{1j}	(4) Population Per Sq. M. x_{2j}	(5) $x_{1j}x_{2j}$	(6) $x_{1j}y_j$	(7) $x_{2j}y_j$	(8) x_{1j}^2	(9) x_{2j}^2	(10) y_j^2
1	3.0	21.7	47.8	1,037.26	65.10	143.40	470.89	2,284.84	9.00
2	3.3	24.1	51.3	1,236.33	79.53	169.29	580.81	2,631.69	10.89
3	4.7	37.4	76.8	2,872.32	175.78	360.96	1,398.76	5,898.24	22.09
4	3.9	29.4	66.2	1,946.28	114.66	258.18	864.36	4,382.44	15.21
5	3.2	22.6	51.9	1,172.94	72.32	166.08	510.76	2,693.61	10.24
6	4.1	32.0	65.3	2,089.60	131.20	267.73	1,024.00	4,264.09	16.81
7	3.6	26.4	57.4	1,515.36	95.04	206.64	696.96	3,294.76	12.96
8	4.3	31.6	66.8	2,110.88	135.88	287.24	998.56	4,462.24	18.49
9	4.7	35.5	76.4	2,712.20	166.85	359.08	1,260.25	5,836.96	22.09
10	3.5	25.1	53.0	1,330.30	87.85	185.50	630.01	2,809.00	12.25
11	4.0	30.8	66.9	2,060.52	123.20	267.60	948.64	4,475.61	16.00
12	3.5	25.8	55.9	1,442.22	90.30	195.65	665.64	3,124.81	12.25
13	4.0	30.3	66.5	2,014.95	121.20	266.00	918.09	4,422.25	16.00
14	3.0	22.2	45.3	1,005.66	66.60	135.90	492.84	2,052.09	9.00
15	4.5	35.7	73.6	2,627.52	160.65	331.20	1,274.49	5,416.96	20.25
16	4.1	30.9	65.1	2,011.59	126.69	266.91	954.81	4,238.01	16.81
17	4.8	35.5	75.2	2,669.60	170.40	360.96	1,260.25	5,655.04	23.04
18	3.4	24.2	54.6	1,321.32	82.28	185.64	585.64	2,981.16	11.56
19	4.3	33.4	68.7	2,294.58	143.62	295.41	1,115.56	4,719.69	18.49
20	4.0	30.0	64.8	1,944.00	120.00	259.20	900.00	4,199.04	16.00
21	4.6	35.1	74.7	2,621.97	161.46	343.62	1,232.01	5,580.09	21.16
22	3.9	29.4	62.7	1,843.38	114.66	244.53	864.36	3,931.29	15.21
23	4.3	32.5	67.6	2,197.00	139.75	290.68	1,056.25	4,569.76	18.49
24	3.1	24.0	51.3	1,231.20	74.40	159.03	576.00	2,631.69	9.61
25	4.4	33.9	70.8	2,400.12	149.16	311.52	1,149.21	5,012.64	19.36
Total	98.2	739.5	1,576.6	47,709.10	2,968.58	6,317.95	22,429.15	101,568.00	393.26
Mean	3.928	29.580	63.064						

y'_j, x'_{1j}, and x'_{2j}. This procedure gives us

(10.9.8)
$$y'_j = y_j - \bar{y}, \qquad x'_{1j} = x_{1j} - \bar{x}_1, \qquad x'_{2j} = x_{2j} - \bar{x}_2$$

Therefore, we can rewrite the sums of squares and cross products in Equations 10.9.6 and 10.9.7 as follows:

$$\Sigma x'^2_{1j} = \Sigma(x_{1j} - \bar{x}_1)^2 = \Sigma x^2_{1j} - \frac{(\Sigma x_{1j})^2}{n}$$

$$\Sigma x'^2_{2j} = \Sigma(x_{2j} - \bar{x}_2)^2 = \Sigma x^2_{2j} - \frac{(\Sigma x_{2j})^2}{n}$$

$$\Sigma x'_{1j}x'_{2j} = \Sigma(x_{1j} - \bar{x}_1)(x_{2j} - \bar{x}_2) = \Sigma x_{1j}x_{2j} - \frac{\Sigma x_{1j}\Sigma x_{2j}}{n}$$

$$\Sigma x'_{1j}y'_j = \Sigma(x_{1j} - \bar{x}_1)(y_j - \bar{y}) = \Sigma x_{1j}y_j - \frac{\Sigma x_{1j}\Sigma y_j}{n}$$

$$\Sigma x'_{2j}y'_j = \Sigma(x_{2j} - \bar{x}_2)(y_j - \bar{y}) = \Sigma x_{2j}y_j - \frac{\Sigma x_{2j}\Sigma y_j}{n}$$

FORMULAS FOR SST, SSR, AND SSE

In Chapter 9, you learned that the total sum of squares is equal to the explained sum of squares, plus the unexplained, or error, sum of squares. This relationship can be expressed as

(10.9.9)
$$\Sigma(y_j - \bar{y})^2 = \Sigma(\hat{y}_j - \bar{y})^2 + \Sigma(y_j - \hat{y}_j)^2$$

or

(10.9.10)
$$\text{SST} = \text{SSR} + \text{SSE}$$

The degrees of freedom associated with the total, explained, and error sums of squares are $n - 1$, k, and $n - k - 1$, respectively.

We can find the total sum of squares from

(10.9.11)
$$\text{SST} = \Sigma(y_j - \bar{y})^2 = \Sigma y'^2_j = \Sigma y^2_j - \frac{(\Sigma y_j)^2}{n}$$

We can find the explained sum of squares from

(10.9.12)
$$\text{SSR} = \Sigma(\hat{y}_j - \bar{y})^2 = b_1\Sigma x'_{1j}y'_j + b_2\Sigma x'_{2j}y'_j + \cdots + b_k\Sigma x'_{kj}y'_j$$

We can find the error sum of squares by subtraction. That is,

(10.9.13)
$$SSE = SST - SSR$$

CALCULATING SST, SSR, AND SSE FOR EXAMPLE 10.3.1

Using data from Table 10.9.1, we use Equation 10.9.11 to get

$$SST = \Sigma(y_j - \bar{y})^2 = \Sigma y_j'^2 = 393.26 - \frac{(98.2)^2}{25} = 7.53$$

Using Equation 10.9.12 and the results of previous calculations, we find that

$$SSR = \Sigma(\hat{y}_j - \bar{y})^2 = 0.067(63.82) + 0.025(125.07) = 7.40$$

By subtraction, we obtain

$$SSE = \Sigma(y_j - \hat{y}_j)^2 = 7.53 - 7.40 = 0.13$$

A FORMULA FOR s_{b_i}

When the assumptions discussed in Section 10.2 are met, the b_i are each normally distributed with mean β_i and variance $c_{ii}\sigma^2$. Since σ^2, the variance common to the subpopulations of Y values, is usually unknown, it is estimated by $s_{y.12...k}^2$. The estimated standard error of b_i, then, is

(10.9.14)
$$s_{b_i} = s_{y.12...k} \sqrt{c_{ii}}$$

In Equation 10.9.14, $s_{y.12...k}$ is the square root of the unexplained variance, or the error mean square, from the analysis-of-variance table. The quantity c_{ii} is called a *Gauss multiplier*. When the analysis involves only three variables, we may obtain it by inverting the matrix of sums of squares and cross products that we can construct from the left-hand terms of the normal equations. The c_{ii} are the diagonal elements of the inverse. We may obtain the c values by solving the following two sets of equations:

(10.9.15)
$$c_{11}\Sigma x_{1j}'^2 + c_{12}\Sigma x_{1j}'x_{2j}' = 1, \qquad c_{11}\Sigma x_{1j}'x_{2j}' + c_{12}\Sigma x_{2j}'^2 = 0$$

(10.9.16)
$$c_{21}\Sigma x_{1j}'^2 + c_{22}\Sigma x_{1j}'x_{2j}' = 0, \qquad c_{21}\Sigma x_{1j}'x_{2j}' + c_{22}\Sigma x_{2j}'^2 = 1$$

where $c_{12} = c_{21}$. For a large number of independent variables, we expand Equations 10.9.15 and 10.9.16 so that there are as many sets of equations as there are independent variables and an equal number of individual equations within each set. We place a 1 to the right of the equal sign in all equations of the form $c_{ii}\Sigma x'^2_{ij}$. In Equation 10.9.15, for example, there is a 1 to the right of the equal sign in the equation containing $c_{11}\Sigma x'^2_{1j}$.

CALCULATING THE s_{b_i} FOR EXAMPLE 10.3.1

We may find the c values for our newspaper-circulation example by substituting the results of the calculations we performed on page 591 into Equations 10.9.15 and 10.9.16. The equations for the example are

$$554.74c_{11} + 1073.27c_{12} = 1, \qquad 1073.27c_{11} + 2141.30c_{12} = 0$$
$$554.74c_{21} + 1073.27c_{22} = 0, \qquad 1073.27c_{21} + 2141.30c_{22} = 1$$

When we solve these equations, we find

$$c_{11} = 0.0595529, \qquad c_{12} = c_{21} = -0.0298493, \qquad c_{22} = 0.0154282$$

Now that we have the c values, we can compute the estimated standard errors of the b_i. This will enable us to construct confidence intervals for and test hypotheses about individual β's.

For Example 10.3.1, then, the estimated standard errors of the b_i are as follows:

$$s_{b_1} = s_{y.12}\sqrt{c_{11}}$$
$$= \sqrt{0.0059}\sqrt{0.0595529} = 0.0187447$$
$$s_{b_2} = s_{y.12}\sqrt{c_{22}}$$
$$= \sqrt{0.0059}\sqrt{0.0154282} = 0.0095408$$

FORMULAS FOR $s_{\hat{y}.12}$ AND $s_{\hat{\mu}_{y.12}}$ FOR THE THREE-VARIABLE CASE

The formula for $s_{\hat{y}.12}$, the estimated standard error of $\hat{y}$ when $\hat{y}$ is used as a predictor of a single value of Y for given values of the independent variables, is as follows:

(10.9.17)
$$s_{\hat{y}.12} = s_{y.12}\sqrt{1 + \frac{1}{n} + c_{11}x'^2_{1j} + c_{22}x'^2_{2j} + 2c_{12}x'_{1j}x'_{2j}}$$

The formula for $s_{\hat{\mu}_{y.12}}$, the estimated standard error of $\hat{y}$ when $\hat{y}$ is used as an estimate of the mean value of Y for given values of the independent variables, is as follows:

(10.9.18)
$$s_{\hat{\mu}_{y.12}} = s_{y.12} \sqrt{\frac{1}{n} + c_{11}x_{1j}'^2 + c_{22}x_{2j}'^2 + 2c_{12}x_{1j}'x_{2j}'}$$

CALCULATING $s_{\hat{y}.12}$ AND $s_{\hat{\mu}_{y.12}}$ FOR EXAMPLE 10.3.1

To calculate $s_{\hat{y}.12}$ by Equation 10.9.17, we require the value of $s_{\hat{y}.12} = \sqrt{MSE}$, which we find in Table 10.4.2 to be $\sqrt{0.0059} = 0.0768$. The other quantities needed for the formula were calculated earlier in this section. Thus, we have

$$s_{\hat{y}.12} = (\sqrt{0.0059})\,\sqrt{1 + \tfrac{1}{25} + (0.0595529)(-4.58)^2 + 0.0154282(-11.064)^2 + 2(-0.0298493)(-4.58)(-11.064)}$$
$$= (0.0768)(1.0736) = 0.0824525$$

To calculate $s_{\hat{\mu}_{y.12}}$ by Equation 10.9.18, we need $\sqrt{MSE}$ and the quantities calculated earlier in this section. The result is

$$s_{\hat{\mu}_{y.12}} = (\sqrt{0.0059})\,\sqrt{\tfrac{1}{25} + (0.0595529)(-4.58)^2 + 0.0154282(-11.064)^2 + 2(-0.0298493)(-4.58)(-11.064)}$$
$$= 0.03001$$

FORMULAS FOR COMPUTING PARTIAL CORRELATION COEFFICIENTS

Before we compute the partial correlation coefficients, we must first compute *simple correlation coefficients*. For the three-variable case, there are three simple sample correlation coefficients, as follows:

r_{y1}, the simple correlation between Y and X_1
r_{y2}, the simple correlation between Y and X_2
r_{12}, the simple correlation between X_1 and X_2

We can compute the simple correlation coefficients, in terms of deviations from means, as follows:

(10.9.19)
$$r_{y1} = \frac{\Sigma x_{1j}'y_j'}{\sqrt{\Sigma x_{1j}'^2 \, \Sigma y_j'^2}}$$

(10.9.20)
$$r_{y2} = \frac{\Sigma x_{2j}'y_j'}{\sqrt{\Sigma x_{2j}'^2 \, \Sigma y_j'^2}}$$

(10.9.21)
$$r_{12} = \frac{\Sigma x'_{1j} x'_{2j}}{\sqrt{\Sigma x'^2_{1j} \, \Sigma x'^2_{2j}}}$$

The partial correlation coefficients that we can compute now are:

1. The partial correlation between Y and X_1 when X_2 is held constant:

(10.9.22)
$$r_{y1.2} = \frac{(r_{y1} - r_{y2}r_{12})}{\sqrt{(1 - r^2_{y2})(1 - r^2_{12})}}$$

2. The partial correlation between Y and X_2 when X_1 is held constant:

(10.9.23)
$$r_{y2.1} = \frac{(r_{y2} - r_{y1}r_{12})}{\sqrt{(1 - r^2_{y1})(1 - r^2_{12})}}$$

3. The partial correlation between X_1 and X_2 when Y is held constant:

(10.9.24)
$$r_{12.y} = \frac{(r_{12} - r_{y1}r_{y2})}{\sqrt{(1 - r^2_{y1})(1 - r^2_{y2})}}$$

PARTIAL CORRELATION COEFFICIENTS FOR EXAMPLE 10.3.1

We can calculate the simple correlation coefficients using the numerical values that were calculated on pages 591 and 594.

$$r_{y1} = \frac{63.82}{\sqrt{(554.74)(7.53)}} = 0.9874$$

$$r_{y2} = \frac{125.07}{\sqrt{(2,141.30)(7.53)}} = 0.9850$$

$$r_{12} = \frac{1073.27}{\sqrt{(554.74)(2,141.30)}} = 0.9847$$

The partial correlation coefficients, then, are

$$r_{y1.2} = \frac{[0.9874 - (0.9850)(0.9847)]}{\sqrt{(1 - 0.9850^2)(1 - 0.9847^2)}} = 0.5810$$

$$r_{y2.1} = \frac{[0.9850 - (0.9874)(0.9847)]}{\sqrt{(1 - 0.9874^2)(1 - 0.9847^2)}} = 0.4608$$

$$r_{12.y} = \frac{[0.9847 - (0.9874)(0.9850)]}{\sqrt{(1 - 0.9874^2)(1 - 0.9850^2)}} = 0.44$$

SUMMARY

This chapter discusses the concepts and techniques of multiple regression analysis and multiple-correlation analysis. It shows the differences between the assumptions underlying the two models.

We use an example to illustrate descriptive and inferential procedures. We suggest that regression analysis should include the following steps:

1. Specification of the model
2. Review of the assumptions
3. Obtaining the equation
4. Evaluating the equation
5. Using the equation

You learned that the multiple regression and multiple-correlation models are straightforward extensions of the simple linear models. For each additional independent variable, we add an additional term to the basic model.

The assumptions for multiple regression and correlation are also extensions of those for the simple linear models. The geometric interpretations of the model involve planes and hyperplanes, rather than straight lines.

We can estimate the parameters in the multiple regression and multiple-correlation models by the method of least squares. When the assumptions are met, we evaluate the resulting equation by applying analysis of variance. We use t tests to evaluate the individual regression coefficients.

A multiple regression equation, like a simple linear regression equation, is used for prediction and estimation.

In correlation analysis, we are often not interested in the equation. We are interested in the strength of the relationship among the variables as measured by the multiple-correlation coefficient and the various partial correlation coefficients.

REVIEW EXERCISES

1. Write out the multiple regression model and explain each component.

2. State the assumptions underlying the multiple regression model.

3. Explain fully the following terms: (a) coefficient of multiple determination, (b) multiple-correlation coefficient, (c) simple correlation coefficient, (d) partial correlation coefficient.

4. Explain the differences between the assumptions of the regression model and those of the correlation model.

5. Explain the difference between a prediction interval and a confidence interval.

6. What is a multivariate normal distribution?

7. Describe a situation in your area of interest in which multiple regression analysis would be useful. Use real or realistic data, and do a complete regression analysis.

8. Describe a situation in your area of interest in which multiple-correlation analysis would be useful. Use real or realistic data, and do a complete correlation analysis.

9. C An industrial psychologist conducts a study to examine those variables thought to be related to on-the-job performance of technical employees. A random sample of 15 employees gives the following results.   (a) Find the multiple regression equation describing the relationship among these variables.   (b) Compute the coefficient of multiple determination and do an analysis of variance. In the table, Y denotes the employees' job performance ratings, X_1 denotes their scores on a job aptitude test, and X_2 denotes the number of in-service training units earned.

Y	54	37	30	48	37	37	31	49	43	12	30	37	61	31	31
X_1	15	13	15	15	10	14	8	12	1	3	15	14	14	9	4
X_2	8	1	1	7	4	2	3	7	9	1	1	2	10	1	5

10. C In a study of job satisfaction among assembly-line employees of The Maitland Manufacturing Company, you collect the following data for a sample of 12 employees. Compute $R_{y.12}$ and test for significance at the 0.05 level. Determine the p value. In the table, Y denotes the employee's score on a job-satisfaction measure, X_1 denotes the supervisor's score on a job-satisfaction measure, and X_2 denotes the employee's self-confidence score.

Y	45	35	35	40	55	50	38	55	38	45	70	60
X_1	39	40	40	42	45	43	44	47	49	48	50	50
X_2	51	51	55	57	57	61	65	64	63	61	65	68

11. C The personnel director with Noyes Power and Light Company wants to know whether level of skill in a certain job can be predicted, using as predictor variables the age and experience of the employee. The following data are obtained on a random sample of 15 employees.   (a) Find the least-squares multiple regression equation.   (b) Compute $R_{y.12}^2$ and test for significance at the 0.05 level. Determine the p value for the test.   (c) Test H_0: $\beta_1 = 0$ and H_0: $\beta_2 = 0$. Let $\alpha = 0.05$. Compute the p value for each test. (d) Compute a 95% confidence interval for β_2.   (e) Let $x_1 = 2$ and $x_2 = 25$ and compute $\hat{y}$.   (f) Find the 95% prediction interval for Y.   (g) Find the 95% confidence interval for the mean of Y when $x_1 = 2$ and $x_2 = 25$.

Skill Level (Y)	Experience (X_1)	Age (X_2)	Skill Level (Y)	Experience (X_1)	Age (X_2)
15	0	21	30	2	25
15	0	18	45	2	38
21	0	22	50	3	44
28	1	24	60	3	51
30	1	25	45	4	39
35	1	25	60	4	54
40	1	26	50	5	55
35	2	34			

12. ⓒ The following table shows the tensile strengths Y of ten specimens of plastic. The independent variables are the amounts of two ingredients included in the formula. (X_1 is the amount of Ingredient 1 and X_2 is the amount of Ingredient 2.)   **(a)** Find the least-squares multiple regression equation.   **(b)** Compute $R^2_{y.12}$ and test for overall regression, using ANOVA. Let $\alpha = 0.05$.   **(c)** Test $H_0: \beta_1 = 0$ and $H_0: \beta_2 = 0$. Let $\alpha = 0.05$, and determine the p value for each test.   **(d)** Suppose that the amounts of Ingredient 1 and Ingredient 2 added to the formula are 5 and 3, respectively. Construct a 95% prediction interval for the tensile strength of a single specimen of plastic.   **(e)** Using the values of x_1 and x_2 specified in (d), construct a 95% confidence interval for all specimens of plastic produced.

Y	1,361	1,588	1,815	2,087	2,268	2,404	3,402	3,629	3,765	4,083
X_1	8	7	4	5	5	4	3	3	2	1
X_2	4	3	4	3	2	2	2	1	1	1

13. ⓒ The following table shows the end-of-month balance (Y) of 15 young couples with charge accounts with Patterson Department Stores. The independent variables are number of years married (X_1) and age of wife (X_2).   **(a)** Do a complete regression analysis of these data. Let $\alpha = 0.05$, and determine the p value for each test.   **(b)** Let $x_1 = 2$ and $x_2 = 20$, and construct a 95% prediction interval for Y.   **(c)** Using the values of x_1 and x_2 specified in (b), construct a 95% confidence interval for the mean of Y.

End-of-Month Balance (Y)	Number of Years Married (X₁)	Age of Wife (X₂)	End-of-Month Balance (Y)	Number of Years Married (X₁)	Age of Wife (X₂)
110	1	25	98	3	25
115	1	24	99	4	30
120	1	22	98	4	24
118	1	24	100	5	29
110	2	20	90	5	30
108	2	20	93	5	30
105	2	20	90	6	28
104	3	24			

14. ⓒ The following data are based on a survey conducted in ten market areas. The dependent variable is the proportion of adults who say that they prefer a certain brand of toothpaste. The independent variables are per capita income (X_1) and a measure of the educational level (X_2) of residents of the market areas.   **(a)** Do a complete regression analysis of these data. Let $\alpha = 0.05$, and determine the p value for each test.   **(b)** Let $x_1 = 5$ and $x_2 = 6$, and construct a 95% prediction interval for Y.   **(c)** Using the same values of x_1 and x_2 specified in (b), construct a 95% confidence interval for the mean of Y.

Market Area	Proportion Preferring the Brand (Y)	Per Capita Income (× 5,000)(X₁)	Index of Education (X₂)
1	61.6	6.0	6.3
2	53.2	4.4	5.5
3	65.5	9.1	3.6

Market Area	Proportion Preferring the Brand (Y)	Per Capita Income (× 5,000)(X_1)	Index of Education (X_2)
4	64.9	8.1	5.8
5	72.7	9.7	6.8
6	52.2	4.8	7.9
7	50.2	7.6	4.2
8	44.0	4.4	6.0
9	53.8	9.1	2.8
10	53.5	6.7	6.7

15. Ⓒ In a study of the sales of a certain product by market area, a marketing researcher collects the following data on a sample of market areas. All observations are coded for ease of calculation. (a) Find the sample multiple-correlation coefficient, and test the null hypothesis that $\rho_{y.12} = 0$. (b) Find each of the partial correlation coefficients, and test each for significance. Let $\alpha = 0.05$ for all tests. (c) Determine the p value for each test. (d) State your conclusions.

Sales (Y)	Advertising Expenditures (X_1)	Market Share (X_2)	Sales (Y)	Advertising Expenditures (X_1)	Market Share (X_2)
149.0	21.00	42.50	169.0	24.92	48.95
152.0	21.79	43.70	172.0	25.50	49.90
155.7	22.40	44.75	174.5	25.80	50.30
159.0	23.00	46.00	176.1	26.01	50.90
163.3	23.70	47.00	176.5	26.15	50.85
166.0	24.30	47.90	179.0	26.30	51.10

16. Ⓒ An education researcher collects the following data on a sample of 11 college seniors majoring in accounting. (a) Compute the multiple-correlation coefficient, and test it for significance. (b) Compute each of the partial correlation coefficients, and test $r_{12.y}$ for significance. Let $\alpha = 0.05$ for all tests. (c) Determine the p value for each test. (d) What are your conclusions? In the table, Y denotes students' scores on a verbal reasoning test, X_1 their scores on a mathematics aptitude test, and X_2 their IQ scores.

Y	162.2	158.0	157.0	155.0	156.0	154.1	169.1	181.0	174.9	180.2	174.0
X_1	51.0	52.9	56.0	56.5	58.0	60.1	58.0	61.0	59.4	56.1	61.2
X_2	108	111	115	116	117	120	124	127	122	121	125

17. In a study of variables thought to be related to scholastic aptitude, a team of education researchers collects data on a sample of 15 students in their first year of college. The variables are as follows.

SAT = Y = scholastic aptitude test scores of students entering college
PTR = X_1 = pupil–teacher ratio in high school from which student graduated
INC = X_2 = median family income of student's community of residence
SIZE = X_3 = size of high school graduating class
GPA = X_4 = student's high school grade-point average

The following is a partial computer printout of the results of the multiple regression analysis. Prepare a verbal interpretation of these results.

Variable I	B(I)	XBAR(I)	S(I)
SAT	2.0886	10.0667	2.40743
PTR	- .244325E-02	30.2666	6.75783
INC	.175112	12.4	6.60102
SIZE	.259161	4.53333	2.9409
GPA	1.72162	2.73333	.771729

Index of determination (R-SQ) = .91937

Correlation Matrix

	SAT	PTR	INC	SIZE	GPA
SAT	1	- .771389	.875112	.420715E-01	.870786
PTR	-.771389	1	- .68683	- .171496	- .689374
INC	.875112	- .686831	1	- .241071	.845416
SIZE	.420715E-01	- .171495	- .241071	1	- .289815
GPA	.870786	- .689374	.845416	- .289815	1

ACTUAL VS CALCULATED

Actual	Calculated	Difference	PCT Differ
14	14.9571	- .957058	-6.3
13	11.4745	1.52546	13.2
6	6.85242	- .852423	-12.4
11	11.8923	- .892345	- 7.5
10	9.28295	.717051	7.7
9	9.10082	- .100823	- 1.1
8	8.39517	- .395173	- 4.7
11	10.5895	.410474	3.8
13	12.2341	.765889	6.2
12	12.313	- .312957	- 2.5
7	7.44439	- .44439	- 5.9
7	6.99089	.911331E-02	.1
8	7.43738	.562624	7.5
12	11.705	.294983	2.5
10	10.3304	- .330365	- 3.1

ANALYSIS OF VARIANCE

Source	SS	DF	MS	F
Regression	79.9264	4	19.9816	28.5059**
Error	7.00964	10	.700964	
Total	86.936	14		

**Significant at 1% level

Variable	Coefficient	STD Error	T Statistic
PTR	- .244325E-02	.550838E-01	- .443552E-01
INC	.175112	.645715E-01	2.71191
SIZE	.259161	.922597E-01	2.80904
GPA	1.72162	.584559	2.94516
DF = 10			

18. A management consultant conducts a study of the performance of salespersons at Raeburn Industries. Data are collected on a sample of ten salespersons. The following variables are studied:

SALES $= Y =$ annual sales (in \$10,000 units)

EXP $= X_1 =$ sales experience (in years)

SCORE $= X_2 =$ score on a sales aptitude test

A partial computer printout of the results of multiple regression analysis follows. Prepare a verbal interpretation of these results.

Variable I	B(I)	XBAR(I)	S(I)
SALES	.395081	20.5	7.00368
EXP	.257827	7.79999	3.68241
SCORE	2.96621	6.09999	1.81387

Index of Determination (R-SQ) = .7526

Correlation Matrix

	Sales	EXP	Score
SALES	1	.666929	.861978
EXP	.66693	1	.691797
SCORE	.86198	.691697	1

ACTUAL VS CALCULATED

Actual	Calculated	Difference	PCT Differ	
22	16.7731	5.22693	31.1	
15	13.0334	1.96661	15	
18	13.8069	4.19312	30.3	
10	15.9996	-5.9996		-37.4
16	19.4814	-3.48145		-17.8
29	26.1873	2.81265	10.7	
35	33.6667	1.33327	3.9	
15	18.32	-3.32004		-18.1
22	23.479	-1.47897		-6.2
23	24.2525	-1.25246		-5.1

ANALYSIS OF VARIANCE

Source	SS	DF	MS	F
Regression	369.162	2	184.581	10.6472*
Error	121.354	7	17.3362	
Total	490.516	9		

*Significant at 1% level

Variable	Coefficient	STD Error	T Statistic
EXP	.257827	. 495103	.520753
SCORE	2.96621	1.00514	2.95103

DF = 7

19. A health research team collects data on ten communities. Measurements are obtained on the following variables:

INDEX $= Y =$ health-care facility utilization index

INC $= X_1 =$ median family income

INS $= X_2 =$ proportion of workers with health insurance

DPR $= X_3 =$ doctor–population ratio

A partial computer printout of the results of multiple regression analysis follows. Prepare a verbal interpretation of these results.

Variable I	B(I)	XBAR(I)	S(I)
INDEX	7.62552	20.1	6.90586
INC	.621658	8.19999	4.42268
INS	16.9724	.574999	.202794
DPR	- .313452	7.59999	4.07923

Index of determination (R-SQ) = .814088

Correlation Matrix

	INDEX	INC	INS	DPR
INDEX	1	.804793	.805102	- .49909
INC	.804794	1	.646684	- .455618
INS	.805102	.646684	1	- .265937
DPR	- .499089	- .455618	- .265937	1

ACTUAL VS CALCULATED

Actual	Calculated	Difference	PCT Differ
20	12.691	7.309	57.5
15	15.5608	- .560793	- 3.6
17	19.6529	-2.65291	-13.4
10	13.1827	-3.18268	-24.1
16	19.026	-3.02602	-15.9
28	26.7931	1.20692	4.5
35	34.1717	.828293	2.4
15	16.3832	-1.38318	- 8.4
22	22.5882	- .588226	- 2.6
23	20.9502	2.04979	9.7

ANALYSIS OF VARIANCE

Source	SS	DF	MS	F
Regression	388.246	3	129.415	8.75775*
Error	88.6636	6	14.7773	
Total	476.91	9		

*Significant at 5% level

Variable	Coefficient	STD Error	T Statistic
INC	.621658	.390581	1.59162
INS	16.9724	7.86578	2.15774
DPR	- .313452	.33507	- .935481

DF = 6

20. Ⓒ A sample survey is conducted to study the relationship between the amount of life insurance held by business executives and several other variables. The following data are collected. (a) Find the least-squares multiple regression equation. (b) Compute $R^2_{y.123}$ and test for significance at the 0.05 level. Determine the p value. (c) Test H_0: $\beta_1 = 0$, H_0: $\beta_2 = 0$, H_0: $\beta_3 = 0$. Let $\alpha = 0.05$, and determine the p value for each test. In the table, Y denotes the amount of life insurance held by the executives ($\times$ \$10,000), X_1 denotes their annual incomes ($\times$ \$1000), X_2 denotes the number of children, and X_3 denotes their ages.

Y	30	60	75	70	50	50	20	40	45	50	50	20	20	30	25
X_1	25	42	37	57	52	48	28	53	51	52	54	32	29	29	25
X_2	2	3	3	3	4	2	1	4	3	2	4	2	1	1	1
X_3	31	35	42	60	58	49	28	55	52	35	38	41	31	32	30

21. C Select a simple random sample size of 40 from the population of employed heads of households in Appendix II. Do a complete multiple regression analysis of the data, using size of residence as the dependent variable and age, salary, education, length of time with current employer, and size of family as the independent variables.

22. C The following data were collected on a simple random sample of 40 assembly-line employees who participated in a time and motion study. Each employee in the sample performed the same task 50 times. The dependent variable is a measure of the average quality of the completed task. The quantitative independent variable is the average number of seconds required to complete the task, and the qualitative independent variable is the shift on which the task was performed.

Average Quality of Completed Task	Average Time to Complete Task (Seconds)	Shift
1.4	30	First
0.9	27	Second
1.2	33	First
1.1	29	Third
1.3	35	First
0.8	27	Second
1.0	32	First
0.7	26	First
1.2	30	Third
0.8	28	First
1.5	32	Second
1.3	31	First
1.4	32	Third
1.5	33	Second
1.0	27	First
1.8	35	Second
1.4	36	Third
1.2	34	First
1.1	28	Second
1.2	30	Second
1.0	29	Third
1.4	33	Third
0.9	28	First
1.0	28	Third
1.9	36	Second
1.3	29	Second
1.7	35	Third
1.0	30	First
0.9	28	First
1.0	31	First

(continues on next page)

Average Quality of Completed Task	Average Time to Complete Task (Seconds)	Shift
1.6	31	Second
1.6	33	Second
1.7	34	Second
1.6	35	Third
1.2	28	First
1.5	30	Second
1.8	34	Second
1.5	34	Third
1.2	30	First
1.2	32	Third

Use dummy-variable coding and multiple regression techniques to analyze these data. May we conclude that the three sampled shift populations differ with respect to quality of completed task when time required to perform the task is taken into account? May we conclude that there is interaction between shift and time required to complete the task? Plot the original data and the fitted regression equations.

23. Ⓒ The management of Sabbatini Enterprises would like to know something about employee morale and the other variables to which it may be related. To study these relationships, each employee in a simple random sample of 27 employees is interviewed and tested to obtain information concerning morale level and the average number of satisfying extra-work social contacts experienced during a week. Whether or not the duties that the employee usually performs are appropriate to the job title is also determined. The results are shown in the following table.

Measure of Morale	Average Number of Social Contacts	Duties Agree with Job Title?	Measure of Morale	Average Number of Social Contacts	Duties Agree with Job Title?
795	13	Yes	1000	11	No
1590	16	No	1100	14	Yes
1250	15	Yes	1500	20	No
1680	21	Yes	1450	19	Yes
800	10	No	1100	14	Yes
2100	26	Yes	950	12	No
1700	25	No	2400	26	Yes
1260	16	Yes	1600	24	No
1370	18	No	2400	30	Yes
1695	26	No	2600	31	Yes
1510	21	No	3000	37	Yes
2000	27	No	1900	25	No
3200	33	Yes	2200	30	No
1050	14	No			

Let morale level be the dependent variable, and use dummy-variable coding to quantify the qualitative variable. Analyze the data using regression techniques. Explain the results. Plot the original data and the fitted regression equations.

24. Ⓒ As part of a study designed to investigate the relationship between amount of exposure to television advertising and the ability of viewers to recall facts regarding the advertised products, researchers collect the following data.

Recall	Exposure	Age Group	Recall	Exposure	Age Group
4.0	0.21	C	5.1	0.48	A
7.5	0.91	A	6.0	0.74	A
3.0	0.22	A	5.7	0.70	A
8.9	0.60	C	14.2	1.60	C
5.1	0.59	A	4.1	0.30	A
5.8	0.50	C	4.0	0.25	A
9.1	0.99	C	6.1	0.22	C
3.5	0.23	A	6.2	0.61	A
7.2	0.51	C	4.9	0.45	A
14.0	1.55	C	7.1	0.83	A
12.9	1.11	C	8.0	0.61	C
11.3	1.45	C	8.1	0.82	C
5.7	0.50	A	9.0	1.15	A
15.0	1.61	C	6.1	0.39	C

The dependent variable is a measure of recall, the quantitative independent variable is a measure of exposure to television advertising, and the qualitative independent variable indicates whether the viewer is a child or an adult. Use dummy-variable coding, and analyze the data by regression techniques. Explain the results. Plot the original data and the fitted regression equations.

25. Ⓒ Tromp Electronics is interested in knowing what variables are associated with consumers' knowledge of a new personal computer that the company recently placed on the market. In a survey of potential purchasers of the computer, information was collected on the following variables:

1. Knowledge of the computer (Y)

2. Education (X_1)

3. Age (X_2)

4. Knowledge of current events (X_3)

5. Distance of residence from major retailing center (X_4)

6. Income of household (X_5)

The results were as follows:

			Variable			
Respondent	Y	X_1	X_2	X_3	X_4	X_5
1	76	12	33	65	11	19
2	65	10	51	74	6	21
3	73	15	59	86	15	40
4	76	11	33	67	15	21
5	68	10	35	65	19	28
6	69	8	23	55	16	12

(continues on next page)

		Variable				
Respondent	Y	X_1	X_2	X_3	X_4	X_5
7	56	7	34	59	12	33
8	70	11	43	73	11	27
9	60	12	43	50	17	33
10	73	11	33	76	16	40
11	60	10	53	68	15	24
12	64	8	26	56	12	30
13	80	14	56	91	4	31
14	88	13	22	69	6	40
15	61	9	43	68	9	30
16	80	12	33	73	12	28
17	69	11	39	72	13	32
18	75	13	41	68	11	33
19	48	6	43	55	16	24
20	79	10	25	80	13	44
21	62	10	43	53	5	21
22	80	15	46	82	21	31
23	69	10	37	66	8	26
24	67	10	43	68	1	35
25	70	9	23	53	4	36
26	81	11	26	74	9	40
27	43	7	44	39	8	23
28	88	11	14	64	1	36
29	60	7	37	64	15	17
30	72	11	32	64	14	36
31	64	9	45	72	10	22
32	92	12	31	97	3	34
33	85	12	36	94	6	32
34	67	10	45	74	9	23
35	65	11	48	73	10	42
36	94	15	33	81	2	38
37	77	14	54	83	9	27
38	83	13	40	82	13	31
39	70	8	33	68	5	19
40	78	11	24	64	5	42
41	68	11	36	65	19	28
42	60	12	44	50	17	33
43	88	13	23	69	7	41
44	76	14	42	68	11	33
45	60	8	37	64	15	17
46	65	11	48	74	10	42

Obtain the sample least-squares regression equation for these data.

26. C Refer to Exercise 25. What is the coefficient of multiple determination for these data?

27. C Refer to Exercise 25. Construct the ANOVA table for these data. At the 0.01 level of significance, can we conclude that there is a linear relationship among the six variables? What is the p value for the test?

28. C Refer to Exercise 25. Test each of the individual sample slope coefficients for significance. Let $\alpha = 0.01$ for each test, and find the p value.

29. C Refer to Exercise 25. Let $X_1 = 10$, $X_2 = 50$, $X_3 = 70$, $X_4 = 15$, and $X_5 = 25$. Estimate the mean of Y, and construct the 95% confidence interval.

30. C Refer to Exercise 25. Let $X_1 = 10$, $X_2 = 50$, $X_3 = 70$, $X_4 = 15$, and $X_5 = 25$. Predict Y, and find the 95% prediction interval.

31. The following is a computer printout for a multiple regression analysis involving 15 observations on each variable. Fill in the blanks.

```
Variable I          B(I)           XBAR(I)            S(I)
   1             - .44611955      14.253333        3.2178409
   2             4.3041468E-04    1052.7333        348.72498
   3             1.3191057E-02    1079.9999        232.58006
Index of determination (R-SQ) =      .98589776
Correlation Matrix
1                 .84735172          .99260055
 .84735172       1                   .83981949
 .99260055        .83981949          1
                ANALYSIS OF VARIANCE
Source           SS                DF          MS           F
Regression     153.12718      b. ____     e. ____     g. ____

Error      a. ____            c. ____     f. ____

Total          155.3175       d. ____

** Significant at 1% level
Variable       Coefficient        STD         T
                                  Error      Statistic
2              4.3041468E-        5.8269672E-   h. ____
               04                 04

3              1.3191057E-        8.7368234E-   i. ____
               02                 04

DF = j. ____
```

32. C A broker with Victoria Properties is interested in knowing what variables are associated with the appraised selling price of single-family dwellings located in a certain area. The data shown in Data Set 8 of Appendix IV were collected on each of the 1,050 dwellings in the population. The variables are as follows:

Y = appraised selling price in thousands of dollars
X_1 = size in 100-square-foot units
X_2 = age in years
X_3 = lot size in acres

Select a simple random sample of size 25 from the population, and find the sample least-squares regression equation.

33. C Refer to Exercise 32. Find the coefficient of multiple determination. What does this measure tell you about your sample? Compare your results with those of your classmates.

34. C Refer to Exercise 32. Use your sample data to construct an ANOVA table. Can we conclude that in the population the four variables are related? Let $\alpha = 0.05$, and find the p value.

35. C Refer to Exercise 32. Test each of your sample slope coefficients for significance. Let $\alpha = 0.05$ for each test, and find the p value.

36. C Refer to Exercise 32. Use your sample regression equation to estimate the mean Y value for selected values of the independent variables. Construct a confidence interval for the mean of Y.

37. C Refer to Exercise 32. Use your sample regression equation to predict Y for selected values of the independent variables.

38. C Select a simple random sample from the population of companies listed in Appendix III. (Ask your instructor how large your sample should be.) Do a multiple regression analysis of the data, with sales as the dependent variable. Cover at least the following calculations and procedures. (a) Find the multiple regression equation. (b) Compute R^2 and R. (c) Use ANOVA to determine whether the six variables are linearly related in the population. (d) Use a t test to test H_0: $\beta = 0$ for each slope coefficient. (e) Use the sample regression equation to predict values of Y for selected values of the X's. (f) Use the sample regression equation to estimate the means of the subpopulations of Y for selected values of the X's.

39. C Repeat Exercise 38 with cash flow as the dependent variable.

40. C Repeat Exercise 38 with net profits as the dependent variable.

*41. We see in Figure 10.3.2 that the STAT+ multiple regression printout contains a column labeled BETA(I). The entries in this column are variously known as *standardized regression coefficients*, *beta coefficients*, and *beta weights*. They are calculated by multiplying a given partial regression coefficient by a fraction obtained by dividing the standard deviation of the associated independent variable by the standard deviation of the dependent variable; that is, BETA(I) = BETA(i) = $b_i(s_{x_i}/s_y)$. From the information given in the printout in Figure 10.3.2, for example, we may compute the standardized regression coefficient associated with the variable RETSAL as follows: BETA(1) = $0.067754(4.710566/0.548826) = 0.581531$, which is the first numerical entry in the BETA(I) column of the printout. One of the purposes of standardized regression coefficients is to allow for their comparison with each other when the observations of the associated independent variables are measured in different units. For example, the observations of one independent variable might be measured in pounds while those of another independent variable might be measured in inches. The two resulting unstandardized regression coefficients are not directly comparable because of the different units of measurement involved. The manner in which the standardized regression coefficients are calculated makes them dimensionless and, therefore, directly comparable. The standardized regression coefficients shown in Figure 10.3.2 may be interpreted as follows: BETA(1) tells us that when there is a 1 standard deviation change in RETSAL, there is a 0.581531 standard deviation change in CIRC. BETA(2) tells us that when there is a 1 standard deviation change in POP, there is a 0.412238 standard deviation change in CIRC. Refer to Review Exercise 9 and calculate and interpret the standardized regression coefficients.

STATISTICS AT WORK

STATISTICS AT WORK

STATISTICS AT

1. USING REGRESSION ANALYSIS TO HELP SELECT STORE LOCATIONS

Deciding where to locate a new retail store is one of the most important decisions that the managers of such firms have to make. Lord and Lynds review the use of regression techniques in research on the location of stores and present a case study of location of a new liquor store.

Their study used regression techniques to identify location variables related to the sales performance of a sample of 16 liquor stores located in a certain area. The dependent variable was volume of sales. The predictor variables were population within 1.5 miles of the store (POP), mean household income of this population (MHI), distance from subject store to nearest other liquor store (DIS), daily volume of traffic on the street on which the store was located (TFL), and amount of employment within 1.5 miles of the store (EMP). They obtained the following results.

Variable	Regression Coefficient	t
POP	0.09460	5.20
MHI	0.06129	2.98
DIS	4.88524	2.83
TFL	−2.59040	−2.11
EMP	−0.00245	−0.54
$R^2 = 0.69$		

What conclusions can you draw from these results? Let $\alpha = 0.05$. What assumptions are necessary? What other variables do you think might be worth considering as predictors of sales volume of a retail store? Why do you think the regression coefficient for TFL is negative?

Source: Dennis J. Lord and Charles D. Lynds, "The Use of Regression Models in Store Location Research: A Review and Case Study," *Akron Business and Economic Review* 12 (Summer 1981), 13–19.

2. REGRESSION ANALYSIS AND ASPHALT CHARACTERISTICS

Researchers at Montana State University developed a high-pressure gel permeation chromatography (HPGPC) technique for separating the components in asphalt cement according to their molecular size. An article by Chollar et al. in *Public Roads* addresses the correlation among HPGPC properties and the physical properties of asphalts. Twenty-eight asphalts were analyzed with the HPGPC technique. The results obtained by the investigators are shown in the following table.

Chromatography data and physical properties of asphalt samples

Lab Number	LMS	DUCT45	DUCT77	SG	SHR SUS	ASPH	REF IND	LST
B2908	32.23	31	130	1.004	0.36	19.0	1.4827	−46
B2909	32.15	9	221	1.007	0.39	20.5	1.4826	−45
B2910	27.01	9	200	1.012	0.51	21.6	1.4817	−41
B2921	12.70	8	250	1.004	0.42	15.5	1.4837	−39
B2922	9.43	0	250	1.007	0.62	18.1	1.4844	−39
B2960	23.96	11	160	1.034	0.42	27.9	1.4775	−51
B2962	17.75	150	155	1.010	0.21	19.3	1.4815	−51
B2963	17.24	150	250	1.015	0.31	20.2	1.4819	−48
B2964	15.98	10	241	1.021	0.44	21.6	1.4822	−44
B2975	8.79	0	215	1.005	0.66	16.5	1.4851	−20
B3009	15.57	12	230	0.994	0.41	17.8	1.4833	−50
B3010	23.07	7	205	0.995	0.49	20.1	1.4813	−54
B3013	26.88	150	245	1.021	0.32	20.8	1.4810	−39
B3014	14.58	14	250	1.025	0.39	21.6	1.4814	−42
B3028	16.09	3	152	1.011	0.30	19.5	1.4806	−53
B3030	12.40	5	250	1.028	0.59	29.3	1.4812	−41
B3036	12.64	11	210	1.026	0.42	16.7	1.4827	−56
B3051	16.13	150	250	1.028	0.18	26.1	1.4769	−46
B3056	11.52	3	250	1.020	0.64	19.2	1.4806	−34
B3058	22.61	150	140	1.021	0.31	22.4	1.4790	−46
B3108	16.27	244	167	1.011	0.23	17.3	1.4851	−40
B3109	18.43	19	250	1.014	0.43	18.6	1.4850	−33
B3110	14.93	9	250	1.018	0.54	19.7	1.4821	−36
B3578	14.11	150	205	1.015	0.21	18.1	1.4890	−35
B3579	11.66	150	245	1.010	0.40	18.0	1.4897	−35
B3601	6.96	250	171	1.011	0.29	9.7	1.4863	−30
B3602	16.50	12	250	1.016	0.50	11.0	1.4867	−23
B3603	3.47	4	250	1.021	0.65	12.2	1.4868	−22

LMS = Large Molecular Size Content (%)
DUCT = Ductility at 45°F and 77°F
SG = Specific Gravity
SHR SUS = Shear Susceptability
ASPH = Asphaltene Content (%)
REF IND = Refractive Index
LST = Limiting Stiffness Temperature (°C)

°F = 1.8°C + 32

Perform a multiple regression analysis of these data, with LMS as the dependent variable. Prepare a narrative report of your results. What conclusions are justified on the basis of your analysis?

Source: Brian H. Chollar, et al., "Chemical and Physical Characterization of Binder Materials," *Public Roads*, 49(June 1985), 7–12.

3. SMALL BUSINESS MANAGERS' PERFORMANCE

Gul examined the interacting effects of management accounting systems (MAS) and perceived environmental uncertainty (PEU) on small business managers' perceptions of their performance (PER). Participants in the study were managers/owners of light engineering manufacturing firms in Australia. Gul hypothesized that the positive effects of sophisticated MAS information on PER would be higher when the level of PEU is greater. He used a model that included, in addition to MAS and PEU, an independent variable whose measurements were the product of the measurements for the other two independent variables. The purpose of the third variable was to reflect the interaction of MAS and PEU. The following measurements were obtained.

PER	MAS	PEU
6.556	3.957	4.833
5.778	4.448	4.143
6.667	4.182	5.875
5.778	4.500	5.500
5.778	4.066	4.875
5.944	5.204	3.500
5.333	3.222	3.375
5.444	4.783	3.500
7.222	5.050	6.000
5.889	5.174	4.625
6.375	5.155	2.000
7.111	6.478	6.000
5.667	4.159	4.143
5.111	3.357	5.875
5.333	4.864	3.875
5.333	4.250	4.625
6.333	5.238	3.400
7.111	5.225	4.000
6.667	4.625	4.750
6.444	5.435	4.500
5.556	4.714	3.625
8.000	3.118	3.750
4.889	4.684	5.571
4.889	4.048	5.571
5.333	5.500	4.625
7.778	2.304	3.625
4.889	3.479	2.750
6.778	4.591	4.375
5.444	3.512	5.875
6.000	4.800	3.625

(continues on next page)

PER	MAS	PEU
6.111	4.154	4.000
6.143	4.091	4.000
6.556	5.067	3.286
6.000	4.217	4.250
7.000	5.069	5.143
7.111	4.304	4.500
5.667	4.726	4.625
7.222	6.212	5.000
6.444	3.109	3.600
5.778	3.587	3.143

Source: Professor Ferdinand A. Gul. Used by permission.

Do a complete regression analysis of these data and state your conclusions.

See: Ferdinand A. Gul, "The Effects of Management Accounting Systems and Environmental Uncertainty on Small Business Managers' Performance," *Accounting and Business Research*, 22 (1991), 57–61.

SUGGESTIONS FOR FURTHER READING

The topics covered in this chapter, as well as others, are discussed in detail in the textbooks listed at the end of Chapter 9. Two additional books of interest are

Cohen, Jacob, and Patricia Cohen (1983). *Applied Multiple Regression/Correlation Analysis for the Behavioral Sciences*, 2nd ed. Lawrence Erlbaum Associates, Hillsdale, N.J.

Pedhazur, Elazar J. (1982). *Multiple Regression in Behavioral Research*, 2nd ed. Holt, Rinehart and Winston, New York.

The following journal articles and bibliographies are also useful:

Allen, David M. (1971). "Mean Square Error of Prediction as a Criterion for Selecting Variables," *Technometrics* 13:469–475.

Daniel, Wayne W. (1979). *The Use of Dummy Variables in Regression Analysis: A Selected Bibliography with Annotations*. Vance Bibliographies, Monticello, Ill.

—— (1980). *Ridge Regression: A Selected Bibliography*. Vance Bibliographies, Monticello, Ill.

Garside, M. J. (1965). "The Best Sub-Set in Multiple Regression Analysis," *Applied Statistics* 14:196–200.

Geary, R. C., and C. E. V. Leser (1968). "Significance Tests in Multiple Regression," *American Statistician* 22 (Feb.):20–21.

Gorman, J. W., and R. J. Toman (1966). "Selection of Variables for Fitting Equations to Data," *Technometrics* 8:27–52.

Hocking, R. R. (1972). "Criteria for Selection of a Subset Regression: Which One Should It Be?" *Technometrics* 14:967–970.

Hocking, R. R., and R. N. Leslie (1967). "Selection of the Best Sub-Set in Regression Analysis," *Technometrics* 9:531–540.

Jaech, J. L. (1966). "Understanding Multiple Regression," *Industrial Quality Control* 23:260–264.

Weiss, S. Neil (1970). "A Graphical Representation of the Relationships Between Multiple Regression and Multiple Correlation," *American Statistician* 24 (April):25–29.

11

Regression Analysis: Model Building

Chapter Objectives: In this chapter, you become acquainted with some additional aspects of regression analysis. Your understanding of the concepts and techniques introduced in this chapter will greatly enhance your ability to analyze problems encountered in the business world and will provide you with additional tools for solving them. After studying this chapter and working the exercises, you should be able to

1. Incorporate the ideas of model building into your strategy for solving problems requiring statistical analysis.
2. Recognize those situations that can be represented by a curvilinear regression model.
3. Apply the techniques of curvilinear regression analysis, when appropriate, to the solution of business problems.
4. Recognize situations that can be represented by a nonlinear regression model.
5. Apply, in the case of a simple nonlinear regression model, appropriate problem-solving techniques.
6. Employ, in a simple situation, a variable transformation to simplify the solution of a problem.
7. Employ some useful techniques for selecting independent variables to be included in a regression model.

11.1   INTRODUCTION

In Chapters 9 and 10, you learned the basic concepts of regression analysis and became acquainted with techniques that can be used to solve problems for which a simple regression model provides an adequate representation.

In Chapter 9, you were introduced to the concepts and techniques of simple linear regression analysis. You learned that the simple linear regression model may be expressed as follows:

$$y_i = \alpha + \beta\, x_i + e_i$$

(11.1.1)

In Chapter 10, you encountered the concepts and techniques of multiple linear regression analysis. You learned that the multiple linear regression model may be expressed as follows:

$$y_j = \beta_0 + \beta_1\, x_{1j} + \beta_2\, x_{2j} + \cdots + \beta_k\, x_{kj} + e_j$$

(11.1.2)

To illustrate the techniques of regression analysis, we assume in Chapter 9 that the simple linear regression model is the appropriate model for the situation at hand. The discussion of regression analysis in Chapter 10 is based on the assumption that the multiple linear regression model was the appropriate one. The procedure by which we arrive at an appropriate model to represent a given situation is called *model building*. In the present chapter, we discuss some model-building techniques and introduce some additional regression models.

11.2   MODEL BUILDING

The objective of model building is to develop, for a real-world situation, a representation (called a model) that will provide a vehicle for obtaining useful results when the model is employed in the analysis of data generated by the modeled situation. The two primary activities in model building in regression analysis are determining the form of the model and selecting the variables to be included in the model. The form of the model may be *linear, curvilinear,* or *nonlinear*.

> A *linear model* is a model that is linear in the parameters, that is, in the regression coefficients and the error term.

The simple linear regression model (Equation 11.1.1), discussed in Chapter 9, and the multiple regression model (Equation 11.1.2), discussed in Chapter 10, exemplify linear models.

A model that is linear in the parameters may be nonlinear with respect to the independent variables. We refer to such a model as a curvilinear model. The following are some examples of curvilinear models:

$$y_j = \beta_0 + \beta_1 x_{1j} + \beta_2 x_{1j}^2 + \beta_3 x_{1j} x_{2j} + \beta_4 x_{2j}^2 + e_j$$

(11.2.1)

(11.2.2)
$$y_j = \beta_0 + \beta_1 x_{1j} + \beta_2 x_{1j}^2 + \beta_3 x_{1j}^3 + e_j$$

(11.2.3)
$$y_j = \beta_0 + \beta_1 \log x_{1j} + \beta_2 \log x_{2j} + e_j$$

(11.2.4)
$$y_j = \beta_0 + \beta_1 x_{1j} + \beta_2 \frac{1}{x_{1j}} + e_j$$

(11.2.5)
$$y_j = \beta_0 + \beta_1 x_{1j} + \beta_2 x_{2j} + \beta_3 x_{1j} x_{2j} + e_j$$

To obtain estimates of the parameters in a curvilinear model, we redefine the independent variables to make the model linear in the redefined variables. The method of least squares, discussed in Chapter 10, can then be used to estimate the parameters of the model.

Suppose, for example, that a situation can be represented adequately by the following model (Equation 11.2.1):

$$y_j = \beta_0 + \beta_1 x_{1j} + \beta_2 x_{1j}^2 + \beta_3 x_{1j} x_{2j} + \beta_4 x_{2j}^2 + e_j$$

We may redefine the independent variables as follows:

$$z_1 = x_1$$
$$z_2 = x_1^2$$
$$z_3 = x_1 x_2$$
$$z_4 = x_2^2$$

The model is now written as

(11.2.6)
$$y_j = \beta_0 + \beta_1 z_{1j} + \beta_2 z_{2j} + \beta_3 z_{3j} + \beta_4 z_{4j} + e_j$$

which is linear in the independent variables.

The value of the highest power of an independent variable in a model is referred to as the *order* of the model. Thus, the model

$$y_i = \alpha + \beta x_i + e_i$$

is called a *simple first-order model with one independent variable*. The model

$$y_j = \beta_0 + \beta_1 x_{1j} + \beta_2 x_{1j}^2 + \beta_3 x_{1j} x_{2j} + \beta_4 x_{2j}^2 + e_j$$

is called a *second-order model with two independent variables*. The variable $x_{1j} x_{2j}$ is included in this second-order model to account for the possible effects of the variables x_{1j} and x_{2j} working together. You learned in Chapter 10 that such an effect is called interaction.

We reserve the term *nonlinear regression model* to designate any regression model that is not linear in the parameters.

The following are some examples of nonlinear regression models:

(11.2.7) $y_i = \alpha\beta^x e_i$ (exponential growth curve)

(11.2.8) $y_i = \alpha\beta^{-x} e_i$ (exponential decay curve)

(11.2.9) $y_i = \alpha - \beta\rho^x + e_i$ (asymptotic regression curve, $0 < \rho < 1$)

(11.2.10) $y_i = \alpha/(1 + \beta\rho^x) + e_i$ (logistic growth curve, $0 < \rho < 1$)

The shapes of the curves defined by Equations 11.2.7 through 11.2.10 are shown in Figure 11.2.1.

FIGURE 11.2.1   Examples of curvilinear regression

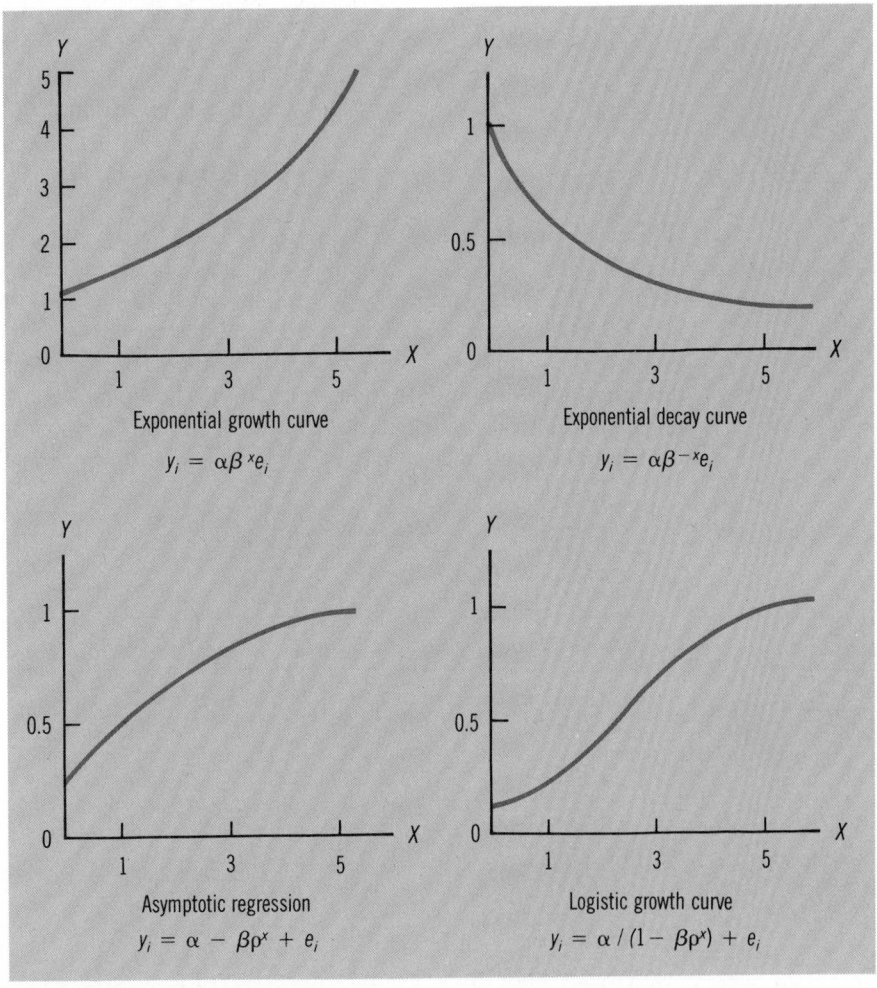

11.3 CURVILINEAR REGRESSION MODELS – AN EXAMPLE

The following example illustrates the method of analysis employed when the second-order model with one independent variable is appropriate.

EXAMPLE 11.3.1 Walton Chemicals is interested in studying the effect of different levels of soil acidity on the yield of a certain crop. One of the objectives of the study is to develop a model that can be used to predict yield when different levels of acidity are present in the soil. The crop was grown on 20 different plots of soil. The yields and soil acidity values are shown in Table 11.3.1.

SOLUTION When we plot the data of Table 11.3.1 as the scatter diagram of Figure 11.3.1, we see that the two variables do not appear to be linearly related. The scatter diagram suggests that some curvilinear model may provide a good fit to the data. Suppose that we try a second-order model by adding the square of x as the second independent variable. The model is written as

$$y_j = \beta_0 + \beta_1 x_{1j} + \beta_2 x_{1j}^2 + e_j$$
(11.3.1)

If we let $z_{1j} = x_{1j}$ and $z_{2j} = x_{1j}^2$, the model is rewritten as

$$y_j = \beta_0 + \beta_1 z_{1j} + \beta_2 z_{2j} + e_j$$
(11.3.2)

We recognize the model of Equation 11.3.2 as the multiple regression model discussed in Chapter 10. We may use the techniques learned in Chapter 10 to estimate the parameters β_0, β_1, and β_2 and thus obtain the sample multiple regression equation. We also may use the procedures learned in Chapter 10 to evaluate the sample equation to see if it is likely to provide good predictions and estimates. If the evaluation indicates that the chosen model provides a satisfactory representation of the population, we may use the equation to predict crop yield for different levels of soil acidity.

TABLE 11.3.1 Crop yield and soil acidity data for Example 11.3.1

Yield (Y)	Soil Acidity (X)	Yield (Y)	Soil Acidity (X)
35.0	7.0	13.8	25.0
28.8	10.0	5.0	29.0
45.0	3.0	20.0	19.0
45.0	5.0	15.0	21.5
55.0	3.0	15.0	16.5
25.0	10.0	25.0	12.5
37.5	4.0	12.5	19.0
27.5	14.0	20.0	16.0
30.0	5.5	7.5	24.0
27.5	8.0	10.0	27.0

FIGURE 11.3.1   Crop yield and soil acidity data for Example 11.3.1

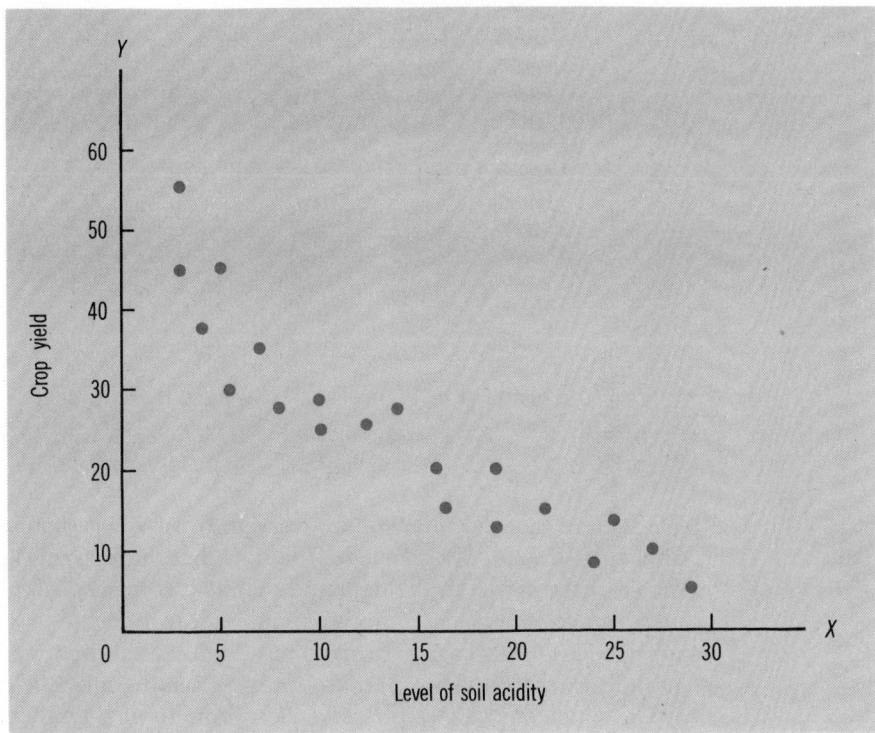

COMPUTER **ANALYSIS**

OBTAINING THE MULTIPLE-REGRESSION EQUATION

The first step in obtaining the sample multiple regression equation is to add the x^2 term, as shown in Table 11.3.2.

We may use either the MINITAB or the STAT+ software package to analyze these data. If we use MINITAB, we may enter the command READ C1 C2 C3 to put the dependent variable into column 1 and the two independent variables into columns 2 and 3, respectively. The commands

MINITAB

```
BRIEF 3
REGRESS C1 2 C2 C3
```

yield an extensive analysis of the data. Part of the resulting printout is given in Figure 11.3.2.

TABLE 11.3.2 The data of Table 11.3.1 with added x^2 term

y	x	x^2	y	x	x^2
35.0	7.0	49.0	13.8	25.0	625.0
28.8	10.0	100.0	5.0	29.0	841.0
45.0	3.0	9.0	20.0	19.0	361.0
45.0	5.0	25.0	15.0	21.5	462.25
55.0	3.0	9.0	15.0	16.5	272.25
25.0	10.0	100.0	25.0	12.5	156.25
37.5	4.0	16.0	12.5	19.0	361.0
27.5	14.0	196.0	20.0	16.0	256.0
30.0	5.5	30.25	7.5	24.0	576.0
27.5	8.0	64.0	10.0	27.0	729.0

From the printout in Figure 11.3.2, we see that the regression equation is

(11.3.3)
$$\hat{y}_j = 53.0 - 2.88x + 0.0464x^2$$

We also see that the t statistic for testing $H_0 : \beta_2 = 0$ is significant at a reasonable level ($p = 0.023$). We conclude from this that the x^2 term significantly improves the fit of the model to the data and that as a representation of the data a curvilinear model is more appropriate than a linear model.

The STAT+ package gives us some additional information, as shown in Figure 11.3.3, which contains a partial printout from the multiple regression program.

The simple and nonlinear regression program in STAT+ allows us to obtain

FIGURE 11.3.2 MINITAB commands and partial printout for Example 11.3.1

```
MTB > BRIEF 3
MTB > REGRESS C1 2 C2 C3

The regression equation is
C1 = 53.0 - 2.88 C2 + 0.0464 C3

Predictor        Coef        Stdev       t-ratio        p
Constant        53.009        3.643        14.55       0.000
C2              -2.8781       0.5769       -4.99       0.000
C3               0.04637      0.01860       2.49       0.023

s = 4.794       R-sq = 88.7%      R-sq(adj) = 87.4%

                ANALYSIS OF VARIANCE

    Source       DF         SS          MS          F         p
Regression        2      3,080.4      1,540.2      67.00     0.000
Error            17        390.8        23.0
Total            19      3,471.1

    Source       DF       SEQ SS
C2                1      2,937.5
C3                1        142.9
```

FIGURE 11.3.3   Partial STAT+ printout for Example 11.3.1

```
VARIABLE I        B(I)       BETA(I)     XBAR(I)     S(I)
YIELD      1    53.00947     N.D.        25.00500   13.17408
ACID       2    -2.878114   -1.792203   13.95000    8.203506
ACIDSQ     3     0.046374    0.895558   261.9000   254.4159

INDEX OF DETERMINATION (R-SQ) = 0.88742

CORRELATION COEFFICIENT (R) = 0.94203
            CORRELATION MATRIX
          Yield        ACID        ACIDSQ
YIELD     1.0000      -0.9199      -0.8501
ACID     -0.9199       1.0000       0.9740
ACIDSQ   -0.8501       0.9740       1.0000
            ANALYSIS OF VARIANCE
   Source        SS          DF         MS            F
REGRESSION   3,080.352775     2    1,540.176388    67.002 @
ERROR          390.777344    17       22.986903
TOTAL        3,471.130127    19

STANDARD DEVIATION OF ERROR TERM 4.7944658

@ BEYOND BOUNDS OF MY TABLE - CONSULT F TABLE TO DETERMINE
SIGNIFICANCE
                                            95%
                                         CONFIDENCE
                               STD         LIMITS
VARIABLE    COEFFICIENT      ERROR   T STATISTIC  (+,-)

ACID    2   -2.878114      0.57689   -4.98899     1.21713
ACIDSQ  3    0.046374      0.01860    2.49298     0.03925

D.F.= 17

DURBIN-WATSON STATISTIC = 2.2865
```

Equation 11.3.3 by simply entering the X and Y values of Table 11.3.1. The program fits the second-order equation to the data without our having to enter the x^2 values. The printout from this program for Example 11.3.1 is shown in Figure 11.3.4. Equation 11.3.3 is Equation 7 on the printout. The printout also shows us that the coefficient of determination (r^2) for the second-order model fit of 0.88742 is larger than the r^2 of 0.84626 for the simple linear regression model.

Let us also compare the adjusted coefficients of determination. In Figure 11.3.2, we see that $\tilde{r}_2 = 0.874$ for the second-order model. From MINITAB regression analysis, we find that for the simple linear model $\tilde{r}_2 = 0.838$. We take these results as evidence that the second-order model provides a better fit to the data than the simple linear model.

The F of 67.00 with an associated p value of 0.000 (to three-decimal-place accuracy) and the two significant t values that allow us to reject $H_0:\beta_1 = 0$ and $H_0:\beta_2 = 0$ justifies our using Equation 11.3.3 to predict and to estimate crop

FIGURE 11.3.4 STAT+ printout showing the estimated parameters of the second-order regression equation fitted to the data of Example 11.3.1

```
Y = YIELD     X = ACID
              SIMPLE AND NONLINEAR REGRESSION RESULTS
                                    STD
     Equation            R^2       ERR        A           B            C
  1. Y=A+B*X            +0.84626   5.445     45.614     -1.477317
  2. Y=A*EXP(B*X)       +0.89487   4.512     56.521     -0.070177
  3. Y=A*(X^B)          +0.81980   5.897    134.362     -0.764151
  4. Y=A+B/X            +0.83323   5.671   9.76635002  129.920743
  7. Y=A+B*X+C*X^2      +0.88742   4.794     53.009     -2.878109   0.0463733
```

yield for specified levels of soil acidity. Suppose that we want to predict crop yield when the measure of soil acidity is 15. We may obtain point estimates, 95% prediction intervals, and 95% confidence intervals by using either STAT+ or MINITAB. In the process of analyzing the data STAT+ asks the user if prediction and confidence intervals are desired. If so, the program asks for values for each of the independent variables. In the present example, we would enter 15 and 225. The resulting printout is shown in Figure 11.3.5.

If we use MINITAB to construct prediction and confidence intervals, we must supply an appropriate subcommand at the time we ask for the regression analysis. For the present example, the appropriate command and subcommand are

MINITAB

```
MTB  REGRESS C1  2  C2 C3
SUBC PREDICT 15, 225.
```

The confidence interval (C. I.) and prediction interval (P. I.) calculated by MINITAB are shown on page 625.

FIGURE 11.3.5 STAT+ printout of confidence interval and prediction interval for Example 11.3.1

```
CONFIDENCE INTERVALS ON YIELD

Enter observed value of X2, ACID      15
Enter observed value of X3, ACIDSQ    225

THE 95% CONFIDENCE LIMITS ON THE EXPECTED VALUE OF X1
(YIELD) ARE:

X1 = 20.27179+/- 3.5287        UPPER = 23.80049
LOWER = 16.74309

THE 95% PREDICTION LIMITS ON THE EXPECTED VALUE OF X1
(YIELD) ARE:

X1 = 20.27179 +/- 10.713       UPPER = 30.98498
LOWER = 9.558610
```

```
 Fit      Stdev.Fit        95% C.I.          95% P.I.
20.27       1.67        (16.74, 23.80)    (9.56, 30.99)
```

We see that both packages provide the same intervals.

We interpret the confidence interval as follows: given a population of land plots, all of which have a soil acidity value of 15, we are 95% confident that the mean yield for the population of plots will be somewhere between 16.74 and 23.80. Our interpretation of the prediction interval is this: given a plot of land with a soil acidity value of 15, we are 95% confident that the yield for this plot will be somewhere between 9.56 and 30.99.

EXERCISES

11.3.1   Ⓒ The following are measurements of wear (Y) sustained by a movable engine part at different engine speeds (X). The data have been coded for ease of calculation. Fit a second-order model to these data.

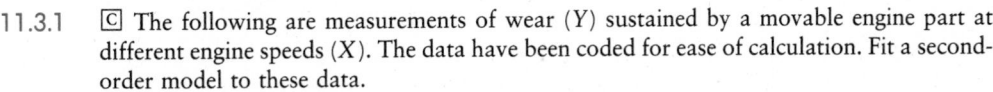

Y	20	10	30	45	45	62	60	80	70	85	75	90	75	85	75
X	20	25	35	40	50	60	80	90	95	105	110	115	130	145	150

Exercises 11.3.2 through 11.3.9 are based on the results of Exercise 11.3.1.

11.3.2   Write out the multiple regression prediction equation showing numerical values for the regression coefficients.

11.3.3   What is the numerical value of the coefficient of determination?

11.3.4   Perform an analysis of variance to determine the level of significance of the overall regression. What is the computed value of F? What is the p value for the test?

11.3.5   What is the numerical value of the computed t statistic for testing the null hypothesis that the slope coefficient associated with the variable speed is 0? What is the p value for the test?

11.3.6   What is the numerical value of the computed t statistic for testing the null hypothesis that the slope coefficient associated with speed squared is equal to 0? What is the p value for the test?

11.3.7   Compute and plot the residuals. What impression regarding the appropriateness of the model do you form by a visual inspection of the residual plot?

11.3.8   Use the regression equation to predict the amount of wear when the engine speed is 75. What are the 95% prediction limits for this prediction?

11.3.9   Use the regression equation to estimate the mean wear for a population of parts subjected to engine speeds of 75. What are the 95% confidence limits for this estimate?

11.3.10   Ⓒ A researcher with a fertilizer manufacturer studied the growth of a certain plant receiving weekly applications of an experimental fertilizer over a ten-week period. The results were as follows (X = weeks elapsing since first application of fertilizer; Y = height, in inches, of plant):

Y	4.00	5.10	6.00	6.50	7.60	12.25	17.75	23.90	27.80	30.25	33.40
X	0	1	2	3	4	5	6	7	8	9	10

Fit a second-order model to these data.

Exercises 11.3.11 through 11.3.17 are based on Exercise 11.3.10.

11.3.11 Write out the multiple regression equation with numerical values for the slope coefficients and the y intercept.

11.3.12 What is the numerical value of the coefficient of determination?

11.3.13 Perform an analysis of variance to test the null hypothesis of no overall regression. What is the numerical value of the F statistic? What is the p value for the test?

11.3.14 What is the numerical value of the t statistic for testing the null hypothesis that the slope coefficient associated with weeks is equal to 0? What is the p value for the test?

11.3.15 What is the numerical value of the t statistic for testing the null hypothesis that the slope coefficient associated with weeks squared is equal to 0? What is the p value for the test?

11.3.16 Compute and plot the residuals. What impression do you get regarding the appropriateness of the second-order model from an inspection of the residual plot?

11.3.17 Use the multiple regression equation to predict the growth at the end of six weeks of a plant treated with weekly applications of the fertilizer.

11.3.18 Ⓒ The operations manager of Yamashita Electronics which produces a component for automotive computers conducted a study to determine the relationship between the production rate of the plant and the number of defective items produced. The following data show the volume (in hundreds of units) of production (X) and number of defective items (Y) for 12 randomly selected days.

X	4	7	3	6	8	9	5.5	2	4.5	9.5	10	3.5
Y	18	24	16	25	29	40	20	9	21	36	39	19

Fit a second-order model to these data.

Exercises 11.3.19 through 11.3.26 are based on Exercise 11.3.18.

11.3.19 Write out the multiple regression equation with numerical values for the slope coefficients and the y intercept.

11.3.20 What is the numerical value of the coefficient of determination?

11.3.21 Perform an analysis of variance to test the null hypothesis of no overall regression. What is the numerical value of the F statistic? What is the p value for the test?

11.3.22 What is the numerical value of the t statistic for testing the null hypothesis that the slope coefficient associated with X is equal to 0? What is the p value for the test?

11.3.23 What is the numerical value of the t statistic for testing the null hypothesis that the slope coefficient associated with X^2 is equal to 0? What is the p value for the test?

11.3.24 Compute and plot the residuals. What impression do you get regarding the appropriateness of the second-order model from an inspection of the residual plot?

11.3.25 Use the multiple regression equation to predict the number of defective items when the production is 500 units.

11.3.26 What are the 95% prediction limits for the prediction obtained in Exercise 11.3.25?

11.4 NONLINEAR REGRESSION MODELS—AN EXAMPLE

The exponential models specified in Equations 11.2.7 and 11.2.8 provide adequate representations of many situations encountered in practice. Measurements taken on many phenomena and tracked over time, for example, do not increase or decrease by a constant amount during each time period. A straight-line model, therefore, does not provide a suitable representation of such data. What one frequently observes is that, over time, measurements on some variables change at either a decreasing or an increasing rate. In such cases an exponential model provides an appropriate representation of the data.

The exponential model is an example of a model that is nonlinear in the parameters. Such nonlinear models are sometimes divided into two categories—those that are *intrinsically linear* and those that are not.

A model is said to be intrinsically linear if it can be made linear through the use of an appropriate *transformation*.

A transformation that can be made when the exponential model is employed is the *logarithmic transformation*. To use the logarithmic transformation with the models specified in Equations 11.2.7 and 11.2.8, for example, we take the logarithm of both sides of the equation. If the original model is

$$y_j = \alpha \beta^x e_j$$

of Equation 11.2.7, the transformed model, using the logarithmic transformation, is

(11.4.1)
$$\log y_j = \log \alpha + (\log \beta)x + \log e_j$$

We recognize the model of Equation 11.4.1 as a linear model.

In the world of business, a frequently encountered example of the exponential model is the *learning curve*.

Learning curves describe the relationships between output quantities and the quantities of certain inputs, such as direct-labor hours in the presence of an incentive for learning.

The fundamental concept in learning-curve theory is that workers learn as they work, and the more times they repeat an operation the more efficient they become. Consequently, over time, there is a decline in the direct labor input per unit produced.

Learning curves provide suitable models in a wide variety of situations in which production planning and control is of interest. The theory of learning curves is applicable in both machine-intensive operations and those operations involving mainly manual labor. The model may be used in situations involving a person who repeatedly performs a task, as well as in situations in which a factory produces many units of a particular product. Generally, learning-curve analysis is used only in the earlier phases of mass production and is not ordinarily considered an appropriate analytical tool for long-term ongoing mass production.

The following example illustrates the use of the exponential model in a situation in which the learning curve is applicable.

EXAMPLE 11.4.1 A firm that manufactures exercise equipment recently began production of a machine that simulates stair climbing. Marketing department forecasts indicate that 200 of these machines can be sold over the next five years. During the first year of production, 30 machines were manufactured. Table 11.4.1 shows the direct-labor hours required to produce the fifth, seventh, eleventh, sixteenth, twentieth, and thirtieth of these 30 machines.

The data of Table 11.4.1 are plotted in Figure 11.4.1.

SOLUTION The pattern of points in the scatter diagram of Figure 11.4.1 suggests that the exponential model

(11.4.2)
$$y_j = \alpha j^\beta e_j$$

would provide an appropriate representation of the data. In the model

y_j = direct-labor hours

α = labor hours to produce the first machine

j = number of completed machine

β = rate of reduction in labor hours

This model is known as the learning-curve model.

TABLE 11.4.1 Direct-labor hours required to produce the jth exercise machine in a series of 30 exercise machines produced

Machine Number (j)	Direct-Labor Hours to Produce jth Machine
5	244
7	196
11	155
16	135
20	99
30	80

FIGURE 11.4.1   Number of exercise machines produced and direct-labor hours

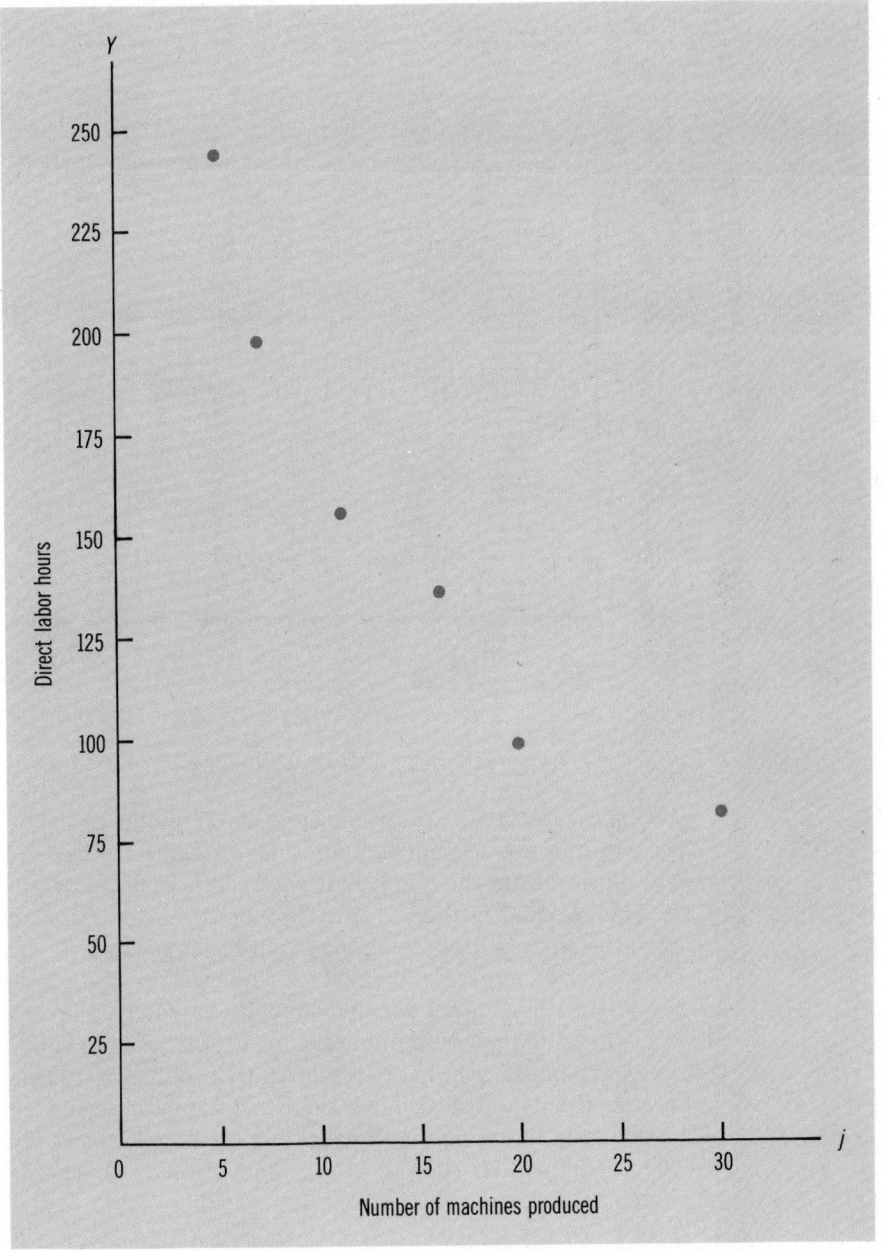

FIGURE 11.4.2 STAT+ printout showing scatter diagram and fitted regression curve for data of Example 11.4.1. (Note that the vertical and horizontal axis labels differ from those of Figure 11.4.1.)

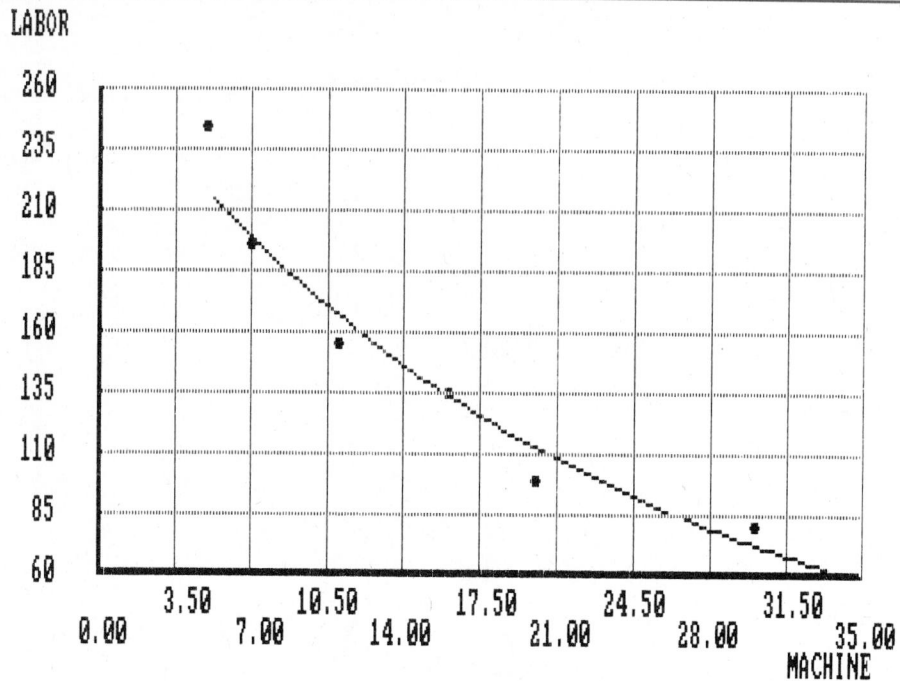

We may use STAT+ to fit the exponential model to the data of Table 11.4.1. The graph of the original data and the fitted line are shown in Figure 11.4.2.

It appears from the graph that the exponential model provides a good fit to the data. We find further evidence in support of the exponential model when we graph the original data on log-log graph paper as has been done in Figure 11.4.3. The scatter of points in Figure 11.4.3 suggests a straight line, as is always the case when such an exponential model adequately represents the data. These results indicate that we should take logarithms of both sides of Equation 11.4.2 in order to linearize it. In other words, we use the logarithmic transformation to linearize the data. When this is done we may use, on the transformed data, the least-squares techniques with which we are familiar to estimate the two parameters, α (the y intercept) and β (the slope of the line). The transformed model is written as

(11.4.3)
$$\log y_j = \log \alpha + \beta \log j + e_j$$

The logarithms of the machine numbers (j) and direct-labor hours (Y) are shown in Table 11.4.2.

FIGURE 11.4.3 Data of Example 11.4.1 plotted on log-log graph paper (Note that the scatter of points suggests a straight line.)

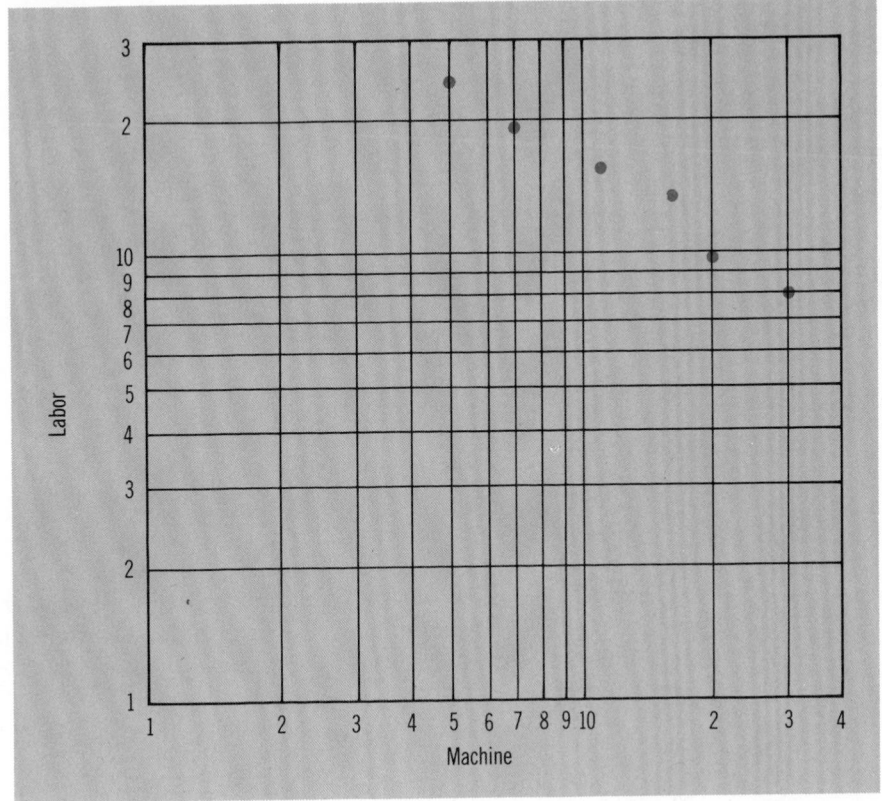

We may use the regression programs of either MINITAB or STAT + to obtain the estimates of α and β and other useful analyses by entering $\log j$ and $\log y$. The MINITAB printout is shown in Figure 11.4.4.

TABLE 11.4.2 Logarithms of data for Example 11.4.1

Machine Number (j)	Log j	Direct-Labor Hours (Y)	Log Y
5	0.69897	244	2.38739
7	0.84510	196	2.29226
11	1.04139	155	2.19033
16	1.20412	135	2.13033
20	1.30103	99	1.99564
30	1.47712	80	1.90309

FIGURE 11.4.4   MINITAB printout of regression analysis of transformed data for Example 11.4.1

```
The regression equation is logY = 2.82 - 0.615 logj
Predictor        Coef        Stdev      t-ratio      p
Constant       2.82346      0.05036      56.07      0.000
logj          -0.61539      0.04471     -13.76      0.000
s = 0.02906   R-sq = 97.9%  R-sq(adj) = 97.4%
                 ANALYSIS OF VARIANCE
    Source      DF       SS         MS        F        p
Regression       1    0.16002    0.16002   189.45    0.000
Error            4    0.00338    0.00084
Total            5    0.16340
Obs.   logj   logY     Fit    Stdev.Fit  Residual  St.Resid
  1    0.70  2.3874  2.3933    0.0213    -0.0059    -0.30
  2    0.85  2.2923  2.3034    0.0163    -0.0111    -0.46
  3    1.04  2.1903  2.1826    0.0121     0.0077     0.29
  4    1.20  2.1303  2.0825    0.0128     0.0479     1.84
  5    1.30  1.9956  2.0228    0.0150    -0.0272    -1.09
  6    1.48  1.9031  1.9145    0.0208    -0.0114    -0.56
```

The MINITAB printout shows that $r^2 = 0.979$, indicating that the learning-curve model fits the data quite well. The printout also shows that the y intercept and slope are 2.82346 and -0.61539, respectively, so that the fitted equation is

(11.4.4)
$$\log y_j = 2.82346 - 0.61539 \log j$$

We may use Equation 11.4.4 to predict the number of direct-labor hours to produce the thirty-fifth machine. We substitute 35 into the equation to estimate y. Following this procedure, we have

$$\log y_j = 2.82346 - 0.61539 \log(35)$$

Since the logarithm of 35 is 1.54407, the equation becomes

$$\log y_j = 2.82346 - 0.61539(1.54407)$$
$$= 1.87325$$

Since the antilogarithm of 1.87325 is 74.7, $\hat{y} = 74.7$. We predict that 74.7 hours will be required to produce the thirty-fifth machine.

The information from analyses such as we have performed may be combined with other data to form the basis for making decisions in such areas as product design and production, corporate strategy, pricing and cost recovery, capital investment, and aggregate planning.

EXERCISES

11.4.1   Ⓒ A food scientist with Quickie Cuisine conducted a study to evaluate the effect of cooking time in a certain oven on the growth of bacteria. A random sample of ten hamburger patties was infected with a constant dose of a particular common bacterium. After the patties were cooked a different length of time (COOKTIME), ranging from 1 to 18 minutes, they were individually prepared as inoculants for a culture medium. After a common period of incubation, the number of bacteria colonies per culture were counted (BACCOUNT). The results were as follows:

BACCOUNT Y	750	425	215	106	50	28	12	7	3	1
COOKTIME X	1	2	4	6	8	10	12	14	16	18

Graph the data. Does it appear from the graph that an exponential model would provide an appropriate representation of the data?

Exercises 11.4.2 through 11.4.7 are based on Exercise 11.4.1.

11.4.2   Take logarithms of X and Y and plot the results. What model do the transformed data suggest?

11.4.3   Do a regression analysis of the transformed data, and write out the regression equation, supplying numerical values for the slope and y intercept.

11.4.4   What is the numerical value of the coefficient of determination?

11.4.5   Perform an analysis of variance to test the null hypothesis of no relationship between the two transformed variables. What is the computed F statistic for the test? What is the p value?

11.4.6   Use the regression equation to predict the number of bacteria colonies in a hamburger patty cooked for five minutes.

11.4.7   What is the expected number of bacteria colonies in hamburger patties that are cooked for 15 minutes?

11.4.8   Ⓒ For its product, a manufacturer reports the following data on marginal cost (in dollars) per unit produced (MARGCOST) and cumulative production (in millions of units) (CUMPROD).

MARGCOST Y	89	62	50	47	41	37	36	33	32	30
CUMPROD X	1	2	3	4	5	6	7	8	9	10

Use a logarithmic transformation on the variables and fit a linear model to the transformed data.

Exercises 11.4.9 through 11.4.16 are based on Exercise 11.4.8.

11.4.9   Plot the original data. What type of model does the graph suggest?

11.4.10   Plot the transformed data. Does this graph suggest a linear relationship between log X and log Y?

11.4.11   Write out the linear equation, supplying numerical values for the slope and y intercept.

11.4.12 Perform an analysis of variance. What is the computed F value? What is the p value associated with this F?

11.4.13 What is the numerical value of the coefficient of determination?

11.4.14 What is the numerical value of the correlation coefficient?

11.4.15 What is the estimated marginal unit cost of production when the cumulative production reaches 12 million units?

11.4.16 Construct the 95% confidence interval for the estimate obtained in Exercise 11.4.15.

11.4.17 ⓒ Attila Aerospace Industries is completing a contract for a government agency to produce 50 units of a specialized piece of equipment. They have been asked to submit a proposal to produce an additional 250 units and wish to use the learning-curve concept in preparing their proposal. Direct-labor hours required to produce the fourth, tenth, fifteenth, twenty-fifth, and thirty-fifth units were as follows:

Unit Number (j)	Direct-Labor Hours Required to Produce Unit j
4	304
10	241
15	184
25	110
35	98

Fit a linear model to the data after they have been transformed by means of the logarithmic transformation. Use a logarithmic transformation on the variables and fit a linear model to the transformed data.

Exercises 11.4.18 through 11.4.25 are based on Exercise 11.4.17.

11.4.18 Plot the original data. What type of model does the graph suggest?

11.4.19 Plot the transformed data. Does this graph suggest a linear relationship between log X and log Y?

11.4.20 Write out the linear equation, supplying numerical values for the slope and y intercept.

11.4.21 Perform an analysis of variance. What is the computed F value? What is the p value associated with this F?

11.4.22 What is the numerical value of the coefficient of determination?

11.4.23 What is the numerical value of the correlation coefficient?

11.4.24 What is the estimate of the number of direct-labor hours required to produce the hundredth unit of the additional 250 units?

11.4.25 Construct a 95% confidence interval for the estimate obtained in Exercise 11.4.24.

11.5 VARIABLE SELECTION PROCEDURES

Managers and other investigators contemplating the use of multiple regression analysis to solve problems usually find that they have a large number of variables from which to select the independent variables to be employed as predictors of the dependent variable. Such investigators will want to include in their model as many variables as possible in order to maximize the model's predictive abilities. The investigator must realize, however, that adding another independent variable to a set of independent variables always increases the coefficient of determination R^2. Therefore, independent variables should not be added to the model indiscriminately, but for good reason. In most situations, for example, some potential predictor variables are more expensive than others in terms of data collection costs. The cost-conscious investigator, therefore, will not want to include an expensive variable in a model unless there is evidence that it makes a worthwhile contribution to the predictive ability of the model.

The investigator who wishes to use multiple regression analysis most effectively must be able to employ some strategy for making intelligent selections from among those potential predictor variables that are available. Many such strategies are in current use, and each has its proponents. The strategies vary in terms of complexity and the tedium involved in their employment. Unfortunately, when applied to the same problem, the strategies do not always lead to the same solution. In the discussion that follows we focus on four variable-selection strategies: (1) *all possible regressions*, (2) *stepwise regression*, (3) *forward selection*, and (4) *backward elimination*. The interested reader will find discussions of other strategies in the Suggestions for Further Reading at the end of this chapter.

ALL-POSSIBLE-REGRESSIONS

When the all-possible-regression strategy is used to select the variables to be included in the prediction equation, every possible regression equation containing every possible combination of the independent variables must be formulated and evaluated. If we have k independent variables, we will have $2^k - 1$ equations to formulate and evaluate. Suppose, for example, that we have one dependent variable and six variables that are candidates for inclusion in the model as independent variables. We would have to consider the following $2^6 - 1 = 64 - 1 = 63$ equations:

6 equations with one independent variable (model: $y_j = \beta_0 + \beta_1 x_{1j} + e_j$)

15 equations with two independent variables (model: $y_j = \beta_0 + \beta_1 x_{1j} + \beta_2 x_{2j} + e_j$)

20 equations with three independent variables (model: $y_j = \beta_0 + \beta_1 x_{1j} + \beta_2 x_{2j} + \beta_3 x_{3j} + e_j$)

15 equations with four independent variables (model: $y_j = \beta_0 + \beta_1 x_{1j} + \beta_2 x_{2j} + \beta_3 x_{3j} + \beta_4 x_{4j} + e_j$)

6 equations with five independent variables (model: $y_j = \beta_0 + \beta_1 x_{1j} + \beta_2 x_{2j} + \beta_3 x_{3j} + \beta_4 x_{4j} + \beta_5 x_{5j} + e_j$)

1 equation with all six independent variables (model: $y_j = \beta_0 + \beta_1 x_{1j} + \beta_2 x_{2j} + \beta_3 x_{3j} + \beta_4 x_{4j} + \beta_5 x_{5j} + \beta_6 x_{6j} + e_j$)

In these models, the numerical subscripts on the x's indicate the positions of the variables in the model and not necessarily the locations of the variables in the list of candidate predictor variables.

After the all-possible-regression models have been fitted to the data at hand, the resulting equations are partitioned into sets in which, within each set, the equations contain 1, 2, . . . , k independent variables. The equations within each set are then ordered on the basis of some criterion for measuring the goodness-of-fit of the model to the data. The coefficient of determination, R^2, is frequently used as the evaluative criterion. For comparing models of different size the adjusted coefficient, $\tilde{R}^2$, introduced in Section 10.4, is a more appropriate criterion. From each set of equations, the leaders, based on the evaluative criterion, say the size of $\tilde{R}^2$, are chosen for further consideration. The following example illustrates the application of the all-possible-regression strategy for selecting independent variables for a regression model.

EXAMPLE 11.5.1 A sales manager wishes to develop a regression model for predicting (on the basis of personal characteristics) the job performance (JOBPER) of potential salespersons. The following variables are available from which to choose the independent variables to include in the model:

X_1 = aggressiveness (AGG)

X_2 = enthusiasm (ENTH)

X_3 = ambition (AMB)

X_4 = communication skills (COMM)

X_5 = congeniality (CONG)

X_6 = initiative (INIT)

SOLUTION Table 11.5.1 shows the measurements taken on the dependent variable, JOBPER, and each of the six independent variables for a sample of 30 salespersons. Table 11.5.2 shows the R^2 and adjusted R^2 values for each of the 63 all-possible-regression equations that can be formulated from the seven variables (one dependent variable and six independent variables) in Example 11.5.1. This table was obtained through the use of the SAS statistical software package.

At this point, the investigator examines the printout in search of the best models based on the chosen criterion. Suppose that we examine Table 11.5.2 to determine which are the four best models based on their adjusted R^2 values. We find that they are the four-predictor-variable model with AGG, ENTH, AMB, and INIT as the predictor variables ($\tilde{R} = 0.82221666$); the five-predictor-variable model with predictor variables AGG, ENTH, AMB, COMM, and INIT ($\tilde{R}^2 = 0.81638473$); the five-predictor-variable model with AGG, ENTH, AMB, CONG, and INIT ($\tilde{R}^2 = 0.81484634$); and the six-predictor-variable model ($\tilde{R}^2 = 0.80879622$). In practice, we would analyze these models in more detail before deciding which one to use eventually for prediction purposes.

TABLE 11.5.1 Measurements on seven variables for Example 11.5.1

Salesperson	Y	X_1 (AGG)	X_2 (ENTH)	X_3 (AMB)	X_4 (COMM)	X_5 (CONG)	X_6 (INIT)
1	45	74	29	40	66	93	47
2	65	65	50	64	68	74	49
3	73	71	67	79	81	87	33
4	63	64	44	57	59	85	37
5	83	79	55	76	76	84	33
6	45	56	48	54	59	50	42
7	60	68	41	66	71	69	37
8	73	76	49	65	75	67	43
9	74	83	71	77	76	84	33
10	69	62	44	57	67	81	43
11	66	54	52	67	63	68	36
12	69	61	46	66	64	75	43
13	71	63	56	67	60	64	35
14	70	84	82	68	64	78	37
15	79	78	53	82	84	78	39
16	83	65	49	82	65	55	38
17	75	86	63	79	84	80	41
18	67	61	64	75	60	81	45
19	67	71	45	67	80	86	48
20	52	59	67	64	69	79	54
21	52	71	32	44	48	65	43
22	66	62	51	72	71	81	43
23	55	67	51	60	68	81	39
24	42	65	41	45	55	58	51
25	65	55	41	58	71	76	35
26	68	78	65	73	93	77	42
27	80	76	57	84	85	79	35
28	50	58	43	55	56	84	40
29	87	86	70	81	82	75	30
30	84	83	38	83	69	79	41

As the preceding discussion demonstrates, this particular all-possible-regression strategy for selecting independent variables is a time-consuming task. If the number of potential independent variables is seven, just one more than the number under consideration in the preceding example, the number of all-possible regressions to be evaluated is $2^7 - 1 = 127$, more than twice the number that had to be evaluated in our example. A major shortcoming of this strategy is the fact that, once the models have been listed, we have to search through the list to find the best ones. Since, in real-life situations, the number of potential independent variables is often ten or more, it is easily seen that this all-possible-regression strategy is not one that is used without good reason. Other less tedious and time-consuming strategies are more commonly used.

An alternative strategy is to make use of a different statistical software package. Another popular computer program for use in model building is BMDP9R, "All

TABLE 11.5.2 All-possible-regression equations, R^2, and adjusted R^2 for Example 11.5.1 (obtained with SAS® software package)

N = 30	Regression Models for Dependent Variable: Y Model: Model 1		
Number in Model	R-Square	Adjusted R-Square	Variables in Model
1	0.02419552	−.01065465	CONG
1	0.18018277	0.15090358	ENTH
1	0.29434831	0.26914647	AGG
1	0.33374313	0.30994824	INIT
1	0.34508617	0.32169639	COMM
1	0.77210421	0.76396507	AMB
2	0.18903323	0.12896162	ENTH CONG
2	0.29439643	0.24212950	AGG CONG
2	0.34813509	0.29984880	CONG INIT
2	0.35013985	0.30200206	COMM CONG
2	0.35037302	0.30225250	AGG ENTH
2	0.37814693	0.33208374	ENTH COMM
2	0.39896864	0.35444780	ENTH INIT
2	0.40788370	0.36402323	AGG COMM
2	0.48432256	0.44612423	AGG INIT
2	0.53505315	0.50061264	COMM INIT
2	0.77211172	0.75523111	AMB COMM
2	0.77316458	0.75636195	AMB CONG
2	0.78744304	0.77169808	ENTH AMB
2	0.79388255	0.77861459	AGG AMB
2	0.80676177	0.79244783	AMB INIT
3	0.35063153	0.27570440	AGG ENTH CONG
3	0.38257983	0.31133904	ENTH COMM CONG
3	0.40642062	0.33793069	ENTH CONG INIT
3	0.41766927	0.35047726	AGG COMM CONG
3	0.42800913	0.36201019	AGG ENTH COMM
3	0.48435873	0.42486166	AGG CONG INIT
3	0.50408314	0.44686196	AGG ENTH INIT
3	0.53775068	0.48441422	COMM CONG INIT
3	0.54231895	0.48950960	ENTH COMM INIT
3	0.56538217	0.51523396	AGG COMM INIT
3	0.77327622	0.74711579	AMB COMM CONG
3	0.78760600	0.76309900	ENTH AMB COMM
3	0.78925812	0.76494174	ENTH AMB CONG
3	0.79393194	0.77015485	AGG AMB CONG
3	0.79759748	0.77424334	AGG AMB COMM
3	0.80699943	0.78473014	AMB COMM INIT
3	0.80787889	0.78571107	AMB CONG INIT
3	0.81515778	0.79382983	AGG ENTH AMB
3	0.82360183	0.80324820	AGG AMB INIT
3	0.82448451	0.80423273	ENTH AMB INIT
4	0.43661539	0.34647385	AGG ENTH COMM CONG
4	0.50408343	0.42473678	AGG ENTH CONG INIT

TABLE 11.5.2   (*Continued*)

N = 30	**Regression Models for Dependent Variable: Y Model: Model 1**		
Number in Model	R-Square	Adjusted R-Square	Variables in Model
4	0.54488297	0.47206425	ENTH COMM CONG INIT
4	0.56933107	0.50042405	AGG ENTH COMM INIT
4	0.57073366	0.50205105	AGG COMM CONG INIT
4	0.78927175	0.75555523	ENTH AMB COMM CONG
4	0.79776046	0.76540213	AGG AMB COMM CONG
4	0.80788664	0.77714850	AMB COMM CONG INIT
4	0.81515802	0.78558330	AGG ENTH AMB CONG
4	0.81839923	0.78934311	AGG ENTH AMB COMM
4	0.82360394	0.79538057	AGG AMB CONG INIT
4	0.82519870	0.79723049	ENTH AMB COMM INIT
4	0.82528108	0.79732605	AGG AMB COMM INIT
4	0.82644302	0.79867391	ENTH AMB CONG INIT
4	0.84673850	0.82221666	AGG ENTH AMB INIT
5	0.57440193	0.48573567	AGG ENTH COMM CONG INIT
5	0.81873306	0.78096912	AGG ENTH AMB COMM CONG
5	0.82542415	0.78905418	AGG AMB COMM CONG INIT
5	0.82655757	0.79042372	ENTH AMB COMM CONG INIT
5	0.84676938	0.81484634	AGG ENTH AMB CONG INIT
5	0.84804254	0.81638473	AGG ENTH AMB COMM INIT
6	0.84835562	0.80879622	AGG ENTH AMB COMM CONG INIT

Possible Subsets Regression," to be found in the BMDP statistical software package. The user of this program specifies the number, k, of best subsets desired, along with one of three available criteria. The program then generates, on the basis of the specified criterion, the best k subsets out of all possible regressions. The program also produces the best k subsets with one predictor variable, the best k subsets with two predictor variables, and so on, up to the single equation that contains all the predictor variables that are under consideration. The use of the BMDP9R program eliminates the need for the searching procedure that we had to use when we generated all possible regressions.

Let us now examine some additional strategies for selecting predictor variables.

THE BACKWARD ELIMINATION STRATEGY

The backward elimination strategy for selecting independent variables for a multiple regression model begins with a model containing all potential independent variables. On the basis of some evaluative criterion, such as a minimum F statistic, variables that do not satisfy a cutoff value are eliminated one at a time.

The backward elimination procedure ends when no variable in the model has an associated F statistic less than some designated value. Once a variable has been removed from the model, it cannot be considered again for inclusion in the model. Many statistical software computer packages, including MINITAB, are capable of performing the backward elimination procedure. We illustrate the technique with the following example.

EXAMPLE 11.5.2 Consider the data on job performance and the six potential independent variables shown in Table 11.5.1. We wish to use the MINITAB backward elimination procedure to select the best independent variables.

SOLUTION The 30 observations on each of the seven variables are entered into MINITAB columns as follows:

Column 1 = JOBPER (Y)
Column 2 = AGG (X_1)
Column 3 = ENTH (X_2)
Column 4 = AMB (X_3)
Column 5 = COMM (X_4)
Column 6 = CONG (X_5)
Column 7 = INIT (X_6)

Through the use of appropriate subcommands, MINITAB performs backward elimination by means of the STEPWISE procedure, which we discuss in more detail later. The first subcommand necessary for execution of the backward elimination procedure is FENTER = 100000, which prevents re-entry into the model of any variable that is once removed. The second subcommand is ENTER C . . . C, which specifies those variables from which the model's independent variables are to be selected. Figure 11.5.1 shows the MINITAB commands and printout when the backward elimination procedure is applied to the data of Table 11.5.1.

We see in Figure 11.5.1 that there are five columns of information corresponding to the five steps that MINITAB executed to obtain the best model. We also see that the relevant information for each step is the t statistic associated with each variable in the model that is evaluated at that particular step. Recall that the t statistic with k degrees of freedom is the square root of an F statistic with 1 numerator and k denominator degrees of freedom. The investigator accustomed to evaluating the contribution of a variable on the basis of its associated F statistic may obtain the desired F statistics by squaring the t ratios on the printout. Unless otherwise instructed through the FREMOVE = K command, MINITAB eliminates in each step a variable whose associated F statistic is less than 4 (or equivalently an associated t ratio with an absolute value of less than 2). In step 1 of Figure 11.5.1, we see that the variable with the smallest associated F statistic is CONG (column 6). It is eliminated from the model, and a new model consisting of the remaining five variables is evaluated. The results are shown as step 2 of the printout. The variable in this model with the smallest associated F statistic

FIGURE 11.5.1 MINITAB printout of backward elimination procedure for data in Table 11.5.1

MINITAB
```
MTB > STEPWISE 'y' c2-c7;
SUBC> FENTER = 100000;
SUBC> ENTER c2-c7.
```

STEPWISE REGRESSION OF   y   ON 6 PREDICTORS,
WITH N = 30

Step	1	2	3	4	5
Constant	22.91	24.08	23.74	34.73	31.96
C1	0.23	0.24	0.21		
T-RATIO	1.82	1.90	1.91		
C3	-0.189	-0.189	-0.190	-0.165	
T-RATIO	-1.86	-1.90	-1.94	-1.62	
C4	0.859	0.854	0.825	0.884	0.787
T-RATIO	6.45	6.63	7.48	7.94	8.13
C5	-0.07	-0.06			
T-RATIO	-0.49	-0.45			
C6	0.02				
T-RATIO	0.22				
C7	-0.42	-0.42	-0.43	-0.46	-0.45
T-RATIO	-2.12	-2.16	-2.27	-2.34	-2.20
S	5.31	5.21	5.12	5.37	5.53
R-SQ	84.84	84.80	84.67	82.45	80.68

is COMM (column 5). It is eliminated from the model, and a new model consisting of the remaining four variables is evaluated. The procedure continues until the model contains no variable with an associated F statistic of less than 4. We see that this occurs in step 5 of the printout, where the two independent variables selected are AMB (column 4) and INIT (column 7). We see also that the R^2 value for this model is 0.8068. The model recommended by the backward elimination procedure, then, is one that contains AMB and INIT as the predictor variables. The estimated regression equation is

$$y = 31.96 + 0.787x_3 - 0.45x_6$$

in which the regression coefficients are obtained from the printout in Figure 11.5.1.

THE FORWARD SELECTION STRATEGY

The forward selection strategy is the reverse of the backward elimination strategy. The forward selection procedure begins with a model containing one independent variable—the one most highly correlated with the dependent variable. Each of the remaining six variables is entered into the model, one at a time, and the associated F statistic for each is calculated. The one with the largest associated F is offered as a candidate for the second independent variable. If the F associated with this variable satisfies the evaluative criterion, it is added to the model. This procedure is continued until none of the variables not in the model satisfy the evaluative criterion for inclusion in the model. Once a variable is added to the model, it is never removed. The following example illustrates the use of the forward selection strategy for selecting independent variables for a multiple regression model.

EXAMPLE 11.5.3 Refer to the job performance data given in Table 11.5.1. We wish to obtain the best model using job performance as the dependent variable, with independent variables selected by the forward selection procedure from the six potential independent variables whose measurements appear in Table 11.5.1.

SOLUTION Through the use of appropriate subcommands within the STEPWISE procedure, we may use MINITAB to obtain our model by the forward selection procedure.

The measurements on the dependent variable JOBPER (job performance) and the six candidate independent variables are, as before, stored in MINITAB columns 1 through 7, respectively. We use the subcommand FREMOVE = 0, which guarantees that no variable, once added to the model, will be removed. The procedure does not remove from the model any variable with an associated F statistic equal to or greater than 4 (which is equivalent to a t statistic greater than 2 or less than -2). Likewise, unless otherwise specified, MINITAB will not let a variable enter the model unless it has an associated F statistic of 4 or more. Figure 11.5.2 shows the required commands and resulting printout when we use MINITAB with our present data to select a model by the forward selection procedure.

We see in Figure 11.5.2 that MINITAB required two steps to arrive at a model meeting our specified criteria. In step 1, AMB (column 4) entered the model since, of the six potential independent variables, it had the largest associated F statistic that was also greater than 4. In step 2, INIT (column 7) entered the model since, of the five remaining potential independent variables, it had the largest associated F statistic that was also larger than 4. The model chosen by the forward selection procedure, then, is a two-independent-variable model, with AMB and INIT as the two independent variables. The R^2 value for this model is 0.8068. Using the regression coefficients provided by the printout in Figure 11.5.2, we see that the estimated regression equation is the same as before:

$$y = 31.96 + 0.787x_3 - 0.45x_6$$

STEPWISE REGRESSION

Perhaps the most widely used strategy for selecting independent variables for a multiple regression model is the stepwise procedure. At each step of the procedure, each variable then in the model is evaluated to see if, according to specified

FIGURE 11.5.2   MINITAB printout of forward selection procedure for the data of Table 11.5.1

MINITAB

```
MTB > STEPWISE 'y' c2-c7;
SUBC> FREMOVE = 0.
        STEPWISE REGRESSION OF   y   ON  6 PREDICTORS,
                         WITH N = 30
Step                    1           2
Constant            7.226      31.955

C4                  0.888       0.787
T-RATIO             9.74        8.13

C7                             -0.45
T-RATIO                        -2.20

S                   5.90        5.53
R-SQ               77.21       80.68
 MORE? (YES, NO, SUBCOMMAND, OR HELP)
SUBC> yes

 NO VARIABLES ENTERED OR REMOVED

 MORE? (YES, NO SUBCOMMAND, OR HELP)

SUBC> NO

MTB >
```

criteria, it should remain in the model. Suppose, for example, that we wish to perform stepwise regression for a model containing k predictor variables. The criterion measure is computed for each variable. Of all the variables that do not satisfy the criterion for inclusion in the model, the one that least satisfies the criterion is removed from the model. If a variable is removed in this step, the regression equation for the smaller model is calculated, and the criterion measure is computed for each variable now in the model. If any of these variables fail to satisfy the criterion for inclusion in the model, the one that least satisfies the criterion is removed. If a variable is removed at this step, the variable that was removed in the first step is re-entered into the model, and the evaluation procedure is continued. This process continues until no more variables can be entered or removed. The nature of the stepwise procedure is such that, although a variable may be deleted from the model in one step, it is evaluated for possible re-entry into the model in subsequent steps.

MINITAB's STEPWISE procedure uses the associated F statistic as the evaluative criterion for deciding whether a variable should be deleted or added to the model. Unless otherwise specified, the cutoff value is $F = 4$. The printout of the STEPWISE results contains t statistics (the square root of F) rather than F statistics. At each step, MINITAB calculates an F statistic for each variable then in the model. If the F statistic for any of these variables is less than the specified cutoff value (4 if some other value is not specified), the variable with the smallest F is removed from the model. The regression equation is refitted for the reduced model, the results are printed, and the procedure goes to the next step. If no variable can be removed, the procedure tries to add a variable. An F statistic is calculated for each variable not then in the model. Of these variables, the one with the largest associated F statistic is added, provided its F statistic is larger than the specified cutoff value (4 if some other value is not specified). The regression equation is refitted for the new model, the results are printed, and the procedure goes on to the next step. The procedure stops when no variable can be added or deleted.

To change from 4 to some other value K, the criterion for allowing a variable to enter the model, we use the subcommand FENTER = K. The new criterion F statistic, then, is K rather than 4. To change from 4 to some other value K, the criterion for deleting a variable from the model, we use the subcommand FREMOVE = K. We must choose FENTER to be greater than or equal to FREMOVE. The following example illustrates the use of the stepwise procedure for selecting variables for a multiple regression model.

EXAMPLE 11.5.4   Consider the job performance data presented in Table 11.5.1. We wish to use the stepwise procedure for selecting independent variables from those available in the table to construct a multiple regression model for predicting job performance.

SOLUTION   We use MINITAB to obtain a useful model by the stepwise procedure. Observations on the dependent variable job performance (JOBPER) and the six candidate independent variables are stored, as before, in MINITAB columns 1 through 7, respectively. Figure 11.5.3 shows the appropriate MINITAB command and the printout of the results.

FIGURE 11.5.3   MINITAB printout of stepwise procedure for the data of Table 11.5.1

MINITAB
```
MTB > STEPWISE 'y' C2-C7
        STEPWISE REGRESSION OF   y   ON  6 PREDICTORS,
                          WITH N = 30
Step           1           2
Constant    7.226      31.955

C4          0.888       0.787
T-RATIO      9.74        8.13

C7                      -0.45
T-RATIO                 -2.20

S           5.90        5.53
R-SQ       77.21       80.68
  MORE? (YES, NO, SUBCOMMAND, OR HELP)
SUBC> yes

 NO VARIABLES ENTERED OR REMOVED

  MORE? (YES, NO SUBCOMMAND, OR HELP)

SUBC> no

MTB >
```

We see in Figure 11.5.3 that the values of FENTER and FREMOVE both were set automatically at 4. In step 1, there are no variables to be considered for deletion from the model. The variable AMB (column 4) has the largest associated F statistic, which is $F = (9.74)^2 = 94.8676$. Since 94.8676 is greater than 4, AMB is added to the model. In step 2, the variable INIT (column 7) qualifies for addition to the model since its associated F of $(-2.2)^2 = 4.84$ is greater than 4 and it is the variable with the largest associated F statistic. It is added to the model. After step 2, no other variables could be added or deleted, and the procedure stopped. We see, then, that the model chosen by the stepwise procedure is a two-independent-variable model, with AMB and INIT as the independent variables. The estimated regression equation is as before

$$y = 31.96 + 0.787x_3 - 0.45x_6$$

We see that, in the case of our job performance example, the backward elimination, the forward selection, and the stepwise strategies all select the same model. This will not always happen.

USE OF THE F TEST TO DETERMINE WHEN TO ADD OR DELETE VARIABLES

Frequently, an investigator wishes to know whether or not it is advantageous in terms of predictive ability to add one or more predictor variables to an existing model. When this is the objective, a procedure that employs the familiar F statistic may be employed. The procedure consists of determining the amount by which the error sum of squares is reduced when one or more independent variables are added to the model. We illustrate the procedure with the data from our now familiar job performance example.

On the basis of the R^2 value, the leaders from each set of equations shown in Table 11.5.2 are shown in Table 11.5.3.

We see in Table 11.5.3 that, among the models with a single independent variable, ambition (AMB) is the independent variable that individually explains

TABLE 11.5.3   Leading equations from Table 11.5.2 by independent variable(s) and R^2 value

Number of Variables in Model	R^2	Variables in Model
1	0.77210421	AMB
2	0.80676177	AMB, INIT
3	0.82448451	ENTH, AMB, INIT
4	0.84673850	AGG, ENTH, AMB, INIT
5	0.84804254	AGG, ENTH, AMB, COMM, INIT
6	0.84835562	AGG, ENTH, AMB, COMM, CONG, INIT

the highest proportion ($R^2 = 0.77210421$) of the variability in job performance (JOBPER). Of the two-independent-variable equations, the one with ambition (AMB) and initiative (INIT) has the highest R^2 value, which is 0.80676177.

A reasonable question to ask at this time is whether the addition of initiative into the model significantly improves predictability. In other words, we wonder if the R^2 of 0.80676177 is significantly greater than the R^2 of 0.77210421. We obtain the answer to our question by testing the null hypothesis that the slope coefficient associated with the variable INIT in the two-variable equation is equal to 0 against the alternative that it is not equal to 0. The test statistic for the test is an F statistic, computed as follows:

$$F = \frac{\dfrac{\text{SSE(AMB)} - \text{SSE(AMB, INIT)}}{1}}{\dfrac{\text{SSE(AMB, INIT)}}{27}}$$

where SSE(AMB) is the error sum of squares obtained from the analysis of the one-variable model; SSE(AMB, INIT) is the error sum of squares obtained from the analysis of the two-variable model; 1 is the difference between the regression degrees of freedom of the two models; and 27 is the error degrees of freedom for the two-variable model. By using the STAT+ software package, we find that SSE(AMB) = 975.211548, and SSE(AMB, INIT) = 826.905029. The computed F statistic, then, is

$$F = \frac{\dfrac{975.211548 - 826.905029}{1}}{\dfrac{826.905029}{27}}$$

$$= 4.8425$$

Since 4.8425 is greater than 4.21, the tabulated F for 1 and 27 degrees of freedom and $\alpha = 0.05$, we reject the null hypothesis that the slope coefficient associated with INIT in the two-variable model is 0. We conclude, at the 0.05 level of significance, that the inclusion of the variable INIT in the model significantly increases the value of R^2. We conclude that the two-variable model, with AMB and INIT as independent variables, is a better model than the one-variable model, with only AMB as the independent variable.

We may also use the F statistic to compare the R^2 value (0.82448451) of the three-variable model, which has ENTH, AMB, and INIT as the independent variables, with the R^2 value of the two-variable model, which has AMB and INIT as the independent variables. The additional quantity needed is SSE(ENTH, AMB, INIT), which, by using STAT+, we find to be 751.065857. The computed F, then, is

$$F = \frac{\dfrac{826.905029 - 751.065857}{1}}{\dfrac{751.065857}{26}}$$

$$= 2.6254$$

Since 2.6254 is less than 4.23, the tabulated F for $\alpha = 0.05$ and 1 and 26 degrees of freedom, we conclude that the addition of the dependent variable ENTH into the model does not significantly (at the 0.05 level) increase the size of R^2. We have no basis for believing that the three-variable model has better predictive ability than the two-variable model.

To see if we can conclude that the four-variable model has a significantly larger R^2 value than the two-variable model, we use STAT+ to obtain SSE(AGG, ENTH, AMB, INIT) = 655.836670 and compute the following F statistic:

$$F = \frac{\dfrac{826.905029 - 655.836670}{2}}{\dfrac{655.836670}{25}}$$

$$= 3.26$$

Since the computed F of 3.26 is smaller than 3.39, the tabulated value of F for 2 and 25 degrees of freedom and $\alpha = 0.05$, we conclude that there is no reason to believe that the four-independent-variable model will provide significantly better predictions than the two-independent-variable model. Since the R^2 values for the five-independent-variable model and the six-independent-variable model are so close, there seems to be no point in continuing the testing procedure. We conclude, on the basis of this analysis, that the two-variable model is the best model for predicting job performance using the best predictor variables from the six that are available. A subjective analysis of the situation might lead some investigators to choose the four-variable model. The difference between the two R^2 values is approximately 0.04, an amount that an investigator might consider to be nonnegligible. If to this fact one could add the argument that aggressiveness (AGG) and enthusiasm (ENTH) are logical and natural variables to take into consideration when evaluating job performance potential, and if the cost of obtaining measurements on these variables is minimal, the case for using the four-independent-variable model would be strengthened.

By now you may have surmised that the general formula for comparing the R^2 values of two models is

(11.5.1)
$$F = \frac{\dfrac{\text{SSE}(x_1, x_2, \ldots, x_q) - \text{SSE}(x_1, x_2, \ldots, x_q, x_{q+1}, \ldots, x_k)}{k - q}}{\dfrac{\text{SSE}(x_1, x_2, \ldots, x_q, x_{q+1}, \ldots, x_k)}{n - k - 1}}$$

In Equation 11.5.1, $x_{q+1}, \ldots, x_k$ are the independent variables added to a model containing q independent variables to obtain a model that contains k independent variables. Note that q is less than k. The computed F is compared for significance with the tabulated F for selected α and $k - q$ numerator and $n - k - 1$ denominator degrees of freedom.

CRITERIA FOR SELECTING INDEPENDENT VARIABLES

In our discussion of variable selection, we have used the multiple coefficient of determination, R^2 and adjusted R^2 as the criteria for evaluating the adequacy of a model. Although these criteria are frequently employed by model builders, they are not the only ones available. In an article entitled "The Analysis and Selection of Variables in Linear Regression," which appeared in the journal *Biometrics*, R. R. Hocking describes eight commonly used criteria (see the Suggestions for Further Reading at the end of this chapter). He recommends that the choice of criterion be determined by the use that is to be made of the final regression equation. He lists the following potential uses of a multiple regression equation:

(a) Pure description
(b) Prediction and estimation
(c) Extrapolation
(d) Estimation of parameters
(e) Control
(f) Model building

EXERCISES

11.5.1 C The following data were obtained from Benson Fibers, a firm that manufactures a synthetic fabric. The variables are defined as follows:

QUALPROD (Y) = a measure of the quality of the finished product
TEMPI (X_1) = maximum temperature attained during phase I of the manufacturing process
TEMPII (X_2) = maximum temperature attained during phase II of the manufacturing process
RECYCLE (X_3) = percentage of recycled material used
QUALRAW (X_4) = a measure of the quality of the raw material used

QUALPROD	TEMPI	TEMPII	RECYCLE	QUALRAW
18.1	270	317	0.3	22.1
16.2	310	268	1.9	14.5
34.8	346	191	8.7	31.5

QUALPROD	TEMPI	TEMPII	RECYCLE	QUALRAW
33.7	411	221	6.2	38.5
26.7	348	211	3.6	34.2
45.8	408	191	8.7	50.9
7.0	236	221	6.2	12.1
7.5	213	218	6.2	8.0
8.1	219	211	3.5	10.3
5.1	206	275	1.3	7.0
10.1	220	237	5.3	11.3
26.9	368	232	4.9	24.5
14.8	280	317	1.3	18.0
22.4	300	191	8.7	27.6
26.1	366	221	6.2	31.5
18.3	273	218	6.2	23.0
27.7	415	266	1.7	30.2
30.3	400	216	6.0	35.5
31.6	401	265	5.1	32.1
32.0	443	273	1.1	38.0
13.0	272	209	3.4	16.1
23.1	323	283	2.3	32.1
34.8	394	230	4.7	40.2
24.7	359	235	5.1	32.1
14.3	260	230	4.7	13.4
8.4	235	315	1.0	13.7
2.7	195	266	1.7	4.1
15.1	299	219	6.0	19.0
13.9	250	283	2.3	19.2
6.3	214	266	1.7	9.9

Use one or more of the potential predictor variables $(X_1 - X_4)$ to determine the best model for predicting the quality of the finished product.

11.5.2 $\boxed{\text{C}}$ Cardozo Industries conducts an ongoing training program for potential assembly-line employees. At the end of the training period, trainees are given a test to measure the effectiveness of the training program. The firm would like to be able to screen out potential trainees who are likely not to benefit from the training program. The following data were collected on a sample of recent adolescent high school dropouts who completed the training program. The variables are defined as follows:

   JTS = job-training test score, the score made on the test given at the end of the training program. This score presumably is a measure of the trainee's suitability for a job.

   INC = income of the trainee's household as a percentage above the poverty level.

   EDUC = functional educational grade level of the trainee's head of household.

   DISC = number of disciplinary infractions by the trainee during the last two years in school.

   WEEKS = number of weeks between dropping out of high school and beginning training program.

   JOBS = number of jobs held since dropping out of high school.

Subject	JTS	INC	EDUC	DISC	WEEKS	JOBS
1	100	3	2	12	36	4
2	120	4	4	12	41	4
3	125	1	3	13	36	4
4	138	2	3	11	57	6
5	196	1	2	12	34	3
6	195	4	3	11	40	4
7	219	5	4	12	25	3
8	230	3	3	11	39	4
9	250	6	4	10	48	5
10	304	6	3	11	31	3
11	315	10	4	10	46	5
12	375	13	5	10	41	4
13	405	16	4	9	46	5
14	425	14	6	9	35	4
15	465	21	5	9	23	2
16	490	17	6	9	23	2
17	510	25	4	8	29	3
18	520	18	7	8	53	5
19	535	23	6	8	24	2
20	642	22	6	7	45	4
21	659	31	7	6	31	3
22	674	27	5	6	46	5
23	681	34	6	4	49	5
24	690	32	7	5	29	3
25	704	30	7	7	60	5
26	722	38	8	6	24	2
27	738	26	7	5	41	4
28	750	33	6	5	55	6
29	820	33	8	5	20	2
30	850	44	7	5	21	2
31	914	39	9	4	35	4
32	974	47	9	4	58	6
33	989	45	10	3	49	5
34	992	50	8	3	59	6
35	998	48	9	3	47	5

Determine the best model for predicting JTS using one or more of the other variables as predictors.

SUMMARY

In this chapter, we present some topics that, when combined with the topics covered in Chapters 9 and 10, provide the decision-maker with a wealth of information for developing a useful regression model. We recommend that the manager or researcher contemplating the use of regression analysis consider the following:

1. The assumptions underlying regression analysis
2. The meaning and uses of such descriptive measures as the slope and y intercept

3. The meaning and uses of such evaluative criteria as R^2

4. The methods and uses of residual analysis

5. The purposes of regression analysis

6. Some common potential pitfalls, such as extrapolation, which one should avoid in the use of regression analysis

7. The use of qualitative independent variables

8. The kinds of regression models—linear, curvilinear, and nonlinear

9. The use of transformations

10. Variable selection techniques

11. The availability and merits of various computer software packages that perform regression analyses

REVIEW EXERCISES

1. What is model building?

2. What is a model?

3. What is a linear model?

4. What is meant by the term "order of the model"?

5. Write in symbolic notation a simple first-order model with one independent variable.

6. Write in symbolic notation a second-order model with two independent variables.

7. What is interaction?

8. What is a nonlinear regression model?

9. Explain the difference between R^2 and adjusted R^2.

10. What is meant by the term "intrinsically linear"?

11. What is a learning curve?

12. Explain the all-possible-regression technique for model building.

13. Explain the stepwise regression procedure for model building.

14. Explain the forward selection procedure for model building.

15. Explain the backward elimination procedure for model building.

16. A manager wishes to build a model for predicting employee turnover. There are nine potential predictor variables. How many regression models will have to be considered if the manager uses a computer program to generate all possible models?

17. Refer to Exercise 16. How many models will be in each subset defined on the basis of the number of predictor variables in the model?

18. List the 11 points that should be considered by a manager or researcher who wishes to use regression analysis.

 19. Ⓒ The following data were collected by a synthetic-fiber manufacturer during an experiment preliminary to the production of a fiber that is a blend of natural and synthetic materials. The dependent variable (Y) is a measure of the durability of the finished product

(DURAB). The independent variable (X) is the percentage of natural material in a given batch of raw material (CONCEN). Sixteen specimens of the product, each representing a different concentration of natural material, were tested.

Specimen	DURAB	CONCEN
	Y	X
1	7	1
2	10	2
3	23	3
4	20	4
5	33	5
6	30	6
7	40	7
8	37	8
9	38	9
10	51	10
11	42	11
12	47	12
13	40	13
14	45	14
15	35	15
16	32	16

Construct a scatter diagram of the data. What type of model does the scatter diagram suggest?

20. Fit a second-order model to the data of Exercise 19. What is the coefficient of determination?

21. Construct an analysis of variance from the information provided by the second-order regression analysis of the data in Exercise 19. What is the numerical value of F? What is the p value for the computed F?

22. What is the predicted durability score for a specimen of fiber containing a natural material concentration of 10%?

23. ⓒ Dillon Sanitary Products has found that within certain bounds the strength of a heavy-duty cleansing agent increases in strength with age. The following data show the strength, in terms of cleansing ability, and the age, in days, of ten specimens of the cleanser. Construct a scatter diagram of these data. What regression model does the scatter diagram suggest as an appropriate representation of the data?

Specimen	1	2	3	4	5	6	7	8	9	10
Strength Y	2	10	12	20	25	36	50	70	110	160
Age X	1	2	3	4	5	6	7	8	9	10

24. Refer to Exercise 23. Take logarithms of the measurements on both variables and fit a simple linear model to the data. What is the numerical value of the coefficient of determination?

25. Refer to Exercise 23. Construct an analysis of variance table from the regression analysis. What is the numerical value of the F statistic? What is the p value for the computed F?

26. Refer to Exercise 23. Use the regression equation to predict the strength of a batch of cleanser that is five days old.

*27. Once a predictive model has been decided upon, it is considered good practice to employ some method of model validation. Validation procedures are designed to answer the question "How well can the model be expected to predict Y for a new set of measurements on the independent variables?" Several methods are available for this purpose. One is referred to as the *data-splitting* procedure since the data are split into two parts. One part is used to develop the model and the other part to validate it. Most often the data are divided into two equal parts. The question arises as to how to divide the data. When the data have been collected over time, a frequently followed practice is to divide the data on the basis of time. If, for example, data have been collected over a four-year period with the same number of data points per year, the data for the first two years may be used to develop the model and those for the last two years to validate it. When the data represent essentially the same point in time, called *cross-sectional data*, a problem arises regarding how the data should be divided. Methods for dealing with this problem are beyond the scope of this text, but the interested reader may find help on the matter in an article by Snee (Ronald J. Snee, "Validation of Regression Models: Methods and Examples," *Technometrics*, 19 [1977], 415–428). Before using the data-splitting procedure, one must make sure that the sample is of sufficient size. A rule of thumb sometimes used is that data splitting should not be used unless $n \geq 2p + 20$, where n is the total sample size and p is the number of parameters in the model. A possible criterion for judging predictive ability is the sum of the squared residuals obtained by using the model derived from the model-building part of the data to predict Y from the values of the independent variables in the validation part of the data. To demonstrate the calculations involved in the procedure and to illustrate how different ways of dividing the data affect the criterion, do the following using a data set of your choice found in this book or one from another source. (a) Randomly select half of the data points and use them to select a model. Use the model to predict Y from the remaining values of the independent variables we call the validation sample. Compute the criterion, the sum of the squared residuals. (b) Reverse the roles of the two halves of data identified in (a); that is, use the data from the original validation sample to select the model and use it to predict Y from the values of the independent variables in the original model-building sample. Compute the criterion measure from the resulting residuals. (c) Arbitrarily divide the data in half on the basis of the order in which they are available. Call one half the model-building sample and the other half the validation sample. Proceed as instructed in (a) and (b) above. (d) Compare the criterion measure from the four predictions.

STATISTICS AT WORK

1. ASPHALT AND PUBLIC ROADS

Researchers at Montana State University theorized that a direct relationship exists between the amount of a certain large molecular size (LMS) material in an asphalt and the thermal cracking properties of pavements incorporating that asphalt. The following table shows the LMS content (as percent) and physical data for 28 asphalt specimens. Determine the best model for predicting LMS using one or more of the other variables as potential predictors.

Chromatography Data and Physical Properties of Asphalt Samples

Lab Number	LMS	DUCT45	DUCT77	SG	SHR SUS	ASPH	REF IND	LST
B2908	32.23	31	130	1.004	0.36	19.0	1.4827	−46
B2909	32.15	9	221	1.007	0.39	20.5	1.4826	−45
B2910	27.01	9	200	1.012	0.51	21.6	1.4817	−41
B2921	12.70	8	250	1.004	0.42	15.5	1.4837	−39
B2922	9.43	0	250	1.007	0.62	18.1	1.4844	−39
B2960	23.96	11	160	1.034	0.42	27.9	1.4775	−51
B2962	17.75	150	155	1.010	0.21	19.3	1.4815	−51
B2963	17.24	150	250	1.015	0.31	20.2	1.4819	−48
B2964	15.98	10	241	1.021	0.44	21.6	1.4822	−44
B2975	8.79	0	215	1.005	0.66	16.5	1.4851	−20
B3009	15.57	12	230	0.994	0.41	17.8	1.4833	−50
B3010	23.07	7	205	0.995	0.49	20.1	1.4813	−54
B3013	26.88	150	245	1.021	0.32	20.8	1.4810	−39
B3014	14.58	14	250	1.025	0.39	21.6	1.4814	−42
B3028	16.09	3	152	1.011	0.30	19.5	1.4806	−53
B3030	12.40	5	250	1.028	0.59	29.3	1.4812	−41
B3036	12.64	11	210	1.026	0.42	16.7	1.4827	−56
B3051	16.13	150	250	1.028	0.18	26.1	1.4769	−46
B3056	11.52	3	250	1.020	0.64	19.2	1.4806	−34
B3058	22.61	150	140	1.021	0.31	22.4	1.4790	−46
B3108	16.27	244	167	1.011	0.23	17.3	1.4851	−40
B3109	18.43	19	250	1.014	0.43	18.6	1.4850	−33
B3110	14.93	9	250	1.018	0.54	19.7	1.4821	−36
B3578	14.11	150	205	1.015	0.21	18.1	1.4890	−35
B3579	11.66	150	245	1.010	0.40	18.0	1.4897	−35
B3601	6.96	250	171	1.011	0.29	9.7	1.4863	−30
B3602	16.50	12	250	1.016	0.50	11.0	1.4867	−23
B3603	3.47	4	250	1.021	0.65	12.2	1.4868	−22

LMS = Large Molecular Size Content (%)   °F = 1.8°C + 32
DUCT = Ductility at 45°F and 77°F
SG = Specific Gravity
SHR SUS = Shear Susceptibility
ASPH = Asphaltene Content (%)
REF IND = Refractive Index
LST = Limiting Stiffness Temperature (°C)

Source: Brian H. Chollar, John G. Boone, Warren E. Cuff, and Ernest F. Bailey (June 1985). "Chemical and Physical Characterization of Binder Materials," *Public Roads*, 49:7–12.

2. MEASURING TECHNOLOGICAL CHANGE IN JET FIGHTER AIRCRAFT

Stanley and Miller, in a 1979 Rand Corporation report prepared for the U.S. Air Force, describe an approach for comparing the level of technology of one jet fighter aircraft with that of another. They provide a quantitative framework to characterize the level of and change in the technology of jet fighter aircraft. The authors assembled design and performance information for 39 American and 13 Soviet fighter aircraft, identified parameters that described the performance consequences of some important advances in fighter technology of the previous 30 years, and, by subjecting these parameters to multiple regression analysis, developed expressions relating the time of appearance of an aircraft design to its level of technology.

Among the variables considered by Stanley and Miller were

FFD—first flight date (measured in months since January 1, 1940).

SPR—specific power (thrust $\times$ maximum velocity/combat weight $\times$ 100).

SLF—sustained load factor (the maximum load factor that the aircraft can sustain in level flight at an altitude of 25,000 feet and a Mach number of 0.8 at its combat weight).

RGF—flight range factor (the maximum value of the product of the average cruise speed and lift-to-drag ratio divided by the specific fuel consumption; the reported measurements are the original measurements divided by 1,000).

PLF—payload fraction (the difference in the maximum gross weight and the full internal weight, all divided by the maximum gross weight of the aircraft).

CAR—carrier capability (denotes whether aircraft can operate from carriers: 1 = no, 0 = yes).

The following table contains observations on these variables as reported by Stanley and Miller for 22 U.S. jet fighters.

Jet Fighter Data

Case	Aircraft Type	FFD	SPR	RGF	PLF	SLF	CAR
1	FH-1	82	1.468	3.300	0.166	0.10	0
2	FJ-1	89	1.605	3.640	0.154	0.10	0
3	F-86A	101	2.168	4.870	0.177	2.90	1
4	F9F-2	107	2.054	4.720	0.275	1.10	0
5	F-94A	115	2.467	4.110	0.298	1.00	1
6	F3D-1	122	1.294	3.750	0.150	0.90	0
7	F-89A	127	2.183	3.970	0.000	2.40	1
8	XF10F-1	137	2.426	4.650	0.117	1.80	0
9	F9F-6	147	2.607	3.840	0.155	2.30	0
10	F-100A	166	4.567	4.920	0.138	3.20	1
11	F4D-1	174	4.588	3.820	0.249	3.50	0
12	F11F-1	175	3.618	4.320	0.143	2.80	0

Jet Fighter Data

Case	Aircraft Type	FFD	SPR	RGF	PLF	SLF	CAR
13	F-101A	177	5.855	4.530	0.172	2.50	1
14	F3H-2	184	2.898	4.480	0.178	3.00	0
15	F-102A	187	3.880	5.390	0.101	3.00	1
16	F-8A	189	4.522	4.990	0.008	2.64	0
17	F-104A	194	8.088	4.500	0.251	2.70	1
18	F-105B	197	6.502	5.200	0.366	2.90	1
19	YF-107A	201	6.081	5.650	0.106	2.90	1
20	F-106A	204	7.105	5.400	0.089	3.20	1
21	F-4B	255	8.548	4.200	0.222	2.90	0
22	F-111A	328	6.321	6.450	0.187	2.00	1

Use these data to build a model in which FFD is the dependent variable.

Source: William L. Stanley, and Michael D. Miller (1979). *Measuring Technological Change in Jet Fighter Aircraft*, R-2249-AF. Santa Monica, Calif., The Rand Corporation.

3.   DIESEL ENGINE EMISSIONS

Charles T. Hare, of the Southwest Research Institute in San Antonio, Texas, conducted research designed to characterize diesel engine emissions. Although it is known that ambient air temperature, humidity, and barometric pressure influence the emission rates of pollutants from gasoline engine passenger cars, no such information relating to diesel-powered passenger cars was available at the time of the study.

The following table shows part of the data collected during the research. The variables are

NOX—nitrous oxide emissions (grams/km).

HUMID—humidity (grains H_2O/lb_m air).

TEMP—temperature (degrees F).

APRES—atmospheric pressure (in Hg).

Emission measurements were taken on a light-duty pickup truck at different times with varying environmental conditions.

Time	NOX	HUMID	TEMP	APRES
1	0.90	72.4	76.3	29.18
2	0.91	41.6	70.3	29.35
3	0.96	34.3	77.1	29.24
4	0.89	35.1	68.0	29.27
5	1.00	10.7	79.0	29.78
6	1.10	12.9	67.4	29.39
7	1.15	8.3	66.8	29.69
8	1.03	20.1	76.9	29.48
9	0.77	72.2	77.7	29.09

(table continues on next page)

Time	NOX	HUMID	TEMP	APRES
10	1.07	24.0	67.7	29.60
11	1.07	23.2	76.8	29.38
12	0.94	47.4	86.6	29.35
13	1.10	31.5	76.9	29.63
14	1.10	10.6	86.3	29.56
15	1.10	11.2	86.0	29.48
16	0.91	73.3	76.3	29.40
17	0.87	75.4	77.9	29.28
18	0.78	96.6	78.7	29.29
19	0.82	107.4	86.8	29.03
20	0.95	54.9	70.9	29.37
21	0.96	58.2	68.9	29.35
22	0.87	90.3	70.1	29.02
23	0.84	95.0	70.2	29.05
24	0.77	94.6	76.3	29.04
25	0.83	74.5	77.3	28.83
26	0.85	69.4	68.4	29.14
27	0.86	105.9	75.1	28.98
28	0.83	71.2	85.8	29.02
29	1.01	36.3	87.3	29.37
30	1.00	52.7	77.7	29.43
31	0.85	78.7	86.8	29.09
32	0.98	83.1	87.8	29.12
33	0.97	120.7	86.8	29.15
34	1.01	118.1	86.4	29.08
35	0.92	114.6	86.8	29.12
36	0.96	135.2	87.0	28.95
37	0.93	106.8	86.9	29.21
38	0.97	90.3	84.8	29.17
39	0.78	147.2	88.6	28.95
40	0.82	137.6	86.1	29.16
41	0.76	134.9	86.4	29.16
42	0.86	90.4	87.4	29.15
43	0.94	88.7	87.4	29.13
44	0.86	140.5	87.5	29.07
45	0.81	158.1	87.0	29.06

Use these data to construct a model for predicting emission levels of nitrous oxide.

Source: Charles T. Hare (1977). *Light-Duty Diesel Emission Correction Factors for Ambient Conditions*, EPA–600/2-77–116, U.S. Environmental Protection Agency, Research Triangle Park, N.C.

4. SOLID WASTE MANAGEMENT

As part of a study of solid waste management, Golueke and McGauhey reported data on several variables thought to be potential determiners of the amount of solid waste produced in a region. In addition to solid waste production (WASTE), reported here in millions of tons, the variables studied included the following, for which the measure is the number of acres devoted to the indicated use:

INDUS—miscellaneous industrial
METAL—fabricated metals manufacturing
WHOLE—trucking and wholesale trade
RETAIL—retail trade
REST—restaurants and hotels
FINAN—finance, insurance, and real estate
MISC—miscellaneous services
RESID—residential

The data reported on each of these variables for 40 disposal service areas in a nine-county region of California are shown in the following table.

Area	Waste	Indus	Metal	Whole	Retail	Rest	Finan	Misc	Resid
1	.3574	102	69	133	125	36	53	106	5,326
2	1.9673	1,220	723	2,616	953	132	252	574	36,138
3	.1862	139	138	46	35	6	9	27	2,594
4	.3816	221	637	153	115	16	41	83	10,346
5	.1512	12	0	1	9	1	2	7	381
6	.1449	1	50	3	25	2	7	7	3,440
7	.4711	1,046	127	313	392	56	62	212	14,559
8	.6512	2,032	44	409	540	98	106	289	40,182
9	.6624	895	54	168	117	32	20	76	4,600
10	.3457	0	0	2	0	1	0	7	1,540
11	.3355	25	2	24	78	15	25	50	6,516
12	.3982	97	12	91	135	24	28	59	6,011
13	.2044	1	0	15	46	11	35	40	1,922
14	.2969	4	1	18	23	8	13	28	931
15	1.1515	42	4	78	41	61	85	49	538
16	.5609	87	162	599	11	3	3	23	199
17	.1104	2	0	26	24	6	11	50	419
18	.0863	2	9	29	11	2	8	25	1,093
19	.1952	48	18	101	25	4	24	8	328
20	.1688	131	126	387	6	0	2	4	797
21	.0786	4	0	103	49	9	18	59	1,855
22	.0955	1	4	46	16	2	16	24	1,572
23	.0486	0	0	468	56	2	11	21	998
24	.0867	7	0	52	37	5	24	43	2,804
25	.1403	5	1	6	95	11	39	29	2,879
26	.3786	174	113	685	69	18	11	43	6,810
27	.0761	0	0	6	35	4	9	23	3,242
28	.8927	233	153	682	404	85	133	270	26,013
29	.3621	155	56	94	75	17	32	66	4,469
30	.1758	120	74	55	120	8	12	49	2,436

(table continues on next page)

Area	Waste	Indus	Metal	Whole	Retail	Rest	Finan	Misc	Resid
31	.2699	8,983	37	236	77	38	18	49	4,400
32	.2762	59	54	138	55	11	13	18	3,351
33	.3240	72	112	169	228	39	38	99	13,979
34	.3737	571	78	254	162	43	46	147	20,138
35	.9114	853	1,002	1,017	418	57	116	182	19,356
36	.2594	5	0	17	14	13	3	8	1,050
37	.4284	11	34	3	20	4	5	14	2,207
38	.1905	258	1	33	48	13	18	28	810
39	.2341	69	14	126	108	20	95	41	1,017
40	.7759	4,790	2,046	3,719	31	7	6	18	962

Use these data to construct a model for predicting WASTE, using the other variables as potential predictors.

Source: C. G. Golueke, and P. H. McGauhey (1970). *Comprehensive Studies of Solid Waste Management*, Public Health Service Publication No. 2039, U.S. Department of Health, Education, and Welfare, Bureau of Solid Waste Management, Washington, D.C.

5. SPARTINA BIOMASS PRODUCTION IN THE CAPE FEAR ESTUARY

For his doctoral dissertation at North Carolina State University, Dr. Rick Linthurst conducted research to identify the important soil characteristics influencing aerial biomass production of the marsh grass *Spartina alterniflora* in the Cape Fear Estuary of North Carolina.

One phase of his research consisted of sampling three types of Spartina vegetation (revegetated "dead" areas, "short" Spartina areas, and "tall" Spartina areas) in each of three locations (Oak Island, Smith Island, and Snows Marsh). Samples of the soil substrate from five random sites within each location-vegetation type (giving 45 total samples) were analyzed for 14 soil physico-chemical characteristics each month for several months. In addition, above-ground biomass at each sample site was measured each month. The data reproduced here involve only the September sampling and the following five substrate measurements:

SAL = Salinity 0/00

pH = Acidity as measured in water

K = Potassium ppm

Na = Sodium ppm

Zn = Zinc ppm

The dependent variable (BIO) is aerial biomass, gm^{-2}.

Observation	Location	Type	BIO	SAL	pH	K	Na	Zn
1	OI	DVEG	676	33	5.00	1,441.67	35,184.5	16.4524
2	OI	DVEG	516	35	4.75	1,299.19	28,170.4	13.9852
3	OI	DVEG	1,052	32	4.20	1,154.27	26,455.0	15.3276
4	OI	DVEG	868	30	4.40	1,045.15	25,072.9	17.3128
5	OI	DVEG	1,008	33	5.55	521.62	31,664.2	22.3312
6	OI	SHRT	436	33	5.05	1,273.02	25,491.7	12.2778
7	OI	SHRT	544	36	4.25	1,346.35	20,877.3	17.8225
8	OI	SHRT	680	30	4.45	1,253.88	25,621.3	14.3516
9	OI	SHRT	640	38	4.75	1,242.65	27,587.3	13.6826
10	OI	SHRT	492	30	4.60	1,282.95	26,511.7	11.7566
11	OI	TALL	984	30	4.10	553.69	7,886.5	9.8820
12	OI	TALL	1,400	37	3.45	494.74	14,596.0	16.6752
13	OI	TALL	1,276	33	3.45	526.97	9,826.8	12.3730
14	OI	TALL	1,736	36	4.10	571.14	11,978.4	9.4058
15	OI	TALL	1,004	30	3.50	408.64	10,368.6	14.9302
16	SI	DVEG	396	30	3.25	646.65	17,307.4	31.2865
17	SI	DVEG	352	27	3.35	514.03	12,822.0	30.1652
18	SI	DVEG	328	29	3.20	350.73	8,582.6	28.5901
19	SI	DVEG	392	34	3.35	496.29	12,369.5	19.8795
20	SI	DVEG	236	36	3.30	580.92	14,731.9	18.5056
21	SI	SHRT	392	30	3.25	535.82	15,060.6	22.1344
22	SI	SHRT	268	28	3.25	490.34	11,056.3	28.6101
23	SI	SHRT	252	31	3.20	552.39	8,118.9	23.1908
24	SI	SHRT	236	31	3.20	661.32	13,009.5	24.6917
25	SI	SHRT	340	35	3.35	672.15	15,003.7	22.6758
26	SI	TALL	2,436	29	7.10	525.65	10,225.0	0.3729
27	SI	TALL	2,216	35	7.35	563.13	8,024.2	0.2703
28	SI	TALL	2,096	35	7.45	497.96	10,393.0	0.3205
29	SI	TALL	1,660	30	7.45	458.38	8,711.6	0.2648
30	SI	TALL	2,272	30	7.40	498.25	10,239.6	0.2105
31	SM	DVEG	824	26	4.85	936.26	20,436.0	18.9875
32	SM	DVEG	1,196	29	4.60	894.79	12,519.9	20.9687
33	SM	DVEG	1,960	25	5.20	941.36	18,979.0	23.9841
34	SM	DVEG	2,080	26	4.75	1,038.79	22,986.1	19.9727
35	SM	DVEG	1,764	26	5.20	898.05	11,704.5	21.3864
36	SM	SHRT	412	25	4.55	989.87	17,721.0	23.7063
37	SM	SHRT	416	26	3.95	951.28	16,485.2	30.5589
38	SM	SHRT	504	26	3.70	939.83	17,101.3	26.8415
39	SM	SHRT	492	27	3.75	925.42	17,849.0	27.7292
40	SM	SHRT	636	27	4.15	954.11	16,949.6	21.5699
41	SM	TALL	1,756	24	5.60	720.72	11,344.6	19.6531
42	SM	TALL	1,232	27	5.35	782.09	14,752.4	20.3295
43	SM	TALL	1,400	26	5.50	773.30	13,649.8	19.5880
44	SM	TALL	1,620	28	5.50	829.26	14,533.0	20.1328
45	SM	TALL	1,560	28	5.40	856.96	16,892.2	19.2420

Use these data to develop the best model for predicting BIO.

Source: J. O. Rawlings, *Applied Regression Analysis*, Copyright (c) 1988 by Wadsworth, Inc. Reprinted by permission of Wadsworth & Brooks/Cole Advanced Books & Software, Pacific Grove, CA 93950.

6. HIGH AND LOW COMPUTER USER ORGANIZATIONS

In a journal article, Zeffane illustrates the use of stepwise regression analysis. Read the article and write a report that answers the following questions:

(a) What was the purpose of the research described in the article?

(b) How were the data collected?

(c) What were the variables on which data were obtained?

(d) What was the unit of association?

(e) What was the specific purpose of stepwise regression in the analysis?

(f) What are the author's conclusions?

Source: Rachid Zeffane, "Patterns of Structural Control in High and Low Computer User Organizations," *Information & Management*, 23 (1992), 159–170.

7. SMALL BUSINESS LENDING

Apilado and Millington used stepwise regression as part of the analysis in a research project reported on in the *Journal of Small Business Management*. Read the article and write a report that answers the following questions:

(a) What was the purpose of the research?

(b) What were the authors' hypotheses?

(c) How were the data collected?

(d) What were the variables on which data were collected?

(e) What was the unit of association?

(f) What information did the stepwise regression procedure provide?

(g) What were the authors' conclusions?

Source: Vincent P. Apilado and J. Kent Millington, "Restrictive Loan Covenants and Risk Adjustment in Small Business Lending," *Journal of Small Business Management*, 30 (January 1992), 38–48.

SUGGESTIONS FOR FURTHER READING

Besides the books listed at the end of Chapter 9 and the end of Chapter 10, the following may be consulted for further discussions of the topics presented in this chapter:

Atkinson, A. C. (1985). *Plots, Transformations, and Regression*. Clarendon Press, Oxford.

Bates, Douglas M., and Donald G. Watts (1988). *Nonlinear Regression Analysis and Its Applications*. Wiley, New York.

Cook, R. Dennis, and Sanford Weisberg (1982). *Residuals and Influence in Regression*. Chapman and Hall, New York.

Gallant, A. Ronald (1987). *Nonlinear Statistical Models*. Wiley, New York.

Ratkowsky, David A. (1983). *Nonlinear Regression Modeling*. Marcel Dekker, New York.

Rawlings, John O. (1988). *Applied Regression Analysis: A Research Tool*. Wadsworth, Pacific Grove, Calif.

Sprent, Peter (1969). *Models in Regression and Related Topics*. Methuen, London.

Wittink, Dick R. (1988). *The Application of Regression Analysis*. Allyn and Bacon, Boston.

Also of interest are the following journal articles:

Gallant, A. R. (1975). "Nonlinear Regression," *American Statistician* 29(May):73–81.

Hocking, R. R. (1976). "The Analysis and Selection of Variables in Linear Regression," *Biometrics* 32(March):1–49.

Those who wish to know more about learning-curve applications will find the following journal articles worth consulting:

Andress, Frank J. (1954). "The Learning Curve As a Production Tool," *Harvard Business Review* 32(January–February):87–97.

Katz, Richard (1969). "Understanding and Applying Learning Curves," *Automation* 16(November):50–53.

Morse, Wayne J. (1972). "Reporting Production Costs That Follow the Learning Curve Phenomenon," *The Accounting Review* 47(October):761–773.

12

The Chi-Square Distribution and the Analysis of Frequencies

Chapter Objectives: In this chapter, you will learn to extend the concepts of statistical hypothesis testing involving attributes to cover situations in which sampling is from populations whose elements can be classified into one of three or more categories. You will find that the testing procedures are simplified if you use the chi-square distribution as an approximate sampling distribution to compare observed frequencies with those expected under the null hypothesis. After studying this chapter and working the exercises, you should be able to

1. Justify the use of the chi-square distribution as an approximate sampling distribution in comparing observed frequencies with expected frequencies.
2. Calculate expected frequencies for goodness-of-fit tests, tests of independence, and tests of homogeneity.
3. Explain how to determine degrees of freedom for each of the above tests.
4. Use the chi-square distribution to conduct statistical tests of hypotheses for goodness-of-fit tests, tests of independence, and tests of homogeneity.

12.1 INTRODUCTION

For most of the statistical techniques discussed in Chapters 8 through 11, you need *measurements,* such as weight, length, diameter, distance, amount of money, or scores on some type of test. But often the data available for analysis consist of *frequency counts* rather than measurements. The following examples illustrate the point.

Suppose that a market analyst wishes to evaluate the effectiveness of three different advertising strategies. The analyst selects three samples of 100 people each, and exposes each sample to one of the three strategies. Effectiveness is measured in terms of the proportion in each sample that buys the advertised product. The pertinent question is whether there would be differences in the corresponding population proportions if three populations of people were similarly exposed to the three strategies.

In another situation, we may hypothesize that the number of defective items coming off an assembly line during each eight-hour shift has a Poisson distribution. For several shifts, we count the number of defective items. Do the observed data provide sufficient evidence to cause rejection of the hypothesis?

Or consider the case in which two factories produce some product under supposedly identical conditions. We examine a sample of items from each factory. For each sample, we count the number of items that fail to meet certain quality standards. Based on these results, should we conclude that the two samples really come from two different populations? That is, can we conclude that the factories are different?

These examples have at least two things in common: (1) The raw data consist of *counts,* or *frequencies,* and (2) under the implied or stated hypotheses, there are *expected frequencies* with which we can compare the *observed frequencies.* Such a comparison can lead to some useful conclusions.

If the three advertising strategies do not differ in effectiveness, for example, we would expect about the same number of people from each sample of 100 to buy the product, all other things being equal. Or if the number of defective items coming off an assembly line during an eight-hour shift is in fact Poisson-distributed, we would expect a sample of shifts to yield data compatible with the hypothesis. Finally, if conditions in two factories producing the same product are identical, we would expect, in samples of equal size from the two factories, about the same number of items to fail to meet the standards.

We compare observed frequencies with expected frequencies.

The question to be answered in each of these cases is whether the discrepancies between observed and expected frequencies are so large as to cast doubt on the assumptions that gave rise to the expected frequencies.

The statistical techniques we use to provide answers to such questions are based on the *chi-square distribution.* These techniques are called the *chi-square test of homogeneity,* the *chi-square test of goodness of fit,* and the *chi-square test of independence.* The basic technique was introduced in 1900 by Karl Pearson.

12.2 MATHEMATICAL PROPERTIES OF THE CHI-SQUARE DISTRIBUTION

Chapter 6 introduces the chi-square distribution in connection with the construction of confidence intervals for a population variance. We can express this distribution mathematically as

(12.2.1)
$$f(u) = \frac{1}{\left(\dfrac{n}{2} - 1\right)! \, 2^{n/2}} \, u^{(n/2)-1} e^{-u/2}, \qquad u > 0$$

where $u = \sum_{i=1}^{n} \left(\dfrac{x_i - \mu_i}{\sigma_i}\right)^2$ and $e = 2.71828\ldots$

and n is called the *degrees of freedom*. The x_i are normally and independently distributed with means μ_i and standard deviations σ_i. The subscript i on μ and σ indicates that it is possible for each observation to be drawn from a different population. When we draw all the observations from the same population, we drop the subscripts on μ and σ. The mean and variance of the distribution are n and $2n$, respectively. This distribution is usually designated by the Greek letter χ^2 (chi squared).

The chi-square distribution is a sampling distribution.

The chi-square distribution is the sampling distribution that results when we draw n values of the normally distributed random variable X repeatedly and at random, transform each value of x to the standard normal, and square and sum the resulting n variables. Suppose, for example, that the random variable X is normally distributed with mean μ and standard deviation σ. Let us draw a large number of independent random samples of size n from this population. Then let us transform each value of x within each sample to the standard normal in the usual manner, as follows:

$$z = \frac{x_i - \mu}{\sigma}$$

Let us square this equation and add overall observations within each individual sample. Then for each sample we have

(12.2.2)
$$u = \sum_{i=1}^{n} z^2 = \sum_{i=1}^{n} \left(\frac{x_i - \mu}{\sigma}\right)^2$$

If we make a list of the different values of u, along with their relative frequency of occurrence, we will have the sampling distribution of $u = \Sigma z^2$, which is the chi-square distribution with n degrees of freedom. Figures 6.11.1 and 6.11.2 show chi-square distributions for several degrees of freedom.

The importance of the chi-square distribution rests on the fact that for large samples the quantity

(12.2.3)
$$X^2 = \sum_{i=1}^{k} \left[\frac{(O_i - E_i)^2}{E_i} \right]$$

Degrees of freedom will always be $k - 1$ or less.

is distributed approximately as χ^2 with degrees of freedom that vary according to the circumstances. In some cases the number of degrees of freedom is equal to $k - 1$. Under other conditions, the degrees of freedom may be fewer. In general, the number of degrees of freedom is equal to $k - r$, where r is the number of constraints imposed on the data. Possible constraints are (1) forcing the sum of the expected frequencies to equal the sum of the observed frequencies and (2) estimating parameters from the sample data. Since we always force the sum of the expected frequencies to equal the sum of the observed frequencies, r will always be at least equal to 1, and the number degrees of freedom will be at most $k - 1$. If parameters have to be estimated from sample data, we lose 1 degree of freedom for each parameter estimated.

Critical values for chi-square tests are obtained from Table F of Appendix I. We enter the table with our chosen level of significance and the appropriate degrees of freedom. The chi-square table is set up like the t table in that values in the body of the table are those that have an amount of the area under the curve to their left equal to the subscript on the statistic at the head of the column. For example, the critical value for a significance level of 0.05 and 6 degrees of freedom is located at the intersection of the row labeled 6 and the column labeled $\chi^2_{0.95}$ and is equal to 12.592. We find p values for chi-square tests in much the same way as we find them for t tests.

In Equation 12.2.3, $O_i = $ an observed frequency, $E_i = $ an expected frequency, and $k = $ the number of pairs of observed and expected frequencies. Observed and expected frequencies arise from situations such as those described in Section 12.1. The quantity X^2 is a measure of the extent to which, in a given situation, pairs of observed and expected frequencies agree. As we shall see, the nature of X^2 is such that when there is close agreement between observed and expected frequencies, it is small, and when the agreement is poor, it is large. Consequently, only a sufficiently large value of X^2 will cause rejection of the null hypothesis. Later sections will show how we can use Equation 12.2.3 to test hypotheses of a practical nature. Note that X^2 will always be positive.

All the chi-square tests discussed in this chapter are one-sided tests, with the rejection region in the right tail of the distribution of the test statistic.

We may rewrite Equation 12.2.3 as

(12.2.4)
$$X^2 = \sum \frac{O_i^2}{E_i} - n$$

This equation may make the calculations easier to perform by hand or on a calculator. One disadvantage of Equation 12.2.4 is the fact that it does not clearly indicate which categories contribute most to the overall lack of agreement between observed and expected frequencies.

A more extensive discussion of the mathematical properties of the chi-square distribution can be found in most textbooks on mathematical statistics.

12.3   TESTS FOR GOODNESS OF FIT

Here we want to determine whether sample data are compatible with the hypothesis that they were drawn from a population that follows some specified functional form—the uniform distribution or the normal distribution, for example. We can reach decisions in this type of case by means of a chi-square *goodness-of-fit test*. To carry out this test, we specify a set of k mutually exclusive categories and note the *observed* frequency of occurrence of sample values in each category. We use the properties of the distribution from which we hypothesize that the sample was drawn to determine *expected* frequencies for each category. The magnitude of the discrepancy between the observed and expected frequencies forms the basis of the test.

In general, the specific steps involved in calculating X^2 for a goodness-of-fit test are as follows:

1. The categories of the variable of interest are specified.
2. Observed frequencies for each category are determined.
3. On the basis of the theory stated or implied in the null hypothesis, expected relative frequencies for each category are determined.
4. For each category, expected frequencies, given that the null hypothesis is true, are determined from the knowledge of the expected relative frequencies.
5. Observed and expected frequencies are entered into Equation 12.2.3 to obtain the computed value of X^2.

EXAMPLE 12.3.1   *The Uniform Distribution.* Everett/Sawyer Communications asks each member of a random sample of 60 viewers to indicate which of 6 television programs he or she prefers. The results are as follows.

Program Number	1	2	3	4	5	6	Total
	5	8	10	12	12	13	60

Can we conclude from these data that the programs are not equally preferred?

SOLUTION   If there is no preference, we would expect the same number of votes for each program. In other words, we would expect the total number of votes to be distributed uniformly among the 6 programs. Pursuing this line of reasoning, we may conduct the following hypothesis test:

1. *Hypotheses.*

H_0: The 6 programs are equally preferred.

H_1: The 6 programs are not equally preferred.

2. *Test statistic.* The test statistic is given by Equation 12.2.3.
3. *Significance level.* Let $\alpha = 0.05$.
4. *Decision rule.* The number of degrees of freedom is equal to the number of categories minus 1, or $6 - 1 = 5$. From Table F of Appendix I, the critical value of chi square for $\alpha = 0.05$ and 5 degrees of freedom is 11.070. The decision rule, then, is: Reject H_0 if the computed value of X^2 is ≥ 11.070.
5. *Calculations.* Under the null hypothesis, the expected number of votes for each program is $60/6 = 10$. By Equation 12.2.3, we may now compute the following value of X^2:

$$X^2 = \frac{(5 - 10)^2}{10} + \frac{(8 - 10)^2}{10} + \frac{(10 - 10)^2}{10} + \frac{(12 - 10)^2}{10}$$
$$+ \frac{(12 - 10)^2}{10} + \frac{(13 - 10)^2}{10} = 4.6$$

6. *Statistical decision.* Since 4.6 is less than 11.070, we cannot reject H_0.
7. *Conclusion.* We conclude that the distribution of votes may be uniformly distributed $(p > 0.10)$.

The assumption of a normally distributed population underlies many of the hypothesis-testing procedures we have discussed. The chi-square goodness-of-fit test provides a means of testing this assumption.

EXAMPLE 12.3.2 *The Normal Distribution.* A simple random sample of 700 assembly-line workers took part in an experiment to determine how much time they needed for a certain task after they had taken a certain training course. Table 12.3.1 shows the frequency distribution of the time in seconds that the subjects needed to complete the task. We wish to determine whether these data provide sufficient evidence to indicate that the observations were not drawn from a normal population.

SOLUTION

1. *Hypotheses.*

H_0: The sample data come from a normally distributed population.

H_1: The sample data do not come from a normally distributed population.

2. *Test statistic.* Equation 12.2.3 provides the test statistic. In this example, k is equal to the number of specified class intervals, and the O_i are the observed frequencies. The E_i are yet to be determined.

TABLE 12.3.1 Frequency distribution of time (in seconds) required to complete a task

Time	Number of Subjects
0–9.99	38
10–19.99	51
20–29.99	62
30–39.99	74
40–49.99	83
50–59.99	91
60–69.99	81
70–79.99	72
80–89.99	61
90–99.99	52
100–109.99	35
	700

$\bar{x} = 54.71, \quad s = 27.61$

3. *Significance level.* Let $\alpha = 0.05$.
4. *Decision rule.* Reject H_0 if the computed value of X^2 is $\geq$ the critical value of χ^2. The critical value of the test statistic is the value of χ^2 from Table F corresponding to $\alpha = 0.05$ and the appropriate degrees of freedom. It can be shown that when the null hypothesis is true, X^2 defined by Equation 12.2.3 is distributed approximately as χ^2 with $k - r$ degrees of freedom. In determining the degrees of freedom, as we have noted, k is the number of categories into which the observed and expected frequencies are cast, and r is the number of restrictions, or constraints, imposed on the data.
5. *Calculations.* Before we can compute the value of the test statistic X^2, we must determine the expected frequencies. According to the principles of probability distributions, we can find the relative frequency of occurrence of values of a given magnitude by finding the area under the curve defined by the distribution. In the case of the normal distribution, for example, the relative frequency of occurrence of values equal to or less than some specified value x_0 is equivalent to the area under the curve and to the left of x_0. See Figure 12.3.1. We find the numerical value corresponding to this area by converting x_0 to a standard normal deviate by the formula $z_0 = (x_0 - \mu)/\sigma$ and finding the area in the standard normal table.

FIGURE 12.3.1 Normal distribution showing $P(x \geq x_0)$

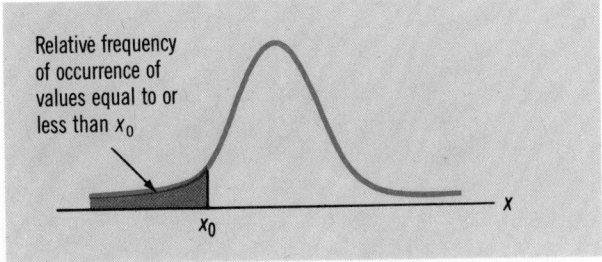

The present null hypothesis has not specified the mean and variance of the hypothesized normal distribution. Using the sample mean of 54.71 and the sample standard deviation of 27.61 as estimates of μ and σ, we can compute the area under the normal distribution between the boundaries of each of the specified class intervals.

For example, to compute the area, and hence the relative frequency of occurrence of values, corresponding to the interval 10–19.99, we proceed as follows: The z corresponding to $x = 10$ is equal to $(10 - 54.71)/27.61 = -1.62$. The z corresponding to $x = 20$ is equal to $(20 - 54.71)/27.61 = -1.26$. The area between -1.62 and -1.26 is equal to 0.0512. Thus, 5.12% of the values are expected (under the null hypothesis that the population is normally distributed) to fall between 10 and 20. The expected frequency is $(0.0512)(700) = 35.84$. Using this procedure, we may construct columns 3 through 5 of Table 12.3.2. From the data in these columns, we compute the entries in column 6 as follows:

$$X^2 = \frac{(38 - 36.82)^2}{36.82} + \frac{(51 - 35.84)^2}{35.84} + \cdots + \frac{(35 - 35.35)^2}{35.35}$$
$$= 20.3558$$

If the null hypothesis is true, there should be close agreement between the observed and expected frequencies. This close agreement leads to a relatively "small" value of X^2. If, on the other hand, the null hypothesis is false, there is no basis for expecting close agreement between the observed and expected frequencies. Consequently, the computed value of X^2 is likely to be relatively "large." In order to determine whether the computed value of X^2 is "small"

TABLE 12.3.2 Class intervals, expected frequencies, observed frequencies, and $(O_i - E_i)^2/E_i$ for Example 12.3.2

1 Class Interval	2 Observed Frequency O_i	3 $z = (x - \bar{x})/s$ at Lower Limit of Interval	4 Area under Normal Curve (Expected Relative Frequency)	5 Expected Frequency E_i	6 $\dfrac{(O_i - E_i)^2}{E_i}$
Less than 10	38	—	0.0526	36.82	0.0378
10–19.99	51	−1.62	0.0512	35.84	6.4125
20–29.99	62	−1.26	0.0829	58.03	0.2716
30–39.99	74	−0.89	0.1114	77.98	0.2031
40–49.99	83	−0.53	0.1344	94.08	1.3049
50–59.99	91	−0.17	0.1428	99.96	0.8031
60–69.99	81	0.19	0.1335	93.45	1.6587
70–79.99	72	0.55	0.1124	78.68	0.5671
80–89.99	61	0.92	0.0785	54.95	0.6661
90–99.99	52	1.28	0.0498	34.86	8.4274
100 or more	35	1.64	0.0505	35.35	0.0035
	700		1.0000	700.00	20.3558

or "large," we must have some criterion with which to compare it. This criterion is the tabulated value of χ^2 for $\alpha = 0.05$ and the appropriate degrees of freedom. To determine the degrees of freedom, consider the number of constraints r that have been imposed on the data. As Table 12.3.2 indicates, the expected frequencies must add to 700, the sample size. This is one constraint. We have imposed two additional constraints on the data because we had to estimate μ and σ from the sample data. Thus, $r = 3$, and the degrees of freedom are $k - r = 11 - 3 = 8$. If μ and σ had been specified in the null hypothesis, we would not have needed to estimate these parameters from the sample data. Thus, r would have been equal to 1. In general, in goodness-of-fit tests of this type, the number of degrees of freedom is equal to the number of categories, less 1 for forcing the sum of the expected frequencies to equal the sum of the observed frequencies, less 1 for each parameter that has to be estimated from sample data.

6. *Statistical decision.* In the present example, the critical value of χ^2 is 15.507. Since the computed value of $X^2 = 20.3558$ is larger than this, we reject the null hypothesis.

7. *Conclusion.* We conclude that the sample data did not come from a normally distributed population $(0.01 > p > 0.005)$.

Warning If you estimate parameters from ungrouped sample data rather than from grouped data as in our example, the distribution of X^2 may not be sufficiently approximated by the chi-square distribution to give good results. We encounter the same problem when parameters are estimated independently of the sample.

Small Expected Frequencies A word of caution regarding the use of the chi-square test with small expected frequencies is appropriate here. It is generally agreed that approximating the distribution of X^2 by χ^2 is not strictly valid when there are small expected frequencies. There is no general agreement, however, on what constitutes small expected frequencies. Many statisticians follow the rule of W. G. Cochran, who states that in goodness-of-fit tests of the type covered in this chapter no expected frequency should be below 1. Others require a minimum expected frequency of 5. This text follows Cochran's rule.

If some categories have expected frequencies below the minimum, we may combine them with adjacent categories to achieve the minimum required frequency. If we do this, we must reduce k accordingly when we determine degrees of freedom.

EXAMPLE 12.3.3 *The Binomial Distribution.* Fawkes Marketing Group is conducting a study on the attitudes of grocery shoppers toward savings stamps. The study involves interviewing a random sample of 25 regular shoppers at each of 100 supermarkets. The analyst interviews each shopper to determine whether that shopper would prefer some form of savings other than stamps. Table 12.3.3 shows the results. We wish to know whether we may conclude that the variable of interest is not binomially distributed.

TABLE 12.3.3 Sample results, Example 12.3.3

Number of shoppers preferring some other form of savings	0	1	2	3	4	5	6	7	8	9	10 or more
Number of stores	4	5	8	10	14	15	12	16	10	6	0 Total: 100

SOLUTION   The analyst conducts the following hypothesis test:

1. Hypotheses.

H_0: The number of shoppers in samples of size 25 preferring some other form of savings is binomially distributed.

H_1: The number of shoppers in samples of size 25 preferring some other form of savings is not distributed as a binomial.

2. Test statistic. The test statistic is provided by Equation 12.2.3.
3. Significance level. Let $\alpha = 0.05$.
4. Decision rule. Reject H_0 if the computed value of X^2 is $\geq$ the critical value of χ^2.
5. Calculations. Since the binomial parameter p is not specified, we must estimate it from the sample data, with a resulting loss of 1 degree of freedom. We estimate p as follows:

$$\hat{p} = \frac{4(0) + 5(1) + 8(2) + \cdots + 16(7) + 10(8) + 6(9)}{2,500} = 0.20$$

Since the analyst interviewed 25 shoppers at each of 100 stores, a total of 2,500 shoppers were interviewed, as indicated in the denominator of $\hat{p}$. The numerator of $\hat{p}$ shows how many of the 2,500 shoppers prefer some other form of savings.

We can find the expected relative frequencies by evaluating the following function for $x = 0, \ldots, 25$:

$$f(x) = {}_{25}C_x(0.2)^x(0.8)^{25-x}$$

where x is the number of shoppers at a given store who prefer some other form of savings. We may use Table A of Appendix I for this purpose. Multiplying each of these probabilities by 100 gives the expected frequencies. For example, the table shows that the probability of observing no shoppers favoring some other form of savings when the null hypothesis is true is 0.0038. Multiplying 0.0038 by 100 gives an expected frequency of 0.38. We can compute the other expected frequencies in a like manner. Columns 3 and 4 of Table 12.3.4 show the results.

TABLE 12.3.4 Observed frequencies, expected relative frequencies, and expected frequencies, Example 12.3.3

Number Preferring Some other Form of Savings	Number of Stores O_i	Binomial Probability (Expected Relative Frequency)	Expected Number of Stores E_i	$\dfrac{(O_i - E_i)^2}{E_i}$
0	4 ⎱ 9	0.0038 ⎱ 0.0274	0.38 ⎱ 2.74	14.302
1	5 ⎰	0.0236 ⎰	2.36 ⎰	0.120
2	8	0.0708	7.08	
3	10	0.1358	13.58	0.944
4	14	0.1867	18.67	1.168
5	15	0.1960	19.60	1.080
6	12	0.1633	16.33	1.148
7	16	0.1109	11.09	2.174
8	10	0.0623	6.23	2.281
9	6	0.0295	2.95	3.153
10 or more	0	0.0173	1.73	1.730
Total	100	1.0000	100.00	28.100

The first expected frequency in the table is less than 1. Therefore, following Cochran's rule for small expected frequencies, we combine the first two categories, as shown in the table. The computed value of the test statistic, then, is

$$X^2 = \frac{(9 - 2.74)^2}{2.74} + \frac{(8 - 7.08)^2}{7.08} + \cdots + \frac{(0 - 1.73)^2}{1.73} = 28.100$$

6. *Statistical decision.* The associated degrees of freedom are 10 (the number of categories after combining), less 1 for forcing the total of the expected frequencies to agree with the total of the observed frequencies, less 1 because p had to be estimated from the sample data. Thus, the degrees of freedom are $10 - 2 = 8$. The critical value of χ^2 for $\alpha = 0.05$ and 8 degrees of freedom is 15.507. Since the computed value of X^2 is greater than the critical value of χ^2, we reject the null hypothesis.

7. *Conclusion.* We conclude that the data did not come from a binomial distribution ($p < 0.005$).

EXAMPLE 12.3.4   *The Poisson Distribution.* The manager of Goodyear Hotels studies the pattern of cancellations over a 90-day period. She observes the results shown in Table 12.3.5. Are these data compatible with the hypothesis that the number of daily cancellations follows a Poisson distribution?

TABLE 12.3.5 Resort hotel cancellation data, Example 12.3.4

Number of cancellations	0	1	2	3	4	5	6	7	8	9 or more
Number of days this number of cancellations was received	9	17	25	15	11	7	2	2	2	0 Total: 90

SOLUTION

1. *Hypotheses.*

   H_0: The sample data came from a population that follows a Poisson distribution.

   H_1: The sample data did not come from a population that follows a Poisson distribution.

2. *Test statistic.* Equation 12.2.3 is the appropriate test statistic.
3. *Significance level.* Let $\alpha = 0.05$.
4. *Decision rule.* Reject H_0 if the computed value of the test statistic is $\geq$ the critical value of χ^2.
5. *Calculations.* Since the Poisson parameter λ is not given, we estimate it from the data as follows:

$$\hat{\lambda} = \frac{0(9) + 1(17) + 2(25) + 3(15) + 4(11) + 5(7) + 6(2) + 7(2) + 8(2)}{90}$$

$$= \frac{233}{90} = 2.6$$

We use the sample mean to estimate λ, since, as you will recall from Chapter 4, λ is the mean of the Poisson distribution. You will also recall that the Poisson distribution is expressed by

$$f(x) = \frac{e^{-\lambda}\lambda^x}{x!}, \qquad x = 0, 1, 2, 3, \ldots, \infty$$

Using the estimate of λ, 2.6, and assuming a Poisson distribution, we can find the probabilities for the different values of X in Appendix Table B. Multiplying each of these probabilities by 90 gives the expected frequency for each value of X. We then compute the value of X^2 in the usual way. Table 12.3.6 shows the probabilities and expected frequencies. From these data, we compute

$$X^2 = \frac{(9 - 6.66)^2}{6.66} + \frac{(17 - 17.37)^2}{17.37} + \cdots + \frac{(4 - 1.53)^2}{1.53} = 6.674$$

6. *Statistical decision.* The degrees of freedom for this example are 6. The number of categories after combining to adjust for the small expected frequencies was 8. One degree of freedom was lost for each of two constraints: (1) forcing the total of the expected frequencies to agree with the total of the observed frequencies, and (2) estimating λ from the sample data. Referring to Table F, we find that the critical value of χ^2 is 12.592. We cannot reject the null

TABLE 12.3.6 Observed frequencies, probabilities, and expected frequencies, Example 12.3.4

Number of Cancellations (1)	Number of Days this Number was Observed (O_i) (2)	Probability, Assuming a Poisson Distribution with $\lambda = 2.6$ (3)	Expected Frequencies, col. (3) × 90 (E_i) (4)	$\dfrac{(O_i - E_i)^2}{E_i}$ (5)
0	9	0.074	6.66	0.822
1	17	0.193	17.37	0.008
2	25	0.251	22.59	0.257
3	15	0.218	19.62	1.088
4	11	0.141	12.69	0.225
5	7	0.074	6.66	0.017
6	2	0.032	2.88	0.269
7	2⎫	0.012⎫	1.08⎫	
8	2⎬4	0.004⎬0.017	0.36⎬1.53	3.988
9 or more	0⎭	0.001⎭	0.09⎭	
Total	90	1.000	90.00	6.674

FIGURE 12.3.2 STAT+ Printout for Example 12.3.4

```
          CHI-SQUARE GOODNESS OF FIT EXPECTED FREQUENCIES
                    DATA SET IS HOTCANCL
Cate-     Class       Hypothesized   Observed      Expected      Cate-
gory      Interv <    Rel. Freq.     Frequencies   Frequencies   gory
1         0.0         0.0740         9             6.7           1
2         1.0         0.1930         17            17.4          2
3         2.0         0.2510         25            22.6          3
4         3.o         0.2180         15            19.6          4
5         4.0         0.1410         11            12.7          5
6         5.0         0.0740         7             6.7           6
7         6.0         0.0320         2             2.9           7
8         7.0         0.0170         4             1.5           8
9         0.0         0.0000         0             0.0           9
10        0.0         0.0000         0             0.0           10
11        0.0         0.0000         0             0.0           11
12        0.0         0.0000         0             0.0           12
13        0.0         0.0000         0             0.0           13
14        0.0         0.0000         0             0.0           14
15        0.0         0.0000         0                           15
Totals
26                    1.000          90            90.0          26
COMPUTED RESULTS FROM CHI-SQUARE GOODNESS OF FIT TEST

In the HOTCANCL problem, how many parameters are estimated from
sample data ? 1

Chi-Square analysis of the 8 category HOTCANL problem yields
Chi-Square = 6.67 with 6 degrees of freedom.
```

hypothesis that the data came from a Poisson distribution at the $\alpha = 0.05$ level of significance, since $6.674 < 12.592$.

7. *Conclusion.* We conclude that the data are compatible with the null hypothesis ($p > 0.10$).

COMPUTER **ANALYSIS**

We may use STAT+ to calculate a chi-square goodness-of-fit statistic. The user inputs the class interval or category labels (optional), the hypothesized relative frequency for each class interval or category, and the observed frequencies. STAT+ then computes the expected frequencies and the chi-square statistic. The program warns the user about small expected frequencies and provides an opportunity to combine categories to bring the expected frequencies up to the necessary levels. Figure 12.3.2 shows the STAT+ printout for Example 12.3.4.

EXERCISES

For each of the following exercises, perform the chi-square test at the indicated level of significance. Determine the p value.

 12.3.1 The following table shows the distribution of a sample of 223 employees by score on an aptitude test. The mean and variance computed from the sample data are 74.47 and 386.4252, respectively. Test the goodness of fit of these data to a normal distribution. Let $\alpha = 0.05$.

Score	Number of Employees
<40.0	10
40.0–49.9	12
50.0–59.9	17
60.0–69.9	37
70.0–79.9	55
80.0–89.9	51
90.0–99.9	34
100.0–109.9	5
110.0 or greater	2
	223

 12.3.2 The manager of Hillmart Variety Stores, during a 300-day observation period, finds that a particular item is called for as follows. Test the goodness of fit of these data to a Poisson distribution. Let $\alpha = 0.05$.

No. of times called for	0	1	2	3	4	5	6	7	8	9	10	11	12	13	
No. of days item was called for this number of times	3	9	21	38	46	54	49	34	20	16	6	3	1	0	Total: 300

12.3.3 A certain clerical operation involves processing forms in batches of 20. A supervisor examines a sample of 100 batches for errors, with the following results. Test the goodness of fit of these data to a binomial distribution with $p = 0.20$. Let $\alpha = 0.05$.

No. of errors	0	1	2	3	4	5	6	7	8	9	10	11	
No. of batches with this no. of errors (O_i)	1	5	12	15	30	21	8	4	2	1	1	0	Total: 100

12.3.4 A new 25-bed hospital shows the following experience relative to the number of beds occupied during the first 134 days of operation. Test the goodness of fit of these data to a binomial distribution. Let $\alpha = 0.05$.

No. of beds occupied	<8	8	9	10	11	12	13	14	15	16	17	18	19	20	21	22	23	
No. of days this no. of beds occupied	0	1	1	2	6	8	17	22	24	21	15	9	5	1	1	1	0	Total: 134

12.3.5 Interviewers ask each of a sample of 300 shoppers which day he or she prefers to shop. The results are as follows. Do these data indicate that not all days are equally preferred by grocery shoppers? Let $\alpha = 0.05$.

Mon.	Tue.	Wed.	Thur.	Fri.	Sat.	Sun.	Total
10	20	40	40	80	60	50	300

12.3.6 A market researcher believes that in a certain population the proportions of persons preferring brands A, B, C, and D of toothpaste are 0.30, 0.60, 0.08, and 0.02, respectively. A simple random sample of 600 people drawn from the population reveals the following preferences. Do these data provide sufficient evidence to cast doubt on the researcher's belief? Let $\alpha = 0.01$.

Brand	A	B	C	D
No. preferring this brand	192	342	44	22

12.3.7 Researchers ask each member of a random sample of 360 residents of a community to list which local television station he or she prefers to watch for national and international news. The results are as follows. Do these data provide sufficient evidence to indicate that the three stations are not equally preferred? Let $\alpha = 0.10$.

Station	A	B	C
No. preferring this station	190	30	140

12.4   TESTS OF INDEPENDENCE

Two variables are independent if knowing the value of one does not help us make a better "guess" of the value of the other.

One of the most frequent uses of χ^2 is for testing the null hypothesis that two criteria of classification, when applied to a population of subjects (or objects), are *independent*. Two criteria of classification are said to be independent if the distribution of one criterion in no way depends on the distribution of the other. If two criteria of classification are *not* independent, there is an *association* between them. Suppose, for example, that two criteria of classification are age and type of television program preferred. Suppose that, for some population of people, knowing a person's age is of no help in predicting the type of program preferred, or vice versa. In such a case, age and type of program preferred are independent.

Typically, we make decisions about the independence of criteria in a population on the basis of sample data. We draw a random sample from the population of interest and cross-classify the subjects according to the two criteria. We display the cross-classification in a table, called a *contingency table*.

In a *contingency table*, the *levels* of one criterion provide row headings, and the levels of the other criterion provide the column headings.

Table 12.4.1 shows a contingency table in which a sample of n subjects has been cross-classified according to two criteria. There are r levels of the criterion forming the rows and c levels of the criterion forming the columns. We place the observed number O_{ij} of subjects that may be characterized by one level of each criterion in the cell formed by the intersection of the ith row and jth column. The cell entries are referred to as *observed cell frequencies*.

EXPECTED FREQUENCIES

To find the *expected cell frequencies* needed to calculate an X^2 value, we use the principles of probability. For the population represented by the sample in Table 12.4.1, suppose that we wish to know the probability that a subject picked at random is characterized by level 1 of the first (column) criterion. The best estimator of this probability is $n_{.1}/n$. Similarly, the estimator of the probability that a subject picked at random is characterized by level 1 of the second (row) criterion is given by $n_{1.}/n$. We can compute similar estimators for each level of each criterion. We call these probabilities *marginal probabilities* because they are computed from marginal totals. Now suppose that we wish to estimate the probability that a subject picked at random is characterized by the level 1 of both criteria. In the absence of any hypothesis about the two criteria of classification, we estimate this probability by O_{11}/n. We call this a *joint probability*. Our objective, however, is to test the null hypothesis that the two criteria of classification are *independent*. Chapter 3 shows that if two events are independent the probability of their joint occurrence is equal to the product of their individual probabilities. Applying this rule to a contingency table, we say the following:

TABLE 12.4.1 Two-way classification of a sample of subjects

Second Criterion of Classification	First Criterion of Classification					
	Level					
Level	1	2	3	$\cdots$	c	Total
1	O_{11}	O_{12}	O_{13}	$\cdots$	O_{1c}	$n_{1\cdot}$
2	O_{21}	O_{22}	O_{23}	$\cdots$	O_{2c}	$n_{2\cdot}$
3	O_{31}	O_{32}	O_{33}	$\cdots$	O_{3c}	$n_{3\cdot}$
$\vdots$	$\vdots$	$\vdots$	$\vdots$	$\vdots$	$\vdots$	$\vdots$
r	O_{r1}	O_{r2}	O_{r3}	$\cdots$	O_{rc}	$n_{r\cdot}$
Total	$n_{\cdot1}$	$n_{\cdot2}$	$n_{\cdot3}$	$\cdots$	$n_{\cdot c}$	n

If two criteria of classification are independent, a *joint probability* is equal to the product of the two corresponding marginal probabilities.

Under the hypothesis of independence, then, the probability that a subject picked at random is characterized by level 1 of both criteria is estimated by $(n_{1\cdot}/n)(n_{\cdot1}/n)$. We can find the probability for every other cell in the same way.

To convert any estimated or expected cell probability to an *expected cell frequency, we multiply the probability* by n. The expected frequency for the first cell, which is the expected number of subjects characterized by level 1 of both criteria, is

(12.4.1)
$$E_{11} = \left(\frac{n_{1\cdot}}{n}\right)\left(\frac{n_{\cdot1}}{n}\right) n$$

if the criteria are independent. The n in the numerator will cancel one of the denominator n's, so that Equation 12.4.1 reduces to

(12.4.2)
$$E_{11} = \frac{(n_{1\cdot})(n_{\cdot1})}{n}$$

This leads to the short-cut procedure for computing expected cell frequencies. We simply divide the product of corresponding marginal totals by n.

Once we have computed the expected frequency for each cell, we compute X^2 by Equation 12.2.3. The analysis then proceeds as explained in Section 12.3. The following example illustrates the chi-square test for independence.

EXAMPLE 12.4.1 Employees of Ibanez Market Analysts wish to know whether they can conclude that, for adults in a certain city, the make of car driven is associated with the driver's area of residence. A random sample of 500 adult drivers is interviewed to determine what make of car they drive and in what area of the city they live. Table 12.4.2 shows the results.

TABLE 12.4.2   Five hundred drivers classified according to make of car driven and area of residence

Area of Residence	Make of Automobile			
	A	B	C	Total
1	52	64	24	140
2	60	59	52	171
3	50	65	74	189
Total	162	188	150	500

SOLUTION

1. *Hypotheses.*

H_0: Make of car driven and area of residence are independent.

H_1: The two criteria of classification are not independent.

2. *Test statistic.* Equation 12.2.3 is the appropriate test statistic.
3. *Significance level.* Let $\alpha = 0.05$.
4. *Decision rule.* In order to determine the critical value of χ^2, we must decide how many degrees of freedom are at our disposal. In general, for a contingency table consisting of r rows and c columns, the number of degrees of freedom equals $(r - 1)(c - 1)$. We can justify this method of calculating the degrees of freedom as follows. Consider any $r \times c$ contingency table with fixed marginal totals. Within any column, we have complete freedom in assigning numbers to $r - 1$ of the cells of that column. Once we have filled these $r - 1$ cells, the frequency of the rth cell is automatically determined, since the sum of the cell frequencies must equal the fixed total. In other words, we have no freedom in assigning a number to the last cell. Similarly, for any row, we are free to assign numbers to only $c - 1$ of the cells in that row. Thus, we can assign numbers to only $(r - 1) \times (c - 1)$ of the rc cells in the table. Hence, the degrees of freedom associated with the table are $(r - 1)(c - 1)$.

> For a contingency table, df = $(r - 1)(c - 1)$.

   In the present example, $r = 3$ and $c = 3$, so that the number of degrees of freedom available is $(3 - 1)(3 - 1) = 4$. The critical value of $\chi^2_{(0.95,4)}$ is 9.488. We will reject H_0, then, if the computed value of X^2 is equal to or greater than 9.488.
5. *Calculations.* Using the data from Table 12.4.2 and the short-cut rule, we compute the expected cell frequencies as follows:

$$E_{11} = \frac{(162)(140)}{500} = 45.36 \qquad E_{32} = \frac{(188)(189)}{500} = 71.06$$

$$E_{21} = \frac{(162)(171)}{500} = 55.40 \qquad E_{13} = \frac{(150)(140)}{500} = 42.00$$

TABLE 12.4.3   Observed and expected frequencies, Example 12.4.1

Area of Residence	Make of Automobile			
	A	B	C	Total
1	52(45.36)	64(52.64)	24(42.00)	140
2	60(55.40)	59(64.30)	52(51.30)	171
3	50(61.24)	65(71.06)	74(56.70)	189
Total	162	188	150	500

$$E_{31} = \frac{(162)(189)}{500} = 61.24 \qquad E_{23} = \frac{(150)(171)}{500} = 51.30$$

$$E_{12} = \frac{(188)(140)}{500} = 52.64 \qquad E_{33} = \frac{(150)(189)}{500} = 56.70$$

$$E_{22} = \frac{(188)(171)}{500} = 64.30$$

We can display the observed and expected frequencies together in a table, such as Table 12.4.3, where the expected frequencies are enclosed in parentheses. From the data in the table, we compute the following value of the test statistic:

$$X^2 = \sum \frac{(O_{ij} - E_{ij})^2}{E_{ij}} = \frac{(52 - 45.36)^2}{45.36} + \frac{(60 - 55.40)^2}{55.40}$$

$$+ \cdots + \frac{(74 - 56.70)^2}{56.70} = 19.825$$

6. *Statistical decision.* Since the computed value of X^2 is greater than 9.488, we reject the null hypothesis.
7. *Conclusion.* We conclude that in the city in which the study was conducted the area of residence and the make of car a person drives are related ($p < 0.005$).

Small Expected Frequencies In contingency-table analysis, some cells may yield small expected frequencies. This poses a possible threat to the validity of a chi-square test. Statisticians disagree as to how to handle this problem. However, many follow the recommendation of Cochran, who says that for tables with more than 1 degree of freedom a minimum expected frequency per cell of 1 is permissible if no more than 20% of the cells have expected frequencies of less than 5. We may combine adjacent rows and/or columns to satisfy this rule, so long as this does not violate the logic of the classification scheme.

THE 2 × 2 CONTINGENCY TABLE

When each criterion of classification has two levels, the resulting contingency table has two rows and two columns. Such a table is called a 2 × 2, or *fourfold, contingency table*. Table 12.4.4 shows a typical 2 × 2 contingency table, where a, b, c, and d are the observed frequencies in the four cells. We compute the X^2 value for a 2 × 2 contingency table by the following short-cut formula:

(12.4.3)
$$X^2 = \frac{n(ad - bc)^2}{(a + c)(b + d)(a + b)(c + d)}$$

This yields the same numerical result as Equation 12.2.3.

The 2 × 2 contingency table is not immune to the problem of small expected frequencies. Again Cochran's recommendations are often followed. According to Cochran, we should not use the χ^2 test with 2 × 2 contingency tables if $n < 20$, or if $20 < n < 40$ and any expected frequency is less than 5. If n is greater than 40, no expected frequency in a 2 × 2 contingency table should be less than 1.

EXAMPLE 12.4.2 Investigating the success of its interviewers, Junot Marketing Solutions finds that 176 out of 225 interviews attempted by trained interviewers are successfully completed. Of 310 interviews attempted by *un*trained interviewers, only 188 are successfully completed. Table 12.4.5 displays these data as a 2 × 2 contingency table.

The firm wishes to know whether these data provide sufficient evidence at the 0.05 level of significance to indicate a relationship between the training level of interviewers and the outcome of attempted interviews.

SOLUTION By Equation 12.4.3, we may compute

$$X^2 = \frac{535[(176)(122) - (188)(49)]^2}{(225)(310)(364)(171)} = 18.522$$

The computed value of X^2 exceeds the critical value of χ^2 in Table F for 1 degree of freedom and $\alpha = 0.05$. We conclude, then, that the two criteria are related ($p < 0.005$).

TABLE 12.4.4 A 2 × 2 contingency table

Second Criterion of Classification	First Criterion of Classification		
	1	2	Total
1	a	b	$a + b$
2	c	d	$c + d$
Total	$a + c$	$b + d$	n

TABLE 12.4.5 Interviews by outcome and training of interviewer

Outcome of Interview	Interviewer Training		
	Trained	Untrained	Total
Successful	176	188	364
Unsuccessful	49	122	171
Total	225	310	535

Yates' Correction In situations in which the chi-square test is used, the observed frequencies are discrete and the chi-square distribution used in the test is continuous. We often "correct" for this for a 2 × 2 contingency table. The correction procedure, conceived by F. Yates in 1934, is usually called *Yates' correction*. This procedure, used only in the 2 × 2 case, involves subtracting 0.5 from the absolute value of the difference between observed and expected frequencies before squaring. When Yates' correction is used, Equation 12.4.3 becomes

(12.4.4)
$$X^2 = \frac{n[|ad - bc| - 0.5n]^2}{(a + c)(b + d)(a + b)(c + d)}$$

Applying the correction procedure to the present example, we have

$$X^2 = \frac{535[|(176)(122) - (188)(49)| - 0.5(535)]^2}{(225)(310)(364)(171)} = 17.7$$

As we might expect with numbers this large, the effect is not dramatic. Although the correction procedure has the greatest effect when n is less than 100, in the past the procedure has been recommended for general use in the 2 × 2 case. Several statisticians, however, have questioned the use of Yates' correction, and many now recommend that the correction not be used. We do not use Yates' correction in the examples and exercises of this text.

STEPS IN TEST FOR INDEPENDENCE

The following is a summary of the steps involved in a chi-square test of independence.

1. From the population of interest, draw a simple random sample.
2. Display the data in a contingency table in which the rows represent one of the criteria of classification and the columns represent the other.
3. Compute the expected frequency for each cell using the probability law for independent events.

4. Compute X^2 by Equation 12.2.3 or 12.4.3 (for a 2×2 contingency table).

5. Determine the critical value of χ^2 from Table F.

6. If the computed X^2 is equal to or greater than the critical χ^2, reject H_0. Otherwise do not reject H_0.

EXERCISES

Perform each test at the indicated level of significance. Determine the p value.

12.4.1 Ⓒ During a market-research survey, Kruger Opinion Services obtains information on the education and socioeconomic status of 375 heads of households. In the following table, the respondents are cross-classified by the two criteria. Test at the 0.05 level the null hypothesis that socioeconomic status and education are independent.

			Education			
Socioeconomic Status	<8 Grades	Grades 8–12	Noncollege, Post–High School Training	Some College	College Degree	Total
1	10	7	3	4	1	25
2	14	10	7	4	2	37
3	9	25	13	18	3	68
4	7	9	38	44	6	104
5	3	8	14	18	62	105
6	2	3	8	10	13	36
Total	45	62	83	98	87	375

12.4.2 Ⓒ A government agency surveys unemployed persons who are seeking work. It prepares the following tabulation, by sex and skill level, of 532 interviewees. Do these data provide sufficient evidence to indicate that skill status is related to sex? Let $\alpha = 0.01$.

	Sex		
Skill Level	Male	Female	Total
Skilled	106	6	112
Semiskilled	93	39	132
Unskilled	215	73	288
Total	414	118	532

12.4.3 Ⓒ A guidance counselor asks a group of 110 junior high school students how much time they spend reading books and how much time they spend watching television. The students are then classified as high or low with respect to each activity. The following table shows the number in each cell when cross-classified. Do these data provide sufficient evidence to suggest, at the 0.05 level of significance, that the amounts of book reading and television viewing are related?

	Book Reading		
Television Viewing	Low	High	Total
Low	11	41	52
High	18	40	58
Total	29	81	110

12.4.4   [C] In a sample of 165 defective items produced in two factories operated by the same company, each item is classified according to whether the defect is due to poor workmanship or inferior material. The data are shown in the following table. Test at the 0.05 level the null hypothesis that cause of defect and factory of production are independent.

		Factory	
Cause of Defect	A	B	Total
Poor workmanship	21	72	93
Inferior material	46	26	72
Total	67	98	165

12.4.5   [C] In a transportation survey, 750 people employed in the downtown area of a large city are interviewed. They are cross-classified by their type of dwelling unit and their mode of travel to and from work. We want to see whether there is an association between the two variables. The following table shows the number of interviewees falling into each cell after they are cross-classified. Test H_0: type of dwelling unit and mode of transportation to work are independent. Let $\alpha = 0.05$.

	Type of Dwelling Unit				
Mode of Transportation	Single-Family	Two-Family	Multiple-Family	Other	Total
Automobile	148	140	102	97	487
Public transportation	49	52	64	60	225
Other	7	8	9	14	38
Total	204	200	175	171	750

12.5 TESTS OF HOMOGENEITY

We often want to explore the proposition that several populations are homogeneous with respect to some characteristic. We may, for example, wish to know whether people in several age groups have the same television-viewing habits. Or we may want to know whether shoppers from different socioeconomic backgrounds have different reasons for buying a certain product. Finally, we may want to know whether some raw material available from several vendors is homogeneous in quality.

Another way of stating the problem is to say that we are interested in testing the null hypothesis that several populations are homogeneous with respect to the proportion of subjects falling into several categories, or levels, of some criterion of classification. We may test the hypothesis by means of a *chi-square test of homogeneity*. We draw a random sample from each of the populations of interest. Then we find the number in each sample falling into each category. We can display the sample data in a contingency table like Table 12.4.1, in which the populations are one of the criteria of classification and the characteristic of interest is the other. In a contingency table constructed from sample data collected in this manner, either the rows or the columns, depending on which we use to indicate the different populations, are *fixed*. The reason is that we determine the sample size before we obtain knowledge about the characteristic of interest. The analytical procedure for performing a chi-square test of homogeneity is identical to that in Section 12.4 for performing a chi-square test of independence.

TESTS OF HOMOGENEITY AND INDEPENDENCE: A COMPARISON

Tests of independence use one sample; tests of homogeneity use two or more samples.

The difference between the chi-square test of homogeneity and the chi-square test of independence comes in the sampling procedure, the rationale underlying the calculation of expected frequencies, and the interpretation of results.

When we are using the chi-square test of independence, the typical sampling procedure is to select a single sample from a population, then cross-classify the sample entities on the basis of two criteria. When we are using the chi-square test of homogeneity, we identify the two or more populations of interest in advance and draw a sample from each. We then place the entities of the resulting samples in the various categories of the single variable of interest.

RATIONALE FOR DETERMINING EXPECTED FREQUENCIES

To get expected frequencies in the test of homogeneity, we pool the sample data.

We saw in Section 12.4 that for the chi-square test of independence the rationale underlying the calculation of expected frequencies is based on the probability of the joint occurrence of independent events. The rationale underlying the calculation of expected frequencies for the test of homogeneity is based on the assumption that, if the sampled populations are homogeneous, we can get the best estimate of the probability that a member of a given population falls into a given category of the variable of interest by pooling the information from the available samples.

Suppose, for example, that the sampled populations are male and female employees of a certain firm and the variable of interest is attitude toward management. Assume that there are two categories of the variable—satisfied with management and dissatisfied with it. Suppose that in a sample of 100 men, 30 are satisfied with management, whereas in a sample of 110 women, 45 are satisfied. If, as hypothesized, men and women are homogeneous with respect to satisfaction, we can pool the two samples and consider them a single sample from the same population with respect to the variable of interest. We would get the best estimate of the true proportion of men and the true proportion of women who are satisfied, then, by pooling the sample information. This gives $(30 + 45)/(100 + 110) = 0.3571$. Applying this proportion to the sample of 100 men gives an expected frequency of $(100)(0.3571) = 35.71$ satisfied men. Applying the proportion to the sample of 110 women yields an expected frequency of $(110)(0.3571) = 39.28$ satisfied women.

Note that the chi-square test of homogeneity is an extension of the procedure for testing hypotheses about the difference between two population proportions (Chapter 7). When there are two populations involved and the characteristic of interest has two categories, the chi-square test of homogeneity is an alternative and equivalent way of testing the null hypothesis that two population proportions are equal.

EXAMPLE 12.5.1 An analyst with Latimer Marketing, Inc., wants to know whether different ethnic groups differ in the types of television programs they prefer. A random sample is selected from each of three ethnic groups. Each person is asked to specify which of three types of television program he or she prefers. Table 12.5.1 shows the results, with expected frequencies in parentheses.

SOLUTION

1. *Hypotheses.*

   H_0: The three ethnic groups are homogeneous
   with respect to type of TV program preferred.

   H_1: The three ethnic groups are not homogeneous.

2. *Test statistic.* Equation 12.2.3 is the appropriate test statistic.
3. *Significance level.* Let $\alpha = 0.05$.
4. *Decision rule.* Reject H_0 if the computed value of X^2 is $\geq$ the critical value of χ^2.
5. *Calculations.* We find the expected frequencies by applying the rationale underlying the test of homogeneity. If the three sampled populations are homogeneous with respect to program preference, the best estimate of the true proportion of subjects in each ethnic group who prefer Type A is given by $140/400 = 0.35$. To find the expected frequency for Type A preference in each ethnic group, we multiply each sample total by 0.35. Thus, $(200)(0.35) = 70$, $(100)(0.35) = 35$, and $(100)(0.35) = 35$. Similar reasoning yields the other two columns of expected frequencies shown in Table 12.5.1.

TABLE 12.5.1 Three samples of persons classified by type of television program preferred (expected frequencies in parentheses)

Population (Ethnic Group)	Type of Program			Total
	A	B	C	
I	120(70)	30(67.50)	50(62.50)	200
II	10(35)	75(33.75)	15(31.25)	100
III	10(35)	30(33.75)	60(31.25)	100
Total	140	135	125	400

From the data in Table 12.5.1, we may compute

$$X^2 = \frac{(120 - 70)^2}{70} + \frac{(10 - 35)^2}{35} + \cdots + \frac{(60 - 31.25)^2}{31.25} = 180.495$$

6. *Statistical decision.* From Table F, the critical value of χ^2 for $\alpha = 0.05$ and 4 degrees of freedom is 9.488. Since the computed value, 180.495, is larger than 9.488, we reject H_0.
7. *Conclusion.* We conclude that the populations are not homogeneous with respect to the type of television program preferred ($p < 0.005$).

   As we have noted, the chi-square test of homogeneity applied to a 2×2 contingency table is equivalent to a test of the equality of two population proportions. To show this, let us refer to Example 7.9.1. We can display the data from that example in the 2×2 contingency table of Table 12.5.2. By Equation 12.4.3, we have

$$X^2 = \frac{400[(54)(123) - (171)(52)]^2}{(106)(294)(175)(225)} = 1.65$$

Since $1.65 < 3.841$, we cannot reject the null hypothesis that the two populations are homogeneous. Recall that in Chapter 7 we computed a z value of -1.28, which did not allow us to reject H_0: $p_1 = p_2$. Note that $(-1.28)^2 = 1.64$, which,

TABLE 12.5.2 Contingency-table display of data from Example 7.9.1

Background	Type of Store		Total
	Chain	Nonchain	
Rural	54	171	225
Urban	52	123	175
Total	106	294	400

except for rounding error, is equal to our computed value of X^2. Also note that the critical value of $\chi^2 = 3.841$ is equal to the square of the critical value of $z = 1.96$. These results should not be surprising in the light of the discussion in Section 12.2. We emphasize that these relationships hold only for a 2×2 contingency table in which X^2 has 1 degree of freedom. One difference between the two procedures is that the test using z can be treated as a one-sided test to reach a conclusion about the direction of the differences in population proportions.

We handle the problem of small expected frequencies in the case of the test of homogeneity in the way suggested in Section 12.4 for tests of independence. The analysis of 2×2 contingency tables is also the same for both tests.

STEPS IN THE TEST OF HOMOGENEITY

The following is a summary of the steps involved in a chi-square test of homogeneity.

1. Identify the two or more populations to be sampled.
2. Draw a simple random sample from each of the populations.
3. For each sample, count the number falling into each category of the variable of interest. These are the observed frequencies.
4. Calculate the expected frequency corresponding to each observed frequency.
5. Compute X^2 by Equation 12.2.3 or, if the data conform to a 2×2 contingency table, by Equation 12.4.3.
6. Determine the critical value of χ^2 by referring to Table F.
7. If the computed value of X^2 is equal to or greater than the critical value of χ^2, reject the null hypothesis that the populations are homogeneous.

COMPUTER **ANALYSIS**

Computers can be used to advantage in chi-square analyses. For instance, the STAT+ package allows the user to perform contingency table analyses and goodness-of-fit tests. After receiving the observed frequencies of a contingency table as input, for example, the program calculates and prints (on demand) the expected frequencies and the X^2 value. Figure 12.5.1 is the printout for the make of automobile/area of residence data of Example 12.4.1.

MINITAB computes expected frequencies for each cell of a contingency table when the data are read into columns a row at the time. The program also gives the degrees of freedom and the computed chi-square value. In addition, MINI-

FIGURE 12.5.1   STAT+ printout for Example 12.4.1

```
            C O N T I N G E N C Y   T A B L E   D A T A
            E X P E C T E D   F R E Q U E N C I E S

                 Autoarea

       Col          A         B          C
       Row                                        Totals

       1           45.4      52.6       42.0       140
       2           55.4      64.3       51.3       171
       3           61.2      71.1       56.7       189
       Totals      162       188        150        500


            C O M P U T E D   R E S U L T S
            F R O M   C H I - S Q U A R E
       C O N T I N G E N C Y   A N A L Y S I S


   Chi-Square analysis of the 3 by 3 AUTOAREA
   problem yields Chi-Square = 19.82 with 4 degrees
   of freedom.
```

FIGURE 12.5.2   MINITAB printout for the data of Example 12.4.1

```
MINITAB    MTB > READ C1-C3
           DATA> 52 64 24
           DATA> 60 59 52
           DATA> 50 65 74
           DATA> END
                  3 ROWS READ
           MTB > CHISQUARE C1-C3

           Expected counts are printed below observed counts
                           C1         C2         C3       Total
                  1         52         64         24        140
                         45.36      52.64      42.00

                  2         60         59         52        171
                         55.40      64.30      51.30

                  3         50         65         74        189
                         61.24      71.06      56.70

           Total         162        188        150        500

           ChiSq = 0.972 + 2.452 + 7.714 +
                   0.381 + 0.436 + 0.010 +
                   2.062 + 0.517 + 5.278 = 19.822

           df = 4
```

TAB prints the $(O - E)^2/E$ quantity for each cell. Figure 12.5.2 shows the data entry and the resulting printout when MINITAB is used with the data of Example 12.4.1.

EXERCISES

Perform each test at the indicated level of significance. Determine the p value.

12.5.1   Ⓒ In a study to evaluate instruction in technical writing, a group of firms submit 110 pieces of technical writing done by members of their staffs who have had training in technical writing. The firms also submit 120 pieces of technical writing by staff members without training in technical writing. A panel of judges rates each article as superior, acceptable, or inferior. The following table shows the number of articles from each group falling into each category. Do the data provide sufficient evidence to indicate that the samples came from different populations? Let $\alpha = 0.05$.

| | **Rating** | | | |
Previous Training	Superior	Acceptable	Inferior	Total
Yes	48	39	23	110
No	12	36	72	120
Total	60	75	95	230

12.5.2   Ⓒ Mandeville Manufacturing Company has a large plant in each of three sections of the country. Six months after a change in working conditions and employee benefits is introduced at the three factories, 250 employees from each plant are randomly selected and asked to rate the degree of their satisfaction with the new system. The following table shows the results. Do these data provide sufficient evidence at the 0.05 level of significance to suggest that the employees at the different plants are not homogeneous with respect to satisfaction with the new system?

| | **Degree of Satisfaction** | | | | |
Factory	Very Satisfied	Satisfied	Dissatisfied	Very Dissatisfied	Total
1	135	70	25	20	250
2	145	80	15	10	250
3	140	75	20	15	250
Total	420	225	60	45	750

12.5.3   Ⓒ Managers may be characterized as traditional or democratic, depending on their management style. A professor of management at a university believes that employees working under democratic managers are more loyal to the organization for which they work than employees working under traditional managers. To find out whether this theory would be supported, the professor conducts a study in which a sample of employees is selected from each of the two populations. Each employee is then classified as loyal or not loyal to the organization for which he or she works. The results are as follows. Can we conclude from these data that the professor's belief is correct? Let $\alpha = 0.05$.

Loyal to Organization?	Management Style		
	Traditional	Democratic	Total
Yes	75	180	255
No	125	70	195
Total	200	250	450

12.5.4 [C] A consultant with Nash Management Concepts wishes to know whether he can conclude that executives with a graduate degree in business administration are more innovative in the performance of their duties than executives who do not hold such a degree. A sample is selected from each of the two populations, and the performance of each executive in the two samples is analyzed by a management consulting firm. On the basis of these analyses, each executive is then categorized as either innovative or not innovative. The results are as follows. Can we conclude from these data that the two populations differ with respect to the proportion of innovative executives? Let $\alpha = 0.05$.

Innovative?	Graduate Degree in Business Administration?		
	Yes	No	Total
Yes	120	90	210
No	50	120	170
Total	170	210	380

SUMMARY

In this chapter, you used the chi-square distribution to analyze frequency data. The chapter presents three types of tests: goodness-of-fit tests, tests of independence, and tests of homogeneity. It also presented methods for handling small expected frequencies.

You learned that the test of goodness of fit is useful for testing the null hypothesis that data available for analysis were drawn from a population that follows some specified distribution, such as the binomial, the Poisson, the normal, or the uniform. Sufficiently poor agreement between observed frequencies and the frequencies we would expect if the null hypothesis is true is taken as an indication that the null hypothesis is false.

The tests of independence and homogeneity are alike in that the arithmetic involved in calculating expected frequencies and the test statistic is the same. The two tests differ, however, with respect to the hypothesis they test, the rationale underlying the computation of expected frequencies, the way in which the data are typically collected, and the interpretation of the results.

The test of independence concerns the relationship between two variables in a single population, whereas the test of homogeneity has to do with whether or not categories of a single variable are represented in the same proportions in two or more populations.

The rationale underlying the calculation of expected frequencies for the test of independence is based on a probability law that states that if two events are independent, the probability of their joint occurrence is equal to the product of the probabilities of the individual occurrences of the two events. The rationale underlying the calculation of expected frequencies for the test of homogeneity is as follows: If, as stated in the null hypothesis, the populations are homogeneous with respect to some variable, we can obtain the best estimates of the probabilities that sample entities fall into the various categories of the variable by pooling the sample data.

When we anticipate a test of independence, we select a random sample from a single population and then cross-classify the sample entities according to the two variables of interest. For the test of homogeneity, we identify two or more populations and draw a sample from each. We then classify sample entities in each sample on the basis of the single variable of interest.

Of course, we interpret the results of independence and homogeneity in terms of independence and homogeneity, respectively.

REVIEW EXERCISES

1. How can a chi-square distribution be derived from a normal distribution?

2. What are the mean and variance of a chi-square distribution?

3. How do you compute degrees of freedom for the chi-square goodness-of-fit test?

4. State Cochran's rule for handling small expected frequencies in (a) goodness-of-fit tests, (b) contingency tables in general, (c) 2×2 contingency tables.

5. What is a contingency table?

6. How are degrees of freedom computed for contingency tables?

7. Explain the rationale behind the method of computing the expected frequencies in a test of independence.

8. Explain the difference between a test of independence and a test of homogeneity.

9. Over a period of three months, Ogden Enterprises observes the following distribution of employee terminations. Test the goodness of fit of these data to a Poisson distribution, using the χ^2 test. Let $\alpha = 0.05$.

No. of terminations	0	1	2	3	4	5	6
No. of days this no. of terminations was observed	7	17	28	20	10	6	2

10. The following is a frequency distribution of the difference between the yearly high and low stock prices for a sample of 115 stocks for a recent year. Test the null hypothesis that these data come from a population of normally distributed values. Let $\alpha = 0.05$. Determine the p value.

Difference	Number of Stocks
0–4.999	3
5.000–9.999	27
10.000–14.999	35
15.000–19.999	25
20.000–24.999	8
25.000–29.999	10
30.000–34.999	4
35.000–39.999	1
40.000–44.999	2
	115

11. Ⓒ The health records of 280 Pegram Laboratories employees who were ill during a year show the following distribution by sex and severity of illness. Do these data provide sufficient evidence at the 0.05 level of significance to indicate that sex and severity of illness are related? Determine the p value.

Severity of Illness	Sex		Total
	Male	Female	
Nondisabling	90	90	180
Disabling but mobile	36	25	61
Confined to bed	24	15	39
Total	150	130	280

12. Ⓒ In a study of the price–quality relationship of certain household products, Rask Market Analysts had a group of homemakers test 135 products and rate them as poor, mediocre, or superior. The following table shows the 135 products cross-classified by the homemakers' ratings and the price category. Test at the 0.05 level the null hypothesis that price and quality are unrelated. Determine the p value.

Rating	Price Category			Total
	Low	Medium	High	
Poor	15	8	7	30
Mediocre	10	40	14	64
Superior	5	12	24	41
Total	30	60	45	135

13. Ⓒ A researcher selects a random sample from the regular customers of each of three shopping centers. The researcher then determines the distance of each customer's residence from the shopping center. The following table shows the distribution by distance of residence for the 500 customers of the three shopping centers. Do these data provide sufficient evidence to suggest that these shopping centers are not homogeneous with respect to distances of residences of their regular shoppers? Let $\alpha = 0.05$. Determine the p value.

	Shopping Center			
Distance of Residence	**A**	**B**	**C**	**Total**
0–5.0	110	80	87	277
5.1–20.0	40	55	57	152
20.1 and over	20	25	26	71
Total	170	160	170	500

14. ☐ In a study of outdoor recreation, researchers select a random sample from among the adult males working in a metropolitan area. Subjects are classified on the basis of their occupation and the extent to which they pursue outdoor activities such as hunting, fishing, camping, and outdoor sports. The results are as given in the following table. Do these data provide sufficient evidence to indicate a lack of independence between occupation and extent of participation in outdoor activities? Let $\alpha = 0.05$, and determine the p value.

	Extent of Participation				
Occupation	**Seldom or Never**	**Occasionally**	**Frequently**	**Very Frequently**	**Total**
Professional	10	10	20	60	100
Executive	10	10	25	65	110
Other white collar	25	30	30	65	150
Skilled labor	25	20	35	40	120
Unskilled labor	45	40	25	20	130
Total	115	110	135	250	610

15. ☐ Market researchers select samples of adults from each of two communities. Respondents are asked to indicate the extent to which they are satisfied with the shopping facilities available to residents of their community. The results are as given in the following table. Do these data provide sufficient evidence to indicate a lack of homogeneity between the two communities with regard to extent of residents' satisfaction with available shopping facilities? Let $\alpha = 0.05$, and determine the p value.

	Community	
Degree of Satisfaction	**A**	**B**
Very satisfied	40	60
Satisfied	70	90
Dissatisfied	60	30
Very dissatisfied	30	20
Total	200	200

16. Ⓒ In a taste test to study the acceptability of a coffee substitute, each member of a panel of 25 coffee drinkers is given coffee (C) and the coffee substitute (S) in six different taste tests. The panelists indicate which of the two they prefer. They are not told which is coffee and which is the coffee substitute. The order in which the two beverages are presented to each panelist is randomized at each test. The results are as given in the following table. Test the null hypothesis that the number of times coffee is chosen follows a binomial distribution. Let $\alpha = 0.05$, and determine the p value.

Taste Test

Panelist	1	2	3	4	5	6	Number of Times C Preferred
1	C	C	S	S	S	S	2
2	S	S	C	C	C	S	3
3	C	C	C	S	C	C	5
4	S	S	C	S	C	S	2
5	S	C	S	S	C	S	2
6	S	C	S	S	S	S	1
7	S	S	S	S	S	C	1
8	S	S	S	C	S	C	2
9	S	S	S	S	S	S	0
10	S	S	C	S	S	C	2
11	S	S	S	S	C	C	2
12	C	S	S	S	S	S	1
13	C	S	S	C	S	C	3
14	S	S	S	C	C	S	2
15	S	C	C	C	C	S	4
16	C	C	S	S	S	C	3
17	S	C	S	S	S	S	1
18	C	C	S	S	C	C	4
19	C	S	S	S	S	S	1
20	C	S	C	S	S	S	2
21	C	C	S	S	S	C	3
22	S	S	S	S	C	S	1
23	C	C	S	S	C	C	4
24	S	S	S	C	S	S	1
25	C	S	S	C	S	S	2

17. In a study of public transportation in a certain city, researchers hypothesize that the distribution of the number of empty seats on buses arriving at a certain point during rush hour follows a Poisson distribution. A check of a random selection of 30 of these buses yields the following results. Do the observed data fail to support the hypothesis? Let $\alpha = 0.05$, and determine the p value.

No. of empty seats	0	1	2	3	4	5	6	7	8	9 or more
Observed frequency	1	6	5	6	5	3	2	1	1	0

18. Ⓒ An economist selects a sample of 200 executives from each of five industries. A questionnaire mailed to each executive asks: "Do you believe the rate of inflation will be higher during the coming year than last year?" The following table shows the results. Can we conclude that there is a lack of homogeneity among industries with regard to the executives' opinions on inflation? Let $\alpha = 0.05$.

			Industry		
Response to Question	**A**	**B**	**C**	**D**	**E**
Yes	150	100	75	170	90
No	50	100	125	30	110
	200	200	200	200	200

19. The following table shows the number of people boarding an elevator during 10–minute intervals. Can we conclude from these data that the sample is not from a Poisson distribution? Let $\alpha = 0.05$, and determine the p value.

No. of persons (x)	0	1	2	3	4	5	6	7	8	9	10	11	12	13	14	15	
No. of periods with x persons	5	10	15	18	20	25	33	28	24	20	17	12	8	4	2	1	Total: 242

20. Sassoon Graphics has found that about 85% of its accounts receivable are paid on time, 8% are paid after becoming 1 through 30 days delinquent, 6% are paid within the 31- through 60-day delinquency period, and 1% are paid after becoming 60 days delinquent or are not paid at all. A random sample of 500 of this year's accounts reveals the following payment status: paid on time, 405; 1–30 days delinquent, 50; 31–60 days delinquent, 40; over 60 days delinquent, 5. Does it appear that current accounts receivable fail to conform to the prior payment experience? Let $\alpha = 0.05$, and determine the p value.

21. In a certain area, the population consists of four ethnic groups in the following proportions:

Ethnic group	A	B	C	D
Proportion of population	0.13	0.05	0.08	0.74

A survey of 1,000 persons in the area employed in managerial and professional positions gives the following results:

Ethnic group	A	B	C	D	
No.	145	45	75	735	Total: 1,000

Do these data indicate that the ethnic-group composition of managers and professionals in the area is different from the ethnic-group composition of the area's population? Let $\alpha = 0.05$, and determine the p value.

22. Ⓒ Market researchers select a random sample from each of two populations of recent purchasers of new cars. Subjects in population A have recently bought a Make A car, and those in population B have recently bought a Make B car. Subjects are asked to indicate the degree to which they are satisfied or dissatisfied with their new car. The results are as given in the following table. Do these data provide sufficient evidence to indicate a lack of homogeneity between the two groups with respect to degree of satisfaction or dissatisfaction? Let $\alpha = 0.05$, and determine the p value.

	Make of Automobile Purchased	
Degree of Satisfaction/Dissatisfaction	A	B
Extremely satisfied	62	28
Mildly satisfied	24	18
Neutral	20	28
Mildly dissatisfied	8	10
Extremely dissatisfied	6	16
	120	100

23. Ⓒ A team of industrial psychologists selects a random sample from among the middle- and lower-echelon white-collar workers in a certain industry. Subjects are asked to indicate the strength of their expectations of achieving a top-level position in their firms. The results by age of respondent are shown in the following table. Do these data provide sufficient evidence to indicate a relationship between age and strength of expectation of achieving a top-level position? Let $\alpha = 0.05$, and determine the p value.

	Strength of Expectation			
Age	Low	High	Uncertain	Total
<25	10	95	20	125
25–34	20	110	20	150
35–44	20	60	20	100
44 or more	50	40	35	125
Total	100	305	95	500

24. Ⓒ A sociologist selects a sample of 200 ads from the media available in a city. The ads are then categorized on the basis of sex orientation and content. The results are as follows. Do these data provide sufficient evidence to indicate a lack of independence between the two variables? Let $\alpha = 0.05$.

	Sex Orientation			
Content	Masculine	Feminine	Neutral	Total
Adventure	60	10	5	75
Domestic	5	50	10	65
Nostalgic	15	10	35	60
Total	80	70	50	200

25. Ⓒ Each of a sample of 400 adults residing in the home city of a professional football team is asked, "Do you think this city should continue to be the home of a professional football team?" The responses by age of respondent are as shown in the following table. Do these data suggest a lack of independence between age and attitude toward the professional football team? Let $\alpha = 0.01$, and determine the p value.

Age of Respondent	Response		Total
	Yes	No	
Under 30	50	75	125
30–49	130	45	175
50 and older	60	40	100
Total	240	160	400

26. C Researchers with Taylor and Taylor Marketing, Inc., conduct a study of shoppers at the four leading department stores of a city. They select independent random samples of shoppers who shop primarily at each store. The following table shows the age distribution of shoppers. Do these data provide sufficient evidence to indicate a lack of homogeneity with respect to age among the sampled populations? Let $\alpha = 0.05$, and determine the p value.

Age Group	Store				Total
	A	B	C	D	
<25	80	40	90	50	260
25–35	60	60	80	40	240
36–45	30	50	45	75	200
Over 45	30	50	35	85	200
Total	200	200	250	250	900

27. C An ecologist investigates the extent to which officials of industrial firms in a certain area are concerned with control of environmental pollution. One of the questions asked is, "Does your firm have a policy regarding the implementation and/or maintenance of environmental pollution-control measures?" The following table shows responses by major industry type. Do these data suggest a lack of independence between type of industry and the presence or absence of a policy on pollution-control measures? Let $\alpha = 0.01$, and find the p value.

Industry Type	Responses		Total
	Yes	No	
A	5	35	40
B	15	15	30
C	10	15	25
D	15	45	60
E	35	15	50
Total	80	125	205

28. C Select a simple random sample of size 100 from the population of employed heads of households in Appendix II. Can you conclude from the information in your sample that sex and occupation are not independent? Let $\alpha = 0.05$, and find the p value.

29. Ⓒ During a market-research survey, Stubbs and Associates obtains information on the social class and major leisure-time activity of 375 heads of households. In the following table, the respondents are cross-classified by the two criteria. Test at the 0.01 level the null hypothesis that social class and major leisure-time activity are independent. What use can be made of the results of this study?

			Social Class			
Leisure-Time Activity	1	2	3	4	5	Total
A	10	7	3	4	1	25
B	14	10	7	4	2	37
C	9	25	13	18	3	68
D	7	9	38	44	6	104
E	3	8	14	18	62	105
F	2	3	8	10	13	36
Total	45	62	83	98	87	375

 30. In a random sample of 150 shoppers, each is allowed to choose one of three brands of facial tissue. The results are as follows: Brand A is chosen 35 times; Brand B, 55 times; and Brand C, 60 times. Do these data provide sufficient evidence to indicate that the three brands are not equally preferred? Let $\alpha = 0.05$.

 31. A random sample of 125 absentee reports filed during a year by employees of a large firm yielded the following information. Do these data provide sufficient evidence to indicate, at the 0.01 level of significance, that employee absenteeism tends to be higher on some days than on others? What use might management make of the results of this study?

Day of absence	M	T	W	Th	F
Number of absences	35	20	15	15	40

 32. Ⓒ One of the biggest problems with which users of sample surveys have to contend is that of nonresponse to mailed surveys. Many solutions to the problem have been proposed. One market-research analyst believes that mailed questionnaires printed on colored paper will be more likely to be returned than those printed on white paper. Each subscriber in a random sample of 500 subscribers to a general-interest magazine was sent the same questionnaire. Half were printed on white paper and half on colored paper. The results were as follows. Do these data provide sufficient evidence to indicate that people are more likely to respond to questionnaires printed on colored paper? Let $\alpha = 0.01$.

		Type of Paper	
Response	White	Colored	Total
Returned	75	158	233
Not returned	175	92	267
Total	250	250	500

33. Ⓒ The president of Trumbull Enterprises wishes to know whether the firm's white-collar and blue-collar employees differ with respect to their opinions on a proposed change in certain fringe benefits. A random sample drawn from each of the two populations yields the following results. Can we conclude from these data that the two populations differ with respect to their opinions regarding the proposal? Let $\alpha = 0.05$.

	Employee Category		
Opinion	White collar	Blue collar	Total
For	70	55	125
Against	30	95	125
Total	100	150	250

 34. Ⓒ A survey is conducted among employees of two different nonunionized firms. One of the questions on the survey is, "Are you in favor of unionization of your firm?" Of the 190 Firm A employees completing the questionnaire, 70 said no. Of 220 Firm B employees completing the questionnaire, 122 said no. On the basis of these results, can we conclude that the two populations differ with respect to their feelings about unionization? Let $\alpha = 0.05$.

 35. Ⓒ Webster Appliances, Inc., includes with each of its products a customer information/warranty card for the purchaser to return to the manufacturer. Two items of information are requested on the card:

1. The appliance was purchased by a
   Man _____
   Woman _____

2. The appliance was purchased at a
   Department store _____
   Other type of store _____

In a random sample of 350 returned cards, 130 stated that the appliance had been purchased by a man. Forty of the purchases by men had been made at department stores. Of the women respondents, 184 indicated that their purchase had been made at a department store. Do these numbers provide sufficient evidence to indicate a lack of independence between place of purchase and gender of purchaser? Let $\alpha = 0.05$.

 36. Ⓒ Data Set 9 in Appendix IV contains information on a population of 2,000 adults. A toothpaste manufacturer collected the data to determine whether the subjects' reaction to a new kind of toothpaste is related to their sex. Variable 1 is sex and is coded as follows:

Male = 1
Female = 2

Variable 2 is the subjects' reaction to the new toothpaste and is coded as follows:

Likes new toothpaste = 1

Indifferent = 2

Does not like new toothpaste = 3

Select a simple random sample of size 50 from this population and perform an appropriate test to determine whether your sample data provide sufficient evidence to enable you to conclude that there is a relationship between sex and reaction to the toothpaste. Let α = 0.05, and find the p value for the test.

For Exercises 37 through 51, do the following. Select a simple random sample of size 200 from the population of companies in Appendix III. Formulate and test an appropriate hypothesis about the independence of pairs of variables as indicated in the exercises that follow. Form appropriate categories for the two variables, and prepare a contingency table containing observed frequencies. Select the level of significance of your choice, follow the seven-step hypothesis-testing procedure, and find the p value for the test.

37. Ⓒ Can we conclude that assets and sales are related?

38. Ⓒ Can we conclude that assets and market value are related?

39. Ⓒ Can we conclude that assets and net profits are related?

40. Ⓒ Can we conclude that assets and cash flow are related?

41. Ⓒ Can we conclude that assets and number employed are related?

42. Ⓒ Can we conclude that sales and market value are related?

43. Ⓒ Can we conclude that sales and net profits are related?

44. Ⓒ Can we conclude that sales and cash flow are related?

45. Ⓒ Can we conclude that sales and number employed are related?

46. Ⓒ Can we conclude that market value and net profits are related?

47. Ⓒ Can we conclude that market value and cash flow are related?

48. Ⓒ Can we conclude that market value and number employed are related?

49. Ⓒ Can we conclude that net profits and cash flow are related?

50. Ⓒ Can we conclude that net profits and number employed are related?

51. Ⓒ Can we conclude that cash flow and number employed are related?

52. Ⓒ Use the data from the simple random sample that you drew for Exercises 37 through 51, and carry out an appropriate test to see whether we can conclude that assets are not a normally distributed variable.

53. Ⓒ Repeat Exercise 52 with sales.

54. Ⓒ Repeat Exercise 52 with market value.

55. Ⓒ Repeat Exercise 52 with net profits.

56. Ⓒ Repeat Exercise 52 with cash flow.

57. Ⓒ Repeat Exercise 52 with number employed.

58. The number of arrivals per hour of tourists at a downtown information center is tallied over a 100-hour period to determine whether the distribution of arrivals seems to

conform to a Poisson distribution. The following table gives the results. At $\alpha = 0.10$, what is your conclusion?

Arrivals per Hour	No. of Hours Observed
0	12
1	21
2	27
3	22
4	13
5	3
6	2
7	0
	100

59. The publisher of Sass Magazine wishes to determine whether or not the public appeal of the magazine differs in different geographic areas. To reach a conclusion, he divides the United States into four regions: north, south, east, and west. In each region, he selects 2,000 families at random to determine whether or not they subscribe to the magazine. The numbers of subscribers, respectively, for the four areas are 263, 321, 248, and 292. At a 0.05 level of significance, what should the publisher conclude?

60. We wish to know whether we can conclude that a single, six-sided die is not fair. In 180 rolls, sides 1 through 6 occurred 39, 28, 35, 24, 32, and 22 times, respectively. Let $\alpha = 0.01$.

61. A spinner with four stopping positions, lettered A, B, C, and D, is designed for use in a game. The specifications require that it be weighted in such a way that B occurs twice as often as A, C twice as often as B, and D twice as often as C. In order to confirm the accuracy of the weighting, the spinner is randomly spun 450 times. If the spinner stops at positions A, B, C, and D 22, 48, 128, and 252 times, respectively, is this sufficient evidence at the 0.05 level of significance to justify the conclusion that the spinner is not properly weighted?

62. You are asked to determine whether the preference for foreign-produced cars versus U.S.-produced cars differs in different geographical areas. To reach a conclusion, you select four cities from across the nation: A, B, C, and D. In each city, you ask 2,000 persons who purchased a new car during the last two years whether the last car they purchased was foreign or U.S.-built. The responses from the four cities are that 831, 726, 769, and 818, respectively, purchased a foreign-built car. At the 0.05 level of significance, what is your conclusion?

63. Refer to Exercise 58. Test for goodness of fit to a Poisson distribution with a mean of two arrivals per hour. With the Poisson parameter given, how are your computations and the results changed?

64. Refer to Exercise 7.9.1, in which there are 36 failures out of $n_A = 225$ trials and 45 failures out of $n_B = 225$ trials. Use a chi-square test to determine whether the sample failure rates are significantly different. Let $\alpha = 0.05$. Compare your results with those obtained when the test statistic was z.

65. Refer to Review Exercise 46 at the end of Chapter 7. In a sample of $n_A = 240$ people, 80 answer yes when asked whether they are bothered by air pollution. In an independent sample of $n_B = 250$ people, 90 answer yes. Use a chi-square test to see whether you can conclude that the two sampled populations differ with respect to air pollution problems. Let $\alpha = 0.05$, and compare your results with those obtained when z was the test statistic.

66. Refer to Review Exercise 57 at the end of Chapter 7. In a sample of 150 white-collar workers and an independent sample of 120 blue-collar workers, the numbers answering yes to a question were 29 and 34, respectively. Use a chi-square test to determine whether the sample results are significant at the 0.05 level. Compare your results with those obtained when the test statistic was z.

67. In a simple random sample of 300 employees of Corporation A, 157 favored a merger with Corporation B. In a random sample of 160 employees of Corporation B, 93 favored a merger with Corporation A. At the 0.10 level, is there a significant difference in the preferences of the two samples of employees regarding a potential merger? Use both the z and the X^2 test statistics to obtain your answer.

*68. As we have seen, the X^2 statistic allows us to decide whether or not there is likely to be an association between two categorical variables. The statistic, however, does not provide a completely satisfactory measure of the strength of the association between two such variables. There are several statistics available that measure the strength of the association, one of which is called the *Cramér statistic* after the man who first proposed it. The Cramér statistic, designated C, is computed from the data of a contingency table as follows: $C = \sqrt{X^2/n(t - 1)}$, where t is the number of rows or columns, whichever is smaller. The significance of C depends on the significance of X^2, which is tested as previously described to provide information regarding the significance of the C computed from it. A useful characteristic of C is the fact that it may be used to compare contingency tables of different sizes with respect to r and c and tables based on different sample sizes. Refer to Review Exercises 23 and 24. Compute C for each exercise and compare the results to decide for which case the association is stronger.

1. SHOPLIFTING

Retailers in the United States annually lose goods worth more than $5 billion because of shoplifting, according to Bellur. He cites other evidence to indicate the mammoth proportions of shoplifting in the United States. With these statistics as background, he designed a questionnaire to reveal more facts about shoplifting, shoplifters, and their victims.

A sample of 106 midwestern retailers completed the questionnaire. The following seven types of stores were represented in the sample: department, grocery, clothing, card and gift, drug, variety and discount, and specialty.

One question asked of retailers was, "Do you have a shoplifting problem?" (Yes or No). In testing the null hypothesis that the type of store is independent of the presence of a shoplifting problem, Bellur obtained an X^2 value of 32.60. What are the degrees of freedom for the test? Should the null hypothesis be rejected at the 0.05 level? Why? What is the p value for the test? What conclusion can one draw from these results? What assumptions are necessary?

Source: Venkatakrishna V. Bellur, "Shoplifting: Can It Be Prevented?" *Journal of the Academy of Marketing Science* 9 (1981), 78–87.

2. POPULAR MUSIC ARTISTS

The recording artist is one of the least examined aspects of the music industry, according to Denisoff and Bridges. They conducted a study that examined the "who-what-where" of performers and their music. They analyzed biographical data on 667 artists, classified as to musical style: (1) rock, (2) soul/rhythm and blues/disco, (3) "easy listening," (4) country and Western, (5) jazz, (6) classical, and (7) "other," which included comedy artists and purely electronic artists. They also classified the musicians in terms of such variables as education, stature (minor, marginal, or major artist), race, geographic region of origin, sex, and age. As part of their statistical analysis, Denisoff and Bridges cross-classified 580 artists on the basis of sex and musical style and computed a chi-square statistic of 41.13. What null hypothesis can one test with these data? Should the null hypothesis be rejected? Why or why not? Let $\alpha = 0.05$. Compute the p value for the test. What assumptions are required?

Source: R. Serge Denisoff and John Bridges, "Popular Music: Who Are the Recording Artists?" *Journal of Communication* 32 (Winter 1982), 132–142.

3. HAZARDS ASSOCIATED WITH ALTERNATIVE HEAT SOURCES

In response to rising fuel prices, many homeowners, landlords, and businesses have invested in improved insulation and alternative sources of heat. In fact, the presence of fuel-burning space heaters—especially those that burn wood— has become a status symbol for some homeowners.

These efforts by conservation-minded people, however, are not without potential hazards. Some authorities fear that improved insulation seals in stale (and possibly polluted) air along with warmth. Studies have also shown that fuel-burning space heaters are a major source of carbon monoxide.

In a study of the problem, Lao and others investigated 27 homes with fuel-burning space heaters. To see whether they could conclude that there is an association between type of fuel burned in the space heater and levels of carbon monoxide, they cross-classified the 27 homes on the basis of these two variables. They set up two categories of heat source (Wood and Other) and two categories of level of carbon monoxide (High and Low). Of the 10 homes using wood-burning heaters, 7 had high levels of carbon monoxide. Five of the homes that burned other types of fuel had high levels of carbon monoxide. What can we conclude from these results? State appropriate null and alternative hypotheses. Compute an appropriate test statistic. Let $\alpha = 0.05$, and find the p value for the test. What assumptions are necessary?

Source: Y. J. Lao, Ronald W. Smith, Terry L. Rich, and Trenton G. Davis, "Carbon Monoxide Levels in Homes with Fuel-Burning Space Heaters," *Journal of Environmental Health* 44 (January–February 1982), 180–182. In this study, a fuel-burning space heater was defined as any heater that burns wood, oil, or gas for the purpose of heating living space.

4. WAITING FOR A PHONE, PART II

Refer to the telephone experiment by Ruback, Pape, and Doriot discussed in the Statistics at Work section of Chapter 8. Because of the wide variability in the length of phone calls, the authors recoded time into two categories: less than three minutes and equal to or greater than three minutes. They then constructed a 2 (time categories) by 3 (experimental conditions) contingency table and performed a chi-square test. Use the raw data to recreate the authors' contingency table, compute the chi-square statistic, and test for significance at the 0.05 level. Is this a test of homogeneity or a test of independence?

Source: R. Barry Ruback, Karen D. Pape, and Philip Doriot, "Waiting for a Phone: Intrusion on Callers Leads to Territorial Defense," *Social Psychology Quarterly* 52 (1989), 232–241.

5. SMOKING IN PUBLIC

Professor Bikram Garcha directed a telephone survey in which 224 adult respondents were asked to provide information regarding their practices and attitudes with respect to cigarette smoking. As part of the survey, respondents were asked to indicate their level of agreement with the statement "Cigarette smoking should be banned in public places." The following table shows the results classified according to the gender of the respondent.

	Level of Agreement				
Gender	Strongly Agree	Agree	Neutral	Disagree	Strongly Disagree
Female	40	38	16	37	5
Male	16	25	11	25	11

Can we conclude on the basis of these data that, in the sampled population, males and females differ with respect to their levels of agreement on the banning of cigarette smoking in public places?

Source: Professor Bikram Garcha, Department of Decision Sciences, Georgia State University, Atlanta, GA. Used by permission.

6.   RISK IN A COMPLEX SOCIETY

"Much concern," says a representative of the Marsh & McLennan Companies, "is currently being expressed about the rapid proliferation of technology and the increased risk associated with contemporary life." In 1979 and 1980, Louis Harris and Associates, Inc., conducted a survey for the Marsh & McLennan Companies, Inc., in which the following broad areas of concern were explored:

> Risk in a Complex Society
> Individual Control of Risk
> Household Risk and Industrial Risk
> Energy and Risk
> Societal Responsibility for Safety
> Risk and Investment

The survey was based on personal interviews with samples from the following groups:

1. Chief executive officers or designated members of their company's executive committee drawn from the 1,506 largest publicly and privately held U.S. corporations ($n = 402$)

2. Institutional investors and corporate bankers ($n = 104$)

3. Members of Congress or their aides ($n = 47$)

4. Members of federal regulatory agencies ($n = 47$)

5. Adult members of the public aged 18 and over ($n = 1,488$)

The 1,488 members of the public, a nationwide sample, were interviewed by telephone for approximately 20 minutes; all other interviews were conducted in person and lasted about 45 minutes.

One of the items on the survey questionnaire was the following: "I would like to read you some statements people have made about various household and personal risks. For each statement please tell me whether you tend to agree or disagree."

WORK
STATISTICS AT WORK
STATISTICS AT WORK
STATISTICS

The following table shows one of the statements and the responses of the interviewees.

(Number of Respondents)	Top Corporate Executives (402)	Investors/ Lenders (104)	Congress (47)	Federal Regulators (47)	Public (1,488)
	%	%	%	%	%
On the whole, business does a good job of protecting the public from dangerous products and substances					
Agree	93	91	66	47	66
Disagree	5	7	30	49	31
Not sure	1	2	4	4	3

Convert the percentages to frequencies and perform a chi-square test to determine if there is a lack of homogeneity among the five groups with respect to their tendency to agree or disagree with the statement.

Source: *Risk in a Complex Society* (1980). Marsh & McLennan Companies, Inc., New York. © Marsh & McLennan 1980. Used by permission.

7. THE TYPE E WOMAN

In her book, *The Type E Woman,* Harriet B. Braiker defines a Type E woman as an overstressed, high-achieving woman caught in the trap of trying to be Everything to Everybody. The book contains a questionnaire designed to help women take stock of their ways of thinking about stress, as well as their typical stress habits and patterns. One of the items (Part I, No. 10) in the questionnaire is the statement "I feel like I'm being pulled in lots of different directions by the needs and expectations of others." The respondent is asked to indicate the frequency with which the statement applies to her by checking one of three responses: usually, sometimes, rarely.

Suppose samples of 100 executives, 150 secretaries, and 125 nonworking mothers complete the questionnaire with the following results with respect to Part I, No. 10.

	Usually	Sometimes	Rarely	Total
Executives	25	60	15	100
Secretaries	80	60	10	150

	Usually	**Sometimes**	**Rarely**	**Total**
Nonworking mothers	60	40	25	125
Total	165	160	50	375

Can we conclude that executives, secretaries, and nonworking mothers differ with respect to the frequency with which they feel as though they are being pulled in lots of different directions by the needs and expectations of others?

Source: Harriet B. Braiker, *The Type E Woman,* New York: Dodd, Mead & Company, 1986.

8.   BANKING INFORMATION SYSTEMS

Dr. Karen D. Loch was the principal investigator in a study of banking information systems. Among the data she collected for a sample of banks were demographic information on top management representatives and their opinions about their bank's information system. The following table shows the age of a top manager at 59 banks and the manager's indicated level of satisfaction with his or her bank's information system's ability to provide assistance in making quicker decisions. The following codes were used to indicate age and level of satisfaction:

Age
1 = 40 and under
2 = 41–50
3 = 51–60
4 = over 60
Level of Satisfaction (LOS)
1 = not at all satisfied
2 = minimally satisfied
3 = mostly satisfied
4 = very satisfied
5 = not sure

Bank	**Age**	**LOS**	**Bank**	**Age**	**LOS**
1	2	3	31	2	1
2	3	2	32	1	3
3	1	4	33	2	3
4	3	2	34	2	2
5	2	4	35	2	3
6	3	4	36	3	5
7	2	2	37	2	4
8	2	3	38	4	4
9	3	3	39	1	3
10	3	3	40	3	3

(table continues on next page)

Bank	Age	LOS	Bank	Age	LOS
11	Not given	3	41	2	4
12	3	3	42	3	3
13	3	4	43	2	4
14	2	3	44	3	4
15	1	4	45	2	2
16	3	4	46	2	3
17	1	3	47	3	3
18	2	2	48	1	4
19	2	3	49	3	4
20	3	3	50	3	3
21	3	3	51	3	4
22	2	2	52	3	3
23	1	2	53	3	2
24	1	4	54	2	4
25	2	3	55	1	3
26	4	4	56	1	2
27	1	2	57	1	3
28	2	3	58	2	3
29	2	3	59	2	3
30	2	2			

On the basis of these data, can we conclude that there is a relationship between age and level of satisfaction?

Source: Professor Karen D. Loch, Georgia State University. Used by permission.

9. HOUSEHOLD STRUCTURE AND WOMEN'S ECONOMIC ACTIVITY

One of the purposes of a study by Wong and Levine was to isolate the effect of a specific characteristic of household structure, the presence of a "mother substitute," as a determinant of participation in economic activity. Subjects were married women who had given birth within the last five years. The data were from a Mexican National Demographic Survey. Among the variables studied were employment status and the presence in the household of another unemployed female thirteen years old or older. The following table shows the study sample cross-classified by these two variables:

Presence of Other Female	Employed		Total
	No (%)	Yes (%)	**Total**
No (%)	1,659 (60.4)	253 (9.2)	1,912 (69.6)
Yes (%)	679 (24.7)	155 (5.7)	834 (30.4)
Total	2,338 (85.1)	408 (14.9)	2,746 (100.0)

May we conclude, on the basis of these data, that the two variables are independent? Let $\alpha = 0.01$, and find the p value.

Source: Rebeca Wong and Ruth E. Levine, "The Effect of Household Structure on Women's Economic Activity and Fertility: Evidence from Recent Mothers in Urban Mexico," *Economic Development and Cultural Change*, 41 (1992), 89–102.

SUGGESTIONS FOR FURTHER READING

The following book presents a thorough treatment of the chi-square distribution.

Lancaster, H. O. (1969). *The Chi-Squared Distribution*. Wiley, New York.

Contingency tables and the analysis of categorical data in general are covered in the following books:

Everitt, B. S. (1977). *The Analysis of Contingency Tables*. Halstead, New York.

Feinberg, Stephen E. (1980). *The Analysis of Cross-Classified Categorical Data*, 2nd ed. MIT Press, Cambridge, Mass.

Fleiss, Joseph L. (1981). *Statistical Methods for Rates and Proportions*, 2nd ed. Wiley, New York.

Gokhale, D. V., and Solomon Kullback (1978). *The Information in Contingency Tables*. Marcel Dekker, New York.

Maxwell, A. E. (1961). *Analysing Qualitative Data*. Wiley, New York.

Plackett, R. L. (1981). *The Analysis of Categorical Data*, 2nd ed. Macmillan, New York.

Upton, Graham J. G. (1978). *The Analysis of Cross-Tabulated Data*. Wiley, New York.

Problems associated with estimating parameters independently of the sample and estimating parameters from ungrouped data for use in goodness-of-fit tests involving grouped data are discussed in the following articles:

Chase, G. R. (1972). "On the Chi-Square Test When the Parameters Are Estimated Independently of the Sample," *Journal of the American Statistical Association* 67:609–611.

Dahiya, Ram C., and John Gurland (1972). "Pearson Chi-squared Test of Fit with Random Intervals," *Biometrika* 59:147–153.

Watson, G. S. (1957). "The χ^2 Goodness-of-Fit Test for Normal Distributions," *Biometrika* 44:336–348.

———— (1958). "On Chi-Square Goodness-of-Fit Tests for Continuous Distributions," *Journal of the Royal Statistical Society* (Series B) 20:44–72.

———— (1959). "Some Recent Results in Chi-Square Goodness-of-Fit Tests," *Biometrics* 15:440–468.

The problems of small expected frequencies are discussed in the following articles:

Cochran, W. G. (1952). "The χ^2 Test of Goodness of Fit," *Annals of Mathematical Statistics* 23:315–345.

———— (1954). "Some Methods for Strengthening the Common χ^2 Tests," *Biometrics* 10:417–451.

Roscoe, John T., and J. A. Byars (1971). "An Investigation of the Restraints with Respect to Sample Size Commonly Imposed on the Use of the Chi-Square Statistic," *Journal of the American Statistical Association* 66:755–759.

Tate, Merle W., and L. A. Hyer (1969). "Significance Values for an Exact Multinomial Test and Accuracy of the Chi-Square Approximation," U.S. Department of Health, Education and Welfare, Office of Education, Bureau of Research, August 1969.

Yarnold, James K. (1970). "The Minimum Expectation in χ^2 Goodness-of-Fit Tests and the Accuracy of Approximations for the Null Distribution," *Journal of the American Statistical Association* 65:864–886.

Yates' correction is discussed in the following articles:

Camilli, Gregory, and Kenneth D. Hopkins (1978). "Applicability of Chi-Square to 2×2 Contingency Tables with Small Expected Cell Frequencies," *Psychological Bulletin* 85:163–167.

Conover, W. J. (1974). "Some Reasons for Not Using the Yates Continuity Correction on 2 × 2 Contingency Tables," *Journal of the American Statistical Association* 69:374–376.

Grizzle, J. E. (1967). "Continuity Correction in the χ^2 Test for 2 × 2 Tables," *American Statistician* 21 (Oct):28–32.

13

Nonparametric Statistics

Chapter Objectives: This chapter introduces you to some statistical techniques that are often characterized as "quick and dirty" because you can usually do the calculations quickly and because the assumptions underlying their use are not as stringent as those underlying most of the other procedures discussed in this text. After studying this chapter and working the exercises, you should be able to

1. List the advantages and disadvantages of nonparametric statistical procedures.
2. Determine when nonparametric statistical procedures are appropriate.
3. Perform the analysis for each of the following statistical procedures: (a) the one-sample runs test, (b) the Wilcoxon test, (c) the Mann-Whitney test, (d) the sign test, (e) the Kruskal-Wallis one-way analysis of variance, (f) the Friedman two-way analysis of variance, (g) the Spearman rank correlation, and (h) nonparametric regression analysis.

13.1   INTRODUCTION

Most of the inferential procedures that we have discussed have two characteristics in common. First, they are concerned with population *parameters*. Second, their validity depends on a set of rigid *assumptions*. (There is one inferential procedure to which this statement does not apply. We discuss it below.) The objectives in estimation and hypothesis testing were to estimate and test hypotheses about such parameters as a population mean, a population proportion, and a population variance. For an example of a set of assumptions underlying an inferential procedure, consider the *t* test for testing the null hypothesis that two population means are equal. The use of this test rests on the assumption that the populations of interest are normally distributed with equal variances.

The one inferential procedure covered earlier that is not concerned with population parameters and does not rest on a rigid set of assumptions is the use of the chi-square distribution in tests of goodness of fit and independence.

We refer to inferential procedures such as the *t* test and analysis-of-variance methods as *parametric procedures* because they are concerned with population parameters. The body of statistical theory and methodology of which they are a part is called *parametric statistics*.

Inferential procedures such as the chi-square tests of goodness of fit and independence, which are not concerned with population parameters or do not depend on rigid assumptions about the distribution of the relevant population, are called *nonparametric procedures*. The body of statistical theory and methodology relating to these procedures is called *nonparametric statistics*.

Some statisticians distinguish between procedures that are not concerned with parameters and procedures that do not depend on the distribution of the parent population. They refer to only the former as nonparametric statistics and call the latter *distribution-free statistics*. At an elementary level of discussion, the two are usually treated under the single heading of nonparametric statistics.

Here we discuss only a few of the more widely used nonparametric procedures. You can find a deeper treatment of the subject in the many textbooks on nonparametric statistics, such as those listed at the end of this chapter.

13.2   WHEN TO USE NONPARAMETRIC STATISTICS

Nonparametric statistics is most often used in four situations.

1. *The data do not meet the assumptions for a parametric test.* For example, the nature of the hypothesis to be tested may suggest the use of the *t* test. But this test may not be appropriate because the sample on which the test is to be based was drawn from a population known to be substantially nonnormally dis-

tributed. In such a case, we may use an alternative nonparametric test that does not depend on the assumption of a normally distributed parent population.

2. *The data consist merely of ranks.* For example, consumers may be asked to indicate how much they like several brands of coffee. They may not be able to assign each brand a numerical score representing how much they like it, but they may be able to rank the brands in order of preference. The analysis, then, is based on ranks. Data consisting of ranks are said to be measured on a weak measurement scale. Most parametric tests require a stronger measurement scale, but generally the nonparametric tests do not. Section 13.3 offers a more complete discussion of measurement scales.

3. *The question to be answered does not involve a parameter.* For example, if we wish to reach a decision about whether a sample is a random sample, we use the appropriate nonparametric test.

4. *We need results quickly.* As a rule, the calculations required by the nonparametric procedures are more quickly and easily carried out than those required by parametric ones. The calculations for some of the nonparametric procedures are so easy that they can be done right at the data-collection site—in a manufacturing plant, for example—by someone relatively unskilled in statistics or mathematics.

13.3 MEASUREMENT AND MEASUREMENT SCALES

We discussed and defined measurement and the various measurement scales—nominal, ordinal, interval, and ratio—in Chapter 1. The issue of measurement and measurement scales frequently comes to the forefront when a decision is being made as to whether one should use a nonparametric statistical technique rather than a parametric technique. In fact, a frequent motivation for considering the use of a nonparametric technique is the manner in which the variable of interest is measured. Many practicing statisticians maintain that parametric techniques should be used only with variables that are measured on either the interval or the ratio scale. At this point, therefore, it is appropriate that readers refer back to Chapter 1 and refresh their memories on the topic of measurement and measurement scales.

13.4 ADVANTAGES AND DISADVANTAGES OF NONPARAMETRIC STATISTICS

There are both advantages and disadvantages associated with the use of nonparametric statistical procedures.

ADVANTAGES

1. The probability statements accompanying the statistical tests are usually exact.
2. The calculations are usually easily and rapidly performed.

3. The assumptions are usually few and easily met.

4. As a consequence of item 3, nonparametric procedures are widely applicable.

5. We can analyze data measured on a weak measurement scale by nonparametric techniques.

DISADVANTAGES

1. Nonparametric procedures, because of their simplicity and ease of computation with small samples, may be applied in cases in which parametric procedures would be more appropriate. Such a practice is inefficient and should be avoided.

2. For large samples, the calculations may become burdensome unless one uses approximations.

INFORMATION CONTENT OF DATA AND CHOICE OF STATISTICAL TECHNIQUE

The person faced with the necessity of making a decision regarding a choice between a parametric statistical technique or a nonparametric technique should consider the information content of the data at hand. Numbers, which are the raw material of statistical analysis, contain information. Generally, the higher the measurement scale that gave rise to the numbers, the richer the information content of the numbers.

EXAMPLE 13.4.1 Management at Brenau Industries has been motivated to take a greater interest in the health of the company's employees as a means of possibly reducing absenteeism, increasing efficiency, and decreasing insurance and related costs. Overweight has been cited as one component of health on which to concentrate. Consider, then, the investigator who must collect and subsequently perform certain analyses on measurements obtained on the variable "weight of employees."

The investigator has several options as to the method of obtaining measurements that will provide information on the variable weight. The first method that comes to mind is the obvious one—have each employee stand on a scale, and record such measurements as 150 pounds, 210 pounds, and so on. The data might be more simply categorized as "overweight" and "not overweight." Finally, for some purposes, it might be useful to rank the employees on the basis of weight from lightest to heaviest.

Thus, we see that the same variable may yield measurements that satisfy the definitions of three of the measurement scales discussed in Chapter 1. The individual weights represent measurement on the ratio scale. Categorization of employees as to whether they are overweight or not overweight results in a nominal scale measurement. When we rank employees on the basis of their weights, the result is an ordinal measurement scale.

Consider now the amount of information conveyed by each of these scales. The individual weights contain the most information, and we have seen through our study of various statistical techniques in preceding chapters how such measurements are used to compute means, variances, and correlation coefficients. The ranks, or ordinal data, contain less information. So far we have not encountered a statistical technique that makes use of ordinal data. Such techniques come under the heading of nonparametric statistical techniques and will be presented in this chapter. The nominal data contain the least amount of information. We have seen that such data may be analyzed by means of the chi-square statistic.

COMPUTER **ANALYSIS**

In many cases, the calculations required in nonparametric statistical procedures may be quickly and easily carried out on a calculator. In other situations, especially when sample sizes are large, the user of nonparametric statistics will find a computer helpful. Most general statistics software packages contain programs for computing selected nonparametric test statistics. There are also many software packages available that are devoted exclusively to nonparametric statistics. On the other hand, users who know how to program may choose to write their own nonparametric statistics programs.

13.5 THE ONE-SAMPLE RUNS TEST

A run is a sequence of like symbols preceded and followed by either a different symbol or no symbol at all.

We have shown the importance of random samples in statistical inference. It is valuable to have a procedure for testing the null hypothesis that a sample is indeed a random sample. This section presents a test based on the number of *runs* present in the sample.

> A *run* is a sequence of like symbols preceded and followed by either a different symbol or no symbol at all.

Two types of symbols are used. One or the other is assigned to each observation in the sample, depending on whether the observation is greater than or less than the sample median or mean. If we display the symbols in the order in which the numerical values they represent were selected, we can easily recognize the number of runs in the data. Suppose, for example, that we observe the following sequence of symbols in a sample of size 10, where *B* stands for a value below the median and *A* represents a value above the median:

$$BBBBB \qquad AAAAA$$

In this sequence there are only two runs. This seems to be too few to support a hypothesis of randomness. By contrast, consider the following sequence:

$$B A B A B A B A B A$$

This sequence contains ten runs. Again we suspect a lack of randomness. Intuitively, it seems that some systematic, rather than random, procedure is operative. In a particular sequence, then, we suspect a lack of randomness if there appear to be either too few or too many runs.

Finally, suppose that we observe the following sequence, which contains six runs:

$$B \quad A \quad BB \quad A \quad BB \quad AAA$$

This sequence seems to be rather well mixed. There does not appear to be any reason to suspect a lack of randomness.

To determine whether an observed number of runs is small enough or large enough to cause rejection of the null hypothesis that the sample is a random one, we can consult Table J of Appendix I. To use Table J, we designate the number of symbols of one kind as n_1 and the number of symbols of the other kind as n_2. (The total sample size is $n_1 + n_2 = n$.) Table J gives critical values of r, the number of runs, for values of n_1 and n_2 through 20. If the observed number of runs is less than or equal to the appropriate critical value of r in Table Ja or greater than or equal to the appropriate critical value of r in Table Jb, we can reject the null hypothesis of randomness at the 0.05 level of significance.

In the first sequence given previously, we have $n_1 =$ number of B's $= 5$, $n_2 =$ number of A's $= 5$, and $r = 2$. Table Ja indicates that we can reject the hypothesis of randomness in that sequence at the 0.05 level of significance, since the critical value is 2. For the second sequence, where $n_1 = 5$, $n_2 = 5$, and $r = 10$, Table Jb shows that we can reject the hypothesis of randomness at the 0.05 significance level, since here the critical value is 10. The last sequence, where $n_1 = 5$, $n_2 = 5$, and $r = 6$, may be in random order, since, by Tables Ja and Jb, $r = 6$ is not significant.

The use of the runs test is not limited to testing the null hypothesis that a sample is random. We can apply it to any sequence for randomness, no matter how the sequence is generated. Sequences that we may test for randomness include, for example, the arrangement of males and females in a cafeteria line, the presence and absence of rain over a period of several days, the wins and losses of an athletic team, or the sequence of correct answers to a true-false quiz. The runs test is frequently used to determine whether the residuals observed as part of a regression are likely to have come from a population in which the assumption of independent error terms is violated. A sufficiently pronounced tendency toward long sequences of observed residuals with the same sign is taken as evidence of a lack of independence of error terms in the population.

EXAMPLE 13.5.1 The quality-control department at Zeno Soap Company requires the mean weight of packages of its product to be 17 ounces. A sample of 20 consecutive packages filled by the same machine is taken from the assembly line and weighed, with the following results (in ounces): 17.9, 17.5, 17.2, 17.3, 16.5, 16.8, 16.7, 17.2, 17.4, 17.6, 17.5, 17.8, 16.8, 16.5, 16.6, 17.7, 17.6, 17.7, 17.8, 17.2. Do these data provide sufficient evidence to indicate a lack of randomness in the pattern of overfills and underfills?

SOLUTION

1. *Hypotheses.*

H_0: Overfills and underfills occur at random.

H_1: Overfills and underfills do not occur at random.

2. *Test statistic.* The test statistic is r, the number of runs present in the sample data.
3. *Significance level.* Let $\alpha = 0.05$.
4. *Decision rule.* Suppose that we let n_1 be the number of weights less than the desired mean of 17 ($n_1 = 6$) and n_2 be the number of weights greater than the desired mean of 17 ($n_2 = 14$). Reference to Table J shows that the critical values of r are 5 and 13. The decision rule, then, is: Reject H_0 if the observed value of r is either ≤ 5 or ≥ 13.
5. *Calculations.* Examination of our sample data shows that they contain 5 runs.
6. *Statistical decision.* We can reject the null hypothesis of randomness at the 0.05 level of significance.
7. *Conclusion.* We conclude that overfills and underfills do not occur at random.

THE LARGE-SAMPLE CASE

When either n_1 or n_2 is larger than 20, we cannot use Table J to test for significance. For samples too large to use Table J, we can compute the following test statistic:

(13.5.1)
$$z = \frac{r - \left(\dfrac{2n_1 n_2}{n_1 + n_2} + 1 \right)}{\sqrt{\dfrac{2n_1 n_2(2n_1 n_2 - n_1 - n_2)}{(n_1 + n_2)^2(n_1 + n_2 - 1)}}}$$

The z of Equation 13.5.1 is compared for significance with tabulated values of the standard normal distribution of Table Ca in Appendix I.

EXAMPLE 13.5.2 At a certain gasoline station, two grades of gasoline are available, A and B. On a certain day, the first 50 gasoline purchases are of grades A and B in the following order: AA B AA B A BB AAA BB A BB A BB A BB A BB A BB AA BBBB AA B A B A B AAA B AAAAA BB. Does this sequence of purchases appear to indicate a random selection of grades of gasoline? (Let $\alpha = 0.05$.)

SOLUTION We have $n_1 = $ number of A's $= 26$, $n_2 = $ number of B's $= 24$, and $r = 28$. Since n_1 and n_2 are both greater than 20, we cannot use Table J.

Thus, we use Equation 13.5.1 to compute

$$z = \frac{28 - \left(\dfrac{2(26)(24)}{26 + 24} + 1\right)}{\sqrt{\dfrac{2(26)(24)[2(26)(24) - 26 - 24]}{(26 + 24)^2(26 + 24 - 1)}}} = 0.58$$

Table Ca shows that a z of 0.58 is not significant at the $\alpha = 0.05$ level of significance. We are therefore unable to reject the null hypothesis that the sequence of gasoline purchases is in random order.

COMPUTER **ANALYSIS**

MINITAB has a program for performing the one-sample runs test. Figure 13.5.1 shows the MINITAB commands and printout for Example 13.5.1. The data were stored in column 1. If the value of K, the value above and below which runs are to be calculated, is not specified, MINITAB sets K equal to the mean of the data set.

FIGURE 13.5.1   MINITAB printout for Example 13.5.1

```
MINITAB   MTB > RUNS 17 C1
          C1
          K =      17.0000
          THE OBSERVED NO. OF RUNS = 5
          THE EXPECTED NO. OF RUNS = 9.4000
          14 OBSERVATIONS ABOVE K      6 BELOW
                    THE TEST IS SIGNIFICANT AT 0.0152
```

EXERCISES

13.5.1   In a large company, the last 15 promotions to top-level jobs were males and females in the following order: M FF MMMMM FFF MMM F. Test for randomness. Let $\alpha = 0.05$.

13.5.2   A sample of 60 consecutively produced bolts is selected from an assembly line and measured. The following are the deviations in thousandths of an inch of the lengths of the bolts from 3.000 inches: $-5, 4, 2, -2, 3, 8, 4, 3, 3, 1, 4, 1, 1, 5, 3, -2, 6, 1, 3, -11,$ $-10, 12, 5, 3, 7, 8, -9, 3, 3, -2, 10, -1, 4, -5, 6, -3, 1, 5, 3, 5, 3, -1, -5, 3, -7,$ $-4, 4, -2, -1, -2, -1, 10, -5, -5, 5, -2, 1, -7, 4, 4.$ Dichotomize the measurements as to whether they are above or below 3.000 inches. Test for randomness. Let $\alpha = 0.05$.

13.5.3 Figure 9.5.5 shows the residuals resulting from the regression analysis of Example 9.4.1. They are -0.7, -11.5, $+6.1$, $+13.3$, -10.6, -4.2, $+15.2$, -9.6, $+7.5$, -5.5. Can we conclude from these data that the residuals are not independent? Use the runs test to test for randomness in the sequence of plus and minus signs. Randomness is compatible with independence. Let $\alpha = 0.05$.

13.6 THE WILCOXON SIGNED-RANK TEST FOR LOCATION

Use the Wilcoxon test for hypotheses about μ when neither t nor z is appropriate.

Sometimes we wish to test a null hypothesis about a population mean, but for some reason we cannot use either z or t as a test statistic. The z statistic may be ruled out, for example, because we have a small (less than 30) sample from a population that is known to be grossly nonnormally distributed. The central limit theorem is not applicable, and the t statistic is not appropriate because the sampled population does not sufficiently approximate a normal distribution. In such a situation, a possible alternative is to use a nonparametric procedure.

A nonparametric procedure that we can often use for the one-sample case in which neither the z statistic nor the t statistic is appropriate is the *Wilcoxon signed-rank test for location.*

THE ASSUMPTIONS

This procedure is based on the following assumptions about the data.

1. The sample is random.
2. The variable is continuous.
3. The population is symmetrically distributed about its mean μ.
4. The measurement scale is at least interval.

THE HYPOTHESES

Here are the null hypotheses about some unknown population mean μ_0 that may be tested, and their alternatives.

$$\text{(a) } H_0: \mu = \mu_0 \qquad \text{(b) } H_0: \mu \geq \mu_0 \qquad \text{(c) } H_0: \mu \leq \mu_0$$
$$H_1: \mu \neq \mu_0 \qquad\quad H_1: \mu < \mu_0 \qquad\quad H_1: \mu > \mu_0$$

THE CALCULATIONS

The calculations involved in applying the Wilcoxon procedure are as follows.

1. Subtract the hypothesized mean μ_0 from each observation x_i, to obtain

$$d_i = x_i - \mu_0$$

If any x_i is equal to the mean, so that $d_i = 0$, eliminate that d_i from the calculations and reduce n accordingly.

2. Rank the usable d_i from the smallest to the largest without regard to the sign of d_i. That is, consider only the absolute value of the d_i, designated by $|d_i|$, when ranking them. If two or more of the $|d_i|$ are equal, assign each tied value the mean of the rank positions that the tied values occupy. If, for example, the three smallest $|d_i|$ are all equal, place them in rank positions 1, 2, and 3, but assign each a rank of $(1 + 2 + 3)/3 = 2$.

3. Assign each rank the sign of the d_i that yields that rank.

4. Find T_+, the sum of the ranks with positive signs, and T_-, the sum of the ranks with negative signs.

THE TEST STATISTIC

The test statistic is either T_+ or T_-, depending on the nature of the alternative hypothesis. To test for significance, enter Table K of Appendix I with the computed test statistic, the sample size n, and the chosen value of α. In Table K, the one-sided significance level is denoted by α' and the two-sided significance level by α''. If the test is two-sided, reject H_0 at the α level of significance if either T_+ or T_- (whichever has the smaller absolute value) is smaller than d for n and tabulated α (two-sided). If the alternative hypothesis is $H_1\colon \mu < \mu_0$, reject H_0 at the α level of significance if T_+ is less than d for n and tabulated α (one-sided). If the alternative hypothesis is $H_1\colon \mu > \mu_0$, reject H_0 at the α level of significance if T_- is less than d for n and tabulated α (one-sided).

THE RATIONALE

Before we look at an example, let us consider the rationale underlying the Wilcoxon signed-rank test. Suppose that H_0 is true, that is, that the population mean μ is equal to the hypothesized mean μ_0. And suppose that the assumptions about the data are met. Then the probability of observing a positive difference d_i of a given magnitude is equal to the probability of observing a negative difference of the same magnitude. For a given sample, then, if H_0 is true, we would expect T_+ and T_- to be about equal. Therefore, a sufficiently small value of T_+ or a sufficiently small value of T_- (depending on the alternative hypothesis) will cause us to reject H_0.

The following example illustrates the use of the Wilcoxon signed-rank test.

EXAMPLE 13.6.1   A market analyst wants to know whether she can conclude, at the 0.05 level of significance, that the mean annual family income in a certain low-income area is less than $15,000. Interviews with heads of household in a random sample of 20 families from the area yield the following incomes (in dollars per year):

8,900	10,300	11,200	12,500	16,200
9,300	12,200	15,300	15,100	13,900
10,100	7,500	17,200	14,900	15,000
18,000	9,900	23,000	14,300	18,000

SOLUTION The market analyst, who believes that the distribution of incomes in the area is symmetrical, conducts the following hypothesis test.

1. *Hypotheses.*

$$H_0: \mu \geq \$15,000, \qquad H_1: \mu < \$15,000$$

2. *Test statistic.* Since the alternative is $\mu < \$15,000$, the test statistic is T_+.
3. *Significance level.* Let $\alpha = 0.05$.
4. *Decision rule.* Reject H_0 if the computed value of T_+ is smaller than the critical value.
5. *Calculations.* Table 13.6.1 gives the calculation of the test statistic.

TABLE 13.6.1   Calculation of the test statistic for Example 13.6.1

Annual Family Income (x_i)	$d_i = x_i - \mu_0$	Rank of $|d_i|$	Signed Rank of $|d_i|$
8,900	−6,100	17	−17
9,300	−5,700	16	−16
10,100	−4,900	14	−14
18,000	+3,000	10.5	+10.5
10,300	−4,700	13	−13
12,200	−2,800	9	− 9
7,500	−7,500	18	−18
9,900	−5,100	15	−15
11,200	−3,800	12	−12
15,300	+ 300	3	+ 3
17,200	+2,200	7	+ 7
23,000	+8,000	19	+19
12,500	−2,500	8	− 8
15,100	+ 100	1.5	+ 1.5
14,900	− 100	1.5	− 1.5
14,300	− 700	4	− 4
16,200	+1,200	6	+ 6
13,900	−1,100	5	− 5
15,000	0	Eliminate from analysis	
18,000	+3,000	10.5	+10.5
			$T_+ = $ 57.5
			$T_- = $ 132.5

The test statistic is $T_+ = 57.5$

6. _Statistical decision._ Reference to Table K, with $n = 19$ and $\alpha' = 0.052$, reveals that, since 57.5 is larger than 55, we cannot reject H_0 at the 0.05 level. In fact, for this test, $p > 0.052$.

7. _Conclusion._ We conclude, then, that the mean annual family income in the area may be \$15,000 or more.

COMPUTER **ANALYSIS**

We may use MINITAB to test hypotheses by means of the Wilcoxon test. For a one-sided alternative, we use a subcommand to specify K equal to $+1$ or -1, depending on the location of the rejection region. If the subcommand is not used, the program performs a two-sided test. If the center is not specified as part of the main command, a center of 0 is assumed. Figure 13.6.1 shows the MINITAB commands and printout for Example 13.6.1, with the data stored in column 1. Note that the MINITAB printout gives an exact p value for the test, whereas use of Table K usually results in an inexact p value.

FIGURE 13.6.1   MINITAB printout for Example 13.6.1

MINITAB
```
MTB > WTEST 15000 C1;
SUBC> ALTERNATIVE = -1.
     TEST OF MEDIAN = 15000 VERSUS MEDIAN L.T. 15000
                  N FOR     WILCOXON                ESTIMATED
           N      TEST      STATISTIC    P-VALUE     MEDIAN
    C1     20      19        57.5         0.068       13550
```

EXERCISES

13.6.1 Sixteen laboratory animals were fed a special diet from birth through the age of 12 weeks. Their weight gains (in grams) were as follows: 64, 69, 80, 66, 65, 64, 66, 65, 77, 75, 67, 67, 68, 74, 70, 77. Can we conclude from these data that the diet results in a mean weight gain of less than 70 grams? Let $\alpha = 0.05$, and find the p value.

13.6.2 [C] A psychologist selects a random sample of 25 handicapped assembly-line workers from among those employed at several factories of a large industry. Their manual dexterity scores were as follows: 32, 52, 21, 39, 23, 55, 36, 27, 37, 41, 34, 51, 51, 35, 46, 40, 31, 19, 41, 33, 52, 36, 34, 46, 41. Do these data provide sufficient evidence to indicate that the mean score for the population is not 45? Let $\alpha = 0.05$. Find the p value.

13.6.3 [C] A population of adolescent laborers who dropped out of high school at age 16 had a mean reading comprehension score of 60. A random sample of 21 adolescents who were still in school at age 16 made the following scores on the same test: 72, 62, 52, 57, 91,

78, 74, 67, 51, 62, 84, 59, 51, 57, 89, 64, 80, 72, 92, 64, 57. Do these data provide sufficient evidence to indicate that the mean score for adolescents still in school at age 16 is greater than that for dropouts employed as laborers? Let $\alpha = 0.05$. Find the p value.

13.7 THE MANN-WHITNEY TEST

Use the Mann-Whitney test with two independent samples when neither t nor z is appropriate.

It is not unusual to have to test a null hypothesis about the difference between two location parameters under conditions that render both z and t inappropriate as test statistics. In such situations, we usually look for an appropriate nonparametric procedure. When the objective is to test for a significant difference between two location statistics computed from independent samples, the nonparametric procedure most often used is the *Mann-Whitney test*. Sometimes, when the test statistic is computed by a formula different from (but related to) the one we give here, the procedure is called the *Mann-Whitney U test*.

The test focuses on the median as the measure of location or central tendency. Recall that when a population is symmetrical, the median and the mean are equal. Therefore, when the two sampled populations are symmetrical, conclusions about their medians based on the Mann-Whitney test also apply to their means.

THE HYPOTHESES

Let M_X = the median of population 1 and M_Y = the median of population 2. The following are the null hypotheses that may be tested, along with their alternatives.

(a) H_0: $M_X = M_Y$
H_1: $M_X \neq M_Y$ Two-sided

(b) H_0: $M_X \geq M_Y$
H_1: $M_X < M_Y$ One-sided

(c) H_0: $M_X \leq M_Y$
H_1: $M_X > M_Y$ One-sided

THE ASSUMPTIONS

The following assumptions underlie the Mann-Whitney test:

1. The samples have been randomly and independently drawn from their respective populations. Let $x_1, x_2, \ldots, x_{n_1}$ represent the sample values drawn from population 1, and let $y_1, y_2, \ldots, y_{n_2}$ represent the sample values drawn from population 2.
2. The variable of interest is continuous.

3. The measurement scale used is at least ordinal.

4. The distributions of the two sampled populations, if they differ at all, differ only with respect to location.

THE CALCULATIONS

If the measurement scale for each sample is ordinal, we must be able to rank the observations of one sample with those of another when the two samples are combined as described here. In practice, we may need an interval scale in order for this to be possible.

To compute the Mann-Whitney test statistic, combine the two samples and rank all sample observations from smallest to largest. Assign tied observations the mean of the rank positions that they would have occupied had there been no ties. Then sum the ranks of the observations from population 1 (that is, the X's). If the location parameter of population 1 is smaller than that of population 2, we expect (for equal sample sizes) the sum of the ranks for population 1 to be smaller than that for population 2. Similarly, if the location parameter of population 1 is larger than the location parameter of population 2, we expect the reverse to be true. The test statistic is based on this rationale. Depending on the null hypothesis, either a sufficiently small or a sufficiently large sum of ranks assigned to sample observations from population 1 causes us to reject the null hypothesis.

THE TEST STATISTIC

The test statistic is

$$(13.7.1) \qquad T = S - \frac{n_1(n_1 + 1)}{2}$$

where S is the sum of the ranks assigned to the sample observations from population 1.

THE DECISION RULES

The appropriate decision rules for an α level of significance are as follows.

1. When we test $H_0: M_X = M_Y$, we reject H_0 for either a sufficiently small or a sufficiently large value of T. Therefore, we reject H_0 if the computed value of T is less than $W_{\alpha/2}$ or greater than $W_{1-\alpha/2}$, where $W_{\alpha/2}$ is the critical value of T given in Table L of Appendix I and $W_{1-\alpha/2}$ is given by

$$(13.7.2) \qquad W_{1-\alpha/2} = n_1 n_2 - W_{\alpha/2}$$

2. When we test $H_0: M_X \geq M_Y$, we reject H_0 for sufficiently small values of T. We reject H_0 if the computed T is less than W_α, the critical value of T given in Table L for n_1, n_2, and α.

3. When we test $H_0: M_X \leq M_Y$, we reject H_0 for sufficiently large values of T. Therefore, we reject H_0 if the computed T is greater than $W_{1-\alpha}$, where

(13.7.3)
$$W_{1-\alpha} = n_1 n_2 - W_\alpha$$

In all cases, when we reject H_0, we conclude that H_1 is true. If we fail to reject H_0, we conclude that H_0 may be true.

LARGE SAMPLES

When either n_1 or n_2 is greater than 20, we cannot use Table L of Appendix I to obtain critical values for the Mann-Whitney test. When this is the case, we may compute

(13.7.4)
$$z = \frac{T - n_1 n_2/2}{\sqrt{n_1 n_2 (n_1 + n_2 + 1)/12}}$$

and compare the results for significance with critical values of the standard normal distribution. The following example illustrates the use of the Mann-Whitney test.

EXAMPLE 13.7.1   A researcher gives a random sample of 15 college men and an independent random sample of 20 college women a test to measure their knowledge of ecological issues. Table 13.7.1 shows the scores. We wish to know whether we can conclude on the basis of these data that the two populations of scores are different with respect to their medians. Let $\alpha = 0.05$.

SOLUTION

1. _Hypotheses._

$$H_0: M_X = M_Y, \qquad H_1: M_X \neq M_Y$$

TABLE 13.7.1   Data for Example 13.7.1

Men's Scores, X			Women's Scores, Y			
18.50	17.00	12.40	25.00	19.10	15.00	18.00
14.00	16.00	15.20	23.00	18.75	21.00	18.25
20.00	12.50	12.50	16.20	21.10	18.50	24.00
19.00	12.00	19.25	19.75	17.50	17.25	18.30
19.50	10.00	11.00	20.00	17.75	16.30	19.20

2. *Test statistic.* Suppose that we are unwilling to assume that the populations are approximately normally distributed. In that case t is not the appropriate test statistic. Since the sample sizes are small, we cannot apply the central limit theorem. Therefore, z is not a valid test statistic. We presume that the assumptions for the Mann-Whitney test statistic are met and use that procedure.
3. *Significance level.* Let $\alpha = 0.05$.
4. *Decision rule.* From Table L, $W_{\alpha/2} = 91$ for $n_1 = 15$, $n_2 = 20$, and $\alpha/2 = 0.025$. By Equation 13.7.2, we compute

$$W_{1-\alpha/2} = 15(20) - 91 = 209$$

We will reject H_0 if the computed value of T is either < 91 or > 209.
5. *Calculations.* Table 13.7.2 shows the scores of Table 13.7.1 in rank order, with the ranks attached. We see in Table 13.7.2 that $S = 186$. By Equation 13.7.1,

TABLE 13.7.2 Data of Table 13.7.1 in rank order, with ranks attached

Men's Scores, X	Ranks	Women's Scores, Y	Ranks
10.00	1		
11.00	2		
12.00	3		
12.40	4		
12.50	5.5		
12.50	5.5		
14.00	7		
		15.00	8
15.20	9		
16.00	10		
		16.20	11
		16.30	12
17.00	13		
		17.25	14
		17.50	15
		17.75	16
		18.00	17
		18.25	18
		18.30	19
18.50	20.5	18.50	20.5
		18.75	22
19.00	23		
		19.10	24
		19.20	25
19.25	26		
19.50	27		
		19.75	28
20.00	29.5	20.00	29.5
		21.00	31
		21.10	32
		23.00	33
		24.00	34
		25.00	35
Total = S = 186			

then, the computed value of the test statistic is

$$T = 186 - \frac{15(15 + 1)}{2} = 66$$

6. *Statistical decision.* Since the computed value of the test statistic, $T = 66$, is less than 91, we reject H_0.
7. *Conclusion.* Since, for our present example, we reject H_0, we conclude that H_1 is true. That is, we conclude that the sampled populations of college men and women differ, on the average, with respect to knowledge of ecological issues.

FINDING THE p VALUE

When the null hypothesis is true, the sampling distribution of the Mann-Whitney test statistic is symmetrical. Since this is the case, we can find the two-sided p value by doubling the one-sided p value. We consult Table L for $n_1 = 15$ and $n_2 = 20$. We find that the computed value of our test statistic, 66, is between 60 and 74. Consequently, for this test,

$$2(0.005) > p > 2(0.001) \qquad \text{or} \qquad 0.010 > p > 0.002$$

Finding the p value in Table L can sometimes be tricky. The following example will help clarify the procedure.

Consider the two-sided test in which the computed value of the test statistic exceeds the largest value in Table L for $\alpha/2$, n_1, and n_2. Suppose that in our example the computed value of the test statistic had been 240. Since 240 exceeds $W_{1-\alpha/2} = (15)(20) - 91 = 209$, we would reject H_0. To find the one-sided p value, we would compute $T' = n_1 n_2 - T_0$, which for this example is $T' = (15)(20) - 240 = 60$. Since the probability, when the null hypothesis is true, of obtaining a value of the test statistic as small as 60 is 0.001, the one-sided p value is 0.001. The two-sided p value, then, would be $2(0.001) = 0.002$. In the one-sided test in which the alternative hypothesis is $M_X > M_Y$, you may have to compute T' in order to determine the p value.

COMPUTER **ANALYSIS**

MINITAB has a program that simultaneously performs the Mann-Whitney test and constructs a confidence interval for the difference between two population location parameters. The alternative subcommand ($+1$ or -1) allows the user to do a one-sided test. The user may specify the level of confidence desired for the interval estimate. If no confidence coefficient is given in the command, MINITAB uses 0.95. Figure 13.7.1 shows the MINITAB commands and printout for Example 13.7.1 when the data have been stored in columns 1 and 2.

FIGURE 13.7.1   MINITAB commands and printout for Example 13.7.1

MINITAB   MTB > MANN-WHITNEY C1 C2

Mann-Whitney Confidence Interval and Test

```
C1            N =  15     Median =        15.200
C2            N =  20     Median =        18.625
Point estimate for ETA1-ETA2 is       -4.000
95.3 pct c.i. for ETA1-ETA2 is (-6.250,-1.249)
W = 186.0
Test of ETA1 = ETA2 vs. ETA1 n.e. ETA2 is signficant
at 0.0054
The test is significant at 0.0054 (adjusted for ties)
```

EXERCISES

13.7.1   Ⓒ Allston Materials wishes to compare two methods of communicating information about a new product. Two groups of subjects are chosen to take part in the experiment. Subjects in the first group learn about the new product by Method A. Subjects in the second group learn about it by Method B. At the end of the experiment, each subject is given a test to measure knowledge of the new product. The results are shown in the following table. Do these data provide sufficient evidence to indicate a difference in median scores among the two groups? Let $\alpha = 0.05$. Determine the p value.

Method A scores	50	59	60	71	80	81	80	78	72	77	73	75	75	77	76
Method B scores	52	54	58	78	65	69	61	60	72	60	59	65	69	68	65

13.7.2   Ⓒ The following table gives the Brinell hardness numbers of specimens in random samples from two competing potential raw materials for a certain product. Can an investigator conclude that Material B has a higher Brinell hardness number, on the average, than Material A?

A	160	162	165	171	162	170	168	165	166	172	160	162	168	171	170
B	167	168	170	172	174	168	171	170	172	171	172	175	172	168	163	169

13.7.3   Ⓒ The following table shows the monthly salaries of independent samples of 20 men and 20 women who do the same type of work. Do these data suggest that there is a difference in the median salaries for men and women doing this particular job? Let $\alpha = 0.05$. Determine the p value.

Men		Women	
$818	$954	$841	$886
942	946	795	955
963	881	887	983
893	788	836	970
819	863	892	894

(table continued on next page)

Men		Women	
941	891	875	877
935	749	960	763
865	847	934	767
840	902	771	961
973	965	715	800

13.7.4 $\boxed{\text{C}}$ A team of industrial psychologists draws a sample of the records of those applicants for a certain job who have completed high school. They select an independent random sample of the records of applicants for the same job who were high school dropouts. The following table shows the emotional maturity test scores of the applicants in the two groups. Do these data provide sufficient evidence to indicate that the two sampled populations have different medians? Let $\alpha = 0.05$. Determine the p value.

High School Graduates				High School Dropouts		
89	79	62	85	85	72	65
97	56	63	67	59	78	51
69	82	96	56	85	47	57
71	72	94	77	58	49	63
67	79	62		66	54	41
64	78	69		65	74	58
86	83	57		64	49	67

13.8 THE SIGN TEST

We may use the sign test with paired samples.

We perform the Mann-Whitney test, presented in Section 13.7, with data from two independent samples. We often want to analyze two sets of data that are not the results of two independently drawn samples. Such data may be "before and after" scores for the same subject or scores for matched subjects that have been treated in different ways. We speak of such data as *data from two related samples.* When the necessary assumptions are met, we can analyze the data of two related samples by the parametric paired-comparisons test that is used to test null hypotheses about the mean difference in the two sets of observations. (See Chapter 7.)

When the assumptions underlying the parametric paired-comparisons test are not met, or when the observations are based on a weak measurement scale, we must use an alternative test. A simple nonparametric test that we can use is the *sign test*, which focuses on the median, rather than the mean, as a measure of central tendency. As we have seen, the median and mean coincide in symmetrical distributions. Specifically, we use the sign test to test hypotheses about median differences, where we obtain differences by comparing pairs of sample observations. Let us call one score in the ith pair X_i and the other score in the pair Y_i. We observe the differences $X_i - Y_i$. If $X_i > Y_i$, we record the difference as $+$. If $X_i < Y_i$, we record the difference as $-$. The test uses the resulting sample of pluses and minuses.

THE HYPOTHESES

Perhaps the most common use of the sign test is to test the null hypothesis that the median difference is 0. This may be stated more compactly as follows:

$$H_0: P(X_i > Y_i) = P(X_i < Y_i) = 0.5$$

The null hypothesis states that a positive difference is as likely to occur as a negative one. In a random sample of pluses and minuses obtained by computing $(X_i - Y_i)$ for each pair of observations, then, we would expect about as many pluses as minuses when the null hypothesis is true. Alternatively, we can state the null hypothesis as

$$H_0: P(+) = P(-) = 0.5$$

We can think of obtaining a series of pluses and minuses in this manner as a binomial experiment with parameters n and p, where n is the number of pairs of observations and $p = 0.5$.

THE TEST STATISTIC

The test statistic for the sign test is either the observed number of plus signs or the observed number of minus signs. The nature of the alternative hypothesis determines which of these test statistics is appropriate.

In a given test, any one of the following alternative hypotheses is possible:

$$H_1: P(+) > P(-) \qquad \text{One-sided alternative}$$
$$H_1: P(+) < P(-) \qquad \text{One-sided alternative}$$
$$H_1: P(+) \neq P(-) \qquad \text{Two-sided alternative}$$

If the alternative hypothesis is

$$H_1: P(+) > P(-)$$

a sufficiently large number of plus signs causes rejection of H_0. The test statistic is the number of plus signs. Suppose that the chosen level of significance is α. We reject H_0 if the probability (when H_0 is true) of obtaining as many or more plus signs than we actually obtain is equal to or less than α. Thus, if $\alpha = 0.05$ and we observe 7 plus signs, we reject H_0 if the probability (when H_0 is true) of obtaining 7 or more plus signs is equal to or less than 0.05.

Similarly, if the alternative hypothesis is

$$H_1: P(+) < P(-)$$

a sufficiently large number of minus signs causes rejection of H_0. The test statistic is the number of minus signs.

If the alternative hypothesis is

$$H_1: P(+) \neq P(-)$$

either a sufficiently large number of plus signs or a sufficiently large number of minus signs causes rejection of the null hypothesis. We may take as the test statistic the more frequently occurring sign or the less frequently occurring sign. For a two-sided test with a significance level α, we reject H_0 if the probability, when H_0 is true, of obtaining as many or more of the more frequently occurring sign than we actually obtained is equal to or less than $\alpha/2$. Alternatively, for a one-sided test, we may consider as the test statistic the less frequently occurring sign. In that case we reject H_0 if the probability, when H_0 is true, of obtaining as few or fewer of the less frequently occurring sign than we actually obtained is equal to or less than α.

If a difference $X_i - Y_i$ is equal to 0, we eliminate the pair from the sample and reduce the value of n accordingly.

EXAMPLE 13.8.1   The following experiment is designed to compare the effectiveness of two detergents in cleaning cotton fabric. Twelve pieces of fabric are uniformly soiled and then cut in half. One half of each piece is randomly assigned to be washed in Detergent A. The other half is washed in Detergent B. After the fabric specimens have been washed and dried, each piece is tested to determine the effectiveness of the detergent. We wish to know whether we can conclude that the median difference is negative. The results are shown in Table 13.8.1.

SOLUTION

1. *Hypotheses.*

   H_0: The median of the differences is 0. $[P(+) = P(-)]$

   H_1: The median of the differences is negative. $[P(+) < P(-)]$

2. *Test statistic.* Since the alternative hypothesis is $P(+) < P(-)$, we have a one-sided test, and the test statistic is the number of minus signs.
3. *Significance level.* Let $\alpha = 0.05$.
4. *Decision rule.* Reject H_0 if the probability, when H_0 is true, of obtaining as many or more minus signs than we observe is ≤ 0.05.
5. *Calculations.* Table 13.8.1 shows one 0, which we eliminate from the analysis, and 9 minus signs.

TABLE 13.8.1   Results of experiment described in Example 13.8.1

Specimen	1	2	3	4	5	6	7	8	9	10	11	12
Detergent A (X)	9	8	7	9	7	7	7	8	7	9	7	8
Detergent B (Y)	8	10	8	8	9	9	8	10	9	9	8	9
Sign of ($X_i - Y_i$)	+	−	−	+	−	−	−	−	−	0	−	−

6. *Statistical decision.* We wish to know the probability of obtaining 9 or more minus signs when the probability of a minus sign is 0.5. That is, we wish to determine $P(k \geq 9|11, 0.5)$, where k is the test statistic, the number of minus signs. Table A of Appendix I shows this probability to be 0.0327. Since 0.0327 is less than 0.05, we reject H_0.

7. <u>Conclusion.</u> We conclude that the median of the differences is negative. The p value is 0.0327.

LARGE SAMPLES

For samples of size 11 or larger, we can use the normal approximation to the binomial (recall Chapters 5, 6, and 7). The transformed test statistic is

(13.8.1)
$$z = \frac{(k \pm 0.5) - 0.5n}{0.5\sqrt{n}}$$

where k = the original test statistic, the number of plus or minus signs, whichever is appropriate. In Equation 13.8.1, $k + 0.5$ is used when $k < n/2$, and $k - 0.5$ is used when $k > n/2$. We compare the computed z with the appropriate z value from the standard normal distribution for significance.

The following example illustrates the use of Equation 13.8.1 with a large sample.

EXAMPLE 13.8.2   To investigate the effectiveness of different kinds of advertising, the market research department of Baldwin Discount Stores conducts the following experiment in a random sample of 15 stores. During a certain week, automotive department specials are advertised by periodic announcements over the stores' loudspeaker systems. During the following week, automotive department specials are advertised by window displays and other storewide visual advertising. The variable of interest is total dollar sales volume for the automotive department during the week. Table 13.8.2 shows the results.

SOLUTION   The hypotheses are as follows. Let $\alpha = 0.05$.

H_0: The median of the differences is 0. $[P(+) = P(-)]$
H_1: The median of the differences is not 0. $[P(+) \neq P(-)]$

By Equation 13.8.1, we compute

$$z = \frac{(11 - 0.5) - 0.5(15)}{0.5\sqrt{15}} = 1.55$$

Since the computed value of $z = 1.55 < 1.96$, we do not reject the null hypothesis. We conclude that the two methods of advertising may have equal effects $[p = 2(0.0606) = 0.1212]$.

We can use the Wilcoxon signed-rank test with paired data when the population of sampled differences satisfies the test's assumptions. After we find the

TABLE 13.8.2 Dollar volume of sales for automotive departments of 15 discount stores under two experimental advertising conditions

Store Number	Announcements (X)	Visual Displays (Y)	Sign of $(X_i - Y_i)$
1	$4,127	$4,147	−
2	4,288	4,048	+
3	4,024	4,853	−
4	3,627	4,865	−
5	4,813	4,376	+
6	3,925	4,838	−
7	4,840	3,526	+
8	3,731	4,300	−
9	3,779	4,672	−
10	4,229	4,721	−
11	3,977	4,770	−
12	3,778	4,484	−
13	3,602	4,389	−
14	3,959	4,560	−
15	4,918	3,848	+

signed difference between each pair of observations, we proceed just as we do for the single-sample case. An advantage of the Wilcoxon test over the sign test is the fact that the Wilcoxon test uses more of the information inherent in the data than the sign test does. However, if the sampled population is not symmetrical, the sign test is preferable.

COMPUTER **ANALYSIS**

MINITAB performs the sign test. After the data have been entered, we may indicate the hypothesized value of the median in the command for performing the test. If no value is indicated, the program uses 0. Unless otherwise specified by the subcommand ALTERNATIVE = +1 or ALTERNATIVE = −1, the program assumes that a two-sided test is wanted. Figure 13.8.1 shows the data entry, the commands, and the printout for Example 13.8.1 when MINITAB is used.

FIGURE 13.8.1 MINITAB analysis of Example 13.8.1

MINITAB

```
MTB > SET C1
DATA> 1 -2 -1 1 -2 -2 -1 -2 -2 0 -1 -1
DATA> END
MTB > STEST C1;
SUBC> ALTERNATIVE = -1.

    SIGN TEST OF MEDIAN = 0.00000 VERSUS L.T. 0.00000
          N    BELOW    EQUAL    ABOVE    P-VALUE    MEDIAN
C1       12      9        1        2       0.0327    -1.000
```

EXERCISES

13.8.1 Ⓒ Castlereagh International wants to study the effect of piped-in music on the productivity of employees. One department of a certain factory is selected at random to receive piped-in music for 30 working days. There are 10 employees in the department. The following table shows the average daily output for 30 days before the introduction of music and the average daily output for the 30 days during which music is piped into the department. Can we conclude from these data that music increases productivity? Let $\alpha = 0.05$. Determine the p value.

Employee	A	B	C	D	E	F	G	H	I	J
Before music	90	80	92	85	81	85	72	85	70	88
During music	99	85	98	83	88	99	80	91	80	94

13.8.2 Ⓒ In a study designed to test the effect of packaging on consumer acceptance of a certain candy bar, 27 candy bars are wrapped in a colorful wrapper (Method A) and 27 identical candy bars are wrapped in a plain wrapper (Method B). Twenty-seven subjects are asked to eat each of the bars and indicate their preference. The following table shows the results. Let the event "A preferred over B" be designated by a plus, and the event "B preferred over A" by a minus. Test to see whether the data provide sufficient evidence to indicate that the candy bar packaged by Method A is preferred over the bar in the plain wrapper. Let $\alpha = 0.05$. Determine the p value. (n.p. = no preference)

Subject	Bar Preferred	Subject	Bar Preferred	Subject	Bar Preferred	Subject	Bar Preferred
1	A	8	A	15	n.p.	22	A
2	A	9	A	16	A	23	A
3	A	10	A	17	A	24	A
4	B	11	A	18	A	25	A
5	B	12	B	19	A	26	A
6	n.p.	13	A	20	A	27	B
7	A	14	A	21	B		

13.8.3 A consumer affairs investigator conducts an experiment to probe the possibility of differential pricing by retail stores in a metropolitan area. At different times two subjects visit 12 retail stores in which prices are not posted. One subject projects the image of a member of the upper socioeconomic stratum of the area. The second subject projects the image of a member of the lower socioeconomic stratum of the area. In 10 instances the upper socioeconomic subject is quoted a lower price. Do these data provide sufficient evidence to indicate that more than 50% of the sampled firms practice differential pricing? Let $\alpha = 0.05$, and determine the p value.

13.9 THE KRUSKAL-WALLIS ONE-WAY ANALYSIS OF VARIANCE BY RANKS

Chapter 8 shows that by means of analysis of variance we may test the null hypothesis that several population means are equal. The simplest application of this technique is the use of one-way analysis of variance. However, the use of the one-way ANOVA presented in Chapter 8 rests on the assumptions that the sampled populations are normally distributed with equal variances.

When either of these assumptions is not met, we need an alternative test. Perhaps the most widely used nonparametric alternative is the *Kruskal-Wallis one-way analysis of variance by ranks*, which uses ranks rather than original observations. (If the original observations themselves are ranks, they are used.) We use the Kruskal-Wallis test only if the samples are independent.

THE TEST STATISTIC

We replace the observations by ranks from 1, corresponding to the smallest observation, to n, corresponding to the largest observation *in the combined set of data*. In the event of ties, we replace each tied observation by the mean of the ranks for which it is tied. We compute the following statistic:

$$(13.9.1) \qquad H = \frac{12}{n(n+1)} \sum_{j=1}^{k} \frac{R_j^2}{n_j} - 3(n+1)$$

where k = the number of samples, n_j = the number of observations in the jth sample, $n = \Sigma n_j$, the total number of observations in all samples, and R_j = the sum of the ranks in the jth sample.

A large value of H tends to cast doubt on the null hypothesis that the k samples are drawn from identically distributed populations. When there are only three groups and five or fewer observations in each group, we determine the significance of the statistic H by referring to Table M of Appendix I. For values of n_j and k not included in Table M, we compare the computed value of H for significance with tabulated values of χ^2 with $k - 1$ degrees of freedom.

If there are ties, we can adjust H by dividing by

$$(13.9.2) \qquad 1 - \frac{\Sigma T}{n^3 - n}$$

where $T = t^3 - t$. The t designates the number of observations in a group of tied observations. The effect of the adjustment is to inflate H, so that if the unadjusted H is significant, the adjustment is not necessary.

EXAMPLE 13.9.1   Researchers conduct an experiment to determine whether different methods of producing a certain molded part result in different mean tensile strengths. Since the researchers are unwilling to make the assumptions necessary for the parametric one-way analysis of variance, they use the Kruskal-Wallis test. Table 13.9.1 shows the tensile strengths of the parts produced by the different methods, with the ranks in parentheses.

TABLE 13.9.1 Tensile strengths (psi) of molded parts produced by four different methods

A	B	C	D
80(10.5)	99(32.5)	89(24)	76(5.5)
88(22.5)	91(26)	82(14)	77(7)
87(21)	98(30)	81(13)	75(3.5)
86(18.5)	98(30)	80(10.5)	78(8)
90(25)	99(32.5)	86(18.5)	76(5.5)
88(22.5)	96(28)	86(18.5)	73(2)
85(16)	92(27)	86(18.5)	71(1)
	98(30)	84(15)	80(10.5)
			75(3.5)
			80(10.5)
$R_1 = 136$	$R_2 = 236$	$R_3 = 132$	$R_4 = 57$

> SOLUTION

1. *Hypotheses.*

   H_0: The mean tensile strengths are the same for all methods.

   H_1: The mean tensile strengths are not the same for all methods.

2. *Test statistic.* The test statistic is given by Equation 13.9.1.
3. *Significance level.* Let $\alpha = 0.05$.
4. *Decision rules.* Since at least one of the samples has more than 5 observations, we obtain the critical value of the test statistic from the chi-square table. Since we have 4 treatments, we have 3 degrees of freedom. The decision rule, then, is: Reject H_0 if the computed value of H is ≥ 7.815.
5. *Calculations.* The value of H that we may compute by Equation 13.9.1 is

$$H = \frac{12}{33(33 + 1)} \left[\frac{(136)^2}{7} + \frac{(236)^2}{8} + \frac{(132)^2}{8} + \frac{(57)^2}{10} \right] - 3(33 + 1) = 27.49$$

6. *Statistical decision.* Since $27.49 > 7.815$, the computed value of H is significant. Consequently, we can reject the hypothesis that the methods yield equal mean tensile strengths ($p < 0.005$).
7. *Conclusion.* We conclude that at least one of the methods yields a mean tensile strength that is different from that yielded by at least one of the other methods.

Since the computed H is significant, we would not in practice go to the trouble of adjusting for the ties that occurred in the assigning of ranks. To demonstrate the method, however, we compute an adjusted H. There were seven groups of ties. In four groups, two observations are tied. In one group, three are tied. In two groups, four are tied. From these ties, we compute

$$\Sigma T = 4(2^3 - 2) + (3^3 - 3) + 2(4^3 - 4) = 168$$

TABLE 13.9.2   Yields (bu/acre) of grain receiving three types of fertilizer

A	B	C
45(6)	42(3)	53(9)
40(1)	44(5)	56(12)
41(2)	43(4)	54(10)
46(7)	47(8)	55(11)
$R_1 = 16$	$R_2 = 20$	$R_3 = 42$

so that the correction factor is

$$1 - \frac{168}{33^3 - 33} = 0.9953$$

and the computed statistic is

$$H_c = \frac{27.49}{0.9953} = 27.62$$

THREE SMALL SAMPLES

To understand the use of Table M, consider the following example.

EXAMPLE 13.9.2   We wish to know whether we can conclude that 3 types of fertilizer have different effects on the mean yield in bushels per acre of a certain grain. Each of the 3 types of fertilizer is applied to 4 one-acre plots of ground. These plots are as alike with respect to relevant variables as possible. The plots are all treated alike during the growing season. Table 13.9.2 shows the yields of the 12 plots.

SOLUTION   From the data in Table 13.9.2, we compute

$$H = \frac{12}{12(12 + 1)} \left[\frac{(16)^2 + (20)^2 + (42)^2}{4} \right] - 3(12 + 1) = 7.54$$

From Table M, the probability of obtaining a value of H as large as 7.54 when the samples are drawn from identical populations is 0.011. Thus, we may reject a null hypothesis of equal treatment means at the 0.05 level of significance. We conclude that the fertilizers have different effects ($p = 0.011$).

COMPUTER **ANALYSIS**

We may use MINITAB to compute the Kruskal-Wallis statistic. The input consists of two columns: one column contains the observations and the other column indicates the treatment group (1, 2, 3, and so on) to which the observations

FIGURE 13.9.1   MINITAB analysis of Example 13.9.1 showing data entry, commands, and output

```
MINITAB    MTB > READ C1 C2
           DATA> 80 1
           DATA> 88 1
             .    .  .
             .    .  .
             .    .  .
           DATA> 85 1
           DATA> 99 2
           DATA> 91 2
             .    .  .
             .    .  .
             .    .  .
           DATA> 98 2
           DATA> 89 3
           DATA> 82 3
             .    .  .
             .    .  .
             .    .  .
           DATA> 84 3
           DATA> 76 4
           DATA> 77 4
             .    .  .
             .    .  .
             .    .  .
           DATA> 75 4
           DATA> 80 4
MINITAB    MTB > KRUSKAL-WALLIS C1 C2
           Level      Nobs     Median    Ave. Rank     Z Value
             1          7      87.00       19.4          0.75
             2          8      98.00       29.5          4.20
             3          8      85.00       16.5         -0.17
             4         10      76.00        5.7         -4.43
           OVERALL     33                  17.0

           H = 27.49 d.f. = 3 p = 0.000
           H = 27.62 d.f. = 3 p = 0.000 (adj. for ties)
```

belong. Figure 13.9.1 shows the data entry, the commands, and the output when we use MINITAB with the data of Example 13.9.1.

EXERCISES

13.9.1 [C] A subject is asked to rank 15 samples of coffee in order of preference from least preferred (1) to most preferred (15). Unknown to the subject, the 15 samples consist of 5 samples of each of 3 brands. The following table shows the rankings by brand. Test the null hypothesis that the three brands are equally preferred. Let $\alpha = 0.05$. Determine the p value.

Brand A	9	10	11	12	13
Brand B	14	1	5	7	8
Brand C	2	3	4	15	6

13.9.2 ⓒ Clarendon Mills wants to compare four new formulas for cake mix. Five cakes are baked from each of the four formulas. A panel of judges, unaware of the differences in formulas, gives each cake a score, as shown in the following table. Test the null hypothesis of no difference among cake mixes. Let $\alpha = 0.05$. Determine the p value.

Formula A	72	88	70	87	71
Formula B	85	89	86	82	88
Formula C	94	94	88	87	89
Formula D	91	93	92	95	94

13.9.3 ⓒ Officials with Digby Utilities wish to compare the bill-paying habits of customers living in four neighborhoods. They analyze random samples of bills from each of the four neighborhoods to determine the number of days between the date the bill is mailed and the date payment is received. The results are as shown in the following table. Do these data provide sufficient evidence to indicate that the bill-paying habits of the populations differ? Let $\alpha = 0.01$. Determine the p value.

Community A	27	17	21	26	25	18	17	23	17	23
Community B	13	13	14	11	13	13	9	13	14	10
Community C	11	13	19	13	16	13	12	17	19	16
Community D	7	13	14	9	12	8	12	12	9	13

13.9.4 ⓒ Researchers run an experiment to evaluate the effectiveness of three different methods of teaching problem solving. The following table shows, by treatment, the 15 participating subjects ranked on the basis of ability to solve problems after training. Do these data provide sufficient evidence to indicate that the three teaching methods differ in effectiveness? Let $\alpha = 0.05$.

Method A	5	7	9	3	6
Method B	4	1	8	2	10
Method C	15	13	11	12	14

13.9.5 ⓒ Ericson Manufacturing conducts a study to compare the characteristics of assembly-line employees. Employees are categorized into three performance groups: high, average, and low. Researchers select a random sample from each group and interview and test them in depth. The following table shows the self-concept scores of subjects in the three groups. Do these data provide sufficient evidence to indicate that the population groups differ with respect to median level of self-concept? Let $\alpha = 0.05$, and find the p value.

Low performers	50	60	58	63	
Average performers	81	87	85		
High performers	96	90	94	99	90

13.10 THE FRIEDMAN TWO-WAY ANALYSIS OF VARIANCE BY RANKS

The Kruskal-Wallis test (Section 13.9) is appropriate when the samples are independently drawn from their respective populations. But we often want to analyze data from nonindependent, or related, samples. For two dependent samples, the sign test is an appropriate nonparametric method for testing the null hypothesis that the median difference is 0. When we wish to test the null hypothesis of no difference in treatment effects among three or more related samples, we often use the *Friedman two-way analysis of variance by ranks*.

This is called a two-way analysis of variance because it provides a nonparametric analogue to the parametric two-way analysis-of-variance technique used to analyze data from a randomized complete block experiment. The data are cast in a table in which the rows correspond to blocks and the columns correspond to treatments or vice versa. Each block may represent a different individual subjected to several experimental conditions. Or it may represent a different batch of some material, portions of which are treated in a different manner.

The original observations may consist of ranks. For example, the blocks may represent subjects who rank several different machines (the treatments) in order of preference. If the original observations consist of scores, we convert them to ranks. We rank the observations in each of the n blocks separately, from 1, which is assigned to the smallest observation in the block, to k, which is assigned to the largest in the block. We assign tied observations the average of the ranks for which they are tied. Suppose that the rows represent blocks and the columns represent treatments. If the null hypothesis is true—that is, if there is no difference in treatment (column) effects—the assignment of ranks to the columns will be the result of chance factors. On the other hand, if there *are* differences, we would expect a preponderance of large or small ranks in at least one of the columns. The Friedman statistic, then, measures the extent to which the ranks within the columns depart from randomness by focusing on the sum of the ranks in each column.

THE TEST STATISTIC

The test statistic, denoted by Friedman as χ_r^2, is

(13.10.1)
$$\chi_r^2 = \frac{12}{nk(k + 1)} \sum_{j=1}^{k} R_j^2 - 3n(k + 1)$$

where n is the number of blocks, k is the number of treatments, and R_j is the sum of the ranks in the jth treatment group. A large value of χ_r^2 reflects a large difference among the rank sums. It tends to cast doubt on the hypothesis of equal treatment effects. To determine whether or not a computed value of χ_r^2 is large enough to cause rejection of the null hypothesis, we can consult Table N in

TABLE 13.10.1 Five technicians' rankings of three brands of calculators (A, B, C)

Technician	A	B	C
1	1	2	3
2	1	2	3
3	2	1	3
4	1	2	3
5	1	3	2
R_j	6	10	14

Appendix I when n and k are small. For values of k and n that are not given in Table N, we can compare the computed χ_r^2 for significance with tabulated values of χ^2 with $k - 1$ degrees of freedom.

EXAMPLE 13.10.1 To reach a decision about the relative merits of three brands of calculators, five technicians rank three brands in order of preference. A rank of 1 indicates first preference. Table 13.10.1 shows the results. We wish to know whether we can conclude that the three brands are not equally preferred.

SOLUTION

1. _Hypotheses._

    H_0: The three brands of calculators are equally preferred.
    H_1: The three brands of calculators are not equally preferred.

2. _Test statistic._ The test statistic is given by Equation 13.10.1.
3. _Significance level._ Let $\alpha = 0.05$.
4. _Decision rule._ Reject H_0 if the computed value of χ_r^2 is ≥ 6.2 (obtained by interpolation). Alternatively, we may state the decision rule in terms of α and the p value as follows: Reject H_0 if the computed p value for the test is ≤ 0.05.
5. _Calculations._ From the data in Table 13.10.1, we may compute

$$\chi_r^2 = \frac{12}{5(3)(3+1)} [(6)^2 + (10)^2 + (14)^2] - 3(5)(3+1) = 6.4$$

6. _Statistical decision._ We reject H_0, since Table N indicates that the probability of obtaining a value of χ_r^2 as large as 6.4 when the null hypothesis is true is 0.039.
7. _Conclusion._ We may conclude that the three brands of calculators are not equally preferred ($p = 0.039$).

LARGE SAMPLES

In the following example, the samples are large.

TABLE 13.10.2 Health ratings of 45 puppies fed different formulas (A, B, C)

Litter	1	2	3	4	5	6	7	8	9	10	11	12	13	14	15	R_j
A	3	3	3	2.5	1	3	3	2	2.5	3	2	3	3	2	2	38
B	2	1	2	2.5	3	2	2	3	2.5	1	3	1	1	3	3	32
C	1	2	1	1	2	1	1	1	1	2	1	2	2	1	1	20

EXAMPLE 13.10.2   The makers of Top Dog puppy food want to compare the effects of three formulas on the health of young puppies. The subjects consist of 3 litter mates of the same sex from each of 15 litters. One litter mate from each set is fed Formula A, one is fed Formula B, and the third is fed Formula C. At the end of the experimental period, a veterinarian rates the health of the puppies. The manufacturers wish to know whether they can conclude on the basis of these results, shown in Table 13.10.2, that the three formulas have different effects.

SOLUTION   From the data in Table 13.10.2, we may compute

$$\chi_r^2 = \frac{12}{15(3)(3 + 1)} [(38)^2 + (32)^2 + (20)^2] - 3(15)(3 + 1) = 11.2$$

Table F reveals that we can reject the null hypothesis of equal treatment effects, since $11.2 > 5.991$. We conclude, then, that at least one formula is better than at least one of the others ($p < 0.005$).

COMPUTER **ANALYSIS**

MINITAB has a program for computing the Friedman test statistic. The data are stored in three columns. The first column contains the observations, the second contains a number indicating the treatment (1, 2, 3, and so on) to which the observation belongs, and the third column contains a number indicating the block (1, 2, 3, and so on) to which the observation belongs. MINITAB prints the test statistic (both adjusted and unadjusted for ties), the associated degrees of freedom, and the p value. The following example illustrates the method of data entry, the commands, and the printout when MINITAB is used to compute the Friedman statistic.

EXAMPLE 13.10.3   Table 13.10.3 shows the stress levels of 15 assembly-line employees classified according to the shift they work and the specific job they perform. We wish to know if there is a difference in stress levels among the shifts when the effects of the different jobs are used as the blocking factor.

SOLUTION   Figure 13.10.1 shows the data entry, commands, and printout when MINITAB is used to compute the Friedman statistic.

TABLE 13.10.3 Stress levels of 15 assembly-line employees classified by shift and job

		Shift	
Job	A(1)	B(2)	C(3)
1	76	90	90
2	77	73	93
3	78	86	99
4	74	81	95
5	82	93	87

FIGURE 13.10.1 MINITAB solution for Example 13.10.3

```
MINITAB   MTB > READ C1-C3
          DATA> 76 1 1
          DATA> 77 1 2
            .     . . .
            .     . . .
            .     . . .
          DATA> 90 2 1
          DATA> 73 2 2
            .     . . .
            .     . . .
            .     . . .
          DATA> 90 3 1
          DATA> 93 3 2
            .     . . .
            .     . . .
            .     . . .
          DATA> 95 3 4
          DATA> 87 3 5
          DATA> END
              15 ROWS READ
MINITAB   MTB > FRIEDMAN C1 C2 C3

          Friedman test of C1 by C2 blocked by C3

          S = 5.70  d.f. = 2  p = 0.058
          S = 6.00  d.f. = 2  p = 0.050 (adjusted for ties)
                                Est.    Sum of
                  C2      N    Median   Ranks
                   1      5    76.000    6.0
                   2      5    82.333   10.5
                   3      5    93.667   13.5
          Grand median = 84.000
```

EXERCISES

13.10.1 [C] Fifteen management trainees with a large company are asked to rank five U.S. cities in order of preference as a place for permanent assignment. The results are as shown in the

following table. Test the null hypothesis that the five cities are equally preferred. Let $\alpha = 0.05$. Determine the p value.

Trainee no.	1	2	3	4	5	6	7	8	9	10	11	12	13	14	15
City A	2	3	3.5	2	3.5	3	5	5	2	2	3	4	1.5	5	5
City B	3	2	3.5	1	3.5	4	1	3	5	5	5	2	1.5	4	4
City C	1	4	5	3	1	1	4	1	1	3	4	1	3	3	2
City D	4	5	2	4	5	5	3	2	4	1	2	3	4	2	3
City E	5	1	1	5	2	2	2	4	3	4	1	5	5	1	1

13.10.2 Ⓒ Fischer Mills is considering three dye formulas for a certain synthetic fiber. Its managers wish to know whether they can conclude that the three do in fact differ in quality. To aid in their decision, they conduct an experiment in which five specimens of fabric are cut into thirds. One third is randomly assigned to be dyed by each of the three dyes. Each piece of fabric is later graded and assigned a score measuring the quality of the dye. The results are as follows. Test the null hypothesis that the dyes are of equal quality. Let $\alpha = 0.05$. Determine the p value.

Fabric specimen	1	2	3	4	5
Dye A	74	78	76	82	77
Dye B	81	86	90	93	73
Dye C	95	99	90	87	93

13.10.3 Ⓒ Ten subjects suffering from arthritis take part in an experiment to evaluate the relative effectiveness of three pain-relieving drugs. The following table shows how the subjects ranked the three drugs in order of preference as pain relievers. Do these data provide sufficient evidence to indicate that the three drugs are not equally preferred? Let $\alpha = 0.05$, and determine the p value.

Subject	1	2	3	4	5	6	7	8	9	10
Drug A	1	1	1	1	1	1	2	1	2	1
Drug B	2	2	2	3	2	3	1	3	1	3
Drug C	3	3	3	2	3	2	3	2	3	2

13.10.4 Ⓒ The production engineer for Graham Business Systems carries out an experiment to evaluate the effect of music on production. Randomly selected assembly-line employees of five branch plants participate. For one month slow, quiet music is piped into the assembly-line area. The next month the music is louder and faster. During the third month there is no music at all. The following table shows the number of units produced per employee per hour under the three conditions. Can it be concluded on the basis of these data that the different conditions have a different effect on production? Let $\alpha = 0.05$. Find the p value.

Plant	Slow, Quiet Music	Loud, Fast Music	No Music
1	750	725	760
2	1,000	850	900
3	800	825	830
4	950	875	925
5	925	900	890

13.11 THE SPEARMAN RANK CORRELATION COEFFICIENT

When the assumptions underlying the parametric correlation analysis introduced in Chapter 9 are not met, we can turn to several other measures of correlation. One of the simplest and most widely used is the *Spearman rank correlation coefficient*, designated by r_S. As the name implies, r_S is computed from data consisting of ranks. Suppose that the observations in their original form are not ranks. Then we can use the Spearman rank correlation coefficient as a measure of correlation if we can rank the observations according to magnitude from smallest to largest.

We rank the X's and Y's separately.

The data consist of a bivariate random sample of size n. One variable is designated X, and the ranks consist of 1 (the observation on X that is smallest in magnitude), 2, . . . , i, . . . , n (the observation on X that is largest). The other variable is designated Y and ranked 1, 2, . . . , i, . . . , n, according to the relative magnitude of the observations. Alternatively, we may assign the rank of 1 to the largest value of X (and Y), and so on to the rank of n, which we assign to the smallest value of X (and Y). The direction of the ranking is immaterial so long as we rank both X and Y in the same direction.

If the two rankings are perfectly and directly correlated, the rank of X will equal the rank of Y for all pairs. If the rankings are perfectly and inversely correlated, the smallest X rank will be paired with the largest Y rank, and so on, until finally, the largest X rank will be paired with the smallest Y rank.

THE TEST STATISTIC

The Spearman rank correlation coefficient focuses on the differences between X and Y ranks (denoted d_i) as a measure of the extent to which the paired rankings depart from perfect direct or inverse correlation. Except in the case of perfect direct correlation, some of the d_i will be negative. Because of the difficulty of working with negative numbers, we use the values of the d_i^2 in the computation of r_S, which is given by

(13.11.1)
$$r_S = 1 - \frac{6\Sigma d_i^2}{n(n^2 - 1)}$$

The larger the differences between the ranks of X and Y, the larger Σd_i^2 will be. If all the differences are 0, Σd_i^2 will equal 0, r_S will equal 1, and we consider the rankings perfectly and directly correlated. If we observe the maximum possible differences between the ranks of X and Y—that is, if the ranking of X is the reverse of the ranking of Y in each case—Σd_i^2 will be a maximum and r_S will equal -1. When the rankings are less than perfectly correlated, r_S will be somewhere between $+1$ and -1. Remember that r_S measures the strength of the association between ranks, not the values of the variates that have been ranked.

If the data do not contain ties, the result of Equation 13.11.1 is equal to the result obtained using Equation 9.8.2 when the original observations are replaced by their ranks.

THE HYPOTHESES

We can use the Spearman rank correlation coefficient to test any one of the following hypotheses:

1. H_0: The X_i and Y_i are mutually independent.
   H_1: Either large values of X_i tend to be paired with large values of Y_i or large values of X_i tend to be paired with small values of Y_i.
2. H_0: The X_i and Y_i are mutually independent.
   H_1: Large values of X_i tend to be paired with large values of Y_i.
3. H_0: The X_i and Y_i are mutually independent.
   H_1: Large values of X_i tend to be paired with small values of Y_i.

The first pair of hypotheses specifies a two-sided test. The last two pairs specify one-sided tests. If we wish to know whether we can conclude that large values of X_i tend to be paired with small values of Y_i, we test the H_0 specified in 3. If we wish to know whether we can conclude that large values of X_i tend to be paired with large values of Y_i, we test the H_0 specified in 2. If we wish to detect a departure from independence in either direction, we test the H_0 specified in 1.

The procedure for testing r_S for significance depends on the sample size. If n is less than or equal to 30, we can consult Table O of Appendix I. Table O contains critical values of r_S for various values of α. For values of n greater than 30, we can compute the statistic

(13.11.2)
$$z = r_S\sqrt{n - 1}$$

and compare it for significance with values of the standard normal distribution.

Ties may occur in the rankings of X, Y, or both. In such cases, the mean of the ranks that would have been assigned had no ties occurred is assigned to the tied ranks.

EXAMPLE 13.11.1   A random sample of 15 assembly-line employees at Hemingway Factories are evaluated by their peers and their supervisors as to congeniality and cooperativeness on the job. Table 13.11.1 shows the scores. The firm's

TABLE 13.11.1   Scores of 15 employees evaluated by peers (X) and supervisors (Y)

Employee	1	2	3	4	5	6	7	8	9	10	11	12	13	14	15
Peers (X)	90	83	60	95	84	68	93	55	79	78	71	80	87	76	89
Supervisors (Y)	90	89	63	87	85	57	81	68	60	65	67	76	70	55	69

TABLE 13.11.2   Fifteen employees ranked as to congeniality and cooperativeness by peers and supervisors

Employee	1	2	3	4	5	6	7	8	9	10	11	12	13	14	15
X rank	13	9	2	15	10	3	14	1	7	6	4	8	11	5	12
Y rank	15	14	4	13	12	2	11	7	3	5	6	10	9	1	8
d_i	-2	-5	-2	2	-2	1	3	-6	4	1	-2	-2	2	4	4
d_i^2	4	25	4	4	4	1	9	36	16	1	4	4	4	16	16

personnel director wishes to know whether he can conclude that the two measures are directly correlated.

SOLUTION   Table 13.11.2 shows the resulting ranks.

1. *Hypotheses.*

   H_0: The X_i and Y_i are mutually independent.

   H_1: Large values of X_i tend to be paired with large values of Y_i.

2. *Test statistic.* The test statistic is given by Equation 13.11.1.
3. *Significance level.* Let $\alpha = 0.05$.
4. *Decision rule.* Reject H_0 if the computed value of r_S is ≥ 0.4429.
5. *Calculations.* By Equation 13.11.1, we compute

$$r_S = 1 - \frac{6(148)}{15(15^2 - 1)} = 0.7357$$

6. *Statistical decision.* Table O indicates that the probability of obtaining a value of r_S as large as or larger than 0.7357 when the null hypothesis is true is less than 0.005. Therefore, we reject the null hypothesis at the 0.05 level of significance.
7. *Conclusion.* We conclude that the two rankings are directly correlated ($0.005 > p > 0.001$).

   One may use the Spearman rank correlation coefficient as the test statistic in a test to detect a lack of homogeneity of variances among the populations of Y variables represented in regression analysis. In such a test, each residual is paired with the corresponding sample value of the independent variable. Rejection of the null hypothesis that the residuals are independent of the independent variable provides the basis for concluding that the populations of Y values do not have equal variances.

EXERCISES

   13.11.1   [C] The personnel department of Kenworthy Technologies gives 20 employees a test to measure their degree of job satisfaction. The following table shows the results, along with the employees' average daily production (in units) during the past year. Convert the original observations to ranks, and test to see whether we can conclude that the two rankings are directly correlated. Let $\alpha = 0.05$. Find the p value.

Employee	1	2	3	4	5	6	7	8	9	10
Job-satis. score	97	83	73	88	69	70	76	60	73	99
Avg. daily production	166	174	111	189	106	129	159	136	153	160

Employee	11	12	13	14	15	16	17	18	19	20
Job-satis. score	97	62	87	89	98	93	85	79	64	85
Avg. daily production	165	121	166	169	189	161	195	145	138	174

13.11.2   C   A panel of five men and another panel of five women are asked to rank ten ideas for a new television program on the basis of their relative appeal to a general audience. The results appear in the following table. Test the null hypothesis that the rankings are mutually independent against the alternative that they are inversely correlated. Let $\alpha = 0.05$. Determine the p value.

Program idea	1	2	3	4	5	6	7	8	9	10
Men	6	4	8	7	2	1	3	5	9	10
Women	6	10	8	2	7	1	5	9	4	3

13.11.3   C   A panel of small-business experts ranks 15 small businesses on the basis of their employees' job-satisfaction scores and the growth potential of the businesses. The results are given in the following table. Can we conclude from these data that there is a direct relationship between employee satisfaction within a firm and that firm's growth potential? Let $\alpha = 0.01$. Find the p value.

Employee satisfaction	1	2	3	4	5	6	7	8	9	10	11	12	13	14	15
Potential for growth	6	3	1	2	4	5	11	10	7	8	12	9	14	13	15

13.11.4   C   The following table shows, for a random sample of college sophomores, grades made in a statistics course and the scores that the students assigned the course on a course evaluation form. Can we conclude from these data that the two variables are directly correlated? Let $\alpha = 0.05$. Find the p value.

Statistics grade	70	88	85	84	90	95
Course evaluation score	4	8	6	5	9	2

13.11.5   C   A random sample of ten employees take part in a study to assess the relationship between the employees' scores on a job-aptitude test and supervisors' evaluations of the employees' job performance. Compute r_S and test to determine whether the two variables are directly related. Let $\alpha = 0.05$. Find the p value. The data are as follows.

Aptitude score	13	41	72	24	57	100	84	36	92	63
Supervisors' evaluation	31	19	81	43	50	74	63	24	100	96

13.12 NONPARAMETRIC LINEAR REGRESSION

Regression analysis is one of the most widely used statistical techniques. In Chapters 9, 10, and 11, you studied simple linear regression and multiple-regression analysis. In Chapter 9, you learned to use the method of least squares to compute, from sample data, a and b, the y intercept and slope, respectively, of a sample regression line. One can use this line to estimate the true regression line that describes the linear relationship between two variables X and Y for the population from which the sample was drawn. As you have seen, the resulting equation,

$$\hat{y} = a + bx$$

can be used for prediction and estimation. But it can be so used only if certain assumptions about the data (given in Chapter 9) are met and if we can conclude from the sample data that X and Y are indeed related. To determine whether we may conclude that X and Y are related, we test $H_0: \beta = 0$ against $H_1: \beta \neq 0$. If we reject H_0, we conclude that, in the sampled population, X and Y are related, since if they are not related, $\beta = 0$. In other situations we may wish to test the null hypothesis that β is of some magnitude other than 0. To repeat, the test is strictly valid *only* if the assumptions in Chapter 9 are met. If we suspect that the data do not conform to the necessary assumptions for the application of the techniques described in Chapter 9, we must use an alternative procedure.

A METHOD BASED ON r_s

W. J. Conover describes a nonparametric test for β that is an appropriate alternative when the regression of Y on X is linear and the residuals are independent of the X's. The procedure is valid when X is random. It is also valid when X is nonrandom, provided that the Y's are independent and their populations are identically distributed. We find point estimates of the sample slope and y intercept by applying Formulas 9.11.3 and 9.11.4, respectively. Usually, the statistics a and b are part of the output of computer programs for simple linear regression analysis.

THE HYPOTHESES

We may use this technique to test any of the following null hypotheses against their accompanying alternatives.

1. $H_0: \beta = \beta_0$, $H_1: \beta \neq \beta_0$
2. $H_0: \beta = \beta_0$, $H_1: \beta > \beta_0$
3. $H_0: \beta = \beta_0$, $H_1: \beta < \beta_0$

THE CALCULATIONS

The calculations are as follows.

1. For each pair of measurements (x_i, y_i), compute $y_i - \beta_0 x_i = u_i$.
2. Compute the Spearman rank correlation coefficient r_S for the pairs (x_i, u_i) as described in Section 13.11.

THE DECISION RULE

The decision rules are as follows. For $H_1: \beta > \beta_0$, reject H_0 at the α level of significance if the computed r_S is greater than r_S^* for given n and α as shown in Table O of Appendix I. For $H_1: \beta < \beta_0$, reject H_0 at the α level of significance if the computed r_S is less than $-r_S^*$ for given n and α. For $H_1: \beta \neq \beta_0$, reject H_0 at the α level of significance if the computed r_S is either greater than r_S^* for n and $\alpha/2$ or less than $-r_S^*$ for n and $\alpha/2$.

The following example shows the use of the technique.

EXAMPLE 13.12.1   Researchers for the Lemoyne Agrichemical Company conducted an experiment in which specified amounts of nitrogen (X) were added to pots containing house-plant seedlings. Later they determined the amounts of nitrogen in the mature plants (Y). Table 13.12.1 shows the results. We wish to know whether we can conclude, at the $\alpha = 0.05$ level, that the slope of the population regression line describing the relationship between X and Y is greater than 0.5.

SOLUTION   We proceed as follows.

1. *Hypotheses.*

$$H_0: \beta = 0.5, \qquad H_1: \beta > 0.5$$

2. *Test statistic.* The test statistic is r_S as given by Equation 13.11.1.
3. *Significance level.* Let $\alpha = 0.05$.
4. *Decision rule.* We will reject H_0 if the computed r_S is greater than 0.4965, the value of r_S^* in Table O corresponding to $n = 12$ and $\alpha = 0.05$.
5. *Calculations.* The u_i are as follows.

TABLE 13.12.1   Data for Example 13.12.1

Plant	1	2	3	4	5	6	7	8	9	10	11	12
Y	0.33	0.62	0.35	0.75	0.66	0.22	0.83	0.73	0.42	0.79	0.94	0.36
X	0.20	0.60	0.40	0.90	0.70	0.10	1.10	0.80	0.30	1.00	1.20	0.50

TABLE 13.12.2 Ranks of x_i and u_i and intermediate calculations for Example 13.12.1

	1	2	3	4	5	6	7	8	9	10	11	12
x_i	0.20	0.60	0.40	0.90	0.70	0.10	1.10	0.80	0.30	1.00	1.20	0.50
u_i	0.23	0.32	0.15	0.30	0.31	0.17	0.28	0.33	0.27	0.29	0.34	0.11
$R(x_i)$	2	6	4	9	7	1	11	8	3	10	12	5
$R(u_i)$	4	10	2	8	9	3	6	11	5	7	12	1
d_i	-2	-4	2	1	-2	-2	5	-3	-2	3	0	4
d_i^2	4	16	4	1	4	4	25	9	4	9	0	16

$$u_1 = 0.33 - (0.5)(0.20) = 0.23 \qquad u_7 = 0.83 - (0.5)(1.10) = 0.28$$
$$u_2 = 0.62 - (0.5)(0.60) = 0.32 \qquad u_8 = 0.73 - (0.5)(0.80) = 0.33$$
$$u_3 = 0.35 - (0.5)(0.40) = 0.15 \qquad u_9 = 0.42 - (0.5)(0.30) = 0.27$$
$$u_4 = 0.75 - (0.5)(0.90) = 0.30 \qquad u_{10} = 0.79 - (0.5)(1.00) = 0.29$$
$$u_5 = 0.66 - (0.5)(0.70) = 0.31 \qquad u_{11} = 0.94 - (0.5)(1.20) = 0.34$$
$$u_6 = 0.22 - (0.5)(0.10) = 0.17 \qquad u_{12} = 0.36 - (0.5)(0.50) = 0.11$$

Table 13.12.2 shows the array of the x's and u's, their ranks, the d_i, and the d_i^2. The computed value of the test statistic, from Equation 13.11.1, is

$$r_S = 1 - \frac{6(96)}{12(144 - 1)} = 0.6643$$

6. *Statistical decision.* Since 0.6643 is greater than 0.4965, we reject H_0.
7. *Conclusion.* We conclude that the slope of the population regression line is greater than 0.5. Since $0.6713 > 0.6643 > 0.5804$, the p value for this test is $0.01 < p < 0.025$.

THEIL'S METHOD

When the assumptions underlying simple linear regression analysis as discussed in Chapter 9 are not met, we may employ a nonparametric procedure suggested by H. Theil. In this section, we present estimators of the slope and intercept that are robust, efficient, and easy-to-calculate alternatives to the least-squares estimators described in Chapter 9.

Theil's Slope Estimator Theil proposes a method for obtaining a point estimate of the slope coefficient β. We assume that the data conform to the classical regression model

$$Y_i = \alpha + \beta x_i + e_i, \qquad i = 1, \ldots, n$$

where the x_i are known constants, α and β are unknown parameters, and y_i is an observed value of the continuous random variable Y at x_i. For each value of x_i, we assume a subpopulation of Y values, and the e_i are mutually independent. The x_i are all distinct (no ties), and we take $x_1 < x_2 < \ldots < x_n$.

The data consist of n pairs of sample observations, (x_1, y_1), (x_2, y_2), $\ldots$, (x_n, y_n), where the ith pair represents measurements taken on the ith unit of association.

To obtain Theil's estimator of β, we first form all possible sample slopes $S_{ij} = (Y_j - y_i)/(x_j - x_i)$, where $i < j$. There will be $N = {}_nC_2$ values of S_{ij}. The estimator of β, which we designate by $\hat{\beta}$, is the median of the S_{ij} values. That is,

(13.12.1)
$$\hat{\beta} = \text{median } \{S_{ij}\}$$

The following example illustrates the calculation of $\hat{\beta}$.

EXAMPLE 13.12.2   In Table 13.12.3 are the calories (Y) and sodium content in a sample of eight fast-food items. We wish to compute the estimate of the population regression slope coefficient by Theil's method.

SOLUTION   The $N = {}_8C_2 = 28$ ordered values of S_{ij} are shown in Table 13.12.4.

TABLE 13.12.3   Number of Calories and Sodium Content in Fast-Food Items

Calories	230	175	315	290	275	150	360	425
Sodium content	421	278	618	482	465	105	550	750

TABLE 13.12.4   Ordered Values of S_{ij} for Example 13.12.2

−0.6618	0.5037
0.1445	0.5263
0.1838	0.5297
0.2532	0.5348
0.2614	0.5637
0.3216	0.5927
0.325	0.6801
0.3472	0.8333
0.3714	0.8824
0.3846	0.9836
0.4118	1.0000
0.4264	1.0078
0.4315	1.0227
0.4719	1.0294

The median of the S_{ij} values is 0.4878. Consequently, our estimate of the population slope coefficient is $\hat{\beta} = 0.4878$.

An Estimator of the Intercept Coefficient Professor E. Jacquelin Dietz recommends two intercept estimators. The first, designated $\hat{\alpha}_{1,M}$, is the median of the n terms $y_i - \hat{\beta}x_i$ in which $\hat{\beta}$ is the Theil estimator. It is recommended when the researcher is not willing to assume that the error terms are symmetrical about 0. If the researcher is willing to assume a symmetrical distribution of error terms, Dietz recommends the estimator $\hat{\alpha}_{2,M}$, which is the median of the $n(n + 1)/2$ pairwise averages of the $y_i - \hat{\beta}x_i$ terms. These averages include the average of each term with each other term and with itself. We illustrate the calculation of each in the following example.

EXAMPLE 13.12.3 Refer to Example 13.12.2. Let us compute $\hat{\alpha}_{1,M}$ and $\hat{\alpha}_{2,M}$ from the data on calories and sodium content.

SOLUTION The ordered $y_i - 0.4878x_i$ terms are 13.5396 24.6362 39.3916 48.1730 54.8804 59.1500 91.7100 98.7810. The median, 51.5267, is the estimator $\hat{\alpha}_{1,M}$.

The $8(8 + 1)/2 = 36$ ordered pairwise averages of the $y_i - 0.4878x_i$ are:

13.5396	53.6615
19.0879	54.8804
24.6362	56.1603
26.4656	57.0152
30.8563	58.1731
32.0139	59.15
34.21	61.7086
36.3448	65.5508
36.4046	69.0863
39.3916	69.9415
39.7583	73.2952
41.8931	73.477
43.7823	75.43
47.136	76.8307
48.173	78.9655
49.2708	91.71
51.5267	95.2455
52.6248	98.781

The median of these averages, 53.1432, is the estimator $\hat{\alpha}_{2,M}$. The estimating equation, then, is $y_i = 53.1432 + 0.4878x_i$ if we are willing to assume that the distribution of error terms is symmetrical about 0. If we are not willing to make the assumption of symmetry, the estimating equation is $y_i = 51.5267 + 0.4878x_i$.

For a more extensive discussion of nonparametric regression analysis, see the Suggestions for Further Reading at the end of this chapter.

EXERCISES

13.12.1   C The following are scores made by a random sample of college students who had just completed their sophomore year. Can we conclude on the basis of these data that $\beta \neq 0$? Let $\alpha = 0.05$. Find the p value.

Verbal fluency	224	280	522	370	391	605	420	291
Academic achievement	5.87	3.40	8.90	4.24	6.20	8.73	17.30	5.00
Verbal fluency	168	211	531	439	303	516	233	429
Academic achievement	4.31	7.21	19.41	11.60	12.30	16.61	3.51	13.99

13.12.2   C Researchers are studying the relationship between visual discrimination and reading ability. They use a sample of 25 employees randomly selected from a large company. A visual discrimination test and a reading test given to the subjects yield the following results. Can we conclude on the basis of these data that $\beta > 0.70$? Let $\alpha = 0.05$, and find the p value. Here X denotes the visual discrimination score and Y denotes the reading ability score.

X	91	91	94	92	87	91	93	89	94	87	90	93	94
Y	525	600	600	575	480	575	595	530	545	535	575	540	625

X	90	87	92	88	89	89	88	89	92	90	89	94
Y	545	440	490	460	545	600	525	510	510	495	480	525

13.12.3   The following table shows the number of added employees (X) and percent increase in production (Y) for nine manufacturing firms during a recent year.

X	163	164	156	151	152	167	165	153	155
Y	53.9	57.4	41.0	40.0	42.0	64.4	59.1	49.9	43.2

Compute $\hat{\beta}$, $\hat{\alpha}_{1,M}$, and $\hat{\alpha}_{2,M}$.

13.12.4   The following are the number of miles driven in a week (X) and total sales (in thousands of dollars) for that week (Y) reported by nine salespersons.

X	660.2	706.0	924.0	936.0	992.1	888.9	999.4	890.3	841.2
Y	781.7	888.7	1,038.1	1,040.0	1,120.0	1,071.5	1,134.5	965.3	925.0

Compute the slope estimator and two intercept estimators by Theil's method.

SUMMARY

This chapter introduces a variety of statistical techniques that you may use under the following conditions:

1. When the assumptions underlying the parametric procedures, presented in previous chapters, are not met

2. When the data represent measurements on a weak measurement scale

3. When you need results in a hurry

4. When the hypothesis does not involve a parameter

You learned to test appropriate hypotheses using the following nonparametric procedures:

1. The one-sample runs test

2. The Wilcoxon test

3. The Mann-Whitney test

4. The sign test

5. The Kruskal-Wallis one-way analysis of variance

6. The Friedman two-way analysis of variance

7. The Spearman rank correlation

8. Nonparametric regression analysis

These procedures are characterized by either the fact that they do not depend on the form of the distribution from which the samples are drawn or the fact that the hypotheses tested are not statements about population parameters. Procedures of the former type are called distribution-free procedures. Those of the latter type are called nonparametric procedures. For convenience, as well as by convention, we refer to both types as nonparametric procedures.

Except for the runs test, the procedures presented in this chapter are nonparametric analogues of parametric procedures presented in previous chapters.

REVIEW EXERCISES

1. Define (a) parametric statistics, (b) nonparametric statistics, (c) distribution-free statistics.

2. Under what conditions are nonparametric procedures used?

3. Define (a) measurement, (b) nominal scale, (c) ordinal scale, (d) interval scale, (e) ratio scale.

4. List the advantages and disadvantages of nonparametric statistics.

5. Describe a situation from your area of interest in which each of the following nonparametric procedures could be used: (a) runs test, (b) Mann-Whitney test, (c) sign test, (d) Kruskal-Wallis test, (e) Friedman test, (f) Spearman rank correlation, (g) Wilcoxon test, (h) nonparametric regression analysis. Use real or realistic data, and carry out an appropriate hypothesis-testing procedure for each test.

 6. Langley Sporting Goods is testing a new material that can be used in the production of tennis balls. An attractive feature of the new material is the fact that it is less expensive than the material currently in use. To evaluate the new material, the company gives 15 expert tennis players a supply of balls made from both the new and the old materials.

The players use each type of ball during 10 hours of practice. Then they say which of the two they prefer. Twelve of the 15 players say that they prefer the balls made from the new material. Would you recommend that the company switch to the new material? Support your answer with an appropriate statistical analysis. Let $\alpha = 0.05$. Find the p value.

7. ⓒ The desired mean length of a certain bolt produced by Madison Bolt and Nut Company is 80 mm. Slight random deviations from the desired mean are tolerable. Twenty consecutive bolts are measured, with the following results. Do these data provide sufficient evidence to indicate that deviations above and below the mean do not occur at random? Let $\alpha = 0.05$, and find the p value.

80.3	80.5	80.4	79.5	79.3	80.2	79.7	80.7	79.8	80.8
79.9	80.1	79.2	80.6	80.1	79.9	79.9	79.9	79.6	79.1

8. Each of 16 randomly selected homemakers in a small town is given a complimentary case of soft drinks for participating in a taste test. They have a choice of either "no-deposit, no-return" or returnable bottles. Thirteen choose the returnable bottles. Do these data provide sufficient evidence to indicate that homemakers in the town prefer soft drinks in returnable bottles? Let $\alpha = 0.05$, and find the p value.

9. A market research team asks each member of a panel of consumers to guess the retail price of 16 small household items on the basis of a simple inspection of the items. The following table gives the actual retail price and the average prices guessed by members of the panel. Compute the rank correlation coefficient between the average guessed price and the actual retail price. Test for significance. Let $\alpha = 0.01$, and determine the p value.

Item	Average Guessed Price ($)	Actual Retail Price ($)	Item	Average Guessed Price ($)	Actual Retail Price ($)
1	1.29	1.45	9	2.05	1.99
2	1.10	1.19	10	3.25	3.79
3	2.40	2.29	11	4.75	4.25
4	2.25	1.65	12	2.25	2.89
5	1.95	2.49	13	4.05	3.90
6	4.00	4.79	14	2.15	3.00
7	2.98	3.75	15	2.60	3.78
8	1.65	1.59	16	4.10	4.70

10. ⓒ Ten applicants for credit cards are ranked on their credit-risk potential by two officials (denoted X and Y) of the issuing bank. The results are given in the following table. Do these data suggest a lack of independence between the two officials' assessments of applicants' credit-risk potentials? Let $\alpha = 0.05$, and find the p value.

Applicant	A	B	C	D	E	F	G	H	I	J
X	3	4	9	10	6	1	7	2	5	8
Y	5	3	7	9	6	2	8	4	1	10

11. ⓒ The following table shows data (in rank form) collected on 15 line managers with Nast Industries. The X variable is the number of years of management experience. The Y variable is the quality of the managers' decision-making abilities as assessed by their

supervisors. Do these data provide sufficient evidence to indicate a lack of independence between the two variables? Let $\alpha = 0.01$, and determine the p value.

Rank of X	1	2	3	4.5	4.5	6	7	8	9.5	9.5	11	12	13	14	15
Rank of Y	3	2	1	7	8	5	4	6	14	15	12	9	10	11	13

12. Ⓒ A research team hired by Phyfe Pharmaceuticals wants to compare the effects of 5 different drugs on the reaction times of experimental animals. They randomly assign 20 animals to receive one of the 5 drugs. The following table shows the animals' decreases in reaction times (in milliseconds) to a standard stimulus after the drugs have been administered. Do these data provide sufficient evidence to indicate a difference among the drugs? Let $\alpha = 0.05$, and determine the p value.

Drug A	4.8	4.6	4.7	4.6
Drug B	4.9	5.2	4.5	4.1
Drug C	5.3	5.2	5.2	5.2
Drug D	5.2	5.1	5.0	5.0
Drug E	4.5	4.2	4.7	4.7

13. Ⓒ Rathenau Chemical Company hires a researcher to conduct an experiment comparing the effects of three different fertilizer formulas on the yield of tomato plants. The researcher applies each formula at random to each of five plots of ground of uniform size in which tomatoes have been planted. Yields, in pounds per plot, are as shown in the following table. Do these data provide sufficient evidence to indicate a difference in the three formulas? Let $\alpha = 0.05$, and determine the p value.

Formula A	78.0	77.5	50.0	76.0	69.1
Formula B	51.0	61.0	49.5	55.4	51.5
Formula C	56.0	43.1	59.5	56.4	52.5

14. Ⓒ An official with the Pizarro fast-food chain conducts an experiment to compare four methods of storing hamburger meat. The variable of interest is a measure of the bacteria growth after 48 hours of storage. Source of supply of raw meat is used as a blocking factor. Four batches of meat from each source are randomly assigned, one to each storage method (Methods A, B, C, and D). The results are as shown in the following table. After we eliminate the variability due to the source, do these data provide sufficient evidence to indicate a difference in storage methods? Let $\alpha = 0.01$, and determine the p value.

Source of raw meat	V	W	X	Y	Z
Method A	20	70	80	50	30
Method B	10	60	40	30	10
Method C	40	110	100	50	50
Method D	10	60	40	30	10

15. Ⓒ Each of a random sample of ten students ranks five accounting professors on the basis of teaching ability. The following table shows the results. Do these data provide sufficient evidence to indicate that some professors are preferred over others? Let $\alpha = 0.05$, and determine the p value.

Student	1	2	3	4	5	6	7	8	9	10
Prof. A	1	2	1	1	2	2	1	2	1	2
Prof. B	3	3	4	2	1	3	2	1	2	1
Prof. C	2	1	2	3	3	1	4	3	4	3
Prof. D	4	5	3	5	4	5	3	4	3	4
Prof. E	5	4	5	4	5	4	5	5	5	5

16. Ⓒ A team of research psychologists believes that male college students are more assertive than female college students. A random sample of $n_1 = 16$ college males made the following scores on a test designed to measure assertiveness (X): 22.3, 24.1, 28.9, 32.6, 29.3, 15.0, 39.9, 36.8, 21.3, 32.3, 27.0, 33.0, 25.5, 22.5, 33.3, 33.7. The scores (Y) made by a random sample of $n_2 = 19$ college females were 18.1, 22.9, 10.0, 10.5, 19.1, 10.0, 10.0, 26.9, 12.5, 10.9, 19.1, 11.7, 14.6, 19.2, 11.4, 29.8, 33.4, 27.0, 25.3. Use the Mann-Whitney test to determine whether or not the psychologists are justified in their belief. Let $\alpha = 0.05$. Compute the p value. Higher scores indicate greater assertiveness.

17. Ⓒ Twelve randomly selected employees scheduled for transfer to a new and unfamiliar job take a test designed to measure their level of anxiety. The results by ethnic group are as follows. We wish to know whether these data provide sufficient evidence to indicate that population median anxiety scores differ among the three ethnic groups. Let $\alpha = 0.05$. Determine the p value.

Group A	52	61	58	64	
Group B	74	83	88		
Group C	90	88	89	65	77

18. Ⓒ The following table categorizes 15 randomly selected white-collar employees according to the area in which they were reared and their rank on a test of verbal reasoning ability. Do these data provide sufficient evidence to indicate that the three populations differ with regard to median verbal reasoning ability? Let $\alpha = 0.05$. Determine the p value.

Suburban	13	15	14	11	12
Rural	1	6	10	2	3
Inner city	8	5	9	7	4

19. Ⓒ Seven randomly selected college seniors majoring in statistics are asked to rank three models of pocket calculator in order of preference. The results are shown in the following table. The investigator wishes to know whether the models differ in their appeal to students. Let $\alpha = 0.05$. Determine the p value.

Student	1	2	3	4	5	6	7
Model A	2	1	3	3	2	1	2
Model B	1	2	1	1	1	2	1
Model C	3	3	2	2	3	3	3

20. Ⓒ Select a simple random sample of size 20 from the population of employed heads of household given in Appendix II. Use the rank correlation technique to see whether you can conclude that there is a direct relationship between age and annual income. Let $\alpha = 0.05$. Find the p value.

21. Ⓒ The following data are measures of cardiac well-being of eight hospitalized patients before and after treatment with an experimental drug. A larger value indicates a more desirable condition. Use the Wilcoxon test to determine whether we can conclude that the treatment is effective. Let $\alpha = 0.05$. Find the p value.

Patient	1	2	3	4	5	6	7	8
After	48	67	104	60	52	63	46	52
Before	50	41	51	36	39	57	44	35

22. Ⓒ A random sample of 12 executives aged 50 or older participate in a physical-fitness program for six months. The following are the subjects' serum cholesterol levels at the beginning and end of the program. Do these data provide sufficient evidence to indicate that the physical-fitness program is effective in lowering serum cholesterol values? Use the Wilcoxon test. Let $\alpha = 0.05$. Find the p value.

Subject	1	2	3	4	5	6	7	8	9	10	11	12
Before	210	231	225	260	235	240	326	235	240	267	284	201
After	195	236	210	220	220	210	296	195	201	237	210	220

23. Ⓒ At the end of the physical-fitness program, the 12 executives in Exercise 22 took a test to measure their endurance, with the following results: 936, 977, 891, 883, 844, 975, 978, 873, 945, 946, 826, 855. Can we conclude on the basis of these data that the population mean is not 900? Let $\alpha = 0.05$. Find the p value. Use the Wilcoxon test.

24. Select a simple random sample from the population of companies in Appendix III. (Ask your instructor how large the sample should be.) Formulate an appropriate hypothesis about the assets variable that can be tested by means of the Wilcoxon signed-rank test. Select a level of significance, carry out the seven-step hypothesis-testing procedure, and find the p value for the test.

25. Repeat Exercise 24 with the sales variable.

26. Repeat Exercise 24 with the market value variable.

27. Repeat Exercise 24 with the net profits variable.

28. Repeat Exercise 24 with the cash flow variable.

29. Repeat Exercise 24 with the number employed variable.

30. Select a simple random sample from the population of companies in Appendix III. (Ask your instructor how large the sample should be.) Formulate an appropriate hypothesis about assets and sales that can be tested by means of the Spearman rank correlation procedure. Choose a level of significance, carry out the seven-step hypothesis-testing procedure, and find the p value for the test.

31. Repeat Exercise 30 with assets and market value.

32. Repeat Exercise 30 with assets and net profits.

33. Repeat Exercise 30 with assets and cash flow.

34. Repeat Exercise 30 with assets and number employed.

35. Repeat Exercise 30 with sales and market value.

36. Repeat Exercise 30 with sales and net profits.

37. Repeat Exercise 30 with sales and cash flow.

38. Repeat Exercise 30 with sales and number employed.

39. Repeat Exercise 30 with market value and net profits.

40. Repeat Exercise 30 with market value and cash flow.

41. Repeat Exercise 30 with market value and number employed.

42. Repeat Exercise 30 with net profits and cash flow.

43. Repeat Exercise 30 with net profits and number employed.

44. Repeat Exercise 30 with cash flow and number employed.

*45. In Chapter 8 you learned to use Tukey's HSD statistic to compare individual pairs of means to help decide which treatments are different from which others when the one-way analysis of variance allows you to conclude that at least one difference exists. We may also perform such multiple comparison tests following the application of nonparametric analysis of variance. One such procedure is appropriate to use in conjunction with the Kruskal-Wallis one-way analysis of variance by ranks. When we use the procedure, we employ what is known as an *experiment-wise error rate* in an attempt to overcome the problem, as discussed in Section 8.3, that arises when we use the same data to conduct multiple tests. The essence of the approach is that we select a larger-than-usual value of α and divide it by the number of comparisons to be made. In general, when the experiment involves k samples, there will be a total of $k(k - 1)/2$ pairs of sample means that can be compared. To use the nonparametric multiple comparison procedure, we first obtain the mean of the ranks for each sample (treatment). Suppose that from among the k sample means we wish to compare the ith one and the jth one for significance. We let $\overline{R}_i$ be the mean of the ranks of the ith sample and $\overline{R}_j$ be the mean of the ranks of the jth sample. Next, when the test is, as usual, two-sided, we find in Table C the value of z that has $\alpha/k(k - 1)$ to its right. Finally, we form the following inequality:

$$|\overline{R}_i - \overline{R}_j| \leq z_{\alpha/k(k-1)}\sqrt{[n(n + 1)/12][(1/n_i) + (1/n_j)]}$$

If the samples are all of the same size, the inequality is $|\overline{R}_i - \overline{R}_j| \leq z_{\alpha/k(k-1)}$ $\sqrt{k(n + 1)/6}$. Any difference $|\overline{R}_i - \overline{R}_j|$ that is larger than the right-hand side of the applicable inequality is declared significant at the α level. We illustrate the procedure by comparing Treatments A and B of the $4(3)/2 = 6$ comparisons that can be made from the data in Example 13.9.1. There we have $k = 4$, $n = 33$, $n_A = 7$, $n_B = 8$, $\overline{R}_A = 136/7 = 19.4286$, and $\overline{R}_B = 236/8 = 29.5$. Suppose we choose an experiment-wise error rate of 0.20. The desired z, then, is the one with $0.20/12 = 0.0167$ of the area to its right. Reference to Table C reveals that the z we seek is 2.53. We now compute the right-hand side of the inequality: $2.53\sqrt{[4(4 + 1)/12][(1/7) + (1/8)]} = 1.6904$. Since $|19.4286 - 29.5| = 10.0714$ is larger than 1.6904, we conclude that Treatments A and B have different effects. Since Sample C also had 8 observations, we may use the same criterion to reach a conclusion about the difference between Treatment A and Treatment C. We compute $|\overline{R}_A - \overline{R}_C| = |19.4286 - 16.5| = 2.9286$. Since 2.9286 is greater than 1.6904, we conclude that Treatments A and C have different effects. We follow the same procedure for making the four remaining possible comparisons. Keep in mind that the right-hand side of the relevant inequality must be recalculated when the sample sizes and/or the experiment-wise error rate are different. Now, do the following: (a) Make the four remaining possible comparisons for Example 13.9.1 using the same experiment-wise error rate. (b) Refer to Exercise 13.9.3. Make all possible comparisons with an experiment-wise error rate of 0.15.

1.   MAGAZINE ADS AND THE FOG INDEX

Robert Gunning, in his book *The Technique of Clear Writing* (McGraw-Hill, 1968), uses what he calls the Fog Index to measure the readability of printed materials. Anyone can measure the Fog Index for a given book or article just by using the following three-step procedure.

1. Find the average sentence length. You do this by counting off a number of sentences and then dividing the total number of words in them by the number of sentences. For books and long articles, several 100-word passages are examined this way.

2. For every 100 words of text, count the total number of words with three or more syllables. Do not count proper names, combinations of short easy words (such as fairyland), or three-syllable words that are created by adding *-es, -ed,* or *-ing.*

3. Add the results of steps 1 and 2 and multiply by 0.4 to obtain the Fog Index value.

Shuptrine and McVicker hypothesized that there is a high correlation between the educational level of magazine audiences and the readability of the ads appearing in these magazines. To see whether their hypothesis would be supported, they selected a sample of nine magazines. For each magazine, they computed a measure of the educational level of its readers. They selected at random six advertisements from each magazine and computed the Fog Index for each of the ads. They then averaged the six scores, to obtain a summary Fog Index for the magazine's ads. Finally, they ranked the magazines on the basis of readers' educational level and the Fog Index. They obtained a Spearman rank correlation coefficient of 0.183. Is their hypothesis supported? Let $\alpha = 0.05$. Find the p value for the test. What assumptions are necessary?

Source: F. Kelly Shuptrine and Daniel D. McVicker, "Readability Levels of Magazine Ads," *Journal of Advertising Research* 21 (October 1981), 45–51.

2.   BUSINESS ETHICS OF TOP VERSUS MIDDLE MANAGERS

We are all aware that ethics are concerned with the right and wrong aspects of an action. But in today's fiercely competitive business world, what do managers consider "right" and what "wrong"? Where do they draw the line? To find out, Kam-Hon Lee did a study of ethical standards of marketing managers. He asked practicing managers to evaluate certain statements and practices. One aspect of the topic with which he was concerned was whether top and middle managers both had the same beliefs about ethics.

Participants in the study indicated the extent to which they agreed with ten statements having to do with ethical behavior. As an example, here is one of the statements: "You produce an anti-dandruff shampoo that is effective with one application. Your assistant says that the product would turn over faster if the instructions on the label recommended two applications. Do you agree that you would recommend two applications?" From subjects' responses, Lee constructed the following ranking (from most agreeable, 1, to least agreeable, 10) of the statements by top managers (TM) and middle managers (MM).

Statement	1	2	4	4	5	6	7	8	9	10
Rank by TM	2	4	5	6	8	1	10	3	9	7
Rank by MM	1	3	6	5	8	2	10	4	9	7

Compute a measure of the agreement among ranks. What do you conclude from these results? What assumptions are required?

Source: Kam-Hon Lee, "Ethical Beliefs in Marketing Management: A Cross-Cultural Study," *European Journal of Marketing* 15, 1 (1981), 58–67.

3. WAITING FOR A PHONE, PART III

Refer to the telephone experiment by Ruback, Pape, and Doriot described in the Statistics at Work section of Chapter 8. The authors state that the amount of time subjects spend on the phone is not normally distributed, a condition that causes concern about the validity of the parametric analysis of variance as a technique for analyzing the data. The authors' solution to the problem of nonnormality was to use a logarithmic transformation of the data. Doing this did not alter their conclusions. An alternative strategy for overcoming the problem of nonnormality is to use a nonparametric statistical technique to analyze the data. What nonparametric procedure discussed in this chapter would be appropriate for the telephone data? Use the appropriate nonparametric procedure and see if you reach the same conclusions arrived at by the use of parametric analysis of variance.

Source: R. Barry Ruback, Karen D. Pape, and Philip Doriot, "Waiting for a Phone: Intrusion on Callers Leads to Territorial Defense," *Social Psychology Quarterly* 52 (1989), 232–241.

4. PUBLIC ATTITUDES TOWARD SCIENCE AND TECHNOLOGY

In 1972, the Opinion Research Corporation conducted a survey for the National Science Foundation to determine public attitudes toward science and technology. The sample consisted of 2,209 persons 18 years of age or older. The survey focused on three general aspects of the attitudes of the public: its regard for science and technology, its assessment of their impacts, and its expectations and desires for their future role in dealing with national problems. As part of the survey, respondents were given a list of nine occupations and instructed to "Choose the statement (excellent, good, average, below average, poor) that best gives your own personal opinion of the prestige or general standing that each job has." Ratings were assigned in which excellent = 100, good = 80, average = 60, below average = 40, and poor = 20. The average of the ratings are shown in the first column of the following table.

In a previous study, conducted in 1963, Hodge, Siegel, and Rossi reported the scores shown in the second column of the table. Compute a measure of the agreement between the two sets of scores and perform a test to see if you can conclude that the public's perception of the nine occupations was the same in 1972 as in 1963.

Ratings of Nine Occupations

| | **Total Score** | |
Occupation	1972	1963
Physician	90	93
Scientist	86	92
Minister	83	87
Engineer	83	86
Lawyer	82	89
Architect	81	88
Banker	81	85
Accountant	78	81
Businessman	77	80

Source: *Science Indicators 1972, Report of the National Science Board, 1973.* National Science Board, National Science Foundation, Washington, D.C., pp. 96–100. R. W. Hodge, P. M. Siegel, and P. H. Rossi (1964). "Occupational Prestige in the United States, 1925–63," *American Journal of Sociology,* 70 (November):286–302.

5. GEOGRAPHIC PATTERNS: R & D IN THE UNITED STATES

The National Science Foundation (NSF) collects and maintains data on the resources devoted to research and development (R & D) in the United States. A special NSF report contains information on expenditures on R & D by state and the sector or organization performing the R & D. The following table shows the 50 states and the District of Columbia ranked according to 1985 R & D performance in two sectors. Determine from these data if there is an association between performance in the two sectors.

State rank by R & D–performing sector: 1985

State	Federal	Academia
Alabama	8	27
Alaska	35	43
Arizona	18	21
Arkansas	38	41
California	3	1
Colorado	17	16
Connecticut	14	18
Delaware	50	46
District of Columbia	2	33
Florida	9	17
Georgia	23	14
Hawaii	42	36
Idaho	44	47
Illinois	22	5
Indiana	27	23
Iowa	40	24
Kansas	46	32
Kentucky	33	37
Louisiana	31	25
Maine	49	48
Maryland	1	7
Massachusetts	13	3
Michigan	25	9
Minnesota	32	19
Mississippi	16	38
Missouri	28	22
Montana	41	45
Nebraska	45	34
Nevada	24	49
New Hampshire	29	39
New Jersey	5	10
New Mexico	4	4
New York	20	2
North Carolina	15	12
North Dakota	43	40
Ohio	7	11
Oklahoma	36	30
Oregon	30	26
Pennsylvania	11	8
Rhode Island	12	35
South Carolina	39	31
South Dakota	48	51
Tennessee	21	29
Texas	10	6
Utah	26	28
Vermont	41	44
Virginia	6	20
Washington	19	15
West Virginia	34	42
Wisconsin	37	13
Wyoming	47	50

Source: *Geographic Patterns: R & D in the United States* (NSF 89-317), National Science Foundation, Washington, D.C., 1989.

SUGGESTIONS FOR FURTHER READING

Bradley, James V. (1968). *Distribution-Free Statistics*. Prentice-Hall, Englewood Cliffs, N.J.

Conover, W. J. (1980). *Practical Nonparametric Statistics*, 2nd ed. Wiley, New York.

Daniel, Wayne W. (1990). *Applied Nonparametric Statistics*, 2nd ed. PWS-Kent, Boston.

Dietz, E. Jacquelin. (1989). "Teaching Regression in a Nonparametric Statistics Course," *American Statistician* 43:35–40.

Gibbons, Jean D. (1985). *Nonparametric Methods for Quantitative Analysis*, 2nd ed. American Sciences Press, Columbus, Ohio.

Hollander, Myles, and Douglas A. Wolfe (1973). *Nonparametric Statistical Methods*. Wiley, New York.

Lehmann, E. L. (1975). *Nonparametrics: Statistical Methods Based on Ranks*. Holden-Day, San Francisco.

Marascuilo, Leonard A., and Maryellen McSweeney (1977). *Nonparametric and Distribution-free Methods for the Social Sciences*. Brooks/Cole, Monterey, Calif.

Mosteller, Frederick, and R. E. K. Rourke (1973). *Sturdy Statistics: Nonparametrics and Order Statistics*. Addison-Wesley, Reading, Mass.

Noether, G. E. (1976). *Introduction to Statistics: A Nonparametric Approach*, 2nd ed. Houghton Mifflin, Boston.

Siegel, Sidney (1956). *Nonparametric Statistics for the Behavioral Sciences*. McGraw-Hill, New York.

Theil, H. (1950). "A Rank-Invariant Method of Linear and Polynomial Regression Analysis. III," *Koninklijke Nederlandse Akademie Van Wetenschappen, Proceedings, Series A* 53:1397–1412.

14

Time-Series Analysis and Forecasting

Chapter Objectives: This chapter introduces you to some of the tools that are useful in the analysis of time-series data. These tools will help you identify the underlying trends and patterns that exist in time-series data and will give you a basis for forecasting the values for future time periods. After studying this chapter and working the exercises, you should be able to

1. Construct a linear trend line for time-series data.
2. Use the Durbin-Watson statistic to test for auto-correlation.
3. Use the method of moving averages to smooth time-series data.
4. Use exponential smoothing techniques to smooth time-series data.
5. Calculate measures of seasonal variation.
6. Calculate measures of cyclical variation.
7. Use smoothed averages, trend values, and/or seasonal index values to obtain forecasts for future time periods.
8. Use Winters' method to forecast.
9. Evaluate forecasting methods to determine which are better.

14.1   INTRODUCTION

A *time series* is a sequence of values of some variable, or composite of variables, taken at successive time periods. Examples of time series include the monthly sales volume of a department store, the annual production of steel in the United States, the annual births in a given state, and the weekly price of pork. In time-series analysis, interest focuses on the variability from one time period to another exhibited by the variable of interest. Why are there more births one year than another? Why is the price of pork higher this week than last? Why are sales of a department store not the same for December as for February?

The analysis of time-series data is of interest to those who wish to understand the nature of past and present data and to those who want to use knowledge of past data to forecast the future. This chapter tries to convey an idea of the nature of time-series data by presenting some analytical techniques and showing how we use time-series data for forecasting.

Accurate forecasts are useful for planning.

Accurate forecasts are very important to both the short-range and long-range planning of a business firm. Good forecasting techniques are needed, for example, in the areas of production, capital investment, personnel management, and inventory control. We have a variety of techniques for obtaining forecasts. A firm may base its forecasts on the individual or collective opinions of its executives, the hunches of its sales directors, or the convictions of its chief accountants. Alternatively, the firm may incorporate statistical procedures in its forecasting methods. The sections that follow discuss some of the procedures appropriate for this purpose.

14.2   COMPONENTS OF TIME-SERIES DATA

The classical approach to time-series analysis begins with the premise that a typical time series has the following four components.

1. *Long-term trend* is the general behavior of a given variable over a long period of time. By observing the long-term trend, we can characterize a time series as showing a downward trend, showing an upward trend, or being stationary. A stationary time series has neither an upward nor a downward trend. Long-term trend is sometimes called *secular trend*.

2. *Seasonal variation* refers to variation of a periodic nature. It is not limited to periodic variation associated with the seasons of the year, although variation of this type is certainly important. Some examples of variables subject to seasonal variation are production of certain farm products, sales volume of department stores, boating accidents, and the number of cars passing a certain point between downtown and suburbia. The unit of time referred to in discussing seasonal variation is less than a year. It may be a quarter, a month, a week, a day, or part of a day.

3. *Cyclical variation* refers to those up-and-down fluctuations that are observable over extended periods of time. These wavelike fluctuations, called *business cycles*, are different from seasonal fluctuations in that they cover longer periods of time, have different causes, and are less predictable.
4. *Erratic variation* is that variation not accounted for by trend, cycle, or seasonal factors. Sometimes called *random variation* or *irregular variation*, this component is not systematic like the other components. In this discussion, random variation is considered to be due to a host of unpredictable influences. Some feel that this definition is an oversimplification. Nevertheless, we can get worthwhile results from analyses based on this concept.

Given these four components of a time series, let us investigate the nature of the relationship among them. The relationship is usually described by one of two models: the *multiplicative model* or the *additive model*. We may present the additive model as

$$Y = T + S + C + E$$

where Y is an observed value of the variable of interest, T is the trend component, S is the seasonal component, C is the cyclical component, and E is the erratic component.

In the additive model, S, C, and E are quantitative deviations about T. This model assumes that the components are independent of one another.

The most widely used model is the *multiplicative model*:

$$Y = T \cdot S \cdot C \cdot E$$

The symbols refer to the same sources of variation as in the additive model, but they are expressed differently and are not numerically equivalent. In the additive model, all the values are expressed in original units. But in the multiplicative model, only one component, usually trend, is expressed in original units. The other three components are expressed as *relatives*, or *percentages*.

We use the multiplicative model in this chapter. In Sections 14.3, 14.4, and 14.5 we cover procedures that are helpful in identifying the components in a set of time-series data. Sections 14.6, 14.7, and 14.8 discuss methods for estimating these components. We begin in Section 14.6 with a consideration of procedures for estimating the trend component T for each of the time periods for which actual data are available. Section 14.7 deals with estimating seasonal components, and Section 14.8 is concerned with cyclical variation.

COMPUTER **ANALYSIS**

We may use either MINITAB or STAT+ to perform time-series analyses. MINITAB's capabilities are extensive and include a wide variety of calculations and graph construction. For further information, consult the MINITAB *Hand-*

FIGURE 14.2.1   STAT+ time-series menu

```
              STAT +         Version 2.0
              TIME SERIES DECOMPOSITION
= 1) DATA HANDLING
  2) PRINT THE DATA SET TO PRINTER OR TEXT FILE
  3) COMPUTE OR IMPOSE SEASONAL INDICES AND DESEASONALIZE DATA
  4) FIT LEAST SQUARES TREND TO DESEASONALIZED DATA
  5) USE TREND AND SEASONAL INDICES TO FORECAST
  6) PRINT THE FORECAST TO PRINTER OR TEXT FILE
  7) GRAPH TIME SERIES
  8) RETURN TO  STAT +  SYSTEM MENU
              MAKE A CHOICE,  THEN  PRESS ENTER
```

book or the MINITAB *Reference Manual.* The menu in Figure 14.2.1 shows the STAT+ capabilities in the area of basic time-series analysis.

14.3   GRAPHS AND FREEHAND FITTING

A useful first step in the analysis of time-series data is the construction of a graph to portray the behavior over time of the variable of interest Y. We may think of the variable of interest as the dependent variable, since its values are "dependent" on time. If, for example, we are interested in annual sales over some period of time, say 1975 to 1985, annual sales is the dependent variable and time, which has the values 1975, 1976, and so on, is thought of as the independent variable. We sometimes refer to Y as the "time-series variable."

We represent time on the horizontal axis and the dependent variable on the vertical axis.

When we graph time-series data, we plot the values of the dependent variable on the vertical axis and represent the time periods on the horizontal axis. The resulting graph is a scatter diagram, such as those discussed in Chapter 9. Visual inspection of the scatter diagram may suggest the presence in the data of one or more of the time-series components—trend, seasonal variation, cyclical variation, and erratic variation. Such a preliminary examination of the data can be very helpful in determining the appropriate model to use in further analysis and may aid in the development of forecasts of the dependent variable for future time periods.

Suppose that a scatter diagram suggests the presence of a long-term trend. If it appears that the trend can reasonably be approximated by a linear equation, we most likely would want to fit a straight line to the data. By plotting, on the scatter diagram, such a straight line that "fits" the data reasonably well, we highlight the general behavior of the variable of interest over time.

OBTAINING A FREEHAND LINEAR EQUATION

In Section 9.4, we mention two methods for obtaining a linear regression equation: (1) freehand fitting of a straight line and (2) the method of least squares. In that section, we use the method of least squares to obtain a regression equation. In this section, we demonstrate the use of the freehand method of fitting a straight line to the observations of a time-series variable. We then use that line to obtain a linear equation that we can use for further trend analysis. The procedure consists of three steps:

1. Construction of a scatter diagram.
2. Visual determination of the location of what appears to be the straight line that best "fits" the data, and the actual drawing of that line. (This line will vary depending on the judgment of the individual drawing the line.)
3. Use of two points on this straight line to obtain the values of a, the Y intercept, and b, the slope for the linear equation.

The procedure is illustrated by the following example.

EXAMPLE 14.3.1   The Midas Software Company reports the following quarterly demand for a certain software package over a three-year period (12 quarters): 37, 22, 62, 80, 77, 95, 94, 131, 148, 155, 126, and 161. We wish to prepare a scatter diagram, visually fit a straight line to the data, and obtain a linear equation for the straight line.

SOLUTION   The scatter diagram for the data is shown in Figure 14.3.1. A "best"-fitting freehand line has been drawn. In the judgment of the person who drew it, this line represents the nature of the relationship between time and quarterly demand better than any other straight line that can be drawn through the data. The line that would result from someone else's attempt to draw the "best"-fitting line would probably be somewhat different. To obtain an estimate of the equation for the line, we proceed as follows. We arbitrarily select two values of the time period t, and for each we determine a value of Y such that when the Y's are paired with the selected values of t they yield the coordinates of two points on the line. By substituting the values of each of these coordinates into the general formula for a linear equation,

$$(14.3.1) \qquad Y = a + bt$$

we obtain estimates of the values of a and b for our equation. For convenience, we choose 0 as the first value of t. From Figure 14.3.1, we see that when $t = 0$, the coordinate value of Y is 24. That is, (0, 24) are the coordinates of a point on the line. Substituting this pair of coordinates into Equation 14.3.1 yields $24 = a + b(0)$. Therefore, the value of a, the Y intercept, is 24. In order to improve the accuracy of the estimate of b, we select, as our second value of t,

FIGURE 14.3.1   Quarterly demand (in thousands of units) for a product over a three-year period

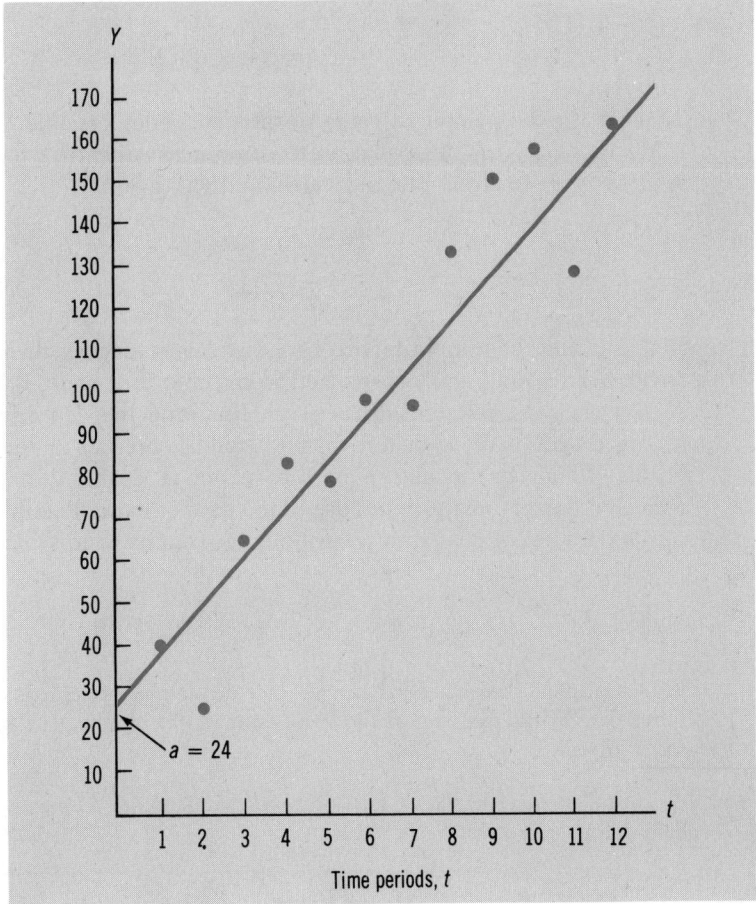

one of the larger t values. Suppose that we let $t = 12$. Again from Figure 14.3.1, we find that the coordinate value of Y is 160. That is, (12, 160) are the coordinates of another point falling on the line. Substituting these coordinates into Equation 14.3.1 gives $160 = a + b(12)$, or $160 = a + 12b$. Since from the previous substitution we found that $a = 24$, we can make the following substitution in our last equation:

$$160 = 24 + 12b$$

Solving for b yields

$$12b = 136$$
$$b = 11.33$$

Thus, our linear equation estimated from the freehand-fitted line in Figure 14.3.1 is

$$Y_c = 24 + 11.33t$$

where Y_c = the computed value of the time-series variable.

We may now use our equation to compute a value of Y for each value of t. If we let $t = 1$, for example, our calculated value of Y is

$$Y_c = 24 + 11.33(1)$$
$$= 35.33$$

The scatter diagram in Figure 14.3.1 strongly suggests the presence of a linear trend. Scatter diagrams constructed from other time-series data may not suggest such a clear-cut relationship between time and the dependent variable. Other scatter diagrams may suggest that no trend is present or that the trend is nonlinear. Whatever the nature of the scatter diagram, it provides useful clues regarding further analysis and use of the data at hand. Possible analyses and uses of the data are discussed in the following sections of this chapter.

EXERCISES

In each of the following exercises, (a) plot the data as presented; (b) fit a straight line to the data by the freehand method and estimate the trend equation; and (c) compute Y_c for each year.

14.3.1 C The following table shows, for Rosebery Manufacturing Company, the number of items damaged in shipment, 1970–1984.

Year	No. of Items	Year	No. of Items
1970	533	1978	291
1971	373	1979	228
1972	132	1980	204
1973	555	1981	349
1974	168	1982	234
1975	281	1983	209
1976	72	1984	176
1977	175		

14.3.2 C The following table shows the volume of sales, in thousands of dollars, of Sands Department Store, 1971–1984.

Year	Sales (× $1,000)	Year	Sales (× $1,000)
1971	815	1978	12,529
1972	1,276	1979	12,824

Year	Sales (× **$1,000**)	Year	Sales (× **$1,000**)
1973	4,752	1980	13,777
1974	7,535	1981	15,379
1975	10,122	1982	18,705
1976	9,642	1983	17,632
1977	14,100	1984	16,571

14.3.3 C The following table shows the number of items repaired under warranty by Todd Service and Repair Company, 1971–1984.

Year	Number	Year	Number
1971	749	1978	611
1972	709	1979	600
1973	700	1980	574
1974	678	1981	559
1975	611	1982	543
1976	641	1983	534
1977	631	1984	524

14.3.4 C The following table shows the annual sales of Uhland and Associates over 11 years.

Year	Sales (Millions of Dollars)	Year	Sales (Millions of Dollars)
1972	12	1978	20
1973	14	1979	22
1974	18	1980	27
1975	20	1981	24
1976	18	1982	30
1977	16		

14.4 MOVING AVERAGES

One of the effects of fitting a trend line to a set of time-series data is a "smoothing" of the seasonal and erratic variation. We may be able to discern the general behavior of the dependent variable over time more easily by observing the trend line than by inspecting the original data. Figure 14.4.1, which shows the trend line visually fitted to the data of Example 14.3.1, illustrates these points. The original observations have been connected by straight lines to emphasize the magnitude of the variability present in the data.

Other smoothing techniques are available for use with time-series data. One such method that is frequently used to obtain smoothed values is the *method of moving averages*. This method is nonlinear in the sense that it does not result in a straight line. However, it does temper, or smooth out, peaks and valleys in a set of observations. A moving average is defined as follows:

FIGURE 14.4.1   Quarterly demand (in thousands of units) for a product over a three-year period
(original data and visually fitted trend line)

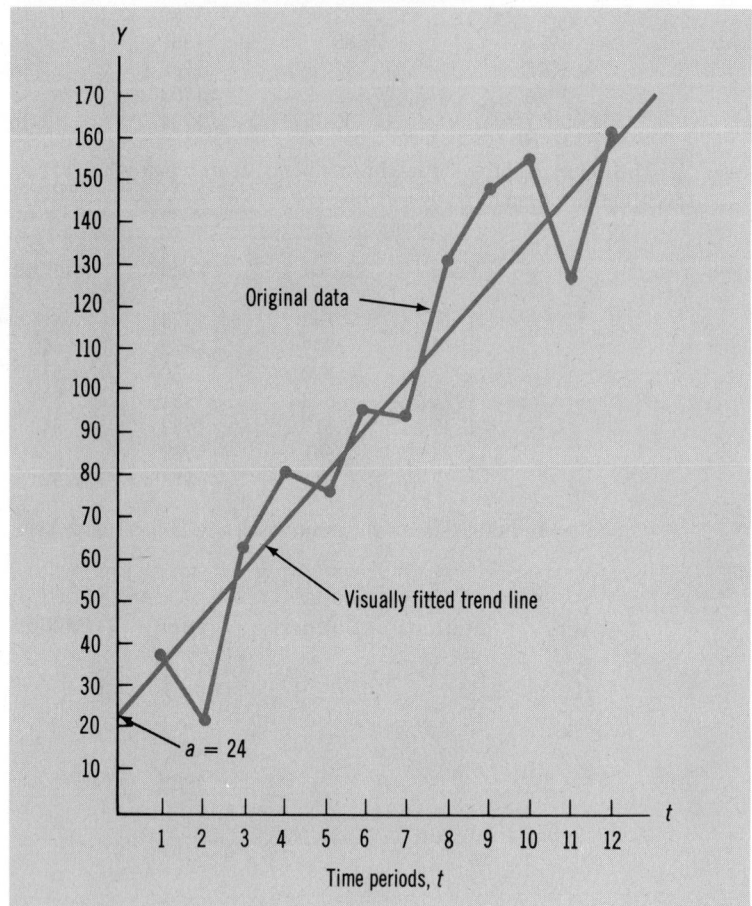

> A *moving average* is an artificially constructed time series in which the value
> for a given time period is replaced by the mean of that value and the
> values for some number of preceding and succeeding time periods.

For example, suppose that we have a time series consisting of annual data for
the years 1910 to 1980. We wish to compute the three-year moving average. We
take the value for 1911, add to it the values for 1910 and 1912, and divide by
3. We then use the resulting average in place of the original value for the year
1911. We continue this procedure through 1979. We cannot compute a three-
year average for the year 1980 (since there is no succeeding value to add to the
values for 1979 and 1980), nor for the year 1910 (since there is no preceding

year to add to the years 1910 and 1911). We can compute a moving average for any number of years. In general, the greater the number of time periods covered, the smoother the resulting curve. The objective in constructing a moving average is to bring out the trend by eliminating any obscuring seasonal, cyclical, or random fluctuations.

Although the moving-average technique is useful under certain conditions, it has drawbacks. One of these is that we lose values for some time periods at the beginning and end of the series. In the example just cited, we lost one year at the beginning and one year at the end of the series. If we compute a five-year moving average, we lose two years at each end, and so on. Another disadvantage is the fact that the method of moving averages does not yield an actual equation. Consequently, the method of moving averages is not, in general, very useful as a forecasting tool. In a limited number of instances, however, the last moving average may be used as a forecast.

A moving average is tedious to compute. The main reason we present the method here is that we use its computational techniques in Sections 14.6 and 14.7. As we show, the computation of a 12-period moving average is an integral step in one method of eliminating seasonal variation from monthly data.

The following example shows the techniques for computing a moving average.

EXAMPLE 14.4.1 Table 14.4.1 shows the number of units of real estate sold by Wallach Realty during the years 1952–1982. The objective is to compute the five-year moving average for these data.

SOLUTION Table 14.4.2 shows the original data, along with the five-year moving totals and five-year moving-average values. Figure 14.4.2 plots the original data and the moving average.

The moving averages computed in Example 14.4.1 contain an odd number of time periods. The procedure must be modified when it is necessary to use an even number of time periods in computing a moving average. This is the case when the time periods are quarters (4 in a year) or months (12 in a year). The result obtained using this modified procedure is called a centered moving average. It is discussed and illustrated in Section 14.7.

TABLE 14.4.1 Number of units of real estate sold by a certain broker, 1952–1982

Year	1952	1953	1954	1955	1956	1957	1958	1959	1960	1961	1962
No. units	1	14	14	24	25	19	8	17	15	44	40

Year	1963	1964	1965	1966	1967	1968	1969	1970	1971	1972	
No. units	25	9	35	35	55	22	48	76	75	199	

Year	1973	1974	1975	1976	1977	1978	1979	1980	1981	1982	
No. units	83	96	96	142	46	86	16	156	143	32	

TABLE 14.4.2   Five-year moving totals and five-year moving average, Example 14.4.1

Year	1952	1953	1954	1955	1956	1957	1958	1959	1960	1961
Annual sales	1	14	14	24	25	19	8	17	15	44
5-year moving totals			78	96	90	93	84	103	124	141
5-year moving average			15.6	19.2	18.0	18.6	16.8	20.6	24.8	28.2

Year	1962	1963	1964	1965	1966	1967	1968	1969	1970	1971
Annual sales	40	25	9	35	35	55	22	48	76	75
5-year moving totals	133	153	144	159	156	195	236	276	420	481
5-year moving average	26.6	30.6	28.8	31.8	31.2	39.0	47.2	55.2	84.0	96.2

Year	1972	1973	1974	1975	1976	1977	1978	1979	1980	1981	1982
Annual sales	199	83	96	96	142	46	86	16	156	143	32
5-year moving totals	529	549	616	463	466	386	446	447	433		
5-year moving average	105.8	109.8	123.2	92.6	93.2	77.2	89.2	89.4	86.6		

FIGURE 14.4.2   Number of units of real estate sold by a broker, 1952–1982, original data and five-year moving average

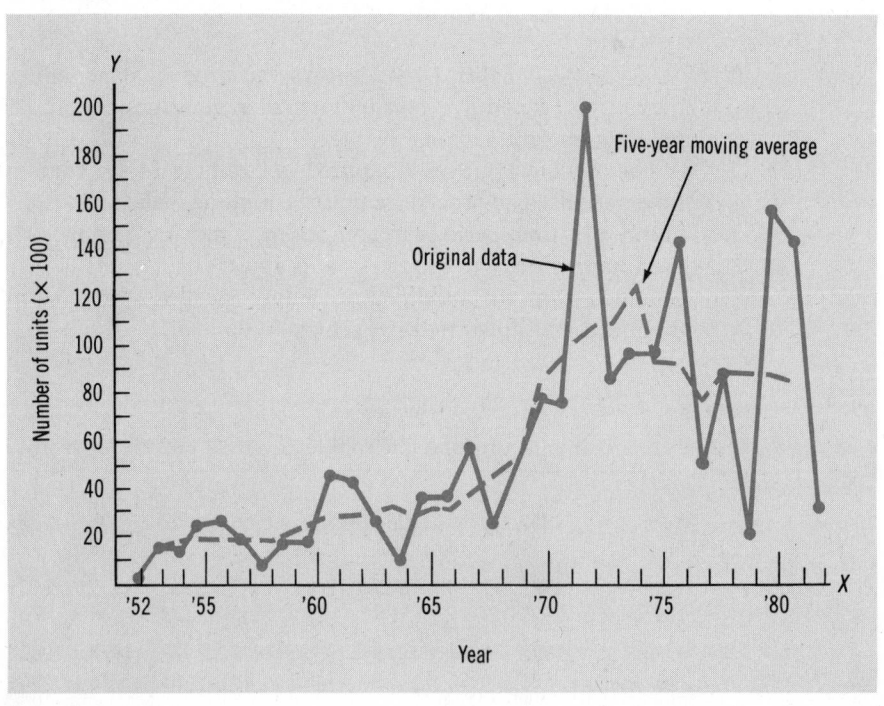

EXERCISES

14.4.1   Ⓒ Compute a five-year moving average using the data of Exercise 14.3.1.

14.4.2   Ⓒ Compute a three-year moving average using the data of Exercise 14.3.2.

14.4.3   Ⓒ Compute a three-year moving average using the data of Exercise 14.3.3.

14.4.4   Ⓒ Compute a three-year moving average using the data of Exercise 14.3.4.

14.5   EXPONENTIAL SMOOTHING

Although the moving-average method of smoothing time-series data, discussed in the preceding section, is satisfactory for some situations, the shortcomings we mentioned earlier limit the usefulness of the technique. In this section, we discuss another method of smoothing time-series data, which does not have these drawbacks. The method is called *exponential smoothing*. As we have seen, the moving-average procedure uses the observed values of a time series in such a way that they are weighted equally in the averaging process. Exponential smoothing weights the observed values of the time series unequally, so that more recent observations are weighted more heavily than older observations.

Exponential smoothing weights recent observations more heavily than older observations.

Exponential smoothing has some important advantages over other smoothing techniques. The computations are simple, and the data-storage requirements are minimal. Exponential smoothing techniques are readily available in computer software packages. The use of exponential smoothing allows us to compute a smoothed average at the end of any time period. The average obtained provides an estimate of the mean of the time-series variable when only random variation is present in the data. Appropriate adjustments for trend and/or seasonal components may be made, however, and these procedures are relatively simple and straightforward. As we see in Section 14.9, exponential smoothing is one of the most widely used forecasting techniques. In this section, we will limit our discussion to its use in the analysis of time-series data rather than as a forecasting tool.

SIMPLE EXPONENTIAL SMOOTHING

Simple exponential smoothing, or first-order exponential smoothing, as it is sometimes called, is the least complicated form of exponential smoothing. When applied to a set of time-series data as a smoothing technique to isolate the trend component, it eliminates or reduces fluctuations that are due to seasonal, cyclical, or random variability. The procedure is based on a period-by-period adjustment of the latest smoothed average, $\overline{Y}_{t-1}$. We accomplish the adjustment by adding or subtracting a portion α of the difference between the observed value for the current period Y_t and the latest smoothed average $\overline{Y}_{t-1}$. The result is a new smoothed average for the current time period, which we designate $\overline{Y}_t$. The procedure is summarized in the following formula:

(14.5.1)
$$\overline{Y}_t = \overline{Y}_{t-1} + \alpha(Y_t - \overline{Y}_{t-1})$$

The quantity α in the equation is called the exponential *smoothing factor* or exponential *smoothing coefficient* or exponential *smoothing constant*. Its value must be between 0 and 1, inclusive. The most commonly used value of α is one between 0.1 and 0.3. We can make calculation of the smoothed average for the current time period easier if we rearrange Equation 14.5.1 to obtain

(14.5.2)
$$\overline{Y}_t = \alpha Y_t + (1 - \alpha)\overline{Y}_{t-1}$$

We may express Equation 14.5.2 in words as follows:

(14.5.3)
$$\begin{pmatrix} \text{The average} \\ \text{for the} \\ \text{current} \\ \text{time period} \end{pmatrix} = \alpha \begin{pmatrix} \text{most recently} \\ \text{observed} \\ \text{value} \end{pmatrix} + (1 - \alpha) \begin{pmatrix} \text{the average} \\ \text{for the} \\ \text{previous} \\ \text{time period} \end{pmatrix}$$

That is, the average for the current time period is equal to the sum of the most recently observed value of the variable of interest and the average for the previous time period, each weighted by an appropriate factor.

Equation 14.5.2 provides a weighted average of all past data, but this fact is not immediately apparent from the formula. We may gain insight into the nature of the formula if we consider the following. If $\overline{Y}_t$ is the average for the current time period, we can use Equation 14.5.2 to write an equation for the smoothed average for time period $t - 1$, computed at time period $t - 1$. It is as follows:

(14.5.4)
$$\overline{Y}_{t-1} = \alpha Y_{t-1} + (1 - \alpha)\overline{Y}_{t-2}$$

Similarly, we may write the smoothed average for time period $t - 2$ as

(14.5.5)
$$\overline{Y}_{t-2} = \alpha Y_{t-2} + (1 - \alpha)\overline{Y}_{t-3}$$

that for time period $t - 3$ as

(14.5.6)
$$\overline{Y}_{t-3} = \alpha Y_{t-3} + (1 - \alpha)\overline{Y}_{t-4}$$

and so on.

We can now show why the smoothing or averaging procedure under discussion is called exponential smoothing. Suppose that we substitute the right-hand side of Equation 14.5.4 for its equivalent $\overline{Y}_{t-1}$ in Equation 14.5.2. The result is

(14.5.7)
$$\overline{Y}_t = \alpha Y_t + (1 - \alpha)[\alpha Y_{t-1} + (1 - \alpha)\overline{Y}_{t-2}]$$
$$= \alpha Y_t + \alpha(1 - \alpha)Y_{t-1} + (1 - \alpha)^2\overline{Y}_{t-2}$$

The right-hand side of Equation 14.5.5 may now be substituted for $\overline{Y}_{t-2}$ in Equation 14.5.7 to give

(14.5.8)
$$\overline{Y}_t = \alpha Y_t + \alpha(1 - \alpha)Y_{t-1} + (1 - \alpha)^2[\alpha Y_{t-2} + (1 - \alpha)\overline{Y}_{t-3}]$$
$$= \alpha Y_t + \alpha(1 - \alpha)Y_{t-1} + \alpha(1 - \alpha)^2 Y_{t-2} + (1 - \alpha)^3\overline{Y}_{t-3}$$

Finally, we may substitute the right-hand side of Equation 14.5.6 for $\overline{Y}_{t-3}$ in Equation 14.5.8 to get the following result:

(14.5.9)
$$\overline{Y}_t = \alpha Y_t + \alpha(1 - \alpha)Y_{t-1} + \alpha(1 - \alpha)^2 Y_{t-2}$$
$$+ (1 - \alpha)^3[\alpha Y_{t-3} + (1 - \alpha)\overline{Y}_{t-4}]$$
$$= \alpha Y_t + \alpha(1 - \alpha)Y_{t-1} + \alpha(1 - \alpha)^2 Y_{t-2}$$
$$+ \alpha(1 - \alpha)^3 Y_{t-3} + (1 - \alpha)^4\overline{Y}_{t-4}$$

We can continue this expansion as far back in time as we wish by making appropriate substitutions for $\overline{Y}_{t-4}$, $\overline{Y}_{t-5}$, and so on. Equation 14.5.9, however, is sufficient to illustrate the nature of exponential smoothing. In arriving at a new average, this equation shows the magnitudes of the weights assigned to each previous time period's actual value.

We recall that $0 \leq \alpha \leq 1$. Therefore, the terms α, $\alpha(1 - \alpha)$, $\alpha(1 - \alpha)^2$, $\alpha(1 - \alpha)^3$, and $\alpha(1 - \alpha)^4$ are successively smaller. The most recent value of Y is given the most weight, whereas values for more remote time periods receive progressively smaller weights, with the value for the most remote time period receiving the smallest weight. Suppose, for example, that $\alpha = 0.3$. Then $\alpha(1 - \alpha) = 0.21$, $\alpha(1 - \alpha)^2 = 0.147$, $\alpha(1 - \alpha)^3 = 0.1029$, and $\alpha(1 - \alpha)^4 = 0.07203$. Thus, if data are available for a total of n time periods, the weight assigned to the value of the first, or oldest, time period would be $\alpha(1 - \alpha)^{n-1}$. Since the weights decrease exponentially (or geometrically), they are said to be exponentially distributed; hence the term exponential smoothing.

CHOOSING THE SMOOTHING CONSTANT

The choice of the smoothing constant α greatly influences the end result in the smoothing technique, and you should exercise care in selecting it.

Let us illustrate the use of Equation 14.5.2 with an example.

EXAMPLE 14.5.1 The sales of musical instruments by Rhythm Ranch, a local music store, for the past 10 months are as follows: 74, 69, 80, 91, 76, 83, 79, 87, 89, and 92. The owners of the store are interested in using exponential smoothing to aid in analyzing these data.

SOLUTION   Let us compute the exponentially smoothed average for each month. When we begin the smoothing calculations, no data are available prior to period 1, so we should set the smoothed average for period 1, $\overline{Y}_1$, equal to some reasonable value, such as the actual value for period 1. That is, we can let $\overline{Y}_1 = Y_1$. Suppose that we let $\alpha = 0.3$ and set $\overline{Y}_1 = Y_1 = 74$. The use of Equation 14.5.2 yields the following smoothed averages:

$$\overline{Y}_2 = 0.3(69) + 0.7(74) = 72.50$$
$$\overline{Y}_3 = 0.3(80) + 0.7(72.50) = 74.75$$
$$\overline{Y}_4 = 0.3(91) + 0.7(74.75) = 79.62$$
$$\overline{Y}_5 = 0.3(76) + 0.7(79.62) = 78.53$$
$$\overline{Y}_6 = 0.3(83) + 0.7(78.53) = 79.87$$
$$\overline{Y}_7 = 0.3(79) + 0.7(79.87) = 79.61$$
$$\overline{Y}_8 = 0.3(87) + 0.7(79.61) = 81.83$$
$$\overline{Y}_9 = 0.3(89) + 0.7(81.83) = 83.98$$
$$\overline{Y}_{10} = 0.3(92) + 0.7(83.98) = 86.39$$

The owners of the store can use these smoothed averages to help them understand the pattern of sales over the 10-month period. They might even want to consider using exponential smoothing to forecast future sales. This use of exponential smoothing is discussed in Section 14.9.

SMOOTHING-FACTOR SELECTION

As Equation 14.5.9 shows, no observed value of the time-series variable is ever dropped from the calculation of the smoothed average $\overline{Y}_t$, but the weight attached to a given value becomes less and less as the values for later time periods enter into the calculation. The rate at which this reduction in influence occurs for a given value depends on the smoothing factor α. When α is large (that is, near 1), the most recent value of Y is weighted much more heavily than the older values. On the other hand, a small value of α (that is, a value near 0) causes the weights assigned to the older values of Y to be closer in size to the weights assigned to recent values of Y. The influence that the value of α has on the weights is illustrated by the following example.

EXAMPLE 14.5.2   We wish to determine and compare the sets of weights that would be assigned to the latest five values of a time-series variable for α values of 0.1 and 0.9, respectively.

SOLUTION   The two sets of weights are shown in Table 14.5.1.

When deciding on a value for α, we must realize that a large change in the value of our time-series variable from one time period to another may be due to random variation, or it may indicate a real change in the underlying forces af-

TABLE 14.5.1 Weights for the latest five values of a time-series variable for specified α values

Time Period	Weights Assigned for α Values of	
	0.1	0.9
t	0.1	0.9
$t - 1$	0.09	0.09
$t - 2$	0.081	0.009
$t - 3$	0.0729	0.0009
$t - 4$	0.06561	0.00009
$t - 5$	0.059049	0.000009

As a rule, use a small value of α when random variation is large and a large value of α when random variation is small.

fecting the variable itself, such as, for example, a change in demand for a product. If the random-variation component is very large, we would want to use a small value of α so that our smoothed values would represent a slower response to a real change. However, if the random-variation component is small, we would probably want the smoothed values to respond rapidly to such a change, and consequently we would choose a larger value of α. When selecting a value of α, we should try to achieve a reasonable balance between two kinds of error: (1) responding too slowly to a real change in the variable and (2) overresponding to random variation. A frequently used method for determining α is to compute a set of smoothed averages using each of several values of α and then choose the value that yields the most satisfactory results according to a predetermined criterion. A computer program that calculates an optimal value of α for a given set of data is included in the book by Gross and Peterson listed at the end of this chapter.

EXERCISES

In each of the following exercises, compute exponentially smoothed averages for each year.

14.5.1 Use the data of Exercise 14.3.1 and let $\alpha = 0.2$.

14.5.2 Use the data of Exercise 14.3.2 and let $\alpha = 0.3$.

14.5.3 Use the data of Exercise 14.3.3 and let $\alpha = 0.4$.

14.5.4 Use the data of Exercise 14.3.4 and let $\alpha = 0.1$.

14.6 MEASURING TREND

So far we have discussed the components of time series (trend, seasonal variation, cyclical variation, and random variation) and certain techniques that may be useful in identifying which of these components may exist in a set of time-series data. The techniques we have discussed are the construction of graphs in the form of scatter diagrams, the fitting of linear equations, and two smoothing techniques, the method of moving averages and simple exponential smoothing. We now turn our attention to methods for decomposing a set of time-series data into the various components so that they may be numerically measured. We begin by considering the measurement of trend.

LINEAR TREND

If we can estimate the trend value for a time period, we can eliminate this component from the original value. Doing this will help to reveal the presence and magnitudes of the other components. The increase or decrease in a series of observed values of some variable over consecutive time periods may be fairly constant. If so, a straight line may provide an adequate means of describing the trend. We can express linear trend as

(14.6.1)
$$Y_c = a + bt$$

where Y_c is the value of the trend for a given time period t. The letter a represents the Y intercept of the trend line, or the trend value when $t = 0$, and b is the slope of the trend line. Note that Equation 14.6.1 is the same equation used in Chapter 9 and Section 14.3.

We may use the freehand method or the method of least squares to obtain a trend equation.

In order to obtain an equation that we can use in describing linear trend, we must obtain numerical values for a and b. We may obtain these values in a variety of ways. In Section 14.3, we mention two methods: (1) freehand fitting and (2) the method of least squares. We demonstrate the freehand-fitting method in Section 14.3. We will now use the method of least squares to obtain values of a and b.

The study of regression in Chapter 9 shows that if we can express the relationship between two variables such as Y and t by an equation of the form

(14.6.2)
$$Y = \alpha + \beta t + e$$

where α and β are constants and e is a random variable with a mean of 0 and variance σ^2, then the method of least squares provides unbiased sample estimates of α and β, which are designated a and b, respectively. The computational formulas for a and b are as follows:

(14.6.3)
$$b = \frac{n\Sigma t_i Y_i - \Sigma t_i \Sigma Y_i}{n\Sigma t_i^2 - (\Sigma t_i)^2}$$

(14.6.4)
$$a = \bar{Y} - b\bar{t}$$

Note that the notation in this chapter is different from that in Chapter 9. In this chapter, we use Y_i instead of y_i and t_i instead of x_i.

For convenience in computing values of a and b, we label the time periods with consecutive integers, beginning with 1 for the oldest time period, 2 for the next oldest, and so on. The following example illustrates the computational procedure.

EXAMPLE 14.6.1   Table 14.6.1 shows the annual volume of timber cut from national forest areas for commercial sale for the years 1956–1970. The data are rounded to the nearest tenth of a billion board feet. We wish to fit a least-squares trend line to the data.

SOLUTION   As a first step, we replace the years with codes, as previously mentioned. That is, 1 replaces 1956, 2 replaces 1957, and so on, until 15 replaces 1970. Table 14.6.2 shows the codes, along with the other necessary computations. The data are plotted in Figure 14.6.1. Substituting appropriate values from Table 14.6.2 into Equations 14.6.3 and 14.6.4 gives

$$b = \frac{15(1303.8) - 120(148.3)}{15(1240) - (120)^2} = 0.4193$$

$$a = 9.8867 - (0.4193)(8) = 6.5323$$

TABLE 14.6.1   Volume (billions of board feet) of timber cut from national forest system areas, 1956–1970

Year	1956	1957	1958	1959	1960	1961	1962	1963
Volume	7.0	7.1	6.5	8.5	9.5	8.5	9.2	10.2

Year	1964	1965	1966	1967	1968	1969	1970
Volume	11.1	11.4	12.3	11.0	12.3	12.0	11.7

Source: Historical Statistics of the United States, Colonial Times to 1970, Bicentennial Edition, Part 1, Washington, D.C., 1975. (Original data have been rounded.)

TABLE 14.6.2   Computations for Example 14.6.1

Year	Year Code, t	Volume, Y_i	tY_i	t^2	Y_c
1956	1	7.0	7.0	1	7.0
1957	2	7.1	14.2	4	7.4
1958	3	6.5	19.5	9	7.8
1959	4	8.5	34.0	16	8.2
1960	5	9.5	47.5	25	8.6
1961	6	8.5	51.0	36	9.0
1962	7	9.2	64.4	49	9.5
1963	8	10.2	81.6	64	9.9
1964	9	11.1	99.9	81	10.3
1965	10	11.4	114.0	100	10.7
1966	11	12.3	135.3	121	11.1
1967	12	11.0	132.0	144	11.6
1968	13	12.3	159.9	169	12.0
1969	14	12.0	168.0	196	12.4
1970	15	11.7	175.5	225	12.8
Total	120	148.3	1303.8	1240	

FIGURE 14.6.1 Volume (billions of board feet) of timber cut from national forest system areas, 1956–1970

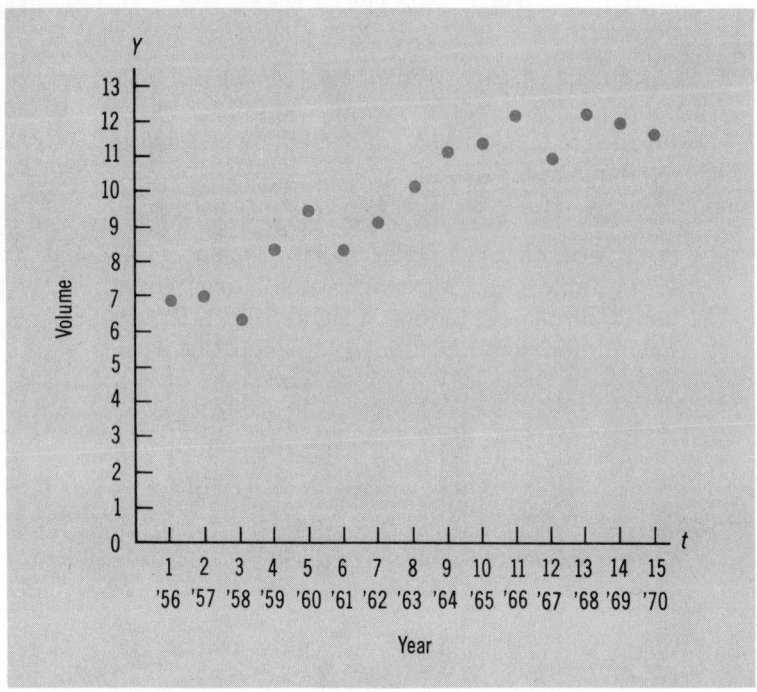

We can now write the equation of the trend line as

$$Y_c = 6.5323 + 0.4193t$$

The next step in the analysis is to substitute the various observed values of t into the equation in order to obtain the values of Y_c shown in the last column of Table 14.6.2. Figure 14.6.2 shows the plotted calculated trend line, along with the original data.

A straight line is not always the line of best fit for a set of time-series data. Other types of curves might be useful, depending on the data. Examples include the parabola, exponential curves, the Gompertz curve, and the Pearl-Reed, or logistic, curve. The last two are widely used for describing growth.

Trend analysis is of primary importance in business forecasting, an activity that is vital to any business. One use of forecasting is to estimate future demand (or sales) for a product. As we have seen, trend analysis consists of applying certain statistical procedures to historical data. A firm may use the results of this analysis to make estimates or projections into the future. The value of such estimates depends on how well past experience represents future experience, after proper adjustment for trend, seasonal, cyclical, and erratic influences. It is mean-

FIGURE 14.6.2 Volume (billions of board feet) of timber cut from national forest system areas, 1956–1970, original data and trend line

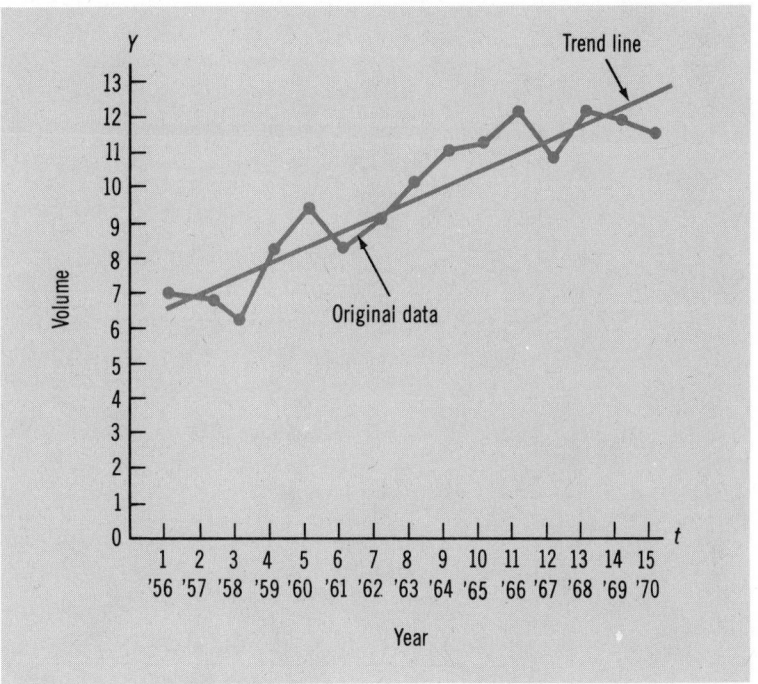

ingless—and even dangerous—for a firm to make such projections unless it seems that the future will be fairly much like the past.

THE MOVING AVERAGE

We may also use the moving-average technique discussed in Section 14.4 to estimate the trend value for a given time period. This procedure, as we have seen, yields a set of averages, each of which is centered on a certain time period. We can treat the average computed for a given time period as the trend value for that time period and use it in eliminating the trend component for that period. We discuss this use of a moving average in Section 14.7.

EXPONENTIALLY SMOOTHED AVERAGE

As we learned in Section 14.5, exponential smoothing yields a smoothed average of the dependent variable for each time period. We may use each of these smoothed averages as an estimate of the trend value for the associated time

FIGURE 14.6.3 Relationship between actual trend and exponentially smoothed average under two conditions

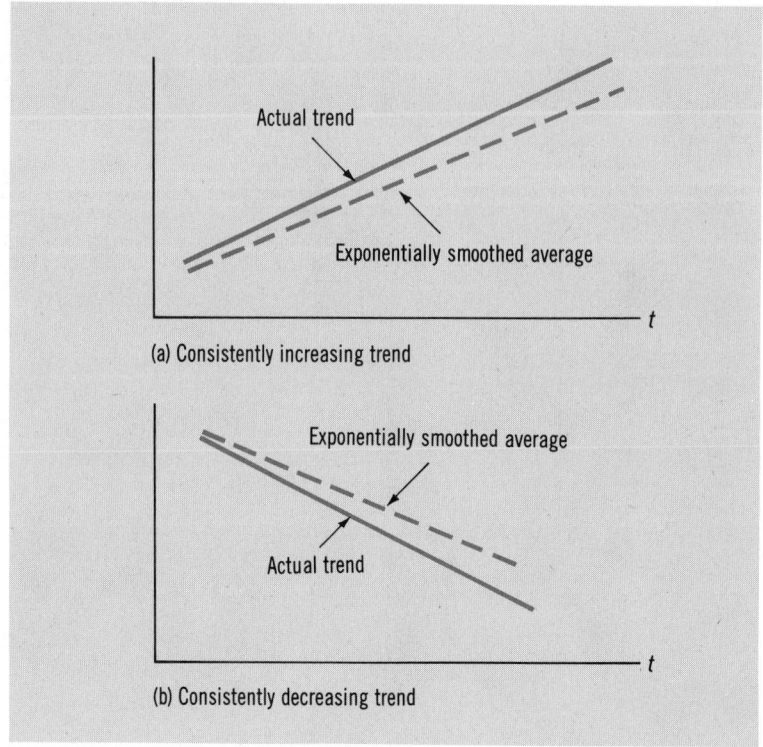

(a) Consistently increasing trend

(b) Consistently decreasing trend

period. When there is a consistently increasing or decreasing trend in a set of time-series data, an exponentially smoothed average will lag behind the actual values of the time series. If there is an increasing trend, the smoothed average will run low. When the trend is decreasing, the smoothed average will run high. This phenomenon is illustrated graphically in Figure 14.6.3(a) for a time-series variable that increases consistently and in Figure 14.6.3(b) for one that decreases consistently.

The amount of lag that occurs depends on both the amount of trend that is present and the value of the smoothing factor α. An adjustment for trend can help in reducing this lag problem. The adjustment is accomplished through the use of the following formula:

(14.6.5)
$$\overline{Y}_{t_a} = \overline{Y}_t + \left(\frac{1 - \alpha}{\alpha}\right) \overline{b}_t$$

where $\overline{Y}_{t_a}$ = smoothed average adjusted for trend
$\overline{Y}_t$ = smoothed average for time period t
$\overline{b}_t$ = average, or smoothed, trend value
α = smoothing factor

We obtain a trend value b_t for each time period by subtracting the smoothed average for the previous period, $\overline{Y}_{t-1}$, from the smoothed average for the period involved, $\overline{Y}_t$. Thus,

(14.6.6)
$$b_t = \overline{Y}_t - \overline{Y}_{t-1}$$

The average or smoothed trend value $\overline{b}_t$ is likely to be obtained in one or the other of the following two ways:

1. By computing a simple arithmetic average of all past trend values (or an average of some of the more recent trend values)
2. By obtaining an exponentially smoothed trend value computed in the same manner as the smoothed average, using the following formula:

(14.6.7)
$$\overline{b}_t = \alpha b_t + (1 - \alpha)\overline{b}_{t-1}$$

Both procedures are illustrated in the following example.

EXAMPLE 14.6.2   Refer to Example 14.5.1. We wish to compute the trend-adjusted smoothed averages using   (a) the arithmetic average of all trend values and   (b) the exponentially smoothed trend value.

SOLUTION   Table 14.6.3 shows the actual values, the smoothed averages, and the trend values b_t for each of the ten time periods.

Now let us calculate, for each time period, $\overline{Y}_{t_a}$, the smoothed averages adjusted for trend. First we obtain $\overline{b}_t$ by computing the arithmetic mean of the nine values of b_t shown in column 3 of Table 14.6.3. We find that

$$\overline{b}_t = \frac{\Sigma b_t}{n} = \frac{12.39}{9} = 1.377$$

TABLE 14.6.3   Actual values, smoothed averages, and trend values for the sale of musical instruments for a ten-month period

Month	Y_t (1)	$\overline{Y}_t$ (2)	$b_t = \overline{Y}_t - \overline{Y}_{t-1}$ (3)
1	74	74.00	—
2	69	72.50	−1.50
3	80	74.75	2.25
4	91	79.62	4.87
5	76	78.53	−1.09
6	83	79.87	1.34
7	79	79.61	−0.26
8	87	81.83	2.22
9	89	83.98	2.15
10	92	86.39	2.41
			12.39

Recall that in Example 14.5.1 we let $\alpha = 0.3$. The rightmost term of Equation 14.6.5, then, is

$$\left(\frac{1 - \alpha}{\alpha}\right) \bar{b}_t = \left(\frac{1 - 0.3}{0.3}\right) 1.377 = 3.21$$

Thus, we add 3.21 to each smoothed average for months 2 through 10 to obtain the trend-adjusted arithmetic average. These values, along with the data of Table 14.6.3, are shown in Table 14.6.4.

We now compute the $\bar{b}_t$ values by the exponential smoothing method using Equation 14.6.7. The results are shown in column 3 of Table 14.6.5. We next calculate the rightmost term of Equation 14.6.5 and display the results in column 4 of Table 14.6.5.

TABLE 14.6.4   Actual values, smoothed averages, trend values, and trend-adjusted smoothed averages (arithmetic method) for the sale of musical instruments for a ten-month period

Month	Y_t	$\bar{Y}_t$	$b_t = \bar{Y}_t - \bar{Y}_{t-1}$	$\bar{Y}_t + \left(\frac{1-\alpha}{\alpha}\right) b_t$ Arithmetic
	(1)	(2)	(3)	(4)
1	74	74.00	—	74.00
2	69	72.50	−1.50	75.71
3	80	74.75	2.25	77.96
4	91	79.62	4.87	82.83
5	76	78.53	−1.09	81.74
6	83	79.87	1.34	83.08
7	79	79.61	−0.26	82.82
8	87	81.83	2.22	85.04
9	89	83.98	2.15	87.19
10	92	86.39	2.41	89.60
			12.39	

TABLE 14.6.5   Calculation of $\bar{b}_t$ by Equation 14.6.7

Month	b_t	$\bar{b}_t = 0.3b_t + 0.7\bar{b}_{t-1}$	$\left(\frac{1-0.3}{0.3}\right) \bar{b}_t$
(1)	(2)	(3)	(4)
2	−1.50	−1.500	−3.50
3	2.25	−0.375	−0.88
4	4.87	1.198	2.80
5	−1.09	0.512	1.19
6	1.34	0.760	1.77
7	−0.26	0.454	1.06
8	2.22	0.984	2.30
9	2.15	1.334	3.11
10	2.41	1.657	3.87

These trend adjustments are added to the appropriate smoothed averages shown in column 2 of Table 14.6.3. The resulting trend-adjusted smoothed averages are shown in column 5 of Table 14.6.6, which also contains the data of Table 14.6.4 for purposes of comparison. We note that neither the arithmetic average method nor the exponential method of obtaining $\overline{b}_t$ assumes a knowledge of the trend component for the first time period.

Since we do not have actual values of Y for time periods prior to period 1, we cannot compute $\overline{Y}$ for time period 1. However, we let $\overline{Y}_1 = Y_1$, as shown in column 2 of Tables 14.6.3, 14.6.4, and 14.6.6. Furthermore, because we do not have actual Y values prior to time period 1, we cannot compute b_t for time period 1. Therefore, b_t for time period 1 is missing from column 3 of Tables 14.6.3 through 14.6.6.

In summary, we note that at this point we have recognized the existence of a trend component, computed the trend value, and adjusted the smoothed average for the presence of this trend. Since this information is now available, we could use it to obtain a trend-adjusted forecast F_{t+1} for the next period, $t + 1$, by means of the following formula:

(14.6.8)
$$F_{t+1} = \overline{Y}_{t_a} + \overline{b}_t$$

A forecast for any future time period $t + k$ can be obtained by the general formula

(14.6.9)
$$F_{t+k} = \overline{Y}_{t_a} + k\overline{b}_t$$

Note that Equations 14.6.8 and 14.6.9 are linear projections or extrapolations for future time periods.

TABLE 14.6.6   Actual values, smoothed averages, trend values, and trend-adjusted smoothed averages (arithmetic and exponential smoothing methods) for the sale of musical instruments for a ten-month period

Month	Y_t	$\overline{Y}_t$	$b_t = \overline{Y}_t - \overline{Y}_{t-1}$	$\overline{Y}_t + \left(\dfrac{1-\alpha}{\alpha}\right)\overline{b}_t$	
				Arithmetic	Smoothed
	(1)	(2)	(3)	(4)	(5)
1	74	74.00	—	74.00	74.00
2	69	72.50	−1.50	75.71	69.00
3	80	74.75	2.25	77.96	73.87
4	91	79.62	4.87	82.83	82.42
5	76	78.53	−1.09	81.74	79.72
6	83	79.87	1.34	83.08	81.64
7	79	79.61	−0.26	82.82	80.67
8	87	81.83	2.22	85.04	84.13
9	89	83.98	2.15	87.19	87.09
10	92	86.39	2.41	89.60	90.26
			12.39		

AUTOCORRELATION

As we have already noted, an assumption for the valid application of the linear trend model is an independent error component. When this assumption is violated because the error terms are correlated, the data exhibit a characteristic known as autocorrelation, a concept that was discussed briefly in Chapter 9. Since, in the analysis and interpretation of time-series data, many problems arise from the presence of autocorrelation, the topic merits additional comment at this time.

There are two types of autocorrelation that one may encounter—*positive autocorrelation* and *negative autocorrelation*. We say that positive autocorrelation is present in error terms occurring over time in two situations: (1) if a positive error term in time period t tends to be followed by a positive error term at one or more later time periods and (2) if a negative error term at time period t tends to be followed by a negative error term at one or more later time periods. We would thus expect to observe positive autocorrelation in a series of sales data for an item experiencing a high level of consumer demand over several time periods followed by several time periods in which demand for the item experienced a steady decline. The residual plot of Figure 14.6.4 illustrates the presence of positive autocorrelation.

We say that a series of error terms exhibits negative autocorrelation if a positive

FIGURE 14.6.4 Residual plot showing the presence of positive autocorrelation

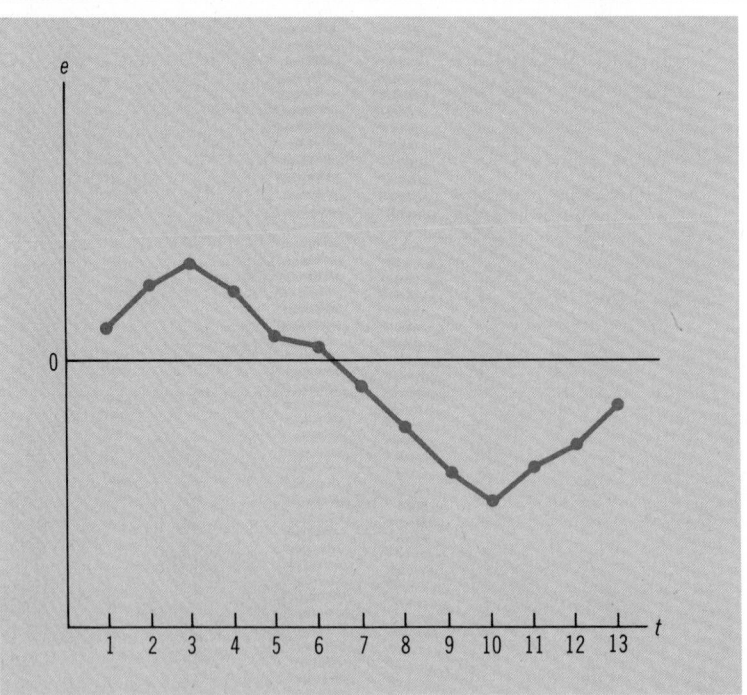

error term in time period t tends to be followed by a negative error term at one or more future time periods and if a negative error term at time period t tends to be followed by a positive error term at one or more future time periods. One expects, for example, to observe negative autocorrelation among error terms arising from data that are subject to the so-called *cobweb theorem* of economics. According to this theorem, the prices of some items, notably certain farm commodities, in a given year are forced up as a result of limited supply. The high prices encourage increased production the following year, thereby driving prices down. Low prices then result in decreased production, which in turn forces prices up again. This repeating cyclical pattern, when graphed, yields a picture that looks something like a stylized cobweb. The graph of the resulting residuals produces a pattern such as that shown in Figure 14.6.5.

TESTING FOR AUTOCORRELATION

Several objective techniques, including the runs test discussed in Chapter 13, are available for use in testing for the presence of autocorrelation in a population of time-series data. The most frequently used procedure for this purpose, however,

FIGURE 14.6.5   Residual plot showing presence of negative autocorrelation

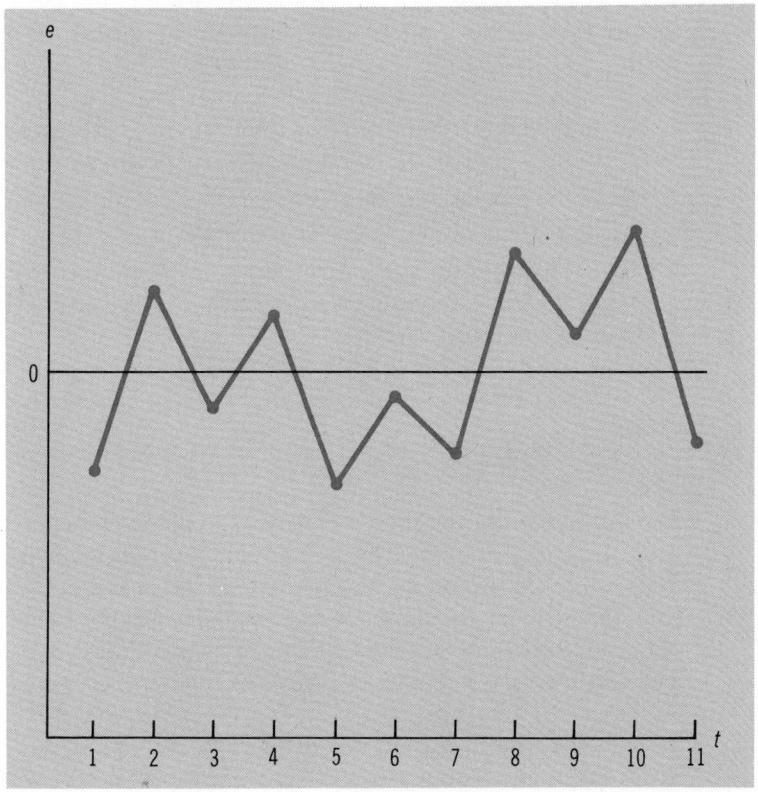

is the Durbin-Watson test statistic, named for its developers, who first published their methodology in 1951, in *Biometrika* (38, pp. 159–178). The Durbin-Watson test statistic is

(14.6.10)
$$d = \frac{\sum_{t=1}^{n} (e_t - e_{t-1})^2}{\sum_{t=1}^{n} e_t^2}$$

where $e_1, e_2, \ldots, e_n$ are the sample residuals ordered according to time.

Most statistics software packages, including STAT+ and MINITAB, contain a program for calculating the Durbin-Watson statistic.

Durbin and Watson included tables of critical values of d for various sample sizes, numbers of independent variables, and levels of significance. These tables appear as Table P in Appendix I.

AUTOCORRELATION HYPOTHESES

The null hypothesis that the error terms are not autocorrelated can be tested against each of three alternatives through the use of the Durbin-Watson test statistic.

1. H_0: In the population, the error terms are not autocorrelated.
   H_1: In the population, the error terms are positively autocorrelated.
2. H_0: In the population, the error terms are not autocorrelated.
   H_1: In the population, the error terms are negatively autocorrelated.
3. H_0: In the population, the error terms are not autocorrelated.
   H_1: In the population, the error terms are either positively autocorrelated or negatively autocorrelated.

THE DECISION RULES

The decision rules for the three sets of hypotheses require the determination, from the tables published by Durbin and Watson, of two critical values of d. They are called d_L and d_U. For hypothesis sets 1 and 2, d_L and d_U are obtained from the table for the chosen level of significance. For hypothesis set 3, they are obtained from the table corresponding to one-half the chosen level of significance. The decision rules may then be stated as follows:

1. Reject H_0 if $d < d_L$. Do not reject H_0 if $d > d_U$. If $d_L \leq d \leq d_U$, the test is inconclusive.

2. Reject H_0 if $(4 - d) < d_L$. Do not reject H_0 if $(4 - d) > d_U$. If $d_L \leq (4 - d) \leq d_U$, the test is inconclusive.
3. Reject H_0 if $d < d_L$ or if $(4 - d) < d_L$. Do not reject H_0 if $d > d_U$ or if $(4 - d) > d_U$. If $d_L \leq d \leq d_U$ or if $(4 - d_U) \leq d \leq (4 - d_L)$, the test is inconclusive.

EXAMPLE 14.6.3   We wish to know if the annual numbers of passengers carried by American railroads in consecutive years are positively autocorrelated.

SOLUTION   Table 14.6.7 shows the relevant data for the years 1965 through 1980. When we employ STAT+ to analyze these data, we get the graph of residuals shown in Figure 14.6.6. STAT+ also computes the Durbin-Watson test statistic. It is $d = 0.6856016$. We now perform the following hypothesis test:

1. *Hypotheses.*

   H_0: In the population, the error terms are not autocorrelated.

   H_1: In the population, the error terms are positively autocorrelated.

2. *Test statistic.* The test statistic is the Durbin-Watson statistic, d.
3. *Significance level.* Let $\alpha = 0.05$.
4. *Decision rule.* Reject H_0 if $d < 1.10$. Do not reject H_0 if $d > 1.37$. If $1.10 \leq d \leq 1.37$, the test is inconclusive. We obtain $d_L = 1.10$ and $d_U = 1.37$ from Table Pa of Appendix I when we enter the table with $n = 16$ and $k = 1$, the number of independent variables.
5. *Calculations.* As already noted, STAT+ calculates $d = 0.6856016$.
6. *Statistical decision.* Since $0.6856016 < 1.10$, we reject H_0.
7. *Conclusion.* In the population, the error terms are positively autocorrelated.

TABLE 14.6.7   Passengers carried by American railroads, 1965–1980

Year	Number of Passengers (Millions)
1965	306
1966	308
1967	304
1968	301
1969	302
1970	289
1971	276
1972	262
1973	255
1974	275
1975	270
1976	272
1977	276
1978	262
1979	274
1980	281

Source: Selected editions of *Statistical Abstract of the United States*.

FIGURE 14.6.6   Residual plot for Example 14.6.3

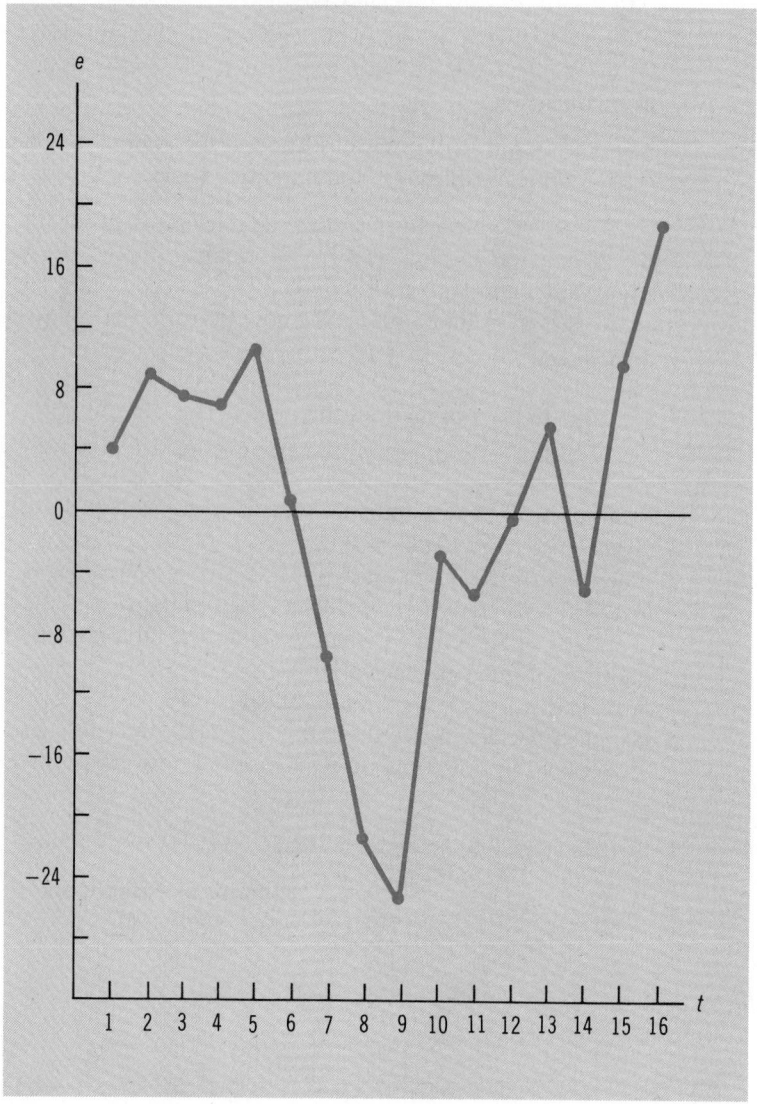

OTHER NONLINEAR METHODS

The moving average and exponentially smoothed averages are trend measures that are nonlinear in the sense that they do not result in a straight line. There are numerous other nonlinear methods and equations that we can use in obtaining trend estimates. There are many computer programs that will fit several different equations and methods to a set of time-series data and provide an evaluation of each, usually in terms of variances or standard errors.

EXERCISES

For Exercises 14.6.1 to 14.6.4, do the following. (a) Compute the least-squares trend equation for the data. (b) Compute Y_c for each year.

14.6.1 Ⓒ Use the data of Exercise 14.3.1.

14.6.2 Ⓒ Use the data of Exercise 14.3.2.

14.6.3 Ⓒ Use the data of Exercise 14.3.3.

14.6.4 Ⓒ Use the data of Exercise 14.3.4.

For each of the following exercises, compute the trend-adjusted exponentially smoothed average for each year.

14.6.5 Use the data of Exercise 14.5.1.

14.6.6 Use the data of Exercise 14.5.2.

14.6.7 Use the data of Exercise 14.5.3.

14.6.8 Use the data of Exercise 14.5.4.

14.6.9 Consult some recent issues of *Statistical Abstract of the United States*. Select a set of time-series data, perform a linear trend analysis of the data, compute d, and perform an appropriate hypothesis test for autocorrelated error terms.

14.6.10 Repeat Exercise 14.6.9 using your choice of time-series data from *Historical Statistics of the United States from Colonial Times to 1970*.

14.6.11 Repeat Exercise 14.6.9 using time-series data of your choice of variable from those appearing over several years in *Forbes* magazine. Select a company and a variable from those in Appendix III, and consult the appropriate issues of the magazine for previous years to build your set of time-series data.

14.6.12 Repeat Exercise 14.6.9 using data from the "*Fortune* 500" listing published in *Fortune* magazine. From the most recent available listing, select a company and variable of your choice, and consult appropriate issues of the magazine for previous years to build your time-series data set. The listing usually appears in May each year.

14.7 MEASURING SEASONAL VARIATION

The term *seasonal variation* brings to mind those fluctuations associated with climate and seasonally related activities and customs. Climate causes variation in the production of farm products and the availability of other raw materials. It also affects the flow of goods and human patterns of consumption in other ways. The seasonal aspect of recreational activities is an obvious example. Social customs related to holidays have an influence on such variables as department-store sales and the production of certain farm products.

Conceivably, we could make time-series data available for any time period desired. Most business data, however, are organized by days, weeks, months, or quarters.

Let us now broaden our concept of seasonal variation. If our data represent the daily sales of a large restaurant, for example, we may notice a considerable variation depending on the day of the week, whereas another organization, say the publisher of a monthly magazine, may be concerned with monthly variations in sales throughout the year. The restaurant owner is concerned with the day of the week that is involved. Each week represents a new set of time periods or a new seasonal cycle. The second organization is concerned with which month of the year is involved, and in this case, each year represents a new set of time periods or a new seasonal cycle.

A *seasonal cycle* is a set (fixed number) of time periods in which the value of a time period is related to its position in the set.

For example, the restaurant's Friday sales are usually considerably higher than Thursday sales. The *seasonal cycle* for the restaurant is a week, and the days of the week are the *seasons*. For the monthly magazine publisher, months are the seasons, and a year is the seasonal cycle. We use the letter L to designate the number of seasons (periods) in a seasonal cycle. For example, when the seasonal cycle is a year and the seasons are months, $L = 12$.

When we analyze time-series data, we can use a number of methods for measuring seasonal variation. However, since our objective here is just to introduce the subject, we do not cover all of them. We limit our discussion to the *ratio-to-trend* method. With this method, a trend value is computed for each time period, using a procedure such as one of those discussed in the preceding sections. The method for measuring seasonal variations would be the same regardless of the procedure used in obtaining the trend values. We illustrate this method using trend values obtained by the moving-average technique. Accordingly, we call this the *ratio-to-moving-average* method. The technique has the additional advantage of being widely used. It consists of two basic steps:

1. Calculating a somewhat sophisticated 12-month moving average for each time period
2. Dividing this moving average for each time period into the original value to obtain the ratio-to-moving-average value

We can use these results to calculate *seasonal indexes*, which can then be used to deseasonalize data, as the following example shows.

EXAMPLE 14.7.1 Column 1 of Table 14.7.1 shows the monthly sales, in bushels, of a certain variety of apple by a farmers' cooperative for the years 1979 through 1983.

SOLUTION Columns 2 through 5 contain the computations needed to carry out the ratio-to-moving-average method for computing indexes of seasonal variation. The data are plotted in Figure 14.7.1 (shown on page 804).

The seasonal pattern associated with the sales of apples can be readily seen in Figure 14.7.1. The peak periods are from October through March. The lowest point on the curve each year occurs in August.

TABLE 14.7.1 Monthly sales of apples by a farmers' cooperative, 1979–1983

Year	Month	(1) Number of Bushels	(2) 12-Month Moving Total	(3) Sum of Two 12-Month Moving Totals	(4) Centered 12-Month Moving Average	(5) Ratio to Moving Average
1979	Jan.	2,406				
	Feb.	2,604				
	Mar.	3,112				
	Apr.	2,915				
	May	2,033				
	June	643				
			20,852			
	July	291		40,913	1,704.7	0.171
			20,061			
	Aug.	67		39,151	1,631.3	0.041
			19,090			
	Sept.	491		37,167	1,548.6	0.317
			18,077			
	Oct.	2,394		35,046	1,460.2	1.640
			16,969			
	Nov.	2,085		32,925	1,371.9	1.520
			15,956			
	Dec.	1,811		31,535	1,314.0	1.378
			15,579			
1980	Jan.	1,615		31,011	1,292.1	1.250
			15,432			
	Feb.	1,633		30,853	1,285.5	1.270
			15,421			
	Mar.	2,099		31,159	1,298.3	1.617
			15,738			
	Apr.	1,807		32,548	1,356.2	1.332
			16,810			
	May	1,020		34,303	1,429.3	0.714
			17,493			
	June	266		36,387	1,516.1	0.175
			18,894			
	July	144		39,367	1,640.3	0.088
			20,473			
	Aug.	56		42,414	1,767.2	0.032
			21,941			
	Sept.	808		45,279	1,886.6	0.428
			23,338			
	Oct.	3,466		46,995	1,958.1	1.770
			23,657			
	Nov.	2,768		47,650	1,985.4	1.394
			23,993			
	Dec.	3,212		48,169	2,007.0	1.600
			24,176			

(table continues on next page)

TABLE 14.7.1 *(continued)*

Year	Month	(1) Number of Bushels	(2) 12-Month Moving Total	(3) Sum of Two 12-Month Moving Totals	(4) Centered 12-Month Moving Average	(5) Ratio to Moving Average
1981	Jan.	3,194		48,355	2,014.8	1.585
			24,179			
	Feb.	3,101		48,335	2,014.0	1.540
			24,156			
	Mar.	3,496		48,342	2,014.2	1.736
			24,186			
	Apr.	2,126		47,272	1,969.7	1.079
			23,086			
	May	1,356		45,194	1,883.1	0.720
			22,108			
	June	449		43,498	1,812.4	0.248
			21,390			
	July	147		41,722	1,738.4	0.085
			20,332			
	Aug.	33		39,559	1,648.3	0.020
			19,227			
	Sept.	838		37,172	1,548.8	0.541
			17,945			
	Oct.	2,366		36,034	1,501.4	1.576
			18,089			
	Nov.	1,790		36,379	1,515.8	1.181
			18,290			
	Dec.	2,494		37,025	1,542.7	1.617
			18,735			
1982	Jan.	2,136		37,912	1,579.7	1.352
			19,177			
	Feb.	1,996		38,505	1,604.4	1.244
			19,328			
	Mar.	2,214		38,149	1,589.5	1.393
			18,821			
	Apr.	2,270		36,794	1,533.1	1.481
			17,973			
	May	1,557		35,682	1,486.8	1.047
			17,709			
	June	894		35,224	1,467.7	0.609
			17,515			
	July	589		34,519	1,438.3	0.410
			17,004			
	Aug.	184		33,779	1,407.5	0.131
			16,775			
	Sept.	331		33,466	1,394.4	0.237
			16,691			
	Oct.	1,518		32,778	1,365.8	1.111
			16,087			
	Nov.	1,526		32,052	1,335.5	1.143
			15,965			
	Dec.	2,300		31,462	1,310.9	1.755
			15,497			

TABLE 14.7.1   *(continued)*

Year	Month	(1) Number of Bushels	(2) 12-Month Moving Total	(3) Sum of Two 12-Month Moving Totals	(4) Centered 12-Month Moving Average	(5) Ratio to Moving Average
1983	Jan.	1,625		30,524	1,271.8	1.278
			15,027			
	Feb.	1,767		29,886	1,245.2	1.419
			14,859			
	Mar.	2,130		29,618	1,234.1	1.726
			14,759			
	Apr.	1,666		29,087	1,212.0	1.375
			14,328			
	May	1,435		28,623	1,192.6	1.203
			14,295			
	June	426		28,008	1,167.0	0.365
			13,713			
	July	119				
	Aug.	16				
	Sept.	231				
	Oct.	1,087				
	Nov.	1,493				
	Dec.	1,718				

OBTAINING MEASURES OF SEASONAL VARIATION

The ratio-to-moving-average method may proceed according to the following six steps. (All column references are to Table 14.7.1.) The ultimate objective is to produce a seasonal index, a number for each month showing the original value for that month as a proportion of the average month. The method we use rests on the multiplicative model, $Y = T \cdot S \cdot C \cdot E$, discussed earlier. The calculations consist of obtaining an estimate of the $T \cdot C$ component, which is divided into each observed value of Y to obtain an estimate of $S \cdot E$. Finally, we obtain an estimate of S by a method designed to eliminate E.

1. We first obtain the *12-month moving totals*. The first figure in column 2 is the total for the 12 months of 1979. This value falls between the months of June and July and is so placed in the table. The second figure in column 2 is the sum of values from February 1979 through January 1980, inclusive. In this manner, we obtain the 12-month moving totals shown in column 2.

FIGURE 14.7.1   Monthly sales of apples, 1979–1983

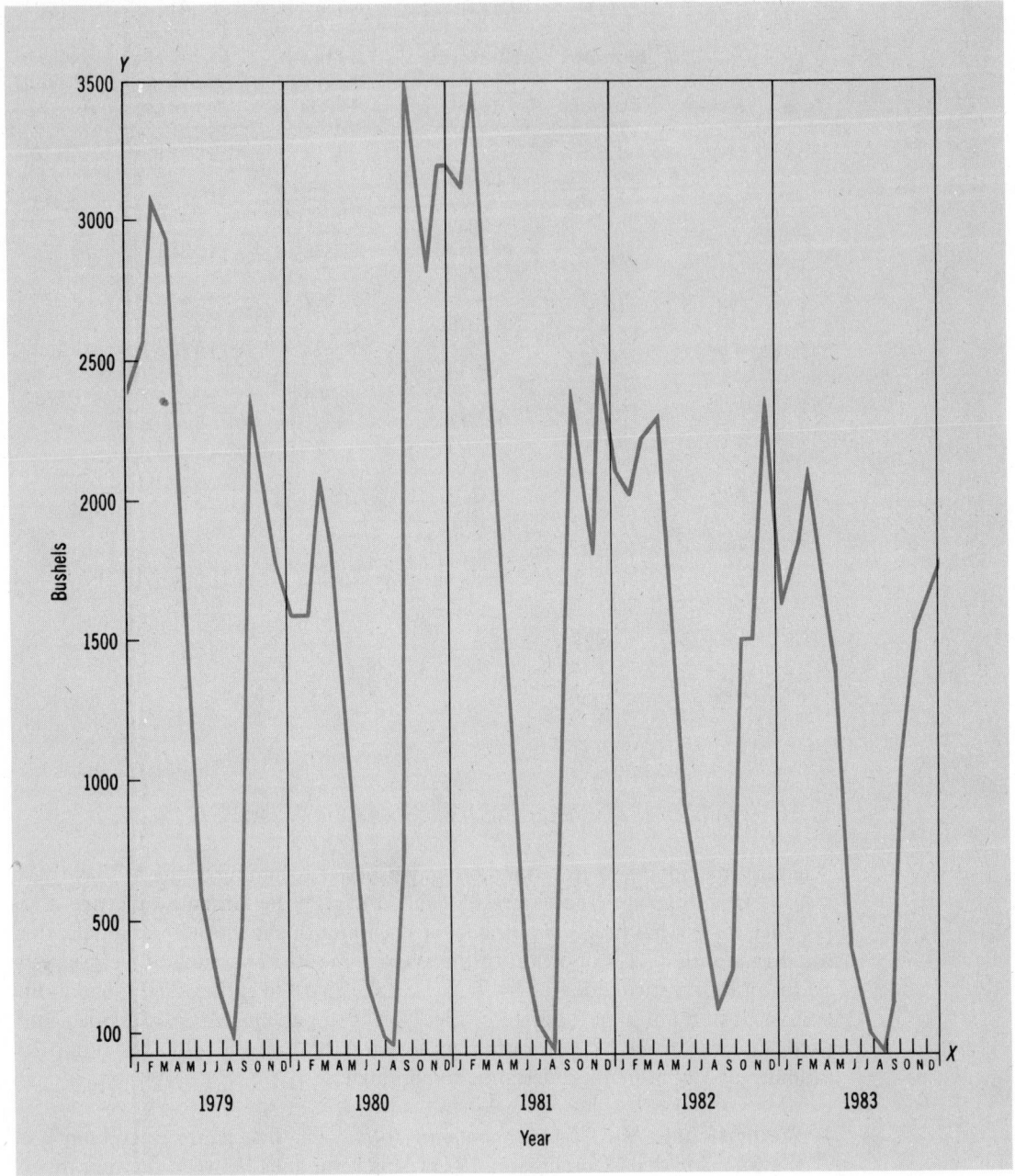

2. Column 3 gives the sum of two consecutive 12-month moving totals. We get these by adding the figures in column 2, a pair at a time, in such a way that, beginning with the second, we add each figure once to the preceding figure and once to the succeeding figure. Thus, the first entry in column 3 is the sum of the first and second figures in column 2. The second entry in column 3 is the sum of the second and third figures in column 2.

3. We find the centered 12-month moving averages of column 4 by dividing the entries in column 3 by 24. We find the 12-month moving average in order to get an estimate of the $T \cdot C$ component. Dividing both sides of the model equation by $T \cdot C$ yields an estimate of the $S \cdot E$ component. Column 5 shows the result. The next step explains its calculation.

4. To obtain column 5, we divide the original monthly entries in column 1 by the corresponding entries in column 4.

5. We next obtain for each month an "average" of the ratio-to-moving-average values in column 5. We can use any legitimate quantitative average—for example, the median or mean—depending on the nature of the data. The objective in averaging is to obtain for each month a value that represents the typical seasonal effect for that month. A common method is to compute a *modified mean*, which is the arithmetic mean of the values when extreme values have been discarded. We use that method of averaging here. Rearranging the data of column 5 as in Table 14.7.2 makes the work easier.

We use a modified mean rather than, say, the arithmetic mean of all the values in order to eliminate the problem of the influence of extreme values. If we eliminate an equal number of the smallest and largest values, the resulting mean is based on central values. In Table 14.7.2, we found the modified mean by computing the mean of the ratio-to-moving-average values for each month after we eliminated the largest and smallest values.

TABLE 14.7.2   Ratio-to-moving-average values, Example 14.7.1

Month	Year					Modified Mean	Seasonal Index
	1979	1980	1981	1982	1983		
January		1.250	1.585	1.352	1.278	1.315	1.324
February		1.270	1.540	1.244	1.419	1.344	1.353
March		1.617	1.736	1.393	1.726	1.672	1.684
April		1.332	1.079	1.481	1.375	1.354	1.363
May		0.714	0.720	1.047	1.203	0.884	0.890
June		0.175	0.248	0.609	0.365	0.306	0.308
July	0.171	0.088	0.085	0.410		0.130	0.131
August	0.041	0.032	0.020	0.131		0.036	0.036
September	0.317	0.428	0.541	0.237		0.372	0.375
October	1.640	1.770	1.576	1.111		1.608	1.619
November	1.520	1.394	1.181	1.143		1.288	1.297
December	1.378	1.600	1.617	1.755		1.608	1.619
Total						11.917	11.999

6. Finally, we get the seasonal indexes by adjusting the modified means so that their sum is 12.00. To do so, we multiply each modified mean by 12.00/11.917 = 1.0069648. The last column of Table 14.7.2 shows the seasonal indexes.

USING MEASURES OF SEASONAL VARIATION

Once we have obtained a measure of seasonal variation, the question is: How can we use it? Two general uses are (1) to analyze past data, and (2) to plan future activity.

We can deseasonalize data.

First of all, we can remove seasonal variation from a series in order to see how things might have been had there been no seasonal fluctuation. The results of such calculations are *deseasonalized data*. In order to show how a series is deseasonalized, let us apply the method to the 1983 data of Example 14.7.1. The computations consist of dividing each observed monthly value by the corresponding seasonal index. For example, the January 1983 index for the sale of apples series is 1.324. This means that the sales for January are 1.324 times the average monthly sales. If we divide the January 1983 sales, which were 1,625, by 1.324, we have

$$\frac{1,625}{1.324} = 1,227$$

We say, then, that had there been no seasonal variation, January 1983 sales would have been 1,227 bushels. We divide each of the seasonal indexes into the corresponding monthly sales figures for the year 1983 to obtain deseasonalized data. Table 14.7.3 shows the deseasonalized data.

TABLE 14.7.3 Deseasonalized data, Example 14.7.1

Month	Sales 1983 (Bushels)	Seasonal Index	Deseasonalized Sales
January	1,625	1.324	1,227
February	1,767	1.353	1,306
March	2,130	1.684	1,265
April	1,666	1.363	1,222
May	1,435	0.890	1,612
June	426	0.308	1,383
July	119	0.131	908
August	16	0.036	444
September	231	0.375	616
October	1,087	1.619	671
November	1,493	1.297	1,151
December	1,718	1.619	1,061

TABLE 14.7.4   Estimates of monthly sales of apples for 1984

Month	Seasonal Index	Estimated Sales (833 × Seasonal Index)
January	1.324	1,103
February	1.353	1,127
March	1.684	1,403
April	1.363	1,135
May	0.890	741
June	0.308	257
July	0.131	109
August	0.036	30
September	0.375	312
October	1.619	1,349
November	1.297	1,080
December	1.619	1,349

We can
seasonalize data.

Suppose that it is estimated that total sales for 1984 will be 10,000 bushels. What might we expect the month-by-month sales to be? If we did not know about seasonal variation, we might estimate each month's sales to be 1/12 of the yearly figure, or 833 bushels. Such estimates would not allow for the seasonal or monthly variation that we know exists and, therefore, would be considered to be *deseasonalized* estimates or forecasts. Since we have measurements of the variation from month to month, we can use this information to *seasonalize* the estimates or forecasts. For example, we expect January sales to be about 1.324 times the average monthly sales. For an estimate of the January sales that takes seasonal variation into account, we multiply 833 by 1.324 to obtain 1103. Assuming that the same seasonal pattern persists into 1984, we obtain the estimates of monthly sales shown in Table 14.7.4.

EXERCISES

14.7.1   Ⓒ The following table gives the number of pairs of water skis sold by Vogler Sporting Goods, by month and year, 1979–1983.   (a) Plot the data.   (b) Compute the seasonal indexes from these data, as in Example 14.7.1.   (c) Compute the deseasonalized values for 1983.

Year	J	F	M	A	M	J	J	A	S	O	N	D
1979	0	2	10	4	89	33	11	4	17	5	17	0
1980	3	0	5	4	14	23	7	11	11	4	4	8
1981	9	2	46	11	14	30	22	4	7	4	0	2
1982	13	4	56	30	90	20	15	11	6	5	1	7
1983	4	12	6	10	17	32	24	9	10	5	17	1

14.7.2   In 1984, the dealer sold 180 pairs of water skis. Using the results of Exercise 14.7.1, estimate the number of sales by month (seasonalized estimates).

14.7.3 In 1984, the sales by month were as follows. (a) How well do you think your estimates agree with the actual data? (b) How do you explain the discrepancies? (c) How would you suggest improving your estimates?

J	F	M	A	M	J	J	A	S	O	N	D
0	8	29	26	42	29	20	8	13	2	3	0

14.7.4 C The following table shows monthly sales for Tot's Toys, × $10,000, over a period of 5 years. (a) Plot the data. (b) Compute the seasonal indexes. (c) Compute the deseasonalized values for 1983. (d) In 1984, total sales were $2,050,000. Estimate the sales by month (seasonalized estimates).

	Month											
Year	J	F	M	A	M	J	J	A	S	O	N	D
1979	10	12	12	14	12	15	14	10	10	13	16	28
1980	8	12	12	12	13	16	15	9	9	12	18	31
1981	7	10	10	13	14	16	15	8	8	14	17	37
1982	10	14	14	14	15	17	14	10	10	15	20	38
1983	12	14	13	14	15	17	15	10	11	15	20	40

14.8 MEASURING CYCLICAL VARIATION

Business cycles are fluctuations in the total economic activity that are beyond the control of the businessperson. Cycles include periods of rapid growth followed by periods of slower growth or recession. There is no regularity to business cycles, in the sense that they do not occur at regular time intervals and are not of a fixed duration.

For these reasons, we cannot forecast cycles as we can seasonal fluctuations. We can, however, isolate them, and we have a number of methods of doing so. We can measure cyclical variation in data reported either on a monthly basis or annually. If we use monthly data, we can eliminate the seasonal component. In Example 14.8.1, we show how to measure cyclical variation when we have only annual data available. Example 14.8.2 demonstrates the method using monthly data.

The method for dealing with annual data that we give here is commonly used, computationally simple, and easily understood. It rests on the fact that in annual data there are only two components, trend and cycle. Seasonal fluctuations do not appear because all seasons are represented. The method also assumes that irregular variations have little influence on annual data. We can express the model that remains as

(14.8.1)
$$Y = T \cdot C$$

If we divide both sides of the equation by T, we have

(14.8.2)
$$C = \frac{Y}{T}$$

This indicates that dividing the values in the original series by the corresponding trend values yields a measure of the cycle. This measure, when multiplied by 100, is called a *cyclical relative*.

EXAMPLE 14.8.1   We wish to isolate the cyclical component from a series composed of the annual production of pairs of shoes by Warner Shoes from 1944 to 1982. Table 14.8.1 gives the original data.

SOLUTION   The first steps in the procedure are to find a trend equation and compute the trend values. We do this by the method of least squares. Table 14.8.1 also shows the intermediate computations. From the data in the table, we obtain

$$b = \frac{39(379,767) - (780)(18,565)}{39(20,540) - (780)^2} = 1.714$$

$$a = \frac{18,565}{39} - 1.714 \left(\frac{780}{39}\right) = 441.75$$

The trend equation, then, is

$$Y_c = 441.75 + 1.714t$$

Substituting the year codes into the equation yields the trend values shown in column 6 of Table 14.8.1. The original values and the trend line are plotted in Figure 14.8.1.

Column 4 of Table 14.8.2 shows the cyclical relatives, obtained by dividing observed production by trend and multiplying by 100. The cyclical relatives are plotted in Figure 14.8.2.

In monthly data, the seasonal factor is present, as are any irregular fluctuations. To eliminate both the trend and the seasonal component, we divide the original observations by both the trend value and the seasonal index. We may express this as

(14.8.3)
$$\frac{Y}{T \cdot S} = \frac{T \cdot S \cdot C \cdot E}{T \cdot S}$$

which leads to

(14.8.4)
$$C \cdot E = \frac{Y}{T \cdot S}$$

TABLE 14.8.1 Pairs of shoes produced ($\times$ 1,000) by a shoe manufacturer, 1944–1982

(1) Year	(2) Year Code t	(3) Production Y	(4) tY	(5) t^2	(6) Y_c
1944	1	380	380	1	443
1945	2	417	834	4	445
1946	3	406	1,218	9	447
1947	4	450	1,800	16	449
1948	5	478	2,390	25	450
1949	6	423	2,538	36	452
1950	7	443	3,101	49	454
1951	8	503	4,024	64	455
1952	9	552	4,968	81	457
1953	10	579	5,790	100	459
1954	11	466	5,126	121	461
1955	12	569	6,828	144	462
1956	13	416	5,408	169	464
1957	14	422	5,908	196	466
1958	15	565	8,475	225	467
1959	16	484	7,744	256	469
1960	17	520	8,840	289	471
1961	18	573	10,314	324	473
1962	19	518	9,842	361	474
1963	20	501	10,020	400	476
1964	21	535	11,235	441	478
1965	22	468	10,296	484	479
1966	23	382	8,786	529	481
1967	24	310	7,440	576	483
1968	25	334	8,350	625	485
1969	26	359	9,334	676	486
1970	27	372	10,044	729	488
1971	28	439	12,292	784	490
1972	29	446	12,934	841	491
1973	30	349	10,470	900	493
1974	31	395	12,245	961	495
1975	32	461	14,752	1,024	497
1976	33	514	16,962	1,089	498
1977	34	583	19,822	1,156	500
1978	35	590	20,650	1,225	502
1979	36	620	22,320	1,296	503
1980	37	578	21,386	1,369	505
1981	38	534	20,292	1,444	507
1982	39	631	24,609	1,521	509
Total	780	18,565	379,767	20,540	

TABLE 14.8.2   Pairs of shoes produced annually ($\times$ 1,000) by a shoe manufacturer (adjustment for secular trend)

Year (1)	Production ($\times$ 1000) (2)	Trend (3)	Cyclical Relatives (Column 2 Divided by Column 3 Times 100)
1944	380	443	85.8
1945	417	445	93.7
1946	406	447	90.8
1947	450	449	100.2
1948	478	450	106.2
1949	423	452	93.6
1950	443	454	97.6
1951	503	455	110.5
1952	552	457	120.8
1953	579	459	126.1
1954	466	461	101.1
1955	569	462	123.2
1956	416	464	89.7
1957	422	466	90.6
1958	565	467	121.0
1959	484	469	103.2
1960	520	471	110.4
1961	573	473	121.1
1962	518	474	109.3
1963	501	476	105.3
1964	535	478	111.9
1965	468	479	97.7
1966	382	481	79.4
1967	310	483	64.2
1968	334	485	68.9
1969	359	486	73.9
1970	372	488	76.2
1971	439	490	89.6
1972	446	491	90.8
1973	349	493	70.8
1974	395	495	79.8
1975	461	497	92.8
1976	514	498	103.2
1977	583	500	116.6
1978	590	502	117.5
1979	620	503	123.3
1980	578	505	114.5
1981	534	507	105.3
1982	631	509	124.0

FIGURE 14.8.1   Annual production of pairs of shoes (×1,000), 1944–1982, original data and trend line

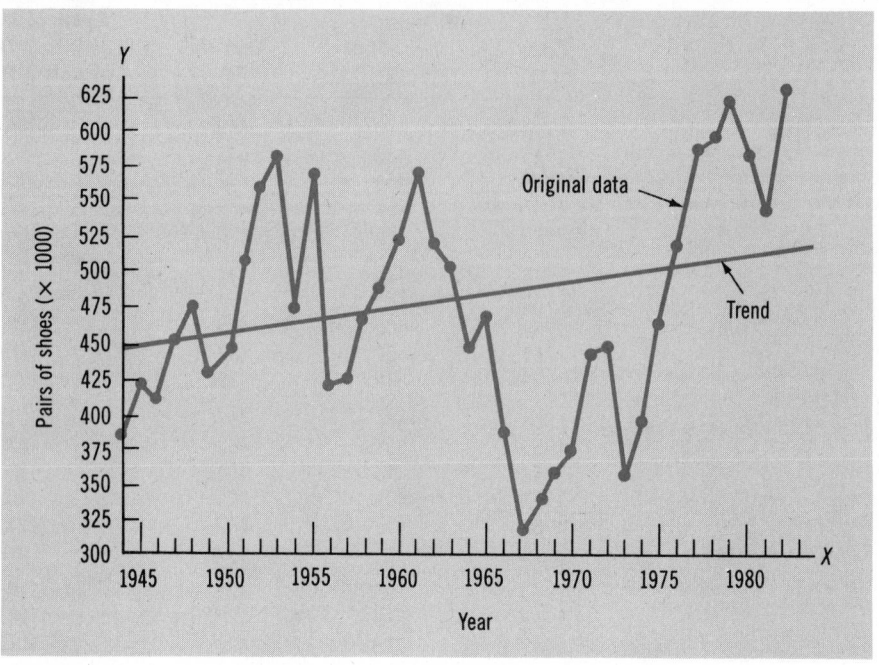

FIGURE 14.8.2   Cyclical relatives, pairs of shoes produced (×1,000) by a shoe manufacturer, 1944–1982

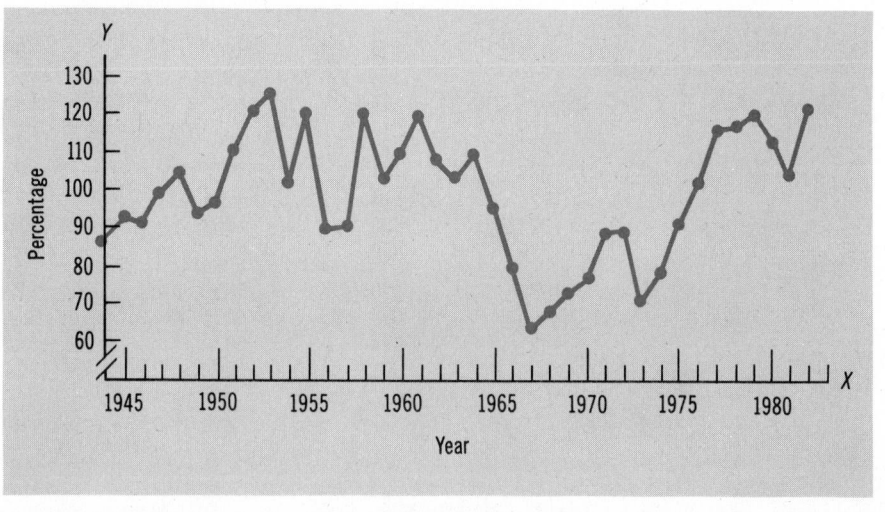

Cyclical irregulars
contain random
variation.

If we multiply $C \cdot E$ by 100, we get what are called the *cyclical irregulars*. As you can see, we have not eliminated the irregular movements. We try to eliminate them by computing a weighted moving average from the cyclical irregulars. The resulting averages are the cyclical relatives. We compute the weighted moving average as follows. Assume that for a series of data beginning in January we want a three-month weighted moving average. We find it by adding the cyclical irregular for January once, the cyclical irregular for February twice, and the cyclical irregular for March once. We then divide the total by $1 + 2 + 1 = 4$. We continue in a similar manner throughout the series. A five-month weighted moving average would use the values for January through May, weighted 1, 4, 6, 4, 1, respectively, where these weights—as were the weights 1, 2, 1—are binomial coefficients. We can use other numbers of months, with the appropriate binomial coefficients as weights. The weighted moving average lets us control the extent of smoothing by the choice of weights.

EXAMPLE 14.8.2   We can use the data of Example 14.7.1 to show how to measure cyclical variation from monthly data. Although the study of cyclical variation would ordinarily cover a longer period of time, we limit our illustration to a single year, 1979.

SOLUTION   The first step is to obtain monthly trend values. Under certain conditions, we can get these from the trend equation based on annual data. In this example, however, it seems better to compute monthly values directly from the data. When we want the least-squares trend line, the procedure we use is identical to that for annual data presented in Section 14.3, except that we use months rather than years as the time periods. We can compute the following least-squares equation from these data:

$$Y_c = 1{,}930.1 - 12.811t$$

If we successively substitute 1, 2, ..., 60 into the least-squares equation, the result is the corresponding monthly trend values. These are shown for the year 1979 in column 2 of Table 14.8.3.

The next components we need are the seasonal indexes. These are given in Table 14.7.2 and recorded again in column 3 of Table 14.8.3. We multiply each of the monthly trend values by the corresponding seasonal index. This product is called the *normal*, since it represents the value that we would expect for each month if trend and seasonal variation were the only components present. That is, $T \times S$ gives the values that we would expect if the cyclical and irregular factors were not present. Finally, we find the cyclical irregulars by dividing the observed values of Y by $(T \times S)$ and multiplying by 100. This is the step indicated by Equation 14.8.4.

Now we can remove the irregular component by means of a three-month moving average. The results of this step give the cyclical relatives, which represent the cyclical effect alone. That is, we have eliminated the effects of trend, season, and erratic variation. Table 14.8.4 gives the results.

TABLE 14.8.3 Calculations for cyclical irregulars for the year 1979, Example 14.8.2

Month	(1) Sales (Y)	(2) Trend (T)	(3) Seasonal Index (S)	(4) Normal (T × S)	(5) Cyclical Irregulars $100 \dfrac{Y}{(T \times S)}$
January	2,406	1,917.3	1.324	2,538.5	94.8
February	2,604	1,904.5	1.353	2,576.8	101.1
March	3,112	1,891.7	1.684	3,185.6	97.7
April	2,915	1,878.9	1.363	2,560.9	113.8
May	2,033	1,866.1	0.890	1,660.8	122.4
June	643	1,853.3	0.308	570.8	112.6
July	291	1,840.4	0.131	241.1	120.7
August	67	1,827.6	0.036	65.8	101.8
September	491	1,814.8	0.375	680.6	72.1
October	2,394	1,802.0	1.619	2,917.4	82.1
November	2,085	1,789.2	1.297	2,320.6	89.8
December	1,811	1,776.4	1.619	2,876.0	63.0

TABLE 14.8.4 Calculation of cyclical relatives by three-month moving average, Example 14.8.2

Month	(1) Cyclical Irregulars C × E	(2) Weighted Three-Month Moving total (1, 2, 1)	(3) Cyclical Relatives C = Column 2/4
January	94.8		
February	101.1	394.7	98.7
March	97.7	410.3	102.6
April	113.8	447.7	111.9
May	122.4	471.2	117.8
June	112.6	468.3	117.1
July	120.7	455.8	114.0
August	101.8	396.4	99.1
September	72.1	328.1	82.0
October	82.1	326.1	81.5
November	89.8	324.7	81.2
December	63.0		

EXERCISES

14.8.1 Ⓒ The following table contains figures on cotton production (bales) on a southern farm from 1930 through 1979. (a) Plot the original data and the least-squares trend line. (b) Compute and plot the cyclical relatives.

Year	Cotton Production	Year	Cotton Production	Year	Cotton Production
1930	309	1947	249	1964	234
1931	360	1948	286	1965	339
1932	369	1949	124	1966	386
1933	256	1950	173	1967	401
1934	398	1951	331	1968	491
1935	377	1952	301	1969	436

Year	Cotton Production	Year	Cotton Production	Year	Cotton Production
1936	258	1953	165	1970	234
1937	381	1954	90	1971	322
1938	398	1955	142	1972	397
1939	327	1956	48	1973	432
1940	350	1957	72	1974	369
1941	360	1958	135	1975	370
1942	151	1959	204	1976	331
1943	299	1960	188	1977	297
1944	248	1961	160	1978	393
1945	140	1962	228	1979	414
1946	310	1963	209		

14.8.2   C Using the data of Example 14.7.1,   (a) compute the cyclical irregulars for 1980 through 1983;   (b) compute the cyclical relatives by means of a weighted three-month moving average.

14.8.3   C The following table shows the annual sales of Arnold's Department Store.   (a) Plot the original data and the least-squares trend line.   (b) Compute and plot the cyclical relatives.

Year	1970	1971	1972	1973	1974	1975	1976	1977	1978	1979	1980	1981	1982	1983	1984
Annual sales ($\times$ \$10,000)	5	7	8	6	4	8	12	12	12	17	22	20	17	22	27

14.9 BUSINESS FORECASTING

Forecasting needs arise at both the corporate and the functional levels of a firm.

The ability to forecast the future with a reasonable degree of accuracy is a skill that is in great demand among those entrusted with the operation of a business firm or other similar organization. The need for expertise in forecasting exists at both the corporate and functional levels of a business organization. Most important management decisions are based on information obtained through forecasting. Also, long-range strategic planning, so vital to the life of a business, requires, as one of its inputs, information obtained through forecasting. Within the functional areas, we find that finance and accounting executives make use of forecasts for budgetary planning and cost control purposes. The marketing department relies on forecasting to provide information on expected sales volume, and also uses the technique in such activities as planning new products, expanding sales territories, and staffing regional sales offices. Those responsible for production and operations management find that forecasts are necessary for activities like aggregate production planning, scheduling, and inventory control.

TYPES OF FORECASTING

A wide variety of forecasting methods is available to the modern manager, and which ones are selected for use will depend on perceived needs and available resources.

TIME-SERIES METHODS

In this text, we focus on the use of time-series methods for forecasting. Sections 14.3 through 14.8 deal with techniques for analyzing historical data for a time-series variable. In some situations, the only purpose of such analysis may be to improve our understanding of the underlying pattern of changes in the data over time. However, in most instances, the primary purpose of such analyses is to obtain information that we can use as the basis for forecasting values of the variable of interest for future time periods. The use of time-series analysis in forecasting is our concern throughout the rest of this section.

The model that we use in the analysis of time-series data Y, starting with Section 14.2, is the multiplicative model, in which the four components trend T, seasonal variation S, cyclical variation C, and random variation E are represented as follows:

$$Y = T \cdot S \cdot C \cdot E$$

As indicated previously, the cyclical and random components are not usually predictable and therefore cannot, as a rule, be forecasted. Thus, our basic forecasting equation will be of the form

$$F = T \cdot S$$

In this equation, the trend and the appropriate seasonal factor, when they are present, are estimated from an analysis of historical data. Since each of these components (trend and seasonal variation) may be either present or not present in a given set of time-series data, our forecasting procedures must consider the following situations:

1. No trend and no seasonal component present
2. Only a trend component present
3. Only a seasonal component present
4. Both a trend and a seasonal component present

NO TREND OR SEASONAL COMPONENT PRESENT

In Sections 14.4 and 14.5, we discuss moving averages and exponential smoothing. You will recall that these smoothing techniques help reduce or eliminate the effects of variability in a set of observations. In those sections, we illustrate their use in isolating the trend component by eliminating fluctuations due to seasonal, cyclical, or random components. These techniques may also be used for forecasting. For example, if no trend component can be isolated, the final value of a moving average might be used as a forecast for a future time period. The simple exponentially smoothed average also may be used for this purpose.

THE MOVING AVERAGE

The following example illustrates the use of moving averages for forecasting.

EXAMPLE 14.9.1   Let us refer to Example 14.4.1 and use the results we obtained to forecast 1983 sales of real estate units.

SOLUTION   The best estimate of sales for 1983 (or any later year) is simply the most recent moving average, which, in this case, is the moving average for 1980. That is,

$$F_{83} = 86.6 \approx 87$$

We round the forecast to 87 since the number of units must be an integer.

SIMPLE EXPONENTIAL SMOOTHING

You should be aware that the moving-average technique is not often used for forecasting because of the limitations mentioned in Section 14.4. However, simple exponential smoothing is frequently used as a forecasting tool. In fact, it is the most commonly used technique when there are neither trend nor seasonal components in a set of time-series data.

COMPUTER **ANALYSIS**

It is convenient to have a computer perform the calculations needed for exponential smoothing. STAT+, for example, contains a subroutine for performing the calculations for simple exponential smoothing, as well as other smoothing techniques and other time-series procedures.

The procedure of simple exponential smoothing is illustrated by the following example.

EXAMPLE 14.9.2   Refer to Example 14.5.1. Let us assume that there are no trend or seasonal components, and let us use simple exponential smoothing to obtain a forecast for the next month (month 11).

SOLUTION   Just as with the moving average, the best estimate of sales for the next month (or any future month) is the most recent smoothed average. That is,

$$F_{11} = \overline{Y}_{10} = 86.39 \approx 86$$

Again, we round the forecast to the nearest integer.

When we use simple exponential smoothing to make forecasts, the smoothed average for the current period, $\overline{Y}_t$, provides the forecast for the next period, $t + 1$. In like manner, F_t, the forecast for period t, would be the smoothed average for the preceding period, $t - 1$. Thus, $F_{t+1} = \overline{Y}_t$ and $F_t = \overline{Y}_{t-1}$. If, in Equation 14.5.2, we substitute F_{t+1} and F_t for $\overline{Y}_t$ and $\overline{Y}_{t-1}$, respectively, we obtain the following forecasting equation:

(14.9.1)
$$F_{t+1} = \alpha Y_t + (1 - \alpha)F_t$$

Equation 14.9.1 is used for updating forecasts in exactly the same way that Equation 14.5.2 is used to update exponentially smoothed averages.

Exponential smoothing is one of the best-known and most widely used forecasting techniques. As you will see later, the basic model can be expanded to cover more complex situations, such as the presence of trend and seasonal components. The use of simple exponential smoothing for forecasting is illustrated more thoroughly by the following example.

EXAMPLE 14.9.3 Baylor Appliances is interested in a procedure for forecasting monthly sales of electric can openers. Table 14.9.1 shows the actual monthly sales of this appliance for the past two years.

Let us assume that the current time is December 31 of year 2. That is, December of year 2 is time period t, and $t = 24$. We want to use simple exponential smoothing to forecast sales, month by month, for each forthcoming month of years 3 and 4, that is, months 25 through 48.

SOLUTION To obtain these forecasts, we make use of Equation 14.9.1. In order to proceed, we need three items of information to substitute into the equation: (1) a value of the smoothing constant α, (2) Y_t, the actual value of Y for the current time period, and (3) F_t, the forecasted value for the current time period. We see in Table 14.9.1 that $Y_t = 2{,}795$.

TABLE 14.9.1 Monthly sales of electric can openers during a two-year period (time periods 1–24)

	Year	
Month	1	2
January	2,000	2,110
February	2,500	2,415
March	2,290	2,611
April	2,110	2,814
May	2,325	2,500
June	2,320	2,500
July	1,705	2,301
August	2,130	2,102
September	2,502	2,300
October	2,200	2,874
November	2,099	2,705
December	2,356	2,795

There are several ways by which we may obtain a value for F_t. In this example, we employ the commonly used procedure of letting F_t equal the mean of several previous actual values of Y_t. Specifically, we use the first 24 months of accumulated data shown in Table 14.9.1. Our value of F_t, then, is

$$F_t = (2,000 + 2,500 + \cdots + 2,795)/24 = 2,356.83 \approx 2,357$$

We now need a value for α. Suppose that we let $\alpha = 0.1$. Remember how important the value of the smoothing constant is. Criteria for choosing it are discussed in Section 14.5.

We are now ready to use Equation 14.9.1 to forecast sales for time period 25, which is January of year 3. Proper substitution yields

$$F_{25} = 0.1(2,795) + (1 - 0.1)(2,357) = 2,401$$

Now let us assume that it is February 1 of year 3. Actual sales data for January of year 3 are now available, and we can compare this figure with our forecast. Suppose that actual sales for time period 25 (January of year 3) were 2,850. Our *forecast error* for this period, then, was $2,850 - 2,401 = 449$.

We now have the necessary inputs for forecasting sales for time period 26 (February of year 3). Our latest actual value of Y is 2,850, the actual sales for January of year 3. Our latest forecast is 2,401, the forecast for January of year 3, and our smoothing constant is still 0.1. Again making use of Equation 14.9.1, we obtain the following forecast for February of year 3:

$$F_{26} = 0.1(2,850) + 0.9(2,401) = 2,446$$

Suppose that the actual sales figure for time period 26 was 2,620. Our forecast error for this period, then, is $2,620 - 2,446 = 174$.

Now let us assume that two years have elapsed since we began using exponential smoothing to forecast sales of electric can openers. We are now at the end of year 4, and we can compare, for the past 24 months, our forecasts with actual sales. The results are shown in Table 14.9.2 and Figure 14.9.1. The differences between our forecasts and the actual sales are our forecast errors. We discuss their use in Section 14.10.

TREND COMPONENT ONLY PRESENT

In Section 14.6, we discuss the use of time-series analysis to measure trend. We employ the linear trend model, the moving average, and exponential smoothing to obtain trend values. In this section, we discuss the use of both the least-squares linear trend model and exponential smoothing in obtaining forecasts when a trend component is present.

TABLE 14.9.2 Monthly forecasts and corresponding monthly sales of electric can openers during a two-year period (Example 14.9.3)

Time Period	Actual Y_t	Forecast F_t	Error $(Y_t - F_t)$
25	2,850	2,401	449
26	2,620	2,446	174
27	2,500	2,463	37
28	2,301	2,467	-166
29	2,570	2,450	120
30	2,710	2,462	248
31	2,809	2,487	322
32	2,924	2,519	405
33	2,802	2,560	242
34	2,611	2,584	27
35	2,709	2,587	122
36	2,500	2,599	-99
37	2,241	2,589	-348
38	2,533	2,554	-21
39	2,400	2,552	-152
40	2,710	2,537	173
41	2,602	2,554	48
42	2,898	2,559	339
43	2,499	2,593	-94
44	2,316	2,584	-268
45	2,105	2,557	-452
46	2,330	2,512	-182
47	2,750	2,494	256
48	2,902	2,520	382

The basic forecasting equation for the least-squares linear trend model is

(14.9.2)
$$F_t = a + bt$$

We can obtain the values of a and b in a variety of ways. Once they are determined, we make forecasts by substituting, for t, integers corresponding to the desired future time periods. Consider the following example.

EXAMPLE 14.9.4 Refer to Example 14.6.1. Let us use the trend-line equation to obtain forecasts for 1971 and 1972.

SOLUTION The forecasting equation is

(14.9.3)
$$F_t = 6.5323 + 0.4193t$$

The years 1971 and 1972 are represented by t values of 16 and 17, respectively. Substituting these values into Equation 14.9.3 yields the following forecasts (billions of board feet):

$$F_{16} = 6.5323 + 0.4193(16) = 13.2411$$
$$F_{17} = 6.5323 + 0.4193(17) = 13.6604$$

FIGURE 14.9.1 Monthly forecasts and corresponding monthly sales of electric can openers during a two-year period (Example 14.9.3)

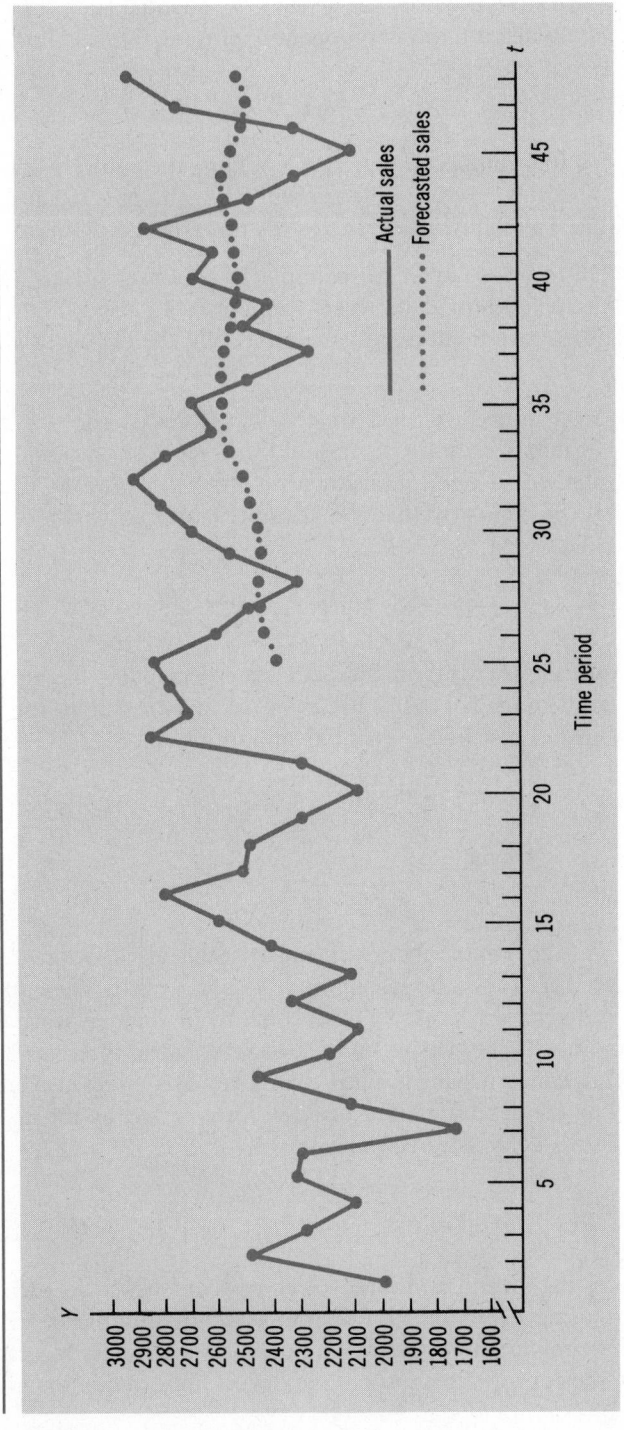

Equation 14.6.9 provides the general exponential smoothing forecasting equation for use when a trend component is present. We recall that this equation is

$$F_{t+k} = \overline{Y}_{t_a} + k\overline{b}_t$$

where k is the number of time periods into the future for which a forecast is desired, $\overline{Y}_{t_a}$ is the average, adjusted for trend, and $\overline{b}_t$ is the average, or smoothed, trend value. The following example illustrates the use of this forecasting equation.

EXAMPLE 14.9.5 Refer to Example 14.6.2. We wish to use Equation 14.6.9 to obtain trend-adjusted forecasts for month 11 using both methods: (a) the arithmetic average of all trend values and (b) the exponentially smoothed trend value.

SOLUTION Since we wish to obtain a forecast for one time period (from period 10) into the future, $k = 1$. Table 14.6.6 shows that, for the arithmetic average method of trend adjustment, $\overline{Y}_{t_a} = 89.60$ and $\overline{b}_{t_i}$, calculated in Section 14.6, is 1.377. When we use the arithmetic average method, then, we have, by Equation 14.6.9,

$$F_{11} = 89.60 + (1)1.377 = 90.977 \approx 91$$

In Table 14.6.6, we find that, for time period 10, $\overline{Y}_{t_a}$, by the exponentially smoothed method, is 90.26. Table 14.6.5 shows that $\overline{b}_t$ for time period 10 is 1.657. Our forecast by exponential smoothing, then, is

$$F_{11} = 90.26 + (1)1.657 = 91.917 \approx 92$$

SEASONAL COMPONENT ONLY PRESENT

Section 14.7 covers the measurement of seasonal variation. A seasonal index is calculated there for each season in our seasonal cycle. These indexes can be used in two different ways: (1) to deseasonalize or remove seasonal variation from the actual time-series values and (2) to seasonalize forecasts for future time periods. Our concern here is with this latter use. We seasonalize a forecast by multiplying the deseasonalized forecast for a period by the appropriate seasonal index. This is demonstrated in Table 14.7.4.

BOTH TREND AND SEASONAL COMPONENTS PRESENT

Sometimes both trend and seasonal components exist. In such cases, the results obtained using Equation 14.9.2 (the least-squares linear trend equation) are called *deseasonalized forecasts*. We can *seasonalize* these forecasts by multiplying them by the appropriate seasonal factors, as indicated in the following equation:

(14.9.4)
$$F_t = (a + bt)S_{t-L}$$

We can see that Equation 14.9.4 is the same as Equation 14.9.2, except for the fact that the forecast in Equation 14.9.4 is multiplied by the seasonal factor S_{t-L}. In Equation 14.9.4, L is the number of time periods in a seasonal cycle. For quarterly data, for example, $L = 4$, and for monthly data, $L = 12$. Since the forecast obtained using Equation 14.9.4 represents an adjustment for the seasonal component, it may be either greater or smaller than the forecast provided by Equation 14.9.2.

The simplicity of this approach to seasonal adjustment and the ease of obtaining forecasts by its use are appealing. However, it has a significant problem: as time passes, the terms of the equation must be updated on a scheduled basis. When we are forecasting many items, this can cause difficulty in terms of data storage, time, and expense. A happy solution is provided by a method developed by Peter R. Winters. Winters' method incorporates the linear trend equation, the multiplicative seasonal factor of Equation 14.9.4, and the simplicity of exponential smoothing to update the terms of the forecasting equation.

WINTERS' METHOD

We can extend the basic concept of exponential smoothing to a model that includes seasonal and/or trend components. When appropriate, we can use such a model as a basis for forecasting values of some variable, such as demand for a product or service, for future time periods.

The Model The model can be expressed in the following form:

(14.9.5)
$$Y_t = (A + Bt)S_t + e_t$$

where Y_t = actual value of the time-series variable for time period t
A = deseasonalized average (trend value)
B = unit trend component (slope)
S_t = multiplicative seasonal factor
e_t = random error component

In the discussion that follows, we use the concepts and terminology relating to seasonal variation that were covered in Section 14.7. Assume that data for a time-series variable (such as demand for a product or service) are available for time period t and a number of preceding time periods. In this case, a forecast for the next time period, $t + 1$, is given by

(14.9.6)
$$F_{t+1} = (a_t + b_t)S_{t-L+1}$$

and a forecast for k periods into the future by

(14.9.7)
$$F_{t+k} = (a_t + b_t k)S_{t-L+k}$$

In Equations 14.9.6 and 14.9.7, a_t and b_t are estimates, respectively, of A and B in Equation 14.9.5. Note also that both equations consider the current time period t to be the origin as far as forecasts are concerned. This means that the origin will move forward one period at a time as additional data become available and the forecasting-equation components are updated.

Beginning values for a_t, b_t, and the seasonal factors are obtained in a variety of ways, which usually involve fairly simple calculations.

The Equations Winters' method provides a procedure for updating these values as new information becomes available by means of the following exponential smoothing equations:

1. Deseasonalized average (trend estimate)

$$a_t = \alpha \left(\frac{Y_t}{S_{t-L}} \right) + (1 - \alpha)(a_{t-1} + b_{t-1})$$

(14.9.8)

2. Average unit trend

$$b_t = \beta(a_t - a_{t-1}) + (1 - \beta)b_{t-1}$$

(14.9.9)

Note: b_t in this model plays the same role that $\bar{b}_t$ plays in Section 13.6.3.

3. Seasonal factor(s)

$$S_t = \sigma \left(\frac{Y_t}{a_t} \right) + (1 - \sigma)S_{t-L}$$

(14.9.10)

where t = latest time period for which data are available

Y_t = actual observed value of the variable of interest at time period t

a_t = estimated deseasonalized average for period t (trend estimate)

b_t = estimated unit trend of the linear equation at time t (slope)

L = number of time periods in a seasonal cycle (4 with quarterly data, for example)

S_t = estimated seasonal factor for period t

S_{t-L} = immediately preceding estimate of seasonal factor for corresponding period in last seasonal cycle

α, β, σ = smoothing constants (they may be the same or different)

Again, we emphasize the importance of judicious selection of the values of the smoothing constants. A computer program for obtaining optimal values of these constants is given in one of the references listed at the end of this chapter.

Before proceeding, let us examine the components of Equation 14.9.7 more closely. The term $a_t + b_t k$ provides a trend value, or deseasonalized forecast, for a future time period. We start with a constant a_t and add to it the same constant amount b_t each time we move one period into the future, regardless of which season is being forecasted. Therefore this term, $a_t + b_t k$, can be viewed as a linear trend equation in which the estimated coefficients a_t (intercept) and b_t (slope) are updated as additional data become available. The deseasonalized forecast $(a_t + b_t k)$ must then be multiplied by the appropriate seasonal factor for the period being forecasted (S_{t-L+k}). You should recall that there is a different seasonal factor for each of the seasons in a seasonal cycle. For quarterly data, for example, there will be 4 seasonal factors, and for monthly data, there will be 12 seasonal factors. As additional data become available, one of the seasonal factors is updated at each time period. Consequently, any given seasonal factor is updated only once during a seasonal cycle. On the other hand, the estimated coefficients a_t and b_t are both updated each time period as additional data become available.

We illustrate the use of Equations 14.9.7 through 14.9.10 by means of the following example.

EXAMPLE 14.9.6   Table 14.9.3 contains data on Gracious Greetings' sales of boxes of greeting cards by quarter for a 6-year period. Assume that we are at the end of year 4 (period 16) and that we want to use Winters' method to forecast

TABLE 14.9.3   Sales of greeting cards by quarter for a six-year period

Year	Quarter	Period	Sales
1	1	1	222
	2	2	339
	3	3	336
	4	4	878
2	1	5	443
	2	6	413
	3	7	398
	4	8	1,143
3	1	9	695
	2	10	698
	3	11	737
	4	12	1,648
4	1	13	1,141
	2	14	1,036
	3	15	938
	4	16	2,168
5	1	17	1,489
	2	18	1,372
	3	19	1,805
	4	20	2,678
6	1	21	2,013
	2	22	1,860
	3	23	2,002
	4	24	3,135

quarterly sales for years 5 and 6 (periods 17 through 24) based on the sales data for the first 4 years.

SOLUTION   A useful first step in analyzing time-series data in which we suspect that trend and seasonal components exist is to plot the data in order to verify that these trend and seasonal components do, in fact, exist. Figure 14.9.2 shows the data for the first 16 time periods. The next step is to obtain an estimated linear trend equation that disregards seasonal variation. As we have seen, there are various ways of obtaining such an equation. For purposes of illustration, we use the least-squares method in the present example. Other methods are discussed later.

Data for the first 16 time periods (4 years) yield the following least-squares equation:

(14.9.11)
$$Y_c = 107.675 + 84.634t$$

This trend line is shown in Figure 14.9.3.

We can obtain the trend estimate for any time period by substituting the period number (from 1 through 16) into this equation. We estimate seasonal indexes by dividing the actual sales values by the trend estimate for each period and then averaging these values for each season. For example, the trend estimate for period 1 is

$$Y_c = 107.675 + 84.634(1) = 192.309$$

FIGURE 14.9.2   Sales of greeting cards by quarter for a 4-year period (16 quarters)

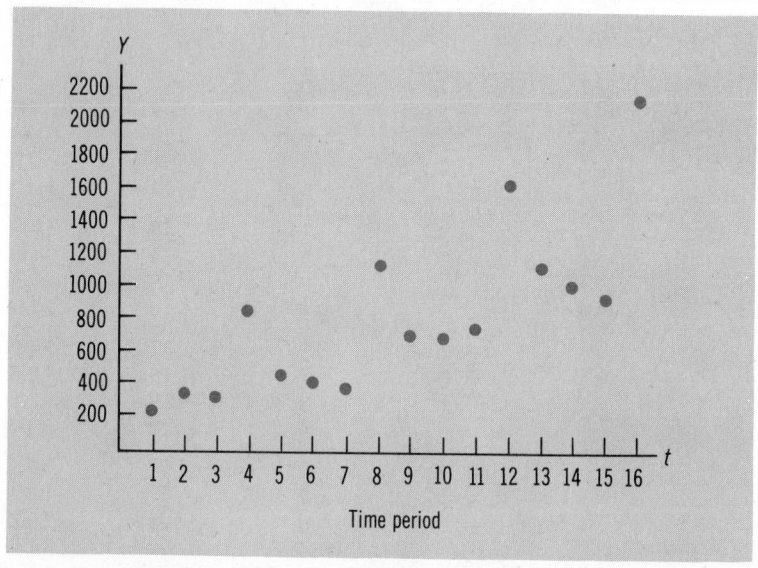

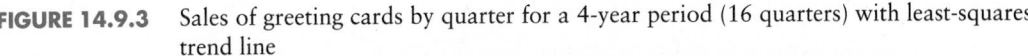

FIGURE 14.9.3   Sales of greeting cards by quarter for a 4-year period (16 quarters) with least-squares trend line

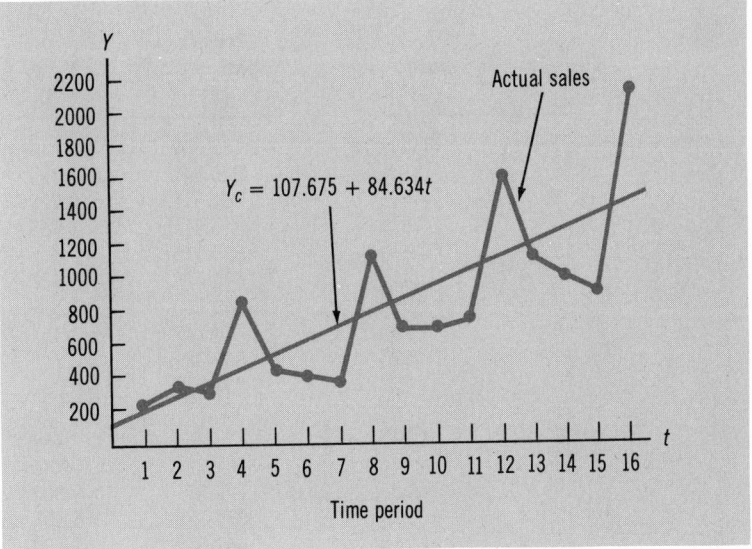

Dividing the actual sales for period 1 by this value yields $222/192.309 = 1.154$. Table 14.9.4 shows calculations for all 16 time periods. Since we have quarterly data, there are 4 seasonal indexes. We obtain initial values of the seasonal indexes by averaging the actual-to-trend ratios. For the first seasonal index (quarter 1), this estimate is

$$(1.154 + 0.835 + 0.799 + 0.945)/4 = 0.933$$

Initial estimates of all four seasonal factors are shown in column 4 of Table 14.9.4.

At this point, we are ready to use Equation 14.9.7 to obtain the desired forecasts for periods 17 through 24. Since the current period, $t = 16$, is considered the origin for developing forecasts, $a_{16} = 107.675 + 84.634(16) = 1461.819$, which is the trend estimate for period 16. The slope, b_{16}, is the same slope used in the regression equation. That is, $b_{16} = 84.634$. The number of the period being forecasted, $t + k$ on the original scale, is equal to k on the forecast time scale. The seasonal index, S_{16-4+k}, is the appropriate one of the four indexes in column 4 of Table 14.9.4. Thus, the forecasting equation is

$$F_{t+k} = (a_t + b_t k)S_{t-L+k}$$

or, in the present case,

$$F_{16+k} = (a_{16} + b_{16}k)S_{16-4+k}$$
$$= (1461.819 + 84.634k)S_{12+k}$$

TABLE 14.9.4 Sales of greeting cards by quarter, trend estimate ($Y_c = 107.675 + 84.634t$), actual-to-trend ratio, and initial seasonal factors

Time (t)	Sales (Y_t) (1)	Trend Estimate (Y_c) (2)	Y_t/Y_c (3)	Initial Seasonal Factors (4)
1	222	192.309	1.154	
2	339	276.943	1.224	
3	336	361.577	0.929	
4	878	446.211	1.968	
5	443	530.845	0.835	
6	413	615.479	0.671	
7	398	700.113	0.568	
8	1,143	784.747	1.457	
9	695	869.381	0.799	
10	698	954.015	0.732	
11	737	1,038.649	0.710	
12	1,648	1,123.283	1.467	
13	1,141	1,207.917	0.945	0.933
14	1,036	1,292.551	0.802	0.857
15	938	1,377.185	0.681	0.722
16	2,168	1,461.819	1.483	1.594
17		1,546.453		
18		1,631.087		
19		1,715.721		
20		1,800.355		
21		1,884.989		
22		1,969.623		
23		2,054.257		
24		2,138.891		

The forecasts for periods 17 through 24 are as follows:

$$F_{17} = [1,461.819 + 84.634(1)](0.933) = 1,546.453(0.933) = 1,442.841$$
$$F_{18} = [1,461.819 + 84.634(2)](0.857) = 1,631.087(0.857) = 1,397.842$$
$$F_{19} = [1,461.819 + 84.634(3)](0.722) = 1,715.721(0.722) = 1,238.751$$
$$F_{20} = [1,461.819 + 84.634(4)](1.594) = 1,800.355(1.594) = 2,869.766$$
$$F_{21} = [1,461.819 + 84.634(5)](0.933) = 1,884.989(0.933) = 1,758.695$$
$$F_{22} = [1,461.819 + 84.634(6)](0.857) = 1,969.623(0.857) = 1,687.967$$
$$F_{23} = [1,461.819 + 84.634(7)](0.722) = 2,054.257(0.722) = 1,483.174$$
$$F_{24} = [1,461.819 + 84.634(8)](1.594) = 2,138.891(1.594) = 3,409.392$$

Forecasts for periods beyond period 24 would be obtained in the same manner.

Now that we have the desired forecasts, let us demonstrate how we can use Equations 14.9.8 through 14.9.10 to update the components of our forecasting equation as additional data become available. Refer to Table 14.9.3, and assume that the sales information for period 17 is now available. The current period t becomes 17, and the previous period $t - 1$ becomes 16. The actual sales Y_{17} for the current period, as shown in the table, is 1,489. The new origin for forecasts, once the components of the forecasting equation are updated, will be period 17. The smoothing equations require values for the smoothing constants α, β, and σ. For simplicity's sake, let $\alpha = \beta = \sigma = 0.20$. The components are updated as follows:

1. Deseasonalized average (by Equation 14.9.8)

$$
\begin{aligned}
a_{17} &= \alpha \left(\frac{Y_{17}}{S_{17-4}} \right) + (1 - \alpha)(a_{16} + b_{16}) \\
&= (0.2)(1489/0.933) + (0.8)(1461.819 + 84.634) \\
&= 319.1854 + 1237.1624 = 1556.348
\end{aligned}
$$

2. Average unit trend (by Equation 14.9.9)

$$
\begin{aligned}
b_{17} &= \beta(a_{17} - a_{16}) + (1 - \beta)b_{16} \\
&= (0.2)(1556.348 - 1461.819) + (0.8)(84.634) \\
&= 18.9058 + 67.7072 = 86.613
\end{aligned}
$$

3. Seasonal factor (by Equation 14.9.10)

$$
\begin{aligned}
S_{17} &= \sigma \left(\frac{Y_{17}}{a_{17}} \right) + (1 - \sigma)S_{17-4} \\
&= (0.2)(1489/1556.348) + (0.8)(0.933) \\
&= 0.1913 + 0.7464 = 0.938
\end{aligned}
$$

We now use Equation 14.9.7 and the updated values of a_{17} and b_{17} to obtain the following forecasting equation for period 18:

$$
\begin{aligned}
F_{17+k} &= (a_{17} + b_{17}k)S_{17-4+k} \\
&= (1556.348 + 86.613k)S_{13+k}
\end{aligned}
$$

The use of this new equation and $k = 1$ gives the following forecast for the next time period (period $17 + 1 = 18$):

$$
\begin{aligned}
F_{18} &= [1556.348 + 86.613(1)](0.857) \\
&= (1642.961)(0.857) \\
&= 1408.018
\end{aligned}
$$

We will use the updated seasonal factor, 0.938, computed by Equation 14.9.10 the next time we make a first-quarter forecast.

The frequency with which forecasts should be prepared will depend on the needs of the firm or organization and on the resources that are available for forecasting purposes. In situations in which forecasts for a number of different variables are needed, this frequency may vary, depending on the number of variables involved. In any case, when Winters' method is used, it is advisable to update the components of the forecasting equation before generating the forecasts.

It is worth noting that Winters' method is a direct and computationally simple procedure for forecasting data with seasonal and/or trend components. If there appears to be no seasonal component in a set of data but a linear trend is present, Equation 14.9.10 is not used and the seasonal factor S_{t-L} is dropped from Equation 14.9.8. On the other hand, should there be a seasonal component but no trend component, Equation 14.9.9 would not be used, and the trend value b_{t-1} would be eliminated from Equation 14.9.8. Should neither of the components exist, then both Equations 14.9.9 and 14.9.10 would be dropped, and both the seasonal factor S_{t-L} and the trend value b_{t-1} would be eliminated from Equation 14.9.8. In this case, Equation 14.9.8 is reduced to the simple exponential smoothing equation discussed previously. We can view Winters' method as a procedure for expanding the simple exponential smoothing technique to include trend and/or seasonal components, then incorporating these components into forecasts for future time periods.

THE BOX-JENKINS FORECASTING METHOD

One of the most widely used and discussed forecasting methods is the *Box-Jenkins method*, so named for the two men—George E. P. Box and Gwilym M. Jenkins—most responsible for developing the method. The Box-Jenkins forecasting procedure consists of three stages:

Stage 1. Identification. In this stage, the forecaster selects a tentative model from a family of available models. Selection of a model relies on two statistical measures called an estimated *autocorrelation function* and an estimated *partial autocorrelation function*. These measures are computed from the data series available for analysis. If, in a later stage, the selected model proves to be inadequate, the forecaster generally returns to Stage 1 to select another tentative model.

Stage 2. Estimation. In this stage, the forecaster estimates the parameters of the tentative model that is fitted to the sample data.

Stage 3. Diagnostic Checking. Diagnostic checks suggested by Box and Jenkins are employed at this stage. The purpose of this stage is to determine if the estimated model is statistically adequate for the job it has been designed to accomplish. If a model fails the tests imposed in this stage, it is rejected, and the forecaster returns to stage 1 and repeats the process. When a model proves worthy in stage 3, it is used for forecasting.

ARIMA Models Box-Jenkins models are often referred to as ARIMA models. ARIMA is an acronym for Auto-Regressive Integrated Moving Average. In the present discussion, we assume a single-series, or univariate, situation. That is, we assume that the anticipated forecasts will be based on only *one* variable. The measurements to be used in building the model consist of past values of the variable to be forecasted. For this reason, the models are sometimes called UBJ-ARIMA models. UBJ stands for univariate Box-Jenkins.

When to Use UBJ-ARIMA models are especially suited for making *short-term* forecasts. The reason for this is the fact that most ARIMA models place more emphasis on observations from the recent past than on observations from the distant past.

Data UBJ-ARIMA models are suitable for both discrete and continuous variables. However, measurements on the variable of interest must be made at equally spaced, discrete time intervals.

Sample Size Relatively large samples are required for building ARIMA models. The generally recommended minimum number of observations is 50. If, for some reason, fewer observations are used, the results should be interpreted with caution.

Stationary Series UBJ-ARIMA models are appropriate only for *stationary* time-series data. A stationary time series may be defined nonrigorously as a time series that has a mean, variance, and autocorrelation function that are essentially constant through time.

Use of Computer The calculations involved in building UBJ-ARIMA models are quite complex. Most forecasters would not attempt the procedure without the aid of a computer. MINITAB, among many other statistical software packages, contains a routine for use in building UBJ-ARIMA models.

Further Reading Books by Anderson, Bowerman and O'Connell, Box and Jenkins, Hoff, and Pankratz, listed in the Suggestions for Further Reading at the end of this chapter, provide additional information on UBJ-ARIMA models.

OTHER TIME-SERIES FORECASTING PROCEDURES

In addition to the time-series forecasting methods discussed in this chapter, others are frequently used.

Adaptive Filtering Another exponential smoothing model, called *adaptive exponential smoothing* or *adaptive filtering*, allows for a change in the value of the smoothing constant α at any time period. Users of this technique have the option of changing or not changing α as they see fit. The use of adaptive filtering has met with success when applied to seasonal data.

Multiple Linear Regression The simple linear regression approach may be extended to include additional independent variables, as discussed in Chapter 10. The inclusion of additional independent variables frequently leads to better forecasts of the dependent variable.

Double and Triple Exponential Smoothing As noted earlier, the use of simple exponential smoothing results in forecasts that lag behind the actual time-series changes over time if a trend is present. To compensate for this phenomenon, we can use double exponential smoothing with time-series data that exhibit a trend. Double exponential smoothing involves two smoothing operations. In the first operation, the original time series is smoothed. We perform the second smoothing operation on the smoothed values obtained from the first smoothing operation. Further appropriate adjustment of the results from these smoothing operations frequently leads to satisfactory forecasts. Triple exponential smoothing is appropriate for use when the data follow a long-term trend pattern that is curvilinear rather than linear.

Autoregressive Techniques When appropriate tests, such as the one involving the Durbin-Watson statistic, lead to the conclusion that the error terms generated by a set of time-series data are autocorrelated, it is possible to exploit this characteristic of the data to obtain better forecasts. A model, known as an *autoregressive model*, may be developed to accomplish this goal. In such a model, the dependent variable is lagged one or more time periods and used as an additional independent variable in the forecasting model. In other words, an autoregressive model states that an individual forecast is a function of previous values of the time series under study. Autoregressive models and techniques are discussed in most textbooks on forecasting.

Historical Correlation Close observers of the economy and related phenomena frequently arrive at their own individualized economic indicators. It has been reported (*The Atlanta Journal*, March 10, 1988, p. 1A), for example, that the chairman of the Coca-Cola Company "watches fountain sales at fast-food restaurants to forecast what the economy will do six to nine months down the road"; that the chairman of Home Depot Inc. considers toilets "one of his more useful in-house indicators" of economic trends; and that a bank executive can foretell the future behavior of the stock market by keeping a record of how long it takes him to find a parking space at an upscale regional shopping mall.

QUALITATIVE TECHNIQUES

In addition to the quantitative forecasting techniques, some of which we have discussed, numerous qualitative forecasting techniques are employed from time to time under various circumstances. Qualitative forecasting techniques are characterized by the use of the opinion of one or more experts and/or the use of subjective probabilities to arrive at a forecast. Such techniques are helpful when historical data are either unavailable or are of questionable quality. A qualitative forecasting technique may be employed, for example, to forecast sales of a new product for which prior sales data do not exist. Among the qualitative techniques that have been used, the following are frequently mentioned.

The Delphi Method Developed in the 1940s by the Rand Corporation, the Delphi method of forecasting relies on a panel of experts who respond to a series of questionnaires relevant to the subject at hand. A panel coordinator collects the first round of questionnaires, relays to all panel members the opinions of the group as a whole, and uses the information contained in the questionnaires to develop a second questionnaire, which is distributed to panel members. The objective of the method is to have the panel reach a consensus after responding to a reasonable number of questionnaires. It is felt that the Delphi method, in which the panel members are physically separated, eliminates the bandwagon effect, which might occur if experts, in an effort to reach an informal opinion to be used as a forecast, dealt with the questions in a panel discussion format.

Technological Comparisons This method, which is frequently used to predict technological change, is based on the premise that appropriate analyses of changes taking place in one area are useful in predicting changes in another area.

Subjective Probabilities Certain forecast needs may be effectively met through the use of subjective probabilities and Bayes' theorem, discussed in Chapter 3.

The Cross-Impact Method This method is based on the assessment of interrelationships among events called *cross-impacts*. Subjective probabilities are employed in the procedure.

More complete discussions of these and other qualitative forecasting techniques are to be found in the books by Bowerman and O'Connell and Sullivan and Claycombe, mentioned at the end of this chapter.

EXERCISES

The following data represent the monthly sales (in thousands) of Chamberlin Tire Company for the year 1985.

	J	F	M	A	M	J	J	A	S	O	N	D
1985	51	53	56	61	59	65	63	60	54	56	53	46

Use these data to work Exercises 14.9.1 through 14.9.4.

 14.9.1   Use a three-month moving average to forecast sales for January and February 1986. Does the technique seem appropriate? Why?

14.9.2   Use a five-month moving average to forecast sales for January and February 1986. Is a five-month moving average more appropriate than a three-month moving average? Why?

14.9.3   Use simple exponential smoothing to forecast sales for January and February 1986. Let $\alpha = 0.1$. Begin by calculating an arithmetic average for January through June 1985. Thereafter, use exponential smoothing.

14.9.4   Refer to Exercise 14.9.3. Repeat the procedure using $\alpha = 0.7$. Which smoothing factor seems to give better results?

For the years 1981 through 1985, the quarterly sales of a major distributor of home central air conditioners were as follows:

	Quarters			
Year	1	2	3	4
1981	1,488	3,915	4,172	540
1982	1,861	5,037	4,918	613
1983	2,198	5,682	5,424	768
1984	2,643	6,104	6,293	834
1985	2,819	7,311	7,547	1,052

Use these data to work Exercises 14.9.5 through 14.9.7.

14.9.5   Construct a scatter diagram and visually fit a straight line to the data. Use this line to estimate the "best" linear equation.

14.9.6   Compute the least-squares linear trend equation and plot the trend line. Calculate Y_c and the ratio-to-trend value for each quarter. Compute the seasonal indexes using an arithmetic average of appropriate ratio-to-trend values. Use the available data to obtain trend-adjusted seasonalized quarterly forecasts for 1986.

14.9.7   Assume that actual quarterly sales for 1986 are 1,326, 7,649, 7,892, and 1,214, respectively. Use Winters' method with smoothing factors of $\alpha = 0.3$, $\beta = 0.4$, and $\sigma = 0.2$ to update components of the forecasting equation quarter by quarter. After each update, obtain a new forecast for the next quarter. Compare these forecasts with those obtained in Exercise 14.9.6.

14.9.8   Refer to Exercise 14.3.1. Use simple exponential smoothing to forecast the number of items damaged for 1985, 1986, and 1987. Begin by calculating an arithmetic average for 1970 through 1974, and use exponential smoothing thereafter. Use a smoothing constant of 0.3.

14.10   MEASURING FORECAST ERROR AND EVALUATING MODELS

Any time that we attempt to forecast the values of a variable, we should be concerned with how "good" our forecasts are. Ideally, we would like our forecasts to be exactly equal to the actual values that occur. However, in practice, we realize that forecasts will not be perfect and that forecasting errors will occur. The forecasting error for any given time period t is the difference between the forecasted value and the actual observed value. That is,

$$\text{Forecast error} = Y_t - F_t$$

The smaller the difference between Y_t and F_t, the better the forecast. We focus on a method of evaluating these errors for each of several alternative models that we may be considering.

MEAN SQUARED ERROR

The errors $Y_t - F_t$ can be evaluated in several different ways. The one that we use for illustrative purposes is the *mean squared error* (MSE). In formula form, the mean squared error is

(14.10.1)

$$\text{MSE} = \frac{\sum\limits_{t=1}^{n} (Y_t - F_t)^2}{n}$$

where n = the number of time periods covered. You will note the similarity between Equation 14.10.1 and the formula for the calculation of a variance.

EXAMPLE 14.10.1   We wish to use Equation 14.10.1 in the evaluation of two models. Refer to Example 14.9.3. A smoothing constant of 0.1 is used to generate forecasts for periods 25 through 48. The actual values, forecasts, and forecast errors are shown in Table 14.9.2.

SOLUTION   For purposes of comparison, let us now change the model by using a different smoothing constant. We use Equation 14.9.1 and a smoothing constant of 0.9 to forecast sales for time periods 25 through 48. The results are shown in Table 14.10.1 and plotted in Figure 14.10.1. The figure also shows the actual sales data for time periods 1 through 24 and the results we obtained previously when we let $\alpha = 0.1$. The impression one gets from Figure 14.10.1 is that the forecasted sales using $\alpha = 0.9$ are closer to the actual sales values than the forecasts obtained when $\alpha = 0.1$. That is, it appears that the forecasting errors $Y_t - F_t$ tend to be smaller when $\alpha = 0.9$ than when $\alpha = 0.1$. The criterion we use for comparing the two models with the different values of α is the magnitude of the mean squared error, MSE.

A close agreement between Y_t and F_t—that is, a good forecasting procedure—will yield a small MSE. In general, then, when we have a choice among forecasting equations, we choose the one that yields the smallest MSE. Let us compute the MSE for the present example using the errors that resulted when the smoothing constant in our forecasting equation was 0.1 and compare it with the MSE that results when $\alpha = 0.9$. The errors for the two cases are shown in the last column of Table 14.9.2 and Table 14.10.1. Table 14.10.2 shows the calculation of the two MSE values. From this table, we see that the MSE of 49,606.58 obtained when $\alpha = 0.9$ is smaller than the MSE of 62,906, which resulted from $\alpha = 0.1$. Our feeling that the use of $\alpha = 0.9$ provides better forecasts, therefore, is confirmed. There may be other values of α that would lead to even smaller MSE values. Of all values of α that we could use, we want to employ the one

TABLE 14.10.1 Actual and forecasted sales values for time periods 25 through 48 for Example 14.9.3 with $\alpha = 0.9$

Time Period	Y_t	F_t	$Y_t - F_t$
25	2,850	2,751	99
26	2,620	2,840	-220
27	2,500	2,642	-142
28	2,301	2,514	-213
29	2,570	2,322	248
30	2,710	2,545	165
31	2,809	2,694	115
32	2,924	2,798	126
33	2,802	2,911	-109
34	2,611	2,813	-202
35	2,709	2,631	78
36	2,500	2,701	-201
37	2,241	2,520	-279
38	2,533	2,269	264
39	2,400	2,507	-107
40	2,710	2,411	299
41	2,602	2,680	-78
42	2,898	2,610	288
43	2,499	2,869	-370
44	2,316	2,536	-220
45	2,105	2,338	-233
46	2,330	2,128	202
47	2,750	2,310	440
48	2,902	2,706	196

that leads to the smallest MSE. In practice, the common procedure is to obtain forecasts on preliminary data using a large number of α values and select, for future forecasting use, the value of α that resulted in the smallest MSE. Such a procedure is practical only when a computer is available to perform the calculations. We can also evaluate models that do not involve simple exponential smoothing using the MSE criterion.

The mean squared error is the most frequently used criterion for evaluating forecasting methods, but it is not the only one. In some instances, we use the square root of the mean squared error, $\sqrt{\text{MSE}}$, since it results in a number that is expressed in the same units of measure as the actual observations. Three other criteria can also aid in evaluating forecasting methods:

1. MAD = mean absolute deviation = $\dfrac{\displaystyle\sum_{t=1}^{n} |Y_t - F_t|}{n}$

This measure is the mean of the absolute values of the forecasting errors.

FIGURE 14.10.1 Actual sales for time periods 1 through 48 and forecasted sales values for time periods 25 through 48 for Example 14.9.3

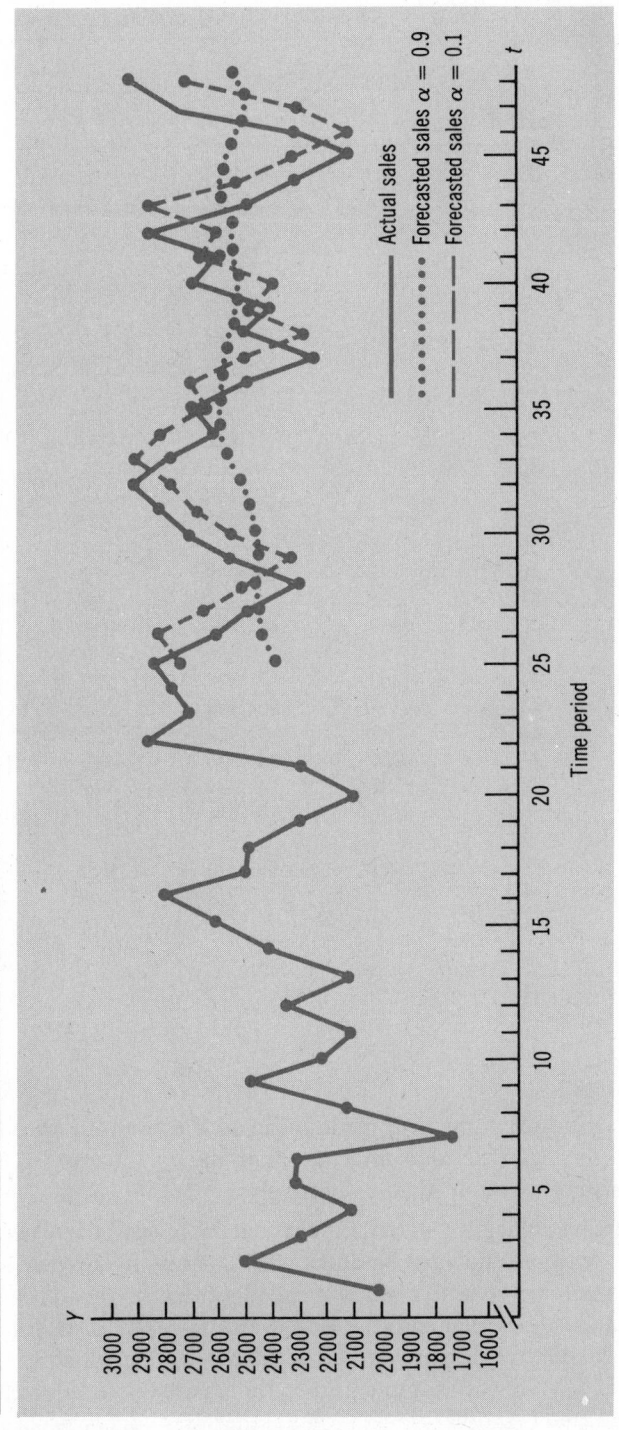

TABLE 14.10.2   Calculation of MSE for $\alpha = 0.1$ and $\alpha = 0.9$, Example 14.9.3

Time Period	$\alpha = 0.1$		$\alpha = 0.9$	
	$Y_t - F_t$	$(Y_t - F_t)^2$	$Y_t - F_t$	$(Y_t - F_t)^2$
25	449	201,601	99	9,801
26	174	30,276	−220	48,400
27	37	1,369	−142	20,164
28	−166	27,556	−213	45,369
29	120	14,400	248	61,504
30	248	61,504	165	27,225
31	322	103,684	115	13,225
32	405	164,025	126	15,876
33	242	58,564	−109	11,881
34	27	729	−202	40,804
35	122	14,884	78	6,084
36	−99	9,801	−201	40,401
37	−348	121,104	−279	77,841
38	−21	441	264	69,696
39	−152	23,104	−107	11,449
40	173	29,929	299	89,401
41	48	2,304	−78	6,084
42	339	114,921	288	82,944
43	−94	8,836	−370	136,900
44	−268	71,824	−220	48,400
45	−452	204,304	−233	54,289
46	−182	33,124	202	40,804
47	256	65,536	440	193,600
48	382	145,924	196	38,416
Total		1,509,744		1,190,558

$$\text{MSE} = \frac{1,509,744}{24} \qquad\qquad \text{MSE} = \frac{1,190,558}{24}$$

$$= 62,906 \qquad\qquad\qquad = 49,606.58$$

2. BIAS $= \dfrac{\sum\limits_{t=1}^{n} (Y_t - F_t)}{n}$

This measure is the arithmetic mean of the errors. Either a large positive or a large negative value indicates that the method yields forecasts that run consistently low or high, respectively.

3. Tracking signals. A measurement that indicates how well the forecasts keep pace with real upward or downward changes in the demand variable over a large number of time periods is called a *tracking signal*. One form of tracking signal assumes that forecast errors are normally distributed with a mean of 0. The allowable forecast error might be set at some value, $\pm 2\sqrt{\text{MSE}}$ or $\pm 3\sqrt{\text{MSE}}$, for example. If these limits are exceeded, a change in the model is indicated. Another tracking signal that uses adaptive exponential smoothing

has been proposed by D. W. Trigg and A. G. Leach. This tracking signal is defined as

$$\text{Tracking signal} = \frac{\text{smoothed signed error}}{\text{smoothed absolute error}}$$

The maximum range of this tracking signal is ± 1. Ideally, the tracking signal should fluctuate around 0. Perhaps the most widely used tracking signal is

$$\text{Tracking signal} = \frac{\text{sum of forecast errors}}{\text{mean absolute deviation}} = \frac{\sum_{t=1}^{n} (Y_t - F_t)}{\text{MAD}}$$

EXERCISES

14.10.1   Refer to Example 14.6.2. Use the trend-adjusted smoothed averages in columns 4 and 5 of Table 14.6.6 to compare the arithmetic and exponentially smoothed methods of computing trend values. Compute the MSE for each column and determine which method is "better." Note that the computational procedures used initially allowed no error in period 1 for the arithmetic method and no error in the first two periods for the exponentially smoothed method.

14.10.2   Refer to Exercises 14.9.6 and 14.9.7. Compute the MSE for each. Which model provides the "better" forecasts?

14.10.3   Refer to Exercises 14.3.1 and 14.6.1. Determine which model is "better" by computing the MSE for each.

14.10.4   Refer to Exercises 14.3.2 and 14.6.2. Compute the MSE for each, and determine which model is "better."

SUMMARY

This chapter is concerned with the analysis of time-series data and forecasting. The focus is on the multiplicative time-series model, $Y = T \cdot S \cdot C \cdot E$, which assumes that an observed value of the variable of interest Y can be expressed as the product of the measures of the following four factors: trend T, seasonal variability S, cyclical variability C, and random error E. You learned in this chapter how you can measure the variability that results from these factors and use it to help you understand the behavior of a variable over time.

This chapter also deals with the nature and use of various techniques for smoothing data and for making forecasts. The techniques discussed are least-squares and other methods of trend analysis, the method of moving averages, and exponential smoothing. Winters' method of exponential smoothing and forecasting is covered in considerable detail. The chapter also discusses methods for evaluating various forecasting models.

REVIEW EXERCISES

1. What is a time series?

2. Why is time-series analysis of interest to the businessperson?

3. List and briefly discuss the four components of time series.

4. Explain $Y = T \cdot S \cdot C \cdot E$.

5. What are the disadvantages of the ratio-to-moving-average method for measuring trend?

6. Define the following terms: (a) moving average, (b) deseasonalized data, (c) cyclical relatives, (d) cyclical irregulars, and (e) modified mean.

7. Of what use is a scatter diagram in time-series analysis?

8. Explain how to fit a freehand line to time-series data.

9. What are the disadvantages of a line obtained by the freehand method?

10. What is the purpose of smoothing time-series data?

11. What are the disadvantages of the moving-average method of smoothing time-series data and forecasting?

12. What is exponential smoothing?

13. In what sense is exponential smoothing exponential?

14. Explain in words the formula that is used in simple exponential smoothing.

15. Why is the choice of the value of the smoothing constant so important in exponential smoothing?

16. What factors should one consider when choosing the smoothing constant?

17. Explain each of the terms in the least-squares trend equation.

18. Explain the word *lag* as it is used in exponential smoothing and discuss its behavior when there is an increasing trend and when there is a decreasing trend in the data.

19. What is a seasonal cycle?

20. What are the two steps in the ratio-to-moving-average method of measuring seasonal variation?

21. Explain the difference between seasonalized and deseasonalized data.

22. What is meant by the term *business forecasting*?

23. Why is forecasting an important function of a business organization?

24. What are the basic components of Winters' method of forecasting?

25. What is adaptive filtering?

26. Describe the Box-Jenkins forecasting method.

27. Name and briefly describe three other forecasting methods.

28. What is meant by the term *forecast error*?

29. Explain the mean-squared-error technique for measuring forecast error.

30. Explain the MAD and BIAS techniques for measuring forecast error.

31. What is a tracking signal?

32. Explain the use of tracking signals in measuring forecast error.

33. Discuss the advantages and disadvantages of each of the forecasting methods discussed in this chapter.

34. Obtain some time-series data relevant to your area of interest and analyze them by as many of the analytical procedures of this chapter as seem appropriate.

 35. Ⓒ The following table lists the annual dividends per share as given in the annual report of De La Rey Communications. (a) Plot the raw data. (b) Compute and plot the least-squares trend line. (c) Compute y_t for each year. (d) Compute a three-year moving average. (e) Compute and plot the cyclical relatives.

Year	Dividends Per Share	Year	Dividends Per Share
1972	1.62	1979	2.20
1973	1.70	1980	2.30
1974	1.75	1981	2.32
1975	1.85	1982	2.42
1976	2.00	1983	2.48
1977	2.10	1984	2.50
1978	2.10		

 36. Ⓒ The following table shows the average amount of an ordinary life policy issued by Fielding Insurance Company between 1969 and 1983. (a) Plot the raw data. (b) Compute and plot the least-squares trend line. (c) Compute y_t for each year. (d) Compute a five-year moving average. (e) Compute and plot the cyclical relatives.

Year	Average Ordinary Policy Amount	Year	Average Ordinary Policy Amount
1969	$3,650	1977	$5,780
1970	3,910	1978	6,100
1971	4,120	1979	6,450
1972	4,450	1980	6,775
1973	4,690	1981	7,240
1974	4,950	1982	7,680
1975	5,210	1983	8,100
1976	5,430		

 37. Ⓒ The following table shows the percentage of its assets that Glasser International invested in government securities for the years 1969 through 1983. (a) Plot the raw data. (b) Compute and plot the least-squares trend line. (c) Compute y_t for each year. (d) Compute a three-year moving average. (e) Compute and plot the cyclical relatives.

Year	Percent of Assets	Year	Percent of Assets
1969	9.6	1977	5.8
1970	9.5	1978	5.4
1971	9.0	1979	5.1
1972	8.5	1980	4.7

Year	Percent of Assets	Year	Percent of Assets
1973	7.7	1981	4.4
1974	7.0	1982	4.5
1975	6.5	1983	4.3
1976	6.0		

38. Refer to Exercises 14.3.3 and 14.6.3. Compute the MSE for each, and determine which method is "better."

39. Refer to Exercises 14.3.4 and 14.6.4. Compute the MSE for each, and determine which method is "better."

For the following exercises, use simple linear regression, moving averages, simple exponential smoothing, and Winters' method to analyze past data and to forecast the future. Graph the original data, then select the smoothing constants, initial starting values, and, for the moving averages, number of periods. It is recommended that these exercises not be attempted without the use of a computer.

40. Ⓒ The following are the number of clients served per month by Red Dot Personnel Services during its first eight years of operation.

				Year				
Month	1	2	3	4	5	6	7	8
J	103	298	724	811	1,171	1,343	1,451	1,611
F	112	251	733	812	1,155	1,362	1,462	1,623
M	121	341	744	869	1,194	1,386	1,481	1,632
A	133	409	754	856	1,239	1,394	1,501	1,645
M	143	466	764	966	1,270	1,402	1,512	1,658
J	151	484	775	924	1,221	1,422	1,526	1,671
J	161	551	785	958	1,290	1,474	1,551	1,682
A	172	556	794	991	1,298	1,378	1,563	1,698
S	183	558	801	1,020	1,306	1,444	1,581	1,701
O	192	645	804	1,023	1,370	1,446	1,601	1,711
N	201	673	805	1,035	1,346	1,421	1,611	1,722
D	221	715	806	1,130	1,347	1,446	1,614	1,743

41. Ⓒ The following are the number of food processors sold each month by Able Appliance Company.

			Year				
Month	1	2	3	4	5	6	7
J	106	108	116	156	155	154	161
F	115	120	126	154	157	154	159
M	110	103	124	132	128	130	137
A	106	114	114	138	144	141	150
M	107	105	127	145	136	145	147
J	99	100	133	155	144	148	151

				Year			
Month	1	2	3	4	5	6	7
J	79	95	119	126	119	122	128
A	91	96	132	124	120	126	129
S	106	111	148	152	111	117	129
O	99	129	133	146	120	122	125
N	111	112	148	154	124	123	138
D	116	119	150	151	119	127	128

42. Ⓒ Thrifty Threads reported the following number of irregular knit shirts produced each week during the past 108 weeks of operation.

1. 34	19. 30	37. 23	55. 28	73. 35	91. 29
2. 22	20. 35	38. 21	56. 29	74. 29	92. 22
3. 27	21. 33	39. 28	57. 23	75. 33	93. 28
4. 29	22. 34	40. 25	58. 26	76. 26	94. 33
5. 36	23. 39	41. 35	59. 21	77. 27	95. 34
6. 36	24. 31	42. 33	60. 25	78. 30	96. 35
7. 37	25. 31	43. 31	61. 34	79. 31	97. 30
8. 30	26. 34	44. 24	62. 36	80. 32	98. 27
9. 26	27. 31	45. 26	63. 36	81. 33	99. 27
10. 32	28. 31	46. 31	64. 37	82. 28	100. 33
11. 32	29. 37	47. 30	65. 29	83. 34	101. 29
12. 29	30. 40	48. 34	66. 30	84. 30	102. 35
13. 28	31. 29	49. 33	67. 30	85. 21	103. 35
14. 30	32. 30	50. 35	68. 31	86. 17	104. 32
15. 27	33. 34	51. 29	69. 32	87. 27	105. 31
16. 29	34. 30	52. 25	70. 29	88. 35	106. 26
17. 29	35. 34	53. 31	71. 36	89. 37	107. 28
18. 32	36. 32	54. 35	72. 36	90. 30	108. 35

43. Ⓒ A beachfront drugstore reported the following number of pairs of a certain brand of sunglasses sold each quarter since the product first came on the market.

Year	Sales by Quarter	Year	Sales by Quarter	Year	Sales by Quarter
1	29	4	53	7	54
	38		72		71
	46		84		84
	35		65		66
2	36	5	54	8	56
	49		73		70
	60		84		85
	47		67		67
3	48	6	53	9	58
	66		72		74
	72		82		90
	56		65		71

*44. The sign test discussed in Chapter 13 is the basis for a nonparametric procedure available for detecting trend in time-series data. To apply the procedure, we pair early observations with late. When, within a pair, the late observation is greater than the early observation, we replace the pair with a minus sign. When the early observation exceeds the late observation, we replace the pair with a plus sign. A sufficiently large number of plus signs suggests a downward trend, and we consider a sufficiently excessive number of minus signs as an indication of an upward trend. Near equal numbers of minus and plus signs are compatible with the conclusion that no trend is present. Theoretically, if there is no trend, $p = P(+) = P(-) = 0.5$. If the number of observations is odd, we discard the middle observation before proceeding. In other words, we always work with an even number of observations. Keeping the observations in their natural time-series sequence, we divide the usable observations into two equal groups. We then pair the observations. Pair number one consists of the first observation from group 1 and the first observation from group 2, pair number two consists of the second observation from group 1 and the second observation from group 2, and so on, to the last pair, which consists of the last observation from group 1 and the last observation from group 2. We then replace the pairs with plus and minus signs as described earlier. Omit pairs yielding zero differences, and designate the number of plus and minus signs combined as n. We may test one of the three following possible null hypotheses: (a) H_0: There is no trend present, H_1: There is either an upward trend or a downward trend; (b) H_0: There is no upward trend, H_1: There is an upward trend; (c) H_0: There is no downward trend, H_1: There is a downward trend. For a specified α and sample size n, the decision rules for the three tests are as follows: (a) Reject H_0 if the probability, given that H_0 is true, of observing as few (or fewer) of the less frequently occurring sign as were actually observed is less than or equal to $\alpha/2$; (b) Reject H_0 if the probability, given that H_0 is true, of observing as few (or fewer) plus signs as were actually observed is less than or equal to α; (c) Reject H_0 if the probability, given that H_0 is true, of observing as few (or fewer) minus signs as were actually observed is less than or equal to α. We obtain the probabilities from Table A of Appendix I in the same manner as described for the sign test. Let us refer to Example 14.6.1 and test H_0 that there is no upward trend with an α of 0.01. The pairs obtained by following the instructions given earlier are: (7.0, 11.1), (7.1, 11.4), (6.5, 12.3), (8.5, 11.0), (9.5, 12.3), (8.5, 12.0), and (9.2, 11.7). Since, in each pair, the early observation is smaller than the late observation, each pair is replaced with a minus sign. Entering Table A with $n = 7$ and $p = 0.5$, we find that the probability, if H_0 happens to be true, of observing zero plus signs is 0.0078. Since 0.0078 is less than 0.01, we reject H_0 and conclude that there is evidence of an upward trend. Refer to Exercise 14.3.1 and test the null hypothesis of no trend at the 0.05 level.

1. THE SEASONAL NATURE OF CHIMNEY SWEEP REVENUE

The Atlanta Chimney Sweep Company experiences seasonal business that is almost completely dependent on cold weather for the generation of revenue. Some people have their chimneys cleaned in the fall for the coming cold weather, while others wait until they actually want to use the fireplace. A few others think ahead far enough to take advantage of off-season rates and a less-crowded scheduling situation and have the work done in the spring in preparation for the next year. The following revenue data were reported for 13 consecutive quarters.

Year	Quarter	Revenue
1	4	$3,516
2	1	2,302
2	2	806
2	3	1,773
2	4	6,280
3	1	2,897
3	2	222
3	3	904
3	4	9,249
4	1	2,580
4	2	771
4	3	3,191
4	4	13,222

Use simple linear regression, moving averages, simple exponential smoothing, and Winters' method to analyze past data and to forecast the future.

Source: David Duffey, Atlanta Chimney Sweep Company.

2. RESIDENTIAL CONSTRUCTION IN SOUTH CAROLINA

The following table shows the number of residential units constructed in South Carolina by month and year for the years 1972 through 1984.

Residential Construction (Number of Units)

Year	Jan	Feb	Mar	Apr	May	Jun	Jul	Aug	Sep	Oct	Nov	Dec
1972	3,665	3,285	3,803	3,109	3,769	3,162	3,085	4,163	4,041	3,449	5,384	2,399
1973	3,824	3,549	3,741	3,622	3,381	3,064	3,174	3,131	2,639	2,263	2,443	1,788
1974	2,707	2,765	2,378	2,119	2,638	1,886	2,188	1,924	1,794	1,561	1,382	1,307
1975	1,434	1,256	1,917	1,664	1,864	1,930	1,967	1,781	1,828	1,756	1,437	1,248

Residential Construction (Number of Units)

Year	Jan	Feb	Mar	Apr	May	Jun	Jul	Aug	Sep	Oct	Nov	Dec
1976	1,536	1,863	2,119	2,082	2,483	1,976	2,162	2,041	2,012	2,066	1,887	1,479
1977	1,751	1,713	2,186	2,257	2,315	2,620	2,199	2,394	2,558	2,061	2,546	1,759
1978	1,851	2,037	2,495	2,769	3,782	3,115	1,980	2,376	1,931	3,443	2,438	2,245
1979	2,251	2,070	2,626	2,693	2,760	3,283	2,549	2,698	2,499	3,171	1,600	1,550
1980	1,882	1,891	1,783	1,604	2,350	2,250	2,411	2,843	2,242	3,170	1,701	2,298
1981	1,633	1,796	2,746	1,717	2,230	1,871	1,696	1,714	1,492	1,665	1,774	1,085
1982	1,587	1,091	1,782	1,516	1,784	1,237	1,760	2,100	1,501	1,884	1,393	2,470
1983	2,155	2,051	2,748	2,156	2,638	2,691	2,791	3,156	2,536	2,318	2,160	2,147
1984	2,096	2,209	3,500	3,218	2,662	2,596	2,396	2,970	2,604	3,720	3,217	2,294

Use simple linear regression, moving averages, simple exponential smoothing, and Winters' method to analyze past data and to forecast the future.

Source: *South Carolina Economic Indicators*, Division of Research, College of Business Administration, the University of South Carolina, Columbia, South Carolina, Volume 21, Number 2, February 15, 1986.

3. UNEMPLOYMENT RATES BY AGE AND GENDER

The following table shows the unemployment rates by year, age group, and gender for the United States for the years 1960 through 1990.

Unemployment rates of all persons, teenagers, and adults by sex, 1960–90 annual averages (Percent of labor force that is unemployed)

Year	Women			Men		
	Total, 16 years and over	16 to 19 years	20 years and over	Total, 16 years and over	16 to 19 years	20 years and over
1960	5.9	13.9	5.1	5.4	15.3	4.7
1961	7.2	16.3	6.3	6.4	17.1	5.7
1962	6.2	14.6	5.4	5.2	14.7	4.6
1963	6.5	17.2	5.4	5.2	17.2	4.5
1964	6.2	16.6	5.2	4.6	15.8	3.9
1965	5.5	15.7	4.5	4.0	14.1	3.2
1966	4.8	14.1	3.8	3.2	11.7	2.5
1967	5.2	13.5	4.2	3.1	12.3	2.3
1968	4.8	14.0	3.8	2.9	11.6	2.2
1969	4.7	13.3	3.7	2.8	11.4	2.1
1970	5.9	15.6	4.8	4.4	15.0	3.5
1971	6.9	17.2	5.7	5.3	16.6	4.4
1972	6.6	16.7	5.4	5.0	15.9	4.0

	Women			Men		
Year	Total, 16 years and over	16 to 19 years	20 years and over	Total, 16 years and over	16 to 19 years	20 years and over
1973	6.0	15.3	4.9	4.2	13.9	3.3
1974	6.7	16.6	5.5	4.9	15.6	3.8
1975	9.3	19.7	8.0	7.9	20.1	6.8
1976	8.6	18.7	7.4	7.1	19.2	5.9
1977	8.2	18.3	7.0	6.3	17.3	5.2
1978	7.2	17.1	6.0	5.3	15.8	4.3
1979	6.8	16.4	5.7	5.1	15.9	4.2
1980	7.4	17.2	6.4	6.9	18.3	5.9
1981	7.9	19.0	6.8	7.4	20.1	6.3
1982	9.4	21.9	8.3	9.9	24.4	8.8
1983	9.2	21.3	8.1	9.9	23.3	8.9
1984	7.6	18.0	6.8	7.4	19.6	6.6
1985	7.4	17.6	6.6	7.0	19.5	6.2
1986	7.1	17.6	6.2	6.9	19.0	6.1
1987	6.2	15.9	5.4	6.2	17.8	5.4
1988	5.6	14.4	4.9	5.5	16.0	4.8
1989	5.4	14.0	4.7	5.2	15.9	4.5
1990	5.4	14.7	4.8	5.6	16.3	4.9

Use simple linear regression, moving averages, simple exponential smoothing, and Winters' method to analyze past data and to forecast the future.

Source: *Working Women: A Chartbook*, Bulletin 2385, Bureau of Labor Statistics, U.S. Department of Labor, Washington, D.C., August 1991.

SUGGESTIONS FOR FURTHER READING

General discussions of forecasting, along with detailed explanations of a variety of forecasting techniques, are to be found in the following books:

Bails, Dale G., and Larry C. Peppers (1982). *Business Fluctuations: Forecasting Techniques and Applications*. Prentice-Hall, Englewood Cliffs, N.J.

Brillinger, David R. (1975). *Time Series: Data Analysis and Theory*. Holt, Rinehart and Winston, New York.

Brown, Robert Goodell (1963). *Smoothing, Forecasting and Prediction of Discrete Time Series*. Prentice-Hall, Englewood Cliffs, N.J.

Granger, C. W. G. (1989). *Forecasting in Business and Economics*, 2nd ed. Academic Press, New York.

Levenbach, Hans, and James P. Cleary (1981). *The Beginning Forecaster*. Lifetime Learning Publications, Belmont, Calif.

Makridakis, Spyros, and Steven C. Wheelwright (1978). *Interactive Forecasting,* 2nd ed. Holden-Day, San Francisco.

Montgomery, Douglas C., and Lynwood A. Johnson (1990). *Forecasting and Time Series Analysis,* 2nd ed. McGraw-Hill, New York.

Nelson, Charles R. (1973). *Applied Time Series Analysis for Managerial Forecasting.* Holden-Day, San Francisco.

Pindyck, Robert S., and Daniel L. Rubinfeld (1981). *Econometric Models and Economic Forecasts,* 2nd ed. McGraw-Hill, New York.

Sullivan, William G., and W. Wayne Claycombe (1977). *Fundamentals of Forecasting.* Reston, Reston, Va.

Thomopoulos, Nick T. (1980). *Applied Forecasting Methods.* Prentice-Hall, Englewood Cliffs, N.J.

Wheelwright, Steven C., and Spyros Makridakis (1980). *Forecasting Methods for Management,* 3rd ed. Wiley, New York.

The Box-Jenkins method is discussed in detail in the following books:

Anderson, O. D. (1977). *Time Series Analysis and Forecasting, The Box-Jenkins Approach.* Butterworth, London.

Bowerman, Bruce L., and Richard T. O'Connell (1987). *Time Series Analysis and Forecasting,* 2nd ed. Duxbury, North Scituate, Mass.

Box, George E. P., and Gwilym M. Jenkins (1976). *Time Series Analysis.* Holden-Day, San Francisco.

Hoff, John C. (1983). *A Practical Guide to Box-Jenkins Forecasting.* Lifetime Learning Publications, Belmont, Calif.

Pankratz, Alan (1983). *Forecasting with Univariate Box-Jenkins Models.* Wiley, New York.

Computer programs for use in forecasting are given in the books by Anderson, Montgomery and Johnson, and Sullivan and Claycombe, and the two books by Makridakis and Wheelwright. The following book contains a computer program for determining optimal values of the constants in simple exponential smoothing and Winters' method:

Gross, Charles W., and Robin T. Peterson (1983). *Business Forecasting,* 2nd ed. Houghton Mifflin, Boston.

The following article may also be of interest:

Trigg, D. W., and A. G. Leach (1967). "Exponential Smoothing with an Adaptive Response Rate," *Operational Research Quarterly* 18 (March 7):53–59.

15

Elementary Survey Sampling

Chapter Objectives: Sampling plays a crucial role in statistical-inference procedures. We have emphasized this point in previous chapters. In this chapter, you get a more extensive look into the topic of sampling. After studying this chapter and working the exercises, you should be able to

1. Understand and appreciate the basic concepts and procedures used in a sample survey.
2. Draw the following kinds of samples: (a) stratified, (b) cluster, and (c) systematic.
3. Estimate means and totals from the data resulting from each of the three sampling plans.
4. Compute sample sizes for each of the three sampling plans.

15.1 INTRODUCTION

What qualities do the homemakers of a particular section of a city value most in a laundry detergent? One way to find out is to ask them. What proportion of the items produced by a certain machine are defective? We can examine all the items produced by the machine and keep a record of defective items found. What is the average age of adults living in a certain section of a city? We can interview each adult living in the area and ask for his or her age.

Needless to say, such methods of getting answers to these questions are in most cases impractical. This is because if a large number of homemakers live in the area of interest, if the machine produces thousands of items, or if we want the age of several thousand adults, the cost of interviewing every person or examining every item is usually prohibitive. Therefore we get answers to these questions by sampling.

Sampling is not new or even recent in human experience. The common practice of taking a small portion of food or other material for tasting or testing undoubtedly precedes recorded history. However, until recent years, people have paid little attention to developing sampling methods that have desirable properties. The method of sampling does not matter as long as the material or population being sampled is uniform, since, in this case, any kind of sample gives about the same result. When the material is *not* uniform, as is usually the case, the method by which we obtain the sample is crucial. Then the study of techniques to ensure a trustworthy sample becomes very important.

Sampling error is the difference between an estimate and the true value of the parameter being estimated.

One objective of sampling is to obtain estimates of one or more population characteristics—*parameters*. The "goodness" of a sample depends on how well it estimates the parameters of interest. The difference between an estimate and the true value of the parameter being estimated is called the *sampling error*. The sampling error for any given estimate is usually unknown, since the parameter being estimated is surely unknown, or else there would be no reason for sampling. We can get around this problem of an unknown sampling error to a large extent if we use probability sampling, since we can get estimates of the sampling error from the sample itself. If we use any method of selecting samples that does not involve probability sampling, there is no known way of estimating the sampling error. Therefore, this chapter deals entirely with probability sampling.

Note that sampling as described in this chapter is only one way of obtaining useful information for decision making. Chapter 8 introduced you to another type of special study, designed experiments. Through sampling, we try to determine the status of an existing population or universe without affecting the units involved. In designed experiments, on the other hand, we carefully select units to be included in the study, determine control variables and their levels, and, usually, determine the different treatments (production techniques, advertising techniques, and so on) to be randomly assigned to the units. The greatest difference between the two types of studies is that in sampling the investigator is limited to the role of an *observer*. He or she exercises no control over the observations made or measurements taken.

15.2   APPLICATIONS

In recent years sampling techniques have been used more and more to obtain information in many areas, such as the following.

1. Public opinion on the outcome of political elections before the elections, television ratings, war issues, taxes, and so on
2. Market research to determine consumer preferences and the effectiveness of a variety of advertising policies
3. Quality-control procedures for manufacturing processes
4. Accounting and auditing
5. Forecasts of crop production
6. Determinations of the incidence and prevalence of specific diseases or conditions within a given geographic area—city, county, state, region, or nation, for example—through the National Health Survey
7. Research relating to many social and economic problems
8. Determinations of such population characteristics as employment status, income, and education

15.3   BASIC THEORY

We discuss the basic concepts of simple random sampling (both replacement and nonreplacement) in previous chapters. We have used statistics calculated from sample results to estimate several population parameters and the associated standard errors. We have shown how the central limit theorem lets us approximate the sampling distributions involved in the statistical inference procedures of constructing confidence intervals and testing hypotheses. In fact, we can apply all the inferential procedures described in this text to data obtained by sampling, using either the techniques in this chapter or simple random sampling as discussed in Chapter 5.

We use the concepts, definitions, and theory of simple random sampling as the foundation for the additional concepts that you will need in order to understand the sample designs covered in this chapter.

15.4   ADDITIONAL CONCEPTS

We have to expand the concepts and terminology used in basic sampling theory when we discuss sample surveys in general. This is because (1) in practice, we use random, nonreplacement sampling almost exclusively; (2) we must identify separately the units on which we perform the sampling operation and the units on which we take measurements; and (3) we must take into account a variety of possible sample designs.

The following terms are important in the consideration of survey sampling.

1. *Observational unit.* An observational unit is the unit (entity) on which some measurement is taken or some classificatory assignment is made. In Chapter 1, we refer to an observational unit as an entity. We use the term *observational unit* in this chapter since it is more common.
2. *Sampling unit.* The sampling unit is the unit on which the sampling operation is based. It may be the individual elements (observational units) of the universe, or it may be groups (clusters) of these individual elements. For example, the sampling unit may be a household instead of an individual.
3. *Universe* (universe of inquiry or investigation). A universe is that set of elements whose characteristics we wish to study. If we can examine only a sample of elements, the universe is the set of elements about which we wish to generalize from the sample.
4. *Population.* This term refers to a set of characteristics of a universe. If a universe is a certain set of individuals, the sets of ages and weights would be two different populations, respectively, for the single universe. Throughout the rest of this chapter, we use the terms *population* and *universe* interchangeably. However, if multiple measurements are involved, the ability to distinguish between an observational unit and the measurement taken on it can be very important.
5. *Sample.* A sample is a fraction or portion of the elements in a universe. The word is also used to refer to a part of a population.
6. *Sampling frame.* A sampling frame is a list or other representation of the sampling units. A given universe may contain several different frames.
7. *Sampling fraction.* This term indicates the proportion of the sampling frame included in the sample.
8. *Cluster.* A cluster is a group of elements from a universe that can be treated as a single sampling unit for sampling purposes.
9. *Cluster sampling.* Cluster sampling is a sampling method that uses groups or clusters of elements in the universe as sampling units.
10. *Stratified sampling.* In stratified sampling, we divide the universe into strata (subuniverses) and select a sample independently from each stratum.
11. *Size of sample.* This term refers to the number of sampling units included in the study.
12. *Probability sampling.* This term refers to sampling plans in which the probabilities of selection are known and nonzero for every sampling unit in the universe.
13. *Gap.* The gap is the difference between the elements contained in the universe of interest and those contained in the sampling frame. The difference between the population of school-age children as shown on the school rolls (the universe) and children actually in school on a given day (the frame) is an example of a gap.

15.5   STEPS INVOLVED IN A SAMPLE SURVEY

A sample survey is a scientific study. Therefore, we should plan and conduct it in a systematic manner. The main steps in a sample survey are as follows:

1. *Statement of objectives.* The statement of objectives must be specific. Without a clear statement of the questions to be answered, we can become so engrossed in the details of planning and conducting a complex survey that we make decisions that are not in accord with the true aims of the study.
2. *General considerations of survey design.* This step deals with questions such as the following: Is the information needed already available, either within or outside the organization? Is a sampling study appropriate? How are measurements to be made? Are measurements both possible and practical? What degree of accuracy is required? What funds and other resources are available?
3. *Sample design.* If we are using sampling methods, the design of the sample is extremely important. We must consider such things as choice of sampling unit, possibility of stratification, size of sample, methods of dealing with hard-to-get observations, and the cost of each operation.
4. *Making the determinations.* The accuracy and usefulness of the results of any study are limited by the accuracy of the raw data. Results from a sample can be better than those obtained from surveying an entire population only if the raw data obtained by sampling are better. Therefore the method of making the determinations, the construction and use of questionnaires, the methods of training and controlling the investigator (the interviewer or the observer), and the detailed methods of dealing with hard-to-get determinations are all important to the validity of the results.
5. *Summary and analysis.* Often, the expense and work involved in processing, analyzing, and presenting data exceed the work and expense needed to obtain them. We should plan for the analysis and estimate its cost when we plan the survey—not after we have collected the data. The planning and conducting of a sample survey are not to be taken lightly. We should realize that the theoretical problems are only one aspect of such an undertaking.

This chapter presents three methods of sampling: *stratified random sampling, cluster sampling,* and *systematic sampling.* Since we cover simple random sampling, its methods, and the inferential procedures based on it in considerable detail in Chapters 5, 6, and 7, we do not discuss them in this chapter.

15.6   STRATIFIED RANDOM SAMPLING

In simple random sampling, the observational unit is the sampling unit, and the sampling frame is the population of interest (if no gap exists).

In *stratified sampling,* the observational unit is still the sampling unit. However, the population of interest is subdivided into subpopulations (strata) based on a known variable that is associated with the measurement to be made on the observational units.

Stratification is similar to blocking in experimental design.

Stratification is similar to blocking in experimental design. The units in a stratum should be more like each other (homogeneous) relative to the measurement of interest than they are like the units in other strata. If a population is to be effectively stratified, we must have information on the variable to be used for stratification purposes for every element in the entire population. In practice, then, we must be able to identify every element in the population, and we must be able to use the stratification variable to assign each element to its proper stratum.

For example, if we are interested in the average income for a population of individuals, a representative sample might contain some laborers, some business-persons, and some professional people. Simple random sampling would not ensure that each of these groups was represented. By stratifying the population into the three occupational groups and selecting some individuals from each group, we can assure the representation of each. The reason we thought of occupational groups in the first place is that we recognized an association between income and occupation.

As another example, consider a study designed to estimate gross sales of a certain type of retail store. What known variable is associated with sales? We might use floor space or the number of employees per store as a basis for stratification.

Effective stratification provides estimators that have smaller variances than those that result from simple random sampling.

Effective stratification provides estimators that have smaller variances than estimators that result from simple random sampling. This is because effective stratification produces subgroups that are more homogeneous than the original population. Other advantages that often result from stratified random sampling are reduced costs and greater administrative convenience. This occurs because we can usually locate the observational unit more easily in stratified random sampling than in simple random sampling. For example, the strata involved may be subdivisions of a larger geographic area that is under study. Such an arrangement lets individual surveyors or teams of surveyors be assigned to a relatively small area. This enables a person to concentrate on a small area rather than the total geographic area of interest. In addition, smaller geographic areas mean shorter distances and reduced travel time for individual surveyors.

The fundamental concept involved is the ability to improve the efficiency of sampling by using a known variable that is associated with the variable of interest (unknown) to form subpopulations, with the units in each subpopulation (stratum) being as alike as possible. We then draw a simple random sample from each stratum and pool the results to get an estimate of the parameter(s) of interest for the total population.

In simple random sampling, we call the ith observation in the population x_i. In stratified sampling, for each observation, we use a label that denotes both the stratum containing the observation and the observation in the stratum that is being referred to. A typical observation is labeled x_{hi}. This label indicates that we are referring to the ith observation in the hth stratum.

ESTIMATING A POPULATION TOTAL

We estimate the population total T by obtaining a separate estimate $\hat{T}_h$ of each stratum total (this is the reason for obtaining a separate sample from each stratum). We then sum these estimates to get the estimated total for the entire population. In formula form,

$$\hat{T}_{st} = \hat{T}_1 + \hat{T}_2 + \cdots + \hat{T}_h + \cdots + \hat{T}_L \tag{15.6.1}$$

where $\hat{T}_{st}$ = estimated population total using stratified sampling

L = number of strata

$\hat{T}_1 = N_1\bar{x}_1$ = the mean of the sample drawn from stratum 1 multiplied by the number of units in stratum 1

$\hat{T}_2 = N_2\bar{x}_2$ = the mean of the sample drawn from stratum 2 multiplied by the number of units in stratum 2

$\hat{T}_h = N_h\bar{x}_h$ = the mean of the sample drawn from stratum h multiplied by the number of units in stratum h

$\hat{T}_L = N_L\bar{x}_L$ = the mean of the last stratum multiplied by the number of units in the last stratum

The form that we will normally use for calculation purposes is

$$\hat{T}_{st} = N_1\bar{x}_1 + N_2\bar{x}_2 + \cdots + N_h\bar{x}_h + \cdots + N_L\bar{x}_L = \sum_{h=1}^{L} N_h\bar{x}_h \tag{15.6.2}$$

The variance of $\hat{T}_{st}$ is given by

$$V(\hat{T}_{st}) = \sum_{h=1}^{L} N_h^2 \frac{N_h - n_h}{N_h} \frac{S_h^2}{n_h} = \sum_{h=1}^{L} N_h(N_h - n_h) \frac{S_h^2}{n_h} \tag{15.6.3}$$

where N_h = number of units in the hth stratum

n_h = number of units in the sample drawn from the hth stratum

$S_h^2 = [1/(N_h - 1)]\Sigma_{i=1}^{N_h}(x_{hi} - \mu_h)^2$, that is, the variance of the units contained in the hth stratum

   The term $(N_h - n_h)/N_h$ in Equation 15.6.3 is called the *finite population correction factor* (fpc). It is always appropriate when sampling is from a finite population. The fpc as used here is comparable to the fpc discussed in Chapter 5, although the formulas are different. The fpc of Chapter 5 is appropriate when σ^2 is used for the population variance, whereas the fpc of this chapter is used when S^2 is used for the population variance. When N_h is large relative to n_h, n_h/N_h becomes small. The fpc then approaches unity and may be omitted. As noted before, we can omit the fpc when $n_h/N_h \leq 0.05$.

Note that the variance of $\hat{T}_h$ is

(15.6.4)
$$V(\hat{T}_h) = N_h(N_h - n_h)\frac{S_h^2}{n_h}$$

We obtain $V(\hat{T}_{st})$ by summing these variances over all strata.

ESTIMATING A POPULATION MEAN

We estimate the mean for the total population by

(15.6.5)
$$\bar{x}_{st} = \frac{\hat{T}_{st}}{N}$$

The variance of $\bar{x}_{st}$ is given by

(15.6.6)
$$V(\bar{x}_{st}) = \frac{1}{N^2}V(\hat{T}_{st}) = \frac{1}{N^2}\sum_{h=1}^{L} N_h(N_h - n_h)\frac{S_h^2}{n_h}$$

where $N = \sum_{h=1}^{L} N_h$

We obtain estimates of the variances given in Equations 15.6.3 and 15.6.6 by estimating each stratum variance and substituting these estimates for the actual stratum variances, as follows:

(15.6.7)
$$\hat{V}(\hat{T}_{st}) = \sum_{h=1}^{L} N_h(N_h - n_h)\frac{s_h^2}{n_h}$$

(15.6.8)
$$\hat{V}(\bar{x}_{st}) = \frac{1}{N^2}\sum_{h=1}^{L} N_h(N_h - n_h)\frac{s_h^2}{n_h}$$

where $s_h^2 = \dfrac{1}{n_h - 1}\displaystyle\sum_{i=1}^{n_h} (x_{hi} - \bar{x}_h)^2$

CONFIDENCE INTERVALS FOR T AND μ

We can construct interval estimates of the population mean μ and the population total T by applying the following general formula, introduced in Chapter 6:

Estimate ± (reliability factor) × (standard error)

In applying this formula here, we shall assume that conditions are suitable for the application of normal theory. Thus, we can use a value from the standard normal distribution as the reliability factor.

The $100(1 - \alpha)\%$ confidence intervals for the population mean and total, respectively, are

(15.6.9)
$$\bar{x}_{st} \pm z_{\alpha/2} \sqrt{V(\bar{x}_{st})}$$

and

(15.6.10)
$$N\bar{x}_{st} \pm z_{\alpha/2} \sqrt{V(\hat{T}_{st})}$$

When population variances are unknown, we use sample variances as estimators.

| EXAMPLE 15.6.1 | The personnel director of Forrestal Technologies wants to estimate the mean and total number of days employees were absent during the past year. The sampling frame consists of an alphabetically arranged card file containing one card for each employee. Since the personnel director has noted in the past that the number of absences appears to be related to length of time on the job, she decides to draw a sample of employees stratified on that basis. Three strata are used: under three years, three through nine years, and ten years or longer. These strata are constructed by sorting the cards according to length of employment. Table 15.6.1 shows the results.

| SOLUTION | By Equation 15.6.2, we have

$$\hat{T}_{st} = 500(2) + 700(4) + 1,000(5) = 8,800$$

The estimated variance of $\hat{T}_{st}$, by Equation 15.6.7, is

$$\hat{V}(\hat{T})_{st} = \frac{(500)(500 - 50)(4)}{50} + \frac{(700)(700 - 70)(5)}{70}$$
$$+ \frac{(1,000)(1,000 - 100)(6)}{100} = 103,500$$

The mean and its variance, by Equations 15.6.5 and 15.6.8, respectively, are

TABLE 15.6.1   Results of the stratified random sample of Example 15.6.1

Stratum	N_h	n_h	$\bar{x}_h$	s_h^2
Under 3 years	500	50	2	4
3–9 years	700	70	4	5
10 years or longer	1,000	100	5	6
Total	2,200	220		

$$\bar{x}_{st} = \frac{8,800}{2,200} = 4 \quad \text{and} \quad \hat{V}(\bar{x}_{st}) = \frac{103,500}{(2,200)^2} = 0.02$$

The 95% confidence interval for the population mean is

$$4 \pm 1.96\sqrt{0.02}, \quad 3.7, 4.3$$

The 95% confidence interval for the population total is

$$8,800 \pm 1.96\sqrt{103,500}; \quad 8,169; 9,431$$

EXERCISES

15.6.1   Given the following results of a stratified random sample, find   (a) $\hat{T}_{st}$,   (b) $\bar{x}_{st}$, (c) $\hat{V}(\hat{T}_{st})$, and   (d) $\hat{V}(\bar{x}_{st})$. Construct the 95% confidence interval for   (e) μ and (f) T.

Stratum	N_h	n_h	$\bar{x}_h$	s_h^2
1	100	10	35	9
2	200	20	45	10
3	300	30	60	8
Total	600	60		

15.6.2   Given the following results of a stratified random sample, find   (a) $\hat{T}_{st}$,   (b) $\bar{x}_{st}$, (c) $\hat{V}(\hat{T}_{st})$, and   (d) $\hat{V}(\bar{x}_{st})$. Construct the 95% confidence interval for   (e) μ and   (f) T.

Stratum	N_h	n_h	$\bar{x}_h$	s_h^2
1	500	50	60	10
2	700	70	75	20
3	1,000	100	100	35
Total	2,200	220		

15.6.3   Mohave Marketing wants information on the amount of money the families of a certain county spend for recreation. The firm decides that it should use a stratified random sample. Stratification is based on the four identifiable groups within the county: rural families, blue-collar families, middle-class suburban families, and upper-class suburban families. The variable of interest is the amount a household spent for recreation during the past year. The results of the survey are given in the following table. Construct 95% confidence intervals for μ and T.

Stratum	N_h	n_h	$\bar{x}_h$	s_h^2
Rural	200	20	75	150
Blue-collar	300	30	150	300
Middle-class	150	15	500	1,000
Upper-class	50	5	900	1,200
Total	700	70		

15.6.4 A universe consists of 1,000 trucking firms. We want to estimate the mean and total amount of money these firms spend on safety and insurance. Using tons hauled as a stratifying variable, we identify three strata and take a random sample from each stratum as follows. Compute (a) $\hat{T}_{st}$, (b) $\bar{x}_{st}$, (c) $\hat{V}(\hat{T}_{st})$, and (d) $\hat{V}(\bar{x}_{st})$. Construct the 95% confidence interval for (e) μ and (f) T.

Stratum	N_h	n_h	Amount Spent for Safety and Insurance by Firms in Sample (Thousands of Dollars)
Small	500	25	12, 20, 15, 21, 12, 7, 26, 13, 23, 15, 18, 24, 20, 24, 20, 25, 16, 6, 7, 17, 9, 19, 12, 21, 12
Medium	300	15	23, 31, 30, 31, 34, 26, 25, 28, 30, 33, 29, 19, 32, 41, 37
Large	200	10	85, 83, 68, 48, 37, 32, 36, 48, 64, 68
Total	1,000	50	

15.7 CLUSTER SAMPLING

As suggested by the definitions stated earlier, sampling units are either single observational units, such as individual people, or groups of observational units, such as households. Often, it is difficult or impossible to identify the individual units making up the population of interest, as is required in constructing a sampling frame for either simple random sampling or stratified sampling. For example, if we wish to sample residents of a large city to obtain opinion data, we can be certain that no one can identify every individual in order to construct a sampling frame of individuals. However, the individual units may all be contained in geographic areas, such as voting districts or city blocks. In this case, we use this set of units (voting districts or city blocks) as our sampling frame.

Other groups that may prove helpful in sample surveys in which we wish information on elementary units include the following:

Group	Elementary Unit
Household	household member
Classroom	student
File cabinet	file folder
Invoice	item

In *cluster sampling*, we select a sample of groups from the sampling frame and obtain information on all the individual elementary units in the groups selected. Such groups are called *clusters*.

If, for each cluster selected in a sample, we retain in the sample all the individual units in that cluster, we refer to the procedure as *simple cluster sampling*. If, from each cluster selected, we draw a sample of individual units for inclusion in the sample, we call the procedure *two-stage cluster sampling.*

WHEN TO USE CLUSTER SAMPLING

Often we must use cluster sampling because we have no sampling frame for the observational units available and cannot construct one. When we have a choice of sampling plans, administrative convenience and economic considerations often present overriding arguments in favor of cluster sampling. In fact, we may have to choose a sampling plan from among plans utilizing different types of clusters. For example, when the observational unit is a household, the choice may be between city blocks and census tracts.

In stratified sampling, we arranged (classified) the population into groups based on a known variable in order to improve the efficiency of the sampling. We then selected a simple random sample from each group (stratum). In order to deal with the theory for stratified sampling, we had to label (number) each individual in a stratum. Identifying an individual required knowledge of both labels (h and i), not just the single label (i) used in simple random sampling. Like stratified sampling, cluster sampling requires two labels to identify a given observational unit, one to identify the cluster containing the observational unit and the other to identify the proper unit within the cluster (x_{ij}). We should stress that we need this double labeling to provide a way of thinking about clusters that lends itself to the development of the necessary theory. In practice we normally do not know how many observational units are in a cluster unless we select it in the sample. For example, in obtaining information from residents of a given city block selected in a sample, we would find out how many people live on that block, but we would not bother to find out how many people live on blocks that are *not* in the sample.

In cluster sampling, then, we describe the population as being composed of M clusters, with the ith cluster containing N_i observational units. Using this new labeling, we note

(15.7.1)
$$N = \sum_{i=1}^{M} N_i \quad \text{(even though the } N_i\text{'s are unknown)}$$

(15.7.2)
$$T = \sum_{i=1}^{M} \sum_{j=1}^{N_i} x_{ij}$$

(We add the values of observational units to obtain cluster totals and then add cluster totals.)

(15.7.3)
$$\mu = \frac{T}{N} = \frac{1}{N} \sum_{i=1}^{M} \sum_{j=1}^{N_i} x_{ij}$$

(15.7.4)

$$T_{i.} = \sum_{j=1}^{N_i} x_{ij}$$

(We obtain the total of the ith cluster by adding the values of all observational units in the ith cluster.)

In simple cluster sampling, we are dealing with clusters and cluster totals. We select m out of M clusters as the sample. For each cluster selected, we use all observational units in the cluster. If we draw repeated samples, the variation in sample results will be due solely to which clusters we select. At this point, therefore, it is useful to define the variance of cluster totals.

We noted in Equation 15.7.4 that a cluster total is the value we obtain by adding the values of all observational units in a cluster. The variance of cluster totals is given by

(15.7.5)

$$S_b^2 = \frac{1}{M-1} \sum_{i=1}^{M} (T_{i.} - \overline{T}..)^2$$

where $\overline{T}..$ is the average of the cluster totals. The subscript b indicates that the variance is the variance *between* clusters.

ESTIMATING A POPULATION TOTAL

Suppose that we want to estimate the total consumption T of a competitor's product in a large city. We take a sample of m city blocks and question all persons living on each block about the amount of the competitor's product used during a specified time period. We estimate the population total T as follows:

1. We use Equation 15.7.4 to obtain the total consumption of persons living in each block selected in our sample.
2. We obtain the total for the sample by adding the cluster totals ($T_{i.}$) for all clusters in the sample (Equation 15.7.2).
3. We estimate the average cluster total by dividing the sample total by the number of clusters in the sample. That is,

$$\hat{\overline{T}}.. = \frac{1}{m} \sum_{i=1}^{m} T_{i.} = \frac{1}{m} \sum_{i=1}^{m} \sum_{j=1}^{N_i} x_{ij}$$

4. Finally, we estimate the population total by multiplying the estimated average cluster total by the number of clusters in the entire population. That is,

$$\hat{T}_{cl} = M \left(\frac{1}{m} \sum_{i=1}^{m} T_{i.} \right) = \frac{M}{m} \sum_{i=1}^{m} \sum_{j=1}^{N_i} x_{ij}$$

We obtain the variance of the estimator from the following:

$$(15.7.6) \qquad V(\hat{T}_{cl}) = M^2 \left[\frac{M - m}{M} \right] \frac{S_b^2}{m}$$

Since S_b^2 is usually unknown, we must estimate it from the sample, as follows:

$$(15.7.7) \qquad s_b^2 = \frac{1}{m - 1} \sum_{i=1}^{m} (T_{i.} - \hat{\bar{T}}..)^2$$

so that

$$(15.7.8) \qquad \hat{V}(\hat{T}_{cl}) = M^2 \left[\frac{M - m}{M} \right] \frac{s_b^2}{m}$$

ESTIMATING A POPULATION MEAN

We can use these results as the basis for estimating the population mean. However, calculations of variances are unwieldy unless all clusters contain approximately the same number of units. In the case of equal cluster sizes,

$$(15.7.9) \qquad N_i = \overline{N} = \frac{N}{M} \qquad \text{for all clusters}$$

$$\bar{x}_{cl} = \frac{\hat{T}_{cl}}{N} = \frac{\hat{T}_{cl}}{M\overline{N}} = \frac{1}{m\overline{N}} \sum_{i=1}^{m} \sum_{j=1}^{N_i} x_{ij}$$

and

$$(15.7.10) \qquad V(\bar{x}_{cl}) = \left(\frac{1}{M\overline{N}} \right)^2 V(\hat{T}_{cl}) = \frac{M^2}{M^2\overline{N}^2} \left(\frac{M - m}{M} \right) \frac{S_b^2}{m} = \frac{1}{\overline{N}^2} \left(\frac{M - m}{M} \right) \frac{S_b^2}{m}$$

In general, we must estimate both S_b^2 and $\overline{N}$ from the sample results.

CONFIDENCE INTERVALS FOR T AND μ

The $100(1 - \alpha)\%$ confidence intervals for the population mean and total, respectively, are given by

$$(15.7.11) \qquad \bar{x}_{cl} \pm z_{\alpha/2} \sqrt{V(\bar{x}_{cl})}$$

and

$$(15.7.12) \qquad \hat{T}_{cl} \pm z_{\alpha/2} \sqrt{V(\hat{T}_{cl})}$$

We use sample values to estimate unknown quantities.

EXAMPLE 15.7.1   The manager of a chain of 300 fast-food establishments would like to know the average age of the sales personnel. Each establishment employs about 6 salespersons. The manager selects a random sample of 10 clusters (establishments) and determines the ages of the employees in these 10 establishments. Table 15.7.1 shows the results.

SOLUTION   By Equation 15.7.9, the estimate of the mean age of the sales personnel is

$$\bar{x}_{cl} = \frac{101 + 109 + \cdots + 115}{10(6)} = \frac{1,080}{60} = 18$$

In order to construct a confidence interval, we must first compute an estimate of the between-cluster variance. Since $\hat{\bar{T}}.. = 1,080/10 = 108$, by Equation 15.7.7 we have

$$s_b^2 = \frac{(101 - 108)^2 + (109 - 108)^2 + \cdots + (115 - 108)^2}{10 - 1} = 19.56$$

We can now compute, by substituting our estimate of S_b^2 into Equation 15.7.10,

$$\hat{V}(\bar{x}_{cl}) = \frac{1}{6^2} \left(\frac{300 - 10}{300} \right) \frac{19.56}{10} = 0.0525$$

The 95% confidence interval for the mean is

$$18 \pm 1.96 \sqrt{0.0525}, \qquad 17.55, \ 18.45$$

TABLE 15.7.1   Ages of sales personnel in ten fast-food establishments

	1	2	3	4	Establishment 5	6	7	8	9	10
	16	21	18	15	16	19	19	16	19	21
	18	20	18	17	21	15	15	15	20	16
	17	18	18	20	17	18	20	16	16	20
	19	16	18	20	19	18	17	21	22	21
	16	19	17	21	19	16	19	24	16	21
	15	15	15	18	17	18	15	17	20	16
Total	101	109	104	111	109	104	105	109	113	115

TABLE 15.7.2 Dollar value of bad checks received from customers, Example 15.7.2

Store	1	2	3	4	5	6	7	8	9	10	
Total amount, $	125	100	130	95	110	105	100	110	115	120	Total: 1,110

EXAMPLE 15.7.2 The chief accountant of a chain of 100 variety stores wishes to estimate the total dollar value of bad checks received from customers during the week before Christmas. Table 15.7.2 shows the information from a random sample of 10 stores (clusters).

SOLUTION We first find

$$\hat{\bar{T}} = \frac{\$1,110}{10} = \$111$$

from which we compute our estimate of the total,

$$\hat{T}_{cl} = 100(\$111) = \$11,100$$

To construct a confidence interval for the population total T, we first compute

$$s_b^2 = \frac{(125 - 111)^2 + (100 - 111)^2 + \cdots + (120 - 111)^2}{(10 - 1)} = 132.22$$

By Equation 15.7.8, we may now compute

$$\hat{V}(\hat{T}_{cl}) = 100^2 \left(\frac{100 - 10}{100}\right) \frac{132.22}{10} = 118,998$$

The 95% confidence interval for T, then, is

$$\$11,100 \pm 1.96 \sqrt{118,998}$$
$$\$11,100 \pm 676, \quad \$10,424; \$11,776$$

There is one big distinction between cluster sampling and stratified random sampling. When we use stratification, the main goal is to reduce sampling error. The result, when we realize the objective, is a narrower confidence-interval estimate of estimated parameters. By contrast, we normally use cluster sampling to reduce costs and increase administrative efficiency. For a given sample size, cluster sampling usually results in a less precise estimate (wider confidence interval) than simple and stratified random sampling.

EXERCISES

15.7.1   Given: $M = 25$, $N_i = \overline{N} = N/M$ for all clusters, $m = 5$

The following observations are obtained. Find   (a) $\hat{T}_{cl}$, (b) $\hat{V}(\hat{T}_{cl})$, (c) $\overline{x}_{cl}$, (d) $\hat{V}(\overline{x}_{cl})$. Construct the 95% confidence interval for   (e) T and   (f) μ.

Sampled Cluster	x_{ij}
1	5, 3, 2, 5, 6, 3, 4, 4, 3, 5
2	5, 9, 9, 10, 2, 2, 3, 4, 2, 1
3	3, 5, 4, 6, 3, 2, 4, 3, 7, 6
4	3, 3, 4, 3, 2, 1, 4, 7, 9, 8
5	8, 1, 3, 4, 5, 7, 2, 4, 5, 8

15.7.2   In a study of radio advertising rates in a certain large area, Granville Advertising divides the area into 20 smaller areas (clusters), each of which contains about 10 radio stations. The agency selects a sample of 6 clusters and obtains the unit charges for a certain type of spot announcement for each station in each cluster. The following data are collected. Find   (a) $\overline{x}_{cl}$ and   (b) $\hat{V}(\overline{x}_{cl})$. Construct the 95% confidence interval for μ.

Sampled Cluster Number

1	2	3	4	5	6
$2.50	$1.50	$4.40	$3.50	$1.50	$4.00
3.50	1.50	6.00	3.60	3.10	3.40
4.00	2.00	2.40	3.65	4.00	6.00
5.00	2.00	3.00	4.00	4.40	5.00
7.00	2.00	4.00	5.00	5.25	4.40
7.00	2.25	3.00	7.50	3.00	6.50
12.00	2.50	5.00	9.00	3.75	7.00
3.00	3.50	9.00	4.00	6.00	5.30
3.00	7.50	9.00	3.50	7.00	12.50
3.00	10.00	10.00	15.00	12.00	9.25

15.8   SYSTEMATIC SAMPLING

Suppose that the head of a department store wants to obtain a rapid estimate of gross sales by checking 2% of the sales slips each week. The sales slips are filed chronologically by cash register each day. Developing a sampling frame and selecting a sample by any of the techniques discussed so far would be time-consuming and costly. An alternative way of selecting a sample in this situation is called *systematic sampling*. Since we want a sample of 1 out of every 50 sales slips, we randomly select 1 of the first 50 sales slips, say number 7, and every fiftieth sales slip after that (57, 107, . . .) until we cover the entire population.

In general, if we want a sample that is $1/M$ of the total population, we select one of the first M items and every Mth item thereafter. The result is called a *1-in-M systematic sample*.

TYPES OF POPULATIONS

When we contemplate systematic sampling, we consider the nature of the population to be sampled. We can identify the following types.

1. A *random population* is one in which the sampling units as represented by the frame are in random order.
2. A *periodic population* is one in which the sampling units as represented by the frame exhibit some type of cyclical variation.
3. An *ordered population* is one in which the sampling units as represented by the frame are ordered according to magnitude.

When we draw a single systematic sample from a random population, the formulas for the estimators, their variances, and the corresponding confidence intervals are the same as for simple random sampling.

When we sample from an ordered or periodic population, the formulas for simple random sampling do not give satisfactory estimates. We may avoid the problem by the technique of *repeated systematic sampling*, in which we draw more than one systematic sample.

Suppose, for example, that we have a population of $N = 1,600$ sampling units, from which we wish to select a sample of size $n = 80$. Suppose that we know that the population is in random order. We can draw a single systematic sample by selecting a random starting point from among the first $M = 1,600/80 = 20$ items, then drawing every twentieth item thereafter. If we suspect that the population is *not* in random order, we draw more than one systematic sample. Suppose that we want to draw $m = 10$ systematic samples. Since we want a total sample size of $n = 80$, each of the 10 systematic samples must contain 8 observations. We also know that under these conditions there are a total of $M = 1,600/8 = 200$ possible systematic samples from which to draw the $m = 10$ we want. We select 10 random numbers between 1 and 200 to provide the starting points for our 10 systematic samples. To each of these starting points we add the constant 200 until we have 10 samples of size 8. Suppose that the 10 random starting points are 74, 37, 91, 18, 120, 162, 27, 176, 24, and 145. Table 15.8.1 shows the random numbers designating which sampling units we would select in each of the 10 systematic samples.

If we think of the $M = 200$ possible systematic samples of size 8 as clusters in the population and the $m = 10$ systematic samples as sample clusters, we may use the formulas of Section 15.7 to obtain estimates of the parameters, their variances, and the corresponding confidence intervals.

EXAMPLE 15.8.1 A firm employing 200 persons wishes to estimate the average age of its employees. Each employee's date of birth is recorded in the personnel record. These records are filed alphabetically by department in a filing cabinet. Table 15.8.2 shows the 200 employees' ages as they would be found in the filing cabinet.

TABLE 15.8.1   Random numbers for selecting ten systematic samples of size 8

Sample Number	Random Starting Point	Second Element in Sample	Third Element in Sample		Eighth Element in Sample
1	18	218	418	· · ·	1,418
2	24	224	424	· · ·	1,424
3	27	227	427	· · ·	1,427
4	37	237	437	· · ·	1,437
5	74	274	474	· · ·	1,474
6	91	291	491	· · ·	1,491
7	120	320	520	· · ·	1,520
8	145	345	545	· · ·	1,545
9	162	362	562	· · ·	1,562
10	176	376	576	· · ·	1,576

TABLE 15.8.2   Ages of 200 employees

001. 23	041. 59	081. 65	121. 47	161. 62
002. 38	042. 58	082. 42	122. 64	162. 17
003. 43	043. 65	083. 50	123. 55	163. 37
004. 49	044. 50	084. 44	124. 50	164. 23
005. 36	045. 46	085. 54	125. 65	165. 36
006. 43	046. 61	086. 17	126. 53	166. 43
007. 61	047. 30	087. 49	127. 32	167. 30
008. 31	048. 55	088. 38	128. 44	168. 41
009. 57	049. 26	089. 22	129. 38	169. 59
010. 61	050. 26	090. 56	130. 37	170. 63
011. 25	051. 62	091. 46	131. 24	171. 35
012. 64	052. 25	092. 27	132. 44	172. 32
013. 60	053. 28	093. 64	133. 27	173. 32
014. 37	054. 34	094. 19	134. 40	174. 31
015. 47	055. 53	095. 64	135. 43	175. 35
016. 38	056. 25	096. 46	136. 45	176. 22
017. 32	057. 33	097. 59	137. 33	177. 58
018. 56	058. 25	098. 60	138. 22	178. 31
019. 49	059. 25	099. 46	139. 62	179. 23
020. 43	060. 25	100. 27	140. 42	180. 29
021. 48	061. 34	101. 59	141. 51	181. 43
022. 38	062. 19	102. 43	142. 49	182. 17
023. 47	063. 23	103. 50	143. 31	183. 53
024. 47	064. 42	104. 51	144. 64	184. 64
025. 57	065. 48	105. 18	145. 36	185. 38
026. 54	066. 37	106. 59	146. 59	186. 36
027. 31	067. 26	107. 33	147. 54	187. 59
028. 36	068. 55	108. 60	148. 24	188. 48
029. 54	069. 36	109. 26	149. 60	189. 26
030. 31	070. 65	110. 18	150. 65	190. 59

(table continues on next page)

TABLE 15.8.2   (*Continued*)

031. 57	071. 63	111. 25	151. 36	191. 29
032. 35	072. 48	112. 18	152. 25	192. 23
033. 24	073. 50	113. 20	153. 25	193. 22
034. 62	074. 49	114. 19	154. 56	194. 63
035. 44	075. 17	115. 31	155. 51	195. 48
036. 32	076. 31	116. 56	156. 53	196. 57
037. 30	077. 26	117. 37	157. 40	197. 25
038. 33	078. 23	118. 49	158. 33	198. 50
039. 50	079. 63	119. 55	159. 26	199. 60
040. 62	080. 37	120. 57	160. 42	200. 28

SOLUTION   The firm decides to take a 10% sample, which will result in a total sample size of 20. It also decides to use systematic sampling. It chooses 4 systematic samples of size 5. Since $200/5 = 40$ possible systematic samples of size 5 can be drawn from a population of size 200, the firm needs 4 random starting points between 1 and 40. Using a table of random numbers, it selects the following starting points: 10, 37, 8, and 12. The samples consist of the elements shown in Table 15.8.3.

Our estimate of the population mean, by Equation 15.7.9, is

$$\bar{x}_{cl} = \frac{243 + 158 + 209 + 192}{20} = 40.1$$

In order to construct a confidence interval for μ, we first compute

$$\hat{\bar{T}}.. = \frac{243 + 158 + 209 + 192}{4} = 200.5$$

TABLE 15.8.3   Four systematic samples of size 5 selected from Table 15.8.2

1		2		3		4	
File No.	Age	File No.	Age	File No.	Age	File No.	Age
10	61	37	30	8	31	12	64
50	26	77	26	48	55	52	25
90	56	117	37	88	38	92	27
130	37	157	40	128	44	132	44
170	63	197	25	168	41	172	32
Total	243		158		209		192

By Equation 15.7.7 we compute

$$s_b^2 = \frac{(243 - 200.5)^2 + (158 - 200.5)^2 + \cdots + (192 - 200.5)^2}{4 - 1}$$

$$= 1{,}252.33$$

and by Equation 15.7.10,

$$\hat{V}(\bar{x}_{cl}) = \frac{1}{(5)^2}\left(\frac{40 - 4}{40}\right)\frac{1{,}252.33}{4} = 11.27$$

The 95% confidence interval for μ, then, is

$$40.1 \pm 1.96\sqrt{11.27}$$
$$40.1 \pm 6.6, \quad 33.5, 46.7$$

Because we can draw a systematic sample with relative ease and efficiency, it is an attractive alternative to other sampling procedures when there is a readily available sampling frame. Although other sampling procedures require us to actually assign a number to each sampling unit, systematic sampling requires only that we count sampling units. For example, a systematic sampling plan may call for the selection of the seventh, the twenty-seventh, and the forty-seventh sampling unit, and so on, until the entire population has been covered. To select a sample in this manner, we do not even need to know the population size. However, sampling units must actually be available for counting. In practice, systematic sampling is widely used as an alternative to simple random sampling because of its convenience and simplicity. As a rule, we analyze the systematic sample as though it were a simple random sample. As we have indicated, for this approach to be valid, the sampling units in the frame must be in random order. The investigator, therefore, should use caution when following this approach, since it is often hard to find out for certain that the sampling units in a frame are indeed in random order. In general, the best practice is to draw several systematic samples, as illustrated in Example 15.8.1.

EXERCISES

15.8.1 Using a table of random numbers, select from Table 15.8.2 four new systematic samples. Construct a 95% confidence interval for μ, using the results of the new samples.

15.8.2 Refer to Exercise 15.8.1. Suppose that you want to take a 15% sample. How many systematic samples would you suggest taking? Randomly select the number of starting points indicated by your answer and use the sample data to construct a 95% confidence interval for μ.

15.9 COSTS, EFFICIENCY, AND SAMPLE SIZE

Up to this point, we have disregarded costs and the efficiency of sampling procedures. Both are important practical considerations. If we are to use sampling to obtain needed data, we need at least rough estimates of the costs of sampling and the quality of the estimate that we will obtain. The desired quality of the estimate dictates the sample size, which, in turn, determines costs. For the types of sampling we have discussed, we can break the total cost C for a sampling study into two basic components: one part that is a function of the number of *observational units*, C_u, and another part, fixed cost, that is relatively independent of the number of observational units, C_f. In stratified sampling, the unit cost may vary considerably from one stratum to another. For example, one stratum may be a rural area and a second stratum an urban area. When there is no cost differential, we can use the formula for simple random sampling.

DETERMINING COSTS

Cost formulas for the different sample designs are as follows.

(15.9.1)   Simple random sampling: $C = C_f + nC_u$

(15.9.2)   Stratified sampling: $C = C_f + \sum_{h=1}^{L} n_h C_{u_h}$

(15.9.3)   Cluster sampling: $C = C_f + \sum_{i=1}^{m} N_i C_{u_i}$

(15.9.4)   Systematic sampling: $C = C_f + \sum_{i=1}^{m} N_i C_{u_i}$

The efficiency of a sample design is associated directly with the variance of the estimator involved. In choosing between alternative sample designs—for example, simple random sampling and cluster sampling—the design that has the smaller variance for its estimator for the same cost would be considered the better design.

SAMPLE SIZE FOR A FIXED BUDGET

When we have a fixed budget for a sampling study, we calculate the sample size in the following manner:

(15.9.5) $n = \dfrac{C - C_f}{C_u}$ (simple random sampling)

(15.9.6) $$m = \frac{C - C_f}{\overline{N}C_{u_i}}$$ (cluster sampling and systematic sampling— if all C_{u_i} are constant)

(15.9.7) $$n = \frac{C - C_f}{C_{u_h}}$$ (stratified sampling—if all C_{u_h} are constant)

In situations in which the quality of the estimator obtained, rather than the cost, is the main consideration, we determine sample size as described in the following paragraphs.

SIMPLE RANDOM SAMPLING

In simple random sampling, the formula for n is given by

(15.9.8) $$n = \frac{Nz^2S^2}{Nd^2 + z^2S^2}$$

where d = maximum desirable sampling error, z = value of normal deviate as determined by portion of time d can be exceeded, S^2 = population variance, and N = size of population. When S^2 is unknown, we use its estimator s^2, computed from a pilot sample, instead.

Equation 15.9.8 differs from the formula for n given in Chapter 6. Equation 15.9.8 incorporates the finite population correction factor. In Chapter 6, we assumed that $n/N \leq 0.05$ and that therefore we could use a simpler formula. Equation 15.9.8 also differs from Equation 6.9.4 in its use of S^2 rather than σ^2.

STRATIFIED SAMPLING

In stratified sampling, the total sample size depends not only on the nature of the population being sampled, but also on the way in which we distribute (allocate) the observational units among the various strata. There are a number of ways to allocate a given total sample size to the different strata. Which of these is the best method depends on the population being sampled. The determination of total sample size and allocation of sample sizes to strata are shown here for the four most commonly used allocation methods.

1. Equal size subsamples selected from each stratum:

(15.9.9) $$n_h = \frac{n}{L}$$ (allocation formula)

(15.9.10) $$n = \frac{z^2 L \Sigma_{h=1}^{L} N_h^2 S_h^2}{N^2 d^2 + z^2 \Sigma_{h=1}^{L} N_h S_h^2}$$ (total-sample-size formula)

2. Subsamples allocated to the strata in proportion to the stratum sizes:

(15.9.11)
$$n_h = \frac{N_h}{N}(n) \qquad \text{(allocation formula)}$$

(15.9.12)
$$n = \frac{z^2 N \Sigma_{h=1}^{L} N_h S_h^2}{N^2 d^2 + z^2 \Sigma_{h=1}^{L} N_h S_h^2} \qquad \text{(total-sample-size formula)}$$

3. Optimal allocation, which allows for variation in both cost and variance across strata:

(15.9.13)
$$n_h = \frac{N_h S_h / \sqrt{C_{u_h}}}{\Sigma_{h=1}^{L} (N_h S_h) / \sqrt{C_{u_h}}}(n) \qquad \text{(allocation formula)}$$

(15.9.14)
$$n = \frac{z^2 (\Sigma_{h=1}^{L} N_h S_h \sqrt{C_{u_h}})(\Sigma_{h=1}^{L} N_h S_h / \sqrt{C_{u_h}})}{N^2 d^2 + z^2 \Sigma_{h=1}^{L} N_h S_h^2}$$

(total-sample-size formula)

4. Neyman allocation, which provides only for variability in variances across strata; all C_{u_h} assumed equal for all strata:

(15.9.15)
$$n_h = \frac{N_h S_h}{\Sigma_{h=1}^{L} N_h S_h}(n) \qquad \text{(allocation formula)}$$

(15.9.16)
$$n = \frac{z^2 (\Sigma_{h=1}^{L} N_h S_h)^2}{N^2 d^2 + z^2 \Sigma_{h=1}^{L} N_h S_h^2} \qquad \text{(total-sample-size formula)}$$

In practice, we substitute s_h^2, sample estimates of stratum variances, for S_h^2 in these formulas, since we usually do not know the population variances.

CLUSTER AND SYSTEMATIC SAMPLING

In our treatment of cluster sampling, we have limited the discussion to studies in which we want to estimate population totals and, in the case of clusters that are approximately equal in size, population means. Systematic sampling qualifies as a special type of cluster sampling, in which it is appropriate to estimate either totals or means. For these situations, we determine sample size in terms of number of clusters (or starting points) as follows:

(15.9.17)
$$m = \frac{M z^2 S_b^2}{M d_{cl}^2 + z^2 S_b^2}$$

where $d_{cl} = \overline{N}d$ = maximum desirable sampling error in estimating the average cluster total.

EXERCISES

15.9.1   Compute the total cost of conducting a sample survey under the following conditions. (a) Simple random sampling, where fixed costs are $1,000, each sampling unit costs $10 to obtain, and a sample of size 150 is required.   (b) Stratified sampling, with fixed costs of $1,500 and information regarding strata as follows.

Stratum	n_h	Cost Per Unit
1	60	$ 5
2	75	10
3	50	8

(c) Cluster sampling, with $1,200 fixed costs, in which we select 5 clusters, each containing 10 sampling units and with costs as follows.

Cluster	1	2	3	4	5
Cost per unit, $	3	7	8	5	5

(d) Systematic sampling, with fixed costs of $500, in which we select 5 random starting points, each of the 5 samples contains 20 sampling units, and the costs per unit are as follows.

Systematic sample	1	2	3	4	5
Cost per unit, $	10	10	10	5	5

15.9.2   Determine what size sample can be taken under each of the following circumstances. (a) Simple random sampling: (1) total budget = $3,500; (2) fixed costs = $1,000; (3) cost per sampling unit = $15.   (b) Cluster sampling: (1) total budget = $5,000; (2) fixed costs = $1,500; (3) cost per observational unit = $5; (4) number of observational units per cluster = 7.   (c) Stratified random sampling: (1) total budget = $3,500; (2) fixed costs = $1,500; (3) C_{u_h} and S_h^2 equal for all strata; (4) cost per sampling unit = $10.

15.9.3   Determine the sample size to be taken under the following circumstances.   (a) Simple random sampling: (1) a 95% confidence interval for μ is desired; (2) a precision of 2.5 units is desired; (3) an estimate of S^2 from a previous study is $s^2 = 100$; (4) $N = 5,000$. (b) Cluster sampling (determine m): (1) $M = 30$; (2) $d_{cl} = 5$; (3) a 95% confidence interval for μ is desired; (4) an estimate of S_b^2 is 100.

15.9.4   Determine the sample size needed when we use stratified sampling and the method of allocation is as indicated.   (a) Equal allocation: (1) a 95% confidence interval for μ is desired; (2) desired precision = 3.0: (3) the following data are available.

Stratum	1	2	3	4	5	
N_h	100	150	200	225	250	Total: 925
S_h^2	75	110	150	200	275	

(b) Proportional allocation: (1) a 95% confidence interval for μ is desired; (2) desired precision = 3; (3) the following information is available.

Stratum	1	2	3	
N_h	500	300	200	Total: 1,000
S_h^2	400	800	2,600	

(c) Optimal allocation: (1) a 95% confidence interval for μ is required; (2) desired precision = 5; (3) the following information is available.

Stratum	1	2	3	
N_h	400	700	900	Total: 2,000
C_h	2	4	6	
S_h^2	200	800	3,100	

(d) Neyman allocation: (1) a 95% confidence interval for μ is desired; (2) desired precision = 5; (3) the following information is available.

Stratum	1	2	3	
N_h	400	700	900	Total: 2,000
S_h^2	200	800	3,100	

15.9.5 Using the values of n found in parts (a), (b), (c), and (d) of Exercise 15.9.4, allocate the sample to the strata by the equal, proportional, optimal, and Neyman methods, respectively.

15.10 NONPROBABILITY SAMPLING PROCEDURES

Nonprobability samples include *judgment samples, quota samples,* and *convenience samples.*

> When the subjective judgment of the sampler determines which items make up the sample, we call the result a *judgment sample.*

Suppose that a market-research team wishes to use a judgment sample as the basis for making inferences about the buying habits of families living in a certain town. The researchers select what, in their judgment, is a sample of families representative of all families in the town. Another team of researchers would, no doubt, select a different judgment sample. It is unlikely that any two teams would ever agree on what constitutes a representative sample.

A quota sample is selected on the basis of more specific guidelines about which items should be drawn. The quota sampler must know, for the population of interest, the proportion of the items with certain characteristics. Suppose, for example, that a real estate appraiser wants to estimate the mean value of the houses in a population of single-family dwellings. If quota sampling is to be used, the appraiser may need to know, for the population, what proportion of houses are two-story, what proportion are split-level, what proportion have central air conditioning, and what proportion have swimming pools. A quota sample should contain dwellings with these characteristics in the same proportions as the population. Within each category, the appraiser, who must know which houses in the population have these characteristics, can use subjective judgment in deciding which ones to include in the sample.

As the name implies, convenience samples are used because of their convenience. A market researcher who wishes to draw a sample of families living in some subdivision might find it convenient to select those families living on the main street of the subdivision. Although convenience samples may serve some specialized purposes, we cannot, in general, depend on them for making inferences about populations.

Nonprobability samples do not have the objectivity of selection that is an essential characteristic of probability samples. Unlike probability samples, nonprobability samples do not yield estimates to which we can attach statements of confidence. This is why probability samples rather than nonprobability samples are the primary focus of attention in this text.

SUMMARY

Probability sampling is one of the most useful management tools. It is being used increasingly to obtain information needed for decision making. We have discussed only the basic techniques and fundamental concepts of probability sampling. You should be aware that you may need far more sophisticated sample designs and estimation techniques to provide the information you need in many situations.

The discussion in this chapter is limited to the estimation of population means and totals. We are often interested in estimating other parameters from the data of stratified, cluster, and systematic samples. The population proportion, for example, is of considerable interest. Although, in the interest of space, this chapter does not cover the procedures for estimating population proportions, the techniques are logical extensions of those that we use for estimating population means. See the references in Suggestions for Further Reading at the end of the chapter for a detailed discussion of the procedures.

REVIEW EXERCISES

1. Define each of the following terms: (a) observational unit, (b) sampling unit, (c) universe, (d) population, (e) sample, (f) sampling frame, (g) sampling fraction, (h) cluster, (i) cluster sampling, (j) stratified sampling, (k) variance, (l) variance of an estimator, (m) probability sampling, (n) gap.

2. List and discuss the steps involved in a sample survey.

3. Explain why the formulas used in cluster sampling are also applicable in systematic sampling.

4. What considerations dictate the use of stratified random sampling rather than simple random sampling?

5. When is it advantageous to use cluster sampling?

6. When is the use of systematic sampling desirable?

7. Describe a business-oriented situation in which stratified random sampling would be appropriate. Identify the variable of interest and the stratified variable. Be able to justify the appropriateness of stratified random sampling to the situation and your choice of a stratifying variable. Use real or realistic data and follow the procedure of constructing a frame, drawing a stratified sample, and constructing a confidence interval for the population mean and/or total.

8. Describe a business situation in which cluster sampling would be appropriate. Justify the use of cluster sampling. Use real or realistic data to carry out the procedure of constructing a frame, drawing a cluster sample, and constructing a confidence interval for the population mean and/or total.

9. Describe a business situation in which systematic sampling would be appropriate. Justify the use of systematic sampling, and carry out the procedure of constructing a frame, drawing a systematic sample, and constructing a confidence interval for the population mean and/or total.

10. An agricultural economist wishes to analyze farmers' annual expenditures for veterinary services in a certain state. Since the amount spent for veterinary services varies greatly with farm size, the economist decides to use stratified sampling, with farm size as the stratifying variable. The economist obtains the following data (coded for ease of calculation). Find **(a)** $\hat{T}_{st}$, **(b)** $\bar{x}_{st}$, **(c)** $\hat{V}(\hat{T}_{st})$, **(d)** $\hat{V}(\bar{x}_{st})$. Construct the 95% confidence interval for **(e)** μ and **(f)** T.

Stratum	N_h	n_h	$\bar{x}_h$	s_h^2
I	85	17	15	20
II	75	15	20	15
III	54	11	30	20
IV	36	7	40	15
	250	50		

11. A representative of Hickok Industries wishes to estimate the mean number of sick-leave days accrued by industry employees in managerial positions. The industry consists of 300 manufacturing firms located throughout the United States. Each firm employs about 6 people in management positions. The investigator wants to obtain the results quickly and cheaply and thus uses cluster sampling, with each firm serving as a cluster. A simple random sample of 10 firms is selected. The following table shows the number of sick-leave days accrued by the management personnel. Find **(a)** $\bar{x}_{cl}$ and **(b)** $\hat{V}(\bar{x}_{cl})$. Construct the 95% confidence interval for μ.

				Firm					
1	2	3	4	5	6	7	8	9	10
15	21	18	17	19	15	18	18	20	16
19	21	18	19	16	19	21	16	16	15
17	16	15	19	15	16	20	18	22	16

				Firm					
1	2	3	4	5	6	7	8	9	10
20	21	18	17	17	18	20	18	16	21
15	16	18	21	18	20	17	15	20	24
19	20	17	16	16	21	15	19	19	17
105	115	104	109	101	109	111	104	113	109

12. The head of Jarvis Laboratories' accounting department wants to estimate the mean length (in minutes) of outgoing long-distance telephone calls. An accounting clerk selects five systematic samples of size 9 from the past year's long-distance records and records the length of each call in the samples. The results are as follows. Construct a 95% confidence interval for μ ($M = 100$).

Sample			Length of Call (Minutes)						
1	7.1	10.4	3.6	2.4	1.9	4.6	6.3	3.4	2.9
2	10.3	7.0	4.0	9.8	4.1	9.2	12.1	8.5	8.0
3	4.8	7.1	2.5	6.2	12.2	2.8	9.6	1.6	5.8
4	3.7	6.9	5.1	3.1	2.4	5.4	5.5	6.7	2.6
5	2.3	2.8	8.3	3.1	8.7	7.6	4.0	15.5	1.4

13. Kelly Properties wants to estimate the mean value per acre of farmland in a certain area. It uses stratified random sampling, with distance from a major recreation center as the stratifying variable. The investigation yields the following results. Compute $\bar{x}_{st}$ and construct the 95% confidence interval for μ.

Stratum	N_h	n_h	$\bar{x}_h$	s_h^2
A	150	15	$500	$1,000
B	80	8	700	1,200
C	70	7	1,000	2,500
D	50	5	2,000	4,000
E	50	5	3,000	5,000
	400	40		

14. The manufacturers of plastic trash bags wish to estimate the mean tensile strength of a shipment of 1,000 packages of their product. They employ cluster sampling, with a package of bags serving as a cluster. There are 40 bags per package. A random sample of 10 packages (clusters) yields the following results (coded for ease of computation). Compute $\bar{x}_{cl}$ and construct the 95% confidence interval for μ.

Package	1	2	3	4	5	6	7	8	9	10
Cluster total	100	105	99	101	98	95	102	100	103	97

15. From the population of employed heads of households in Appendix II, select a single systematic sample of size 50. Construct a 95% confidence interval for the mean annual salary of the persons in the population. Assume that the population is in random order. Use the table of random numbers to select your starting point.

16. From the population of employed heads of households in Appendix II, select 5 systematic samples in such a way that you get a total of 50 units. Use the results to construct a 95% confidence interval for the mean number of years with current employer for the persons in the population.

17. Select a stratified random sample from the population of employed heads of households in Appendix II. Use occupation as the stratifying variable, and construct a 95% confidence interval for the mean annual salary of the persons in the population. Use a total sample size of 60, and use proportional allocation. (Without the aid of a computer, this exercise may require considerable time.)

18. ⒸData Set 10 in Appendix IV gives two kinds of data about the assembly-line workers at Lee Enterprises: the age at the nearest birthday and the number of days they were absent from work because of illness during the past year. The firm has a factory in each of four geographic locations, as indicated. Select a simple random sample of size 50 from this population (all four factories combined) and construct a 95% confidence interval for the mean number of days of absence from work because of illness. Compare your results with those of your classmates.

19. Ⓒ Refer to Exercise 18. From the population of employees, select 5 systematic samples in such a way that you get a total of at least 50 employees. Use the results to construct a 95% confidence interval for the population mean number of days absent. Compare your results with those of your classmates and with the results of Exercise 18.

20. Ⓒ Refer to Exercise 18. Select a stratified random sample from the population of employees. Use a total sample of at least 50, and use age as the stratifying variable. Use four strata as follows:

Stratum 1—employees less than 30 years of age

Stratum 2—employees between 30 and 39 years of age, inclusive

Stratum 3—employees between 40 and 49 years of age, inclusive

Stratum 4—employees 50 years of age and older

Use proportional allocation and construct a 95% confidence interval for the population mean number of days absent from work. Compare the results with those of your classmates and with your results from Exercises 18 and 19.

21. Ⓒ Refer to Exercise 18. Select a stratified sample of at least 50 employees from the population. Use the four factory locations as the basis for stratification as follows:

Stratum 1—location A   Stratum 3—location C

Stratum 2—location B   Stratum 4—location D

Use proportional allocation and construct a 95% confidence interval for the mean number of days absent for the population. Compare the results with those of your classmates and with your results from Exercises 18, 19, and 20.

22. Ⓒ Refer to Exercise 18. Disregard the four factory locations. Consider each group of five employees as a cluster; that is, consider employees 1–5 as cluster 1, employees 6–10 as cluster 2, and so on. Select a simple random sample of 10 clusters and use cluster-sampling procedures to construct a 95% confidence interval for the mean number of days absent for the population. Compare your results with those of your classmates and with your results from Exercises 18, 19, 20, and 21.

*23. The concept of using information about one variable to help us reach conclusions about another variable is, as we have seen, basic to the theory and application of regression analysis. The concept may also be employed in the ordinary estimation of such parameters as population means and totals. One method of estimation based on the concept is called *ratio estimation*. Suppose, for example, that, from the results of a survey of a large population of households, we wish to estimate the mean monthly income of the households. Realizing that respondents might be reluctant to divulge their incomes, we decide to obtain income information from a simple random sample of respondents. From all respondents we obtain information regarding monthly expenditure for food, a variable that we assume to be highly correlated with income and one about which respondents would be willing to provide accurate information. We then use the method of ratio estimation to obtain an estimate of the mean monthly household income. Suppose that from our survey we find that the mean monthly expenditure for food for the population is $400, for the subsample it is $300, and for the subsample the mean monthly income is $1500. From the subsample data we compute the ratio of income to food expenditure as $1500/$300 = 5. Multiplying this result times the population mean monthly expenditure for food yields a value of $5 \times \$400 = \$2,000$, which is our estimate of the mean monthly income for the entire population. The procedure we followed to obtain this estimate, along with its estimated variance, may be expressed in symbols as follows:

$$Y = \text{variable of interest, } X = \text{related variable}$$
$$r = \bar{y}/\bar{x} = \text{estimate of the population ratio } R$$
$$\hat{\mu}_y = r\mu_x$$

$$\hat{V}(\hat{\mu}_y) = \left(\frac{1}{n}\right)\frac{\sum_{i=1}^{n}(y_i - rx_i)^2}{n-1} = \text{estimated variance of } \hat{\mu}_y$$

when the finite population correction factor can be ignored.

The sum of squares in the variance formula may be conveniently computed by the following formula:

$$\sum_{i=1}^{n}(y_i - rx_i)^2 = \sum_{i=1}^{n}y_i^2 + r^2\sum_{i=1}^{n}x_i^2 - 2r\sum_{i=1}^{n}x_iy_i$$

To illustrate the use of these formulas, we refer to Example 10.3.1. The objective is to estimate the mean weekend circulation of daily newspapers per trade area (Y). We choose as the related variable, population per square mile (X). Suppose we know from previous research that $\mu_x = 65$ persons per square mile. We obtain the remainder of the numbers for substitution into the formulas from Tables 10.3.1 and 10.9.1.

$$r = 3.928/63.064 = 0.0622859$$
$$\hat{\mu}_y = 0.0622859(65) = 4.0485835 \text{ or } 4,049 \text{ newspapers per weekend.}$$

$$\sum_{i=1}^{n}(y_i - rx_i)^2 = 393.26 + (0.0622859^2)(101,568.00) - 2(0.0622859)(6,317.95)$$

$$= 0.258038346$$

$$\hat{V}(\hat{\mu}_y) = (1/25)(0.258038346/24) = 0.000430063$$

The 95% confidence interval for μ_y is

$$4.0485835 \pm 1.96\sqrt{0.000430063}$$
$$4.0079, 4.0892, \text{ or } 4,008, 4,089$$

Refer again to Example 10.3.1. Use total retail sales as the related variable and estimate the mean weekend circulation of daily newspapers per trade area. Construct a 95% confidence interval around the estimate.

STATISTICS AT WORK

STATISTICS AT WORK

STATISTICS AT

1. HOW LONG SHOULD A QUESTIONNAIRE BE?

The length of a questionnaire is itself a question that plagues the questioners. What effect does length of questionnaire have on quality of response? Some researchers feel that there is a maximum length for questionnaires, which—if it is exceeded—impairs the quality of the responses. Others believe that under certain conditions questionnaires can be quite lengthy without any adverse effect on the quality of the responses.

Herzog and Bachman report the results obtained when both long and short questionnaires were administered to high school seniors. They found that "on the whole, the comparisons of long and short forms revealed rather little evidence of systematic differences. . . ." Do these results surprise you?

The short form was designed to be completed in 45 minutes. The long form required, on the average, more than 2 hours. What sort of incentives do you think one would have to offer to high school seniors to ensure that they would give careful, correct responses to a questionnaire of this length? The high school students who completed Herzog and Bachman's long questionnaire were paid $5 and given released time from class. In your opinion, would these incentives provide adequate motivation for high-quality responses?

Herzog and Bachman did find that for long sets of items using the same response scales the students tended to use the same response category for all items in such a set. Herzog and Bachman call this kind of response "straight-line" responding. Why do you think students would respond this way?

What other factors—besides monetary rewards and incentives like released time from class—do you think would motivate students to give high-quality responses to long questionnaires?

Have you had any experience in filling out survey questionnaires? How do you feel about the effect of the length of a questionnaire on the quality of your responses? Have you ever refused to fill out a questionnaire because you thought it was too long? Would you consider a questionnaire that takes 45 minutes to complete a "short" questionnaire?

Source: A. Regula Herzog and Jerald G. Bachman, "Effects of Questionnaire Length on Response Quality," *Public Opinion Quarterly* 45 (Winter 1981), 549–559.

2. THE ORDER OF QUESTIONS IN A QUESTIONNAIRE

The design of questionnaires is an important aspect of sample surveys. One should design questionnaires with care, so that responses will accurately reflect the knowledge and/or opinions of respondents. It goes without saying that questions should be clear, unambiguous, and couched in language appropriate to the respondents' education and socioeconomic status. But, according to McFarland, there is another important consideration when one is designing a questionnaire: *the order in which the questions are asked*. He conducted a telephone survey of 516 respondents, in which he studied the effects on respondents' attitudes toward certain issues when (1) a general question preceded specific questions and (2) specific questions preceded the general question.

McFarland found that respondents expressed significantly more interest in certain issues (politics and religion) when the general question *followed* specific questions on the same issues. Why do you think this was the case? Or do you think that respondents are more likely to give "true" responses to a general question when it precedes specific questions?

McFarland also found that the effects of order of questions were consistent for both sexes and across education levels. What implications do these findings have for the design of questionnaires?

McFarland's findings applied to politics and religion. What other issues do you think would yield the same results with respect to order of questions? What issues do you think would yield opposite results?

Source: Sam G. McFarland, "Effects of Question Order on Survey Responses," *Public Opinion Quarterly* 45 (Summer 1981), 208–215.

3. MANAGEMENT INFORMATION SYSTEMS

In a study of management information systems in public and private organizations, Bretschneider used a stratified sampling design. Read his article and prepare a report in which you answer the following questions: **(a)** Why was stratified sampling used? **(b)** What were the strata? **(c)** Was the use of stratification effective? **(d)** Do you think the study could have been designed differently? If so, how?

Source: Stuart Bretschneider, "Management Information Systems in Public and Private Organizations," *Public Administration Review* 50 (1990), 536–545.

4. MARKETING AND SATISFACTION WITH LIFE

Leelakulthanit et al. used cluster sampling in a study and reported their findings. Read their article and prepare a report in which you answer the following questions: **(a)** Why was cluster sampling used? **(b)** What were the clusters? **(c)** Was the use of cluster sampling effective? **(d)** Do you think the study could have been designed differently? If so, how?

Source: Orose Leelakulthanit, Ralph Day, and Rockney Walters, "Investigating the Relationship Between Marketing and Overall Satisfaction with Life in a Developing Country," *Journal of Macromarketing* 11 (Spring 1991), 3–23.

STATI ... AT WORK

5. ORGANIZATIONAL CONTROL AND MARKETING IN MULTIHOSPITAL SYSTEMS

Tucker and Zaremba used stratified sampling in a study they reported. Read their article and prepare a report in which you answer the following questions: **(a)** Why was stratified sampling used? **(b)** What were the strata? **(c)** Was the use of stratification effective? **(d)** Do you think the study could have been designed differently? If so, how?

Source: Lewis R. Tucker and Roger A. Zaremba, "Organizational Control and the Status of Marketing in Multihospital Systems," *Health Care Management Review* 16 (Winter 1991), 41–56.

SUGGESTIONS FOR FURTHER READING

Cochran, W. G. (1977). *Sampling Techniques,* 3rd ed. Wiley, New York.

Dillman, Don A. (1978). *Mail and Telephone Surveys.* Wiley, New York.

Ferber, Robert, et al. (1980). *What Is a Survey?* American Statistical Association, Washington, D.C.

Guy, Dan M. (1981). *An Introduction to Statistical Sampling in Auditing.* Wiley, New York.

McCall, Chester H. (1982). *Sampling and Statistical Handbook for Research.* Iowa State University Press, Ames.

Scheaffer, Richard L., William Mendenhall, and Lyman Ott (1986). *Elementary Survey Sampling,* 3rd ed. Duxbury, North Scituate, Mass.

Slonim, Morris James (1960). *Sampling.* Simon and Schuster, New York.

Sudman, Seymour (1976). *Applied Sampling.* Academic Press, New York.

Warwick, Donald P., and Charles A. Lininger (1975). *The Sample Survey: Theory and Practice.* McGraw-Hill, New York.

Williams, William Howard (1978). *A Sampler on Sampling.* Wiley, New York.

Yamane, Taro (1967). *Elementary Sampling Theory.* Prentice-Hall, Englewood Cliffs, N.J.

16

Statistical Decision Theory

Chapter Objectives: The main objective of this text is to give you some tools that will help you, as a businessperson, to make decisions. In this chapter, you get a closer look at the decision process and add some more techniques to your arsenal of decision-making tools. After a careful study of this chapter, you should understand the following concepts and be able to use them in making decisions.

1. The payoff table
2. The maximin criterion
3. The minimax criterion
4. The maximax criterion
5. The Hurwicz criterion
6. The Bayes criterion
7. Utility theory

16.1 INTRODUCTION

In Chapter 7, you learned about hypothesis testing, one of the two major areas of statistical inference, in considerable detail. This type of inference is known as *classical statistical inference*. The final step in the proposed hypothesis-testing procedure is designated as "drawing a conclusion," a step that involves the making of a decision. Classical statistical inference thus provides a theory and methodology that we can use to obtain information on which to base a decision.

This chapter considers another theory and methodology that the decision-maker can use. This alternative to classical statistical inference as a decision-making tool is known as *statistical decision theory*. We have already discussed two concepts basic to the theory. These are the concept of subjective probability and the concept underlying Bayes' theorem, including the mathematical formula from which the theory gets its name.

Bayes' theorem is covered in some detail in Chapter 3. In Section 16.2, we see the use that Bayesian practitioners make of this theorem.

16.2 SOME BASIC IDEAS

THE ENVIRONMENT OF UNCERTAINTY

The typical decision-maker in a business organization operates in an environment characterized by some degree of *uncertainty*. This uncertainty may concern the present situation, the future outcome of a decision, or both.

The following are examples of the types of decisions that management may face and that typically contain some degree of uncertainty: How will potential consumers react to a new product that is ready to be placed on the market? Should a company spend more money on television advertising than on newspaper advertising? A firm is moving into a new building. Should the old building be sold or leased? How many units of a product should a manufacturer produce? How many units of a particular part should be kept in inventory? The list of examples is endless.

In each situation calling for a decision, there are *alternative acts* that may be pursued. A firm can place a new product on the market, withhold it from the market, or make a decision after obtaining more information. A firm may channel most of its advertising budget into television advertising, or it may spend less on television advertising and more on newspaper advertising, or it may decide to do further research and then make the decision. An old building may be leased, sold, or leased for a while and then sold. A firm can increase production, cut back, or hold the line. Inventory can be kept at a high level, it can be kept at a low level, or parts may be ordered or manufactured as needed. Choosing the best act from the alternatives available is the decision-maker's responsibility.

Associated with each act is a *payoff,* or consequence, resulting from the particular act. The payoff may be positive, negative, or zero. In an environment of uncertainty, the nature of the payoff is unknown in advance.

The nature of the payoff is determined by the *event,* or outcome of the decision that is made. We can refer to outcomes of decisions as *states of nature.* If a firm places a new product on the market, the product may be well received, or it may not appeal to the consumer. Potential customers for a firm's line may be primarily television viewers, or they may be non-watchers of television who spend a lot of time reading the newspaper. An old building may command a good rent over a long period, or it may be located in a part of town that is beginning to deteriorate and thus is less attractive to potential tenants. Future demand for a certain product may be such that it would be profitable to increase production, or it may be such that the most profitable course of action would be to maintain the present level of production or slow down. The price of parts may go up in the future, so that it may be most economical to carry as large a quantity in stock as possible. Storage costs per item, however, may be greater than any expected future price increase.

The decision-maker needs to have the most potent tools available in order to make the best choices. Previous topics in this text have provided many of these tools. In this chapter, we suggest additional ones.

THE PAYOFF TABLE

A convenient way to visualize the relationships between acts, events, and the consequences of any combination of act and event is to prepare a *payoff table.* Table 16.2.1 shows a generalized payoff table. The column headings of the table indicate the various acts from which the decision-maker may choose. The row headings show the possible events, or states of nature, that may exist after the act has been executed. In the body of the table, the symbol p_{ij} indicates the payoffs for the various act-event combinations, where i tells in what row and j tells in what column a particular p is located. The symbol p stands for payoff. To determine the payoff when act A_1 is taken and event E_1 occurs, we locate the

TABLE 16.2.1   Payoff table

		Acts				
Events	A_1	A_2	A_3	$\cdots$	A_n
E_1	p_{11}	p_{12}	p_{13}	$\cdots$	p_{1n}
E_2	p_{21}	p_{22}	p_{23}	$\cdots$	p_{2n}
E_3	p_{31}	p_{32}	p_{33}	$\cdots$	p_{3n}
.	.	.	.	.	.
.	.	.	.	.	.
E_m	p_{m1}	p_{m2}	p_{m3}	$\cdots$	p_{mn}

FIGURE 16.2.1   Tree diagram for a three-act, two-event decision situation

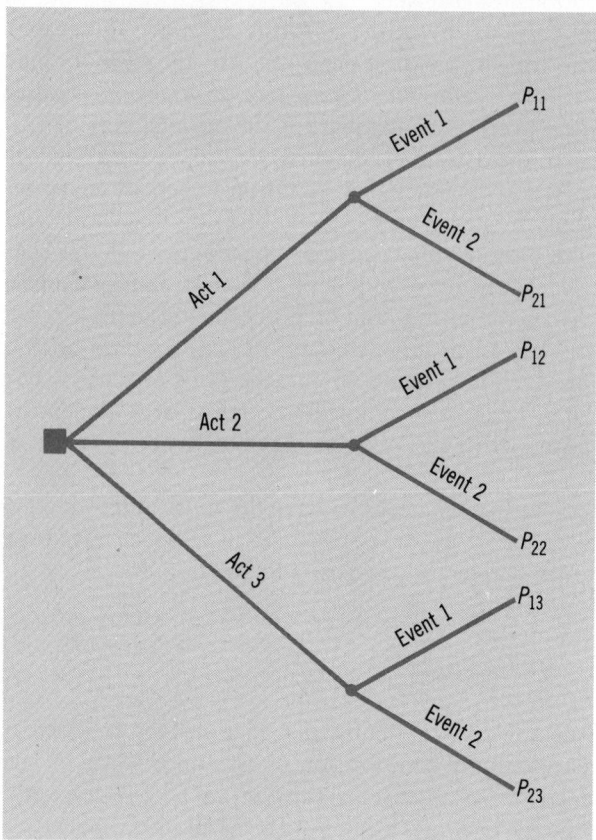

intersection of row 1 and column 1 and find the payoff to be p_{11}. The payoff for act A_3 and event E_2 is located at the intersection of row 2 and column 3, and we see that it is p_{23}. We can find payoffs for all act-event combinations in a similar manner.

We can show a decision-analysis situation graphically by means of a tree diagram. When we construct such tree diagrams, the possible acts appear as the first branches. The possible events associated with each act are shown as second-level branches emanating from the appropriate act branch. Figure 16.2.1 shows a tree diagram for a decision involving three acts and two events. The following examples explain the construction and use of payoff tables.

EXAMPLE 16.2.1   The MacNeil Group is about to place a new product on the market. There are two possible courses of action: (1) place the product on the market, or (2) do not place it on the market. For simplicity, assume that three events are possible: (1) demand for the product will be high, (2) demand

TABLE 16.2.2   Payoff table for Example 16.2.1

Events	Acts	
	Market Product	Do Not Market Product
Demand strong	$10,000	0
Demand weak	2,000	0
No demand	−3,000	0

will be weak, or (3) there will be no demand. Suppose that it has been determined that if the company places the product on the market and demand is strong the payoff will be $10,000. If the demand is weak, the payoff will be $2,000. If there is no demand, the payoff will be −$3,000, the cost of marketing the product. Of course, if the company does not market the product, the payoff will be 0 in any event. Table 16.2.2 shows the situation. Figure 16.2.2 represents the possible act-event combinations by a tree diagram.

The role of the decision-maker is to select a course of action. If the decision-maker knows the event, or state of nature, that will exist after the act has been

FIGURE 16.2.2   Tree diagram for Example 16.2.1

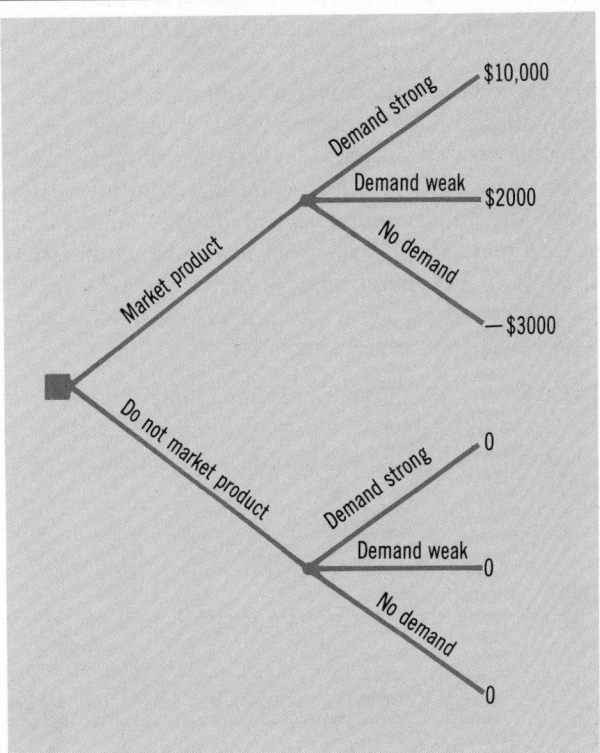

TABLE 16.2.3 Payoff table for Example 16.2.2

	Acts		
Event	All TV Adv.	All Newspaper Adv.	Half-and-half
Most customers watch TV only	$60,000	$ 2,000	$30,000
Most read newspapers only	3,000	40,000	10,000

chosen, there is no problem in making a decision. A decision-maker who knows with certainty, for example, that demand will be strong will market the product. Even if the demand is weak, it would be more profitable to market the product than not to. Only when there is no demand would it be more profitable not to market it.

EXAMPLE 16.2.2 Nelson and Associates has an advertising budget of $20,000 with which to promote a certain product. The firm can spend the entire $20,000 on television advertising, spend it all on newspaper advertising, or divide it between the two. Assume that the decision-maker knows that, if a large proportion of the potential customers watch television and all the budget is spent on TV advertising, the payoff will be $60,000. This is the payoff in cell 1 of the payoff table. Assume further that the decision-maker has been able to prepare additional entries, as shown in Table 16.2.3. Figure 16.2.3 shows a tree diagram for this situation.

The firm could divide the advertising between the two media in a proportion other than half-and-half. However, we will assume that for some reason this seems to be the best allocation. Likewise, for simplicity, we will assume that no other event is possible. Again, having infallible information about the future would make the choice simple. If the decision-maker knew that most of the potential customers watch television, he or she would select the act "spend the entire $20,000 on TV advertising." If the decision-maker knew that newspapers could reach more prospective customers, he or she would spend the entire $20,000 on newspaper advertising.

EXAMPLE 16.2.3 A company moving out of a building has been able to construct the payoff table shown in Table 16.2.4 relative to the acts "sell" or "lease" the old building and the events "the area deteriorates" or "the area does not deteriorate."

TABLE 16.2.4 Payoff table for Example 16.2.3

	Acts	
Events	Sell	Lease
Area deteriorates	$250,000	$ 95,000
Area does not deteriorate	250,000	1,000,000

FIGURE 16.2.3   Tree diagram for Example 16.2.2

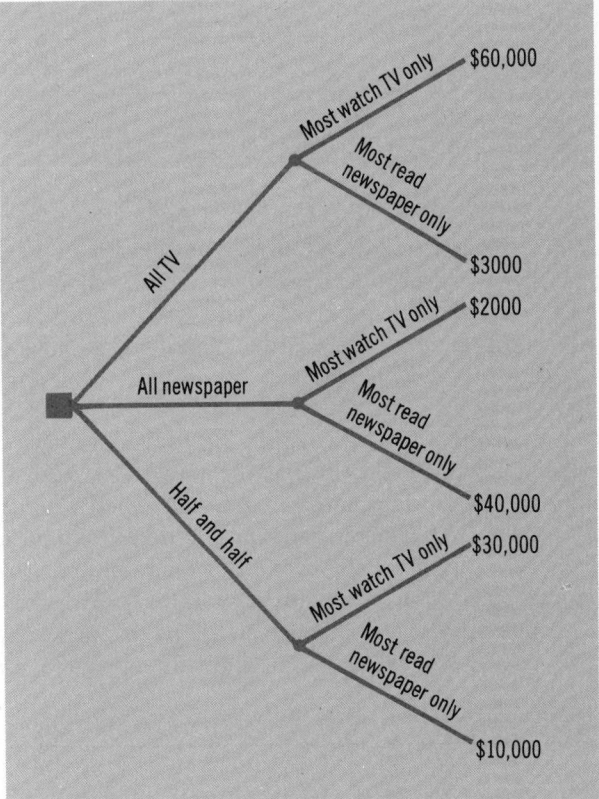

The decision-maker must decide whether to sell or lease. If the decision-maker knows that the area is not going to deteriorate, the decision will be to lease the building. If, however, the decision-maker knows for sure that the area is on the verge of rapid deterioration, the decision will be to sell.

Unfortunately, typical decision-makers do not know for sure what event will take place. They must therefore make decisions in the face of uncertainty. With this responsibility, they need some criteria for making a choice among acts.

THE MAXIMIN CRITERION

Maximin criterion: maximum of the minimum payoffs

The *maximin criterion* for choosing among acts assumes that the worst will happen. That is, it assumes that the most undesirable state of nature will prevail at that time in the future when the decision-maker has selected the act. Given this assumption, then, the decision-maker chooses the act that gives the *maxi*mum of the *min*imum payoffs. Combining appropriate syllables from these words gives us the word *maximin*.

TABLE 16.2.5   Payoff table for Example 16.2.2

Event	Acts		
	All TV Adv.	All Newspaper Adv.	Half-and-half
Most customers watch TV	$60,000	$ 2,000	$30,000
Most read newspapers only	3,000	40,000	10,000

Let us apply this criterion to our previous examples. In the case of the company about to market a new product, we would assume, under the maximin criterion, that if the new product is marketed, there will be no demand. The payoff will thus be −$3,000. If the product is not marketed, the payoff is 0 in any event. The act to choose would be the act "do not market the product," since 0 is greater than −$3,000.

Consider Example 16.2.2, in which the firm must decide how to spend its advertising budget. In Table 16.2.5, the payoff for each act under the most undesirable state of nature is enclosed in a box. These are the minimum payoffs. The largest is $10,000. Thus the maximin criterion would lead to the decision to divide the advertising equally between TV and newspapers.

In Example 16.2.3 the firm with a building to dispose of would sell if it followed the maximin criterion, since a sure payoff of $250,000 is greater than the $95,000 payoff that would result from the worst possible event, given the act "lease."

THE MINIMAX CRITERION

Minimax criterion: minimum of the maximum opportunity losses

We may also construct a payoff table with *opportunity losses* rather than payoffs in the body of the table. An opportunity loss is the difference between the payoff for a particular event and the payoff that we would have realized had we selected the best act for that event. When the payoff is dollars, opportunity loss represents the amount of profit that we lost because we did not select the most profitable act. Under the minimax criterion, the decision-maker expects the worst event to happen and so selects the act that will give the *mini*mum of the *max*imum opportunity losses.

EXAMPLE 16.2.4   Paulus Technologies, which wants to increase production of a product, can choose between two courses of action. The firm can add an extra shift and produce the additional items, or it can subcontract to another firm. Future demand for the product may be strong, or it may be weak. From these contingencies, the manufacturer can construct Table 16.2.6.

SOLUTION   From Table 16.2.6 we may construct Table 16.2.7, the opportunity-loss table. Using the minimax criterion, if the firm adds a shift, the expectation is weak demand and a maximum opportunity loss of $2,000. If the firm subcontracts, the expectation is strong demand and a maximum opportunity

TABLE 16.2.6   Payoff table for Example 16.2.4

	Acts	
Event	Add Shift	Subcontract
Strong demand	$30,000	$20,000
Weak demand	3,000	5,000

TABLE 16.2.7   Opportunity-loss table for Example 16.2.4

	Acts	
Event	Add Shift	Subcontract
Strong demand	0	$10,000
Weak demand	$2000	0

loss of $10,000. The minimum of these opportunity losses is $2,000. Hence the manufacturer chooses to add a shift.

THE MAXIMAX CRITERION

Maximum payoff will take place.

As we have seen, the minimax criterion is a criterion for the pessimist. A decision rule for optimists is the *maximax* criterion, which assumes that for any act the event with the maximum payoff will take place. The optimistic decision-maker then chooses the act that will yield the maximum of these maximum payoffs. Using this criterion in the problems posed in Examples 16.2.1, 16.2.2, and 16.2.3, we would choose the following acts:

1. In the case of the firm trying to decide whether or not to market a product, we would decide to market the product.
2. In trying to decide where to spend the advertising budget, we would optimistically believe that most customers watch TV only and therefore spend our entire advertising budget on TV.
3. The firm with the surplus building would elect to lease the building.

HURWICZ CRITERION

The Hurwicz criterion: a weighted average of the maximum and minimum payoffs.

For those whose outlook lies between the extremes of the pessimists and the optimists, Leonid Hurwicz has suggested a compromise. Using the Hurwicz criterion, the decision-maker takes a weighted average of the maximum and minimum payoffs for each act, then chooses the act with the largest weighted average. The weights used represent what the decision-maker feels are the probabilities of occurrence of the maximum and minimum payoffs. Given the payoff matrix of

Table 16.2.3 (shown on page 888), suppose that the decision-maker feels that the probability of a maximum payoff is 0.75 and, consequently, that the probability of a minimum payoff is 0.25. The decision-maker would evaluate the three acts as follows:

Spend entire budget on TV advertising:
$60,000 (0.75) + $3,000 (0.25) = $45,750

Spend entire budget on newspaper advertising:
$2,000 (0.25) + $40,000 (0.75) = $30,500

Spend half on TV and half on newspaper:
$30,000 (0.75) + $10,000 (0.25) = $25,000

The decision-maker would then choose the first act, since it gives the maximum weighted average. Figure 16.2.4 shows the tree diagram reflecting this decision situation. The dollar values shown at the right end of the event branches are the

FIGURE 16.2.4   Tree diagram for Example 16.2.2, showing application of Hurwicz criterion

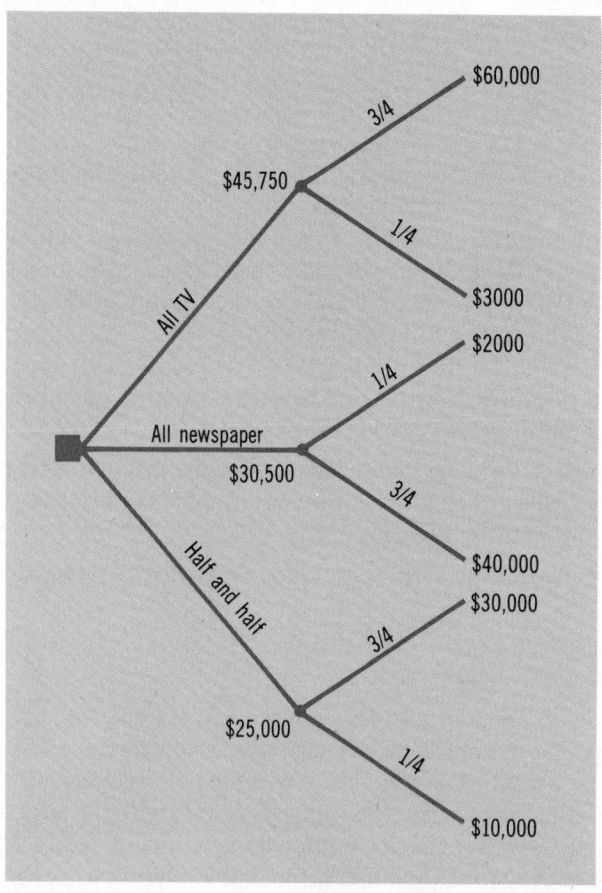

payoffs. The weighted averages for each act are shown at the origin of the event branches. The probabilities appear on their respective event branches.

THE BAYES CRITERION

The Bayes criterion maximizes expected profit.

The Bayes criterion, which enables us to apply the subjective probability concepts discussed in Chapter 3, is a decision rule that gives the decision-maker a mechanism for *maximizing expected profit* or *minimizing expected opportunity loss,* depending on the situation. To use the Bayes criterion, the decision-maker must be able to assign a probability to each specified event, or state of nature. The sum of these probabilities must be 1. These probabilities represent the strength of the decision-maker's feeling about the likelihood of occurrence of the various events. Because the process generating these probabilities is usually subjective, many people reject the Bayes criterion and the related theory.

After identifying the relevant future events and assigning the probabilities, the decision-maker computes the expected payoff for each act and chooses the act with the best expected payoff. If the payoffs represent income or profit, the decision-maker chooses the act with the highest expected payoff. If, on the other hand, the payoffs represent opportunity losses, or costs, the decision-maker selects the act with the lowest expected payoff.

EXAMPLE 16.2.5 Rayleigh Realty has a piece of land adjacent to a larger tract of land, which is soon to be zoned for industrial, office park, or residential use. The firm must decide how to develop the property before the zoning decision for the larger tract has been made. It can develop the property for a grocery store, a restaurant, or a service station.

SOLUTION To evaluate the situation, the firm's managers have constructed Table 16.2.8, in which payoffs represent net realizable profit over the next five years.

Their analysis has also led them to have a fairly strong opinion about the probabilities of the various outcomes of the zoning decision. They feel that it is twice as likely that the adjacent tract of land will be zoned for residential use as for an office park. They feel that an office park is as likely as an industrial park.

TABLE 16.2.8 Payoff table for Example 16.2.5

	Acts		
Events	Construct Grocery Store	Construct Restaurant	Construct Service Station
Industrial park	$10,000	$18,000	$25,000
Office park	10,000	50,000	15,000
Residential	60,000	15,000	20,000

In other words, they assign the probabilities 0.50, 0.25, and 0.25 to the events residential, office park, and industrial park, respectively.

We compute the expected payoff for each of the three acts by multiplying the payoff for each event by the assigned probability and summing these products. Performing these calculations leads to the following expected payoffs.

Act	Computations	Expected Payoff
Grocery store	$10,000(0.25) + $10,000(0.25) + $60,000(0.5) =	$35,000
Restaurant	18,000(0.25) + 50,000(0.25) + 15,000(0.5) =	24,500
Service station	25,000(0.25) + 15,000(0.25) + 20,000(0.5) =	20,000

Rayleigh Realty decides to construct a grocery store because the maximum expected payoff is associated with that act. Because the firm selects this act under conditions of uncertainty, the expected profit, $35,000, is referred to as the *expected profit under uncertainty*. The act is referred to as the *optimal act*.

Section 16.3 contains more examples of the use of the Bayes criterion.

EXERCISES

16.2.1 Rittenhouse Cereals is considering whether to sponsor a certain television program. It constructs the following payoff table.   (a) The firm's advertising manager applies the maximin criterion. What course of action is indicated?   (b) The manager applies the minimax criterion. What course of action is indicated?   (c) The manager applies the maximax criterion. What course of action is indicated?   (d) The firm decides to use the Hurwicz criterion. What act results? Let P (maximum payoff) = 0.5 and P (minimum payoff) = 0.5.   (e) The advertising manager feels that the probabilities associated with events E_1, E_2, and E_3 are 0.4, 0.3, and 0.3, respectively. Apply the Bayes criterion. What act is suggested?

	Acts	
Events	Sponsor Program (A_1)	Do Not Sponsor Program (A_2)
Very favorable viewer reaction (E_1)	$400,000	$0
Favorable viewer reaction (E_2)	150,000	0
Unfavorable viewer reaction (E_3)	−250,000	0

16.2.2 Shelly Mills wants to reach a decision about adopting a new package for its corn crisps. The possible acts are (1) adopt the new package, (2) stick with the old package, and (3) give buyers a choice by packaging half the production in the new and half in the old. The possible customer reactions (events) are (1) preference for the new package, (2) preference for the old package, and (3) indifference. The manufacturer constructs the following payoff table. Determine the appropriate course of action using   (a) the maximin criterion, (b) the minimax criterion,   (c) the maximax criterion,   (d) the Hurwicz criterion, letting P(max payoff) = 0.7 and P(min payoff) = 0.3,   (e) the Bayes criterion, assuming that the probabilities associated with the three events—prefer new, prefer old, and indifferent— are 0.7, 0.2, and 0.1, respectively.

	Acts		
Events	New (A$_1$)	Old (A$_2$)	Half-and-half (A$_3$)
Prefer new (E$_1$)	$4,000,000	$1,000,000	$2,000,000
Prefer old (E$_2$)	400,000	3,500,000	1,500,000
Indifferent (E$_3$)	3,000,000	3,000,000	3,000,000

16.2.3   Given the following payoff table, determine the appropriate act under the   (a) maximin criterion,   (b) minimax criterion,   (c) maximax criterion,   (d) Hurwicz criterion, with $P(\text{max payoff}) = 0.8$, $P(\text{min payoff}) = 0.2$,   (e) Bayes criterion.

	Acts			
Events	A$_1$	A$_2$	A$_3$	P(E$_i$)
E$_1$	100	50	80	.0.5
E$_2$	75	150	25	0.3
E$_3$	25	50	160	0.2

16.2.4   Consider the following payoff table. What is the appropriate act when applying the (a) maximin   criterion,   (b) minimax   criterion,   (c) maximax   criterion,   (d) Hurwicz criterion, with $P(\text{max payoff}) = 0.7$, $P(\text{min payoff}) = 0.3$,   (e) Bayes criterion?

	Acts			
Events	A$_1$	A$_2$	A$_3$	P(E$_i$)
E$_1$	100	50	80	0.6
E$_2$	75	150	25	0.3
E$_3$	25	50	160	0.1

16.2.5   Describe a business situation in which decision theory might be appropriate. Construct a payoff table and do steps (a) through (e) as in Exercise 16.2.3.

16.3   APPLICATION OF THE BAYES CRITERION

Bayes' theorem, as discussed in Chapter 3, has recently assumed an important role in statistical decision theory. In fact, the terms "Bayesian theory" and "statistical decision theory" are often used interchangeably. However, Bayesian theory is only a subset of statistical decision theory. Other subsets include utility theory, discussed in Section 16.4, and payoff analysis, covered in Section 16.2.

This section illustrates the use of the Bayesian decision criterion by extending Example 16.2.5. We discuss three possible phases of a business decision process and illustrate them by means of this example. These three phases, in order of their occurrence, are *prior analysis, preposterior analysis,* and *posterior analysis.*

First, you need to understand the concept known as the *expected value of perfect information* (EVPI). The EVPI in a given situation is the maximum amount of money that you should spend for additional information. For example, if you can get additional information through sampling, the EVPI figure indicates the maximum amount of money that you should spend on the sampling process.

You find the expected value of perfect information in a given situation by subtracting the *expected profit under uncertainty* from the *expected profit with perfect information (EPPI)*. In Example 16.2.5, we calculated the expected profit under uncertainty for the three available acts. We found these quantities to be $35,000, $24,500, and $20,000 for the acts "build a grocery store," "build a restaurant," and "build a service station," respectively. We found that the decision-maker should choose the first act, since it promised the maximum profit.

We now need to find the expected profit, given perfect information. This is calculated on the assumption that the decision-maker has a perfect predictor available. When this perfect predictor indicates that a certain event will occur, the decision-maker chooses the optimal act for that event. We now attach a slightly different interpretation to the probabilities assigned to the events. We interpret each one as the relative frequency with which the perfect predictor predicts the associated event. For example, we would now say that, when faced with the present situation a great many times, the predictor would predict residential zoning 50% of the time, office-park zoning 25% of the time, and industrial-park zoning 25% of the time. Table 16.3.1 shows the calculation of the expected profit with perfect information for Example 16.2.5.

The figure $48,750 is the expected profit with perfect information, EVPI. We can interpret this as the average profit that would be realized in the long run if the decision-maker, repeatedly faced with this same problem, each time took the optimal act associated with the event predicted by the predictor. Some writers call this value the *expected profit under certainty*. We now have enough information to compute EVPI = expected profit with perfect information − expected profit under uncertainty = $48,750 − $35,000 = $13,750.

Note that the expected value of perfect information is, in general, equal to the expected opportunity loss of selecting the optimum act in an uncertain environment. (We discuss opportunity loss in Section 16.2.) Computing the expected opportunity loss under uncertainty using the Bayesian criterion is like computing the expected profit under uncertainty. Comparing that quantity for the present

TABLE 16.3.1   Calculation of expected profit with perfect information for Example 16.2.5

Event	Profit for Optimal Act	Probability	Weighted Profit
Industrial park	$25,000	0.25	$ 6,250
Office park	50,000	0.25	12,500
Residential	60,000	0.50	30,000
			$48,750

example, we find that it is equal to $13,750, the expected value of perfect information that we just computed. When we convert the payoff table, Table 16.2.8, to an opportunity-loss table, we have Table 16.3.2.

The optimal act, considering expected opportunity losses, would be to build a grocery store, since that would minimize the expected opportunity loss. This value, $13,750, is equal to the expected value of perfect information. Some

TABLE 16.3.2   Opportunity-loss table for real-estate developer

	Acts		
Events	Construct Grocery Store	Construct Restaurant	Construct Service Station
Industrial park	$15,000	$ 7,000	$ 0
Office park	40,000	0	35,000
Residential	0	45,000	40,000

Expected opportunity loss for each of the three acts

ACT: CONSTRUCT GROCERY STORE

Event	Probability	Opportunity Loss	Weighted Opportunity Loss
Industrial park	0.25	$15,000	$ 3,750
Office park	0.25	40,000	10,000
Residential	0.50	0	0
Expected opportunity loss		=	$13,750

ACT: CONSTRUCT RESTAURANT

Event	Probability	Opportunity Loss	Weighted Opportunity Loss
Industrial park	0.25	$ 7,000	$ 1,750
Office park	0.25	0	0
Residential	0.50	45,000	22,500
Expected opportunity loss		=	$24,250

ACT: CONSTRUCT SERVICE STATION

Event	Probability	Opportunity Loss	Weighted Opportunity Loss
Industrial park	0.25	$ 0	$ 0
Office park	0.25	35,000	8,750
Residential	0.50	40,000	20,000
Expected opportunity loss		=	$28,750

writers refer to the expected opportunity loss for the optimal act under uncertainty as the *cost of uncertainty*. Thus, the following three terms mean the same thing: *expected value of perfect information, expected opportunity loss for the optimal act under uncertainty,* and *cost of uncertainty*.

PRIOR ANALYSIS

In the foregoing illustrations, the probabilities that we assigned to events were *prior probabilities*. They are called *prior* because the decision-maker formulated them prior to acquiring experimental or sampling information. As a rule, these prior probabilities are subjective, representing decision-makers' best estimates of the relative likelihood of the various events. The analysis that is carried out using these prior probabilities is called *prior analysis*.

Following the prior analysis, decision-makers must decide either to get more information or to take the final action indicated by the prior analysis. They can get more information by conducting a survey, by carrying out an experiment, or by some other means. This additional information is usually called *sample information,* no matter how they acquire it.

If decision-makers elect to take the action indicated by the prior analysis, no further analyses are necessary. They forge ahead and await the consequences. If, however, they decide to get more information, they may find that this new information causes them to substitute new probabilities for the prior ones. With new probabilities for the various events, decision-makers will perform another analysis using this new information. They recompute the expected profit for the various acts. They obtain these new probabilities, called *posterior probabilities,* by using Bayes' theorem. The subsequent analysis with the new probabilities is called *posterior analysis*.

The question here is whether it is worthwhile to obtain further information. In general, additional information is bought at a price. Decision-makers must decide whether the potential result is worth the cost.

PREPOSTERIOR ANALYSIS

The objective in preposterior analysis is to find out before taking final action whether it is worthwhile to gather further information (to sample).

EXAMPLE 16.3.1 The owner of Tyler Nursing Homes wants to open a new facility in a certain area. He usually builds 25-, 50-, or 100-bed facilities, depending on whether anticipated demand is low, medium, or high. What analyses should the owner perform?

SOLUTION The owner constructs Table 16.3.3 on the basis of past experience. The payoffs in the table are short-range net profits.

TABLE 16.3.3   Payoff table for Example 16.3.1

	Acts		
Events	Build 25-bed Facility	Build 50-bed Facility	Build 100-bed Facility
Low demand	$30,000	−$20,000	−$40,000
Medium demand	35,000	50,000	−10,000
High demand	40,000	55,000	75,000

On the basis of his information about the area, the owner feels that the probabilities of low demand (E_1), medium demand (E_2), and high demand (E_3) are 0.1, 0.4, and 0.5, respectively. Formally, we may write $P(E_1) = 0.1$, $P(E_2) = 0.4$, and $P(E_3) = 0.5$. The expected payoffs for each act are as follows.

Act	**Expected Payoff**
Build 25-bed facility	$30,000(0.1) + 35,000(0.4) + 40,000(0.5) = \$37,000$
Build 50-bed facility	$(-20,000)(0.1) + 50,000(0.4) + 55,000(0.5) = \$45,500$
Build 100-bed facility	$(-40,000)(0.1) + (-10,000)(0.4) + 75,000(0.5) = \$29,500$

Suppose that the owner decides not to collect additional information. That is, he will base his decision on this prior analysis. His decision would be to build a 50-bed facility, since that has the highest expected payoff. Figure 16.3.1 is a tree diagram for the decision options and possible outcomes for this situation.

We can now compute the expected value of perfect information. However, we first need to calculate the expected profit with perfect information, as shown in Table 16.3.4. Thus, we find EVPI = $\$60,500 - \$45,500 = \$15,000$.

Recall that we can also interpret this value, $15,000, both as the expected opportunity loss for the optimal act under uncertainty and as the cost of uncertainty. Since the decision-maker can do no better than obtain perfect information, this figure places an upper bound on the amount that he will be willing to pay for sample information that he knows will be something less than perfect.

At this point, the owner of the chain of nursing homes decides to look into the idea of conducting a survey in the area to get an updated estimate of demand. A research firm will conduct the survey for $5,000 and provide information that will be translated into an estimate of low demand (X_1), medium demand (X_2),

TABLE 16.3.4   Calculation of expected profit with perfect information, Example 16.3.1

Event	**Profit for Optimal Act**	**Probability**	**Weighted Profit**
Low demand	$30,000	0.1	$ 3,000
Medium demand	50,000	0.4	20,000
High demand	75,000	0.5	37,500
Expected profit with perfect information		=	$60,500

FIGURE 16.3.1   Tree diagram for decision options and possible outcomes for Example 16.3.1 without collecting additional information

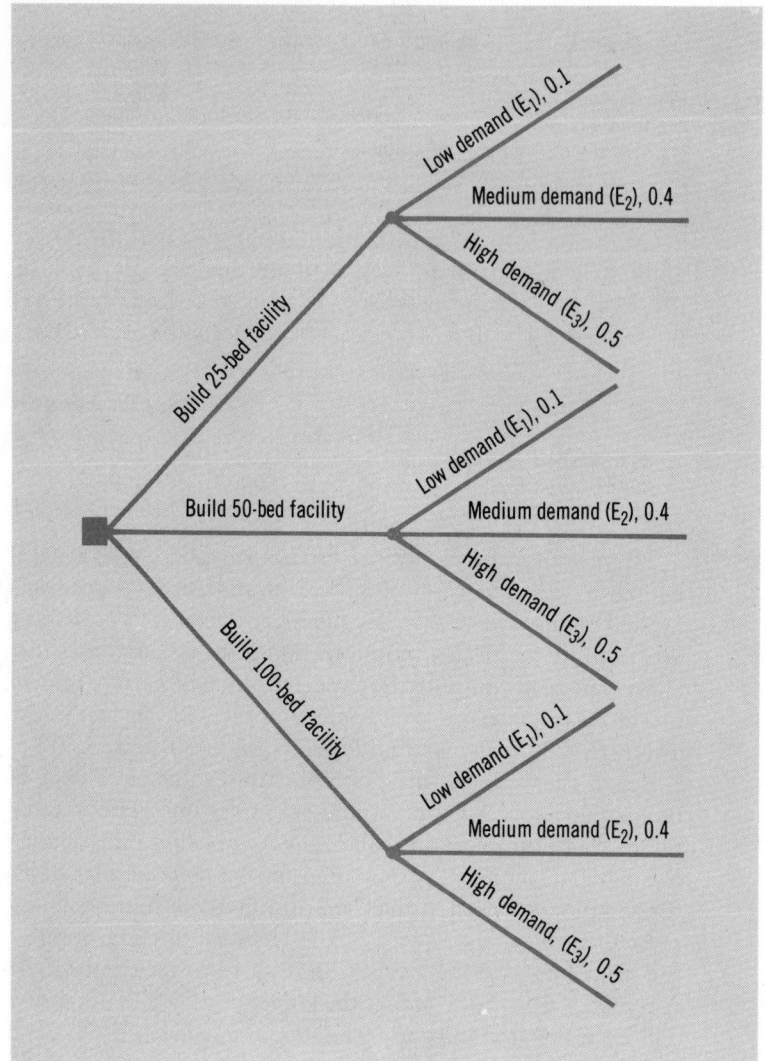

or high demand (X_3), depending on the results of the survey. The research firm describes the reliability of these estimates as follows. Over many years of doing such surveys, the firm has found that when the true demand for a thing is low, sample evidence indicates a low demand about 75% of the time. The evidence indicates a medium demand about 15% of the time, and a high demand about 10% of the time. These are the conditional probabilities of a sample estimate, given a specific event. For example, 0.75 is the conditional probability of a sample

TABLE 16.3.5   Conditional probabilities for Example 16.3.1

	Sample Estimates		
True Events	Low Demand (X_1)	Medium Demand (X_2)	High Demand (X_3)
Low demand (E_1)	0.75	0.15	0.10
Medium demand (E_2)	0.08	0.80	0.12
High demand (E_3)	0.05	0.10	0.85

estimate of low demand, given that the true event or state of nature is low demand. When the true demand is medium, the sample evidence indicates medium demand about 80% of the time, low demand about 8% of the time, and high demand about 12% of the time. When the true demand is high, sample estimates of low, medium, and high demand occur with relative frequencies of 0.05, 0.10, and 0.85, respectively. Table 16.3.5 displays the research firm's evaluation of the conditional probabilities, where the cell entries are the $P(X_j|E_i)$'s.

Next the decision-maker wants to know the probability that a given event is the true state of nature and that the sample estimates it as such. These probabilities are the joint probabilities of each state of nature and each sample estimate. They are found by multiplying the prior probability of the event by the conditional probability of the sample estimate, given the event. For example, we find the probability of the true event being low demand and the sample evidence indicating low demand by multiplying 0.1 by 0.75 to give 0.075. Symbolically,

$$P(E_1 \cap X_1) = P(E_1)P(X_1|E_1)$$

Table 16.3.6 displays these joint probabilities. In the table, note that the row totals are the marginal probabilities of the respective events. These are equal to the prior probabilities. The column totals are the marginal probabilities for the respective sample estimates, given all events.

At this point, we use Bayes' theorem to incorporate information that may be provided by the possible outcomes of sampling. Applying Bayes' theorem yields what are called *posterior probabilities*. Given a particular sample estimate, we

TABLE 16.3.6   Joint probabilities for Example 16.3.1

Event	Prior Probability	Joint Probabilities			Total $P(E_i)$
		$P(E_i \cap X_1)$	$P(E_i \cap X_2)$	$P(E_i \cap X_3)$	
E_1	0.1	0.075	0.015	0.010	0.1
E_2	0.4	0.032	0.320	0.048	0.4
E_3	0.5	0.025	0.050	0.425	0.5
Total	1.0	0.132	0.385	0.483	1.0

TABLE 16.3.7 Posterior probabilities of specific events, given a particular sample estimate, Example 16.3.1

Event E_i	Posterior Probabilities		
	$P(E_i|X_1)$	$P(E_i|X_2)$	$P(E_i|X_3)$
E_1	0.5682	0.0390	0.0207
E_2	0.2424	0.8312	0.0994
E_3	0.1894	0.1299	0.8799
Total	1.0000	1.0000	1.0000

find the probability that a specific event is the true event. Symbolically, we evaluate

(16.3.1)
$$P(E_i|X_j) = \frac{P(E_i)P(X_j|E_i)}{\Sigma P(E_i)P(X_j)|E_i)}$$

For example, the probability of low demand (E_1), given a sample estimate of low demand (X_1), is

$$P(E_1|X_1) = \frac{0.075}{0.132} = 0.5682$$

Table 16.3.7 shows the posterior probabilities arrived at from the data of this example.

The next step in preposterior analysis is to use the posterior probabilities from Table 16.3.7 to find the expected payoffs for each act, given the various possible sample estimates. Table 16.3.8 shows the computation and results of this analysis.

Suppose that the owner decides to engage the research firm. We know that he will get one of three possible results: an indication that the demand is low, high, or medium. If the sample estimates a low demand, the expected payoffs are as follows:

Act	Expected Payoff
Build 25-bed facility	$33,106.00
Build 50-bed facility	11,173.00
Build 100-bed facility	−10,947.00

This indicates that if the survey is made and the results indicate a low demand, the owner should choose the act "build 25-bed facility," since it yields the maximum of the expected payoffs.

The research firm carries out the survey and estimates that demand will be medium. What should the owner do? Since the expected payoffs are $35,458.00, $47,924.50, and −$129.50 for the acts "build 25-bed facility," "build 50-bed

TABLE 16.3.8   Expected payoffs, preposterior analysis, Example 16.3.1

ACT: BUILD A 25-BED FACILITY

1. Low demand

(30,000)(0.5682)	=	$17,046.00
(35,000)(0.2424)	=	8,484.00
(40,000)(0.1894)	=	7,576.00
Expected payoff:		$33,106.00

2. Medium demand

(30,000)(0.0390)	=	$ 1,170.00
(35,000)(0.8312)	=	29,092.00
(40,000)(0.1299)	=	5,196.00
		$35,458.00

3. High demand

(30,000)(0.0207)	=	$ 621.00
(35,000)(0.0994)	=	3,479.00
(40,000)(0.8799)	=	35,196.00
		$39,296.00

ACT: BUILD A 50-BED FACILITY

1. Low demand

(−20,000)(0.5682)	=	$−11,364.00
(50,000)(0.2424)	=	12,120.00
(55,000)(0.1894)	=	10,417.00
Expected payoff:		$11,173.00

2. Medium demand

(−20,000)(0.0390)	=	$ −780.00
(50,000)(0.8312)	=	41,560.00
(55,000)(0.1299)	=	7,144.50
		$47,924.50

3. High demand

(−20,000)(0.0207)	=	$−414.00
(50,000)(0.0994)	=	4,970.00
(55,000)(0.8799)	=	48,394.50
		$52,950.50

ACT: BUILD A 100-BED FACILITY

1. Low demand

(−40,000)(0.5682)	=	$−22,728.00
(−10,000)(0.2424)	=	−2,424.00
(75,000)(0.1894)	=	14,205.00
Expected payoff:		$−10,947.00

2. Medium demand

(−40,000)(0.0390)	=	$−1,560.00
(−10,000)(0.8312)	=	−8,312.00
(75,000)(0.1299)	=	9,742.50
		$−129.50

3. High demand

(−40,000)(0.0207)	=	$−828.00
(−10,000)(0.0994)	=	−994.00
(75,000)(0.8799)	=	65,992.50
		$64,170.50

facility," and "build 100-bed facility," respectively, he should build a 50-bed facility, since that yields the maximum expected payoff. If the sample estimate had shown high demand, the act "build 100-bed facility" would yield the maximum expected payoff. The outcome of a survey is uncertain. What we need is a single figure that indicates what the expected payoff is if a survey is done and if we select the optimal act after we get the survey estimates. We get such a figure by multiplying the maximum payoff for each sample result by the marginal probabilities of this result and summing the products. For the present example,

$$\$33,106.00(0.132) + \$47,924.50(0.385)$$
$$+ \$64,170.50(0.483) = \$53,815.28$$

This indicates that if a survey is conducted, the resulting payoff may be as great as $53,815.28. The maximum expected payoff (when a 50-bed facility is built) without benefit of a survey, as we have seen, is only $45,500.

Should the owner have the research firm carry out the survey? Yes, because the expected payoff *with* a survey is greater than the expected payoff without one. The difference is $53,815 − 45,500 = $8,315. This figure is called the *expected value of sample information* (EVSI). It indicates how much a person should be willing to pay for sample information. In this example, the survey is to cost $5,000. Since the *expected net gain from sampling* (ENGS) is $8,315 − $5,000 = $3,315, the owner should spend the money to have the survey done.

Expected value of sample information (EVSI): the maximum one should be willing to pay for sample information

FIGURE 16.3.2 Tree diagram for Example 16.3.1

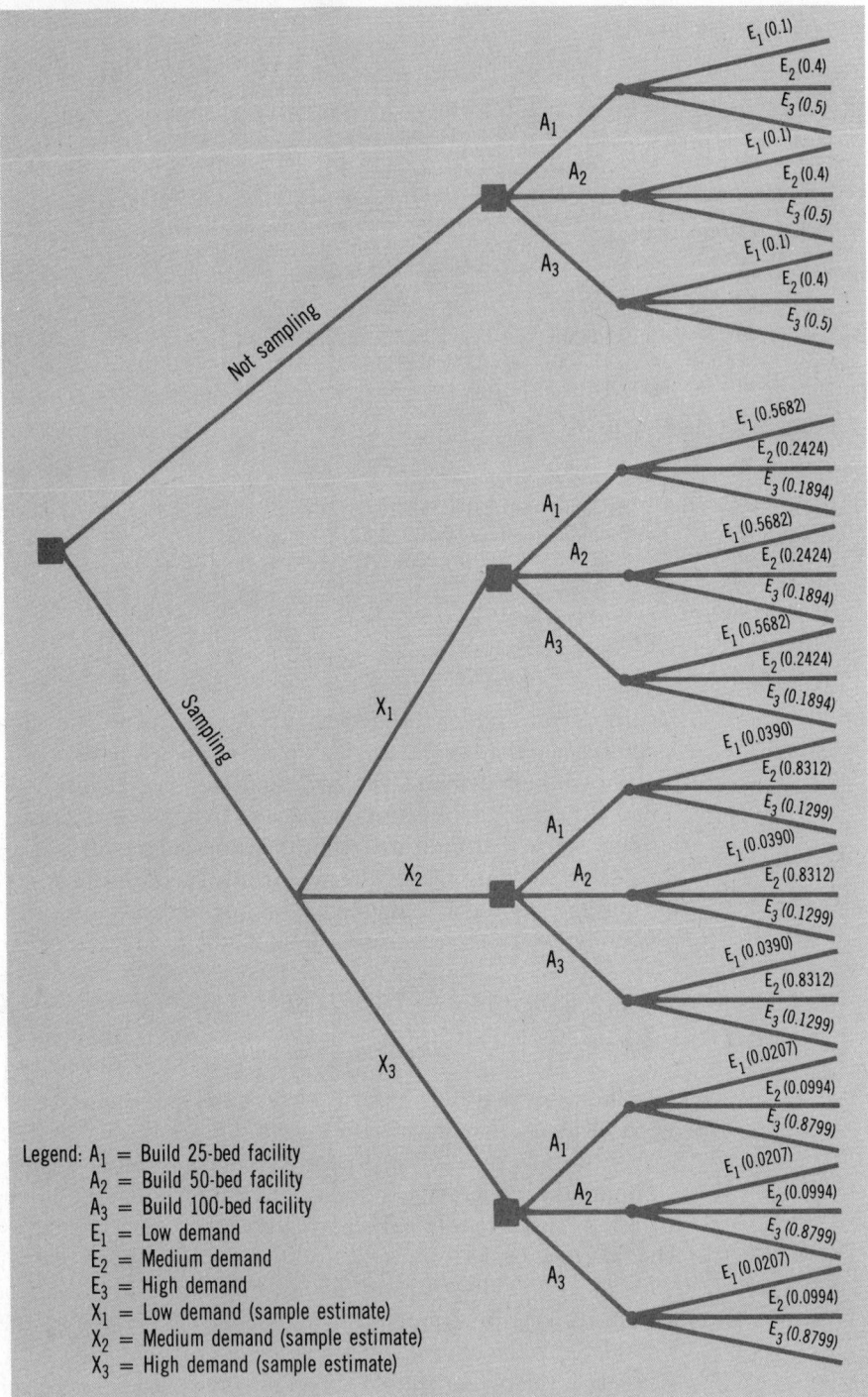

Legend: A_1 = Build 25-bed facility
A_2 = Build 50-bed facility
A_3 = Build 100-bed facility
E_1 = Low demand
E_2 = Medium demand
E_3 = High demand
X_1 = Low demand (sample estimate)
X_2 = Medium demand (sample estimate)
X_3 = High demand (sample estimate)

Figure 16.3.2 is a tree diagram for Example 16.3.1. This diagram compares the alternatives of (1) not collecting more information (not sampling) and (2) collecting more information (sampling). Note that the alternative of not sampling results in a decision situation of the type discussed in Section 16.2.

The probabilities shown on the terminal branches of the "Not sampling" major branch of Figure 16.3.2 are the prior probabilities of the events "low demand" (E_1), "medium demand" (E_2), and "high demand" (E_3). The probabilities shown on the terminal branches of the "Sampling" major branch are revised probabilities, based on the sample results shown in Table 16.3.7.

POSTERIOR ANALYSIS

Once decision-makers have decided to sample, carried out the survey, and know the results, they are ready to carry out *posterior analysis*. Posterior analysis is the method whereby we combine sample information with prior information to obtain revised probabilities for various events. This method of incorporating sample information into the analysis is the same as that explained in the section on preposterior analysis. In preposterior analysis, we find revised probabilities for every possible sample outcome. In posterior analysis, we compute revised probabilities for the single sample outcome that actually occurred. For example, suppose that the owner of the nursing homes obtained an estimate of medium demand from his sample survey. He would use the middle column of probabilities from Table 16.3.7. These are the only ones of interest to him now, since they are associated with the actual outcome of the survey. A decision-maker who is now ready to choose an act is interested in the expected payoffs. The owner need look only at the middle column of Table 16.3.8. He should choose the second act, "build a 50-bed facility," since that act yields the largest expected payoff.

Sometimes the costs of sampling may be slight. In this case the decision-maker would probably get sample information and do a posterior analysis, bypassing the preposterior step.

Note that, after an initial survey, a decision-maker may wish to look into the possibility of getting still more sample information. If so, the posterior probabilities become the prior probabilities for purposes of preposterior and posterior analysis connected with the second sampling activity. One can continue this process as long as it is profitable to do so. Such a course of action is a *sequential decision-making* procedure.

EXERCISES

16.3.1 A farmer may choose one of three main crops, c_1, c_2, and c_3, for planting in the spring. The yield of the crops—and consequently the income from them—depends on the weather conditions during the growing season. One can describe three categories of weather conditions, w_1, w_2, and w_3. Condition w_1 is better for c_1 and unfavorable to c_2 and c_3, although not completely ruinous. The same relationship exists between w_2, c_2, c_1, and c_3

and between w_3, c_3, c_1, and c_2. The farmer does not know which weather condition will prevail during the coming season. Therefore, she must decide what crop to plant in an environment of uncertainty. She has been able to construct the following payoff table. (a) Compute the expected opportunity loss for each of the three acts. (b) Compute the EVPI. (c) What act do these computations pinpoint as the optimal act? (d) Which act has the highest expected payoff? (e) Compute the expected profit with perfect information. (f) Does the expected profit with perfect information, less the expected profit under uncertainty, equal the expected opportunity loss of selecting the optimum act in an uncertain environment? (g) Without further analysis, which crop would the farmer plant? (h) What is the maximum amount the farmer would be willing to pay for "sample" information?

Event (Weather Condition w_i Will Prevail)	Act (Plant Crop c_i)			
	c_1	c_2	c_3	$P(w_i)$
w_1	$50,000	$30,000	$25,000	0.6
w_2	40,000	60,000	35,000	0.3
w_3	45,000	55,000	70,000	0.1

16.3.2 An operator of a chain of coin-operated laundries is planning to open a new laundry in another section of the city. He is trying to decide whether to install 10, 15, or 25 washing machines. He envisions three levels of demand that may exist in the area. He has been able to come up with subjective probabilities associated with each. His payoff table is as follows. Answer questions (a) through (f) as in Exercise 16.3.1.

Event: Demand	Act (Install)			
	10 Machines (A_1)	15 Machines (A_2)	25 Machines (A_3)	$P(E_i)$
High	$6,000	$10,000	$15,000	0.40
Medium	5,000	9,000	8,000	0.35
Low	4,800	3,000	2,000	0.25

(g) Without further analysis, which act would the laundry operator pursue? (h) What is the maximum amount he would be willing to pay for "sample" information? (i) A research firm, for $1,000, will conduct a survey to estimate demand. The firm provides the following data relative to past experience with similar surveys.

When the True Event is	The Sample Estimates the Demand to be as Follows the Indicated Proportion of Times		
	High Demand (X_1)	Medium Demand (X_2)	Low Demand (X_3)
High demand (E_1)	0.82	0.15	0.03
Medium demand (E_2)	0.09	0.74	0.17
Low demand (E_3)	0.03	0.12	0.85

Find the probability that each event is the true event and that the sample estimates it as such. That is, find the joint probabilities $P(E_i \cap X_j) = P(E_i)P(X_j|E_i)$.   (j) Compute the posterior probabilities of each event, given each sample estimate.   (k) Use the posterior probabilities from step (j) to obtain the expected payoffs for each act, given each of the sample estimates.   (l) Suppose that a survey is taken. What action should be taken if the survey estimates high demand? If the survey estimates medium demand? If the survey estimates low demand?   (m) What is the expected payoff if a survey is done and the laundry operator chooses the optimal act after acquiring the survey estimates?   (n) Should a survey be done?   (o) What is the expected value of sample information?   (p) In the light of the analysis to this point, what should the operator do?

16.3.3   Describe a business situation in which prior, preposterior, and perhaps posterior analysis would be appropriate. Use real or realistic data to provide the necessary inputs, and do a complete analysis as called for in Exercise 16.3.2. If appropriate, carry the analysis further to include a posterior analysis.

16.4   UTILITY THEORY

In Sections 16.2 and 16.3, we express payoffs—both profits and losses—in dollar amounts. Clearly, however, not all decision-makers attach the same value to money. Consider Businessperson A, who has total capital of $100,000. An investment opportunity arises that requires an expenditure of $100,000. This investment will either double the money or leave A with none. That is, A will either gain $100,000 or lose all the capital. The probability of the latter event is 0.25. The probability of the former is 0.75. The expected result from this investment is then

$$0.75(\$200,000) + 0.25(-\$100,000) = \$125,000$$

Also available to A is another investment opportunity that requires an expenditure of $100,000. The profit on this investment is a certain $20,000.

Consider another businessperson, B, whose capital assets are $10,000,000. Suppose that B has the same investment opportunities as A. We would not expect identical behavior on the part of A and B. Whereas A stands to lose everything by electing to take "advantage" of the opportunity involving a gamble, B stands to lose only 1% of total capital by deciding on this course of action. Thus, $100,000 appears to represent different levels of value to these two people. We would expect A to forgo the gamble and B to take it.

By following this line of reasoning, we have, by implication, cast A and B in the roles of prudent people. Suppose, on the other hand, that A is a pathological gambler and B is conservative to a fault. We might then find A passing up a sure $20,000 out of preference for a 0.75 chance of realizing a profit of $100,000. Likewise B, if conservative enough, would find the chance that we have described unthinkable.

Therefore, we may conclude that the actions a decision-maker takes depend on at least two conditions: level of assets and attitude toward risk. We know that these conditions are not the same for all decision-makers.

Absolute dollar amounts of money may not be adequate criteria on which to base decisions of this sort. This fact was recognized as far back as 1738, when mathematician Daniel Bernoulli concluded that not all people use the same rule when evaluating a gamble. Bernoulli proposed that the value of an item should be determined by the *utility* it yields, not by its price. A person's utility is determined by the *preference* that person exhibits for the choices available in circumstances involving risk. In fact, some authorities prefer the term *preference* theory in referring to the concept we shall call *utility theory*.

The following sections show how to incorporate utility theory into a decision-making procedure.

THE STANDARD GAMBLE

We illustrate an application of utility theory in the following example.

EXAMPLE 16.4.1 Suppose that we confront an executive with a situation in which she may expend $50,000 in one of two investments: (1) investment A will yield a profit of $100,000 with probability 0.5 and a loss of the $50,000 with probability 0.5; and (2) investment B will yield a profit of $10,000 with probability 1.

For reasons that will soon become apparent, we need, at this point, to assign an arbitrary *utility index* to the amounts of $100,000 and $-$50,000 specified in the gamble.

> The *utility index* is a subjective measure of the decision-maker's preference for an outcome of some action.

We shall assign a utility index of 0 to $-$50,000 and a utility index of 1 to $100,000. We express this symbolically as $U(\$100,000) = 1$ and $U(-\$50,000) = 0$. We could have used any other numbers, so long as the index for $100,000 was greater than the index for $-$50,000.

Now we ask the executive which investment she would prefer, A or B. Suppose that she prefers Investment B. We then ask for what probability of receiving $100,000 her choice would be Investment A. She may tell us that if the probability of a profit of $100,000 were 1 (and consequently the probability of losing $50,000 were 0) she would prefer Investment A. We then try to determine whether there is some lesser probability for which she would take the gamble. In fact, we try to find some probability to which she is *indifferent*. The point of indifference is represented by the probability figure p. The value of p is chosen so that for any probability greater than p, the decision-maker would prefer the investment involving a gamble. For any probability less than p, she would prefer the investment with a certain profit. Let us suppose that the value of p is 0.85. We can now compute the decision-maker's utility index for $10,000, the sure profit associated with Investment B. We can do this on the assumption that the point at which the decision-maker is indifferent between the two choices is the point at which the expected utilities of the choices are the same. Thus,

$$U(\$10,000) = 0.85[U(\$100,000)] + 0.15[U(-\$50,000)]$$
$$= 0.85(1) + 0.15(0) = 0.85$$

We persuade the executive to play the game once more. We ask her what value of p would make her indifferent between the gamble and a sure profit of $50,000. Suppose that she says that p in this case is 0.95. From this information, we calculate the utility of $50,000 to be

$$U(\$50,000) = 0.95(1) + 0.05(0) = 0.95$$

What if we change the consequences of Investment B so that now this act yields a certain *loss* of $20,000? She must now arrive at a value of p for the gamble. She must tell us what likelihood of realizing a profit of $100,000 she would require before she would be indifferent between choosing the sure loss of $20,000 and taking the gamble. We would expect the value of p to be lower than for the situations mentioned previously. Assume that she says that the probability of getting the $100,000 on the gamble would have to be 0.52. The utility for $-\$20,000$ is then

$$U(-\$20,000) = 0.52(1) + 0.48(0) = 0.52$$

In a similar manner, we can determine the decision-maker's utility for any sum of money between $-\$50,000$ and $100,000.

THE UTILITY FUNCTION

The conversation with the decision-maker results in the following set of monetary amounts and their associated utilities: $(-\$50,000, 0)$, ($100,000, 1), ($10,000, 0.85), ($50,000, 0.95), and $(-\$20,000, 0.52)$. We can plot these on a *utility–money graph*, as shown in Figure 16.4.1. We may find additional points and connect them to produce a curve that corresponds to the decision-maker's *utility function*. Assume that the utility curve for our decision-maker in this example is that in Figure 16.4.1. With the utility curve, we can determine her utility for any amount between $-\$50,000$ and $100,000. We do this by locating the dollar amount on the horizontal axis of Figure 16.4.1, moving up to the curve, and moving across to the utility on the vertical axis. For example, the utility for $30,000 is 0.92. In general, a point on the vertical axis (a utility) means that the decision-maker is indifferent between (1) having for certain the amount of money on the horizontal axis below the point on the curve corresponding to that utility, and (2) taking a gamble involving the highest amount on the horizontal axis with probability equal to the utility value, and the lowest amount on the hori-

FIGURE 16.4.1   Utility—money graph for Example 16.4.1

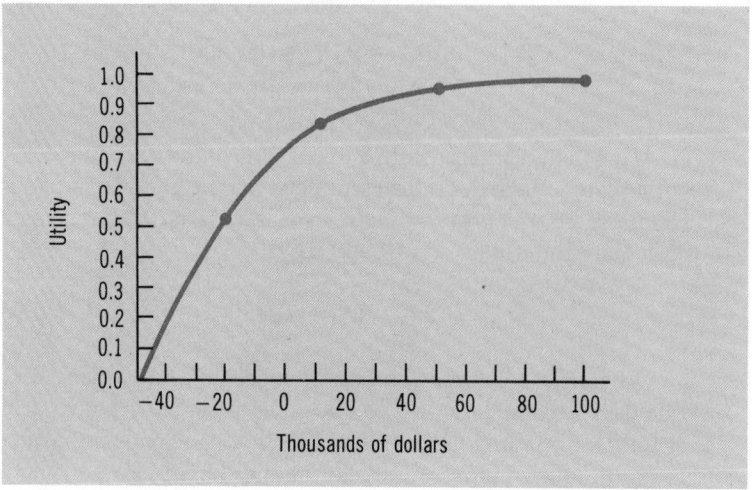

zontal axis with probability equal to 1 minus the utility value. The decision-maker's utility is equal to the probabilities we asked her to assign to the larger amount in the gamble. This is the convenience we achieved by assigning a utility index of 1 to $100,000 and 0 to −$50,000.

Note that the utility curve generated by the decision-maker is not a straight line, but a curve that is concave downward. From this we may conclude that she tends to be conservative. This type of curve is characteristic of the *risk avoider*. A decision-maker whose utility curve is a straight line is known as an averages player, or a *risk-neutral* decision-maker. However, the decision-maker with a utility curve that is concave upward is one who tends to prefer the gamble to the sure thing. This type of decision-maker is called a *risk preferrer*. Figure 16.4.2 illustrates these three types of utility curves.

These are not the only types of utility curves that decision-makers can generate. There are many variations on these basic shapes.

In general, a decision-maker wants to maximize expected utility rather than expected monetary value. However, when a decision-maker's utility curve is linear, the act that maximizes expected utility and the act that maximizes expected monetary value are the same. For those decisions in which the money involved is small relative to the assets of the organization, we can usually consider the utility curves to be linear. Thus, maximizing expected monetary value is usually a valid procedure. If, however, the money amounts are relatively large, we may have no basis for assuming a linear utility curve. In such cases, the decision-maker wants a utility curve that is specific to the situation and that maximizes expected utility.

FIGURE 16.4.2   Three types of utility curve

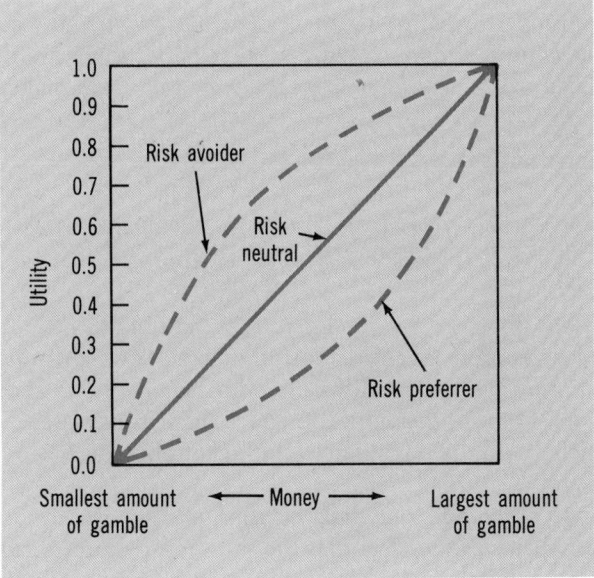

ASSUMPTIONS UNDERLYING UTILITY THEORY

The validity of utility theory as we have presented it here depends on the following assumptions:

1. When confronted with two alternatives, such as those we have discussed, the decision-maker is either indifferent between the two, prefers the first to the second, or prefers the second to the first.

2. When a decision-maker prefers alternative A to alternative B and prefers alternative B to alternative C, then he or she prefers alternative A to alternative C. This is called *transitivity* of preference.

3. When the decision-maker prefers a gamble to some outcome A when $p = 1$, but prefers A to the gamble when $p = 0$, then there exists some value of p such that the decision-maker is indifferent between the gamble and the outcome A. This is referred to as the *continuity* of preference assumption.

4. When a decision-maker is indifferent as to the choice between two acts, then one may be substituted for the other, and the utilities of the two acts can be considered equal. This is known as the principle of *substitution*.

5. When two gambles have identical payoffs, but the more attractive payoff of one has a probability different from the more attractive payoff of the other, the decision-maker will prefer the gamble with the highest such probability.

Prescriptive Versus Descriptive Role of Utility Theory Some authorities feel that utility theory is well suited to *describing* the behavior of the decision-maker. Thus, the proper use of utility theory lets one *predict* how a decision-maker will behave in a given situation. On the other hand, there are those who see utility theory as directing, or *prescribing*, the way a decision-maker *should* behave.

16.5 BAYESIAN DECISION THEORY AND CLASSICAL STATISTICAL INFERENCE

Bayesian decision theory and classical inference both have the same objective — guiding a decision-maker to choose the best of two or more courses of action. There are, however, some differences in their methods and their philosophical foundations. Some of the points on which there is a difference of opinion between the classicists and the Bayesians include the following.

1. <u>Subjective probability.</u> Bayesian decision-makers readily use subjective probabilities whenever they feel that the situation requires them. A frequent source of prior probabilities is the decision-maker's best evaluation of the likelihood of certain events. Classicists cannot accept the validity and usefulness of subjective probabilities. They require that probabilities be generated by objective means.

2. <u>The choice of the significance level in hypothesis testing.</u> Advocates of the Bayesian approach contend that classicists often arbitrarily select a significance level without putting much thought into the underlying assumptions or consequences.

3. <u>Costs.</u> The Bayesians also criticize the classicists because they do not incorporate cost considerations into the hypothesis-testing and estimation procedures.

SUMMARY

This chapter covers some of the basic concepts and techniques of decision theory and analysis. It discusses the use of payoff tables and decision trees as aids in the decision-making process. It also presents the following criteria for making choices that may be used when one is faced with the necessity of making a decision: the maximin criterion, the minimax criterion, the maximax criterion, the Hurwicz criterion, and the Bayes criterion. Application of the Bayes criterion is discussed in detail. You were also told how to incorporate utility theory into the decision-making procedure. Finally, the chapter compared Bayesian decision theory and classical statistical inference.

REVIEW EXERCISES

1. Define   (**a**) payoff,   (**b**) event,   (**c**) state of nature,   (**d**) payoff table.

2. Explain   (**a**) the maximin criterion,   (**b**) the minimax criterion,   (**c**) the maximax criterion,   (**d**) the Hurwicz criterion,   (**e**) the Bayes criterion.

3. Explain or define   (**a**) prior analysis,   (**b**) preposterior analysis,   (**c**) posterior analysis,   (**d**) expected profit under uncertainty,   (**e**) expected profit with perfect information,   (**f**) expected value of perfect information,   (**g**) cost of uncertainty,   (**h**) expected value of sample information.

4. What is meant by utility theory?

5. What is meant by utility index?

6. How is a utility function constructed?

7. How is a utility function used?

8. Describe the utility curve of   (**a**) the risk avoider,   (**b**) the risk-neutral decision-maker,   (**c**) the risk preferrer.

9. What assumptions underlie utility theory?

10. Locate in a business-oriented journal an article discussing an application of statistical decision theory. Write a critique of the article.

11. Describe a situation in your area of interest in which the Bayes criterion could be applied. Use realistic data, and carry out the calculations necessary to arrive at a decision.

12. A small soft-drink company is about to begin operation, with distribution limited to a single state. The management wishes to know whether the company should use "no deposit–no return" bottles or returnable bottles. There is a rumor that the state legislature may pass a law banning no-return bottles. If it does, and if the company has decided to use no-return bottles, the switch to returnable bottles will be expensive. Management's preliminary payoff table is as follows. (Payoffs are in millions of dollars.)   (**a**) Compute the expected payoff for each of the two acts.   (**b**) Compute the EVPI.   (**c**) What is the optimal act?   (**d**) Which act has the higher expected payoff?   (**e**) Without further analysis, which act should management follow?   (**f**) What is the maximum amount management should pay for "sample" information?

	Act		
	Use No-return Bottles	Use Returnable Bottles	
Event (E$_i$)	(A$_1$)	(A$_2$)	**P(E$_1$)**
Law is passed	$10	$15	0.8
Law is not passed	20	15	0.2

13. There are three possible actions, A$_1$ through A$_3$, and three possible states of nature, E$_1$ through E$_3$. The payoffs, all of which are positive, are as follows. Determine the optimum action and calculate the expected value of perfect information (EVPI) using both the expected monetary value (EMV) and the expected opportunity-loss (EOL) methods.

E	P(E)	A₁	A₂	A₃
1	0.24	36.7	81.6	47.8
2	0.48	53.5	20.4	46.9
3	0.28	28.6	37.5	52.1

14. There are four possible actions A_1 through A_4, and four possible states of nature, E_1 through E_4. The payoffs are as follows. Determine the optimum action and calculate the expected value of perfect information using the expected opportunity-loss method.

E	P(E)	A₁	A₂	A₃	A₄
1	0.29	27.2	−16.8	123.5	57.6
2	0.17	−20.3	40.4	−30.7	19.2
3	0.34	88.6	31.5	55.1	−82.3
4	0.20	−3.8	10.6	−32.1	61.4

15. Vernon Industries is deciding whether to market a new product. Company officials believe that either 20% or 40% of its customers will buy this product.   (a) If the company assigns the following payoffs and probabilities, what should the company do based on these data alone?

			Payoffs	
State of Nature (θ)	P(θ)		Market	Do Not Market
20% will purchase	0.70		− $30,000	0
40% will purchase	0.30		50,000	0

(b) The company is considering the merits of surveying a sample of ten customers. Design a decision tree that could be used to illustrate the optimum strategy and the expected value of such a survey.   (c) If the company completed the survey of ten customers and determined that six of the ten would buy the product, revise the probabilities and complete the decision-tree calculations.   (d) What should the company do under these circumstances?

16. The decision tree on the following page lists probabilities, the cost of sampling, and the positive terminal payoffs. Calculate the expected values at each node, (a) through (g). In addition, calculate   (h) the expected value of sampling information and   (i) the expected net gain from sampling.

*****17.** We may use Bayes' theorem as a basis for estimating a population mean. We assume that we have the following *prior* beliefs about the population of interest: the mean, μ, of the population is a normally distributed random variable with a mean of μ' and a variance of σ'^2. If we draw a simple random sample of size n from the population of interest and compute the sample mean, $\bar{x}$, we may use the concept of Bayes' theorem to arrive at a conclusion regarding the *posterior* probability distribution of the population mean, μ. Specifically, the posterior distribution of μ is a normal distribution with a mean μ'' and variance σ''^2 given by the following formulas:

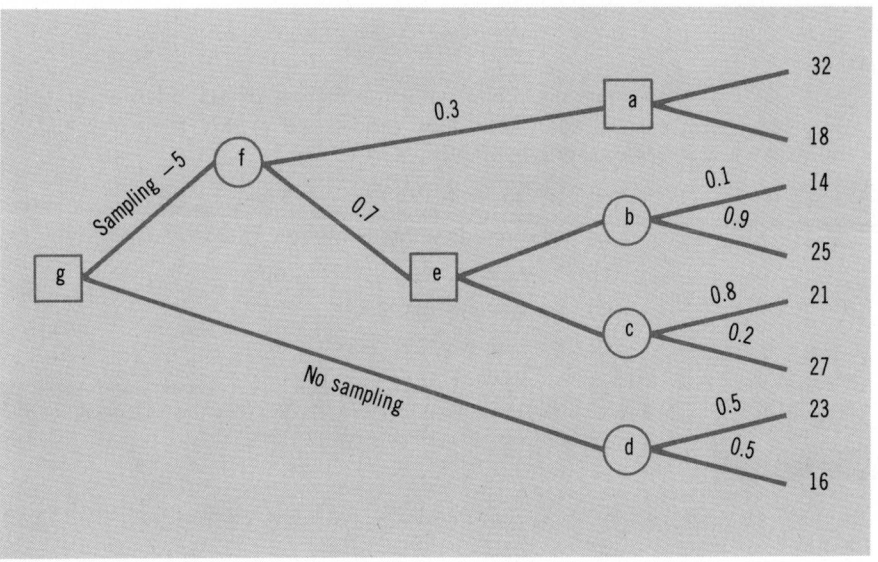

$$\mu'' = \frac{(1/\sigma'^2)\mu' + (n/\sigma^2)\bar{x}}{(1/\sigma'^2) + (n/\sigma^2)}$$

$$\sigma''^2 = \frac{1}{(1/\sigma'^2) + (n/\sigma^2)}$$

When the population variance, σ^2, is unknown, we use the sample variance, s^2, to estimate it. The logic behind this procedure is that we are using *prior* information plus sample information to obtain *posterior* information. We see that μ'' is the weighted average of μ' and $\bar{x}$ in which the weights are the reciprocals of the variances of the two measures. The marketing director of a large manufacturing firm is interested in future annual demand of a new household product. He believes that mean demand is a normally distributed variable with a mean of 25 units and a standard deviation of 5 units. A simple random sample of 100 households revealed that the mean number of items the household plans to purchase during the next year is 30. The sample standard deviation is 15. Describe the posterior distribution of annual demand for the product.

1. DECISION AND RISK ANALYSIS IN DU PONT

Krumm and Rolle report on the use of risk decision and risk analysis (D&RA) in Du Pont. Read their article and write a report on it in which you cover at least the following points:

(a) what officials at Du Pont think of D&RA,

(b) what made implementation of D&RA worthwhile for Du Pont,

(c) how D&RA works at Du Pont,

(d) the benefits of D&RA,

(e) the future of D&RA at Du Pont.

Source: F. V. Krumm and C. F. Rolle, "Management and Application of Decision and Risk Analysis in Du Pont," *Interfaces* 22 (November–December 1992), 84–93.

2. DECISION ANALYSIS AND THE MILITARY

Applications of decision analysis in the military are the topic of a journal article by Buede and Bresnick. Read their article and write a report on it in which you cover at least the following points:

(a) how decision analysis is used,

(b) the specific area of application,

(c) complications encountered in implementation,

(d) contributions of the studies that were conducted.

Source: Dennis M. Buede and Terry A. Bresnick, "Applications of Decision Analysis to the Military Systems Acquisition Process," *Interfaces* 22 (November–December 1992), 110–125.

3. DECISION ANALYSIS AND UTILITY ENVIRONMENTAL RISK

A journal article by Balson et al. discusses the use of decision analysis and risk analysis to manage utility environmental risk. Read the article and write a report on it in which you cover at least the following points:

(a) the authors' definition of risk analysis,

(b) the components of risk analysis,

(c) the environmental risks to which electric utilities are subject,

(d) specific applications of risk analysis,

(e) the authors' conclusions,

(f) current topics being addressed.

Source: William E. Balson, Justin L. Welsh, and Donald S. Wilson, "Using Decision Analysis and Risk Analysis to Manage Utility Environmental Risk," *Interfaces* 22 (November–December 1992), 126–139.

STATISTICS AT

4. OPERATIONS RISK MANAGEMENT AND BANKING

Engemann and Miller write in a journal article about the use of operations risk management at a major bank. Read the article and write a report on it in which you cover at least the following points:

(a) the problem,

(b) the risk management methodology developed,

(c) specific projects in which the methodology has been used,

(d) the authors' conclusions.

Source: Kurt J. Engemann and Holmes E. Miller, "Operations Risk Management at a Major Bank," *Interfaces* 22 (November–December 1992), 140–149.

SUGGESTIONS FOR FURTHER READING

Braverman, Jerome D. (1980). *Management Decision Making: A Formal/Intuitive Approach*. AMACOM, New York.

Byrd, Jack, Jr., and L. Ted Moore (1982). *Decision Models for Management*. McGraw-Hill, New York.

Eden, Colin, and John Harris (1975). *Management Decisions and Decision Analysis*. Macmillan, New York.

Fishburn, Peter C. (1970). *Utility Theory for Decision Making*. Wiley, New York.

Gordon, Gilbert, and Israel Pressman (1983). *Quantitative Decision Making for Business*, 2nd ed. Prentice-Hall, Englewood Cliffs, N.J.

Harrison, E. Frank (1987). *The Managerial Decision-Making Process*, 3rd ed. Houghton Mifflin, Boston.

Hill, Percy H., et al. (1979). *Making Decisions: A Multidisciplinary Approach*. Addison-Wesley, Reading, Mass.

Holloway, Charles A. (1979). *Decision Making Under Uncertainty: Models and Choices*. Prentice-Hall, Englewood Cliffs, N.J.

Interfaces, Volume 22, Number 6 (November–December 1992). The entire issue is devoted to decision and risk analysis.

Morris, William T. (1977). *Decision Analysis*. Grid, Columbus, Ohio.

Trueman, Richard E. (1981). *Quantitative Methods for Decision Making in Business*. Dryden, New York.

Ungson, Gerardo R., and Daniel N. Braunstein, eds. (1982). *Decision Making: An Interdisciplinary Approach*. Kent, Boston.

17

Some Statistical Applications in Quality Control

Chapter Objectives: In this chapter you become acquainted with an important concern of business in which statistical methodology is used to great advantage. You will learn additional ways in which to apply the basic concepts and techniques that you learned in the preceding chapters. After studying this chapter and working the exercises, you should be able to

1. Understand the meaning of quality, total quality, and total quality management.
2. Construct and use control charts for variables.
3. Construct and use control charts for attributes.
4. Develop and use acceptance sampling plans for attributes.
5. Develop and use acceptance sampling plans for variables.
6. Understand and apply the concept of process capability.

17.1   INTRODUCTION

For the past few years, experts in the field of quality control have been telling us that we are experiencing "a quality revolution in the world marketplace," that attention must be paid to "new technical and educational directions for managing product quality," and that there are very good reasons "why quality has to be measured."

Behind this wave of concern for higher quality is the recognition on the part of American goods producers that, to be competitive, their products must match in quality those of their foreign counterparts, who in recent years have earned a reputation for turning out merchandise of high quality. Robert R. Irving has stated that "American industry is beginning to wake up to the realization that it will not get anywhere in this economic battle for survival without a well engineered and carefully orchestrated quality assurance program." The experts agree that acceptable levels of quality will never be reached without an effective statistical quality-control program.

The concept of quality control, in its broadest sense, has many facets. Quality control is a concern of most, if not all, of the areas of a business organization. In fact, the life and health of a business depend on the quality of the product it produces and the services it renders. It is no wonder, then, that management is concerned with measuring and controlling the quality of its product and services.

Management should establish company policy concerning the quality of the product. The standard must be based on the performance of the product in actual use by customers. It must be at a level that is acceptable to customers, comparable to that of competitors, and economically feasible from the standpoint of cost of production and service.

Design engineers must have quality in mind when they design a product. Those responsible for buying raw materials must keep an eye on quality. (The quality of the finished product depends on the quality of the raw materials from which it is made.) The accounting department watches over the cost of achieving high quality. The marketing department is deeply concerned with the quality of the product the company places on the market. Thus, companies strive at all levels to obtain the "best" balance between cost and quality.

This concern with good quality—and its measurement and control—is present in a business organization whether or not it has a formal quality-control department. When a business does have a quality-control department, however, that department performs a variety of functions. It collects samples, takes measurements, performs tests, makes arithmetical and statistical computations, keeps records, prepares reports, and makes decisions.

WHAT IS QUALITY?

The concept of quality is so pervasive and so ingrained in the human psyche that it may seem strange that the word *quality* requires defining. The meaning of the word *quality,* however, depends on the context in which the word is used. Standard dictionaries provide definitions that are satisfactory for everyday use. The unabridged *Random House Dictionary of the English Language,* second edition, for example, lists nineteen definitions for *quality.* Among the words used in these definitions are *high grade, superiority,* and *excellence.*

In the industrial setting, one finds that different definitions are in use. A production supervisor with a manufacturer may consider quality as the characteristic of a product that meticulously meets certain specifications. On the other hand, a business manager attuned to customer relationships and goodwill might define quality in terms of what it takes to satisfy purchasers. In his book *Managing Quality,*[1] David Garvin lists definitions of *quality* categorized under the following five headings:

1. *Transcendent.* This definition is concerned with the abstract, universal, non-technical concept of quality.

2. *Product-based.* The traditional, industrial quality-control manager can relate to this definition, in which quality is conceived of as a precise and measurable characteristic. According to this definition, for example, the amount of impuritiesin some manufactured product orraw material can be determined.

3. *User-based.* This is the definition that businesspersons concerned with customer relations and customer satisfaction would use as a criterion of quality.

4. *Manufacturing-based.* Those in the industrial setting who are charged with the responsibility of seeing that standards and specifications for their product are met are expected to find this definition meaningful.

5. *Value-based.* This definition takes into consideration the "value for price" concept. Consumers do not expect the same level and type of quality in the physical structure of a throwaway camera that they expect in a high-tech camera designed to last a lifetime. Neither do they expect to pay as much for the disposable camera as for the more durable one.

TOTAL QUALITY (TQ)

The pages of industrial history may someday show that the 1980s were the years in which America turned around in the matter of quality of goods and services. This decade witnessed the emergence of a quality movement in the world of business that touched every aspect of its existence, from boardrooms to assembly lines. Total quality became the battle cry of those engaged in the business of providing the world with products and services. Thousands of reams of paper have been devoted to discussions, definitions, explanations, and analyses of the

---

[1]David A. Garvin, *Managing Quality: The Strategies and Competitive Edge* (New York: The Free Press, 1988), pp. 39–46.

topic of TQ. David Hutchins in his book *Achieve Total Quality* describes TQ as "everything that an organization, a society or a community does, which in the eyes of others determines its reputation on a comparative basis with the best alternatives."[2] The author emphasizes that the word *organization* as used in his definition is not restricted to a business organization. The organization may be an industry in one country in comparison to a like industry in another country. It may be a public institution, a government agency, a community, or a nation. Whenever an organization is engaged in providing goods and/or services, the quality of the manner in which it does this as well as the end result will be judged by those that the organization wishes to reach.

According to Hutchins, there are four key elements to TQ:

1. Systems
2. Process control
3. Management
4. People

The first two elements have to do with the structures, tools, and mechanisms that an organization puts in place to ensure the quality of its goods or services. The last two have to do with the manner in which the first two are utilized. The systems and process control elements must be piloted by effective management policies and high-caliber personnel at all levels of operation.

TOTAL QUALITY MANAGEMENT (TQM)

Reflecting the fact that management is crucial to the achievement of quality, the term *total quality management (TQM)* is in wide use today. According to Hutchins, TQM is a subelement of TQ that is composed of the managerial and organizational features of a TQ program. The concept of TQM, according to Hutchins, does not include an organization's philosophical or strategic concerns. Total quality management has been the subject of many books, journal articles, seminars, speeches, and courses of study. Proponents of TQM have mustered every conceivable resource and exercised great feats of ingenuity in an effort to imbue their audiences with the philosophy, techniques, and wisdom of the concept.

In their book *Putting Total Quality Management to Work,* Marshall Sashkin and Kenneth J. Kiser suggest that the reader conceive of the delivery of goods and services as a flowing stream whose status can be ascertained at strategic

---

[2]David Hutchins, *Achieve Total Quality* (Cambridge, England: Director Books, 1992).

points along its course.[3] These authors identify the following five checkpoints at which the quality of the product or service can be monitored.

1. *The Customer.* The consumer is the most important point along the flow of the goods and services delivery stream. An organization dedicated to quality must have available at any point in time the latest information on the needs, desires, and expectations of its customers.

2. *The "Shipping Dock."* This checkpoint is where the product or service leaves the organization that produced it. This stage of production and delivery has been the traditional point at which quality-control efforts have been concentrated. The objective of TQM is to reduce the importance of this checkpoint through an increased emphasis on ensuring high quality at the other checkpoints.

3. *"In the Shop."* This is the point where goods are produced and services are planned. Historically this point in the delivery stream has been the scene of intensive quality-control efforts. An objective of TQM is to divert some of the quality-control activity from this area to the other checkpoints.

4. *The "Receiving Dock."* Providers of goods and services must see to it that their raw materials are of sufficient quality to ensure an outcome of acceptable quality.

5. *Design and Production.* Executing TQM principles at this checkpoint involves such activities as designing and producing raw materials, parts, and supplies that meet specifications; providing vendors and suppliers with the information required for them to meet the organization's needs; and attending to the needs, desires, and expectations of the consumer via checkpoint 1.

Those organizations that have attempted to adopt the principles and philosophy of TQM have not always met with success. A great deal has been written about the failures with the result that, as one writing team puts it, TQM "is getting a bad reputation."[4] According to these authors, failure in implementing TQM is often the result of the failure of an organization to recognize the importance of being customer-driven. They offer the following five suggestions to assist organizations in setting customer-driven priorities and measuring results effectively:

1. Determine what is important to customers.

2. Solicit complaints.

3. Integrate and reconcile problem data.

4. Track the results of quality initiatives.

---

[3]Marshall Sashkin and Kenneth J. Kiser, *Putting Total Quality Management to Work* (San Francisco: Berrett-Koehler Publishers, 1993).

[4]John A. Goodman, Gary F. Bargatze, and Cynthia Grimm, "The Key Problem with TQM," *Quality Progress* (January 1994), 45–48.

5. Educate the staff on the link between customer problems and customer loyalty, extra costs, and employee frustration.

An article by Rahul Jacob in *Fortune* magazine states that up to two-thirds of American managers think that TQM has failed in their companies.[5] Despite this seemingly gloomy situation, the author concludes, "Thoughtfully applied and modified, total quality's principles still represent a sound way to run a company." His suggestions for achieving an effective TQ program emphasize the importance of CEO involvement, the need to focus on customer satisfaction, and the desirability of customizing the principles and concepts of TQ to the individual organization.

TQ PRINCIPLES ARE UNIVERSAL

We emphasize that the concepts and techniques of quality control are not limited to manufacturing processes. They are equally appropriate for use in most other operational areas of a business. Other functions that can profit from the application of quality-control measures include computer operations, accounting, customer relations, and research and development.

STATISTICS AND TOTAL QUALITY

This chapter presents some of the statistical concepts and techniques used in the statistical component of quality control. Most of the statistical concepts and techniques that we employ in our discussion of quality control are ones that you have learned about in earlier chapters of this book. There are many components of a comprehensive quality-control program. Our discussion will be limited to three of these: (1) control charts, (2) acceptance sampling, and (3) process capability.

Space does not permit an exhaustive cataloguing of the concepts and techniques or a complete treatment of the ideas that we do present. For additional reading in this area of statistical application, see Suggestions for Further Reading at the end of this chapter.

COMPUTER **APPLICATIONS**

Throughout this text we have emphasized the use of computers in the application of statistical techniques. Their use is no less important in the application of quality-control methodology. Donald W. Marquardt, of E. I. du Pont de Nemours & Co., states that "to achieve excellence in managing product quality,

---

[5]Rahul Jacob, "TQM More than a Dying Fad?" *Fortune* (October 18, 1993), 66–72.

the latest technology in using computers must inevitably play a decisive role." In the area of quality control, computers are used to do more than just statistical calculations. Some of the other applications of computers include computer-controlled robots, computerized design, and computer-aided inspection.

An extensive directory of software for quality control appears annually in the journal *Quality Progress*. The 1993 directory, for example, contains a list of 235 packages.[6]

17.2 CONTROL CHARTS—VARIABLES

Walter A. Shewhart of Bell Telephone Laboratories, in a memorandum dated May 16, 1924, introduced the concept of the *control chart*. Further development of the technique is chronicled in a number of articles by Shewhart and in his 1931 landmark book, *Economic Control of Quality of Manufactured Product*.

The control chart is a decision-making device that gives the user information about the quality of product resulting from a manufacturing process. A control chart usually consists of three horizontal lines. The top line represents the *upper control limit*, the bottom line the *lower control limit*, and the center line an acceptable average for the process based on specifications or historical data. The control chart is constructed in such a way that we can plot the results of assessing the quality of the manufactured product through periodic monitoring of the manufacturing process. Each time the process is monitored, a point is placed on the control chart. As long as the points fall within the two control limits, we do not question the quality of the product. But when a plotted point falls *outside* the control limits, this alerts the production manager to the possibility that the quality of the product is unacceptable. Figure 17.2.1 shows a basic control chart.

Variation in quality may be due either to *chance* or to some *assignable cause*.

In any manufacturing process, not all items produced are exactly alike. The various forces and conditions of the manufacturing environment result in variations from item to item in any measurement that we can take. There are two types of variation in quality control—variation due to *chance* and variation due to some *assignable cause*.

Variation due to chance is called *random variation*. It is a characteristic of almost every imaginable process encountered in business. Within reasonable limits, such variability is usually of little or no concern to the consumer.

Assignable cause, or *assignable variation* as it is sometimes called, is the result of some fixed or recurring (nonrandom) activity or physical property that can be identified and changed. Some common sources of assignable variation are machines that are out of adjustment, tools that are wearing out, or operators who are fatigued, poorly trained, or inadequately motivated. Assignable variation is the target of much that goes on in the operation of a quality-control program.

---

[6]Tricia Kelly, "Quality Progress' Tenth Annual QA/QC Software Directory," *Quality Progress*, 26 (March 1993), 21–84.

FIGURE 17.2.1   A basic control chart

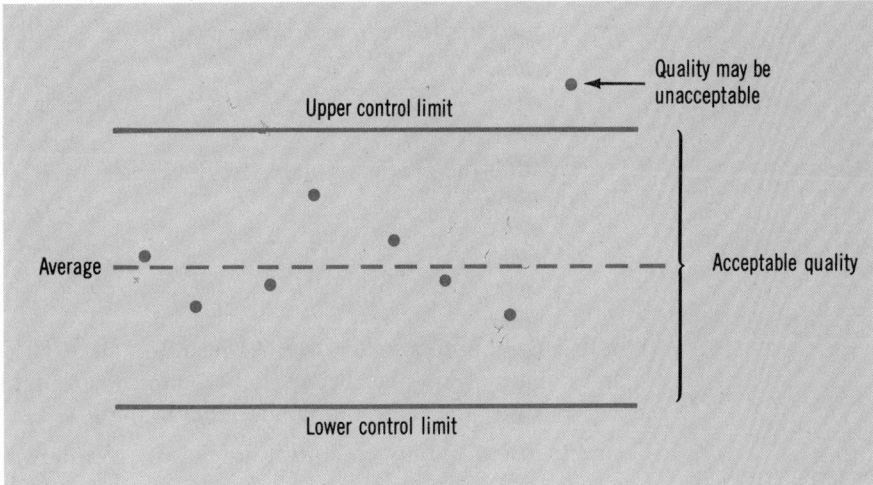

Once they are constructed, we consult control charts from time to time to determine the type of observable variation present. If the control chart indicates that the observed variation is due to chance alone, we say that the process is "in control." On the other hand, if the control chart indicates that the observed variation is not due to chance—that is, if it indicates that some other cause seems to be operating—we conclude that the process is "out of control." In this event, we halt the process. Then we look for and correct apparent causes.

We keep separate variable-control charts for each variable (measurement) of interest. We use them to indicate whether, for these variables, the manufacturing process is in control with respect to the population mean and population dispersion. A control chart for the mean is called an $\bar{x}$ *chart*. When control of dispersion is the objective, the measure used is the range. The resulting chart is called an *R chart*.

When we construct control charts for detecting a shift in population dispersion, we use the range, rather than the standard deviation, of the sample. The reason is that the range is easier to compute. Furthermore, persons not trained in statistics understand the *range* better than the standard deviation. We should use standard deviations when $n \geq 10$ and/or when each measurement is comparatively expensive and we want the maximum information from the data. Remember that the construction of *R* charts as presented here assumes that the distribution of values making up the population is normal. However, good results have been reported even when this assumption does not hold.

STEPS IN CONSTRUCTING AND USING VARIABLE-CONTROL CHARTS

The basic steps in constructing and utilizing variable-control charts are as follows.

1. Select a random sample of n items from the manufacturing process and take measurements $x_1, x_2, \ldots, x_n$.

2. Compute the sample mean and range as follows:

$$\bar{x} = \frac{\sum_{i=1}^{n} x_i}{n}, \qquad R = x_{max} - x_{min}$$

3. If you feel that the process is stable, select k successive samples and compute the following values:

$$\bar{\bar{x}} = \frac{\sum_{i=1}^{k} \bar{x}_i}{k}, \qquad \bar{R} = \frac{\sum_{i=1}^{k} R_i}{k}$$

You usually choose a value of k between 20 and 30. The value of $\bar{\bar{x}}$, which is an estimate of $\mu_{\bar{x}} = \mu$, becomes the center horizontal line on the $\bar{x}$ chart, and $\bar{R}$ becomes the center horizontal line on the R chart.

4. Compute lower and upper control limits for $\bar{x}$ as follows:

$$LCL_{\bar{x}} = \bar{\bar{x}} - A_2 \bar{R}, \qquad UCL_{\bar{x}} = \bar{\bar{x}} + A_2 \bar{R}$$

You can find the constant A_2 in Table 17.2.1.

TABLE 17.2.1 Factors useful in the construction of control charts

	Chart for Averages	Chart for Ranges			
	Factor for Control Limit	Factor for Central Line	Factors for Control Limits		
n	A_2	d_2	D_3	D_4	d_3
2	1.880	1.128	0	3.267	0.8525
3	1.023	1.693	0	2.575	0.8884
4	0.729	2.059	0	2.282	0.8798
5	0.577	2.326	0	2.115	0.8641
6	0.483	2.534	0	2.004	0.8480
7	0.419	2.704	0.076	1.924	0.833
8	0.373	2.847	0.136	1.864	0.820
9	0.337	2.970	0.184	1.816	0.808
10	0.308	3.078	0.223	1.777	0.797
11	0.285	3.173	0.256	1.744	0.787
12	0.266	3.258	0.284	1.716	0.778
13	0.249	3.336	0.308	1.692	0.770
14	0.235	3.407	0.329	1.671	0.762
15	0.223	3.472	0.348	1.652	0.755
16	0.212	3.532	0.364	1.636	0.749
17	0.203	3.588	0.379	1.621	0.743
18	0.194	3.640	0.392	1.608	0.738
19	0.187	3.689	0.404	1.596	0.733
20	0.180	3.735	0.414	1.586	0.729

TABLE 17.2.1   *(Continued)*

n	Chart for Averages	Chart for Ranges			
	Factor for Control Limit A_2	Factor for Central Line d_2	Factors for Control Limits D_3	D_4	d_3
21	0.173	3.778	0.425	1.575	0.724
22	0.167	3.819	0.434	1.566	0.720
23	0.162	3.858	0.443	1.557	0.716
24	0.157	3.895	0.452	1.548	0.712
25	0.153	3.931	0.459	1.541	0.709

Values of d_2 and d_3 are from E. S. Pearson, "The Percentage Limits for the Distribution of Range in Samples from a Normal Population," Biometrika, 24 (1932), p. 416. Used by permission of the Biometrika trustees. $A_2 = 3/(d_2\sqrt{n})$, $D_3 = 1 - 3(d_3/d_2)$, $D_4 = 1 + 3(d_3/d_2)$.

CHARACTERISTICS OF THE SAMPLING DISTRIBUTION OF $\bar{x}$

Remember these essential principles of the sampling distribution of sample means:

(a) When the population from which the samples are drawn is normally distributed, the distribution of sample means is normal, with a mean $\mu_{\bar{x}}$ equal to the population mean and a standard deviation equal to $\sigma/\sqrt{n}$.

(b) If the sample size is large, the central limit theorem tells us that, regardless of the functional form of the parent population (provided that it has a mean and a finite variance), the distribution of the sample means that we can compute from samples drawn from such a population is approximately normal, with $\mu_{\bar{x}} = \mu$ and $\sigma_{\bar{x}} = \sigma/\sqrt{n}$. Although a sample size of about 30 is generally thought necessary for a satisfactory approximation, some people use the approximation for samples as small as 5 or 10.

(c) Approximately 68% of the area lies under the curve of $f(\bar{x})$ and above the $\bar{x}$ axis between the points $\mu_{\bar{x}} \pm 1\sigma_{\bar{x}}$; approximately 95% of the area lies between the points $\mu_{\bar{x}} \pm 2\sigma_{\bar{x}}$; and approximately 99.7% of the area lies between the points $\mu_{\bar{x}} \pm 3\sigma_{\bar{x}}$. These points are referred to as the *1-, 2-, and 3-sigma limits* on $\bar{x}$. The probability that a single sample picked at random from the population will yield an $\bar{x}$ within these limits is equal to the area under the curve between the points defining the limits. In control limits for $\bar{x}$, $A_2\bar{R}$ is an estimate of $3\sigma_{\bar{x}}$. Therefore, the control limits previously specified are called the *3-sigma control limits for $\bar{x}$.*

5. Compute the lower and upper 3-sigma control limits for R as follows:

$$\text{LCL}_R = D_3\bar{R}, \qquad \text{UCL}_R = D_4\bar{R}$$

Values for D_3 and D_4 are found in Table 17.2.1.

6. Compute lower and upper *3-sigma process tolerance limits* for individual values of x as follows:

$$\text{LTL}_x = \bar{\bar{x}} - \frac{3\bar{R}}{d_2}, \qquad \text{UTL}_x = \bar{\bar{x}} + \frac{3\bar{R}}{d_2}$$

Again, the constant d_2 is found in Table 17.2.1.

These limits are usually called the *natural tolerance limits* for the process. When a process is in good control, these limits include almost all the individual values. If these limits are within the manufacturer's specifications, we may conclude that most of the items are of satisfactory quality. If they are outside the manufacturer's specifications, we question the quality of the product.

In constructing $\bar{x}$ and R charts, the most frequently used sample size is either 4 or 5. The following example illustrates the construction and use of $\bar{x}$ and R charts.

EXAMPLE 17.2.1 Consider a manufacturing process that produces 20 bolts every minute. Table 17.2.2 shows the measurements of each bolt in terms of the deviation above or below 3.000 inches. From these data, we wish to construct an $\bar{x}$ chart and an R chart.

SOLUTION We use the first 25 time periods to establish control limits. We draw a random sample of size 4 from each time period. We then calculate the mean and range for each sample. Table 17.2.3 shows the results.

From the data in Table 17.2.3, we compute the following:

$$\bar{\bar{x}} = \frac{1.0 + 0.75 + \cdots + (-1.0)}{25} = \frac{5.25}{25} = 0.21$$

$$\bar{R} = \frac{7 + 11 + \cdots + 4}{25} = \frac{236}{25} = 9.44$$

$$\text{LCL}_{\bar{x}} = 0.21 - 0.729(9.44) = 0.21 - 6.88 = -6.67$$

$$\text{UCL}_{\bar{x}} = 0.21 + 0.729(9.44) = 7.09$$

$$\text{LCL}_R = (0)(9.44) = 0, \qquad \text{UCL}_R = (2.282)(9.44) = 21.54$$

Figure 17.2.2 shows the resulting control charts, along with the plotted values of $\bar{x}$ and R computed from the first 25 samples.

None of the sample values falls outside the control limits. This indicates that the process is under control during this period. Therefore, we can use the central lines and control limits of these charts as a standard for future reference. Let us now continue to draw samples of size 4 from each time period and observe whether or not the process continues to be in control. We sample time periods 26 through 40 (shown in Table 17.2.2). Table 17.2.3 shows the mean and range

TABLE 17.2.2 Lengths of 1,000 consecutively produced bolts (measurements represent deviations in thousandths of an inch above or below 3.000 inches)

Time Period										Bolt Number										
	1	2	3	4	5	6	7	8	9	10	11	12	13	14	15	16	17	18	19	20
1	7	3	4	4	-5	5	1	11	-2	-8	1	-1	4	-5	-3	0	6	9	4	1
2	6	7	1	0	-1	-7	-7	3	5	-4	5	0	-2	-1	-1	2	-9	5	1	-1
3	-1	-11	-1	-1	-1	-6	-7	-4	-2	-9	-14		6	-10	-1	-2	-2	-2	0	-1
4	-9	-2	-4	5	2	5	-1	5	5	-9	-3	-8	0	0	6	1	6	-5	3	11
5	8	11	-2	0	4	-3	-1	9	0	-1	-8	-11	6	8	-4	10	1	2	-2	5
6	-2	2	4	-4	3	-4	-8	3	4	4	3	5	-5	-2	-3	0	-10	-4	1	-1
7	-7	13	0	7	0	4	-6	-3	-2	-7	-3	-2	0	3	10	0	-8	2	-1	-2
8	-8	3	9	-2	3	12	-5	-6	-14	-1	0	9	4	-1	1	-5	4	-9	2	-5
9	-1	-4	-1	-3	4	-4	8	-1	-2	-5	-4	-7	-7	-5	-5	5	-2	3	-4	0
10	-7	-9	-3	0	1	-3	2	1	-2	0	5	-5	-7	-5	0	7	2	2	-2	3
11	-4	-12	3	-3	-6	-5	-12	5	-3	3	5	8	2	-6	2	2	-10	-2	0	-4
12	-5	4	2	-2	3	8	4	3	3	1	4	1	1	5	3	-2	6	0	3	-11
13	-10	12	5	3	7	8	-9	3	3	-2	10	0	4	-5	6	-3	0	5	3	5
14	3	-1	-5	3	-7	-4	4	-2	-1	-2	0	10	-5	-5	5	-2	1	-7	4	4
15	-7	-1	5	1	-6	13	-3	6	-1	-1	9	5	1	-3	2	-2	-4	-6	-3	-7
16	-5	-5	6	8	-2	10	6	1	4	5	-16	-2	-3	-1	3	1	1	5	-3	3
17	-2	-7	4	0	2	-10	-2	3	5	8	-8	-2	-6	0	-2	9	7	-2	-1	8
18	7	0	-4	6	8	5	-2	2	0	2	3	1	-3	0	-3	0	3	2	-4	1
19	-6	-4	10	3	3	3	5	-6	0	6	5	7	7	-5	-5	-2	-2	-1	2	-1
20	0	6	5	13	1	6	-7	1	6	2	7	-8	0	1	-3	-3	-2	0	-2	4
21	-6	3	2	2	1	-2	-4	-12	3	2	-6	6	4	-8	7	-5	-11	4	2	-2
22	3	8	2	-9	12	-4	0	-6	-1	-2	-2	1	5	-7	1	-2	0	1	6	-6
23	0	4	2	-7	-1	4	-3	6	9	-6	5	5	4	-4	-9	-8	-3	-1	-3	0
24	-5	-2	0	0	12	-1	-6	-8	4	5	8	-7	4	-3	4	2	-3	3	10	0
25	-9	8	-1	-5	2	-2	-4	1	2	1	-1	7	6	1	0	1	-3	11	3	8

(table continues on next page)

TABLE 17.2.2 (*Continued*)

Bolt Number

Time Period	1	2	3	4	5	6	7	8	9	10	11	12	13	14	15	16	17	18	19	20
26	-5	-5	-1	-2	-7	-4	-1	-1	2	6	-3	0	1	2	10	1	-2	-2	-4	9
27	-1	-5	4	2	-5	6	-2	9	-12	-2	2	2	2	13	10	2	-2	1	-4	0
28	-12	11	-2	-5	-2	7	-1	-3	-3	10	4	-5	1	7	-1	2	-5	-3	-7	-3
29	9	10	13	8	12	2	6	16	10	10	13	1	14	10	9	4	18	9	12	21
30	-10	4	-2	-14	1	-5	7	3	-4	-6	6	3	-9	1	6	4	4	-2	0	-3
31	4	-5	-4	0	7	0	-1	-12	-8	-3	2	-3	1	-8	-3	16	4	-5	-3	-2
32	5	-2	-1	-2	5	2	-3	2	7	-1	7	-1	3	3	-1	-7	-10	-3	-4	-3
33	1	-3	0	2	-8	-3	0	1	-4	-1	-2	-2	1	0	-1	5	1	-3	-3	4
34	-11	-1	1	8	3	-2	1	-3	9	3	-6	-7	4	-10	0	-1	5	11	17	-1
35	0	-18	-11	-4	-17	-2	-14	-14	-11	-11	-10	-9	-9	-12	-8	-5	-16	-16	-7	-5
36	1	10	0	5	-3	1	-5	5	-2	-4	-1	5	-9	-7	11	10	-4	4	-2	5
37	8	2	2	-2	-1	4	-4	-3	4	0	-4	-10	-4	-3	5	3	1	2	9	14
38	24	8	-35	14	-25	-1	-11	-34	36	-46	-13	7	20	-26	23	6	9	-21	-13	1
39	-4	13	0	5	4	4	-6	1	8	2	6	-3	1	3	0	-1	-1	2	3	-6
40	5	-1	-3	-3	2	6	-3	6	1	8	2	3	4	-3	6	1	-1	5	-6	-8
41	-20	14	-19	3	-34	32	68	6	-33	-27	-60	17	12	5	-6	4	-29	24	0	3
42	-2	3	4	0	-6	-7	9	-3	7	1	2	-6	4	-1	-1	2	-5	-4	4	5
43	3	-4	-3	4	-4	3	-9	-1	6	1	-1	4	-3	-7	-2	3	-9	-7	-2	-6
44	15	48	27	-13	34	-49	13	-41	-1	-15	15	-12	-40	7	12	-12	-26	4	-20	-13
45	-4	-7	0	-2	-4	-5	3	-4	5	-1	4	-2	-5	-3	5	-3	-3	-1	0	2
46	-3	-2	11	-4	-5	6	-9	0	-1	-1	-3	-2	3	6	-9	-1	-3	0	6	0
47	0	-9	-6	-13	-11	-17	-4	-11	-15	-6	-17	-8	-2	-14	0	-15	-9	-5	-7	-10
48	-8	1	3	5	-2	1	2	7	5	-7	4	7	2	-6	0	-5	1	-1	7	-3
49	9	-2	6	15	11	7	10	11	-1	4	13	12	14	6	10	9	-2	11	5	5
50	4	-4	4	1	6	3	-1	-2	-1	-2	1	8	-1	8	-1	-5	3	1	0	8

TABLE 17.2.3   Mean and range computed from random samples drawn from time periods
shown in Table 17.2.2

Sample Number	x_1	x_2	x_3	x_4	Total	$\bar{x}$	R
1	5	0	−2	1	4	1.0	7
2	1	−1	7	−4	3	0.75	11
3	−14	−1	1	−1	−15	−3.75	15
4	−1	5	1	−3	2	0.5	8
5	11	4	9	−3	21	5.25	14
6	−2	4	0	−3	−1	−0.25	7
7	−2	0	2	0	0	0.0	4
8	3	−6	3	−2	−2	−0.5	9
9	5	−7	−3	−4	−9	−2.25	12
10	1	−3	2	−7	−7	−1.75	9
11	−12	−12	−5	5	−24	−6.0	17
12	−2	3	3	−2	2	0.5	5
13	5	8	0	0	13	3.25	8
14	−5	3	−5	−7	−14	−3.5	10
15	−3	9	−2	2	6	1.5	12
16	3	5	−5	10	13	3.25	15
17	−2	2	0	−7	−7	−1.75	9
18	−3	6	0	−3	0	0.0	9
19	0	−2	2	7	7	1.75	9
20	−7	6	13	0	12	3.0	20
21	7	4	2	3	16	4.0	5
22	2	2	1	0	5	1.25	2
23	−3	5	0	4	6	1.5	8
24	−3	2	0	−5	−6	−1.5	7
25	0	1	−2	−3	−4	−1.0	4
26	2	−5	10	−1	6	1.5	15
27	2	0	10	13	25	6.25	13
28	−5	7	1	−1	2	0.5	12
29	9	18	4	1	32	8.0	17
30	4	−5	3	1	3	0.75	9
31	1	−5	4	−1	−1	−0.25	9
32	5	−1	2	−1	5	1.25	6
33	1	−2	1	−1	−1	−0.25	3
34	−6	−1	8	−1	0	0.0	14
35	−18	−14	−11	−16	−59	−14.75	7
36	4	−1	5	5	13	3.25	6
37	9	−4	−4	0	1	0.25	13
38	−34	6	−26	−1	−55	−13.75	40
39	0	13	1	2	16	4.0	13
40	4	−1	−3	2	2	0.5	7

(table continues on next page)

TABLE 17.2.3 *(Continued)*

Sample Number	x_1	x_2	x_3	x_4	Total	$\bar{x}$	R
41	24	3	−34	12			
42	−2	−4	2	−3			
43	−9	−1	2	3			
44	27	−13	−49	−12			
45	−7	0	3	−4			
46	−9	−3	6	−9			
47	−9	−17	−13	−10			
48	2	−2	−3	−1			
49	7	6	9	11			
50	8	1	4	3			

FIGURE 17.2.2 Control charts for $\bar{x}$ and R, using data from Tables 17.2.2 and 17.2.3

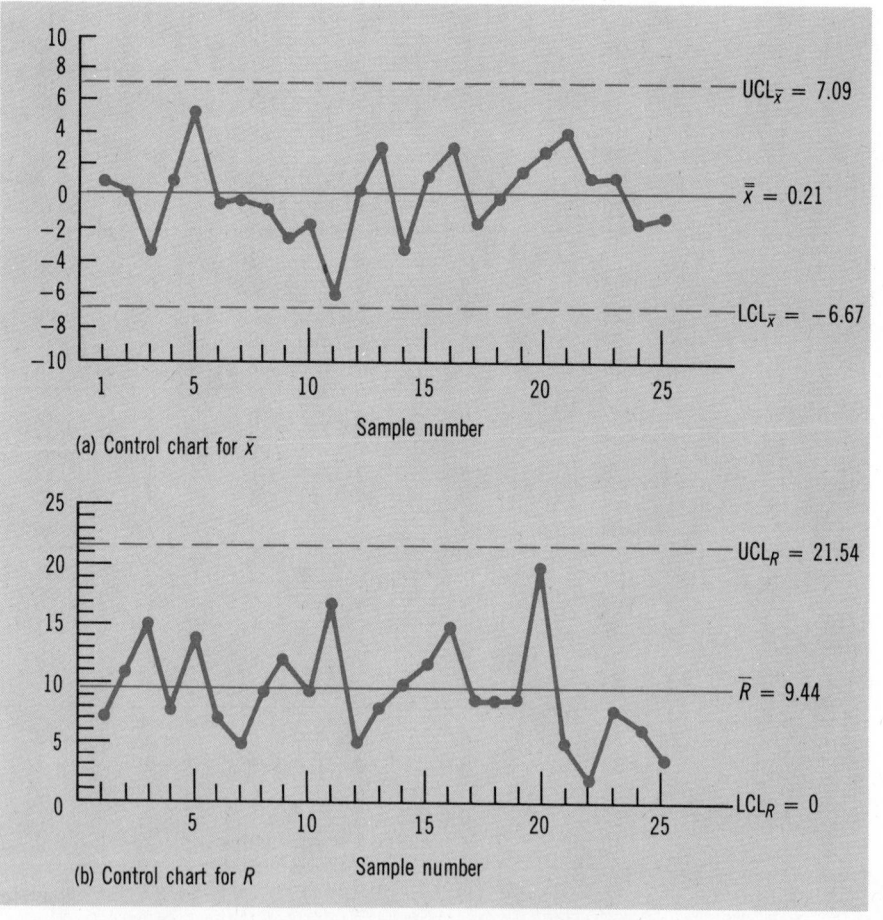

(a) Control chart for $\bar{x}$

(b) Control chart for R

FIGURE 17.2.3   Control chart for $\bar{x}$, showing location of $\bar{x}$ for samples 26 through 40, as shown in Table 17.2.3.

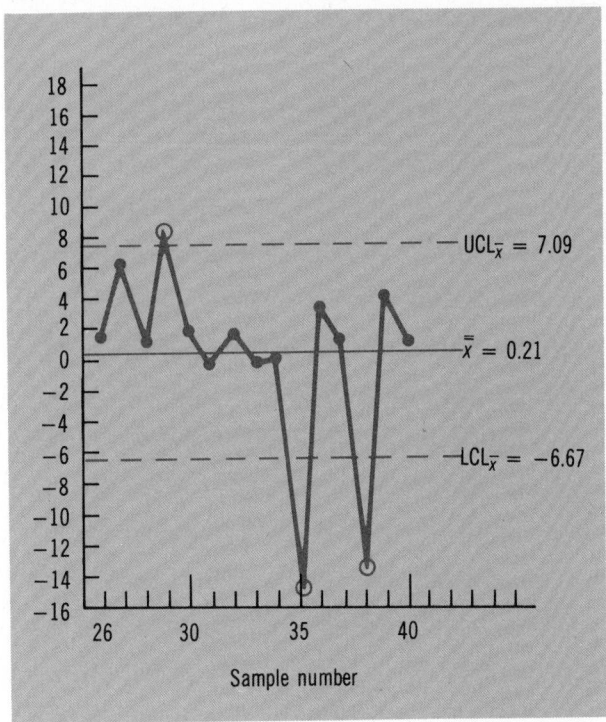

for each of these samples. Figures 17.2.3 and 17.2.4 show the locations of the sample values of $\bar{x}$ and R on the control charts.

Samples 29, 35, and 38 produce means that fall outside the control limits. We assume that each mean that fell outside the control limits was considered to be an indication that the process mean had changed. We assume that the process was stopped each time, and then an assignable cause for the change was found and corrected.

The process variation seems to have changed at the time of drawing sample number 38, since this sample value of R falls outside the control limit for R. Again, we assume that an assignable cause was found and corrected.

EXERCISES

17.2.1   Using the sample values in Table 17.2.3, compute the mean and range for samples 41 through 50. Plot them on the $\bar{x}$ and R charts that were constructed from the first 25 samples of the table. Explain the results.

17.2.2   Using the data of Table 17.2.2, draw samples of size 5 from each of the first 25 time periods. Construct an $\bar{x}$ chart and an R chart based on these samples.

FIGURE 17.2.4   Control chart for R, showing location of R for samples 26 through 40, as shown in Table 17.2.3

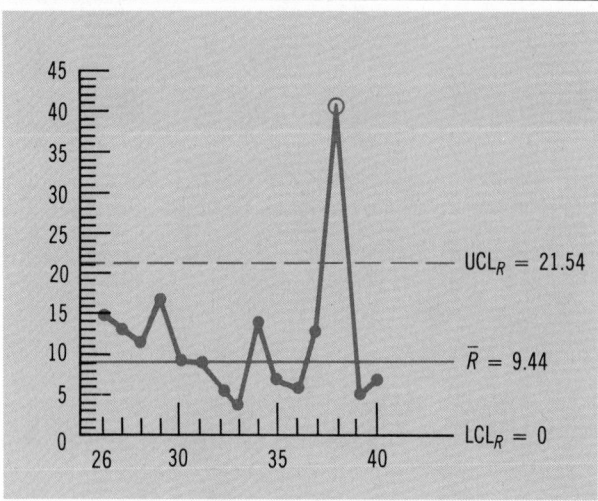

17.2.3   Draw samples of size 5 from each of the remaining time periods. Compute the sample mean and range for each. Plot them on the control charts.

17.3   CONTROL CHARTS — ATTRIBUTES

Sometimes it is not possible to determine the quality of an item of product by measuring such things as length, weight, or temperature. Alternatively, we can classify the quality of an item of product as either *acceptable* or *nonacceptable*. In other words, the *attribute* of the product determines its quality. We may consider an item that has the attribute of being *defective* as *nonacceptable*. We may consider an item that has the attribute of being *without defect* as *acceptable*.

Two types of control charts based on attributes are generally used. These are the *p chart* for *fraction defective* and the *c chart* for *number of defects per item*. We consider only the p chart in this text.

In constructing p charts, we define the value of p as

$$p = \frac{\text{number of defective items in a sample}}{\text{total number of items in the sample}}$$

and

$$\bar{p} = \frac{\text{total number of defective items in several samples}}{\text{total number of items inspected from several samples}}$$

Corresponding to the statistic p, we call the fraction of defective items in the population p'. We may use $\bar{p}$ to estimate p'.

THE SAMPLING DISTRIBUTION OF p

Recall some basic facts about the sampling distribution of p:

1. When we draw samples of size n from a large finite population with a fraction of defective items equal to p', the sampling distribution of p, the fraction of defective items observed in the samples, is distributed as the binomial probability distribution. We find the probability of observing in a sample a fraction of defective items equal to p by evaluating

$$f(p) = \frac{n!}{(np)!(n - np)!} (p')^{np}(1 - p')^{n-np}, \qquad p = \frac{0}{n}, \frac{1}{n}, \frac{2}{n}, \ldots, \frac{n}{n}$$

2. The mean of all possible sample values of the fraction of defective items is equal to p', the fraction of defective items in the population.

3. The standard deviation of the distribution of sample p values is given by

$$\sigma_p = \sqrt{\frac{p'(1 - p')}{n}}$$

To estimate σ_p, we use

$$\hat{\sigma}_p = \sqrt{\frac{\bar{p}(1 - \bar{p})}{n}}$$

4. When n is large and neither p' nor $1 - p'$ is too close to 1, the distribution of sample p values is closely approximated by a normal distribution. We generally consider these conditions to be met when both np' and $n(1 - p')$ > 5.

The following example shows how to construct a p chart.

EXAMPLE 17.3.1   Wentworth International produces plastic toy cars. The manufacturing process is a continuous one. Samples of size 50 are periodically taken from the output and inspected. The process is deemed currently to be under control, since much effort has gone into training the operators, adjusting the machines, and ensuring that only high-quality raw material is used. Table 17.3.1 shows the number of defective items discovered in the first 25 samples taken from the output after these efforts to improve the quality. We wish to see whether the process is, in fact, now in control.

SOLUTION   A preliminary control chart will aid in this decision. The first step in constructing the preliminary control chart for the fraction of defective items is to compute $\bar{p}$, the average fraction of defective items found in 25 samples taken from the existing process.

TABLE 17.3.1 Number of defective items observed in 25 samples of size 50 from a manufacturing process

Time Period (Sample Number)	Number of Defective Items	p	Time Period (Sample Number)	Number of Defective Items	p
1	12	0.24	14	9	0.18
2	12	0.24	15	9	0.18
3	22	0.44	16	22	0.44
4	12	0.24	17	3	0.06
5	6	0.12	18	11	0.22
6	12	0.24	19	9	0.18
7	13	0.26	20	9	0.18
8	12	0.24	21	11	0.22
9	13	0.26	22	12	0.24
10	7	0.14	23	10	0.20
11	10	0.20	24	24	0.48
12	8	0.16	25	10	0.20
13	13	0.26	Total	291	

$$\bar{p} = \frac{\text{total number of defective items}}{\text{total number of items inspected}} = \frac{291}{1,250} = 0.2328$$

We now use $\bar{p}$ as an estimate of p', the fraction of defective items, and use it as the center line of our preliminary control chart.

To obtain our $3\sigma_p$ control limits, we add to and subtract from 0.2328 the quantity

$$3\hat{\sigma}_p = 3\sqrt{\frac{\bar{p}(1 - \bar{p})}{n}} = 3\sqrt{\frac{(0.2328)(0.7672)}{50}} = 0.1793$$

We now have

$$LCL_p = 0.2328 - 0.1793 = 0.0535$$
$$UCL_p = 0.2328 + 0.1793 = 0.4121$$

From these data, we construct the preliminary control chart shown in Figure 17.3.1. A total of three points are outside the control limits on the chart. We conclude from this that the process is not under control.

Our objective is to get the process under control. Thus, we investigate the points that fell outside the control limits to discover some assignable cause. Let us assume that we found the following causes for the points that were out of control: during the time period in which sample 3 was drawn, several employees were out sick, and employees from another department were brought in as temporary replacements. The supervisor feels that this caused the large proportion of defective items in sample 3. During the period in which sample 16 was drawn,

FIGURE 17.3.1 A p chart for analyzing past data

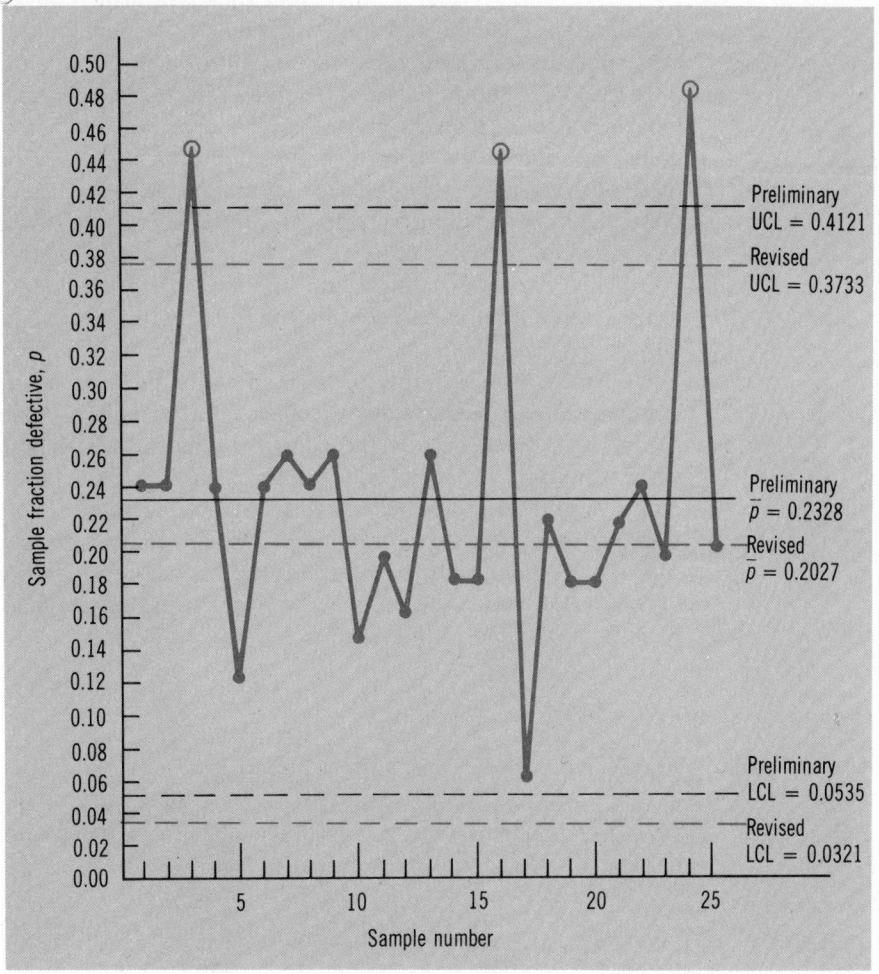

a machine got out of adjustment and caused a larger-than-usual proportion of defective items to be produced. Sample 24 was taken just after a new machine was installed and while it was being broken in.

As a result of these investigations, we decide to discard the data for which we have found an assignable cause. We compute a new value of $\bar{p}$ and new control limits based on the remainder of the data. These revised values are as follows:

$$\bar{p} = \frac{223}{1{,}100} = 0.2027$$

$$\text{UCL}_p = 0.2027 + 3\sqrt{\frac{(0.2027)(0.7973)}{50}} = 0.2027 + 0.1706 = 0.3733$$

$$\text{LCL}_p = 0.2027 - 0.1706 = 0.0321$$

Figure 17.3.1 shows these revised values as the revised UCL_p and LCL_p, respectively. No sample values, other than those for which an assignable cause was found, fall outside the new limits. We take these new limits, along with the new center line, as standards for controlling production in the future.

Table 17.3.2 shows the sample results for the time periods 26 through 50. We plot the values of p on the revised control chart as shown in Figure 17.3.2. Three points fall outside the control limits, two above and one below. When we see these outlying points, we look for an assignable cause. Assume that for each of these values of p falling outside the control limits, we find an assignable cause and make the necessary corrections. We are especially interested in the value that falls below the lower control limit. Perhaps the cause is one that we can use to bring about a general reduction in the fraction of defective items in the factory's output.

We have considered only the case in which the sample size n is constant. But at times we may need to have a p chart for a variable n. Furthermore, even when points do not fall outside the control limits, in actual practice their behavior within the limits is watched. In particular, if a larger number of consecutive points appear to fall either above or below the center line, the quality-control manager investigates the situation. There are tests to determine whether or not such a pattern indicates a real trend. For further consideration of this point, and of the case in which the sample size is not constant, see Suggestions for Further Reading at the end of this chapter.

EXERCISES

17.3.1   The daily production of window air conditioners is 1,000 units. A random sample of 50 units is inspected each day. After 28 days, a quality-control technician finds a total of 182 defective units. Assume that the production process is in control. Compute the center line and 3-sigma control limits for a p chart.

TABLE 17.3.2   Sample data from time periods 26–50

Time Period (Sample Number)	Number of Defective Items	p	Time Period (Sample Number)	Number of Defective Items	p
26	10	0.20	39	8	0.16
27	19	0.38	40	6	0.12
28	5	0.10	41	13	0.26
29	8	0.16	42	20	0.40
30	12	0.24	43	9	0.18
31	9	0.18	44	8	0.16
32	11	0.22	45	5	0.10
33	8	0.16	46	14	0.28
34	7	0.14	47	1	0.02
35	11	0.22	48	9	0.18
36	16	0.32	49	11	0.22
37	11	0.22	50	10	0.20
38	7	0.14			

FIGURE 17.3.2   Revised p chart, showing values of p for samples 26 through 50

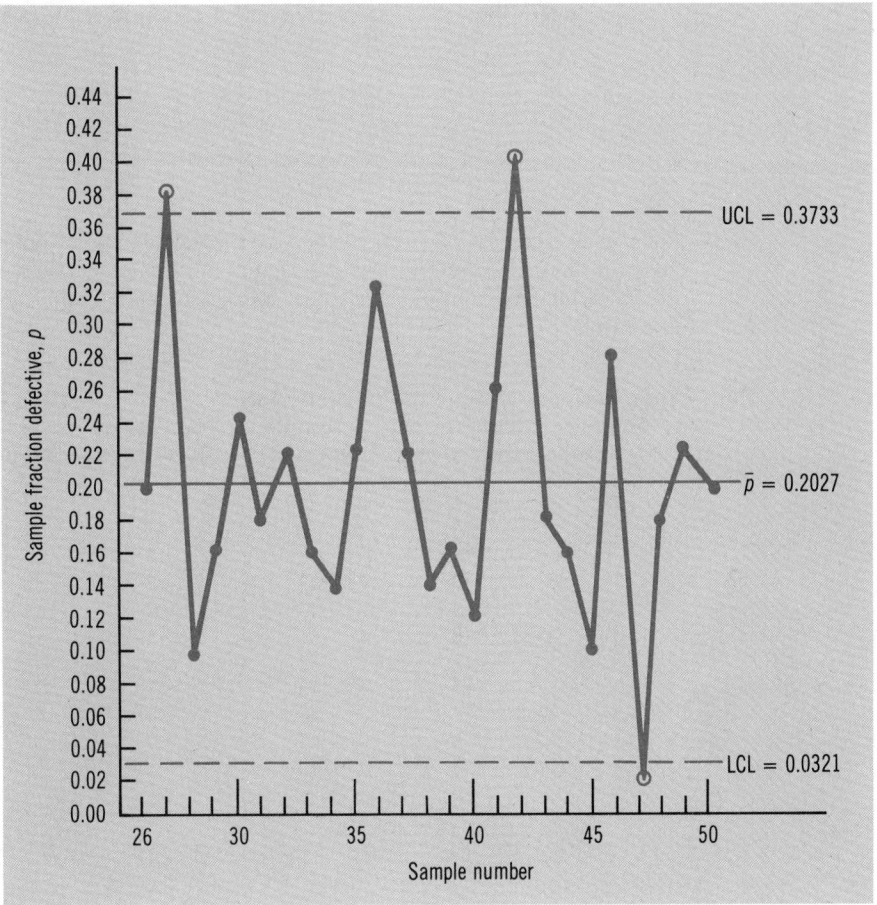

17.3.2   The following table shows the number of defective items in 25 samples of size 50 drawn from a manufacturing process. One sample was drawn from each of 25 time periods. (a) Use these data to construct a p chart for analyzing past data.   (b) Plot the 25 values of p on the chart. Suggest possible causes for any values lying outside the control limits.

Time Period (Sample Number)	Number of Defectives	Time Period (Sample Number)	Number of Defectives
1	10	8	19
2	10	9	9
3	11	10	7
4	10	11	8
5	12	12	8
6	10	13	7
7	12	14	11

(table continues on next page)

Time Period (Sample Number)	Number of Defectives	Time Period (Sample Number)	Number of Defectives
15	12	21	12
16	3	22	9
17	20	23	9
18	10	24	12
19	7	25	10
20	21		

17.3.3   Refer to Exercise 17.3.2.   (a) Discard the data giving rise to points outside the control limits (if any). Construct a revised p chart.   (b) Compute values of p from the data in the following table and plot the values on the revised p chart. Does the process remain in control?

Time Period (Sample Number)	Number of Defectives	Time Period (Sample Number)	Number of Defectives	Time Period (Sample Number)	Number of Defectives
26	6	36	10	46	10
27	10	37	13	47	9
28	7	38	18	48	20
29	19	39	9	49	6
30	4	40	12	50	10
31	8	41	6		
32	11	42	3		
33	7	43	11		
34	9	44	8		
35	5	45	9		

17.4   ACCEPTANCE SAMPLING FOR ATTRIBUTES

During the production of any item, from time to time questions of acceptability arise. Is the incoming raw material acceptable? After the first stages of manufacture are completed, is the semifinished product acceptable for further processing? Is the quality of the outgoing product acceptable? The logical response to such questions is to inspect the items and find out. The questions and the response imply that (1) the product can be inspected, (2) we have established criteria whereby we can classify an item of product as either acceptable or not, and (3) the results of an inspection will lead to some type of action.

Suppose that we decide to inspect a product at one of the stages mentioned, to find out whether it is acceptable. We can follow one of several paths. First, we decide whether to inspect 100% of the product or only a part of it. Typically we decide on the latter. That is, we decide to sample. Sampling requires less time, money, and effort. If the test to which we subject our product is destructive, sampling is the only way of ensuring that there will remain a product to sell. In short, the considerations that favor sampling are applicable within the context of quality control. Furthermore, inspecting 100% of the product does not mean that we will recognize all unacceptable items. When inspectors have to examine every item produced, fatigue and monotony surely impair their efficiency.

Assume that the items of product are available in groups, called *inspection lots*. The sampling procedure, called *lot-by-lot sampling inspection*, may proceed. Inspection of an item results in its being classified as either *acceptable (nondefective)* or *not acceptable (defective)*. In other words, an item of product possesses one or the other *attribute: defective* or *nondefective*. Therefore, we call the procedure *attribute sampling*. When we carry out a sampling procedure, we draw the sampled items at random from the inspection lots, without replacement. Depending on the results, we either accept or reject the lots.

SAMPLING PLANS

The actual sampling procedure is called a *sampling plan*. The three standard plans are as follows.

Single Sampling Plan As the name implies, a single sampling plan requires the drawing of only one sample. The following is an example.

EXAMPLE 17.4.1   Inspection lots consist of 1,000 items of product. An inspector selects from a lot a sample of size 80, and examines each. When she finds 7 or fewer defective items out of the 80 in the sample, she considers the lot acceptable, and *accepts* it. When she finds 8 or more defective, she considers the lot unacceptable, and *rejects* it.

Double Sampling Plan A double sampling plan allows an inspector to draw two samples, if needed, before reaching a decision to accept or reject a lot. The following is an example.

EXAMPLE 17.4.2   We examine a sample of 50 items. When we find 3 or fewer defective items, we accept the lot. When we find 7 or more defective items, we reject the lot. When we find more than 3 but fewer than 7 defective items, we neither accept nor reject. Instead, we select a second sample of 50 items from the same lot, and examine these items. If the number of defectives in the second sample, plus those in the first, is equal to or less than 6, we accept the lot. If the number of defectives in the second sample, plus those in the first, is equal to or greater than 7, we reject the lot.

Multiple Sampling Plan Multiple sampling plans allow for the drawing of more than two samples, if the inspector needs to do so in order to reach a decision to reject or accept a lot. The following is an example.

EXAMPLE 17.4.3   We select a sample of size 20 from an inspection lot. When examination reveals no defective items, we accept the lot. When we find 4 or more defectives, we reject the lot. When we find 1, 2, or 3 defective items, we

FIGURE 17.4.1 Flow diagram illustrating a multiple sampling plan

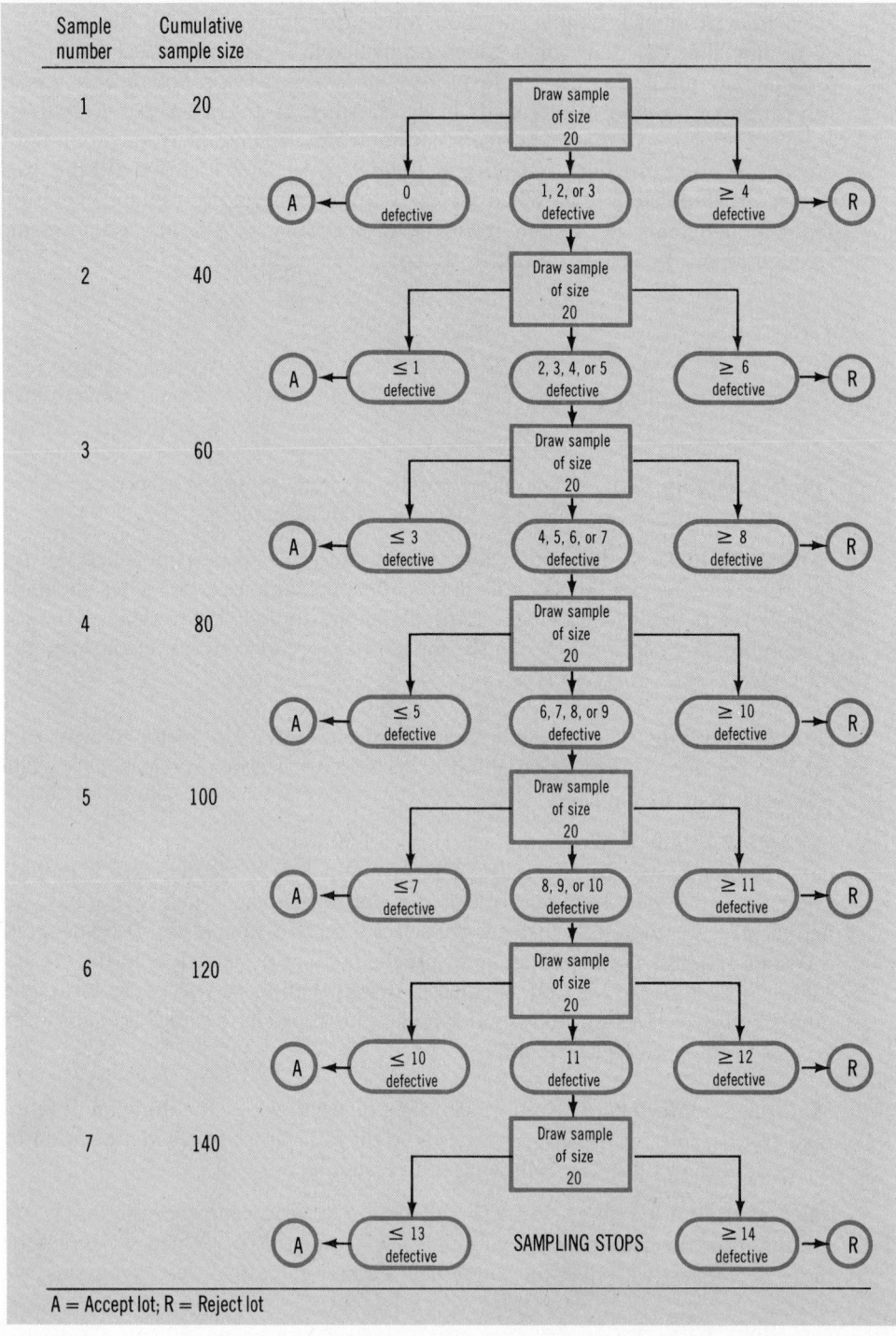

Sample number	Cumulative sample size
1	20
2	40
3	60
4	80
5	100
6	120
7	140

Draw sample of size 20

A ← 0 defective | 1, 2, or 3 defective | ≥ 4 defective → R

Draw sample of size 20

A ← ≤ 1 defective | 2, 3, 4, or 5 defective | ≥ 6 defective → R

Draw sample of size 20

A ← ≤ 3 defective | 4, 5, 6, or 7 defective | ≥ 8 defective → R

Draw sample of size 20

A ← ≤ 5 defective | 6, 7, 8, or 9 defective | ≥ 10 defective → R

Draw sample of size 20

A ← ≤ 7 defective | 8, 9, or 10 defective | ≥ 11 defective → R

Draw sample of size 20

A ← ≤ 10 defective | 11 defective | ≥ 12 defective → R

Draw sample of size 20

A ← ≤ 13 defective | SAMPLING STOPS | ≥ 14 defective → R

A = Accept lot; R = Reject lot

select another sample of size 20. When examination of both samples (40 items) turns up only 1 defective, we accept the lot. When we find 6 or more defectives, we reject the lot. When we find 2, 3, 4, or 5 defectives, we take another sample of size 20. This process continues until we decide to reject or accept the lot. We reach a decision at least by the time we examine the seventh sample of size 20. The flow diagram in Figure 17.4.1 shows the number of defectives required for a decision at each stage of the process.

These sampling plans are from a compilation of sampling plans and procedures for inspection by attributes prepared by the Department of Defense. (The title is *Military Standard Sampling Procedures and Tables for Inspection by Attributes*, MIL-STD-105D, 29 April 1963.) It is sold by the Superintendent of Documents, U.S. Government Printing Office, Washington, D.C. 20402.

SAMPLING PLAN NOTATION

Here we consider single and double sampling plans only. We do not discuss multiple sampling, although that is important. It is convenient to adopt the following notation:

$$N = \text{the size of the lot}$$
$$n = \text{the size of the sample, single sampling}$$
$$n_1 = \text{the size of the first sample, double sampling}$$
$$n_2 = \text{the size of the second sample, double sampling}$$
$$d = \text{the number of defective items in the sample, single sampling}$$
$$d_1 = \text{the number of defective items in the first sample, double sampling}$$
$$d_2 = \text{the number of defective items in the second sample, double sampling}$$
$$c = \text{acceptance number, single sampling}$$
$$c + 1 = \text{rejection number, single sampling}$$
$$c_1 = \text{acceptance number on first sample, double sampling}$$
$$c_2 = \text{acceptance number on second sample, double sampling}$$
$$c_2 + 1 = \text{rejection number, double sampling}$$
$$p' = \text{lot fraction defective (sometimes expressed as percentage)}$$
$$P_a = \text{probability of acceptance of a lot}$$

CRITERIA FOR ACCEPTANCE AND REJECTION

We write the criteria for acceptance and rejection in the single and double sampling plans in condensed form as follows.

Single sampling, d defective items in n:

$$d \leq c, \text{ accept lot}, \qquad d > c, \text{ reject lot}$$

Double sampling, d_1 defective items in n_1:

$$d_1 \leq c_1, \text{ accept lot}, \qquad d_1 > c_2, \text{ reject lot},$$
$$c_1 < d_1 \leq c_2, \text{ take second sample of size } n_2$$

Double sampling, $d_1 + d_2$ defective items in $n_1 + n_2$:

$$d_1 + d_2 \leq c_2, \text{ accept lot}, \qquad d_1 + d_2 > c_2, \text{ reject lot}$$

In order to use MIL-STD-105D, one must be able to specify the lot size, the *acceptable quality level* (AQL), the type of sampling plan (single, double, or multiple), and the *inspection level* desired. The AQL is the maximum percentage defective that we can consider satisfactory as a *process average* (average percentage defective in the production process), or *lot percent defective*. The purpose of sampling inspection is to judge whether or not this AQL is, in fact, exceeded.

Three levels of inspection are available: *level I*, for use when we need less discrimination; *level II*, for normal inspection; and *level III*, for use when we need more discrimination. We use level I when the supplier of the product has a reputation for providing a high-quality product. We use level III when the product is from a supplier with a reputation for submitting a poor-quality product. We use level II for the cases in between.

To illustrate the use of MIL-STD-105D, consider the following example.

EXAMPLE 17.4.4   Company A buys parts from Company B. The parts are received in lots of size $N = 1,000$ and inspected at Company A's *receiving inspection* station. The company uses a single sampling plan selected from MIL-STD-105D, with an AQL of 4% for a normal inspection level (level II).

SOLUTION   The use of MIL-STD-105D consists of the following steps.

1. Enter Table 17.4.1 (Table I of MIL-STD-105D) with the lot size of 1000 and general inspection level II, to obtain a sample size code letter. For lot sizes from 501 to 1200 and general inspection level II, the sample size code letter is J.
2. Enter Table 17.4.2 (Table II-A of MIL-STD-105D) with the sample size code letter and the AQL, to determine the sample size and acceptance and rejection numbers.

Step 1 revealed the sample size code letter to be J. Table 17.4.2 tells us that the sample size should be 80. Our AQL was designated as 4. Locating in Table 17.4.2 the intersection of the column headed 4.0 and the row labeled J, we find that the acceptance and rejection numbers are 7 and 8, respectively. This tells us to accept a lot if the random sample of size 80 yields 7 or fewer defective items, and to reject it if it yields 8 or more defective items.

TABLE 17.4.1   Sample size code letters, Table I of MIL-STD-105D

Lot or Batch Size	Special Inspection Levels				General Inspection Levels		
	S-1	S-2	S-3	S-4	I	II	III
2 to 8	A	A	A	A	A	A	B
9 to 15	A	A	A	A	A	B	C
16 to 25	A	A	B	B	B	C	D
26 to 50	A	B	B	C	C	D	E
51 to 90	B	B	C	C	C	E	F
91 to 150	B	B	C	D	D	F	G
151 to 280	B	C	D	E	E	G	H
281 to 500	B	C	D	E	F	H	J
501 to 1,200	C	C	E	F	G	J	K
1,201 to 3,200	C	D	E	G	H	K	L
3,201 to 10,000	C	D	F	G	J	L	M
10,001 to 35,000	C	D	F	H	K	M	N
35,001 to 150,000	D	E	G	J	L	N	P
150,001 to 500,000	D	E	G	J	M	P	Q
500,001 and over	D	E	H	K	N	Q	R

Source: *Military Standard Sampling Procedures and Tables for Inspection by Attributes, MIL-STD-105D, Department of Defense, 29 April 1963.*

Operating Characteristic (OC) Curves   We can summarize any sampling plan graphically by means of an *operating characteristic (OC) curve*. The OC curve indicates the probability P_a that a lot of submitted product is accepted if it is of a given quality, as indicated by p', the fraction of defective items in the lot. Stated another way, the operating characteristic curve of a sampling plan indicates the percentage of lots that may be expected to be accepted if they are of a given quality. MIL-STD-105D gives OC curves for various combinations of p', P_a, AQL, and sample size.

EXAMPLE 17.4.5   Find the OC curve for the single sampling plan described earlier.

SOLUTION   To locate the curve, recall that the code letter for the sample size is J. Accordingly, we go to Chart J in MIL-STD-105D (see Figure 17.4.2). Since the AQL is 4, we locate the curve labeled 4 in Chart J of Figure 17.4.2. On the horizontal axis, we can find various values of p' (percent defective, in our case) for a submitted lot. Following the line up to the curve and reading from this point on the curve across to the vertical axis, we read the probability P_a of the lot's being accepted. Suppose that 6% of the items are defective. We locate the figure 6 on the horizontal axis, move up the vertical line drawn at 6 until we reach the curve labeled 4.0, and read across to the vertical axis. There we find

TABLE 17.4.2 Single sampling plans for normal inspection (master table), Table II-A of MIL-STD-105D

Acceptable quality levels (normal inspection)

Sample size code letter	Sample size	0.010		0.015		0.025		0.040		0.065		0.10		0.15		0.25		0.40		0.65		1.0		1.5		2.5		4.0		6.5		10		15		25		40		65		100		150		250		400		650		1000	
		Ac	Re	Ac	Re	Ac	Re	Ac	Re	Ac	Re	Ac	Re	Ac	Re	Ac	Re	Ac	Re	Ac	Re	Ac	Re	Ac	Re	Ac	Re	Ac	Re	Ac	Re	Ac	Re	Ac	Re	Ac	Re	Ac	Re	Ac	Re	Ac	Re	Ac	Re	Ac	Re	Ac	Re	Ac	Re
A	2	↓		↓		↓		↓		↓		↓		↓		↓		↓		↓		↓		↓		↓		↓		↓		↓		↓		1	2	2	3	3	4	5	6	7	8	10	11	14	15	21	22	30	31
B	3	↓		↓		↓		↓		↓		↓		↓		↓		↓		↓		↓		↓		↓		↓		↓		↓		1	2	2	3	3	4	5	6	7	8	10	11	14	15	21	22	30	31	44	45
C	5	↓		↓		↓		↓		↓		↓		↓		↓		↓		↓		↓		↓		↓		↓		0	1	1	2	2	3	3	4	5	6	7	8	10	11	14	15	21	22	30	31	44	45	↑	
D	8	↓		↓		↓		↓		↓		↓		↓		↓		↓		↓		↓		↓		↓		0	1	1	2	2	3	3	4	5	6	7	8	10	11	14	15	21	22	30	31	44	45	↑		↑	
E	13	↓		↓		↓		↓		↓		↓		↓		↓		↓		↓		↓		↓		0	1	1	2	2	3	3	4	5	6	7	8	10	11	14	15	21	22	30	31	44	45	↑		↑		↑	
F	20	↓		↓		↓		↓		↓		↓		↓		↓		↓		↓		↓		0	1	1	2	2	3	3	4	5	6	7	8	10	11	14	15	21	22	30	31	44	45	↑		↑		↑		↑	
G	32	↓		↓		↓		↓		↓		↓		↓		↓		↓		↓		0	1	1	2	2	3	3	4	5	6	7	8	10	11	14	15	21	22	30	31	44	45	↑		↑		↑		↑		↑	
H	50	↓		↓		↓		↓		↓		↓		↓		↓		↓		0	1	1	2	2	3	3	4	5	6	7	8	10	11	14	15	21	22	30	31	44	45	↑		↑		↑		↑		↑		↑	
J	80	↓		↓		↓		↓		↓		↓		↓		↓		0	1	1	2	2	3	3	4	5	6	7	8	10	11	14	15	21	22	30	31	44	45	↑		↑		↑		↑		↑		↑		↑	
K	125	↓		↓		↓		↓		↓		↓		↓		0	1	1	2	2	3	3	4	5	6	7	8	10	11	14	15	21	22	30	31	44	45	↑		↑		↑		↑		↑		↑		↑		↑	
L	200	↓		↓		↓		↓		↓		↓		0	1	1	2	2	3	3	4	5	6	7	8	10	11	14	15	21	22	30	31	44	45	↑		↑		↑		↑		↑		↑		↑		↑		↑	
M	315	↓		↓		↓		↓		↓		0	1	1	2	2	3	3	4	5	6	7	8	10	11	14	15	21	22	30	31	44	45	↑		↑		↑		↑		↑		↑		↑		↑		↑		↑	
N	500	↓		↓		↓		↓		0	1	1	2	2	3	3	4	5	6	7	8	10	11	14	15	21	22	30	31	44	45	↑		↑		↑		↑		↑		↑		↑		↑		↑		↑		↑	
P	800	↓		↓		↓		0	1	1	2	2	3	3	4	5	6	7	8	10	11	14	15	21	22	30	31	44	45	↑		↑		↑		↑		↑		↑		↑		↑		↑		↑		↑		↑	
Q	1250	↓		↓		0	1	1	2	2	3	3	4	5	6	7	8	10	11	14	15	21	22	30	31	44	45	↑		↑		↑		↑		↑		↑		↑		↑		↑		↑		↑		↑		↑	
R	2000	↓		0	1	1	2	2	3	3	4	5	6	7	8	10	11	14	15	21	22	30	31	44	45	↑		↑		↑		↑		↑		↑		↑		↑		↑		↑		↑		↑		↑		↑	

↓ = Use first sampling plan below arrow. If sample size equals, or exceeds, lot or batch size, do 100% inspection.
↑ = Use first sampling plan above arrow.
Ac = Acceptance number
Re = Rejection number

Source: Military Standard Sampling Procedures and Tables for Inspection by Attributes, MIL-STD-105D, Department of Defense, 29 April 1963.

FIGURE 17.4.2   Tables for sample size code letter J, Table X-J of MIL-STD-105D

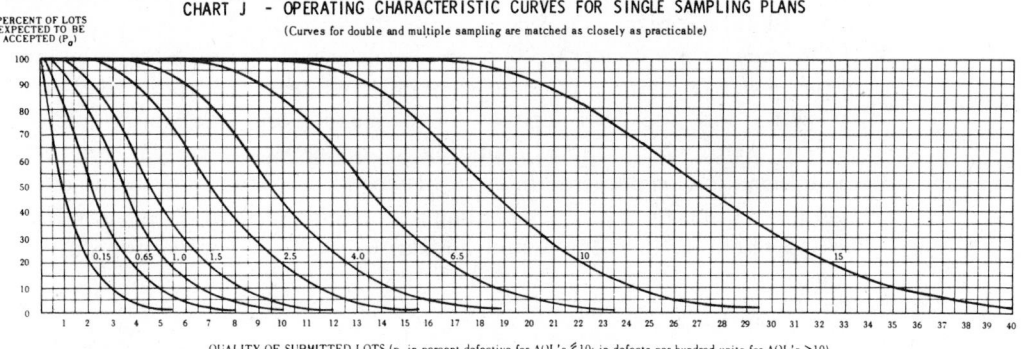

CHART J - OPERATING CHARACTERISTIC CURVES FOR SINGLE SAMPLING PLANS

(Curves for double and multiple sampling are matched as closely as practicable)

QUALITY OF SUBMITTED LOTS (p, in percent defective for AQL's ≤10; in defects per hundred units for AQL's >10)

Note: Figures on curves are Acceptable Quality Levels (AQL's) for normal inspection.

TABLE X-J-1 - TABULATED VALUES FOR OPERATING CHARACTERISTIC CURVES FOR SINGLE SAMPLING PLANS

P_a	Acceptable Quality Levels (normal inspection)																		
	0.15	0.65	1.0	1.5	2.5	4.0	✕	6.5	✕	10	0.15	0.65	1.0	1.5	2.5	4.0	✕	6.5	✕	10	✕	15
	p (in percent defective)										p (in defects per hundred units)								
99.0	0.013	0.188	0.550	1.05	2.30	3.72		4.50	6.13	7.88	9.75	0.013	0.186	0.545	1.03	2.23	3.63	4.38	5.96	7.62	9.35	12.9	15.7
95.0	0.064	0.444	1.03	1.73	3.32	5.06		5.98	7.91	9.89	11.9	0.064	0.444	1.02	1.71	3.27	4.98	5.87	7.71	9.61	11.6	15.6	18.6
90.0	0.132	0.666	1.38	2.20	3.98	5.91		6.91	8.95	11.0	13.2	0.131	0.665	1.38	2.18	3.94	5.82	6.79	8.78	10.8	12.9	17.1	20.3
75.0	0.359	1.202	2.16	3.18	5.30	7.50		8.62	10.9	13.2	15.5	0.360	1.20	2.16	3.17	5.27	7.45	8.55	10.8	13.0	15.3	19.9	23.4
50.0	0.863	2.09	3.33	4.57	7.06	9.55		10.8	13.3	15.8	18.3	0.866	2.10	3.34	4.59	7.09	9.59	10.8	13.3	15.8	18.3	23.3	27.1
25.0	1.72	3.33	4.84	6.31	9.14	11.9		13.3	16.0	18.6	21.3	1.73	3.37	4.90	6.39	9.28	12.1	13.5	16.3	19.0	21.8	27.2	31.2
10.0	2.84	4.78	6.52	8.16	11.3	14.2		15.7	18.6	21.4	24.2	2.88	4.86	6.65	8.35	11.6	14.7	16.2	19.3	22.2	25.2	30.9	35.2
5.0	3.68	5.80	7.66	9.39	12.7	15.8		17.3	20.3	23.2	26.0	3.75	5.93	7.87	9.69	13.1	16.4	18.0	21.2	24.3	27.4	33.4	37.8
1.0	5.59	8.00	10.1	12.0	15.6	18.9		20.5	23.6	26.5	29.5	5.76	8.30	10.5	12.6	16.4	20.0	21.8	25.2	28.5	31.8	38.2	42.9
	0.25	1.0	1.5	2.5	4.0	✕	6.5	✕	10	✕	0.25	1.0	1.5	2.5	4.0	✕	6.5	✕	10	✕	15	✕
	Acceptable Quality Levels (tightened inspection)																		

Note: All values given in above table based on Poisson distribution as an approximation to the Binomial.

Source: Military Standard Sampling Procedures and Tables for Inspection by Attributes, MIL-STD-105D, Department of Defense, 29 April 1963.

that P_a is equal to 0.90. This means that the probability of the lot's being accepted is 0.90. In other words, if lots are submitted with a consistent 6% defective, we accept 90% of them in the long run.

Alternatively, we can get the same information for selected values of P_a from Table X-J-1 (Figure 17.4.2). This table shows that 90% of lots with 5.91 defectives are accepted. We can attribute this slight difference from the value read from the chart to the loss in precision that is usual in graphs of mathematical data.

OTHER CURVES

In addition to the OC curve, we can construct other curves to describe a sampling plan. These are listed here with a brief description.

1. *The average outgoing quality (AOQ) curve.* This curve makes it easier to determine the quality in all lots after we have examined the rejected lots 100% and removed all defectives.
2. *The average sample number (ASN) curve.* This curve shows the average number of pieces per lot that we must inspect before we reach a decision to reject or accept the lot. The ASN depends on the quality of the incoming lot. This curve is useful when double or multiple sampling plans are used.
3. *The average total inspection (ATI) curve.* If we want to know the average total amount of inspection per lot, including the sampling inspection and any 100% sorting required, then we would find an average total inspection curve of value.

EXERCISES

17.4.1   Find a single sampling plan for normal inspection to fit the following situations: (a) Inspection lots of size 600 and an AQL of 0.15;   (b) inspection lots of size 800 and an AQL of 2.5;   (c) inspection lots of size 900 and an AQL of 10;   (d) inspection lots of size 1,000 and an AQL of 1.5;   (e) inspection lots of size 1,200 and an AQL of 4.

17.4.2   For each of the plans in Exercise 17.4.1, find the quality of the process for which we may expect 95% of the lots to be accepted.

17.5   ACCEPTANCE SAMPLING BY VARIABLES

Often the characteristic we want to study in quality control is measurable on a continuous scale. It is reasonable to assume that the characteristic follows, at least approximately, some specific distribution, say the normal. When this is the case, we may want to use a sampling plan based on measurements, such as the sample mean or the sample mean and standard deviation. Sampling plans of this type are called *variables sampling plans*. Their use in acceptance sampling is called *acceptance sampling by variables*.

We discuss two types of variables sampling plans: (1) *known sigma plans*, used when the variable of interest has a specified distribution and the standard deviation is known, and (2) *unknown sigma plans*, used when the variable of interest has a specified distribution and the standard deviation is *un*known. In each case, we develop a plan that indicates how large a sample to inspect and gives some criterion against which to compare the results in order to determine whether to reject the lot.

KNOWN SIGMA PLANS

Assume that the variable of interest is normally distributed and that the standard deviation σ is known and constant from lot to lot. This is not an unrealistic assumption for many manufacturing processes. By a known σ, we mean an estimate based on a large amount of previous data, since, in general, the true σ cannot be known.

The following three types of plans are available:

1. A plan that protects us from *too small* a lot mean. In this type, we specify a *minimum* value of X. That is, we determine for the lot mean an acceptable value located enough standard deviations above the specification to ensure that very few values of X are below the specification. Likewise, we choose a *rejectable value* for the lot mean so close (as measured in standard deviations) to the *minimum specification* that we are certain to reject lots with a mean this low.

2. A plan that protects us from *too large* a lot mean. The procedure is similar to the first plan, except that we specify a *maximum* value of X.

3. A plan that provides protection against a lot mean that deviates too far in either direction. This type of plan is a logical extension of the first two.

The following example illustrates the case in which we are interested in protection against a too-small lot mean.

EXAMPLE 17.5.1   The tensile strength of a certain type of wire is normally distributed. We estimate the true variance from extensive past data. For practical purposes, we consider that we have a known sigma, which we call σ', of $\sqrt{30}$ = 5.48. A roll of wire with a tensile strength less than 87 is not strong enough to do the job for which it is intended. We would like 1% or fewer of our rolls of wire to be below 87 in tensile strength. In other words, if no more than 1% of the items in a lot are defective, we will accept the lot. What will the value of the lot mean $\overline{X}'$ have to be in order for us to achieve this state of affairs in the long run?

SOLUTION   Table C of Appendix I shows that, under the standard normal curve, the value of z to the left of which lies 0.01 of the area is -2.33. We can use the relationship

$$z = \frac{X - \overline{X}'}{\sigma'}$$

to determine the needed value of $\overline{X}'$. When we substitute known quantities into this expression, we have

$$-2.33 = \frac{87 - \overline{X}'}{5.48}$$

which yields $\overline{X}' = 99.7684$. We designate this our *acceptable* quality and call it $\overline{X}'_2$. Let us now find a *rejectable* value of $\overline{X}'$, which we shall call $\overline{X}'_1$. We begin by specifying some proportion of X values for which, if this proportion lies below 87 in a given lot, we would want to be sure of rejecting the lot. Assume that we would want to reject lots with 5% defective items. The desired proportion is 0.05. We now find the rejectable $(\overline{X}_1')$ value by noting that Table C indicates that the z value to the left of which 0.05 of the area under the standard normal curve lies is -1.645. This leads to

$$-1.645 = \frac{87 - \overline{X}_1'}{5.48}$$

and $\overline{X}_1' = 96.0146$, the rejectable value of $\overline{X}'$. We must now answer two questions: (1) what risk do we wish to run of accepting a lot with a mean tensile strength of 96.0146, if a lot of this quality should be offered; and (2) what risk do we want to take of rejecting a lot with a mean tensile strength of 99.7684?

The risk of rejecting a lot of acceptable quality is designated α. The risk of accepting a lot of rejectable quality is designated β. For the present example, α is specified as 0.01, and β as 0.10. We want a plan that meets these requirements and, at the same time, tells us how large a sample to take and the minimum sample mean $\overline{X}$ for which we will accept a lot. This minimum value of the sample mean is called K. Suppose that the sample comes from a population with a mean $\overline{X}'$ of 96.0146 and $\sigma' = 5.48$. We know that the sampling distribution of the means from all possible samples is normal, with a mean of 96.0146 and a standard deviation equal to

$$\frac{\sigma'}{\sqrt{n}} = \frac{5.48}{\sqrt{n}}$$

Similarly, suppose that the sample comes from a population with a mean of 99.7684 and a standard deviation of 5.48. We know that the sampling distribution of means computed from samples from this population is normal, with a mean of 99.7684 and a standard deviation of $5.48/\sqrt{n}$. Figure 17.5.1 shows these two distributions, as well as α and β.

FIGURE 17.5.1   Sampling distributions of $\overline{x}$ from populations of acceptable and rejectable quality with corresponding risks, tensile strength of wire

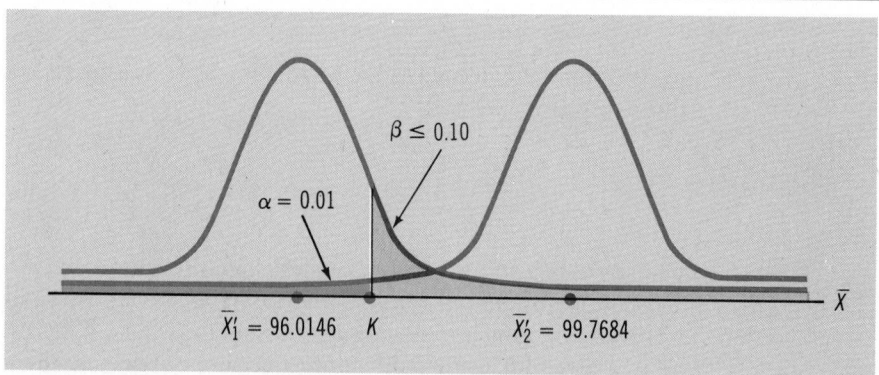

Considering, in turn, each of the two sampling distributions shown in Figure 17.5.1, we can make the following observations. We can convert the sampling distribution on the left to the standard normal distribution using the relationship

(17.5.1)

$$z = \frac{K - \overline{X}_1}{\sigma'/\sqrt{n}}$$

Table C shows that the value of z to the right of which 0.10 of the area under the standard normal curve lies is $+1.28$. Substituting this and other known quantities into Equation 17.5.1 yields

$$1.28 = \frac{K - 96.0146}{5.48/\sqrt{n}}$$

If we proceed in the same manner with the sampling distribution shown on the right, we find that the appropriate z value is -2.33. This leads to

$$-2.33 = \frac{K - 99.7684}{5.48/\sqrt{n}}$$

Solving these two equations simultaneously for n gives $n = 27.77$.

To find K, we can either substitute 27.77 into the first equation, which was derived from the distribution with which we associated β, or substitute it into the equation arising from the distribution with which we associated α. Both are illustrated here. Of course, in actual practice, we would select one or the other only. Substituting into the first equation, we have

$$1.28 = \frac{K - 96.0146}{5.48/\sqrt{27.77}}$$
$$1.3311 = K - 96.0146, \qquad K = 97.3457$$

Substituting into the second equation, we have

$$-2.33 = \frac{K - 99.7684}{5.48/\sqrt{27.77}}$$
$$-2.4230 = K - 99.7684, \qquad K = 97.3454 \text{ (note rounding error)}$$

We always round up the actual sample size used, in this case to 28. In solving for K, we always use the calculated sample size, not the rounded value, to obtain the correct K value. The sampling plan now reads as follows: "Select 28 specimens at random and test each for tensile strength. If the mean tensile strength is greater than or equal to 97.3457, accept the lot. If the mean tensile strength is less than 97.3457, reject the lot."

The procedure for obtaining a sampling plan when we are interested in protection against too large a lot mean is, as we have noted, analogous to this procedure. We can outline it briefly as follows.

1. Determine the specification value.

2. Choose an acceptable value for a lot mean; call it $\overline{X}'_1$. The same considerations as were previously noted should go into its selection.

3. Choose a rejectable value for a lot mean; call it $\overline{X}'_2$. Note that the notation is reversed from what it was when we were interested in protection against a too-small mean. Whereas $\overline{X}'_1$ previously referred to rejectable quality and $\overline{X}'_2$ referred to acceptable quality, $\overline{X}'_1$ now refers to acceptable quality and $\overline{X}'_2$ to rejectable quality. The purpose of this notation is to retain the relationship $\overline{X}'_2 > \overline{X}'_1$.

4. Choose values for α, the risk of rejecting lots of acceptable quality, and β, the risk of accepting lots of rejectable quality.

5. Solve for n and K as before.

6. The plan specifies n, and indicates acceptance of the lot if $\overline{X} \leq K$ and rejection if $\overline{X} > K$. (For an example of determining this type of plan, see Exercise 17.5.2.)

In some situations, we want to reject lots with either too large a mean or too small a mean. In other words, there may be both an upper and a lower specification. For a discussion of plans of this type, which are called *double-specification plans*, see Suggestions for Further Reading at the end of this chapter.

The value of n initially specified by a sampling plan may be larger than desired from a practical or economical point of view. If this occurs, we must increase either α or β or both. Alternatively, we must increase the distance between acceptable and rejectable means in the single-specification case, or we must increase the distance between the two rejectable means in double-specification plans.

UNKNOWN SIGMA PLANS

We may not always know the lot standard deviation, as we did in the situations just discussed. When the standard deviation is unknown, we proceed in essentially the same manner as for a known sigma plan, except that we use some sample estimate in place of σ'. A larger sample size is the price we pay for using an estimate of σ'.

STANDARD VARIABLES SAMPLING PLANS

A number of standard sampling plans for variables sampling are available in published form. You may select from among these plans the particular one that best fits your needs and situation. Among the available published plans are those contained in *Military Standard* 414 (MIL-STD-414), published by the United States Department of Defense.

MIL-STD-414 has four sections. Section A gives a general description of the plans. Section B contains variables plans based on the sample standard deviation for the case in which σ' is unknown. Section C contains plans based on the sample range. Section D gives plans based on the sample mean for the case in which σ' is known. The use of MIL-STD-414 lets us (1) calculate a maximum allowable percentage of defective items in a given lot and (2) estimate the percentage of defective items in the presented lot. If the latter exceeds the former, we reject the lot; otherwise we accept it.

The use of MIL-STD-414 is illustrated by the following example, in which there is a double-specification limit, the variability is unknown, and the sample standard deviation is used as the basis for determining the sample plan. There are five inspection levels available. For this example, we use level IV, normal inspection.

EXAMPLE 17.5.2   The specifications on the diameter of a certain type of wire cable call for an upper limit of 0.363 and a lower limit of 0.357, with a nominal diameter of 0.360. The AQL is 2% for both upper and lower specification limits combined. We want a sampling plan for incoming lots of size 800. As already indicated, we assume that the variability is unknown, that we wish to use the normal (IV) inspection level, and that we wish to use a plan that utilizes the standard-deviation method rather than the range method.

SOLUTION   The first step is to consult Table A-1 of MIL-STD-414 (see Table 17.5.1) to see what AQL value to use. We have specified an AQL value of 2.

TABLE 17.5.1   AQL conversion table, Table A-1 of MIL-STD-414

For Specified AQL Values Falling Within these Ranges		Use this AQL Value
——	to 0.049	0.04
0.050	to 0.069	0.065
0.070	to 0.109	0.10
0.110	to 0.164	0.15
0.165	to 0.279	0.25
0.280	to 0.439	0.40
0.440	to 0.699	0.65
0.700	to 1.09	1.0
1.10	to 1.64	1.5
1.65	to 2.79	2.5
2.80	to 4.39	4.0
4.40	to 6.99	6.5
7.00	to 10.9	10.0
11.00	to 16.4	15.0

Source: MIL-STD-414, 11 June 1957.

TABLE 17.5.2 Sample size code letters,[1] Table A-2 of MIL-STD-414

Lot Size		Inspection Levels				
		I	II	III	IV	V
3 to	8	B	B	B	B	C
9 to	15	B	B	B	B	D
16 to	25	B	B	B	C	E
26 to	40	B	B	B	D	F
41 to	65	B	B	C	E	G
66 to	110	B	B	D	F	H
111 to	180	B	C	E	G	I
181 to	300	B	D	F	H	J
301 to	500	C	E	G	I	K
501 to	800	D	F	H	J	L
801 to	1,300	E	G	I	K	L
1,301 to	3,200	F	H	J	L	M
3,201 to	8,000	G	I	L	M	N
8,001 to	22,000	H	J	M	N	O
22,001 to	110,000	I	K	N	O	P
110,001 to	550,000	I	K	O	P	Q
550,001 and over		I	K	P	Q	Q

[1]Sample size code letters given in body of table are applicable when the indicated inspection levels are to be used.

Source: MIL-STD-414, 11 June 1957.

Since this falls between 1.65 and 2.79, it should be replaced (according to Table A-1) by 2.5 for future use in obtaining the sampling plan.

We next consult Table A-2 of MIL-STD-414 (see Table 17.5.2) to determine the code letter for our sample size. The table indicates that, when lots of size 800 are presented and inspection level IV is used, the sample size code letter is J.

We now consult Table B-3 of MIL-STD-414 (see Table 17.5.3). It shows that for code letter J and an AQL of 2.5 the sample size is 30, and the value of M, the maximum allowable percentage of defective items, is 5.86%.

We now know that we must take from each lot a sample of size 30, compute an estimate of the percentage of defective items in the lot, and compare this value with 5.86. If the estimate of the percentage of defective items in the lot is less than or equal to 5.86, we accept the lot. Otherwise we reject it.

Suppose that a lot is presented and a sample of size 30 yields the diameter measurements in Table 17.5.4. From the sample data of Table 17.5.4, we compute $\bar{x} = 0.362$ and $s = 0.0006$. Next, we calculate the upper and lower *quality indices* Q_U and Q_L as follows:

(17.5.2)
$$Q_U = \frac{U - \overline{X}}{s}$$

and

TABLE 17.5.3   Master table for normal and tightened inspection for plans based on variability unknown (double-specification limit and form 2—single-specification limit), standard-deviation method, Table B-3 of MIL-STD-414

Sample Size Code Letter	Sample Size	.04	.065	.10	.15	.25	.40	.65	1.00	1.50	2.50	4.00	6.50	10.00	15.00
		M	**M**	**M**	**M**	**M**	**M**	**M**	**M**	**M**	**M**	**M**	**M**	**M**	**M**
B	3	↓	↓	↓	↓	↓	↓	↓	↓	↓	7.59	18.86	26.94	33.69	40.47
C	4							↓	1.53	5.50	10.92	16.45	22.86	29.45	36.90
D	5	↓	↓	↓	↓	↓	↓	1.33	3.32	5.83	9.80	14.39	20.19	26.56	33.99
E	7					0.422	1.06	2.14	3.55	5.35	8.40	12.20	17.35	23.29	30.50
F	10	↓	↓	↓	0.349	0.716	1.30	2.17	3.26	4.77	7.29	10.54	15.17	20.74	27.57
G	15	0.099	0.186	0.312	0.503	0.818	1.31	2.11	3.05	4.31	6.56	9.46	13.71	18.94	25.61
H	20	0.135	0.228	0.365	0.544	0.846	1.29	2.05	2.95	4.09	6.17	8.92	12.99	18.03	24.53
I	25	0.155	0.250	0.380	0.551	0.877	1.29	2.00	2.86	3.97	5.97	8.63	12.57	17.51	23.97
J	30	0.179	0.280	0.413	0.581	0.879	1.29	1.98	2.83	3.91	5.86	8.47	12.36	17.24	23.58
K	35	0.170	0.264	0.388	0.535	0.847	1.23	1.87	2.68	3.70	5.57	8.10	11.87	16.65	22.91
L	40	0.179	0.275	0.401	0.566	0.873	1.26	1.88	2.71	3.72	5.58	8.09	11.85	16.61	22.86
M	50	0.163	0.250	0.363	0.503	0.789	1.17	1.71	2.49	3.45	5.20	7.61	11.23	15.87	22.00
N	75	0.147	0.228	0.330	0.467	0.720	1.07	1.60	2.29	3.20	4.87	7.15	10.63	15.13	21.11
O	100	0.145	0.220	0.317	0.447	0.689	1.02	1.53	2.20	3.07	4.69	6.91	10.32	14.75	20.66
P	150	0.134	0.203	0.293	0.413	0.638	0.949	1.43	2.05	2.89	4.43	6.57	9.88	14.20	20.02
Q	200	0.135	0.204	0.294	0.414	0.637	0.945	1.42	2.04	2.87	4.40	6.53	9.81	14.12	19.92
		.065	.10	.15	.25	.40	.65	1.00	1.50	2.50	4.00	6.50	10.00	15.00	

Acceptable quality levels (tightened inspection)

All AQL and table values are in percent defective.

↓ Use first sampling plan below arrow, that is, sample size as well as M value. When sample size equals or exceeds lot size, every item in the lot must be inspected.

Source: MIL-STD-414, 11 June 1957.

TABLE 17.5.4   Diameter measurements obtained in sample of size 30, Example 17.5.2

0.362	0.362	0.362	0.362	0.361	0.363
0.363	0.361	0.362	0.362	0.362	0.361
0.363	0.363	0.363	0.362	0.362	0.362
0.362	0.361	0.362	0.362	0.362	0.361
0.362	0.362	0.362	0.361	0.362	0.362

(17.5.3)
$$Q_L = \frac{\overline{X} - L}{s}$$

Here U = the upper specification limit and L = the lower specification limit. For the present example, we have

$$Q_U = \frac{0.363 - 0.362}{0.0006} = 1.67, \qquad Q_L = \frac{0.362 - 0.357}{0.0006} = 8.33$$

The next step is to enter Table B-5 of MIL-STD-414 (see Table 17.5.5) with these values to find the estimated percentage of defective items in the lot for Q_U and Q_L. For Q_U, we find the estimated percentage of defective items in the lot

TABLE 17.5.5 Table for estimating the lot percentage defective using standard-deviation method[1]

Q_U or Q_L	Sample Size 10	Sample Size 20	Sample Size 30	Q_U or Q_L	Sample Size 10	Sample Size 20	Sample Size 30
0	50.00	50.00	50.00	2.20	0.437	0.968	1.120
0.1	46.16	46.08	46.05	2.23	0.366	0.875	1.023
0.2	42.35	42.19	42.15	2.25	0.324	0.816	0.962
0.3	38.60	38.37	38.31	2.30	0.233	0.685	0.823
0.40	34.93	34.65	34.58	2.40	0.109	0.473	0.594
0.50	31.37	31.06	30.98	2.50	0.041	0.317	0.421
0.60	27.94	27.63	27.55	2.60	0.011	0.207	0.293
0.70	24.67	24.38	24.31	2.70	0.001	0.130	0.200
0.80	21.57	21.33	21.27	2.80	0.000	0.079	0.133
0.90	18.67	18.50	18.46	2.90	0.000	0.046	0.087
1.00	15.97	15.89	15.88	3.00	0.000	0.025	0.055
1.10	13.50	13.52	13.53	3.10	0.000	0.013	0.034
1.20	11.24	11.38	11.42	3.20	0.000	0.006	0.020
1.30	9.22	9.48	9.55	3.30	0.000	0.003	0.012
1.40	7.44	7.80	7.90	3.40	0.000	0.001	0.007
1.50	5.87	6.34	6.46	3.50	0.000	0.000	0.003
1.60	4.54	5.09	5.23	3.60	0.000	0.000	0.002
1.67	3.73	4.32	4.48	3.70	0.000	0.000	0.001
1.70	3.41	4.02	4.18	3.80	0.000	0.000	0.000
1.80	2.49	3.13	3.30	3.90	0.000	0.000	0.000
1.85	2.09	2.75	2.92				
1.90	1.75	2.40	2.57				
1.95	1.44	2.09	2.26				
2.00	1.17	1.81	1.98				
2.10	0.74	1.34	1.50				

[1]Values tabulated are read in percent.

Source: Abridged from Table B-5 of MIL-STD-414, 11 June 1957.

FIGURE 17.5.2   Operating characteristic curves for sampling plans based on standard-deviation method, Table A-3 of MIL-STD-414

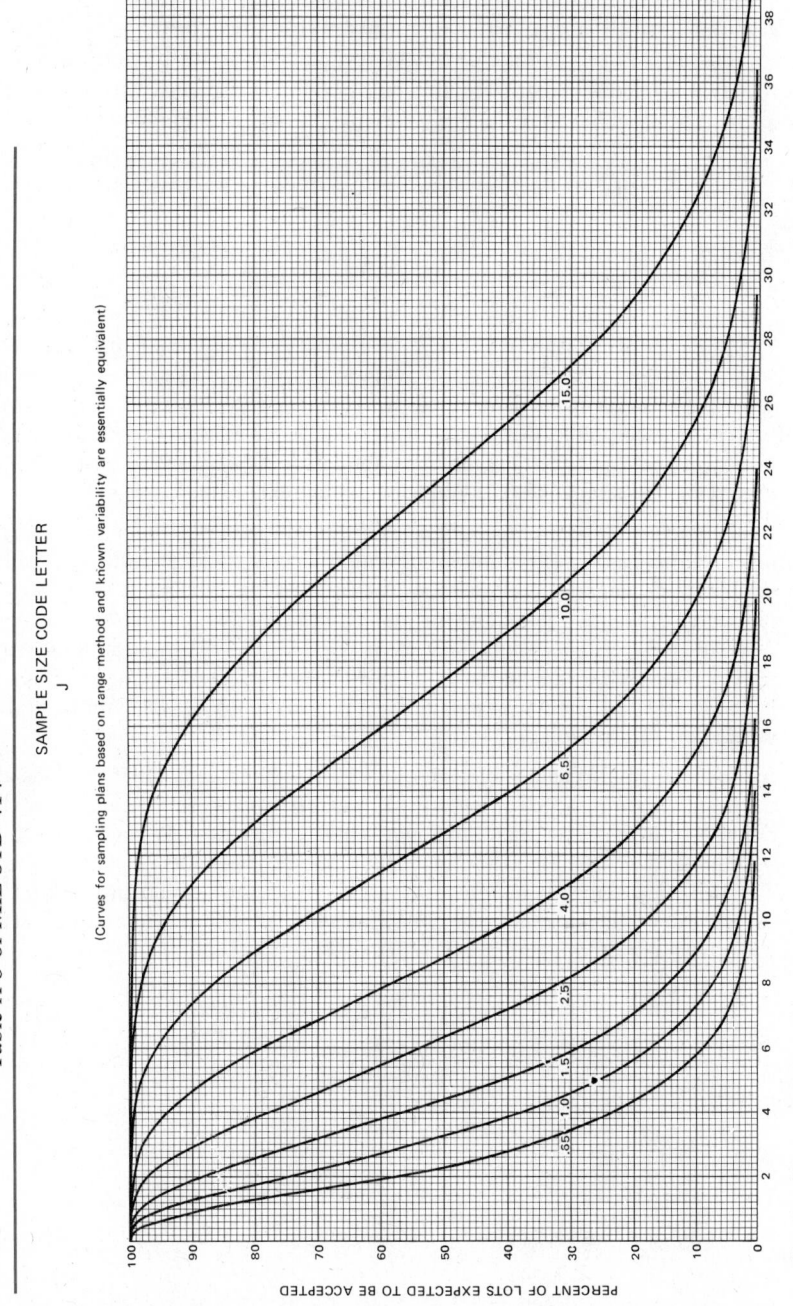

SAMPLE SIZE CODE LETTER
J

(Curves for sampling plans based on range method and known variability are essentially equivalent)

PERCENT OF LOTS EXPECTED TO BE ACCEPTED

QUALITY OF SUBMITTED LOTS (In percent defective)

Note: Figures on curves are Acceptable Quality Levels for normal inspection.

The values of the percent of lots expected to be accepted are valid only when measurements are selected at random from a normal distribution.

Source: MIL-STD-414, *Sampling Procedures and Tables for Inspection by Attributes,* Department of Defense, 11 June 1957.

above U by locating the intersection of the row for 1.67 and the column for sample size 30. The value we seek is 4.48%. In like manner, we find that the estimated percentage of defective items in the lot below L is 0. We now find the total estimated percentage of defective items in the lot by adding 4.48% and 0% to get 4.48%. We compare this with 5.86%, the previously found maximum allowable percentage of defective items in the lot. Since $4.48 < 5.86$, we accept the lot.

Table A-3 of MIL-STD-414 gives the OC curve for our plan (see Figure 17.5.2).

EXERCISES

17.5.1   The amounts of pressure required to rupture a certain type of fuel tank, in pounds per square inch, are normally distributed. Given past data, we accept a value of $\sigma'^2 = 9,200$ as the population variance. Any tank that ruptures when subjected to 2,500 psi of pressure or less is unacceptable. We would like 1% or fewer unacceptable tanks in accepted lots. If more than 5% of the tanks in a lot are defective, we want to reject the lot. Using the procedure of Example 17.5.1, find a single sampling plan. Let $\alpha = 0.01$, $\beta = 0.10$.

17.5.2   A manufacturer of frozen meat pies requires that the ingredients have a moisture content not exceeding 20%. The standard deviation among packages is known to be 0.05; 1% or less of packages per lot with a moisture content greater than 20% is acceptable. However, if lots in which 2.5% or more packages have a moisture content in excess of 20% are presented, we want them to be rejected. Use the procedure of Example 17.5.1 to find a suitable sampling plan. Let $\alpha = 0.025$ and $\beta = 0.05$. What assumptions are necessary? Do they seem reasonable? If the preliminary sample size is intolerable, what would you suggest doing?

17.5.3   A certain length of metal chain is considered to be unacceptable if readings above 381 or below 327.5 are recorded when it is subjected to a stress test. Readings are known to be normally distributed with an unknown standard deviation. Assume an AQL of 1.5% for both upper and lower specification limits combined, and lots of size 600. Use MIL-STD-414 to find a single sampling plan that employs the normal inspection level and the standard-deviation method. The following sample measurements are observed. Indicate whether or not the lot should be accepted.

364	382	353	370	353	373
359	346	350	366	327	375
366	349	340	372	336	356
356	364	367	342	342	358
345	376	346	355	361	353

17.6   PROCESS CAPABILITY

Once it has been determined through the use of control charts and other techniques that a process is in control, the focus of attention shifts to another area of concern—*process capability*.

Process capability refers to the ability of a process to produce a product that conforms to specification limits.

Process capability studies are widely used as tools for understanding the capability and variability of the processes that are the object of quality-control programs.

Three basic techniques are used in process capability studies: (1) histograms, (2) control charts, and (3) designed experiments. We shall discuss the first two. The reader interested in learning about the use of designed experiments in process capability studies may consult the references in Suggestions for Further Reading, such as the book by Montgomery, at the end of the chapter.

HISTOGRAMS

The use of histograms in process capability studies involves the selection of a sample of measurements, the construction of a frequency distribution and histogram, the calculation of the sample mean and standard deviation, and an appropriate analysis of these sample results. Runger (see Suggestions for Further Reading at the end of this chapter) emphasizes that the most critical component of a process capability study is the strategy used in collecting the sample data. Measurements should be taken on items selected at random in such a way that they are representative of the populations of possible sources of variation, such as machines, workstations, relevant operating conditions (temperature, humidity, speeds, and so on), shifts, and operators. Measurements must be taken over a long period of time if long-term variability is to be taken into account. Runger states that the omission of long-term variability in a process capability study is a serious error. We illustrate the use of histograms by means of the following example.

EXAMPLE 17.6.1   Morosgo Manufacturing collected the measurements on the tensile strength (p.s.i.) of 100 plastic containers as shown in Table 17.6.1. The measurements have been coded for ease of calculation. We wish to use a histo-

TABLE 17.6.1   Tensile strength measurements of 100 plastic containers

52.0	92.5	108.0	70.5	76.5	67.0	121.0	80.5	73.5
74.5	103.0	71.0	78.5	110.0	96.5	113.5	81.0	72.0
86.5	84.5	83.5	83.0	99.5	74.5	79.5	87.5	116.5
89.5	74.5	78.0	66.5	82.0	43.0	78.5	67.0	84.0
82.0	76.0	76.5	89.5	57.0	108.5	85.0	96.0	88.0
94.5	91.0	78.5	87.0	75.0	48.0	86.5	65.0	90.0
56.5	89.5	79.5	63.5	99.0	83.0	49.5	72.5	97.5
81.5	67.0	82.0	85.0	100.0	86.5	93.0	88.5	82.0
98.5	54.5	84.0	80.0	79.5	118.0	88.5	86.5	60.0
73.5	65.0	89.5	85.5	82.0	90.0	61.0	103.5	91.0
122.5	70.5	87.5	53.5	81.5	82.0	81.0	59.5	79.5
99.0								

TABLE 17.6.2   Frequency distribution of tensile strength measurements of 100 plastic containers

Class Interval	Frequency
40–49	3
50–59	6
60–69	9
70–79	22
80–89	35
90–99	14
100–109	5
110–119	4
120–129	2
Total	100

gram to reach a conclusion regarding the process capability of the manufacturing process.

SOLUTION   The frequency distribution of the data is shown in Table 17.6.2, and the histogram appears in Figure 17.6.1. The mean tensile strength computed from the 100 measurements is $\bar{x} = 82.36$, and the standard deviation is $s = 15.87$. From these measurements we estimate the process capability to be

$$\bar{x} \pm 3s$$
$$82.36 \pm 3(15.87)$$
$$82.36 \pm 47.61$$

The histogram of the data suggests that the population of measurements is approximately normally distributed. Consequently we estimate that approximately 99.7% of the containers will fall somewhere between $82.36 - 47.61 = 34.75$ p.s.i. and $82.36 + 47.61 = 129.97$ p.s.i. As we have seen, these limits are sometimes called the *natural tolerance limits* for the process.

The histogram is a visual representation of the data that provides the investigator with a clue regarding likely process performance. What one looks for is the location of the histogram in relation to the lower specification limit (LSL) and the upper specification limit (USL). A histogram constructed from data generated by a capable process is expected to be centered between LSL and USL and have as its smallest value one that is well above LSL and as its largest value one that is well below USL. Figure 17.6.2 shows three possible histograms that sample data from a process capability study may yield.

THE PROCESS CAPABILITY INDEX C_p

Useful as the histogram may be, objective measures of process capability are usually desired. One such measure is the *process capability index*, designated C_p.

FIGURE 17.6.1   Histogram of tensile strength measurements of 100 specimens of electrical wire

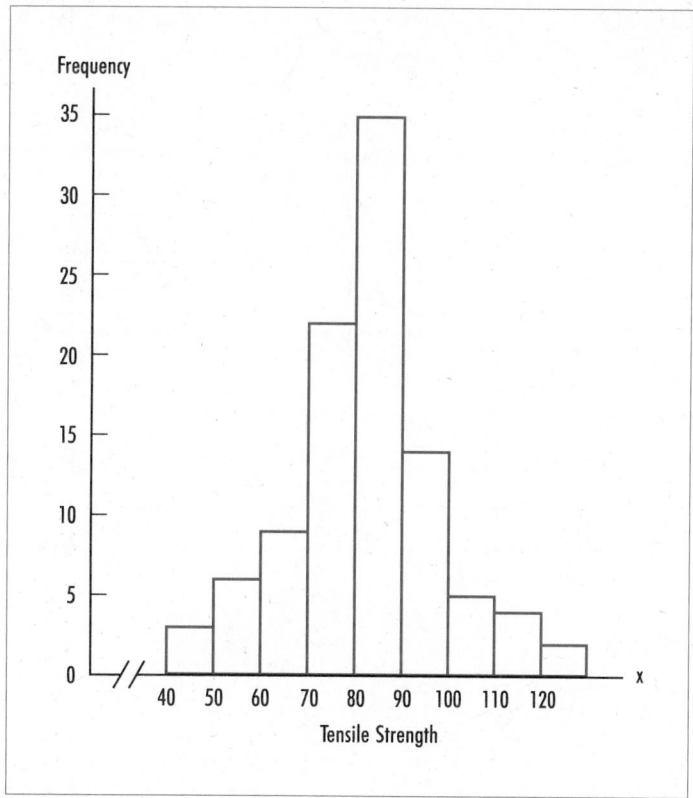

Sometimes called the *process capability ratio,* the index is computed by the following formula:

(17.6.1)
$$C_p = (USL - LSL)/6s$$

A C_p value less than 1 indicates that the process is not capable of meeting its specifications. A value of 1 indicates that the process is just barely capable. A C_p value greater than 1 is more desirable since such a value indicates that the process is more likely to produce a product whose measurements are consistently within the specification limits.

The process capability index serves several purposes. It can be used to establish specification limits, to evaluate processes in relationship to the required specification limits, and to help set requirements on processes. For example, a manufacturer may require as part of its purchase agreements with vendors of raw materials and parts that the C_p value be of a specified size. A requirement that is frequently specified by manufacturers is $C_p \geq 1.33$.

FIGURE 17.6.2 Three possible histograms that may result from the data obtained as part of a process capability study: (a) Suggests that the process is capable (b) Suggests that the process is not capable because the data are poorly located (c) Suggests that the process is not capable because the data exhibit excessive variability

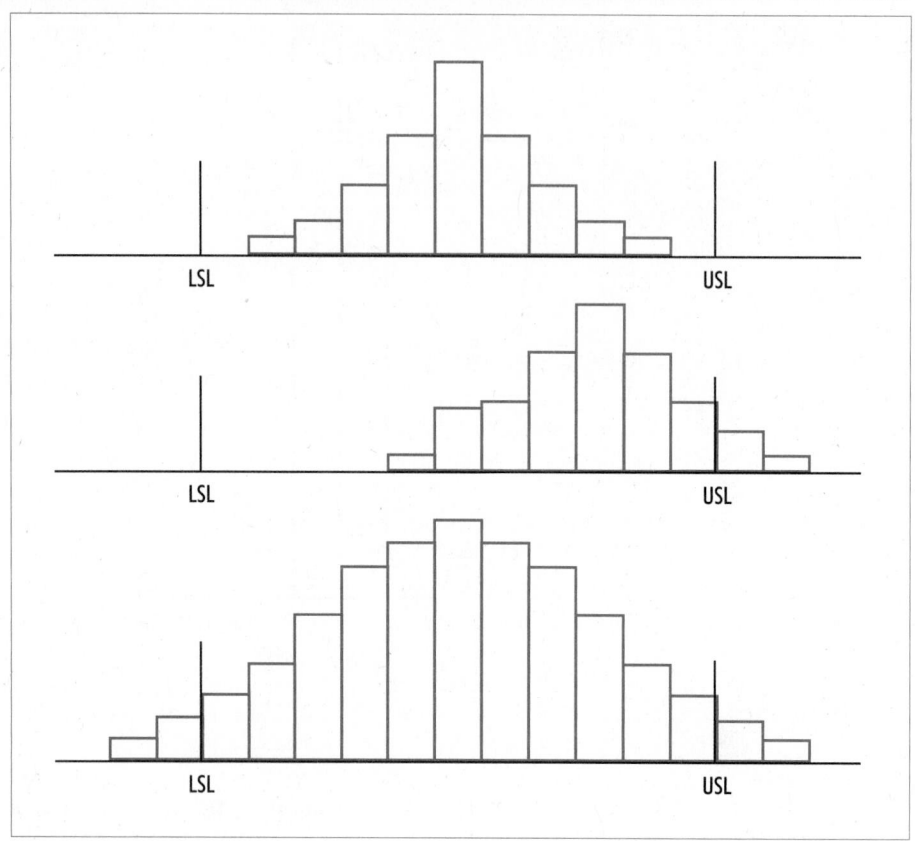

ONE-SIDED SPECIFICATIONS

Equation 17.6.1 is for use when both upper and lower specification limits are critical. In some cases only one limit is of interest. For example, for some raw material we might not care how strong it is as long as it meets some minimum strength specification. In that case LSL is of concern, but USL is of no interest. A USL, but not an LSL, may be critical to the characteristic of some raw material used in the manufacture of a plastic product. The raw material might be capable of achieving a degree of toughness that makes it incapable of being processed. In such a case the manufacturer would want to guard against purchasing raw materials that exceeded the maximum desirable degree of toughness. The process capability indexes for such one-sided specifications are

(17.6.2)
$$UC_p = (\text{USL} - \bar{x})/3s$$

for upper specifications, and

(17.6.3)
$$LC_p = (\bar{x} - \text{LSL})/3s$$

for lower specifications.

A generally recommended C_p value for one-sided specifications is 1.25.

EXAMPLE 17.6.2 Suppose, for our example, that the lower specification limit on container strength is 20. We wish to compute the process capability index.

SOLUTION By Equation 17.6.3 we compute the process capability index to be

$$LC_p = (82.36 - 20)/3(15.87) = 1.31$$

We see that this value is above the recommended value of 1.25. We conclude that the process is capable of meeting specifications.

Under the assumption that strength measurements are approximately normally distributed, we may use our sample results to estimate the proportion of containers that we can expect to fail to meet specifications. We compute $z = (20 - 82.36)/15.87 = -3.93$. In Table C we find that the area to the left of -3.93 is 0.0000. That is, we estimate that for every 10,000 containers manufactured, the process will produce less than 1 container that does not meet specifications.

CONTROL CHARTS

Process capability studies should be undertaken only when the process of interest is in a state of control. As we have seen, the control chart is the device usually used to determine the status of a process relative to whether or not it is out of control. When the control chart indicates that the process is under control, we may use the data by which it was constructed to compute the process capability index, C_p.

EXAMPLE 17.6.3 Let us refer to Example 17.2.1, in which the process of interest is the production of bolts. Suppose the specification limits are -8 and $+8$. We wish to compute C_p for this process.

SOLUTION The control charts for the example shown in Figure 17.2.2 show that $\overline{\overline{x}} = 0.21$ and $\overline{R} = 9.44$. To get an estimate of s we compute $\overline{R}/d_2$ where d_2 is obtained from Table 17.2.1. For our example, in which the individual sample sizes were $n = 4$, we find in Table 17.2.1 that $d_2 = 2.059$. Consequently we estimate s to be $9.44/2.059 = 4.5847$. Since the situation calls for two-sided specifications, we use Equation 17.6.1 to compute

$$C_p = [8 - (-8)]/6(4.5847) = 0.58$$

Since our computed value of 0.58 is less than the recommended value of 1.33, we conclude that the process is not capable of meeting specifications. This is an example of a situation in which the process may be in control but not capable of meeting specifications.

EXERCISES

17.6.1   The manufacturer of a lawn fertilizer wishes to establish a control chart for a machine that delivers a raw ingredient into a mixing chamber. The following are the amounts in pounds of the ingredient delivered on a sample of 110 occasions.

137	131	143	138	136	148	135	136	133	144	131
149	142	133	141	136	150	134	123	134	138	138
132	140	142	142	138	143	133	143	147	131	136
139	144	149	136	142	131	152	136	135	132	133
125	135	134	149	134	123	137	124	136	133	142
138	136	136	127	127	139	129	141	150	135	142
140	140	134	133	136	141	139	137	135	127	140
128	136	126	138	138	139	132	145	135	134	129
131	132	136	124	136	134	149	131	145	139	134
146	136	125	139	138	144	131	132	137	136	150

Construct a histogram of these data and estimate process capability. Assume that a normal distribution provides a satisfactory model for the process.

17.6.2   Refer to Exercise 17.6.1. Compute the process capability index for specification limits of 127 and 147. What are your conclusions regarding the process?

17.6.3   Refer to Exercise 17.6.1. Compute the process capability index for specification limits of 120 and 160. What are your conclusions regarding the process capability relative to these specification limits?

17.6.4   Refer to Exercise 17.6.1. What are the tightest symmetrical specification limits that will yield a value of C_p no smaller than 1.33?

17.6.5   The manufacturer of a drug requires periodic monitoring to control the level of alcohol, which is one of the ingredients. Twenty samples of five bottles each of the drug yielded the following measurements:

Sample Observation	1	2	3	4	5	6	7
1	7.3	6.5	6.6	7.2	7.1	6.6	6.5
2	6.8	7.1	7.3	7.0	6.8	7.3	7.2
3	7.1	7.2	6.8	6.9	7.3	6.9	7.5
4	7.4	7.6	7.0	7.1	7.1	6.5	6.6
5	7.0	7.1	6.4	7.1	6.5	7.0	7.2

Sample Observation	8	9	10	11	12	13	14
1	6.9	6.7	7.1	6.8	7.7	7.3	7.4
2	7.1	7.2	6.8	6.4	7.4	6.8	7.4
3	7.0	6.7	6.7	7.1	7.0	6.8	6.7
4	7.2	7.0	7.1	7.1	6.9	7.2	6.9
5	6.8	7.2	6.7	6.9	6.6	6.5	7.0

Sample Observation	15	16	17	18	19	20
1	6.6	6.6	7.1	7.1	7.3	6.8
2	6.6	6.5	6.9	7.5	7.1	7.2
3	6.5	7.1	6.8	7.1	6.9	7.5
4	6.6	6.8	6.7	7.1	6.8	7.1
5	7.0	6.9	7.0	6.7	7.0	7.3

Construct $\bar{x}$ and R charts from these data. Compute C_p when LSL = 6 and USL = 8. What are your conclusions?

17.6.6 Refer to Exercise 17.6.5. What are the tightest symmetrical specification limits that will yield a C_p value of 1.33 or larger?

SUMMARY

This chapter introduces the subject of quality control as a logical and meaningful area in which to apply the concepts and techniques of statistical inference. We limit treatment of the subject to the concepts of acceptance sampling and control charts, and we cover the use of these techniques for both variables and attributes. We also introduce the concept of the operating characteristic curve and process capability.

In evaluating an organization's quality program, one would do well to consider Richard M. Balano's "10 Commandments of Quality," which he lists and elaborates on in an article in *Quality Progress* as follows:[7]

1. Identify and reduce variation.

2. Experiment to optimize.

---

[7]Richard M. Balano, "The 10 Commandments of Quality," *Quality Progress* (January 1994), 41–42.

3. Establish and maintain data bases.

4. Embrace statistics.

5. Standardize procedures and audit for compliance.

6. Design for manufacturability.

7. Communicate with suppliers.

8. Plan for quality.

9. Teach quality.

10. Document improvements and corrective actions.

REVIEW EXERCISES

1. Define (a) quality, (b) total quality, (c) total quality management, (d) inspection lot, (e) attribute sampling, (f) sampling plan.

2. Explain, by means of an example, each of the following: (a) single sampling plan, (b) double sampling plan, (c) multiple sampling plan.

3. What is MIL-STD-105D?

4. What is an operating characteristic curve? How is it used?

5. What is a variables sampling plan?

6. Explain the difference between known- and unknown-sigma plans.

7. What is MIL-STD-414?

8. What is a control chart?

9. What is meant by the term "assignable cause"?

10. What is an $\bar{x}$ chart?

11. What is an R chart?

12. Why is the range used in constructing control charts for detecting a shift in population dispersion?

13. Briefly outline the steps involved in constructing and using variables control charts.

14. What is a p chart?

15. List the basic facts about the sampling distribution of p.

16. What is process capability?

17. What are the three basic techniques used in process capability studies?

18. How should measurements for a process capability study be collected?

19. What is the formula for computing an estimate of process capability?

20. What is the process capability index?

21. How is the process capability index computed for two-sided specifications? for one-sided specifications when LSL is critical? for one-sided specifications when USL is critical?

22. How is the process capability index used?

23. What is the recommended C_p value for two-sided specifications?

24. What is the recommended C_p value for one-sided specifications?

25. A manufacturer keeps control charts on the weights of 24-ounce packages of a breakfast cereal filled by an automatic packaging machine. The sample size is 5. Values of $\bar{x}$ and R are computed for each sample. After 25 samples, $\Sigma\bar{x} = 602.5$ ounces and $\Sigma R = 17.5$ ounces. Assume that the process is in control. Compute 3-sigma control limits for $\bar{x}$ and R charts.

26. A p chart is to be used to monitor the fraction of defective items in the manufacture of a certain valve. Random samples of size 100 are selected from each day's production and inspected. At the end of 25 days, the following results are obtained. (a) Construct a preliminary control chart for p. (b) Plot the 25 p values on the preliminary control chart. (c) Are any values outside the control limits? What suggestions would you make if the p chart is to be used to monitor the process for the fraction of defective valves?

Day	Number of Defectives	Day	Number of Defectives	Day	Number of Defectives
1	9	10	12	18	6
2	12	11	10	19	14
3	10	12	14	20	17
4	13	13	11	21	11
5	11	14	10	22	9
6	12	15	16	23	25
7	10	16	12	24	12
8	14	17	11	25	10
9	22				

27. In acceptance sampling for attributes, select a single sampling plan, using normal inspection, for each of the following situations: (a) inspection lots of 100 and an AQL of 4.0; (b) inspection lots of 400 and an AQL of 0.25; (c) inspection lots of 5,000 and an AQL of 0.15; (d) inspection lots of 700 and an AQL of 10; (e) inspection lots of 1,500 and an AQL of 0.65.

28. The manager of a soft-drink bottling plant wants to monitor and warrant the average amount of cola put in 16-ounce bottles that are filled in the bottling operation. She plans to select a random sample of the bottles filled each day, measure the volume of cola in each, and compute the mean amount per bottle. If the mean volume for all bottles filled during a day is equal to or greater than 16.04 fluid ounces, she wants to be 95% sure of classifying the day's operation as acceptable. If the mean is less than 16 fluid ounces, she wants to be 99% sure of classifying the day's operation as unacceptable. The standard deviation is 0.14 fluid ounce. Find a suitable sampling plan.

*29. Quality-control managers sometimes find that they are also responsible for the life-testing activities of their organizations. Life testing is motivated by a concern for the longevity of a product, a component part, or raw material. Life-testing experiments are designed to answer questions regarding such item characteristics as their average life, the probability that one of them will fail within some specified interval of time, and how their expected failure experience compares with that of similar items such as a competing product. In 1963 Lloyd S. Nelson introduced the precedence life test, which allows an experimenter to reach a conclusion about the difference between two samples of items subjected at the same time to a life test procedure.[8] Suppose, for example, that a sample of 10 flashlight batteries from a shipment of Brand A batteries and a sample of 10 from a shipment of Brand B batteries are placed on life test at the same time. Suppose 4 of the Brand A batteries failed before any failure occurred among the Brand B batteries. What can we conclude about the average life of Brand A batteries relative to the average life of Brand B batteries? What we wish to do is to test the null hypothesis that the two populations of batteries have equal average lifetimes. Given that the null hypothesis is true, we will reject it if the probability of the occurrence of the phenomenon just described is less than some preselected significance level. The test statistic is given by

$$p = [1/_{n_1 + n_2}C_{n_1}] \sum_{j=x}^{n_i} [(_{x+r-1}C_j)(_{n_1+n_2-r+1-x}C_{n_i-j})]$$

where $i = 1$ if x is the number of failures in the smaller sample n_1 that precede the rth failure in the larger sample n_2, and $i = 2$ otherwise. When, in solving for p, a negative factorial is called for, the summation stops. The resulting value of p is for a one-sided test. For a two-sided test, double p when the sample sizes are equal. Because of this convenience and to maximize power, it is recommended that $n_1 = n_2$. The precedence test is a distribution-free test. Referring again to the flashlight battery problem, we may compute $p = [1/_{20}C_{10}][_4C_4][_{16}C_6] = (0.000005412)(1)(8,008) = 0.043339$. Thus, in this case, we may reject the null hypothesis at the 0.05 level and conclude that Brand B batteries have a longer average life than Brand A batteries. In another paper, Nelson provides a computer program based on the equation given above for p. The program allows the user to analyze the results of any precedence test.[9]

The shelf life of a certain ingredient is of interest to a drug manufacturer. Twelve specimens randomly selected from shipments from each of two competing suppliers are put on life test at the same time. Four specimens from Supplier A failed before the first failure occurred among Supplier B specimens. Can we conclude, on the basis of these data, that Supplier B's product has a longer average shelf life than Supplier A's? Let $\alpha = 0.05$.

[8]Lloyd S. Nelson, "Tables for a Precedence Life Test," *Technometrics,* 5 (November 1963), 491–499.

[9]Lloyd S. Nelson, "Tests on Early Failures—The Precedence Test," *Journal of Quality Technology,* 25 (April 1993), 140–143.

STATISTICS AT WORK

STATISTICS AT WORK

STATISTICS AT

STATISTICS AT

1. CONTROL CHARTS FOR INDIVIDUAL MEASUREMENTS

Control charts for individual measurements are desirable in many situations. A control chart for individual measurements is equivalent to using samples of size 1 for process control. Such charts are appropriate in a factory in which every unit produced is analyzed or in cases where the manufacturing process is so slow that it is not convenient to draw samples larger than 1. Cryer and Ryan suggest that the upper and lower control limits of a three-sigma control chart for individual measurements be obtained by use of the following formula:

$$\bar{x} \pm 3 \left(\frac{s}{c_4} \right)$$

where s is the sample standard deviation and c_4 is a constant that may be obtained from certain statistical tables or approximated (for $n > 25$) from the following formula:

$$c_4 \approx \frac{4(n - 1)}{4n - 3}$$

The center line of the control chart for individual measurements is the sample mean.

Cryer and Ryan use actual data from a chemical process to illustrate the construction of a control chart for individual measurements. The variable is a color property, and they use the following 35 measurements in their computations.

0.67	0.63	0.76	0.66	0.69	0.71	0.72
0.71	0.72	0.72	0.83	0.87	0.76	0.79
0.74	0.81	0.76	0.77	0.68	0.68	0.74
0.68	0.69	0.75	0.80	0.81	0.86	0.86
0.79	0.78	0.77	0.77	0.80	0.76	0.67

We assume that the data come from a process yielding measurements that are independent, and identically and normally distributed. Use these data to construct a control chart for individual measurements. To obtain the authors' results, round the sample mean and c_4 to four decimal places and the sample standard deviation to three decimal places.

Source: Jonathan D. Cryer, and Thomas P. Ryan, "The Estimation of Sigma for an X Chart: $\overline{MR}/d_2$ or S/c_4?" *Journal of Quality Technology*, 22 (July 1990), 187–192. © 1990 American Society for Quality Control. Reprinted by permission. For further information on control charts for individual measurements, see the book by Montgomery listed in Suggestions for Further Reading at the end of this chapter.

2. A CONTROL CHART FOR RATIOS

Andrew W. Spisak, a mathematical statistician with the U.S. Department of Labor in Washington, D.C., discusses the construction of a control chart for the ratio of two variables. He lists the following examples of ratios for which such control charts can be used:

1. The ratio of charges underbilled or overbilled to total billings in a firm's accounts receivable

2. The ratio of employees' time spent correcting errors or reworking faulty products to time devoted to productive work

3. Financial ratios such as savings to disposable income, price to earnings, or debt to equity

To illustrate the construction of a control chart for ratios, Spisak uses data collected through the Labor Department's Unemployment Insurance Quality Control program. The two variables are

$$Y = \text{dollars of unemployment insurance benefits overpaid}$$
$$X = \text{total unemployment insurance benefits paid}$$

The ratio of interest is $R = Y/X$, which is estimated by $\hat{r}$ computed as follows:

$$\hat{r} = \frac{\sum\limits_{h=1}^{H} y_h}{\sum\limits_{h=1}^{H} x_h}$$

where $y_h = \sum\limits_{i=1}^{n_h} y_{hi}$ is the amount of unemployment insurance benefits overpaid in the n_h payments in the sample for week h, and $x_h = \sum\limits_{i=1}^{n_h} x_{hi}$ is the total amount of unemployment insurance benefits paid in the n_h payments.

The variance of $\hat{r}$ is

$$\text{var}(\hat{r}) = \frac{1}{X^2}\left\{ \sum_{h=1}^{H}\left[\frac{N_h^2}{n_h}(n_h - 1) \right] \sum_{i=1}^{n_h}(y_{hi} - \hat{r}x_{hi})^2 \right\}$$

where N_h is the number of unemployment insurance payments in week h, from which the sample was selected, and X is the total amount of benefits paid during the H weeks.

Under certain conditions, a finite population correction factor may be needed in the formula for the variance. The 3-sigma control limits are

$$\text{UCL} = \hat{r} + 3\sqrt{\text{var}(\hat{r})}$$
$$\text{LCL} = \hat{r} + 3\sqrt{\text{var}(\hat{r})}$$

where UCL is the upper control limit and LCL is the lower control limit. Spisak uses the following data to illustrate the construction of his ratio control chart:

Sample	Sample Size	$ Paid (x)	$ Error (y)
1	14	1,863	257
2	14	1,773	116
3	14	1,897	316
4	14	1,824	257
5	14	1,846	552
6	14	1,838	652
7	14	1,944	250
8	14	1,859	683
9	13	1,563	86
10	13	1,529	136
11	13	1,716	222
12	14	1,823	417
Total	165	21,475	3,944

From the data, he computes $\text{var}(\hat{r}) = 0.001024$. Use these data to construct a ratio control chart.

Source: Andrew W. Spisak, "A Control Chart for Ratios," *Journal of Quality Technology*, 22 (January 1990), 34–37. © 1990 American Society for Quality Control. Reprinted by permission. To learn more about ratio estimates, consult the textbooks on sampling listed at the end of Chapter 15 and the following journal articles:
Hartley, H.O., and A. Ross (1954). "Unbiased Ratio Estimators," *Nature* 174:270–271.
Koop, J. C. (1968). "An Exercise in Ratio Estimation." *The American Statistician* 22:29–30.

3. SIX-SIGMA QUALITY PROGRAMS

In an article in *Quality Progress*, Fred R. McFadden discusses a quality management program called six sigma that was developed and pursued by Motorola, Inc. Read the article and write a report on it in which you cover at least the following points:

(a) What is six sigma?

(b) What is the goal of a six-sigma program?

(c) What are the components of a six-sigma program?

(d) Describe the metrics of a six-sigma program.

(e) Discuss process capability in a six-sigma program.

(f) What are the assumptions of a six-sigma program?

Source: Fred R. McFadden, "Six-Sigma Quality Programs," *Quality Progress*, 26 (June 1993), 37–41.

SUGGESTIONS FOR FURTHER READING

Alloway, James A., Jr. (1994). "Laying the Groundwork for Total Quality," *Quality Progress* (January), 65–66.

Banks, Jerry (1989). *Principles of Quality Control.* Wiley, New York.

Broh, Robert A. (1982). *Managing Quality for Higher Profits.* McGraw-Hill, New York.

Caudron, Shari (1993). "Change Keeps TQM Programs Thriving," *Personnel Journal* (October), 104–109.

Friesecke, Raymond F. (1983). "The Quality Revolution: A Challenge to Management," *Managerial Planning* 32:7–9, 26.

Irving, Robert R. (1983). "Is America Turning It Around in Quality?" *Iron Age* (July 22), 40–44.

———— (1983). "Quality in Design, That's Where It All Starts," *Iron Age* (Aug. 1), 35–40.

———— (1983). "Quality Control by the Numbers," *Iron Age* (Aug. 19), 37–44.

———— (1983). "Why Quality Has to Be Measured," *Iron Age* (Sept. 5), 58–63.

———— (1983). "NDT: Quality's Ace in the Hole," *Iron Age* (Sept. 23), 56–59.

Juran, J. M., and Frank M. Gryna, Jr. (1980). *Quality Planning and Analysis,* 2nd ed. McGraw-Hill, New York.

Lester, Ronald H., Norbert L. Enrick, and Harry E. Mottley, Jr. (1977). *Quality Control for Profit.* Industrial Press, New York.

Marquardt, Donald W. (1984). "New Technical and Educational Directions for Managing Product Quality," *The American Statistician* 38:8–14.

Merron, Keith A. (1994). "Creating TQM Organizations," *Quality Progress* (January), 51–54.

Montgomery, Douglas C. (1991). *Introduction to Statistical Quality Control,* 2nd ed. Wiley, New York.

Ott, Ellis R. (1975). *Process Quality Control.* McGraw-Hill, New York.

Runger, George C. (1993). "Designing Process Capability Studies," *Quality Progress* 26 (July), 31–32.

Schilling, Edward G. (1982). *Acceptance Sampling in Quality Control.* Marcel Dekker, New York.

Soin, Sarv Singh (1992). *Total Quality Control Essentials.* McGraw-Hill, New York.

Townsend, Patrick L. and Joan E. Gebhardt (1992). *Quality in Action: 93 Lessons in Leadership, Participation, and Measurement.* Wiley, New York.

Walton, M. (1986). *The Deming Management Method.* Dodd, Mead, & Company, New York.

Wheeler, D. J. and D. S. Chambers (1986). *Understanding Statistical Process Control,* Statistical Process Controls, Inc., Knoxville, Tennessee.

Appendix I

TABLES

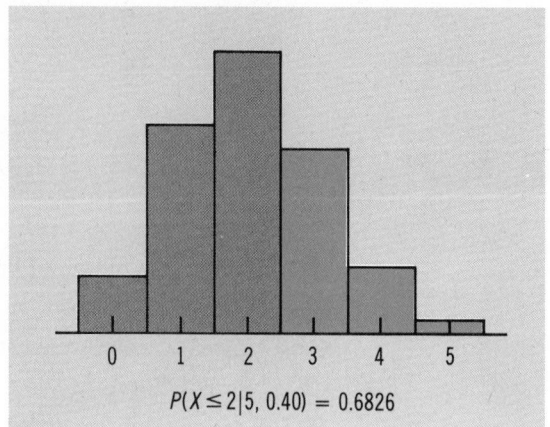

$$P(X \le x | n, p) = \sum_{x=0}^{x} {_nC_x}\, p^x q^{n-x}$$

$P(X \le 2 | 5, 0.40) = 0.6826$

TABLE A   Cumulative binomial probability distribution

$n = 5$

x \ p	0.01	0.02	0.03	0.04	0.05	0.06	0.07	0.08	0.09	0.10
0	0.9510	0.9039	0.8587	0.8154	0.7738	0.7339	0.6957	0.6591	0.6240	0.5905
1	0.9990	0.9962	0.9915	0.9852	0.9774	0.9681	0.9575	0.9456	0.9326	0.9185
2	1.0000	0.9999	0.9997	0.9994	0.9988	0.9980	0.9969	0.9955	0.9937	0.9914
3	1.0000	1.0000	1.0000	1.0000	1.0000	0.9999	0.9999	0.9998	0.9997	0.9995
4	1.0000	1.0000	1.0000	1.0000	1.0000	1.0000	1.0000	1.0000	1.0000	1.0000

x \ p	0.11	0.12	0.13	0.14	0.15	0.16	0.17	0.18	0.19	0.20
0	0.5584	0.5277	0.4984	0.4704	0.4437	0.4182	0.3939	0.3707	0.3487	0.3277
1	0.9035	0.8875	0.8708	0.8533	0.8352	0.8165	0.7973	0.7776	0.7576	0.7373
2	0.9888	0.9857	0.9821	0.9780	0.9734	0.9682	0.9625	0.9563	0.9495	0.9421
3	0.9993	0.9991	0.9987	0.9983	0.9978	0.9971	0.9964	0.9955	0.9945	0.9933
4	1.0000	1.0000	1.0000	0.9999	0.9999	0.9999	0.9999	0.9998	0.9998	0.9997
5	1.0000	1.0000	1.0000	1.0000	1.0000	1.0000	1.0000	1.0000	1.0000	1.0000

x \ p	0.21	0.22	0.23	0.24	0.25	0.26	0.27	0.28	0.29	0.30
0	0.3077	0.2887	0.2707	0.2536	0.2373	0.2219	0.2073	0.1935	0.1804	0.1681
1	0.7167	0.6959	0.6749	0.6539	0.6328	0.6117	0.5907	0.5697	0.5489	0.5282
2	0.9341	0.9256	0.9164	0.9067	0.8965	0.8857	0.8743	0.8624	0.8499	0.8369
3	0.9919	0.9903	0.9886	0.9866	0.9844	0.9819	0.9792	0.9762	0.9728	0.9692
4	0.9996	0.9995	0.9994	0.9992	0.9990	0.9988	0.9986	0.9983	0.9979	0.9976
5	1.0000	1.0000	1.0000	1.0000	1.0000	1.0000	1.0000	1.0000	1.0000	1.0000

TABLE A   (*continued*)

n = 5 (continued)

x \ p	0.31	0.32	0.33	0.34	0.35	0.36	0.37	0.38	0.39	0.40
0	0.1564	0.1454	0.1350	0.1252	0.1160	0.1074	0.0992	0.0916	0.0845	0.0778
1	0.5077	0.4875	0.4675	0.4478	0.4284	0.4094	0.3907	0.3724	0.3545	0.3370
2	0.8234	0.8095	0.7950	0.7801	0.7648	0.7491	0.7330	0.7165	0.6997	0.6826
3	0.9653	0.9610	0.9564	0.9514	0.9460	0.9402	0.9340	0.9274	0.9204	0.9130
4	0.9971	0.9966	0.9961	0.9955	0.9947	0.9940	0.9931	0.9921	0.9910	0.9898
5	1.0000	1.0000	1.0000	1.0000	1.0000	1.0000	1.0000	1.0000	1.0000	1.0000

x \ p	0.41	0.42	0.43	0.44	0.45	0.46	0.47	0.48	0.49	0.50
0	0.0715	0.0656	0.0602	0.0551	0.0503	0.0459	0.0418	0.0380	0.0345	0.0312
1	0.3199	0.3033	0.2871	0.2714	0.2562	0.2415	0.2272	0.2135	0.2002	0.1875
2	0.6651	0.6475	0.6295	0.6114	0.5931	0.5747	0.5561	0.5375	0.5187	0.5000
3	0.9051	0.8967	0.8879	0.8786	0.8688	0.8585	0.8478	0.8365	0.8247	0.8125
4	0.9884	0.9869	0.9853	0.9835	0.9815	0.9794	0.9771	0.9745	0.9718	0.9688
5	1.0000	1.0000	1.0000	1.0000	1.0000	1.0000	1.0000	1.0000	1.0000	1.0000

n = 6

x \ p	0.01	0.02	0.03	0.04	0.05	0.06	0.07	0.08	0.09	0.10
0	0.9415	0.8858	0.8330	0.7828	0.7351	0.6899	0.6470	0.6064	0.5679	0.5314
1	0.9985	0.9943	0.9875	0.9784	0.9672	0.9541	0.9392	0.9227	0.9048	0.8857
2	1.0000	0.9998	0.9995	0.9988	0.9978	0.9962	0.9942	0.9915	0.9882	0.9841
3	1.0000	1.0000	1.0000	1.0000	0.9999	0.9998	0.9997	0.9995	0.9992	0.9987
4	1.0000	1.0000	1.0000	1.0000	1.0000	1.0000	1.0000	1.0000	1.0000	0.9999
5	1.0000	1.0000	1.0000	1.0000	1.0000	1.0000	1.0000	1.0000	1.0000	1.0000

x \ p	0.11	0.12	0.13	0.14	0.15	0.16	0.17	0.18	0.19	0.20
0	0.4970	0.4644	0.4336	0.4046	0.3771	0.3513	0.3269	0.3040	0.2824	0.2621
1	0.8655	0.8444	0.8224	0.7997	0.7765	0.7528	0.7287	0.7044	0.6799	0.6554
2	0.9794	0.9739	0.9676	0.9605	0.9527	0.9440	0.9345	0.9241	0.9130	0.9011
3	0.9982	0.9975	0.9966	0.9955	0.9941	0.9925	0.9906	0.9884	0.9859	0.9830
4	0.9999	0.9999	0.9998	0.9997	0.9996	0.9995	0.9993	0.9990	0.9987	0.9984
5	1.0000	1.0000	1.0000	1.0000	1.0000	1.0000	1.0000	1.0000	1.0000	0.9999
6	1.0000	1.0000	1.0000	1.0000	1.0000	1.0000	1.0000	1.0000	1.0000	1.0000

x \ p	0.21	0.22	0.23	0.24	0.25	0.26	0.27	0.28	0.29	0.30
0	0.2431	0.2252	0.2084	0.1927	0.1780	0.1642	0.1513	0.1393	0.1281	0.1176
1	0.6308	0.6063	0.5820	0.5578	0.5339	0.5104	0.4872	0.4644	0.4420	0.4202
2	0.8885	0.8750	0.8609	0.8461	0.8306	0.8144	0.7977	0.7804	0.7626	0.7443
3	0.9798	0.9761	0.9720	0.9674	0.9624	0.9569	0.9508	0.9443	0.9372	0.9295
4	0.9980	0.9975	0.9969	0.9962	0.9954	0.9944	0.9933	0.9921	0.9907	0.9891

TABLE A   (*continued*)

	n = 6 (continued)									
x \ p	**0.21**	**0.22**	**0.23**	**0.24**	**0.25**	**0.26**	**0.27**	**0.28**	**0.29**	**0.30**
5	0.9999	0.9999	0.9999	0.9998	0.9998	0.9997	0.9996	0.9995	0.9994	0.9993
6	1.0000	1.0000	1.0000	1.0000	1.0000	1.0000	1.0000	1.0000	1.0000	1.0000

x \ p	**0.31**	**0.32**	**0.33**	**0.34**	**0.35**	**0.36**	**0.37**	**0.38**	**0.39**	**0.40**
0	0.1079	0.0989	0.0905	0.0827	0.0754	0.0687	0.0625	0.0568	0.0515	0.0467
1	0.3988	0.3780	0.3578	0.3381	0.3191	0.3006	0.2828	0.2657	0.2492	0.2333
2	0.7256	0.7064	0.6870	0.6672	0.6471	0.6268	0.6063	0.5857	0.5650	0.5443
3	0.9213	0.9125	0.9031	0.8931	0.8826	0.8714	0.8596	0.8473	0.8343	0.8208
4	0.9873	0.9852	0.9830	0.9805	0.9777	0.9746	0.9712	0.9675	0.9635	0.9590
5	0.9991	0.9989	0.9987	0.9985	0.9982	0.9978	0.9974	0.9970	0.9965	0.9959
6	1.0000	1.0000	1.0000	1.0000	1.0000	1.0000	1.0000	1.0000	1.0000	1.0000

x \ p	**0.41**	**0.42**	**0.43**	**0.44**	**0.45**	**0.46**	**0.47**	**0.48**	**0.49**	**0.50**
0	0.0422	0.0381	0.0343	0.0308	0.0277	0.0248	0.0222	0.0198	0.0176	0.0156
1	0.2181	0.2035	0.1895	0.1762	0.1636	0.1515	0.1401	0.1293	0.1190	0.1094
2	0.5236	0.5029	0.4823	0.4618	0.4415	0.4214	0.4015	0.3820	0.3627	0.3437
3	0.8067	0.7920	0.7768	0.7610	0.7447	0.7280	0.7107	0.6930	0.6748	0.6562
4	0.9542	0.9490	0.9434	0.9373	0.9308	0.9238	0.9163	0.9083	0.8997	0.8906
5	0.9952	0.9945	0.9937	0.9927	0.9917	0.9905	0.9892	0.9878	0.9862	0.9844
6	1.0000	1.0000	1.0000	1.0000	1.0000	1.0000	1.0000	1.0000	1.0000	1.0000

	n = 7									
x \ p	**0.01**	**0.02**	**0.03**	**0.04**	**0.05**	**0.06**	**0.07**	**0.08**	**0.09**	**0.10**
0	0.9321	0.8681	0.8080	0.7514	0.6983	0.6485	0.6017	0.5578	0.5168	0.4783
1	0.9980	0.9921	0.9829	0.9706	0.9556	0.9382	0.9187	0.8974	0.8745	0.8503
2	1.0000	0.9997	0.9991	0.9980	0.9962	0.9937	0.9903	0.9860	0.9807	0.9743
3	1.0000	1.0000	1.0000	0.9999	0.9998	0.9996	0.9993	0.9988	0.9982	0.9973
4	1.0000	1.0000	1.0000	1.0000	1.0000	1.0000	1.0000	0.9999	0.9999	0.9998
5	1.0000	1.0000	1.0000	1.0000	1.0000	1.0000	1.0000	1.0000	1.0000	1.0000

x \ p	**0.11**	**0.12**	**0.13**	**0.14**	**0.15**	**0.16**	**0.17**	**0.18**	**0.19**	**0.20**
0	0.4423	0.4087	0.3773	0.3479	0.3206	0.2951	0.2714	0.2493	0.2288	0.2097
1	0.8250	0.7988	0.7719	0.7444	0.7166	0.6885	0.6604	0.6323	0.6044	0.5767
2	0.9669	0.9584	0.9487	0.9380	0.9262	0.9134	0.8995	0.8846	0.8687	0.8520
3	0.9961	0.9946	0.9928	0.9906	0.9879	0.9847	0.9811	0.9769	0.9721	0.9667
4	0.9997	0.9996	0.9994	0.9991	0.9988	0.9983	0.9978	0.9971	0.9963	0.9953
5	1.0000	1.0000	1.0000	1.0000	0.9999	0.9999	0.9999	0.9998	0.9997	0.9996
6	1.0000	1.0000	1.0000	1.0000	1.0000	1.0000	1.0000	1.0000	1.0000	1.0000

TABLE A (*continued*)

n = 7 (continued)

x \ p	0.21	0.22	0.23	0.24	0.25	0.26	0.27	0.28	0.29	0.30
0	0.1920	0.1757	0.1605	0.1465	0.1335	0.1215	0.1105	0.1003	0.0910	0.0824
1	0.5494	0.5225	0.4960	0.4702	0.4449	0.4204	0.3965	0.3734	0.3510	0.3294
2	0.8343	0.8159	0.7967	0.7769	0.7564	0.7354	0.7139	0.6919	0.6696	0.6471
3	0.9606	0.9539	0.9464	0.9383	0.9294	0.9198	0.9095	0.8984	0.8866	0.8740
4	0.9942	0.9928	0.9912	0.9893	0.9871	0.9847	0.9819	0.9787	0.9752	0.9712
5	0.9995	0.9994	0.9992	0.9989	0.9987	0.9983	0.9979	0.9974	0.9969	0.9962
6	1.0000	1.0000	1.0000	1.0000	0.9999	0.9999	0.9999	0.9999	0.9998	0.9998
7	1.0000	1.0000	1.0000	1.0000	1.0000	1.0000	1.0000	1.0000	1.0000	1.0000

x \ p	0.31	0.32	0.33	0.34	0.35	0.36	0.37	0.38	0.39	0.40
0	0.0745	0.0672	0.0606	0.0546	0.0490	0.0440	0.0394	0.0352	0.0314	0.0280
1	0.3086	0.2887	0.2696	0.2513	0.2338	0.2172	0.2013	0.1863	0.1721	0.1586
2	0.6243	0.6013	0.5783	0.5553	0.5323	0.5094	0.4866	0.4641	0.4419	0.4199
3	0.8606	0.8466	0.8318	0.8163	0.8002	0.7833	0.7659	0.7479	0.7293	0.7102
4	0.9668	0.9620	0.9566	0.9508	0.9444	0.9375	0.9299	0.9218	0.9131	0.9037
5	0.9954	0.9945	0.9935	0.9923	0.9910	0.9895	0.9877	0.9858	0.9836	0.9812
6	0.9997	0.9997	0.9996	0.9995	0.9994	0.9992	0.9991	0.9989	0.9986	0.9984
7	1.0000	1.0000	1.0000	1.0000	1.0000	1.0000	1.0000	1.0000	1.0000	1.0000

x \ p	0.41	0.42	0.43	0.44	0.45	0.46	0.47	0.48	0.49	0.50
0	0.0249	0.0221	0.0195	0.0173	0.0152	0.0134	0.0117	0.0103	0.0090	0.0078
1	0.1459	0.1340	0.1228	0.1123	0.1024	0.0932	0.0847	0.0767	0.0693	0.0625
2	0.3983	0.3771	0.3564	0.3362	0.3164	0.2973	0.2787	0.2607	0.2433	0.2266
3	0.6906	0.6706	0.6502	0.6294	0.6083	0.5869	0.5654	0.5437	0.5219	0.5000
4	0.8937	0.8831	0.8718	0.8598	0.8471	0.8337	0.8197	0.8049	0.7895	0.7734
5	0.9784	0.9754	0.9721	0.9684	0.9643	0.9598	0.9549	0.9496	0.9438	0.9375
6	0.9981	0.9977	0.9973	0.9968	0.9963	0.9956	0.9949	0.9941	0.9932	0.9922
7	1.0000	1.0000	1.0000	1.0000	1.0000	1.0000	1.0000	1.0000	1.0000	1.0000

n = 8

x \ p	0.01	0.02	0.03	0.04	0.05	0.06	0.07	0.08	0.09	0.10
0	0.9227	0.8508	0.7837	0.7214	0.6634	0.6096	0.5596	0.5132	0.4703	0.4305
1	0.9973	0.9897	0.9777	0.9619	0.9428	0.9208	0.8965	0.8702	0.8423	0.8131
2	0.9999	0.9996	0.9987	0.9969	0.9942	0.9904	0.9853	0.9789	0.9711	0.9619
3	1.0000	1.0000	0.9999	0.9998	0.9996	0.9993	0.9987	0.9978	0.9966	0.9950
4	1.0000	1.0000	1.0000	1.0000	1.0000	1.0000	0.9999	0.9999	0.9997	0.9996
5	1.0000	1.0000	1.0000	1.0000	1.0000	1.0000	1.0000	1.0000	1.0000	1.0000

TABLE A *(continued)*

	$n = 8$ (continued)									
x \ p	0.11	0.12	0.13	0.14	0.15	0.16	0.17	0.18	0.19	0.20
0	0.3937	0.3596	0.3282	0.2992	0.2725	0.2479	0.2252	0.2044	0.1853	0.1678
1	0.7829	0.7520	0.7206	0.6889	0.6572	0.6256	0.5943	0.5634	0.5330	0.5033
2	0.9513	0.9392	0.9257	0.9109	0.8948	0.8774	0.8588	0.8392	0.8185	0.7969
3	0.9929	0.9903	0.9871	0.9832	0.9786	0.9733	0.9672	0.9603	0.9524	0.9437
4	0.9993	0.9990	0.9985	0.9979	0.9971	0.9962	0.9950	0.9935	0.9917	0.9896
5	1.0000	0.9999	0.9999	0.9998	0.9998	0.9997	0.9995	0.9993	0.9991	0.9988
6	1.0000	1.0000	1.0000	1.0000	1.0000	1.0000	1.0000	1.0000	0.9999	0.9999
7	1.0000	1.0000	1.0000	1.0000	1.0000	1.0000	1.0000	1.0000	1.0000	1.0000

x \ p	0.21	0.22	0.23	0.24	0.25	0.26	0.27	0.28	0.29	0.30
0	0.1517	0.1370	0.1236	0.1113	0.1001	0.0899	0.0806	0.0722	0.0646	0.0576
1	0.4743	0.4462	0.4189	0.3925	0.3671	0.3427	0.3193	0.2969	0.2756	0.2553
2	0.7745	0.7514	0.7276	0.7033	0.6785	0.6535	0.6282	0.6027	0.5772	0.5518
3	0.9341	0.9235	0.9120	0.8996	0.8862	0.8719	0.8567	0.8406	0.8237	0.8059
4	0.9871	0.9842	0.9809	0.9770	0.9727	0.9678	0.9623	0.9562	0.9495	0.9420
5	0.9984	0.9979	0.9973	0.9966	0.9958	0.9948	0.9936	0.9922	0.9906	0.9887
6	0.9999	0.9998	0.9998	0.9997	0.9996	0.9995	0.9994	0.9992	0.9990	0.9987
7	1.0000	1.0000	1.0000	1.0000	1.0000	1.0000	1.0000	1.0000	0.9999	0.9999
8	1.0000	1.0000	1.0000	1.0000	1.0000	1.0000	1.0000	1.0000	1.0000	1.0000

x \ p	0.31	0.32	0.33	0.34	0.35	0.36	0.37	0.38	0.39	0.40
0	0.0514	0.0457	0.0406	0.0360	0.0319	0.0281	0.0248	0.0218	0.0192	0.0168
1	0.2360	0.2178	0.2006	0.1844	0.1691	0.1548	0.1414	0.1289	0.1172	0.1064
2	0.5264	0.5013	0.4764	0.4519	0.4278	0.4042	0.3811	0.3585	0.3366	0.3154
3	0.7874	0.7681	0.7481	0.7276	0.7064	0.6847	0.6626	0.6401	0.6172	0.5941
4	0.9339	0.9250	0.9154	0.9051	0.8939	0.8820	0.8693	0.8557	0.8414	0.8263
5	0.9866	0.9841	0.9813	0.9782	0.9747	0.9707	0.9664	0.9615	0.9561	0.9502
6	0.9984	0.9980	0.9976	0.9970	0.9964	0.9957	0.9949	0.9939	0.9928	0.9915
7	0.9999	0.9999	0.9999	0.9998	0.9998	0.9997	0.9996	0.9996	0.9995	0.9993
8	1.0000	1.0000	1.0000	1.0000	1.0000	1.0000	1.0000	1.0000	1.0000	1.0000

x \ p	0.41	0.42	0.43	0.44	0.45	0.46	0.47	0.48	0.49	0.50
0	0.0147	0.0128	0.0111	0.0097	0.0084	0.0072	0.0062	0.0053	0.0046	0.0039
1	0.0963	0.0870	0.0784	0.0705	0.0632	0.0565	0.0504	0.0448	0.0398	0.0352
2	0.2948	0.2750	0.2560	0.2376	0.2201	0.2034	0.1875	0.1724	0.1581	0.1445
3	0.5708	0.5473	0.5238	0.5004	0.4770	0.4537	0.4306	0.4078	0.3854	0.3633
4	0.8105	0.7938	0.7765	0.7584	0.7396	0.7202	0.7001	0.6795	0.6584	0.6367
5	0.9437	0.9366	0.9289	0.9206	0.9115	0.9018	0.8914	0.8802	0.8682	0.8555
6	0.9900	0.9883	0.9864	0.9843	0.9819	0.9792	0.9761	0.9728	0.9690	0.9648

TABLE A   (*continued*)

| | | | | | n = 8 (continued) | | | | | |
| | | | | | | | | | | |

x \ p	0.41	0.42	0.43	0.44	0.45	0.46	0.47	0.48	0.49	0.50
7	0.9992	0.9990	0.9988	0.9986	0.9983	0.9980	0.9976	0.9972	0.9967	0.9961
8	1.0000	1.0000	1.0000	1.0000	1.0000	1.0000	1.0000	1.0000	1.0000	1.0000

| | | | | | n = 9 | | | | | |

x \ p	0.01	0.02	0.03	0.04	0.05	0.06	0.07	0.08	0.09	0.10
0	0.9135	0.8337	0.7602	0.6925	0.6302	0.5730	0.5204	0.4722	0.4279	0.3874
1	0.9966	0.9869	0.9718	0.9522	0.9288	0.9022	0.8729	0.8417	0.8088	0.7748
2	0.9999	0.9994	0.9980	0.9955	0.9916	0.9862	0.9791	0.9702	0.9595	0.9470
3	1.0000	1.0000	0.9999	0.9997	0.9994	0.9987	0.9977	0.9963	0.9943	0.9917
4	1.0000	1.0000	1.0000	1.0000	1.0000	0.9999	0.9998	0.9997	0.9995	0.9991
5	1.0000	1.0000	1.0000	1.0000	1.0000	1.0000	1.0000	1.0000	1.0000	0.9999
6	1.0000	1.0000	1.0000	1.0000	1.0000	1.0000	1.0000	1.0000	1.0000	1.0000

x \ p	0.11	0.12	0.13	0.14	0.15	0.16	0.17	0.18	0.19	0.20
0	0.3504	0.3165	0.2855	0.2573	0.2316	0.2082	0.1869	0.1676	0.1501	0.1342
1	0.7401	0.7049	0.6696	0.6343	0.5995	0.5652	0.5315	0.4988	0.4670	0.4362
2	0.9327	0.9167	0.8991	0.8798	0.8591	0.8371	0.8139	0.7895	0.7643	0.7382
3	0.9883	0.9842	0.9791	0.9731	0.9661	0.9580	0.9488	0.9385	0.9270	0.9144
4	0.9986	0.9979	0.9970	0.9959	0.9944	0.9925	0.9902	0.9875	0.9842	0.9804
5	0.9999	0.9998	0.9997	0.9996	0.9994	0.9991	0.9987	0.9983	0.9977	0.9969
6	1.0000	1.0000	1.0000	1.0000	1.0000	0.9999	0.9999	0.9998	0.9998	0.9997
7	1.0000	1.0000	1.0000	1.0000	1.0000	1.0000	1.0000	1.0000	1.0000	1.0000

x \ p	0.21	0.22	0.23	0.24	0.25	0.26	0.27	0.28	0.29	0.30
0	0.1199	0.1069	0.0952	0.0846	0.0751	0.0665	0.0589	0.0520	0.0458	0.0404
1	0.4066	0.3782	0.3509	0.3250	0.3003	0.2770	0.2548	0.2340	0.2144	0.1960
2	0.7115	0.6842	0.6566	0.6287	0.6007	0.5727	0.5448	0.5171	0.4898	0.4628
3	0.9006	0.8856	0.8696	0.8525	0.8343	0.8151	0.7950	0.7740	0.7522	0.7297
4	0.9760	0.9709	0.9650	0.9584	0.9511	0.9429	0.9338	0.9238	0.9130	0.9012
5	0.9960	0.9949	0.9935	0.9919	0.9900	0.9878	0.9851	0.9821	0.9787	0.9747
6	0.9996	0.9994	0.9992	0.9990	0.9987	0.9983	0.9978	0.9972	0.9965	0.9957
7	1.0000	1.0000	0.9999	0.9999	0.9999	0.9999	0.9998	0.9997	0.9997	0.9996
8	1.0000	1.0000	1.0000	1.0000	1.0000	1.0000	1.0000	1.0000	1.0000	1.0000

x \ p	0.31	0.32	0.33	0.34	0.35	0.36	0.37	0.38	0.39	0.40
0	0.0355	0.0311	0.0272	0.0238	0.0207	0.0180	0.0156	0.0135	0.0117	0.0101
1	0.1788	0.1628	0.1478	0.1339	0.1211	0.1092	0.0983	0.0882	0.0790	0.0705
2	0.4364	0.4106	0.3854	0.3610	0.3373	0.3144	0.2924	0.2713	0.2511	0.2318

TABLE A *(continued)*

x \ p	0.31	0.32	0.33	0.34	0.35	0.36	0.37	0.38	0.39	0.40
3	0.7065	0.6827	0.6585	0.6338	0.6089	0.5837	0.5584	0.5331	0.5078	0.4826
4	0.8885	0.8748	0.8602	0.8447	0.8283	0.8110	0.7928	0.7738	0.7540	0.7334
5	0.9702	0.9652	0.9596	0.9533	0.9464	0.9388	0.9304	0.9213	0.9114	0.9006
6	0.9947	0.9936	0.9922	0.9906	0.9888	0.9867	0.9843	0.9816	0.9785	0.9750
7	0.9994	0.9993	0.9991	0.9989	0.9986	0.9983	0.9979	0.9974	0.9969	0.9962
8	1.0000	1.0000	1.0000	0.9999	0.9999	0.9999	0.9999	0.9998	0.9998	0.9997
9	1.0000	1.0000	1.0000	1.0000	1.0000	1.0000	1.0000	1.0000	1.0000	1.0000

x \ p	0.41	0.42	0.43	0.44	0.45	0.46	0.47	0.48	0.49	0.50
0	0.0087	0.0074	0.0064	0.0054	0.0046	0.0039	0.0033	0.0028	0.0023	0.0020
1	0.0628	0.0558	0.0495	0.0437	0.0385	0.0338	0.0296	0.0259	0.0225	0.0195
2	0.2134	0.1961	0.1796	0.1641	0.1495	0.1358	0.1231	0.1111	0.1001	0.0898
3	0.4576	0.4330	0.4087	0.3848	0.3614	0.3386	0.3164	0.2948	0.2740	0.2539
4	0.7122	0.6903	0.6678	0.6449	0.6214	0.5976	0.5735	0.5491	0.5246	0.5000
5	0.8891	0.8767	0.8634	0.8492	0.8342	0.8183	0.8015	0.7839	0.7654	0.7461
6	0.9710	0.9666	0.9617	0.9563	0.9502	0.9436	0.9363	0.9283	0.9196	0.9102
7	0.9954	0.9945	0.9935	0.9923	0.9909	0.9893	0.9875	0.9855	0.9831	0.9805
8	0.9997	0.9996	0.9995	0.9994	0.9992	0.9991	0.9989	0.9986	0.9984	0.9980
9	1.0000	1.0000	1.0000	1.0000	1.0000	1.0000	1.0000	1.0000	1.0000	1.0000

x \ p	0.01	0.02	0.03	0.04	0.05	0.06	0.07	0.08	0.09	0.10
0	0.9044	0.8171	0.7374	0.6648	0.5987	0.5386	0.4840	0.4344	0.3894	0.3487
1	0.9957	0.9838	0.9655	0.9418	0.9139	0.8824	0.8483	0.8121	0.7746	0.7361
2	0.9999	0.9991	0.9972	0.9938	0.9885	0.9812	0.9717	0.9599	0.9460	0.9298
3	1.0000	1.0000	0.9999	0.9996	0.9990	0.9980	0.9964	0.9942	0.9912	0.9872
4	1.0000	1.0000	1.0000	1.0000	0.9999	0.9998	0.9997	0.9994	0.9990	0.9984
5	1.0000	1.0000	1.0000	1.0000	1.0000	1.0000	1.0000	1.0000	0.9999	0.9999
6	1.0000	1.0000	1.0000	1.0000	1.0000	1.0000	1.0000	1.0000	1.0000	1.0000

x \ p	0.11	0.12	0.13	0.14	0.15	0.16	0.17	0.18	0.19	0.20
0	0.3118	0.2785	0.2484	0.2213	0.1969	0.1749	0.1552	0.1374	0.1216	0.1074
1	0.6972	0.6583	0.6196	0.5816	0.5443	0.5080	0.4730	0.4392	0.4068	0.3758
2	0.9116	0.8913	0.8692	0.8455	0.8202	0.7936	0.7659	0.7372	0.7078	0.6778
3	0.9822	0.9761	0.9687	0.9600	0.9500	0.9386	0.9259	0.9117	0.8961	0.8791
4	0.9975	0.9963	0.9947	0.9927	0.9901	0.9870	0.9832	0.9787	0.9734	0.9672
5	0.9997	0.9996	0.9994	0.9990	0.9986	0.9980	0.9973	0.9963	0.9951	0.9936
6	1.0000	1.0000	0.9999	0.9999	0.9999	0.9998	0.9997	0.9996	0.9994	0.9991

TABLE A *(continued)*

n = 10 (continued)

x \ p	0.11	0.12	0.13	0.14	0.15	0.16	0.17	0.18	0.19	0.20
7	1.0000	1.0000	1.0000	1.0000	1.0000	1.0000	1.0000	1.0000	0.9999	0.9999
8	1.0000	1.0000	1.0000	1.0000	1.0000	1.0000	1.0000	1.0000	1.0000	1.0000

x \ p	0.21	0.22	0.23	0.24	0.25	0.26	0.27	0.28	0.29	0.30
0	0.0947	0.0834	0.0733	0.0643	0.0563	0.0492	0.0430	0.0374	0.0326	0.0282
1	0.3464	0.3185	0.2921	0.2673	0.2440	0.2222	0.2019	0.1830	0.1655	0.1493
2	0.6474	0.6169	0.5863	0.5558	0.5256	0.4958	0.4665	0.4378	0.4099	0.3828
3	0.8609	0.8413	0.8206	0.7988	0.7759	0.7521	0.7274	0.7021	0.6761	0.6496
4	0.9601	0.9521	0.9431	0.9330	0.9219	0.9096	0.8963	0.8819	0.8663	0.8497
5	0.9918	0.9896	0.9870	0.9839	0.9803	0.9761	0.9713	0.9658	0.9596	0.9527
6	0.9988	0.9984	0.9979	0.9973	0.9965	0.9955	0.9944	0.9930	0.9913	0.9894
7	0.9999	0.9998	0.9998	0.9997	0.9996	0.9994	0.9993	0.9990	0.9988	0.9984
8	1.0000	1.0000	1.0000	1.0000	1.0000	1.0000	0.9999	0.9999	0.9999	0.9999
9	1.0000	1.0000	1.0000	1.0000	1.0000	1.0000	1.0000	1.0000	1.0000	1.0000

x \ p	0.31	0.32	0.33	0.34	0.35	0.36	0.37	0.38	0.39	0.40
0	0.0245	0.0211	0.0182	0.0157	0.0135	0.0115	0.0098	0.0084	0.0071	0.0060
1	0.1344	0.1206	0.1080	0.0965	0.0860	0.0764	0.0677	0.0598	0.0527	0.0464
2	0.3566	0.3313	0.3070	0.2838	0.2616	0.2405	0.2206	0.2017	0.1840	0.1673
3	0.6228	0.5956	0.5684	0.5411	0.5138	0.4868	0.4600	0.4336	0.4077	0.3823
4	0.8321	0.8133	0.7936	0.7730	0.7515	0.7292	0.7061	0.6823	0.6580	0.6331
5	0.9449	0.9363	0.9268	0.9164	0.9051	0.8928	0.8795	0.8652	0.8500	0.8338
6	0.9871	0.9845	0.9815	0.9780	0.9740	0.9695	0.9644	0.9587	0.9523	0.9452
7	0.9980	0.9975	0.9968	0.9961	0.9952	0.9941	0.9929	0.9914	0.9897	0.9877
8	0.9998	0.9997	0.9997	0.9996	0.9995	0.9993	0.9991	0.9989	0.9986	0.9983
9	1.0000	1.0000	1.0000	1.0000	1.0000	1.0000	1.0000	0.9999	0.9999	0.9999
10	1.0000	1.0000	1.0000	1.0000	1.0000	1.0000	1.0000	1.0000	1.0000	1.0000

x \ p	0.41	0.42	0.43	0.44	0.45	0.46	0.47	0.48	0.49	0.50
0	0.0051	0.0043	0.0036	0.0030	0.0025	0.0021	0.0017	0.0014	0.0012	0.0010
1	0.0406	0.0355	0.0309	0.0269	0.0233	0.0201	0.0173	0.0148	0.0126	0.0107
2	0.1517	0.1372	0.1236	0.1111	0.0996	0.0889	0.0791	0.0702	0.0621	0.0547
3	0.3575	0.3335	0.3102	0.2877	0.2660	0.2453	0.2255	0.2067	0.1888	0.1719
4	0.6078	0.5822	0.5564	0.5304	0.5044	0.4784	0.4526	0.4270	0.4018	0.3770
5	0.8166	0.7984	0.7793	0.7593	0.7384	0.7168	0.6943	0.6712	0.6474	0.6230
6	0.9374	0.9288	0.9194	0.9092	0.8980	0.8859	0.8729	0.8590	0.8440	0.8281
7	0.9854	0.9828	0.9798	0.9764	0.9726	0.9683	0.9634	0.9580	0.9520	0.9453
8	0.9979	0.9975	0.9969	0.9963	0.9955	0.9946	0.9935	0.9923	0.9909	0.9893
9	0.9999	0.9998	0.9998	0.9997	0.9997	0.9996	0.9995	0.9994	0.9992	0.9990
10	1.0000	1.0000	1.0000	1.0000	1.0000	1.0000	1.0000	1.0000	1.0000	1.0000

TABLE A *(continued)*

n = 11

x \ p	0.01	0.02	0.03	0.04	0.05	0.06	0.07	0.08	0.09	0.10
0	0.8953	0.8007	0.7153	0.6382	0.5688	0.5063	0.4501	0.3996	0.3544	0.3138
1	0.9948	0.9805	0.9587	0.9308	0.8981	0.8618	0.8228	0.7819	0.7399	0.6974
2	0.9998	0.9988	0.9963	0.9917	0.9848	0.9752	0.9630	0.9481	0.9305	0.9104
3	1.0000	1.0000	0.9998	0.9993	0.9984	0.9970	0.9947	0.9915	0.9871	0.9815
4	1.0000	1.0000	1.0000	1.0000	0.9999	0.9997	0.9995	0.9990	0.9983	0.9972
5	1.0000	1.0000	1.0000	1.0000	1.0000	1.0000	1.0000	0.9999	0.9998	0.9997
6	1.0000	1.0000	1.0000	1.0000	1.0000	1.0000	1.0000	1.0000	1.0000	1.0000

x \ p	0.11	0.12	0.13	0.14	0.15	0.16	0.17	0.18	0.19	0.20
0	0.2775	0.2451	0.2161	0.1903	0.1673	0.1469	0.1288	0.1127	0.0985	0.0859
1	0.6548	0.6127	0.5714	0.5311	0.4922	0.4547	0.4189	0.3849	0.3526	0.3221
2	0.8880	0.8634	0.8368	0.8085	0.7788	0.7479	0.7161	0.6836	0.6506	0.6174
3	0.9744	0.9659	0.9558	0.9440	0.9306	0.9154	0.8987	0.8803	0.8603	0.8389
4	0.9958	0.9939	0.9913	0.9881	0.9841	0.9793	0.9734	0.9666	0.9587	0.9496
5	0.9995	0.9992	0.9988	0.9982	0.9973	0.9963	0.9949	0.9932	0.9910	0.9883
6	1.0000	0.9999	0.9999	0.9998	0.9997	0.9995	0.9993	0.9990	0.9986	0.9980
7	1.0000	1.0000	1.0000	1.0000	1.0000	1.0000	0.9999	0.9999	0.9998	0.9998
8	1.0000	1.0000	1.0000	1.0000	1.0000	1.0000	1.0000	1.0000	1.0000	1.0000

x \ p	0.21	0.22	0.23	0.24	0.25	0.26	0.27	0.28	0.29	0.30
0	0.0748	0.0650	0.0564	0.0489	0.0422	0.0364	0.0314	0.0270	0.0231	0.0198
1	0.2935	0.2667	0.2418	0.2186	0.1971	0.1773	0.1590	0.1423	0.1270	0.1130
2	0.5842	0.5512	0.5186	0.4866	0.4552	0.4247	0.3951	0.3665	0.3390	0.3127
3	0.8160	0.7919	0.7667	0.7404	0.7133	0.6854	0.6570	0.6281	0.5989	0.5696
4	0.9393	0.9277	0.9149	0.9008	0.8854	0.8687	0.8507	0.8315	0.8112	0.7897
5	0.9852	0.9814	0.9769	0.9717	0.9657	0.9588	0.9510	0.9423	0.9326	0.9218
6	0.9973	0.9965	0.9954	0.9941	0.9924	0.9905	0.9881	0.9854	0.9821	0.9784
7	0.9997	0.9995	0.9993	0.9991	0.9988	0.9984	0.9979	0.9973	0.9966	0.9957
8	1.0000	1.0000	0.9999	0.9999	0.9999	0.9998	0.9998	0.9997	0.9996	0.9994
9	1.0000	1.0000	1.0000	1.0000	1.0000	1.0000	1.0000	1.0000	1.0000	1.0000

x \ p	0.31	0.32	0.33	0.34	0.35	0.36	0.37	0.38	0.39	0.40
0	0.0169	0.0144	0.0122	0.0104	0.0088	0.0074	0.0062	0.0052	0.0044	0.0036
1	0.1003	0.0888	0.0784	0.0690	0.0606	0.0530	0.0463	0.0403	0.0350	0.0302
2	0.2877	0.2639	0.2413	0.2201	0.2001	0.1814	0.1640	0.1478	0.1328	0.1189
3	0.5402	0.5110	0.4821	0.4536	0.4256	0.3981	0.3714	0.3455	0.3204	0.2963
4	0.7672	0.7437	0.7193	0.6941	0.6683	0.6419	0.6150	0.5878	0.5603	0.5328
5	0.9099	0.8969	0.8829	0.8676	0.8513	0.8339	0.8153	0.7957	0.7751	0.7535
6	0.9740	0.9691	0.9634	0.9570	0.9499	0.9419	0.9330	0.9232	0.9124	0.9006

TABLE A   *(continued)*

$n = 11$ (continued)

x \ p	0.31	0.32	0.33	0.34	0.35	0.36	0.37	0.38	0.39	0.40
7	0.9946	0.9933	0.9918	0.9899	0.9878	0.9852	0.9823	0.9790	0.9751	0.9707
8	0.9992	0.9990	0.9987	0.9984	0.9980	0.9974	0.9968	0.9961	0.9952	0.9941
9	0.9999	0.9999	0.9999	0.9998	0.9998	0.9997	0.9996	0.9995	0.9994	0.9993
10	1.0000	1.0000	1.0000	1.0000	1.0000	1.0000	1.0000	1.0000	1.0000	1.0000

x \ p	0.41	0.42	0.43	0.44	0.45	0.46	0.47	0.48	0.49	0.50
0	0.0030	0.0025	0.0021	0.0017	0.0014	0.0011	0.0009	0.0008	0.0006	0.0005
1	0.0261	0.0224	0.0192	0.0164	0.0139	0.0118	0.0100	0.0084	0.0070	0.0059
2	0.1062	0.0945	0.0838	0.0740	0.0652	0.0572	0.0501	0.0436	0.0378	0.0327
3	0.2731	0.2510	0.2300	0.2100	0.1911	0.1734	0.1567	0.1412	0.1267	0.1133
4	0.5052	0.4777	0.4505	0.4236	0.3971	0.3712	0.3459	0.3213	0.2974	0.2744
5	0.7310	0.7076	0.6834	0.6586	0.6331	0.6071	0.5807	0.5540	0.5271	0.5000
6	0.8879	0.8740	0.8592	0.8432	0.8262	0.8081	0.7890	0.7688	0.7477	0.7256
7	0.9657	0.9601	0.9539	0.9468	0.9390	0.9304	0.9209	0.9105	0.8991	0.8867
8	0.9928	0.9913	0.9896	0.9875	0.9852	0.9825	0.9794	0.9759	0.9718	0.9673
9	0.9991	0.9988	0.9986	0.9982	0.9978	0.9973	0.9967	0.9960	0.9951	0.9941
10	0.9999	0.9999	0.9999	0.9999	0.9998	0.9998	0.9998	0.9997	0.9996	0.9995
11	1.0000	1.0000	1.0000	1.0000	1.0000	1.0000	1.0000	1.0000	1.0000	1.0000

$n = 12$

x \ p	0.01	0.02	0.03	0.04	0.05	0.06	0.07	0.08	0.09	0.10
0	0.8864	0.7847	0.6938	0.6127	0.5404	0.4759	0.4186	0.3677	0.3225	0.2824
1	0.9938	0.9769	0.9514	0.9191	0.8816	0.8405	0.7967	0.7513	0.7052	0.6590 .
2	0.9998	0.9985	0.9952	0.9893	0.9804	0.9684	0.9532	0.9348	0.9134	0.8891
3	1.0000	0.9999	0.9997	0.9990	0.9978	0.9957	0.9925	0.9880	0.9820	0.9744
4	1.0000	1.0000	1.0000	0.9999	0.9998	0.9996	0.9991	0.9984	0.9973	0.9957
5	1.0000	1.0000	1.0000	1.0000	1.0000	1.0000	0.9999	0.9998	0.9997	0.9995
6	1.0000	1.0000	1.0000	1.0000	1.0000	1.0000	1.0000	1.0000	1.0000	0.9999
7	1.0000	1.0000	1.0000	1.0000	1.0000	1.0000	1.0000	1.0000	1.0000	1.0000

x \ p	0.11	0.12	0.13	0.14	0.15	0.16	0.17	0.18	0.19	0.20
0	0.2470	0.2157	0.1880	0.1637	0.1422	0.1234	0.1069	0.0924	0.0798	0.0687
1	0.6133	0.5686	0.5252	0.4834	0.4435	0.4055	0.3696	0.3359	0.3043	0.2749
2	0.8623	0.8333	0.8023	0.7697	0.7358	0.7010	0.6656	0.6298	0.5940	0.5583
3	0.9649	0.9536	0.9403	0.9250	0.9078	0.8886	0.8676	0.8448	0.8205	0.7946
4	0.9935	0.9905	0.9867	0.9819	0.9761	0.9690	0.9607	0.9511	0.9400	0.9274
5	0.9991	0.9986	0.9978	0.9967	0.9954	0.9935	0.9912	0.9884	0.9849	0.9806
6	0.9999	0.9998	0.9997	0.9996	0.9993	0.9990	0.9985	0.9979	0.9971	0.9961

TABLE A *(continued)*

					n = 12 (continued)					

x \ *p*	0.11	0.12	0.13	0.14	0.15	0.16	0.17	0.18	0.19	0.20
7	1.0000	1.0000	1.0000	1.0000	0.9999	0.9999	0.9998	0.9997	0.9996	0.9994
8	1.0000	1.0000	1.0000	1.0000	1.0000	1.0000	1.0000	1.0000	1.0000	0.9999
9	1.0000	1.0000	1.0000	1.0000	1.0000	1.0000	1.0000	1.0000	1.0000	1.0000

x \ *p*	0.21	0.22	0.23	0.24	0.25	0.26	0.27	0.28	0.29	0.30
0	0.0591	0.0507	0.0434	0.0371	0.0317	0.0270	0.0229	0.0194	0.0164	0.0138
1	0.2476	0.2224	0.1991	0.1778	0.1584	0.1406	0.1245	0.1100	0.0968	0.0850
2	0.5232	0.4886	0.4550	0.4222	0.3907	0.3603	0.3313	0.3037	0.2775	0.2528
3	0.7674	0.7390	0.7096	0.6795	0.6488	0.6176	0.5863	0.5548	0.5235	0.4925
4	0.9134	0.8979	0.8808	0.8623	0.8424	0.8210	0.7984	0.7746	0.7496	0.7237
5	0.9755	0.9696	0.9626	0.9547	0.9456	0.9354	0.9240	0.9113	0.8974	0.8822
6	0.9948	0.9932	0.9911	0.9887	0.9857	0.9822	0.9781	0.9733	0.9678	0.9614
7	0.9992	0.9989	0.9984	0.9979	0.9972	0.9964	0.9953	0.9940	0.9924	0.9905
8	0.9999	0.9999	0.9998	0.9997	0.9996	0.9995	0.9993	0.9990	0.9987	0.9983
9	1.0000	1.0000	1.0000	1.0000	1.0000	0.9999	0.9999	0.9999	0.9998	0.9998
10	1.0000	1.0000	1.0000	1.0000	1.0000	1.0000	1.0000	1.0000	1.0000	1.0000

x \ *p*	0.31	0.32	0.33	0.34	0.35	0.36	0.37	0.38	0.39	0.40
0	0.0116	0.0098	0.0082	0.0068	0.0057	0.0047	0.0039	0.0032	0.0027	0.0022
1	0.0744	0.0650	0.0565	0.0491	0.0424	0.0366	0.0315	0.0270	0.0230	0.0196
2	0.2296	0.2078	0.1876	0.1687	0.1513	0.1352	0.1205	0.1069	0.0946	0.0834
3	0.4619	0.4319	0.4027	0.3742	0.3467	0.3201	0.2947	0.2704	0.2472	0.2253
4	0.6968	0.6692	0.6410	0.6124	0.5833	0.5541	0.5249	0.4957	0.4668	0.4382
5	0.8657	0.8479	0.8289	0.8087	0.7873	0.7648	0.7412	0.7167	0.6913	0.6652
6	0.9542	0.9460	0.9368	0.9266	0.9154	0.9030	0.8894	0.8747	0.8589	0.8418
7	0.9882	0.9856	0.9824	0.9787	0.9745	0.9696	0.9641	0.9578	0.9507	0.9427
8	0.9978	0.9972	0.9964	0.9955	0.9944	0.9930	0.9915	0.9896	0.9873	0.9847
9	0.9997	0.9996	0.9995	0.9993	0.9992	0.9989	0.9986	0.9982	0.9978	0.9972
10	1.0000	1.0000	1.0000	0.9999	0.9999	0.9999	0.9999	0.9998	0.9998	0.9997
11	1.0000	1.0000	1.0000	1.0000	1.0000	1.0000	1.0000	1.0000	1.0000	1.0000

x \ *p*	0.41	0.42	0.43	0.44	0.45	0.46	0.47	0.48	0.49	0.50
0	0.0018	0.0014	0.0012	0.0010	0.0008	0.0006	0.0005	0.0004	0.0003	0.0002
1	0.0166	0.0140	0.0118	0.0099	0.0083	0.0069	0.0057	0.0047	0.0039	0.0032
2	0.0733	0.0642	0.0560	0.0487	0.0421	0.0363	0.0312	0.0267	0.0227	0.0193
3	0.2047	0.1853	0.1671	0.1502	0.1345	0.1199	0.1066	0.0943	0.0832	0.0730
4	0.4101	0.3825	0.3557	0.3296	0.3044	0.2802	0.2570	0.2348	0.2138	0.1938
5	0.6384	0.6111	0.5833	0.5552	0.5269	0.4986	0.4703	0.4423	0.4145	0.3872
6	0.8235	0.8041	0.7836	0.7620	0.7393	0.7157	0.6911	0.6657	0.6396	0.6128

TABLE A   (*continued*)

| | | | | | $n = 12$ (continued) | | | | | |

x \ p	0.41	0.42	0.43	0.44	0.45	0.46	0.47	0.48	0.49	0.50
7	0.9338	0.9240	0.9131	0.9012	0.8883	0.8742	0.8589	0.8425	0.8249	0.8062
8	0.9817	0.9782	0.9742	0.9696	0.9644	0.9585	0.9519	0.9445	0.9362	0.9270
9	0.9965	0.9957	0.9947	0.9935	0.9921	0.9905	0.9886	0.9863	0.9837	0.9807
10	0.9996	0.9995	0.9993	0.9991	0.9989	0.9986	0.9983	0.9979	0.9974	0.9968
11	1.0000	1.0000	1.0000	0.9999	0.9999	0.9999	0.9999	0.9999	0.9998	0.9998
12	1.0000	1.0000	1.0000	1.0000	1.0000	1.0000	1.0000	1.0000	1.0000	1.0000

| | | | | | $n = 13$ | | | | | |

x \ p	0.01	0.02	0.03	0.04	0.05	0.06	0.07	0.08	0.09	0.10
0	0.8775	0.7690	0.6730	0.5882	0.5133	0.4474	0.3893	0.3383	0.2935	0.2542
1	0.9928	0.9730	0.9436	0.9068	0.8646	0.8186	0.7702	0.7206	0.6707	0.6213
2	0.9997	0.9980	0.9938	0.9865	0.9755	0.9608	0.9422	0.9201	0.8946	0.8661
3	1.0000	0.9999	0.9995	0.9986	0.9969	0.9940	0.9897	0.9837	0.9758	0.9658
4	1.0000	1.0000	1.0000	0.9999	0.9997	0.9993	0.9987	0.9976	0.9959	0.9935
5	1.0000	1.0000	1.0000	1.0000	1.0000	0.9999	0.9999	0.9997	0.9995	0.9991
6	1.0000	1.0000	1.0000	1.0000	1.0000	1.0000	1.0000	1.0000	0.9999	0.9999
7	1.0000	1.0000	1.0000	1.0000	1.0000	1.0000	1.0000	1.0000	1.0000	1.0000

x \ p	0.11	0.12	0.13	0.14	0.15	0.16	0.17	0.18	0.19	0.20
0	0.2198	0.1898	0.1636	0.1408	0.1209	0.1037	0.0887	0.0758	0.0646	0.0550
1	0.5730	0.5262	0.4814	0.4386	0.3983	0.3604	0.3249	0.2920	0.2616	0.2336
2	0.8349	0.8015	0.7663	0.7296	0.6920	0.6537	0.6152	0.5769	0.5389	0.5017
3	0.9536	0.9391	0.9224	0.9033	0.8820	0.8586	0.8333	0.8061	0.7774	0.7473
4	0.9903	0.9861	0.9807	0.9740	0.9658	0.9562	0.9449	0.9319	0.9173	0.9009
5	0.9985	0.9976	0.9964	0.9947	0.9925	0.9896	0.9861	0.9817	0.9763	0.9700
6	0.9998	0.9997	0.9995	0.9992	0.9987	0.9981	0.9973	0.9962	0.9948	0.9930
7	1.0000	1.0000	0.9999	0.9999	0.9998	0.9997	0.9996	0.9994	0.9991	0.9988
8	1.0000	1.0000	1.0000	1.0000	1.0000	1.0000	1.0000	0.9999	0.9999	0.9998
9	1.0000	1.0000	1.0000	1.0000	1.0000	1.0000	1.0000	1.0000	1.0000	1.0000

x \ p	0.21	0.22	0.23	0.24	0.25	0.26	0.27	0.28	0.29	0.30
0	0.0467	0.0396	0.0334	0.0282	0.0238	0.0200	0.0167	0.0140	0.0117	0.0097
1	0.2080	0.1846	0.1633	0.1441	0.1267	0.1111	0.0971	0.0846	0.0735	0.0637
2	0.4653	0.4301	0.3961	0.3636	0.3326	0.3032	0.2755	0.2495	0.2251	0.2025
3	0.7161	0.6839	0.6511	0.6178	0.5843	0.5507	0.5174	0.4845	0.4522	0.4206
4	0.8827	0.8629	0.8415	0.8184	0.7940	0.7681	0.7411	0.7130	0.6840	0.6543
5	0.9625	0.9538	0.9438	0.9325	0.9198	0.9056	0.8901	0.8730	0.8545	0.8346
6	0.9907	0.9880	0.9846	0.9805	0.9757	0.9701	0.9635	0.9560	0.9473	0.9376
7	0.9983	0.9976	0.9968	0.9957	0.9944	0.9927	0.9907	0.9882	0.9853	0.9818

TABLE A *(continued)*

					$n = 13$ (continued)					
x \ p	0.21	0.22	0.23	0.24	0.25	0.26	0.27	0.28	0.29	0.30
8	0.9998	0.9996	0.9995	0.9993	0.9990	0.9987	0.9982	0.9976	0.9969	0.9960
9	1.0000	1.0000	0.9999	0.9999	0.9999	0.9998	0.9997	0.9996	0.9995	0.9993
10	1.0000	1.0000	1.0000	1.0000	1.0000	1.0000	1.0000	1.0000	0.9999	0.9999
11	1.0000	1.0000	1.0000	1.0000	1.0000	1.0000	1.0000	1.0000	1.0000	1.0000

x \ p	0.31	0.32	0.33	0.34	0.35	0.36	0.37	0.38	0.39	0.40
0	0.0080	0.0066	0.0055	0.0045	0.0037	0.0030	0.0025	0.0020	0.0016	0.0013
1	0.0550	0.0473	0.0406	0.0347	0.0296	0.0251	0.0213	0.0179	0.0151	0.0126
2	0.1815	0.1621	0.1443	0.1280	0.1132	0.0997	0.0875	0.0765	0.0667	0.0579
3	0.3899	0.3602	0.3317	0.3043	0.2783	0.2536	0.2302	0.2083	0.1877	0.1686
4	0.6240	0.5933	0.5624	0.5314	0.5005	0.4699	0.4397	0.4101	0.3812	0.3530
5	0.8133	0.7907	0.7669	0.7419	0.7159	0.6889	0.6612	0.6327	0.6038	0.5744
6	0.9267	0.9146	0.9012	0.8865	0.8705	0.8532	0.8346	0.8147	0.7935	0.7712
7	0.9777	0.9729	0.9674	0.9610	0.9538	0.9456	0.9365	0.9262	0.9149	0.9023
8	0.9948	0.9935	0.9918	0.9898	0.9874	0.9846	0.9813	0.9775	0.9730	0.9679
9	0.9991	0.9988	0.9985	0.9980	0.9975	0.9968	0.9960	0.9949	0.9937	0.9922
10	0.9999	0.9999	0.9998	0.9997	0.9997	0.9995	0.9994	0.9992	0.9990	0.9987
11	1.0000	1.0000	1.0000	1.0000	1.0000	1.0000	0.9999	0.9999	0.9999	0.9999
12	1.0000	1.0000	1.0000	1.0000	1.0000	1.0000	1.0000	1.0000	1.0000	1.0000

x \ p	0.41	0.42	0.43	0.44	0.45	0.46	0.47	0.48	0.49	0.50
0	0.0010	0.0008	0.0007	0.0005	0.0004	0.0003	0.0003	0.0002	0.0002	0.0001
1	0.0105	0.0088	0.0072	0.0060	0.0049	0.0040	0.0033	0.0026	0.0021	0.0017
2	0.0501	0.0431	0.0370	0.0316	0.0269	0.0228	0.0192	0.0162	0.0135	0.0112
3	0.1508	0.1344	0.1193	0.1055	0.0929	0.0815	0.0712	0.0619	0.0536	0.0461
4	0.3258	0.2997	0.2746	0.2507	0.2279	0.2065	0.1863	0.1674	0.1498	0.1334
5	0.5448	0.5151	0.4854	0.4559	0.4268	0.3981	0.3701	0.3427	0.3162	0.2905
6	0.7476	0.7230	0.6975	0.6710	0.6437	0.6158	0.5873	0.5585	0.5293	0.5000
7	0.8886	0.8736	0.8574	0.8400	0.8212	0.8012	0.7800	0.7576	0.7341	0.7095
8	0.9621	0.9554	0.9480	0.9395	0.9302	0.9197	0.9082	0.8955	0.8817	0.8666
9	0.9904	0.9883	0.9859	0.9830	0.9797	0.9758	0.9713	0.9662	0.9604	0.9539
10	0.9983	0.9979	0.9973	0.9967	0.9959	0.9949	0.9937	0.9923	0.9907	0.9888
11	0.9998	0.9998	0.9997	0.9996	0.9995	0.9993	0.9991	0.9989	0.9986	0.9983
12	1.0000	1.0000	1.0000	1.0000	1.0000	1.0000	0.9999	0.9999	0.9999	0.9999
13	1.0000	1.0000	1.0000	1.0000	1.0000	1.0000	1.0000	1.0000	1.0000	1.0000

					$n = 14$					
x \ p	0.01	0.02	0.03	0.04	0.05	0.06	0.07	0.08	0.09	0.10
0	0.8687	0.7536	0.6528	0.5647	0.4877	0.4205	0.3620	0.3112	0.2670	0.2288

TABLE A   (*continued*)

| | | | | | | $n = 14$ (continued) | | | | |

x \ p	0.01	0.02	0.03	0.04	0.05	0.06	0.07	0.08	0.09	0.10
1	0.9916	0.9690	0.9355	0.8941	0.8470	0.7963	0.7436	0.6900	0.6368	0.5846
2	0.9997	0.9975	0.9923	0.9833	0.9699	0.9522	0.9302	0.9042	0.8745	0.8416
3	1.0000	0.9999	0.9994	0.9981	0.9958	0.9920	0.9864	0.9786	0.9685	0.9559
4	1.0000	1.0000	1.0000	0.9998	0.9996	0.9990	0.9980	0.9965	0.9941	0.9908
5	1.0000	1.0000	1.0000	1.0000	1.0000	0.9999	0.9998	0.9996	0.9992	0.9985
6	1.0000	1.0000	1.0000	1.0000	1.0000	1.0000	1.0000	1.0000	0.9999	0.9998
7	1.0000	1.0000	1.0000	1.0000	1.0000	1.0000	1.0000	1.0000	1.0000	1.0000

x \ p	0.11	0.12	0.13	0.14	0.15	0.16	0.17	0.18	0.19	0.20
0	0.1956	0.1670	0.1423	0.1211	0.1028	0.0871	0.0736	0.0621	0.0523	0.0440
1	0.5342	0.4859	0.4401	0.3969	0.3567	0.3193	0.2848	0.2531	0.2242	0.1979
2	0.8061	0.7685	0.7292	0.6889	0.6479	0.6068	0.5659	0.5256	0.4862	0.4481
3	0.9406	0.9226	0.9021	0.8790	0.8535	0.8258	0.7962	0.7649	0.7321	0.6982
4	0.9863	0.9804	0.9731	0.9641	0.9533	0.9406	0.9259	0.9093	0.8907	0.8702
5	0.9976	0.9962	0.9943	0.9918	0.9885	0.9843	0.9791	0.9727	0.9651	0.9561
6	0.9997	0.9994	0.9991	0.9985	0.9978	0.9968	0.9954	0.9936	0.9913	0.9884
7	1.0000	0.9999	0.9999	0.9998	0.9997	0.9995	0.9992	0.9988	0.9983	0.9976
8	1.0000	1.0000	1.0000	1.0000	1.0000	0.9999	0.9999	0.9998	0.9997	0.9996
9	1.0000	1.0000	1.0000	1.0000	1.0000	1.0000	1.0000	1.0000	1.0000	1.0000

x \ p	0.21	0.22	0.23	0.24	0.25	0.26	0.27	0.28	0.29	0.30
0	0.0369	0.0309	0.0258	0.0214	0.0178	0.0148	0.0122	0.0101	0.0083	0.0068
1	0.1741	0.1527	0.1335	0.1163	0.1010	0.0874	0.0754	0.0648	0.0556	0.0475
2	0.4113	0.3761	0.3426	0.3109	0.2811	0.2533	0.2273	0.2033	0.1812	0.1608
3	0.6634	0.6281	0.5924	0.5568	0.5213	0.4864	0.4521	0.4187	0.3863	0.3552
4	0.8477	0.8235	0.7977	0.7703	0.7415	0.7116	0.6807	0.6490	0.6168	0.5842
5	0.9457	0.9338	0.9203	0.9051	0.8883	0.8699	0.8498	0.8282	0.8051	0.7805
6	0.9848	0.9804	0.9752	0.9690	0.9617	0.9533	0.9437	0.9327	0.9204	0.9067
7	0.9967	0.9955	0.9940	0.9921	0.9897	0.9868	0.9833	0.9792	0.9743	0.9685
8	0.9994	0.9992	0.9989	0.9984	0.9978	0.9971	0.9962	0.9950	0.9935	0.9917
9	0.9999	0.9999	0.9998	0.9998	0.9997	0.9995	0.9993	0.9991	0.9988	0.9983
10	1.0000	1.0000	1.0000	1.0000	1.0000	0.9999	0.9999	0.9999	0.9998	0.9998
11	1.0000	1.0000	1.0000	1.0000	1.0000	1.0000	1.0000	1.0000	1.0000	1.0000

x \ p	0.31	0.32	0.33	0.34	0.35	0.36	0.37	0.38	0.39	0.40
0	0.0055	0.0045	0.0037	0.0030	0.0024	0.0019	0.0016	0.0012	0.0010	0.0008
1	0.0404	0.0343	0.0290	0.0244	0.0205	0.0172	0.0143	0.0119	0.0098	0.0081
2	0.1423	0.1254	0.1101	0.0963	0.0839	0.0729	0.0630	0.0543	0.0466	0.0398
3	0.3253	0.2968	0.2699	0.2444	0.2205	0.1982	0.1774	0.1582	0.1405	0.1243
4	0.5514	0.5187	0.4862	0.4542	0.4227	0.3920	0.3622	0.3334	0.3057	0.2793

TABLE A   (*continued*)

n = 14 (continued)

x \ p	0.31	0.32	0.33	0.34	0.35	0.36	0.37	0.38	0.39	0.40
5	0.7546	0.7276	0.6994	0.6703	0.6405	0.6101	0.5792	0.5481	0.5169	0.4859
6	0.8916	0.8750	0.8569	0.8374	0.8164	0.7941	0.7704	0.7455	0.7195	0.6925
7	0.9619	0.9542	0.9455	0.9357	0.9247	0.9124	0.8988	0.8838	0.8675	0.8499
8	0.9895	0.9869	0.9837	0.9800	0.9757	0.9706	0.9647	0.9580	0.9503	0.9417
9	0.9978	0.9971	0.9963	0.9952	0.9940	0.9924	0.9905	0.9883	0.9856	0.9825
10	0.9997	0.9995	0.9994	0.9992	0.9989	0.9986	0.9981	0.9976	0.9969	0.9961
11	1.0000	0.9999	0.9999	0.9999	0.9999	0.9998	0.9997	0.9997	0.9995	0.9994
12	1.0000	1.0000	1.0000	1.0000	1.0000	1.0000	1.0000	1.0000	1.0000	0.9999
13	1.0000	1.0000	1.0000	1.0000	1.0000	1.0000	1.0000	1.0000	1.0000	1.0000

x \ p	0.41	0.42	0.43	0.44	0.45	0.46	0.47	0.48	0.49	0.50
0	0.0006	0.0005	0.0004	0.0003	0.0002	0.0002	0.0001	0.0001	0.0001	0.0001
1	0.0066	0.0054	0.0044	0.0036	0.0029	0.0023	0.0019	0.0015	0.0012	0.0009
2	0.0339	0.0287	0.0242	0.0203	0.0170	0.0142	0.0117	0.0097	0.0079	0.0065
3	0.1095	0.0961	0.0839	0.0730	0.0632	0.0545	0.0468	0.0399	0.0339	0.0287
4	0.2541	0.2303	0.2078	0.1868	0.1672	0.1490	0.1322	0.1167	0.1026	0.0898
5	0.4550	0.4246	0.3948	0.3656	0.3373	0.3100	0.2837	0.2585	0.2346	0.2120
6	0.6645	0.6357	0.6063	0.5764	0.5461	0.5157	0.4852	0.4549	0.4249	0.3953
7	0.8308	0.8104	0.7887	0.7656	0.7414	0.7160	0.6895	0.6620	0.6337	0.6047
8	0.9320	0.9211	0.9090	0.8957	0.8811	0.8652	0.8480	0.8293	0.8094	0.7880
9	0.9788	0.9745	0.9696	0.9639	0.9574	0.9500	0.9417	0.9323	0.9218	0.9102
10	0.9951	0.9939	0.9924	0.9907	0.9886	0.9861	0.9832	0.9798	0.9759	0.9713
11	0.9992	0.9990	0.9987	0.9983	0.9978	0.9973	0.9966	0.9958	0.9947	0.9935
12	0.9999	0.9999	0.9999	0.9998	0.9997	0.9997	0.9996	0.9994	0.9993	0.9991
13	1.0000	1.0000	1.0000	1.0000	1.0000	1.0000	1.0000	1.0000	1.0000	0.9999
14	1.0000	1.0000	1.0000	1.0000	1.0000	1.0000	1.0000	1.0000	1.0000	1.0000

n = 15

x \ p	0.01	0.02	0.03	0.04	0.05	0.06	0.07	0.08	0.09	0.10
0	0.8601	0.7386	0.6333	0.5421	0.4633	0.3953	0.3367	0.2863	0.2430	0.2059
1	0.9904	0.9647	0.9270	0.8809	0.8290	0.7738	0.7168	0.6597	0.6035	0.5490
2	0.9996	0.9970	0.9906	0.9797	0.9638	0.9429	0.9171	0.8870	0.8531	0.8159
3	1.0000	0.9998	0.9992	0.9976	0.9945	0.9896	0.9825	0.9727	0.9601	0.9444
4	1.0000	1.0000	0.9999	0.9998	0.9994	0.9986	0.9972	0.9950	0.9918	0.9873
5	1.0000	1.0000	1.0000	1.0000	0.9999	0.9999	0.9997	0.9993	0.9987	0.9978
6	1.0000	1.0000	1.0000	1.0000	1.0000	1.0000	1.0000	0.9999	0.9998	0.9997
7	1.0000	1.0000	1.0000	1.0000	1.0000	1.0000	1.0000	1.0000	1.0000	1.0000

TABLE A   (*continued*)

					n = 15 (continued)					
x \ *p*	0.11	0.12	0.13	0.14	0.15	0.16	0.17	0.18	0.19	0.20
0	0.1741	0.1470	0.1238	0.1041	0.0874	0.0731	0.0611	0.0510	0.0424	0.0352
1	0.4969	0.4476	0.4013	0.3583	0.3186	0.2821	0.2489	0.2187	0.1915	0.1671
2	0.7762	0.7346	0.6916	0.6480	0.6042	0.5608	0.5181	0.4766	0.4365	0.3980
3	0.9258	0.9041	0.8796	0.8524	0.8227	0.7908	0.7571	0.7218	0.6854	0.6482
4	0.9813	0.9735	0.9639	0.9522	0.9383	0.9222	0.9039	0.8833	0.8606	0.8358
5	0.9963	0.9943	0.9916	0.9879	0.9832	0.9773	0.9700	0.9613	0.9510	0.9389
6	0.9994	0.9990	0.9985	0.9976	0.9964	0.9948	0.9926	0.9898	0.9863	0.9819
7	0.9999	0.9999	0.9998	0.9996	0.9994	0.9990	0.9986	0.9979	0.9970	0.9958
8	1.0000	1.0000	1.0000	1.0000	0.9999	0.9999	0.9998	0.9997	0.9995	0.9992
9	1.0000	1.0000	1.0000	1.0000	1.0000	1.0000	1.0000	1.0000	0.9999	0.9999
10	1.0000	1.0000	1.0000	1.0000	1.0000	1.0000	1.0000	1.0000	1.0000	1.0000

x \ *p*	0.21	0.22	0.23	0.24	0.25	0.26	0.27	0.28	0.29	0.30
0	0.0291	0.0241	0.0198	0.0163	0.0134	0.0109	0.0089	0.0072	0.0059	0.0047
1	0.1453	0.1259	0.1087	0.0935	0.0802	0.0685	0.0583	0.0495	0.0419	0.0353
2	0.3615	0.3269	0.2945	0.2642	0.2361	0.2101	0.1863	0.1645	0.1447	0.1268
3	0.6105	0.5726	0.5350	0.4978	0.4613	0.4258	0.3914	0.3584	0.3268	0.2969
4	0.8090	0.7805	0.7505	0.7190	0.6865	0.6531	0.6190	0.5846	0.5500	0.5155
5	0.9252	0.9095	0.8921	0.8728	0.8516	0.8287	0.8042	0.7780	0.7505	0.7216
6	0.9766	0.9702	0.9626	0.9537	0.9434	0.9316	0.9183	0.9035	0.8870	0.8689
7	0.9942	0.9922	0.9896	0.9865	0.9827	0.9781	0.9726	0.9662	0.9587	0.9500
8	0.9989	0.9984	0.9977	0.9969	0.9958	0.9944	0.9927	0.9906	0.9879	0.9848
9	0.9998	0.9997	0.9996	0.9994	0.9992	0.9989	0.9985	0.9979	0.9972	0.9963
10	1.0000	1.0000	0.9999	0.9999	0.9999	0.9998	0.9998	0.9997	0.9995	0.9993
11	1.0000	1.0000	1.0000	1.0000	1.0000	1.0000	1.0000	1.0000	0.9999	0.9999
12	1.0000	1.0000	1.0000	1.0000	1.0000	1.0000	1.0000	1.0000	1.0000	1.0000

x \ *p*	0.31	0.32	0.33	0.34	0.35	0.36	0.37	0.38	0.39	0.40
0	0.0038	0.0031	0.0025	0.0020	0.0016	0.0012	0.0010	0.0008	0.0006	0.0005
1	0.0296	0.0248	0.0206	0.0171	0.0142	0.0117	0.0096	0.0078	0.0064	0.0052
2	0.1107	0.0962	0.0833	0.0719	0.0617	0.0528	0.0450	0.0382	0.0322	0.0271
3	0.2686	0.2420	0.2171	0.1940	0.1727	0.1531	0.1351	0.1187	0.1039	0.0905
4	0.4813	0.4477	0.4148	0.3829	0.3519	0.3222	0.2938	0.2668	0.2413	0.2173
5	0.6916	0.6607	0.6291	0.5968	0.5643	0.5316	0.4989	0.4665	0.4346	0.4032
6	0.8491	0.8278	0.8049	0.7806	0.7548	0.7278	0.6997	0.6705	0.6405	0.6098
7	0.9401	0.9289	0.9163	0.9023	0.8868	0.8698	0.8513	0.8313	0.8098	0.7869
8	0.9810	0.9764	0.9711	0.9649	0.9578	0.9496	0.9403	0.9298	0.9180	0.9050
9	0.9952	0.9938	0.9921	0.9901	0.9876	0.9846	0.9810	0.9768	0.9719	0.9662
10	0.9991	0.9988	0.9984	0.9978	0.9972	0.9963	0.9953	0.9941	0.9925	0.9907

TABLE A (*continued*)

$n = 15$ (continued)

x \ p	0.31	0.32	0.33	0.34	0.35	0.36	0.37	0.38	0.39	0.40
11	0.9999	0.9998	0.9997	0.9996	0.9995	0.9994	0.9991	0.9989	0.9985	0.9981
12	1.0000	1.0000	1.0000	1.0000	0.9999	0.9999	0.9999	0.9998	0.9998	0.9997
13	1.0000	1.0000	1.0000	1.0000	1.0000	1.0000	1.0000	1.0000	1.0000	1.0000

x \ p	0.41	0.42	0.43	0.44	0.45	0.46	0.47	0.48	0.49	0.50
0	0.0004	0.0003	0.0002	0.0002	0.0001	0.0001	0.0001	0.0001	0.0000	0.0000
1	0.0042	0.0034	0.0027	0.0021	0.0017	0.0013	0.0010	0.0008	0.0006	0.0005
2	0.0227	0.0189	0.0157	0.0130	0.0107	0.0087	0.0071	0.0057	0.0046	0.0037
3	0.0785	0.0678	0.0583	0.0498	0.0424	0.0359	0.0303	0.0254	0.0212	0.0176
4	0.1948	0.1739	0.1546	0.1367	0.1204	0.1055	0.0920	0.0799	0.0690	0.0592
5	0.3726	0.3430	0.3144	0.2869	0.2608	0.2359	0.2125	0.1905	0.1699	0.1509
6	0.5786	0.5470	0.5153	0.4836	0.4522	0.4211	0.3905	0.3606	0.3316	0.3036
7	0.7626	0.7370	0.7102	0.6824	0.6535	0.6238	0.5935	0.5626	0.5314	0.5000
8	0.8905	0.8746	0.8573	0.8385	0.8182	0.7966	0.7735	0.7490	0.7233	0.6964
9	0.9596	0.9521	0.9435	0.9339	0.9231	0.9110	0.8976	0.8829	0.8667	0.8491
10	0.9884	0.9857	0.9826	0.9789	0.9745	0.9695	0.9637	0.9570	0.9494	0.9408
11	0.9975	0.9968	0.9960	0.9949	0.9937	0.9921	0.9903	0.9881	0.9855	0.9824
12	0.9996	0.9995	0.9993	0.9991	0.9989	0.9986	0.9982	0.9977	0.9971	0.9963
13	1.0000	1.0000	0.9999	0.9999	0.9999	0.9998	0.9998	0.9997	0.9996	0.9995
14	1.0000	1.0000	1.0000	1.0000	1.0000	1.0000	1.0000	1.0000	1.0000	1.0000

$n = 16$

x \ p	0.01	0.02	0.03	0.04	0.05	0.06	0.07	0.08	0.09	0.10
0	0.8515	0.7238	0.6143	0.5204	0.4401	0.3716	0.3131	0.2634	0.2211	0.1853
1	0.9891	0.9601	0.9182	0.8673	0.8108	0.7511	0.6902	0.6299	0.5711	0.5147
2	0.9995	0.9963	0.9887	0.9758	0.9571	0.9327	0.9031	0.8688	0.8306	0.7892
3	1.0000	0.9998	0.9989	0.9968	0.9930	0.9868	0.9779	0.9658	0.9504	0.9316
4	1.0000	1.0000	0.9999	0.9997	0.9991	0.9981	0.9962	0.9932	0.9889	0.9830
5	1.0000	1.0000	1.0000	1.0000	0.9999	0.9998	0.9995	0.9990	0.9981	0.9967
6	1.0000	1.0000	1.0000	1.0000	1.0000	1.0000	0.9999	0.9999	0.9997	0.9995
7	1.0000	1.0000	1.0000	1.0000	1.0000	1.0000	1.0000	1.0000	1.0000	0.9999
8	1.0000	1.0000	1.0000	1.0000	1.0000	1.0000	1.0000	1.0000	1.0000	1.0000

x \ p	0.11	0.12	0.13	0.14	0.15	0.16	0.17	0.18	0.19	0.20
0	0.1550	0.1293	0.1077	0.0895	0.0743	0.0614	0.0507	0.0418	0.0343	0.0281
1	0.4614	0.4115	0.3653	0.3227	0.2839	0.2487	0.2170	0.1885	0.1632	0.1407
2	0.7455	0.7001	0.6539	0.6074	0.5614	0.5162	0.4723	0.4302	0.3899	0.3518
3	0.9093	0.8838	0.8552	0.8237	0.7899	0.7540	0.7164	0.6777	0.6381	0.5981

TABLE A   (*continued*)

n = 16 (continued)

x \ p	0.11	0.12	0.13	0.14	0.15	0.16	0.17	0.18	0.19	0.20
4	0.9752	0.9652	0.9529	0.9382	0.9209	0.9012	0.8789	0.8542	0.8273	0.7982
5	0.9947	0.9918	0.9880	0.9829	0.9765	0.9685	0.9588	0.9473	0.9338	0.9183
6	0.9991	0.9985	0.9976	0.9962	0.9944	0.9920	0.9888	0.9847	0.9796	0.9733
7	0.9999	0.9998	0.9996	0.9993	0.9989	0.9984	0.9976	0.9964	0.9949	0.9930
8	1.0000	1.0000	0.9999	0.9999	0.9998	0.9997	0.9996	0.9993	0.9990	0.9985
9	1.0000	1.0000	1.0000	1.0000	1.0000	1.0000	0.9999	0.9999	0.9998	0.9998
10	1.0000	1.0000	1.0000	1.0000	1.0000	1.0000	1.0000	1.0000	1.0000	1.0000

x \ p	0.21	0.22	0.23	0.24	0.25	0.26	0.27	0.28	0.29	0.30
0	0.0230	0.0188	0.0153	0.0124	0.0100	0.0081	0.0065	0.0052	0.0042	0.0033
1	0.1209	0.1035	0.0883	0.0750	0.0635	0.0535	0.0450	0.0377	0.0314	0.0261
2	0.3161	0.2827	0.2517	0.2232	0.1971	0.1733	0.1518	0.1323	0.1149	0.0994
3	0.5582	0.5186	0.4797	0.4417	0.4050	0.3697	0.3360	0.3041	0.2740	0.2459
4	0.7673	0.7348	0.7009	0.6659	0.6302	0.5940	0.5575	0.5212	0.4853	0.4499
5	0.9008	0.8812	0.8595	0.8359	0.8103	0.7831	0.7542	0.7239	0.6923	0.6598
6	0.9658	0.9568	0.9464	0.9342	0.9204	0.9049	0.8875	0.8683	0.8474	0.8247
7	0.9905	0.9873	0.9834	0.9786	0.9729	0.9660	0.9580	0.9486	0.9379	0.9256
8	0.9979	0.9970	0.9959	0.9944	0.9925	0.9902	0.9873	0.9837	0.9794	0.9743
9	0.9996	0.9994	0.9992	0.9988	0.9984	0.9977	0.9969	0.9959	0.9945	0.9929
10	0.9999	0.9999	0.9999	0.9998	0.9997	0.9996	0.9994	0.9992	0.9989	0.9984
11	1.0000	1.0000	1.0000	1.0000	1.0000	0.9999	0.9999	0.9999	0.9998	0.9997
12	1.0000	1.0000	1.0000	1.0000	1.0000	1.0000	1.0000	1.0000	1.0000	1.0000

x \ p	0.31	0.32	0.33	0.34	0.35	0.36	0.37	0.38	0.39	0.40
0	0.0026	0.0021	0.0016	0.0013	0.0010	0.0008	0.0006	0.0005	0.0004	0.0003
1	0.0216	0.0178	0.0146	0.0120	0.0098	0.0079	0.0064	0.0052	0.0041	0.0033
2	0.0856	0.0734	0.0626	0.0533	0.0451	0.0380	0.0319	0.0266	0.0222	0.0183
3	0.2196	0.1953	0.1730	0.1525	0.1339	0.1170	0.1018	0.0881	0.0759	0.0651
4	0.4154	0.3819	0.3496	0.3187	0.2892	0.2613	0.2351	0.2105	0.1877	0.1666
5	0.6264	0.5926	0.5584	0.5241	0.4900	0.4562	0.4230	0.3906	0.3592	0.3288
6	0.8003	0.7743	0.7469	0.7181	0.6881	0.6572	0.6254	0.5930	0.5602	0.5272
7	0.9119	0.8965	0.8795	0.8609	0.8406	0.8187	0.7952	0.7702	0.7438	0.7161
8	0.9683	0.9612	0.9530	0.9436	0.9329	0.9209	0.9074	0.8924	0.8758	0.8577
9	0.9908	0.9883	0.9852	0.9815	0.9771	0.9720	0.9659	0.9589	0.9509	0.9417
10	0.9979	0.9972	0.9963	0.9952	0.9938	0.9921	0.9900	0.9875	0.9845	0.9809
11	0.9996	0.9995	0.9993	0.9990	0.9987	0.9983	0.9977	0.9970	0.9962	0.9951
12	1.0000	0.9999	0.9999	0.9999	0.9998	0.9997	0.9996	0.9995	0.9993	0.9991
13	1.0000	1.0000	1.0000	1.0000	1.0000	1.0000	1.0000	0.9999	0.9999	0.9999
14	1.0000	1.0000	1.0000	1.0000	1.0000	1.0000	1.0000	1.0000	1.0000	1.0000

TABLE A   (*continued*)

					n = 16 (continued)					
x \ *p*	0.41	0.42	0.43	0.44	0.45	0.46	0.47	0.48	0.49	0.50
0	0.0002	0.0002	0.0001	0.0001	0.0001	0.0001	0.0000	0.0000	0.0000	0.0000
1	0.0026	0.0021	0.0016	0.0013	0.0010	0.0008	0.0006	0.0005	0.0003	0.0003
2	0.0151	0.0124	0.0101	0.0082	0.0066	0.0053	0.0042	0.0034	0.0027	0.0021
3	0.0556	0.0473	0.0400	0.0336	0.0281	0.0234	0.0194	0.0160	0.0131	0.0106
4	0.1471	0.1293	0.1131	0.0985	0.0853	0.0735	0.0630	0.0537	0.0456	0.0384
5	0.2997	0.2720	0.2457	0.2208	0.1976	0.1759	0.1559	0.1374	0.1205	0.1051
6	0.4942	0.4613	0.4289	0.3971	0.3660	0.3359	0.3068	0.2790	0.2524	0.2272
7	0.6872	0.6572	0.6264	0.5949	0.5629	0.5306	0.4981	0.4657	0.4335	0.4018
8	0.8381	0.8168	0.7940	0.7698	0.7441	0.7171	0.6889	0.6596	0.6293	0.5982
9	0.9313	0.9195	0.9064	0.8919	0.8759	0.8584	0.8393	0.8186	0.7964	0.7728
10	0.9766	0.9716	0.9658	0.9591	0.9514	0.9426	0.9326	0.9214	0.9089	0.8949
11	0.9938	0.9922	0.9902	0.9879	0.9851	0.9817	0.9778	0.9732	0.9678	0.9616
12	0.9988	0.9984	0.9979	0.9973	0.9965	0.9956	0.9945	0.9931	0.9914	0.9894
13	0.9998	0.9998	0.9997	0.9996	0.9994	0.9993	0.9990	0.9987	0.9984	0.9979
14	1.0000	1.0000	1.0000	1.0000	0.9999	0.9999	0.9999	0.9999	0.9998	0.9997
15	1.0000	1.0000	1.0000	1.0000	1.0000	1.0000	1.0000	1.0000	1.0000	1.0000

					n = 17					
x \ *p*	0.01	0.02	0.03	0.04	0.05	0.06	0.07	0.08	0.09	0.10
0	0.8429	0.7093	0.5958	0.4996	0.4181	0.3493	0.2912	0.2423	0.2012	0.1668
1	0.9877	0.9554	0.9091	0.8535	0.7922	0.7283	0.6638	0.6005	0.5396	0.4818
2	0.9994	0.9956	0.9866	0.9714	0.9497	0.9218	0.8882	0.8497	0.8073	0.7618
3	1.0000	0.9997	0.9986	0.9960	0.9912	0.9836	0.9727	0.9581	0.9397	0.9174
4	1.0000	1.0000	0.9999	0.9996	0.9988	0.9974	0.9949	0.9911	0.9855	0.9779
5	1.0000	1.0000	1.0000	1.0000	0.9999	0.9997	0.9993	0.9985	0.9973	0.9953
6	1.0000	1.0000	1.0000	1.0000	1.0000	1.0000	0.9999	0.9998	0.9996	0.9992
7	1.0000	1.0000	1.0000	1.0000	1.0000	1.0000	1.0000	1.0000	1.0000	0.9999
8	1.0000	1.0000	1.0000	1.0000	1.0000	1.0000	1.0000	1.0000	1.0000	1.0000

x \ *p*	0.11	0.12	0.13	0.14	0.15	0.16	0.17	0.18	0.19	0.20
0	0.1379	0.1138	0.0937	0.0770	0.0631	0.0516	0.0421	0.0343	0.0278	0.0225
1	0.4277	0.3777	0.3318	0.2901	0.2525	0.2187	0.1887	0.1621	0.1387	0.1182
2	0.7142	0.6655	0.6164	0.5676	0.5198	0.4734	0.4289	0.3867	0.3468	0.3096
3	0.8913	0.8617	0.8290	0.7935	0.7556	0.7159	0.6749	0.6331	0.5909	0.5489
4	0.9679	0.9554	0.9402	0.9222	0.9013	0.8776	0.8513	0.8225	0.7913	0.7582
5	0.9925	0.9886	0.9834	0.9766	0.9681	0.9577	0.9452	0.9305	0.9136	0.8943
6	0.9986	0.9977	0.9963	0.9944	0.9917	0.9882	0.9837	0.9780	0.9709	0.9623
7	0.9998	0.9996	0.9993	0.9989	0.9983	0.9973	0.9961	0.9943	0.9920	0.9891
8	1.0000	0.9999	0.9999	0.9998	0.9997	0.9995	0.9992	0.9988	0.9982	0.9974
9	1.0000	1.0000	1.0000	1.0000	1.0000	0.9999	0.9999	0.9998	0.9997	0.9995

TABLE A (*continued*)

n = 17 (continued)

x \ p	0.11	0.12	0.13	0.14	0.15	0.16	0.17	0.18	0.19	0.20
10	1.0000	1.0000	1.0000	1.0000	1.0000	1.0000	1.0000	1.0000	1.0000	0.9999
11	1.0000	1.0000	1.0000	1.0000	1.0000	1.0000	1.0000	1.0000	1.0000	1.0000

x \ p	0.21	0.22	0.23	0.24	0.25	0.26	0.27	0.28	0.29	0.30
0	0.0182	0.0146	0.0118	0.0094	0.0075	0.0060	0.0047	0.0038	0.0030	0.0023
1	0.1004	0.0849	0.0715	0.0600	0.0501	0.0417	0.0346	0.0286	0.0235	0.0193
2	0.2751	0.2433	0.2141	0.1877	0.1637	0.1422	0.1229	0.1058	0.0907	0.0774
3	0.5073	0.4667	0.4272	0.3893	0.3530	0.3186	0.2863	0.2560	0.2279	0.2019
4	0.7234	0.6872	0.6500	0.6121	0.5739	0.5357	0.4977	0.4604	0.4240	0.3887
5	0.8727	0.8490	0.8230	0.7951	0.7653	0.7339	0.7011	0.6671	0.6323	0.5968
6	0.9521	0.9402	0.9264	0.9106	0.8929	0.8732	0.8515	0.8279	0.8024	0.7752
7	0.9853	0.9806	0.9749	0.9680	0.9598	0.9501	0.9389	0.9261	0.9116	0.8954
8	0.9963	0.9949	0.9930	0.9906	0.9876	0.9839	0.9794	0.9739	0.9674	0.9597
9	0.9993	0.9989	0.9984	0.9978	0.9969	0.9958	0.9943	0.9925	0.9902	0.9873
10	0.9999	0.9998	0.9997	0.9996	0.9994	0.9991	0.9987	0.9982	0.9976	0.9968
11	1.0000	1.0000	1.0000	0.9999	0.9999	0.9998	0.9998	0.9997	0.9995	0.9993
12	1.0000	1.0000	1.0000	1.0000	1.0000	1.0000	1.0000	1.0000	0.9999	0.9999
13	1.0000	1.0000	1.0000	1.0000	1.0000	1.0000	1.0000	1.0000	1.0000	1.0000

x \ p	0.31	0.32	0.33	0.34	0.35	0.36	0.37	0.38	0.39	0.40
0	0.0018	0.0014	0.0011	0.0009	0.0007	0.0005	0.0004	0.0003	0.0002	0.0002
1	0.0157	0.0128	0.0104	0.0083	0.0067	0.0054	0.0043	0.0034	0.0027	0.0021
2	0.0657	0.0556	0.0468	0.0392	0.0327	0.0272	0.0225	0.0185	0.0151	0.0123
3	0.1781	0.1563	0.1366	0.1188	0.1028	0.0885	0.0759	0.0648	0.0550	0.0464
4	0.3547	0.3222	0.2913	0.2622	0.2348	0.2094	0.1858	0.1640	0.1441	0.1260
5	0.5610	0.5251	0.4895	0.4542	0.4197	0.3861	0.3535	0.3222	0.2923	0.2639
6	0.7464	0.7162	0.6847	0.6521	0.6188	0.5848	0.5505	0.5161	0.4818	0.4478
7	0.8773	0.8574	0.8358	0.8123	0.7872	0.7605	0.7324	0.7029	0.6722	0.6405
8	0.9508	0.9405	0.9288	0.9155	0.9006	0.8841	0.8659	0.8459	0.8243	0.8011
9	0.9838	0.9796	0.9746	0.9686	0.9617	0.9536	0.9443	0.9336	0.9216	0.9081
10	0.9957	0.9943	0.9926	0.9905	0.9880	0.9849	0.9811	0.9766	0.9714	.9652
11	0.9991	0.9987	0.9983	0.9977	0.9970	0.9960	0.9949	0.9934	0.9916	0.9894
12	0.9998	0.9998	0.9997	0.9996	0.9994	0.9992	0.9989	0.9985	0.9981	0.9975
13	1.0000	1.0000	1.0000	0.9999	0.9999	0.9999	0.9998	0.9998	0.9997	0.9995
14	1.0000	1.0000	1.0000	1.0000	1.0000	1.0000	1.0000	1.0000	1.0000	0.9999
15	1.0000	1.0000	1.0000	1.0000	1.0000	1.0000	1.0000	1.0000	1.0000	1.0000

x \ p	0.41	0.42	0.43	0.44	0.45	0.46	0.47	0.48	0.49	0.50
0	0.0001	0.0001	0.0001	0.0001	0.0000	0.0000	0.0000	0.0000	0.0000	0.0000
1	0.0016	0.0013	0.0010	0.0008	0.0006	0.0004	0.0003	0.0002	0.0002	0.0001

TABLE A *(continued)*

n = 17 (continued)

x \ p	0.41	0.42	0.43	0.44	0.45	0.46	0.47	0.48	0.49	0.50
2	0.0100	0.0080	0.0065	0.0052	0.0041	0.0032	0.0025	0.0020	0.0015	0.0012
3	0.0390	0.0326	0.0271	0.0224	0.0184	0.0151	0.0123	0.0099	0.0080	0.0064
4	0.1096	0.0949	0.0817	0.0699	0.0596	0.0505	0.0425	0.0356	0.0296	0.0245
5	0.2372	0.2121	0.1887	0.1670	0.1471	0.1288	0.1122	0.0972	0.0838	0.0717
6	0.4144	0.3818	0.3501	0.3195	0.2902	0.2623	0.2359	0.2110	0.1878	0.1662
7	0.6080	0.5750	0.5415	0.5079	0.4743	0.4410	0.4082	0.3761	0.3448	0.3145
8	0.7762	0.7498	0.7220	0.6928	0.6626	0.6313	0.5992	0.5665	0.5333	0.5000
9	0.8930	0.8764	0.8581	0.8382	0.8166	0.7934	0.7686	0.7423	0.7145	0.6855
10	0.9580	0.9497	0.9403	0.9295	0.9174	0.9038	0.8888	0.8721	0.8538	0.8338
11	0.9867	0.9835	0.9797	0.9752	0.9699	0.9637	0.9566	0.9483	0.9389	0.9283
12	0.9967	0.9958	0.9946	0.9931	0.9914	0.9892	0.9866	0.9835	0.9798	0.9755
13	0.9994	0.9992	0.9989	0.9986	0.9981	0.9976	0.9969	0.9960	0.9950	0.9936
14	0.9999	0.9999	0.9998	0.9998	0.9997	0.9996	0.9995	0.9993	0.9991	0.9988
15	1.0000	1.0000	1.0000	1.0000	1.0000	1.0000	0.9999	0.9999	0.9999	0.9999
16	1.0000	1.0000	1.0000	1.0000	1.0000	1.0000	1.0000	1.0000	1.0000	1.0000

n = 18

x \ p	0.01	0.02	0.03	0.04	0.05	0.06	0.07	0.08	0.09	0.10
0	0.8345	0.6951	0.5780	0.4796	0.3972	0.3283	0.2708	0.2229	0.1831	0.1501
1	0.9862	0.9505	0.8997	0.8393	0.7735	0.7055	0.6378	0.5719	0.5091	0.4503
2	0.9993	0.9948	0.9843	0.9667	0.9419	0.9102	0.8725	0.8298	0.7832	0.7338
3	1.0000	0.9996	0.9982	0.9950	0.9891	0.9799	0.9667	0.9494	0.9277	0.9018
4	1.0000	1.0000	0.9998	0.9994	0.9985	0.9966	0.9933	0.9884	0.9814	0.9718
5	1.0000	1.0000	1.0000	0.9999	0.9998	0.9995	0.9990	0.9979	0.9962	0.9936
6	1.0000	1.0000	1.0000	1.0000	1.0000	1.0000	0.9999	0.9997	0.9994	0.9988
7	1.0000	1.0000	1.0000	1.0000	1.0000	1.0000	1.0000	1.0000	0.9999	0.9998
8	1.0000	1.0000	1.0000	1.0000	1.0000	1.0000	1.0000	1.0000	1.0000	1.0000

x \ p	0.11	0.12	0.13	0.14	0.15	0.16	0.17	0.18	0.19	0.20
0	0.1227	0.1002	0.0815	0.0662	0.0536	0.0434	0.0349	0.0281	0.0225	0.0180
1	0.3958	0.3460	0.3008	0.2602	0.2241	0.1920	0.1638	0.1391	0.1176	0.0991
2	0.6827	0.6310	0.5794	0.5287	0.4797	0.4327	0.3881	0.3462	0.3073	0.2713
3	0.8718	0.8382	0.8014	0.7618	0.7202	0.6771	0.6331	0.5888	0.5446	0.5010
4	0.9595	0.9442	0.9257	0.9041	0.8794	0.8518	0.8213	0.7884	0.7533	0.7164
5	0.9898	0.9846	0.9778	0.9690	0.9581	0.9449	0.9292	0.9111	0.8903	0.8671
6	0.9979	0.9966	0.9946	0.9919	0.9882	0.9833	0.9771	0.9694	0.9600	0.9487
7	0.9997	0.9994	0.9989	0.9983	0.9973	0.9959	0.9940	0.9914	0.9880	0.9837
8	1.0000	0.9999	0.9998	0.9997	0.9995	0.9992	0.9987	0.9980	0.9971	0.9957
9	1.0000	1.0000	1.0000	1.0000	0.9999	0.9999	0.9998	0.9996	0.9994	0.9991

TABLE A   (*continued*)

n = 18 (continued)

x \ p	0.11	0.12	0.13	0.14	0.15	0.16	0.17	0.18	0.19	0.20
10	1.0000	1.0000	1.0000	1.0000	1.0000	1.0000	1.0000	0.9999	0.9999	0.9998
11	1.0000	1.0000	1.0000	1.0000	1.0000	1.0000	1.0000	1.0000	1.0000	1.0000

x \ p	0.21	0.22	0.23	0.24	0.25	0.26	0.27	0.28	0.29	0.30
0	0.0144	0.0114	0.0091	0.0072	0.0056	0.0044	0.0035	0.0027	0.0021	0.0016
1	0.0831	0.0694	0.0577	0.0478	0.0395	0.0324	0.0265	0.0216	0.0176	0.0142
2	0.2384	0.2084	0.1813	0.1570	0.1353	0.1161	0.0991	0.0842	0.0712	0.0600
3	0.4586	0.4175	0.3782	0.3409	0.3057	0.2728	0.2422	0.2140	0.1881	0.1646
4	0.6780	0.6387	0.5988	0.5586	0.5187	0.4792	0.4406	0.4032	0.3671	0.3327
5	0.8414	0.8134	0.7832	0.7512	0.7174	0.6824	0.6462	0.6093	0.5719	0.5344
6	0.9355	0.9201	0.9026	0.8829	0.8610	0.8370	0.8109	0.7829	0.7531	0.7217
7	0.9783	0.9717	0.9637	0.9542	0.9431	0.9301	0.9153	0.8986	0.8800	0.8593
8	0.9940	0.9917	0.9888	0.9852	0.9807	0.9751	0.9684	0.9605	0.9512	0.9404
9	0.9986	0.9980	0.9972	0.9961	0.9946	0.9927	0.9903	0.9873	0.9836	0.9790
10	0.9997	0.9996	0.9994	0.9991	0.9988	0.9982	0.9975	0.9966	0.9954	0.9939
11	1.0000	0.9999	0.9999	0.9998	0.9998	0.9997	0.9995	0.9993	0.9990	0.9986
12	1.0000	1.0000	1.0000	1.0000	1.0000	0.9999	0.9999	0.9999	0.9998	0.9997
13	1.0000	1.0000	1.0000	1.0000	1.0000	1.0000	1.0000	1.0000	1.0000	1.0000

x \ p	0.31	0.32	0.33	0.34	0.35	0.36	0.37	0.38	0.39	0.40
0	0.0013	0.0010	0.0007	0.0006	0.0004	0.0003	0.0002	0.0002	0.0001	0.0001
1	0.0114	0.0092	0.0073	0.0058	0.0046	0.0036	0.0028	0.0022	0.0017	0.0013
2	0.0502	0.0419	0.0348	0.0287	0.0236	0.0193	0.0157	0.0127	0.0103	0.0082
3	0.1432	0.1241	0.1069	0.0917	0.0783	0.0665	0.0561	0.0472	0.0394	0.0328
4	0.2999	0.2691	0.2402	0.2134	0.1886	0.1659	0.1451	0.1263	0.1093	0.0942
5	0.4971	0.4602	0.4241	0.3889	0.3550	0.3224	0.2914	0.2621	0.2345	0.2088
6	0.6889	0.6550	0.6202	0.5849	0.5491	0.5133	0.4776	0.4424	0.4079	0.3743
7	0.8367	0.8122	0.7859	0.7579	0.7283	0.6973	0.6651	0.6319	0.5979	0.5634
8	0.9280	0.9139	0.8981	0.8804	0.8609	0.8396	0.8165	0.7916	0.7650	0.7368
9	0.9736	0.9671	0.9595	0.9506	0.9403	0.9286	0.9153	0.9003	0.8837	0.8653
10	0.9920	0.9896	0.9867	0.9831	0.9788	0.9736	0.9675	0.9603	0.9520	.0.9424
11	0.9980	0.9973	0.9964	0.9953	0.9938	0.9920	0.9898	0.9870	0.9837	0.9797
12	0.9996	0.9995	0.9992	0.9989	0.9986	0.9981	0.9974	0.9966	0.9956	0.9942
13	0.9999	0.9999	0.9999	0.9998	0.9997	0.9996	0.9995	0.9993	0.9990	0.9987
14	1.0000	1.0000	1.0000	1.0000	1.0000	0.9999	0.9999	0.9999	0.9998	0.9998
15	1.0000	1.0000	1.0000	1.0000	1.0000	1.0000	1.0000	1.0000	1.0000	1.0000

x \ p	0.41	0.42	0.43	0.44	0.45	0.46	0.47	0.48	0.49	0.50
0	0.0001	0.0001	0.0000	0.0000	0.0000	0.0000	0.0000	0.0000	0.0000	0.0000
1	0.0010	0.0008	0.0006	0.0004	0.0003	0.0002	0.0002	0.0001	0.0001	0.0001

TABLE A   *(continued)*

n = 18 (continued)

x \ p	0.41	0.42	0.43	0.44	0.45	0.46	0.47	0.48	0.49	0.50
2	0.0066	0.0052	0.0041	0.0032	0.0025	0.0019	0.0015	0.0011	0.0009	0.0007
3	0.0271	0.0223	0.0182	0.0148	0.0120	0.0096	0.0077	0.0061	0.0048	0.0038
4	0.0807	0.0687	0.0582	0.0490	0.0411	0.0342	0.0283	0.0233	0.0190	0.0154
5	0.1849	0.1628	0.1427	0.1243	0.1077	0.0928	0.0795	0.0676	0.0572	0.0481
6	0.3418	0.3105	0.2807	0.2524	0.2258	0.2009	0.1778	0.1564	0.1368	0.1189
7	0.5287	0.4938	0.4592	0.4250	0.3915	0.3588	0.3272	0.2968	0.2678	0.2403
8	0.7072	0.6764	0.6444	0.6115	0.5778	0.5438	0.5094	0.4751	0.4409	0.4073
9	0.8451	0.8232	0.7996	0.7742	0.7473	0.7188	0.6890	0.6579	0.6258	0.5927
10	0.9314	0.9189	0.9049	0.8893	0.8720	0.8530	0.8323	0.8098	0.7856	0.7597
11	0.9750	0.9693	0.9628	0.9551	0.9463	0.9362	0.9247	0.9117	0.8972	0.8811
12	0.9926	0.9906	0.9882	0.9853	0.9817	0.9775	0.9725	0.9666	0.9598	0.9519
13	0.9983	0.9978	0.9971	0.9962	0.9951	0.9937	0.9921	0.9900	0.9875	0.9846
14	0.9997	0.9996	0.9994	0.9993	0.9990	0.9987	0.9983	0.9977	0.9971	0.9962
15	1.0000	0.9999	0.9999	0.9999	0.9999	0.9998	0.9997	0.9996	0.9995	0.9993
16	1.0000	1.0000	1.0000	1.0000	1.0000	1.0000	1.0000	1.0000	0.9999	0.9999
17	1.0000	1.0000	1.0000	1.0000	1.0000	1.0000	1.0000	1.0000	1.0000	1.0000

n = 19

x \ p	0.01	0.02	0.03	0.04	0.05	0.06	0.07	0.08	0.09	0.10
0	0.8262	0.6812	0.5606	0.4604	0.3774	0.3086	0.2519	0.2051	0.1666	0.1351
1	0.9847	0.9454	0.8900	0.8249	0.7547	0.6829	0.6121	0.5440	0.4798	0.4203
2	0.9991	0.9939	0.9817	0.9616	0.9335	0.8979	0.8561	0.8092	0.7585	0.7054
3	1.0000	0.9995	0.9978	0.9939	0.9868	0.9757	0.9602	0.9398	0.9147	0.8850
4	1.0000	1.0000	0.9998	0.9993	0.9980	0.9956	0.9915	0.9853	0.9765	0.9648
5	1.0000	1.0000	1.0000	0.9999	0.9998	0.9994	0.9986	0.9971	0.9949	0.9914
6	1.0000	1.0000	1.0000	1.0000	1.0000	0.9999	0.9998	0.9996	0.9991	0.9983
7	1.0000	1.0000	1.0000	1.0000	1.0000	1.0000	1.0000	0.9999	0.9999	0.9997
8	1.0000	1.0000	1.0000	1.0000	1.0000	1.0000	1.0000	1.0000	1.0000	1.0000

x \ p	0.11	0.12	0.13	0.14	0.15	0.16	0.17	0.18	0.19	0.20
0	0.1092	0.0881	0.0709	0.0569	0.0456	0.0364	0.0290	0.0230	0.0182	0.0144
1	0.3658	0.3165	0.2723	0.2331	0.1985	0.1682	0.1419	0.1191	0.0996	0.0829
2	0.6512	0.5968	0.5432	0.4911	0.4413	0.3941	0.3500	0.3090	0.2713	0.2369
3	0.8510	0.8133	0.7725	0.7292	0.6841	0.6380	0.5915	0.5451	0.4995	0.4551
4	0.9498	0.9315	0.9096	0.8842	0.8556	0.8238	0.7893	0.7524	0.7136	0.6733
5	0.9865	0.9798	0.9710	0.9599	0.9463	0.9300	0.9109	0.8890	0.8643	0.8369
6	0.9970	0.9952	0.9924	0.9887	0.9837	0.9772	0.9690	0.9589	0.9468	0.9324
7	0.9995	0.9991	0.9984	0.9974	0.9959	0.9939	0.9911	0.9874	0.9827	0.9767

TABLE A   (*continued*)

n = 19 (continued)

x \ p	0.11	0.12	0.13	0.14	0.15	0.16	0.17	0.18	0.19	0.20
8	0.9999	0.9998	0.9997	0.9995	0.9992	0.9986	0.9979	0.9968	0.9953	0.9933
9	1.0000	1.0000	1.0000	0.9999	0.9999	0.9998	0.9996	0.9993	0.9990	0.9984
10	1.0000	1.0000	1.0000	1.0000	1.0000	1.0000	0.9999	0.9999	0.9998	0.9997
11	1.0000	1.0000	1.0000	1.0000	1.0000	1.0000	1.0000	1.0000	1.0000	1.0000

x \ p	0.21	0.22	0.23	0.24	0.25	0.26	0.27	0.28	0.29	0.30
0	0.0113	0.0089	0.0070	0.0054	0.0042	0.0033	0.0025	0.0019	0.0015	0.0011
1	0.0687	0.0566	0.0465	0.0381	0.0310	0.0251	0.0203	0.0163	0.0131	0.0104
2	0.2058	0.1778	0.1529	0.1308	0.1113	0.0943	0.0795	0.0667	0.0557	0.0462
3	0.4123	0.3715	0.3329	0.2968	0.2631	0.2320	0.2035	0.1776	0.1542	0.1332
4	0.6319	0.5900	0.5480	0.5064	0.4654	0.4256	0.3871	0.3502	0.3152	0.2822
5	0.8071	0.7749	0.7408	0.7050	0.6677	0.6295	0.5907	0.5516	0.5125	0.4739
6	0.9157	0.8966	0.8751	0.8513	0.8251	0.7968	0.7664	0.7343	0.7005	0.6655
7	0.9693	0.9604	0.9497	0.9371	0.9225	0.9059	0.8871	0.8662	0.8432	0.8180
8	0.9907	0.9873	0.9831	0.9778	0.9713	0.9634	0.9541	0.9432	0.9306	0.9161
9	0.9977	0.9966	0.9953	0.9934	0.9911	0.9881	0.9844	0.9798	0.9742	0.9674
10	0.9995	0.9993	0.9989	0.9984	0.9977	0.9968	0.9956	0.9940	0.9920	0.9895
11	0.9999	0.9999	0.9998	0.9997	0.9995	0.9993	0.9990	0.9985	0.9980	0.9972
12	1.0000	1.0000	1.0000	0.9999	0.9999	0.9999	0.9998	0.9997	0.9996	0.9994
13	1.0000	1.0000	1.0000	1.0000	1.0000	1.0000	1.0000	1.0000	0.9999	0.9999
14	1.0000	1.0000	1.0000	1.0000	1.0000	1.0000	1.0000	1.0000	1.0000	1.0000

x \ p	0.31	0.32	0.33	0.34	0.35	0.36	0.37	0.38	0.39	0.40
0	0.0009	0.0007	0.0005	0.0004	0.0003	0.0002	0.0002	0.0001	0.0001	0.0001
1	0.0083	0.0065	0.0051	0.0040	0.0031	0.0024	0.0019	0.0014	0.0011	0.0008
2	0.0382	0.0314	0.0257	0.0209	0.0170	0.0137	0.0110	0.0087	0.0069	0.0055
3	0.1144	0.0978	0.0831	0.0703	0.0591	0.0495	0.0412	0.0341	0.0281	0.0230
4	0.2514	0.2227	0.1963	0.1720	0.1500	0.1301	0.1122	0.0962	0.0821	0.0696
5	0.4359	0.3990	0.3634	0.3293	0.2968	0.2661	0.2373	0.2105	0.1857	0.1629
6	0.6294	0.5927	0.5555	0.5182	0.4812	0.4446	0.4087	0.3739	0.3403	0.3081
7	0.7909	0.7619	0.7312	0.6990	0.6656	0.6310	0.5957	0.5599	0.5238	0.4878
8	0.8997	0.8814	0.8611	0.8388	0.8145	0.7884	0.7605	0.7309	0.6998	0.6675
9	0.9595	0.9501	0.9392	0.9267	0.9125	0.8965	0.8787	0.8590	0.8374	0.8139
10	0.9863	0.9824	0.9777	0.9720	0.9653	0.9574	0.9482	0.9375	0.9253	0.9115
11	0.9962	0.9949	0.9932	0.9911	0.9886	0.9854	0.9815	0.9769	0.9713	0.9648
12	0.9991	0.9988	0.9983	0.9977	0.9969	0.9959	0.9946	0.9930	0.9909	0.9884
13	0.9998	0.9998	0.9997	0.9995	0.9993	0.9991	0.9987	0.9983	0.9977	0.9969
14	1.0000	1.0000	0.9999	0.9999	0.9999	0.9998	0.9998	0.9997	0.9995	0.9994
15	1.0000	1.0000	1.0000	1.0000	1.0000	1.0000	1.0000	1.0000	0.9999	0.9999
16	1.0000	1.0000	1.0000	1.0000	1.0000	1.0000	1.0000	1.0000	1.0000	1.0000

TABLE A (*continued*)

n = 19 (continued)

x \ p	0.41	0.42	0.43	0.44	0.45	0.46	0.47	0.48	0.49	0.50
0	0.0000	0.0000	0.0000	0.0000	0.0000	0.0000	0.0000	0.0000	0.0000	0.0000
1	0.0006	0.0005	0.0004	0.0003	0.0002	0.0001	0.0001	0.0001	0.0001	0.0000
2	0.0043	0.0033	0.0026	0.0020	0.0015	0.0012	0.0009	0.0007	0.0005	0.0004
3	0.0187	0.0151	0.0122	0.0097	0.0077	0.0061	0.0048	0.0037	0.0029	0.0022
4	0.0587	0.0492	0.0410	0.0340	0.0280	0.0229	0.0186	0.0150	0.0121	0.0096
5	0.1421	0.1233	0.1063	0.0912	0.0777	0.0658	0.0554	0.0463	0.0385	0.0318
6	0.2774	0.2485	0.2213	0.1961	0.1727	0.1512	0.1316	0.1138	0.0978	0.0835
7	0.4520	0.4168	0.3824	0.3491	0.3169	0.2862	0.2570	0.2294	0.2036	0.1796
8	0.6340	0.5997	0.5647	0.5294	0.4940	0.4587	0.4238	0.3895	0.3561	0.3238
9	0.7886	0.7615	0.7328	0.7026	0.6710	0.6383	0.6046	0.5701	0.5352	0.5000
10	0.8960	0.8787	0.8596	0.8387	0.8159	0.7913	0.7649	0.7369	0.7073	0.6762
11	0.9571	0.9482	0.9379	0.9262	0.9129	0.8979	0.8813	0.8628	0.8425	0.8204
12	0.9854	0.9817	0.9773	0.9720	0.9658	0.9585	0.9500	0.9403	0.9291	0.9165
13	0.9960	0.9948	0.9933	0.9914	0.9891	0.9863	0.9829	0.9788	0.9739	0.9682
14	0.9991	0.9988	0.9984	0.9979	0.9972	0.9964	0.9954	0.9940	0.9924	0.9904
15	0.9999	0.9998	0.9997	0.9996	0.9995	0.9993	0.9990	0.9987	0.9983	0.9978
16	1.0000	1.0000	1.0000	0.9999	0.9999	0.9999	0.9999	0.9998	0.9997	0.9996
17	1.0000	1.0000	1.0000	1.0000	1.0000	1.0000	1.0000	1.0000	1.0000	1.0000

n = 20

x \ p	0.01	0.02	0.03	0.04	0.05	0.06	0.07	0.08	0.09	0.10
0	0.8179	0.6676	0.5438	0.4420	0.3585	0.2901	0.2342	0.1887	0.1516	0.1216
1	0.9831	0.9401	0.8802	0.8103	0.7358	0.6605	0.5869	0.5169	0.4516	0.3917
2	0.9990	0.9929	0.9790	0.9561	0.9245	0.8850	0.8390	0.7879	0.7334	0.6769
3	1.0000	0.9994	0.9973	0.9926	0.9841	0.9710	0.9529	0.9294	0.9007	0.8670
4	1.0000	1.0000	0.9997	0.9990	0.9974	0.9944	0.9893	0.9817	0.9710	0.9568
5	1.0000	1.0000	1.0000	0.9999	0.9997	0.9991	0.9981	0.9962	0.9932	0.9887
6	1.0000	1.0000	1.0000	1.0000	1.0000	0.9999	0.9997	0.9994	0.9987	0.9976
7	1.0000	1.0000	1.0000	1.0000	1.0000	1.0000	1.0000	0.9999	0.9998	0.9996
8	1.0000	1.0000	1.0000	1.0000	1.0000	1.0000	1.0000	1.0000	1.0000	0.9999
9	1.0000	1.0000	1.0000	1.0000	1.0000	1.0000	1.0000	1.0000	1.0000	1.0000

x \ p	0.11	0.12	0.13	0.14	0.15	0.16	0.17	0.18	0.19	0.20
0	0.0972	0.0776	0.0617	0.0490	0.0388	0.0306	0.0241	0.0189	0.0148	0.0115
1	0.3376	0.2891	0.2461	0.2084	0.1756	0.1471	0.1227	0.1018	0.0841	0.0692
2	0.6198	0.5631	0.5080	0.4550	0.4049	0.3580	0.3146	0.2748	0.2386	0.2061
3	0.8290	0.7873	0.7427	0.6959	0.6477	0.5990	0.5504	0.5026	0.4561	0.4114
4	0.9390	0.9173	0.8917	0.8625	0.8298	0.7941	0.7557	0.7151	0.6729	0.6296
5	0.9825	0.9740	0.9630	0.9493	0.9327	0.9130	0.8902	0.8644	0.8357	0.8042

TABLE A (*continued*)

n = 20 (continued)

x \ p	0.11	0.12	0.13	0.14	0.15	0.16	0.17	0.18	0.19	0.20
6	0.9959	0.9933	0.9897	0.9847	0.9781	0.9696	0.9591	0.9463	0.9311	0.9133
7	0.9992	0.9986	0.9976	0.9962	0.9941	0.9912	0.9873	0.9823	0.9759	0.9679
8	0.9999	0.9998	0.9995	0.9992	0.9987	0.9979	0.9967	0.9951	0.9929	0.9900
9	1.0000	1.0000	0.9999	0.9999	0.9998	0.9996	0.9993	0.9989	0.9983	0.9974
10	1.0000	1.0000	1.0000	1.0000	1.0000	0.9999	0.9999	0.9998	0.9996	0.9994
11	1.0000	1.0000	1.0000	1.0000	1.0000	1.0000	1.0000	1.0000	0.9999	0.9999
12	1.0000	1.0000	1.0000	1.0000	1.0000	1.0000	1.0000	1.0000	1.0000	1.0000

x \ p	0.21	0.22	0.23	0.24	0.25	0.26	0.27	0.28	0.29	0.30
0	0.0090	0.0069	0.0054	0.0041	0.0032	0.0024	0.0018	0.0014	0.0011	0.0008
1	0.0566	0.0461	0.0374	0.0302	0.0243	0.0195	0.0155	0.0123	0.0097	0.0076
2	0.1770	0.1512	0.1284	0.1085	0.0913	0.0763	0.0635	0.0526	0.0433	0.0355
3	0.3690	0.3289	0.2915	0.2569	0.2252	0.1962	0.1700	0.1466	0.1256	0.1071
4	0.5858	0.5420	0.4986	0.4561	0.4148	0.3752	0.3375	0.3019	0.2685	0.2375
5	0.7703	0.7343	0.6965	0.6573	0.6172	0.5765	0.5357	0.4952	0.4553	0.4164
6	0.8929	0.8699	0.8442	0.8162	0.7858	0.7533	0.7190	0.6831	0.6460	0.6080
7	0.9581	0.9464	0.9325	0.9165	0.8982	0.8775	0.8545	0.8293	0.8018	0.7723
8	0.9862	0.9814	0.9754	0.9680	0.9591	0.9485	0.9360	0.9216	0.9052	0.8867
9	0.9962	0.9946	0.9925	0.9897	0.9861	0.9817	0.9762	0.9695	0.9615	0.9520
10	0.9991	0.9987	0.9981	0.9972	0.9961	0.9945	0.9926	0.9900	0.9868	0.9829
11	0.9998	0.9997	0.9996	0.9994	0.9991	0.9986	0.9981	0.9973	0.9962	0.9949
12	1.0000	1.0000	0.9999	0.9999	0.9998	0.9997	0.9996	0.9994	0.9991	0.9987
13	1.0000	1.0000	1.0000	1.0000	1.0000	1.0000	0.9999	0.9999	0.9998	0.9997
14	1.0000	1.0000	1.0000	1.0000	1.0000	1.0000	1.0000	1.0000	1.0000	1.0000

x \ p	0.31	0.32	0.33	0.34	0.35	0.36	0.37	0.38	0.39	0.40
0	0.0006	0.0004	0.0003	0.0002	0.0002	0.0001	0.0001	0.0001	0.0001	0.0000
1	0.0060	0.0047	0.0036	0.0028	0.0021	0.0016	0.0012	0.0009	0.0007	0.0005
2	0.0289	0.0235	0.0189	0.0152	0.0121	0.0096	0.0076	0.0060	0.0047	0.0036
3	0.0908	0.0765	0.0642	0.0535	0.0444	0.0366	0.0300	0.0245	0.0198	0.0160
4	0.2089	0.1827	0.1589	0.1374	0.1182	0.1011	0.0859	0.0726	0.0610	0.0510
5	0.3787	0.3426	0.3082	0.2758	0.2454	0.2171	0.1910	0.1671	0.1453	0.1256
6	0.5695	0.5307	0.4921	0.4540	0.4166	0.3803	0.3453	0.3118	0.2800	0.2500
7	0.7409	0.7078	0.6732	0.6376	0.6010	0.5639	0.5265	0.4892	0.4522	0.4159
8	0.8660	0.8432	0.8182	0.7913	0.7624	0.7317	0.6995	0.6659	0.6312	0.5956
9	0.9409	0.9281	0.9134	0.8968	0.8782	0.8576	0.8350	0.8103	0.7837	0.7553
10	0.9780	0.9721	0.9650	0.9566	0.9468	0.9355	0.9225	0.9077	0.8910	0.8725
11	0.9931	0.9909	0.9881	0.9846	0.9804	0.9753	0.9692	0.9619	0.9534	0.9435
12	0.9982	0.9975	0.9966	0.9955	0.9940	0.9921	0.9898	0.9868	0.9833	0.9790
13	0.9996	0.9994	0.9992	0.9989	0.9985	0.9979	0.9972	0.9963	0.9951	0.9935

TABLE A (*continued*)

n = 20 (continued)

x \ p	0.31	0.32	0.33	0.34	0.35	0.36	0.37	0.38	0.39	0.40
14	0.9999	0.9999	0.9999	0.9998	0.9997	0.9996	0.9994	0.9991	0.9988	0.9984
15	1.0000	1.0000	1.0000	1.0000	1.0000	0.9999	0.9999	0.9998	0.9998	0.9997
16	1.0000	1.0000	1.0000	1.0000	1.0000	1.0000	1.0000	1.0000	1.0000	1.0000

x \ p	0.41	0.42	0.43	0.44	0.45	0.46	0.47	0.48	0.49	0.50
0	0.0000	0.0000	0.0000	0.0000	0.0000	0.0000	0.0000	0.0000	0.0000	0.0000
1	0.0004	0.0003	0.0002	0.0002	0.0001	0.0001	0.0001	0.0000	0.0000	0.0000
2	0.0028	0.0021	0.0016	0.0012	0.0009	0.0007	0.0005	0.0004	0.0003	0.0002
3	0.0128	0.0102	0.0080	0.0063	0.0049	0.0038	0.0029	0.0023	0.0017	0.0013
4	0.0423	0.0349	0.0286	0.0233	0.0189	0.0152	0.0121	0.0096	0.0076	0.0059
5	0.1079	0.0922	0.0783	0.0660	0.0553	0.0461	0.0381	0.0313	0.0255	0.0207
6	0.2220	0.1959	0.1719	0.1499	0.1299	0.1119	0.0958	0.0814	0.0688	0.0577
7	0.3804	0.3461	0.3132	0.2817	0.2520	0.2241	0.1980	0.1739	0.1518	0.1316
8	0.5594	0.5229	0.4864	0.4501	0.4143	0.3793	0.3454	0.3127	0.2814	0.2517
9	0.7252	0.6936	0.6606	0.6264	0.5914	0.5557	0.5196	0.4834	0.4474	0.4119
10	0.8520	0.8295	0.8051	0.7788	0.7507	0.7209	0.6896	0.6568	0.6229	0.5881
11	0.9321	0.9190	0.9042	0.8877	0.8692	0.8489	0.8266	0.8024	0.7762	0.7483
12	0.9738	0.9676	0.9603	0.9518	0.9420	0.9306	0.9177	0.9031	0.8867	0.8684
13	0.9916	0.9893	0.9864	0.9828	0.9786	0.9735	0.9674	0.9603	0.9520	0.9423
14	0.9978	0.9971	0.9962	0.9950	0.9936	0.9917	0.9895	0.9867	0.9834	0.9793
15	0.9996	0.9994	0.9992	0.9989	0.9985	0.9980	0.9973	0.9965	0.9954	0.9941
16	0.9999	0.9999	0.9999	0.9998	0.9997	0.9996	0.9995	0.9993	0.9990	0.9987
17	1.0000	1.0000	1.0000	1.0000	1.0000	0.9999	0.9999	0.9999	0.9999	0.9998
18	1.0000	1.0000	1.0000	1.0000	1.0000	1.0000	1.0000	1.0000	1.0000	1.0000

n = 21

x \ p	0.01	0.02	0.03	0.04	0.05	0.06	0.07	0.08	0.09	0.10
0	0.8097	0.6543	0.5275	0.4243	0.3406	0.2727	0.2178	0.1736	0.1380	0.1094
1	0.9815	0.9347	0.8701	0.7956	0.7170	0.6382	0.5622	0.4906	0.4246	0.3647
2	0.9988	0.9919	0.9760	0.9503	0.9151	0.8716	0.8213	0.7663	0.7081	0.6484
3	0.9999	0.9993	0.9968	0.9911	0.9811	0.9659	0.9449	0.9181	0.8856	0.8480
4	1.0000	1.0000	0.9997	0.9988	0.9968	0.9930	0.9867	0.9775	0.9646	0.9478
5	1.0000	1.0000	1.0000	0.9999	0.9996	0.9988	0.9975	0.9950	0.9912	0.9856
6	1.0000	1.0000	1.0000	1.0000	1.0000	0.9998	0.9996	0.9991	0.9982	0.9967
7	1.0000	1.0000	1.0000	1.0000	1.0000	1.0000	0.9999	0.9999	0.9997	0.9994
8	1.0000	1.0000	1.0000	1.0000	1.0000	1.0000	1.0000	1.0000	1.0000	0.9999
9	1.0000	1.0000	1.0000	1.0000	1.0000	1.0000	1.0000	1.0000	1.0000	1.0000

TABLE A   (*continued*)

						$n = 21$ (continued)					

x \ p	0.11	0.12	0.13	0.14	0.15	0.16	0.17	0.18	0.19	0.20
0	0.0865	0.0683	0.0537	0.0421	0.0329	0.0257	0.0200	0.0155	0.0120	0.0092
1	0.3111	0.2637	0.2222	0.1861	0.1550	0.1285	0.1059	0.0869	0.0709	0.0576
2	0.5887	0.5302	0.4739	0.4205	0.3705	0.3243	0.2820	0.2437	0.2093	0.1787
3	0.8060	0.7604	0.7122	0.6622	0.6113	0.5604	0.5103	0.4616	0.4148	0.3704
4	0.9269	0.9017	0.8724	0.8392	0.8025	0.7629	0.7208	0.6769	0.6317	0.5860
5	0.9777	0.9672	0.9538	0.9372	0.9173	0.8940	0.8674	0.8375	0.8047	0.7693
6	0.9944	0.9910	0.9862	0.9797	0.9713	0.9606	0.9474	0.9316	0.9130	0.8915
7	0.9988	0.9980	0.9966	0.9945	0.9917	0.9877	0.9825	0.9758	0.9674	0.9569
8	0.9998	0.9996	0.9993	0.9988	0.9980	0.9968	0.9951	0.9928	0.9897	0.9856
9	1.0000	0.9999	0.9999	0.9998	0.9996	0.9993	0.9989	0.9982	0.9973	0.9959
10	1.0000	1.0000	1.0000	1.0000	0.9999	0.9999	0.9998	0.9996	0.9994	0.9990
11	1.0000	1.0000	1.0000	1.0000	1.0000	1.0000	1.0000	0.9999	0.9999	0.9998
12	1.0000	1.0000	1.0000	1.0000	1.0000	1.0000	1.0000	1.0000	1.0000	1.0000

x \ p	0.21	0.22	0.23	0.24	0.25	0.26	0.27	0.28	0.29	0.30
0	0.0071	0.0054	0.0041	0.0031	0.0024	0.0018	0.0013	0.0010	0.0008	0.0006
1	0.0466	0.0375	0.0301	0.0240	0.0190	0.0150	0.0118	0.0093	0.0072	0.0056
2	0.1517	0.1281	0.1075	0.0898	0.0745	0.0615	0.0506	0.0413	0.0336	0.0271
3	0.3286	0.2898	0.2540	0.2213	0.1917	0.1650	0.1413	0.1202	0.1018	0.0856
4	0.5403	0.4951	0.4509	0.4083	0.3674	0.3287	0.2923	0.2584	0.2271	0.1984
5	0.7316	0.6920	0.6509	0.6090	0.5666	0.5242	0.4822	0.4411	0.4011	0.3627
6	0.8672	0.8400	0.8103	0.7780	0.7436	0.7073	0.6695	0.6305	0.5907	0.5505
7	0.9444	0.9295	0.9122	0.8924	0.8701	0.8452	0.8179	0.7883	0.7566	0.7230
8	0.9803	0.9737	0.9655	0.9556	0.9439	0.9300	0.9140	0.8958	0.8752	0.8523
9	0.9941	0.9917	0.9885	0.9845	0.9794	0.9731	0.9654	0.9561	0.9452	0.9324
10	0.9985	0.9978	0.9968	0.9954	0.9936	0.9912	0.9881	0.9843	0.9795	0.9736
11	0.9997	0.9995	0.9992	0.9989	0.9983	0.9976	0.9966	0.9952	0.9935	0.9913
12	0.9999	0.9999	0.9998	0.9998	0.9996	0.9994	0.9992	0.9988	0.9983	0.9976
13	1.0000	1.0000	1.0000	1.0000	0.9999	0.9999	0.9998	0.9997	0.9996	0.9994
14	1.0000	1.0000	1.0000	1.0000	1.0000	1.0000	1.0000	1.0000	0.9999	0.9999
15	1.0000	1.0000	1.0000	1.0000	1.0000	1.0000	1.0000	1.0000	1.0000	1.0000

x \ p	0.31	0.32	0.33	0.34	0.35	0.36	0.37	0.38	0.39	0.40
0	0.0004	0.0003	0.0002	0.0002	0.0001	0.0001	0.0001	0.0000	0.0000	0.0000
1	0.0043	0.0033	0.0025	0.0019	0.0014	0.0011	0.0008	0.0006	0.0004	0.0003
2	0.0218	0.0174	0.0139	0.0110	0.0086	0.0067	0.0052	0.0041	0.0031	0.0024
3	0.0716	0.0596	0.0492	0.0405	0.0331	0.0269	0.0217	0.0174	0.0139	0.0110
4	0.1723	0.1487	0.1277	0.1089	0.0924	0.0779	0.0652	0.0543	0.0449	0.0370
5	0.3261	0.2914	0.2590	0.2288	0.2009	0.1753	0.1521	0.1312	0.1124	0.0957
6	0.5103	0.4705	0.4314	0.3934	0.3567	0.3216	0.2882	0.2568	0.2275	0.2002

TABLE A *(continued)*

$n = 21$ (continued)

x \ p	0.31	0.32	0.33	0.34	0.35	0.36	0.37	0.38	0.39	0.40
7	0.6877	0.6511	0.6135	0.5752	0.5365	0.4978	0.4595	0.4218	0.3851	0.3495
8	0.8272	0.7998	0.7704	0.7390	0.7059	0.6713	0.6355	0.5988	0.5614	0.5237
9	0.9177	0.9009	0.8820	0.8609	0.8377	0.8123	0.7848	0.7554	0.7243	0.6914
10	0.9665	0.9580	0.9480	0.9363	0.9228	0.9074	0.8901	0.8707	0.8492	0.8256
11	0.9884	0.9849	0.9805	0.9751	0.9687	0.9610	0.9519	0.9413	0.9291	0.9151
12	0.9966	0.9954	0.9938	0.9918	0.9892	0.9861	0.9821	0.9774	0.9716	0.9648
13	0.9992	0.9988	0.9984	0.9977	0.9969	0.9958	0.9944	0.9927	0.9905	0.9877
14	0.9998	0.9998	0.9996	0.9995	0.9993	0.9990	0.9986	0.9980	0.9973	0.9964
15	1.0000	1.0000	0.9999	0.9999	0.9999	0.9998	0.9997	0.9996	0.9994	0.9992
16	1.0000	1.0000	1.0000	1.0000	1.0000	1.0000	1.0000	0.9999	0.9999	0.9998
17	1.0000	1.0000	1.0000	1.0000	1.0000	1.0000	1.0000	1.0000	1.0000	1.0000

x \ p	0.41	0.42	0.43	0.44	0.45	0.46	0.47	0.48	0.49	0.50
0	0.0000	0.0000	0.0000	0.0000	0.0000	0.0000	0.0000	0.0000	0.0000	0.0000
1	0.0002	0.0002	0.0001	0.0001	0.0001	0.0000	0.0000	0.0000	0.0000	0.0000
2	0.0018	0.0014	0.0010	0.0008	0.0006	0.0004	0.0003	0.0002	0.0002	0.0001
3	0.0087	0.0068	0.0053	0.0041	0.0031	0.0024	0.0018	0.0014	0.0010	0.0007
4	0.0302	0.0245	0.0198	0.0158	0.0126	0.0099	0.0078	0.0061	0.0047	0.0036
5	0.0810	0.0681	0.0569	0.0472	0.0389	0.0319	0.0259	0.0209	0.0167	0.0133
6	0.1752	0.1523	0.1316	0.1130	0.0964	0.0816	0.0687	0.0574	0.0476	0.0392
7	0.3155	0.2830	0.2524	0.2237	0.1971	0.1725	0.1500	0.1295	0.1111	0.0946
8	0.4860	0.4487	0.4119	0.3760	0.3413	0.3079	0.2761	0.2461	0.2179	0.1917
9	0.6572	0.6219	0.5856	0.5488	0.5117	0.4746	0.4377	0.4015	0.3661	0.3318
10	0.8000	0.7724	0.7429	0.7118	0.6790	0.6449	0.6097	0.5736	0.5369	0.5000
11	0.8992	0.8814	0.8616	0.8398	0.8159	0.7900	0.7622	0.7325	0.7011	0.6682
12	0.9567	0.9472	0.9362	0.9236	0.9092	0.8930	0.8749	0.8547	0.8326	0.8083
13	0.9843	0.9802	0.9752	0.9692	0.9621	0.9538	0.9441	0.9328	0.9200	0.9054
14	0.9953	0.9938	0.9920	0.9897	0.9868	0.9833	0.9791	0.9740	0.9680	0.9608
15	0.9989	0.9984	0.9979	0.9972	0.9963	0.9951	0.9936	0.9918	0.9895	0.9867
16	0.9998	0.9997	0.9996	0.9994	0.9992	0.9989	0.9985	0.9979	0.9973	0.9964
17	1.0000	1.0000	0.9999	0.9999	0.9999	0.9998	0.9997	0.9996	0.9995	0.9993
18	1.0000	1.0000	1.0000	1.0000	1.0000	1.0000	1.0000	0.9999	0.9999	0.9999
19	1.0000	1.0000	1.0000	1.0000	1.0000	1.0000	1.0000	1.0000	1.0000	1.0000

$n = 22$

x \ p	0.01	0.02	0.03	0.04	0.05	0.06	0.07	0.08	0.09	0.10
0	0.8016	0.6412	0.5117	0.4073	0.3235	0.2563	0.2026	0.1597	0.1256	0.0985
1	0.9798	0.9290	0.8598	0.7808	0.6982	0.6163	0.5381	0.4652	0.3988	0.3392
2	0.9987	0.9907	0.9728	0.9441	0.9052	0.8576	0.8032	0.7442	0.6826	0.6200
3	0.9999	0.9991	0.9962	0.9895	0.9778	0.9602	0.9362	0.9059	0.8696	0.8281

TABLE A (*continued*)

					$n = 22$ (continued)					
x \ p	0.01	0.02	0.03	0.04	0.05	0.06	0.07	0.08	0.09	0.10
4	1.0000	0.9999	0.9996	0.9985	0.9960	0.9913	0.9838	0.9727	0.9575	0.9379
5	1.0000	1.0000	1.0000	0.9998	0.9994	0.9985	0.9967	0.9936	0.9888	0.9818
6	1.0000	1.0000	1.0000	1.0000	0.9999	0.9998	0.9995	0.9988	0.9976	0.9956
7	1.0000	1.0000	1.0000	1.0000	1.0000	1.0000	0.9999	0.9998	0.9996	0.9991
8	1.0000	1.0000	1.0000	1.0000	1.0000	1.0000	1.0000	1.0000	0.9999	0.9999
9	1.0000	1.0000	1.0000	1.0000	1.0000	1.0000	1.0000	1.0000	1.0000	1.0000

x \ p	0.11	0.12	0.13	0.14	0.15	0.16	0.17	0.18	0.19	0.20
0	0.0770	0.0601	0.0467	0.0362	0.0280	0.0216	0.0166	0.0127	0.0097	0.0074
1	0.2864	0.2403	0.2003	0.1659	0.1367	0.1120	0.0913	0.0740	0.0597	0.0480
2	0.5582	0.4983	0.4412	0.3877	0.3382	0.2929	0.2520	0.2154	0.1830	0.1545
3	0.7821	0.7328	0.6812	0.6283	0.5752	0.5226	0.4715	0.4224	0.3758	0.3320
4	0.9136	0.8847	0.8515	0.8144	0.7738	0.7305	0.6850	0.6318	0.5905	0.5429
5	0.9721	0.9593	0.9432	0.9235	0.9001	0.8730	0.8424	0.8086	0.7719	0.7326
6	0.9926	0.9881	0.9820	0.9738	0.9632	0.9499	0.9338	0.9147	0.8924	0.8670
7	0.9984	0.9971	0.9952	0.9925	0.9886	0.9834	0.9766	0.9679	0.9570	0.9439
8	0.9997	0.9994	0.9989	0.9982	0.9970	0.9954	0.9930	0.9898	0.9854	0.9799
9	1.0000	0.9999	0.9998	0.9996	0.9993	0.9989	0.9982	0.9972	0.9958	0.9939
10	1.0000	1.0000	1.0000	0.9999	0.9999	0.9998	0.9996	0.9994	0.9990	0.9984
11	1.0000	1.0000	1.0000	1.0000	1.0000	1.0000	0.9999	0.9999	0.9998	0.9997
12	1.0000	1.0000	1.0000	1.0000	1.0000	1.0000	1.0000	1.0000	1.0000	0.9999
13	1.0000	1.0000	1.0000	1.0000	1.0000	1.0000	1.0000	1.0000	1.0000	1.0000

x \ p	0.21	0.22	0.23	0.24	0.25	0.26	0.27	0.28	0.29	0.30
0	0.0056	0.0042	0.0032	0.0024	0.0018	0.0013	0.0010	0.0007	0.0005	0.0004
1	0.0383	0.0305	0.0241	0.0190	0.0149	0.1116	0.0090	0.0069	0.0053	0.0041
2	0.1296	0.1081	0.0897	0.0740	0.0606	0.0495	0.0401	0.0323	0.0259	0.0207
3	0.2915	0.2542	0.2203	0.1897	0.1624	0.1381	0.1168	0.0981	0.0820	0.0681
4	0.4958	0.4499	0.4057	0.3634	0.3235	0.2861	0.2515	0.2197	0.1907	0.1645
5	0.6914	0.6486	0.6050	0.5608	0.5168	0.4733	0.4309	0.3899	0.3507	0.3134
6	0.8387	0.8075	0.7736	0.7375	0.6994	0.6597	0.6189	0.5774	0.5357	0.4942
7	0.9282	0.9098	0.8888	0.8650	0.8385	0.8094	0.7779	0.7441	0.7085	0.6712
8	0.9728	0.9640	0.9533	0.9405	0.9254	0.9080	0.8881	0.8657	0.8408	0.8135
9	0.9912	0.9877	0.9832	0.9776	0.9705	0.9619	0.9515	0.9392	0.9249	0.9084
10	0.9976	0.9964	0.9949	0.9928	0.9900	0.9865	0.9820	0.9764	0.9695	0.9613
11	0.9994	0.9991	0.9987	0.9980	0.9971	0.9959	0.9943	0.9922	0.9894	0.9860
12	0.9999	0.9998	0.9997	0.9995	0.9993	0.9990	0.9985	0.9978	0.9969	0.9957
13	1.0000	1.0000	0.9999	0.9999	0.9999	0.9998	0.9997	0.9995	0.9992	0.9989
14	1.0000	1.0000	1.0000	1.0000	1.0000	1.0000	0.9999	0.9999	0.9998	0.9998
15	1.0000	1.0000	1.0000	1.0000	1.0000	1.0000	1.0000	1.0000	1.0000	1.0000

TABLE A (*continued*)

$n = 22$ (continued)

x \ p	0.31	0.32	0.33	0.34	0.35	0.36	0.37	0.38	0.39	0.40
0	0.0003	0.0002	0.0001	0.0001	0.0001	0.0001	0.0000	0.0000	0.0000	0.0000
1	0.0031	0.0023	0.0018	0.0013	0.0010	0.0007	0.0005	0.0004	0.0003	0.0002
2	0.0164	0.0129	0.0101	0.0079	0.0061	0.0047	0.0036	0.0027	0.0021	0.0016
3	0.0562	0.0461	0.0376	0.0304	0.0245	0.0196	0.0156	0.0123	0.0097	0.0076
4	0.1411	0.1202	0.1018	0.0856	0.0716	0.0595	0.0491	0.0403	0.0328	0.0266
5	0.2784	0.2458	0.2156	0.1880	0.1629	0.1402	0.1200	0.1020	0.0861	0.0722
6	0.4532	0.4132	0.3745	0.3374	0.3022	0.2689	0.2379	0.2091	0.1826	0.1584
7	0.6327	0.5933	0.5534	0.5134	0.4736	0.4344	0.3961	0.3591	0.3236	0.2898
8	0.7840	0.7522	0.7186	0.6833	0.6466	0.6089	0.5704	0.5315	0.4926	0.4540
9	0.8896	0.8686	0.8452	0.8195	0.7916	0.7615	0.7296	0.6959	0.6607	0.6244
10	0.9514	0.9397	0.9262	0.9107	0.8930	0.8732	0.8511	0.8269	0.8005	0.7720
11	0.9816	0.9763	0.9698	0.9619	0.9526	0.9417	0.9290	0.9145	0.8979	0.8793
12	0.9941	0.9920	0.9894	0.9861	0.9820	0.9770	0.9710	0.9637	0.9550	0.9449
13	0.9984	0.9977	0.9969	0.9957	0.9942	0.9923	0.9899	0.9869	0.9831	0.9785
14	0.9996	0.9995	0.9992	0.9989	0.9984	0.9978	0.9970	0.9960	0.9947	0.9930
15	0.9999	0.9999	0.9998	0.9998	0.9997	0.9995	0.9993	0.9990	0.9986	0.9981
16	1.0000	1.0000	1.0000	1.0000	0.9999	0.9999	0.9999	0.9998	0.9997	0.9996
17	1.0000	1.0000	1.0000	1.0000	1.0000	1.0000	1.0000	1.0000	0.9999	0.9999
18	1.0000	1.0000	1.0000	1.0000	1.0000	1.0000	1.0000	1.0000	1.0000	1.0000

x \ p	0.41	0.42	0.43	0.44	0.45	0.46	0.47	0.48	0.49	0.50
0	0.0000	0.0000	0.0000	0.0000	0.0000	0.0000	0.0000	0.0000	0.0000	0.0000
1	0.0001	0.0001	0.0001	0.0001	0.0000	0.0000	0.0000	0.0000	0.0000	0.0000
2	0.0012	0.0009	0.0006	0.0005	0.0003	0.0002	0.0002	0.0001	0.0001	0.0001
3	0.0059	0.0045	0.0035	0.0026	0.0020	0.0015	0.0011	0.0008	0.0006	0.0004
4	0.0214	0.0171	0.0135	0.0107	0.0083	0.0065	0.0050	0.0038	0.0029	0.0022
5	0.0602	0.0498	0.0409	0.0334	0.0271	0.0218	0.0174	0.0138	0.0108	0.0085
6	0.1366	0.1170	0.0995	0.0841	0.0705	0.0587	0.0486	0.0399	0.0325	0.0262
7	0.2580	0.2281	0.2005	0.1750	0.1518	0.1307	0.1118	0.0949	0.0800	0.0669
8	0.4161	0.3791	0.3433	0.3090	0.2764	0.2456	0.2168	0.1901	0.1656	0.1431
9	0.5870	0.5491	0.5109	0.4728	0.4350	0.3979	0.3618	0.3269	0.2935	0.2617
10	0.7415	0.7092	0.6753	0.6401	0.6037	0.5665	0.5289	0.4910	0.4532	0.4159
11	0.8585	0.8356	0.8106	0.7834	0.7543	0.7233	0.6905	0.6562	0.6207	0.5841
12	0.9331	0.9196	0.9041	0.8867	0.8672	0.8456	0.8219	0.7961	0.7682	0.7383
13	0.9730	0.9663	0.9584	0.9491	0.9383	0.9258	0.9115	0.8953	0.8771	0.8569
14	0.9908	0.9881	0.9848	0.9807	0.9757	0.9697	0.9626	0.9543	0.9445	0.9331
15	0.9974	0.9965	0.9953	0.9939	0.9920	0.9897	0.9868	0.9833	0.9790	0.9738
16	0.9994	0.9992	0.9988	0.9984	0.9979	0.9971	0.9962	0.9950	0.9935	0.9915
17	0.9999	0.9998	0.9998	0.9997	0.9995	0.9994	0.9991	0.9988	0.9984	0.9978
18	1.0000	1.0000	1.0000	0.9999	0.9999	0.9999	0.9998	0.9998	0.9997	0.9996

TABLE A   (*continued*)

					n = 22 (continued)					

p / *x*	0.41	0.42	0.43	0.44	0.45	0.46	0.47	0.48	0.49	0.50
19	1.0000	1.0000	1.0000	1.0000	1.0000	1.0000	1.0000	1.0000	1.0000	0.9999
20	1.0000	1.0000	1.0000	1.0000	1.0000	1.0000	1.0000	1.0000	1.0000	1.0000

					n = 23					

p / *x*	0.01	0.02	0.03	0.04	0.05	0.06	0.07	0.08	0.09	0.10
0	0.7936	0.6283	0.4963	0.3911	0.3074	0.2410	0.1884	0.1469	0.1143	0.0886
1	0.9780	0.9233	0.8493	0.7658	0.6794	0.5947	0.5146	0.4408	0.3742	0.3151
2	0.9985	0.9895	0.9695	0.9376	0.8948	0.8431	0.7846	0.7219	0.6570	0.5920
3	0.9999	0.9990	0.9955	0.9877	0.9742	0.9541	0.9269	0.8930	0.8528	0.8073
4	1.0000	0.9999	0.9995	0.9981	0.9951	0.9895	0.9805	0.9674	0.9496	0.9269
5	1.0000	1.0000	1.0000	0.9998	0.9992	0.9981	0.9958	0.9920	0.9860	0.9774
6	1.0000	1.0000	1.0000	1.0000	0.9999	0.9997	0.9993	0.9984	0.9968	0.9942
7	1.0000	1.0000	1.0000	1.0000	1.0000	1.0000	0.9999	0.9997	0.9994	0.9988
8	1.0000	1.0000	1.0000	1.0000	1.0000	1.0000	1.0000	1.0000	0.9999	0.9998
9	1.0000	1.0000	1.0000	1.0000	1.0000	1.0000	1.0000	1.0000	1.0000	1.0000

p / *x*	0.11	0.12	0.13	0.14	0.15	0.16	0.17	0.18	0.19	0.20
0	0.0685	0.0529	0.0406	0.0312	0.0238	0.0181	0.0138	0.0104	0.0079	0.0059
1	0.2634	0.2186	0.1803	0.1478	0.1204	0.0976	0.0786	0.0630	0.0502	0.0398
2	0.5283	0.4673	0.4099	0.3566	0.3080	0.2640	0.2247	0.1900	0.1596	0.1332
3	0.7575	0.7047	0.6500	0.5946	0.5396	0.4859	0.4342	0.3851	0.3391	0.2965
4	0.8991	0.8665	0.8294	0.7883	0.7440	0.6972	0.6487	0.5993	0.5497	0.5007
5	0.9656	0.9504	0.9313	0.9082	0.8811	0.8502	0.8157	0.7779	0.7374	0.6947
6	0.9903	0.9847	0.9769	0.9667	0.9537	0.9376	0.9183	0.8956	0.8695	0.8402
7	0.9977	0.9960	0.9935	0.9899	0.9848	0.9780	0.9693	0.9583	0.9447	0.9285
8	0.9995	0.9991	0.9985	0.9974	0.9958	0.9934	0.9902	0.9858	0.9800	0.9727
9	0.9999	0.9998	0.9997	0.9994	0.9990	0.9983	0.9973	0.9959	0.9938	0.9911
10	1.0000	1.0000	0.9999	0.9999	0.9998	0.9996	0.9994	0.9990	0.9984	0.9975
11	1.0000	1.0000	1.0000	1.0000	1.0000	0.9999	0.9999	0.9998	0.9996	0.9994
12	1.0000	1.0000	1.0000	1.0000	1.0000	1.0000	1.0000	1.0000	0.9999	0.9999
13	1.0000	1.0000	1.0000	1.0000	1.0000	1.0000	1.0000	1.0000	1.0000	1.0000

p / *x*	0.21	0.22	0.23	0.24	0.25	0.26	0.27	0.28	0.29	0.30
0	0.0044	0.0033	0.0025	0.0018	0.0013	0.0010	0.0007	0.0005	0.0004	0.0003
1	0.0314	0.0247	0.0193	0.0150	0.0116	0.0089	0.0068	0.0052	0.0039	0.0030
2	0.1105	0.0911	0.0746	0.0608	0.0492	0.0396	0.0317	0.0252	0.0200	0.0157
3	0.2575	0.2221	0.1903	0.1620	0.1370	0.1151	0.0961	0.0797	0.0657	0.0538
4	0.4529	0.4069	0.3630	0.3217	0.2832	0.2477	0.2151	0.1857	0.1592	0.1356

TABLE A   (*continued*)

n = 23 (continued)

x \ p	0.21	0.22	0.23	0.24	0.25	0.26	0.27	0.28	0.29	0.30
5	0.6503	0.6049	0.5591	0.5134	0.4685	0.4247	0.3825	0.3423	0.3043	0.2688
6	0.8077	0.7725	0.7348	0.6951	0.6537	0.6113	0.5682	0.5249	0.4821	0.4399
7	0.9094	0.8873	0.8623	0.8344	0.8037	0.7705	0.7349	0.6975	0.6584	0.6181
8	0.9634	0.9521	0.9384	0.9223	0.9037	0.8823	0.8583	0.8317	0.8025	0.7709
9	0.9873	0.9825	0.9763	0.9687	0.9592	0.9479	0.9344	0.9186	0.9005	0.8799
10	0.9963	0.9945	0.9922	0.9891	0.9851	0.9801	0.9738	0.9660	0.9566	0.9454
11	0.9991	0.9985	0.9978	0.9968	0.9954	0.9935	0.9910	0.9878	0.9837	0.9786
12	0.9998	0.9997	0.9995	0.9992	0.9988	0.9982	0.9973	0.9962	0.9947	0.9928
13	1.0000	0.9999	0.9999	0.9998	0.9997	0.9996	0.9993	0.9990	0.9985	0.9979
14	1.0000	1.0000	1.0000	1.0000	0.9999	0.9999	0.9999	0.9998	0.9997	0.9995
15	1.0000	1.0000	1.0000	1.0000	1.0000	1.0000	1.0000	1.0000	0.9999	0.9999
16	1.0000	1.0000	1.0000	1.0000	1.0000	1.0000	1.0000	1.0000	1.0000	1.0000

x \ p	0.31	0.32	0.33	0.34	0.35	0.36	0.37	0.38	0.39	0.40
0	0.0002	0.0001	0.0001	0.0001	0.0000	0.0000	0.0000	0.0000	0.0000	0.0000
1	0.0022	0.0017	0.0012	0.0009	0.0007	0.0005	0.0004	0.0003	0.0002	0.0001
2	0.0123	0.0095	0.0074	0.0057	0.0043	0.0033	0.0025	0.0018	0.0014	0.0010
3	0.0438	0.0355	0.0285	0.0228	0.0181	0.0143	0.0112	0.0087	0.0067	0.0052
4	0.1148	0.0965	0.0806	0.0669	0.0551	0.0451	0.0367	0.0297	0.0238	0.0190
5	0.2358	0.2056	0.1781	0.1532	0.1309	0.1112	0.0938	0.0785	0.0653	0.0540
6	0.3990	0.3596	0.3221	0.2866	0.2534	0.2226	0.1942	0.1684	0.1450	0.1240
7	0.5771	0.5357	0.4944	0.4535	0.4136	0.3748	0.3376	0.3021	0.2686	0.2373
8	0.7371	0.7014	0.6641	0.6255	0.5860	0.5460	0.5059	0.4660	0.4267	0.3884
9	0.8569	0.8313	0.8034	0.7732	0.7408	0.7066	0.6707	0.6334	0.5952	0.5562
10	0.9932	0.9170	0.8995	0.8797	0.8575	0.8330	0.8062	0.7771	0.7460	0.7129
11	0.9722	0.9646	0.9554	0.9445	0.9318	0.9170	0.9002	0.8812	0.8599	0.8364
12	0.9902	0.9870	0.9829	0.9779	0.9717	0.9643	0.9554	0.9450	0.9328	0.9187
13	0.9971	0.9959	0.9944	0.9925	0.9900	0.9868	0.9829	0.9780	0.9722	0.9651
14	0.9992	0.9989	0.9984	0.9978	0.9970	0.9958	0.9944	0.9925	0.9902	0.9872
15	0.9998	0.9998	0.9996	0.9995	0.9992	0.9989	0.9985	0.9979	0.9971	0.9960
16	1.0000	1.0000	0.9999	0.9999	0.9998	0.9998	0.9996	0.9995	0.9993	0.9990
17	1.0000	1.0000	1.0000	1.0000	1.0000	1.0000	0.9999	0.9999	0.9999	0.9998
18	1.0000	1.0000	1.0000	1.0000	1.0000	1.0000	1.0000	1.0000	1.0000	1.0000

x \ p	0.41	0.42	0.43	0.44	0.45	0.46	0.47	0.48	0.49	0.50
0	0.0000	0.0000	0.0000	0.0000	0.0000	0.0000	0.0000	0.0000	0.0000	0.0000
1	0.0001	0.0001	0.0000	0.0000	0.0000	0.0000	0.0000	0.0000	0.0000	0.0000
2	0.0007	0.0005	0.0004	0.0003	0.0002	0.0001	0.0001	0.0001	0.0000	0.0000
3	0.0039	0.0030	0.0022	0.0017	0.0012	0.0009	0.0007	0.0005	0.0003	0.0002
4	0.0150	0.0118	0.0092	0.0071	0.0055	0.0042	0.0032	0.0024	0.0018	0.0013

TABLE A   (*continued*)

					$n = 23$ (continued)					
x \ *p*	0.41	0.42	0.43	0.44	0.45	0.46	0.47	0.48	0.49	0.50
5	0.0443	0.0361	0.0292	0.0234	0.0186	0.0147	0.0116	0.0090	0.0069	0.0053
6	0.1053	0.0888	0.0743	0.0618	0.0510	0.0417	0.0339	0.0273	0.0219	0.0173
7	0.2082	0.1815	0.1571	0.1350	0.1152	0.0976	0.0821	0.0685	0.0567	0.0466
8	0.3513	0.3157	0.2819	0.2500	0.2203	0.1927	0.1674	0.1444	0.1236	0.1050
9	0.5170	0.4777	0.4389	0.4007	0.3636	0.3278	0.2936	0.2612	0.2308	0.2024
10	0.6782	0.6420	0.6046	0.5665	0.5278	0.4890	0.4503	0.4122	0.3749	0.3388
11	0.8105	0.7825	0.7524	0.7204	0.6865	0.6512	0.6145	0.5769	0.5386	0.5000
12	0.9025	0.8843	0.8639	0.8413	0.8164	0.7893	0.7602	0.7289	0.6959	0.6612
13	0.9566	0.9467	0.9351	0.9217	0.9063	0.8889	0.8694	0.8477	0.8237	0.7976
14	0.9835	0.9789	0.9734	0.9668	0.9589	0.9495	0.9386	0.9260	0.9115	0.8950
15	0.9947	0.9930	0.9908	0.9881	0.9847	0.9805	0.9755	0.9693	0.9621	0.9534
16	0.9986	0.9980	0.9973	0.9964	0.9952	0.9937	0.9918	0.9894	0.9864	0.9827
17	0.9997	0.9996	0.9994	0.9991	0.9988	0.9983	0.9977	0.9970	0.9960	0.9947
18	0.9999	0.9999	0.9999	0.9998	0.9998	0.9996	0.9995	0.9993	0.9990	0.9987
19	1.0000	1.0000	1.0000	1.0000	1.0000	0.9999	0.9999	0.9999	0.9998	0.9998
20	1.0000	1.0000	1.0000	1.0000	1.0000	1.0000	1.0000	1.0000	1.0000	1.0000

					$n = 24$					
x \ *p*	0.01	0.02	0.03	0.04	0.05	0.06	0.07	0.08	0.09	0.10
0	0.7857	0.6158	0.4814	0.3754	0.2920	0.2265	0.1752	0.1352	0.1040	0.0798
1	0.9761	0.9174	0.8388	0.7508	0.6608	0.5735	0.4918	0.4173	0.3508	0.2925
2	0.9983	0.9982	0.9659	0.9307	0.8841	0.8282	0.7657	0.6994	0.6316	0.5643
3	0.9999	0.9988	0.9947	0.9857	0.9702	0.9474	0.9170	0.8793	0.8352	0.7857
4	1.0000	0.9999	0.9994	0.9977	0.9940	0.9873	0.9767	0.9614	0.9409	0.9149
5	1.0000	1.0000	0.9999	0.9997	0.9990	0.9975	0.9947	0.9900	0.9827	0.9723
6	1.0000	1.0000	1.0000	1.0000	0.9999	0.9996	0.9990	0.9979	0.9958	0.9925
7	1.0000	1.0000	1.0000	1.0000	1.0000	0.9999	0.9998	0.9996	0.9992	0.9983
8	1.0000	1.0000	1.0000	1.0000	1.0000	1.0000	1.0000	0.9999	0.9999	0.9997
9	1.0000	1.0000	1.0000	1.0000	1.0000	1.0000	1.0000	1.0000	1.0000	0.9999
10	1.0000	1.0000	1.0000	1.0000	1.0000	1.0000	1.0000	1.0000	1.0000	1.0000

x \ *p*	0.11	0.12	0.13	0.14	0.15	0.16	0.17	0.18	0.19	0.20
0	0.0610	0.0465	0.0354	0.0268	0.0202	0.0152	0.0114	0.0085	0.0064	0.0047
1	0.2420	0.1987	0.1621	0.1315	0.1059	0.0849	0.0676	0.0535	0.0422	0.0331
2	0.4992	0.4375	0.3800	0.3274	0.2798	0.2374	0.1999	0.1671	0.1388	0.1145
3	0.7323	0.6762	0.6188	0.5613	0.5049	0.4504	0.3986	0.3500	0.3050	0.2639
4	0.8835	0.8471	0.8061	0.7612	0.7134	0.6634	0.6122	0.5607	0.5097	0.4599
5	0.9583	0.9403	0.9180	0.8914	0.8606	0.8257	0.7873	0.7458	0.7017	0.6559
6	0.9876	0.9806	0.9710	0.9585	0.9428	0.9236	0.9008	0.8744	0.8444	0.8111

TABLE A (*continued*)

	$n = 24$ (continued)									
x \ p	0.11	0.12	0.13	0.14	0.15	0.16	0.17	0.18	0.19	0.20
7	0.9969	0.9947	0.9913	0.9866	0.9801	0.9716	0.9606	0.9470	0.9304	0.9108
8	0.9993	0.9988	0.9978	0.9963	0.9941	0.9910	0.9866	0.9809	0.9733	0.9638
9	0.9999	0.9998	0.9995	0.9991	0.9985	0.9976	0.9961	0.9941	0.9912	0.9874
10	1.0000	1.0000	0.9999	0.9998	0.9997	0.9994	0.9990	0.9984	0.9975	0.9962
11	1.0000	1.0000	1.0000	1.0000	0.9999	0.9999	0.9998	0.9996	0.9994	0.9990
12	1.0000	1.0000	1.0000	1.0000	1.0000	1.0000	1.0000	0.9999	0.9999	0.9998
13	1.0000	1.0000	1.0000	1.0000	1.0000	1.0000	1.0000	1.0000	1.0000	1.0000

x \ p	0.21	0.22	0.23	0.24	0.25	0.26	0.27	0.28	0.29	0.30
0	0.0035	0.0026	0.0019	0.0014	0.0010	0.0007	0.0005	0.0004	0.0003	0.0002
1	0.0258	0.0200	0.0154	0.0118	0.0090	0.0069	0.0052	0.0039	0.0029	0.0022
2	0.0939	0.0765	0.0619	0.0498	0.0398	0.0316	0.0250	0.0196	0.0153	0.0119
3	0.2266	0.1933	0.1637	0.1377	0.1150	0.0955	0.0787	0.0645	0.0524	0.0424
4	0.4119	0.3662	0.3233	0.2834	0.2466	0.2132	0.1830	0.1560	0.1321	0.1111
5	0.6089	0.5614	0.5140	0.4674	0.4222	0.3786	0.3373	0.2984	0.2622	0.2288
6	0.7747	0.7356	0.6944	0.6515	0.6074	0.5627	0.5180	0.4738	0.4305	0.3886
7	0.8880	0.8621	0.8330	0.8009	0.7662	0.7291	0.6899	0.6492	0.6073	0.5647
8	0.9521	0.9378	0.9209	0.9012	0.8787	0.8533	0.8250	0.7941	0.7607	0.7250
9	0.9823	0.9758	0.9676	0.9575	0.9453	0.9308	0.9138	0.8943	0.8721	0.8472
10	0.9944	0.9919	0.9886	0.9842	0.9787	0.9717	0.9631	0.9527	0.9403	0.9258
11	0.9985	0.9977	0.9965	0.9949	0.9928	0.9900	0.9863	0.9817	0.9758	0.9686
12	0.9996	0.9994	0.9991	0.9986	0.9979	0.9969	0.9956	0.9938	0.9915	0.9885
13	0.9999	0.9999	0.9998	0.9997	0.9995	0.9992	0.9988	0.9982	0.9974	0.9964
14	1.0000	1.0000	1.0000	0.9999	0.9999	0.9998	0.9997	0.9996	0.9993	0.9990
15	1.0000	1.0000	1.0000	1.0000	1.0000	1.0000	0.9999	0.9999	0.9999	0.9998
16	1.0000	1.0000	1.0000	1.0000	1.0000	1.0000	1.0000	1.0000	1.0000	1.0000

x \ p	0.31	0.32	0.33	0.34	0.35	0.36	0.37	0.38	0.39	0.40
0	0.0001	0.0001	0.0001	0.0000	0.0000	0.0000	0.0000	0.0000	0.0000	0.0000
1	0.0016	0.0012	0.0009	0.0006	0.0005	0.0003	0.0002	0.0002	0.0001	0.0001
2	0.0092	0.0070	0.0053	0.0040	0.0030	0.0023	0.0017	0.0012	0.0009	0.0007
3	0.0341	0.0272	0.0215	0.0170	0.0133	0.0103	0.0080	0.0061	0.0046	0.0035
4	0.0928	0.0770	0.0634	0.0519	0.0422	0.0340	0.0273	0.0217	0.0171	0.0134
5	0.1983	0.1707	0.1459	0.1239	0.1044	0.0874	0.0727	0.0600	0.0491	0.0400
6	0.3484	0.3103	0.2746	0.2413	0.2106	0.1825	0.1571	0.1342	0.1139	0.0960
7	0.5219	0.4794	0.4375	0.3968	0.3575	0.3200	0.2845	0.2513	0.2204	0.1919
8	0.6875	0.6484	0.6081	0.5670	0.5275	0.4844	0.4436	0.4037	0.3650	0.3279
9	0.8197	0.7898	0.7574	0.7230	0.6867	0.6488	0.6097	0.5698	0.5295	0.4891
10	0.9089	0.8896	0.8678	0.8435	0.8167	0.7875	0.7560	0.7225	0.6872	0.6502
11	0.9598	0.9493	0.9369	0.9225	0.9058	0.8868	0.8654	0.8416	0.8155	0.7870

TABLE A   (*continued*)

n = 24 (continued)

x \ p	0.31	0.32	0.33	0.34	0.35	0.36	0.37	0.38	0.39	0.40
12	0.9846	0.9798	0.9738	0.9665	0.9577	0.9473	0.9350	0.9207	0.9043	0.8857
13	0.9949	0.9931	0.9906	0.9875	0.9836	0.9787	0.9727	0.9655	0.9568	0.9465
14	0.9986	0.9979	0.9971	0.9960	0.9945	0.9926	0.9901	0.9870	0.9831	0.9783
15	0.9997	0.9995	0.9992	0.9989	0.9984	0.9978	0.9970	0.9958	0.9944	0.9925
16	0.9999	0.9999	0.9998	0.9997	0.9996	0.9994	0.9992	0.9989	0.9984	0.9978
17	1.0000	1.0000	1.0000	1.0000	0.9999	0.9999	0.9998	0.9997	0.9996	0.9995
18	1.0000	1.0000	1.0000	1.0000	1.0000	1.0000	1.0000	1.0000	0.9999	0.9999
19	1.0000	1.0000	1.0000	1.0000	1.0000	1.0000	1.0000	1.0000	1.0000	1.0000

x \ p	0.41	0.42	0.43	0.44	0.45	0.46	0.47	0.48	0.49	0.50
0	0.0000	0.0000	0.0000	0.0000	0.0000	0.0000	0.0000	0.0000	0.0000	0.0000
1	0.0001	0.0000	0.0000	0.0000	0.0000	0.0000	0.0000	0.0000	0.0000	0.0000
2	0.0005	0.0003	0.0002	0.0002	0.0001	0.0001	0.0001	0.0000	0.0000	0.0000
3	0.0026	0.0020	0.0014	0.0011	0.0008	0.0006	0.0004	0.0003	0.0002	0.0001
4	0.0105	0.0081	0.0062	0.0047	0.0036	0.0027	0.0020	0.0015	0.0011	0.0008
5	0.0323	0.0259	0.0206	0.0162	0.0127	0.0099	0.0076	0.0058	0.0044	0.0033
6	0.0803	0.0666	0.0549	0.0449	0.0364	0.0293	0.0234	0.0185	0.0146	0.0113
7	0.1660	0.1425	0.1215	0.1028	0.0863	0.0719	0.0594	0.0487	0.0396	0.0320
8	0.2926	0.2593	0.2282	0.1994	0.1730	0.1490	0.1273	0.1080	0.0908	0.0758
9	0.4490	0.4097	0.3714	0.3344	0.2991	0.2657	0.2343	0.2052	0.1783	0.1537
10	0.6121	0.5730	0.5333	0.4935	0.4539	0.4148	0.3767	0.3397	0.3043	0.2706
11	0.7563	0.7235	0.6889	0.6526	0.6151	0.5766	0.5374	0.4979	0.4584	0.4194
12	0.8648	0.8416	0.8160	0.7881	0.7580	0.7258	0.6917	0.6560	0.6188	0.5806
13	0.9345	0.9205	0.9045	0.8863	0.8659	0.8431	0.8181	0.7907	0.7611	0.7294
14	0.9725	0.9654	0.9569	0.9469	0.9352	0.9217	0.9061	0.8884	0.8685	0.8463
15	0.9901	0.9871	0.9833	0.9787	0.9731	0.9663	0.9581	0.9485	0.9373	0.9242
16	0.9970	0.9959	0.9945	0.9927	0.9905	0.9876	0.9841	0.9798	0.9745	0.9680
17	0.9992	0.9989	0.9985	0.9979	0.9972	0.9962	0.9949	0.9933	0.9913	0.9887
18	0.9998	0.9998	0.9997	0.9995	0.9993	0.9990	0.9987	0.9982	0.9975	0.9967
19	1.0000	1.0000	0.9999	0.9999	0.9999	0.9998	0.9997	0.9996	0.9994	0.9992
20	1.0000	1.0000	1.0000	1.0000	1.0000	1.0000	1.0000	0.9999	0.9999	0.9999
21	1.0000	1.0000	1.0000	1.0000	1.0000	1.0000	1.0000	1.0000	1.0000	1.0000

n = 25

x \ p	0.01	0.02	0.03	0.04	0.05	0.06	0.07	0.08	0.09	0.10
0	0.7778	0.6035	0.4670	0.3604	0.2774	0.2129	0.1630	0.1244	0.0946	0.0718
1	0.9742	0.9114	0.8280	0.7358	0.6424	0.5527	0.4696	0.3947	0.3286	0.2712
2	0.9980	0.9868	0.9620	0.9235	0.8729	0.8129	0.7466	0.6768	0.6063	0.5371
3	0.9999	0.9986	0.9938	0.9835	0.9659	0.9402	0.9064	0.8649	0.8169	0.7636
4	1.0000	0.9999	0.9992	0.9972	0.9928	0.9850	0.9726	0.9549	0.9314	0.9020

TABLE A   (*continued*)

n = 25 (continued)

x \ p	0.01	0.02	0.03	0.04	0.05	0.06	0.07	0.08	0.09	0.10
5	1.0000	1.0000	0.9999	0.9996	0.9988	0.9969	0.9935	0.9987	0.9790	0.9666
6	1.0000	1.0000	1.0000	1.0000	0.9998	0.9995	0.9987	0.9972	0.9946	0.9905
7	1.0000	1.0000	1.0000	1.0000	1.0000	0.9999	0.9998	0.9995	0.9989	0.9977
8	1.0000	1.0000	1.0000	1.0000	1.0000	1.0000	1.0000	0.9999	0.9998	0.9995
9	1.0000	1.0000	1.0000	1.0000	1.0000	1.0000	1.0000	1.0000	1.0000	0.9999
10	1.0000	1.0000	1.0000	1.0000	1.0000	1.0000	1.0000	1.0000	1.0000	1.0000

x \ p	0.11	0.12	0.13	0.14	0.15	0.16	0.17	0.18	0.19	0.20
0	0.0543	0.0409	0.0308	0.0230	0.0172	0.0128	0.0095	0.0070	0.0052	0.0038
1	0.2221	0.1805	0.1457	0.1168	0.0931	0.0737	0.0580	0.0454	0.0354	0.0274
2	0.4709	0.4088	0.3517	0.3000	0.2537	0.2130	0.1774	0.1467	0.1204	0.0982
3	0.7066	0.6475	0.5877	0.5286	0.4711	0.4163	0.3648	0.3171	0.2734	0.2340
4	0.8669	0.8266	0.7817	0.7332	0.6821	0.6293	0.5759	0.5228	0.4708	0.4207
5	0.9501	0.9291	0.9035	0.8732	0.8385	0.7998	0.7575	0.7125	0.6653	0.6167
6	0.9844	0.9757	0.9641	0.9491	0.9305	0.9080	0.8815	0.8512	0.8173	0.7800
7	,0.9959	0.9930	0.9887	0.9827	0.9745	0.9639	0.9505	0.9339	0.9141	0.8909
8	0.9991	0.9983	0.9970	0.9950	0.9920	0.9879	0.9822	0.9748	0.9652	0.9532
9	0.9998	0.9996	0.9993	0.9987	0.9979	0.9965	0.9945	0.9917	0.9878	0.9827
10	1.0000	0.9999	0.9999	0.9997	0.9995	0.9991	0.9985	0.9976	0.9963	0.9944
11	1.0000	1.0000	1.0000	1.0000	0.9999	0.9998	0.9997	0.9994	0.9990	0.9985
12	1.0000	1.0000	1.0000	1.0000	1.0000	1.0000	0.9999	0.9999	0.9998	0.9996
13	1.0000	1.0000	1.0000	1.0000	1.0000	1.0000	1.0000	1.0000	1.0000	0.9999
14	1.0000	1.0000	1.0000	1.0000	1.0000	1.0000	1.0000	1.0000	1.0000	1.0000

x \ p	0.21	0.22	0.23	0.24	0.25	0.26	0.27	0.28	0.29	0.30
0	0.0028	0.0020	0.0015	0.0010	0.0008	0.0005	0.0004	0.0003	0.0002	0.0001
1	0.0211	0.0162	0.0123	0.0093	0.0070	0.0053	0.0039	0.0029	0.0021	0.0016
2	0.0796	0.0640	0.0512	0.0407	0.0321	0.0252	0.0196	0.0152	0.0117	0.0090
3	0.1987	0.1676	0.1403	0.1166	0.0962	0.0789	0.0642	0.0519	0.0417	0.0332
4	0.3730	0.3282	0.2866	0.2484	0.2137	0.1826	0.1548	0.1304	0.1090	0.0905
5	0.5675	0.5184	0.4701	0.4233	0.3783	0.3356	0.2956	0.2585	0.2245	0.1935
6	0.7399	0.6973	0.6529	0.6073	0.5611	0.5149	0.4692	0.4247	0.3817	0.3407
7	0.8642	0.8342	0.8011	0.7651	0.7265	0.6858	0.6435	0.6001	0.5560	0.5118
8	0.9386	0.9212	0.9007	0.8772	0.8506	0.8210	0.7885	0.7535	0.7162	0.6769
9	0.9760	0.9675	0.9569	0.9440	0.9287	0.9107	0.8899	0.8662	0.8398	0.8106
10	0.9918	0.9883	0.9837	0.9778	0.9703	0.9611	0.9498	0.9364	0.9205	0.9022
11	0.9976	0.9964	0.9947	0.9924	0.9893	0.9852	0.9801	0.9736	0.9655	0.9558
12	0.9994	0.9990	0.9985	0.9977	0.9966	0.9951	0.9931	0.9904	0.9870	0.9825
13	0.9999	0.9998	0.9996	0.9994	0.9991	0.9986	0.9979	0.9970	0.9957	0.9940
14	1.0000	1.0000	0.9999	0.9999	0.9998	0.9997	0.9995	0.9992	0.9988	0.9982

TABLE A   (*continued*)

						$n = 25$ (continued)					

x \ p	0.21	0.22	0.23	0.24	0.25	0.26	0.27	0.28	0.29	0.30
15	1.0000	1.0000	1.0000	1.0000	1.0000	0.9999	0.9999	0.9998	0.9997	0.9995
16	1.0000	1.0000	1.0000	1.0000	1.0000	1.0000	1.0000	1.0000	0.9999	0.9999
17	1.0000	1.0000	1.0000	1.0000	1.0000	1.0000	1.0000	1.0000	1.0000	1.0000

x \ p	0.31	0.32	0.33	0.34	0.35	0.36	0.37	0.38	0.39	0.40
0	0.0001	0.0001	0.0000	0.0000	0.0000	0.0000	0.0000	0.0000	0.0000	0.0000
1	0.0011	0.0008	0.0006	0.0004	0.0003	0.0002	0.0002	0.0001	0.0001	0.0001
2	0.0068	0.0051	0.0039	0.0029	0.0021	0.0016	0.0011	0.0008	0.0006	0.0004
3	0.0263	0.0207	0.0162	0.0126	0.0097	0.0074	0.0056	0.0043	0.0032	0.0024
4	0.0746	0.0610	0.0496	0.0400	0.0320	0.0255	0.0201	0.0158	0.0123	0.0095
5	0.1656	0.1407	0.1187	0.0994	0.0826	0.0682	0.0559	0.0454	0.0367	0.0294
6	0.3019	0.2657	0.2321	0.2013	0.1734	0.1483	0.1258	0.1060	0.0886	0.0736
7	0.4681	0.4253	0.3837	0.3439	0.3061	0.2705	0.2374	0.2068	0.1789	0.1536
8	0.6361	0.5943	0.5518	0.5092	0.4668	0.4252	0.3848	0.3458	0.3086	0.2735
9	0.7787	0.7445	0.7081	0.6700	0.6303	0.5896	0.5483	0.5067	0.4653	0.4246
10	0.8812	0.8576	0.8314	0.8025	0.7712	0.7375	0.7019	0.6645	0.6257	0.5858
11	0.9440	0.9302	0.9141	0.8956	0.8746	0.8510	0.8249	0.7964	0.7654	0.7323
12	0.9770	0.9701	0.9617	0.9515	0.9396	0.9255	0.9093	0.8907	0.8697	0.8462
13	0.9917	0.9888	0.9851	0.9804	0.9745	0.9674	0.9588	0.9485	0.9363	0.9222
14	0.9974	0.9964	0.9950	0.9931	0.9907	0.9876	0.9837	0.9788	0.9729	0.9656
15	0.9993	0.9990	0.9985	0.9979	0.9971	0.9959	0.9944	0.9925	0.9900	0.9868
16	0.9998	0.9998	0.9996	0.9995	0.9992	0.9989	0.9984	0.9977	0.9968	0.9957
17	1.0000	1.0000	0.9999	0.9999	0.9998	0.9997	0.9996	0.9994	0.9992	0.9988
18	1.0000	1.0000	1.0000	1.0000	1.0000	0.9999	0.9999	0.9999	0.9998	0.9997
19	1.0000	1.0000	1.0000	1.0000	1.0000	1.0000	1.0000	1.0000	1.0000	0.9999
20	1.0000	1.0000	1.0000	1.0000	1.0000	1.0000	1.0000	1.0000	1.0000	1.0000

x \ p	0.41	0.42	0.43	0.44	0.45	0.46	0.47	0.48	0.49	0.50
0	0.0000	0.0000	0.0000	0.0000	0.0000	0.0000	0.0000	0.0000	0.0000	0.0000
1	0.0000	0.0000	0.0000	0.0000	0.0000	0.0000	0.0000	0.0000	0.0000	0.0000
2	0.0003	0.0002	0.0002	0.0001	0.0001	0.0000	0.0000	0.0000	0.0000	0.0000
3	0.0017	0.0013	0.0009	0.0007	0.0005	0.0003	0.0002	0.0002	0.0001	0.0001
4	0.0073	0.0055	0.0042	0.0031	0.0023	0.0017	0.0012	0.0009	0.0006	0.0005
5	0.0233	0.0184	0.0144	0.0112	0.0086	0.0066	0.0050	0.0037	0.0028	0.0020
6	0.0606	0.0495	0.0401	0.0323	0.0258	0.0204	0.0160	0.0124	0.0096	0.0073
7	0.1308	0.1106	0.0929	0.0773	0.0639	0.0523	0.0425	0.0342	0.0273	0.0216
8	0.2407	0.2103	0.1823	0.1569	0.1340	0.1135	0.0954	0.0795	0.0657	0.0539
9	0.3849	0.3465	0.3098	0.2750	0.2424	0.2120	0.1840	0.1585	0.1354	0.1148
10	0.5452	0.5044	0.4637	0.4235	0.3843	0.3462	0.3098	0.2751	0.2426	0.2122
11	0.6971	0.6603	0.6220	0.5826	0.5426	0.5022	0.4618	0.4220	0.3829	0.3450

TABLE A (*continued*)

	p									
x	0.41	0.42	0.43	0.44	0.45	0.46	0.47	0.48	0.49	0.50

n = 25 (continued)

x	0.41	0.42	0.43	0.44	0.45	0.46	0.47	0.48	0.49	0.50
12	0.8203	0.7920	0.7613	0.7285	0.6937	0.6571	0.6192	0.5801	0.5402	0.5000
13	0.9059	0.8873	0.8664	0.8431	0.8173	0.7891	0.7587	0.7260	0.6914	0.6550
14	0.9569	0.9465	0.9344	0.9203	0.9040	0.8855	0.8647	0.8415	0.8159	0.7878
15	0.9829	0.9780	0.9720	0.9647	0.9560	0.9457	0.9337	0.9197	0.9036	0.8852
16	0.9942	0.9922	0.9897	0.9866	0.9826	0.9778	0.9719	0.9648	0.9562	0.9461
17	0.9983	0.9977	0.9968	0.9956	0.9942	0.9923	0.9898	0.9868	0.9830	0.9784
18	0.9996	0.9994	0.9992	0.9988	0.9984	0.9977	0.9969	0.9959	0.9945	0.9927
19	0.9999	0.9999	0.9998	0.9997	0.9996	0.9995	0.9992	0.9989	0.9985	0.9980
20	1.0000	1.0000	1.0000	1.0000	0.9999	0.9999	0.9998	0.9998	0.9997	0.9995
21	1.0000	1.0000	1.0000	1.0000	1.0000	1.0000	1.0000	1.0000	0.9999	0.9999
22	1.0000	1.0000	1.0000	1.0000	1.0000	1.0000	1.0000	1.0000	1.0000	1.0000

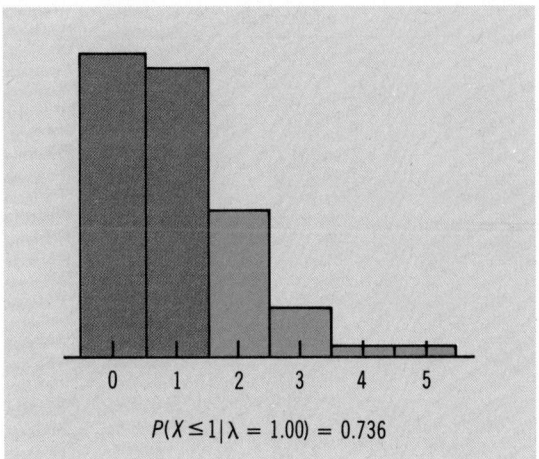

$P(X \le 1 | \lambda = 1.00) = 0.736$

TABLE B   Cumulative Poisson distribution $P(X \le x/\lambda)$

A thousand times the probability of x or fewer occurrences of an event that has an average number of occurrences equal to λ

x \ λ	0.02	0.04	0.06	0.08	0.10	0.15	0.20	0.25
0	980	961	942	923	905	861	819	779
1	1000	999	998	997	995	990	982	974
2		1000	1000	1000	1000	999	999	998
3						1000	1000	1000

x \ λ	0.30	0.35	0.40	0.45	0.50	0.55	0.60	0.65
0	741	705	670	638	607	577	549	522
1	963	951	938	925	910	894	878	861
2	996	994	992	989	986	982	977	972
3	1000	1000	999	999	998	998	997	996
4			1000	1000	1000	1000	1000	999
5								1000

x \ λ	0.70	0.75	0.80	0.85	0.90	0.95	1.0	1.1
0	497	472	449	427	407	387	368	333
1	844	827	809	791	772	754	736	699
2	966	959	953	945	937	929	920	900
3	994	993	991	989	987	984	981	974
4	999	999	999	998	998	997	996	995
5	1000	1000	1000	1000	1000	1000	999	999
6							1000	1000

TABLE B (*continued*)

x \ λ	1.2	1.3	1.4	1.5	1.6	1.7	1.8	1.9
0	301	273	247	223	202	183	165	150
1	663	627	592	558	525	493	463	434
2	879	857	833	809	783	757	731	704
3	966	957	946	934	921	907	891	875
4	992	989	986	981	976	970	964	956
5	998	998	997	996	994	992	990	987
6	1000	1000	999	999	999	998	997	997
7			1000	1000	1000	1000	999	999
8							1000	1000

x \ λ	2.0	2.2	2.4	2.6	2.8	3.0	3.2	3.4
0	135	111	091	074	061	050	041	033
1	406	355	308	267	231	199	171	147
2	677	623	570	518	469	423	380	340
3	857	819	779	736	692	647	603	558
4	947	928	904	877	848	815	781	744
5	983	975	964	951	935	916	895	871
6	995	993	988	983	976	966	955	942
7	999	998	997	995	992	988	983	977
8	1000	1000	999	999	998	996	994	992
9			1000	1000	999	999	998	997
10					1000	1000	1000	999
11								1000

x \ λ	3.6	3.8	4.0	4.2	4.4	4.6	4.8	5.0
0	027	022	018	015	012	010	008	007
1	126	107	092	078	066	056	048	040
2	303	269	238	210	185	163	143	125
3	515	473	433	395	359	326	294	265
4	706	668	629	590	551	513	476	440
5	844	816	785	753	720	686	651	616
6	927	909	889	867	844	818	791	762
7	969	960	949	936	921	905	887	867
8	988	984	979	972	964	955	944	932
9	996	994	992	989	985	980	975	968
10	999	998	997	996	994	992	990	986
11	1000	999	999	999	998	997	996	995
12		1000	1000	1000	999	999	999	998
13					1000	1000	1000	999
14								1000

x \ λ	5.2	5.4	5.6	5.8	6.0	6.2	6.4	6.6
0	006	005	004	003	002	002	002	001
1	034	029	024	021	017	015	012	010
2	109	095	082	072	062	054	046	040

TABLE B (*continued*)

x \ λ	5.2	5.4	5.6	5.8	6.0	6.2	6.4	6.6
3	238	213	191	170	151	134	119	105
4	406	373	342	313	285	259	235	213
5	581	546	512	478	446	414	384	355
6	732	702	670	638	606	574	542	511
7	845	822	797	771	744	716	687	658
8	918	903	886	867	847	826	803	780
9	960	951	941	929	916	902	886	869
10	982	977	972	965	957	949	939	927
11	993	990	988	984	980	975	969	963
12	997	996	995	993	991	989	986	982
13	999	999	998	997	996	995	994	992
14	1000	999	999	999	999	998	997	997
15		1000	1000	1000	999	999	999	999
16					1000	1000	1000	999
17								1000

x \ λ	6.8	7.0	7.2	7.4	7.6	7.8	8.0	8.5
0	001	001	001	001	001	000	000	000
1	009	007	006	005	004	004	003	002
2	034	030	025	022	019	016	014	009
3	093	082	072	063	055	048	042	030
4	192	173	156	140	125	112	100	074
5	327	301	276	253	231	210	191	150
6	480	450	420	392	365	338	313	256
7	628	599	569	539	510	481	453	386
8	755	729	703	676	648	620	593	523
9	850	830	810	788	765	741	717	653
10	915	901	887	871	854	835	816	763
11	955	947	937	926	915	902	888	849
12	978	973	967	961	954	945	936	909
13	990	987	984	980	976	971	966	949
14	996	994	993	991	989	986	983	973
15	998	998	997	996	995	993	992	986
16	999	999	999	998	998	997	996	993
17	1000	1000	999	999	999	999	998	997
18			1000	1000	1000	1000	999	999
19							1000	999
20								1000

x \ λ	9.0	9.5	10.0	10.5	11.0	11.5	12.0	12.5
1	001	001	000	000	000	000	000	000
2	006	004	003	002	001	001	001	000
3	021	015	010	007	005	003	002	002
4	055	040	029	021	015	011	008	005
5	116	089	067	050	038	028	020	015
6	207	165	130	102	079	060	046	035

TABLE B (*continued*)

x \ λ	9.0	9.5	10.0	10.5	11.0	11.5	12.0	12.5
7	324	269	220	179	143	114	090	070
8	456	392	333	279	232	191	155	125
9	587	522	458	397	341	289	242	201
10	706	645	583	521	460	402	347	297
11	803	752	697	639	579	520	462	406
12	876	836	792	742	689	633	576	519
13	926	898	864	825	781	733	682	628
14	959	940	917	888	854	815	772	725
15	978	967	951	932	907	878	844	806
16	989	982	973	960	944	924	899	869
17	995	991	986	978	968	954	937	916
18	998	996	993	988	982	974	963	948
19	999	998	997	994	991	986	979	969
20	1000	999	998	997	995	992	988	983
21		1000	999	999	998	996	994	991
22			1000	999	999	998	997	995
23				1000	1000	999	999	998
24						1000	999	999
25							1000	999
26								1000

x \ λ	13.0	13.5	14.0	14.5	15	16	17	18
3	001	001	000	000	000	000	000	000
4	004	003	002	001	001	000	000	000
5	011	008	006	004	003	001	001	000
6	026	019	014	010	008	004	002	001
7	054	041	032	024	018	010	005	003
8	100	079	062	048	037	022	013	007
9	166	135	109	088	070	043	026	015
10	252	211	176	145	118	077	049	030
11	353	304	260	220	185	127	085	055
12	463	409	358	311	268	193	135	092
13	573	518	464	413	363	275	201	143
14	675	623	570	518	466	368	281	208
15	764	718	669	619	568	467	371	287
16	835	798	756	711	664	566	468	375
17	890	861	827	790	749	659	564	469
18	930	908	883	853	819	742	655	562
19	957	942	923	901	875	812	736	651
20	975	965	952	936	917	868	805	731
21	986	980	971	960	947	911	861	799
22	992	989	983	976	967	942	905	855
23	996	994	991	986	981	963	937	899
24	998	997	995	992	989	978	959	932
25	999	998	997	996	994	987	975	955
26	1000	999	999	998	997	993	985	972
27		1000	999	999	998	996	991	983

TABLE B   (*continued*)

x \ λ	13.0	13.5	14.0	14.5	15	16	17	18
28			1000	999	999	998	995	990
29				1000	1000	999	997	994
30						999	999	997
31						1000	999	998
32							1000	999
33								1000

x \ λ	19	20	21	22	23	24	25
6	001	000	000	000	000	000	000
7	002	001	000	000	000	000	000
8	004	002	001	001	000	000	000
9	009	005	003	002	001	000	000
10	018	011	006	004	002	001	001
11	035	021	013	008	004	003	001
12	061	039	025	015	009	005	003
13	098	066	043	028	017	011	006
14	150	105	072	048	031	020	012
15	215	157	111	077	052	034	022
16	292	221	163	117	082	056	038
17	378	297	227	169	123	087	060
18	469	381	302	232	175	128	092
19	561	470	384	306	238	180	134
20	647	559	471	387	310	243	185
21	725	644	558	472	389	314	247
22	793	721	640	556	472	392	318
23	849	787	716	637	555	473	394
24	893	843	782	712	635	554	473
25	927	888	838	777	708	632	553
26	951	922	883	832	772	704	629
27	969	948	917	877	827	768	700
28	980	966	944	913	873	823	763
29	988	978	963	940	908	868	818
30	993	987	976	959	936	904	863
31	996	992	985	973	956	932	900
32	998	995	991	983	971	953	929
33	999	997	994	989	981	969	950
34	999	999	997	994	988	979	966
35	1000	999	998	996	993	987	978
36		1000	999	998	996	992	985
37			999	999	997	995	991
38			1000	999	999	997	994
39				1000	999	998	997
40					1000	999	998
41						999	999
42						1000	999
43							1000

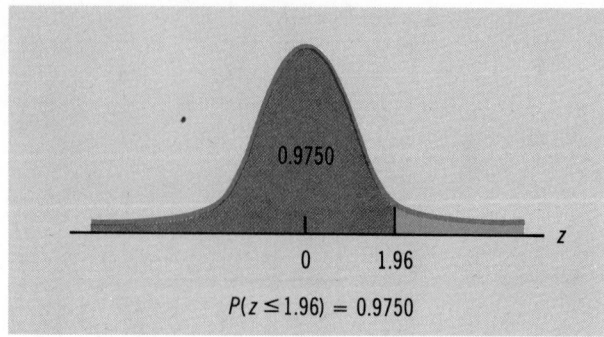

$P(z \le 1.96) = 0.9750$

TABLE Ca Normal curve areas $P(z \le z_0)$

Entries in the body of the table are areas between $-\infty$ and z.

z	Area	z	Area	z	Area	z	Area
-3.89	.0000	-3.39	.0003	-3.14	.0008	-2.89	.0019
$\vdots$	$\vdots$	-3.38	.0004	-3.13	.0009	-2.88	.0020
-3.62	.0001	-3.37	.0004	-3.12	.0009	-2.87	.0021
-3.61	.0002	-3.36	.0004	-3.11	.0009	-2.86	.0021
-3.60	.0002	-3.35	.0004	-3.10	.0010	-2.85	.0022
-3.59	.0002	-3.34	.0004	-3.09	.0010	-2.84	.0023
-3.58	.0002	-3.33	.0004	-3.08	.0010	-2.83	.0023
-3.57	.0002	-3.32	.0005	-3.07	.0011	-2.82	.0024
-3.56	.0002	-3.31	.0005	-3.06	.0011	-2.81	.0025
-3.55	.0002	-3.30	.0005	-3.05	.0011	-2.80	.0026
-3.54	.0002	-3.29	.0005	-3.04	.0012	-2.79	.0026
-3.53	.0002	-3.28	.0005	-3.03	.0012	-2.78	.0027
-3.52	.0002	-3.27	.0005	-3.02	.0013	-2.77	.0028
-3.51	.0002	-3.26	.0006	-3.01	.0013	-2.76	.0029
-3.50	.0002	-3.25	.0006	-3.00	.0013	-2.75	.0030
-3.49	.0002	-3.24	.0006	-2.99	.0014	-2.74	.0031
-3.48	.0003	-3.23	.0006	-2.98	.0014	-2.73	.0032
-3.47	.0003	-3.22	.0006	-2.97	.0015	-2.72	.0033
-3.46	.0003	-3.21	.0007	-2.96	.0015	-2.71	.0034
-3.45	.0003	-3.20	.0007	-2.95	.0016	-2.70	.0035
-3.44	.0003	-3.19	.0007	-2.94	.0016	-2.69	.0036
-3.43	.0003	-3.18	.0007	-2.93	.0017	-2.68	.0037
-3.42	.0003	-3.17	.0008	-2.92	.0018	-2.67	.0038
-3.41	.0003	-3.16	.0008	-2.91	.0018	-2.66	.0039
-3.40	.0003	-3.15	.0008	-2.90	.0019	-2.65	.0040

TABLE Ca   (*continued*)

Entries in the body of the table are areas between $-\infty$ and z.

z	Area	z	Area	z	Area	z	Area
−2.64	.0041	−2.24	.0125	−1.84	.0329	−1.44	.0749
−2.63	.0043	−2.23	.0129	−1.83	.0336	−1.43	.0764
−2.62	.0044	−2.22	.0132	−1.82	.0344	−1.42	.0778
−2.61	.0045	−2.21	.0136	−1.81	.0351	−1.41	.0793
−2.60	.0047	−2.20	.0139	−1.80	.0359	−1.40	.0808
−2.59	.0048	−2.19	.0143	−1.79	.0367	−1.39	.0823
−2.58	.0049	−2.18	.0146	−1.78	.0375	−1.38	.0838
−2.57	.0051	−2.17	.0150	−1.77	.0384	−1.37	.0853
−2.56	.0052	−2.16	.0154	−1.76	.0392	−1.36	.0869
−2.55	.0054	−2.15	.0158	−1.75	.0401	−1.35	.0885
−2.54	.0055	−2.14	.0162	−1.74	.0409	−1.34	.0901
−2.53	.0057	−2.13	.0166	−1.73	.0418	−1.33	.0918
−2.52	.0059	−2.12	.0170	−1.72	.0427	−1.32	.0934
−2.51	.0060	−2.11	.0174	−1.71	.0436	−1.31	.0951
−2.50	.0062	−2.10	.0179	−1.70	.0446	−1.30	.0968
−2.49	.0064	−2.09	.0183	−1.69	.0455	−1.29	.0985
−2.48	.0066	−2.08	.0188	−1.68	.0465	−1.28	.1003
−2.47	.0068	−2.07	.0192	−1.67	.0475	−1.27	.1020
−2.46	.0069	−2.06	.0197	−1.66	.0485	−1.26	.1038
−2.45	.0071	−2.05	.0202	−1.65	.0495	−1.25	.1056
−2.44	.0073	−2.04	.0207	−1.64	.0505	−1.24	.1075
−2.43	.0075	−2.03	.0212	−1.63	.0516	−1.23	.1093
−2.42	.0078	−2.02	.0217	−1.62	.0526	−1.22	.1112
−2.41	.0080	−2.01	.0222	−1.61	.0537	−1.21	.1131
−2.40	.0082	−2.00	.0228	−1.60	.0548	−1.20	.1151
−2.39	.0084	−1.99	.0233	−1.59	.0559	−1.19	.1170
−2.38	.0087	−1.98	.0239	−1.58	.0571	−1.18	.1190
−2.37	.0089	−1.97	.0244	−1.57	.0582	−1.17	.1210
−2.36	.0091	−1.96	.0250	−1.56	.0594	−1.16	.1230
−2.35	.0094	−1.95	.0256	−1.55	.0606	−1.15	.1251
−2.34	.0096	−1.94	.0262	−1.54	.0618	−1.14	.1271
−2.33	.0099	−1.93	.0268	−1.53	.0630	−1.13	.1292
−2.32	.0102	−1.92	.0274	−1.52	.0643	−1.12	.1314
−2.31	.0104	−1.91	.0281	−1.51	.0655	−1.11	.1335
−2.30	.0107	−1.90	.0287	−1.50	.0668	−1.10	.1357
−2.29	.0110	−1.89	.0294	−1.49	.0681	−1.09	.1379
−2.28	.0113	−1.88	.0301	−1.48	.0694	−1.08	.1401
−2.27	.0116	−1.87	.0307	−1.47	.0708	−1.07	.1423
−2.26	.0119	−1.86	.0314	−1.46	.0721	−1.06	.1446
−2.25	.0122	−1.85	.0322	−1.45	.0735	−1.05	.1469

TABLE Ca (*continued*)

Entries in the body of the table are areas between $-\infty$ and z.

z	Area	z	Area	z	Area	z	Area
−1.04	.1492	−0.64	.2611	−0.24	.4052	0.16	.5636
−1.03	.1515	−0.63	.2643	−0.23	.4090	0.17	.5675
−1.02	.1539	−0.62	.2676	−0.22	.4129	0.18	.5714
−1.01	.1562	−0.61	.2709	−0.21	.4168	0.19	.5753
−1.00	.1587	−0.60	.2743	−0.20	.4207	0.20	.5793
−0.99	.1611	−0.59	.2776	−0.19	.4247	0.21	.5832
−0.98	.1635	−0.58	.2810	−0.18	.4286	0.22	.5871
−0.97	.1660	−0.57	.2843	−0.17	.4325	0.23	.5910
−0.96	.1685	−0.56	.2877	−0.16	.4364	0.24	.5948
−0.95	.1711	−0.55	.2912	−0.15	.4404	0.25	.5987
−0.94	.1736	−0.54	.2946	−0.14	.4443	0.26	.6026
−0.93	.1762	−0.53	.2981	−0.13	.4483	0.27	.6064
−0.92	.1788	−0.52	.3015	−0.12	.4522	0.28	.6103
−0.91	.1814	−0.51	.3050	−0.11	.4562	0.29	.6141
−0.90	.1841	−0.50	.3085	−0.10	.4602	0.30	.6179
−0.89	.1867	−0.49	.3121	−0.09	.4641	0.31	.6217
−0.88	.1894	−0.48	.3156	−0.08	.4681	0.32	.6255
−0.87	.1922	−0.47	.3192	−0.07	.4721	0.33	.6293
−0.86	.1949	−0.46	.3228	−0.06	.4761	0.34	.6331
−0.85	.1977	−0.45	.3264	−0.05	.4801	0.35	.6368
−0.84	.2005	−0.44	.3300	−0.04	.4840	0.36	.6406
−0.83	.2033	−0.43	.3336	−0.03	.4880	0.37	.6443
−0.82	.2061	−0.42	.3372	−0.02	.4920	0.38	.6480
−0.81	.2090	−0.41	.3409	−0.01	.4960	0.39	.6517
−0.80	.2119	−0.40	.3446	0.00	.5000	0.40	.6554
−0.79	.2148	−0.39	.3483	0.01	.5040	0.41	.6591
−0.78	.2177	−0.38	.3520	0.02	.5080	0.42	.6628
−0.77	.2206	−0.37	.3557	0.03	.5120	0.43	.6664
−0.76	.2236	−0.36	.3594	0.04	.5160	0.44	.6700
−0.75	.2266	−0.35	.3632	0.05	.5199	0.45	.6736
−0.74	.2296	−0.34	.3669	0.06	.5239	0.46	.6772
−0.73	.2327	−0.33	.3707	0.07	.5279	0.47	.6808
−0.72	.2358	−0.32	.3745	0.08	.5319	0.48	.6844
−0.71	.2389	−0.31	.3783	0.09	.5359	0.49	.6879
−0.70	.2420	−0.30	.3821	0.10	.5398	0.50	.6915
−0.69	.2451	−0.29	.3859	0.11	.5438	0.51	.6950
−0.68	.2483	−0.28	.3897	0.12	.5478	0.52	.6985
−0.67	.2514	−0.27	.3936	0.13	.5517	0.53	.7019
−0.66	.2546	−0.26	.3974	0.14	.5557	0.54	.7054
−0.65	.2578	−0.25	.4013	0.15	.5596	0.55	.7088

TABLE Ca   (*continued*)

Entries in the body of the table are areas between $-\infty$ and z.

z	Area	z	Area	z	Area	z	Area
0.56	.7123	0.96	.8315	1.36	.9131	1.76	.9608
0.57	.7157	0.97	.8340	1.37	.9147	1.77	.9616
0.58	.7190	0.98	.8365	1.38	.9162	1.78	.9625
0.59	.7224	0.99	.8389	1.39	.9177	1.79	.9633
0.60	.7257	1.00	.8413	1.40	.9192	1.80	.9641
0.61	.7291	1.01	.8438	1.41	.9207	1.81	.9649
0.62	.7324	1.02	.8461	1.42	.9222	1.82	.9656
0.63	.7357	1.03	.8485	1.43	.9236	1.83	.9664
0.64	.7389	1.04	.8508	1.44	.9251	1.84	.9671
0.65	.7422	1.05	.8531	1.45	.9265	1.85	.9678
0.66	.7454	1.06	.8554	1.46	.9279	1.86	.9686
0.67	.7486	1.07	.8577	1.47	.9292	1.87	.9693
0.68	.7517	1.08	.8599	1.48	.9306	1.88	.9699
0.69	.7549	1.09	.8621	1.49	.9319	1.89	.9706
0.70	.7580	1.10	.8643	1.50	.9332	1.90	.9713
0.71	.7611	1.11	.8665	1.51	.9345	1.91	.9719
0.72	.7642	1.12	.8686	1.52	.9357	1.92	.9726
0.73	.7673	1.13	.8708	1.53	.9370	1.93	.9732
0.74	.7704	1.14	.8729	1.54	.9382	1.94	.9738
0.75	.7734	1.15	.8749	1.55	.9394	1.95	.9744
0.76	.7764	1.16	.8770	1.56	.9406	1.96	.9750
0.77	.7794	1.17	.8790	1.57	.9418	1.97	.9756
0.78	.7823	1.18	.8810	1.58	.9429	1.98	.9761
0.79	.7852	1.19	.8830	1.59	.9441	1.99	.9767
0.80	.7881	1.20	.8849	1.60	.9452	2.00	.9772
0.81	.7910	1.21	.8869	1.61	.9463	2.01	.9778
0.82	.7939	1.22	.8888	1.62	.9474	2.02	.9783
0.83	.7967	1.23	.8907	1.63	.9484	2.03	.9788
0.84	.7995	1.24	.8925	1.64	.9495	2.04	.9793
0.85	.8023	1.25	.8944	1.65	.9505	2.05	.9798
0.86	.8051	1.26	.8962	1.66	.9515	2.06	.9803
0.87	.8078	1.27	.8980	1.67	.9525	2.07	.9808
0.88	.8106	1.28	.8997	1.68	.9535	2.08	.9812
0.89	.8133	1.29	.9015	1.69	.9545	2.09	.9817
0.90	.8159	1.30	.9032	1.70	.9554	2.10	.9821
0.91	.8186	1.31	.9049	1.71	.9564	2.11	.9826
0.92	.8212	1.32	.9066	1.72	.9573	2.12	.9830
0.93	.8238	1.33	.9082	1.73	.9582	2.13	.9834
0.94	.8264	1.34	.9099	1.74	.9591	2.14	.9838
0.95	.8289	1.35	.9115	1.75	.9599	2.15	.9842

TABLE Ca (*continued*)

Entries in the body of the table are areas between $-\infty$ and z.

z	Area	z	Area	z	Area	z	Area
2.16	.9846	2.56	.9948	2.96	.9985	3.36	.9996
2.17	.9850	2.57	.9949	2.97	.9985	3.37	.9996
2.18	.9854	2.58	.9951	2.98	.9986	3.38	.9996
2.19	.9857	2.59	.9952	2.99	.9986	3.39	.9997
2.20	.9861	2.60	.9953	3.00	.9987	3.40	.9997
2.21	.9864	2.61	.9955	3.01	.9987	3.41	.9997
2.22	.9868	2.62	.9956	3.02	.9987	3.42	.9997
2.23	.9871	2.63	.9957	3.03	.9988	3.43	.9997
2.24	.9875	2.64	.9959	3.04	.9988	3.44	.9997
2.25	.9878	2.65	.9960	3.05	.9989	3.45	.9997
2.26	.9881	2.66	.9961	3.06	.9989	3.46	.9997
2.27	.9884	2.67	.9962	3.07	.9989	3.47	.9997
2.28	.9887	2.68	.9963	3.08	.9990	3.48	.9997
2.29	.9890	2.69	.9964	3.09	.9990	3.49	.9998
2.30	.9893	2.70	.9965	3.10	.9990	3.50	.9998
2.31	.9896	2.71	.9966	3.11	.9991	3.51	.9998
2.32	.9898	2.72	.9967	3.12	.9991	3.52	.9998
2.33	.9901	2.73	.9968	3.13	.9991	3.53	.9998
2.34	.9904	2.74	.9969	3.14	.9992	3.54	.9998
2.35	.9906	2.75	.9970	3.15	.9992	3.55	.9998
2.36	.9909	2.76	.9971	3.16	.9992	3.56	.9998
2.37	.9911	2.77	.9972	3.17	.9992	3.57	.9998
2.38	.9913	2.78	.9973	3.18	.9993	3.58	.9998
2.39	.9916	2.79	.9974	3.19	.9993	3.59	.9998
2.40	.9918	2.80	.9974	3.20	.9993	3.60	.9998
2.41	.9920	2.81	.9975	3.21	.9993	3.61	.9998
2.42	.9922	2.82	.9976	3.22	.9994	3.62	.9999
2.43	.9925	2.83	.9977	3.23	.9994	⋮	⋮
2.44	.9927	2.84	.9977	3.24	.9994	3.89	1.0000
2.45	.9929	2.85	.9978	3.25	.9994		
2.46	.9931	2.86	.9979	3.26	.9994		
2.47	.9932	2.87	.9979	3.27	.9995		
2.48	.9934	2.88	.9980	3.28	.9995		
2.49	.9936	2.89	.9981	3.29	.9995		
2.50	.9938	2.90	.9981	3.30	.9995		
2.51	.9940	2.91	.9982	3.31	.9995		
2.52	.9941	2.92	.9982	3.32	.9995		
2.53	.9943	2.93	.9983	3.33	.9996		
2.54	.9945	2.94	.9984	3.34	.9996		
2.55	.9946	2.95	.9984	3.35	.9996		

TABLE Cb   Percentiles of the Normal Distribution $P(z \leq z_0)$

z	0.00	0.01	0.02	0.03	0.04	0.05	0.06	0.07	0.08	0.09	z
0.00	.5000	.5040	.5080	.5120	.5160	.5199	.5239	.5279	.5319	.5359	0.00
0.10	.5398	.5438	.5478	.5517	.5557	.5596	.5636	.5675	.5714	.5753	0.10
0.20	.5793	.5832	.5871	.5910	.5948	.5987	.6026	.6064	.6103	.6141	0.20
0.30	.6179	.6217	.6255	.6293	.6331	.6368	.6406	.6443	.6480	.6517	0.30
0.40	.6554	.6591	.6628	.6664	.6700	.6736	.6772	.6808	.6844	.6879	0.40
0.50	.6915	.6950	.6985	.7019	.7054	.7088	.7123	.7157	.7190	.7224	0.50
0.60	.7257	.7291	.7324	.7357	.7389	.7422	.7454	.7486	.7517	.7549	0.60
0.70	.7580	.7611	.7642	.7673	.7704	.7734	.7764	.7794	.7823	.7852	0.70
0.80	.7881	.7910	.7939	.7967	.7995	.8023	.8051	.8078	.8106	.8133	0.80
0.90	.8159	.8186	.8212	.8238	.8264	.8289	.8315	.8340	.8365	.8389	0.90
1.00	.8413	.8438	.8461	.8485	.8508	.8531	.8554	.8577	.8599	.8621	1.00
1.10	.8643	.8665	.8686	.8708	.8729	.8749	.8770	.8790	.8810	.8830	1.10
1.20	.8849	.8869	.8888	.8907	.8925	.8944	.8962	.8980	.8997	.9015	1.20
1.30	.9032	.9049	.9066	.9082	.9099	.9115	.9131	.9147	.9162	.9177	1.30
1.40	.9192	.9207	.9222	.9236	.9251	.9265	.9279	.9292	.9306	.9319	1.40
1.50	.9332	.9345	.9357	.9370	.9382	.9394	.9406	.9418	.9429	.9441	1.50
1.60	.9452	.9463	.9474	.9484	.9495	.9505	.9515	.9525	.9535	.9545	1.60
1.70	.9554	.9564	.9573	.9582	.9591	.9599	.9608	.9616	.9625	.9633	1.70
1.80	.9641	.9649	.9656	.9664	.9671	.9678	.9686	.9693	.9699	.9706	1.80
1.90	.9713	.9719	.9726	.9732	.9738	.9744	.9750	.9756	.9761	.9767	1.90
2.00	.9772	.9778	.9783	.9788	.9793	.9798	.9803	.9808	.9812	.9817	2.00
2.10	.9821	.9826	.9830	.9834	.9838	.9842	.9846	.9850	.9854	.9857	2.10
2.20	.9861	.9864	.9868	.9871	.9875	.9878	.9881	.9884	.9887	.9890	2.20
2.30	.9893	.9896	.9898	.9901	.9904	.9906	.9909	.9911	.9913	.9916	2.30
2.40	.9918	.9920	.9922	.9925	.9927	.9929	.9931	.9932	.9934	.9936	2.40
2.50	.9938	.9940	.9941	.9943	.9945	.9946	.9948	.9949	.9951	.9952	2.50
2.60	.9953	.9955	.9956	.9957	.9959	.9960	.9961	.9962	.9963	.9964	2.60
2.70	.9965	.9966	.9967	.9968	.9969	.9970	.9971	.9972	.9973	.9974	2.70
2.80	.9974	.9975	.9976	.9977	.9977	.9978	.9979	.9979	.9980	.9981	2.80
2.90	.9981	.9982	.9982	.9983	.9984	.9984	.9985	.9985	.9986	.9986	2.90
3.00	.9987	.9987	.9987	.9988	.9988	.9989	.9989	.9989	.9990	.9990	3.00
3.10	.9990	.9991	.9991	.9991	.9992	.9992	.9992	.9992	.9993	.9993	3.10
3.20	.9993	.9993	.9994	.9994	.9994	.9994	.9994	.9995	.9995	.9995	3.20
3.30	.9995	.9995	.9995	.9996	.9996	.9996	.9996	.9996	.9996	.9997	3.30
3.40	.9997	.9997	.9997	.9997	.9997	.9997	.9997	.9997	.9997	.9998	3.40
3.50	.9998	.9998	.9998	.9998	.9998	.9998	.9998	.9998	.9998	.9998	3.50
3.60	.9998	.9998	.9999	.9999	.9999	.9999	.9999	.9999	.9999	.9999	3.60
3.70	.9999	.9999	.9999	.9999	.9999	.9999	.9999	.9999	.9999	.9999	3.70
3.80	.9999	.9999	.9999	.9999	.9999	.9999	.9999	.9999	.9999	.9999	3.80

TABLE D   Random digits

Column Row	00000 12345	00001 67890	11111 12345	11112 67890	22222 12345	22223 67890	33333 12345	33334 67890	44444 12345	44445 67890
01	85967	73152	14511	85285	36009	95892	36962	67835	63314	50162
02	07483	51453	11649	86348	76431	81594	95848	36738	25014	15460
03	96283	01898	61414	83525	04231	13604	75339	11730	85423	60698
04	49174	12074	98551	37895	93547	24769	09404	76548	05393	96770
05	97366	39941	21225	93629	19574	71565	33413	56087	40875	13351
06	90474	41469	16812	81542	81652	45554	27931	93994	22375	00953
07	28599	64109	09497	76235	41383	31555	12639	00619	22909	29563
08	25254	16210	89717	65997	82667	74624	36348	44018	64732	93589
09	28785	02760	24359	99410	77319	73408	58993	61098	04393	48245
10	84725	86576	86944	93296	10081	82454	76810	52975	10324	15457
11	41059	66456	47679	66810	15941	84602	14493	65515	19251	41642
12	67434	41045	82830	47617	36932	46728	71183	36345	41404	81110
13	72766	68816	37643	19959	57550	49620	98480	25640	67257	18671
14	92079	46784	66125	94932	64451	29275	57669	66658	30818	58353
15	29187	40350	62533	73603	34075	16451	42885	03448	37390	96328
16	74220	17612	65522	80607	19184	64164	66962	82310	18163	63495
17	03786	02407	06098	92917	40434	60602	82175	04470	78754	90775
18	75085	55558	15520	27038	25471	76107	90832	10819	56797	33751
19	09161	33015	19155	11715	00551	24909	31894	37774	37953	78837
20	75707	48992	64998	87080	39333	00767	45637	12538	67439	94914
21	21333	48660	31288	00086	79889	75532	28704	62844	92337	99695
22	65626	50061	42539	14812	48895	11196	34335	60492	70650	51108
23	84380	07389	87891	76255	89604	41372	10837	66992	93183	56920
24	46479	32072	80083	63868	70930	89654	05359	47196	12452	38234
25	59847	97197	55147	76639	76971	55928	36441	95141	42333	67483
26	31416	11231	27904	57383	31852	69137	96667	14315	01007	31929
27	82066	83436	67914	21465	99605	83114	97885	74440	99622	87912
28	01850	42782	39202	18582	46214	99228	79541	78298	75404	63648
29	32315	89276	89582	87138	16165	15984	21466	63830	30475	74729
30	59388	42703	55198	80380	67067	97155	34160	85019	03527	78140
31	58089	27632	50987	91373	07736	20436	96130	73483	85332	24384
32	61705	57285	30392	23660	75841	21931	04295	00875	09114	32101
33	18914	98982	60199	99275	41967	35208	30357	76772	92656	62318
34	11965	94089	34803	48941	69709	16784	44642	89761	66864	62803
35	85251	48111	80936	81781	93248	67877	16498	31924	51315	79921
36	66121	96986	84844	93873	46352	92183	51152	85878	30490	15974
37	53972	96642	24199	58080	35450	03482	66953	49521	63719	57615
38	14509	16594	78883	43222	23093	58645	60257	89250	63266	90858
39	37700	07688	65533	72126	23611	93993	01848	03910	38552	17472
40	85466	59392	72722	15473	73295	49759	56157	60477	83284	56367
41	52969	55863	42312	67842	05673	91878	82738	36563	79540	61935
42	42744	68315	17514	02878	97291	74851	42725	57894	81434	62041
43	26140	13336	67726	61876	29971	99294	96664	52817	90039	53211
44	95589	56319	14563	24071	06916	59555	18195	32280	79357	04224
45	39113	13217	59999	49952	83021	47709	53105	19295	88318	41626
46	41392	17622	18994	98283	07249	52289	24209	91139	30715	06604
47	54684	53645	79246	70183	87731	19185	08541	33519	07223	97413
48	89442	61001	36658	57444	95388	36682	38052	46719	09428	94012
49	36751	16778	54888	15357	68003	43564	90976	58904	40512	07725
50	98159	02564	21416	74944	53049	88749	02865	25772	89853	88714

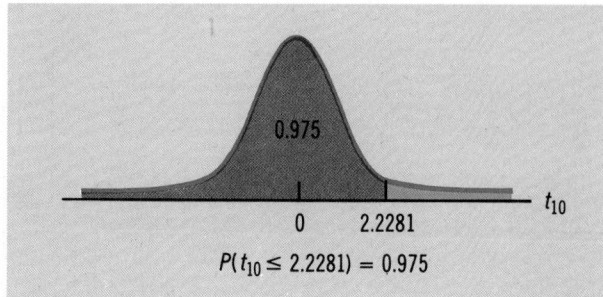

$P(t_{10} \le 2.2281) = 0.975$

TABLE E   Percentiles of the t distribution $P(t \le t_0)$

df	$t_{0.90}$	$t_{0.95}$	$t_{0.975}$	$t_{0.99}$	$t_{0.995}$
1	3.078	6.3138	12.706	31.821	63.657
2	1.886	2.9200	4.3027	6.965	9.9248
3	1.638	2.3534	3.1825	4.541	5.8409
4	1.533	2.1318	2.7764	3.747	4.6041
5	1.476	2.0150	2.5706	3.365	4.0321
6	1.440	1.9432	2.4469	3.143	3.7074
7	1.415	1.8946	2.3646	2.998	3.4995
8	1.397	1.8595	2.3060	2.896	3.3554
9	1.383	1.8331	2.2622	2.821	3.2498
10	1.372	1.8125	2.2281	2.764	3.1693
11	1.363	1.7959	2.2010	2.718	3.1058
12	1.356	1.7823	2.1788	2.681	3.0545
13	1.350	1.7709	2.1604	2.650	3.0123
14	1.345	1.7613	2.1448	2.624	2.9768
15	1.341	1.7530	2.1315	2.602	2.9467
16	1.337	1.7459	2.1199	2.583	2.9208
17	1.333	1.7396	2.1098	2.567	2.8982
18	1.330	1.7341	2.1009	2.552	2.8784
19	1.328	1.7291	2.0930	2.539	2.8609
20	1.325	1.7247	2.0860	2.528	2.8453
21	1.323	1.7207	2.0796	2.518	2.8314
22	1.321	1.7171	2.0739	2.508	2.8188
23	1.319	1.7139	2.0687	2.500	2.8073
24	1.318	1.7109	2.0639	2.492	2.7969
25	1.316	1.7081	2.0595	2.485	2.7874
26	1.315	1.7056	2.0555	2.479	2.7787
27	1.314	1.7033	2.0518	2.473	2.7707
28	1.313	1.7011	2.0484	2.467	2.7633
29	1.311	1.6991	2.0452	2.462	2.7564
30	1.310	1.6973	2.0423	2.457	2.7500
35	1.3062	1.6896	2.0301	2.438	2.7239
40	1.3031	1.6839	2.0211	2.423	2.7045
45	1.3007	1.6794	2.0141	2.412	2.6896
50	1.2987	1.6759	2.0086	2.403	2.6778
60	1.2959	1.6707	2.0003	2.390	2.6603
70	1.2938	1.6669	1.9945	2.381	2.6480
80	1.2922	1.6641	1.9901	2.374	2.6388
90	1.2910	1.6620	1.9867	2.368	2.6316
100	1.2901	1.6602	1.9840	2.364	2.6260
120	1.2887	1.6577	1.9799	2.358	2.6175
140	1.2876	1.6558	1.9771	2.353	2.6114
160	1.2869	1.6545	1.9749	2.350	2.6070
180	1.2863	1.6534	1.9733	2.347	2.6035
200	1.2858	1.6525	1.9719	2.345	2.6006
∞	1.282	1.645	1.96	2.326	2.576
One-tail α	0.10	0.05	0.025	0.01	0.005
Two-tail α	0.20	0.10	0.05	0.02	0.01

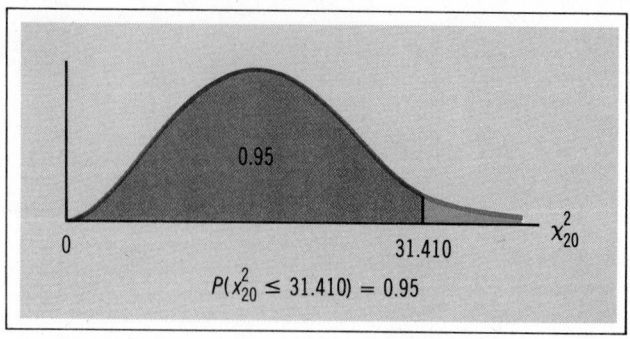

$$P(\chi^2_{20} \leq 31.410) = 0.95$$

TABLE F Percentiles of the chi-square distribution $P(X^2 \leq \chi^2)$

df	$\chi^2_{0.005}$	$\chi^2_{0.025}$	$\chi^2_{0.05}$	$\chi^2_{0.90}$	$\chi^2_{0.95}$	$\chi^2_{0.975}$	$\chi^2_{0.99}$	$\chi^2_{0.995}$
1	0.0000393	0.000982	0.00393	2.706	3.841	5.024	6.635	7.879
2	0.0100	0.0506	0.103	4.605	5.991	7.378	9.210	10.597
3	0.0717	0.216	0.352	6.251	7.815	9.348	11.345	12.838
4	0.207	0.484	0.711	7.779	9.488	11.143	13.277	14.860
5	0.412	0.831	1.145	9.236	11.070	12.832	15.086	16.750
6	0.676	1.237	1.635	10.645	12.592	14.449	16.812	18.548
7	0.989	1.690	2.167	12.017	14.067	16.013	18.475	20.278
8	1.344	2.180	2.733	13.362	15.507	17.535	20.090	21.955
9	1.735	2.700	3.325	14.684	16.919	19.023	21.666	23.589
10	2.156	3.247	3.940	15.987	18.307	20.483	23.209	25.188
11	2.603	3.816	4.575	17.275	19.675	21.920	24.725	26.757
12	3.074	4.404	5.226	18.549	21.026	23.336	26.217	28.300
13	3.565	5.009	5.892	19.812	22.362	24.736	27.688	29.819
14	4.075	5.629	6.571	21.064	23.685	26.119	29.141	31.319
15	4.601	6.262	7.261	22.307	24.996	27.488	30.578	32.801
16	5.142	6.908	7.962	23.542	26.296	28.845	32.000	34.267
17	5.697	7.564	8.672	24.769	27.587	30.191	33.409	35.718
18	6.265	8.231	9.390	25.989	28.869	31.526	34.805	37.156
19	6.844	8.907	10.117	27.204	30.144	32.852	36.191	38.582
20	7.434	9.591	10.851	28.412	31.410	34.170	37.566	39.997
21	8.034	10.283	11.591	29.615	32.671	35.479	38.932	41.401
22	8.643	10.982	12.338	30.813	33.924	36.781	40.289	42.796
23	9.260	11.688	13.091	32.007	35.172	38.076	41.638	44.181
24	9.886	12.401	13.848	33.196	36.415	39.364	42.980	45.558
25	10.520	13.120	14.611	34.382	37.652	40.646	44.314	46.928
26	11.160	13.844	15.379	35.563	38.885	41.923	45.642	48.290
27	11.808	14.573	16.151	36.741	40.113	43.194	46.963	49.645
28	12.461	15.308	16.928	37.916	41.337	44.461	48.278	50.993
29	13.121	16.047	17.708	39.087	42.557	45.722	49.588	52.336
30	13.787	16.791	18.493	40.256	43.773	46.979	50.892	53.672
35	17.192	20.569	22.465	46.059	49.802	53.203	57.342	60.275
40	20.707	24.433	26.509	51.805	55.758	59.342	63.691	66.766
45	24.311	28.366	30.612	57.505	61.656	65.410	69.957	73.166
50	27.991	32.357	34.764	63.167	67.505	71.420	76.154	79.490
60	35.535	40.482	43.188	74.397	79.082	83.298	88.379	91.952
70	43.275	48.758	51.739	85.527	90.531	95.023	100.425	104.215
80	51.172	57.153	60.391	96.578	101.879	106.629	112.329	116.321
90	59.196	65.647	69.126	107.565	113.145	118.136	124.116	128.299
100	67.328	74.222	77.929	118.498	124.342	129.561	135.807	140.169

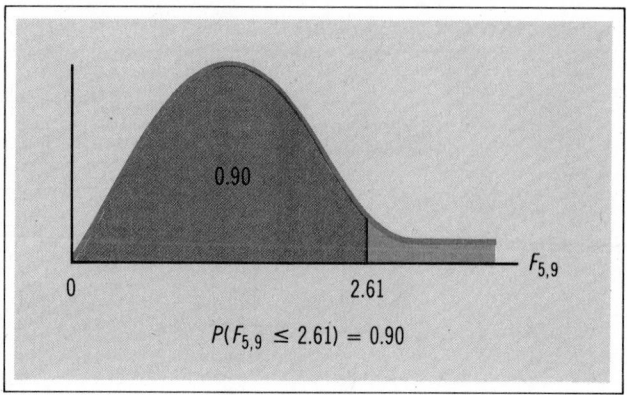

$$P(F_{5,9} \le 2.61) = 0.90$$

TABLE G   Percentiles of the F distribution $P(F \le F_0)$

$F_{0.90}$

Denominator degrees of freedom	\multicolumn{9}{c}{Numerator degrees of freedom}
	1	2	3	4	5	6	7	8	9
1	39.86	49.50	53.59	55.83	57.24	58.20	58.91	59.44	59.86
2	8.53	9.00	9.16	9.24	9.29	9.33	9.35	9.37	9.38
3	5.54	5.46	5.39	5.34	5.31	5.28	5.27	5.25	5.24
4	4.54	4.32	4.19	4.11	4.05	4.01	3.98	3.95	3.94
5	4.06	3.78	3.62	3.52	3.45	3.40	3.37	3.34	3.32
6	3.78	3.46	3.29	3.18	3.11	3.05	3.01	2.98	2.96
7	3.59	3.26	3.07	2.96	2.88	2.83	2.78	2.75	2.72
8	3.46	3.11	2.92	2.81	2.73	2.67	2.62	2.59	2.56
9	3.36	3.01	2.81	2.69	2.61	2.55	2.51	2.47	2.44
10	3.29	2.92	2.73	2.61	2.52	2.46	2.41	2.38	2.35
11	3.23	2.86	2.66	2.54	2.45	2.39	2.34	2.30	2.27
12	3.18	2.81	2.61	2.48	2.39	2.33	2.28	2.24	2.21
13	3.14	2.76	2.56	2.43	2.35	2.28	2.23	2.20	2.16
14	3.10	2.73	2.52	2.39	2.31	2.24	2.19	2.15	2.12
15	3.07	2.70	2.49	2.36	2.27	2.21	2.16	2.12	2.09
16	3.05	2.67	2.46	2.33	2.24	2.18	2.13	2.09	2.06
17	3.03	2.64	2.44	2.31	2.22	2.15	2.10	2.06	2.03
18	3.01	2.62	2.42	2.29	2.20	2.13	2.08	2.04	2.00
19	2.99	2.61	2.40	2.27	2.18	2.11	2.06	2.02	1.98
20	2.97	2.59	2.38	2.25	2.16	2.09	2.04	2.00	1.96
21	2.96	2.57	2.36	2.23	2.14	2.08	2.02	1.98	1.95
22	2.95	2.56	2.35	2.22	2.13	2.06	2.01	1.97	1.93
23	2.94	2.55	2.34	2.21	2.11	2.05	1.99	1.95	1.92
24	2.93	2.54	2.33	2.19	2.10	2.04	1.98	1.94	1.91

TABLE G (*continued*)

$F_{0.90}$

Denominator degrees of freedom	1	2	3	4	5	6	7	8	9
				Numerator degrees of freedom					
25	2.92	2.53	2.32	2.18	2.09	2.02	1.97	1.93	1.89
26	2.91	2.52	2.31	2.17	2.08	2.01	1.96	1.92	1.88
27	2.90	2.51	2.30	2.17	2.07	2.00	1.95	1.91	1.87
28	2.89	2.50	2.29	2.16	2.06	2.00	1.94	1.90	1.87
29	2.89	2.50	2.28	2.15	2.06	1.99	1.93	1.89	1.86
30	2.88	2.49	2.28	2.14	2.05	1.98	1.93	1.88	1.85
40	2.84	2.44	2.23	2.09	2.00	1.93	1.87	1.83	1.79
60	2.79	2.39	2.18	2.04	1.95	1.87	1.82	1.77	1.74
120	2.75	2.35	2.13	1.99	1.90	1.82	1.77	1.72	1.68
∞	2.71	2.30	2.08	1.94	1.85	1.77	1.72	1.67	1.63

$F_{0.90}$

Denominator degrees of freedom	10	12	15	20	24	30	40	60	120	∞
					Numerator degrees of freedom					
1	60.19	60.71	61.22	61.74	62.00	62.26	62.53	62.79	63.06	63.33
2	9.39	9.41	9.42	9.44	9.45	9.46	9.47	9.47	9.48	9.49
3	5.23	5.22	5.20	5.18	5.18	5.17	5.16	5.15	5.14	5.13
4	3.92	3.90	3.87	3.84	3.83	3.82	3.80	3.79	3.78	3.76
5	3.30	3.27	3.24	3.21	3.19	3.17	3.16	3.14	3.12	3.10
6	2.94	2.90	2.87	2.84	2.82	2.80	2.78	2.76	2.74	2.72
7	2.70	2.67	2.63	2.59	2.58	2.56	2.54	2.51	2.49	2.47
8	2.54	2.50	2.46	2.42	2.40	2.38	2.36	2.34	2.32	2.29
9	2.42	2.38	2.34	2.30	2.28	2.25	2.23	2.21	2.18	2.16
10	2.32	2.28	2.24	2.20	2.18	2.16	2.13	2.11	2.08	2.06
11	2.25	2.21	2.17	2.12	2.10	2.08	2.05	2.03	2.00	1.97
12	2.19	2.15	2.10	2.06	2.04	2.01	1.99	1.96	1.93	1.90
13	2.14	2.10	2.05	2.01	1.98	1.96	1.93	1.90	1.88	1.85
14	2.10	2.05	2.01	1.96	1.94	1.91	1.89	1.86	1.83	1.80
15	2.06	2.02	1.97	1.92	1.90	1.87	1.85	1.82	1.79	1.76
16	2.03	1.99	1.94	1.89	1.87	1.84	1.81	1.78	1.75	1.72
17	2.00	1.96	1.91	1.86	1.84	1.81	1.78	1.75	1.72	1.69
18	1.98	1.93	1.89	1.84	1.81	1.78	1.75	1.72	1.69	1.66
19	1.96	1.91	1.86	1.81	1.79	1.76	1.73	1.70	1.67	1.63
20	1.94	1.89	1.84	1.79	1.77	1.74	1.71	1.68	1.64	1.61
21	1.92	1.87	1.83	1.78	1.75	1.72	1.69	1.66	1.62	1.59
22	1.90	1.86	1.81	1.76	1.73	1.70	1.67	1.64	1.60	1.57
23	1.89	1.84	1.80	1.74	1.72	1.69	1.66	1.62	1.59	1.55
24	1.88	1.83	1.78	1.73	1.70	1.67	1.64	1.61	1.57	1.53
25	1.87	1.82	1.77	1.72	1.69	1.66	1.63	1.59	1.56	1.52
26	1.86	1.81	1.76	1.71	1.68	1.65	1.61	1.58	1.54	1.50
27	1.85	1.80	1.75	1.70	1.67	1.64	1.60	1.57	1.53	1.49
28	1.84	1.79	1.74	1.69	1.66	1.63	1.59	1.56	1.52	1.48
29	1.83	1.78	1.73	1.68	1.65	1.62	1.58	1.55	1.51	1.47

TABLE G   (*continued*)

$F_{0.90}$

Denominator degrees of freedom	Numerator degrees of freedom									
	10	12	15	20	24	30	40	60	120	∞
30	1.82	1.77	1.72	1.67	1.64	1.61	1.57	1.54	1.50	1.46
40	1.76	1.71	1.66	1.61	1.57	1.54	1.51	1.47	1.42	1.38
60	1.71	1.66	1.60	1.54	1.51	1.48	1.44	1.40	1.35	1.29
120	1.65	1.60	1.55	1.48	1.45	1.41	1.37	1.32	1.26	1.19
∞	1.60	1.55	1.49	1.42	1.38	1.34	1.30	1.24	1.17	1.00

$F_{0.95}$

Denominator degrees of freedom	Numerator degrees of freedom								
	1	2	3	4	5	6	7	8	9
1	161.4	199.5	215.7	224.6	230.2	234.0	236.8	238.9	240.5
2	18.51	19.00	19.16	19.25	19.30	19.33	19.35	19.37	19.38
3	10.13	9.55	9.28	9.12	9.01	8.94	8.89	8.85	8.81
4	7.71	6.94	6.59	6.39	6.26	6.16	6.09	6.04	6.00
5	6.61	5.79	5.41	5.19	5.05	4.95	4.88	4.82	4.77
6	5.99	5.14	4.76	4.53	4.39	4.28	4.21	4.15	4.10
7	5.59	4.74	4.35	4.12	3.97	3.87	3.79	3.73	3.68
8	5.32	4.46	4.07	3.84	3.69	3.58	3.50	3.44	3.39
9	5.12	4.26	3.86	3.63	3.48	3.37	3.29	3.23	3.18
10	4.96	4.10	3.71	3.48	3.33	3.22	3.14	3.07	3.02
11	4.84	3.98	3.59	3.36	3.20	3.09	3.01	2.95	2.90
12	4.75	3.89	3.49	3.26	3.11	3.00	2.91	2.85	2.80
13	4.67	3.81	3.41	3.18	3.03	2.92	2.83	2.77	2.71
14	4.60	3.74	3.34	3.11	2.96	2.85	2.76	2.70	2.65
15	4.54	3.68	3.29	3.06	2.90	2.79	2.71	2.64	2.59
16	4.49	3.63	3.24	3.01	2.85	2.74	2.66	2.59	2.54
17	4.45	3.59	3.20	2.96	2.81	2.70	2.61	2.55	2.49
18	4.41	3.55	3.16	2.93	2.77	2.66	2.58	2.51	2.46
19	4.38	3.52	3.13	2.90	2.74	2.63	2.54	2.48	2.42
20	4.35	3.49	3.10	2.87	2.71	2.60	2.51	2.45	2.39
21	4.32	3.47	3.07	2.84	2.68	2.57	2.49	2.42	2.37
22	4.30	3.44	3.05	2.82	2.66	2.55	2.46	2.40	2.34
23	4.28	3.42	3.03	2.80	2.64	2.53	2.44	2.37	2.32
24	4.26	3.40	3.01	2.78	2.62	2.51	2.42	2.36	2.30
25	4.24	3.39	2.99	2.76	2.60	2.49	2.40	2.34	2.28
26	4.23	3.37	2.98	2.74	2.59	2.47	2.39	2.32	2.27
27	4.21	3.35	2.96	2.73	2.57	2.46	2.37	2.31	2.25
28	4.20	3.34	2.95	2.71	2.56	2.45	2.36	2.29	2.24
29	4.18	3.33	2.93	2.70	2.55	2.43	2.35	2.28	2.22
30	4.17	3.32	2.92	2.69	2.53	2.42	2.33	2.27	2.21
40	4.08	3.23	2.84	2.61	2.45	2.34	2.25	2.18	2.12
60	4.00	3.15	2.76	2.53	2.37	2.25	2.17	2.10	2.04
120	3.92	3.07	2.68	2.45	2.29	2.17	2.09	2.02	1.96
∞	3.84	3.00	2.60	2.37	2.21	2.10	2.01	1.94	1.88

TABLE G (*continued*)

$$F_{0.95}$$

Denominator degrees of freedom	10	12	15	20	24	30	40	60	120	∞
				Numerator degrees of freedom						
1	241.9	243.9	245.9	248.0	249.1	250.1	251.1	252.2	253.3	254.3
2	19.40	19.41	19.43	19.45	19.45	19.46	19.47	19.48	19.49	19.50
3	8.79	8.74	8.70	8.66	8.64	8.62	8.59	8.57	8.55	8.53
4	5.96	5.91	5.86	5.80	5.77	5.75	5.72	5.69	5.66	5.63
5	4.74	4.68	4.62	4.56	4.53	4.50	4.46	4.43	4.40	4.36
6	4.06	4.00	3.94	3.87	3.84	3.81	3.77	3.74	3.70	3.67
7	3.64	3.57	3.51	3.44	3.41	3.38	3.34	3.30	3.27	3.23
8	3.35	3.28	3.22	3.15	3.12	3.08	3.04	3.01	2.97	2.93
9	3.14	3.07	3.01	2.94	2.90	2.86	2.83	2.79	2.75	2.71
10	2.98	2.91	2.85	2.77	2.74	2.70	2.66	2.62	2.58	2.54
11	2.85	2.79	2.72	2.65	2.61	2.57	2.53	2.49	2.45	2.40
12	2.75	2.69	2.62	2.54	2.51	2.47	2.43	2.38	2.34	2.30
13	2.67	2.60	2.53	2.46	2.42	2.38	2.34	2.30	2.25	2.21
14	2.60	2.53	2.46	2.39	2.35	2.31	2.27	2.22	2.18	2.13
15	2.54	2.48	2.40	2.33	2.29	2.25	2.20	2.16	2.11	2.07
16	2.49	2.42	2.35	2.28	2.24	2.19	2.15	2.11	2.06	2.01
17	2.45	2.38	2.31	2.23	2.19	2.15	2.10	2.06	2.01	1.96
18	2.41	2.34	2.27	2.19	2.15	2.11	2.06	2.02	1.97	1.92
19	2.38	2.31	2.23	2.16	2.11	2.07	2.03	1.98	1.93	1.88
20	2.35	2.28	2.20	2.12	2.08	2.04	1.99	1.95	1.90	1.84
21	2.32	2.25	2.18	2.10	2.05	2.01	1.96	1.92	1.87	1.81
22	2.30	2.23	2.15	2.07	2.03	1.98	1.94	1.89	1.84	1.78
23	2.27	2.20	2.13	2.05	2.01	1.96	1.91	1.86	1.81	1.76
24	2.25	2.18	2.11	2.03	1.98	1.94	1.89	1.84	1.79	1.73
25	2.24	2.16	2.09	2.01	1.96	1.92	1.87	1.82	1.77	1.71
26	2.22	2.15	2.07	1.99	1.95	1.90	1.85	1.80	1.75	1.69
27	2.20	2.13	2.06	1.97	1.93	1.88	1.84	1.79	1.73	1.67
28	2.19	2.12	2.04	1.96	1.91	1.87	1.82	1.77	1.71	1.65
29	2.18	2.10	2.03	1.94	1.90	1.85	1.81	1.75	1.70	1.64
30	2.16	2.09	2.01	1.93	1.89	1.84	1.79	1.74	1.68	1.62
40	2.08	2.00	1.92	1.84	1.79	1.74	1.69	1.64	1.58	1.51
60	1.99	1.92	1.84	1.75	1.70	1.65	1.59	1.53	1.47	1.39
120	1.91	1.83	1.75	1.66	1.61	1.55	1.50	1.43	1.35	1.25
∞	1.83	1.75	1.67	1.57	1.52	1.46	1.39	1.32	1.22	1.00

$$F_{0.975}$$

Denominator degrees of freedom	1	2	3	4	5	6	7	8	9
				Numerator degrees of freedom					
1	647.8	799.5	864.2	899.6	921.8	937.1	948.2	956.7	963.3
2	38.51	39.00	39.17	39.25	39.30	39.33	39.36	39.37	39.39
3	17.44	16.04	15.44	15.10	14.88	14.73	14.62	14.54	14.47
4	12.22	10.65	9.98	9.60	9.36	9.20	9.07	8.98	8.90

TABLE G   (*continued*)

$$F_{0.975}$$

Denominator degrees of freedom	1	2	3	4	5	6	7	8	9
				Numerator degrees of freedom					
5	10.01	8.43	7.76	7.39	7.15	6.98	6.85	6.76	6.68
6	8.81	7.26	6.60	6.23	5.99	5.82	5.70	5.60	5.52
7	8.07	6.54	5.89	5.52	5.29	5.12	4.99	4.90	4.82
8	7.57	6.06	5.42	5.05	4.82	4.65	4.53	4.43	4.36
9	7.21	5.71	5.08	4.72	4.48	4.32	4.20	4.10	4.03
10	6.94	5.46	4.83	4.47	4.24	4.07	3.95	3.85	3.78
11	6.72	5.26	4.63	4.28	4.04	3.88	3.76	3.66	3.59
12	6.55	5.10	4.47	4.12	3.89	3.73	3.61	3.51	3.44
13	6.41	4.97	4.35	4.00	3.77	3.60	3.48	3.39	3.31
14	6.30	4.86	4.24	3.89	3.66	3.50	3.38	3.29	3.21
15	6.20	4.77	4.15	3.80	3.58	3.41	3.29	3.20	3.12
16	6.12	4.69	4.08	3.73	3.50	3.34	3.22	3.12	3.05
17	6.04	4.62	4.01	3.66	3.44	3.28	3.16	3.06	2.98
18	5.98	4.56	3.95	3.61	3.38	3.22	3.10	3.01	2.93
19	5.92	4.51	3.90	3.56	3.33	3.17	3.05	2.96	2.88
20	5.87	4.46	3.86	3.51	3.29	3.13	3.01	2.91	2.84
21	5.83	4.42	3.82	3.48	3.25	3.09	2.97	2.87	2.80
22	5.79	4.38	3.78	3.44	3.22	3.05	2.93	2.84	2.76
23	5.75	4.35	3.75	3.41	3.18	3.02	2.90	2.81	2.73
24	5.72	4.32	3.72	3.38	3.15	2.99	2.87	2.78	2.70
25	5.69	4.29	3.69	3.35	3.13	2.97	2.85	2.75	2.68
26	5.66	4.27	3.67	3.33	3.10	2.94	2.82	2.73	2.65
27	5.63	4.24	3.65	3.31	3.08	2.92	2.80	2.71	2.63
28	5.61	4.22	3.63	3.29	3.06	2.90	2.78	2.69	2.61
29	5.59	4.20	3.61	3.27	3.04	2.88	2.76	2.67	2.59
30	5.57	4.18	3.59	3.25	3.03	2.87	2.75	2.65	2.57
40	5.42	4.05	3.46	3.13	2.90	2.74	2.62	2.53	2.45
60	5.29	3.93	3.34	3.01	2.79	2.63	2.51	2.41	2.33
120	5.15	3.80	3.23	2.89	2.67	2.52	2.39	2.30	2.22
∞	5.02	3.69	3.12	2.79	2.57	2.41	2.29	2.19	2.11

$$F_{0.975}$$

Denominator degrees of freedom	10	12	15	20	24	30	40	60	120	∞
				Numerator degrees of freedom						
1	968.6	976.7	984.9	993.1	997.2	1001	1006	1010	1014	1018
2	39.40	39.41	39.43	39.45	39.46	39.46	39.47	39.48	39.49	39.50
3	14.42	14.34	14.25	14.17	14.12	14.08	14.04	13.99	13.95	13.90
4	8.84	8.75	8.66	8.56	8.51	8.46	8.41	8.36	8.31	8.26
5	6.62	6.52	6.43	6.33	6.28	6.23	6.18	6.12	6.07	6.02
6	5.46	5.37	5.27	5.17	5.12	5.07	5.01	4.96	4.90	4.85
7	4.76	4.67	4.57	4.47	4.42	4.36	4.31	4.25	4.20	4.14
8	4.30	4.20	4.10	4.00	3.95	3.89	3.84	3.78	3.73	3.67
9	3.96	3.87	3.77	3.67	3.61	3.56	3.51	3.45	3.39	3.33

TABLE G   (*continued*)

$$F_{0.975}$$

Denominator degrees of freedom	10	12	15	20	24	30	40	60	120	∞
				Numerator degrees of freedom						
10	3.72	3.62	3.52	3.42	3.37	3.31	3.26	3.20	3.14	3.08
11	3.53	3.43	3.33	3.23	3.17	3.12	3.06	3.00	2.94	2.88
12	3.37	3.28	3.18	3.07	3.02	2.96	2.91	2.85	2.79	2.72
13	3.25	3.15	3.05	2.95	2.89	2.84	2.78	2.72	2.66	2.60
14	3.15	3.05	2.95	2.84	2.79	2.73	2.67	2.61	2.55	2.49
15	3.06	2.96	2.86	2.76	2.70	2.64	2.59	2.52	2.46	2.40
16	2.99	2.89	2.79	2.68	2.63	2.57	2.51	2.45	2.38	2.32
17	2.92	2.82	2.72	2.62	2.56	2.50	2.44	2.38	2.32	2.25
18	2.87	2.77	2.67	2.56	2.50	2.44	2.38	2.32	2.26	2.19
19	2.82	2.72	2.62	2.51	2.45	2.39	2.33	2.27	2.20	2.13
20	2.77	2.68	2.57	2.46	2.41	2.35	2.29	2.22	2.16	2.09
21	2.73	2.64	2.53	2.42	2.37	2.31	2.25	2.18	2.11	2.04
22	2.70	2.60	2.50	2.39	2.33	2.27	2.21	2.14	2.08	2.00
23	2.67	2.57	2.47	2.36	2.30	2.24	2.18	2.11	2.04	1.97
24	2.64	2.54	2.44	2.33	2.27	2.21	2.15	2.08	2.01	1.94
25	2.61	2.51	2.41	2.30	2.24	2.18	2.12	2.05	1.98	1.91
26	2.59	2.49	2.39	2.28	2.22	2.16	2.09	2.03	1.95	1.88
27	2.57	2.47	2.36	2.25	2.19	2.13	2.07	2.00	1.93	1.85
28	2.55	2.45	2.34	2.23	2.17	2.11	2.05	1.98	1.91	1.83
29	2.53	2.43	2.32	2.21	2.15	2.09	2.03	1.96	1.89	1.81
30	2.51	2.41	2.31	2.20	2.14	2.07	2.01	1.94	1.87	1.79
40	2.39	2.29	2.18	2.07	2.01	1.94	1.88	1.80	1.72	1.64
60	2.27	2.17	2.06	1.94	1.88	1.82	1.74	1.67	1.58	1.48
120	2.16	2.05	1.94	1.82	1.76	1.69	1.61	1.53	1.43	1.31
∞	2.05	1.94	1.83	1.71	1.64	1.57	1.48	1.39	1.27	1.00

$$F_{0.99}$$

Denominator degrees of freedom	1	2	3	4	5	6	7	8	9
				Numerator degrees of freedom					
1	4052	4999.5	5403	5625	5764	5859	5928	5981	6022
2	98.50	99.00	99.17	99.25	99.30	99.33	99.36	99.37	99.39
3	34.12	30.82	29.46	28.71	28.24	27.91	27.67	27.49	27.35
4	21.20	18.00	16.69	15.98	15.52	15.21	14.98	14.80	14.66
5	16.26	13.27	12.06	11.39	10.97	10.67	10.46	10.29	10.16
6	13.75	10.92	9.78	9.15	8.75	8.47	8.26	8.10	7.98
7	12.25	9.55	8.45	7.85	7.46	7.19	6.99	6.84	6.72
8	11.26	8.65	7.59	7.01	6.63	6.37	6.18	6.03	5.91
9	10.56	8.02	6.99	6.42	6.06	5.80	5.61	5.47	5.35
10	10.04	7.56	6.55	5.99	5.64	5.39	5.20	5.06	4.94
11	9.65	7.21	6.22	5.67	5.32	5.07	4.89	4.74	4.63
12	9.33	6.93	5.95	5.41	5.06	4.82	4.64	4.50	4.39
13	9.07	6.70	5.74	5.21	4.86	4.62	4.44	4.30	4.19
14	8.86	6.51	5.56	5.04	4.69	4.46	4.28	4.14	4.03

TABLE G (*continued*)

$F_{0.99}$

Denominator degrees of freedom	1	2	3	Numerator degrees of freedom 4	5	6	7	8	9
15	8.68	6.36	5.42	4.89	4.56	4.32	4.14	4.00	3.89
16	8.53	6.23	5.29	4.77	4.44	4.20	4.03	3.89	3.78
17	8.40	6.11	5.18	4.67	4.34	4.10	3.93	3.79	3.68
18	8.29	6.01	5.09	4.58	4.25	4.01	3.84	3.71	3.60
19	8.18	5.93	5.01	4.50	4.17	3.94	3.77	3.63	3.52
20	8.10	5.85	4.94	4.43	4.10	3.87	3.70	3.56	3.46
21	8.02	5.78	4.87	4.37	4.04	3.81	3.64	3.51	3.40
22	7.95	5.72	4.82	4.31	3.99	3.76	3.59	3.45	3.35
23	7.88	5.66	4.76	4.26	3.94	3.71	3.54	3.41	3.30
24	7.82	5.61	4.72	4.22	3.90	3.67	3.50	3.36	3.26
25	7.77	5.57	4.68	4.18	3.85	3.63	3.46	3.32	3.22
26	7.72	5.53	4.64	4.14	3.82	3.59	3.42	3.29	3.18
27	7.68	5.49	4.60	4.11	3.78	3.56	3.39	3.26	3.15
28	7.64	5.45	4.57	4.07	3.75	3.53	3.36	3.23	3.12
29	7.60	5.42	4.54	4.04	3.73	3.50	3.33	3.20	3.09
30	7.56	5.39	4.51	4.02	3.70	3.47	3.30	3.17	3.07
40	7.31	5.18	4.31	3.83	3.51	3.29	3.12	2.99	2.89
60	7.08	4.98	4.13	3.65	3.34	3.12	2.95	2.82	2.72
120	6.85	4.79	3.95	3.48	3.17	2.96	2.79	2.66	2.56
∞	6.63	4.61	3.78	3.32	3.02	2.80	2.64	2.51	2.41

$F_{0.99}$

Denominator degrees of freedom	10	12	15	Numerator degrees of freedom 20	24	30	40	60	120	∞
1	6056	6106	6157	6209	6235	6261	6287	6313	6339	6366
2	99.40	99.42	99.43	99.45	99.46	99.47	99.47	99.48	99.49	99.50
3	27.23	27.05	26.87	26.69	26.60	26.50	26.41	26.32	26.22	26.13
4	14.55	14.37	14.20	14.02	13.93	13.84	13.75	13.65	13.56	13.46
5	10.05	9.89	9.72	9.55	9.47	9.38	9.29	9.20	9.11	9.02
6	7.87	7.72	7.56	7.40	7.31	7.23	7.14	7.06	6.97	6.88
7	6.62	6.47	6.31	6.16	6.07	5.99	5.91	5.82	5.74	5.65
8	5.81	5.67	5.52	5.36	5.28	5.20	5.12	5.03	4.95	4.86
9	5.26	5.11	4.96	4.81	4.73	4.65	4.57	4.48	4.40	4.31
10	4.85	4.71	4.56	4.41	4.33	4.25	4.17	4.08	4.00	3.91
11	4.54	4.40	4.25	4.10	4.02	3.94	3.86	3.78	3.69	3.60
12	4.30	4.16	4.01	3.86	3.78	3.70	3.62	3.54	3.45	3.36
13	4.10	3.96	3.82	3.66	3.59	3.51	3.43	3.34	3.25	3.17
14	3.94	3.80	3.66	3.51	3.43	3.35	3.27	3.18	3.09	3.00
15	3.80	3.67	3.52	3.37	3.29	3.21	3.13	3.05	2.96	2.87
16	3.69	3.55	3.41	3.26	3.18	3.10	3.02	2.93	2.84	2.75
17	3.59	3.46	3.31	3.16	3.08	3.00	2.92	2.83	2.75	2.65
18	3.51	3.37	3.23	3.08	3.00	2.92	2.84	2.75	2.66	2.57
19	3.43	3.30	3.15	3.00	2.92	2.84	2.76	2.67	2.58	2.49

TABLE G   (*continued*)

$F_{0.99}$

Denominator degrees of freedom	Numerator degrees of freedom									
	10	12	15	20	24	30	40	60	120	∞
20	3.37	3.23	3.09	2.94	2.86	2.78	2.69	2.61	2.52	2.42
21	3.31	3.17	3.03	2.88	2.80	2.72	2.64	2.55	2.46	2.36
22	3.26	3.12	2.98	2.83	2.75	2.67	2.58	2.50	2.40	2.31
23	3.21	3.07	2.93	2.78	2.70	2.62	2.54	2.45	2.35	2.26
24	3.17	3.03	2.89	2.74	2.66	2.58	2.49	2.40	2.31	2.21
25	3.13	2.99	2.85	2.70	2.62	2.54	2.45	2.36	2.27	2.17
26	3.09	2.96	2.81	2.66	2.58	2.50	2.42	2.33	2.23	2.13
27	3.06	2.93	2.78	2.63	2.55	2.47	2.38	2.29	2.20	2.10
28	3.03	2.90	2.75	2.60	2.52	2.44	2.35	2.26	2.17	2.06
29	3.00	2.87	2.73	2.57	2.49	2.41	2.33	2.23	2.14	2.03
30	2.98	2.84	2.70	2.55	2.47	2.39	2.30	2.21	2.11	2.01
40	2.80	2.66	2.52	2.37	2.29	2.20	2.11	2.02	1.92	1.80
60	2.63	2.50	2.35	2.20	2.12	2.03	1.94	1.84	1.73	1.60
120	2.47	2.34	2.19	2.03	1.95	1.86	1.76	1.66	1.53	1.38
∞	2.32	2.18	2.04	1.88	1.79	1.70	1.59	1.47	1.32	1.00

$F_{0.995}$

Denominator degrees of freedom	Numerator degrees of freedom								
	1	2	3	4	5	6	7	8	9
1	16211	20000	21615	22500	23056	23437	23715	23925	24091
2	198.5	199.0	199.2	199.2	199.3	199.3	199.4	199.4	199.4
3	55.55	49.80	47.47	46.19	45.39	44.84	44.43	44.13	43.88
4	31.33	26.28	24.26	23.15	22.46	21.97	21.62	21.35	21.14
5	22.78	18.31	16.53	15.56	14.94	14.51	14.20	13.96	13.77
6	18.63	14.54	12.92	12.03	11.46	11.07	10.79	10.57	10.39
7	16.24	12.40	10.88	10.05	9.52	9.16	8.89	8.68	8.51
8	14.69	11.04	9.60	8.81	8.30	7.95	7.69	7.50	7.34
9	13.61	10.11	8.72	7.96	7.47	7.13	6.88	6.69	6.54
10	12.83	9.43	8.08	7.34	6.87	6.54	6.30	6.12	5.97
11	12.23	8.91	7.60	6.88	6.42	6.10	5.86	5.68	5.54
12	11.75	8.51	7.23	6.52	6.07	5.76	5.52	5.35	5.20
13	11.37	8.19	6.93	6.23	5.79	5.48	5.25	5.08	4.94
14	11.06	7.92	6.68	6.00	5.56	5.26	5.03	4.86	4.72
15	10.80	7.70	6.48	5.80	5.37	5.07	4.85	4.67	4.54
16	10.58	7.51	6.30	5.64	5.21	4.91	4.69	4.52	4.38
17	10.38	7.35	6.16	5.50	5.07	4.78	4.56	4.39	4.25
18	10.22	7.21	6.03	5.37	4.96	4.66	4.44	4.28	4.14
19	10.07	7.09	5.92	5.27	4.85	4.56	4.34	4.18	4.04
20	9.94	6.99	5.82	5.17	4.76	4.47	4.26	4.09	3.96
21	9.83	6.89	5.73	5.09	4.68	4.39	4.18	4.01	3.88
22	9.73	6.81	5.65	5.02	4.61	4.32	4.11	3.94	3.81
23	9.63	6.73	5.58	4.95	4.54	4.26	4.05	3.88	3.75
24	9.55	6.66	5.52	4.89	4.49	4.20	3.99	3.83	3.69

TABLE G   (*continued*)

$$F_{0.995}$$

Denominator degrees of freedom	Numerator degrees of freedom								
	1	2	3	4	5	6	7	8	9
25	9.48	6.60	5.46	4.84	4.43	4.15	3.94	3.78	3.64
26	9.41	6.54	5.41	4.79	4.38	4.10	3.89	3.73	3.60
27	9.34	6.49	5.36	4.74	4.34	4.06	3.85	3.69	3.56
28	9.28	6.44	5.32	4.70	4.30	4.02	3.81	3.65	3.52
29	9.23	6.40	5.28	4.66	4.26	3.98	3.77	3.61	3.48
30	9.18	6.35	5.24	4.62	4.23	3.95	3.74	3.58	3.45
40	8.83	6.07	4.98	4.37	3.99	3.71	3.51	3.35	3.22
60	8.49	5.79	4.73	4.14	3.76	3.49	3.29	3.13	3.01
120	8.18	5.54	4.50	3.92	3.55	3.28	3.09	2.93	2.81
∞	7.88	5.30	4.28	3.72	3.35	3.09	2.90	2.74	2.62

$$F_{0.995}$$

Denominator degrees of freedom	Numerator degrees of freedom									
	10	12	15	20	24	30	40	60	120	∞
1	24224	24426	24630	24836	24940	25044	25148	25253	25359	25465
2	199.4	199.4	199.4	199.4	199.5	199.5	199.5	199.5	199.5	199.5
3	43.69	43.39	43.08	42.78	42.62	42.47	42.31	42.15	41.99	41.83
4	20.97	20.70	20.44	20.17	20.03	19.89	19.75	19.61	19.47	19.32
5	13.62	13.38	13.15	12.90	12.78	12.66	12.53	12.40	12.27	12.14
6	10.25	10.03	9.81	9.59	9.47	9.36	9.24	9.12	9.00	8.88
7	8.38	8.18	7.97	7.75	7.65	7.53	7.42	7.31	7.19	7.08
8	7.21	7.01	6.81	6.61	6.50	6.40	6.29	6.18	6.06	5.95
9	6.42	6.23	6.03	5.83	5.73	5.62	5.52	5.41	5.30	5.19
10	5.85	5.66	5.47	5.27	5.17	5.07	4.97	4.86	4.75	4.64
11	5.42	5.24	5.05	4.86	4.76	4.65	4.55	4.44	4.34	4.23
12	5.09	4.91	4.72	4.53	4.43	4.33	4.23	4.12	4.01	3.90
13	4.82	4.64	4.46	4.27	4.17	4.07	3.97	3.87	3.76	3.65
14	4.60	4.43	4.25	4.06	3.96	3.86	3.76	3.66	3.55	3.44
15	4.42	4.25	4.07	3.88	3.79	3.69	3.58	3.48	3.37	3.26
16	4.27	4.10	3.92	3.73	3.64	3.54	3.44	3.33	3.22	3.11
17	4.14	3.97	3.79	3.61	3.51	3.41	3.31	3.21	3.10	2.98
18	4.03	3.86	3.68	3.50	3.40	3.30	3.20	3.10	2.99	2.87
19	3.93	3.76	3.59	3.40	3.31	3.21	3.11	3.00	2.89	2.78
20	3.85	3.68	3.50	3.32	3.22	3.12	3.02	2.92	2.81	2.69
21	3.77	3.60	3.43	3.24	3.15	3.05	2.95	2.84	2.73	2.61
22	3.70	3.54	3.36	3.18	3.08	2.98	2.88	2.77	2.66	2.55
23	3.64	3.47	3.30	3.12	3.02	2.92	2.82	2.71	2.60	2.48
24	3.59	3.42	3.25	3.06	2.97	2.87	2.77	2.66	2.55	2.43
25	3.54	3.37	3.20	3.01	2.92	2.82	2.72	2.61	2.50	2.38
26	3.49	3.33	3.15	2.97	2.87	2.77	2.67	2.56	2.45	2.33
27	3.45	3.28	3.11	2.93	2.83	2.73	2.63	2.52	2.41	2.29
28	3.41	3.25	3.07	2.89	2.79	2.69	2.59	2.48	2.37	2.25
29	3.38	3.21	3.04	2.86	2.76	2.66	2.56	2.45	2.33	2.21

TABLE G *(continued)*

$F_{0.995}$

Denominator degrees of freedom	Numerator degrees of freedom									
	10	12	15	20	24	30	40	60	120	∞
30	3.34	3.18	3.01	2.82	2.73	2.63	2.52	2.42	2.30	2.18
40	3.12	2.95	2.78	2.60	2.50	2.40	2.30	2.18	2.06	1.93
60	2.90	2.74	2.57	2.39	2.29	2.19	2.08	1.96	1.83	1.69
120	2.71	2.54	2.37	2.19	2.09	1.98	1.87	1.75	1.61	1.43
∞	2.52	2.36	2.19	2.00	1.90	1.79	1.67	1.53	1.36	1.00

TABLE H   Percentage points of the Studentized range for 2 through 20 treatments

Error					Upper 1% points				
df	2	3	4	5	6	7	8	9	10
1	90.03	135.0	164.3	185.6	202.2	215.8	227.2	237.0	245.6
2	14.04	19.02	22.29	24.72	26.63	28.20	29.53	30.68	31.69
3	8.26	10.62	12.17	13.33	14.24	15.00	15.64	16.20	16.69
4	6.51	8.12	9.17	9.96	10.58	11.10	11.55	11.93	12.27
5	5.70	6.98	7.80	8.42	8.91	9.32	9.67	9.97	10.24
6	5.24	6.33	7.03	7.56	7.97	8.32	8.61	8.87	9.10
7	4.95	5.92	6.54	7.01	7.37	7.68	7.94	8.17	8.37
8	4.75	5.64	6.20	6.62	6.96	7.24	7.47	7.68	7.86
9	4.60	5.43	5.96	6.35	6.66	6.91	7.13	7.33	7.49
10	4.48	5.27	5.77	6.14	6.43	6.67	6.87	7.05	7.21
11	4.39	5.15	5.62	5.97	6.25	6.48	6.67	6.84	6.99
12	4.32	5.05	5.50	5.84	6.10	6.32	6.51	6.67	6.81
13	4.26	4.96	5.40	5.73	5.98	6.19	6.37	6.53	6.67
14	4.21	4.89	5.32	5.63	5.88	6.08	6.26	6.41	6.54
15	4.17	4.84	5.25	5.56	5.80	5.99	6.16	6.31	6.44
16	4.13	4.79	5.19	5.49	5.72	5.92	6.08	6.22	6.35
17	4.10	4.74	5.14	5.43	5.66	5.85	6.01	6.15	6.27
18	4.07	4.70	5.09	5.38	5.60	5.79	5.94	6.08	6.20
19	4.05	4.67	5.05	5.33	5.55	5.73	5.89	6.02	6.14
20	4.02	4.64	5.02	5.29	5.51	5.69	5.84	5.97	6.09
24	3.96	4.55	4.91	5.17	5.37	5.54	5.69	5.81	5.92
30	3.89	4.45	4.80	5.05	5.24	5.40	5.54	5.65	5.76
40	3.82	4.37	4.70	4.93	5.11	5.26	5.39	5.50	5.60
60	3.76	4.28	4.59	4.82	4.99	5.13	5.25	5.36	5.45
120	3.70	4.20	4.50	4.71	4.87	5.01	5.12	5.21	5.30
∞	3.64	4.12	4.40	4.60	4.76	4.88	4.99	5.08	5.16

Error										
df	11	12	13	14	15	16	17	18	19	20
1	253.2	260.0	266.2	271.8	277.0	281.8	286.3	290.4	294.3	298.0
2	32.59	33.40	34.13	34.81	35.43	36.00	36.53	37.03	37.50	37.95
3	17.13	17.53	17.89	18.22	18.52	18.81	19.07	19.32	19.55	19.77
4	12.57	12.84	13.09	13.32	13.53	13.73	13.91	14.08	14.24	14.40
5	10.48	10.70	10.89	11.08	11.24	11.40	11.55	11.68	11.81	11.93
6	9.30	9.48	9.65	9.81	9.95	10.08	10.21	10.32	10.43	10.54
7	8.55	8.71	8.86	9.00	9.12	9.24	9.35	9.46	9.55	9.65
8	8.03	8.18	8.31	8.44	8.55	8.66	8.76	8.85	8.94	9.03
9	7.65	7.78	7.91	8.03	8.13	8.23	8.33	8.41	8.49	8.57
10	7.36	7.49	7.60	7.71	7.81	7.91	7.99	8.08	8.15	8.23
11	7.13	7.25	7.36	7.46	7.56	7.65	7.73	7.81	7.88	7.95
12	6.94	7.06	7.17	7.26	7.36	7.44	7.52	7.59	7.66	7.73
13	6.79	6.90	7.01	7.10	7.19	7.27	7.35	7.42	7.48	7.55
14	6.66	6.77	6.87	6.96	7.05	7.13	7.20	7.27	7.33	7.39
15	6.55	6.66	6.76	6.84	6.93	7.00	7.07	7.14	7.20	7.26
16	6.46	6.56	6.66	6.74	6.82	6.90	6.97	7.03	7.09	7.15
17	6.38	6.48	6.57	6.66	6.73	6.81	6.87	6.94	7.00	7.05
18	6.31	6.41	6.50	6.58	6.65	6.73	6.79	6.85	6.91	6.97
19	6.25	6.34	6.43	6.51	6.58	6.65	6.72	6.78	6.84	6.89
20	6.19	6.28	6.37	6.45	6.52	6.59	6.65	6.71	6.77	6.82
24	6.02	6.11	6.19	6.26	6.33	6.39	6.45	6.51	6.56	6.61
30	5.85	5.93	6.01	6.08	6.14	6.20	6.26	6.31	6.36	6.41
40	5.69	5.76	5.83	5.90	5.96	6.02	6.07	6.12	6.16	6.21
60	5.53	5.60	5.67	5.73	5.78	5.84	5.89	5.93	5.97	6.01
120	5.37	5.44	5.50	5.56	5.61	5.66	5.71	5.75	5.79	5.83
∞	5.23	5.29	5.35	5.40	5.45	5.49	5.54	5.57	5.61	5.65

TABLE H (*continued*)

Upper 5% points

Error df	2	3	4	5	6	7	8	9	10
1	17.97	26.98	32.82	37.08	40.41	43.12	45.40	47.36	49.07
2	6.08	8.33	9.80	10.88	11.74	12.44	13.03	13.54	13.99
3	4.50	5.91	6.82	7.50	8.04	8.48	8.85	9.18	9.46
4	3.93	5.04	5.76	6.29	6.71	7.05	7.35	7.60	7.83
5	3.64	4.60	5.22	5.67	6.03	6.33	6.58	6.80	6.99
6	3.46	4.34	4.90	5.30	5.63	5.90	6.12	6.32	6.49
7	3.34	4.16	4.68	5.06	5.36	5.61	5.82	6.00	6.16
8	3.26	4.04	4.53	4.89	5.17	5.40	5.60	5.77	5.92
9	3.20	3.95	4.41	4.76	5.02	5.24	5.43	5.59	5.74
10	3.15	3.88	4.33	4.65	4.91	5.12	5.30	5.46	5.60
11	3.11	3.82	4.26	4.57	4.82	5.03	5.20	5.35	5.49
12	3.08	3.77	4.20	4.51	4.75	4.95	5.12	5.27	5.39
13	3.06	3.73	4.15	4.45	4.69	4.88	5.05	5.19	5.32
14	3.03	3.70	4.11	4.41	4.64	4.83	4.99	5.13	5.25
15	3.01	3.67	4.08	4.37	4.59	4.78	4.94	5.08	5.20
16	3.00	3.65	4.05	4.33	4.56	4.74	4.90	5.03	5.15
17	2.98	3.63	4.02	4.30	4.52	4.70	4.86	4.99	5.11
18	2.97	3.61	4.00	4.28	4.49	4.67	4.82	4.96	5.07
19	2.96	3.59	3.98	4.25	4.47	4.65	4.79	4.92	5.04
20	2.95	3.58	3.96	4.23	4.45	4.62	4.77	4.90	5.01
24	2.92	3.53	3.90	4.17	4.37	4.54	4.68	4.81	4.92
30	2.89	3.49	3.85	4.10	4.30	4.46	4.60	4.72	4.82
40	2.86	3.44	3.79	4.04	4.23	4.39	4.52	4.63	4.73
60	2.83	3.40	3.74	3.98	4.16	4.31	4.44	4.55	4.65
120	2.80	3.36	3.68	3.92	4.10	4.24	4.36	4.47	4.56
∞	2.77	3.31	3.63	3.86	4.03	4.17	4.29	4.39	4.47

Error df	11	12	13	14	15	16	17	18	19	20
1	50.59	51.96	53.20	54.33	55.36	56.32	57.22	58.04	58.83	59.56
2	14.39	14.75	15.08	15.38	15.65	15.91	16.14	16.37	16.57	16.77
3	9.72	9.95	10.15	10.35	10.52	10.69	10.84	10.98	11.11	11.24
4	8.03	8.21	8.37	8.52	8.66	8.79	8.91	9.03	9.13	9.23
5	7.71	7.32	7.47	7.60	7.72	7.83	7.93	8.03	8.12	8.21
6	6.65	6.79	6.92	7.03	7.14	7.24	7.34	7.43	7.51	7.59
7	6.30	6.43	6.55	6.66	6.76	6.85	6.94	7.02	7.10	7.17
8	6.05	6.18	6.29	6.39	6.48	6.57	6.65	6.73	6.80	6.87
9	5.87	5.98	6.09	6.19	6.28	6.36	6.44	6.51	6.58	6.64
10	5.72	5.83	5.93	6.03	6.11	6.19	6.27	6.34	6.40	6.47
11	5.61	5.71	5.81	5.90	5.98	6.06	6.13	6.20	6.27	6.33
12	5.51	5.61	5.71	5.80	5.88	5.95	6.02	6.09	6.15	6.21
13	5.43	5.53	5.63	5.71	5.79	5.86	5.93	5.99	6.05	6.11
14	5.36	5.46	5.55	5.64	5.71	5.79	5.85	5.91	5.97	6.03
15	5.31	5.40	5.49	5.57	5.65	5.72	5.78	5.85	5.90	5.96
16	5.26	5.35	5.44	5.52	5.59	5.66	5.73	5.79	5.84	5.90
17	5.21	5.31	5.39	5.47	5.54	5.61	5.67	5.73	5.79	5.84
18	5.17	5.27	5.35	5.43	5.50	5.57	5.63	5.69	5.74	5.79
19	5.14	5.23	5.31	5.39	5.46	5.53	5.59	5.65	5.70	5.75
20	5.11	5.20	5.28	5.36	5.43	5.49	5.55	5.61	5.66	5.71
24	5.01	5.10	5.18	5.25	5.32	5.38	5.44	5.49	5.55	5.59
30	4.92	5.00	5.08	5.15	5.21	5.27	5.33	5.38	5.43	5.47
40	4.82	4.90	4.98	5.04	5.11	5.16	5.22	5.27	5.31	5.36
60	4.73	4.81	4.88	4.94	5.00	5.06	5.11	5.15	5.20	5.24
120	4.64	4.71	4.78	4.84	4.90	4.95	5.00	5.04	5.09	5.13
∞	4.55	4.62	4.68	4.74	4.80	4.85	4.89	4.93	4.97	5.01

TABLE I   Transformation of r to z

The body of the table contains values of $z = 0.5 \ln [(1 + r)/(1 - r)] = \tanh^{-1}$ for corresponding values of r, the correlation coefficient. For negative values of r, put a minus sign in front of the tabled numbers.

r	0.00	0.01	0.02	0.03	0.04	0.05	0.06	0.07	0.08	0.09
0.0	0.00000	0.01000	0.02000	0.03001	0.04002	0.05004	0.06007	0.07011	0.08017	0.09024
0.1	0.10034	0.11045	0.12058	0.13074	0.14093	0.15114	0.16139	0.17167	0.18198	0.19234
0.2	0.20273	0.21317	0.22366	0.23419	0.24477	0.25541	0.26611	0.27686	0.28768	0.29857
0.3	0.30952	0.32055	0.33165	0.34283	0.35409	0.36544	0.37689	0.38842	0.40006	0.41180
0.4	0.42365	0.43561	0.44769	0.45990	0.47223	0.48470	0.49731	0.51007	0.52298	0.53606
0.5	0.54931	0.56273	0.57634	0.59015	0.60416	0.61838	0.63283	0.64752	0.66246	0.67767
0.6	0.69315	0.70892	0.72501	0.74142	0.75817	0.77530	0.79281	0.81074	0.82911	0.84796
0.7	0.86730	0.88718	0.90764	0.92873	0.95048	0.97296	0.99622	1.02033	1.04537	1.07143
0.8	1.09861	1.12703	1.15682	1.18814	1.22117	1.25615	1.29334	1.33308	1.37577	1.42193
0.9	1.47222	1.52752	1.58903	1.65839	1.73805	1.83178	1.94591	2.09230	2.29756	2.64665

TABLE Ja   Table of critical values of r in the runs test

Table Ja and Table Jb contain various critical values of r for various values of n_1 and n_2. For the one-sample runs test, any value of r that is equal to or smaller than that shown in Table Ja or equal to or larger than that shown in Table Jb is significant at the 0.05 level.

n_1 \ n_2	2	3	4	5	6	7	8	9	10	11	12	13	14	15	16	17	18	19	20
2											2	2	2	2	2	2	2	2	2
3					2	2	2	2	2	2	2	2	2	3	3	3	3	3	3
4				2	2	2	3	3	3	3	3	3	3	3	4	4	4	4	4
5			2	2	3	3	3	3	3	4	4	4	4	4	4	4	5	5	5
6		2	2	3	3	3	3	4	4	4	4	5	5	5	5	5	5	6	6
7		2	2	3	3	3	4	4	5	5	5	5	5	6	6	6	6	6	6
8		2	3	3	3	4	4	5	5	5	6	6	6	6	6	7	7	7	7
9		2	3	3	4	4	5	5	5	6	6	6	7	7	7	7	8	8	8
10		2	3	3	4	5	5	5	6	6	7	7	7	7	8	8	8	8	9
11		2	3	4	4	5	5	6	6	7	7	7	8	8	8	9	9	9	9
12	2	2	3	4	4	5	6	6	7	7	7	8	8	8	9	9	9	10	10
13	2	2	3	4	5	5	6	6	7	7	8	8	9	9	9	10	10	10	10
14	2	2	3	4	5	5	6	7	7	8	8	9	9	9	10	10	10	11	11
15	2	3	3	4	5	6	6	7	7	8	8	9	9	10	10	11	11	11	12
16	2	3	4	4	5	6	6	7	8	8	9	9	10	10	11	11	11	12	12
17	2	3	4	4	5	6	7	7	8	9	9	10	10	11	11	11	12	12	13
18	2	3	4	5	5	6	7	8	8	9	9	10	10	11	11	12	12	13	13
19	2	3	4	5	6	6	7	8	8	9	10	10	11	11	12	12	13	13	13
20	2	3	4	5	6	6	7	8	9	9	10	10	11	12	12	13	13	13	14

TABLE Jb   Table of critical values of r in the runs test

n_1 \ n_2	2	3	4	5	6	7	8	9	10	11	12	13	14	15	16	17	18	19	20
2																			
3																			
4				9	9														
5			9	10	10	11	11												
6			9	10	11	12	12	13	13	13	13								
7				11	12	13	13	14	14	14	14	15	15	15					
8				11	12	13	14	14	15	15	16	16	16	16	17	17	17	17	17
9					13	14	14	15	16	16	16	17	17	18	18	18	18	18	18
10					13	14	15	16	16	17	17	18	18	18	19	19	19	20	20
11					13	14	15	16	17	17	18	19	19	19	20	20	20	21	21
12					13	14	16	16	17	18	19	19	20	20	21	21	21	22	22
13						15	16	17	18	19	19	20	20	21	21	22	22	23	23
14						15	16	17	18	19	20	20	21	22	22	23	23	23	24
15						15	16	18	18	19	20	21	22	22	23	23	24	24	25
16							17	18	19	20	21	21	22	23	23	24	25	25	25
17							17	18	19	20	21	22	23	23	24	25	25	26	26
18							17	18	19	20	21	22	23	24	25	25	26	26	27
19							17	18	20	21	22	23	23	24	25	26	26	27	27
20							17	18	20	21	22	23	24	25	25	26	27	27	28

TABLE K *d*-factors for the Wilcoxon signed-rank test

(α' = one-sided significance level, α'' = two-sided significance level)

n	d	α''	α'	n	d	α''	α'	n	d	α''	α'
3	1	.250	.125	13	10	.008	.004	20	38	.009	.005
4	1	.125	.063		11	.010	.005		39	.011	.005
5	1	.062	.031		18	.048	.024		53	.048	.024
	2	.125	.063		19	.057	.029		54	.053	.027
6	1	.031	.016		22	.094	.047		61	.097	.049
	2	.063	.031		23	.110	.055		62	.105	.053
	3	.094	.047	14	13	.009	.004	21	43	.009	.005
	4	.156	.078		14	.011	.005		44	.010	.005
7	1	.016	.008		22	.049	.025		59	.046	.023
	2	.031	.016		23	.058	.029		60	.050	.025
	4	.078	.039		26	.091	.045		68	.096	.048
	5	.109	.055		27	.104	.052		69	.103	.052
8	1	.008	.004	15	16	.008	.004	22	49	.009	.005
	2	.016	.008		17	.010	.005		50	.010	.005
	4	.039	.020		26	.048	.024		66	.046	.023
	5	.055	.027		27	.055	.028		67	.050	.025
	6	.078	.039		31	.095	.047		76	.098	.049
	7	.109	.055		32	.107	.054		77	.105	.053
9	2	.008	.004	16	20	.009	.005	23	55	.009	.005
	3	.012	.006		21	.011	.006		56	.010	.005
	6	.039	.020		30	.044	.022		74	.048	.024
	7	.055	.027		31	.051	.025		75	.052	.026
	9	.098	.049		36	.093	.047		84	.098	.049
	10	.129	.065		37	.105	.052		85	.105	.052
10	4	.010	.005	17	24	.009	.005	24	62	.010	.005
	5	.014	.007		25	.011	.006		63	.011	.005
	9	.049	.024		35	.045	.022		82	.049	.025
	10	.064	.032		36	.051	.025		83	.053	.026
	11	.084	.042		42	.098	.049		92	.095	.048
	12	.105	.053		43	.109	.054		93	.101	.051
11	6	.010	.005	18	28	.009	.005	25	69	.010	.005
	7	.014	.007		29	.010	.005		70	.011	.005
	11	.042	.021		41	.048	.024		90	.048	.024
	12	.054	.027		42	.054	.027		91	.052	.026
	14	.083	.042		48	.099	.049		101	.096	.048
	15	.102	.051		49	.108	.054		102	.101	.051
12	8	.009	.005	19	33	.009	.005				
	9	.012	.006		34	.011	.005				
	14	.042	.021		47	.049	.025				
	15	.052	.026		48	.055	.027				
	18	.092	.046		54	.096	.048				
	19	.110	.055		55	.104	.052				

Note: For $n > 25$ use $d \approx \frac{1}{2}[\frac{1}{2}n(n + 1) + 1 - z\sqrt{n(n + 1)(2n + 1)/6}]$, where z is read from Table Ca.

TABLE L Quantiles of the Mann–Whitney test statistic

n_1	p	$n_2=2$	3	4	5	6	7	8	9	10	11	12	13	14	15	16	17	18	19	20
	.001	0	0	0	0	0	0	0	0	0	0	0	0	0	0	0	0	0	0	0
	.005	0	0	0	0	0	0	0	0	0	0	0	0	0	0	0	0	0	1	1
2	.01	0	0	0	0	0	0	0	0	0	0	0	1	1	1	1	1	1	2	2
	.025	0	0	0	0	0	0	1	1	1	1	2	2	2	2	2	3	3	3	3
	.05	0	0	0	1	1	1	2	2	2	2	3	3	4	4	4	4	5	5	5
	.10	0	1	1	2	2	2	3	3	4	4	5	5	5	6	6	7	7	8	8
	.001	0	0	0	0	0	0	0	0	0	0	0	0	0	0	0	1	1	1	1
	.005	0	0	0	0	0	0	0	1	1	1	2	2	2	3	3	3	3	4	4
3	.01	0	0	0	0	0	1	1	2	2	2	3	3	3	4	4	5	5	5	6
	.025	0	0	0	1	2	2	3	3	4	4	5	5	6	6	7	7	8	8	9
	.05	0	1	1	2	3	3	4	5	5	6	6	7	8	8	9	10	10	11	12
	.10	1	2	2	3	4	5	6	6	7	8	9	10	11	11	12	13	14	15	16
	.001	0	0	0	0	0	0	0	0	1	1	1	2	2	2	3	3	4	4	4
	.005	0	0	0	0	1	1	2	2	3	3	4	4	5	6	6	7	7	8	9
4	.01	0	0	0	1	2	2	3	4	4	5	6	6	7	9	8	9	10	10	11
	.025	0	0	1	2	3	4	5	5	6	7	8	9	10	11	12	12	13	14	15
	.05	0	1	2	3	4	5	6	7	8	9	10	11	12	13	15	16	17	18	19
	.10	1	2	4	5	6	7	8	10	11	12	13	14	16	17	18	19	21	22	23
	.001	0	0	0	0	0	0	1	2	2	3	3	4	4	5	6	6	7	8	8
	.005	0	0	0	1	2	2	3	4	5	6	7	8	8	9	10	11	12	13	14
5	.01	0	0	1	2	3	4	5	6	7	8	9	10	11	12	13	14	15	16	17
	.025	0	1	2	3	4	6	7	8	9	10	12	13	14	15	16	18	19	20	21
	.05	1	2	3	5	6	7	9	10	12	13	14	16	17	19	20	21	23	24	26
	.10	2	3	5	6	8	9	11	13	14	16	18	19	21	23	24	26	28	29	31
	.001	0	0	0	0	0	0	2	3	4	5	5	6	7	8	9	10	11	12	13
	.005	0	0	1	2	3	4	5	6	7	8	10	11	12	13	14	16	17	18	19
6	.01	0	0	2	3	4	5	7	8	9	10	12	13	14	16	17	19	20	21	23
	.025	0	2	3	4	6	7	9	11	12	14	15	17	18	20	22	23	25	26	28
	.05	1	3	4	6	8	9	11	13	15	17	18	20	22	24	26	27	29	31	33
	.10	2	4	6	8	10	12	14	16	18	20	22	24	26	28	30	32	35	37	39
	.001	0	0	0	0	1	2	3	4	6	7	8	9	10	11	12	14	15	16	17
	.005	0	0	1	2	4	5	7	8	10	11	13	14	16	17	19	20	22	23	25
7	.01	0	1	2	4	5	7	8	10	12	13	15	17	18	20	22	24	25	27	29
	.025	0	2	4	6	7	9	11	13	15	17	19	21	23	25	27	29	31	33	35
	.05	1	3	5	7	9	12	14	16	18	20	22	25	27	29	31	34	36	38	40
	.10	2	5	7	9	12	14	17	19	22	24	27	29	32	34	37	39	42	44	47
	.001	0	0	0	1	2	3	5	6	7	9	10	12	13	15	16	18	19	21	22
	.005	0	0	2	3	5	7	8	10	12	14	16	18	19	21	23	25	27	29	31
8	.01	0	1	3	5	7	8	10	12	14	16	18	21	23	25	27	29	31	33	35
	.025	1	3	5	7	9	11	14	16	18	20	23	25	27	30	32	35	37	39	42
	.05	2	4	6	9	11	14	16	19	21	24	27	29	32	34	37	40	42	45	48
	.10	3	6	8	11	14	17	20	23	25	28	31	34	37	40	43	46	49	52	55

TABLE L (*continued*)

n_1	p	$n_2=2$	3	4	5	6	7	8	9	10	11	12	13	14	15	16	17	18	19	20
9	.001	0	0	0	2	3	4	6	8	9	11	13	15	16	18	20	22	24	26	27
	.005	0	1	2	4	6	8	10	12	14	17	19	21	23	25	28	30	32	34	37
	.01	0	2	4	6	8	10	12	15	17	19	22	24	27	29	32	34	37	39	41
	.025	1	3	5	8	11	13	16	18	21	24	27	29	32	35	38	40	43	46	49
	.05	2	5	7	10	13	16	19	22	25	28	31	34	37	40	43	46	49	52	55
	.10	3	6	10	13	16	19	23	26	29	32	36	39	42	46	49	53	56	59	63
10	.001	0	0	1	2	4	6	7	9	11	13	15	18	20	22	24	26	28	30	33
	.005	0	1	3	5	7	10	12	14	17	19	22	25	27	30	32	35	38	40	43
	.01	0	2	4	7	9	12	14	17	20	23	25	28	31	34	37	39	42	45	48
	.025	1	4	6	9	12	15	18	21	24	27	30	34	37	40	43	46	49	53	56
	.05	2	5	8	12	15	18	21	25	28	32	35	38	42	45	49	52	56	59	63
	.10	4	7	11	14	18	22	25	29	33	37	40	44	48	52	55	59	63	67	71
11	.001	0	0	1	3	5	7	9	11	13	16	18	21	23	25	28	30	33	35	38
	.005	0	1	3	6	8	11	14	17	19	22	25	28	31	34	37	40	43	46	49
	.01	0	2	5	8	10	13	16	19	23	26	29	32	35	38	42	45	48	51	54
	.025	1	4	7	10	14	17	20	24	27	31	34	38	41	45	48	52	56	59	63
	.05	2	6	9	13	17	20	24	28	32	35	39	43	47	51	55	58	62	66	70
	.10	4	8	12	16	20	24	28	32	37	41	45	49	53	58	62	66	70	74	79
12	.001	0	0	1	3	5	8	10	13	15	18	21	24	26	29	32	35	38	41	43
	.005	0	2	4	7	10	13	16	19	22	25	28	32	35	38	42	45	48	52	55
	.01	0	3	6	9	12	15	18	22	25	29	32	36	39	43	47	50	54	57	61
	.025	2	5	8	12	15	19	23	27	30	34	38	42	46	50	54	58	62	66	70
	.05	3	6	10	14	18	22	27	31	35	39	43	48	52	56	61	65	69	73	78
	.10	5	9	13	18	22	27	31	36	40	45	50	54	59	64	68	73	78	82	87
13	.001	0	0	2	4	6	9	12	15	18	21	24	27	30	33	36	39	43	46	49
	.005	0	2	4	8	11	14	18	21	25	28	32	35	39	43	46	50	54	58	61
	.01	1	3	6	10	13	17	21	24	28	32	36	40	44	48	52	56	60	64	68
	.025	2	5	9	13	17	21	25	29	34	38	42	46	51	55	60	64	68	73	77
	.05	3	7	11	16	20	25	29	34	38	43	48	52	57	62	66	71	76	81	85
	.10	5	10	14	19	24	29	34	39	44	49	54	59	64	69	75	80	85	90	95
14	.001	0	0	2	4	7	10	13	16	20	23	26	30	33	37	40	44	47	51	55
	.005	0	2	5	8	12	16	19	23	27	31	35	39	43	47	51	55	59	64	68
	.01	1	3	7	11	14	18	23	27	31	35	39	44	48	52	57	61	66	70	74
	.025	2	6	10	14	18	23	27	32	37	41	46	51	56	60	65	70	75	79	84
	.05	4	8	12	17	22	27	32	37	42	47	52	57	62	67	72	78	83	88	93
	.10	5	11	16	21	26	32	37	42	48	53	59	64	70	75	81	86	92	98	103
15	.001	0	0	2	5	8	11	15	18	22	25	29	33	37	41	44	48	52	56	60
	.005	0	3	6	9	13	17	21	25	30	34	38	43	47	52	56	61	65	70	74
	.01	1	4	8	12	16	20	25	29	34	38	43	48	52	57	62	67	71	76	81
	.025	2	6	11	15	20	25	30	35	40	45	50	55	60	65	71	76	81	86	91
	.05	4	8	13	19	24	29	34	40	45	51	56	62	67	73	78	84	89	95	101
	.10	6	11	17	23	28	34	40	46	52	58	64	69	75	81	87	93	99	105	111

TABLE L   (*continued*)

n_1	p	$n_2=2$	3	4	5	6	7	8	9	10	11	12	13	14	15	16	17	18	19	20
	.001	0	0	3	6	9	12	16	20	24	28	32	36	40	44	49	53	57	61	66
	.005	0	3	6	10	14	19	23	28	32	37	42	46	51	56	61	66	71	75	80
16	.01	1	4	8	13	17	22	27	32	37	42	47	52	57	62	67	72	77	83	88
	.025	2	7	12	16	22	27	32	38	43	48	54	60	65	71	76	82	87	93	99
	.05	4	9	15	20	26	31	37	43	49	55	61	66	72	78	84	90	96	102	108
	.10	6	12	18	24	30	37	43	49	55	62	68	75	81	87	94	100	107	113	120
	.001	0	1	3	6	10	14	18	22	26	30	35	39	44	48	53	58	62	67	71
	.005	0	3	7	11	16	20	25	30	35	40	45	50	55	61	66	71	76	82	87
17	.01	1	5	9	14	19	24	29	34	39	45	50	56	61	67	72	78	83	89	94
	.025	3	7	12	18	23	29	35	40	46	52	58	64	70	76	82	88	94	100	106
	.05	4	10	16	21	27	34	40	46	52	58	65	71	78	84	90	97	103	110	116
	.10	7	13	19	26	32	39	46	53	59	66	73	80	86	93	100	107	114	121	128
	.001	0	1	4	7	11	15	19	24	28	33	38	43	47	52	57	62	67	72	77
	.005	0	3	7	12	17	22	27	32	38	43	48	54	59	65	71	76	82	88	93
18	.01	1	5	10	15	20	25	31	37	42	48	54	60	66	71	77	83	89	95	101
	.025	3	8	13	19	25	31	37	43	49	56	62	68	75	81	87	94	100	107	113
	.05	5	10	17	23	29	36	42	49	56	62	69	76	83	89	96	103	110	117	124
	.10	7	14	21	28	35	42	49	56	63	70	78	85	92	99	107	114	121	129	136
	.001	0	1	4	8	12	16	21	26	30	35	41	46	51	56	61	67	72	78	83
	.005	1	4	8	13	18	23	29	34	40	46	52	58	64	70	75	82	88	94	100
19	.01	2	5	10	16	21	27	33	39	45	51	57	64	70	76	83	89	95	102	108
	.025	3	8	14	20	26	33	39	46	53	59	66	73	79	86	93	100	107	114	120
	.05	5	11	18	24	31	38	45	52	59	66	73	81	88	95	102	110	117	124	131
	.10	8	15	22	29	37	44	52	59	67	74	82	90	98	105	113	121	129	136	144
	.001	0	1	4	8	13	17	22	27	33	38	43	49	55	60	66	71	77	83	89
	.005	1	4	9	14	19	25	31	37	43	49	55	61	68	74	80	87	93	100	106
20	.01	2	6	11	17	23	29	35	41	48	54	61	68	74	81	88	94	101	108	115
	.025	3	9	15	21	28	35	42	49	56	63	70	77	84	91	99	106	113	120	128
	.05	5	12	19	26	33	40	48	55	63	70	78	85	93	101	108	116	124	131	139
	.10	8	16	23	31	39	47	55	63	71	79	87	95	103	111	120	128	136	144	152

TABLE M   Critical values of the Kruskal-Wallis test statistic

n_1	n_2	n_3	Critical value	α	n_1	n_2	n_3	Critical value	α
2	1	1	2.7000	0.500	4	3	3	6.7455	0.010
2	2	1	3.6000	0.200				6.7091	0.013
2	2	2	4.5714	0.067				5.7909	0.046
			3.7143	0.200				5.7273	0.050
3	1	1	3.2000	0.300				4.7091	0.092
3	2	1	4.2857	0.100	4	3	3	4.7000	0.101
			3.8571	0.133	4	4	1	6.6667	0.010
3	2	2	5.3572	0.029				6.1667	0.022
			4.7143	0.048				4.9667	0.048
			4.5000	0.067				4.8667	0.054
			4.4643	0.105				4.1667	0.082
3	3	1	5.1429	0.043				4.0667	0.102
			4.5714	0.100	4	4	2	7.0364	0.006
			4.0000	0.129				6.8727	0.011
3	3	2	6.2500	0.011				5.4545	0.046
			5.3611	0.032				5.2364	0.052
			5.1389	0.061				4.5545	0.098
			4.5556	0.100				4.4455	0.103
			4.2500	0.121	4	4	3	7.1439	0.010
3	3	3	7.2000	0.004				7.1364	0.011
			6.4889	0.011				5.5985	0.049
			5.6889	0.029				5.5758	0.051
			5.6000	0.050				4.5455	0.099
			5.0667	0.086				4.4773	0.102
			4.6222	0.100	4	4	4	7.6538	0.008
4	1	1	3.5714	0.200				7.5385	0.011
4	2	1	4.8214	0.057				5.6923	0.049
			4.5000	0.076				5.6538	0.054
			4.0179	0.114				4.6539	0.097
4	2	2	6.0000	0.014				4.5001	0.104
			5.3333	0.033	5	1	1	3.8571	0.143
			5.1250	0.052	5	2	1	5.2500	0.036
			4.4583	0.100				5.0000	0.048
			4.1667	0.105				4.4500	0.071
4	3	1	5.8333	0.021				4.2000	0.095
			5.2083	0.050				4.0500	0.119
			5.0000	0.057	5	2	2	6.5333	0.008
			4.0556	0.093				6.1333	0.013
			3.8889	0.129				5.1600	0.034
4	3	2	6.4444	0.008				5.0400	0.056
			6.3000	0.011				4.3733	0.090
			5.4444	0.046				4.2933	0.122
			5.4000	0.051	5	3	1	6.4000	0.012
			4.5111	0.098				4.9600	0.048
			4.4444	0.102				4.8711	0.052

TABLE M (*continued*)

n₁	n₂	n₃	Critical value	α	n₁	n₂	n₃	Critical value	α
5	3	1	4.0178	0.095	5	4	4	5.6571	0.049
			3.8400	0.123				5.6176	0.050
5	3	2	6.9091	0.009				4.6187	0.100
			6.8218	0.010				4.5527	0.102
			5.2509	0.049	5	5	1	7.3091	0.009
			5.1055	0.052				6.8364	0.011
			4.6509	0.091				5.1273	0.046
			4.4945	0.101				4.9091	0.053
5	3	3	7.0788	0.009				4.1091	0.086
			6.9818	0.011				4.0364	0.105
			5.6485	0.049	5	5	2	7.3385	0.010
			5.5152	0.051				7.2692	0.010
			4.5333	0.097				5.3385	0.047
			4.4121	0.109				5.2462	0.051
5	4	1	6.9545	0.008				4.6231	0.097
			6.8400	0.011				4.5077	0.100
			4.9855	0.044	5	5	3	7.5780	0.010
			4.8600	0.056				7.5429	0.010
			3.9873	0.098				5.7055	0.046
			3.9600	0.102				5.6264	0.051
5	4	2	7.2045	0.009				4.5451	0.100
			7.1182	0.010				4.5363	0.102
			5.2727	0.049	5	5	4	7.8229	0.010
			5.2682	0.050				7.7914	0.010
			4.5409	0.098				5.6657	0.049
			4.5182	0.101				5.6429	0.050
5	4	3	7.4449	0.010				4.5229	0.099
			7.3949	0.011				4.5200	0.101
			5.6564	0.049	5	5	5	8.0000	0.009
			5.6308	0.050				7.9800	0.010
			4.5487	0.099				5.7800	0.049
			4.5231	0.103				5.6600	0.051
5	4	4	7.7604	0.009				4.5600	0.100
			7.7440	0.011				4.5000	0.102

TABLE Na Exact distribution of χ_r^2 for tables with 2 to 9 sets of three ranks ($k = 3$; $n = 2, 3, 4,$ 5, 6, 7, 8, 9)

p is the probability of obtaining a value of χ_r^2 as great as or greater than the corresponding value of χ_r^2.

| \multicolumn{2}{c}{n = 2} | | \multicolumn{2}{c}{n = 3} | | \multicolumn{2}{c}{n = 4} | | \multicolumn{2}{c}{n = 5} | |

χ_r^2	p	χ_r^2	p	χ_r^2	p	χ_r^2	p
0	1.000	0.000	1.000	0.0	1.000	0.0	1.000
1	0.833	0.667	0.944	0.5	0.931	0.4	0.954
3	0.500	2.000	0.528	1.5	0.653	1.2	0.691
4	0.167	2.667	0.361	2.0	0.431	1.6	0.522
		4.667	0.194	3.5	0.273	2.8	0.367
		6.000	0.028	4.5	0.125	3.6	0.182
				6.0	0.069	4.8	0.124
				6.5	0.042	5.2	0.093
				8.0	0.0046	6.4	0.039
						7.6	0.024
						8.4	0.0085
						10.0	0.00077

χ_r^2	p	χ_r^2	p	χ_r^2	p	χ_r^2	P
\multicolumn{2}{c}{n = 6}		\multicolumn{2}{c}{n = 7}		\multicolumn{2}{c}{n = 8}		\multicolumn{2}{c}{n = 9}	
0.00	1.000	0.000	1.000	0.00	1.000	0.000	1.000
0.33	0.956	0.286	0.964	0.25	0.967	0.222	0.971
1.00	0.740	0.857	0.768	0.75	0.794	0.667	0.814
1.33	0.570	1.143	0.620	1.00	0.654	0.889	0.865
2.33	0.430	2.000	0.486	1.75	0.531	1.556	0.569
3.00	0.252	2.571	0.305	2.25	0.355	2.000	0.398
4.00	0.184	3.429	0.237	3.00	0.285	2.667	0.328
4.33	0.142	3.714	0.192	3.25	0.236	2.889	0.278
5.33	0.072	4.571	0.112	4.00	0.149	3.556	0.187
6.33	0.052	5.429	0.085	4.75	0.120	4.222	0.154
7.00	0.029	6.000	0.052	5.25	0.079	4.667	0.107
8.33	0.012	7.143	0.027	6.25	0.047	5.556	0.069
9.00	0.0081	7.714	0.021	6.75	0.038	6.000	0.057
9.33	0.0055	8.000	0.016	7.00	0.030	6.222	0.048
10.33	0.0017	8.857	0.0084	7.75	0.018	6.889	0.031
12.00	0.00013	10.286	0.0036	9.00	0.0099	8.000	0.019
		10.571	0.0027	9.25	0.0080	8.222	0.016
		11.143	0.0012	9.75	0.0048	8.667	0.010
		12.286	0.00032	10.75	0.0024	9.556	0.0060
		14.000	0.000021	12.00	0.0011	10.667	0.0035
				12.25	0.00086	10.889	0.0029
				13.00	0.00026	11.556	0.0013
				14.25	0.000061	12.667	0.00066
				16.00	0.0000036	13.556	0.00035
						14.000	0.00020
						14.222	0.000097
						14.889	0.000054
						16.222	0.000011
						18.000	0.0000006

TABLE Nb   Exact distribution of χ_r^2 for tables with 2 to 4 sets of four ranks ($k = 4$; $n = 2, 3, 4$)

p is the probability of obtaining a value of χ_r^2 as great as or greater than the corresponding value of χ_r^2.

$n = 2$		$n = 3$		$n = 4$			
χ_r^2	p	χ_r^2	p	χ_r^2	p	χ_r^2	p
0.0	1.000	0.2	1.000	0.0	1.000	5.7	0.141
0.6	0.958	0.6	0.958	0.3	0.992	6.0	0.105
1.2	0.834	1.0	0.910	0.6	0.928	6.3	0.094
1.8	0.792	1.8	0.727	0.9	0.900	6.6	0.077
2.4	0.625	2.2	0.608	1.2	0.800	6.9	0.068
3.0	0.542	2.6	0.524	1.5	0.754	7.2	0.054
3.6	0.458	3.4	0.446	1.8	0.677	7.5	0.052
4.2	0.375	3.8	0.342	2.1	0.649	7.8	0.036
4.8	0.208	4.2	0.300	2.4	0.524	8.1	0.033
5.4	0.167	5.0	0.207	2.7	0.508	8.4	0.019
6.0	0.042	5.4	0.175	3.0	0.432	8.7	0.014
		5.8	0.148	3.3	0.389	9.3	0.012
		6.6	0.075	3.6	0.355	9.6	0.0069
		7.0	0.054	3.9	0.324	9.9	0.0062
		7.4	0.033	4.5	0.242	10.2	0.0027
		8.2	0.017	4.8	0.200	10.8	0.0016
		9.0	0.0017	5.1	0.190	11.1	0.00094
				5.4	0.158	12.0	0.000072

TABLE O   Critical values of the Spearman test statistic

Approximate upper-tail critical values, r_s^*, where $P(r_s > r_s^*) \le \alpha$, $n = 4(1)30$

			Significance Level, α			
n	0.001	0.005	0.010	0.025	0.050	0.100
4	——	——	——	——	.8000	.8000
5	——	——	.9000	.9000	.8000	.7000
6	——	.9429	.8857	.8286	.7714	.6000
7	.9643	.8929	.8571	.7450	.6786	.5357
8	.9286	.8571	.8095	.7143	.6190	.5000
9	.9000	.8167	.7667	.6833	.5833	.4667
10	.8667	.7818	.7333	.6364	.5515	.4424
11	.8364	.7545	.7000	.6091	.5273	.4182
12	.8182	.7273	.6713	.5804	.4965	.3986
13	.7912	.6978	.6429	.5549	.4780	.3791
14	.7670	.6747	.6220	.5341	.4593	.3626
15	.7464	.6536	.6000	.5179	.4429	.3500
16	.7265	.6324	.5824	.5000	.4265	.3382
17	.7083	.6152	.5637	.4853	.4118	.3260
18	.6904	.5975	.5480	.4716	.3994	.3148
19	.6737	.5825	.5333	.4579	.3895	.3070
20	.6586	.5684	.5203	.4451	.3789	.2977
21	.6455	.5545	.5078	.4351	.3688	.2909
22	.6318	.5426	.4963	.4241	.3597	.2829
23	.6186	.5306	.4852	.4150	.3518	.2767
24	.6070	.5200	.4748	.4061	.3435	.2704
25	.5962	.5100	.4654	.3977	.3362	.2646
26	.5856	.5002	.4564	.3894	.3299	.2588
27	.5757	.4915	.4481	.3822	.3236	.2540
28	.5660	.4828	.4401	.3749	.3175	.2490
29	.5567	.4744	.4320	.3685	.3113	.2443
30	.5479	.4665	.4251	.3620	.3059	.2400

Note: The corresponding lower-tail critical value for r_s is $-r_s^*$.

TABLE Pa Critical Values for the Durbin-Watson d Statistic, $\alpha = 0.05$

n	k = 1 d_L	k = 1 d_U	k = 2 d_L	k = 2 d_U	k = 3 d_L	k = 3 d_U	k = 4 d_L	k = 4 d_U	k = 5 d_L	k = 5 d_U
15	1.08	1.36	0.95	1.54	0.82	1.75	0.69	1.97	0.56	2.21
16	1.10	1.37	0.98	1.54	0.86	1.73	0.74	1.93	0.62	2.15
17	1.13	1.38	1.02	1.54	0.90	1.71	0.78	1.90	0.67	2.10
18	1.16	1.39	1.05	1.53	0.93	1.69	0.82	1.87	0.71	2.06
19	1.18	1.40	1.08	1.53	0.97	1.68	0.86	1.85	0.75	2.02
20	1.20	1.41	1.10	1.54	1.00	1.68	0.90	1.83	0.79	1.99
21	1.22	1.42	1.13	1.54	1.03	1.67	0.93	1.81	0.83	1.96
22	1.24	1.43	1.15	1.54	1.05	1.66	0.96	1.80	0.86	1.94
23	1.26	1.44	1.17	1.54	1.08	1.66	0.99	1.79	0.90	1.92
24	1.27	1.45	1.19	1.55	1.10	1.66	1.01	1.78	0.93	1.90
25	1.29	1.45	1.21	1.55	1.12	1.66	1.04	1.77	0.95	1.89
26	1.30	1.46	1.22	1.55	1.14	1.65	1.06	1.76	0.98	1.88
27	1.32	1.47	1.24	1.56	1.16	1.65	1.08	1.76	1.01	1.86
28	1.33	1.48	1.26	1.56	1.18	1.65	1.10	1.75	1.03	1.85
29	1.34	1.48	1.27	1.56	1.20	1.65	1.12	1.74	1.05	1.84
30	1.35	1.49	1.28	1.57	1.21	1.65	1.14	1.74	1.07	1.83
31	1.36	1.50	1.30	1.57	1.23	1.65	1.16	1.74	1.09	1.83
32	1.37	1.50	1.31	1.57	1.24	1.65	1.18	1.73	1.11	1.82
33	1.38	1.51	1.32	1.58	1.26	1.65	1.19	1.73	1.13	1.81
34	1.39	1.51	1.33	1.58	1.27	1.65	1.21	1.73	1.15	1.81
35	1.40	1.52	1.34	1.58	1.28	1.65	1.22	1.73	1.16	1.80
36	1.41	1.52	1.35	1.59	1.29	1.65	1.24	1.73	1.18	1.80
37	1.42	1.53	1.36	1.59	1.31	1.66	1.25	1.72	1.19	1.80
38	1.43	1.54	1.37	1.59	1.32	1.66	1.26	1.72	1.21	1.79
39	1.43	1.54	1.38	1.60	1.33	1.66	1.27	1.72	1.22	1.79
40	1.44	1.54	1.39	1.60	1.34	1.66	1.29	1.72	1.23	1.79
45	1.48	1.57	1.43	1.62	1.38	1.67	1.34	1.72	1.29	1.78
50	1.50	1.59	1.46	1.63	1.42	1.67	1.38	1.72	1.34	1.77
55	1.53	1.60	1.49	1.64	1.45	1.68	1.41	1.72	1.38	1.77
60	1.55	1.62	1.51	1.65	1.48	1.69	1.44	1.73	1.41	1.77
65	1.57	1.63	1.54	1.66	1.50	1.70	1.47	1.73	1.44	1.77
70	1.58	1.64	1.55	1.67	1.52	1.70	1.49	1.74	1.46	1.77
75	1.60	1.65	1.57	1.68	1.54	1.71	1.51	1.74	1.49	1.77
80	1.61	1.66	1.59	1.69	1.56	1.72	1.53	1.74	1.51	1.77
85	1.62	1.67	1.60	1.70	1.57	1.72	1.55	1.75	1.52	1.77
90	1.63	1.68	1.61	1.70	1.59	1.73	1.57	1.75	1.54	1.78
95	1.64	1.69	1.62	1.71	1.60	1.73	1.58	1.75	1.56	1.78
100	1.65	1.69	1.63	1.72	1.61	1.74	1.59	1.76	1.57	1.78

TABLE Pb Critical Values of the Durbin-Watson d Statistic, $\alpha = 0.025$

n	$k = 1$		$k = 2$		$k = 3$		$k = 4$		$k = 5$	
	d_L	d_U	d_L	d_U	d_L	d_U	d_L	d_U	d_L	d_U
15	0.95	1.23	0.83	1.40	0.71	1.61	0.59	1.84	0.48	2.09
16	0.98	1.24	0.86	1.40	0.75	1.59	0.64	1.80	0.53	2.03
17	1.01	1.25	0.90	1.40	0.79	1.58	0.68	1.77	0.57	1.98
18	1.03	1.26	0.93	1.40	0.82	1.56	0.72	1.74	0.62	1.93
19	1.06	1.28	0.96	1.41	0.86	1.55	0.76	1.72	0.66	1.90
20	1.08	1.28	0.99	1.41	0.89	1.55	0.79	1.70	0.70	1.87
21	1.10	1.30	1.01	1.41	0.92	1.54	0.83	1.69	0.73	1.84
22	1.12	1.31	1.04	1.42	0.95	1.54	0.86	1.68	0.77	1.82
23	1.14	1.32	1.06	1.42	0.97	1.54	0.89	1.67	0.80	1.80
24	1.16	1.33	1.08	1.43	1.00	1.54	0.91	1.66	0.83	1.79
25	1.18	1.34	1.10	1.43	1.02	1.54	0.94	1.65	0.86	1.77
26	1.19	1.35	1.12	1.44	1.04	1.54	0.96	1.65	0.88	1.76
27	1.21	1.36	1.13	1.44	1.06	1.54	0.99	1.64	0.91	1.75
28	1.22	1.37	1.15	1.45	1.08	1.54	1.01	1.64	0.93	1.74
29	1.24	1.38	1.17	1.45	1.10	1.54	1.03	1.63	0.96	1.73
30	1.25	1.38	1.18	1.46	1.12	1.54	1.05	1.63	0.98	1.73
31	1.26	1.39	1.20	1.47	1.13	1.55	1.07	1.63	1.00	1.72
32	1.27	1.40	1.21	1.47	1.15	1.55	1.08	1.63	1.02	1.71
33	1.28	1.41	1.22	1.48	1.16	1.55	1.10	1.63	1.04	1.71
34	1.29	1.41	1.24	1.48	1.17	1.55	1.12	1.63	1.06	1.70
35	1.30	1.42	1.25	1.48	1.19	1.55	1.13	1.63	1.07	1.70
36	1.31	1.43	1.26	1.49	1.20	1.56	1.15	1.63	1.09	1.70
37	1.32	1.43	1.27	1.49	1.21	1.56	1.16	1.62	1.10	1.70
38	1.33	1.44	1.28	1.50	1.23	1.56	1.17	1.62	1.12	1.70
39	1.34	1.44	1.29	1.50	1.24	1.56	1.19	1.63	1.13	1.69
40	1.35	1.45	1.30	1.51	1.25	1.57	1.20	1.63	1.15	1.69
45	1.39	1.48	1.34	1.53	1.30	1.58	1.25	1.63	1.21	1.69
50	1.42	1.50	1.38	1.54	1.34	1.59	1.30	1.64	1.26	1.69
55	1.45	1.52	1.41	1.56	1.37	1.60	1.33	1.64	1.30	1.69
60	1.47	1.54	1.44	1.57	1.40	1.61	1.37	1.65	1.33	1.69
65	1.49	1.55	1.46	1.59	1.43	1.62	1.40	1.66	1.36	1.69
70	1.51	1.57	1.48	1.60	1.45	1.63	1.42	1.66	1.39	1.70
75	1.53	1.58	1.50	1.61	1.47	1.64	1.45	1.67	1.42	1.70
80	1.54	1.59	1.52	1.62	1.49	1.65	1.47	1.67	1.44	1.70
85	1.56	1.60	1.53	1.63	1.51	1.65	1.49	1.68	1.46	1.71
90	1.57	1.61	1.55	1.64	1.53	1.66	1.50	1.69	1.48	1.71
95	1.58	1.62	1.56	1.65	1.54	1.67	1.52	1.69	1.50	1.71
100	1.59	1.63	1.57	1.65	1.55	1.67	1.53	1.70	1.51	1.72

TABLE Pc   Critical Values of the Durbin-Watson d Statistic, $\alpha = 0.01$

n	k = 1		k = 2		k = 3		k = 4		k = 5	
	d_L	d_U	d_L	d_U	d_L	d_U	d_L	d_U	d_L	d_U
15	0.81	1.07	0.70	1.25	0.59	1.46	0.49	1.70	0.39	1.96
16	0.84	1.09	0.74	1.25	0.63	1.44	0.53	1.66	0.44	1.90
17	0.87	1.10	0.77	1.25	0.67	1.43	0.57	1.63	0.48	1.85
18	0.90	1.12	0.80	1.26	0.71	1.42	0.61	1.60	0.52	1.80
19	0.93	1.13	0.83	1.26	0.74	1.41	0.65	1.58	0.56	1.77
20	0.95	1.15	0.86	1.27	0.77	1.41	0.68	1.57	0.60	1.74
21	0.97	1.16	0.89	1.27	0.80	1.41	0.72	1.55	0.63	1.71
22	1.00	1.17	0.91	1.28	0.83	1.40	0.75	1.54	0.66	1.69
23	1.02	1.19	0.94	1.29	0.86	1.40	0.77	1.53	0.70	1.67
24	1.04	1.20	0.96	1.30	0.88	1.41	0.80	1.53	0.72	1.66
25	1.05	1.21	0.98	1.30	0.90	1.41	0.83	1.52	0.75	1.65
26	1.07	1.22	1.00	1.31	0.93	1.41	0.85	1.52	0.78	1.64
27	1.09	1.23	1.02	1.32	0.95	1.41	0.88	1.51	0.81	1.63
28	1.10	1.24	1.04	1.32	0.97	1.41	0.90	1.51	0.83	1.62
29	1.12	1.25	1.05	1.33	0.99	1.42	0.92	1.51	0.85	1.61
30	1.13	1.26	1.07	1.34	1.01	1.42	0.94	1.51	0.88	1.61
31	1.15	1.27	1.08	1.34	1.02	1.42	0.96	1.51	0.90	1.60
32	1.16	1.28	1.10	1.35	1.04	1.43	0.98	1.51	0.92	1.60
33	1.17	1.29	1.11	1.36	1.05	1.43	1.00	1.51	0.94	1.59
34	1.18	1.30	1.13	1.36	1.07	1.43	1.01	1.51	0.95	1.59
35	1.19	1.31	1.14	1.37	1.08	1.44	1.03	1.51	0.97	1.59
36	1.21	1.32	1.15	1.38	1.10	1.44	1.04	1.51	0.99	1.59
37	1.22	1.32	1.16	1.38	1.11	1.45	1.06	1.51	1.00	1.59
38	1.23	1.33	1.18	1.39	1.12	1.45	1.07	1.52	1.02	1.58
39	1.24	1.34	1.19	1.39	1.14	1.45	1.09	1.52	1.03	1.58
40	1.25	1.34	1.20	1.40	1.15	1.46	1.10	1.52	1.05	1.58
45	1.29	1.38	1.24	1.42	1.20	1.48	1.16	1.53	1.11	1.58
50	1.32	1.40	1.28	1.45	1.24	1.49	1.20	1.54	1.16	1.59
55	1.36	1.43	1.32	1.47	1.28	1.51	1.25	1.55	1.21	1.59
60	1.38	1.45	1.35	1.48	1.32	1.52	1.28	1.56	1.25	1.60
65	1.41	1.47	1.38	1.50	1.35	1.53	1.31	1.57	1.28	1.61
70	1.43	1.49	1.40	1.52	1.37	1.55	1.34	1.58	1.31	1.61
75	1.45	1.50	1.42	1.53	1.39	1.56	1.37	1.59	1.34	1.62
80	1.47	1.52	1.44	1.54	1.42	1.57	1.39	1.60	1.36	1.62
85	1.48	1.53	1.46	1.55	1.43	1.58	1.41	1.60	1.39	1.63
90	1.50	1.54	1.47	1.56	1.45	1.59	1.43	1.61	1.41	1.64
95	1.51	1.55	1.49	1.57	1.47	1.60	1.45	1.62	1.42	1.64
100	1.52	1.56	1.50	1.58	1.48	1.60	1.46	1.63	1.44	1.65

ACKNOWLEDGMENTS FOR TABLES

D. From the Rand Corporation, *A Million Random Digits with 100,000 Normal Deviates*. Glencoe, Ill.: The Free Press, 1955. Used by permission of The Rand Corporation.

E. Reproduced from *Documenta Geigy Scientific Tables,* 7th ed., Basel, 1970. Courtesy CIBA-GEIGY Limited, Basel, Switzerland.

F. From A. Hald and S. A. Sinkbaek, "A Table of Percentage Points of the χ^2 Distribution," *Skandinavisk Aktuarietidskrift* 33(1950):168–175. Used by permission.

G. From *Biometrika Tables for Statisticians,* 3rd ed., vol. I, London: Bentley House, 1970. Reprinted by permission of the Biometrika Trustees.

H. From E. S. Pearson and H. O. Hartley, eds. *Biometrika Tables for Statisticians,* 3rd ed., vol. I, London: The Syndics of the Cambridge University Press, 1970. Used by permission of the Biometrika Trustees.

J. Tables Ja and Jb adapted from Frieda S. Swed and C. Eisenhart, "Tables for Testing Randomness of Grouping in a Sequence of Alternatives," *Annals of Mathematical Statistics* 14(1943):66–87. Used by permission.

K. F. Wilcoxon, S. Katti, and R. A. Wilcox, *Critical Values and Probability Levels for the Wilcoxon Rank Sum Test and the Wilcoxon Signed Rank Test,* Pearl River, N.Y.; American Cyanamid Co., 1949; reproduced with the permission of American Cyanamid Company.

L. Adapted from L. R. Verdooren, "Extended Tables of Critical Values for Wilcoxon's Test Statistic," *Biometrika* 50(1963):177–186. Used by permission of the Biometrika Trustees.

M. From W. H. Kruskal and W. A. Wallis, "Use of Ranks in One-Criterion Analysis of Variance," *Journal of the American Statistical Association* 47(1952):583–621; errata, ibid., 48(1953):907–911. Reprinted by permission of the American Statistical Association.

N. From M. Friedman, "The Use of Ranks to Avoid the Assumption of Normality Implicit in the Analysis of Variance," *Journal of the American Statistical Association* 32(1937):675–701. Reprinted by permission of the American Statistical Association.

O. From Gerald J. Glasser and Robert Winter, "Critical Values of the Coefficient of Rank Correlation for Testing the Hypothesis of Independence," *Biometrika* 48(1961):444–448. Used by permission of the Biometrika Trustees. The table as reprinted here contains corrections given in W. J. Conover, *Practical Nonparametric Statistics,* © 1971 by John Wiley & Sons, Inc., New York.

P. From J. Durbin, and G. S. Watson, "Testing for Serial Correlation in Least Squares Regression," *Biometrika* 38 (1951):159–178. Reprinted by permission of the *Biometrika* Trustees.

Appendix II
Hypothetical
Population of
Employed Heads
of Households

VARIABLE

1. **Sex**
   1 = male
   2 = female

2. **Marital status**
   1 = single
   2 = married
   3 = widowed or divorced

3. **Age**

4. **Occupation**
   1 = professional
   2 = managerial
   3 = sales
   4 = clerical and technical
   5 = other

5. **Education** (years of school completed)

6. **Commuting distance to work** (miles)

7. **Number of years with current employer**

8. **Annual income** (thousands of dollars)

9. **Family size** (number of persons)

10. **Size of residence** (hundreds of square feet of floor space)

					Variable					
Subject	1	2	3	4	5	6	7	8	9	10
1	1	2	29	4	14	12	5	24	4	26
2	1	2	48	1	16	34	10	27	4	22
3	1	2	41	5	12	12	11	16	4	20
4	1	2	54	4	14	18	20	23	3	20
5	1	2	44	4	12	5	20	21	3	19
6	1	2	57	3	16	30	21	44	2	36
7	1	1	45	2	16	22	22	48	1	8
8	1	2	59	2	12	20	29	32	2	25
9	1	1	18	3	12	17	1	12	1	6
10	1	2	49	3	14	24	24	37	3	32
11	1	2	43	2	16	7	18	38	3	33
12	1	2	44	4	16	14	20	31	4	30
13	1	2	43	2	12	29	15	28	4	29
14	1	2	45	5	12	28	14	17	3	18
15	1	2	50	1	16	17	23	24	3	20
16	1	1	44	4	14	28	20	22	1	19
17	1	2	52	3	12	17	21	30	3	30
18	1	2	60	2	16	22	25	60	2	39
19	1	2	43	2	16	9	12	39	4	31
20	1	2	53	4	12	26	16	18	3	17
21	1	3	45	5	16	21	20	29	1	28
22	1	2	55	3	12	5	30	27	2	20
23	1	3	20	5	14	33	2	10	1	6
24	1	2	58	4	14	32	16	24	2	19
25	1	2	43	4	12	31	21	17	4	17
26	1	3	43	3	12	34	24	24	1	26
27	2	1	21	3	12	13	2	10	1	5
28	1	2	41	2	16	31	14	38	4	32
29	1	2	44	2	16	17	12	42	3	4
30	1	2	40	4	16	17	10	29	4	28
31	1	2	56	2	12	13	16	23	2	20
32	1	2	47	3	16	29	18	41	4	34
33	1	2	51	2	12	24	16	30	3	32
34	2	3	26	2	16	17	3	16	2	24
35	2	1	18	4	12	6	1	11	1	6
36	1	2	30	2	16	5	1	31	3	27
37	1	2	49	2	12	32	9	28	3	31
38	1	2	42	4	16	33	12	24	4	20
39	1	2	50	4	14	25	14	20	3	18
40	1	2	54	3	16	5	13	37	3	34
41	1	2	45	4	14	31	23	24	4	20
42	1	2	57	2	16	11	20	60	2	38
43	2	3	25	1	17	20	3	18	2	12
44	2	1	24	1	18	10	1	19	1	5
45	1	2	59	2	16	10	19	51	2	36
46	2	1	34	1	16	13	7	14	1	7

					Variable					
Subject	1	2	3	4	5	6	7	8	9	10
47	1	2	43	2	12	25	16	21	4	20
48	2	3	30	2	16	14	5	12	3	12
49	1	2	45	4	16	17	15	22	3	19
50	1	2	58	3	15	33	20	31	2	33
51	2	1	25	1	16	4	3	15	1	5
52	1	2	29	3	16	32	2	34	5	30
53	1	2	52	2	14	32	7	28	3	25
54	1	2	18	4	12	23	1	10	2	4
55	1	2	53	4	14	12	11	21	2	20
56	1	2	55	3	16	27	15	41	2	34
57	2	3	35	3	13	19	10	12	2	9
58	1	2	40	2	12	16	10	26	4	27
59	2	1	42	4	16	30	6	13	1	5
60	1	2	44	2	16	32	15	32	3	34
61	1	2	48	4	16	27	21	30	3	32
62	1	1	20	5	12	28	2	12	1	6
63	1	2	42	2	16	9	12	38	4	34
64	1	2	60	3	14	8	20	27	2	28
65	1	3	21	3	12	16	1	12	1	5
66	1	2	56	2	15	32	26	29	2	27
67	1	2	41	2	16	20	15	34	4	33
68	1	2	51	4	14	30	20	21	3	19
69	1	2	44	4	12	20	12	20	4	18
70	1	2	47	5	12	29	17	16	3	17
71	1	2	31	2	13	14	6	35	4	38
72	1	2	20	4	13	35	3	11	3	6
73	1	2	50	3	12	34	22	27	4	23
74	1	2	47	4	16	16	16	25	3	22
75	1	2	54	4	14	32	28	23	3	21
76	2	1	31	5	12	7	11	11	1	6
77	1	2	57	4	14	27	22	24	2	21
78	2	3	29	1	18	21	5	20	2	24
79	1	2	59	5	12	9	31	17	2	27
80	1	2	42	3	16	28	19	41	3	38
81	1	2	42	3	16	9	14	38	4	37
82	2	2	48	5	12	9	8	12	4	10
83	2	2	49	4	12	7	14	13	5	16
84	1	2	55	2	16	8	15	44	3	36
85	1	2	49	4	12	16	10	17	4	18
86	1	1	21	5	12	32	2	12	1	7
87	1	2	30	4	14	20	3	29	4	27
88	2	1	26	1	16	29	4	17	1	70
89	2	1	35	3	14	28	12	10	1	5
90	1	2	52	4	14	30	12	19	2	18
91	1	1	18	3	12	20	1	10	1	6
92	1	2	53	5	12	29	24	15	3	16

					Variable					
Subject	1	2	3	4	5	6	7	8	9	10
93	1	2	43	2	16	14	21	38	4	37
94	1	2	58	3	16	35	16	37	2	39
95	2	1	44	2	18	11	20	19	1	11
96	1	2	40	2	12	34	12	27	4	34
97	1	2	41	2	16	11	11	36	3	37
98	1	2	48	4	16	34	10	28	3	27
99	1	2	40	2	14	25	12	30	4	28
100	1	1	60	4	14	10	24	25	1	21
101	2	3	31	1	18	24	7	19	3	15
102	1	2	56	3	16	20	20	42	2	38
103	1	2	51	3	12	9	21	31	3	23
104	2	1	33	1	16	28	10	20	1	23
105	1	2	29	1	18	15	5	29	3	27
106	1	2	22	1	16	29	1	22	2	12
107	1	1	29	5	12	17	4	28	1	6
108	2	1	36	2	16	25	11	17	1	12
109	1	2	32	1	16	26	2	30	4	27
110	1	2	21	4	13	10	2	11	3	7
111	1	2	48	1	16	23	14	20	4	29
112	1	2	43	2	12	29	12	24	3	30
113	1	2	50	2	12	22	30	27	3	21
114	2	1	37	3	14	26	10	14	1	8
115	1	2	54	1	16	19	26	22	2	29
116	2	2	48	4	14	23	8	13	6	11
117	1	2	57	3	16	9	20	38	2	34
118	2	1	38	5	16	28	3	12	1	7
119	1	1	59	4	14	9	32	21	1	19
120	1	2	47	2	16	31	24	32	3	33
121	1	3	58	4	16	32	20	24	2	20
122	1	2	55	1	16	34	25	29	3	22
123	1	2	52	3	14	30	22	27	4	24
124	1	2	31	1	16	33	4	32	4	27
125	2	1	43	1	16	16	3	17	1	10
126	2	1	27	4	12	15	8	10	1	5
127	1	2	53	2	12	15	18	30	2	24
128	2	3	28	5	13	5	8	12	3	18
129	1	2	40	2	12	6	15	21	4	19
130	1	2	41	4	14	17	17	19	3	16
131	1	2	42	2	16	29	14	35	4	34
132	1	1	20	5	12	19	2	14	1	8
133	1	2	43	4	12	16	18	21	3	19
134	1	2	42	3	16	12	14	40	3	34
135	1	2	60	3	12	32	27	30	2	30
136	1	2	56	2	16	15	28	38	2	33
137	1	2	18	3	12	26	1	12	3	6
138	1	2	51	2	16	30	19	44	3	37

					Variable					
Subject	1	2	3	4	5	6	7	8	9	10
139	1	2	49	2	12	34	10	32	5	30
140	1	2	30	3	12	14	8	34	3	27
141	1	2	30	4	14	26	5	25	5	17
142	1	2	38	3	12	5	10	38	3	35
143	1	2	49	2	14	35	11	24	3	30
144	1	3	50	2	16	22	15	38	4	33
145	2	2	47	3	14	15	20	16	2	23
146	1	2	54	3	16	9	21	41	3	35
147	1	2	43	4	16	8	20	26	4	30
148	1	1	57	3	12	34	24	27	1	31
149	1	1	18	3	12	21	1	14	1	5
150	1	2	59	2	14	17	32	28	2	30
151	1	2	40	2	12	13	20	24	5	31
152	1	2	20	5	14	14	2	16	2	5
153	1	1	49	4	16	9	22	22	1	19
154	1	3	55	5	12	20	26	18	1	5
155	1	1	22	2	16	31	2	20	1	6
156	1	1	21	4	15	9	2	15	1	6
157	1	2	29	3	15	28	1	37	6	18
158	1	1	23	2	16	11	1	20	1	7
159	1	2	32	2	16	33	1	41	5	18
160	1	1	20	5	12	30	1	11	1	5
161	1	1	52	5	12	28	27	17	1	8
162	1	3	41	4	16	13	14	20	1	6
163	1	2	53	3	16	13	21	35	3	34
164	1	2	44	5	14	33	20	18	4	20
165	1	2	58	4	14	14	30	21	2	19
166	1	1	47	2	16	32	22	33	3	32
167	1	2	60	5	12	23	28	15	2	15
168	1	2	42	4	16	9	20	22	4	20
169	2	2	47	5	12	25	22	18	4	12
170	1	2	43	3	16	11	14	42	3	33
171	1	2	48	2	16	23	17	45	2	34
172	1	1	56	2	12	6	21	30	1	30
173	1	2	42	5	12	12	22	18	4	20
174	1	2	51	4	14	27	20	21	3	20
175	1	2	31	2	16	16	5	45	5	38
176	1	2	31	4	14	10	7	30	3	26
177	1	2	21	4	12	27	3	16	3	8
178	1	2	48	3	14	35	20	20	3	20
179	1	1	42	2	16	10	20	31	1	33
180	1	2	50	4	16	20	16	24	3	21
181	1	2	44	1	16	26	20	22	4	19
182	1	1	54	4	12	34	26	17	1	12
183	2	1	28	2	16	5	3	20	1	5
184	1	2	34	2	16	28	7	40	3	36

	Variable									
Subject	1	2	3	4	5	6	7	8	9	10
185	1	2	56	3	14	29	26	30	2	20
186	2	1	32	3	12	12	6	14	1	6
187	1	2	55	2	16	22	22	24	2	24
188	1	2	41	2	14	24	13	20	3	19
189	1	2	53	4	16	23	20	21	3	20
190	2	3	27	2	18	29	5	22	2	19
191	2	1	18	5	12	15	1	11	1	5
192	1	3	30	5	12	20	3	30	1	5
193	2	1	22	1	16	24	1	17	1	7
194	1	2	33	2	12	34	7	29	2	36
195	1	1	24	1	16	21	2	21	1	4
196	1	2	18	5	12	11	1	12	2	4
197	1	2	49	4	14	20	28	19	4	18
198	1	2	52	5	12	35	26	16	3	17
199	1	2	23	2	15	30	2	15	3	12
200	1	2	51	2	16	10	28	42	3	23
201	1	1	20	3	12	31	2	10	1	5
202	1	2	47	3	16	27	20	31	4	20
203	1	2	45	2	12	23	25	22	3	18
204	1	2	22	3	12	10	3	12	2	6
205	1	2	43	2	12	35	19	20	4	19
206	2	3	36	4	14	10	9	13	3	18
207	2	3	32	1	16	25	8	16	4	12
208	1	2	32	2	18	7	5	42	2	39
209	1	1	20	4	12	25	1	10	1	7
210	1	2	29	2	16	30	4	38	2	29
211	1	2	20	3	12	10	2	11	2	4
212	1	1	25	1	16	14	2	18	1	7
213	1	2	29	3	12	31	6	27	3	28
214	1	1	18	4	12	15	1	10	1	5
215	1	1	32	1	16	14	10	30	1	9
216	1	1	22	4	14	32	2	12	1	4
217	1	2	35	4	14	12	5	26	4	15
218	1	2	34	3	16	30	4	42	4	29
219	1	2	20	5	12	27	2	14	3	6
220	1	2	36	2	15	14	4	27	3	16
221	1	3	23	1	16	15	1	21	1	15
222	1	2	47	2	12	13	17	22	3	19
223	1	2	41	2	16	7	16	34	3	31
224	1	2	49	3	16	9	19	37	2	33
225	1	2	42	4	12	8	14	18	4	27
226	1	2	50	3	12	17	29	24	3	30
227	2	1	42	2	16	21	15	22	1	8
228	1	2	31	1	17	8	1	39	2	9
229	1	3	53	4	12	16	27	21	1	19
230	1	1	21	3	12	8	3	14	1	4

	Variable									
Subject	1	2	3	4	5	6	7	8	9	10
231	1	2	54	3	16	10	16	36	3	35
232	1	2	48	2	16	19	20	41	3	37
233	2	1	32	3	16	25	8	21	1	14
234	2	3	25	2	16	11	2	23	2	14
235	1	2	52	2	12	14	30	24	2	21
236	1	2	44	3	12	20	21	30	3	33
237	2	1	29	2	16	27	3	24	1	14
238	1	2	51	2	16	16	26	55	3	39
239	1	2	43	2	12	31	19	22	4	20
240	1	2	24	3	12	7	1	17	3	20
241	1	2	46	3	16	10	16	37	3	23
242	1	2	45	2	16	31	19	35	4	29
243	1	2	33	3	16	24	6	45	4	39
244	1	2	30	1	17	16	3	32	4	28
245	2	3	33	4	12	9	12	14	4	12
246	2	3	27	4	12	15	4	12	1	8
247	1	2	26	1	16	12	2	25	3	28
248	1	2	21	3	12	22	3	10	2	4
249	1	2	30	2	12	13	7	28	4	16
250	1	2	24	2	16	35	3	24	3	24
251	1	2	33	2	16	5	4	42	3	30
252	2	1	33	5	12	15	9	11	1	6
253	1	2	35	3	12	34	14	22	3	15
254	2	3	45	5	12	5	15	12	3	17
255	1	2	34	4	14	35	9	22	4	15
256	1	2	46	5	16	22	17	24	4	20
257	2	3	26	1	18	25	2	18	1	18
258	1	2	48	4	12	23	24	17	2	21
259	1	2	42	4	14	8	20	22	3	20
260	1	1	20	5	13	11	2	12	1	6
261	1	2	36	3	16	6	5	40	4	38
262	1	3	29	4	15	17	6	30	1	8
263	1	1	25	2	12	7	1	14	1	7
264	1	2	18	4	12	18	1	10	2	5
265	1	2	32	4	14	12	8	31	4	17
266	1	2	47	2	16	13	25	42	2	32
267	2	1	25	3	14	10	3	19	1	8
268	2	3	34	3	12	16	7	19	2	12
269	2	3	35	2	16	10	7	26	3	19
270	2	3	37	5	12	15	14	13	4	20
271	1	2	45	3	16	32	24	41	4	33
272	1	2	22	2	16	8	1	14	3	10
273	1	2	44	3	12	19	21	31	3	31
274	2	3	40	4	12	22	10	13	5	14
275	1	3	43	2	16	17	19	49	1	26
276	1	2	37	2	12	7	12	29	4	15

Subject	1	2	3	4	5	6	7	8	9	10
					Variable					
277	1	1	20	4	13	20	2	12	1	6
278	1	2	41	3	16	16	20	30	4	24
279	1	1	23	4	16	26	1	19	1	7
280	1	3	31	5	12	32	1	25	1	7
281	1	1	18	5	12	27	1	12	1	6
282	1	1	18	4	12	22	2	10	1	4
283	1	1	18	3	12	17	1	10	1	7
284	2	3	46	3	12	9	21	15	3	16
285	1	2	23	2	16	13	2	22	3	20
286	1	2	27	1	17	16	3	20	4	19
287	2	1	26	4	14	21	2	14	1	6
288	1	2	31	2	16	12	3	28	3	15
289	1	1	20	3	14	8	3	10	1	6
290	1	2	34	1	18	24	2	21	3	16
291	1	3	22	5	15	10	3	15	1	7
292	1	2	35	2	16	23	10	46	5	39
293	2	1	31	2	16	7	3	16	1	5
294	1	2	42	2	16	15	11	47	2	34
295	1	2	45	3	16	20	16	52	3	35
296	2	3	27	5	12	15	5	12	1	13
297	1	2	26	4	12	12	6	15	3	18
298	1	2	30	3	16	11	5	45	5	39
299	1	1	33	1	17	28	3	35	1	19
300	1	1	21	5	15	18	1	12	1	6
301	1	2	36	4	14	33	9	24	4	16
302	2	1	41	1	18	8	12	19	1	5
303	2	1	39	2	16	19	9	21	1	6
304	1	1	44	1	18	26	20	20	1	6
305	1	1	41	2	16	12	13	36	1	8
306	1	3	43	4	12	28	17	19	1	7
307	1	1	18	5	12	25	1	12	1	5
308	1	2	38	3	16	25	14	45	5	20
309	1	2	20	3	12	26	3	13	3	12
310	1	2	36	3	16	12	10	45	5	38
311	1	2	32	3	12	10	7	30	5	25
312	2	3	34	4	15	11	10	13	3	12
313	1	1	24	2	16	5	1	20	1	15
314	1	2	25	3	14	10	3	15	3	16
315	1	2	29	2	13	28	8	32	3	27
316	1	1	18	4	12	11	1	14	1	6
317	2	3	18	3	12	9	1	16	1	6
318	1	2	25	5	12	8	3	18	4	18
319	1	1	20	4	12	31	1	15	1	6
320	1	2	28	5	12	20	2	20	5	19
321	1	2	29	2	16	15	7	30	4	27
322	2	3	47	3	16	14	20	14	4	17

					Variable					
Subject	1	2	3	4	5	6	7	8	9	10
323	2	1	34	5	13	10	13	15	1	6
324	2	3	25	4	12	16	9	13	2	6
325	2	1	40	1	16	9	16	19	1	7
326	1	2	32	3	16	13	6	45	5	34
327	2	1	27	1	16	13	1	17	1	5
328	1	1	34	2	16	25	7	36	1	15
329	2	3	33	1	18	24	11	20	3	19
330	1	2	35	1	16	35	7	21	4	16
331	1	2	21	3	12	16	2	14	2	10
332	1	2	23	1	16	29	1	20	2	21
333	1	2	36	4	12	9	8	29	5	27
334	1	1	19	5	12	12	1	12	1	6
335	1	2	27	2	13	15	5	19	3	18
336	1	2	24	3	14	16	2	16	2	20
337	1	2	31	4	15	19	5	30	5	36
338	2	3	38	3	12	6	9	14	2	17
339	2	3	48	5	12	13	16	11	4	18
340	1	2	20	4	14	8	3	14	3	11
341	1	2	38	2	12	25	16	31	5	29
342	1	2	37	2	16	8	11	52	4	38
343	1	1	22	2	16	22	1	18	1	7
344	1	2	33	4	14	15	2	32	5	28
345	1	2	30	1	16	9	4	34	3	39
346	1	2	26	3	15	25	2	14	3	15
347	2	1	49	4	13	11	26	11	1	6
348	1	1	20	5	12	32	2	10	1	4
349	1	1	19	5	12	27	1	12	1	7
350	2	3	28	2	16	18	3	24	3	18
351	1	1	21	4	12	21	1	12	1	6
352	1	1	24	1	16	20	3	19	1	20
353	1	2	26	2	16	28	3	27	4	19
354	1	1	20	3	12	25	1	14	1	4
355	1	2	30	3	16	7	4	42	5	38
356	1	2	33	2	16	7	5	41	4	37
357	1	3	34	3	16	26	7	50	5	31
358	1	2	19	5	12	10	2	15	2	12
359	1	2	45	2	16	30	15	45	2	34
360	1	2	39	2	12	6	12	30	3	30
361	1	2	43	3	16	32	10	41	4	38
362	1	1	22	4	14	28	2	14	1	6
363	1	2	34	3	12	29	10	37	5	38
364	1	2	44	4	14	33	22	21	3	21
365	1	2	40	2	13	7	12	18	5	20
366	1	3	32	3	12	26	5	32	1	17
367	2	3	29	2	16	20	5	14	1	5
368	1	2	25	4	16	28	2	22	3	18

	Variable									
Subject	**1**	**2**	**3**	**4**	**5**	**6**	**7**	**8**	**9**	**10**
369	1	2	28	4	14	12	3	24	6	19
370	1	2	29	3	16	6	7	40	4	30
371	1	1	36	1	16	14	6	21	1	8
372	1	2	20	4	14	23	2	15	3	12
373	1	3	42	4	12	20	16	17	1	4
374	2	3	32	2	18	15	3	22	2	14
375	1	1	41	3	16	19	14	31	1	4
376	2	1	23	1	16	21	1	19	1	6
377	2	1	28	2	16	8	4	20	1	7
378	1	2	38	1	18	32	12	22	3	18
379	1	2	37	4	12	5	16	20	5	14
380	1	1	18	3	12	27	1	10	1	4
381	1	2	31	4	16	30	2	35	4	38
382	1	2	27	3	16	13	4	24	5	28
383	1	1	23	3	12	9	3	19	1	7
384	2	3	41	1	16	19	17	16	4	12
385	2	1	30	2	18	25	4	23	1	8
386	1	1	20	4	12	22	2	12	1	4
387	1	2	27	4	12	9	3	18	4	16
388	1	1	23	5	13	10	4	17	1	8
389	2	1	39	3	14	25	12	14	1	6
390	1	2	31	3	16	12	7	45	4	39
391	1	2	35	5	12	7	1	15	2	15
392	2	3	21	5	12	12	2	11	2	9
393	1	2	38	4	14	34	14	20	4	18
394	1	2	45	2	12	24	10	22	3	20
395	1	2	43	4	14	12	23	19	2	19
396	1	1	18	4	12	27	1	13	1	5
397	1	2	46	3	16	18	22	55	2	36
398	1	2	34	2	16	14	11	45	4	38
399	1	3	22	1	16	23	1	16	1	6
400	1	2	30	5	12	21	4	32	5	27
401	1	2	33	3	14	31	6	34	3	38
402	2	1	19	3	12	7	1	13	1	5
403	1	1	26	5	13	33	4	17	1	7
404	1	2	36	3	16	16	5	42	5	30
405	1	2	40	2	16	9	20	39	3	31
406	1	2	39	2	12	7	18	28	2	29
407	1	2	44	3	16	30	14	40	4	32
408	1	1	19	3	12	31	2	12	1	4
409	1	2	42	4	15	30	12	18	3	19
410	1	2	21	5	12	25	2	11	2	10
411	1	2	41	5	14	8	13	17	3	18
412	1	3	37	5	12	11	8	22	1	8
413	1	1	20	3	12	21	1	11	1	4
414	1	2	32	5	12	31	4	28	4	16

Subject	Variable									
	1	2	3	4	5	6	7	8	9	10
415	1	2	29	2	18	13	5	43	5	39
416	1	2	28	1	16	6	6	21	3	18
417	1	3	24	2	15	33	2	18	1	6
418	1	3	25	5	15	6	1	20	1	6
419	2	1	35	5	12	14	9	14	1	6
420	2	1	29	3	12	7	7	12	1	7
421	1	1	25	2	16	33	3	24	1	18
422	1	2	28	2	18	24	1	32	2	26
423	1	2	29	1	16	23	3	30	4	36
424	1	1	18	4	12	12	1	10	1	5
425	1	2	32	5	12	9	2	21	4	22
426	1	2	35	4	14	34	3	29	3	25
427	1	2	19	4	12	26	2	11	2	9
428	1	3	38	5	12	5	7	18	1	7
429	1	3	23	4	15	23	5	15	1	6
430	1	3	41	2	16	35	20	52	1	20
431	1	2	46	2	12	22	16	29	3	21
432	2	3	25	4	16	15	2	14	2	14
433	1	2	34	3	16	28	4	35	5	38
434	1	1	43	3	16	27	14	37	1	22
435	1	2	24	4	16	33	3	21	3	22
436	1	1	20	4	12	29	2	12	1	4
437	1	2	27	5	12	27	5	21	2	19
438	1	2	31	3	12	30	6	42	3	28
439	1	1	21	4	12	29	3	14	1	6
440	1	2	36	2	12	8	7	28	4	28
441	1	2	42	1	18	18	13	26	4	28
442	1	2	39	4	16	30	12	28	5	22
443	1	3	47	4	14	13	21	24	3	21
444	2	1	25	5	12	13	3	16	1	5
445	1	2	48	2	12	16	19	22	4	20
446	1	3	44	5	12	25	20	15	1	6
447	1	2	40	3	16	30	17	35	3	34
448	1	2	45	3	12	34	20	23	3	20
449	1	2	37	2	16	33	9	28	4	28
450	1	2	33	3	12	14	2	31	2	26
451	1	2	20	5	12	17	1	13	2	10
452	2	3	24	4	14	13	4	14	2	12
453	1	1	30	3	16	18	3	41	1	14
454	1	1	22	5	13	11	3	15	1	6
455	1	2	26	4	13	17	8	18	3	15
456	1	1	20	5	13	15	2	12	1	4
457	1	2	26	2	16	28	1	26	4	21
458	1	2	22	2	16	35	1	18	2	5
459	1	2	30	4	13	30	2	30	4	18
460	1	2	33	3	16	28	10	48	3	30

	Variable									
Subject	**1**	**2**	**3**	**4**	**5**	**6**	**7**	**8**	**9**	**10**
461	2	1	36	4	12	15	11	11	1	6
462	1	2	35	5	12	6	3	18	2	7
463	1	2	37	3	16	7	14	45	5	35
464	2	3	31	1	17	6	8	18	2	13
465	1	1	39	2	12	21	9	21	1	7
466	1	2	44	2	16	28	14	34	3	23
467	1	2	21	3	12	8	2	11	2	5
468	1	1	34	5	12	22	3	20	1	7
469	1	1	23	1	16	9	1	22	1	9
470	1	2	28	3	14	16	3	32	4	30
471	2	3	26	4	13	15	4	12	2	9
472	1	2	25	3	12	5	3	20	3	17
473	2	1	26	3	14	19	2	11	1	4
474	1	2	29	2	16	8	4	42	4	21
475	1	2	32	3	16	30	4	45	5	39
476	2	1	38	2	18	8	13	20	1	5
477	1	2	36	2	18	13	12	36	4	16
478	1	2	24	4	14	6	1	17	3	18
479	1	1	18	4	12	13	1	12	1	4
480	1	2	40	4	14	12	15	21	2	20
481	2	3	39	3	16	13	13	13	2	10
482	1	2	43	3	16	6	18	38	3	31
483	1	1	42	2	12	10	17	18	1	6
484	1	2	19	4	12	34	1	13	2	6
485	1	2	41	4	16	9	11	31	4	25
486	1	2	20	3	12	20	2	14	1	5
487	1	2	37	1	18	24	6	19	3	15
488	1	2	31	5	12	11	7	38	4	27
489	2	1	48	4	12	11	18	12	1	5
490	1	2	27	4	14	22	7	22	4	16
491	2	3	30	3	12	8	6	14	2	14
492	2	1	27	3	14	22	3	11	1	4
493	1	1	22	2	16	25	1	20	1	7
494	1	2	24	5	12	9	2	16	3	17
495	1	1	19	5	12	26	1	10	1	4
496	1	1	27	2	18	12	3	25	1	8
497	2	1	34	4	14	9	3	10	1	4
498	1	1	31	1	18	26	2	26	1	9
499	2	3	27	4	12	8	5	11	2	9
500	1	1	35	3	16	19	6	48	5	37
501	1	2	38	2	16	34	15	32	5	30
502	2	1	47	1	18	25	12	21	1	11
503	1	2	33	2	16	17	11	50	4	37
504	1	2	23	2	16	34	1	23	2	19
505	1	2	34	5	12	33	1	21	3	15
506	1	2	26	1	16	23	2	23	3	21

					Variable					
Subject	1	2	3	4	5	6	7	8	9	10
507	1	2	30	2	16	9	4	44	2	30
508	1	1	20	5	12	14	2	10	i	4
509	1	3	36	5	12	14	5	18	1	7
510	1	2	39	1	18	13	12	20	5	20
511	1	1	40	2	16	15	17	30	1	8
512	2	1	46	2	18	15	10	24	1	11
513	2	1	37	2	16	5	7	22	1	5
514	1	2	43	3	16	32	13	46	2	26
515	1	1	21	4	15	10	1	15	1	6
516	1	2	42	4	12	16	16	17	3	21
517	1	1	20	4	14	7	1	12	1	4
518	1	2	44	2	12	18	20	22	3	20
519	1	2	41	2	14	35	20	23	4	19
520	1	2	37	2	12	8	12	27	4	26
521	1	1	18	3	12	28	1	13	1	4
522	1	3	32	2	16	21	6	44	1	9
523	1	2	29	3	14	25	2	39	3	29
524	1	1	28	1	18	25	5	24	1	4
525	1	2	25	4	13	11	1	19	3	18
526	1	1	25	2	16	15	2	26	1	20
527	2	1	37	3	14	8	6	13	1	4
528	1	2	28	2	16	34	2	34	4	31
529	1	2	32	2	12	18	8	30	3	16
530	2	3	28	3	14	25	2	12	3	14
531	2	3	39	1	18	14	4	15	1	5
532	1	2	21	5	12	23	2	15	3	6
533	1	2	35	2	12	34	14	27	4	16
534	2	3	31	4	13	23	6	11	2	6
535	1	2	38	4	12	10	17	21	5	19
536	1	2	23	2	14	5	2	16	3	18
537	1	2	42	2	16	24	16	49	4	32
538	1	1	18	3	12	23	2	10	1	4
539	1	2	34	2	16	31	6	48	5	38
540	1	2	43	1	12	31	15	25	3	18
541	1	3	20	5	12	32	1	12	1	6
542	1	1	22	3	12	35	3	17	1	7
543	1	2	27	3	14	10	4	27	5	20
544	1	2	31	4	14	16	5	22	4	24
545	2	3	42	1	16	24	4	24	3	12
546	1	2	36	3	12	21	9	28	3	25
547	1	1	19	4	12	23	2	13	1	6
548	1	1	24	2	13	23	2	15	1	7
549	1	2	44	3	12	5	24	24	2	19
550	1	2	41	5	16	25	15	34	3	29
551	1	2	20	4	12	25	3	14	3	4
552	1	2	40	4	12	24	16	15	4	16

	Variable									
Subject	1	2	3	4	5	6	7	8	9	10
553	1	2	39	2	12	12	13	12	5	18
554	1	1	37	3	16	32	11	47	1	10
555	1	3	33	2	13	8	1	25	1	15
556	2	1	24	1	16	25	2	20	1	6
557	1	3	30	4	14	32	8	35	1	10
558	1	2	29	4	13	20	4	27	4	17
559	2	1	28	2	16	18	5	21	1	5
560	1	2	26	3	14	16	5	28	4	22
561	2	3	48	2	18	22	15	24	4	20
562	1	3	26	4	12	23	8	20	1	7
563	1	1	20	4	12	15	1	12	1	4
564	1	2	29	2	16	26	6	45	5	38
565	1	2	30	1	16	11	4	28	4	26
566	2	3	38	3	14	16	8	14	4	18
567	1	2	33	1	16	35	3	29	5	27
568	1	2	35	1	18	23	5	23	3	25
569	1	1	19	5	12	29	1	15	1	6
570	1	2	38	3	16	5	14	52	5	38
571	1	2	42	2	16	18	14	25	3	20
572	1	1	20	5	14	5	2	13	1	6
573	1	2	34	2	12	5	10	28	5	29
574	1	2	24	2	16	33	3	20	3	16
575	1	3	25	1	16	11	1	20	1	7
576	2	3	31	4	13	20	8	12	2	6
577	2	3	49	4	12	13	13	10	3	10
578	2	3	49	3	14	18	20	14	5	16
579	2	3	32	2	16	6	5	21	1	5
580	1	2	28	3	16	9	4	25	2	16
581	1	2	32	1	16	26	10	29	2	25
582	2	1	29	4	14	7	4	13	1	6
583	1	2	36	2	16	27	9	35	5	38
584	1	2	40	4	12	22	15	19	2	18
585	2	1	36	1	18	8	3	19	1	11
586	1	1	41	3	16	21	12	32	1	9
587	2	3	29	3	12	14	9	15	2	6
588	1	2	39	4	14	13	10	21	3	18
589	1	2	37	4	14	13	15	22	5	17
590	1	2	23	2	12	30	4	16	3	17
591	1	1	18	3	12	33	2	14	1	6
592	1	1	21	5	12	29	3	10	1	4
593	1	2	31	3	16	35	4	47	4	39
594	1	1	22	2	16	35	1	19	1	7
595	1	2	27	1	18	10	2	20	3	18
596	1	2	22	2	12	8	3	18	2	12
597	1	2	27	3	15	12	5	22	4	17
598	2	3	32	1	18	18	6	18	2	13

Subject	1	2	3	4	5	6	7	8	9	10
						Variable				
599	2	3	37	4	12	20	7	13	3	13
600	1	2	31	2	16	31	6	41	4	39
601	1	2	21	3	14	11	2	12	2	6
602	1	2	35	4	12	9	10	25	4	17
603	2	3	33	3	14	21	11	15	1	7
604	1	2	38	2	16	12	13	40	5	34
605	2	3	43	2	16	17	16	19	3	14
606	1	3	34	3	16	15	8	39	1	8
607	1	1	39	2	16	23	14	37	1	9
608	2	1	25	3	16	10	2	14	1	9
609	1	2	29	3	16	35	4	46	5	38
610	1	2	30	3	15	32	7	40	4	38
611	1	2	33	4	12	19	5	32	2	16
612	2	1	33	4	12	24	9	15	1	6
613	1	2	26	4	14	33	3	19	3	18
614	1	2	41	3	12	18	19	21	4	21
615	2	1	19	4	12	14	1	12	1	4
616	1	2	36	2	16	11	5	38	5	27
617	1	2	24	1	16	9	1	18	4	18
618	1	1	19	4	13	6	2	10	1	4
619	1	2	20	4	12	6	3	13	2	6
620	1	3	42	3	16	26	14	23	1	7
621	1	3	18	4	12	12	1	14	1	7
622	1	2	40	2	14	35	12	38	3	22
623	1	2	20	4	14	33	2	15	3	5
624	1	2	37	2	16	10	10	45	5	38
625	2	1	38	3	12	18	9	11	1	5
626	1	2	32	2	12	19	9	27	3	17
627	2	3	29	4	12	18	3	10	2	5
628	1	1	23	1	16	5	2	21	1	9
629	1	2	28	4	12	17	6	20	3	15
630	1	2	25	4	14	23	3	22	2	16
631	1	1	20	4	12	15	2	12	1	4
632	1	2	25	5	12	8	3	19	4	15
633	1	1	23	3	12	18	1	17	1	5
634	1	2	28	2	12	17	5	21	4	17
635	1	2	32	3	14	32	7	24	4	16
636	1	3	18	3	12	7	1	13	1	6
637	1	2	35	2	16	20	9	40	2	10
638	1	2	38	3	16	26	12	52	4	36
639	1	1	21	5	12	33	1	15	1	4
640	1	2	44	2	16	29	21	32	4	24
641	1	2	45	3	16	11	20	40	3	35
642	1	2	19	4	13	9	2	14	2	6
643	1	2	34	4	14	32	3	19	3	16
644	1	3	40	3	12	7	19	26	1	9

		Variable							
Subject	1	2	3	4	5	6	7	8	9	10
645	1	3	20	4	14	11	2	12	1	4
646	1	1	24	5	16	35	2	22	1	7
647	1	2	27	2	16	31	1	25	5	20
648	2	1	32	1	18	7	5	17	1	8
649	1	1	31	3	14	10	7	24	1	7
650	1	1	22	3	12	24	4	17	1	6
651	1	1	36	3	12	33	7	27	1	9
652	2	1	45	2	17	11	12	22	1	8
653	1	2	46	4	14	25	22	20	3	19
654	1	2	42	3	12	25	17	24	4	20
655	2	3	28	4	14	6	4	12	1	4
656	1	2	43	2	16	8	19	31	3	32
657	1	2	39	2	16	21	12	33	4	33
658	1	2	41	5	12	5	11	16	3	19
659	1	2	33	5	16	19	7	41	3	39
660	2	1	26	4	14	12	1	13	1	6
661	2	3	34	1	18	17	3	21	2	19
662	1	2	37	3	15	24	17	20	4	16
663	1	2	30	3	16	5	4	45	4	38
664	1	1	29	1	17	14	4	29	1	14
665	1	2	26	5	16	14	1	25	4	20
666	2	3	47	3	14	24	19	14	5	14
667	2	1	39	2	18	16	8	25	1	12
668	1	3	24	2	15	19	2	19	1	7
669	1	2	26	5	13	25	6	20	3	18
670	1	1	30	4	14	33	5	37	1	9
671	2	3	27	4	14	5	3	12	1	4
672	1	2	33	1	18	5	9	30	4	17
673	2	3	36	4	13	22	11	11	2	12
674	1	3	35	2	12	29	2	20	1	9
675	1	2	38	4	14	17	14	26	5	20
676	1	1	20	5	12	5	3	12	1	4
677	1	2	42	4	12	35	22	19	4	17
678	1	2	41	2	14	31	16	21	3	16
679	1	2	34	1	18	34	4	19	3	16
680	2	1	27	3	12	12	4	12	1	4
681	2	3	44	4	12	19	16	10	3	13
682	1	1	25	3	14	35	5	18	1	6
683	1	1	19	3	12	17	2	10	1	4
684	1	2	28	3	16	5	4	35	5	30
685	1	2	32	4	15	23	5	22	4	16
686	1	3	18	3	12	29	1	10	1	4
687	1	2	36	1	16	13	9	19	4	15
688	2	1	31	2	16	7	5	18	1	5
689	1	2	40	2	16	17	17	38	2	18
690	2	1	35	1	18	5	8	19	1	8

					Variable					
Subject	1	2	3	4	5	6	7	8	9	10
691	1	2	21	5	15	7	1	15	3	8
692	1	2	20	5	12	6	2	12	2	6
693	1	2	39	3	12	30	15	20	4	19
694	1	3	22	1	16	26	1	21	1	8
695	2	3	33	3	16	5	6	17	2	16
696	1	1	37	1	18	32	2	16	1	7
697	1	2	23	5	12	6	3	15	3	20
698	2	3	34	1	18	18	7	20	3	14
699	1	2	31	2	16	11	3	38	4	37
700	1	2	27	1	16	28	3	21	3	17
701	1	2	27	4	16	19	4	28	4	20
702	1	1	22	2	13	9	2	20	1	5
703	1	3	31	3	16	34	1	44	1	10
704	1	1	20	4	12	5	2	14	1	6
705	1	2	35	3	14	14	5	34	3	36
706	1	1	21	4	12	6	1	15	1	6
707	1	1	38	5	12	17	1	17	1	7
708	1	2	46	2	16	17	17	28	3	20
709	1	2	39	2	16	14	18	30	4	20
710	1	2	45	4	14	26	14	21	3	20
711	2	1	28	3	12	28	3	12	1	4
712	1	1	50	2	12	11	23	23	2	19
713	1	2	42	3	16	16	20	40	3	35
714	1	2	34	2	16	26	1	47	4	39
715	1	1	19	4	12	26	1	10	1	4
716	1	2	24	3	16	20	2	18	2	17
717	1	2	26	1	16	19	2	23	4	19
718	1	2	33	2	15	31	2	40	3	38
719	1	2	36	5	12	15	4	19	4	14
720	1	2	48	4	16	7	22	26	3	21
721	2	3	22	4	12	10	2	11	1	4
722	1	3	51	3	16	5	16	42	2	34
723	1	2	43	3	14	32	15	29	3	20
724	2	1	23	4	12	17	1	12	1	4
725	1	3	49	2	12	25	19	27	1	21
726	1	2	47	3	16	22	21	42	4	33
727	1	2	40	2	16	15	14	31	4	24
728	1	3	44	2	12	10	24	25	1	20
729	1	2	37	5	12	27	15	19	4	15
730	1	2	32	4	14	34	3	30	4	27
731	2	3	26	4	14	6	2	12	2	10
732	1	2	28	5	12	20	3	21	3	25
733	1	2	25	2	16	24	2	26	3	29
734	2	3	32	3	14	9	7	10	2	5
735	1	3	23	4	12	5	2	17	1	4
736	1	3	25	4	12	11	6	17	1	5

					Variable					
Subject	1	2	3	4	5	6	7	8	9	10
737	1	3	27	1	18	16	2	19	1	6
738	1	2	28	3	16	24	1	33	3	27
739	2	1	30	2	16	27	3	21	1	5
740	1	2	23	2	16	14	2	23	3	22
741	1	1	32	3	16	7	1	40	1	15
742	1	2	35	3	16	24	4	48	5	39
743	2	3	31	4	12	29	4	14	3	19
744	1	2	46	2	12	27	14	28	3	21
745	1	2	38	1	18	18	7	38	4	27
746	1	2	48	2	16	16	19	32	3	20
747	1	1	45	2	16	27	16	26	1	5
748	1	2	22	5	16	22	1	22	3	13
749	1	2	34	5	12	7	2	19	4	14
750	1	2	36	2	16	18	7	32	5	18
751	1	2	49	3	16	9	22	41	3	33
752	1	3	39	4	14	15	14	22	5	23
753	1	2	47	3	12	27	19	29	3	22
754	2	1	29	2	16	8	6	20	1	5
755	1	2	50	4	16	12	28	23	2	20
756	1	1	43	3	16	33	13	34	1	15
757	1	2	51	3	12	35	28	27	2	20
758	1	2	20	4	12	7	1	12	2	6
759	1	2	52	2	16	24	22	52	3	36
760	1	1	19	4	12	9	2	13	1	6
761	1	2	53	3	16	20	27	36	3	31
762	1	2	40	3	12	22	21	24	4	22
763	1	2	52	5	16	8	22	27	2	20
764	1	2	33	3	12	9	4	35	2	16
765	2	3	25	4	14	12	1	13	2	5
766	1	2	44	1	16	7	22	22	3	18
767	2	3	31	1	18	21	7	19	1	12
768	1	1	24	1	16	22	1	20	1	5
769	1	2	37	3	16	19	16	51	5	20
770	1	2	26	3	14	15	4	21	4	17
771	1	2	24	2	12	6	2	17	2	16
772	1	1	26	2	15	7	3	21	1	7
773	1	1	33	2	16	32	6	38	1	9
774	1	2	35	5	12	15	6	27	4	6
775	1	2	52	2	12	14	22	24	3	20
776	1	2	38	3	16	14	11	52	5	36
777	1	2	53	4	16	21	26	20	3	19
778	1	2	48	3	16	24	22	27	4	24
779	2	1	30	2	16	19	6	26	1	10
780	1	2	50	4	14	27	25	21	3	19
781	1	2	54	3	16	10	27	39	4	36
782	2	3	30	4	12	21	5	13	2	14

					Variable					
Subject	**1**	**2**	**3**	**4**	**5**	**6**	**7**	**8**	**9**	**10**
783	1	2	55	2	16	34	30	34	3	31
784	1	3	51	3	12	24	29	30	3	30
785	1	2	34	4	12	23	9	22	5	15
786	2	3	44	3	12	10	16	11	3	8
787	2	1	31	4	13	25	4	12	1	6
788	1	2	25	5	12	35	4	19	4	15
789	1	2	23	3	14	35	3	18	3	21
790	1	2	27	2	12	22	7	22	5	19
791	1	1	22	4	13	13	2	15	1	6
792	1	2	36	4	14	32	8	29	3	27
793	1	2	49	3	12	12	24	22	2	19
794	1	2	39	3	12	16	19	24	4	31
795	1	2	47	2	16	33	18	21	3	20
796	1	1	40	3	16	15	16	32	1	32
797	1	2	46	4	16	34	24	30	4	30
798	1	1	20	5	12	20	1	12	1	5
799	1	2	45	4	14	31	24	22	4	29
800	1	1	19	5	12	5	1	10	1	4
801	1	2	44	4	16	35	22	26	4	30
802	2	1	35	3	14	25	11	12	1	6
803	2	1	44	2	18	23	10	25	1	5
804	1	2	37	4	13	20	16	18	3	16
805	1	3	28	4	12	31	2	22	1	5
806	1	1	19	4	12	30	1	10	1	4
807	1	2	28	2	16	10	3	31	4	29
808	1	2	35	4	14	31	12	29	4	26
809	2	1	32	1	18	7	4	20	1	5
810	1	1	20	4	12	23	1	11	1	6
811	1	2	49	2	12	16	14	24	4	21
812	1	2	45	3	16	29	15	32	3	24
813	2	3	31	3	14	17	6	12	3	10
814	1	1	50	4	14	21	22	20	1	20
815	1	2	38	2	16	11	14	30	4	30
816	1	2	51	2	16	35	20	35	3	33
817	1	2	39	2	16	28	16	41	4	36
818	1	1	48	3	16	15	21	30	1	20
819	1	1	47	2	12	33	20	20	1	19
820	1	1	34	3	12	29	13	32	1	10
821	2	3	35	2	16	5	4	19	2	12
822	1	2	26	3	12	35	8	22	4	16
823	1	2	36	3	16	13	9	36	3	37
824	2	1	20	3	12	16	2	10	1	4
825	1	2	52	4	12	23	18	19	2	17
826	1	2	53	3	16	34	17	41	2	30
827	2	3	46	4	14	22	11	12	2	4
828	2	1	34	1	18	20	9	22	1	4

					Variable					
Subject	1	2	3	4	5	6	7	8	9	10
829	1	2	54	2	12	35	24	29	3	20
830	1	2	40	2	16	28	16	31	4	21
831	1	2	55	1	16	7	27	21	2	20
832	1	2	23	1	16	24	2	20	2	19
833	1	2	56	4	16	25	26	25	2	20
834	1	1	24	3	15	13	2	16	1	7
835	1	2	46	3	14	14	20	31	3	23
836	1	3	37	2	16	12	13	39	1	14
837	2	3	30	2	16	20	6	23	2	15
838	1	2	27	3	16	10	4	29	5	20
839	1	2	25	3	16	17	2	26	3	20
840	2	1	39	3	12	24	13	15	1	5
841	1	2	27	4	14	25	5	26	4	18
842	2	3	45	4	14	19	14	12	2	5
843	1	1	35	1	18	11	5	23	1	9
844	1	1	49	2	16	26	16	43	2	26
845	1	2	50	2	12	5	14	27	3	19
846	2	3	43	4	14	10	9	13	2	5
847	1	3	54	3	16	23	12	32	1	22
848	1	1	38	3	16	35	14	54	1	38
849	1	2	57	2	14	25	30	23	3	20
850	1	2	39	4	16	14	14	27	5	23
851	1	2	59	2	16	10	21	28	2	22
852	1	3	60	2	12	15	30	21	2	20
853	1	2	40	4	16	15	19	20	3	19
854	1	2	55	4	14	33	14	18	3	17
855	2	3	31	3	14	7	3	17	3	25
856	1	3	36	2	12	25	11	22	1	10
857	1	2	24	2	16	29	2	22	4	19
858	1	2	28	3	15	15	5	32	4	38
859	1	2	48	5	12	14	13	16	3	20
860	1	2	52	4	14	18	20	18	3	19
861	2	1	33	2	17	7	8	21	1	12
862	1	2	46	4	14	28	18	19	4	20
863	1	2	58	3	16	10	16	38	3	36
864	2	3	39	1	18	13	13	18	3	24
865	1	3	56	2	12	35	14	24	2	23
866	1	2	53	2	16	29	14	29	4	23
867	2	3	35	1	17	20	8	19	2	20
868	1	2	51	3	16	31	23	37	5	36
869	1	1	19	4	12	16	2	10	1	4
870	1	2	47	2	16	25	20	43	3	38
871	1	2	37	2	12	7	17	28	5	27
872	2	3	34	2	16	6	5	27	2	26
873	1	2	26	2	12	19	5	24	5	17
874	2	3	32	4	12	7	4	12	1	6

Subject	\multicolumn{10}{c}{Variable}									
	1	2	3	4	5	6	7	8	9	10
875	1	1	25	2	15	20	3	19	1	5
876	1	3	25	5	12	15	2	16	1	7
877	2	3	32	4	12	8	7	13	4	18
878	1	2	26	3	12	29	2	20	4	15
879	1	2	49	2	12	18	14	31	3	24
880	1	1	19	3	12	21	2	11	1	6
881	1	2	50	2	16	26	22	38	4	36
882	1	2	38	2	16	13	12	32	4	30
883	1	2	54	3	16	18	20	40	3	37
884	1	2	47	2	16	25	19	33	3	32
885	1	2	56	4	14	5	16	18	2	17
886	2	1	24	1	16	15	1	19	1	11
887	1	2	57	2	12	9	21	21	2	20
888	2	1	34	3	12	8	6	14	1	7
889	1	2	27	5	16	32	3	27	4	20
890	1	1	55	2	16	10	22	34	1	23
891	1	2	40	4	14	5	14	18	4	20
892	1	1	58	2	12	11	31	21	1	20
893	2	1	33	3	12	17	5	10	1	5
894	1	3	59	2	16	29	20	42	2	24
895	1	2	52	2	16	14	16	37	3	32
896	2	3	36	2	16	12	3	21	4	27
897	1	2	60	3	12	19	32	23	2	20
898	2	3	23	1	16	17	1	18	2	18
899	2	3	38	2	16	13	8	24	4	30
900	2	3	20	4	12	9	1	11	1	6
901	1	2	40	2	12	7	16	24	4	24
902	1	2	48	2	16	25	14	41	4	37
903	2	1	43	1	18	11	7	19	1	5
904	2	1	38	4	12	20	14	13	1	7
905	1	1	51	3	14	9	20	24	1	22
906	1	3	39	2	15	12	12	25	5	23
907	1	1	53	3	14	30	14	20	1	20
908	1	2	37	2	16	33	14	40	4	39
909	2	3	33	1	18	7	4	20	2	6
910	1	2	28	4	14	11	3	21	2	15
911	2	3	34	2	18	10	8	28	3	28
912	1	3	28	2	16	33	6	34	1	15
913	1	2	49	3	16	9	11	42	3	24
914	1	2	38	5	12	16	9	17	3	16
915	1	2	54	2	12	11	21	29	3	19
916	2	1	37	4	12	12	13	13	1	6
917	2	3	34	3	12	8	7	16	2	12
918	1	3	48	2	12	8	22	27	1	23
919	1	2	56	2	16	17	14	35	2	25
920	2	3	37	3	12	20	8	17	1	6

		Variable								
Subject	1	2	3	4	5	6	7	8	9	10
921	1	2	57	4	14	11	24	24	2	21
922	1	2	47	3	16	22	21	32	3	22
923	1	3	50	3	12	27	28	26	1	5
924	1	2	58	2	16	28	33	30	2	21
925	1	3	40	2	16	12	10	35	1	20
926	1	2	55	1	16	8	14	27	2	19
927	1	1	19	3	12	31	1	10	1	4
928	1	2	59	4	14	22	21	21	2	20
929	1	2	60	4	15	33	29	22	2	19
930	2	1	30	1	18	6	3	18	1	8
931	1	2	40	2	16	34	11	41	4	34
932	1	2	42	4	16	6	12	28	3	19
933	2	3	37	4	12	16	5	13	4	10
934	1	2	43	2	16	13	14	34	4	25
935	1	2	44	3	12	33	21	29	4	19
936	1	2	37	2	12	8	15	26	5	18
937	2	3	42	2	16	15	14	25	2	24
938	1	2	36	4	12	25	16	19	5	15
939	1	2	53	3	16	20	25	33	4	20
940	1	2	39	2	16	23	16	35	4	37
941	1	3	52	2	14	24	12	26	3	19
942	2	1	36	3	14	15	7	16	1	5
943	1	2	51	4	12	34	15	24	3	20
944	1	3	27	2	16	19	3	31	1	10
945	1	3	26	5	16	5	2	27	1	5
946	1	1	19	4	12	14	1	11	1	6
947	1	1	27	3	14	34	5	30	1	9
948	1	3	49	2	16	16	17	40	1	19
949	1	2	54	2	16	17	12	45	3	24
950	2	3	33	2	18	19	4	27	3	21
951	1	1	57	3	12	9	17	30	1	8
952	1	2	47	4	14	33	17	26	4	20
953	1	2	59	5	12	10	29	18	2	19
954	1	2	48	2	16	22	22	37	4	21
955	1	2	60	4	12	23	24	20	2	19
956	1	2	52	3	16	18	21	32	3	30
957	1	2	40	2	16	35	14	35	4	33
958	2	1	32	1	18	15	8	23	1	6
959	1	2	58	2	12	24	30	26	2	20
960	1	2	55	4	14	23	15	21	2	18
961	2	3	33	4	12	13	11	14	2	14
962	1	2	28	1	18	6	4	27	4	17
963	1	2	43	2	12	33	13	25	4	20
964	1	2	45	2	16	7	17	35	3	32
965	1	2	49	3	16	27	12	40	4	34
966	1	2	39	1	16	21	10	28	5	18

| | Variable | | | | | | | | | |
Subject	1	2	3	4	5	6	7	8	9	10
967	1	2	50	4	16	15	21	30	3	21
968	1	2	48	3	12	35	22	24	3	19
969	2	3	39	3	12	8	14	13	4	19
970	2	3	41	4	12	8	13	14	3	15
971	2	1	31	1	18	9	4	21	1	6
972	1	2	44	2	14	12	14	26	4	20
973	2	3	36	2	16	11	5	24	2	30
974	1	2	42	2	12	11	14	25	3	19
975	1	2	40	4	12	23	15	20	4	18
976	1	2	56	2	14	16	16	27	2	20
977	1	2	39	3	12	35	19	26	4	21
978	1	2	53	3	16	29	23	45	3	37
979	2	3	38	1	16	13	6	20	2	8
980	1	2	51	4	16	23	25	33	3	24
981	1	3	47	3	16	14	17	33	1	24
982	1	1	48	2	16	22	19	37	1	25
983	1	2	49	2	12	28	20	28	3	20
984	2	3	40	2	16	20	14	22	2	18
985	1	2	54	4	16	7	24	21	3	19
986	1	2	57	3	14	33	28	30	2	22
987	2	3	35	3	14	10	7	18	1	7
988	1	2	56	3	12	25	32	26	2	19
989	1	2	55	4	16	5	24	24	2	18
990	1	2	40	3	16	23	16	32	4	23
991	1	2	53	2	16	7	20	29	3	21
992	2	3	39	4	12	8	9	13	1	6
993	2	1	22	1	16	9	1	20	1	6
994	1	2	52	2	12	20	24	21	3	20
995	2	3	24	5	12	19	1	12	2	6
996	1	2	51	2	14	5	20	20	3	19
997	1	2	50	3	12	35	19	27	3	22
998	1	3	19	5	12	15	1	10	1	4
999	1	1	28	3	16	11	1	36	1	10
1000	2	3	32	4	12	9	3	13	2	6

Appendix III
Ranking the *Forbes* 500s (Data on 785 Different Companies)

Listed below are data on the 785 American firms that were included in at least one of the *Forbes* 500s 1994 lists—Sales, Net Profits, Assets, Market Value, Jobs, and Productivity. Each firm is one of the nation's top 500 firms in at least one of the six categories.

Company	Sales ($mil)	Net Profits ($mil)	Assets ($mil)	Market Value ($mil)	Cash Flow ($mil)	Number Employees (thou)
1. Abbott Laboratories	8,408	1,399.1	7,689	23,160	1,883.2	48.9
2. Advanced Micro Devices	1,648	228.8	1,929	2,750	403.8	11.8
3. Aetna Life & Casualty	17,118	−588.3	100,037	6,452	−388.9	42.8
4. Aflac	5,001	243.9	15,443	3,259	243.9	3.8
5. HF Ahmanson	3,100	−138.0	50,871	2,089	−21.6	10.4
6. Air Products & Chemicals	3,342	207.0	4,752	6,027	551.8	14.3
7. Albertson's	11,284	339.7	3,295	7,353	536.1	73.1
8. Alco Standard	6,916	6.0	3,437	2,992	88.9	26.0
9. Alex Brown	628	89.2	1,283	443	96.2	2.0
10. Alleghany	1,908	97.6	6,285	981	139.8	10.5
11. Allegheny Power System	2,332	215.8	5,949	2,839	426.2	6.0
12. Allergan	859	108.9	940	1,472	155.7	5.0
13. AlliedSignal	11,827	656.0	10,829	10,928	1,203.0	87.9
14. Allmerica Property & Casualty	1,953	252.4	5,198	1,128	252.4	5.3
15. Alltel	2,342	262.0	4,270	5,108	534.5	13.9
16. Aluminum Co of America	9,056	4.8	11,597	6,849	715.9	63.4
17. ALZA	214	42.9	622	1,908	55.1	1.1
18. Ambac	328	179.4	3,807	1,399	185.1	0.5
19. Amerada Hess	5,852	−297.7	8,642	4,556	682.7	10.2
20. American Brands	8,288	668.2	16,339	6,355	977.1	46.3
21. American Cyanamid	4,277	−163.7	6,057	4,043	55.1	26.5
22. American Electric Power	5,269	353.8	15,341	5,928	909.2	20.4
23. American Express	14,173	1,605.0	94,132	14,756	2,016.0	63.6
24. American General	4,829	250.0	43,982	6,114	250.0	11.6
25. American Greetings	1,740	125.4	1,682	2,150	180.4	21.4

Source: Excerpted by permission of Forbes magazine, April 25, 1994, © Forbes Inc., 1994.

Company	Sales ($mil)	Net Profits ($mil)	Assets ($mil)	Market Value ($mil)	Cash Flow ($mil)	Number Employees (thou)
26. American Home Products	8,305	1,469.3	7,687	18,275	1,710.4	51.0
27. American International Group	20,135	1,918.1	101,015	26,921	2,390.3	32.5
28. American Medical Holding	2,255	72.9	2,829	1,773	222.5	27.9
29. American National Insurance	1,329	185.5	5,451	1,377	203.0	5.0
30. American Power Conversion	250	48.6	159	2,612	51.5	0.9
31. American Premier Underwrts[1]	1,763	232.0	4,050	1,234	264.8	5.2
32. American President Cos Ltd	2,594	80.1	1,464	812	189.2	5.3
33. American Re	1,444	110.7	6,231	1,300	122.4	1.2
34. American Savings of Fla FSB	191	30.5	3,117	219	41.4	0.7
35. American Stores	18,763	262.1	6,927	3,722	646.4	130.0
36. American Tel & Tel	67,156	3,974.0	60,766	72,882	7,600.0	310.7
37. Ameritech	11,710	1,512.8	23,428	22,481	3,674.9	69.2
38. Ames Department Stores	2,309	NA	730	101	0.1	23.0
39. Amgen	1,374	374.6	1,766	5,150	425.3	2.7
40. Amoco	25,336	1,820.0	28,486	27,302	4,013.0	46.7
41. AMP	3,451	296.7	3,118	6,715	578.9	26.0
42. AMR	15,816	−96.0	19,326	4,681	1,127.0	111.1
43. AmSouth Bancorporation	971	146.2	12,548	1,565	182.8	5.4
44. Anadarko Petroleum	476	40.0	2,023	2,803	207.7	1.0
45. Anchor Bancorp	531	53.1	8,346	327	64.5	1.4
46. Anheuser-Busch Cos	11,505	594.5	10,880	13,719	1,202.8	44.1
47. Aon	3,845	323.8	16,279	3,444	465.9	23.5
48. Apple Computer	8,446	−34.7	5,042	4,265	134.6	14.9
49. Applied Materials	1,205	122.4	1,142	4,135	164.2	4.3
50. Archer Daniels Midland	10,315	468.7	8,662	8,170	825.7	13.8
51. Argonaut Group	439	89.1	2,183	770	97.5	0.7
52. Arkla	2,950	39.9	3,738	918	190.9	7.2
53. Armstrong World Industries	2,525	63.5	1,929	2,054	193.5	21.7
54. Arrow Electronics	2,536	81.6	1,191	1,294	101.5	3.2
55. Arvin Industries	1,939	40.3	1,246	683	110.3	15.9
56. Asarco	1,736	−70.7	3,152	1,126	10.0	8.7
57. Ashland Oil	9,528	175.9	5,470	2,636	479.0	32.8
58. AST Research	1,971	−49.8	1,011	756	−35.1	5.1
59. Atlantic Energy	866	95.3	2,488	1,107	163.2	1.9
60. Atlantic Richfield	17,189	269.0	23,894	16,155	2,406.0	26.0
61. Automatic Data Processing	2,339	310.8	2,517	7,767	457.2	20.8
62. AutoZone	1,287	91.8	741	4,318	116.8	14.5
63. Avery Dennison	2,609	83.3	1,639	1,672	178.7	16.2
64. Avnet	2,906	70.4	1,673	1,785	96.1	6.6
65. Avon Products	4,008	239.6	1,958	4,110	302.4	29.8
66. Baker Hughes	2,642	71.5	3,273	2,826	259.4	19.0
67. Ball Corp	2,441	−32.5	1,796	755	83.8	13.3
68. Baltimore Gas & Electric	2,669	309.9	7,987	3,368	623.9	9.2
69. Banc One	7,227	1,120.6	79,919	13,229	1,383.3	44.0
70. Bancorp Hawaii	938	132.6	12,462	1,314	158.2	4.4
71. Bank of Boston	7,396	274.8	40,588	2,579	450.1	19.1
72. Bank of New York	3,822	559.0	45,546	4,998	746.0	14.9

NA: Not available.   [1]Formerly Penn Central.

Company	Sales ($mil)	Net Profits ($mil)	Assets ($mil)	Market Value ($mil)	Cash Flow ($mil)	Number Employees (thou)
73. Bank South	435	70.9	5,530	873	85.0	2.7
74. BankAmerica	15,900	1,954.0	186,933	15,170	2,836.0	81.2
75. Bankers Trust New York	7,800	1,070.0	92,082	6,045	1,177.0	13.6
76. BanPonce	897	103.2	11,517	1,048	146.7	7.2
77. Barnett Banks	3,130	421.0	38,331	4,444	558.4	19.7
78. Bausch & Lomb	1,872	156.5	2,512	2,905	241.1	15.2
79. Baxter International	8,879	−268.0	10,773	6,567	226.0	60.9
80. BayBanks	789	67.7	10,111	1,059	91.9	5.5
81. BB&T Financial	671	98.2	9,173	955	121.9	4.1
82. Bear Stearns Cos	3,396	474.3	67,384	2,439	517.4	6.3
83. Becton Dickinson	2,459	215.2	2,995	2,924	409.3	19.1
84. Bell Atlantic	12,990	1,481.6	29,544	22,785	4,026.7	72.5
85. BellSouth	15,880	1,034.1	32,873	27,410	4,137.9	96.1
86. Beneficial Corp	1,958	186.0	12,896	2,024	234.2	8.1
87. Bergen Brunswig	7,058	27.0	2,013	670	56.7	4.2
88. Berkshire Hathaway	3,653	759.1	19,520	19,555	799.6	22.0
89. Best Buy	2,427	31.1	1,169	1,356	51.0	14.0
90. Bethlehem Steel	4,323	−266.3	5,877	1,965	11.2	20.7
91. Beverly Enterprises	2,871	60.3	1,994	1,265	146.4	91.0
92. BHC Communications	412	224.3	2,242	1,971	347.5	1.2
93. Bindley Western Industries	3,426	9.6	735	150	15.2	0.7
94. Black & Decker	4,882	95.2	5,311	1,793	295.7	30.1
95. H&R Block	1,278	189.4	1,132	4,890	251.0	4.1
96. Blockbuster Entertainment	2,227	243.6	3,531	6,463	639.8	34.5
97. BMC Software	274	81.2	398	1,800	90.8	0.8
98. Boatmen's Bancshares	2,107	317.4	26,654	3,033	406.3	13.9
99. Boeing	25,438	1,244.0	20,450	15,991	2,269.0	134.4
100. Boise Cascade	3,958	−77.1	4,513	979	190.6	17.3
101. Borden	5,506	−575.6	3,924	2,086	−351.6	39.5
102. Boston Edison	1,482	118.2	3,477	1,249	279.5	4.5
103. Bradlees	1,881	13.5	958	169	60.5	15.1
104. Briggs & Stratton	1,190	84.0	714	1,269	131.9	7.9
105. Brinker International	740	56.9	485	2,295	99.5	26.4
106. Bristol-Myers Squibb	11,413	1,959.0	12,101	25,579	2,267.0	51.1
107. Brown-Forman	1,409	163.3	1,275	1,955	209.1	6.7
108. Browning-Ferris Industries	3,581	204.1	4,382	5,206	579.0	30.5
109. Bruno's	2,893	36.2	939	644	87.5	17.5
110. Brunswick	2,207	42.3	1,984	2,254	160.1	17.5
111. Burlington Industries	2,071	88.7	1,837	1,082	172.2	23.5
112. Burlington Northern	4,699	296.0	7,045	5,845	648.0	30.5
113. Burlington Resources	1,249	256.3	4,448	6,014	541.6	1.7
114. Cabletron Systems	553	110.1	441	3,671	126.5	2.9
115. Caesars World	1,013	92.5	983	1,315	147.4	10.1
116. Caldor	2,414	41.4	1,006	515	80.0	12.5
117. California Federal Bank	1,084	−145.5	15,326	259	−112.4	3.2
118. Campbell Soup	6,759	595.3	5,025	10,173	849.8	46.9
119. Capital Cities/ABC	5,674	467.4	5,793	10,840	623.8	19.3

Company	Sales ($mil)	Net Profits ($mil)	Assets ($mil)	Market Value ($mil)	Cash Flow ($mil)	Number Employees (thou)
120. **Capital Holding**	2,884	322.7	22,900	3,370	322.7	9.3
121. **Cardinal Health[2]**	2,304	38.5	841	1,154	46.7	1.5
122. **Carolina Power & Light**	2,895	346.5	8,194	4,340	806.6	8.1
123. **Carter Hawley Hale Stores**	2,093	−95.9	1,934	585	−95.9	17.5
124. **Caterpillar**	11,615	681.0	14,807	12,134	1,349.0	51.0
125. **CBS**	3,510	326.2	3,419	4,860	397.2	6.5
126. **CCB Financial**	230	29.2	3,258	335	29.2	1.5
127. **CCP Insurance**	633	107.6	5,298	730	107.6	0.0
128. **Centerior Energy**	2,474	−942.6	10,710	1,691	−599.4	7.6
129. **Centex**	2,996	78.7	2,630	1,131	97.6	6.5
130. **Central & South West**	3,687	262.0	10,623	4,828	628.0	8.7
131. **Central Fidelity Banks**	740	102.9	9,662	1,151	102.9	3.4
132. **Centura Banks**	304	41.1	4,139	411	48.7	1.8
133. **Champion International**	5,069	−134.5	9,143	2,802	309.0	26.3
134. **Charter One Financial**	385	61.4	5,215	432	65.6	1.3
135. **Chase Manhattan**	11,417	466.0	102,103	5,943	727.0	34.5
136. **Chemical Banking**	12,427	1,569.0	149,888	9,719	1,569.0	40.6
137. **Chevron**	32,123	1,265.0	34,736	30,219	3,717.0	48.4
138. **Chiquita Brands International**	2,533	−51.1	2,822	923	−51.1	45.0
139. **Chiron**	318	18.4	969	2,324	43.4	2.0
140. **Chrysler**	43,600	2,415.0	43,830	20,531	4,055.0	115.9
141. **Chubb**	5,500	344.2	19,437	6,491	386.4	10.3
142. **Cigna**	18,402	234.0	84,975	4,530	234.0	51.4
143. **Cincinnati Financial**	1,442	202.2	4,602	2,830	212.6	2.0
144. **Cincinnati Gas & Electric**	1,752	−8.7	5,144	2,136	143.3	5.0
145. **Cipsco**	845	85.5	1,758	976	163.6	2.7
146. **Circuit City Stores**	3,822	125.4	1,833	1,993	176.6	21.8
147. **Circus Circus Enterprises**	955	116.2	1,298	3,272	175.2	16.0
148. **Cisco Systems**	928	241.0	802	10,083	262.8	1.5
149. **Citadel Holding**	304	−67.2	4,390	34	−44.1	0.9
150. **Citicorp**	32,196	1,919.0	216,574	15,170	2,542.0	81.3
151. **Citizens Bancorp**	242	26.8	3,271	430	33.4	1.7
152. **Citizens Utilities**	619	125.6	2,627	2,902	180.3	2.3
153. **City National**	214	−6.9	3,101	372	−2.4	1.5
154. **Clorox**	1,644	204.2	1,587	2,795	286.9	5.3
155. **CMS Energy**	3,482	155.0	6,964	1,853	586.0	10.1
156. **Coast Savings Financial**	576	17.2	8,095	258	28.6	1.8
157. **Coastal Corp**	10,136	118.3	10,227	3,464	477.1	16.3
158. **Coca-Cola**	13,957	2,188.0	12,021	54,248	2,548.0	32.7
159. **Coca-Cola Enterprises**	5,465	−15.0	8,682	2,395	404.0	25.8
160. **Colgate-Palmolive**	7,141	548.1	5,761	9,329	757.7	28.0
161. **Collective Bancorp**	250	57.1	4,022	358	60.8	0.8
162. **Columbia Gas System**	3,391	152.2	6,958	1,491	392.0	10.2
163. **Columbia/HCA Healthcare[3]**	10,252	591.0	10,216	14,814	1,145.0	130.0
164. **Comcast**	1,338	−98.9	4,948	4,947	242.6	5.4
165. **Comdisco**	2,118	70.0	4,929	857	1,016.0	2.0
166. **Comerica**	2,245	340.6	30,295	3,130	340.6	13.0

[2]Formerly Cardinal Distribution.   [3]Formerly Columbia Healthcare.

Company	Sales ($mil)	Net Profits ($mil)	Assets ($mil)	Market Value ($mil)	Cash Flow ($mil)	Number Employees (thou)
167. Commerce Bancshares	582	86.9	8,047	1,035	111.7	4.3
168. Commercial Federal	393	35.0	5,290	251	50.6	1.0
169. Commonwealth Edison	5,260	102.7	23,963	5,771	1,013.8	19.5
170. Compaq Computer	7,191	462.2	4,084	8,730	618.2	10.1
171. Compass Bancshares[4]	625	89.3	7,252	857	115.5	3.6
172. Computer Associates Internatl	2,055	341.6	2,361	6,368	559.5	7.3
173. Computer Sciences	2,502	84.2	1,581	1,987	211.2	26.0
174. ConAgra	23,002	408.4	11,974	7,007	771.1	84.0
175. Conner Peripherals	2,152	−445.3	1,464	954	−340.6	10.9
176. Conrail[5]	3,453	234.0	7,948	4,755	518.0	25.4
177. Conseco	2,637	308.9	13,749	1,509	308.9	2.9
178. Consolidated Edison	6,265	658.5	13,483	7,090	1,062.3	18.2
179. Consolidated Freightways	4,192	50.6	2,307	964	196.9	38.5
180. Consolidated Natural Gas	3,184	188.5	5,410	4,031	483.1	7.6
181. Consolidated Papers	947	64.2	1,467	1,839	167.0	4.9
182. Continental Airlines	5,775	NA	5,107	510	NA	43.3
183. Continental Bank	1,761	258.0	22,601	1,717	274.0	4.2
184. Continental Corp	5,174	208.4	16,221	1,307	247.2	13.1
185. Cooper Industries	6,274	367.1	7,148	4,482	669.9	51.2
186. Cooper Tire & Rubber	1,194	102.2	890	2,288	148.6	7.4
187. CoreStates Financial	2,014	327.9	23,666	3,173	388.3	13.7
188. Corning	4,005	−15.2	5,232	6,782	265.2	35.2
189. Countrywide Credit Industries	1,078	171.4	5,537	1,502	184.7	4.0
190. CPC International	6,738	454.5	5,061	7,191	720.3	38.5
191. Crestar Financial	1,081	140.5	13,287	1,679	180.1	6.1
192. Crown Cork & Seal	4,163	180.9	4,244	3,632	362.2	20.4
193. CSF Holdings	342	58.2	4,437	189	62.4	0.8
194. CSX	8,940	359.0	13,420	9,169	931.0	47.1
195. CUC International	843	80.0	553	3,548	105.8	6.0
196. Cullen/Frost Bankers	266	38.8	3,639	391	55.6	1.8
197. Cummins Engine	4,248	182.6	2,391	1,992	307.7	23.5
198. Cyprus Amax Minerals[6]	1,764	100.2	5,625	3,021	245.0	7.5
199. Dana	5,588	128.5	4,632	2,847	324.2	35.5
200. Dauphin Deposit	360	64.5	4,596	781	71.4	1.9
201. Dayton Hudson	19,233	375.0	10,778	5,373	873.0	172.0
202. Dean Foods	2,352	66.3	1,112	1,312	120.3	10.5
203. Dean Witter Discover & Co	5,822	603.6	27,662	6,099	654.9	26.0
204. Deere & Co	8,057	308.3	11,780	7,722	565.6	34.0
205. Dell Computer	2,873	−35.8	1,140	1,029	−8.2	5.3
206. Delmarva Power & Light	971	111.1	2,594	1,280	224.0	2.8
207. Delta Air Lines	12,295	−225.9	11,600	2,454	467.1	73.5
208. Deluxe	1,582	141.9	1,252	2,549	214.2	17.6
209. Deposit Guaranty	374	66.6	4,898	490	90.6	2.5
210. Detroit Edison	3,555	521.9	11,135	4,081	954.4	9.0
211. Dial	3,000	142.4	3,294	1,847	242.6	25.0
212. Diamond Shamrock	2,555	32.6	1,349	845	96.9	6.0
213. Digital Equipment	13,637	−92.3	10,369	4,533	694.4	104.0

NA: Not available.   [4]Formerly Central Bancshares of the South.   [5]Formerly Consolidated Rail.   [6]Formerly Cyprus Minerals.

Company	Sales ($mil)	Net Profits ($mil)	Assets ($mil)	Market Value ($mil)	Cash Flow ($mil)	Number Employees (thou)
214. Dillard Dept Stores	5,131	241.1	4,430	3,884	412.3	35.5
215. Dime Savings Bank of NY FSB	576	44.6	9,276	502	104.3	2.0
216. Walt Disney	8,865	779.5	12,600	25,238	1,930.9	60.0
217. Dole Food	3,431	77.9	3,388	2,103	210.5	45.0
218. Dominion Resources	4,434	516.6	13,350	6,898	1,110.5	12.1
219. RR Donnelley & Sons	4,388	178.9	3,654	4,760	453.7	32.0
220. Dover	2,484	158.3	1,774	3,801	235.2	19.6
221. Dow Chemical	18,060	644.0	25,505	17,910	2,196.0	58.4
222. Dow Jones	1,932	147.5	2,350	4,109	336.2	9.9
223. Downey Savings & Loan Assn	238	28.6	3,467	293	31.9	0.9
224. DPL	1,151	139.0	3,305	2,109	249.9	3.2
225. DQE	1,196	141.4	4,574	1,696	314.3	4.1
226. Dr Pepper/Seven-Up	707	94.1	680	1,600	673.8	0.9
227. Dresser Industries	4,650	300.6	4,229	4,360	476.2	26.7
228. Dreyfus	386	99.4	915	1,791	109.2	2.0
229. DSC Communications	731	81.7	900	3,033	143.5	3.7
230. EI du Pont de Nemours	32,621	566.0	37,053	39,873	3,399.0	119.5
231. Duke Power	4,282	626.4	12,193	7,733	1,283.5	17.7
232. Dun & Bradstreet	4,710	428.7	5,170	10,320	802.4	51.4
233. Duracell International	1,788	132.2	2,157	4,898	216.2	7.9
234. E-Systems	2,097	121.9	1,279	1,544	176.7	17.6
235. Eastman Chemical	3,903	247.0	4,341	3,314	593.0	18.3
236. Eastman Kodak	16,364	475.0	20,324	14,917	1,586.0	112.3
237. Eaton	4,401	180.0	3,268	4,253	376.0	38.3
238. Echlin	2,037	104.0	1,384	1,873	163.6	18.6
239. Eckerd	4,191	41.4	1,418	716	133.7	32.4
240. AG Edwards	1,262	151.2	1,914	1,237	173.7	9.7
241. EG&G	2,698	79.6	769	1,012	117.4	34.0
242. El Paso Natural Gas	909	91.7	2,270	1,447	145.7	2.5
243. EMC	783	127.1	830	4,215	148.9	1.8
244. Emerson Electric	8,200	838.7	7,778	14,084	1,177.0	71.6
245. Engelhard	2,151	16.7	1,279	2,978	84.8	6.0
246. Enron	10,097	332.5	11,504	8,266	879.9	7.4
247. Enserch	1,902	59.2	2,760	1,008	204.0	5.6
248. Entergy	4,485	458.1	22,780	7,457	901.6	14.6
249. Equifax	1,217	63.5	731	2,016	118.4	12.6
250. Equitable Cos	6,480	234.5	98,991	3,417	420.8	12.0
251. Equitable of Iowa Cos	573	87.2	6,431	1,095	87.7	0.4
252. Ethyl	1,938	90.0	2,009	1,450	217.5	5.5
253. Exxon	97,825	5,280.0	84,145	81,817	10,164.0	93.0
254. Farm & Home Financial	252	15.1	3,742	191	17.4	0.7
255. Federal Express	8,253	179.5	5,959	3,974	766.8	84.1
256. Federal Home Loan Mortgage	5,584	786.0	83,880	10,426	786.0	2.8
257. Federal National Mortge Assn	16,054	2,042.5	216,979	22,565	2,042.5	3.2
258. Federated Department Stores	7,229	196.8	7,419	3,016	426.6	70.2
259. FHP International	2,265	53.1	1,007	891	89.7	11.3
260. Fifth Third Bancorp	954	196.4	11,966	2,920	209.8	4.8

Company	Sales ($mil)	Net Profits ($mil)	Assets ($mil)	Market Value ($mil)	Cash Flow ($mil)	Number Employees (thou)
261. Fina	3,416	70.4	2,511	1,115	280.4	3.3
262. First Alabama Bancshares	688	112.0	10,476	1,365	129.5	5.1
263. First American Corp	517	101.9	7,188	776	118.3	3.1
264. First Bancorporation of Ohio	332	55.2	3,997	656	65.0	2.6
265. First Bank System	2,231	298.0	26,385	3,500	387.0	12.3
266. First Chicago	4,827	804.5	52,560	4,297	992.5	17.2
267. First Citizens BancShares	451	55.6	6,101	416	71.8	3.7
268. First Colony	1,560	203.9	8,335	1,208	277.4	0.9
269. First Commerce	496	95.2	6,660	673	109.2	3.2
270. First Commercial	237	37.5	3,401	367	47.9	1.8
271. First Data	1,490	173.0	4,148	5,144	290.9	19.4
272. First Empire State	851	102.0	10,365	954	118.2	4.3
273. First Fidelity Bancorp	2,429	396.5	33,763	3,635	449.8	11.3
274. First Financial Corp	378	45.2	4,775	354	57.2	1.6
275. First Financial Management	1,670	127.6	1,626	3,462	203.6	12.1
276. First Hawaiian	512	78.2	7,266	882	99.0	3.0
277. First Interstate Bancorp	3,898	561.4	51,461	5,693	685.8	26.8
278. First National of Nebraska	546	70.1	4,272	625	85.4	2.9
279. First of America Bank	1,803	247.4	21,230	2,292	296.1	13.1
280. First Security	812	114.1	10,212	1,398	138.8	6.1
281. First Tennessee National	857	120.7	9,609	1,097	151.0	5.0
282. First Union	5,755	817.5	70,787	7,113	1,176.9	28.2
283. First USA	581	64.1	4,574	1,983	131.9	1.4
284. First Virginia Banks	587	116.0	7,037	1,237	132.5	4.7
285. Firstar	1,209	204.3	13,794	2,140	251.4	8.4
286. FirstFed Financial	241	−2.0	3,661	141	−0.3	0.5
287. FirstFed Michigan	735	41.4	9,264	457	48.8	1.2
288. FirsTier Financial	256	47.9	3,052	542	56.6	1.5
289. Flagstar Cos[7]	3,970	−1,681.5	1,821	519	−1,434.5	118.0
290. Fleet Financial Group	4,678	488.0	47,923	5,124	846.6	26.8
291. Fleetwood Enterprises	2,207	60.0	1,124	1,085	79.5	13.0
292. Fleming Cos	13,092	37.5	3,103	933	138.6	23.1
293. Florida Progress	2,449	195.8	5,639	2,700	495.7	7.6
294. Fluor	8,101	175.1	2,640	4,233	285.5	41.1
295. FMC	3,754	41.0	2,813	1,744	267.6	21.4
296. Food Lion	7,610	3.9	2,504	2,993	146.9	45.3
297. Ford Motor	108,521	2,529.0	198,938	30,699	9,997.0	322.2
298. Forest Laboratories	333	75.7	594	2,258	86.3	1.2
299. Foster Wheeler	2,583	57.7	1,806	1,575	109.2	9.7
300. Fourth Financial	523	65.2	6,743	715	89.6	3.1
301. FPL Group	5,316	428.7	13,078	6,605	1,027.1	13.5
302. Franklin Resources	712	199.8	1,628	4,051	229.3	2.9
303. Freeport-McMoRan	1,611	−96.9	3,714	2,834	126.2	7.2
304. Fruit of the Loom	1,884	212.8	2,734	2,281	334.4	33.1
305. Fund American Enterprises	251	70.4	3,305	647	70.4	1.8
306. Gannett	3,642	397.8	3,824	8,222	607.4	36.6
307. Gap	3,296	258.4	1,763	6,554	400.2	41.5

[7]Formerly TW Holdings.

Company	Sales ($mil)	Net Profits ($mil)	Assets ($mil)	Market Value ($mil)	Cash Flow ($mil)	Number Employees (thou)
308. Gateway 2000	1,732	100.1	564	1,393	105.9	3.4
309. GATX	1,087	72.7	3,392	871	223.4	5.3
310. Gaylord Entertainment	623	36.1	916	2,400	125.3	5.9
311. Geico	2,638	286.4	4,831	3,790	305.8	7.8
312. GenCorp	1,905	43.0	1,164	472	129.0	13.6
313. Genentech	608	58.9	1,469	5,425	103.6	2.4
314. General Dynamics	3,187	885.0	2,580	2,854	944.0	24.8
315. General Electric	60,562	5,177.0	251,506	89,226	6,808.0	226.5
316. General Instrument	1,393	90.4	1,776	2,924	187.8	9.7
317. General Mills	8,381	518.8	4,996	9,001	807.5	121.3
318. General Motors	138,220	2,465.8	188,034	55,376	11,998.3	710.8
319. General Public Utilities	3,596	295.7	8,869	3,377	721.0	12.0
320. General Re	3,560	696.8	18,469	8,938	696.8	2.4
321. Genuine Parts	4,384	258.9	1,871	4,604	293.3	19.5
322. Georgia-Pacific	12,330	−18.0	10,545	6,150	812.0	51.0
323. Gerber Products	1,177	131.0	970	2,185	168.4	9.3
324. Giant Food	3,567	95.0	1,340	1,536	189.8	23.7
325. Gillette	5,411	426.9	5,102	14,582	645.4	32.2
326. Glendale Federal Bank FSB[8]	1,044	NA	17,951	234	0.1	3.7
327. Golden West Financial	1,932	273.9	28,829	2,509	287.8	3.8
328. BF Goodrich	1,818	128.3	2,360	1,116	227.8	13.4
329. Goodyear Tire & Rubber	11,643	488.7	8,436	6,811	881.6	91.8
330. GP Financial	561	95.9	7,377	1,036	102.6	1.3
331. WR Grace	4,408	26.0	6,107	4,059	253.7	42.5
332. WW Grainger	2,628	149.3	1,377	3,383	207.4	9.1
333. Great Atlantic & Pacific Tea	10,384	4.0	3,171	1,013	237.8	90.0
334. Great Lakes Chemical	1,792	272.8	1,901	5,462	362.8	7.0
335. Great Western Financial	2,883	62.0	38,348	2,371	178.5	16.5
336. Grumman	3,225	58.8	2,024	2,197	132.6	19.5
337. GTE	19,748	990.0	41,575	30,450	4,409.0	123.0
338. Halliburton	6,351	−161.0	5,403	3,765	291.0	67.0
339. Hannaford Bros	2,055	54.6	795	1,067	111.0	14.6
340. Harcourt General	3,681	158.6	6,112	2,832	327.4	20.1
341. Harley-Davidson	1,217	18.4	583	1,890	51.7	5.9
342. Harris Corp	3,179	119.6	2,556	2,035	277.0	28.3
343. Hasbro	2,747	200.0	2,293	3,166	300.7	11.8
344. Hawaiian Electric Industries	1,142	48.7	4,522	930	110.4	3.3
345. HealthTrust	2,425	140.7	2,489	2,516	274.9	26.7
346. Hechinger	2,095	24.8	1,277	569	67.5	12.8
347. HJ Heinz	7,135	543.5	6,540	8,402	793.5	37.7
348. Hercules	2,773	208.4	3,162	4,752	377.7	14.8
349. Hershey Foods	3,488	297.2	2,855	4,315	410.3	14.5
350. Hewlett-Packard	21,426	1,284.0	17,201	22,606	2,170.0	94.4
351. Hibernia	367	48.0	4,796	638	66.7	2.5
352. Hillenbrand Industries	1,448	145.8	2,271	2,995	258.6	10.3
353. Hilton Hotels	1,358	102.7	2,675	3,354	221.6	42.0
354. Home Depot	9,239	457.4	4,701	18,929	547.2	44.8

NA: Not available.   [8]Formerly GlenFed.

Company	Sales ($mil)	Net Profits ($mil)	Assets ($mil)	Market Value ($mil)	Cash Flow ($mil)	Number Employees (thou)
355. Homestake Mining	704	52.5	1,121	2,851	155.9	2.1
356. Honeywell	5,963	322.2	4,598	4,572	607.1	53.9
357. Hook-SupeRx	2,304	−3.3	735	188	31.7	18.4
358. Horace Mann Educators	708	77.2	3,148	724	98.6	2.5
359. Hormel Foods	2,888	103.0	1,093	1,571	136.5	9.6
360. Host Marriott[9]	1,354	−60.0	3,848	1,459	118.0	22.9
361. Household International	4,455	298.7	32,962	3,152	541.8	15.8
362. Houston Industries	4,324	416.0	12,230	4,885	882.9	11.5
363. Hubbell	832	66.3	864	2,111	96.4	5.7
364. Humana	3,137	89.0	1,731	3,447	136.0	8.7
365. Huntington Bancshares	1,542	236.9	17,619	2,362	364.4	7.6
366. IBP	11,671	77.5	1,539	1,151	136.2	28.3
367. ICH	968	287.0	3,896	329	305.5	1.5
368. Idaho Power	540	84.5	2,097	1,034	143.2	1.6
369. Illinois Central	565	91.7	1,259	1,593	115.2	3.3
370. Illinois Power	1,581	−55.8	5,424	1,645	111.5	4.6
371. Illinois Tool Works	3,159	206.6	2,337	5,038	338.3	18.4
372. Ingersoll-Rand	4,021	163.5	3,375	4,112	287.0	35.2
373. Inland Steel Industries	3,888	−37.6	3,436	1,415	94.2	16.2
374. Integra Financial	1,114	152.8	14,097	1,572	185.8	5.2
375. Intel	8,782	2,295.3	11,344	30,096	2,991.9	27.7
376. Intelligent Electronics	2,646	42.9	577	939	52.2	0.7
377. International Business Machin	62,716	−7,987.0	81,113	33,212	−1,326.0	278.9
378. International Flavors & Frags	1,189	202.5	1,225	4,183	237.5	4.3
379. International Game Technol	532	113.9	692	4,078	134.3	2.4
380. International Multifoods	2,200	2.2	829	334	31.2	8.4
381. International Paper	13,685	289.0	16,631	8,703	1,187.0	72.8
382. Interpublic Group of Cos	1,740	125.3	2,870	2,344	186.5	17.2
383. Itel	1,909	14.8	2,494	957	96.8	4.5
384. ITT	22,043	963.0	70,560	10,140	1,539.0	102.0
385. IVAX	645	84.7	658	2,174	102.4	2.5
386. James River Corp of Virginia	4,650	−0.3	5,851	1,490	362.8	28.1
387. Jefferson-Pilot	1,247	219.3	5,641	2,418	223.4	4.4
388. John Alden Financial	1,407	80.0	6,116	953	99.4	2.9
389. Johnson & Johnson	14,138	1,787.0	12,242	25,412	2,404.0	83.3
390. Johnson Controls	6,255	143.3	3,261	2,482	383.4	48.5
391. Kansas City Power & Light	857	105.8	2,755	1,385	205.6	2.8
392. Kansas City Southern Indus	961	97.0	1,917	2,183	194.2	6.8
393. Kellogg	6,295	680.7	4,237	11,111	945.9	16.3
394. Kelly Services	1,955	44.6	542	1,019	61.2	4.2
395. Kemper	1,549	247.4	14,038	2,011	247.4	6.7
396. Kerr-McGee	3,281	77.1	3,547	2,408	398.1	5.8
397. KeyCorp[10]	5,186	709.9	59,655	7,888	966.5	29.5
398. Keystone Financial	256	39.4	3,151	561	45.7	1.7
399. Kimberly-Clark	6,973	510.9	6,381	9,134	806.8	42.5
400. King World Productions	498	102.2	637	1,456	106.2	0.3
401. Kmart	34,557	−912.0	17,504	7,466	−209.0	320.0

[9]Formerly Marriott.   [10]Formerly Society.

Company	Sales ($mil)	Net Profits ($mil)	Assets ($mil)	Market Value ($mil)	Cash Flow ($mil)	Number Employees (thou)
402. Knight-Ridder	2,451	148.1	2,431	3,322	289.8	20.4
403. Kohl's	1,306	55.7	571	2,007	78.9	8.7
404. Kroger	22,384	170.8	4,480	2,717	513.9	190.0
405. LDDS Communications	1,145	104.2	2,533	3,400	184.1	3.1
406. Leggett & Platt	1,527	85.9	902	1,860	131.2	12.2
407. Leucadia National	1,408	116.3	4,689	1,144	246.3	4.5
408. LG&E Energy	900	88.3	2,285	1,248	170.9	3.5
409. Liberty Media	841	−0.3	1,445	3,075	37.5	6.0
410. Liberty National Bancorp	382	51.5	4,916	782	73.0	2.2
411. Eli Lilly	6,452	491.1	9,624	15,481	889.4	32.5
412. Limited	7,245	391.0	4,135	6,978	662.4	60.9
413. Lincoln National	8,290	415.3	48,380	4,015	498.9	11.9
414. Litton Industries	3,492	−21.2	3,951	1,469	81.3	18.2
415. Liz Claiborne	2,204	125.3	1,236	1,784	157.6	8.4
416. Lockheed	13,071	422.0	8,961	4,187	920.0	81.5
417. Loews	12,582	594.1	45,850	5,845	729.2	27.6
418. Long Island Lighting	2,881	296.6	13,456	2,462	520.0	6.4
419. Longs Drug Stores	2,499	49.8	795	776	83.0	15.4
420. Loral	3,562	201.4	3,191	3,323	354.3	24.5
421. Lotus Development	981	55.5	905	3,819	142.5	4.6
422. Louisiana-Pacific	2,511	254.4	2,466	4,425	437.6	12.3
423. Lowe's Cos	4,538	131.8	2,202	4,917	213.9	25.1
424. LTV	4,163	386.9	5,795	1,498	627.2	17.4
425. Lubrizol	1,526	85.0	1,183	2,523	146.6	4.6
426. Lyondell Petrochemical	3,850	4.0	1,231	1,860	63.0	2.3
427. Magna Group	290	37.5	4,128	502	46.5	2.2
428. Mallinckrodt Group[11]	1,850	−102.9	2,248	2,526	−4.8	9.8
429. Manor Care	1,119	73.0	1,111	1,806	138.4	24.1
430. Manpower	3,180	−48.9	833	1,495	47.9	6.7
431. Manville	2,276	60.8	3,600	1,070	217.8	16.0
432. Mapco	2,567	127.0	1,941	1,806	224.3	5.8
433. Marion Merrell Dow	2,818	362.0	3,795	4,568	469.0	9.8
434. Marriott International	8,062	161.0	3,092	4,319	272.0	166.0
435. Marsh & McLennan Cos	3,163	332.4	3,547	6,232	452.3	25.7
436. Marshall & Ilsley	787	125.5	7,970	1,280	159.9	6.5
437. Martin Marietta	9,436	450.3	7,775	4,306	800.3	83.0
438. Marvel Entertainment Group	415	56.0	447	2,397	68.1	0.8
439. Masco	3,886	221.1	4,021	5,300	337.1	44.1
440. Mattel	2,704	135.9	2,000	4,377	227.9	21.0
441. Maxxam	2,031	−131.9	3,572	333	−11.1	12.1
442. May Department Stores	11,529	711.0	8,800	11,177	1,059.0	112.0
443. Maytag	2,987	51.3	2,469	2,001	163.1	21.2
444. MBIA	429	246.1	4,106	2,499	254.1	0.3
445. MBNA	1,393	207.8	7,320	3,230	258.0	6.6
446. McCaw Cellular Commun	2,195	−227.3	9,065	10,770	176.3	9.3
447. McCormick & Co	1,584	100.7	1,313	1,886	151.2	8.6
448. McDonald's	7,408	1,082.5	12,035	21,529	1,650.9	166.5

[11]Formerly Imcera Group.

Company	Sales ($mil)	Net Profits ($mil)	Assets ($mil)	Market Value ($mil)	Cash Flow ($mil)	Number Employees (thou)
449. McDonnell Douglas	14,487	396.0	12,026	4,513	719.0	78.7
450. McGraw-Hill	2,195	11.4	3,084	3,557	94.3	14.5
451. MCI Communications	11,921	627.0	11,276	13,728	1,646.0	33.6
452. McKesson	12,203	150.5	3,203	2,683	230.0	14.0
453. Mead	4,790	124.1	4,165	2,567	440.2	20.0
454. Medtronic	1,356	223.6	1,315	4,674	302.2	9.2
455. Mellon Bank	3,237	361.0	36,139	3,666	565.0	20.2
456. Melville	10,435	331.8	4,272	3,911	523.4	113.4
457. Mercantile Bancorporation	893	117.0	10,513	1,237	141.5	5.3
458. Mercantile Bankshares	455	82.4	5,554	897	89.8	2.7
459. Mercantile Stores	2,730	86.6	2,033	1,409	180.1	23.0
460. Merck	10,498	2,166.2	19,928	39,812	2,552.7	42.8
461. Mercury Finance	194	64.7	854	1,952	65.8	1.0
462. Mercury General	534	96.2	864	822	97.9	1.1
463. Meridian Bancorp	1,247	150.5	14,085	1,737	232.4	6.8
464. Merisel	3,086	30.4	936	641	40.9	2.2
465. Merrill Lynch	16,588	1,394.4	152,910	8,772	1,702.9	41.0
466. Metropolitan Financial	563	65.2	7,007	510	76.4	2.5
467. Fred Meyer	2,979	70.9	1,319	1,065	141.5	24.0
468. MFS Communications	141	−15.8	907	2,135	18.9	0.7
469. MGIC Investment	404	127.3	1,343	1,821	129.3	1.2
470. Michigan National	935	27.8	10,173	971	188.9	5.9
471. Micron Technology	1,231	246.6	1,081	3,564	396.2	4.6
472. Microsoft	4,109	1,036.0	4,486	24,235	1,201.0	14.4
473. Midlantic	1,012	131.4	13,947	1,507	161.6	5.4
474. Minnesota Mining & Mfg	14,020	1,263.0	12,197	22,118	2,339.0	86.6
475. Mirage Resorts	953	48.1	1,705	2,186	142.8	14.5
476. Mobil	56,576	2,084.0	40,585	31,654	4,713.0	62.8
477. Molex	900	82.6	985	2,313	167.2	7.6
478. Monsanto	7,902	494.0	8,640	9,133	1,066.0	31.9
479. Montana Power	1,076	107.2	2,386	1,347	188.1	4.1
480. JP Morgan & Co	11,941	1,723.0	133,888	12,502	1,723.0	14.8
481. Morgan Stanley Group	9,176	786.1	97,725	5,148	786.1	7.8
482. Morrison Knudsen	2,723	35.8	1,226	865	73.8	12.2
483. Morton International	2,537	154.4	2,374	5,369	283.7	11.9
484. Motorola	16,963	1,022.0	13,498	30,180	2,218.0	113.5
485. Multimedia	635	85.5	655	1,127	155.2	3.8
486. Murphy Oil	1,637	86.8	2,169	1,983	275.1	1.8
487. Nalco Chemical	1,389	152.7	1,212	2,429	239.2	6.8
488. Nash Finch	2,724	15.9	522	190	45.0	12.1
489. National City	2,702	404.0	31,068	4,287	522.3	19.4
490. National Health Laboratories	761	112.7	533	1,215	144.9	6.6
491. National Intergroup	5,388	8.6	1,668	217	29.8	4.1
492. National Medical Expenses	3,435	−270.1	3,725	2,861	−85.5	42.4
493. National Semiconductor	2,244	222.9	1,626	2,637	390.0	23.4
494. National Service Industries	1,843	77.3	1,073	1,388	140.3	21.2
495. National Steel	2,419	−242.4	2,304	509	−104.9	9.9

Company	Sales ($mil)	Net Profits ($mil)	Assets ($mil)	Market Value ($mil)	Cash Flow ($mil)	Number Employees (thou)
496. NationsBank	10,392	1,301.4	157,686	13,003	1,653.4	54.1
497. Navistar International	4,797	−258.9	4,661	1,922	−187.0	13.8
498. NBD Bancorp	3,208	481.8	40,776	4,641	587.2	18.7
499. New England Electric System	2,234	190.2	4,796	2,412	490.7	5.2
500. New York State Electric & Gas	1,800	166.0	5,276	1,950	330.6	4.8
501. New York Times	2,020	6.1	3,215	2,993	135.0	11.6
502. Newell Co	1,645	165.3	1,953	3,319	229.6	13.3
503. Newmont Mining	634	94.7	1,186	3,749	204.7	2.4
504. Nextel Communications	62	−36.1	1,471	3,867	7.7	0.7
505. Niagara Mohawk Power	3,933	271.8	9,419	2,017	584.4	11.7
506. Nicor	1,674	111.7	2,222	1,494	208.2	3.5
507. NIKE	3,769	306.5	2,375	4,273	335.3	9.6
508. Nipsco Industries	1,678	156.1	3,912	2,000	343.1	4.6
509. Nordstrom	3,590	140.4	2,177	3,303	243.9	33.0
510. Norfolk Southern	4,460	548.8	10,520	9,388	954.2	29.3
511. Northeast Federal	238	−14.1	3,920	84	−9.3	1.0
512. Northeast Utilities	3,629	198.3	10,668	3,238	619.5	9.9
513. Northern States Power	2,404	211.7	5,588	2,867	541.7	7.4
514. Northern Trust	1,259	167.9	16,903	2,252	207.2	6.3
515. Northrop	5,063	96.0	2,939	2,144	310.0	31.7
516. Northwest Airlines	8,649	−115.3	7,571	754	302.0	43.0
517. Norwest	5,277	653.6	50,782	7,122	848.4	32.0
518. Novell	1,174	−33.2	1,439	7,432	12.4	4.0
519. Nucor	2,254	123.5	1,829	5,641	245.8	5.9
520. NWNL Cos	1,490	82.5	9,913	921	92.7	2.6
521. Nynex	13,408	−272.4	29,320	15,142	2,261.6	79.0
522. Occidental Petroleum	8,116	295.0	17,123	5,398	1,202.0	21.7
523. Office Depot	2,580	63.4	1,464	3,705	93.9	15.5
524. Ogden	2,039	62.1	3,313	1,022	147.8	42.5
525. Ohio Casualty	1,670	87.0	3,817	1,146	100.3	4.6
526. Ohio Edison	2,370	24.5	8,918	2,994	302.4	6.1
527. Oklahoma Gas & Electric	1,447	114.3	2,731	1,452	233.8	3.8
528. Old Kent Financial	807	127.9	9,856	1,246	155.1	4.7
529. Old National Bancorp	284	42.5	3,715	710	81.3	1.8
530. Old Republic International	1,736	166.4	6,098	1,264	166.4	5.8
531. Olin	2,423	−92.0	1,930	934	47.0	13.0
532. Olsten	2,158	−11.9	690	1,398	13.7	9.0
533. Omnicom Group	1,516	85.3	2,290	1,602	138.9	13.5
534. OnBancorp	374	58.0	5,770	448	64.5	1.5
535. Oracle Systems	1,693	197.8	1,229	10,079	284.8	9.2
536. Oryx Energy	1,080	−93.0	3,624	1,721	302.0	1.6
537. Owens-Corning Fiberglas	2,944	105.0	3,013	1,728	210.0	16.0
538. Owens-Illinois	3,535	17.6	4,901	1,472	248.4	31.2
539. Paccar	3,542	142.2	3,291	2,186	198.9	11.4
540. Pacific Enterprises	2,899	181.0	5,596	1,852	424.0	9.5
541. Pacific Gas & Electric	10,582	1,065.5	27,163	13,030	2,516.8	24.8
542. Pacific Telesis Group	9,244	191.0	20,563	23,374	1,927.0	56.2
543. PacifiCare Health Systems	2,382	66.7	891	1,486	83.8	2.4
544. PacifiCorp	3,412	475.1	11,959	5,164	943.4	13.1
545. PaineWebber Group	4,005	246.2	37,027	1,464	277.2	14.0

Company	Sales ($mil)	Net Profits ($mil)	Assets ($mil)	Market Value ($mil)	Cash Flow ($mil)	Number Employees (thou)
546. Pall	683	97.2	914	1,973	132.4	6.3
547. Panhandle Eastern	2,121	148.1	6,731	2,643	375.3	5.0
548. Parametric Technology	184	49.3	204	1,840	53.0	0.7
549. Paramount Communications	4,711	171.4	7,417	5,587	1,435.1	12.9
550. Parker Hannifin	2,492	64.5	1,818	1,863	176.9	25.6
551. Payless Cashways	2,650	30.2	1,495	731	87.1	17.9
552. PECO Energy[12]	3,988	590.6	15,032	6,147	1,156.1	9.6
553. Penn Traffic	3,172	8.2	1,625	443	91.0	24.6
554. JC Penney	19,578	944.0	14,788	13,309	1,260.0	192.5
555. Pennsylvania Power & Light	2,727	348.1	9,454	3,575	716.6	7.9
556. Pennzoil	2,477	160.2	4,886	2,508	491.2	9.5
557. People's Bank	497	41.3	6,400	343	57.6	2.4
558. PepsiCo	25,021	1,587.9	23,706	30,055	3,032.1	397.5
559. Perrigo	634	52.4	455	1,840	69.9	3.6
560. Pet	1,564	−100.4	1,161	1,844	−59.4	5.9
561. Pfizer	7,478	657.5	9,331	18,293	915.7	40.6
562. Phelps Dodge	2,596	187.9	3,721	4,197	375.0	14.7
563. PHH	2,116	63.0	4,763	641	880.1	4.8
564. Philip Morris Cos	50,621	3,568.0	51,205	48,248	5,187.0	167.0
565. Phillips Petroleum	12,309	245.0	10,868	7,583	1,208.0	20.4
566. Pinnacle West Capital	1,719	170.0	6,957	1,836	428.6	7.9
567. Pioneer Hi-Bred International	1,342	132.4	1,350	3,217	199.9	4.9
568. Pitney Bowes	3,543	353.2	6,794	7,157	616.2	30.7
569. PNC Bank	4,146	745.3	62,080	6,488	837.1	19.4
570. Polaroid	2,245	67.9	2,212	1,592	168.2	12.2
571. Portland General	947	89.1	3,449	963	181.5	2.9
572. Potomac Electric Power	1,702	241.6	6,665	2,756	405.2	5.0
573. PPG Industries	5,754	295.0	5,652	8,481	645.2	31.4
574. Praxair	2,438	143.0	3,255	2,538	405.0	17.7
575. Premark International	3,097	172.5	2,120	2,536	284.4	24.1
576. Premier Bancorp	336	67.6	4,216	467	86.4	2.7
577. Premier Industrial	713	91.3	484	2,180	99.2	4.4
578. Price/Costco	15,681	145.9	4,317	4,376	262.4	43.0
579. Procter & Gamble	30,067	571.0	25,543	38,675	1,706.0	104.8
580. Progressive	1,955	267.3	4,011	2,237	283.4	5.8
581. Promus Cos	1,252	91.8	1,793	4,793	189.9	24.2
582. Protective Life	760	56.6	5,316	580	56.6	1.0
583. Provident Bancorp	325	51.3	4,698	472	61.0	1.6
584. Provident Life & Accident	2,938	−81.2	16,892	1,251	−38.3	5.3
585. PSI Resources	1,088	96.4	2,664	1,334	223.3	4.3
586. Public Service Co of Colorado	1,999	157.4	4,058	1,863	301.3	6.5
587. Pub Service Enterprise Group	5,706	595.5	16,305	7,160	1,298.5	12.8
588. Puget Sound Power & Light	1,113	138.3	3,341	1,487	254.0	2.7
589. Pulte[13]	1,633	77.8	3,811	906	80.1	3.1
590. Quaker Oats	5,792	304.6	2,805	4,318	471.6	20.2
591. Quantum	2,003	−9.6	888	831	26.8	2.3
592. Ralston-Continental Bak Grp	1,984	27.7	832	138	100.9	21.3
593. Ralston-Ralston Purina Grp	5,949	332.0	4,454	4,465	568.5	38.2
594. Raytheon	9,201	693.0	7,258	9,076	970.9	63.9

[12]Formerly Philadelphia Electric.   [13]Formerly PHM.

Company	Sales ($mil)	Net Profits ($mil)	Assets ($mil)	Market Value ($mil)	Cash Flow ($mil)	Number Employees (thou)
595. Reader's Digest Assn	2,821	271.9	2,053	4,943	317.1	7.4
596. Reebok International	2,894	223.4	1,392	2,940	258.7	4.7
597. Reliance Group Holdings	2,963	85.5	8,969	669	85.5	9.5
598. Republic New York	2,328	301.2	39,493	2,714	349.5	5.1
599. Revco DS	2,420	30.5	1,082	831	81.2	16.5
600. Reynolds Metals	5,269	−322.1	6,709	3,162	−35.1	29.1
601. Rhone-Poulenc Rorer	4,019	421.1	4,050	4,709	589.0	22.7
602. Riggs National	369	−94.2	4,780	321	−81.2	1.9
603. Rite Aid	4,289	126.5	2,055	1,663	229.4	31.1
604. RJR Nabisco	15,104	−3.0	31,295	7,540	1,165.0	64.8
605. Roadway Services	4,156	119.3	1,846	2,751	319.4	46.5
606. Rochester Community Sav Bk	240	−59.4	4,189	222	−51.2	1.8
607. Rockwell International	10,952	583.6	9,758	9,482	1,071.8	77.9
608. Rohm & Haas	3,269	126.0	3,524	3,746	352.0	13.4
609. Roosevelt Financial Group	244	38.1	4,016	263	40.1	0.5
610. Rubbermaid	1,960	211.4	1,513	4,710	292.3	12.0
611. Ryder System	4,217	114.7	4,258	2,157	723.3	37.6
612. Safeco	3,517	425.9	14,807	3,517	458.0	7.2
613. Safeway	15,215	123.3	5,075	2,562	453.5	105.4
614. St Jude Medical	253	109.6	450	1,382	118.6	0.7
615. St Paul Bancorp	289	41.4	3,705	364	46.4	1.0
616. St Paul Cos	4,460	427.6	17,149	3,394	486.2	12.6
617. Sallie Mae	2,617	430.1	46,509	3,793	430.1	4.4
618. Salomon	8,799	864.0	184,835	5,735	1,081.0	8.6
619. San Diego Gas & Electric	1,980	218.7	4,702	2,679	480.5	4.2
620. Santa Fe Pacific	2,726	338.8	5,937	4,493	586.7	16.1
621. Sara Lee	14,963	733.0	11,244	10,346	1,286.0	133.0
622. Scana	1,264	168.0	4,041	2,182	344.2	4.8
623. SCEcorp	7,821	639.0	21,379	7,613	1,668.0	17.2
624. Schering-Plough	4,341	825.0	4,317	11,350	967.4	21.4
625. Charles Schwab	1,097	124.4	6,897	1,741	168.8	5.5
626. Scott Paper	4,749	−289.1	6,625	3,405	11.2	26.2
627. EW Scripps	1,206	128.7	1,676	2,070	249.6	8.2
628. Seagate Technology	3,114	151.3	2,496	2,008	344.2	43.0
629. Sears, Roebuck	50,838	2,409.1	90,808	16,885	3,087.5	382.5
630. Sensormatic Electronics	549	63.2	1,029	2,257	95.4	4.0
631. Service Corp International	899	103.1	3,683	2,323	161.3	12.3
632. Service Merchandise	3,815	82.3	2,012	770	152.0	22.6
633. SFFed Corp	234	9.9	3,389	141	19.3	0.7
634. Shaw Industries	2,476	117.6	1,454	3,110	200.2	21.7
635. Shawmut National	1,931	244.6	27,245	1,980	365.6	10.3
636. Sherwin-Williams	2,949	165.2	1,915	2,855	234.0	17.1
637. Sigma-Aldrich	739	107.2	730	2,665	139.1	4.3
638. Signet Banking	1,169	174.4	11,849	2,174	211.5	5.9
639. Silicon Graphics	1,262	114.7	1,325	3,598	185.6	3.7
640. Smith's Food & Drug Centers	2,807	45.8	1,654	678	128.0	19.0
641. Snap-on Tools	1,132	85.8	1,219	1,830	117.9	9.0
642. Snapple Beverage	516	59.5	239	2,860	69.8	0.2
643. Sonat	1,741	265.1	3,214	2,702	491.1	2.2
644. Sonoco Products	1,947	118.8	1,707	2,124	214.6	16.5

Company	Sales ($mil)	Net Profits ($mil)	Assets ($mil)	Market Value ($mil)	Cash Flow ($mil)	Number Employees (thou)
645. Southern Co	8,489	1,002.0	25,911	12,724	2,013.0	28.9
646. Southern National	438	75.6	5,898	617	85.0	2.4
647. South New England Telecom	1,654	−53.9	3,762	1,963	237.2	10.8
648. Southern Pacific Rail	2,919	−44.9	3,434	3,719	88.3	21.1
649. Southland	5,781	−11.3	1,999	1,716	143.1	34.0
650. SouthTrust	1,102	150.5	14,708	1,539	188.4	6.7
651. Southwest Airlines	2,297	154.3	2,576	5,053	273.6	13.3
652. Southwestern Bell	10,690	1,435.2	24,308	24,372	3,442.2	59.0
653. Southwestern Public Service	826	104.5	1,784	1,182	166.6	2.2
654. Sovereign Bancorp	271	30.6	4,495	364	30.6	0.8
655. Spiegel	2,596	48.7	2,211	2,379	92.2	12.0
656. Springs Industries	2,023	47.3	1,292	690	134.4	20.3
657. Sprint	11,368	468.3	14,149	11,994	1,827.0	51.4
658. Standard Federal Bank	769	115.6	10,905	873	137.7	2.5
659. Stanley Works	2,273	92.6	1,577	1,823	173.3	19.0
660. Star Banc	631	100.3	7,637	1,073	133.8	3.6
661. State Street Boston	1,532	179.8	18,720	2,930	263.9	9.7
662. Statesman Group	379	37.2	4,491	170	38.7	0.3
663. Stone Container	5,060	−319.2	6,837	1,322	27.6	30.1
664. Stop & Shop Companies	3,568	63.7	1,644	1,288	143.3	28.0
665. Sumitomo Bank of California	377	2.3	5,089	191	9.9	1.6
666. Summit Bancorp	304	42.4	4,312	511	50.2	1.6
667. Sun Co	7,297	283.0	5,900	3,707	651.0	14.4
668. Sun Microsystems	4,493	188.2	2,610	2,851	412.1	13.3
669. SunAmerica	884	138.6	15,541	1,354	138.6	1.0
670. Sunbeam-Oster	1,066	88.8	1,006	1,474	121.0	9.4
671. Sundstrand	1,383	145.7	1,512	1,597	233.8	10.1
672. SunTrust Banks	3,089	473.7	40,728	5,688	613.9	19.5
673. Supervalu	16,104	182.6	4,181	2,476	372.8	42.0
674. Sybase	427	44.1	333	2,401	68.5	2.5
675. Synovus Financial	615	74.1	5,627	1,159	74.1	4.7
676. Sysco	10,589	212.2	2,735	5,020	325.8	23.4
677. Tandem Computers	2,023	−510.3	1,630	1,725	−340.8	10.4
678. Tandy	4,103	83.8	3,219	2,750	163.8	43.9
679. TCF Financial	477	38.0	5,026	401	48.2	2.8
680. TECO Energy	1,284	150.3	3,128	2,356	315.7	4.8
681. Tele-Communications	4,047	12.0	16,199	10,180	816.0	22.0
682. Teledyne	2,492	72.8	1,478	1,060	145.5	22.4
683. Telephone & Data Systems	591	33.9	2,259	2,192	161.4	4.1
684. Temple-Inland	2,736	67.4	11,959	2,684	277.1	15.0
685. Tenneco	13,255	451.0	15,373	9,742	960.0	77.0
686. Texaco	33,245	1,068.0	26,626	17,167	2,699.0	33.7
687. Texas Instruments	8,523	476.0	5,993	7,844	1,093.0	59.8
688. Texas Utilities	5,435	368.7	21,518	8,440	912.1	10.8
689. Textron	9,078	379.1	19,658	5,106	659.9	55.0
690. Thermo Electron	1,250	76.6	2,474	2,049	119.0	8.2
691. 3Com	753	−42.6	387	2,015	−17.5	2.0

Company	Sales ($mil)	Net Profits ($mil)	Assets ($mil)	Market Value ($mil)	Cash Flow ($mil)	Number Employees (thou)
692. TIG Holdings	1,881	−128.0	6,253	1,297	−128.0	3.7
693. Time Warner	14,544	−164.0	16,533	16,344	1,169.0	44.0
694. Times Mirror	3,714	317.2	4,606	4,324	583.5	27.6
695. TJX Cos	3,627	127.0	1,427	1,992	194.5	34.0
696. Torchmark	2,177	279.6	7,646	3,134	315.2	2.7
697. Tosco	3,559	80.6	1,493	1,012	145.7	1.9
698. Toys 'R' Us	7,946	483.0	6,150	10,376	616.3	52.2
699. Transamerica	4,833	400.5	36,051	4,106	567.6	10.7
700. Transatlantic Holdings	726	86.7	3,170	1,070	86.7	0.3
701. Transco Energy	2,922	−3.9	4,085	681	183.4	4.6
702. Travelers[14]	6,797	950.0	101,360	11,654	1,073.0	38.0
703. Tribune	1,953	188.6	2,536	4,047	291.4	9.9
704. Trustmark	336	48.6	4,432	514	65.6	2.0
705. TRW	7,948	220.0	5,336	4,775	678.0	62.7
706. Turner Broadcasting System	1,922	72.4	3,245	4,636	651.6	5.3
707. Turner Corp	2,768	−6.2	664	46	3.6	2.6
708. 20th Century Industries	1,104	108.6	1,648	1,107	115.8	2.3
709. Tyco International	3,133	79.2	2,309	2,503	169.2	23.5
710. Tyson Foods	4,777	185.3	3,526	2,968	366.6	49.2
711. UAL	14,511	−31.0	12,840	3,136	733.0	84.9
712. UJB Financial	1,062	74.2	13,411	1,413	101.2	6.3
713. Ultramar	2,438	86.5	1,725	1,075	125.2	3.3
714. Unifi	1,365	114.9	950	1,665	185.2	6.5
715. Union Bank	1,266	83.1	16,391	940	108.8	7.2
716. Union Camp	3,120	50.0	4,685	3,198	311.6	19.6
717. Union Carbide	4,640	165.0	4,689	3,913	441.0	14.1
718. Union Electric	2,066	297.2	6,596	3,651	553.9	6.5
719. Union Pacific	7,561	705.0	15,001	12,307	1,654.0	47.1
720. Union Planters	484	61.3	6,318	503	84.3	2.8
721. Unisys	7,743	361.6	7,519	2,663	838.3	51.7
722. United Carolina Bancshares	242	31.7	3,051	319	39.8	1.9
723. United HealthCare	2,469	194.6	1,494	7,075	240.3	5.4
724. United Missouri Bancshares	415	41.1	6,529	639	60.3	3.5
725. US Bancorp	1,966	257.9	21,415	2,597	364.7	12.4
726. US Healthcare	2,580	299.7	1,344	7,280	321.5	3.1
727. US Shoe	2,626	−15.8	1,079	775	68.9	38.5
728. US Trust	446	42.3	3,186	484	57.2	2.4
729. United Technologies	20,736	487.0	15,618	8,623	1,302.0	173.3
730. Unitrin	1,363	95.0	4,895	2,112	95.0	7.7
731. Universal	2,887	59.9	1,783	708	92.7	25.0
732. Unocal	7,261	343.0	9,254	6,848	1,351.0	14.2
733. UNUM	3,397	312.0	12,437	4,293	312.0	7.0
734. Upjohn	3,653	411.3	4,816	5,181	584.8	18.7
735. US West	10,294	394.4	20,680	17,370	2,348.9	62.2
736. USAir Group	7,083	−349.4	6,878	518	−43.0	48.7
737. USF&G	3,249	127.2	14,335	1,309	150.8	7.0
738. USG	1,916	NA	2,163	1,278	NA	11.9

NA: Not available.   [14]Formerly Primerica.

Company	Sales ($mil)	Net Profits ($mil)	Assets ($mil)	Market Value ($mil)	Cash Flow ($mil)	Number Employees (thou)
739. Uslico	418	23.6	3,412	188	23.6	0.7
740. USLife	1,600	97.2	6,740	920	109.9	2.2
741. UST Inc	1,080	368.9	706	5,573	395.6	3.7
742. USX-Marathon	10,035	−6.0	10,806	5,087	769.0	22.0
743. USX-US Steel	5,612	−169.0	6,616	2,994	145.0	21.5
744. UtiliCorp United	1,572	86.4	2,851	1,276	232.4	4.5
745. Valley Bancorp	377	45.9	4,592	739	63.0	2.7
746. Varity	2,726	76.3	2,028	2,121	161.1	13.6
747. Venture Stores	1,863	43.9	663	387	66.8	15.0
748. VF	4,320	246.4	2,877	3,225	372.2	59.5
749. Viacom	2,005	169.5	6,417	3,926	322.5	5.0
750. Vons Cos	5,075	33.0	2,250	753	148.7	22.1
751. Vulcan Materials	1,133	88.2	1,079	1,857	191.0	6.3
752. Waban	3,589	−18.7	1,073	604	16.8	14.1
753. Wachovia	2,742	492.1	36,526	5,613	585.1	15.8
754. Wal-Mart Stores	67,345	2,333.3	26,302	61,492	3,182.0	472.5
755. Walgreen	8,498	249.9	2,673	5,031	357.1	55.6
756. Warner-Lambert	5,794	285.0	4,828	8,523	455.4	34.5
757. Washington Federal Sav & Loan	295	95.2	3,234	881	100.5	0.5
758. Washington Mutual Sav Bank	1,180	175.3	15,827	1,330	206.6	3.9
759. Washington Post	1,498	153.8	1,623	2,799	248.5	6.5
760. Wellfleet Communications	267	42.2	190	2,607	51.5	0.6
761. WellPoint Health Networks	2,449	186.6	1,927	3,532	190.4	2.8
762. Wells Fargo	4,854	612.0	52,513	8,032	878.0	20.5
763. West One Bancorp	600	83.2	7,671	968	111.5	4.4
764. Western Atlas	1,959	78.2	2,010	1,938	246.2	14.1
765. Western Resources	1,909	177.4	5,412	1,833	370.5	5.2
766. Westinghouse Electric	8,875	−270.0	10,553	4,682	41.0	106.1
767. Westvaco	2,361	51.4	3,943	2,238	252.9	14.5
768. Weyerhaeuser	9,545	527.3	12,638	9,248	1,014.2	37.9
769. Whirlpool	7,533	231.0	6,047	4,969	500.0	39.1
770. Whitman	2,530	106.4	2,103	1,694	201.9	14.6
771. Willamette Industries	2,622	110.7	2,805	2,868	304.9	12.0
772. Williams Cos	2,438	231.8	5,020	2,629	443.1	7.0
773. Wilmington Trust	405	82.8	4,638	898	91.1	2.2
774. Winn-Dixie Stores	11,040	239.7	2,199	4,169	388.9	69.0
775. Wisconsin Energy	1,644	188.5	4,223	2,725	404.1	5.8
776. Witco	2,143	19.8	1,839	1,629	122.3	8.3
777. WMX Technologies[15]	9,136	452.8	16,264	12,328	1,249.5	69.9
778. Woolworth	9,626	−495.0	4,593	2,622	−238.0	95.3
779. Worthen Banking	279	31.4	3,579	370	45.1	2.0
780. Worthington Industries	1,236	81.8	695	1,798	112.4	7.0
781. Wm Wrigley Jr	1,429	174.9	815	6,067	209.5	6.6
782. Xerox	17,334	−126.0	38,750	10,437	503.0	98.2
783. Yellow Corp[16]	2,857	18.8	1,266	734	151.2	35.0
784. York International	2,032	75.5	1,335	1,450	119.5	13.2
785. Zions Bancorporation	346	51.4	4,366	565	62.5	2.5

[15]Formerly Waste Management.   [16]Formerly Yellow Freight System.

Appendix IV
Additional Data Sets For Selected Exercises

DATA SET 1   Data for Chapter 2, Review Exercises 34–36

1. 237	40. 234	79. 195	118. 252	157. 214	196. 184
2. 280	41. 175	80. 258	119. 219	158. 211	197. 235
3. 222	42. 258	81. 236	120. 207	159. 264	198. 187
4. 250	43. 206	82. 188	121. 223	160. 181	199. 196
5. 227	44. 220	83. 225	122. 233	161. 202	200. 209
6. 304	45. 257	84. 251	123. 239	162. 212	201. 214
7. 261	46. 230	85. 197	124. 238	163. 232	202. 205
8. 201	47. 236	86. 197	125. 243	164. 217	203. 188
9. 245	48. 213	87. 309	126. 276	165. 239	204. 223
10. 250	49. 231	88. 226	127. 207	166. 225	205. 213
11. 238	50. 201	89. 232	128. 200	167. 194	206. 190
12. 212	51. 220	90. 205	129. 248	168. 279	207. 274
13. 198	52. 187	91. 312	130. 229	169. 253	208. 237
14. 193	53. 211	92. 221	131. 237	170. 237	209. 149
15. 204	54. 248	93. 162	132. 204	171. 242	210. 193
16. 193	55. 219	94. 231	133. 237	172. 262	211. 232
17. 226	56. 192	95. 182	134. 229	173. 215	212. 246
18. 217	57. 158	96. 209	135. 202	174. 196	213. 177
19. 240	58. 163	97. 209	136. 232	175. 194	214. 271
20. 285	59. 221	98. 233	137. 218	176. 222	215. 228
21. 222	60. 201	99. 239	138. 222	177. 227	216. 219
22. 224	61. 171	100. 197	139. 169	178. 172	217. 200
23. 236	62. 269	101. 239	140. 237	179. 212	218. 226
24. 224	63. 267	102. 194	141. 253	180. 154	219. 199
25. 244	64. 212	103. 263	142. 206	181. 176	220. 219
26. 162	65. 223	104. 223	143. 225	182. 236	221. 229
27. 258	66. 228	105. 231	144. 195	183. 266	222. 166
28. 270	67. 129	106. 212	145. 253	184. 192	223. 222
29. 230	68. 167	107. 230	146. 206	185. 281	224. 189
30. 179	69. 227	108. 236	147. 156	186. 228	225. 239
31. 176	70. 187	109. 224	148. 245	187. 244	226. 203
32. 196	71. 207	110. 224	149. 240	188. 212	227. 227
33. 221	72. 185	111. 232	150. 261	189. 237	228. 223
34. 178	73. 194	112. 238	151. 184	190. 208	229. 241
35. 214	74. 204	113. 187	152. 201	191. 261	230. 247
36. 232	75. 169	114. 222	153. 254	192. 249	231. 217
37. 176	76. 257	115. 260	154. 189	193. 167	232. 228
38. 174	77. 221	116. 221	155. 259	194. 215	233. 217
39. 181	78. 264	117. 215	156. 205	195. 223	234. 189

235. 235	289. 200	343. 241	397. 253	451. 209	505. 225
236. 197	290. 232	344. 187	398. 222	452. 268	506. 259
237. 177	291. 206	345. 237	399. 240	453. 197	507. 159
238. 246	292. 245	346. 184	400. 196	454. 162	508. 267
239. 193	293. 266	347. 224	401. 249	455. 204	509. 189
240. 250	294. 189	348. 194	402. 208	456. 265	510. 183
241. 200	295. 195	349. 236	403. 244	457. 222	511. 256
242. 232	296. 200	350. 213	404. 203	458. 221	512. 197
243. 167	297. 184	351. 230	405. 206	459. 201	513. 259
244. 215	298. 268	352. 224	406. 214	460. 189	514. 231
245. 260	299. 248	353. 280	407. 230	461. 253	515. 238
246. 196	300. 232	354. 200	408. 252	462. 223	516. 234
247. 213	301. 201	355. 208	409. 210	463. 192	517. 200
248. 202	302. 213	356. 250	410. 206	464. 276	518. 202
249. 256	303. 219	357. 183	411. 158	465. 250	519. 273
250. 193	304. 262	358. 243	412. 233	466. 193	520. 187
251. 225	305. 205	359. 253	413. 237	467. 229	521. 207
252. 264	306. 270	360. 263	414. 234	468. 193	522. 254
253. 252	307. 222	361. 226	415. 200	469. 201	523. 227
254. 224	308. 243	362. 243	416. 227	470. 168	524. 293
255. 188	309. 249	363. 251	417. 195	471. 223	525. 175
256. 214	310. 173	364. 234	418. 218	472. 206	526. 249
257. 225	311. 251	365. 235	419. 267	473. 197	527. 267
258. 210	312. 168	366. 286	420. 206	474. 179	528. 233
259. 190	313. 236	367. 227	421. 264	475. 266	529. 270
260. 224	314. 226	368. 229	422. 217	476. 236	530. 224
261. 210	315. 233	369. 188	423. 225	477. 237	531. 212
262. 253	316. 220	370. 250	424. 212	478. 219	532. 238
263. 251	317. 229	371. 243	425. 242	479. 195	533. 236
264. 216	318. 216	372. 231	426. 207	480. 218	534. 211
265. 225	319. 211	373. 192	427. 153	481. 224	535. 195
266. 209	320. 156	374. 216	428. 203	482. 208	536. 207
267. 217	321. 202	375. 187	429. 208	483. 211	537. 254
268. 236	322. 268	376. 237	430. 319	484. 248	538. 189
269. 175	323. 217	377. 239	431. 225	485. 215	539. 252
270. 172	324. 166	378. 261	432. 234	486. 209	540. 248
271. 208	325. 239	379. 251	433. 247	487. 230	541. 218
272. 225	326. 193	380. 224	434. 228	488. 227	542. 256
273. 219	327. 195	381. 222	435. 236	489. 190	543. 165
274. 184	328. 155	382. 238	436. 275	490. 259	544. 215
275. 196	329. 244	383. 195	437. 216	491. 212	545. 205
276. 191	330. 224	384. 249	438. 210	492. 238	546. 197
277. 247	331. 187	385. 196	439. 204	493. 213	547. 216
278. 214	332. 227	386. 240	440. 169	494. 200	548. 221
279. 252	333. 206	387. 236	441. 211	495. 202	549. 244
280. 188	334. 203	388. 261	442. 221	496. 212	550. 206
281. 214	335. 193	389. 250	443. 153	497. 277	551. 213
282. 244	336. 218	390. 163	444. 218	498. 208	552. 216
283. 232	337. 230	391. 180	445. 276	499. 183	553. 255
284. 281	338. 196	392. 187	446. 199	500. 211	554. 199
285. 209	339. 250	393. 238	447. 202	501. 251	555. 216
286. 226	340. 210	394. 235	448. 203	502. 250	556. 225
287. 177	341. 223	395. 214	449. 232	503. 217	557. 188
288. 132	342. 197	396. 245	450. 215	504. 169	558. 261

559. 146	566. 229	573. 249	580. 217	587. 272	594. 187
560. 227	567. 213	574. 204	581. 189	588. 230	595. 216
561. 171	568. 256	575. 166	582. 282	589. 190	596. 222
562. 242	569. 209	576. 220	583. 201	590. 220	597. 234
563. 229	570. 209	577. 213	584. 216	591. 226	598. 245
564. 229	571. 245	578. 264	585. 229	592. 210	599. 245
565. 248	572. 211	579. 244	586. 150	593. 251	600. 247

DATA SET 2   Data Set for Chapter 2, Statistics at Work 4.

Vehicles

26	60	10	168	25	2	2	32	17	28	3
29	21	41	5	5	26	36	3	3	8	3
17	27	12	58	79	1	10	19	1	18	2
28	178	8	2	4	3	13	4	41	2	14
2	3	13	4	12	132	20	5	318	11	4
34	45	6	4	3	24	61	159	2	6	3
9	5	6	42	13	25	102	4	3	2	1
12	627	17	5	8	5	4	6	8	59	5
5	346	8	13	19	7	13	4	18	4	19
14	7	28	54	20	22	163	6	24	13	12
37	2	2	23	111	3	4	5	2	6	67
43	439	44	11	613	29	2	5	1	62	18
42	59	11	8	7	81	14	11	3	7	202
6	25	25	101	5	3	59	56	17	100	57
36	49	52	4	35	11	4	8	29	850	31
44	123	6	9	195	40	9	156	7	24	46
19	2	3	5	13	11	3	12	25	65	908
50	243	15	164	32	30	14	23	295	26	18
14	5	43	20	23	11	21	24	23	52	9
892	30	15	32	21	3	53	778	70	446	23
131	39	22	96	169	8	16	25	15	2	11
5	4	6	30	64	65	8	79	8	2	49
51	15	23	42	35	3	5	172	4	433	20
2	20	15	19	31	48	50	10	21	20	5
10	55	29	24	5	27	14	23	45	17	7
28	10	19	7	20	117	5	194	370	141	75
280	3	62	12	16	32	14	416	80	390	256
241	168	9	154	47	25	8	22	31	167	135
160	33	108	33	25	93	4	42	18	47	13
9	43	4	7	73	250	11	34	100	25	26
6	41	35	97	46	4	13	40	161	2	1
27	3	46	66	46	3	12	210	2	8	15
12	14	4	5	20	45	69	190	559	6	14
59	2	12	17	90	46	2	7	240	7	32
35	27	16	54	25	633	211	12	2	22	3
20	83	2	16	17	31	3	10	6	20	722
35	34	22	65	13	5	33	7	40	33	10
30	2	60	1	2	10	21	45	12	196	450
58	199	34	78	80	20	2	21	30	39	40
17	131	12	22	12	3	49	582	90	8	23
32	11	22	73	184	24	30	6	5	2	54

Vehicles

15	122	6	15	26	34	50	200	243	3	16
8	32	74	22	31	64	29	24	25	590	25
27	70	54	10	6	9	40	6	32	36	149
58	21	30	50	570	42	34	15	200	120	88
11	5	8	22	14	4	43	50	6	11	14
2	13	3	24	71	5	1	14	50	67	44
6	5	4	2	50	6	47	34	2	18	10
9	27	10	20	72	80	158	4	17	143	22
172	69	13	17	19	2	9	76	22	42	28
9	4	13	6	20	47	5	30	32	34	40
4	34	16	12	12	12	40	27	34	41	19
20	40	31	35	2	20	17	90	12	51	18
13	47	30	29	228	26	43	32	22	63	47
29	6	29	11	32	103	60	31	2	66	29
34	34	3	4	10	567	18	2	8	3	59
30	27	3	10	69	39	26	16	49	80	49
88	72	30	36	9	16	15	31	25	53	14
23	24	30	35	108	2	17	9	8	49	77
6	206	4	4	3	13	33	49	4	79	14
15	5	126	34	3	1	71	34	13	2	20
14	40	16	28	49	55	35	250	6	43	15
74	9	42	3	25	22	53	90	40	6	20
5	2	13	8	48	7	3	14	28	9	5
6	26	16	13	75	4	85	22	112	41	40
48	29	13	6	268	16	31	22	38	9	6
10	8	17	15	31	6	7	2	52	16	14
62	19	9	8	24	34	38	4	3	4	5
14	4	40	41	19	5	10	24	13	4	149
14	28	58	4	17	29	4	1	8	22	2
5	7	59	54	27	68	29	9	2	40	5
1	5	63	17	19	3	4	1	45	2	1
20	608	30	2	33	83	11	3	6	9	75
12	4	2	3	2	25	98	5	1	6	7
73	5	57	318	3	4	1	1	21	8	12
8	19	58	3	3	5	30	34	13	5	22
10	17	4	17	7	10	5	12	16	17	74
486	7	8	26	60	6	17	4	6	63	10
106	23	17	40	6	9	22	22	3	12	42
38	38	3	3	889	7	16	2	12	62	1
8	27	25	29	30	12	16	19	64	67	14
10	1	14	20	32	2	32	6	40	5	11
24	15	11	105	11	82	26	10	39	65	5
5	5	54	45	85	3	6	65	60	20	27
132	6	71	103	1	4	58	34	22	17	38
43	10	141	8	49	23	1	20	74	58	12
19	96	24	6	64	60	27	190	83	32	26
20	74	52	80	146	29	13	26	32	42	16
105	107	254	252	104	14	66	34	17	18	117
4	11	4	23	350	2	13	100	16	62	6
6	62	3	26	43	71	8	11	17	46	4
571	430	67	11	7	3	11	87	4	22	4
8	18	5	10	53	56	9	12	70	167	28

Vehicles

4	21	21	7	18	4	15	25	52	31	4
15	32	42	2	90	10	49	15	11	42	10
100	44	9	9	90	1	65	8	37	23	97
3	65	12	31	21	6	50	40	341	17	3
23	2	20	72	27	6	13	43	17	10	21
49	19	25	6	17	27	13	3	83	14	4
10	16	180	32	80	36	100	4	7	33	32
4	13	23	36	59	6	114	47	15	14	11
1	49	2	10	88	46	6	39	8	80	4
20	42	21	658	700	1	43	19	21	35	7
42	8	25	2	6	5	48	40	30	16	17
17	7	17	18	12	2	5	58	24	14	19
3	25	175	2	18	59	19	288	9	10	15
3	1	142	17	6	12	126	1	10	50	48
7	2	46	55	31	18	2	119	67	8	24
30	111	103	94	22	37	26	2	26	3	15
74	55	54	6	151	212	20	1	7	3	9
71	27	28	54	16	80	20	1	33	15	356
154	101	35	426	2	65	43	22	28	18	16
108	55	1	1	2	2	178	50	15	17	2
3	7	42	28	41	26	85	15	3	51	9
33	2	13	5	115	30	20	39	38	36	2
4	12	72	19	4	2	75	6	105	6	178
50	1	29	92	21	24	77	4	43	17	130
51	30	160	5	20	40	78	31	27	28	87
14	65	20	30	138	18	3	5	25	5	29
170	16	7	20	4	4	21	46	4	46	8
8	39	7	79	57	11	2	6	106	24	39
19	15	6	24	1	120	107	6	27	48	2
42	13	9	40	240	45	3	12	43	35	13
19	67	65	10	7	117	50	43	20	80	48
334	32	15	8	40	20	3	23	3	7	473
82	13	107	41	486	8	6	319	24	13	12
96	104	114	43	7	5	76	150	39	56	112
4	57	175	5	63	482	17	50	26	5	250
9	22	195	200	68	22	145	23	25	75	4
22	10	81	216	22	14	162	67	78	325	10
85	37	31	53	20	31	23	6	350	113	19
190	278	8	8	539	28	6	30	455	20	8
6	21	45	7	29	5	258	98	2	75	20
26	38	8	17	3	196	33	30	8	7	28
40	115	63	2	4	39	25	305	230	122	3
22	40	339	13	22	59	45	10	3	42	1
32	7	37	6	100	86	2	36	4	3	33
34	22	16	26	4	41	21	3	27	3	8
19	8	13	4	7	58	48	34	12	18	8
9	34	8	4	15	4	4	18	8	4	92
35	1	8	25	48	36	5	14	3	2	10
13	123	172	24	155	12	10	7	30	5	48
7	18	140	150	8	414	20	31	691	60	45
5	333	16	20	6	9	436	16	3	5	20
9	19	15	31	28	45	15	3	27	21	10

Vehicles

10	2	40	12	10	13	5	22	240	19	10
12	3	9	4	6	55	9	11	6	103	86
4	25	6	36	22	104	92	3	11	93	550
6	69	8	5	10	2	27	2	93	5	4
81	275	54	672	27	6	50	2	2	76	31
83	50	3	24	26	8	36	26	7	78	40
74	32	10	26	7	2	20	85	6	31	9
21	1	6	134	265	14	11	79	14	6	3
10	109	14	26	361	47	14	59	29	25	59
73	21	32	75	4	85	18	22	8	21	39
4	33	64	101	19	4	8	39	3	395	8
14	59	19	4	35	18	8	37	13	103	15
12	67	44	40	12	20	240	12	40	14	7
352	22	5	16	36	50	20	992	21	38	31
6	23	50	102	75	3	112	3	4	40	35
51	29	35	34	6	12	6	12	140	3	22
1	7	34	5	106	4	120	17	82	8	22
65	14	22	4	11	5	2	5	1	19	3
13	61	10	251	510	37	18	8	6	8	10
9	54	62	22	6	6	58	5	4	7	19
8	12	3	15	52	5	39	45	15	65	2
43	54	26	48	9	9	7	11	67	62	4
6	7	33	4	5	22	3	8	8	10	12
40	25	21	112	19	29	2	20	10	219	7
23	7	38	3	137	11	15	7	2	37	12
27	29	12	3	256	135	28	1	28	37	53
760	4	18	19	15	2	1	6	186	5	156
25	10	3	37	18	3	56	10	54	950	85
4	60	5	6	150	46	26	41	64	1	20
9	4	6	22	11	10	22	1	481	9	20
23	11	7	6	42	20	56	15	38	34	366
6	9	11	10	41	50	3	35	15	25	19
3	13	19	28	39	28	12	11	50	23	20
10	8	4	20	7	36	4	133	26	4	4
24	17	25	389	43	14	11	9	5	244	28
14	3	28	5	24	1	35	11	2	50	4

Source: Bus Industry Bus Ride 1986, Volume 9 (July 1986), Friendship Publications, Inc., Spokane, Washington. Used by permission.

DATA SET 3 Data for Chapter 5, Review Exercises 34–36

1. 14	53. 12	105. 15	157. 16	209. 15	261. 13
2. 13	54. 15	106. 13	158. 13	210. 12	262. 11
3. 12	55. 16	107. 12	159. 13	211. 15	263. 14
4. 13	56. 14	108. 17	160. 16	212. 15	264. 12
5. 13	57. 13	109. 14	161. 15	213. 12	265. 15
6. 14	58. 14	110. 13	162. 15	214. 12	266. 13
7. 12	59. 12	111. 13	163. 16	215. 12	267. 14
8. 12	60. 15	112. 14	164. 14	216. 15	268. 13
9. 14	61. 14	113. 15	165. 17	217. 14	269. 13
10. 14	62. 15	114. 15	166. 14	218. 13	270. 14
11. 14	63. 14	115. 14	167. 13	219. 13	271. 16
12. 13	64. 12	116. 15	168. 14	220. 14	272. 14
13. 12	65. 15	117. 15	169. 15	221. 13	273. 16
14. 13	66. 14	118. 13	170. 13	222. 13	274. 13
15. 12	67. 14	119. 14	171. 15	223. 15	275. 15
16. 13	68. 14	120. 14	172. 14	224. 16	276. 17
17. 13	69. 14	121. 13	173. 14	225. 12	277. 13
18. 12	70. 15	122. 13	174. 16	226. 13	278. 11
19. 11	71. 13	123. 13	175. 12	227. 13	279. 12
20. 12	72. 15	124. 13	176. 15	228. 16	280. 15
21. 12	73. 13	125. 14	177. 17	229. 16	281. 16
22. 14	74. 15	126. 13	178. 16	230. 14	282. 15
23. 13	75. 14	127. 12	179. 13	231. 14	283. 11
24. 15	76. 15	128. 13	180. 12	232. 13	284. 14
25. 16	77. 15	129. 15	181. 12	233. 14	285. 13
26. 12	78. 14	130. 16	182. 14	234. 12	286. 13
27. 14	79. 14	131. 17	183. 15	235. 15	287. 11
28. 14	80. 13	132. 14	184. 15	236. 13	288. 12
29. 14	81. 17	133. 14	185. 13	237. 14	289. 14
30. 14	82. 12	134. 14	186. 15	238. 14	290. 14
31. 14	83. 15	135. 18	187. 13	239. 13	291. 14
32. 16	84. 12	136. 16	188. 15	240. 13	292. 16
33. 14	85. 13	137. 17	189. 12	241. 12	293. 15
34. 13	86. 13	138. 10	190. 14	242. 15	294. 15
35. 15	87. 12	139. 14	191. 15	243. 14	295. 16
36. 14	88. 16	140. 14	192. 13	244. 11	296. 17
37. 13	89. 13	141. 12	193. 14	245. 14	297. 14
38. 14	90. 15	142. 13	194. 13	246. 12	298. 12
39. 17	91. 12	143. 15	195. 12	247. 14	299. 13
40. 15	92. 14	144. 14	196. 14	248. 14	300. 17
41. 14	93. 14	145. 13	197. 15	249. 12	301. 11
42. 14	94. 13	146. 14	198. 15	250. 14	302. 14
43. 14	95. 13	147. 13	199. 12	251. 14	303. 14
44. 13	96. 15	148. 14	200. 13	252. 13	304. 14
45. 17	97. 13	149. 15	201. 14	253. 12	305. 13
46. 14	98. 14	150. 14	202. 12	254. 13	306. 14
47. 12	99. 14	151. 14	203. 14	255. 14	307. 16
48. 15	100. 13	152. 16	204. 14	256. 13	308. 13
49. 16	101. 14	153. 14	205. 17	257. 13	309. 13
50. 12	102. 14	154. 12	206. 14	258. 13	310. 11
51. 14	103. 13	155. 15	207. 16	259. 15	311. 12
52. 14	104. 12	156. 15	208. 16	260. 13	312. 11

313. 15	368. 12	423. 13	478. 17	533. 15	588. 18
314. 13	369. 14	424. 16	479. 11	534. 13	589. 14
315. 13	370. 15	425. 13	480. 14	535. 15	590. 13
316. 13	371. 12	426. 14	481. 13	536. 12	591. 14
317. 14	372. 14	427. 14	482. 15	537. 15	592. 11
318. 14	373. 13	428. 15	483. 13	538. 14	593. 13
319. 13	374. 11	429. 15	484. 14	539. 13	594. 13
320. 14	375. 14	430. 15	485. 15	540. 13	595. 14
321. 15	376. 14	431. 12	486. 16	541. 13	596. 14
322. 15	377. 13	432. 13	487. 12	542. 11	597. 12
323. 16	378. 14	433. 16	488. 15	543. 15	598. 12
324. 12	379. 15	434. 13	489. 14	544. 15	599. 12
325. 13	380. 13	435. 14	490. 13	545. 15	600. 12
326. 14	381. 14	436. 12	491. 14	546. 16	601. 15
327. 15	382. 15	437. 15	492. 15	547. 12	602. 14
328. 14	383. 16	438. 16	493. 16	548. 13	603. 15
329. 14	384. 16	439. 12	494. 14	549. 16	604. 14
330. 15	385. 16	440. 15	495. 14	550. 11	605. 13
331. 16	386. 13	441. 13	496. 12	551. 13	606. 13
332. 13	387. 13	442. 12	497. 13	552. 11	607. 14
333. 11	388. 15	443. 13	498. 14	553. 14	608. 16
334. 14	389. 12	444. 13	499. 15	554. 15	609. 13
335. 12	390. 14	445. 15	500. 14	555. 14	610. 16
336. 13	391. 15	446. 14	501. 13	556. 12	611. 12
337. 15	392. 15	447. 15	502. 14	557. 14	612. 17
338. 15	393. 11	448. 14	503. 16	558. 14	613. 16
339. 17	394. 12	449. 16	504. 15	559. 17	614. 14
340. 14	395. 14	450. 14	505. 15	560. 16	615. 13
341. 13	396. 14	451. 13	506. 13	561. 13	616. 15
342. 13	397. 15	452. 15	507. 13	562. 14	617. 14
343. 15	398. 14	453. 17	508. 13	563. 15	618. 16
344. 16	399. 14	454. 15	509. 14	564. 13	619. 13
345. 14	400. 12	455. 13	510. 14	565. 15	620. 16
346. 14	401. 13	456. 12	511. 16	566. 13	621. 15
347. 12	402. 16	457. 12	512. 13	567. 14	622. 12
348. 13	403. 14	458. 12	513. 13	568. 16	623. 17
349. 14	404. 16	459. 14	514. 14	569. 16	624. 13
350. 15	405. 14	460. 14	515. 12	570. 14	625. 14
351. 18	406. 13	461. 15	516. 15	571. 15	626. 13
352. 16	407. 16	462. 15	517. 15	572. 12	627. 14
353. 12	408. 15	463. 14	518. 13	573. 14	628. 11
354. 14	409. 12	464. 15	519. 17	574. 13	629. 14
355. 14	410. 17	465. 13	520. 15	575. 16	630. 12
356. 14	411. 12	466. 12	521. 16	576. 14	631. 13
357. 13	412. 14	467. 15	522. 14	577. 13	632. 14
358. 14	413. 15	468. 12	523. 13	578. 14	633. 11
359. 12	414. 12	469. 13	524. 15	579. 11	634. 17
360. 17	415. 15	470. 16	525. 14	580. 15	635. 13
361. 14	416. 15	471. 14	526. 12	581. 14	636. 14
362. 15	417. 15	472. 14	527. 16	582. 12	637. 14
363. 16	418. 16	473. 16	528. 15	583. 14	638. 13
364. 15	419. 14	474. 14	529. 13	584. 11	639. 15
365. 13	420. 13	475. 13	530. 12	585. 14	640. 14
366. 16	421. 16	476. 13	531. 13	586. 16	641. 16
367. 13	422. 14	477. 13	532. 12	587. 15	642. 14

643. 14	657. 14	671. 15	685. 13	699. 12	713. 15
644. 15	658. 14	672. 15	686. 15	700. 17	714. 14
645. 15	659. 16	673. 16	687. 14	701. 12	715. 14
646. 12	660. 15	674. 14	688. 14	702. 15	716. 16
647. 13	661. 15	675. 14	689. 14	703. 13	717. 16
648. 15	662. 14	676. 14	690. 15	704. 14	718. 14
649. 17	663. 14	677. 13	691. 13	705. 16	719. 16
650. 12	664. 14	678. 13	692. 14	706. 14	720. 13
651. 12	665. 14	679. 14	693. 15	707. 16	721. 14
652. 12	666. 10	680. 16	694. 13	708. 13	722. 11
653. 14	667. 15	681. 15	695. 13	709. 15	723. 14
654. 16	668. 15	682. 12	696. 14	710. 14	724. 14
655. 14	669. 15	683. 14	697. 13	711. 14	
656. 12	670. 15	684. 14	698. 15	712. 14	

DATA SET 4   Data for Chapter 6, Review Exercises 77–81

Respon-dent	Miles Driven	Type of Accom-modations	Respon-dent	Miles Driven	Type of Accom-modations	Respon-dent	Miles Driven	Type of Accom-modations
1	1110	1	33	922	1	65	1399	1
2	1499	1	34	1266	0	66	2018	1
3	1316	0	35	1364	1	67	1722	1
4	1190	0	36	1321	0	68	2420	1
5	1097	0	37	1591	1	69	1078	0
6	842	0	38	1812	0	70	1750	0
7	2144	1	39	1216	0	71	1018	0
8	1596	1	40	1436	0	72	1811	0
9	1713	1	41	1757	1	73	1680	1
10	1791	0	42	1789	1	74	1162	1
11	2047	1	43	1796	0	75	1775	0
12	1463	1	44	1612	1	76	1501	0
13	1417	1	45	950	1	77	1685	1
14	1576	1	46	868	1	78	2130	0
15	991	0	47	1324	0	79	1349	1
16	1931	1	48	1435	0	80	1789	1
17	1794	1	49	1592	0	81	1813	0
18	998	1	50	1253	0	82	1696	1
19	989	0	51	2175	1	83	1742	0
20	994	1	52	1815	1	84	1447	1
21	1129	0	53	980	1	85	2041	0
22	1518	0	54	604	1	86	1396	1
23	1513	1	55	1433	0	87	1632	1
24	1290	0	56	1423	0	88	1666	0
25	1659	1	57	2186	1	89	1306	0
26	1918	1	58	1411	1	90	1546	0
27	1401	0	59	1310	0	91	1246	1
28	1837	0	60	1131	0	92	1333	1
29	1799	1	61	1368	1	93	1755	0
30	1242	0	62	1577	1	94	1521	0
31	1683	1	63	1549	1	95	1473	0
32	1544	1	64	1025	1	96	2068	1

Respon-dent	Miles Driven	Type of Accom-modations	Respon-dent	Miles Driven	Type of Accom-modations	Respon-dent	Miles Driven	Type of Accom-modations
97	1111	0	146	1598	0	195	1364	1
98	1568	1	147	1421	0	196	948	1
99	2099	0	148	1204	1	197	1187	0
100	1713	1	149	1390	1	198	445	1
101	1426	1	150	1442	0	199	1138	1
102	1929	1	151	1085	0	200	1739	1
103	1097	0	152	791	0	201	1088	1
104	1172	0	153	2542	1	202	2065	1
105	1717	1	154	1776	1	203	2188	0
106	1658	1	155	952	0	204	1242	0
107	1968	1	156	1103	0	205	1683	0
108	1402	0	157	1830	0	206	707	1
109	1839	0	158	1364	0	207	1658	0
110	1157	1	159	1355	0	208	1483	1
111	2085	0	160	805	1	209	1251	1
112	1692	1	161	1052	1	210	1707	1
113	959	0	162	1697	1	211	1222	0
114	1007	0	163	1673	1	212	834	0
115	1076	1	164	1591	1	213	843	1
116	1227	0	165	1488	1	214	1404	1
117	1206	0	166	1234	1	215	1344	1
118	2075	0	167	1348	0	216	1905	0
119	1226	1	168	1092	0	217	1258	1
120	1488	1	169	1730	0	218	1654	0
121	1136	1	170	1821	0	219	2191	0
122	1294	1	171	1780	0	220	1788	0
123	1113	1	172	1360	0	221	1045	0
124	1678	1	173	1403	0	222	971	1
125	1888	0	174	682	1	223	1561	0
126	2125	0	175	1728	1	224	1877	1
127	1690	0	176	1748	1	225	1542	1
128	2043	1	177	1877	1	226	758	0
129	1267	1	178	1637	0	227	1059	1
130	1723	0	179	1850	1	228	1529	1
131	1013	1	180	1633	0	229	1605	0
132	1371	0	181	1445	1	230	1619	0
133	1490	0	182	1587	1	231	1615	1
134	1135	0	183	1056	1	232	1339	1
135	2170	1	184	1620	0	233	1579	0
136	1793	1	185	1372	1	234	1851	1
137	950	1	186	1350	0	235	1535	1
138	1464	0	187	1182	0	236	1834	1
139	1897	1	188	1466	1	237	2019	1
140	1456	0	189	1375	1	238	1097	1
141	1687	0	190	1097	1	239	1528	1
142	996	1	191	1620	0	240	1931	1
143	1405	1	192	1763	0	241	1274	1
144	1286	1	193	1422	0	242	886	0
145	1521	1	194	1290	0	243	1282	0

Respon-dent	Miles Driven	Type of Accom-modations	Respon-dent	Miles Driven	Type of Accom-modations	Respon-dent	Miles Driven	Type of Accom-modations
244	1323	1	293	1479	1	342	1603	0
245	1014	1	294	1522	1	343	2291	1
246	2230	0	295	1214	1	344	2123	0
247	1859	0	296	2098	0	345	1126	0
248	1920	1	297	2034	1	346	1483	0
249	2055	0	298	1109	0	347	1836	0
250	1502	1	299	1661	0	348	793	0
251	1037	0	300	1514	1	349	1434	1
252	1477	0	301	1470	0	350	862	1
253	2115	1	302	2069	1	351	1610	0
254	1556	0	303	1376	1	352	2053	1
255	1820	1	304	1342	0	353	1472	0
256	1442	1	305	1878	1	354	1286	1
257	1627	1	306	1773	1	355	1769	1
258	1340	1	307	1023	1	356	1423	1
259	1329	0	308	871	0	357	1793	0
260	1400	1	309	1255	1	358	1724	1
261	1349	1	310	1103	0	359	1570	0
262	1746	0	311	1511	0	360	1200	0
263	793	0	312	1266	0	361	1020	0
264	1383	0	313	1007	1	362	1730	0
265	1451	0	314	1684	1	363	1955	0
266	1280	0	315	1437	1	364	1498	0
267	1420	0	316	756	1	365	1521	0
268	1497	1	317	1823	1	366	1403	1
269	2076	1	318	1451	0	367	1256	1
270	1078	1	319	1450	1	368	1466	1
271	1526	1	320	1513	1	369	1803	0
272	1558	0	321	1995	1	370	2271	1
273	1802	1	322	1468	1	371	1075	0
274	904	1	323	1578	0	372	2031	0
275	858	0	324	905	1	373	1684	0
276	1350	1	325	1865	1	374	750	1
277	1225	0	326	1372	0	375	817	1
278	1740	1	327	1707	1	376	1626	1
279	1075	0	328	696	1	377	1723	1
280	740	1	329	1655	0	378	1220	0
281	1256	1	330	1785	0	379	1679	1
282	1453	0	331	962	0	380	1052	1
283	1167	0	332	2010	0	381	1790	0
284	1583	0	333	712	1	382	1555	0
285	1733	1	334	2128	0	383	1350	1
286	1726	0	335	1146	1	384	1365	0
287	2258	1	336	829	1	385	1429	1
288	1093	0	337	1668	1	386	1418	0
289	1766	0	338	1453	0	387	1484	0
290	706	1	339	880	1	388	1331	1
291	1630	1	340	1551	1	389	1437	0
292	1487	1	341	2186	0	390	1358	1

Respon-dent	Miles Driven	Type of Accom-modations	Respon-dent	Miles Driven	Type of Accom-modations	Respon-dent	Miles Driven	Type of Accom-modations
391	1500	1	440	2085	1	489	1221	1
392	1506	0	441	992	0	490	2169	1
393	1261	1	442	1806	1	491	1691	1
394	1773	1	443	976	0	492	1561	0
395	1131	0	444	336	1	493	1490	0
396	1812	0	445	1196	1	494	1445	0
397	871	0	446	1782	0	495	2380	0
398	1074	1	447	1625	1	496	1865	1
399	1827	1	448	1229	1	497	1214	1
400	2090	1	449	1108	0	498	1475	1
401	1796	1	450	1648	0	499	1049	0
402	1352	0	451	1528	0	500	1550	1
403	1987	0	452	1071	1	501	1819	1
404	1934	1	453	1357	0	502	1214	0
405	1229	1	454	1231	1	503	1651	0
406	1627	1	455	2033	0	504	1288	0
407	1709	0	456	1277	0	505	579	0
408	1317	0	457	1663	1	506	1994	0
409	1029	1	458	1318	0	507	1348	1
410	1540	1	459	1660	0	508	1595	0
411	1794	0	460	1103	0	509	1521	1
412	1718	0	461	1387	0	510	2126	1
413	1339	1	462	1776	1	511	1668	1
414	978	0	463	620	1	512	1257	1
415	150	0	464	1354	0	513	1693	1
416	1703	0	465	2024	0	514	1681	1
417	1879	1	466	1004	1	515	1408	0
418	988	1	467	1749	1	516	1993	0
419	1122	1	468	1166	1	517	1392	1
420	1270	1	469	1848	1	518	1694	1
421	1492	0	470	1393	1	519	464	1
422	1667	0	471	1158	0	520	1607	1
423	2034	0	472	769	0	521	1925	0
424	729	1	473	1060	0	522	1782	1
425	1759	1	474	1301	1	523	1630	0
426	2588	1	475	1711	1	524	1200	0
427	1162	1	476	831	0	525	1659	0
428	1494	1	477	1934	1	526	1518	1
429	1218	0	478	1210	1	527	932	1
430	1364	1	479	1705	1	528	1709	1
431	1359	1	480	988	1	529	1117	1
432	1594	0	481	1606	0	530	1636	0
433	864	0	482	1654	1	531	2730	0
434	1333	1	483	962	0	532	1100	0
435	1046	1	484	1916	1	533	1440	0
436	2057	0	485	1975	1	534	1290	0
437	2131	1	486	1351	1	535	804	1
438	1528	1	487	1854	1	536	1680	1
439	2043	1	488	1723	1	537	2277	1

Respon- dent	Miles Driven	Type of Accom- modations	Respon- dent	Miles Driven	Type of Accom- modations	Respon- dent	Miles Driven	Type of Accom- modations
538	1402	1	587	1139	0	636	2056	1
539	1474	1	588	1915	1	637	1622	0
540	1951	1	589	1512	0	638	1746	1
541	980	1	590	1818	1	639	2124	1
542	1152	1	591	2351	1	640	1430	1
543	638	1	592	1522	0	641	2052	0
544	2357	0	593	1501	1	642	1352	0
545	1814	1	594	1529	1	643	1721	1
546	504	1	595	1891	1	644	924	1
547	1917	0	596	1506	1	645	925	1
548	1633	1	597	905	1	646	1497	1
549	1651	0	598	1884	1	647	1885	0
550	1447	1	599	1000	1	648	1240	1
551	1350	1	600	1359	1	649	1083	1
552	1508	1	601	1004	1	650	1908	1
553	1524	0	602	1555	1	651	1403	0
554	971	1	603	1548	1	652	1484	1
555	1855	0	604	1993	0	653	1606	1
556	1333	1	605	1412	0	654	1490	0
557	1962	1	606	1833	1	655	2147	0
558	1442	1	607	1374	1	656	1045	0
559	1199	1	608	1487	0	657	1545	0
560	1843	1	609	1137	1	658	1818	0
561	1157	1	610	1547	0	659	859	0
562	2135	1	611	1894	1	660	714	1
563	1741	0	612	1454	0	661	1239	1
564	2106	1	613	1835	1	662	1943	0
565	1446	0	614	1575	1	663	1314	1
566	1483	1	615	1124	0	664	1246	1
567	1590	1	616	1944	0	665	1381	0
568	1765	1	617	666	1	666	1988	1
569	967	0	618	1269	0	667	719	1
570	1858	0	619	1578	0	668	726	0
571	1446	1	620	1144	0	669	2219	1
572	889	1	621	1550	1	670	1119	0
573	1418	1	622	1552	1	671	1290	0
574	1802	1	623	1837	0	672	1915	0
575	1817	1	624	2137	1	673	1259	1
576	1456	1	625	1314	0	674	1486	0
577	1395	1	626	1386	1	675	1164	1
578	1577	0	627	2045	1	676	579	1
579	1476	1	628	1485	0	677	1438	0
580	1565	1	629	1895	0	678	2426	1
581	2185	1	630	1764	1	679	1757	1
582	1673	1	631	1913	1	680	1489	1
583	1789	1	632	1586	1	681	1560	0
584	1421	0	633	1217	1	682	916	1
585	2060	1	634	1674	1	683	1971	1
586	1608	1	635	1086	1	684	1339	1

Respon-dent	Miles Driven	Type of Accom-modations	Respon-dent	Miles Driven	Type of Accom-modations	Respon-dent	Miles Driven	Type of Accom-modations
685	751	0	691	1591	1	697	1523	1
686	1220	0	692	1567	1	698	2081	0
687	1720	1	693	1467	0	699	1202	0
688	1463	0	694	1896	1	700	1605	0
689	2236	0	695	1202	0			
690	1861	1	696	1484	0			

DATA SET 5   Data for Chapter 7, Review Exercises 72–76

1 = yes, surgery was performed
0 = no, surgery was not performed

Subject	No. of Days	Surgery?	Subject	No. of Days	Surgery?	Subject	No. of Days	Surgery?
1	11	1	33	15	1	65	8	1
2	6	1	34	14	1	66	12	1
3	15	1	35	10	1	67	10	1
4	10	0	36	10	1	68	11	1
5	13	0	37	12	0	69	11	1
6	13	1	38	10	1	70	9	0
7	12	1	39	8	0	71	12	1
8	14	1	40	9	0	72	9	0
9	12	1	41	13	0	73	12	1
10	10	0	42	11	1	74	12	1
11	15	1	43	7	1	75	12	0
12	12	1	44	8	1	76	6	0
13	13	1	45	9	1	77	10	0
14	9	1	46	8	1	78	7	1
15	16	1	47	12	0	79	9	1
16	14	1	48	11	1	80	8	0
17	5	1	49	14	1	81	14	0
18	12	1	50	12	1	82	6	1
19	11	0	51	13	0	83	16	0
20	8	0	52	13	1	84	17	1
21	14	1	53	8	1	85	13	1
22	8	1	54	6	1	86	12	1
23	8	1	55	6	1	87	17	1
24	6	1	56	16	0	88	15	1
25	13	0	57	12	1	89	14	1
26	11	0	58	2	0	90	8	1
27	10	1	59	14	1	91	4	1
28	16	1	60	10	0	92	5	1
29	7	1	61	12	1	93	13	1
30	12	0	62	8	0	94	7	0
31	11	1	63	10	1	95	11	1
32	9	0	64	9	1	96	8	1

Subject	No. of Days	Surgery?	Subject	No. of Days	Surgery?	Subject	No. of Days	Surgery?
97	7	1	148	8	0	199	16	1
98	10	1	149	10	0	200	11	0
99	12	1	150	5	1	201	4	1
100	4	1	151	10	1	202	10	1
101	5	1	152	9	0	203	10	1
102	9	1	153	11	0	204	6	1
103	12	0	154	7	1	205	9	0
104	6	1	155	7	0	206	9	0
105	13	0	156	11	1	207	15	0
106	14	1	157	6	0	208	17	1
107	8	1	158	7	1	209	15	1
108	8	1	159	10	1	210	8	0
109	7	1	160	14	1	211	7	1
110	12	1	161	13	0	212	11	1
111	13	1	162	7	1	213	9	1
112	12	1	163	7	1	214	15	1
113	9	1	164	3	1	215	11	0
114	10	1	165	13	1	216	8	1
115	7	0	166	13	1	217	6	1
116	7	0	167	7	0	218	12	0
117	8	0	168	6	1	219	6	1
118	12	1	169	10	1	220	8	1
119	9	1	170	7	0	221	11	1
120	8	0	171	9	1	222	6	1
121	9	1	172	9	1	223	17	1
122	11	1	173	11	1	224	9	0
123	6	1	174	5	0	225	7	1
124	18	1	175	6	1	226	10	1
125	6	1	176	12	0	227	13	1
126	7	1	177	10	1	228	9	0
127	4	1	178	10	1	229	10	1
128	12	1	179	15	1	230	1	0
129	8	1	180	7	1	231	9	1
130	10	0	181	12	1	232	5	1
131	6	1	182	10	0	233	9	1
132	14	1	183	15	0	234	14	1
133	7	0	184	9	1	235	11	0
134	13	1	185	8	0	236	11	1
135	16	0	186	11	1	237	8	0
136	7	1	187	12	1	238	6	0
137	9	1	188	15	1	239	12	0
138	12	0	189	9	1	240	14	1
139	10	1	190	8	0	241	12	1
140	9	1	191	5	1	242	9	0
141	11	1	192	5	0	243	11	1
142	6	0	193	13	1	244	7	1
143	8	1	194	6	1	245	8	0
144	10	1	195	4	1	246	8	1
145	4	0	196	13	1	247	9	1
146	10	0	197	8	1	248	9	1
147	4	1	198	7	1	249	11	1

Subject	No. of Days	Surgery?	Subject	No. of Days	Surgery?	Subject	No. of Days	Surgery?
250	13	1	301	11	0	352	13	1
251	14	0	302	15	1	353	8	1
252	13	0	303	12	1	354	14	1
253	10	1	304	11	1	355	8	0
254	10	1	305	12	1	356	11	0
255	12	1	306	6	0	357	12	1
256	8	1	307	11	0	358	12	1
257	11	1	308	5	1	359	8	0
258	7	0	309	17	1	360	9	1
259	9	1	310	13	1	361	11	1
260	8	1	311	11	0	362	12	1
261	4	1	312	13	1	363	14	1
262	12	1	313	6	0	364	9	1
263	8	0	314	11	1	365	10	0
264	3	1	315	12	1	366	5	1
265	7	1	316	5	1	367	8	0
266	9	1	317	10	1	368	10	1
267	10	0	318	12	1	369	6	1
268	10	1	319	11	1	370	11	0
269	12	1	320	9	1	371	9	0
270	11	0	321	12	1	372	11	1
271	14	1	322	11	1	373	10	1
272	13	1	323	10	1	374	6	1
273	11	1	324	14	1	375	6	0
274	7	1	325	8	1	376	7	1
275	11	1	326	7	0	377	13	1
276	5	1	327	9	1	378	7	0
277	8	1	328	15	1	379	13	0
278	11	0	329	5	1	380	21	1
279	8	1	330	9	0	381	15	0
280	8	1	331	16	1	382	17	1
281	8	1	332	9	1	383	10	0
282	7	0	333	8	1	384	8	1
283	9	1	334	5	0	385	10	0
284	10	1	335	9	1	386	6	1
285	12	1	336	11	1	387	5	0
286	11	1	337	5	1	388	9	0
287	15	0	338	11	0	389	8	1
288	12	1	339	10	1	390	9	0
289	8	0	340	14	0	391	7	1
290	15	1	341	11	1	392	11	1
291	8	1	342	10	1	393	10	1
292	10	1	343	11	1	394	8	1
293	14	1	344	6	0	395	8	0
294	6	1	345	6	0	396	12	1
295	9	1	346	14	1	397	10	1
296	14	1	347	7	0	398	12	1
297	10	1	348	7	1	399	9	0
298	9	1	349	9	1	400	8	0
299	8	1	350	10	0	401	12	1
300	12	1	351	11	0	402	17	1

Subject	No. of Days	Surgery?	Subject	No. of Days	Surgery?	Subject	No. of Days	Surgery?
403	8	0	454	13	0	505	5	1
404	11	1	455	10	1	506	14	1
405	9	1	456	8	0	507	7	1
406	7	1	457	13	1	508	11	1
407	8	0	458	10	0	509	11	1
408	13	1	459	18	1	510	7	1
409	11	1	460	9	0	511	11	1
410	9	0	461	13	0	512	14	0
411	7	1	462	13	1	513	7	1
412	7	0	463	5	1	514	10	1
413	11	1	464	10	1	515	11	0
414	13	0	465	10	1	516	7	0
415	9	0	466	8	1	517	7	0
416	10	0	467	9	0	518	12	1
417	12	0	468	8	1	519	8	1
418	11	0	469	9	1	520	7	0
419	3	1	470	8	0	521	10	1
420	11	1	471	12	0	522	14	1
421	14	0	472	15	0	523	12	1
422	12	1	473	10	1	524	8	1
423	8	1	474	8	1	525	12	1
424	8	1	475	7	1	526	9	0
425	6	1	476	11	0	527	14	0
426	13	1	477	7	1	528	5	1
427	10	0	478	16	1	529	9	1
428	4	1	479	6	1	530	14	0
429	8	1	480	8	1	531	10	1
430	16	1	481	8	0	532	12	1
431	7	1	482	13	1	533	15	1
432	8	0	483	7	1	534	5	1
433	8	1	484	14	0	535	7	1
434	6	0	485	10	1	536	18	1
435	8	1	486	12	1	537	10	1
436	8	1	487	13	1	538	7	1
437	8	1	488	7	1	539	10	0
438	11	1	489	10	1	540	9	0
439	9	0	490	4	0	541	12	0
440	9	0	491	11	1	542	11	0
441	9	1	492	8	1	543	16	1
442	6	0	493	11	1	544	10	1
443	10	0	494	9	0	545	10	1
444	11	1	495	9	1	546	5	1
445	10	1	496	11	1	547	12	0
446	11	1	497	17	1	548	9	1
447	14	1	498	9	1	549	13	0
448	9	1	499	13	0	550	13	1
449	5	1	500	16	1	551	7	0
450	12	1	501	9	1	552	12	1
451	11	1	502	7	0	553	10	1
452	10	0	503	9	1	554	2	1
453	13	1	504	11	0	555	12	1

Subject	No. of Days	Surgery?	Subject	No. of Days	Surgery?	Subject	No. of Days	Surgery?
556	11	0	605	11	0	654	17	1
557	17	1	606	7	1	655	5	1
558	9	1	607	7	1	656	11	0
559	9	1	608	6	1	657	8	0
560	11	1	609	9	1	658	9	0
561	14	0	610	6	0	659	9	1
562	15	1	611	13	1	660	11	1
563	10	0	612	10	1	661	13	0
564	11	1	613	17	0	662	9	1
565	11	1	614	10	1	663	11	1
566	7	1	615	12	1	664	10	1
567	5	1	616	11	1	665	8	0
568	14	0	617	16	1	666	16	1
569	6	1	618	11	1	667	12	1
570	7	1	619	9	1	668	10	0
571	14	1	620	9	1	669	11	1
572	11	1	621	12	0	670	10	1
573	11	1	622	10	1	671	10	1
574	6	0	623	14	0	672	5	1
575	3	0	624	15	1	673	6	0
576	10	0	625	11	1	674	12	0
577	15	1	626	3	0	675	16	0
578	11	0	627	11	1	676	5	1
579	13	1	628	10	0	677	11	1
580	8	1	629	11	0	678	10	1
581	19	1	630	14	1	679	7	1
582	11	0	631	11	1	680	7	0
583	12	1	632	6	1	681	6	1
584	7	0	633	10	1	682	11	1
585	11	1	634	4	1	683	15	0
586	9	1	635	6	0	684	11	1
587	8	1	636	12	1	685	12	0
588	4	0	637	14	1	686	6	1
589	11	1	638	9	1	687	7	1
590	8	1	639	10	0	688	13	1
591	12	1	640	8	1	689	13	1
592	4	0	641	12	1	690	15	1
593	10	1	642	12	0	691	2	0
594	6	1	643	11	1	692	9	1
595	10	0	644	16	1	693	9	1
596	13	0	645	5	0	694	7	0
597	11	1	646	13	0	695	10	1
598	7	0	647	11	1	696	16	0
599	12	0	648	9	1	697	4	1
600	12	1	649	11	1	698	10	1
601	9	1	650	12	1	699	14	0
602	11	1	651	7	0	700	12	1
603	7	1	652	11	1			
604	9	0	653	12	1			

DATA SET 6 Data for Chapter 8, Review Exercises 55–56

Population	Subjects
A	Male clerical workers
B	Female clerical workers
C	Male executives
D	Female executives

	Population					Population			
Row No.	A	B	C	D	Row No.	A	B	C	D
1	43	48	71	61	43	55	30	53	82
2	41	55	52	70	44	49	32	75	47
3	51	48	70	60	45	52	38	66	68
4	48	50	67	65	46	54	38	73	63
5	44	28	75	54	47	59	34	66	73
6	30	28	71	69	48	59	54	69	75
7	57	35	66	56	49	47	58	55	62
8	40	34	49	79	50	61	49	65	58
9	46	47	60	78	51	49	36	52	47
10	59	53	71	67	52	43	18	56	65
11	39	42	53	61	53	52	25	64	73
12	48	45	64	72	54	62	44	56	55
13	51	37	76	72	55	52	58	32	70
14	42	34	44	71	56	37	32	75	55
15	51	47	58	64	57	56	23	88	71
16	52	29	51	51	58	51	10	68	57
17	44	38	52	62	59	58	47	66	42
18	55	28	58	68	60	64	51	66	75
19	36	39	60	57	61	48	49	63	80
20	53	32	67	63	62	47	52	70	56
21	41	37	67	61	63	39	46	59	76
22	59	27	73	62	64	62	48	59	76
23	46	39	61	59	65	63	48	78	63
24	65	49	46	79	66	53	39	43	75
25	49	52	65	66	67	41	53	71	69
26	46	44	59	60	68	53	23	76	71
27	57	26	52	70	69	61	50	82	68
28	55	40	74	52	70	35	27	73	88
29	44	45	63	70	71	50	36	72	67
30	47	34	64	76	72	64	26	53	54
31	32	61	92	55	73	44	56	77	59
32	44	37	53	72	74	53	57	69	58
33	43	20	69	64	75	60	56	67	70
34	51	39	74	62	76	55	46	53	53
35	40	49	75	55	77	37	30	64	73
36	44	48	62	69	78	49	43	69	55
37	44	47	81	60	79	40	22	83	65
38	67	36	55	83	80	51	21	50	86
39	42	34	67	76	81	37	55	55	85
40	50	45	61	64	82	40	48	64	74
41	41	54	58	69	83	51	43	89	52
42	44	27	69	66	84	59	45	59	73

Row No.	Population				Row No.	Population			
	A	B	C	D		A	B	C	D
85	48	37	78	64	135	51	39	64	58
86	45	41	51	79	136	56	56	49	68
87	59	41	70	65	137	57	42	65	67
88	50	48	50	85	138	58	41	87	50
89	66	32	67	67	139	52	42	52	62
90	39	35	68	66	140	54	48	64	68
91	66	37	83	68	141	40	30	59	55
92	45	49	72	63	142	52	48	52	60
93	41	27	35	75	143	42	21	84	77
94	60	54	63	49	144	48	39	59	61
95	54	58	70	73	145	59	41	66	80
96	46	30	69	53	146	54	48	58	60
97	46	27	59	69	147	65	35	71	61
98	69	47	58	76	148	72	31	47	60
99	46	40	55	57	149	35	35	68	58
100	44	26	66	61	150	55	42	54	67
101	62	44	62	60	151	34	34	29	58
102	44	25	78	76	152	33	25	88	47
103	60	39	79	66	153	54	48	60	61
104	46	55	66	63	154	54	34	79	62
105	33	32	52	47	155	53	44	80	62
106	48	56	68	58	156	46	39	75	75
107	44	40	56	61	157	57	32	54	51
108	71	45	51	65	158	46	51	59	51
109	60	50	67	59	159	49	42	68	69
110	40	40	63	54	160	39	35	60	56
111	44	42	67	55	161	53	36	83	55
112	40	47	83	75	162	44	36	69	59
113	46	25	45	55	163	44	33	57	60
114	34	37	74	52	164	43	44	64	63
115	54	32	56	94	165	44	52	55	61
116	59	13	69	65	166	37	46	62	58
117	43	47	76	78	167	48	38	69	92
118	43	21	56	75	168	39	70	81	78
119	38	45	60	62	169	39	40	84	61
120	61	35	71	53	170	49	35	58	61
121	32	45	49	61	171	46	33	58	78
122	57	35	42	75	172	43	48	73	69
123	47	37	56	65	173	59	31	60	76
124	57	47	87	53	174	47	52	60	78
125	61	49	64	57	175	38	30	70	75
126	47	44	70	68	176	48	47	62	51
127	53	32	51	75	177	75	29	65	65
128	69	31	71	74	178	36	35	71	56
129	46	41	74	50	179	61	37	68	53
130	58	38	67	77	180	38	25	64	68
131	39	30	70	66	181	41	48	78	66
132	39	36	43	60	182	56	21	61	70
133	70	34	69	73	183	59	28	70	66
134	57	36	95	52	184	38	31	60	67

	Population					Population			
Row No.	A	B	C	D	**Row No.**	A	B	C	D
185	36	42	72	86	235	40	42	73	78
186	44	52	75	90	236	56	34	63	82
187	51	42	62	58	237	74	35	65	63
188	57	50	73	77	238	46	35	64	60
189	54	51	54	62	239	42	54	60	70
190	71	46	62	64	240	32	42	56	68
191	46	35	61	58	241	32	22	77	76
192	54	26	56	66	242	35	37	62	75
193	50	46	72	75	243	54	11	77	64
194	53	45	59	48	244	55	38	76	70
195	58	50	60	71	245	62	38	58	71
196	60	36	83	59	246	38	47	56	69
197	55	39	72	50	247	50	29	64	61
198	41	42	58	61	248	43	45	64	46
199	57	42	46	49	249	49	44	63	76
200	57	33	54	58	250	53	55	60	69
201	63	52	64	71	251	56	34	81	60
202	51	43	76	56	252	55	64	53	75
203	59	38	69	66	253	46	47	51	57
204	40	35	69	69	254	60	59	49	56
205	33	63	66	66	255	40	42	71	58
206	40	36	72	52	256	65	46	54	62
207	33	18	66	67	257	53	35	60	51
208	53	39	56	56	258	54	66	71	74
209	63	39	64	89	259	55	30	58	66
210	54	50	85	76	260	55	42	51	55
211	33	31	49	65	261	37	17	66	67
212	49	49	58	59	262	58	44	52	82
213	43	39	63	70	263	49	42	65	46
214	55	34	80	72	264	25	48	68	71
215	72	34	62	82	265	61	36	80	90
216	46	55	71	61	266	54	33	72	60
217	57	40	56	73	267	41	54	65	64
218	44	30	61	68	268	58	52	69	58
219	53	30	63	67	269	45	38	79	72
220	64	43	67	72	270	58	40	73	82
221	37	39	85	72	271	51	43	73	57
222	49	43	59	70	272	46	51	72	50
223	51	45	58	73	273	47	44	72	62
224	59	30	59	83	274	57	33	63	55
225	55	40	39	66	275	37	38	65	72
226	59	42	69	73	276	63	22	61	75
227	47	33	60	57	277	55	44	71	66
228	58	40	66	79	278	68	49	63	63
229	48	52	80	73	279	53	33	80	67
230	52	47	68	52	280	56	33	60	55
231	41	24	71	55	281	50	37	64	69
232	23	60	63	72	282	68	23	59	58
233	63	48	56	75	283	48	39	64	67
234	72	31	51	57	284	62	25	60	68

Row No.	Population A	B	C	D	Row No.	Population A	B	C	D
285	58	38	77	83	335	30	51	62	60
286	56	11	70	70	336	40	45	72	56
287	48	38	74	75	337	70	35	60	68
288	59	41	86	61	338	40	53	59	71
289	57	47	75	53	339	27	47	45	64
290	56	53	51	76	340	34	44	65	61
291	46	40	69	64	341	53	52	71	63
292	41	47	73	79	342	53	48	64	58
293	40	36	81	69	343	43	60	74	76
294	43	59	70	46	344	38	47	67	75
295	41	39	59	64	345	53	35	65	87
296	44	36	75	76	346	46	48	69	78
297	46	38	63	44	347	47	41	72	63
298	53	36	64	59	348	60	44	55	61
299	55	30	54	67	349	46	35	60	70
300	40	29	64	62	350	44	40	43	63
301	43	44	58	57	351	50	27	65	66
302	35	44	71	91	352	45	36	56	71
303	47	55	61	54	353	61	46	75	57
304	49	26	67	60	354	63	30	58	61
305	63	25	76	66	355	61	30	52	66
306	76	31	75	73	356	58	25	68	63
307	47	40	70	68	357	60	37	70	65
308	48	17	50	54	358	27	37	69	73
309	52	46	66	56	359	34	50	66	68
310	41	27	68	90	360	46	35	90	83
311	58	46	75	78	361	47	22	55	45
312	44	42	72	68	362	46	63	46	60
313	38	46	53	73	363	61	49	49	66
314	55	33	75	74	364	54	30	77	78
315	50	45	65	66	365	32	53	47	63
316	50	48	75	72	366	54	34	72	74
317	62	48	81	72	367	40	38	77	85
318	49	45	47	79	368	65	24	47	67
319	50	33	56	76	369	49	24	64	63
320	34	29	58	67	370	69	46	80	66
321	59	25	64	94	371	55	41	70	76
322	50	40	83	69	372	66	40	64	78
323	59	47	84	57	373	76	47	81	64
324	51	45	62	69	374	44	45	60	69
325	55	39	81	80	375	45	36	58	49
326	45	42	56	64	376	57	37	69	63
327	67	40	73	72	377	48	36	62	59
328	39	57	66	49	378	49	31	81	69
329	46	52	62	57	379	43	47	68	62
330	45	41	72	73	380	59	32	72	70
331	56	39	74	62	381	44	33	59	65
332	49	48	70	69	382	48	30	58	62
333	42	51	79	54	383	45	43	66	81
334	39	47	70	79	384	51	47	56	54

Row No.	Population				Row No.	Population			
	A	B	C	D		A	B	C	D
385	45	27	76	53	435	44	56	57	53
386	66	41	79	72	436	66	33	60	70
387	53	52	59	61	437	58	34	62	58
388	45	27	54	68	438	51	42	78	74
389	50	36	87	76	439	47	34	70	57
390	67	48	49	50	440	57	52	64	76
391	62	29	67	67	441	49	42	73	70
392	49	51	50	62	442	66	43	74	62
393	47	37	50	74	443	55	34	62	58
394	71	47	60	73	444	48	39	61	73
395	50	63	62	56	445	42	26	62	68
396	45	51	63	65	446	50	60	75	76
397	50	49	57	66	447	39	66	70	69
398	62	47	50	78	448	60	43	73	63
399	52	34	62	56	449	59	35	73	73
400	29	51	68	67	450	47	41	57	54
401	59	42	64	51	451	67	38	59	50
402	39	38	62	68	452	42	30	51	63
403	59	35	62	80	453	51	36	60	56
404	56	42	56	73	454	53	29	78	77
405	38	44	70	67	455	39	39	68	71
406	51	34	52	63	456	63	34	64	75
407	43	28	70	58	457	32	57	75	66
408	19	48	62	85	458	53	37	51	59
409	74	37	62	77	459	53	56	68	66
410	61	31	74	62	460	40	37	58	51
411	31	44	70	52	461	60	24	77	63
412	67	42	67	61	462	43	51	85	63
413	54	34	64	49	463	34	41	55	56
414	49	19	59	64	464	54	51	63	74
415	57	22	68	69	465	46	35	64	74
416	56	40	69	72	466	51	46	55	55
417	56	57	66	46	467	35	52	74	73
418	39	44	66	81	468	48	49	65	63
419	65	34	66	71	469	46	24	62	65
420	47	23	81	66	470	39	39	68	61
421	64	17	62	52	471	61	42	61	71
422	38	50	72	50	472	43	29	49	78
423	64	31	65	66	473	58	31	81	71
424	55	41	76	57	474	52	48	58	41
425	56	43	65	67	475	55	55	76	70
426	43	35	73	83	476	28	38	64	60
427	51	28	60	79	477	50	38	55	66
428	64	43	54	49	478	42	37	68	62
429	39	27	67	69	479	59	42	62	59
430	55	27	45	72	480	51	40	66	64
431	43	30	62	84	481	58	39	58	61
432	55	57	68	62	482	62	41	65	59
433	50	21	64	66	483	45	51	60	61
434	26	37	59	80	484	48	31	63	76

	Population					Population			
Row No.	A	B	C	D	Row No.	A	B	C	D
485	40	39	50	67	493	48	64	66	84
486	37	38	74	63	494	53	41	81	85
487	55	38	75	74	495	49	37	47	58
488	44	19	54	75	496	48	44	76	65
489	50	45	74	66	497	67	40	60	79
490	28	37	88	58	498	35	35	64	66
491	51	45	52	69	499	52	54	68	67
492	52	55	63	63	500	68	38	65	35

DATA SET 7   Data for Chapter 9, Review Exercises 35–44

Item No.	X	Y	Item No.	X	Y	Item No.	X	Y
1	166	17.23	37	216	21.41	73	128	11.01
2	143	12.51	38	149	14.71	74	162	12.49
3	263	23.21	39	205	17.40	75	173	17.08
4	177	10.57	40	99	7.29	76	117	15.99
5	147	13.69	41	186	19.13	77	128	15.51
6	184	17.08	42	210	19.23	78	214	19.44
7	158	15.50	43	122	10.82	79	168	17.05
8	149	17.17	44	159	15.99	80	212	17.40
9	203	16.75	45	150	15.04	81	182	13.49
10	144	13.24	46	125	10.99	82	218	23.34
11	162	13.83	47	237	21.95	83	188	15.08
12	175	19.47	48	138	12.64	84	200	15.87
13	173	14.15	49	112	6.52	85	153	10.38
14	163	16.22	50	189	20.59	86	193	15.97
15	148	8.69	51	137	13.97	87	155	15.28
16	146	18.87	52	138	10.07	88	164	13.77
17	79	8.39	53	162	15.65	89	170	16.68
18	166	13.30	54	183	15.44	90	197	11.70
19	174	14.39	55	205	24.24	91	119	14.71
20	161	15.29	56	113	11.30	92	113	6.79
21	211	16.64	57	183	19.03	93	111	8.63
22	166	13.49	58	185	18.58	94	228	17.66
23	121	8.41	59	203	13.95	95	185	12.75
24	171	18.94	60	167	12.94	96	213	20.28
25	167	15.39	61	93	7.99	97	223	15.05
26	221	22.18	62	148	10.04	98	190	16.65
27	103	8.67	63	187	18.49	99	163	16.25
28	173	16.05	64	88	10.25	100	225	21.55
29	170	13.80	65	202	16.56	101	101	6.25
30	187	17.24	66	211	19.76	102	86	8.26
31	165	14.89	67	205	17.47	103	195	16.03
32	228	20.87	68	196	12.00	104	125	11.35
33	143	12.18	69	202	20.82	105	192	17.46
34	141	12.36	70	158	14.46	106	146	14.61
35	152	12.50	71	233	23.47	107	139	14.45
36	167	14.98	72	167	13.66	108	157	13.10

Item No.	X	Y	Item No.	X	Y	Item No.	X	Y
109	213	20.24	161	199	21.00	213	150	15.33
110	203	17.36	162	216	17.01	214	113	9.48
111	202	18.87	163	192	17.28	215	146	14.81
112	211	18.71	164	209	17.54	216	167	17.50
113	170	15.07	165	173	18.06	217	180	15.29
114	198	16.77	166	177	12.96	218	221	18.63
115	124	10.89	167	207	18.72	219	225	18.89
116	125	14.86	168	123	6.32	220	130	10.82
117	191	15.84	169	95	9.35	221	137	6.65
118	229	23.17	170	194	18.10	222	138	14.07
119	156	15.48	171	144	17.76	223	100	14.09
120	132	12.14	172	132	12.34	224	248	23.07
121	143	14.05	173	142	12.45	225	204	18.11
122	126	13.77	174	159	11.14	226	222	11.42
123	143	6.41	175	92	11.30	227	188	19.56
124	155	15.39	176	201	15.11	228	175	11.73
125	175	15.53	177	167	14.49	229	182	16.15
126	133	10.36	178	96	9.41	230	165	13.63
127	172	13.50	179	158	13.74	231	113	8.91
128	130	9.46	180	90	6.53	232	212	19.76
129	156	11.52	181	191	19.69	233	165	16.18
130	183	15.24	182	185	16.44	234	207	15.64
131	205	16.85	183	88	9.53	235	203	16.13
132	126	14.61	184	206	17.81	236	101	8.94
133	184	13.01	185	249	25.29	237	135	10.62
134	208	14.24	186	194	21.57	238	164	15.14
135	112	9.47	187	231	22.38	239	237	23.02
136	207	18.25	188	166	17.82	240	197	18.78
137	143	11.21	189	130	12.62	241	188	16.16
138	218	16.90	190	161	12.94	242	134	12.17
139	137	10.83	191	111	10.56	243	244	23.11
140	191	14.35	192	181	16.32	244	106	11.67
141	182	17.18	193	121	10.70	245	176	15.68
142	163	16.17	194	172	12.93	246	176	15.36
143	134	11.73	195	145	15.57	247	182	12.46
144	125	11.82	196	148	12.75	248	248	18.47
145	154	16.15	197	149	16.37	249	247	25.28
146	173	14.05	198	218	20.57	250	90	3.87
147	100	10.64	199	239	17.59	251	156	16.77
148	160	17.08	200	249	22.90	252	159	14.76
149	193	19.33	201	211	20.26	253	210	18.16
150	178	14.63	202	223	22.95	254	216	19.31
151	108	5.70	203	154	15.23	255	182	18.57
152	147	13.30	204	155	12.36	256	107	8.51
153	172	15.45	205	121	7.59	257	198	18.48
154	174	16.95	206	195	14.56	258	137	9.64
155	162	12.54	207	166	12.19	259	252	20.47
156	194	17.04	208	135	12.03	260	188	16.67
157	170	13.54	209	164	15.49	261	225	17.56
158	176	14.58	210	179	12.08	262	141	10.61
159	176	14.15	211	164	14.76	263	141	13.05
160	165	13.34	212	132	9.74	264	201	20.41

Item No.	X	Y	Item No.	X	Y	Item No.	X	Y
265	187	16.52	317	201	18.66	369	125	12.05
266	167	16.61	318	204	16.16	370	200	15.55
267	88	10.27	319	229	17.14	371	206	17.43
268	238	21.32	320	264	26.48	372	164	16.18
269	107	8.22	321	226	16.95	373	137	12.59
270	121	12.35	322	170	15.61	374	214	16.46
271	160	13.32	323	179	15.92	375	215	15.24
272	222	20.34	324	249	23.14	376	149	12.67
273	125	9.62	325	124	12.86	377	226	19.27
274	167	13.21	326	175	13.06	378	107	10.25
275	167	15.79	327	189	15.12	379	203	15.56
276	127	11.60	328	111	10.14	380	206	18.80
277	213	16.45	329	191	15.86	381	95	9.48
278	114	7.97	330	192	18.57	382	172	16.87
279	215	17.70	331	141	9.06	383	165	11.67
280	147	13.17	332	176	12.11	384	118	11.21
281	170	15.50	333	163	11.45	385	142	11.94
282	178	12.25	334	128	13.02	386	126	10.51
283	142	13.19	335	214	23.67	387	185	15.21
284	158	16.36	336	159	15.58	388	212	20.36
285	189	14.70	337	231	16.72	389	225	15.75
286	191	15.02	338	200	17.74	390	217	25.52
287	143	10.10	339	219	15.97	391	222	15.64
288	217	19.21	340	200	15.55	392	148	18.59
289	245	19.72	341	159	15.62	393	202	16.38
290	253	25.97	342	209	17.55	394	171	13.63
291	233	24.51	343	184	15.17	395	201	17.29
292	200	15.28	344	160	15.75	396	165	10.84
293	184	14.03	345	144	11.18	397	187	14.84
294	153	14.88	346	170	14.47	398	133	13.27
295	218	16.75	347	191	15.40	399	94	12.03
296	181	13.96	348	143	13.81	400	145	14.33
297	217	15.80	349	217	21.86	401	191	16.77
298	139	14.08	350	159	16.52	402	108	12.88
299	226	17.30	351	214	21.32	403	207	18.03
300	151	11.28	352	132	12.37	404	171	13.75
301	164	16.54	353	198	15.61	405	238	14.76
302	157	14.04	354	157	15.81	406	198	14.72
303	208	22.73	355	210	16.49	407	214	16.43
304	176	13.18	356	216	16.11	408	153	10.62
305	184	17.07	357	183	16.53	409	170	14.79
306	176	14.54	358	219	23.80	410	205	17.52
307	209	18.61	359	128	11.10	411	239	19.97
308	205	22.18	360	243	17.56	412	183	9.94
309	150	13.61	361	155	12.57	413	249	20.92
310	183	17.99	362	197	19.15	414	141	11.77
311	176	15.98	363	126	13.04	415	197	15.74
312	208	21.11	364	137	8.01	416	129	10.02
313	126	11.76	365	209	19.91	417	247	20.19
314	217	18.15	366	165	12.10	418	148	13.08
315	127	13.15	367	148	13.64	419	74	8.01
316	174	13.03	368	130	9.44	420	170	16.96

Item No.	X	Y	Item No.	X	Y	Item No.	X	Y
421	220	22.59	473	158	13.03	525	202	19.64
422	144	14.15	474	164	15.89	526	116	2.87
423	136	11.49	475	215	17.42	527	203	17.91
424	154	9.58	476	133	11.07	528	199	16.69
425	250	17.74	477	167	13.71	529	214	18.10
426	220	19.81	478	152	12.46	530	158	14.20
427	204	16.55	479	118	14.13	531	169	10.63
428	168	13.40	480	183	20.19	532	169	13.74
429	169	13.37	481	170	13.86	533	174	16.35
430	180	13.68	482	217	18.48	534	217	19.23
431	223	21.14	483	205	14.21	535	153	15.72
432	179	13.55	484	157	12.71	536	232	21.47
433	108	7.42	485	230	22.86	537	182	8.92
434	117	7.88	486	175	16.27	538	119	7.65
435	200	17.07	487	215	18.53	539	188	15.76
436	105	13.44	488	144	15.32	540	255	20.20
437	155	10.87	489	157	12.05	541	199	16.77
438	169	13.55	490	121	6.41	542	132	10.72
439	100	5.29	491	226	18.28	543	174	14.76
440	206	19.97	492	180	12.30	544	214	14.30
441	93	5.87	493	213	18.27	545	254	19.86
442	181	17.12	494	170	15.97	546	139	9.09
443	88	9.03	495	92	4.33	547	227	24.38
444	184	12.82	496	227	18.76	548	118	8.29
445	190	17.33	497	173	17.96	549	205	21.59
446	236	18.39	498	168	17.76	550	134	5.20
447	198	16.21	499	163	15.48	551	201	13.94
448	105	11.42	500	141	10.85	552	169	14.92
449	175	13.90	501	136	14.07	553	147	13.20
450	141	10.32	502	230	19.99	554	89	9.47
451	98	11.50	503	176	17.18	555	180	16.04
452	132	12.16	504	170	16.28	556	249	21.51
453	164	15.36	505	154	16.15	557	187	19.90
454	122	8.32	506	256	25.40	558	164	15.52
455	155	10.30	507	203	17.40	559	127	14.23
456	172	19.44	508	257	17.72	560	180	16.00
457	169	14.67	509	215	16.58	561	180	16.42
458	130	12.79	510	190	13.67	562	140	14.86
459	115	10.62	511	178	18.55	563	126	15.26
460	169	19.25	512	181	15.49	564	104	8.42
461	122	21.23	513	219	19.16	565	198	16.62
462	150	13.68	514	228	20.86	566	169	16.07
463	197	17.25	515	181	14.33	567	116	9.68
464	117	7.15	516	162	14.95	568	196	16.93
465	171	16.95	517	201	18.84	569	163	15.37
466	220	14.48	518	194	19.79	570	238	18.38
467	143	14.19	519	106	8.45	571	170	17.99
468	178	15.12	520	218	18.92	572	195	15.42
469	138	16.42	521	269	24.01	573	107	9.16
470	145	10.34	522	131	12.15	574	199	18.70
471	190	18.37	523	184	14.05	575	175	14.10
472	173	12.87	524	211	16.86	576	162	17.03

Item No.	X	Y	Item No.	X	Y	Item No.	X	Y
577	211	19.49	629	233	19.87	681	161	14.28
578	129	15.45	630	147	12.48	682	176	18.52
579	158	14.90	631	246	20.23	683	168	17.93
580	165	13.85	632	201	19.03	684	178	17.70
581	155	13.77	633	209	18.39	685	157	13.17
582	216	19.87	634	228	23.59	686	179	18.13
583	153	14.10	635	198	17.02	687	120	7.86
584	141	7.46	636	225	18.27	688	220	19.33
585	104	12.06	637	163	11.29	689	178	14.58
586	182	18.96	638	191	15.31	690	195	13.07
587	170	15.83	639	186	13.78	691	290	29.32
588	141	8.85	640	138	14.14	692	192	13.52
589	176	13.06	641	171	13.89	693	182	13.98
590	121	10.76	642	220	17.67	694	151	15.25
591	169	11.24	643	171	12.78	695	235	20.33
592	214	17.56	644	132	9.52	696	226	16.14
593	230	16.10	645	182	17.52	697	230	19.86
594	123	11.60	646	199	20.82	698	207	16.35
595	166	13.12	647	214	18.46	699	151	13.52
596	184	14.65	648	208	20.95	700	144	12.40
597	182	13.09	649	163	13.96	701	219	18.48
598	199	14.46	650	236	18.38	702	183	13.02
599	148	11.86	651	218	20.43	703	216	20.40
600	157	17.15	652	142	14.35	704	153	10.54
601	219	17.49	653	161	10.77	705	188	17.89
602	170	14.94	654	156	13.97	706	98	10.42
603	196	16.25	655	137	11.50	707	238	17.48
604	191	16.75	656	214	15.88	708	150	10.65
605	163	14.61	657	153	14.37	709	146	13.73
606	191	20.50	658	261	23.25	710	160	17.72
607	137	9.91	659	192	15.91	711	191	19.88
608	234	20.08	660	177	13.56	712	140	13.20
609	87	6.81	661	171	16.75	713	147	13.67
610	131	12.41	662	231	21.74	714	190	19.44
611	120	9.71	663	158	14.57	715	170	13.83
612	185	16.50	664	182	17.04	716	174	15.79
613	161	13.85	665	158	16.12	717	171	16.68
614	131	11.01	666	119	10.46	718	248	21.42
615	139	11.32	667	209	20.75	719	224	19.36
616	195	20.12	668	216	21.38	720	167	10.99
617	197	16.12	669	116	8.83	721	167	16.34
618	153	19.36	670	240	17.01	722	120	11.31
619	134	11.88	671	99	6.38	723	98	8.51
620	175	12.36	672	170	13.22	724	88	6.40
621	182	18.71	673	124	7.82	725	189	15.08
622	164	13.44	674	184	13.82	726	121	15.85
623	130	16.83	675	165	13.93	727	224	18.45
624	172	8.40	676	131	14.05	728	142	11.62
625	164	14.43	677	55	2.57	729	203	18.15
626	202	17.74	678	113	10.88	730	153	13.53
627	195	13.31	679	196	18.30	731	236	23.63
628	147	14.51	680	220	19.89	732	211	17.08

Item No.	X	Y	Item No.	X	Y	Item No.	X	Y
733	146	12.78	786	110	12.10	839	209	15.86
734	188	17.41	787	135	13.39	840	191	19.01
735	107	11.27	788	159	11.29	841	107	11.38
736	199	17.98	789	201	14.85	842	165	16.55
737	208	14.22	790	214	21.06	843	178	15.42
738	189	15.06	791	151	9.24	844	219	19.40
739	201	17.28	792	192	23.04	845	131	12.26
740	154	14.95	793	149	7.85	846	205	16.64
741	170	15.03	794	183	17.07	847	163	10.08
742	192	10.99	795	181	19.39	848	144	12.34
743	139	10.21	796	157	14.53	849	217	18.97
744	171	14.70	797	152	13.89	850	168	16.23
745	137	13.62	798	174	14.48	851	223	19.83
746	136	9.07	799	157	13.03	852	135	12.91
747	186	16.96	800	181	11.90	853	90	9.82
748	104	9.71	801	156	12.36	854	240	21.09
749	165	9.02	802	144	14.94	855	187	16.91
750	200	15.24	803	184	16.54	856	104	8.69
751	240	20.79	804	158	11.16	857	203	15.96
752	253	22.83	805	219	19.31	858	122	8.66
753	198	18.35	806	199	16.72	859	202	16.69
754	207	14.45	807	231	15.54	860	194	16.86
755	174	13.76	808	172	19.81	861	149	10.77
756	119	10.57	809	136	12.79	862	170	13.23
757	151	12.55	810	143	8.84	863	144	12.60
758	193	12.54	811	107	8.93	864	176	16.78
759	168	16.39	812	204	18.22	865	184	18.28
760	225	20.76	813	181	18.75	866	160	14.84
761	150	17.84	814	181	18.69	867	165	15.60
762	124	14.40	815	186	19.91	868	211	21.05
763	140	8.51	816	160	9.21	869	137	10.72
764	201	14.53	817	202	13.82	870	177	14.60
765	193	15.80	818	197	19.96	871	161	14.25
766	191	14.38	819	114	5.40	872	140	12.90
767	210	19.14	820	174	13.18	873	147	11.04
768	94	4.63	821	195	16.04	874	129	10.53
769	175	12.11	822	195	17.99	875	191	16.38
770	182	15.48	823	214	17.34	876	152	8.80
771	125	11.84	824	164	13.94	877	168	12.39
772	146	9.35	825	172	12.70	878	115	8.18
773	241	21.83	826	209	18.90	879	113	11.67
774	165	11.93	827	204	21.79	880	219	17.85
775	181	17.26	828	186	18.73	881	181	16.22
776	200	18.94	829	219	18.81	882	148	14.96
777	248	22.55	830	223	17.86	883	168	15.00
778	167	13.65	831	160	14.53	884	101	8.01
779	177	18.73	832	122	8.96	885	200	15.89
780	173	13.17	833	160	10.03	886	220	16.42
781	110	8.57	834	257	20.39	887	217	19.92
782	214	15.57	835	202	18.41	888	87	3.20
783	163	15.01	836	125	13.62	889	108	10.04
784	77	7.55	837	186	19.46	890	221	21.85
785	171	17.84	838	166	13.76	891	110	4.90

Item No.	X	Y	Item No.	X	Y	Item No.	X	Y
892	229	21.94	945	139	9.78	998	206	17.44
893	254	20.07	946	150	12.44	999	214	16.79
894	175	12.34	947	136	10.16	1,000	162	11.89
895	197	11.87	948	168	13.43	1,001	231	20.72
896	153	14.18	949	219	20.39	1,002	150	15.23
897	139	14.09	950	180	15.23	1,003	125	9.78
898	140	8.84	951	189	10.54	1,004	146	15.40
899	229	24.02	952	172	12.77	1,005	159	15.71
900	185	20.82	953	174	14.95	1,006	123	8.96
901	195	18.57	954	148	15.70	1,007	239	22.35
902	245	17.88	955	130	8.97	1,008	163	12.50
903	194	20.93	956	222	20.17	1,009	200	13.62
904	128	6.93	957	156	14.89	1,010	140	11.70
905	190	14.45	958	131	9.94	1,011	226	21.75
906	222	17.40	959	114	8.39	1,012	196	18.53
907	146	8.51	960	121	12.25	1,013	181	16.05
908	223	19.98	961	204	18.65	1,014	225	19.09
909	146	12.55	962	108	6.87	1,015	166	18.19
910	236	26.19	963	186	17.01	1,016	241	18.70
911	174	20.94	964	175	14.82	1,017	276	25.04
912	148	14.95	965	143	11.09	1,018	178	18.67
913	231	17.26	966	114	9.78	1,019	119	9.76
914	196	20.53	967	130	11.16	1,020	199	18.61
915	184	14.94	968	234	22.25	1,021	140	9.02
916	159	16.88	969	102	8.38	1,022	127	11.11
917	211	14.19	970	198	14.13	1,023	195	13.53
918	102	7.87	971	229	21.00	1,024	221	16.19
919	165	18.27	972	155	12.83	1,025	225	23.33
920	201	14.57	973	260	22.24	1,026	207	17.88
921	133	13.03	974	200	19.57	1,027	175	17.51
922	178	13.54	975	116	10.55	1,028	109	9.05
923	137	12.68	976	215	15.35	1,029	158	9.15
924	138	8.26	977	130	11.41	1,030	273	19.52
925	227	24.31	978	219	17.57	1,031	206	19.20
926	79	4.11	979	196	19.98	1,032	212	18.82
927	167	13.54	980	136	14.12	1,033	121	11.58
928	153	9.49	981	159	12.28	1,034	207	15.91
929	122	8.55	982	142	16.05	1,035	227	18.33
930	219	20.94	983	175	10.98	1,036	125	11.01
931	169	16.44	984	117	9.10	1,037	169	15.89
932	187	17.46	985	151	13.20	1,038	211	15.80
933	124	8.03	986	209	18.43	1,039	175	20.58
934	166	16.36	987	208	20.31	1,040	242	17.18
935	221	15.70	988	214	17.26	1,041	104	8.73
936	232	19.38	989	167	17.05	1,042	190	14.89
937	155	12.95	990	168	14.12	1,043	204	18.14
938	205	19.58	991	159	12.47	1,044	209	19.58
939	180	15.98	992	161	13.07	1,045	147	15.01
940	205	15.92	993	131	12.71	1,046	177	14.70
941	128	14.85	994	224	18.09	1,047	185	14.98
942	175	17.17	995	124	11.71	1,048	119	12.71
943	178	16.50	996	131	11.50	1,049	179	18.70
944	170	15.53	997	188	19.88	1,050	169	13.20

DATA SET 8   Data for Chapter 10, Review Exercises 32–37

Dwelling	Y	X_1	X_2	X_3	Dwelling	Y	X_1	X_2	X_3
1	80	17	12	1.36	51	110	23	19	1.51
2	125	25	15	1.52	52	100	20	19	1.43
3	97	22	11	1.34	53	69	13	14	1.42
4	87	19	11	1.33	54	101	18	28	1.62
5	81	17	19	1.36	55	87	17	19	1.46
6	132	25	20	1.79	56	111	17	19	1.88
7	83	19	23	1.18	57	79	15	15	1.45
8	105	23	24	1.31	58	163	27	21	2.19
9	90	18	24	1.36	59	89	21	21	1.15
10	115	23	25	1.52	60	87	19	19	1.27
11	84	18	24	1.23	61	118	21	19	1.75
12	113	21	22	1.59	62	121	23	20	1.66
13	93	21	20	1.24	63	95	18	17	1.61
14	106	19	21	1.57	64	102	18	18	1.70
15	85	16	11	1.53	65	119	20	19	1.86
16	123	22	16	1.85	66	100	19	22	1.52
17	88	17	22	1.45	67	106	21	24	1.50
18	113	25	19	1.24	68	74	15	19	1.37
19	103	22	17	1.38	69	59	13	19	1.20
20	107	17	10	1.91	70	74	14	21	1.43
21	109	19	18	1.77	71	107	21	21	1.48
22	67	17	23	1.03	72	114	21	21	1.61
23	78	17	24	1.29	73	68	16	19	1.19
24	108	20	19	1.65	74	91	17	21	1.56
25	82	18	28	1.24	75	119	24	20	1.49
26	56	18	14	0.78	76	86	20	14	1.29
27	72	14	20	1.37	77	87	19	21	1.27
28	109	22	22	1.43	78	123	22	21	1.72
29	103	17	23	1.67	79	93	20	15	1.29
30	125	20	16	1.94	80	78	18	12	1.22
31	112	19	16	1.77	81	81	18	23	1.17
32	112	20	21	1.75	82	94	18	19	1.58
33	94	20	17	1.28	83	98	22	14	1.24
34	76	16	25	1.28	84	52	13	15	1.06
35	96	22	14	1.21	85	88	19	19	1.35
36	106	20	20	1.56	86	122	22	19	1.67
37	74	15	27	1.30	87	101	18	21	1.62
38	106	24	18	1.15	88	119	23	26	1.60
39	142	23	29	1.96	89	74	17	16	1.18
40	95	20	20	1.38	90	105	20	14	1.63
41	85	17	14	1.45	91	101	21	18	1.45
42	81	20	18	1.19	92	111	20	16	1.69
43	59	15	15	1.04	93	126	23	26	1.67
44	76	16	20	1.32	94	71	17	21	1.10
45	126	22	21	1.83	95	103	23	19	1.27
46	107	19	19	1.73	96	127	25	23	1.64
47	100	18	25	1.59	97	148	25	23	1.97
48	82	18	22	1.26	98	108	20	23	1.64
49	92	16	16	1.61	99	64	16	18	1.08
50	90	18	16	1.44	100	94	22	23	1.18

Dwelling	Y	X_1	X_2	X_3	Dwelling	Y	X_1	X_2	X_3
101	128	25	25	1.54	153	80	20	14	1.07
102	133	26	17	1.67	154	108	21	15	1.57
103	103	19	27	1.57	155	71	19	12	1.03
104	121	24	13	1.55	156	126	25	20	1.64
105	71	17	20	1.16	157	132	24	27	1.78
106	79	18	18	1.16	158	99	18	14	1.66
107	97	21	25	1.28	159	81	16	22	1.38
108	106	20	18	1.63	160	78	18	12	1.26
109	82	17	21	1.35	161	108	19	26	1.69
110	119	24	27	1.38	162	67	16	20	1.06
111	85	18	23	1.25	163	55	12	13	1.26
112	117	21	19	1.70	164	85	19	19	1.25
113	91	18	21	1.43	165	113	20	20	1.78
114	81	16	19	1.37	166	105	20	11	1.73
115	105	20	21	1.54	167	107	21	29	1.43
116	100	21	19	1.36	168	100	19	20	1.52
117	88	21	23	1.13	169	108	21	20	1.59
118	104	22	18	1.46	170	84	18	20	1.28
119	95	17	20	1.71	171	95	18	22	1.47
120	82	19	21	1.15	172	100	23	17	1.23
121	132	23	21	1.83	173	92	17	28	1.51
122	106	18	22	1.64	174	107	21	22	1.50
123	100	20	18	1.49	175	118	24	18	1.56
124	77	17	18	1.24	176	91	20	17	1.29
125	76	15	23	1.35	177	108	24	18	1.41
126	82	21	16	1.09	178	131	24	17	1.74
127	61	12	17	1.33	179	117	18	26	1.93
128	141	26	24	1.79	180	118	21	19	1.74
129	111	25	14	1.28	181	83	14	21	1.56
130	142	25	18	1.93	182	77	16	19	1.32
131	101	18	18	1.64	183	107	20	15	1.63
132	71	19	13	1.03	184	88	18	19	1.38
133	116	24	23	1.50	185	125	21	12	1.97
134	140	25	28	1.71	186	113	19	21	1.82
135	86	16	16	1.53	187	114	21	23	1.69
136	113	22	22	1.51	188	63	14	14	1.23
137	111	20	17	1.68	189	86	17	21	1.37
138	84	19	15	1.32	190	121	20	20	1.97
139	110	19	25	1.69	191	80	14	23	1.54
140	75	19	12	1.06	192	115	20	18	1.78
141	84	21	20	1.15	193	59	16	19	0.97
142	108	21	16	1.68	194	100	18	27	1.59
143	94	20	26	1.32	195	101	19	24	1.52
144	116	20	10	1.82	196	84	17	23	1.27
145	101	19	18	1.55	197	88	19	17	1.33
146	101	17	22	1.70	198	85	19	20	1.25
147	104	21	10	1.57	199	94	25	21	0.96
148	96	20	21	1.38	200	73	12	18	1.53
149	99	18	12	1.63	201	99	20	21	1.48
150	107	23	20	1.36	202	107	20	25	1.54
151	64	12	20	1.42	203	98	21	18	1.35
152	84	17	17	1.47	204	80	20	24	1.01

Dwelling	Y	X_1	X_2	X_3	Dwelling	Y	X_1	X_2	X_3
205	45	14	23	0.81	257	81	19	21	1.15
206	92	18	13	1.42	258	71	18	16	1.07
207	83	15	14	1.54	259	109	22	15	1.55
208	130	23	19	1.80	260	97	17	18	1.61
209	106	19	24	1.62	261	148	24	18	2.18
210	105	20	20	1.65	262	113	17	17	1.95
211	109	21	15	1.59	263	74	17	14	1.21
212	92	21	13	1.25	264	79	17	15	1.36
213	125	24	22	1.58	265	95	22	15	1.20
214	103	20	21	1.58	266	105	19	21	1.61
215	126	18	18	2.21	267	75	17	25	1.23
216	111	19	20	1.77	268	108	22	11	1.53
217	112	24	24	1.33	269	93	16	21	1.65
218	98	23	19	1.23	270	106	18	21	1.72
219	108	19	19	1.69	271	128	23	20	1.70
220	118	25	17	1.41	272	98	20	20	1.39
221	76	16	17	1.37	273	85	16	15	1.46
222	120	22	19	1.62	274	77	16	23	1.31
223	91	15	19	1.67	275	116	21	22	1.72
224	108	20	12	1.65	276	67	19	12	1.03
225	88	20	19	1.24	277	137	24	15	1.84
226	114	20	20	1.78	278	105	19	20	1.61
227	116	20	21	1.72	279	86	17	18	1.42
228	119	22	20	1.70	280	115	25	22	1.34
229	128	23	22	1.77	281	80	15	22	1.42
230	150	27	20	1.88	282	112	23	22	1.43
231	75	17	20	1.19	283	103	21	22	1.44
232	93	20	24	1.27	284	101	20	25	1.40
233	112	19	24	1.77	285	58	14	11	1.21
234	102	19	17	1.57	286	83	14	30	1.51
235	134	25	25	1.74	287	112	24	23	1.34
236	110	20	24	1.64	288	107	19	23	1.59
237	112	23	19	1.48	289	101	17	18	1.65
238	115	23	25	1.45	290	80	14	20	1.54
239	78	17	17	1.39	291	75	17	16	1.25
240	121	21	21	1.82	292	91	20	18	1.40
241	122	22	21	1.70	293	66	15	26	1.10
242	96	20	18	1.41	294	90	19	22	1.40
243	89	18	21	1.35	295	109	17	20	1.87
244	109	22	23	1.44	296	73	15	15	1.26
245	87	17	15	1.50	297	91	21	21	1.16
246	130	23	18	1.89	298	106	19	17	1.71
247	107	19	22	1.64	299	107	17	22	1.81
248	90	20	19	1.28	300	90	19	22	1.36
249	128	23	22	1.70	301	93	17	26	1.56
250	82	16	22	1.37	302	95	17	13	1.65
251	123	21	23	1.90	303	95	19	20	1.44
252	117	22	23	1.67	304	125	24	16	1.72
253	94	16	20	1.66	305	96	21	18	1.31
254	92	20	22	1.25	306	93	17	15	1.57
255	121	22	21	1.73	307	95	18	22	1.52
256	40	13	13	0.92	308	133	24	21	1.81

Dwelling	Y	X_1	X_2	X_3	Dwelling	Y	X_1	X_2	X_3
309	128	25	20	1.64	361	99	21	14	1.40
310	60	14	18	1.12	362	72	18	16	1.02
311	81	14	25	1.50	363	76	16	16	1.36
312	108	21	16	1.52	364	109	25	19	1.28
313	105	19	19	1.68	365	111	22	19	1.52
314	98	18	18	1.59	366	105	22	21	1.33
315	77	20	17	1.00	367	88	15	21	1.64
316	87	18	28	1.35	368	117	21	24	1.68
317	93	17	18	1.60	369	79	18	18	1.29
318	102	20	17	1.53	370	82	20	17	1.20
319	85	20	15	1.23	371	111	22	22	1.47
320	125	24	20	1.63	372	69	12	16	1.55
321	80	18	17	1.24	373	98	17	23	1.62
322	109	22	16	1.61	374	93	18	23	1.57
323	94	23	26	1.21	375	110	24	27	1.21
324	95	17	23	1.57	376	126	24	25	1.66
325	116	23	22	1.56	377	104	20	24	1.53
326	76	14	20	1.42	378	80	16	29	1.29
327	86	22	14	1.13	379	91	18	18	1.51
328	107	20	17	1.63	380	82	18	23	1.14
329	74	18	21	1.02	381	81	18	17	1.28
330	83	17	24	1.41	382	116	22	25	1.60
331	110	17	22	1.91	383	129	24	18	1.65
332	88	15	18	1.69	384	80	20	25	0.97
333	106	20	24	1.51	385	74	18	13	1.16
334	90	20	25	1.22	386	121	23	24	1.56
335	109	22	16	1.47	387	75	16	15	1.35
336	91	17	17	1.56	388	56	11	10	1.34
337	101	23	19	1.25	389	93	17	20	1.55
338	76	12	20	1.51	390	94	19	15	1.42
339	83	17	19	1.37	391	128	26	22	1.53
340	117	20	17	1.82	392	146	27	19	1.83
341	75	16	24	1.35	393	119	20	14	1.91
342	95	21	14	1.32	394	98	16	18	1.78
343	118	21	13	1.75	395	75	16	17	1.37
344	93	17	23	1.55	396	76	18	17	1.16
345	96	20	13	1.45	397	76	18	22	1.14
346	140	24	24	1.93	398	114	22	16	1.55
347	107	19	14	1.76	399	79	17	22	1.28
348	112	25	21	1.33	400	87	17	18	1.49
349	59	13	20	1.19	401	99	18	18	1.67
350	108	21	19	1.58	402	86	19	17	1.33
351	86	22	17	1.00	403	103	22	18	1.35
352	104	20	18	1.60	404	79	19	24	1.11
353	152	25	27	2.09	405	74	14	23	1.49
354	104	21	17	1.41	406	128	22	16	1.87
355	127	24	29	1.63	407	90	20	16	1.31
356	146	25	26	1.84	408	68	15	18	1.27
357	149	25	26	1.93	409	96	21	18	1.25
358	91	18	18	1.48	410	92	20	19	1.18
359	104	19	26	1.63	411	102	19	12	1.66
360	101	18	12	1.63	412	97	18	17	1.53

Dwelling	Y	X_1	X_2	X_3	Dwelling	Y	X_1	X_2	X_3
413	106	19	19	1.60	465	75	16	16	1.36
414	115	20	23	1.71	466	115	16	17	2.06
415	90	16	17	1.57	467	90	17	20	1.46
416	155	25	18	2.08	468	117	23	20	1.56
417	97	17	10	1.79	469	95	19	15	1.45
418	103	21	23	1.41	470	128	26	23	1.59
419	112	19	24	1.74	471	62	15	14	1.14
420	93	20	21	1.25	472	119	21	22	1.77
421	97	20	25	1.30	473	112	21	15	1.65
422	31	13	19	0.62	474	107	22	22	1.43
423	95	18	16	1.51	475	118	23	17	1.60
424	94	19	22	1.39	476	59	18	15	0.87
425	80	19	17	1.15	477	108	20	14	1.62
426	91	18	21	1.53	478	103	21	27	1.38
427	103	21	23	1.40	479	93	20	17	1.34
428	78	18	14	1.28	480	76	17	27	1.19
429	84	15	21	1.53	481	76	16	13	1.32
430	75	17	17	1.25	482	97	20	23	1.37
431	107	21	18	1.56	483	139	24	21	1.92
432	54	15	14	1.02	484	79	18	18	1.22
433	84	19	16	1.26	485	77	18	17	1.22
434	106	20	25	1.57	486	106	22	16	1.45
435	101	18	22	1.68	487	110	21	21	1.58
436	100	20	20	1.47	488	86	16	18	1.53
437	84	19	21	1.19	489	99	19	15	1.49
438	142	25	26	1.81	490	107	22	23	1.49
439	85	16	23	1.47	491	123	22	21	1.85
440	98	19	21	1.56	492	90	18	14	1.54
441	111	21	23	1.56	493	99	21	13	1.39
442	99	19	22	1.48	494	100	18	19	1.66
443	75	14	20	1.42	495	132	23	15	1.87
444	66	17	19	0.99	496	105	20	18	1.57
445	93	17	25	1.56	497	110	21	18	1.56
446	128	21	25	1.87	498	95	18	15	1.52
447	102	21	24	1.43	499	55	13	15	1.19
448	122	23	17	1.63	500	105	22	21	1.45
449	94	18	22	1.44	501	105	20	14	1.60
450	73	15	17	1.33	502	108	20	21	1.61
451	124	23	17	1.68	503	118	21	13	1.75
452	85	15	16	1.59	504	99	21	23	1.43
453	124	20	27	1.95	505	89	19	21	1.35
454	141	25	17	1.95	506	106	18	23	1.70
455	105	20	18	1.59	507	86	17	21	1.41
456	106	20	19	1.59	508	105	20	20	1.55
457	132	23	17	1.88	509	70	16	17	1.18
458	60	14	20	1.08	510	78	15	15	1.47
459	95	20	29	1.37	511	117	23	21	1.57
460	90	16	22	1.49	512	102	21	15	1.45
461	94	17	21	1.64	513	109	17	21	1.83
462	99	20	26	1.40	514	106	18	22	1.81
463	104	21	17	1.44	515	131	24	18	1.80
464	96	20	18	1.42	516	96	20	21	1.29

Dwelling	Y	X_1	X_2	X_3	Dwelling	Y	X_1	X_2	X_3
517	73	16	21	1.25	569	124	21	17	1.91
518	104	21	13	1.53	570	115	22	20	1.62
519	74	17	10	1.32	571	92	18	17	1.46
520	70	15	15	1.28	572	121	17	21	2.13
521	99	20	12	1.45	573	122	19	18	1.98
522	101	24	22	1.06	574	109	21	17	1.50
523	106	19	24	1.59	575	98	21	11	1.41
524	111	20	16	1.64	576	65	14	13	1.32
525	94	23	19	1.19	577	96	20	19	1.44
526	60	14	23	1.13	578	77	15	15	1.44
527	57	13	13	1.21	579	69	14	20	1.29
528	117	20	23	1.85	580	113	20	23	1.63
529	100	19	22	1.41	581	113	22	16	1.52
530	95	20	17	1.31	582	99	21	13	1.47
531	91	19	18	1.34	583	76	18	11	1.26
532	80	14	21	1.48	584	123	21	18	1.82
533	91	20	21	1.37	585	123	24	20	1.53
534	118	21	23	1.69	586	91	20	20	1.27
535	62	14	20	1.08	587	93	21	16	1.28
536	101	17	15	1.75	588	95	18	24	1.47
537	110	19	21	1.81	589	108	23	15	1.43
538	66	16	14	1.22	590	130	22	19	1.89
539	81	16	16	1.43	591	93	19	15	1.51
540	115	21	17	1.70	592	81	17	27	1.25
541	88	17	14	1.54	593	108	20	17	1.64
542	123	22	19	1.78	594	96	19	23	1.38
543	84	18	22	1.31	595	99	20	26	1.35
544	110	24	20	1.35	596	92	16	18	1.65
545	91	20	20	1.37	597	108	22	21	1.48
546	89	17	15	1.58	598	90	20	16	1.34
547	67	19	17	0.91	599	74	16	18	1.39
548	93	20	19	1.29	600	133	26	24	1.65
549	116	19	16	1.92	601	108	20	26	1.61
550	101	20	23	1.46	602	100	16	21	1.75
551	63	13	20	1.31	603	61	15	19	1.10
552	47	14	10	0.92	604	95	18	18	1.59
553	121	23	15	1.74	605	111	20	20	1.65
554	124	22	33	1.70	606	102	17	23	1.74
555	97	19	12	1.54	607	92	16	15	1.70
556	97	20	22	1.36	608	116	25	23	1.36
557	111	21	19	1.61	609	62	16	18	1.00
558	120	22	12	1.72	610	72	12	23	1.49
559	118	24	17	1.57	611	102	22	22	1.38
560	96	21	23	1.26	612	96	18	25	1.57
561	92	19	17	1.42	613	60	16	14	1.00
562	123	25	27	1.49	614	103	18	16	1.70
563	107	20	23	1.62	615	76	17	14	1.31
564	113	24	21	1.42	616	56	15	17	0.97
565	94	21	12	1.29	617	115	20	23	1.81
566	102	17	21	1.74	618	69	16	19	1.24
567	102	21	17	1.34	619	124	22	19	1.78
568	100	22	17	1.42	620	90	17	17	1.52

Dwelling	Y	X_1	X_2	X_3	Dwelling	Y	X_1	X_2	X_3
621	77	17	20	1.19	673	124	19	26	1.99
622	73	14	21	1.46	674	105	23	23	1.33
623	108	21	18	1.57	675	88	17	21	1.42
624	108	17	13	1.87	676	103	21	15	1.52
625	108	20	24	1.69	677	93	20	22	1.27
626	92	17	23	1.56	678	102	21	24	1.36
627	115	23	12	1.51	679	127	23	22	1.67
628	102	21	19	1.37	680	90	19	14	1.26
629	96	23	21	1.04	681	116	20	22	1.76
630	89	17	19	1.49	682	137	29	14	1.53
631	86	20	16	1.12	683	116	24	27	1.42
632	71	18	16	1.12	684	85	16	13	1.57
633	103	17	18	1.77	685	106	21	13	1.51
634	115	19	32	1.69	686	134	23	24	1.83
635	99	19	26	1.45	687	97	16	15	1.81
636	110	21	29	1.50	688	130	23	27	1.74
637	89	17	23	1.45	689	75	17	16	1.27
638	115	22	21	1.50	690	77	15	23	1.43
639	83	15	18	1.57	691	105	21	17	1.51
640	102	24	16	1.19	692	63	14	20	1.22
641	90	16	16	1.62	693	100	16	19	1.73
642	71	17	18	1.11	694	90	22	19	1.12
643	107	21	21	1.56	695	103	19	18	1.65
644	80	15	18	1.40	696	76	17	21	1.24
645	124	24	22	1.64	697	118	20	19	1.85
646	87	18	21	1.39	698	106	20	21	1.59
647	79	19	11	1.04	699	95	21	28	1.08
648	124	18	31	2.02	700	100	22	18	1.31
649	76	15	18	1.38	701	88	21	16	1.15
650	131	25	24	1.68	702	116	19	24	1.84
651	139	25	23	1.84	703	109	22	23	1.54
652	89	19	28	1.21	704	88	19	24	1.35
653	82	18	22	1.28	705	106	24	8	1.27
654	112	21	19	1.66	706	97	20	18	1.46
655	89	19	22	1.27	707	110	20	18	1.67
656	104	21	24	1.39	708	69	17	20	1.02
657	113	24	24	1.40	709	116	23	10	1.63
658	127	24	19	1.80	710	127	24	20	1.68
659	103	21	15	1.41	711	90	17	20	1.54
660	99	20	17	1.50	712	163	27	23	2.06
661	27	10	13	0.97	713	79	21	16	1.04
662	144	24	27	1.99	714	96	20	19	1.38
663	127	24	16	1.75	715	167	27	22	2.20
664	64	17	14	1.04	716	112	21	19	1.66
665	75	17	27	1.19	717	83	17	19	1.38
666	98	19	25	1.43	718	102	17	26	1.68
667	85	20	18	1.14	719	91	17	19	1.51
668	96	24	14	1.06	720	93	20	17	1.37
669	86	18	25	1.35	721	100	19	22	1.54
670	112	22	15	1.63	722	87	20	19	1.28
671	91	19	25	1.32	723	124	24	27	1.49
672	82	19	20	1.18	724	93	22	14	1.17

Dwelling	Y	X_1	X_2	X_3	Dwelling	Y	X_1	X_2	X_3
725	106	20	20	1.62	777	113	26	20	1.24
726	109	24	22	1.36	778	128	24	25	1.64
727	114	21	19	1.66	779	77	18	21	1.20
728	98	20	25	1.45	780	98	20	17	1.43
729	99	22	18	1.20	781	88	21	22	1.16
730	94	18	10	1.70	782	104	21	17	1.53
731	116	19	23	1.84	783	83	17	19	1.27
732	94	17	20	1.49	784	62	15	16	1.11
733	92	18	16	1.45	785	105	19	18	1.66
734	110	22	17	1.50	786	85	12	20	1.75
735	96	21	17	1.26	787	84	18	20	1.26
736	74	16	12	1.34	788	101	20	24	1.52
737	98	20	24	1.32	789	93	21	18	1.24
738	119	24	17	1.44	790	76	16	15	1.29
739	96	21	18	1.31	791	124	25	13	1.57
740	112	19	22	1.77	792	80	17	12	1.36
741	96	22	15	1.36	793	103	21	19	1.39
742	74	17	12	1.28	794	71	16	15	1.23
743	123	24	27	1.57	795	120	19	22	1.92
744	103	20	20	1.42	796	94	16	26	1.62
745	94	21	19	1.25	797	41	12	15	1.07
746	95	18	18	1.63	798	94	18	20	1.52
747	78	19	23	1.07	799	86	20	18	1.16
748	96	17	20	1.61	800	78	18	17	1.12
749	77	17	11	1.33	801	122	24	23	1.55
750	101	21	16	1.45	802	89	18	24	1.43
751	89	20	14	1.31	803	80	13	16	1.69
752	75	15	19	1.36	804	112	20	22	1.69
753	86	19	14	1.39	805	73	14	21	1.42
754	104	21	19	1.53	806	113	24	23	1.35
755	94	22	30	1.09	807	91	21	20	1.23
756	107	21	16	1.53	808	76	18	18	1.23
757	95	23	26	1.12	809	108	20	21	1.70
758	113	21	22	1.49	810	80	17	23	1.22
759	110	23	16	1.48	811	111	23	22	1.39
760	92	20	17	1.38	812	102	23	23	1.31
761	76	17	20	1.22	813	111	22	17	1.54
762	116	19	23	1.81	814	101	22	18	1.32
763	84	18	23	1.31	815	94	18	20	1.56
764	113	18	18	1.91	816	66	16	18	1.19
765	120	21	25	1.71	817	101	17	29	1.67
766	106	18	20	1.81	818	97	18	30	1.50
767	117	18	28	1.87	819	103	21	18	1.43
768	74	14	18	1.40	820	125	20	21	1.89
769	101	22	19	1.31	821	114	22	19	1.57
770	75	19	14	1.09	822	128	22	17	1.90
771	98	21	21	1.36	823	136	24	17	1.86
772	116	24	18	1.45	824	106	19	21	1.65
773	97	20	18	1.37	825	122	22	21	1.75
774	95	19	14	1.46	826	127	27	20	1.36
775	122	24	19	1.65	827	118	17	19	2.01
776	87	21	17	1.14	828	114	24	26	1.27

Dwelling	Y	X_1	X_2	X_3	Dwelling	Y	X_1	X_2	X_3
829	140	25	17	1.97	881	77	14	10	1.56
830	113	22	16	1.68	882	92	14	25	1.77
831	90	21	19	1.24	883	94	18	14	1.48
832	86	14	13	1.70	884	81	17	21	1.28
833	90	14	15	1.76	885	59	15	20	1.04
834	109	22	17	1.50	886	114	19	22	1.72
835	94	20	19	1.29	887	73	17	21	1.16
836	102	17	20	1.61	888	114	21	23	1.61
837	96	19	22	1.46	889	128	24	22	1.74
838	93	19	16	1.48	890	145	26	17	1.91
839	95	19	16	1.45	891	81	16	11	1.49
840	99	24	17	1.21	892	85	20	19	1.20
841	115	22	22	1.56	893	94	20	17	1.36
842	72	16	27	1.10	894	62	14	20	1.19
843	73	18	24	1.05	895	102	17	17	1.77
844	62	16	21	1.04	896	105	17	18	1.80
845	162	25	29	2.28	897	95	18	30	1.40
846	94	20	24	1.32	898	65	15	12	1.23
847	98	20	19	1.46	899	96	19	20	1.47
848	85	19	18	1.24	900	104	23	25	1.29
849	117	21	19	1.70	901	119	20	17	1.81
850	142	25	19	1.92	902	87	14	17	1.81
851	113	20	30	1.59	903	117	23	14	1.56
852	92	20	24	1.25	904	76	15	18	1.41
853	62	12	18	1.40	905	92	16	15	1.65
854	84	18	18	1.33	906	115	23	20	1.49
855	111	25	13	1.40	907	81	16	27	1.29
856	56	16	17	0.90	908	86	19	19	1.30
857	89	18	11	1.41	909	103	20	15	1.57
858	80	14	20	1.51	910	95	16	16	1.68
859	84	16	15	1.52	911	75	16	19	1.32
860	89	21	17	1.20	912	108	22	20	1.45
861	117	21	13	1.81	913	82	16	19	1.41
862	90	18	15	1.48	914	86	16	31	1.41
863	83	18	18	1.39	915	138	24	17	1.88
864	77	14	14	1.58	916	92	18	16	1.53
865	56	13	16	1.14	917	107	19	15	1.73
866	133	24	14	1.79	918	88	20	19	1.25
867	86	20	21	1.13	919	89	20	22	1.18
868	84	20	19	1.16	920	49	12	12	1.22
869	91	17	24	1.46	921	111	24	14	1.34
870	110	19	21	1.80	922	95	19	23	1.46
871	76	16	18	1.24	923	123	22	23	1.74
872	77	18	23	1.17	924	87	20	17	1.14
873	82	17	26	1.37	925	107	23	11	1.45
874	85	19	12	1.35	926	111	18	17	1.82
875	114	24	18	1.49	927	109	21	14	1.59
876	104	22	22	1.40	928	81	17	27	1.38
877	137	26	24	1.71	929	94	15	15	1.72
878	71	17	14	1.08	930	85	18	19	1.40
879	100	21	9	1.53	931	75	19	18	1.01
880	116	21	27	1.73	932	103	21	23	1.37

Dwelling	Y	X_1	X_2	X_3	Dwelling	Y	X_1	X_2	X_3
933	92	18	16	1.61	985	130	24	18	1.75
934	63	17	11	1.04	986	70	17	16	1.10
935	95	19	19	1.47	987	94	19	23	1.32
936	96	20	18	1.45	988	93	19	16	1.44
937	89	18	13	1.40	989	96	20	25	1.34
938	92	20	12	1.36	990	87	18	18	1.42
939	78	18	20	1.18	991	133	25	20	1.77
940	102	18	17	1.65	992	73	19	17	1.01
941	78	20	18	1.03	993	82	17	14	1.44
942	119	19	17	1.95	994	70	19	23	0.90
943	97	19	22	1.47	995	123	23	20	1.71
944	141	25	27	1.79	996	106	17	23	1.75
945	69	14	19	1.30	997	81	16	12	1.41
946	78	19	17	1.13	998	122	23	22	1.67
947	95	17	15	1.64	999	128	26	23	1.59
948	81	14	23	1.55	1000	129	22	18	1.92
949	87	17	15	1.44	1001	87	18	19	1.26
950	103	21	21	1.49	1002	90	19	19	1.29
951	115	23	23	1.55	1003	114	21	13	1.71
952	133	23	25	1.86	1004	93	20	20	1.28
953	70	17	13	1.21	1005	90	20	12	1.24
954	140	20	21	2.16	1006	88	19	18	1.29
955	101	22	14	1.35	1007	130	25	16	1.65
956	108	20	23	1.54	1008	113	23	24	1.42
957	94	20	14	1.39	1009	98	18	15	1.57
958	102	19	20	1.58	1010	98	18	22	1.61
959	73	16	11	1.23	1011	123	23	19	1.62
960	129	24	26	1.64	1012	93	19	18	1.46
961	97	20	18	1.39	1013	67	19	21	0.85
962	89	19	17	1.39	1014	100	20	19	1.42
963	106	20	17	1.69	1015	139	26	19	1.78
964	67	16	20	1.15	1016	62	19	19	0.76
965	124	24	12	1.67	1017	80	18	9	1.28
966	75	16	18	1.32	1018	103	20	23	1.49
967	113	20	20	1.71	1019	114	22	17	1.60
968	116	20	27	1.66	1020	84	20	18	1.10
969	105	21	20	1.47	1021	124	23	17	1.69
970	105	21	29	1.42	1022	93	20	22	1.38
971	94	21	24	1.27	1023	85	20	18	1.13
972	101	16	16	1.80	1024	81	16	23	1.44
973	101	19	22	1.60	1025	80	19	14	1.23
974	111	21	11	1.72	1026	64	12	22	1.36
975	84	16	21	1.48	1027	111	19	21	1.71
976	119	20	18	1.86	1028	134	23	28	1.77
977	93	20	20	1.31	1029	112	21	21	1.59
978	83	16	19	1.46	1030	89	17	13	1.59
979	81	17	18	1.31	1031	70	16	23	1.20
980	78	14	17	1.51	1032	95	16	25	1.66
981	90	12	18	1.91	1033	102	20	22	1.46
982	104	22	17	1.39	1034	92	22	20	1.18
983	123	21	18	1.87	1035	97	19	21	1.38
984	121	21	12	1.88	1036	98	18	21	1.55

Dwelling	Y	X_1	X_2	X_3	Dwelling	Y	X_1	X_2	X_3
1037	105	22	21	1.43	1044	85	14	22	1.68
1038	94	20	17	1.38	1045	71	17	16	1.16
1039	81	18	22	1.23	1046	91	19	15	1.39
1040	91	19	22	1.38	1047	86	19	27	1.24
1041	139	21	19	2.28	1048	69	15	20	1.29
1042	123	24	19	1.66	1049	88	18	14	1.37
1043	78	16	16	1.33	1050	118	21	20	1.76

DATA SET 9   Data for Chapter 12, Review Exercise 36

Subject	Sex	Reaction	Subject	Sex	Reaction	Subject	Sex	Reaction
1	1	3	41	2	1	81	1	1
2	1	2	42	1	1	82	2	1
3	1	1	43	1	1	83	2	1
4	2	1	44	2	3	84	1	2
5	1	1	45	2	1	85	2	2
6	2	3	46	1	1	86	1	2
7	2	1	47	2	3	87	1	2
8	2	1	48	1	1	88	2	2
9	1	1	49	2	1	89	2	3
10	2	1	50	1	1	90	1	3
11	2	2	51	1	2	91	1	1
12	2	1	52	1	3	92	2	1
13	1	1	53	1	1	93	2	3
14	2	1	54	1	1	94	2	1
15	2	2	55	2	1	95	2	3
16	2	3	56	1	2	96	1	1
17	2	1	57	2	1	97	2	2
18	1	1	58	2	1	98	2	2
19	2	3	59	2	3	99	1	3
20	1	1	60	2	2	100	2	2
21	2	1	61	1	1	101	1	2
22	2	1	62	2	2	102	1	3
23	2	3	63	2	1	103	1	1
24	1	1	64	1	1	104	2	1
25	1	1	65	1	3	105	1	1
26	1	1	66	2	1	106	1	1
27	2	2	67	1	1	107	2	1
28	2	3	68	2	1	108	1	1
29	2	1	69	2	1	109	1	1
30	1	1	70	1	2	110	1	3
31	2	1	71	1	2	111	1	2
32	2	1	72	2	1	112	1	2
33	1	1	73	1	1	113	1	3
34	2	1	74	2	2	114	2	3
35	1	1	75	1	2	115	1	1
36	1	1	76	2	1	116	2	2
37	1	1	77	2	1	117	2	1
38	2	1	78	1	3	118	1	1
39	1	2	79	2	1	119	2	3
40	2	1	80	2	1	120	1	1

Subject	Sex	Reaction	Subject	Sex	Reaction	Subject	Sex	Reaction
121	2	1	173	1	2	225	1	2
122	1	1	174	1	1	226	1	3
123	2	3	175	2	1	227	2	1
124	2	3	176	2	2	228	1	1
125	2	2	177	2	1	229	2	1
126	1	2	178	2	2	230	2	3
127	2	2	179	1	1	231	1	1
128	1	3	180	1	1	232	2	3
129	2	3	181	1	1	233	1	2
130	2	2	182	2	3	234	2	1
131	2	3	183	1	3	235	1	3
132	1	1	184	2	1	236	2	1
133	2	3	185	2	1	237	2	1
134	2	1	186	1	1	238	1	3
135	1	1	187	2	3	239	2	3
136	2	1	188	1	3	240	2	1
137	2	1	189	1	1	241	1	1
138	1	1	190	2	1	242	1	1
139	1	3	191	1	2	243	2	1
140	1	2	192	1	1	244	2	2
141	2	1	193	2	1	245	2	2
142	1	2	194	1	2	246	2	2
143	2	2	195	2	1	247	1	3
144	2	3	196	2	1	248	2	1
145	2	1	197	1	2	249	2	1
146	2	1	198	1	1	250	2	2
147	1	2	199	1	1	251	2	2
148	1	3	200	2	2	252	1	3
149	2	1	201	1	1	253	1	1
150	1	1	202	1	1	254	1	1
151	2	1	203	2	1	255	2	1
152	2	1	204	1	3	256	2	3
153	2	1	205	2	3	257	2	1
154	1	1	206	2	1	258	2	2
155	2	1	207	2	1	259	1	1
156	2	1	208	2	1	260	1	1
157	1	2	209	2	1	261	2	1
158	1	2	210	2	1	262	1	2
159	1	1	211	1	1	263	2	1
160	1	2	212	1	1	264	1	1
161	1	3	213	1	1	265	1	1
162	2	3	214	1	3	266	2	1
163	2	1	215	2	1	267	2	3
164	2	3	216	2	1	268	1	1
165	2	1	217	2	2	269	1	1
166	2	2	218	2	1	270	2	1
167	2	3	219	2	2	271	2	1
168	1	1	220	2	3	272	2	2
169	1	3	221	2	1	273	2	3
170	1	1	222	1	2	274	1	2
171	1	1	223	2	1	275	2	1
172	1	3	224	2	1	276	2	1

Subject	Sex	Reaction	Subject	Sex	Reaction	Subject	Sex	Reaction
277	1	3	329	2	1	381	2	2
278	2	2	330	2	3	382	1	1
279	2	2	331	2	1	383	1	3
280	1	1	332	1	1	384	1	1
281	1	1	333	2	2	385	2	1
282	1	1	334	1	2	386	2	3
283	1	1	335	1	2	387	1	2
284	2	1	336	2	3	388	2	3
285	2	2	337	2	3	389	1	1
286	2	1	338	2	1	390	2	1
287	2	1	339	2	1	391	2	1
288	1	3	340	2	2	392	2	1
289	1	1	341	1	3	393	1	1
290	1	1	342	1	2	394	1	2
291	1	1	343	1	1	395	1	1
292	1	2	344	2	1	396	2	1
293	1	2	345	2	1	397	1	3
294	2	1	346	1	1	398	2	2
295	1	1	347	1	3	399	2	3
296	1	1	348	1	1	400	2	1
297	2	2	349	1	1	401	2	2
298	1	3	350	2	1	402	1	1
299	1	2	351	1	1	403	2	2
300	1	1	352	1	3	404	1	1
301	1	1	353	1	1	405	2	1
302	1	1	354	2	1	406	1	1
303	2	1	355	1	1	407	2	2
304	1	1	356	1	1	408	1	2
305	1	3	357	1	1	409	1	1
306	2	3	358	1	1	410	2	1
307	1	1	359	2	3	411	1	2
308	2	1	360	1	1	412	1	2
309	2	1	361	1	1	413	2	1
310	1	3	362	2	2	414	1	1
311	1	1	363	1	1	415	1	3
312	1	2	364	1	1	416	1	1
313	2	1	365	2	1	417	2	1
314	2	1	366	2	1	418	2	1
315	1	1	367	2	1	419	2	1
316	1	1	368	1	1	420	2	1
317	1	2	369	1	3	421	1	2
318	1	1	370	1	1	422	1	1
319	1	3	371	1	1	423	2	2
320	2	1	372	2	2	424	1	2
321	2	2	373	2	1	425	1	1
322	2	1	374	2	1	426	1	1
323	1	1	375	1	2	427	1	1
324	2	1	376	2	1	428	1	1
325	1	1	377	1	1	429	1	3
326	1	1	378	2	2	430	1	2
327	2	1	379	2	2	431	1	3
328	2	3	380	1	1	432	2	1

Subject	Sex	Reaction	Subject	Sex	Reaction	Subject	Sex	Reaction
433	2	1	485	2	2	537	1	3
434	1	3	486	2	1	538	2	2
435	1	1	487	1	3	539	2	3
436	1	3	488	2	1	540	1	1
437	2	3	489	1	1	541	2	1
438	1	1	490	1	1	542	2	1
439	1	2	491	1	2	543	1	1
440	1	1	492	2	1	544	1	3
441	1	1	493	2	3	545	1	1
442	1	2	494	2	2	546	1	3
443	2	2	495	1	1	547	2	1
444	2	1	496	1	1	548	1	1
445	2	2	497	2	1	549	2	3
446	1	2	498	1	1	550	1	1
447	1	1	499	2	3	551	2	1
448	1	1	500	2	2	552	2	1
449	1	1	501	1	1	553	1	2
450	2	1	502	1	1	554	1	1
451	2	1	503	2	1	555	2	3
452	2	1	504	1	3	556	1	1
453	1	1	505	2	1	557	2	2
454	2	2	506	1	1	558	1	2
455	2	1	507	1	1	559	2	1
456	2	1	508	2	1	560	2	3
457	2	1	509	2	1	561	1	1
458	1	1	510	1	2	562	1	2
459	1	1	511	1	1	563	2	1
460	2	1	512	2	1	564	1	1
461	2	1	513	1	3	565	2	1
462	1	1	514	1	2	566	2	1
463	1	2	515	2	1	567	1	1
464	1	3	516	2	1	568	1	1
465	2	1	517	2	3	569	2	3
466	1	1	518	1	2	570	1	2
467	2	1	519	2	1	571	1	1
468	2	1	520	2	1	572	1	1
469	2	1	521	2	2	573	1	2
470	2	1	522	2	1	574	2	1
471	2	2	523	1	1	575	2	2
472	2	2	524	1	2	576	1	1
473	1	3	525	1	1	577	2	1
474	2	1	526	1	2	578	1	3
475	2	1	527	1	1	579	2	1
476	1	2	528	1	2	580	2	1
477	1	3	529	1	1	581	2	1
478	2	1	530	2	1	582	2	3
479	1	2	531	1	2	583	2	3
480	2	1	532	1	1	584	1	2
481	1	2	533	2	2	585	1	2
482	2	1	534	2	1	586	2	2
483	2	1	535	1	1	587	1	1
484	1	1	536	1	2	588	2	3

Subject	Sex	Reaction	Subject	Sex	Reaction	Subject	Sex	Reaction
589	2	3	641	1	1	693	1	1
590	1	1	642	1	1	694	2	1
591	1	1	643	2	1	695	1	1
592	1	1	644	2	3	696	1	2
593	2	3	645	2	1	697	1	1
594	1	1	646	2	1	698	2	1
595	2	3	647	1	1	699	1	2
596	2	1	648	1	2	700	1	1
597	1	3	649	1	3	701	2	1
598	2	1	650	1	1	702	1	1
599	1	1	651	2	2	703	2	1
600	2	2	652	2	1	704	2	1
601	2	1	653	1	1	705	2	3
602	1	1	654	1	1	706	2	1
603	1	1	655	1	1	707	1	1
604	2	3	656	2	1	708	2	1
605	1	1	657	2	3	709	1	1
606	1	1	658	1	1	710	2	2
607	2	2	659	2	2	711	2	1
608	2	1	660	1	2	712	1	3
609	1	3	661	1	3	713	2	3
610	2	1	662	1	1	714	1	1
611	2	1	663	1	1	715	2	1
612	2	3	664	1	1	716	2	1
613	1	1	665	2	2	717	1	1
614	2	1	666	1	1	718	2	1
615	2	1	667	1	1	719	2	3
616	2	1	668	2	1	720	2	1
617	1	1	669	1	2	721	1	3
618	2	2	670	2	1	722	1	1
619	1	1	671	1	1	723	1	3
620	2	3	672	1	3	724	2	1
621	1	1	673	2	1	725	2	1
622	1	1	674	1	1	726	2	1
623	1	1	675	1	2	727	1	3
624	1	1	676	1	2	728	2	2
625	1	1	677	1	3	729	2	3
626	2	2	678	1	2	730	2	1
627	2	1	679	2	2	731	2	1
628	1	1	680	1	3	732	1	3
629	1	1	681	2	1	733	2	3
630	1	3	682	2	1	734	1	3
631	2	1	683	1	1	735	1	3
632	1	1	684	2	3	736	2	1
633	2	3	685	2	1	737	1	1
634	2	2	686	1	1	738	2	3
635	1	3	687	2	2	739	2	1
636	2	1	688	1	2	740	2	1
637	1	1	689	2	1	741	1	3
638	1	1	690	1	1	742	1	3
639	1	3	691	2	1	743	1	3
640	2	2	692	2	1	744	2	1

Subject	Sex	Reaction	Subject	Sex	Reaction	Subject	Sex	Reaction
745	2	3	797	1	1	849	1	1
746	2	1	798	2	3	850	1	1
747	1	2	799	2	1	851	1	1
748	1	1	800	1	1	852	1	1
749	2	1	801	1	1	853	2	1
750	2	2	802	2	3	854	1	1
751	2	1	803	1	3	855	2	1
752	2	2	804	2	1	856	1	1
753	2	1	805	1	1	857	1	1
754	1	1	806	1	1	858	1	1
755	2	1	807	2	3	859	1	1
756	1	2	808	2	3	860	1	3
757	1	2	809	2	1	861	1	1
758	2	2	810	1	1	862	2	2
759	2	1	811	2	1	863	2	1
760	1	1	812	1	2	864	1	2
761	1	3	813	1	1	865	1	1
762	2	1	814	1	1	866	1	3
763	2	1	815	1	2	867	2	1
764	1	3	816	2	2	868	1	1
765	2	1	817	1	2	869	1	1
766	1	1	818	2	1	870	2	1
767	2	3	819	1	3	871	2	2
768	1	3	820	2	1	872	2	1
769	2	3	821	1	1	873	2	1
770	2	1	822	2	1	874	2	1
771	2	1	823	1	1	875	2	1
772	1	3	824	1	3	876	2	3
773	1	1	825	2	1	877	1	3
774	1	3	826	2	1	878	1	3
775	2	3	827	1	1	879	2	1
776	1	1	828	1	2	880	1	2
777	2	1	829	1	2	881	1	1
778	2	1	830	1	1	882	1	2
779	2	2	831	2	1	883	2	1
780	1	1	832	1	1	884	2	2
781	1	1	833	2	3	885	2	1
782	2	3	834	2	2	886	2	3
783	2	1	835	2	1	887	2	1
784	1	3	836	1	1	888	1	2
785	2	1	837	1	2	889	1	2
786	1	3	838	2	2	890	2	1
787	2	1	839	1	1	891	2	1
788	1	1	840	2	3	892	1	3
789	1	1	841	1	3	893	2	3
790	2	1	842	2	1	894	2	2
791	1	1	843	2	1	895	1	1
792	1	3	844	1	1	896	2	1
793	1	1	845	1	1	897	1	1
794	2	1	846	1	1	898	2	3
795	1	2	847	2	1	899	2	1
796	2	1	848	2	1	900	2	2

Subject	Sex	Reaction	Subject	Sex	Reaction	Subject	Sex	Reaction
901	1	2	953	2	1	1,005	1	1
902	1	3	954	1	1	1,006	2	3
903	2	3	955	2	1	1,007	1	2
904	1	2	956	2	3	1,008	1	1
905	1	1	957	1	3	1,009	1	3
906	1	1	958	2	1	1,010	2	1
907	2	3	959	2	3	1,011	1	3
908	1	1	960	2	1	1,012	1	1
909	2	1	961	2	1	1,013	2	1
910	2	1	962	2	3	1,014	1	1
911	1	3	963	1	1	1,015	1	1
912	1	1	964	1	2	1,016	1	2
913	2	3	965	1	1	1,017	2	3
914	1	2	966	1	3	1,018	1	1
915	2	1	967	1	2	1,019	2	3
916	1	3	968	1	2	1,020	2	1
917	1	1	969	2	1	1,021	2	1
918	1	2	970	1	1	1,022	2	1
919	1	1	971	1	2	1,023	1	1
920	1	3	972	1	1	1,024	1	1
921	2	2	973	1	3	1,025	1	3
922	2	3	974	2	1	1,026	2	2
923	2	1	975	1	1	1,027	1	1
924	1	1	976	1	1	1,028	1	1
925	2	2	977	1	1	1,029	2	1
926	1	2	978	2	3	1,030	2	3
927	2	2	979	2	2	1,031	1	2
928	1	1	980	2	1	1,032	1	3
929	1	1	981	2	2	1,033	2	3
930	2	1	982	1	1	1,034	2	1
931	2	1	983	1	1	1,035	2	1
932	1	1	984	1	1	1,036	1	1
933	1	1	985	2	1	1,037	2	1
934	1	3	986	1	1	1,038	1	1
935	2	2	987	2	3	1,039	1	2
936	1	1	988	1	1	1,040	1	2
937	1	1	989	1	1	1,041	1	1
938	2	1	990	2	1	1,042	1	1
939	2	3	991	2	3	1,043	2	3
940	2	1	992	1	2	1,044	2	3
941	2	1	993	2	1	1,045	1	3
942	2	3	994	2	1	1,046	2	1
943	2	1	995	2	1	1,047	2	1
944	2	2	996	1	1	1,048	1	1
945	2	2	997	1	1	1,049	2	3
946	1	2	998	2	1	1,050	2	1
947	2	1	999	2	3	1,051	2	1
948	2	1	1,000	1	1	1,052	1	1
949	1	1	1,001	2	3	1,053	1	3
950	1	1	1,002	1	1	1,054	1	3
951	1	2	1,003	2	1	1,055	1	2
952	1	1	1,004	2	1	1,056	2	1

Subject	Sex	Reaction	Subject	Sex	Reaction	Subject	Sex	Reaction
1,057	1	1	1,109	1	1	1,161	1	3
1,058	2	1	1,110	2	2	1,162	1	1
1,059	1	2	1,111	2	1	1,163	2	1
1,060	2	1	1,112	2	1	1,164	2	2
1,061	2	1	1,113	2	1	1,165	1	2
1,062	2	1	1,114	1	3	1,166	1	3
1,063	2	3	1,115	2	1	1,167	2	1
1,064	1	2	1,116	2	1	1,168	1	3
1,065	1	1	1,117	2	1	1,169	1	1
1,066	2	1	1,118	1	2	1,170	2	2
1,067	2	1	1,119	1	1	1,171	2	3
1,068	2	1	1,120	2	3	1,172	2	2
1,069	1	1	1,121	2	1	1,173	1	1
1,070	2	1	1,122	1	2	1,174	2	1
1,071	1	1	1,123	1	3	1,175	1	1
1,072	1	3	1,124	1	1	1,176	2	1
1,073	1	2	1,125	1	1	1,177	2	1
1,074	1	1	1,126	2	1	1,178	2	3
1,075	1	1	1,127	1	1	1,179	1	3
1,076	2	1	1,128	1	3	1,180	1	1
1,077	1	3	1,129	2	2	1,181	1	2
1,078	1	1	1,130	2	1	1,182	1	3
1,079	1	1	1,131	2	1	1,183	2	1
1,080	1	1	1,132	1	1	1,184	1	1
1,081	2	3	1,133	1	1	1,185	2	1
1,082	1	1	1,134	1	1	1,186	2	3
1,083	2	1	1,135	1	1	1,187	1	1
1,084	1	1	1,136	1	2	1,188	2	1
1,085	2	1	1,137	1	1	1,189	2	2
1,086	1	1	1,138	2	3	1,190	1	3
1,087	1	1	1,139	1	1	1,191	1	1
1,088	1	2	1,140	1	1	1,192	1	3
1,089	2	2	1,141	1	1	1,193	2	2
1,090	1	1	1,142	1	1	1,194	2	1
1,091	1	2	1,143	2	2	1,195	1	3
1,092	1	3	1,144	2	3	1,196	1	1
1,093	2	1	1,145	2	3	1,197	2	2
1,094	2	1	1,146	1	1	1,198	2	3
1,095	2	1	1,147	1	3	1,199	2	1
1,096	1	1	1,148	1	1	1,200	1	1
1,097	1	1	1,149	1	1	1,201	2	1
1,098	1	1	1,150	2	1	1,202	2	1
1,099	1	1	1,151	2	3	1,203	1	3
1,100	1	1	1,152	1	1	1,204	2	1
1,101	1	1	1,153	2	2	1,205	1	2
1,102	1	1	1,154	2	1	1,206	2	1
1,103	1	2	1,155	1	3	1,207	2	1
1,104	2	1	1,156	2	3	1,208	1	1
1,105	1	3	1,157	2	1	1,209	1	1
1,106	1	3	1,158	2	2	1,210	2	1
1,107	2	1	1,159	1	1	1,211	1	2
1,108	1	1	1,160	2	1	1,212	1	2

Subject	Sex	Reaction	Subject	Sex	Reaction	Subject	Sex	Reaction
1,213	1	1	1,265	1	3	1,317	2	1
1,214	1	3	1,266	1	1	1,318	1	1
1,215	1	1	1,267	2	1	1,319	1	1
1,216	2	1	1,268	2	3	1,320	1	1
1,217	1	3	1,269	2	1	1,321	1	2
1,218	2	1	1,270	2	1	1,322	2	1
1,219	1	1	1,271	2	1	1,323	1	2
1,220	1	1	1,272	2	1	1,324	2	1
1,221	2	2	1,273	2	1	1,325	2	1
1,222	1	1	1,274	2	1	1,326	1	1
1,223	2	1	1,275	1	1	1,327	1	3
1,224	1	2	1,276	2	1	1,328	1	1
1,225	2	1	1,277	2	3	1,329	1	3
1,226	1	1	1,278	1	2	1,330	1	1
1,227	1	2	1,279	1	1	1,331	2	1
1,228	1	3	1,280	1	1	1,332	2	3
1,229	1	2	1,281	1	2	1,333	1	1
1,230	1	3	1,282	2	1	1,334	2	3
1,231	1	2	1,283	2	1	1,335	1	2
1,232	1	1	1,284	2	2	1,336	1	2
1,233	2	2	1,285	2	1	1,337	2	2
1,234	1	1	1,286	1	2	1,338	2	3
1,235	2	1	1,287	1	2	1,339	2	1
1,236	2	3	1,288	2	2	1,340	2	1
1,237	1	3	1,289	2	2	1,341	2	1
1,238	2	1	1,290	2	1	1,342	2	3
1,239	2	2	1,291	1	2	1,343	2	2
1,240	2	1	1,292	2	1	1,344	1	1
1,241	2	2	1,293	2	1	1,345	2	3
1,242	2	1	1,294	1	1	1,346	1	1
1,243	1	2	1,295	1	2	1,347	2	1
1,244	1	1	1,296	2	1	1,348	2	2
1,245	2	1	1,297	2	1	1,349	1	2
1,246	2	1	1,298	1	1	1,350	2	1
1,247	1	1	1,299	1	2	1,351	1	2
1,248	2	1	1,300	1	3	1,352	1	1
1,249	2	2	1,301	1	1	1,353	2	1
1,250	2	1	1,302	1	2	1,354	2	1
1,251	1	1	1,303	1	2	1,355	2	1
1,252	2	2	1,304	2	2	1,356	2	3
1,253	1	1	1,305	2	1	1,357	1	1
1,254	2	3	1,306	1	1	1,358	2	1
1,255	1	2	1,307	2	1	1,359	2	1
1,256	2	1	1,308	2	3	1,360	2	1
1,257	2	2	1,309	2	1	1,361	1	3
1,258	1	3	1,310	2	3	1,362	2	1
1,259	2	1	1,311	2	1	1,363	2	1
1,260	1	3	1,312	2	1	1,364	2	3
1,261	1	1	1,313	2	2	1,365	1	1
1,262	1	1	1,314	2	2	1,366	1	1
1,263	1	3	1,315	1	3	1,367	1	1
1,264	2	3	1,316	1	1	1,368	1	3

Subject	Sex	Reaction	Subject	Sex	Reaction	Subject	Sex	Reaction
1,369	2	1	1,421	2	2	1,473	1	1
1,370	1	1	1,422	2	1	1,474	1	1
1,371	1	1	1,423	1	1	1,475	1	2
1,372	2	1	1,424	2	1	1,476	2	1
1,373	2	1	1,425	2	1	1,477	1	3
1,374	2	1	1,426	2	1	1,478	1	3
1,375	2	1	1,427	2	2	1,479	2	1
1,376	2	2	1,428	2	1	1,480	1	1
1,377	2	2	1,429	1	2	1,481	1	3
1,378	1	2	1,430	2	1	1,482	1	3
1,379	1	2	1,431	2	1	1,483	1	1
1,380	1	1	1,432	2	1	1,484	1	1
1,381	2	2	1,433	1	3	1,485	1	1
1,382	1	1	1,434	2	1	1,486	2	1
1,383	2	1	1,435	2	1	1,487	2	3
1,384	1	3	1,436	2	3	1,488	1	1
1,385	1	1	1,437	2	1	1,489	2	1
1,386	1	2	1,438	1	2	1,490	2	1
1,387	2	1	1,439	2	2	1,491	2	3
1,388	2	1	1,440	2	3	1,492	1	3
1,389	1	1	1,441	1	1	1,493	1	1
1,390	1	1	1,442	1	1	1,494	2	3
1,391	2	2	1,443	1	3	1,495	1	1
1,392	1	1	1,444	1	1	1,496	2	1
1,393	1	1	1,445	1	2	1,497	2	1
1,394	2	3	1,446	2	1	1,498	2	2
1,395	1	3	1,447	2	1	1,499	2	2
1,396	2	1	1,448	2	2	1,500	1	3
1,397	1	1	1,449	2	1	1,501	2	1
1,398	1	3	1,450	1	3	1,502	2	1
1,399	1	1	1,451	1	1	1,503	1	1
1,400	2	1	1,452	2	1	1,504	1	3
1,401	1	3	1,453	1	1	1,505	1	1
1,402	2	2	1,454	2	1	1,506	1	2
1,403	2	1	1,455	1	1	1,507	2	1
1,404	1	3	1,456	2	3	1,508	1	3
1,405	1	1	1,457	1	1	1,509	2	1
1,406	2	1	1,458	1	2	1,510	1	2
1,407	2	3	1,459	1	3	1,511	2	1
1,408	1	1	1,460	2	1	1,512	2	1
1,409	2	1	1,461	1	1	1,513	2	1
1,410	1	3	1,462	2	3	1,514	1	1
1,411	2	3	1,463	2	2	1,515	2	1
1,412	2	3	1,464	2	3	1,516	1	1
1,413	1	1	1,465	1	3	1,517	1	3
1,414	2	1	1,466	1	1	1,518	2	3
1,415	2	2	1,467	1	3	1,519	1	3
1,416	1	1	1,468	2	1	1,520	1	1
1,417	2	1	1,469	2	1	1,521	2	1
1,418	1	3	1,470	2	1	1,522	2	1
1,419	1	3	1,471	1	1	1,523	2	1
1,420	2	1	1,472	1	1	1,524	2	1

Subject	Sex	Reaction	Subject	Sex	Reaction	Subject	Sex	Reaction
1,525	1	1	1,578	2	1	1,631	1	1
1,526	1	1	1,579	2	3	1,632	2	1
1,527	1	1	1,580	1	1	1,633	2	1
1,528	2	3	1,581	1	2	1,634	2	1
1,529	1	2	1,582	2	2	1,635	2	1
1,530	1	1	1,583	2	1	1,636	2	2
1,531	1	1	1,584	1	1	1,637	1	1
1,532	2	2	1,585	2	2	1,638	1	1
1,533	1	2	1,586	1	1	1,639	2	2
1,534	2	1	1,587	2	2	1,640	2	1
1,535	2	1	1,588	2	1	1,641	1	1
1,536	2	1	1,589	1	1	1,642	1	1
1,537	2	1	1,590	2	1	1,643	1	1
1,538	1	2	1,591	2	1	1,644	2	3
1,539	2	3	1,592	1	1	1,645	1	1
1,540	1	2	1,593	1	1	1,646	1	1
1,541	1	1	1,594	2	1	1,647	1	3
1,542	2	2	1,595	2	1	1,648	1	1
1,543	2	3	1,596	1	1	1,649	2	1
1,544	2	1	1,597	1	1	1,650	1	1
1,545	2	3	1,598	1	1	1,651	1	3
1,546	1	2	1,599	2	1	1,652	1	2
1,547	2	1	1,600	1	2	1,653	2	2
1,548	2	1	1,601	1	1	1,654	2	1
1,549	1	1	1,602	1	1	1,655	1	3
1,550	1	1	1,603	1	1	1,656	2	1
1,551	2	1	1,604	2	1	1,657	2	1
1,552	2	1	1,605	2	3	1,658	1	3
1,553	1	3	1,606	2	3	1,659	1	2
1,554	2	1	1,607	2	1	1,660	1	1
1,555	2	1	1,608	2	1	1,661	2	1
1,556	2	3	1,609	2	3	1,662	2	1
1,557	2	1	1,610	1	1	1,663	1	1
1,558	1	2	1,611	1	3	1,664	1	1
1,559	1	2	1,612	1	1	1,665	1	1
1,560	2	1	1,613	2	1	1,666	2	3
1,561	1	2	1,614	1	2	1,667	1	3
1,562	2	1	1,615	2	2	1,668	2	1
1,563	1	3	1,616	1	1	1,669	1	1
1,564	1	1	1,617	1	1	1,670	1	3
1,565	1	1	1,618	1	1	1,671	1	1
1,566	2	3	1,619	2	2	1,672	1	1
1,567	1	1	1,620	1	3	1,673	1	3
1,568	2	1	1,621	1	3	1,674	2	1
1,569	2	1	1,622	2	1	1,675	1	2
1,570	2	1	1,623	2	1	1,676	1	1
1,571	1	3	1,624	1	2	1,677	1	1
1,572	2	1	1,625	1	1	1,678	1	3
1,573	1	2	1,626	1	1	1,679	2	2
1,574	1	1	1,627	1	1	1,680	2	2
1,575	1	1	1,628	2	1	1,681	1	2
1,576	2	1	1,629	1	2	1,682	2	3
1,577	1	3	1,630	2	2	1,683	2	1

Subject	Sex	Reaction	Subject	Sex	Reaction	Subject	Sex	Reaction
1,684	1	1	1,737	1	1	1,790	1	1
1,685	1	1	1,738	1	1	1,791	1	1
1,686	1	1	1,739	2	1	1,792	1	3
1,687	1	1	1,740	2	2	1,793	2	1
1,688	1	1	1,741	2	2	1,794	2	1
1,689	1	1	1,742	1	1	1,795	1	3
1,690	1	2	1,743	2	2	1,796	2	1
1,691	1	1	1,744	1	1	1,797	2	2
1,692	2	2	1,745	1	1	1,798	2	3
1,693	2	1	1,746	2	1	1,799	1	3
1,694	1	1	1,747	2	1	1,800	1	1
1,695	2	1	1,748	2	2	1,801	2	1
1,696	2	3	1,749	1	1	1,802	1	2
1,697	2	2	1,750	2	2	1,803	2	3
1,698	2	1	1,751	2	1	1,804	1	2
1,699	1	1	1,752	2	3	1,805	2	3
1,700	1	1	1,753	2	2	1,806	1	1
1,701	1	2	1,754	2	3	1,807	2	1
1,702	2	1	1,755	1	2	1,808	2	2
1,703	2	3	1,756	1	1	1,809	1	1
1,704	2	1	1,757	2	2	1,810	2	1
1,705	1	1	1,758	2	1	1,811	2	3
1,706	2	1	1,759	2	3	1,812	1	1
1,707	2	2	1,760	1	3	1,813	1	3
1,708	2	1	1,761	1	1	1,814	2	1
1,709	1	1	1,762	1	2	1,815	1	1
1,710	1	1	1,763	1	1	1,816	2	1
1,711	2	3	1,764	1	2	1,817	1	1
1,712	1	1	1,765	1	1	1,818	1	1
1,713	2	3	1,766	2	1	1,819	2	2
1,714	1	2	1,767	1	1	1,820	1	1
1,715	1	3	1,768	1	1	1,821	2	2
1,716	1	1	1,769	2	1	1,822	2	1
1,717	1	1	1,770	1	3	1,823	2	2
1,718	2	3	1,771	1	1	1,824	1	1
1,719	2	1	1,772	1	2	1,825	2	1
1,720	2	1	1,773	2	1	1,826	1	1
1,721	1	1	1,774	2	2	1,827	1	2
1,722	2	1	1,775	1	1	1,828	2	2
1,723	2	1	1,776	2	2	1,829	1	3
1,724	1	3	1,777	2	1	1,830	2	2
1,725	1	1	1,778	1	1	1,831	2	1
1,726	1	1	1,779	1	1	1,832	1	1
1,727	1	1	1,780	2	3	1,833	2	3
1,728	1	2	1,781	2	1	1,834	1	1
1,729	1	3	1,782	1	2	1,835	2	1
1,730	2	3	1,783	1	2	1,836	2	2
1,731	1	1	1,784	1	1	1,837	1	1
1,732	2	3	1,785	1	2	1,838	2	2
1,733	2	2	1,786	1	3	1,839	1	1
1,734	2	1	1,787	2	1	1,840	1	1
1,735	1	3	1,788	2	1	1,841	1	1
1,736	1	1	1,789	2	1	1,842	2	2

Subject	Sex	Reaction	Subject	Sex	Reaction	Subject	Sex	Reaction
1,843	1	3	1,896	1	2	1,949	2	1
1,844	1	1	1,897	2	1	1,950	2	1
1,845	1	1	1,898	1	1	1,951	1	1
1,846	1	1	1,899	2	1	1,952	1	1
1,847	2	1	1,900	1	1	1,953	2	2
1,848	2	1	1,901	2	2	1,954	2	1
1,849	2	2	1,902	2	1	1,955	2	2
1,850	2	1	1,903	1	2	1,956	2	3
1,851	1	2	1,904	1	1	1,957	1	1
1,852	2	1	1,905	2	1	1,958	2	3
1,853	1	3	1,906	2	2	1,959	1	1
1,854	2	1	1,907	2	1	1,960	2	1
1,855	1	1	1,908	2	3	1,961	2	3
1,856	1	1	1,909	1	1	1,962	2	2
1,857	2	2	1,910	2	1	1,963	1	1
1,858	1	2	1,911	2	1	1,964	2	1
1,859	1	1	1,912	1	2	1,965	1	3
1,860	1	1	1,913	2	2	1,966	1	1
1,861	1	1	1,914	1	1	1,967	1	2
1,862	1	1	1,915	1	1	1,968	1	1
1,863	2	1	1,916	2	1	1,969	1	1
1,864	1	1	1,917	1	3	1,970	1	2
1,865	1	1	1,918	2	1	1,971	1	3
1,866	1	3	1,919	1	1	1,972	1	3
1,867	2	1	1,920	2	1	1,973	2	1
1,868	2	1	1,921	2	1	1,974	2	1
1,869	2	3	1,922	1	1	1,975	2	3
1,870	1	1	1,923	2	1	1,976	1	1
1,871	2	1	1,924	2	1	1,977	1	3
1,872	1	1	1,925	1	1	1,978	2	1
1,873	1	3	1,926	2	3	1,979	2	2
1,874	1	3	1,927	2	1	1,980	2	1
1,875	2	1	1,928	2	2	1,981	2	1
1,876	1	1	1,929	1	1	1,982	1	1
1,877	1	2	1,930	2	1	1,983	1	3
1,878	2	1	1,931	2	1	1,984	1	2
1,879	1	1	1,932	1	3	1,985	1	1
1,880	2	1	1,933	1	1	1,986	1	3
1,881	2	3	1,934	1	1	1,987	2	1
1,882	2	2	1,935	1	2	1,988	1	1
1,883	1	1	1,936	1	1	1,989	1	1
1,884	1	1	1,937	2	1	1,990	2	2
1,885	1	3	1,938	1	3	1,991	2	1
1,886	2	1	1,939	2	1	1,992	2	3
1,887	1	2	1,940	2	3	1,993	1	1
1,888	1	1	1,941	1	1	1,994	1	1
1,889	2	1	1,942	1	1	1,995	1	2
1,890	2	1	1,943	2	2	1,996	2	1
1,891	2	1	1,944	1	2	1,997	2	1
1,892	1	1	1,945	1	2	1,998	1	2
1,893	1	2	1,946	2	3	1,999	2	1
1,894	2	1	1,947	2	3	2,000	1	1
1,895	1	3	1,948	1	1			

DATA SET 10   Data for Chapter 15, Review Exercises 18–22

Location A

Subject	Age	Days Absent	Subject	Age	Days Absent	Subject	Age	Days Absent
1	31	2.3	50	28	2.4	99	39	3.8
2	43	3.5	51	40	4.4	100	38	3.4
3	35	2.5	52	31	3.1	101	43	4.5
4	40	3.5	53	28	0.4	102	28	0.9
5	32	1.9	54	35	3.7	103	40	3.2
6	40	3.3	55	38	3.2	104	30	2.8
7	34	3.4	56	40	4.3	105	29	0.8
8	26	0.5	57	39	2.8	106	33	3.1
9	30	1.5	58	44	5.0	107	33	3.0
10	37	3.0	59	24	0.6	108	39	4.4
11	36	3.9	60	37	2.8	109	42	4.2
12	47	5.1	61	41	4.3	110	36	2.9
13	29	1.8	62	31	2.3	111	34	2.1
14	30	2.1	63	38	3.3	112	33	2.9
15	36	4.0	64	37	4.3	113	39	3.6
16	32	2.1	65	27	3.2	114	33	2.4
17	33	2.8	66	36	3.5	115	26	0.9
18	48	4.7	67	37	2.4	116	37	3.6
19	39	4.1	68	39	3.5	117	26	1.5
20	31	2.1	69	47	5.0	118	39	4.2
21	41	3.9	70	34	1.2	119	24	1.6
22	35	3.8	71	35	3.2	120	41	3.9
23	29	2.4	72	40	3.2	121	43	4.6
24	32	1.6	73	44	4.4	122	38	4.6
25	35	3.5	74	29	1.7	123	33	2.1
26	29	2.1	75	44	5.6	124	40	3.9
27	35	3.2	76	33	3.4	125	36	3.6
28	34	3.3	77	28	2.1	126	39	3.5
29	38	4.4	78	32	3.0	127	33	2.0
30	38	4.5	79	38	4.5	128	33	3.0
31	30	1.3	80	28	1.8	129	36	3.1
32	37	3.2	81	37	4.3	130	45	5.5
33	42	5.2	82	39	3.2	131	32	2.6
34	36	2.6	83	46	4.4	132	48	4.9
35	34	3.7	84	31	2.6	133	35	3.7
36	35	2.5	85	47	5.4	134	32	3.0
37	35	2.9	86	33	1.8	135	37	2.7
38	33	3.5	87	31	2.4	136	34	3.4
39	37	3.0	88	33	3.5	137	34	1.6
40	34	4.5	89	39	2.2	138	33	2.5
41	36	3.5	90	36	3.3	139	39	4.0
42	40	2.8	91	35	3.4	140	33	2.4
43	38	3.6	92	37	3.0	141	34	3.1
44	31	1.7	93	37	3.7	142	35	2.8
45	36	3.6	94	36	3.3	143	32	2.9
46	24	1.7	95	34	3.3	144	34	3.1
47	34	3.2	96	41	4.7	145	30	2.3
48	38	3.3	97	31	2.5	146	34	1.6
49	34	3.0	98	33	2.8	147	32	2.6

Location A

Subject	Age	Days Absent	Subject	Age	Days Absent	Subject	Age	Days Absent
148	30	2.3	198	43	3.2	248	45	4.5
149	35	2.1	199	44	3.2	249	47	4.5
150	38	3.0	200	48	4.4	250	47	5.7
151	41	3.5	201	39	3.8	251	34	3.4
152	35	2.9	202	50	4.7	252	30	3.5
153	49	4.8	203	52	4.2	253	34	3.0
154	39	2.4	204	42	3.3	254	39	6.1
155	37	3.5	205	49	4.7	255	29	2.5
156	42	4.3	206	41	4.8	256	28	3.5
157	39	2.4	207	52	6.0	257	30	3.4
158	37	2.3	208	45	4.3	258	32	3.1
159	44	4.3	209	47	3.7	259	40	5.2
160	50	5.5	210	49	5.0	260	31	2.8
161	48	4.0	211	48	5.0	261	32	2.8
162	44	4.0	212	57	6.0	262	31	3.6
163	39	2.7	213	44	3.3	263	35	4.0
164	47	5.1	214	53	4.8	264	29	2.9
165	50	4.2	215	51	4.3	265	25	2.0
166	44	4.5	216	49	4.3	266	35	4.8
167	39	3.1	217	40	3.8	267	33	3.7
168	36	1.6	218	46	4.1	268	30	3.7
169	48	5.2	219	48	5.1	269	23	1.7
170	45	3.1	220	46	3.9	270	23	1.0
171	44	3.6	221	43	3.1	271	28	2.2
172	52	5.3	222	45	3.8	272	31	3.0
173	44	3.7	223	53	4.8	273	29	2.4
174	48	4.1	224	36	4.2	274	39	4.8
175	42	3.7	225	43	3.9	275	37	4.9
176	51	4.4	226	38	3.8	276	32	3.9
177	48	4.8	227	49	5.0	277	38	4.8
178	46	3.5	228	39	3.0	278	32	3.5
179	43	3.6	229	50	5.2	279	31	4.2
180	41	3.7	230	50	4.6	280	34	4.4
181	48	4.6	231	33	2.0	281	35	4.0
182	48	4.7	232	39	3.6	282	27	3.0
183	50	4.3	233	39	2.6	283	29	2.8
184	56	5.8	234	43	4.3	284	30	3.1
185	45	4.1	235	47	4.8	285	34	3.7
186	49	5.7	236	42	3.1	286	24	1.8
187	44	4.1	237	39	2.4	287	47	7.5
188	44	3.6	238	37	2.1	288	32	2.9
189	45	4.3	239	42	3.4	289	27	2.7
190	32	1.8	240	38	2.4	290	29	2.6
191	48	4.1	241	45	4.5	291	24	1.0
192	43	5.2	242	40	3.7	292	37	4.3
193	52	5.6	243	51	5.8	293	33	3.8
194	46	4.4	244	48	3.9	294	29	2.8
195	45	4.2	245	38	2.9	295	30	3.4
196	41	3.5	246	41	3.5	296	30	3.1
197	46	4.7	247	52	4.7	297	28	2.6

Location A

Subject	Age	Days Absent	Subject	Age	Days Absent	Subject	Age	Days Absent
298	25	3.3	316	35	2.6	334	39	3.3
299	31	3.7	317	44	1.7	335	40	3.5
300	25	0.9	318	41	2.9	336	44	3.2
301	44	4.5	319	43	4.2	337	45	4.2
302	41	2.7	320	39	2.9	338	50	4.5
303	39	4.6	321	38	3.3	339	45	3.9
304	49	4.7	322	46	4.1	340	46	3.6
305	40	2.9	323	50	5.0	341	51	5.5
306	31	2.7	324	42	3.7	342	49	4.7
307	53	5.1	325	43	3.8	343	42	3.2
308	41	3.7	326	53	4.9	344	49	4.5
309	44	2.9	327	47	4.1	345	41	3.6
310	47	3.9	328	41	2.7	346	39	3.4
311	44	3.4	329	44	4.2	347	46	3.9
312	57	6.0	330	34	3.2	348	51	5.0
313	43	2.8	331	42	2.1	349	46	4.0
314	52	5.4	332	55	5.5	350	46	4.9
315	40	2.6	333	45	4.9			

Location B

Subject	Age	Days Absent	Subject	Age	Days Absent	Subject	Age	Days Absent
1	18	1.4	26	22	2.2	51	23	3.2
2	25	2.9	27	24	2.7	52	23	3.0
3	24	3.4	28	20	0.8	53	27	3.4
4	28	3.3	29	21	1.4	54	28	4.4
5	20	1.4	30	27	3.4	55	21	1.4
6	26	3.3	31	26	2.6	56	27	3.4
7	23	3.2	32	23	1.1	57	22	1.6
8	24	2.6	33	19	1.7	58	22	2.4
9	21	2.9	34	21	2.1	59	25	3.4
10	27	3.8	35	24	2.1	60	21	0.4
11	24	4.0	36	18	2.0	61	23	2.4
12	23	2.6	37	20	2.3	62	26	3.1
13	18	1.2	38	21	1.4	63	24	3.4
14	28	4.3	39	26	2.5	64	20	1.3
15	23	2.5	40	26	3.7	65	27	4.1
16	25	2.9	41	27	3.6	66	22	1.7
17	25	3.1	42	28	3.3	67	23	3.3
18	25	3.2	43	21	2.9	68	24	2.7
19	22	3.2	44	24	3.2	69	28	4.8
20	31	5.6	45	22	2.0	70	27	4.6
21	32	4.5	46	21	1.8	71	23	2.8
22	24	3.6	47	25	4.5	72	26	3.6
23	24	3.3	48	24	2.2	73	32	4.9
24	24	4.0	49	22	2.8	74	31	5.5
25	27	3.8	50	26	2.9	75	25	3.0

Location B

Subject	Age	Days Absent	Subject	Age	Days Absent	Subject	Age	Days Absent
76	28	3.8	126	27	3.1	176	23	0.5
77	21	2.8	127	24	3.2	177	25	1.8
78	23	3.2	128	23	2.1	178	23	0.7
79	26	2.8	129	26	2.5	179	23	1.4
80	24	3.8	130	22	2.7	180	29	1.5
81	27	3.1	131	24	3.2	181	36	3.9
82	23	2.6	132	22	3.0	182	27	2.7
83	24	2.4	133	25	3.3	183	32	3.5
84	27	4.2	134	21	2.7	184	28	2.4
85	28	4.3	135	17	0.9	185	26	2.1
86	25	2.5	136	20	1.9	186	29	2.5
87	26	3.8	137	22	2.2	187	29	2.8
88	28	3.1	138	26	2.5	188	30	3.3
89	20	0.5	139	23	2.7	189	27	3.0
90	23	2.8	140	27	4.0	190	24	1.6
91	25	2.4	141	23	3.2	191	38	5.1
92	21	1.9	142	24	3.0	192	31	4.5
93	21	2.2	143	25	3.1	193	27	3.2
94	20	2.4	144	25	3.4	194	31	2.5
95	25	1.9	145	22	1.7	195	28	3.0
96	25	3.6	146	25	2.9	196	36	4.5
97	26	2.5	147	22	1.5	197	29	2.7
98	28	4.7	148	24	3.8	198	28	3.5
99	28	3.6	149	22	1.7	199	33	2.9
100	21	1.6	150	24	2.9	200	30	3.1
101	23	2.3	151	31	3.7	201	30	3.2
102	25	2.3	152	29	2.7	202	35	3.4
103	23	3.3	153	38	4.4	203	34	3.1
104	18	2.3	154	31	3.0	204	29	3.1
105	29	3.9	155	32	3.1	205	31	2.0
106	30	5.0	156	26	1.7	206	28	3.2
107	20	2.0	157	24	1.9	207	25	1.8
108	18	1.4	158	30	2.9	208	29	2.6
109	24	3.0	159	25	1.5	209	26	1.4
110	22	2.3	160	36	3.8	210	32	3.8
111	29	3.8	161	26	2.0	211	27	2.6
112	28	5.1	162	28	1.8	212	31	3.0
113	27	4.5	163	29	2.5	213	30	2.8
114	26	4.3	164	24	3.0	214	32	3.8
115	27	3.0	165	32	2.6	215	33	3.5
116	26	3.2	166	30	2.6	216	28	2.7
117	21	0.8	167	29	3.3	217	31	4.1
118	22	2.8	168	29	3.0	218	31	3.5
119	24	3.3	169	29	3.1	219	33	4.0
120	21	2.8	170	24	1.0	220	23	2.3
121	22	1.7	171	22	1.8	221	29	3.5
122	26	3.2	172	27	2.9	222	31	3.6
123	24	2.4	173	38	4.7	223	28	3.2
124	24	3.0	174	26	2.1	224	32	2.9
125	28	3.9	175	25	2.1	225	30	1.9

Location B

Subject	Age	Days Absent	Subject	Age	Days Absent	Subject	Age	Days Absent
226	32	3.5	251	29	2.0	276	40	3.2
227	31	3.3	252	37	3.6	277	39	3.0
228	38	4.1	253	30	1.6	278	26	1.6
229	19	0.8	254	29	1.4	279	24	2.3
230	35	3.5	255	36	3.3	280	32	2.4
231	27	2.2	256	40	4.2	281	25	1.5
232	34	4.6	257	39	4.6	282	36	3.2
233	30	3.3	258	37	3.1	283	44	4.6
234	29	2.8	259	30	3.6	284	40	4.7
235	32	2.7	260	26	1.9	285	41	4.6
236	20	1.4	261	31	2.1	286	42	3.7
237	31	3.7	262	35	3.6	287	36	2.1
238	32	2.4	263	39	4.0	288	36	2.3
239	27	3.0	264	40	4.1	289	26	1.7
240	24	1.6	265	41	3.8	290	30	2.0
241	31	4.3	266	33	1.5	291	42	4.5
242	33	3.7	267	24	1.0	292	32	2.4
243	29	3.3	268	30	2.1	293	28	2.3
244	19	1.2	269	36	2.7	294	27	1.6
245	27	2.5	270	35	3.4	295	19	0.9
246	33	3.2	271	31	2.0	296	42	5.0
247	34	2.9	272	29	2.6	297	25	1.9
248	29	2.2	273	32	3.5	298	28	1.8
249	31	3.5	274	32	3.0	299	35	4.0
250	24	1.0	275	35	3.0	300	48	4.0

Location C

Subject	Age	Days Absent	Subject	Age	Days Absent	Subject	Age	Days Absent
1	34	2.9	19	30	2.1	37	28	1.8
2	30	2.5	20	29	2.2	38	37	3.2
3	31	2.3	21	32	2.7	39	41	3.8
4	33	3.3	22	26	1.5	40	35	3.3
5	40	3.2	23	29	3.1	41	44	4.0
6	49	5.2	24	29	2.4	42	46	4.8
7	21	2.0	25	29	1.7	43	43	4.6
8	38	2.8	26	32	2.2	44	31	1.9
9	39	2.2	27	40	3.6	45	37	3.3
10	36	2.8	28	47	3.7	46	38	3.2
11	35	2.7	29	32	2.3	47	44	4.2
12	40	4.0	30	38	3.0	48	36	3.3
13	20	1.5	31	41	3.3	49	47	4.9
14	30	3.1	32	32	1.9	50	27	1.5
15	36	2.3	33	30	2.1	51	31	1.5
16	42	3.2	34	28	2.0	52	36	2.8
17	40	3.2	35	27	2.4	53	36	3.3
18	49	4.8	36	29	1.4	54	35	2.6

Location C

Subject	Age	Days Absent	Subject	Age	Days Absent	Subject	Age	Days Absent
55	38	3.9	105	30	2.4	155	44	3.2
56	23	1.2	106	32	2.5	156	35	2.1
57	40	3.7	107	34	2.7	157	36	3.3
58	21	0.6	108	33	3.1	158	42	4.6
59	35	3.0	109	31	2.0	159	37	2.8
60	28	2.2	110	25	2.3	160	36	2.9
61	49	5.9	111	41	4.9	161	46	3.9
62	44	2.6	112	36	3.0	162	32	2.5
63	38	4.4	113	28	3.4	163	31	2.2
64	52	5.7	114	29	1.6	164	37	3.2
65	34	3.7	115	46	3.2	165	31	1.4
66	29	1.7	116	31	2.3	166	20	1.2
67	40	3.5	117	50	4.2	167	37	3.2
68	44	4.3	118	23	2.4	168	30	1.2
69	27	2.4	119	31	2.1	169	28	2.5
70	28	1.3	120	36	3.8	170	24	1.8
71	39	4.2	121	21	1.1	171	40	4.4
72	34	3.0	122	45	3.4	172	49	5.3
73	34	3.4	123	38	2.6	173	31	2.7
74	42	3.0	124	43	4.6	174	39	4.5
75	45	4.4	125	32	3.7	175	33	2.8
76	34	3.3	126	25	2.2	176	39	3.0
77	39	4.1	127	39	3.0	177	27	1.9
78	44	3.9	128	31	3.2	178	37	3.6
79	29	3.6	129	44	4.2	179	38	2.1
80	39	3.1	130	22	2.7	180	38	2.9
81	33	3.0	131	22	1.3	181	23	1.0
82	43	3.8	132	34	2.3	182	37	3.2
83	30	1.5	133	27	0.9	183	46	3.9
84	42	4.7	134	34	3.7	184	31	3.1
85	33	2.7	135	30	1.5	185	29	1.6
86	31	2.3	136	46	5.0	186	38	2.7
87	40	3.8	137	31	2.3	187	29	2.5
88	31	3.2	138	46	5.8	188	45	5.0
89	30	3.5	139	30	2.0	189	38	3.6
90	28	2.1	140	27	1.2	190	26	1.5
91	28	0.9	141	46	4.7	191	31	2.2
92	43	4.2	142	43	5.0	192	29	2.3
93	41	3.3	143	33	2.7	193	31	2.5
94	30	2.6	144	38	3.0	194	24	1.3
95	35	3.0	145	38	3.6	195	40	3.5
96	32	3.6	146	31	1.8	196	38	3.9
97	36	3.7	147	34	1.8	197	45	3.3
98	29	4.0	148	31	2.1	198	27	2.3
99	49	4.7	149	40	2.4	199	37	3.7
100	35	3.3	150	38	3.4	200	34	3.7
101	31	2.1	151	22	0.4	201	36	3.5
102	28	2.1	152	35	2.7	202	37	3.6
103	23	1.5	153	33	2.9	203	36	3.4
104	26	1.0	154	46	4.3	204	37	2.9

Location C

Subject	Age	Days Absent	Subject	Age	Days Absent	Subject	Age	Days Absent
205	42	3.5	217	34	2.5	229	31	2.2
206	47	4.9	218	32	2.9	230	32	2.4
207	28	2.5	219	27	2.0	231	45	4.6
208	27	2.8	220	27	1.4	332	39	5.0
209	18	0.9	221	26	1.8	233	22	1.4
210	23	0.8	222	31	3.0	234	35	2.0
211	37	2.3	223	35	2.7	235	26	1.7
212	22	1.2	224	34	3.7	236	38	4.6
213	32	2.4	225	31	1.9	237	33	3.1
214	32	2.5	226	31	2.7	238	23	1.0
215	24	1.6	227	36	3.8	239	25	1.3
216	30	3.2	228	38	3.5	240	30	2.3

Location D

Subject	Age	Days Absent	Subject	Age	Days Absent	Subject	Age	Days Absent
1	36	4.3	32	39	4.6	63	44	6.0
2	33	3.8	33	36	5.5	64	24	2.8
3	29	2.5	34	20	2.0	65	37	4.2
4	53	5.9	35	27	3.4	66	30	3.0
5	25	2.7	36	35	2.5	67	31	4.0
6	45	5.3	37	42	5.4	68	47	5.2
7	29	4.6	38	32	4.9	69	26	3.2
8	22	2.5	39	17	2.8	70	41	4.1
9	30	3.1	40	41	4.7	71	31	3.2
10	24	2.2	41	44	4.9	72	39	5.0
11	32	3.7	42	38	3.8	73	27	2.8
12	28	3.0	43	23	3.5	74	45	5.8
13	38	3.7	44	30	4.6	75	39	4.0
14	34	3.6	45	37	3.6	76	41	4.4
15	34	4.2	46	25	3.6	77	40	4.2
16	33	3.6	47	42	4.6	78	28	3.1
17	25	2.7	48	35	4.1	79	46	5.5
18	42	5.1	49	42	5.2	80	34	3.2
19	50	6.4	50	32	3.0	81	31	3.2
20	38	4.9	51	32	3.1	82	37	3.8
21	32	3.4	52	31	3.2	83	34	5.6
22	37	4.6	53	23	3.2	84	40	4.7
23	29	2.8	54	32	3.3	85	33	5.0
24	37	3.8	55	22	2.3	86	39	3.6
25	27	3.3	56	39	4.3	87	40	4.7
26	40	3.9	57	28	3.6	88	34	3.9
27	31	3.9	58	33	3.3	89	47	4.3
28	39	5.0	59	28	4.0	90	29	2.4
29	30	2.2	60	35	4.4	91	25	1.7
30	35	3.4	61	38	3.8	92	35	4.9
31	31	2.5	62	33	3.1	93	28	3.0

Location D

Subject	Age	Days Absent	Subject	Age	Days Absent	Subject	Age	Days Absent
94	18	2.0	117	38	4.4	140	39	4.0
95	32	3.9	118	24	2.2	141	26	3.0
96	41	4.0	119	23	2.4	142	28	3.8
97	34	4.0	120	40	4.6	143	34	3.9
98	37	4.9	121	39	4.9	144	46	4.5
99	38	4.1	122	36	4.2	145	32	3.7
100	38	5.3	123	32	4.6	146	28	2.9
101	35	3.4	124	27	2.9	147	24	2.7
102	39	4.3	125	51	6.6	148	21	3.4
103	39	4.7	126	26	4.5	149	45	5.6
104	41	5.0	127	37	3.8	150	40	5.4
105	26	2.7	128	36	4.4	151	32	3.1
106	37	3.8	129	37	4.2	152	22	1.1
107	42	6.3	130	29	3.9	153	34	3.2
108	30	2.6	131	32	4.0	154	47	5.3
109	21	2.0	132	35	3.9	155	27	2.1
110	35	4.3	133	55	6.6	156	20	1.2
111	44	6.3	134	33	3.8	157	44	3.2
112	36	4.5	135	29	3.9	158	32	3.0
113	49	4.3	136	40	4.4	159	38	2.5
114	35	4.8	137	41	3.8	160	51	4.8
115	39	4.0	138	43	5.7			
116	30	3.5	139	36	3.7			

Appendix V
Summation
Notation

The symbol Σ, which we use extensively in this text, is mathematical shorthand notation. We use it to indicate that the items following it are to be added. When necessary for clarity, we include an index of summation, usually i, as part of the notation. For example,

$$\sum_{i=1}^{4} x_i$$

instructs us to add the values of x from x_1 through x_4. That is,

$$\sum_{i=1}^{4} x_i = x_1 + x_2 + x_3 + x_4$$

Similarly, Σx or Σx_i instructs us to add all values of x, where the meaning of "all" is apparent from the context.

The following are some algebraic properties of summation that you will find useful.

1. The summation of a constant c is n times the constant, when n is the number of values of the index of summation. That is,

$$\sum_{i=1}^{n} c = nc$$

For example,

$$\sum_{i=1}^{4} 5 = 4(5) = 20$$

2. The summation of a constant times a variable is equal to the constant times the summation of the variable. That is, given that c is a constant, then

$$\sum_{i=1}^{n} cx_i = c \sum_{i=1}^{n} x_i$$

For example,

$$\sum_{i=1}^{4} 5(x_i) = 5 \sum_{i=1}^{4} x_i$$

If $x_1 = 2$, $x_2 = 3$, $x_3 = 6$, and $x_4 = 10$, we have

$$5(2 + 3 + 6 + 10) = 5(21) = 105$$

3. The summation of a sum (or difference) is the sum (or difference) of the individual sums. In symbols,

$$\sum_{i=1}^{n} (x_i \pm y_i) = \sum_{i=1}^{n} x_i \pm \sum_{i=1}^{n} y_i$$

This last property extends to more than two components. For example,

$$\sum_{i=1}^{n} (x_i + y_i - z_i) = \sum_{i=1}^{n} x_i + \sum_{i=1}^{n} y_i - \sum_{i=1}^{n} z_i$$

Double Subscript Notation In some cases, a population may be composed of two or more identifiable groups, or subpopulations. It is frequently convenient in such cases both to distinguish one observation from another and to identify the subpopulation to which each observation belongs. We can accomplish this by using a double subscript on each observation. For example, consider a population consisting of four groups, or subpopulations, each containing three observations, as shown in the following table.

Group			
1	2	3	4
10	8	2	8
15	9	6	11
25	14	1	4
50	31	9	23

We refer to the first observation in group 2 as x_{12}, and we may write $x_{12} = 8$. The second observation in group 4 is designated x_{24}, and we may write $x_{24} = 11$, and so on.

The total of a given group is obtained by adding the observations in that group as shown in the table. The total for the entire population of 12 observations is obtained by adding the group totals. For the population shown in the table, the population total is $50 + 31 + 9 + 23 = 113$. This system of notation and summation may be generalized for the case of k groups as follows.

x_{ij} = the ith observation in the jth group, where j identifies the group and i distinguishes one observation from another within the group

$$\sum_{i=1}^{n_j} x_{ij} = \text{the total for the } j\text{th group}$$

$$\sum_{j=1}^{k}\sum_{i=1}^{n_j} x_{ij} = \text{the grand total of all observations}$$

GREEK ALPHABET

α	Alpha	ι	Iota	ρ	Rho
β	Beta	κ	Kappa	$\sigma\ (\Sigma)$	Sigma
γ	Gamma	λ	Lambda	τ	Tau
δ	Delta	μ	Mu	υ	Upsilon
ϵ	Epsilon	ν	Nu	ϕ	Phi
ζ	Zeta	ξ	Xi	χ	Chi
η	Eta	o	Omicron	ψ	Psi
θ	Theta	π	Pi	ω	Omega

Appendix VI
Some Basic
MINITAB
Data-Handling
Commands

This appendix contains some basic MINITAB data-handling commands and illustrations of their use. However, it is not intended to be a definitive reference manual for the MINITAB software package. Its purpose is to provide the text user who is also a MINITAB user with a quick reference to frequently used commands. For those readers who do not use MINITAB, it serves as an illustration of the ways in which the software package can handle data. The serious user of the MINITAB data analysis system should have available for reference (1) the *MINITAB Statistical Software Reference Manual* for the MINITAB release number being used and (2) the latest edition of the *MINITAB Handbook* by Barbara F. Ryan, Brian L. Joiner, and Thomas A. Ryan, Jr., published by PWS-Kent Publishing Company of Boston.

The following data-handling commands will enable the reader to prepare data for all the MINITAB analyses discussed in this text. Commands for obtaining the various analyses are given and illustrated where the particular analysis is discussed.

READ The READ command allows the user to enter two or more columns of data a row at a time. Suppose, for example, that we have one column of data (column 1) consisting of the observations 24, 34, 44, 15, 24 and a second column of data (column 2) consisting of the observations 33, 16, 27, 22, 32. We use the READ command to enter the data as follows:

```
MTB>   READ C1 C2
DATA>  24 33
DATA>  34 16
DATA>  44 27
DATA>  15 22
DATA>  24 32
DATA>  END
        5 ROWS READ
```

The data are now stored in a matrix containing two columns and five rows. The END command signals the end of the data entry.

SET When we use the READ command, we enter our data a row at a time. When we use the SET command, we enter our data a column at a time. Let us use the SET command to enter our two columns of data.

```
MTB>   SET C1
DATA>  24 34 44 15 24
DATA>  SET C2
DATA>  33 16 27 22 32
DATA>  END
```

PRINT The PRINT command allows us to view the data that we have entered. For example, when we enter the command PRINT C1, C2, the computer responds with a display of our previously entered two columns of data. The following is a printout of the operation:

```
PRINT C1, C2
ROW              C1              C2
1                24              33
2                34              16
3                44              27
4                15              22
5                24              32
```

INSERT We use the INSERT command to add observations to our data sets at various locations in our data matrix. Suppose, for example, that we wish to add the observation 16 between rows 2 and 3 of column 1 and the observation 20 after row 5 of column 2. The commands are as follows:

```
MTB>   INSERT 2 3 C1
DATA>  16
DATA>  INSERT C2
DATA>  20
```

We may use the PRINT command to obtain a display of the edited data:

```
PRINT C1 C2
ROW              C1              C2
1                24              33
2                34              16
3                16              27
4                44              22
5                15              32
6                24              20
```

DELETE The DELETE command is used to remove observations from data sets. As part of the command, we specify the row and column location of each observation to be deleted. Let us use this command to remove the two previously inserted observations: observation 16 now stored in row 3 of column 1 and observation 20 now stored in row 6 of column 2. The commands are as follows:

```
DELETE 3 C1
DELETE 6 C2
```

LET When we want to change an observation we use the LET command. When we use the command we must specify the row and column location of the observation to be changed. Suppose, for example, that after entering our data we discover that observation 34 stored in row 2 of column 1 was incorrectly entered and should be 35. The following display illustrates the use of the LET command to accomplish the change:

```
LET C1(2) = 35
```

NAME In many instances we may wish to give a column of data some descriptive label. For example if the observations in column 1 are heights of people, we might want to label the column with the name HEIGHT. In regression analysis we might want to give our columns of data such labels as Y, X1, X2, and so on. The NAME command permits us to perform this operation. When we use the NAME command, the designated name must be enclosed in single quotes. Suppose we use the NAME command to name our previously entered columns of data X and Y, respectively. The appropriate command is

```
NAME C1 = 'X', C2 = 'Y'
```

The PRINT command allows us to view the data and their new labels as follows:

```
PRINT C1 C2
ROW            X              Y
1              24             33
2              35             16
3              44             27
4              15             22
5              24             32
```

SORT The SORT command allows us to sort a column of observations, carry along any other columns of observations, row by row, with the sorted column, and store the sorted column and "carried along" columns in newly designated columns. Suppose for example, that we wish to sort our previously entered and edited observations now stored in column 1. We wish to retain (carry along) column 2 as part of the data set and store the two columns in columns 3 and 4. The following command accomplishes this objective:

```
SORT C1, CARRY ALONG C2, PUT INTO C3-C4
```

By means of the PRINT command, we may verify that the sorting procedure was carried out:

```
PRINT C3 C4
ROW            C3              C4
1              15              22
2              24              33
3              24              32
4              35              16
5              44              27
```

If we do not wish to carry along other columns, row by row, with the sorted column, we merely issue the SORT command for the column we wish to sort. For example, to sort column 1, we issue the command

```
SORT C1, C1
```

We may view a display of the two columns with the PRINT command as follows:

```
PRINT C1 C2
ROW            X               Y
1              14              33
2              15              16
3              24              27
4              35              22
5              44              32
```

RANK The RANK command replaces the observations in a specified column by their corresponding ranks and stores the ranks in a designated new column. To replace with their ranks the observations previously stored in column 1 and column 2 (and subsequently sorted) and store the ranks in columns 3 and 4, we issue the following commands:

```
RANK C1 C3
RANK C2 C4
```

Through the use of the PRINT command we may view the resulting columns of ranks:

```
PRINT C3 C4
ROW            C3              C4
1              1.0             2
2              2.5             5
3              2.5             4
4              4.0             1
5              5.0             3
```

Answers to Odd-Numbered Exercises

Note: Many of the following answers were obtained by computer and, consequently, may differ from answers obtained by hand calculations because of rounding.

CHAPTER 2

2.5.1 Suggested class intervals: 10–19, 20–29, 30–39, etc. Frequencies: 5, 14, 27, 26, 16, 10, 5, 4, 3

2.5.3 Suggested class intervals: 40–49, 50–59, 60–69, 70–79, 80–89, 90–99. Frequencies: 7, 10, 28, 33, 16, 6

2.5.5

Class Interval	Frequency	Cumulative Frequency	Relative Frequency	Cumulative Relative Frequency
10–14	23	23	0.168	0.168
15–19	29	52	0.212	0.380
20–24	47	99	0.343	0.723
25–29	24	123	0.175	0.898
30–34	9	132	0.066	0.964
35–39	3	135	0.022	0.986
40n44	2	137	0.014	1.000
	137		1.000	

2.6.1

Stem	Leaf
0	7
1	2 8 7 6
2	5 1 7 0 6 7 1
3	0 4 5 6 0 0 5 0 0
4	2 0 6
5	1

2.6.3

	Adult Male		Adult Female	
Stem	**Leaf**	**Stem**	**Leaf**	
17	1	12	5	
18	4	13	5	
19	1 5	14	3 5	
20	1 2 5 1 9	15	2 4 4 0 5	
21	2 3 4 4 3 7	16	5 6 8 7	
22	2 5 2 9	17	8 3	
23	9 8 3	18	6 6 4	
24	9 5 8	19	0 0 5 9	
		20	3	
		21	2 4	

2.7.1

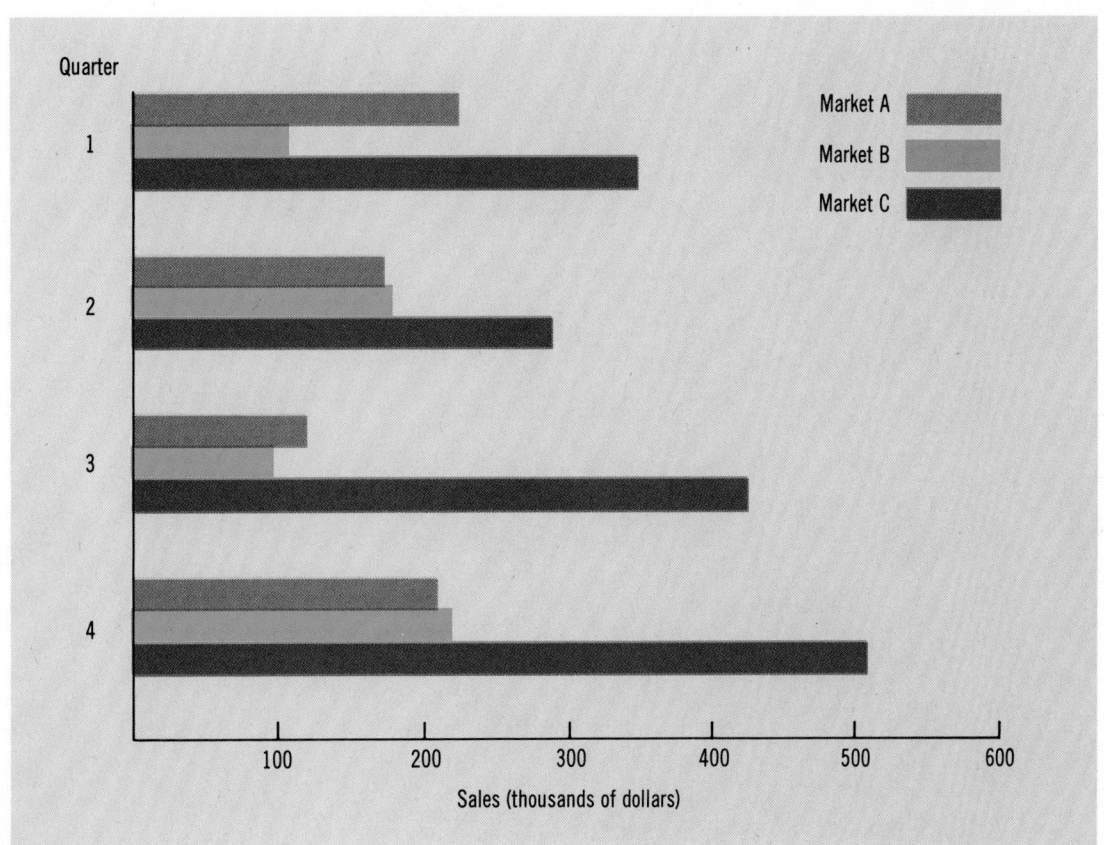

2.7.3

	Percent		
County	Owner-Occupied	Renter-Occupied	Vacant
A	0.70	0.24	0.06
B	0.67	0.32	0.01
C	0.60	0.37	0.03
D	0.53	0.31	0.16
E	0.66	0.33	0.01
F	0.76	0.20	0.04
G	0.62	0.30	0.08
H	0.72	0.22	0.06
I	0.74	0.22	0.04
J	0.69	0.25	0.06
K	0.75	0.20	0.05
L	0.78	0.20	0.02
M	0.70	0.20	0.10
N	0.65	0.23	0.12
O	0.62	0.31	0.07

2.7.3

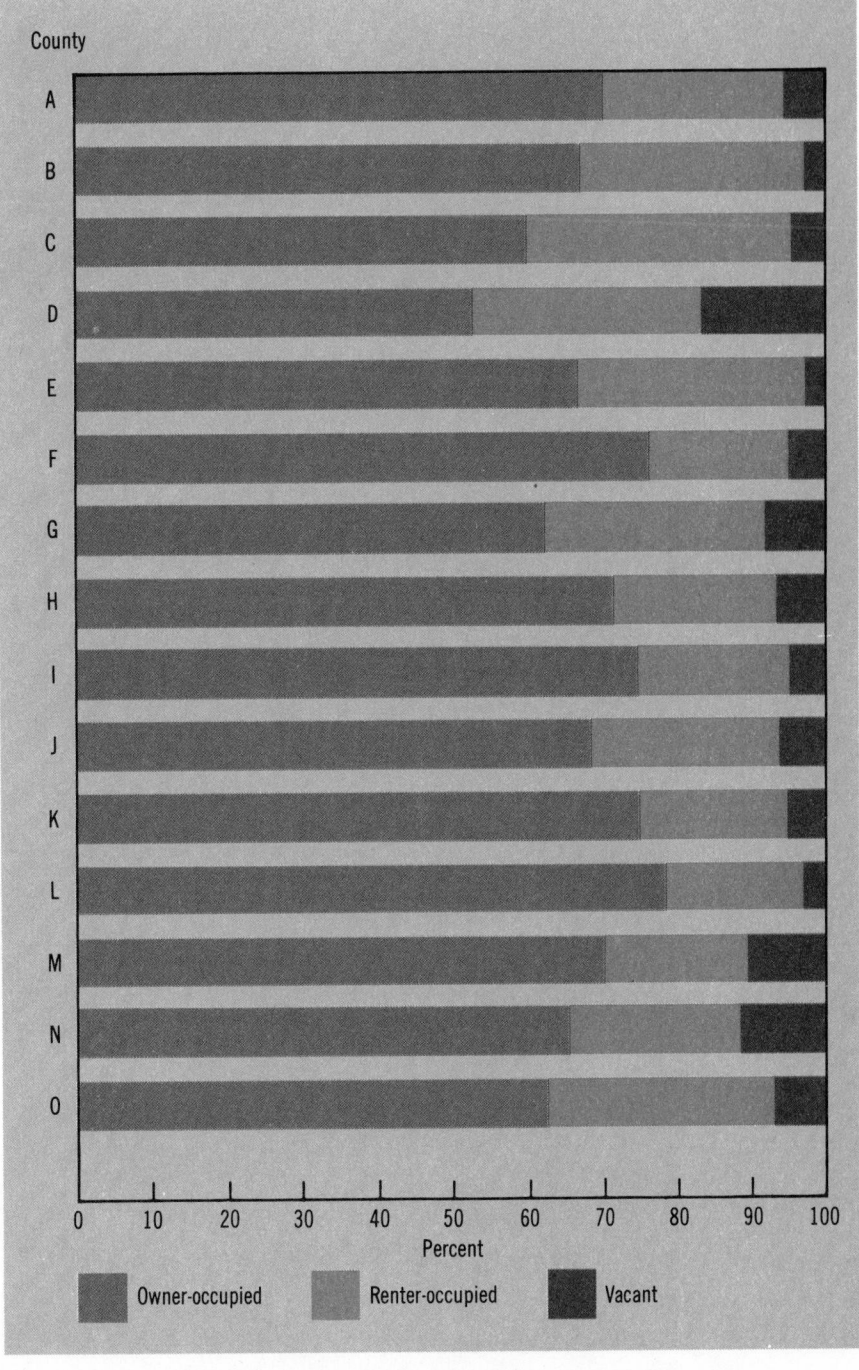

2.7.5

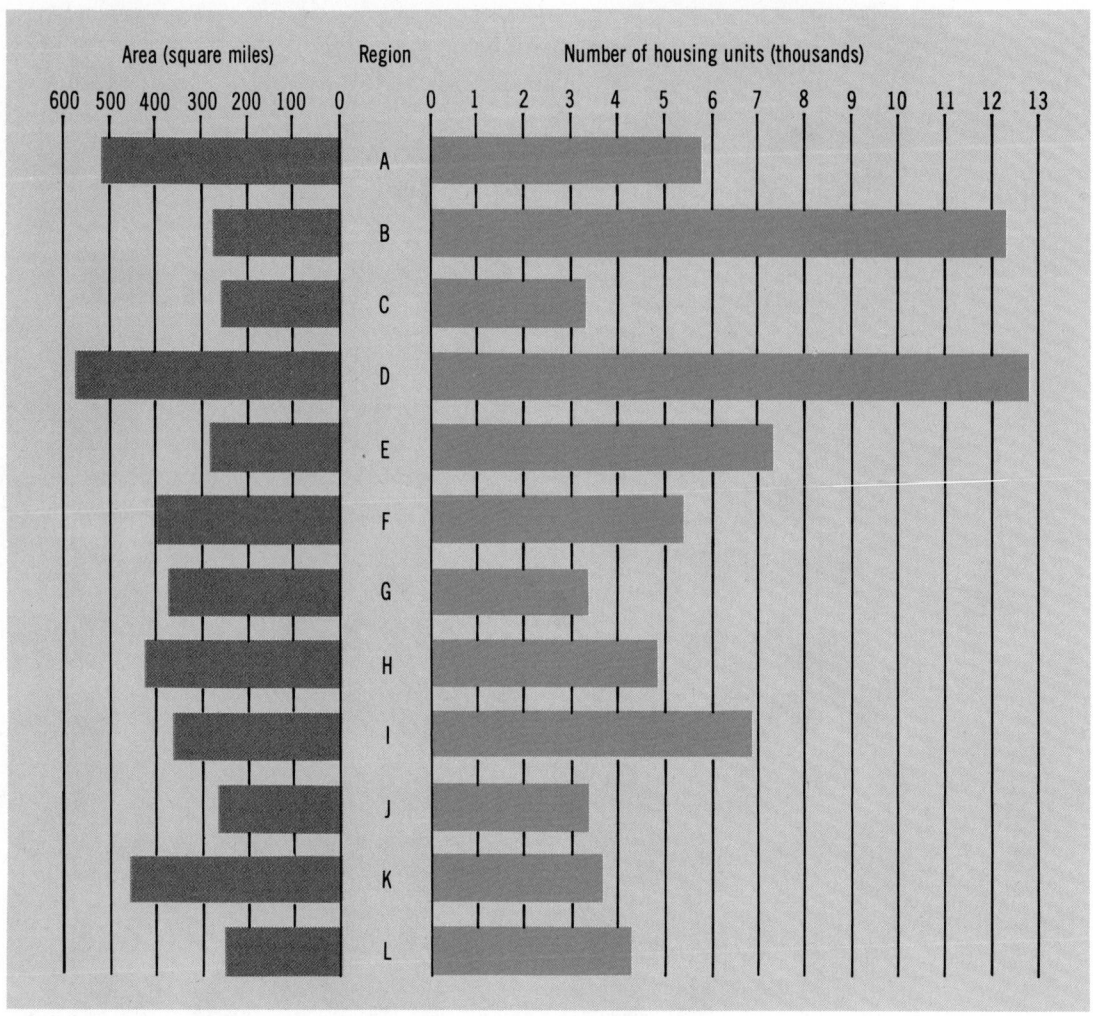

2.8.1   (a) 27.5   (b) 28.5   (c) 30   (d) 20   (e) 38.28   (f) 6.2

2.8.3   (a) 57.1   (b) 56   (c) 56 and 59   (d) 10   (e) 9.0   (f) 3.0

2.8.5   (a) 75   (b) 50–150

2.9.1 $\bar{x} = 45.59$ Median = 42.96 $s^2 = 336.4137$ $s = 18.34$

2.9.3 $\bar{x} = 70.4$ Median = 71.0 $s^2 = 155.75$ $s = 12.5$

2.9.5   Ordered array:

117	134	140	143	146	150	153	158	164	180
119	135	140	143	147	151	154	159	166	183
122	136	140	143	147	151	154	160	169	184
123	137	142	143	148	151	154	161	169	184
124	137	142	143	148	151	155	161	170	187
126	137	142	144	148	152	155	162	171	190
130	139	143	144	148	152	156	162	172	191
130	139	143	145	149	152	156	163	173	191
132	139	143	145	149	153	157	163	175	200
133	139	143	145	150	153	157	164	176	202

$R = 85$ $k \approx 8$ For convenience let class interval width be 10.

Class Interval	f_i	x_i	$x_i f_i$	$x_i^2 f_i$	Cumulative Frequency
110–119	2	114.5	229.0	26,220.50	2
120–129	4	124.5	498.0	62,001.00	6
130–139	14	134.5	1883.0	253,263.50	20
140–149	29	144.5	4190.5	605,527.25	49
150–159	23	154.5	3553.5	549,015.75	72
160–169	12	164.5	1974.0	324,723.00	84
170–179	6	174.5	1047.0	182,701.50	90
180–189	5	184.5	922.5	170,201.25	95
190–199	3	194.5	583.5	113,490.75	98
200–209	2	204.5	409.0	83,640.50	100
	100		15,290.0	2,370,785.00	

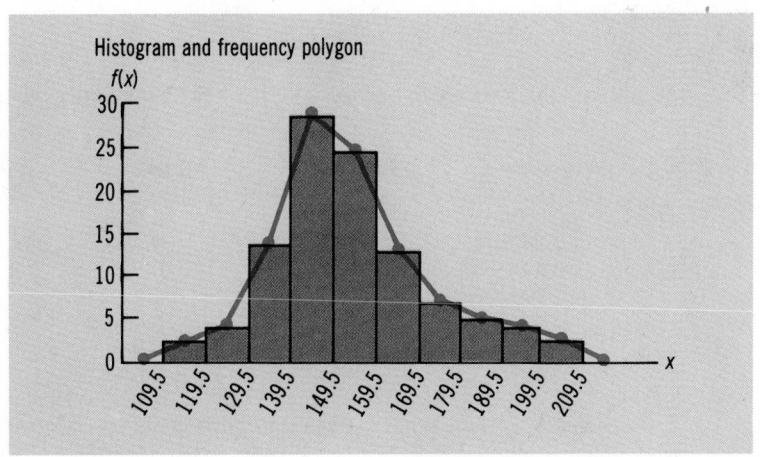

Histogram and frequency polygon

2.9.7

Class Interval	x_i	f_i	$x_i f_i$	$x_i^2 f_i$
100–119	109.5	2	219.00	23,980.5
120–139	129.5	18	2,331.00	301,864.5
140–159	149.5	52	7,774.00	1,162,213.0
160–179	169.5	18	3,051.00	517,144.5
180–199	189.5	8	1,516.00	287,282.0
200–219	209.5	2	419.00	87,780.5
		100	15,310.00	2,380,265.0

$\bar{x} = 153.1$ $s^2 = 366.70707$ $s = 19.1496$ Median $= 151.04$

2.9.9   Ordered array:

19	34	37	46	54	57	67	76
25	35	39	46	54	64	68	76
31	36	40	48	54	64	69	79
31	36	41	51	55	65	69	81
32	36	41	53	55	67	70	93

$Q_1 = 36.25$ Median $= 53.5$ $Q_3 = 67.00$

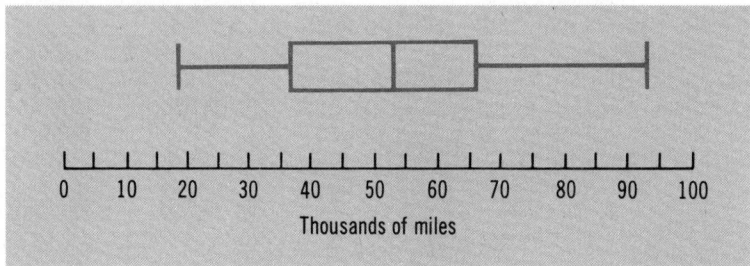

2.11.1   (a) 166.67, 116.67, 133.33, 130.00   (b) 132.00   (c) 132.6   (d) 130.2   (e) 132.6

REVIEW EXERCISES

15.

	(b) Relative frequency		(c) Cumulative relative frequency	
	Magazine A	**Magazine B**	**Magazine A**	**Magazine B**
	0.05	0.04	0.05	0.04
	0.24	0.09	0.29	0.13
	0.29	0.09	0.58	0.22
	0.19	0.14	0.77	0.36
	0.14	0.27	0.91	0.63
	0.05	0.23	0.96	0.86
	0.04	0.14	1.00	1.00

(d) Magazine A, because it has a greater proportion of subscribers in the age groups most likely to have babies.
(e) Magazine B, because it has a greater proportion of subscribers at or nearing retirement age.

17. $\bar{x} = 4.97$ Median = 5 $s^2 = 2.7446$ $s = 1.66$

19. $\bar{x} = 15.2$ Median = 14.5 $s^2 = 6.6222$ $s = 2.57$

21. $\bar{x} = 2.9$ Median = 3.15 $s^2 = 0.88889$ $s = 0.94281$

23. $\bar{x} = 2.28$ Median = 2 $s^2 = 4.0433$ $s = 2.0108$

25. $\bar{x} = 1.204$ Median = 1.2 $s^2 = 0.0529$ $s = 0.23$

27. $\bar{x} = 39.2$ Median = 42 $s^2 = 47.314$ $s = 6.8785$

29. $\bar{x} = 365$ Median = 348.5 $s^2 = 13,754$ $s = 117.28$

31. $\bar{x} = 7.65625$ Median = 7.15 $s^2 = 2.212$ $s = 1.4873$

33. (a)

Community A

Salaries ($1000)	Frequency	Cumulative Frequency	Relative Frequency	Cumulative Relative Frequency
10–19	43	43	0.4095	0.4095
20–29	15	58	0.1429	0.5524
30–39	13	71	0.1238	0.6762
40–49	12	83	0.1143	0.7905
50–59	11	94	0.1048	0.8953
60–69	9	103	0.0857	0.9810
70–79	2	105	0.0190	1.0000

Median = 19.5 + (9.5/15)(10) = 25.83

Community B

Salaries ($1000)	Frequency	Cumulative Frequency	Relative Frequency	Cumulative Relative Frequency
10–19	10	10	0.0917	0.0917
20–29	11	21	0.1009	0.1926
30–39	13	34	0.1193	0.3119
40–49	16	50	0.1468	0.4587
50–59	18	68	0.1651	0.6238
60–69	16	84	0.1468	0.7706
70–79	23	107	0.2110	0.9816
80–89	0	107	0.0000	0.9816
90–99	2	109	0.0183	0.9999

Median = 49.5 + (4.5/18)(10) = 52

(b) *Community B*. A greater percentage of the heads of households have annual salaries equal to or greater than $50,000.

(c) Median for both cases, because both distributions are skewed.

(d) $\sigma_A^2 = 329.7596$ $\sigma_B^2 = 411.3964$

35. Suggested class intervals: 120–139, 140–159, etc. Frequencies 2, 12, 36, 89, 151, 165, 91, 42, 8, 4

37. $s^2 = 893.0440$ $s = 29.88$ $\sigma^2 = 891.5556$ $\sigma = 29.86$

39. 0.003, 0.020, 0.060, 0.148, 0.252, 0.275, 0.152, 0.070, 0.013, 0.007

41. 109.5989

49. $\bar{x} = 40.74$ Median $= 40.1$ $s^2 = 81.81256$ $s = 9.04503$

51.

Class Interval	x_i	f_i	$x_i f_i$	$x_i^2 f_i$
0–999.99	500	3	1,500	750,000
1000–1999.99	1500	15	22,500	33,750,000
2000–2999.99	2500	32	80,000	200,000,000
3000–3999.99	3500	12	42,000	147,000,000
4000–4999.99	4500	9	40,500	182,250,000
5000–5999.99	5500	7	38,500	211,750,000
		78	225,000	775,500,000

$\bar{x} = 2884.62$
Median $= 2656.245$
$s = 1281.55$

53. (a) $\bar{x} = 4298.77$
     $s = 2739.59$
    (b) $0.90(137) \approx 123$ $P_{90} = \$7888.39$

55. $\mu = 36.6769$ Median $= 38$ $\sigma^2 = 73.941774$ $\sigma = 8.5989$

57. $\bar{x} = 1003.2$, Median $= 989.8$, $s = 54.9$, $s^2 = 3014.01$

59. $\bar{x} = 2.999$, Median $= 1.800$, $s = 2.938$, $s^2 = 8.3618$

61. $n = 26$

63.

```
 17    1  00011222235556778
 26    2  344456779
(10)   3  3344477778
 24    4  022568889
 15    5  1228
 11    6  028
  8    7  045
  5    8  027
  2    9  12
```

65. $[(35)(897) + (20)(1244) + (28)(989)] / (35 + 20 + 28) = 1,011.65$

STATISTICS AT WORK

2.

Midpoint	Frequency
12	19
17	84
22	22
27	10
32	7
37	3
42	1

5. = 49.81, Median = 20.00, Variance = 9834.6889

6.

Variances Across Years by Region

10.2216
7.7656
4.2696
1.3080
2.6680
5.6376
2.4304
3.7640
68.5760
8.9216

N	MEAN	MEDIAN	TRMEAN	STDEV	SEMEAN	MIN	MAX	Q1	Q3
10	11.56	4.95	5.71	20.25	6.40	1.31	68.58	2.61	9.25

Range = 68.58 − 1.31 = 67.27
60% of the variances are between Q1 and Q3.

The variance of the variances is 410.0625.

Variances Across Regions by Year

17.0904
14.2325
15.1576
12.7896
23.9765

N	MEAN	MEDIAN	TRMEAN	STDEV	SEMEAN	MIN	MAX	Q1	Q3
5	16.65	15.16	16.65	4.38	1.96	12.79	23.98	13.51	20.53

Range = 23.9765 − 12.7896 = 11.1869
60% of the variances are between Q1 and Q3.

The variance of the variances is 19.1844.

7. Cases

Midpoint	Freq.	Cum. Freq.	Rel. Freq.	Cum. Rel. Freq.
150	10	10	0.1333	0.1333
450	12	22	0.1600	0.2933
750	17	39	0.2267	0.5200
1050	5	44	0.0667	0.5867
1350	9	53	0.1200	0.7067
1650	8	61	0.1067	0.8134
1950	2	63	0.0267	0.8401
2250	4	67	0.0533	0.8934
2550	2	69	0.0267	0.9201
2850	2	71	0.0267	0.9468
3150	1	72	0.0133	0.9601
3450	0	72	0.0000	0.9601
3750	1	73	0.0133	0.9734
4050	0	73	0.0000	0.9734
4350	1	74	0.0133	0.9867
4650	0	74	0.0000	0.9867
4950	0	74	0.0000	0.9867
5250	1	75	0.0133	1.0000
			1.0000	

Controls

Midpoint	Freq.	Cum. Freq.	Rel. Freq.	Cum. Rel. Freq.
150	36	36	0.5625	0.5625
450	17	53	0.2656	0.8281
750	6	59	0.0938	0.9212
1050	3	62	0.0469	0.9688
1350	2	64	0.0312	1.0000
			1.0000	

CHAPTER 3

3.2.1   (a) 5   (b) 0   (c) 2   (d) 44   (e) 89   (f) 125   (g) 190   (h) 45   (i) 12   (j) 218
(k) 0   (l) 18   (m) 80   (n) 100   (o) 80   (p) 18

3.2.3   {0, 1, 2, 3, 4, 5}, {3}

3.3.1   (a) 56   (b) 60   (c) 362,880   (d) 5040   (e) 30   (f) 120   (g) 120   (h) 35   (i) 5   (j) 70

3.3.3   35

3.3.5   (a) 120   (b) 60

3.3.7   (a) 720   (b) 360

3.6.1   **(a) (1)** 0.10 **(2)** 0.142 **(3)** 0.015 **(4)** 0.106 **(5)** 0.3500 **(6)** 0.227 **(b) (1)** 0.075 **(2)** 0.165 **(3)** 0.010 **(4)** 0.010 **(5)** 0.230 **(6)** 0.438 **(7)** 0.600 **(c)** No. $P(A_1 \cap B_1)$ $\neq P(A_1)P(B_1)$, for example.

3.6.3   **(a)** 0.33 **(b)** 0.17 **(c)** 0.50

3.6.5   **(a)** 5/231 **(b)** 0 **(c)** 2/231 **(d)** 44/231 **(e)** 89/231 **(f)** 125/231 **(g)** 190/231 **(h)** 45/23 **(i)** 12/231

3.7.1   **(a)** 0.427 **(b)** 0.256 **(c)** 0.197 **(d)** 0.120

3.7.3   **(a)** 0.2490 **(b)** 0.1120 **(c)** 0.4149 **(d)** 0.2241

REVIEW EXERCISES

11. 4

13. 15,504

15. **(a)** 0.021 **(b)** 0.040 **(c)** 0.004

17. **(a)** Employees who voted in favor of the plan or who have children in school or both **(b)** Employees who voted in favor of the plan and have children in school **(c)** Employees who did not vote in favor of the plan **(d)** Employees who do not have children in school

19. **(a)** $\varnothing$ **(b)** A **(c)** U **(d)** $\overline{A}$

21. $_{12}C_4 = \dfrac{12!}{4!8!} = \dfrac{12 \cdot 11 \cdot 10 \cdot 9 \cdot 8!}{4 \cdot 3 \cdot 2 \cdot 8!} = 495$

23. 12,600

25. **(a)** **(1)** 0.60 **(2)** 0.27, 0.13 **(3)** 0.25 (for each area) **(4)** 0.92 **(5)** 0.35 **(b)** **(1)** 0.01 **(2)** 0.62 **(3)** 0.75 **(4)** 0.48 **(5)** 0.08 **(6)** 0.60

27. 0.0364
0.4545
<u>0.5091</u>
1.0000

29. 0.45

31. **(a)** 15; M_1M_2, M_1F_1, M_1F_2, M_1F_3, M_1F_4, M_2F_1, M_2F_2, M_2F_3, M_2F_4, F_1F_2, F_1F_3, F_1F_4, F_2F_3, F_2F_4, F_3F_4 **(b)** 0.9333 **(c)** 0.5333 **(d)** 0.6000 **(e)** 0.0667

33. **(a)** 0.06 **(b)** 0.50

35. **(a)** 1/504 **(b)** 16/21

37. **(a)** 0.60 **(b)** 0.75 **(c)** 0.25 **(d)** 0.60

39. **(a)** 0.5714 **(b)** 0.3571 **(c)** 0.5556

41. 0.0714

43. **(a)** 0.95 **(b)** 0.53 **(c)** 0.67

45. **(a)** 0.12 **(b)** 0.38 **(c)** 0.4

47. **(a)** $_{15}P_5 = 360,360$ **(b)** $_{15}C_5 = 3003$

49.

Event	Prior Probability	Likelihood	Joint Probability	Posterior Probability
A	0.25	0.8	0.200	0.4706
B	0.75	0.3	0.225	0.5294
	1.00		0.425	1.0000

(a) $P(A) = 0.25$ (b) $P(B) = 0.75$
Joint Probabilities:
$P(A \cap W) = 0.200$ $P(B \cap W) = 0.225$
Posterior Probabilities:
(c) $P(A|W) = 0.4706$ (d) $P(B|W) = 0.5294$ (e) $P(W) = 0.425$ (f) $P(R) = 0.575$

51. (a) $P(A \cap \bar{B}) = 0.10$ (b) $P(A \cup \bar{B}) = 0.55$ (c) $P(A|\bar{B}) = 0.25$ (d) A and B are independent, since the following statements are true: (1) $P(A|B) = P(A)$ (2) $P(B|A) = P(B)$ (3) $P(A \cap B) = P(A)P(B)$ (e) A and B are not mutually exclusive, since $P(A \cap B) \neq 0$

53. (a) 0.250 (b) 0.225 (c) 0.200 (d) 0.595 (e) 0.610

55. (a) $P(R_1|R_2) = 0$ (b) $P(W_1|R_2) = 0.4$ (c) $P(B_1|R_2) = 0.6$ (d) $P(\bar{R}_1 \cap R_2) = 0.1667$

57. (a) $(_5P_5)(_4P_4) = 2880$ (b) 0.4

59. (a) $P[(B_1 \cap B_2)|B_1] = 0.5$ (b) $P[(B_1 \cap B_2)|(B_1 \cap B_2) \cup (B_1 \cap G_2) \cup (G_1 \cap B_2)] = 0.3333$

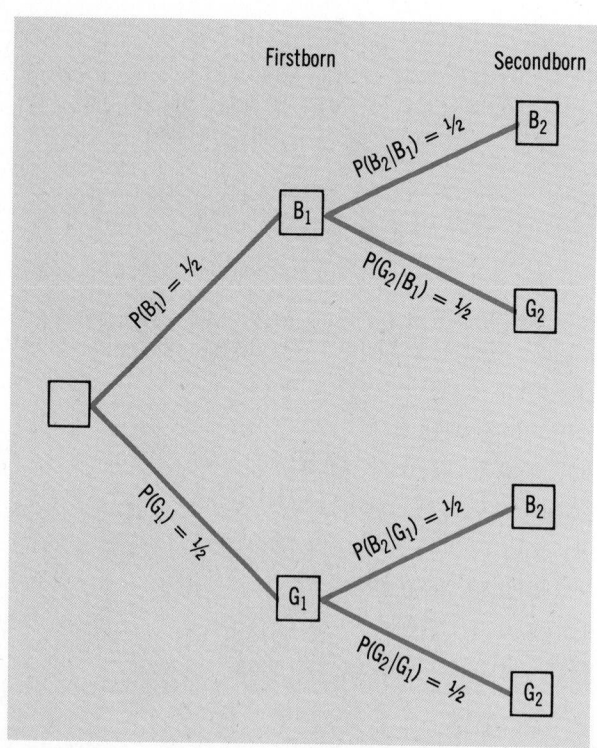

61. (a) 0.6 (b) 0.8 (c) 0.5 (d) 0.83333 (e) 0.3 (f) 0.5

63. Fewer **65.** 0.30 **67.** 0.0303

69. 427,518,000 **71.** 0.625

73. 0.6667 **75.** 12

77. (a) 70/30 = 7 to 3 (b) 70/100 = 0.7 (c) 30/100 = 0.3 (d) 0.7/0.3 = 7 to 3 (e) Odds: numerator = number of successes, denominator = number of failures. Probability: numerator = number of successes, denominator = number of successes + number of failures.

STATISTICS AT WORK

1. $1 - 0.36 = 0.64$

2. a. 372/7776 = 0.0478 **b.** 318/380 = 0.8368 **c.** (5451 + 2123)/7776 = 0.9740 **d.** (873 + 938)/7776 = 0.2329 **e.** $\dfrac{467}{7776} + \dfrac{5451}{7776} - \dfrac{368}{7776} = 0.7137$

3. a. 1148/3496 = 0.328375 **b.** (1148 + 580)/3496 = 0.494279

4. a. $(100 - 27.8)/27.8 = 72.2/27.8$; approximately 7 to 3 **b.** $(100 - 5.9)/5.9 = 94.1/5.9$; approximately 94 to 6

CHAPTER 4

4.2.1 (a) $P(X = x_i)$: 0.05, 0.08, 0.10, 0.12, 0.18, 0.14, 0.10, 0.09, 0.08, 0.04, 0.02 (b) $P(X \le x_i)$: 0.05, 0.13, 0.23, 0.35, 0.53, 0.67, 0.77, 0.86, 0.94, 0.98, 1.00 (c) $\mu = 4.49$ $\sigma^2 = 26.31 - (4.49)^2 = 6.1499$

4.2.3 (a) 0.05 (b) 0.02 (c) 0.33 (d) 0.67 (e) 0.63

4.2.5 (a) $P(X = x)$: 15/80, 27/80, 14/80, 12/80, 6/80, 4/80, 1/80, 1/80 (b) $P(X \le x)$: 15/80, 42/80, 56/80, 68/80, 74/80, 78/80, 79/80, 80/80 (c) (1) 38/80 (2) 15/80 (3) 6/80 (4) 56/80 (d) 1.85, 2.4775

4.3.1 (a) 0.3125 (b) 0.5 (c) 0.5 (d) 0.0312 (e) 0.0312

4.3.3 (a) 0.0170 (b) 0.9984 (c) 0.3430

4.3.5 Yes, since 500 is not contained in the interval

4.3.7 (a) 0.5846 (b) 0.0338 (c) 0.5846 (d) 0.9906

4.3.9 (a) 0.4670 (b) 0.5330 (c) 0.5329 (d) 0.0001 (e) 0

4.3.11 (a) 0.0034 (b) 0.9958 (c) 0.0008 (d) 0.1476

4.4.1 (a) 0.923 (b) 0.077 (c) 0.003

4.4.3 Binomial (a) 0.0054 (b) 0.0380. Poisson (a) 0.006 (b) 0.041

4.4.5 (a) 0.034 (b) 0.001 (c) 0.185

4.5.1 0.4286

4.5.3 (a) 0.00476 (b) 0.5429 (c) 0.9286

4.5.5 (a) 0.4762 (b) 0.9523 (c) 0.5952

4.7.1 (a) $\mu = 275$ (b) $\sigma = 14.4338$ (c) (d) $P(X < 260°) = 0.2$ (e) $P(265° \leq X \leq 280°)$ $= 0.3$

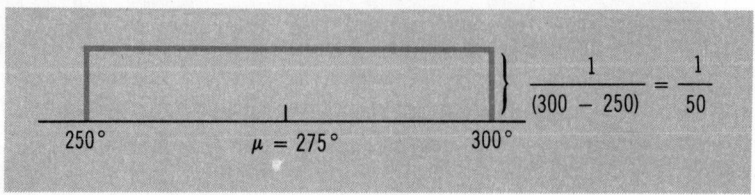

4.7.3 (a) (b) $\mu = 3$ $\sigma^2 = 2.0833$ (c) $P(3 \leq X \leq 4) = 0.20$

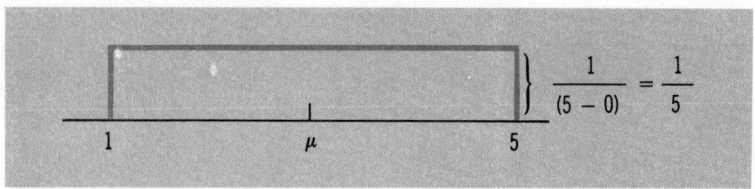

4.8.1	0.4382		**4.8.3**	0.2578
4.8.5	0.0099		**4.8.7**	0.9500
4.8.9	0.8934		**4.8.11**	-2.54
4.8.13	1.77		**4.8.15**	1.32
4.8.17	0.9876		**4.8.19**	0.0505
4.8.21	(a) 0.0228 (b) 0.9525 (c) 0.0099		**4.8.23**	0.9676

REVIEW EXERCISES

17. (a) $P(X = x_i)$: 0.10, 0.15, 0.20, 0.25, 0.15, 0.05, 0.03, 0.02, 0.02, 0.02, 0.01 (c) $P(X \leq x_i)$: 0.10, 0.25, 0.45, 0.70, 0.85, 0.90, 0.93, 0.95, 0.97, 0.99, 1.00

19. (a) 0.0480 (b) 0.0171 (c) 0.7454 (d) 0.0003

21. (a) 0.380 (b) 0.620 (c) 0.895 (d) 0.105 (e) 0.041 (f) 0.959

23. 0.9010   **25.** 3.33

27. 265.30   **29.** (a) 0.0013 (b) 0.0062 (c) 0.7745 (d) 728 (e) 2.28%

31. 0.1320

33. (a) 0.1935 (b) 0.0018 (c) 0.0018 The normal distribution provides a suitable approximation to the binomial, since $25(0.3)$ and $25(0.7)$ are both greater than 5. Normal: (a) 0.1992 (b) 0.0011 (c) 0.0011

35. 0.2131   **37.** 0.8414

39. (a) 0.0228   **41.** (a) 64.75 (b) $k = 118.45$ (c) $k = 130.15$ (b) 309   (d) $k = 131.80$, $k' = 68.20$

43. 14.90   **45.** 10.6

47. (a) 2, 1.8   (b) 4, 3.2   (c) 6, 4.2   (d) 8, 4.8   (e) 10, 5   (f) 12, 4.8   (g) 14, 4.2 (h) 16, 3.2   (i) 18, 1.8 σ^2 largest for $p = 0.5$ σ^2 smallest for $p = 0.1$ and $p = 0.9$

49. (a) 0.875   (b) 0.492   (c) 0.265

51. (a) 0.149   (b) 0.050   (c) 0.801   (d) 0.185

53. (a) 0.933   (b) 0.049   (c) 0.922   (d) 0.220   (e) 0.697

55. 0.080

57. (a) 0.0985   (b) 0.5645   (c) 0.0011   (d) 0.0702

59. 0.0624

61. 0.7081

63. (a) 0.1841   (b) 0.9713   (c) 0.0796

65. 0.238

67. 0.4175

69. Poisson 0.275

71. (a) Hypergeometric   (b) $N = 4000$, $N_1 = 3840$, $N_2 = 160$, $n = 200$ (c) $P(X = 192) = \frac{_{3840}C_{192} \; _{160}C_8}{_{4000}C_{200}}$ (d) Binomial: Because $n \leq 10\%$ of N. $n = 200$, $P = 0.04$, $q = 0.96$. Poisson: Because $p \leq 0.05$, $n \geq 20$. $\lambda = 8$. Normal: Because np and $n(1 - p)$ are both ≥ 5. $\mu = 8$ $\sigma = 2.77$ (e) Binomial: 0.14246. Poisson: 0.140. Normal: 0.1428

73. Poisson 0.070

75. Normal approximation to the binomial. 0.1271

77. 0.4561

79. Poisson 0.60

81. Hypergeometric: $N = 1000$, $N_1 = 327$, $n = 300$. Binomial: $n = 300$, $p = 0.327$. Normal: $\mu = 98.1$ $\sigma = 8.125$. $P(X < 100) = 0.5684$

83. $\mu = 17.5$ $\sigma = 3.37$ $P(25 \leq X \leq 30) = 0.0187$

85. $\mu = 60$ $\sigma = 6.48$ $P(X \leq 75) = 0.9916$

87. $\lambda = 6$ $P(X = 5) = 0.161$

89. $\sigma^2 = 175$

91. $n = 200$
$\sigma = 5.6568$

93. $\mu = 200$

95. $\mu = 24.25$
$\sigma = 5.5396$

STATISTICS AT WORK

1. a. 0.06925   **b.** $P(2 \leq x \leq 5) = 0.6915$ **c.** $1 - P(x \leq 3) = 0.27931$

2. a. $P(x < 800) = P(z < -2.62) = 0.0044$ **b.** $P(x > 1200) = P(z > 1.16) = 0.1230$ **c.** $1 - (0.0044 + 0.1230) = 0.8726$

3. a. 0.0000 **b.** 0.0166 **c.** 0.8179

4. Using formulas from Chapter 2, we find $\bar{x}$ = 4.32, s = 0.81. Median = 4.205 + (303/408)(0.60) = 4.65. Mode = 4.505. 4.32 ± (1)(0.81) → 3.51, 5.13. This interval contains 66.8% of the values. 4.32 ± (2)(0.81) → 2.70, 5.94. This interval contains 95.33% of the values. 4.32 ± (3)(0.81) → 1.89, 6.75. This interval contains 99.4% of the values.

CHAPTER 5

5.4.1	(a) 99.8, 0.548 (b) 0.5554	5.4.3	0.9237
5.4.7	0.0174	5.5.1	0.0071
5.5.3	0.4778	5.6.1	0.8413
5.6.3	0.4658	5.6.5	0.2358
5.7.1	(a) 0.07, 0.05 (b) 0.3811 (c) 0.1587	5.7.3	0.015
5.7.5	0.0029		

REVIEW EXERCISES

13. (a) 32, 1.5 (b) 0.8854 (c) 0.0228 (d) 0.0918 (f) random

15. 0.0475 **17.** 0.0351

19. 0.0089 **21.** 0.0228

23. 0.8764, 0.0618 **25.** 0.0668

27. 0.2005 **29.** 0.0475

33. 0.0034

37. 0.0188

39. (a) 0.3897 (b) 0.0027 (c) $n \approx 22$

41. 0.0838

43. (a) 0.4325 (b) 0.1423 (c) 0.0537 (d) 0.0082 (e) 0.0001 (f) $n \geq 93.84$ or $n \geq 94$

45. $P[(\bar{x}_A - \bar{x}_B) > 2000] = 0.0060$. Similarly, $P[(\bar{x}_A - \bar{x}_B) < -2000] = 0.0060$. Therefore, the probability that the two population means differ by more than $2000 in either direction is 0.0060 + 0.0060 = 0.0120.

47. 300

49. 27.3861 **51.** 0.000007017 **53.** 0.40

55. $z_1 = -1.51$; $z_2 = 0.50$; $P(-1.51 \leq z - 0.50) = 0.626$

CHAPTER 6

6.3.1	8.6, 9.0	6.3.3	63, 67
6.3.5	18.67, 28.67	6.4.1	312, 412
6.4.3	25, 27	6.5.1	52, 68
6.5.3	0.23, 1.27	6.5.5	1.54, 2.78

6.6.1   (a) $s_p^2 = 229.4$; 5.6, 24.6   (b) 5.4, 24.8

6.6.3   (a) $s_p^2 = 0.019$, -0.17, 0.05   (b) -0.17, 0.05

6.7.1	0.45, 0.55	6.7.3	0.64, 0.76
6.8.1	0.14, 0.26	6.8.3	-0.02, 0.16
6.9.1	82	6.9.3	157
6.9.5	157	6.10.1	385
6.10.3	218	6.10.5	162

6.11.1   1.89, 13.33. The sample was randomly selected from a normally distributed population.

6.11.3 $19.45 \leq \sigma^2 \leq 90.26$

6.12.1   0.52, 5.15

6.12.3 $1.6086 \leq \sigma_1^2/\sigma_2^2 \leq 10.5978$

REVIEW EXERCISES

15.	2.482, 2.498	**19.**	0.02, 0.08
21.	0.02, 0.08	**23.**	12, 18
25.	0.07, 0.23	**27.**	0.53, 0.67
29.	5.1, 7.6	**31.**	0.36, 0.44
33.	0.82, 0.92	**35.**	\$34, \$50
37.	$0.45 \leq \sigma_2^2/\sigma_1^2 \leq 4.23$	**39.**	171
41.	7.8, 20.2	**43.**	1476
45.	0.004, 0.216	**47.**	$2.20 \leq \sigma^2 \leq 8.11$
49.	12.706, 23.161	**51.**	167.559, 182.041
53.	0.0724, 0.2610; No	**55.**	32, 36
57.	943	**61.**	3.75, 5.67
63.	0.30, 0.50	**65.**	0.26, 0.42
67.	$\hat{p}_M = 0.30$, $\hat{p}_F = 0.40$	**69.**	62.4, 70.2
71.	50.23, 60.27	**73.**	9.89, 26.95
75.	0.28, 0.52	**77.**	1457.93, 1514.87
95.	3394	**97.**	5.16, 5.58

99. 6.1917

101. (a) $180 - 2.485(11/\sqrt{26}) = 174.6392$ (b) We are 99% confident that the population mean is $\geq 1.74.6392$.   (c) (1) $x + z\sigma/\sqrt{n}, x - z\sigma/\sqrt{n}$ (2) $x + zs/\sqrt{n}, x - zs/\sqrt{n}$ (3) $\hat{p} + z\sqrt{\hat{p}\hat{q}/n}, \hat{p} - z\sqrt{\hat{p}\hat{q}/n}$

STATISTICS AT WORK

1. $s_p^2 = 0.571212; 0.01, 1.19$

2. 0.03, 0.09

3. 0.49, 0.57

4. 18.5, 23.5

5. $2.28 \pm 1.96(0.56)/\sqrt{487}; 2.23, 2.33$
$2.60 \pm 1.96(0.52)/\sqrt{487}; 2.55, 2.65$
$2.37 \pm 1.96(0.54)/\sqrt{487}; 2.32, 2.42$
$2.32 \pm 1.96(0.71)/\sqrt{487}; 2.26; 2.38$
$3.61 \pm 1.96(0.65)/\sqrt{487}; 3.55, 3.67$

CHAPTER 7

7.3.1   Reject null hypothesis, $z = -3.00; p = 0.0026$

7.3.3   Since $3.00 > 1.96$, reject H_0, $p = 0.0026$

7.4.1   Yes, $t = 2.50; 0.01 < p < 0.025$

7.4.3 $t = 3.115; p < 0.005$

7.4.5   Yes; $t = 2.264; 0.025 > p > 0.01$

7.5.1 $z = -2.00; p = 0.0456$

7.5.3 $z = 2; p = 0.0228$

7.5.5   Yes, $z = -2.347; p \approx 0.0094$

7.6.1   (a) $s_p^2 = 11.25$; No, $t = -2.79; 0.01 > p > 0.005$ (b) computed $t' = -2.73$; critical $t' = -1.82$

7.6.3 $t = 5; p < 0.005$

7.6.5   No, $t = 0.1880; p > 0.10$

7.7.1   Yes, $z = 6.35; p < 0.0001$

7.7.3   Yes, $z = -4.00; p < 0.0001$

7.7.5   Yes, $z = -8.5888; p < 0.0002$

7.8.1   No, $z = -1.31; p = 0.0951$

7.8.3   Yes, $z = 2.50; p = 0.0062$

7.9.1   No, $z = -1.11; p = 0.2670$

7.9.3 $z = 0.88; p = 0.1894$

7.10.1   Cannot reject H_0, $X^2 = 13.33$; $p > 0.10$ (one-sided)

7.10.3   No, $X^2 = 33.6$; $0.10 > p > 0.05$

7.11.1   Yes, $F = 3.00$; $0.01 < p < 0.025$ (one-sided)

7.11.3 $F = 1.59$, cannot reject H_0; $p > 0.10$ (one-sided)

7.12.1

Alternative Value of μ	β	Value of Power Function $1 - \beta$
516	0.9500	0.0500
521	0.8461	0.1539
528	0.5596	0.4404
533	0.3156	0.6844
539	0.1093	0.8907
544	0.0314	0.9686
547	0.0129	0.9871

7.12.3

Alternative Value of μ	β	Value of Power Function $1 - \beta$
4.25	0.9900	0.0100
4.50	0.8599	0.1401
4.75	0.4325	0.5675
5.00	0.0778	0.9222
5.25	0.0038	0.9962

7.12.5   Critical value of $\bar{x} = 4.716$; $P(\bar{x} < 4.716 | \mu = 5) = 0.0778$

7.13.1 $n = 548$; $C = 518.25$. Select a sample of size 548 and compute $\bar{x}$. If $\bar{x} \geq 518.25$, reject H_0. If $\bar{x} < 518.25$, do not reject H_0.

7.13.3 $n = 103$; $C = 4.66$. Select a sample of size 103 and compute $\bar{x}$. If $\bar{x} \geq 4.66$, reject H_0. If $\bar{x} < 4.66$, do not reject H_0.

REVIEW EXERCISES

17. Yes, $z = -1.67$; $p = 0.0475$

19. Yes, $t = -2.50$; $0.025 > p > 0.01$

21. Yes, $z = -3.00$; $p = 0.0013$

23. Yes, $t = -4.84$. The samples were randomly and independently drawn from normally distributed populations. $p < 0.005$

27. No, $z \approx 1.00$; $p = 0.1587$

29. $H_0: p_A \leq p_B$; $H_1: p_A > p_B$; No. $\bar{p} = 0.504$, $z = 0.62$, $p = 0.2676$

31. No, $F = 2.03$; $0.025 < p < 0.05$

33. $z = -2.5$; $p = 0.0062$

37. $z = 2.67; p = 0.0038$

39. $t = 1.421; 0.10 > p > 0.05$

43. $t = -2.763; 0.01 > p > 0.005$

45. $z = 1.72; p = 0.0427$

47. Since $z = 3 > 1.645$, we reject H_0. $p = 0.0013$

49. $\chi^2 = 10(1225)/625 = 19.6 < 20.483$, and H_0 cannot be rejected. $0.025 < p < 0.05$ (one-sided)

51. Assume that the two groups are independent random samples from normally distributed populations. Since $F = 81/36 = 2.25 > 1.89$, we reject H_0. $0.01 < p < 0.025$.

53. No, $t = -1.3474; 0.20 > p > 0.10$

55. Yes, $t = -3.5841; p < 0.01$

57. No, $z = -1.7375; p = 0.0818$

59. No, $z = 1.02; p = 0.1539$

61. Yes, $\overline{d} = -5.5, s_d = 4.58, t = -4.160, p < 0.005$

63. Yes, $t = 4.704$

65. No, $t = 1.337; p = 0.0901$

67. $\overline{x}_A = 7.54, s_A^2 = 24.3657, \overline{x}_B = 10.03, s_B^2 = 21.2491$

69. Reject H_0, since $-4.88 < -1.645$. $p < 0.0001$

71. Reject H_0, since $-2.00 < -1.645$. $p = 0.0228$

73. 0.69

75. Reject H_0, since $-3.67 < -1.645$. $p = 0.0001$

89. Reject H_0, since $-2.43 < -1.9432$. $0.025 < p < 0.05$

91. (a) $F = 1.13$. Do not reject H_0.   (b) $t = -1.6511$. Do not reject H_0. $0.20 > p > 0.10$

93. Since $-2.12 > -2.33$, do not reject H_0; $p = 0.0170$

95. If H_0 is false because $\mu = \$210, \beta = 0.0455$. If H_0 is false because $\mu = \$190, \beta = 0.0455$.

97. Critical value of $\hat{p} = 0.2329; \beta = 0.2148$

99. Critical values of $\hat{p} = 0.6729$ and $0.8271; \beta = 0.1762$

101. $t = 2.6833$

103. 2.508

105. $H_0: p \leq 0.20; H_1: p > 0.20; P(x > 6|15, 0.20) = 0.0181$. Since $0.0181 < 0.05$, reject H_0.

STATISTICS AT WORK

1. $t = 8.18$ (authors' results), $p < 0.01$, reject H_0: $\mu_S = \mu_F$.

2. $\bar{d} = -0.0767$, $s_d^2 = 0.1102$, $t = -0.8003$, fail to reject H_0; $\bar{d} = 4.8650$, $s_d^2 = 0.2187$, $t = 36.0370$, reject H_0; $\bar{d} = 5.4733$, $s_d^2 = 0.3362$, $t = 32.6994$, reject H_0.

3. $z = 1.57$, $p = 0.0582$

4. $t = 2.85$, $p < 0.01$

5. The differences, $d_i = T2 - T3$, are:

0 2 1 0 −1 0 0 1 0 2 2 2 1 1 −2 1 1 1 1 3 1 1 2 0

$\bar{d} = 0.783$, $s_d = 1.085$, $s_{\bar{d}} = 0.226$; $t = 3.4646$. Since $3.4646 > 2.8188$, $p/2 < 0.005$, $p < .01$. Reject H_0 and conclude that implementation causes a change.

6. H_0: $\mu_L \geq \mu_S$; H_1: $\mu_L < \mu_S$; $z = -1.94$. Since $-1.94 < -1.645$, reject H_0. Conclude that leavers tend to have a lower level of job satisfaction.

CHAPTER 8

8.2.1 $F = 94.04$; $p < 0.005$

8.2.3   Yes, $F = 10.24$; $p < 0.005$

8.3.1

Table of Differences Between Means

	$\bar{x}_B$	$\bar{x}_C$	$\bar{x}_A$	$\bar{x}_D$
$\bar{x}_B = 2.44$	—	0	4.12**	4.34**
$\bar{x}_C = 2.44$		—	4.12**	4.34**
$\bar{x}_A = 6.56$			—	0.22
$\bar{x}_D = 6.78$				—

8.3.3

Table of Differences Between Means

	$\bar{x}_A$	$\bar{x}_B$	$\bar{x}_C$
$\bar{x}_A = 17.14$	—	2.15	6.29**
$\bar{x}_B = 19.29$		—	4.14**
$\bar{x}_C = 23.43$			—

8.4.1   No, $F = 3.01$; $0.10 > p > 0.05$

8.4.3   Yes, $F = 9.12$; $p < 0.005$

8.5.1   Yes, $F = 59.75$; $p < 0.005$

8.5.3   Yes, $F = 171.86$; $0.005 < p < 0.01$

8.6.1 $F(\text{pressure}) = 0.40$, $F(\text{temp.}) = 6.23$, $F(\text{interaction}) = 35.89$ $p(A) > 0.10$; $p(B) < 0.005$; $p(AB) < 0.005$

8.6.3 F(competitive activity) = 1.54, F(geo, reg.) = 8.29, F(interaction) = 87.19; $p(A) > 0.10$, $p(B) < 0.005$; $p(AB) < 0.005$

REVIEW EXERCISES

19. Since $22.79 > 5.49$, reject H_0. $p < 0.005$

21. No, $F = 2.77$; $p > 0.10$

23.

Table of Differences Between Means

	$\bar{x}_A$	$\bar{x}_B$	$\bar{x}_D$	$\bar{x}_C$	$\bar{x}_E$
$\bar{x}_A = 23.0$	—	2.8	6.1*	6.4*	19.6*
$\bar{x}_B = 25.8$		—	3.3	3.6	16.8*
$\bar{x}_D = 29.1$			—	0.3	13.5*
$\bar{x}_C = 29.4$				—	13.2*
$\bar{x}_E = 42.6$					—

25.

Table of Differences Between Means

	$\bar{x}_A$	$\bar{x}_B$	$\bar{x}_C$
$\bar{x}_A = 60.3$	—	3.7	18.4**
$\bar{x}_B = 64.0$		—	14.7**
$\bar{x}_C = 78.7$			

27. Since $9.77 > 5.14$, reject H_0. $0.01 < p < 0.025$

29. Since $21.41 > 3.26$, reject H_0. $p < 0.005$

31. $F_A = 6.33$, $p < 0.005$, $F_B = 38.87$, $p < 0.005$, $F_{AB} = 4.97$, $0.01 > p > 0.005$

33. $F = 8.30$

35. $F = 18.82$; $p < 0.005$

37. $F = 59.13$; $p < 0.005$

39. $F = 9.83$; $p < 0.005$

41.

Source	SS	df	MS	F	p
Treatments	499.5	3	166.5000	57.6346	< 0.005
Blocks	183.5	3	61.1667		
Error	26.0	9	2.8889		
Total	709.0	15			

43. (a) Analysis for a factorial experiment   (b) There is a significant difference among levels of factor A and among levels of factor B, and there is also a significant interaction effect, since all three p values are < 0.005.

45. (a) Randomized complete block design **(b)** 3 **(c)** 24 **(d)** No, because 2.824 < 3.74.

47. Yes. Since 6.49 > 2.98, reject the null hypothesis of equal population means. Since 6.49 > 5.41, $p < 0.005$.

49.

Source	SS	df	MS	F
Treatments	90.5	2	45.25	7.37
Blocks	260.66663	3	86.888875	
Error	36.833374	6	6.1388956	

51.

Source	SS	df	MS	F
Rows	0.64160538	4	0.16040134	1.3434062
Columns	5.2536058	4	1.3134015	11.000105
Treatments	2.7936049	4	0.69840121	5.8493058
Error	1.4327879	12	0.11939899	

53.

Source	SS	df	MS	F
Diets	90.408	3	30.136	83.02
Exercise	13.796	5	2.759	7.60
Interaction	32.001	15	2.133	5.88
Error	17.447	48	0.363	
Total	153.651	71		

57. (a)

ANOVA Table

Source	SS	df	MS	F
Treatments	70.75	2	35.37	3.04
Error	163.13	14	11.65	
Total	233.88	16		

(b) H_0: The three treatments are equally effective ($\mu_A = \mu_B = \mu_C$); H_1: The three treatments are not equally effective (not all μ's are equal) **(c)** Reject H_0 if the computed F is ≥ 3.74. **(d)** Do not reject H_0, since 3.04 < 3.74. **(e)** $s_y = 3.82$

59. $F = 49.19$

STATISTICS AT WORK

1. $F = 10.47$ (authors' results), HSD $= 0.656401$; differences between means 1 and 2 and 1 and 3 are significant.

2. $F = 15.02$, $p < 0.01$ (authors' results), between df $= 1$, within df $= 2230$.

3. $F = 3.42$, $p = 0.04$

4. ANALYSIS OF VARIANCE   ELABTOT
F (MEDIA) $= 4.5438$, $0.05 > p > 0.025$

F (INVOLVMT) = 0.6173, $p > 0.10$
F (INTERACTION) = 2.8318, $0.10 > p > 0.05$

　　ANALYSIS OF VARIANCE　BRANDCOG
F (MEDIA) = 4.0178, $0.05 > p > 0.025$
F (INVOLVMT) = 7.1428, $0.025 > p > 0.01$
F (INTERACTION) = 4.0178, $0.05 > p > 0.025$

　　ANALYSIS OF VARIANCE　ADCOG
F (MEDIA) = 11.3628, $p < 0.005$
F (INVOLVMT) = 47.1471, $p < 0.005$
F (INTERACTION) = 4.5037, $0.05 > p > 0.025$

5. ANALYSIS OF VARIANCE　MOREIDEA
F (GRP) = 10.2470, $p < 0.005$
F (TECH) = 0.0445, $p > 0.10$
F (INTERACTION) = 0.6113, $p > 0.10$

6.

Source	df	SS	MS	F	P
Treatment	2	3,255	1,627.5	3.9366	$0.025 > p > 0.01$
Error	190	78,551	413.4263		
Total	192	81,806			

CHAPTER 9

9.4.1　$\hat{y} = -0.1329 + 0.0618x$

9.4.3　$\hat{y} = 78.2210 + 1.5161x$

9.5.1　(a) $r^2 = 0.92$　(b) $F = 145.8$; $p < 0.005$　(c) $t = 12.12$; $p < 0.01$　(e) 0.05, 0.07

9.5.3　(a) $r^2 = 0.90$　(b) $F = 122.89$; $p < 0.005$　(c) $t = 11.08$; $p < 0.01$　(e) 1.22, 1.81

9.5.5　$(\hat{y} - \bar{y}) = 4.0976$, $(y_i - \hat{y}) = 15.2024$, $(y_i - \bar{y}) = 19.3$

9.5.7　Standardized residual for observation 3 is -2.65, an outlier. No influential points.

9.5.9　No outliers; no influential points.

9.5.11　$\hat{y} = 7.4 + 0.886x$. Observation 4 identified as influential point. Observation 17 identified as outlier (standardized residual = -2.41).

9.6.1　(a) $2.96 \pm (2.1604)(1.16447)(0.3182)$　(b) $2.96 \pm (2.1604)(1.16447)(1.0494)$

9.6.3　(a) $169.19 \pm (2.1604)(7.1924)(0.2947)$　(b) $169.19 \pm (2.1604)(7.1924)(1.0425)$

9.6.5

Confidence Limits for $\mu_{y|x}$		
x	**Lower**	**Upper**
20	9.06	12.52
30	15.25	18.12
40	21.38	23.77
50	27.42	29.52
60	33.34	35.39
70	39.11	41.40
80	44.79	47.51
25	12.16	15.31
90	50.41	53.68
100	55.99	59.88

9.8.1   **(b)** Reject H_0, since $t = 5.53 > 2.306$; $p < 0.01$ **(c)** $z = -1.08$, $p = 0.1401$

9.8.3   **(b)** Reject H_0; $\rho = 0$, since $t = 6.39 > 2.306$; $p < 0.01$ **(c)** $z = -0.80$, $p = 0.2119$

REVIEW EXERCISES

15. **(a)** $\hat{y} = 54.61229 + 0.394782x$ **(b)** $r = 0.2151$ **(c)** $t = 0.934$ **(d)** $p > 0.20$

17. **(a)** $\hat{y} = 22.6046 + 12.6714x$

(b)

Source	SS	df	MS	F
Regression	18,535.15	1	18.535.15	78.306
Error	3,313.85	14	236.70	
Total	21,849.00	15		

(c) $p < 0.005$ **(d)** $\hat{y} = \$111.30$

19. **(b)** $\hat{y} = 0.78336 + 0.56821x$ **(c)** $t = 18.148$, $p < 0.005$ **(d)** 0.962   **(e)** 22.69, 35.70

23. **(a)** $\hat{y} = 4.78001 + 0.0897939x$

(b)

Source	SS	df	MS	F
Regression	40.476	1	40.476	10.2649
Error	51.2608	13	3.94314	
Total	91.7368	14		

(c) Since $10.2649 > 4.67$, reject H_0.

27. 0.66299079

29. $t = 8.6462$, $p < 0.01$

31. 0.8142425

33. 91.02525

61.

ANOVA Table

Source	SS	df	MS	F
Regression	3962.08	1	3962.08	286.77
Error	663.17	48	13.816089	
Total	4625.25	49		

(a) $s_y = 9.72$ (b) $s_{y|x} = 3.717$ (c) $s_b = 0.0607$ (d) $s_{y|x=20} = 3.8019$ (e) $r = 0.9255$
(f) $F = 286.77$ (g) Reject H_0, since $286.77 > 4.08$ (h) $t = 16.9343$

63. (a) 0.99971   (f) 59.16144

     (b) 1,364.551067   (g) 58.81684

     (c) 0.060027   (h) 59.54578

     (d) 22,732.209   (i) 58.43249

     (e) 150.77211

65. $r = [\text{Cov}(x,y)/\sqrt{s_x^2 s_y^2}$

STATISTICS AT WORK

1. $p < 0.01$ (authors' results), df $= 2648$, $t = -3.3001$, reject H_0.

2. $\hat{y} = 68.12$, $t = 9.2736$, $p < 0.01$.

3. $\hat{y} = 2.43 - 0.354x$; $r^2 = 0.23$; $F = 7.76$.

4. $\hat{y} = 74.7 - 6.44x$; $r^2 = 0.984$; $F = 480.99$.

5. FOI $= 1.43 + 0.115$ MKTSHARE

Predictor	t-ratio	p
Constant	3.12	0.008
MKTSHARE	7.97	0.000

$s = 0.8960$ $R - sq = 83.0\%$ $F = 63.52, p = 0.000$

CHAPTER 10

10.3.1 $\hat{y} = -30.5761 + 1.0406x_{1j} + 0.8390x_{2j}$

10.3.3 $\hat{y} = -3.8162 + 68.9486x_{1j} + 0.2457x_{2j}$

10.4.1 (a) 0.98 (b) $F = 173.77$; $p < 0.005$ (c) $t(b_1) = 5.46$; $p < 0.01$; $t(b_2) = 6.36$;
$p < 0.01$ (d) $1.0406 \pm (2.3646)(0.1905)$; $0.8390 \pm (2.3646)(0.1319)$

10.4.3 (a) 0.98 (b) $F = 146.48$; $p < 0.005$ (c) $t(b_1) = 4.02$; $p < 0.01$; $t(b_2) = 1.31$;
$p > 0.20$ (d) $68.9486 \pm (2.3646)(17.1460)$; $0.2457 \pm (2.3646)(0.1878)$

10.5.1 $52.9979 + (2.3646)(1.47490)^{1/2}[(1/10) + 0.0246(-2.7)^2 + 0.0118(-7.5)^2 + 2(-0.0136)(-2.7)(-7.5)]^{1/2}$. For prediction interval add 1 under the last radical.

10.5.3 $24.7155 \pm (2.3646)(3.39)^{1/2}[(1/10) + 86.7209(-0.13)^2 + 0.0104(-0.9)^2 + 2(-0.9015)(-0.13)(-0.9)]^{1/2}$. For prediction interval add 1 under the last radical.

10.6.1 $\hat{y} = -11.6 + 0.920x_1 + 17.3x_2$; for hypertensive subjects, $\hat{y} = -11.6 + 0.920x_1 + 17.3(1) = 5.7 + 0.920x_1$; for normal subjects, $\hat{y} = -11.6 + 0.920x_1 + 17.3(0) = -11.6 + 0.920x_1$. Hypertensive subjects have a poorer health score, on the average, than normal subjects. The difference in y intercepts is $5.7 - (-11.6) = 17.3$. Since $t = 7.51 > 2.0930$, reject H_0 that $\beta_2 = 0$. Since $7.51 > 2.8609$, $p < 2(0.005) = 0.01$. $17.334 \pm 2.0930(2.309)$; 12.50, 22.17

10.6.3 $X_2 = \begin{cases} 1 \text{ if A} \\ 0 \text{ if otherwise} \end{cases}$ $X_3 = \begin{cases} 1 \text{ if B} \\ 0 \text{ if otherwise} \end{cases}$

$\hat{y} = 257 - 2.01x_1 + 75.9x_2 + 73.5x_3 - 0.754x_1x_2 - 2.02x_1x_3$; for Make A, $\hat{y} = (257 + 75.9) + (-2.01 - 0.754)x_1 = 332.9 - 2.764x_1$; for Make B: $\hat{y} = (257 + 73.5) + (-2.01 - 2.02)x_1 = 330.5 - 4.03x_1$; for Make C: $\hat{y} = 257 - 2.01x_1$. By Equation 10.6.5, the y intercept for Make A is equal to $b_0 + b_2$. H_0: $\beta_2 = 0$; $t = 2.80 > 2.7239$, $p < 0.01$. Reject H_0 and conclude that the population y intercept for Make A is different from that of Make C. By Equation 10.6.6, the y intercept for Make B is equal to $b_0 + b_3$. H_0: $\beta_3 = 0$; $t = 2.82 > 2.7239$, $p < 0.01$. Reject H_0 and conclude that the population y intercept for Make B is different from that of Make C. By Equation 10.6.5, the slope of the regression line for Make A is equal to $b_1 + b_4$. H_0: $\beta_4 = 0$; $t = -1.56 > -1.6896$, $p > 0.10$. Do not reject H_0 and conclude that the slopes of the population regression lines for Makes A and C may not be different. By Equation 10.6.6, the slope of the regression line for Make B is equal to $b_1 + b_5$. H_0: $\beta_5 = 0$; $t = -4.12 < -2.7239$, $p < 0.01$. Reject H_0 and conclude that the slopes of the population regression lines for Makes B and C are different. Thus we conclude that there is interaction between age and make of machine. (Use 35 degrees of freedom to find approximate p values and approximate critical values of t.)

10.7.1 **(a)** 0.9796 **(b)** $F = 83.35$; $p < 0.005$ **(c)** $r_{y1.2} = 0.9518$, $r_{y2.1} = 0.1685$, $r_{12.y} = 0.0658$ **(d)** $t = 8.21$; $p < 0.01$

10.7.3 **(a)** 0.8577 **(b)** $F = 11.13$; $p < 0.005$ **(c)** $r_{y1.2} = -0.8570$, $r_{y2.1} = 0.4405$, $r_{12.y} = 0.4639$ **(d)** $t = -4.70$; $p < 0.01$

REVIEW EXERCISES

9. **(a)** $\hat{y} = 11.43 + 1.26x_1 + 3.11x_2$ **(b)** $R^2_{y.12} = 0.92$

Source	SS	df	MS	F
Regression	1827.0046	2	913.50	69.048
Residual	158.7286	12	13.23	
Total	1985.7332	14		

$p < 0.005$

11. **(a)** $\hat{y} = 2.08 + 0.06x_{1j} + 1.05x_{2j}$ **(b)** $R^2_{y.12} = 0.8506$; $F = 34.1512$; $p < 0.005$ **(c)** $t_1 = 0.023$; $p > 2(0.10) = 0.20$, do not reject H_0. $t_2 = 3.221$; $p < 2(0.005) = 0.01$, reject H_0. **(d)** 0.34, 1.76 **(e)** $\hat{y} = 28.45$ **(f)** 13.44, 43.46 **(g)** 21.26, 35.64.

13. **(a)** $\hat{y} = 117.03 - 5.32x_1 + 0.1118x_2$; $R^2_{y.12} = 0.8635$; $F = 37.95$; $p < 0.005$. $t_1 = 6.03$; $p < 0.01$, reject H_0. $t_2 = 0.27$, $p > 0.20$, do not reject H_0. **(b)** 99.377, 117.875 **(c)** 104.626, 112.626

15. (a) $R = 0.9976$; $F = 933$; $p < 0.005$ (b) $r_{y1.2} = 0.505$; $r_{y2.1} = -0.084$; $r_{12.y} = 0.902$ (c) $t_1 = 1.755$; $0.20 > p > 0.10$; $t_2 = -0.253$; $p > 0.20$; $t_3 = 6.268$; $p < 0.01$

17. $\hat{y}_j = 2.0886 - 0.00244325x_{1j} + 0.175112x_{2j} + 0.259161x_{3j} + 1.72162x_{4j}$; $R^2_{y.1234} = 0.91937$; $r_{y1} = -0.771389$; $r_{y2} = 0.875112$; $r_{y3} = 0.0420715$; $r_{y4} = 0.870786$; $r_{12} = -0.68683$; $r_{13} = -0.171496$; $r_{14} = -0.689374$; $r_{23} = -0.241071$; $r_{24} = 0.845416$; $r_{34} = -0.289815$ The overall regression is significant at the 0.01 level.

t Statistic	p Value
-0.0443552	$p > 0.10$
2.71191	$0.02 < p < 0.05$
2.80904	$0.01 < p < 0.02$
2.94516	$0.01 < p < 0.02$

19. $\hat{y}_j = 7.62552 + 0.621658x_{1j} + 16.9724x_{2j} - 0.313452x_{3j}$; $R_{y.123} = 0.814088$. The overall regression is significant at the 0.05 level. $r_{y1} = 0.804793$; $r_{y2} = 0.805102$; $r_{y3} = -0.49909$; $r_{12} = 0.646684$; $r_{13} = -0.455618$; $r_{23} = -0.265937$

t Statistic	p Value
1.59162	$p > 0.10$
2.15774	$0.10 > p > 0.05$
-0.935481	$p > 0.10$

23. $\hat{y} = -112 + 80.4x_1 + 159x_2$, for the "Yes" group, $\hat{y} = -112 + 80.4x_1 + 159(1) = 47 + 80.4x_1$; for the "No" group, $\hat{y} = -112 + 80.4x_1 + 159(0) = -112 + 80.4x_1$; H_0: $\beta_2 = 0$; $t = 2.12$ is between 2.0639 and 2.492, therefore, $0.05 > p > 0.02$. Reject H_0 at the 0.05 level. 95% confidence interval for β_2: $150 \pm 2.0639(75.28)$; 3.6296, 314.3704

25. $\hat{y} = 43.431767 + 3.0465865x_1 - 0.67852496x_2 + 0.42126156x_3 - 0.29911886x_4 - 0.18493916x_5$

27. Since $787.92794 > 3.51$, reject H_0. Since $787.92794 > 3.99$, $p < 0.005$.

29. $\hat{y} = 60.349432$; 59.708211, 60.990653

31. (a) 2.19032 (b) 2 (c) 12 (d) 14 (e) 76.56359 (f) 0.18252667 (g) 419.46522 (h) 0.73865961 (i) 15.09824 (j) 12

41. $s_{x_1} = 4.798809$; $s_{x_2} = 10.695238$; $s_y = 141.838095$; BETA1 $= 0.042624247$; BETA2 $= 0.234267977$

STATISTICS AT WORK

1. All coefficients significant at 0.05 level except EMP (authors' results).

3. PER $= 5.80 + 0.098$ MAS $- 0.022$ PEU

Predictor	t-ratio	p
Constant	6.80	0.000
MAS	0.62	0.537
PEU	-0.16	0.877

$s = 0.8081$ $R - sq = 1.0\%$ $F = 0.20, p = 0.823$

CHAPTER 11

11.3.1   Regression coefficients: Wear, -14.36511; Speed, 1.540333; Speedsq, -0.006165. $r^2 = 0.92811$, $F = 77.456$.

11.3.3 0.92811

11.3.5 7.21817, $p < 0.01$

11.3.9 $\hat{y} = 66.48396$; 60.31485, 72.65308

11.3.11 $\hat{y}_i = 3.203499 + 0.850241x + 0.240385x^2$

11.3.13 144.375, $p < 0.01$

11.3.15 3.43348, $p < 0.01$

11.3.17 $\hat{y}_i = 16.95881$; 11.79046, 22.12715

11.3.19 $\hat{y}_i = 7.295871 + 2.153196x + 0.104335x^2$

11.3.25 $\hat{y}_i = 20.67022$

11.4.3   Regression coefficients:

```
LOGBAC = 3.302094
LOGCOOK = -2.129899

INDEX OF DETERMINATION (R-SQ) = 0.86689

F = 52.102
```

11.4.7 $\log y_i = 0.797119$; $\hat{y} = 6.27$

11.4.11 $\log y_i = 1.938160 - 0.462011 \log j$

11.4.13 0.99527

11.4.15 $\log y_i = 1.439558$; $\hat{y} = 27.51$

11.4.17   Regression coefficients:

```
LOGHOURS = 2.870655
LOGJ = -0.557841

INDEX OF DETERMINATION (R-SQ) = 0.92932

F = 39.442
```

11.4.21 39.442

11.4.23 -0.96401

11.5.1

Predictor	Coef
Constant	-15.141
TEMPI	0.05094
TEMPII	0.01437
RECYCLE	0.6960
QUALRAW	0.55781

R-sq = 96.3%

F = 160.68

REVIEW EXERCISES

21. 62.883, $p < 0.005$

25. 221.734, $p < 0.005$

CHAPTER 12

12.3.1 $X^2 = 22.94; p < 0.005$

12.3.3 $X^2 = 7.79; p > 0.10$

12.3.5 $X^2 = 78.0001;$ Critical $\chi_6^2 = 12.592.$ Reject $H_0; p < 0.005$

12.3.7 $X^2 = 111.67; p < 0.005$

12.4.1 $X^2 = 206.45; p < 0.005$ Reject H_0.

12.4.3 $X^2 = 1.37883; p > 0.10$ Do not reject H_0.

12.4.5 $X^2 = 17.873; 0.01 > p > 0.005$ Reject H_0.

12.5.1 $X^2 = 46.626; p < 0.005$ Reject H_0.

12.5.3 $X^2 = 53.8575; p < 0.005$ Reject H_0.

REVIEW EXERCISES

9. $X^2 = 2.7019; p > 0.10$

11. $X^2 = 2.64545; p > 0.10$ Do not reject H_0.

13. $X^2 = 9.14807; 0.10 > p > 0.05$ Do not reject H_0.

15. $X^2 = 18.5; p < 0.005$ Reject H_0.

17. $X^2 = 1.9106$ Do not reject H_0. $p > 0.10$

19. $X^2 = 76.3906$ Reject H_0. $p < 0.005$

21. $X^2 = 2.577; p > 0.10$ Do not reject H_0.

23. $X^2 = 71.4431; p < 0.005$ Reject H_0.

25. $X^2 = 33.7143; p < 0.005$ Reject H_0.

27. $X^2 = 38.4759; p < 0.005$ Reject H_0.

29. $X^2 = 206.45; p < 0.005$

31. $X^2 = 22.0; p < 0.005$

33. $X^2 = 26.6667; p < 0.005$ Reject H_0.

35. $X^2 = 99.1259; p < 0.005$ Reject H_0.

59.

Subscribe?	N	S	E	W	Total
Yes	263 (281)	321 (281)	248 (281)	292 (281)	1124
No	1737 (1719)	1679 (1719)	1752 (1719)	1708 (1719)	6876
Total	2000	2000	2000	2000	8000

Expected frequencies are in parentheses. H_0: Appeal of the magazine is the same among geographic areas. Since $X^2 = 12.9762 > 7.815$, reject H_0. Report that there is a difference in appeal among geographic areas.

61.

x	Expected Relative Frequency	E_i	O_i	X^2
A	1/15	30	22	2.133
B	2/15	60	48	2.400
C	4/15	120	128	0.533
D	8/15	240	252	0.600
				5.666

Since $5.666 < 7.815$, we cannot reject the null hypothesis of a proper weighting. We conclude that the spinner may be weighted properly.

63. Since $4.2239 < 9.236$, do not reject H_0.

65.

Answer	A	B	Total
Y	80 (83.27)	90 (86.73)	170
N	160 (156.73)	160 (163.27)	320
Total	240	250	490

$X^2 = 0.3843$

$0.3843 = (0.62)^2$, the square of the z value computed earlier.

67.

	A	B	Total
Yes	157 (163.04)	93 (86.96)	250
No	143 (136.96)	67 (73.04)	210
Total	300	160	460

Expected frequencies are in parentheses. $X^2 = 1.41$. No significant difference in sample results, since $1.41 < 2.706$. $\bar{p} = 0.54348$; $z = -1.1877$ No significant difference, since $-1.1877 < -1.645$. Note: $(-1.1877)^2 = 1.41$ $(-1.645)^2 = 2.706$

STATISTICS AT WORK

1. df = 6, significant at 0.00001 level (authors' results), reject H_0.
2. df = 6, $p < 0.0001$ (authors' results), reject H_0.
3. $X^2 = 4.20$, $p < 0.05$ (authors' results), reject H_0.
4. $X^2 = 6.849$
5. $X^2 = 8.575$
6. $X^2 = 156.294$
7. $X^2 = 31.629$
8. $X^2 = 1.371$
9. ChiSq = 13.153, df = 1, $p < 0.005$

CHAPTER 13

13.5.1 $r = 6$, not significant
13.5.3   Since $2 < 7 < 9$, H_0 cannot be rejected.
13.6.1   Do not reject H_0. $p > 0.054$
13.6.3   Reject H_0. $0.023 > p > 0.005$
13.7.1   Since $178.5 > 160$, reject H_0. $0.01 > p > 0.002$
13.7.3   Since $272 > 227 > 128$, do not reject H_0. $p > 0.20$
13.8.1 $P(k \geq 9|10, 0.5) = 0.0107$; $p = 0.0107$ Reject H_0.
13.8.3 $P(k \geq 10|12, 0.5) = 0.0193$; Reject H_0. $p = 0.0193$
13.9.1 $H = 3.5$ Cannot reject H_0. $p > 0.102$
13.9.3 $H = 24.425$; H_0 can be rejected at 0.01 level. $p < 0.005$
13.9.5 $H = 9.69$; $p < 0.01$ Reject H_0.
13.10.1 $\chi_r^2 = 3.08$ Cannot reject H_0. $p > 0.10$
13.10.3 $\chi_r^2 = 10.4$ Reject H_0. $0.01 > p > 0.005$
13.11.1 $r_S = 0.703$; $p < 0.001$
13.11.3 $r_S = 0.864$; $p < 0.001$ (one-sided test)   Reject H_0.
13.11.5 $r_S = 0.7455$; $0.005 < p < 0.010$
13.12.1 $r_S = 0.6676$; $0.01 > p > 0.002$
13.12.3 $\hat{\beta} = 1.492$, $\hat{\alpha}_{1,M} = -176.685$, $\hat{\alpha}_{2,M} = -176.63$

REVIEW EXERCISES

7. Since $6 < 12 < 16$, do not reject H_0. $p > 0.05$
9. $r_S = 0.918$; $p < 0.001$ (one-sided test)   Reject H_0.
11. $r_S = 0.7804$. Since $0.7804 > 0.7464$, $p < 2(0.001) = 0.002$ Reject H_0.

13. $H = 4.46$ Do not reject H_0. $p > 0.102$

15. $\chi_r^2 = 27.76$ Reject H_0. $p < 0.005$

17. $H = 7.549; p < 0.01$

19. $\chi_r^2 = 7.143; p = 0.027$

21. $T_+ = 34.5; T_- = 1.5; 0.008 > p > 0.004$

23. $T_+ = 49.5; T_- = 28.5; p > 0.110$

45. Example 13.9.1:

A vs D

$2.53\sqrt{[4(5)/12][(1/7)(1/10)]} = 0.39039$

Since $|19.4286 - 5.7| > 0.39039$, conclude that A and D have different effects.

B vs C

$2.53\sqrt{4(34)/6} = 12.0452$

Since $|29.5 - 16.5| > 12.0542$, conclude that B and C have different effects.

B vs D

$2.53\sqrt{[4(5)/12][(1/8)(1/10)]} = 0.36517$

Since $|29.5 - 5.7| > 0.36517$, conclude that B and D have different effects.

C vs D

Since $|16.5 - 5.7| > 0.36517$, conclude that C and D have different effects.

Exercise 13.9.3:

$2.24\sqrt{4(41)/6} = 11.711$. Since $|34.55 - 15.30| > 11.711$, conclude that the two population means differ. Since $|34.55 - 22.00| > 11.711$, conclude that the two population means differ. Since $|34.55 - 10.15| > 11.711$, conclude that the two population means differ. Since $|15.30 - 22.00| < 11.711$, conclude that the two population means may not differ. Since $|15.30 - 10.15| < 11.711$, conclude that the two population means may not differ. Since $|22.00 - 10.15| > 11.711$, conclude that the two population means differ.

STATISTICS AT WORK

1. df $= 8, p > 0.10$

2. $r_S = 0.96, p < 0.01$

3. $H = 6.05$

4. $r_S = 0.84$

5. $r_s = 0.708$

CHAPTER 14

14.4.1 352, 302, 242, 250, 197, 209, 194, 249, 261, 245, 234

14.4.3 719, 696, 663, 643, 628, 628, 614, 595, 578, 559, 545, 534

14.5.1 533.000, 501.000, 427.200, 452.760, 395.808, 372.846, 312.677, 285.142, 286.313, 274.651, 260.521, 278.216, 269.373, 257.299, 241.039

14.5.3 749.000, 733.000, 719.800, 703.080, 666.248, 656.149, 646.089, 632.054, 619.232, 601.139, 584.284, 567.770, 554.262, 542.157

14.6.1   354.7333, 341.9619, 329.1905, 316.4190, 303.6476, 290.8762, 278.1048, 265.3333, 252.5619, 239.7905, 227.0190, 214.2476, 201.4762, 188.7048, 175.9333

14.6.3   724.9143, 708.5978, 692.2813, 675.9648, 659.6484, 643.3319, 627.0154, 610.6989, 594.3824, 578.0659, 561.7494, 545.4330, 529.1165, 512.8000

14.6.5   533.000, 373.000, 265.760, 344.056, 263.284, 248.458, 165.033, 144.998, 175.133, 176.379, 170.601, 220.436, 216.073, 204.999, 186.191

14.6.7   749.0000, 709.0000, 697.4800, 679.6560, 630.0944, 628.3975, 623.4021, 610.0208, 598.3188, 577.7352, 560.1288, 543.3685, 531.5163, 521.2466

14.7.1   **(b)** 59.34, 20.02, 193.53, 101.17, 192.10, 292.19, 93.90, 49.33, 94.62, 37.18, 23.83, 42.78   **(c)** 7, 60, 3, 10, 9, 11, 26, 18, 11, 13, 71, 2

14.7.3   Estimated number of pairs: 9, 3, 29, 15, 29, 44, 14, 7, 14, 6, 4, 6

14.8.1   **(b)** 117.9, 136.8, 139.8, 96.6, 149.7, 141.3, 96.4, 141.8, 147.7, 120.9, 129.0, 132.2, 55.3, 109.1, 90.1, 50.7, 111.9, 89.6, 102.6, 44.3, 61.6, 117.5, 106.5, 58.2, 31.6, 49.8, 16.8, 25.1, 46.9, 70.6, 64.8, 55.0, 78.1, 71.4, 79.7, 115.1, 130.6, 135.3, 165.1, 146.2, 78.2, 107.3, 131.9, 143.1, 121.8, 121.8, 108.6, 97.2, 128.2, 134.6

14.8.3   **(b)** 176.0, 161.6, 137.5, 82.1, 45.5, 77.8, 101.9, 90.5, 81.3, 104.6, 124.1, 104.0, 82.1, 99.1, 114.0

14.9.1   53.33, 56.67, 58.67, 61.67, 62.33, 62.67, 59.00, 56.67, 54.33, 51.67

14.9.3   58.25, 58.725, 58.8525, 58.3673, 58.1306, 57.6175, 56.4558

14.9.7   3019.0578, 5723.715, 6028.9296, 864.1357

14.10.1   MSE (arithmetic) = 17.6359; MSE (smoothed) = 14.4583

14.10.3   14,630.5837

REVIEW EXERCISES

35.

	(c)	(d)	(e)
	Y_c	Three-year Moving Average	Cyclical Relatives
	1.64	—	98.780
	1.72	1.69	98.837
	1.80	1.77	97.222
	1.87	1.87	98.930
	1.95	1.98	102.564
	2.03	2.07	103.448
	2.10	2.13	100.000
	2.18	2.20	100.917
	2.26	2.27	101.770
	2.33	2.35	99.571
	2.41	2.41	100.415
	2.49	2.47	99.598
	2.56	—	97.656

$Y_c = 1.5657 + 0.0768t$ (obtained by computer)

37.

	(c) Y_c	(d) Three-year Moving Average	(e) Cyclical Relatives
	9.46	—	101.480
	9.04	9.37	105.088
	8.62	9.00	104.408
	8.20	8.40	103.659
	7.79	7.73	98.845
	7.37	7.07	94.980
	6.95	6.50	93.525
	6.53	6.10	91.884
	6.11	5.73	94.926
	5.70	5.43	94.737
	5.28	5.07	96.591
	4.86	4.73	96.708
	4.44	4.53	99.099
	4.03	4.40	111.663
	3.61	—	119.114

$Y_c = 9.8762 - 0.41786t$ (obtained by computer)

39. MSE = 4.6701909

CHAPTER 15

15.6.1   (a) 30,500   (b) 50.83   (c) 47,700 (d) 0.13   (e) 50.120, 51.546   (f) 30,072; 30,928

15.6.3   252.3, 262.0; 176,622, 183,378

15.7.1   (a) 1105   (b) 870   (c) 4.42   (d) 0.01392   (e) 1047, 1163   (f) 4.19, 4.65

15.9.1   (a) $2500   (b) $2950   (c) $1480   (d) $1300

15.9.3   (a) 61   (b) 11

15.9.5   (a) 17   (b) 146, 87, 58   (c) 23, 57, 119   (d) 14, 51, 129

REVIEW EXERCISES

11. (a) $\bar{x}_{cl} = 18$ (b) $\hat{V}(\bar{x}_{cl}) = 0.0525$ 17.55, 18.45

13. $\bar{x}_{st} = \$1127.50$ \$1113.78; \$1141.22

23. $r = 3.928/29.580 = 0.132792$; $\hat{\mu}_y = 8.63148$, or 8,631 per weekend; 8.583, 8.680

CHAPTER 16

16.2.1   (a) Do not sponsor program.   (b) Sponsor program.   (c) Sponsor program.   (d) Sponsor program.   (e) Sponsor program.

16.2.3 (a) A_2 (b) A_2 (c) A_3 (d) A_3 (e) A_2

16.3.1 (a) \$8500, \$13,500, \$22,500 (b) \$8500 (c) c_1 (d) c_1 (e) \$55,000 (f) Yes, \$8500 (g) c_1 (h) \$8500

REVIEW EXERCISES

13.

Expected Monetary Value Method

E	A_1	A_2	A_3	EPPI
1	8.808	19.584	11.472	19.584
2	25.68	9.792	22.512	25.680
3	8.008	10.5	14.588	14.588
	42.496	39.876	*48.572	59.852

EVPI $= 59.852 - 48.572 = 11.28$

Expected Opportunity Loss Method

E	A_1	A_2	A_3
1	10.776	0	8.112
2	0	15.888	3.168
3	6.58	4.088	0
	17.356	19.976	11.28*

EVPI $= 11.28$

15. (a) Do not market, since $0 > -6000$. (b) See p. A-227.

(c) θ	$P(\theta)$	$P(x = 6 | n = 10, \theta)$	Joint	$P(\theta | n = 10, x = 6)$
20%	0.7	0.0055	0.00385	*0.1033
40%	0.3	0.1114	0.03342	*0.8967
			*0.03727	1.0

*Values are included in the tree

(d) Market

17. Normally distributed with $\mu'' = 29.587$; $\sigma'^2 = 2.0642$

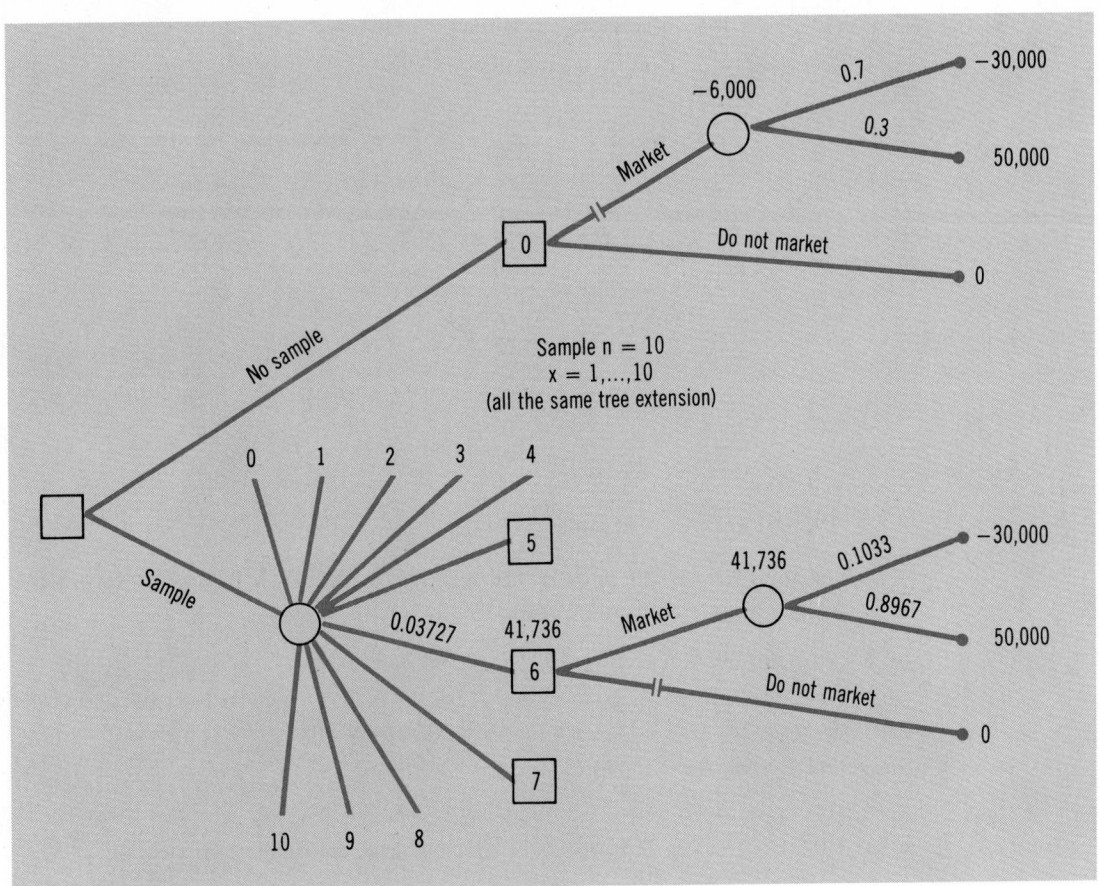

CHAPTER 17

17.2.1

Sample #	$\bar{x}$	R
41	1.25	58
42	−1.75	6
43	−1.25	12
44	−11.75	76
45	−2.00	10
46	−3.75	15
47	−12.25	8
48	−1.00	5
49	8.25	5
50	4.00	7

17.3.1 $\bar{p} = 0.13$ LCL = 0 (cannot be negative)   UCL = 0.27

17.3.3 (a) UCL revised = 0.3675, LCL revised = 0.0291

(b)

Time Period	p	Time Period	p
26	0.12	39	0.18
27	0.20	40	0.24
28	0.14	41	0.12
29	0.38	42	0.06
30	0.08	43	0.22
31	0.16	44	0.16
32	0.22	45	0.18
33	0.14	46	0.20
34	0.18	47	0.18
35	0.10	48	0.40
36	0.20	49	0.12
37	0.26	50	0.20
38	0.36		

Values for samples 29 and 48 fall outside the control limits. Therefore the process does not remain under control.

17.4.1 (a) 80, 0, 1 (b) 80, 5, 6 (c) 80, 14, 15 (d 80, 3, 4 (e) 80, 7, 8

17.5.1 Select 28 items; if the mean psi at failure is greater than or equal to 2681.09, accept the lot. If the mean psi at failure is less than 2681.09, reject the lot.

17.5.3 Since 3.94 > 3.91, reject the lot.

17.6.1 $\bar{x} = 136.77$, $s = 6.41$; $136.77 \pm 3(6.41)$; 117.54, 156.00

17.6.3 $C_p = 1.04$. Conclusion: The process is just capable of meeting its specifications.

17.6.5 $\bar{\bar{x}} = 6.969$; $\bar{R} = 0.68$; LCL = 6.57664; UCL = 7.36136; $C_p = 1.1402$

REVIEW EXERCISES

25. $\bar{\bar{x}} = 24.1$; $\bar{R} = 0.7$; $LCI_{\bar{x}} = 23.6961$; $UCL_{\bar{x}} = 24.5039$; $LCL_R = 0$; $UCL_R = 1.4805$

27. (a) F, 20, 2, 3 (b) H, 50, 0, 1 (c) L, 200, 0, 1 (d) J, 80, 14, 15 (e) K, 125, 2, 3

29. $p = 0.00474903$. Conclude that Supplier B's product has a longer average life than Supplier A's.

STATISTICS AT WORK

1. $\bar{x} = 0.7489$, UCL = 0.9319, LCL = 0.5659

2. $\hat{r} = 0.184$, UCL = 0.280, LCL = 0.088

INDEX